THE DYING OF THE LIGHT

Also by James Tunstead Burtchaell:

Catholic Theories of Biblical Inspiration Since 1810: A Review and Critique, Cambridge University Press, 1969

Philemon's Problem: The Daily Dilemma of the Christian, ACTA, 1973

Philemon's Problem: Jubilee edition, William B. Eerdmans Publishing Co., 1998

Marriage among Christians: A Curious Tradition (ed.), Ave Maria Press, 1977

Bread and Salt: A Cassette Catechism, Credence Cassettes, 1978

Abortion Parley (ed.), Andrews & McMeel, 1980

Rachel Weeping, and Other Essays on Abortion, Andrews & McMeel, 1982

For Better, for Worse: Sober Thoughts on Passionate Promises, Paulist Press, 1985

A Just War No Longer Exists: The Teaching and Trial of Don Lorenzo Milani, University of Notre Dame Press, 1988

The Giving and Taking of Life: Essays Ethical, University of Notre Dame Press, 1989

From Synagogue to Church: Public Services and Offices in the Earliest Christian Communities, Cambridge University Press, 1992

The Dying of the Light

THE DISENGAGEMENT
OF COLLEGES AND UNIVERSITIES
FROM THEIR CHRISTIAN CHURCHES

James Tunstead Burtchaell, C.S.C.

WILLIAM B. EERDMANS PUBLISHING COMPANY
GRAND RAPIDS, MICHIGAN / CAMBRIDGE, U.K.

© 1998 Wm. B. Eerdmans Publishing Co.
255 Jefferson Ave. S.E., Grand Rapids, Michigan 49503 /
P.O. Box 163, Cambridge CB3 9PU U.K.

Printed in the United States of America

03 02 01 00 99 98   7 6 5 4 3 2 1

Library of Congress Cataloging-in-Publication Data

Burtchaell, James Tunstead.
The dying of the light : the disengagement of colleges and universities
from their Christian churches / James Tunstead Burtchaell.
p.   cm.
Includes bibliographical references and index.
ISBN 0-8028-3828-6 (hardcover : alk. paper).
ISBN 0-8028-4481-2 (pbk. : alk. paper).
1. Church and college — United States — History.
2. Universities and colleges — United States — Religion — History.
3. Church colleges — United States — History.
4. Secularization — United States — History.
I. Title.
LC383.B87   1998
371.071 — dc21   98-18064
CIP

For

The Marianites of Holy Cross

my gracious and hospitable sisters

Contents

Preface

Countless colleges and universities in the history of the United States were founded under some sort of Christian patronage, but many which still survive do not claim any relationship with a church or denomination. Even on most of the campuses which are still listed by churches as their affiliates, there is usually some concern expressed today about how authentic or how enduring that tie really is; and often wistful concern is all that remains. This book is an attempt to narrate and understand the dynamics of these church-campus relations, the ways they have tended to wither, and the whys.

I hope to supplement the magisterial work already done by George Marsden, Philip Gleason, and Douglas Sloan. Marsden, in *The Soul of the American University*, recounts how America's most influential universities — Harvard, Yale, Princeton, Columbia, Michigan, Johns Hopkins, Chicago — while still under liberal Protestant influence at the turn of the century, excluded Christian belief as unworthy of study in the new orthodoxy of secularism. My study deals with both colleges and universities, of more diverse ecclesial origins, and discerns the dynamics and rationales at various times whereby the link of mutual patronage between college and church was severed in this century — severed, paradoxically, just at the time when the resources were first in place to allow a vital synergism, and severed by the hand of ecclesiastics and academics who saw themselves as uniting both identities within themselves, but not within their institutions.[1]

Gleason, in *Contending with Modernity*, has studied the Catholic experience in higher education. Though united to the church by few formal ties, the vast enterprise of Catholic education began the century held together by a revived neo-scholastic philosophy and a loyalty to their historically transnational tradition. The Catholic establishment thus fended off both Modernism and Americanism until the destabilizing 1960s, when lay autonomy, an embarrassment about scholarly mediocrity, and the drive for recognition by the then secular American academy and the acceptance of its liberal dogma abruptly destroyed the Catholic self-assuredness of an intellectual advantage. My study of the Protestant experiences offers another angle whereby to see how their much longer and slower disaffection from church followed a similar path decades ahead of the Catholics, who would be unaware that what they were achieving in the 1960s had been familiar to some Protestants since the 1890s.[2]

Sloan's *Faith and Knowledge* studies various attempts by liberal Protestants in this century to reunite faith and knowledge, which had become severed within academe, in his view, not at the Reformation but in the early years of this century. He recounts repeated attempts by theologians to pander to their academic colleagues: by appropriating the humanities and social sciences as the habitat they imagined proper for their Christian "values," and by translating their faith into the language and categories of accepted disciplines. What emerged was neither faith nor knowledge, and it awakened the interest, not of the theologians' cultured despisers, but of their naive disciples.[3] His is the more intellectual history and mine the more circumstantial and eventually theological; mine begins with mainline Protestants and follows their story into the wider experience of other Protestants and of Catholics.

I have chosen to study institutions with historic bonds to the Congregationalists, the Presbyterians, the Methodists, the Baptists, the Lutherans, the Catholics, and the evangelicals because they sponsored the most colleges and universities. Thus I have had to leave aside what may have been even more interesting stories: those of the Mennonites, the Mormons, the Quakers, the Disciples of Christ, the Episcopalians, the Seventh-Day Adventists.

Within the clusters studied, I looked at institutions that emerged from distinctive historical and geographical sectors.[4] Thus for the Congregationalists there is Dartmouth College, a colonial New England foundation, and Beloit College, a missionary venture in the West. The Presbyterians were divided culturally and politically into North and South, which I have ensampled respectively by Lafayette and Davidson Colleges, whose stories also display both Old School and New School loyalties. The Methodists also divided South and North, over sectional and theological differences, and their representatives here are Millsaps College and Ohio Wesleyan University. The Baptist cleavage has been more enduring; Wake Forest University has been chosen from among the Southern Baptist schools, Linfield College from the American Baptists, and Virginia Union University as a foundation of the American Baptists for black freedmen after the Civil War. Three branches of Lutherans are represented here: Gettysburg College for the colonial "Americanist" Lutherans of the eastern seaboard; St. Olaf College for the German-Scandinavian "confessing" churches of the Upper Midwest; and Concordia University for the Missouri Synod. As samples of Catholic foundations, the three largest teaching congregations are exemplified: the Jesuits by Boston College; the Ursulines by the College of New Rochelle, and the Christian Brothers by Saint Mary's College of California. The Coalition of Christian Colleges and Universities, a large working group of evangelical schools, is represented by Azusa Pacific University of the Wesleyan Holiness tradition and Dordt College of the Christian Reformed

Church. There are colleges from New Hampshire to Mississippi, from Oregon to Minnesota; and their foundations run from 1769 to 1955. The campuses range from very compact to rambling; the annual budgets and endowments, from frugal to affluent. I intentionally selected institutions which I had never visited or studied, with one exception: I had once briefly visited the campus of Saint Mary's in Moraga, California, in 1974. They have together proven to be as randomly representational as was reasonably possible, especially in respect of the issue to be studied: the dynamics of their relationships with religious patronage. There were many surprises.

One constant was the universally hospitable welcome the author found at the hands of the archivists. The denominational and church officials responsible for liaison with colleges and universities were also contacted and usually visited, and here, too, there was a wide range in professionalism, resources, experience, religious seriousness, and interaction with the campuses.

The story in the stories is more melancholy than the author had expected. Most of these colleges and universities no longer have a serious, valued, or functioning relationship with their Christian sponsors of the past. Many apparently never did. I call this melancholy for two reasons. One wishes they had all successfully cultivated their denominational affiliations, and that they could have helped their churches intellectually in the process. More importantly, the estrangement between colleges and churches was effected by men and women who said and apparently thought that they wanted them to be partners in both the life of the spirit and the life of the mind. But they concealed from themselves and from some of their constituencies the process of alienation as it was under way. There is considerable self-deception in these narratives, and I have worked to recount them in their wry truth.

The chapters are not written uniformly, because the ways in which the various churches and denominations treated their colleges and universities varied considerably. The shape of the individual narratives differs also because the archival and interview evidence for the various institutions ranges from scanty to pressed down, shaken up, and overflowing in the lap.

These seventeen stories amount to a hefty book, of the size usually reserved for major wars. The subject of our inquiry is a very important one, and to reach a reliable judgment required something of a sojourn at a variety of colleges and universities and their sponsoring churches, not a flying visit or a quick read through a dossier. Most readers will and probably should begin with the stories of the denomination they know best, and then browse through other chapters of special personal interest. Most will want to go to my overview chapter, "The Story within the Stories," after reading two or three of the narrative chapters. If my hunch is correct, they will then find themselves going back to see what differences or similarities the remaining stories will display. The author, who has spent no small amount of time and work on these studies, still finds every one of them distinctively interesting. The stories are told in enough tangle and detail to allow the reader to get some feel for the sensibilities that went into the protagonists' ambitions and decisions. Whoever reads it all will emerge as a journeyman, *honoris causa,* in the knowledge of our country's and churches' educational history.

Beyond its lengthy range, this study also invites reflection on a matter of even more spacious concern: the dynamics whereby any Christian endeavor can unwittingly be decomposed. It offers enough folly at close range for readers to be stimulated to reflection about the circumspection and canniness we all require to review and renew earlier commitments without forfeiting them unawares. So much that is onward is not upward.

NOTES TO PREFACE

1. George M. Marsden, *The Soul of the American University* (New York: Oxford University Press, 1994). A very valuable companion volume is *The Secularization of the Academy,* ed. Marsden and Bradley J. Longfield (New York: Oxford University Press, 1992).

2. Philip Gleason, *Contending with Modernity: Catholic Higher Education in the Twentieth Century* (New York: Oxford University Press, 1995).

3. Douglas Sloan, *Faith and Knowledge: Mainline Protestantism and American Higher Education* (Louisville: Westminster John Knox, 1994).

4. At the threshold of this project I published an exploratory inquiry, examining Vanderbilt University and a variety of Catholic institutions. The former study was based on published sources only, and the latter left all references anonymous; neither has been included here. See James Tunstead Burtchaell, C.S.C., "The Alienation of Christian Higher Education in America: Diagnosis and Prognosis," in *Schooling Christians: "Holy Experiments" in American Education,* ed. Stanley Hauerwas and John H. Westerhoff (Grand Rapids: William B. Eerdmans Publishing Co., 1992), 129-83; also, in a slightly different format, "The Decline and Fall of the Christian College," *First Things* 12 (April 1991): 16-29; 13 (May 1991): 30-38.

Acknowledgments

I owe renewed thanks to the librarians and archivists who have welcomed me to their collections and permitted me to use their historical records:

Harold F. Worthley at the Congregational Library, Boston

Barbara L. Krieger at Special Collections in the Dartmouth College Library

Fred A. Burwell at the Beloit College Archives

Kenneth J. Ross and Susan J. Sullivan at the Presbyterian Historical Society, Philadelphia

Diane Windham Shaw at the Lafayette College Archives

Professor Emeritus and Archivist Emeritus Albert W. Gendebien, Lafayette College

Jan Blodgett at the Davidson College Archives

Mark Shenise at the General Commission on Archives and History, the United Methodist Church, Madison, New Jersey

Marice Wolfe at the Vanderbilt University Archives

Susan J. Cohen at the West Ohio Conference United Methodist Archives and the Ohio Wesleyan University Archives

Debra McIntosh at the J. B. Cain Archives of Mississippi Methodism and the Millsaps College Archives

Beverly Carlson at the American Baptist Historical Society, Valley Forge

John Woodard at the Baptist Historical Collection and the Wake Forest University Archives

Ronald Shelton at the Virginia Union University Archives

Mary Margaret Benson at Special Collections, Northup Library, Linfield College

Elisabeth Wittman at the Archives of the Evangelical Lutheran Church in America, Chicago

John E. Peterson at the Lutheran Archives Center at Philadelphia

David T. Hedrick at Special Collections, Musselman Library, Gettysburg
    College
Joan R. Olson at the St. Olaf College Archives
George R. Nielsen at the Concordia University Archives
John Atteberry at the John J. Burns Library, Boston College
Sister Mary Russo, O.S.U., at the College of New Rochelle Archives
Linda Wobbe Seekamp at the Saint Mary's College of California, College
    Archives
Wendy Clauson Schlereth at the Archives of the University of Notre Dame
Doane Wylie at the Azusa Pacific University Archives
Sandra Heynen at the Dordt College Archives

I am also appreciative to the educational executives of churches and denominations who offered information and perspective:

Rev. James A. Smith, Jr., Minister for Higher Education Relationships for
    the Board for Homeland Ministries, United Church of Christ, Cleveland
Rev. Duncan S. Ferguson, Executive Director, Association of Presbyterian
    Colleges and Universities, Louisville
Dr. Ken Yamada, Associate General Secretary, Division of Higher Education,
    Board of Higher Education and Ministry, the United Methodist Church,
    Nashville
Dr. Arthur L. Walker, Executive Director, Educational Commission of the
    Southern Baptist Convention, Nashville
Dr. Jean Kim, Executive Director of Educational Ministries, American Baptist
    Churches USA, Valley Forge
Dr. Donald A. Stoike, Executive Director, Lutheran Educational Conference
    of North America, Washington
Rev. W. Robert Sorenson, Executive Director, Division for Education, and
    Rev. James M. Unglaube, Director for Colleges and Universities, Evangelical Lutheran Church in America, Chicago
Rev. William F. Meyer, Executive Director, Board for Higher Education
    Services, the Lutheran Church–Missouri Synod, Saint Louis
Dr. Paul Gallagher, Acting Executive Director of the Association of Catholic
    Colleges and Universities, Washington
Revs. Paul Tipton, S.J., and the late James W. Sauvé, S.J., successive Presidents of the Association of Jesuit Colleges and Universities, Washington
Rev. Terrence Toland, S.J., Coordinator in the Department of Education,
    National Conference of Catholic Bishops, Washington
Dr. Karen A. Longman, Vice President, Coalition for Christian Colleges and
    Universities, Washington

Various fellow scholars have been good enough to help me with specific questions and insights in conversation or correspondence, or to read and comment on parts of this manuscript. For this I owe thanks to Diogenes Allen, Scott Appleby, Myron Augsburger, Michael Baxter, C.S.C., Michael Beaty, David Bebbington, Robert Bellah, Earl Brill, Michael Garvey, Darryl Hart, Stanley Hauerwas, Christopher Kauffman, Dean Kelley, Thomas Langford, George Marsden, Albert Meyer, William Narum, David O'Brien, Sheldon Rothblatt, Gerald Sloyan, Timothy Smith, Winton Solberg, Merle Strege, James Turner, John Vander Stelt, Robert Wilken, David Wills, and Robert Wuthnow. Two scholars whose work I have long appreciated have been most kind in reading and offering extensive and helpful criticism upon the entire text: Philip Gleason and Douglas Sloan. For constant encouragement in this project I am indebted to no one more than to Richard John Neuhaus. And for the research grants that have supported this inquiry, thanks are due to the Lilly Endowment and to the Lynde and Harry Bradley Foundation.

Center for the Study of American Religion
Princeton University

List of Acronyms

AACS	Association for the Advancement of Christian Scholarship
AAUP	American Association of University Professors
ABC	American Baptist Convention
ABCA	American Baptist Archives Center, Valley Forge, Pa.
ABC/USA	American Baptist Churches in the USA
ABEC	American Baptist Educational Commission
ABES	American Baptist Education Society
ABHMS	American Baptist Home Mission Society
AC	Azusa College
ACCA	Association of Colleges of Congregational Affiliation
ACCU	Association of Catholic Colleges and Universities
ACE	American Council on Education
ACES	American College and Education Society
ACTION	American Council to Improve Our Neighborhoods
AES	American Education Society
AFL-CIO	American Federation of Labor and Congress of Industrial Organizations
AHMS	American Home Missionary Society
AJCU	Association of Jesuit Colleges and Universities
ALC	American Lutheran Church
APC	Azusa Pacific College
APU	Azusa Pacific University
APUA	Azusa Pacific University Archives
BC	Boston College
BCA	Beloit College Archives
BCA	Boston College Archives (John J. Burns Library, Boston College)
BCE	Board of Christian Education

BEST	*Baptist Education Study Task*
BHEM	Board of Higher Education and Ministry
BHEM/UMC	Board of Higher Education and Ministry/United Methodist Church
BSC	Baptist State Convention
CCCU	Coalition for Christian Colleges and Universities
CES	Congregational Education Society
CIRP	Cooperative Institutional Research Program
CLB	Congregational Library, Boston
CNR	College of New Rochelle
CNRA	College of New Rochelle Archives
CPHS	Papers of Theodore M. Hesburgh, C.S.C.
CRC	Christian Reformed Church in North America
CU	Concordia University (River Forest)
CUA	Concordia University Archive
CUNY	City University of New York
DCA	Dartmouth Christian Association
DCA	Dartmouth College Archives
DCA	Davidson College Archives
DCA	Dordt College Archives
DHE	Division of Higher Education
DOHP	Department of History and Records Management Services (Philadelphia)
EBR	Papers of Edward B. Rooney, S.J.
ELC	Evangelical Lutheran Church
ELCA	Evangelical Lutheran Church in America
FCCB	First Congregational Church, Beloit
FSC	Frères des Écoles Chrétiennes
GA	General Assembly
GC	General Congregation
GCA	Gettysburg College Archives
GEB	General Education Board (Rockefeller)
GPA	grade point average
GRS	Graduate School
IFCU	International Federation of Catholic Universities
IPC	Inter-Province Committee
IWU	Illinois Wesleyan University

JEA	Jesuit Educational Association
JEQ	*Jesuit Educational Quarterly*
LCA	Archives of Linfield College
LCA	Lutheran Church in America
LCMS	Lutheran Church–Missouri Synod
LCSCA	Lafayette College Special Collections and Archives
LECNA	Lutheran Educational Conference of North America
MCA	Millsaps College Archives
MIT	Massachusetts Institute of Technology
NBC	Northern Baptist Convention
NCA	North Central Association of Colleges and Secondary Schools
NCAA	National Collegiate Athletic Association
NYU	New York University
OBSC	Oregon Baptist State Convention
OWCA	Ohio Wesleyan Historical Collection, Ohio Wesleyan University
OWM	Office of World Missions
OWU	Ohio Wesleyan University
PBC	Pacific Bible College
PCCW	Presbyterian and Congregational Convention of Wisconsin
PCUS	Presbyterian Church in the United States (Southern Presbyterian Church)
PCUSA	Presbyterian Church in the United States of America (Northern Presbyterian Church)
PC(USA)	Presbyterian Church (U.S.A.)
PP	Presidents' Papers
PP/MPW	Presidents' Papers, Michael P. Walsh, S.J.
RNS	Religious News Service
ROTC	Reserve Officers' Training Corps
SACS	Southern Association of Colleges and Schools
SAS	School of Arts and Sciences
SBC	Southern Baptist Convention
SCA	Student Christian Association
SEBA	School of Economics and Business Administration
SGA	Student Government Association
SMC	Saint Mary's College

SMCA	Saint Mary's College of California Archives
SNR	School of New Resources
SOCA	St. Olaf College Archives
SON	School of Nursing
SPCTEW	Society for the Promotion of Collegiate and Theological Education at the West
SUNY	State University of New York
TSCW	Training School for Christian Workers
UA	University Archives (BCA)
UCC	United Church of Christ
UCLA	University of California, Los Angeles
ULCA	United Lutheran Church in America
UMC	United Methodist Church
UMCA	United Methodist Church Archives
UNC	University of North Carolina
UNCF	United Negro College Fund
UNDA	University of Notre Dame Archives
UNLC	United Norwegian Lutheran Church
UPCUSA, UPC/USA, UPC(USA)	United Presbyterian Church in the United States of America
USC	University of Southern California
VUU	Virginia Union University
WASC	Western Association of Schools and Colleges
WASP	White Anglo-Saxon Protestant
WFU	Wake Forest University
YMCA	Young Men's Catholic Association
YMCA	Young Men's Christian Association
YWCA	Young Women's Christian Association

CHAPTER 1

The Congregationalists

The colleges founded within the ambit of Congregationalism must be the first in our study, since it was in Congregationalist New England that the American college pattern was first established. Had the rising sentiments of resistance to England arisen later or with less animus, the early foundations associated with the Church of England — such as the College of William and Mary (1693), King's College (1754, now Columbia University), and the Charity School (1740, now the University of Pennsylvania) — might have established the dominant mode, especially in the southern colonies where that church was established and in the riparian cities where Anglicans were well represented. But the surge of anti-Tory hostility swept away all that, and the sponsorship of colonial and early federal higher education fell mostly to the Congregationalists in New England and the Presbyterians in the Middle Atlantic and southern areas. Those two religious communities were separated by a denominational barrier more permeable than the political borders between them, but their two stories are distinctive enough to be narrated and understood separately in our study.

The Congregational story has notable aspects. Except in the earliest years, their colleges' relationship to Congregationalism has been ambiguous and unstable. Second, the Congregational establishment began with a strength of conviction and a great sweep of foundations, yet today it leaves only a handful of institutions willing to be associated with the United Church of Christ (UCC), the residual legatee of their founders.

In our studies of other denominations we list extant colleges and universities which are claimed as church related, and note separately some of the foundations no longer existing or claimed. In the case of the Congregationalists this would distort the picture. Instead we list the extant institutions that were once claimed by the Congregationalists, the great majority of which are now independent of any

This essay was researched and written in 1994, and the statistics and facts it reports as current derive from the latest sources then available.

1

relationship and are designated by italic type in the following table. The eighteen which appear in roman type are presently claimed as related to the United Church of Christ.[1]

1636	*Harvard University*	*Cambridge, Mass.*
1701	*Yale University*	*New Haven, Conn.*
1769	*Dartmouth College*	*Hanover, N.H.*
1793	*Williams College*	*Williamstown, Mass.*
1794	*Bowdoin College*	*Brunswick, Maine*
1800	*Middlebury College*	*Middlebury, Vt.*
1821	*Amherst College*	*Amherst, Mass.*
1829	Illinois College	Jacksonville, Ill.
1833	*Oberlin College*	*Oberlin, Ohio*
1835	*Marietta College*	*Marietta, Ohio*
1837	*Knox College**	*Galesburg, Ill.*
1837	*Mount Holyoke College*	*South Hadley, Mass.*
1844	Olivet College	Olivet, Mich.
1846	Beloit College*	Beloit, Wis.
1846	Grinnell College*	Grinnell, Iowa
1847	*Rockford College**	*Rockford, Ill.*
1849	Pacific University*	Forest Grove, Oreg.
1851	Ripon College*	Ripon, Wis.
1852	*Antioch University*	*Yellow Springs, Ohio*
1855	*Berea College*	*Berea, Ky.*
1859	*Whitman College*	*Walla Walla, Wash.*
1860	*Wheaton College*	*Wheaton, Ill.*
1862	LeMoyne-Owen College	Memphis, Tenn.
1865	*Atlanta University*	*Atlanta, Ga.*
1865	*Washburn University*	*Topeka, Kans.*
1866	Carleton College	Northfield, Minn.
1866	Fisk University	Nashville, Tenn.
1867	Talladega College	Talladega, Ala.
1867	*Howard University*	*Washington, D.C.*
1869	Dillard University	New Orleans, La.
1869	*Smith College*	*Northampton, Mass.*
1871	*Wellesley College*	*Wellesley, Mass.*
1871	Tougaloo University	Tougaloo, Miss.
1872	Doane College	Crete, Nebr.
1873	Drury College	Springfield, Mo.
1874	*Colorado College*	*Colorado Springs, Colo.*

*Originally joint Congregational-Presbyterian ventures under the Society for the Promotion of Collegiate and Theological Education at the West.

2

1875	Huston-Tillotson College	Austin, Tex.
1875	Westminster College of	
	Salt Lake City	Salt Lake City, Utah
1878	Rocky Mountain College[2]	Billings, Mont.
1885	*Rollins College*	*Winter Park, Fla.*
1887	*Pomona College*	*Claremont, Calif.*
1892	Northland College	Ashland, Wisc.
1897	*Piedmont College*	*Demorest, Ga.*
1926	*Scripps College*	*Claremont, Calif.*

Four of these colleges were founded for women only, and eight for black students. In their early determination to sponsor colleges in the West, along with the Presbyterians they cofounded such institutions as Wabash, Western Reserve, Wittenberg, and the College of California (now the University of California, Berkeley). Today some, like Berea and Wheaton, designate themselves as nondenominational Christian colleges. Washburn has become a state institution. Of the eighteen still listed by the United Church of Christ, many publish that affiliation (historically black institutions commonly have one or even two other church affiliations), while Grinnell, Ripon, and Carleton are silent, identifying themselves simply as private and independent. Beloit generally ignores the UCC claim and states that it is "nonsectarian but historically related to Congregationalism." Ambiguity continues.

Before going to our case studies, it is helpful to take note of some features of denominational history which figure in the shifting relationships between Congregationalists and their colleges. Robert Browne and Robert Harrison, influenced by the Reformed theology that predominated in Cambridge, England, in the later sixteenth century, preached around Norfolk a Christian faith without any institutional authority. All authority, they believed, was conferred by the Spirit; none by humans. Whoever had the inspiration for it was thereby authorized to be a preacher. They repudiated both the authority of bishops over churches and the religious authority exercised by the civil magistracy, which had recently been reaffirmed under the Elizabethan Settlement. Since they dissented even from most English Puritans, who still saw themselves as reformers working within the established church, their followers became known instead as Separatists, then as Independents. The cohesive force among Christians, they insisted, could not be any authority rooted in clerical ordination. It was the free covenant wrought by autonomous believers who had been saved by the Spirit. These believers would form a "gathered" (voluntary) assembly that would provide itself with a creed they could all agree upon, and officers to whom they willingly gave authority over themselves. Whatever collaborative activities (e.g., missions, publishing, ministerial training) drew the churches (they knew only "churches" in the plural, for there was no divinely intended entity higher than the local congregations) into joint activity were the creatures, not the masters, of the local churches. In their tradition, worship was much more extemporaneous, since it was the inspiration in the minister which directed it, without any prayer formulae. These ministers were to be supported by freewill offerings — once again, voluntariety was essential — not by tithes or taxes.

They were swiftly hunted out of England, and by the time they made their way from Holland to New England they had already begun to make adjustments in this polity. But its inspiration would remain: a disavowal of institutionalized authority. As numerous disillusioned Puritans lost hope in the established church and sailed to America, they would join their name and faith to the Independents of New England.

Congregational Instability

Congregational doctrine came from Calvin, through Cambridge and the Congregationalists' sojourn in Holland. It professed a God justly wrathful in the face of human sin. Their doctrine had it that we are all born helpless to do good, and capable only of sin. Thus all that we can deserve is eternal punishment. God, the offended and remote Creator, by his inscrutable choice predestines some — but only some — to gratuitous eternal life through the merits of his Son Jesus who died. That salvation occurs through a conversion from sin to grace that brings one from death into an undeserved life. The world being what it is, that life of grace is under constant threat of extinction from surrounding wickedness, and requires periodic revival, also undeserved. And though grace brings gladness, a faithful life is one of abstinence, struggle, and constant vigilance against backsliding.

There were, from the outset, some inevitable stresses in their polity. For one thing, Calvin did believe in authority within the church, and he succumbed to Genevan necessity and accepted superintendence by the civil powers. But the greatest test of Independency's capacity to survive came after many of them migrated to America. They were a people determined to have their freedom, but for themselves only. Their determination was to create a unitary commonwealth which was jointly moderated by both the churches and the civil officers. There was a sort of reciprocal control. On the one hand, no one but certified converts and church members could either vote or hold office in the colony, and the ministers looked closely over the shoulders of the civil authorities and offered from the pulpit strong and explicit guidance as to the will of God for public policy. The civil authorities, on the other hand, were expected to enforce the moral regime by fines and floggings, and the doctrinal regime by banishment or even execution. So, though founded on a fear of submerging God's people to civil regulation in matters spiritual, the Congregationalists (as they were soon called) created a matrix of reciprocal relations wherein the ascendance of the clergy could be, and one day was, reversed in favor of the civil officers. The dictatorship of the saints did not last.

What this produced was one of the more volatile Christian settlements in our history. With a constancy that some might almost be tempted to ascribe to the divine will, every generation threw up its challenge to the central doctrine of original depravity and moral helplessness. The early doctrine of visible sainthood prescribed that only persons who had authenticated a vehemently experiential conversion could present themselves for full membership in the church. They were henceforth subject to the public scrutiny and detailed discipline of the congregation. People began to postpone this step, with the result that membership was dwindling by the second and third generations. A "halfway covenant" was eventually enacted, whereby these members-in-waiting were admitted into an associate status, as were the baptized children of members. This implied a moral state somehow midway between depravity and regeneration, which no one was anxious to explore theoretically. When the issue was pressed, those who thought it a compromise went off to the Baptists and those who thought it too exclusionary found a home with the Presbyterians.

When the Great Awakening ensued in the eighteenth century, its more unrestrained devotees, the New Lights, reaffirmed that without this passage through fire there could be no human righteousness. To the Old Lights, whose experience and observation persuaded them that conversion was a gradual journey, that was all fanaticism. A New Divinity was slowly enunciated by disciples of Jonathan Edwards in the later years of the century, which took to itself from the Enlightenment a large entrée to individualism and compromised the communitarian accents of the original assemblies. And as the insistent doctrine of the wrathful God kept being renewed, an entire wing of the denomination finally rejected the central doctrinal tenet and saw Jesus, not as the willing victim of an irascible Father, but as a gentle and attractive human teacher whose message was what counted, not his status. It was evidently a heresy whose time had come, for Unitarians hemorrhaged forth from a wounded body Congregational.

These are but several of the incidents in which the traditional doctrine, when pressed home by the conservatives, provoked a reaction and then a departure from the ranks. But as the nineteenth century came into middle age, that stopped. Somehow the guardians of the old orthodoxy finally lost a vote of confidence, and when other, more gentle and compromising construals of the Calvinist formula were proposed, the denomination no longer drove them out or suppressed them.

Over the years when Congregational doctrine was subjected to challenge after challenge, so was Congregational polity. There were recurring needs — doctrinal, financial, disciplinary, missionary, educational, ministerial, ecumenical — that required a concerted effort for which there was no seat of initiative or authority. A succession of arrangements was devised that allowed corporate deliberation and definition and management without openly vacating the polity which had given the denomination its name. Ministers formed regional associations, and then began to do the ordaining and to issue the licenses for ministry. Synods met to enunciate creeds that were admittedly "unauthoritative," yet they clearly stated the orthodoxy to which one had better defer. Independent boards were organized to fund and administer missions, ministerial education, and the publication of educational materials and texts for worship. A national council was formed, to meet regularly and broker consensus. What was happening was the formation of an unacknowledged tradition and management and authority, for which no theoretical justification was ever worked out.

The Congregationalists had seemed to be a denomination with a clear self-understanding and a commitment to creating a society that would embody the kingdom of God on earth, and they repeatedly defended and refreshed its identity by pitching out all sorts of alien elements: antinomians, Anabaptists, Quakers, enthusiasts, Arminians, Socinians, Arians, Presbyterians, Anglicans, Separates, and Unitarians. The faithfully preserved tradition repeatedly needed to purge itself of various liberal alternatives because they were unfaithful to the authentic understanding of Christianity confessed throughout the ages.

But over the years they have come to be a very unstable fellowship: not for being narrow but for being broad. In 1865 a plenary convention met in Boston to draw up a confession of faith. They were riven by a pluralism that would not permit the adoption of any normative expression of belief. Eventually they accepted what is called the Burial Hill Declaration. It was framed in vague generalities and became the only formula that a representative gathering of American Congregationalists managed to accept in over two centuries. From 1865 onward there was no longer either the ground or the occasion for anyone to be excluded from church membership on grounds of deviant creed or polity. Successive statements of faith in 1913 and 1959 are evasive about God and silent on the old topics of depravity, salvation, and conversion. The denomination slowly shifted its focus of energy from individual salvation in Christ to the political reconstruction of the social order, its new orthodoxy.

All along, from the banishment of Anne Hutchinson in 1637 for antinomianism to the activist sociopolitical concerns of the United Church of Christ in the 1960s, there has been a custom of accommodation. The federal theology, the Cambridge Platform (1648), the Half-way Covenant (1662), the growth of ministerial associations (1650-1750), the Reforming Synod (1680), the Saybrook Platform (1708), the Northampton deviation (1729), the Great Awakening (1740), the Plan of Union (1801), the disestablishments in Connecticut (1818) and New Hampshire (1819) and Massachusetts (1833), the founding of the various functional societies (1810-), the New Haven Theology (1828), the emergence of Lyman Beecher, Horace Bushnell, Washington Gladden, et al. and the Social Gospel movement (1840s-), the Kansas City Statement (1913), and the Uniting Synod (1957) — all of these accommodations manifest the Congregational ability to adjust normative statements of doctrine and discipline and polity by redefining the grounds of unity. The unity thus defined, however, became thin in texture.

One can see in Congregational history the capacity for this community to accept — often, to welcome — innovation, provided it could be presented as continuity.[3] And though it might seem there was an early phase of firm orthodoxy followed by a tailing off into doctrinal indifference, the earlier period is the more fascinating because of its repeated inclination to modify, to blur, to compromise, yet without apparent awareness of change. It is that capacity to undergo substantial change — of priorities, predilections, and prescriptions — while claiming continuity which was in the background of the Congregationally related colleges we study here, both of which at roughly the same time unwittingly and peaceably disengaged themselves from the denomination.

When the Independents rejected any authority in the believing community as divinely guided to discern and define right belief, they did not thereby free the saints from the need to believe rightly, and to do so as a community. Their device for doing that was the covenantal creed which individuals had to agree upon in order to found a church. These creeds, which from time to time required revision in order to retain the necessary consensus to hold the congregation together, managed in a sort of common-law way to reflect some of the large shifts of doctrine and perspective the denomination experienced. But since they required consensus, and were intended to shape the minds of a people who were relatively well educated but not very proficient in theology, they were very compact, spare, and uncontentious.

What this produced was a "denomination": a fellowship of faith which aggregates individuals and churches but is not a church in itself. A denomination claims no corporate charism to deliberate upon the gospel or to groom a tradition of belief to keep it in communion with its foundational beginnings. Of course there were Congregational divines who worked at this, but since it was not a work in which the entire community had a stake, it rarely contributed to a coherent development of doctrine.

Thus the Congregationalists were not a very coherent theological community. Neither were they a community where intellectual discourse was continuously at work appraising the cultural institutions with a traditional Christian wisdom. From this followed several results which would affect their work in education. When controversy did arise, it was usually provoked by some strong or acerbic personality, and was usually engaged by others equally animated. The community would observe intently, but it would usually not participate. Secondly, there was much more appetite for theological controversy about moral than about doctrinal matters. This was perhaps inevitable in a community with so slight a capacity for corporate inquiry. Thirdly, and much to our point here, although this was the community which founded American colleges and the college model itself, it did not foster divinity in its curriculum, either as a subject in its own right or as a discipline meant to permeate intellectual inquiry.

As the nineteenth century saw a mounting and intransigent conflict between the orthodox Calvinist divines and their liberal rivals, the site for these encounters was usually the divinity schools or the journals, not the colleges. And for want of a shared tradition of such discourse, their liberal companions turned away from dialectic, since they and, as it turned out, so many of their fellow Congregationalists had lost interest in the axioms which the conservatives guarded but did not groom.

7

The religious elements at their colleges which seemed hale and wholesome were those of piety and moral discipline, not religious discourse. They drew their insights and their perspectives from the other sources that fed the minds of their age: political and philosophical and economic theory and advocacy. The longer their minds were no longer engaged by discourse proper to a believing community, the more likely and indeed inevitable it became that their moral convictions were more framed by the manners of their class, region, and political party than secured to the gospel by the tether of a lively faith tradition.

This interesting Congregational knack for a fellowship of unselfconscious accommodation is worthy of notice at the outset of our study. It would be a syndrome that helps explain the instability of their educational ventures, but one that repeatedly emerges in so many other stories of Christian colleges that could not be retained by their churches.

DARTMOUTH COLLEGE

There were nine American schools founded before the Revolution that would survive and reach collegiate status. Each was under the patronage of a clientele identified by religion and located within a geographic concentration of that denomination:

> Harvard, Yale, and Dartmouth served the Congregationalists of New England;
> William and Mary (1693), the Charity School (1740, later the University of Pennsylvania), and King's (1754, later Columbia) all served the Episcopalians in Virginia and the Middle Atlantic cities;
> The College of New Jersey (1746, later Princeton) and Queens (1766, later Rutgers) served the Presbyterians and Dutch Reformed of the Middle Atlantic colonies; and
> Rhode Island (1764, later Brown) served the Baptists who had gathered there.

Because the New England colonies included from the start a significant number of immigrants who arrived with degrees and had the broadest interest in sending their sons to college, and because they were the first to begin the work of higher education in America, the Puritans' colleges were the exemplary models which exerted a cultural and financial ascendancy over their neighbors to the south.

Dartmouth College was founded in 1769, the ninth and last of the colonial schools. Eleazar Wheelock, born in Connecticut in 1711, emerged at the age of eighteen from a Yale education, the first in a long line of Berkeley Scholars. After service as a lay preacher he was called and ordained by the Second Church of Lebanon, then the second-largest town in Connecticut. Congregational pastorates and their associated landholdings and income were protected by law, and young Wheelock could look forward to security and even comfort in his calling. But he

8

was a man called further. He was already a rousing preacher, but he allied himself with the New Lights, the Pietist enthusiasts who laid particular emphasis on a heart-swelling conversion experience as a prerequisite to both church membership and eternal salvation. Already in his twenties he had become a personal friend and protégé of George Whitefield, the perfervid English preacher who brought down fire on so many Americans in the Great Awakening. And already he had begun to attract the hostility of Bostonians like Charles Chauncy who thought of him as a deviant from Calvinism, influenced by a nest of Quakers, and extravagant in the commotions of his piety.[4]

Despite fairly comfortable circumstances, Wheelock had followed the practice of tutoring boys both to supplement his income and to do his share to prepare a new generation of learned preachers. A Mohican woman brought him her son for tutelage, and Samson Occom turned Wheelock's interest from his disappointingly torpid congregation to the prospect of educating and converting the Indians. His attention was directed mostly to the Iroquois federation, the Six Nations. He was not unaware that two British missionary groups were competing with one another to fund evangelical ventures such as this: the Society for the Propagation of the Gospel in Foreign Parts (Anglican) and the Society in Scotland for Propagating Christian Knowledge (Presbyterian). Wheelock recruited other Indian pupils with remarkably assimilated names like John Pumpshire, Jacob Woolley, and Joseph Brant, and although the Connecticut legislature refused to subsidize his evangelical project (probably to protect Yale from competition), the English and Scottish societies sent support. One local contributor, Joshua More, gave so generously that More's Charity School (soon misspelled as Moor's) became the name of the venture, and Wheelock counted first two, then five, then as many as twenty-two Native American scholars, all with their expenses paid from funds Wheelock managed to solicit here and there. The Indian War of 1763, however, drove off both scholars and scholarships. Rather than discouraging Wheelock, this provoked him to enlarge his hopes, and he announced a college "among the Pagans in America." At one point he pleaded with General Gage to spare fifteen to twenty "likely" Indian children from massacre so that he might be provided with a student body. But alongside these unrealistic hopes, Wheelock had noticed that there were still good numbers of white ("English") youngsters who could pay for their education, and he was happy to fill seats with them.

In 1765 a younger parson was sent off to Britain to solicit funds, along with Samson Occom, who had served as a missionary schoolteacher among his own people, then as an ordained minister (who was paid only one-eighth of what his white colleagues received). George Whitefield's endorsement gave them entrée in high circles: George III subscribed £200, and the Earl of Dartmouth, soon to be Secretary of State for the Colonies, served as chair for a supportive committee of noblemen and gentlemen in London. The Scots were approached as well, but the Americans thought it best not to let either their English friends (mostly evangelical Anglicans leaning toward the new Methodist movement) or the Scottish Presby-

9

terians know that their respective rivals were also being canvassed. The expedition lasted two years and yielded a trust of more than £11,000, an extraordinary success.

But all was not well in Moor's Charity School. Drunkenness among the Indian pupils, plus their seeming inability ever to move (or to be invited to move) beyond elementary to college studies, plus the fact that of the forty he had sent out to teach among their own people only twenty had remained at that task, plus the high-handedness of Wheelock's trusted son and agent Ralph, plus the Indians' preference for the less rigorous French Jesuits down from Canada, plus the relentless burden on Wheelock of securing funds to support the entire operation, gradually wrought a mutual disaffection between the Indians and their mentor. By 1769 the school was down to only three in number, and Wheelock was quietly persuaded that the Indians would never become a reliable missionary force for the conversion of their tribes. Yet to turn his back on them openly would incur a great loss. The £11,000 bearing interest in Britain proved a wondrous tonic to Eleazar Wheelock's educational energies, and he offered to move his school to any colony or province that would support his missionary effort.

A Welcome to New Hampshire

He sent out notices in every direction: Virginia, New York, Pennsylvania. But each already had a college to support. In 1768 John Wentworth, the royal Governor of the Province of New Hampshire, began negotiating with him. After adroit bargaining Wheelock came away with more than 22,000 acres of choice wooded land on the Connecticut River. He also won a royal charter under the governor's authority and seal. Lord Dartmouth was gratefully adopted as the college's new namesake, but Wheelock managed to fend off Wentworth's suggestion that the Bishop of London be included on the board of trustees. Wentworth, himself an Anglican, intended this as a gesture toward the English benefactors, but Wheelock said his Calvinist supporters on this side of the ocean would take it as an infringement by the Church of England by law established, which they had come to America to escape.

The charter, said to be the most liberal in the land, stipulated that eight of the twelve trustees be from New Hampshire. There was no requirement that any be clergy; to the contrary, a majority (seven) were required to be laity. The charter noted that Eleazar Wheelock's efforts had caused throngs of Indians to solicit education for their children and to welcome missionaries and schoolmasters in their midst. The Crown's express purpose was "to encourage the laudable and charitable design of spreading Christian Knowledge among the Savages of our American Wilderness and also that the best means of Education be established in our Province of New Hampshire." The only reference to religious affiliation was the injunction against "excluding any Person of any religious denomination whatsoever from free and equal liberty and advantage of Education or from any of the liberties and

privileges or immunities of the said College on account of their speculative sentiments in Religion and of his or their being of a religious profession different from
the said Trustees of the said Dartmouth College." Buried within the charter was
the crucial proviso which allowed that Indians need not be the exclusive beneficiaries of the new college, for "without the least impediment to the said design the
same School may be enlarged and improved to promote Learning among the
English, and be a means to supply a great number of Churches and Congregations
which are likely soon to be formed in that new Country with a learned and orthodox
Ministry . . ."[5]

The fiduciaries of the English fund, who had envisioned their moneys as the
source of scores of Samson Occoms, all britched and wigged in proper pulpits
strewn among the Oneida and Mohawk and Mohican settlements, quickly saw that
Wheelock meant to use their contributions to build himself another Harvard in the
howling wilderness of the North. Critics in Boston and elsewhere also noted that
the intrepid doctor's staff of professors and tutors, as also the Connecticut divines
among the trustees, were almost to a man composed of his family or their in-laws.

The trustees included the governor *ex officio,* three "churchmen" (Anglicans), and nine "Dissenters" (Congregationalists). All the New Hampshire college
graduates among them were Harvard men, and all those from Connecticut were
from Yale. Wheelock did not lack the adroitness required to induce a largely
Anglican group in London and Portsmouth (the provincial capital) to finance what
he never doubted would be a thoroughly Congregational enterprise. He was less
successful in persuading the Scots that he was not now in the pocket of the
Anglicans.

As the chill winter of 1771 took New Hampshire into its stiff embrace,
Wheelock summoned his entire establishment to make the trek from Connecticut
to what was at first a single rough log barn they erected in a clearing near Hanover.
In addition to his family there were thirty frostbitten students. Only three were
Indians. When the Six Nations decided no longer to send any of their children,
Wheelock looked to Canada for more, but learned that the English up there had
promised the Indians free exercise of their religion, and that they had become
"more zealous and bigoted Roman Catholicks than the French and Canadians they
live amongst."[6] By aggressive recruiting he raised the Indian enrollment to its peak
of twenty in 1775. Then the Revolution, which largely cast the Indians as allies or
at least suspect allies of the British, put their presence at Dartmouth in swift decline.
By 1785 there were only three, and after that none came for the remainder of the
century. Simultaneously the complement of white "English" pupils grew to nearly
one hundred. About two-thirds were fee paying; the others were charity students
on condition that they signed a commitment to work as missionaries among the
"pagans" after their departure. Of the 150 Indians who had studied under Eleazar
Wheelock, less than a handful progressed to the point of beginning college-level
studies. Some managed to become schoolteachers, but most lapsed into what their
mentors called dissolute lives (often involving alcohol), and almost all died young.

11

The original purpose of the Charity School was tacitly admitted to be a failure. Missions by the white graduates to Indian villages were discontinued, as was further recruitment of Indian students. Yet it was only on the still-asserted claim that Dartmouth was primarily devoted to the Native Americans that the English funds had continued to build and to maintain the college (Wheelock managed to possess himself of almost all of those capital funds just before Independence), and that the Continental Congress later made three grants to the college.

Critics of Dartmouth took sharp notice of the fact that Wheelock had allotted the choicest landholdings near the college to himself and to his remarkably extended and employed family. Nevertheless, the Wheelock energy managed to double the college's early grants to an eventual 44,000 acres. The enrollments went on increasing, reaching 160 in 1790. By then Dartmouth was graduating nearly twice as many students as either Harvard, Yale, or Princeton. And most of them were paying their own tuition.

All of this was founded on the work of a very doughty man. Eleazar Wheelock, who with mighty hand and outstretched arm created Dartmouth College *ex nihilo,* was appraised ambivalently by Ezra Stiles at Yale:

> Such a mixture of apparent Piety and Eminent Holiness, together with the love of Riches, Dominion & Family Aggrandizement is seldom seen. He was certainly as singular a Character as that of Ignatius Loyola. I was personally acquainted with him, & thought him a sincere Friend of the divine Emmanuel.[7]

Leon Richardson, the college historian, is more focused in his assessment:

> His most serious fault was an arbitrary and dictatorial point of view. His conception of an effective form of government for his undertakings was an autocracy, with himself in the role of a kindly but absolute despot. . . . With entire honesty, he regarded those who opposed him as guilty of a dereliction of the moral law. He had so convinced himself of the righteousness of his projects that he came to regard opposition to himself as opposition to the cause of Christ.[8]

In a word, Wheelock was not untypical of the founders of early American colleges.

During the latter years of the eighteenth century the largest number of students came up from Connecticut. Wheelock's Congregationalism was widely known to be of the New Light variety, nurtured by the Great Awakening, and there was much more sympathy in Connecticut for that religion with the faster heartbeat than there was in the intervening Massachusetts. Hanover, with a population of about twenty families when Dartmouth came into its midst, already had a church, organized as Presbyterian. Wheelock was not constitutionally capable of worshiping with any body over which he did not preside, so he convened a church at the college, also in the Presbyterian communion. In New Hampshire, like Connecticut but unlike Massachusetts, clergy and laity moved back and forth between these two denominations without much sense of having crossed guarded frontiers. The Presbyterian polity, which assigned autonomy somewhat more to the ministry than to the congregation, offered a means whereby Wheelock could maintain as much control over his church as over his college. In time he also gathered the area's clergy into a presbytery, which gave his leadership even wider play.

The state of religion on campus was hardly constant, as was true elsewhere through New England. In the year 1775, it was later recalled with pride, every single member of the graduating class was a "professor of religion." By 1798, however, religion had fallen into a slump: only a single senior that year could be found to profess a public commitment. Despite the charter's prohibition of denominational bias, both the board and the staff comprised all Congregationalists. Were all the students Congregationalists, or at least Calvinists? Apparently not. Philander Chase, '96, went on to become an Episcopal bishop. It may be that the Episcopalians were rather a diminished threat to the Calvinists after the Revolution. But other denominations did continue to be considered with ill-disguised animosity. Roswell Shurtleff, who would serve Dartmouth for years as the Phillips Professor of Theology, is the subject of this anecdote, which refers to the time when Congregationalists were being transmogrified into Unitarians throughout New England:

> Being once drawn into a theological discussion by a gentleman who wearied him by an advocacy of Unitarianism, [Shurtleff] finally inquired, "What have you read on the subject?" "Well, I have read Dr. Channing and I have read the Bible." "Oh," said the professor, "I see you have read both sides," and dropped the subject.[9]

One of the founder's tactics to retain unchallenged power was to secure from Governor Wentworth the right to appoint, by will, his successor this being congruent with his own sense of being more proprietor than president. Not surprisingly his choice fell upon his son John, who had made his career in the Continental Army. Eleazar died in 1779 when the college was but ten years old. The trustees' sense of filial piety to the old man made them swallow strong misgivings and accept the man who would be Dartmouth's most ill-starred president until their successors finally removed him from his offices as president, trustee, and professor in 1815. It was not immaterial to their decision that John Wheelock controlled his father's substantial inheritance and was available therefore to serve virtually without salary.

Enrollments continued to grow, the faculty expanded, and various buildings began to fill in the perimeter of the college green. It was, however, a time of many conflicts. John Wheelock had "inherited from his father an intense will, amounting to a spirit of domination, but . . . the narrowness of his spirit was not offset by scholarship or learning."[10] One of the issues that divided the college, and would eventually bring down its president, was the struggle over the college church.

John Wheelock eventually butted heads with his board, and with the Hanover townsfolk. The latter took the meetinghouse they had built away from him for a new Congregational church, and the former took away his presidency.[11] Wheelock appealed to the New Hampshire government, who amended the Dartmouth College Charter, designating it henceforth a university and putting its governance in politically appointed hands. In essence, they were expropriating Dartmouth to serve as the state university. Thus the struggle came to be seen as one between the trustees' college and Wheelock's university, Congregationalists against Presbyterians, Federalists against Democrats. The campus was claimed and used by rival student bodies, faculties, administrations, and boards. Wheelock, who, though in every way an authoritarian, had managed to persuade the most freethinking Democrats that he was a champion of freedom against rigid orthodoxy, at the same time alienated divines throughout the state, who saw the flood of godless liberal support for the university, and so the clergy arose with newfound interest to support the college. A lawsuit made its way from the state courts (which thoroughly sanctioned the state takeover) to the U.S. Supreme Court, where Dartmouth alumnus Daniel Webster's famous advocacy, a majority vote by six of seven justices, and a magisterial decision by John Marshall all combined to vindicate Dartmouth College and its trustees, and to assert that all charitable institutions became, by their charters, independent legal persons, not state enterprises, and that their charters, status, property, and governance could not be altered unilaterally by state action.

Religion on Campus

Dartmouth reverted, then, to being Congregational, as Eleazar Wheelock's establishment in Connecticut had been. Its shifts of allegiance both to and from Presbyterianism under the Wheelocks, *père et fils,* had been dislocations more of politics than of piety. The presidents who followed John were three Congregational ministers who left office, respectively, by an early death, an immediate nervous breakdown, and a swift return to the pastorate. Dartmouth settled into the pattern of life familiar to the New England colleges. Students were belled from their beds as soon as the seasonal light allowed, though never before 5:00 A.M. Prayers followed in chapel, followed by breakfast at 6:30. Study and recitations commenced at 8:00, lunchtime intervened at midday, and there was chapel again at 6:00 or as late as the light would permit, followed by tea.

The morning chapel was quite simple: an invocation, a Bible reading, and a prayer. Evening chapel included the same, plus a hymn sung by the Handel Society, and once a week a prepared oration by one of the seniors. The president presided, and in his absence the faculty took this duty in turn, one week at a time. On Saturdays the theological professor would present a Bible exercise, and on Sundays there were two services in the church besides the two chapels. There was a lot of time spent at prayer, if not always in prayer.

Dartmouth was thought to be the most conservative of the New England

14

colleges, but there were moments when she stood forth as willful. For instance, in 1825 when the ailing president was convalescing in the South, he and his wife engaged Edward Mitchell, a young black, as coachman and factotum. He returned and lived with them as family. When he applied to the college, he was admitted as a student by the faculty but then turned down by the trustees lest it offend some of the students. The students ardently caucused and argued on his behalf and prevailed on the board to reverse its decision. In the earliest days of Moor's School there had been some blacks among the students; after Mitchell they began to come with some regularity.

As early as 1827 a faculty report proposed a broad and spunky slate of reform. A minimum age would be set for admission (fourteen). Latin and Greek would be given a reduced share of the required courses, and then made altogether elective. "In reference particularly to the Greek language it is believed that this neither so much exercises the mind, nor increases knowledge nor assists conversation, except in the case of those who contemplate the profession of Divinity [an increasingly inconspicuous minority], as many other branches of study. To a very large portion of graduates Greek in a few years is entirely lost, and with it the time devoted to it at college, which might have been improved more usefully for purposes connected with their professions."[12] Most of the proposals were not accepted; Greek remained a required discipline.

The "biblical exercise" was a perennial drudge, and the students did prevail when it was made voluntary and shifted to Sunday afternoon. No one went, so it was again made compulsory. President Nathan Lord, who took office in 1828, admitted that the college had not been notably successful in religious studies. "The whole subject of Biblical instruction is one of no ordinary embarrassment, on which our theoretical reasonings are not always found to bear well and safely in their applications. Whether the Bible should be put on a level with the classics as a text book for study, whether it should be like other studies required of all indiscriminately, and to what extent and in what form it should be used for purposes of literary or moral instruction are all questions which benevolence will be more ready to answer than discretion."[13]

It was this Nathan Lord whose tenure at Dartmouth (1828-63) anchored a long period of administrative leadership that would see it through the greater part of the nineteenth century. Equally important was the presidency of Samuel Colcord Bartlett, who presided from 1877 to 1893. Both these men ended their presidencies by resignation under pressure, but between them they created an institution where Congregationalism was pervasive in its presence, yet had virtually no standing in the unimaginative intellectual life that was defensively preserved on the campus.

Lord, who had come to the presidency from a pastorate in Amherst, proved successful at fund-raising. He was also effective in bringing more students to the campus; in the early 1840s Dartmouth was still graduating more than all the other New England colleges except Yale.[14] But he ruled his college with firm convictions, and it is fair to see his character as a directive force in that formative period of

Dartmouth's development. His own grandson, John King Lord, a career professor at Dartmouth and its historian, is kindest in his judgment:

> Dr. Lord was a Puritan in character but not in conduct, in the intensity and assurance of his beliefs but not in his method of enforcing them, for he approached men by persuasion and not by coercion. His appeal was always first to the conscience, then to reason, rather than to reason first and conscience afterward, and as conscience was in his view only the individual witness to the truth of God, whose final expression was the Bible, he made the Bible the basis of every appeal to conscience and enforced it under a literal interpretation as a rule of life. From its teachings, as he believed them, he never swerved, no matter where they led him, and for thirty-five years with all the power he could command . . .[15]

Let one of his more radical rulings illustrate how Lord appealed to the consciences of his colleagues and students. He announced that Dartmouth would change to a "non-ambitious" system, eliminating all campus honors and academic distinctions. He argued

> that ambition and emulation are selfish principles, that they are consequently immoral & ought not to be appealed to in a private or public discipline, that tho' they exist naturally in man, they are not of Divine origin, but the product and evidence of an apostate & disordered mind; that the work of education should not be to stimulate & train, but, so far as possible, to eradicate them, & that education then only is moral or answers its proper design when it prevails over them & substitutes for them the disinterested virtue of Jesus Christ.[16]

Whatever the prophetic insight in Lord's message for the academic world, neither his argument nor his policy elicited much moral conviction. Eventually the faculty murmured that "some more efficient means of intellectual and moral excitement" had to be found to summon students from their inclination to mediocrity. Ralph Waldo Emerson was less indirect, and called it "an old granny system." Alumni groups marshaled explicit protests. All in vain; the president stood firm, and the board stood behind him.

One reason which might have persuaded the president to discontinue ranking students was the embarrassment Dartmouth encountered in its examinations. The ancient custom of having external examiners share in the assessment of student accomplishment had led the college to draw upon ministers in New Hampshire and Vermont. "Examiners, who, though besought 'to ask questions,' sat through successive examinations without apparent knowledge of a subject, or exhibited total ignorance of it, as when one examiner in German held his book upside down during the whole exercise, brought discredit upon the system and became themselves objects of ridicule."[17]

In the curriculum of instruction Lord conserved what was typical for colleges of the time. In 1860, a student in the course of his sixteen terms on campus would be required to take four courses bearing on religion:

[William] Paley's Natural Theology (Philosophy)
Evidences for Christianity
[Jonathan] Edwards on the Will
[Joseph] Butler's Analogy

Actually none of this presented theology as such; that was offered in the much-disliked biblical exercises given once a week by the Phillips Professor of Theology (whose chair would lie vacant for sixteen years during Lord's presidency). These four courses, which did not figure among the load-bearing elements of the curriculum, consisted for the most part in apologetics. But this was the standard program in antebellum Dartmouth's sister colleges.

Piety, Not Theology

It was piety, not religious learning, that sustained the college's religious identity. It was sustained first of all by the abounding treks to chapel and church. Student restiveness showed itself in various antics which, in themselves, constituted minor outbursts of youthful ennui. It ought to be remembered that in the middle 1850s less than a third of these students who were so regularly expected at worship were on record as being "professors of religion."[18] Eventually there were some adjustments of the prayer schedule (morning prayer was postponed until after breakfast in 1856; and in 1861 evening prayers disappeared), which were often imposed by a lack of clergy or faculty to preside, not by any deference to student tedium. Lest this all be taken as the indifference of distracted juveniles, one must know that from time to time the board of trustees stirred itself to remind the faculty that their presence in church would "exert a healthful moral influence" on their students.

The second support for college piety was a moral code that Lord dutifully enforced. Notably excluded were cards, dice, bowling, dancing, drinking "ardent spirits," and most activities on the Sabbath, including the use of the library.

Some were persuaded that anyone who was regular at church and chapel would make it through Dartmouth safely, no matter what his grades were. This surmise would combine well with other evidence that the piety, though strongly cultivated by the president and his board and probably most of the faculty (notably those in the arts, not those in the newer disciplines of science, medicine, and engineering), had a life of its own and was not amalgamated with the program of learning.

The charter so effectively defended by Webster had provided that no one should incur disadvantage at Dartmouth because of his denominational difference from the trustees or his "speculative sentiments in Religion." This same disposition was echoed in the will of Abiel Chandler, who left a generous legacy to Dartmouth to open a department or school of engineering:

> [F]irst and above all, I would enjoin in connection with the above branches, the careful inculcation of the principles of pure morality, piety and religion, without introducing topics of controversial theology, that the benefits of said department or school may be equally enjoyed by all religious denominations without distinction.[19]

Chandler was only expressing the conventional Pietist conviction that theological inquiry tended to be sectarian and divisive. No one had more evidence of this than the Congregationalists, whose original Puritan program comprised only a few points of doctrine, but those few were quite clear, severe, and separatist. What Chandler asked of Dartmouth was being provided in the typical American colleges of the time. But perhaps not in Dartmouth itself. There are several events in Lord's time that imply an abiding denominational animus on his part, and on that of the trustees. When, in 1847, the Phillips Chair was finally being filled once again after a long vacancy, they selected a Congregational pastor from Concord and attached to his appointment an unusual resolution:

> That the Board have made the appointment of a Professor of Theology in the belief that his religious sentiments are in accordance with the compend of Christian doctrine set forth in the Westminster Assembly of Divines [1643-49] in their Shorter Catechism, and that any material departure from that Platform is deemed by the Board a sufficient ground of removal from office.[20]

The college gave frequent assurances that it was free from sectarian control, but ever since it had re-allied itself with the Congregationalists back in 1815 its patronage and its loyalties had allied it with that denomination. The trustees were Congregationalists and were selected for their doctrinal reliability. Faculty prospects were vetted for their orthodoxy. Letters of recommendation for prospective faculty displayed a more elaborate inquiry into this qualification than any other.

There had been several harsh episodes involving faculty. Benjamin Hale, descended from a Puritan family but now a member and indeed an ordained minister of the Episcopal Church, was appointed professor of chemistry in 1827. He gathered some Episcopal students and a colleague for evening services on campus until he was forced to desist. He continued to hold services at home, however, and drew into his circle several Congregational neighbors whose pastor raised a bitter complaint about this harrying of his flock. Hale stood his ground, and the cry was then taken up by the regional Congregational ministers en masse. The board then moved to relieve itself of such reproach in 1835 by shuffling positions so that no professorship of chemistry any longer existed. The president lacked the nerve even to tell Hale that he had been effectively dismissed, and left town. Trustees let it out abroad that Hale had defaulted on his academic duties by inappropriate promotion of episcopacy. An exchange of published pamphlets blew the controversy onto the pages of the public press. Hale quickly left and became a successful president at Hobart College, and the professorship was swiftly reactivated. Critics of Dartmouth observed that it must now be forbidden to profess the faith of John Wentworth, the governor whose welcome had founded the college.

In 1849 Alpheus Crosby, professor of Greek, published a tract that sympathized with the Universalist doctrine that all people would somehow be given access to salvation. No more mortal attack was imaginable upon the Congregational missionary enterprise, which was animated by the tenet that unless converted to the gospel, all heathens must perish eternally. The board promptly asked for his resignation. Crosby replied that his positions on sectarian controversies were none of their business. Not wishing to be burnt twice by their own fervor, the board asked Lord to work things out quietly with Crosby, who in any case had been on the point of asking for early retirement.

The force of his character and the self-assurance of his convictions regularly served Nathan Lord to rally the support of his board in every controversy. Every controversy, that is, but the one which would bring him down. In his younger years Lord had shared the abolitionist sentiments of his fellow New England Congregationalists. But along the way he encountered the passage in Genesis whereby, as punishment for unfilial treatment of a drunken Noah by his son Ham, the sons of Ham were cursed and condemned to everlasting enslavement by the sons of his two more respectful brothers, Shem and Japheth. The text was justifying a Hebrew claim to rule their Canaanite neighbors, but Lord took it in the meaning assigned by the defenders of slavery: the sons of Ham were the Negroes, and this meant that slavery was a divinely imposed punishment and therefore could never be set aside as immoral. Once Lord got this bit between his teeth he began to publish tractates on the subject, first anonymously and then under his own name.[21] It was not slavery, he argued, but abolition that caused the Civil War. Slavery was "a providential order" accepted by the Law of Moses, Christ and his apostles, the fathers of the church, and common law. The Lord who decreed it might well bring it to an end in the millennium of his grace, but emancipation by human politics would abuse the divine authority of government and make life only worse for the former slaves. "What for should we reject the dictates of religion, the usages of civilized and Christian life, the claims of humanity, the providential enlargement of superior races, and doom, as we necessarily must, an inferior, imbecile, and dependent race, which God has committed to our trust, to a condition worse than slavery — to a lingering, miserable, and hopeless death?"[22]

Not every Congregationalist was as radically opposed to slavery as Ezra Stiles and Edward Beecher and Harriet Beecher Stowe, but Lord lived in the New England which stood foursquare behind the struggle for emancipation, and he served as the president of a college founded to serve what its founders saw as an inferior and dependent race — a college which saw 652 of its students and alumni off to the Union Army (a larger percentage, it was claimed, than from any other college in the North). His dogged exegesis of Genesis 9 was not the first time he had spun a biblical verse or phrase into a cosmic policy, but now he was flying in the face of most of his colleagues in the New England clergy, and most of his trustees. At their first annual board meeting following the Emancipation Proclamation they acknowledged with open satisfaction the resolution by the local Congregational clergy that Dartmouth find itself a new president, and then passed a sonorous resolution of their own, invoking divine support "that American slavery, with all its sin and shame, and the alienations, jealousies, and hostilities between the people of different sections, of which it has been the fruitful source, may find its merited doom in the consequence of the war which it has evoked."[23] The president left the room forthwith and returned with his letter of resignation, all the while denying their right to impose any religious, ethical, or political test upon any officer of the college.

Narrow Congregationalism versus Enlightening Christianity

Some of these particulars of Nathan Lord's lengthy and formative leadership at Dartmouth serve to illustrate the way in which his presidency had consistently invoked orthodox Congregationalism in support of an educational policy wherein fidelity to tradition was rarely the sponsor and often the adversary of enlightened inquiry.

Lord was followed by Asa Dodge Smith, a career pastor, who eventually mended the college's relations with the clergy. His inaugural largely ignored the recent circumstances which had led to his election. Instead, he spoke rather vaguely but unusually of how religion integrated college work:

> The College . . . should be distinctly and eminently *Christian*. Not in the narrow, sectarian sense — that be far from us — but in the broadest evangelical view. . . . Christianity is the great unity. . . . Let the studies which we call moral, have all a Christian baptism; and, with all our getting, let us not stop short of the cardinal points of our most holy faith. Let the Will be still investigated, not as a brute force, or in a merely intellectual light, but in those high spiritual aspects in which our great New England metaphysician delighted to present it. Let Butler, with his curious trestle-work of analogy, bridge, to the forming mind, the chasm between natural and revealed religion. Let the Christian Evidences be fully unfolded. We can hardly dispense with them in an age, when, by means of Westminster Reviews, and other subtle organs of infidelity, the old mode of assault being abandoned, a sapping and mining process is continually going forward. Let Ethical Science, — embracing in its wide sweep, the Economy of Private Life, the Philosophy of Government, and Law, which "hath its seat in the bosom of God," — be all bathed in the light of Calvary.[24]

20

Here the claim is openly made that the standard authors studied in religion-related courses — Edwards, Butler, and Paley — served as an intellectual tethering post for the other disciplines which, left to roam by themselves, would all decamp in various directions. It is not clear how real a claim it was.

Dartmouth suffered the same decline all the colleges felt after the Civil War, and Smith's tenure was not and probably could not be one of academic ascent. Student morality was providentially served by a police raid that closed the popular Frary's Bar. But a new gymnasium in 1867 had an entire floor devoted to bowling, explicitly forbidden back in 1835: "an indication of the changed sentiment of the times," observes the chronicler.[25] Two years later Judge Richard Fletcher of Boston left the college a handsome legacy, $10,000 of which was to finance a biennial prize for a student essay that would "counteract the worldly influences that draw professed Christians into fatal conformity with the world." After several decades of fatally dreary submissions, the college decided to go to court and ask to have the terms of the bequest set aside.[26]

The college pastor was often absent, and the faculty agreed to stand in for him at Sunday services but declined to come in both mornings and afternoons. Morning services were thus discontinued (permanently, it turned out), and to rescue the Sabbath from inevitable student abuse the afternoon service began to feature a brief address from the president.

Bartlett Discredits Academic and Religious Orthodoxy

In 1877 Smith was succeeded by Samuel Colcord Bartlett, whose presidency, ending in 1893, in so many ways closed an age that Nathan Lord had commenced. Bartlett had begun as a pastor but then had been an educator at the college and finally at the seminary level. He had served as a principal speaker at the college's centennial in 1869, and spoke on Dartmouth's relations to the Christian religion. He went right to the point: whatever the college's contributions to statesmanship, jurisprudence, literature, science, medicine, military service, and even education, all this was subservient to its success in bringing men to respect religion and its ordinances. Many of Dartmouth's graduates had gone into ministry or missions: in the early years, always a majority and sometimes as many as five-sixths; but a good fourth of all graduates up to the present. Dartmouth was proud, too, that its long line of permanent faculty contained "no name of an irreligious or even of a non-religious man."

The education there was at once evangelical and catholic. "Conducted chiefly by members of the Congregational communion, it has never protruded its distinctive tenets on its students. The young man has always felt the steady pressure of a religious but never a sectarian hand. It has sent forth two eminent prelates and scores of presbyters of the Episcopal Church. It has educated the educators of the Presbyterian, Baptist, and Freewill Baptist ministry, and its sons have abundantly passed over from the polity of their fathers to other connections . . ." (Later in his talk he spoke of several unfortunate deviations by alumni into Mormonism and Deism, and of one ardent reformer who had called the American churches a "brotherhood of thieves," yet it was "marvelous how few such grapes of gall hung from this goodly vine.") The reason Dartmouth could engender a widely acceptable Christianity was that it avoided overconcern for doctrinal inquiry, which could always be divisive, and concentrated its piety instead on a moral program:

> The influence of the College in religion has also been regulative and conservative. As in its charter, so in its creed, it has stood for the ancient landmarks, and its motion has been chiefly beside the old paths. . . . The moral atmosphere of the College has been eminently — shall I not say permanently — healthy. For a lad far away from his home, there has been, I believe there is, no safer place. Law and order and innocence have reigned. . . . Some of us have seen the reckless and even the profane and profligate here brought to the Cross. A wholesome influence has clung to the great body of those who have not yielded thus. They have largely become respecters if not supporters, of religion.[27]

Bartlett stated upon arrival as president that his intellectual hopes for Dartmouth were conservative. Though the campus now included several schools of professional studies, the central college would follow the English example by inculcating "the exact and exhaustive mastery of certain limited sections of knowledge and thought, as the gymnastic for all other spheres and toils." The central discipline of a liberal education remained the same:

> that great branch of study for which, though often severely assailed because unwisely defended or inadequately pursued, the revised and deliberate judgment of the ablest and wisest men can find no fair substitute, — the study of the classic tongues. Grant that it may be, and often is, mechanically or pedantically pursued. Yet when rightly prosecuted, its benefits are wide, deep, and continuous, more than one can easily set forth — and they range through the whole scale, rising with the gradual expansion of the mind. It comprises subtle distinctions, close analysis, broad generalization, and that balancing of evidence which is the basis of all moral reasoning; it tracks the countless shadings of human thought, and their incarnation in the growths of speech, and seizes, in Comparative Philology, the universal affinities of the race; it passes in incessant review the stores of the mother tongue; it furnishes the constant clew to the meaning of the vernacular, a basis for the easy study of modern European languages, and a key to the terminology of science and art; it familiarizes intimately with many of the most remarkable monuments of genius and culture; and it imbues with the history, life, and thought which have prompted, shaped, and permeated all that is notable in the intellectual achievements of two thousand years, and binds together the whole Republic of Letters.[28]

22

It is instructive to hear Bartlett out at blustery length, for in 1877 this was not the direction in which the universities or the leading colleges were moving. Nor was it even a valid description of what was going on at Dartmouth. The principal mode of formal teaching remained the recitation, wherein students on cue from the professor were to repeat back almost verbatim what they had ingested from their textbook or from the professor's lecture. The college library collection was comprised mostly of textbooks, rather than primary sources. In Lord's time the college did not yet even possess, in their original languages or in translation, many of the documents included in the syllabus. The collection was skimpy and largely uncatalogued, and allowed of no direct student access. Just three years before Bartlett arrived, the book collections of the several campus literary societies, purchased by the students over the years with their own contributions, and significantly richer in intellectual depth and breadth of inquiry, had been amalgamated into the college library.[29] Dartmouth, when Bartlett arrived, had neither the resources nor the practice of offering a liberal education in the ancient languages that delivered what its new president described.

Besides his manifest academic conservatism, Bartlett also saw the educational project as surrounded by forces of subversion. There were the obvious contemporary critics of Christianity: David Hume, David Friedrich Strauss, Auguste Comte, John Tyndall, Thomas Henry Huxley, Joseph Ernest Renan, Ernst Häckel, and their godless ilk. Closer to home there were dangerous writers indiscriminately willing to classify Catholicism, Islam, superstition, malignant passion, obstinate prejudice, "and what not" under the heading of "religion."[30]

Bartlett's years on campus were not peaceful. He had accepted the presidency without being informed that the college labored under $125,000 of accumulated debt. His labors to retire that were arduous and largely successful. Also, after years of waning enrollment he saw it grow from 240 to 423 during his term of service. Understandably he saw his task as setting the house in order. In a style that was rancorous, not entirely honest, and not at all diplomatic, he warmed to that task. He set out to curb what he saw as a wanton and costly independence of the professional schools: the Medical School, the Chandler School of Science and the Arts, the Thayer School of Civil Engineering, and the New Hampshire College of Agriculture and the Mechanic Arts (which Dartmouth administered on behalf of the state). He lectured them on the inferiority of their disciplines to the liberal arts, and they artfully resisted his supervision. He also sat lightly to the opinions of his antagonized faculty on prospective appointments. He turned the practices of student discipline in a more rigorous and confrontational direction. The year of his arrival scholars were required to take a pledge forswearing alcohol, tobacco, dancing, and billiards. The students objected to compulsory chapel services, demanded the replacement of a relentlessly dull pastor, and complained that the biblical exercises were deadening. He waved aside various alumni attempts to intervene, and to have elected representation on the board of trustees.

In 1876 the board did promise, for the next three board elections, to canvass the alumni individually for candidates and "in all probability" to elect one of the persons most highly recommended. The alumni considered this an unsatisfactory response.

By 1880-81 the trustees had received formal requests from faculty, students, and alumni to remove the president. The story had a vigorous life of its own in the press, and eventually both Bartlett and his accusers demanded public hearings. Hearings they had, in what was known as the Dartmouth Trial (not to be confused with the earlier Dartmouth College Case), and lengthy depositions and interrogations were held, and transcribed by court reporters. In the event, the board simply admonished the president to live more peaceably with his constituencies, and left him in office.

Bartlett stood forth as an articulate leader of the conservative wing of the Congregationalists, and he had some supporters on his faculty and his board who were more staunchly conservative than he was. On one occasion, for example, some faculty went around him to the trustees to block the appointment of a nominee for being Episcopalian. But it was Bartlett who, in public view, usually stood for all that resisted liberalization in Congregationalism. His stubborn and reactionary behavior as an administrator seemed all of a piece with his unbending religious orthodoxy.

To see how this came across to the college community, one may contrast his account of Dartmouth's calling with that of Alonzo H. Quint, a minister and veteran Congregational editor and a college trustee. Both had occasion to speak to the same subject at the June exercises in 1885 and 1886. Dartmouth, according to Quint, had been chartered to "spread the knowledge of the great Redeemer," but her "spirit must be broad, unsectarian, not dogmatic in any sense." Bartlett, with clear hostility toward the cultured despisers of the church, and with disdainful allusions to other campuses which were defecting from their Puritan origins, called for "the arrest and reversal of the secularizing tendency" which he saw manifest in the doctrinal indifference in American intellectual life. Quint, in his account of how religion should actually infuse the curriculum, gives one of the few descriptions that concretely describes how religious sophistication might be needed for accomplishment in other disciplines:

> The facts of moral and spiritual life challenge [the student's] attention as strongly as facts of physical science. Is one well educated who is ignorant of them? . . .
>
> These facts have entered into the life of the world. They have necessitated and made philosophies. They have thereby, — for ideas conquer, not guns, — made history. What student would he be, who studies only the pikes with which Cromwell's men swept the royal soldiery over the cliffs at Dunbar, and not study the men who believed they were chosen of God to use those pikes? There are histories of civilization; but a history of civilization which omits the hypothesis of human, organic, sin, is a failure. There are plans of explanation which make

24

characteristics of races follow mountain ranges; but the plan which does not study the religious life which imbues the drifting emigrations, is idle. There are political economies, but the theory of one which forgets the nature of a race, and the remedies for a fallen and degraded life by a spiritual power, has lost an essential element in his calculations. There are theories of government; but one which defies the laws of God or, repentant, has not learned that "without the shedding of blood there is no remission of sin," awakens to the truth only in the sound of shotted guns. History is full of it. Philosophies are filled with it. Literature embodies it. Art takes from it its saints, and the Mother and Child are its inspiration. Because God is all in all.

Quint is learned, but no scholar. Yet he attempts to describe a Christian commitment that works within the actual intellectual inquiry of the college. Bartlett, who is a scholar, is preoccupied about quite other realities when he propounds what religion must do in the college. It must be a Christianity actively defended in the polity of the trustees, energetically and loyally inculcated by a faculty free of atheists or critics ("If that is narrowness or bigotry, then make the most of it"), and a discipline that guides and controls the deportment of the students. Quint speaks as if there were little opposition, and Bartlett sees it all around him.[31] And for Bartlett it is eternal damnation that is at stake, for in his classically Puritan theology every person who fails to enter covenant with Christ, whether through ignorance or intellectual pride or dissolute living or apostasy, is subject to the wrath of God and his unquenchable fire.[32]

Bartlett saw Dartmouth College at serious risk, from cultural hostility without and naïveté within. A secure maintenance of control was essential to her survival, under direct threat by an increasingly well-organized and strident demand by the Dartmouth alumni for the power to elect the college trustees. It was not simply that the alumni had thrice formally demanded his ouster (one year the senior class did the same). It was his immovable conviction that the alumni would definitively destroy Dartmouth's fidelity to her religious calling. But finally, in 1891, the board gave way and agreed that if the alumni would nominate candidates for five of their twelve positions as they came vacant, the trustees would make their elections from those nominees. Bartlett saw that it was all over, and in 1892 he submitted his resignation.

During Bartlett's time of travail at Dartmouth, there were comparable revolts against the presidents on six other New England campuses: Middlebury, Williams, Union, Hamilton, Wesleyan, and Amherst. A large part of the intentional resistance by students was their claim for freedom in their extracurricular activities. Bartlett and his fellow presidents "all stirred up frantic dissent," George Peterson believes, "because they wished to undo liberal practices already in effect, annul independence already granted, or re-instate a religion already dead . . ." After peace had been restored, "evangelical religion had been replaced by a more gentle, more rational, and more socially minded Christianity."[33]

The removal of Samuel Bartlett both closed and discredited a long period of Congregational dominance at Dartmouth. He was followed by William Jewett Tucker, who from then till now has been hailed as the creator of the New Dartmouth, the greatest president the college has ever enjoyed. As we shall see, the praise is not overblown: Tucker was almost too good to be true. But the almost total repudiation of the Congregational conservatives made it smoothly possible for him to guide the college into a new religious liaison, with eventual effects quite beyond anything he is likely to have intended.

Tucker, the Modernist, Arrives

Tucker came to Dartmouth in 1893 from Andover Seminary, which had been a battleground for the Congregationalists. The school owed its beginnings to quarrels within the denomination. By the time Eleazar and John Wheelock were engaged in the struggle to create Dartmouth, the Calvinists had fallen into three camps. The Old Calvinists were traditional followers of New England Puritanism, but in a more amiable and bourgeois fashion than the first colonists. The Westminster Confession of the Presbyterians was their rule of faith. They came to be called the Old Lights. The New Lights, descendants of the Great Awakening, were called Hopkinsians after Samuel Hopkins, a disciple and interpreter of Jonathan Edwards. They preferred to call themselves Consistent Calvinists, but behind their back were known as hyper-Calvinists. They were inclined to pay more attention to matters of doctrine, by comparison with the Old Lights, whose preoccupation was morality.

Old Calvinists and Hopkinsians did not get on very well, except in the presence of the third party, the Liberals, who spoke irresponsibly of God as benevolent and of humans as capable of rational and perhaps even moral behavior. They tended to drift into Unitarianism, and when in 1805 Henry Ware, a Unitarian, was elected to the Hollis Professorship of Divinity at Harvard, the country's oldest endowed chair, the Old Calvinists from Harvard and the Hopkinsians from Yale rivaled one another in their disgust. It was clear that the colleges were too polluted for the training of orthodox clergy, and they began to plan the opening of a seminary. Or, to be more precise, seminaries, for they could not imagine sharing such a trust. The Old Calvinists had chosen Andover, Massachusetts, for their school, in association with the well-established Phillips Academy. The Hopkinsians were planning their school for Newburyport, less than twenty miles away. A generous expenditure of diplomacy, determination, and Calvinist dollars finally led to a legal but very wary union. Its instability was manifest in the simple fact that the institution was defined by a bicameral form of governance; a complex documentation of constitution, associate statutes, and rules which at the outset comprised 140 articles; and a creed containing 36 unalterable articles defining "the fundamental and distinguishing doctrines of the Gospel" to which every professor was obliged to subscribe at five-year intervals. Every professor was to be "a Master of Arts, of the Protestant Reformed Religion, an ordained Minister of the Congregational or Presbyterian denomination, and shall sustain the character of a discreet, honest, learned, and devout Christian." But the Andover Creed made clear that these nervous allies were better defined by all they were against. For instance:

> 33. I will maintain and inculcate the Christian faith, as expressed in the Creed, by me now repeated, together with all the other doctrines and duties of our holy religion, so far as may appertain to my office, according to the best light God shall give me, and in opposition, not only to Atheists and Infidels, but to Jews, Papists, Mahometans, Arians, Pelagians, Antinomians, Arminians, Socinians, Sabellians, Unitarians, and Universalists, and to all heresies and errors, antient or modern, which may be opposed to the Gospel of Christ, or hazardous to the souls of men.[34]

Andover Seminary quickly secured the patronage of the wealthy families of Calvinist New England and acquired a campus, and an endowment that surpassed what most colleges then had.

Three-quarters of a century later, the Liberals had become ever more influential in Congregationalist pulpits and publications, and Andover stood against them, now with a united faculty and ethos. As far as Andover was concerned, the issue was theological. The very embodiment of orthodoxy at the time was Edwards A. Park, who would conclude forty-five years on the faculty in 1881. He had been a colleague of all but two of the professors who had ever taught at Andover, and he saw the Liberals preparing to ravish his seminary. Parks was a precise thinker, and he laid out the four points at issue, as construed by the Orthodox and the Liberals (whom he called "the New Departure"). It is necessary to understand this in order to know who was contending for control of Andover, and only a few years later, of Dartmouth.[35]

The Orthodox	The Liberals
1. The Bible, in all its religious and moral teachings, is entirely trustworthy.	1. We are not authorized to confide in all the biblical teachings; even in all which relate to religion and morality.
2. All the moral actions of every man, before he is converted by the Divine Spirit, are opposed to the divine law, and are sinful.	2. The moral actions of some unrenewed men are sometimes conformed to the divine law, and are holy; even if they are not holy, they may not be sinful in such sense or degree that they can justly or fairly be punished forever.

3. The Son of God took upon himself the office of High Priest, and offered his blood as a sacrifice for all men; his sacrificial pains and death were inflicted by his Father, were representative of the penalty which the Father had threatened to men, were substituted by the Father for the actual punishment of believers, were equivalent to that punishment in honoring and vindicating the Father's holiness, distributive justice, and law; were needed, first of all, on God's account and in order that he may forgive the sins of the penitent; and accordingly the crucifixion of the Lamb of God, and the sufferings preparatory to it, and implied in it, are the sole and exclusive ground on which the penitent are saved; and therefore the grace of Christ, as manifested in his sacrificial pains, is the brightest of all his glories.

3. The atonement of our Lord consists, not mainly in his dying, but mainly in his holy living. Also: The pains of Christ were not *designed* mainly, if at all, to vindicate and honor the retributive justice and the holiness of the supreme Lawgiver. They were not inflicted by the Father as the punishment the law had threatened. The brightest glory of our Lord does not consist in his willingly enduring the pains of the Cross; but it consists in his incarnate personality as distinct from the shedding of his blood, in the person of the God-man as our king. . . .

4. The present state is the only state of probation; the future life is a state, not of probation, but of punishment: the punishment of incorrigible transgressors begins as soon as they die, and continues forever.

4. The future life is not, or perhaps is not, a state in which probation is closed. If men die impenitent, they will not, or perhaps will not, be punished forever.[36]

William Jewett Tucker, a Most Agreeable New Light

In 1881 Park was retired, and when the Liberals came over the walls in the twinkling of an eye, William Jewett Tucker was among them. After finding freedom, stimulus, and personal responsibility at Dartmouth, he had chosen ministry for his career. His call, he admits, "lacked some of the usual motives. But it took account of certain moral and spiritual values which were not then emphasized in the creeds and which had little recognition within the sphere of organized religion. It was a call, though imperfectly apprehended, to that larger ministry which was soon to find its place within the scope of modern Christianity."[37]

Ordained as a Congregationalist in 1867, Tucker ministered to the same church in Manchester that Bartlett had earlier served. Soon he accepted a call to an elegant Presbyterian congregation, the Madison Square Church in Manhattan. In both Manchester and New York his congregations gathered in the people of privilege, but during these incumbencies Tucker became intensely aware of the working class that by now had little presence in Congregational pews. He noticed that churches tended to align themselves with class, but Tucker was moved by the justice denied to the working people, especially in their struggle for collective bargaining. The earlier Protestant social movement, he observed, had been grounded in charity, whereas the social forces in the secular movement were dedicated to claiming economic justice. That was perhaps the agenda the Christians should be serving. He determined to educate himself in social economics, and he did.

Also, his reflections on the Civil War led him to conclude that Puritanism had spent most of its prophetic energy in the abolition movement and that his people had thereby fixed their attitude in a stout defense of individualism. But the injustices wrought in America by individualism, especially in the industrial sphere, required a moral energy that was less individualistic and more inclined toward the general welfare. Thus, when the Social Gospel movement arose in the latter years of the century, he was a ready and enthusiastic supporter.

But the most significant change that came upon him in his years of ministry before going back to Dartmouth was theological. Frederick Robertson, little known in America, was an Anglican divine who had died in 1853 at the age of thirty-seven. Tucker found, through Robertson's published life and letters, a mentor who would profoundly dislocate him as a Congregationalist. In particular, Robertson directly discredited those four pillars of the traditional Puritan faith: the sufficiency of Scripture, total depravity, atonement, and future punishment.

As for the Bible, he believed it was inspired but not dictated: "It is the word of God, — the words of man: as the former, perfect; as the latter, imperfect. God the Spirit, as a Sanctifier, does not produce absolute perfection of human character; God the Spirit, as an Inspirer, does not produce absolute perfection of human knowledge."[38] He regarded bibliolatry as "pernicious, dangerous to true views of God and His revelation to the human race, and the cause of much bitter Protestant Popery, or claims to infallibility of interpretation."[39]

Total depravity had no place in Robertson's view. He noted that Peter had baptized the centurion Cornelius because, while still an unconverted Gentile, he already possessed the Spirit. One of his key pastoral teachings was that baptism does not make a person a child of God; it is the authoritative and symbolic revelation that he or she is already, by dint of creation, God's child. Christians must see all people as God's own, and therefore their brothers and sisters: Greeks and Jews; barbarians and Samaritans; aliens, heretics, and harlots.[40]

Atonement, then, would look quite different. Robertson insists that we are always in God's hand: never hated, always loved. That Christ or any other human was ever the object of the wrath of God, he argues, is a groundless belief. To be a "child of wrath" before conversion means, not that God is hostile, but that the person has not yet come to consciousness of his or her being cherished, and redirected his or her life accordingly.[41] The Evangelicals and Dissenters "make two Gods, a loving one and an angry one, — the former saving from the latter." The medieval Catholics had likewise portrayed anger and love, though resident in different personalities; they used Jesus and Mary instead of the Father and Jesus. Both traditions go astray in the ways they reconcile mercy and justice; the Evangelical scheme Robertson considers to be "the poorest effort ever made by false metaphysics."[42]

Robertson was never a Universalist, but he did admit that everlasting punishment was a doctrine he would happily have disallowed if only he could find grounds to do so.[43] Yet his account of the divine benevolence differed so entirely from the conventional Calvinist understanding that the prospect of a postmortem "second chance" did not much occupy his imagination.

Robertson saw himself flanked on the left by Unitarians, Dissenters, and Evangelicals, while to the right were the Tractarians and the Catholics. And all of them manifested much mutual and disagreeable rancor. He concluded: "I am forced to hope that there is more inclusiveness in the Love of God than in the bitter orthodoxy of sects and churches."[44]

> We do not trust God; we trust ourselves. We do not believe that he seeks us; we fancy we have to seek Him. We are anxious to know *all about* God, and meanwhile we never think of knowing *God*. God, instead of religion, and much more, God, instead of theology, is what we need to believe in.[45]

The truth, he thought, is like poetry: more to be felt than reasoned out or proved. As Robertson's editor says, faith rested "ultimately, not on the authority of the Bible or the church, but on that witness of God's Spirit in the heart of man which is to be realized, not through the cultivation of the understanding, but by the loving obedience of the heart."[46] That, coupled with a requisite largeness of heart, would lead Christians to see that the polar contraries expressed in some of the classical doctrinal quarrels might, if examined together, convey an underlying truth. The Protestant teaching, for instance, is that the sacrifice of Christ was offered once and for all. The Catholic teaching is that it is also offered daily. The Catholics are right, that it is repeated daily, in a spiritual manner, in the hearts of all faithful people; but they have got it muddled by thinking that this occurs only in the Mass. Likewise, Catholics are right that there is an apostolic succession, but they mistakenly associate it with a laying on of hands. "It is not a line of priests; it is a succession of prophets."[47]

Robertson had been accused of latitudinarianism, a distaste for any well-defined belief. He denied this, and also that he was offering another *via media*.[48] The truth, he insisted, was to be found by uniting two contradictory propositions, not by forging some compromise between them. The paradoxical result, at least in his hands, was not a generalization in some reductive terms, but a pastorally guided

30

insight that was friendly to the sensibilities of people on either extreme. Thus he, an Anglican, could write knowingly and appreciatively of American Calvinists across the spectrum who would not themselves have made common cause: Jonathan Edwards, Horace Bushnell, Theodore Parker, and William Ellery Channing.

What makes Frederick Robertson worth our while is his difference from the American who was so attracted by him. Robertson was a Pietist, but the faith-vision Tucker drew from him was highly unstable, and in his hands was degraded into something that the controversial parson who had served the working classes of Brighton would have disavowed.[49] Robertson was exemplary in the sensible way in which he combined the new critical studies of Scripture and a devout and meditative spiritual reading of the Bible, and elaborated an exegesis that was at once academically learned and pastorally nourishing. But Tucker admired so many scholars that Bartlett up at Dartmouth had reviled — Strauss, Darwin, Huxley, Renan — and drifted away from the exposition of Scripture rather than exegeting it in a newly critical yet devout way. His addresses would conventionally begin with a two-line quotation that he would pick up somehow as an aphorism in the course of his remarks, so that the Bible served him more as a source of quotations than as one of doctrine. And while the "underlying truths" that Robertson would extract appreciatively from such opposing sources would be identifiably Christian, Tucker's discourse inclined more to manners and morals without much overt or essential element of faith.

It should be noted that in a community raised on Jonathan Edwards's "Sinners in the Hands of an Angry God" and Dwight L. Moody's "Whatsoever a man soweth that shall he also reap" and hardened by the tough doctrine of Edwards Park and his outgoing regime, for a Congregationalist who was freed, as Tucker so providentially was by Robertson, from a fixation on the divine wrath, from a compulsion to elaborate explicit dogmatic formulations, and from disdain for all Christians beyond the Calvinist palisade, the lighter touch would feel like a liberating improvement. But as such changes often are, this one somehow caused the man who would shortly become Dartmouth's most eloquent and gracious president to be ineffective in passing on religious conviction. Robertson's integrated and engaging doctrine never grafted onto Tucker's Congregational stock. Paradoxically Tucker took it as his pretext to become a modernist. He was an especially instructive example of how a Pietistic Congregationalism, in one generation, began to evaporate as an intellectual endeavor. The Old Lights had flickered and guttered a long while as they burned down; the New Lights, especially on the traditionally Congregational campuses, were simply snuffed out.

Andover gave Tucker thirteen years mostly crowded with strife. Eventually the conservative forces in the denomination targeted the five liberal members of the faculty who edited the *Andover Review,* and the Board of Visitors arraigned them with formal charges of heresy. Their principal delict, especially in the eyes of the denomination's mission board, was to suggest that God might provide otherwise for the salvation of those who never heard the gospel. The universal and unavoidable perdition of the heathen, they insisted, was the necessary basis for missions.[50] The heresy trial, with its various stages of formal review involving the Supreme Court of Massachusetts, endured for six years, after which all charges were finally dismissed.[51] After becoming the consensus choice for president by trustees, faculty, and alumni in 1892, Tucker declined again out of loyalty to his seminary colleagues, whose destiny was still under a cloud; only some months later, after the trial was over, did he accept.

Dartmouth was large-spirited toward Samuel Bartlett after he had finally been eased out of the presidency. At the inauguration of his successor, Bartlett was invited to offer the opening prayer, and his invocation left the Almighty in no doubt as to the protection that would be needed under the new and probably impious management:

> Thou art our God and our fathers' God, and thou, our Lord and Saviour Jesus Christ art the same yesterday, to-day, and forever. We come and we go, but thou abidest. . . .
>
> We thank thee, O Lord, that in the generations past thou didst establish here a distant outpost of thy kingdom, and hast made it a stronghold and an aggressive force. Thou didst set up here the old landmark, not to be removed . . . We thank thee for the good men and true, its faithful guardians, that have held it fast to its origin and aim . . .
>
> May [thy servant, its president elect] be enabled to hold the institution firmly to its ancient moorings of sound learning and thorough training, consecrated by true piety and dedicated to the Master's cause . . . till the kingdom and the dominion and the greatness of the kingdom under the whole heaven shall be given to the people of the saints of the Most High, through Jesus Christ our Lord.[52]

With or without an "Amen" to that minatory supplication, Tucker then declared that America was served with more enlightenment by its educators than by its social or political or even religious institutions. Dartmouth, he gave assurance, was able to be faithful to its original impulse, which was religious. But there was need for religion (which for Tucker was generic and without content) to be present on the campus in new and even discontinuous ways:

> Religion must not be set to do the menial tasks of the college, it must not be made an instrument of discipline, it must not become through any kind of indifference the repository of obsolete opinions or obsolete customs, it must not be used to maintain any artificial relation between the college and the constituency. . . . The college fulfills an office which no man, I take it, will question, as it translates the original and constant religious impulse into terms of current thought and action, making itself a centre of spiritual light, of generous activities, and, above all, of a noble intellectual and religious charity.[53]

The New Dartmouth

There was a severe lurch in the nation's economy in 1893, an inauspicious time to assume a college presidency. But in Hanover there was immediate and enthusiastic talk of the New Dartmouth. In Tucker's first year the largest freshman class in history came to Hanover. Only 12 percent of the student body came from beyond the confines of New England, and none yet from beyond the Rockies. But every year the enrollment net was flung wider. When Tucker came to campus the enrollment stood at 315; when he left it had nearly quadrupled, to 1,136, and they were coming from thirty-two states. The faculty swelled from twenty-two to sixty-nine, and the courses offered grew from 108 to 327. The campus began with fifteen buildings and counted thirty-five when he retired. Total income and annual expenditures quintupled.[54] The State of New Hampshire was prevailed upon to take effective notice of the education so many of its citizens were receiving at a fee well below its actual cost, and in 1893 began a series of biennial appropriations to the college.[55]

The president's own relationship to all this affluence was more than honorable. He was said to have "left a ten-thousand dollar pulpit" at Madison Square when he went to Andover, which paid him only $3,000 (still more than Dartmouth could pay its professors for some years to come). In the spring of 1897, when the Dartmouth board believed it did not have funds available to grant the increases Tucker had proposed for the professors, Tucker insisted that his own salary be reduced from $4,500 to $4,000 for a period of three years. After unanimous objections, they consented.[56] When Tucker arrived on campus Dartmouth had no dean, no treasurer, no registrar, no librarian: all these tasks were allotted to various faculty members. The president was the only full-time administrator: he had no secretary and wrote his own correspondence in longhand.

Tucker recruited faculty who had mostly earned their doctorates and benefited from experience at European universities. The age distribution became so inverted, after years of dominance by elders, that the students referred to them as the "kid faculty." The number of Dartmouth alumni on the faculty doubled, but their proportion fell from three-quarters to one-third. Specialization naturally increased, and finally Dartmouth accepted the institution of academic departments: twenty-eight were in existence when Tucker left. Tucker made peace with the various professional schools, which were either incorporated into the college, given their independence, or financially and academically stabilized.[57]

True to his word, Tucker saw to it that religion was not the Dartmouth disciplinarian. For years the students had complained that Sabbath observance prevented them from access to the library on Sundays. At his first meeting of the board as president, Tucker secured their agreement that the reading room be open on Sunday afternoons.[58] Scholarship holders were no longer required to take the pledge to abstain from tobacco (he thought the lying this was likely to provoke was morally more harmful than the smoking it would curtail). They were, however, still required to take the pledge against alcohol. The college itself built a pool and billiards facility in its student activities building, and dancing classes began to prepare students to taste formerly forbidden fruit. The campus church's superannuated pastor was supplemented in the pulpit by a medley of invited preachers, but when even that failed to breathe life back into Sunday services, Tucker told the board they had, sadly, become "detrimental to the spiritual life of the students," and they became no longer obligatory.[59]

The Sunday afternoon "vesper service" now became the chief act of college piety during the week. Although compulsory chapel had elicited some of the most regularly rowdy behavior among Dartmouth students — reading of newspapers, carving of graffiti into pews, horns, firecrackers, howling — Tucker managed to convene them in an entirely different spirit on these occasions. His talks were remembered with unrelieved affection and awe by alumni, and Tucker himself said they were his most important moments as an educator. At the time of his retirement he recalled his satisfaction:

The service in Rollins Chapel stands for the freedom and unity of religious faith. It is an academic, not an ecclesiastical religious service. I do not recall ever having invited any person outside a member of the faculty to occupy this place in my absence. However much I should have wished to show my personal respect for the representatives of various religious communions, who have been from time to time with us, I have wished to emphasize the fact beyond all controversy, that here is a place where all men who have religious aspirations in any form may unite in religious service, while at the same time honoring in clear and unmistakable terms the faith of the founders of the college.

The Sunday service in Rollins Chapel has been held at an hour when there could be no conflict with the services of the churches of the town. Students have been urged to attend these various services according to their religious training or religious preferences. Loyalty to one's church connection, wherever it exists, has been constantly inculcated, — more constantly illustrated, I ought to say, by students in the Catholic communion than by those in other communions, — but in this service which brings the entire college together there has been a sensitive regard to the rights of varying religious opinions and of religious faiths. It is, of course, too much to expect that the miracle of Pentecost should be repeated and that as we come together day by day, or Sunday by Sunday, we should all hear the truth, or worship "every man in his own language wherein he was born." That is not necessary. What is necessary is that we should recognize those fundamental obligations and incentives of religion in which we are all substantially agreed.[60]

Tucker let it be known how very much he preferred holding the vesper services in Rollins Chapel, instead of the older Webster Hall. Rollins was the first chapel space the college had which was not shared with other assemblies and activities.[61] Yet the talks he gave there had a very attenuated religious aspect. His preference was always to drift away from the explicit language and concerns of faith toward the generic. Those "fundamental obligations and incentives of religion" in which the now diversified student body substantially agreed emerged as a great deal less substantial than what Wheelock, Lord, or Bartlett had expounded:

> Christianity, when it came into the world, struck the note of universality. There was no restriction upon its message. It was the "good tidings of great joy to all the people." But the history of Christianity has proved to be one long struggle, more frequently unsuccessful than successful, to maintain its original scope. It seemed impossible to protect Christianity from falling into bondage to some form of partialism. Now it has been the partialism of doctrine wrought out in the exclusive creed; now the partialism of administration. But in one way and another the Christian church has been continually losing its connection with the universal.[62]

Lest anyone imagine Tucker was exempting his own Congregationalists and Presbyterians, he often quoted one of his seminary teachers who had said: "I teach that Independency is a transient form of Puritanism, that Puritanism is a transient form of Protestantism, that Protestantism is a transient form of Christianity."[63]

Tucker's preoccupation with the sectarian attitudes of his conservative contemporaries made it virtually impossible for him to be worried about retaining a homogeneous faculty. Bartlett had raised that concern in 1886 as a necessary strategy to arrest and reverse "the secularizing tendency." He quoted the *Independent,* which he fairly identified as "an exceedingly liberal religious journal":

> A Christian college has this characteristic, chief above all others, that it does not put into its Faculty men who sneer at or even who disbelieve in the Christian religion. We would despise a College which limits its appointments by denominational lines; but any College is justified in making it a bar against the election of a professor of ethics, or history, or political economy, or Greek, or geology, that he is an atheist. If that is narrowness or bigotry, then make the most of it. More than this, a Christian College has more in view, in the selection of its teachers, than the negative aim of getting men who are not hostile to the Christian faith. It should seek men who are decided in their faith and who love to teach it.[64]

Even Bartlett, who was struggling to keep around him allies who were not merely Congregationalists but conservative and devotedly Calvinist ones, could not bring himself to think or to say that denomination should be taken into account. Tucker, his liberal nemesis, prefers to describe the cultural divide differently, since so many he considers destructive are aggressive Christians and so many he considers enlightened are critical outsiders.

President Tucker, Spokesman of a New Piety

It is worth our while to study William Jewett Tucker, for he is an early exponent of a type of Pietist Congregationalism that provided the text, so to speak, for Dartmouth's religious transition. The guiding force in the transition was not academic, not the striving of lively educators to disentangle themselves from religious stricture. It was religious, and what Tucker said and did at Dartmouth is a model for us, since he was so articulate about it. He focuses his interest, neither on Calvinism nor on Protestantism nor even on Christianity, but on "religion." And if one listens carefully one sees that, as Tucker understands it, the concerns of religion were neither very concrete nor discernibly religious. This can be seen in a Lenten address, "The Religion of the Educator":

> Religion, as the experience of the human soul, needs all which the soul has to offer through reason, and conscience, and heart. It is never at its best except as it expresses in some form the passions of the soul. But if you trace the religious spirit to its sources you will find, I think, that the quality which it draws from the schools, from what I have called academic religion, is reverence. Reverence is more than anything else a habit of the mind. A great many people of religious emotion are singularly irreverent. Contrast the curiosity of the mediæval mind, its sensuous longings after heaven, with the inquiry of the modern mind (which accepts mystery) into the workings of God in nature. Contrast, if you will, the futile but restless questionings about destiny — "Lord, are there few that be saved?" [a classical Calvinist concern] — with the untroubled but passionate search after truth. The conception of God which rises out of the sense of values, is that of Scripture: He is a "faithful Creator"; "He cannot deny himself." Having made the human mind and given it inalienable rights, its entire freedom is guaranteed by one safeguard, and one only, reverence. . . .
>
> The religion of the educator is set on its practical side toward . . . right-mindedness . . . the moral disposition of the mind, the habit not simply of clear, strong, resolute thinking, but of right thinking. The most dangerous thing about education, that which every educator fears most, is the perversion of power. You see the occasional result when some man of highly trained mind does some questionable act, usually in finance or politics, or when he does some flagrantly ungenerous or selfish act, through his personal or corporate relation to the public.

Near the end of this upbeat but vague moralizing, he admits that one might want to know about the *content* of the educator's religious faith:

> I suppose that you do not mean to ask what are his theological holdings, for we do not express ourselves to-day in theological as much as in religious terms. This fact means that we have changed the emphasis from the content of faith to the tone of faith. The question in the popular mind in regard to any man in whom

it is interested religiously is not, so much as formerly, what he believes, but much more than formerly, how he believes. Formerly the distinction was, Is a man orthodox or heterodox? To-day the distinction is, — Is a man an optimist or a pessimist? Our religious beliefs and denials are experienced in shades and colors rather than in sharp and rigid outlines. And this means that we believe, or doubt, or deny, much more according to our experience of the world than according to logic.[65]

The wonderfully renegade power in Tucker's suggestion that authentic religious insight derives from personal experience is tamed by his actual depiction of it, which is unrelievedly mannered, and authentically New England. In one chapel talk, "Moral Maturity," he begins, as usual, with a brief quotation from Scripture: "Whatsoever ye would that men should do to you, even so do ye also to them: for this is the law and the prophets." He then summons his young audience beyond the law and the prophets, and indeed beyond the gospel and any of its derivative creeds, to a higher morality still: "personal standards of conduct and duty," which single out "the stronger and better souls" for a distinctively liberated moral initiative:

> The law still speaks to us as capable of responding to authority. The prophets still speak to us as capable of responding to ideals. Jesus speaks to us as capable of responding to the sense of the human in ourselves and in all men. . . . How do we reach moral maturity? Not by abiding always in the commandments. The literalism of obedience will surely leave us immature morally. Not by living altogether in the freedom and in the comparative irresponsibility of our ideals. The moral power of the idealist is too much like that of an amateur. When we take it into the world men call it academic. The order of moral advance is from commandments to ideals, and then from ideals to those actual personal standards which are wrought out in the contact of man with man.

He closed the address with an account of how the teaching of Jesus gives access to a true, albeit vapid, humanism:

> I count it the great moral obligation of all believing men to have faith in the working power of Christ's sayings. They will be no more true a hundred years hence than they are to-day, but we can make them more evidently true before we are done with them. And to this end, keep your faith, I pray you, in men. Faith in God has been defined as trusting Him against appearances. Do not take men at their word when they talk below themselves. Use the true, never the false, in human nature, and persist in doing this. So shall you gain access, every one of you in his own way, to the heart of humanity.[66]

Tucker publicly deplored the sectarian divisions within Christendom, which he ascribed to a stubborn literalism applied to the Bible. "A Bible set free from the last bondage to literalism, no longer the bulwark of divisive ecclesiastical dogmas, but now become the simple and natural vehicle for the supreme revelation of God to men, has already begun its great constructive work in the Church. . . . The belief which makes a man a Christian has been magnified above any or all beliefs which make him this or that kind of a Christian . . . giving a new conception of Christianity, larger, simpler, and more unifying."[67]

Tucker was typical of the Progressive Orthodoxy wing of Congregationalism, in that he embraced and propounded an articulate social doctrine, but without any Christian base. To appreciate how abruptly the liberal American Congregationalists had wrenched themselves free from the Puritan theology, one need only read Tucker's other hero, Washington Gladden, who wrote this in 1873:

> To teach that God is a being who has a perfect right to bring into this world a creature with faculties impaired, with no power to resist temptation, utterly unable to do right, powerless even to repent of the wrong which he is fated to do, and then send to everlasting misery this helpless creature for the sin which he could not help committing, — to teach such a doctrine as this about God is to inflict upon religion a terrible injury and to subvert the very foundations of morality. To say that God may justly punish a man for the sins of his ancestors, that God does blame us for what happened long before we were born, is to blaspheme God, if there be any such thing as blasphemy. To say that any such thing is clearly taught in the Bible is to say that the Bible clearly teaches a monstrous lie. Yet such theology as this is taught in several of our theological seminaries and preached from many of our pulpits. It is idle to say that it is nothing but a philosophical refinement; that the men who come out of our theological seminaries with these notions in their heads never make any use of them in their pulpits. They do make use of them. They are scattering this atrocious stuff all over the land. They are making infidels faster than they are converting sinners. Men say, "If this is your God, worship him, if you want to, but do not ask us to bow down to your Moloch!" Who can blame them? For our own part, we say, with all emphasis, that between such a theology as this and atheism we should promptly choose the latter.[68]

Tucker was much more gentlemanly in his manner, yet his sensibilities were close to those of Gladden. The doctrine of his denomination had been so traumatically discredited in his mind that all he seemed to be left with, apart from a forthright and able sense of social justice, was a doctrine of gentlemanliness. When, despite old Bartlett's prayer, Tucker did move "the old landmark," it was done smoothly, with no scar to mark the old emplacement.

Dartmouth Knows It Has Changed

His constituencies at Dartmouth, without anyone having taken much notice, had meanwhile begun to change. Tucker several times invited Dartmouth alumni who were bishops to participate in building dedications: surely in a different atmosphere than the phobia toward Anglican bishops of Wheelock's generation.[69] Besides Tucker's backhanded compliment to the Catholic students, we know that he had acquiesced in the changing population patterns in New England; Catholics were beginning to matriculate at Dartmouth. An alumnus who had graduated two years before Tucker's arrival complained another thirty years later: "In my own class there was not a single man who was not of a Protestant variety who remained in college; now it is considered wise to avoid Friday as a day for alumni dinners on account of the attendance of so many who are expected to refrain from eating meat on that day in the week!"[70] It was in Tucker's time that the "so many" began to enroll. In Tucker's first year as president, the YMCA reading room subscribed to the *Congregationalist, Methodist Review, Expository Times* (Anglican), *Catholic World,* and *Lutheran Quarterly.*[71] The Episcopalians began to be served by Saint Thomas Church, built in 1876, unlike the earlier days when Benjamin Hale had been maneuvered out of the college for gathering his fellow Episcopalians to worship. Now they and the Catholic students both had student organizations mentioned in the college catalogue.[72] Also, Jewish students were being admitted at the time. The complexion of the board of trustees had changed as well, and even more abruptly. Tucker's own early nomination by the alumni as a trustee would prove untypical. After the alumni gained virtual control of the board elections in Bartlett's last year, they nominated very few clergy. Of the twenty-two men who served at various times during Tucker's presidency, only five were clergymen. And in 1906, near the end of his incumbency, the Dartmouth board included seven Congregationalists, five Unitarians, and one Presbyterian. Only one trustee was a minister. Even more significant is the disclosure that a majority of them — seven — were not active members of any congregation.[73]

The proposal by the Carnegie Foundation to subsidize pension funds that would allow college and university faculty the wherewithal to retire excluded all institutions having formal denominational connections, or requiring their trustees or officers to belong to a specific denomination. When the first list of forty-six grantee institutions was published in 1906, nearly half were schools of Congregational origin, e.g., Harvard, Yale, Amherst, Williams, Oberlin, Carleton, Beloit, Smith, Middlebury, along with Dartmouth. Dartmouth had sent in its formal denial of any such entanglement: "Dartmouth College has no relation whatsoever with any religious denomination. The choice of trustees, officers, or professors depends in no way upon denominational considerations. In faculty and in students practically all denominations are represented." After the official list was published, the president of the Foundation wrote Tucker a somewhat embarrassed note, observing that some denominations continued to carry on their official rosters of colleges and universities the names of many of the Carnegie beneficiaries, presumably because they made no distinction between "institutions under the control of a denomination and those whose relation to it is merely a sympathetic one." He suggested that Dartmouth might want to do something about its "misleading" inclusion in the *Congregational Year Book*.[74] In the case of Dartmouth and several others, the Carnegie money was an incentive to disown formally, albeit quietly, what the administration now regarded as only a circumstantial relationship. It was in this period, if not by this action, that Dartmouth actually was shrugging off its affiliation with a denomination whose deficits seemed now to outweigh its benefits.

The prospect of a Carnegie grant concentrated the minds of college and university presidents wonderfully, and the Congregationalists had an easier time of it than most, understanding why there was virtually nothing at stake in disavowing a sectarian tie. They looked with admiration at Brown University where a committee had just proposed to discontinue their relationship with the Baptists. The people at Brown had excused themselves: "If we were as a corporation seeking pensions for ourselves, our motive would indeed be selfish or sordid. We want these pensions for the self-sacrificing men who are toiling, in many cases, on a meager salary, and for their wives and children." One article in the *Congregationalist and Christian World,* just at the time of Tucker's retirement, looked over the back fence at Brown. The author insists it was not for the Carnegie money that colleges were casting off their denominational bonds. Well before Mr. Carnegie came round, "many of these colleges had practically come to a non-denominational basis, drawing their constituency from many religious bodies and inculcating in the classroom and pulpit a comprehensive Christianity." The author then mused, in terms quite close to the discussion developing at Dartmouth:

> This is one of the inevitable drifts of our time, over which, it seems to us, it is not worth while to grieve. We dishonor the founders of our colleges when we imply that they toiled and sacrificed chiefly in behalf of denominational aggrandizement. If in the case of any institution the present members of the faculty and the student body are not moved by gratitude to revere the denomination with which the institution is traditionally allied, if their own sense of honor does not prompt them to serve it as they are able, then we see no hope of securing such desirable results through hard and fast restrictions embedded in the charter.[75]

It was not in Tucker's nature to alienate those whom or with whom he served. For instance, the board members were almost to a man economically and socially conservative businessmen or professionals, certainly not inclined to welcome the one set of high-profile political and moral views which Tucker did possess. Yet there is no record of his enjoying anything but the most positive relations with his trustees. Further: the conservative monitors among the Congregationalists who had assailed the liberals at Andover, Tucker included, mounted no campaign against him at Dartmouth. He was an unqualified success in every measurable way, and a gracious man besides. The evidence seems conclusive that his leadership at Dartmouth was well received by all constituencies.[76]

Some sense of how Dartmouth under Tucker was faring religiously may be gained from the condition of its religious societies. These date back to the founding of the Students' Religious Society in 1801, later called the Theological Society (its members informally referred to it as the *Religiosi*). It seems to have been the central undertaking of student piety in those years. It was joined by the Society of Inquiry in 1821, which held meetings "to inquire into the state of the Heathen" and encouraged its members to consider work in the foreign missions. By the time of the Dartmouth centennial in 1869 the Theological Society had enrolled 1,200 members, one-third of all the men who had gone through Dartmouth. More than a third of those had entered the ministry. In the earlier years more than two-thirds had followed that calling.

A retrospective essay written for the 1868-69 centennial gives the feel of the Society then:

> The past is not without its warnings, its voices against illiberality in judgment, and excess of Puritanic sternness. Yet we have little to fear, at the present day, from these errors of the past; but while we may rejoice that these blemishes, which rendered the christian unlovely, have been to so great a degree removed, let us be on our guard, lest with these the sterling uncompromising virtues, which befit a follower of our Lord, be not also defaced or cast aside.[77]

The Theological Society and the Society of Inquiry combined in that year, 1869, to form the Dartmouth Theological and Missionary Society (the name was soon simplified to Christian Fraternity), for "the cultivation of piety and the acquisition of religious knowledge." Discussion topics included: "Is general letter writing on the Sabbath justifiable?" "Shall women preach?" "Can a Christian consistently believe in Darwinism?" "Is it right for Christians to play cards?" "Ought we to oppose the running of railway cars on the Sabbath?" Membership fluctuated. As one of the student societies, it took its turn in inviting the commencement speaker, but it set its sights high on luminaries like Phillips Brooks and Washington Gladden, without success. The postbellum discussion topics seem continuous with the past: "Is betting morally wrong?" "Will it pay to Christianize the Indians?" (this must have given Eleazar Wheelock some postmortem twinge), and "Will Christ's coming precede the Millennium?" This was fairly conventional piety.

The national YMCA had an active evangelical program of college chapters, begun at the University of Virginia in 1858, and in 1881 the Christian Fraternity became the YMCA affiliate at Dartmouth. Membership in an evangelical church was required of all who belonged. The national connection provided inspirational summer camps, and in 1885 brought to Hanover the acclaimed evangelist Dwight L. Moody, who spoke twice a day to audiences of 1,500. Various faculty members, at the request of the Y, began to offer noncredit courses, unavailable in the curriculum, on the life of Christ and the life of Paul. In Samuel Bartlett's later years as president, he personally intervened on their behalf and raised enough money to erect a building for their use. The trustees would make it his memorial after he retired.

Just as William Tucker was arriving (he had been an invited YMCA speaker some years earlier), the boys of the Y began to diversify their program. Besides their meetings of piety, they undertook to publish an annual information source known as the *Freshman Bible*. They fitted out their library, reading room, game room, and parlor as a social center for the college, and invited the fraternities to make use of it as well. Now that the organization was more diversified in its activities and was attracting more members, in 1896 the college helped it to afford a salaried general secretary, usually a recent graduate. In 1905, without dislodging themselves from the YMCA, the local group changed their name again, to the Dartmouth Christian Association (DCA). The president was a member of the football team, a sure sign of mainstream status, later recognized when the DCA president was put on a par with other societies' prexies. They began to support a Dartmouth-in-Turkey missionary project, and students regularly went out to churches around Hanover to help with Sunday school teaching. By 1914 Bartlett Hall's location on the growing campus was no longer socially strategic, and the association moved to a more accessible building. A tutoring service was set up, and then an employment bureau. The DCA provided musical groups to enhance college social functions, and to entertain off campus. They collected used clothing for sailors in Boston and taught English to immigrants. They pointed to the fact that one-fourth of the students enrolled in Bible study were either varsity athletes or leaders of campus organizations, as a plus-value for religious activities. Billy Sunday came to preach in 1917. When the military effectively took over the campus during World War I, the Y facility became the recreational center for the entire student body.

Members joining in 1919 were to make this commitment: "I affirm my desire to have my influence in the College count on the side of clean living and all-around manhood, and to realize in my own life the Christian ideals of character and service." More than 80 percent of the students were ready to make that wholesome undertaking. But three years later the active membership had plunged to less than one-tenth of what it had been. The initiation pledge was revised: "to acknowledge Christ and to try to follow his teachings, interpreting these to mean 'you must love the Lord your God with your whole heart, your whole soul and your whole mind and you must love your neighbor as yourself.' "[78]

Religious activities organized by the students themselves, throughout the nineteenth century, followed a pattern of devout piety, pretty much confined by the doctrinal and moral concerns of the Congregational community — neither of which were very wide. Once they began to be swept into the energetic flow of the YMCA, they were quickened by the evangelical enthusiasm of a national movement. During the Tucker presidency the initiative seems to have passed back to the campus itself, where the Christian Association turned its imagination to a broad medley of service activities, and in return found positive affirmation and social acceptance. The perfect amalgamation seems to have been made then, of a muscular piety compounded with generous service. This seems, however, to have been the peak of a parabolic curve of development, for the vitality began to deplete in the early 1920s.

William Jewett Tucker was obliged by failing health to offer his resignation in 1909. In his sixteen years of leadership he had transformed Dartmouth, and some of his creative reforms would still take some years to display their maturity. He was followed by Ernest Fox Nichols, Dartmouth's first lay president except for John Wheelock, who had been designated by his father. Nichols was a physicist at Columbia University who had spent earlier years on the Dartmouth faculty. Historian Leon Richardson tells us his seven-year presidency was "not marked by events of special significance."[79] He passed on the ordinary responsibility for presiding at chapel to a chaplain, and with the awesome presence of Dr. Tucker no longer at the presiding desk, students resumed their restive dislike for compulsory worship.[80] In 1916 began another presidency which was in many critical respects a sequel to that of Tucker.

With Hopkins, the Banality Is Complete

Ernest Martin Hopkins, the son of Adoniram Judson Hopkins, a Baptist minister with a Harvard degree, had gone to Dartmouth and caught the eye of President Tucker, who hired him at graduation in 1901 as his secretary, and then assistant and confidant. After staying on with President Nichols for a year, he went out into the business world and in 1916 was on the point of accepting a lucrative position in industry when he was invited (at a painful drop in salary) to come back as president. He was an early instance of a pure administrator, lacking the credentials of either clergy or faculty. He was a confessed disciple and admirer of his mentor, Tucker, who lived nearby in retirement for nearly twenty years. Hopkins would serve until 1945, twice as long as Tucker, but very much in the same spirit. It is fair to say that Tucker and Hopkins, in a half-century, transformed the Dartmouth that Lord and Bartlett had formed in their half-century.

Hopkins's first decision which openly affected Dartmouth's religious character was, ironically, one with which Tucker disagreed. But it followed the trajectory of Tucker's own leadership. In 1924 Hopkins finally announced the board's decision to abolish compulsory chapel, and one year later the Sunday vesper service, the last obligatory religious service on campus, was also made voluntary. The student response was manifest: after worship became voluntary, daily attendance shrank to 3 percent of the student body.[81]

Response by the alumni, especially those from before Tucker's time, was strident but not united. One Jewish graduate wrote: "Well, Mrs. ——— and myself think that the abolition of compulsory attendance at chapel [was] a mistake. We believe that the Chapel exercises have a most wholesome influence, and while not *ultra* religiously inclined, yet we feel that some good must result from beginning the school day with the moral and sacred influences which are necessarily associated with such exercises." Another graduate, an attorney, wrote:

> Many authorities, from President Coolidge down to [New York] Police Commissioner Enright have said that the fundamental trouble is the lessening of religious instruction and training. Even Clarence Darrow, the Agnostic, mentioned that as one of the reasons for the plight of his Chicago clients. I share this opinion and believe that lack of religious instruction and training affects unfavorably many who fall short of criminality . . . If left to my own devices I do not think I would have received any religious instruction or training whatever. Fishing attracted me more than Sunday School and in College, I went to Chapel and Church because that was the thing to do, otherwise I would have been more pleasantly employed. I was guilty of all the misconduct that you speak of (yes, I even read a book behind a post) and then some. . . . I am prepared to say that *"compulsory"* religious instruction and training into which I was *coerced* was the best thing that ever happened to me.

This received a quick reply from another alumnus:

> I sat at Dr. Tucker's feet for four years and call him blessed, not for "compulsory required attendance at religious exercises," but because of the influence upon me of his personality and of his Chapel talks, very few of which had any direct relation to religion. He did *not* utilize Chapel services as an agency for the forcible feeding of religion. His use of Chapel services was "for definite and constant access to the mind of the College" — "for interpreting men to themselves" — "to stir the mind of the College to the understanding of the meaning of its own personality" — "to keep its mind open and sensitive to that human world of which it was a part" — "for the development of the sense of the human, that is, of one's part in the life of the world." . . . I venture to say that most of my contemporaries tenderly recall Dr. Tucker as an inspired moulder of character, rather than as a teacher of religion. In so far as I am aware, he never gave religious instruction at Dartmouth.

Some cited William Jennings Bryan, who said in a speech in Hanover that Dartmouth was the most irreligious college in the country. Others thought it strange that chapel was voluntary but that courses on evolution, or citizenship, or industrial society were all compulsory. Another pointed out that in recent years there were usually no more than one or two faculty members at morning chapel. The chairman of AT&T (also a trustee), however, regarded the change as a good one:

A teacher of mine (before College days) used to say, "I wouldn't give a cent for a God I could understand." My conception of religion is something inculcated, something pumped in through a period of years by precept and example rather than something to be accepted through a process of reasoning. It is a very personal matter — for parents to concern themselves with — but not the State and not the College or the School; probably because it cannot be generalized. If it were possible to inculcate religion without preaching a particular religion, the case would be different. Religion is above education or anything else and entitled to so much respect that it ought not to be used as an excuse for getting boys together in the morning.

Another alumnus offered "just a few desultory thoughts":

I miss morning chapel when I go back to Hanover. I want to attend it myself, though I never go to church in any other place, except occasionally to a Christmas Eve service. . . . In my time there was no sense of compulsion any more than in our attendance on mathematics or Latin recitations. The college told us what to do and we did as little of it as we could except in so far as it interested us, but we never felt we had any more of a special grievance because we were made to go to chapel than because we were made to go to the Wednesday afternoon "rhetoricals" which were held in the old chapel.

I am hoping some day to see a church whose services are based on some such simple statement as: — "We do not know whether there is a God. We do not know whether there is any life after this. But these things matter not. We do know that while we are in this life, we should live it like gentlemen. And we are met in a service designed to strengthen us in our determination so to live and enlighten us as to what such a life should be."

Hopkins replied to an avalanche of controversy among the alumni:

Certain . . . colleges, such as Amherst, had largely forsaken anything approximating a religious service or a devotional form of service, in a portion of their chapel exercises, and were holding joint debates on college policy or having faculty monologues in regard to their subjects, or undergraduate discussions of undergraduate subjects. At Brown, they had tided over a period of uneasiness by making the morning chapel a sort of bulletin board descriptive of the undergraduate activities of the day, and periodically, — I think, once a week, — they gave the exercises over to the students for a football rally or for some form of a "bigger, busier and better Brown." . . .

The one thing that the present-day undergraduate is not, and cannot be clubbed into being, is a conformist, and at no point is he more a non-conformist than in the matter of the relationship between churches and religion . . . However, this [is] an eagerness to know God as he actually is and to worship him in spirit and

45

in truth rather than to accept the man-made conceptions of God and the practices which have arisen in recognizing Him through generations not wholly altruistically interested in religion nor religious ideals. . . .

I believe that the purpose of churches and chapels and religious exercises of all kinds is to develop and aid a religious spirit. I believe that a religious spirit is essential to mankind in order that men may be good. If men are good, I have very little concern as to the avenues by which they come to goodness, nor in regard to the forms which they hold.[82]

Dartmouth naturally looked to the precedent of its elders, Harvard and Yale. Harvard had moved forty years earlier to make first church and then chapel voluntary. In 1885, as those changes were under way, they had received sharp comment from the denominational press. The replacement on the Harvard seal of *Christo et Ecclesiæ* by the "glittering generality" of *Veritas* was taken to be an omen of a total change of identity:

These morning prayers, and the motto, *Christo et Ecclesiæ,* on the college seal, are, so far as we can learn, the only Christian things that cling to the university. . . . Things have been drifting toward this result at Harvard since President Eliot defined its policy. His first motive was to escape from the limitations of a Unitarian sect by getting the university onto the broader ground of indifference to denominational distinctions. Unfortunately, the theory he started would not stop at denominational distinctions, nor, in fact, anywhere short of absolute liberty to believe, say, and teach what one would, whether it fell inside or outside the lines of Christianity.

There are natural necessities controlling matters of this nature which may or may not have been foreseen by Mr. Eliot and his friends, but which have certainly proven too strong for them, and have now carried the university into a position whose tenor makes college Prayers, college worship, and college profession of faith an illogical and contradictory survival of a system the university is no longer working on.

We applaud the Overseers' decision as an honest and brave attempt, as far as it goes, to stem the tide. But if they really mean to sustain college Prayers, and to keep the college on a religious foundation, they will have to come to an issue with the entire theory as to religious profession and responsibility into which the university has of late been drifting.

The Overseers say that religion cannot be ignored in college. They would come closer to the point had they said that it cannot be ignored in college education and administration. How can history be taught, for example, without definite theories as to the religious principles which lie at its core? And as to philosophy, what is theology but the philosophy of life? In handling these subjects some theory of religion must be taught. If it is not the Christian theory, it is either a fatal skepticism or some kindred phase of secularism. That the silent pulpit of

Appleton Chapel does not imply silence as to religion in the classroom the recent publication of Mr. Royce's lectures to his Harvard classes demonstrates.[83]

It was not reassuring to some Dartmouth alumni that by 1925 the daily services at Harvard were attracting the voluntary attendance of about only one-half of one percent of its undergraduates.[84] Meanwhile at Yale, the dean was offering gruff comment on the fact that the students had just voted eight-to-one against compulsory chapel, and the faculty (or the minority who bothered to vote) had agreed with them by three-to-one. "For the undergraduate in Yale College everything is 'compulsory' — compulsory recitations, compulsory examinations, compulsory themes, lectures, terms, papers. No undergraduate is left to his own desires in meeting any of these requirements."[85] But copies of the *Harvard Crimson* were fraternally rushed by automobile down to New Haven, arriving just after morning chapel, full of comment by Lucius Beebe, who after two years at Yale had recently transferred to Harvard. Wrote Beebe, his eyes newly opened:

> The only people who desire the retention of chapel [at Yale] are those the least concerned with it: namely, members of the corporation, of which at present four are ministers, and a fringe of hangers-on, uplifters, right thinkers and reformers. . . . [Present Yale services are] of a more or less disorderly nature; late risers appearing tastily attired in pajamas and fur overcoats, where mail from the morning delivery is scanned to the tune of some good, depressing hymns.[86]

The spat in 1925-26 brought to the surface a Dartmouth in which the chapel supporters and the chapel critics made it similarly clear that what was at stake was not the worship of the God of Abraham, Isaac, and Jacob, the Father of Jesus. Nor was it initiation of the juniors by their elders into the faith once handed on to the saints. Least of all was it a revealed wisdom that held together a communion of faith.

The Harvard critic noted that when Charles Eliot withdrew Harvard from its allegiance to Unitarianism, it ended up withdrawing, not from a denomination, but from Christ. When William Jewett Tucker, several decades later, forswore what he saw as the extravagances of Calvinist Congregationalism, what emerged in its place was not an ecumenical Christianity but a mannered civics lesson. Tucker was a powerful and well-placed advocate, but more importantly his perspective was shared by those who would have the ear of Dartmouth in years to come. For example, at the first commencement weekend after Tucker's retirement, the baccalaureate sermon was given by Hugh Black, professor at Union Theological Seminary and popular Calvinist preacher, whose account of religion suggests the primal darkness which covered the face of the deep:

> The approach to God may be by many varied paths, but they must all lead to the same gate of serious thought and honest reflection. The driving power which

brings a man to the point of decision may be vivid emotion, or keen sorrow, or painful repentance, or the impulse of a high resolve, or the wooing of a great love, or a kindled passion after good and purity. But all the roads converge to this point of solemn reflection when a man considers his life in the light of God's presence. . . .

In religion we find the traditional and conventional and seldom the original. By original is meant not the senseless striving after new opinions, but a living faith that is the expression of a man's own thought and experience. We do not often hear a live voice that is more than an echo, speaking out of the depths of personal and experimental knowledge. We are so improved in living that we can respect life.[87]

President Nichols, during the same weekend, spoke in similar vein at the vesper service and offered a deconstruction of the old Sabbath mandate. It is a cameo example of the reductive treatment that the new Congregationalists were applying to their traditional doctrine:

Life gains much of its value and most of its interest through contrasts. Change is one of its most fundamental laws, and changes rightly used by the individual [are] one of the greatest sources of power.

The power to work enthusiastically, intensively, at specific tasks is a strong defense, but then come hours of weariness which cannot all be spent in sleep. One of life's greatest problems is the right use of recreation, and the character of some public entertainments in which many find amusement is, to the thoughtful, one of the most discouraging features of our complex civilization.

In the use of man's rest day, lie the great chances of life, the very roots of good and evil. Let no one be tempted to flee from himself, his own thoughts, or to be led from his own companionship into less worthy. It is the uses of the hours of freedom which make or mar the man. They finally determine him on his largest and noblest side, and work the very temper of the soul.[88]

A decade later, at Dartmouth's sesquicentennial, the anniversary sermon was given by Rev. Ozora Stearns Davis, president of Chicago Theological Seminary. There were three chasms which sundered the human community, he said: class, color, and creed. Dartmouth had done well in assailing racial suspicion and class antagonism with its own resilient spirit of democracy. But tribalism was not yet defeated. It was rooted in a preferential attachment to one's self, family, neighborhood, state, craft, and (here lay his emphasis) church. "From this is born a rabid individualism, class arrogance, neighborhood impertinence, ecclesiastical despotism, and shrieking sectional patriotism. What is the cure for this? It lies in the ideal of universal good will, of sympathetic appreciation of others which produces the true balance for individualism, neighborliness, patriotism, morals, religion." This would have been a timely charge to the undergraduate contemporaries of

Ozora Davis, '89, when the orthodox Congregationalists had Dartmouth in its tight grasp. But it was a different — and much more indifferent — air that one breathed in Hanover thirty years later.

Davis moved to his sermon's climax:

> Today the spiritual interests of humanity are torn by faction and harried by distrust. "So many gods, so many creeds, so many paths that wind and wind," cries out one singer, who shudders at the dark. And we must admit the justice of a deep resentment at this on the part of many earnest souls.
>
> Is the God of Jesus, is the Christ of the Christian's love and hope, great enough to blend and fuse this mass of yearning and unrest into a holy, passionate, loving brotherhood of souls who shall make this world in very truth God's world? Yes.
>
> This is the most imperial, the most audacious, the most exacting faith which a human soul may dare to hold. To believe abstruse propositions concerning a metaphysical trinity is easy in comparison with the conviction that this human race, so vast, so complex, so contradictory, is the subject of the divine redemptive love of God, which cannot finally be defeated, and which will unite mankind into a brotherhood of good will. . . .
>
> This simple resolute confidence that God is in the whole mighty movement of life is far deeper and more sustaining than any expression of it in creed or sacrament, in ritual or institution, although all these are vital to it.[89]

Needless to say, this graciously positive appraisal of human life did not derive from the Calvinism that had begotten Dartmouth. The burden of his message, however, is that sectarian particularities were not at all vital to the generic, Pietist belief in the whole mighty movement of life. This theme was picked up by President Hopkins in his own statement. He had been asked, he said, to enunciate a credo for Dartmouth, a brief account of the college's belief and conviction in these times. Most of what he then said was composed of conventional aspirations for original thought, training for leadership, campus comradeship, high standards, sound mind in a sound body, etc. It is at his conclusion that he reaches his crescendo:

> Finally, the historic colleges of this country are products of religious impulse and in so far as they glory in their birthrights they must glory in this. . . . It would be an affectation for us to define the purpose of Dartmouth College in the pious phrases of the eighteenth century, but it would be an unforgivable omission to ignore the present day equivalents of the motives which actuated Eleazar Wheelock in his unceasing efforts to establish this foundation. The founder's altruistic purpose of converting the heathen savage to the glory of God becomes in modern parlance a desire to convert society to the welfare of man. Either purpose requires the highest idealism, and the highest idealism is the purest religion, the symbol of which is God and the manifestation of which is the spirit of Christ. May this ever be the spirit of Dartmouth College.[90]

Ernest Hopkins, who paid tribute to the venerated Tucker as his mentor, and who was himself not a professional educator, emerged finally as a broadly inquisitive and more eloquent man than his predecessor. His incumbency of three decades gave him the opportunity to stabilize Dartmouth on the new course into which Tucker had steered it. He has been quoted here as one inclined to platitudes in the matter of religion. It was not his general disposition: he was, for example, a dedicated Republican opponent of the New Deal, and when he turned from religion to that subject his discourse hardened from gelatin to steel. What was the source and nature of his diffidence toward Christian inquiry and instruction? On one occasion, referring to the throwaway phrase "the faith of the fathers," he reminded his audience with some heat that it was "the faith of the fathers" that brought hemlock to Socrates and the cross to Jesus, that forced Roger Bacon to lay by his scholarship and Galileo to deny his.[91] Antiquity of tradition conferred no inevitable value.

So he turned from anything that resembled religious categories of thought, much as Tucker had done, and favored generic abstractions: "Friendliness and good will: this is the essence of the religion Jesus taught."[92] He became persuaded that these contemporary reductive banalities, not the discourse of the past, were the normative reference point for Christian belief.

> It is hard doctrine for many a man to accept that what Moses or Isaiah or Jesus said of religion in their respective times, or what Washington or Jefferson or Hamilton said of politics in theirs, is far less important than what these great leaders, with their courage and intelligence and idealism, would respectively say today in a time so different from the times whose thoughts they so defied and so largely molded.[93]

Leon B. Richardson, professor of chemistry, was charged with authorship of a major self-study by the Dartmouth faculty. He published his report in 1924, the year of the chapel debacle. He noted that in this age the colleges were expected to train their students for citizenship, and that had come to mean the development of character. "It is obvious," he wrote, "that the development of intelligence uncontrolled by moral purpose becomes a danger rather than a help to the state." The old college had had a clear idea how character was to be formed: through moral, and particularly religious, instruction. That view still endured in denominational colleges, noted Richardson, with a strong implication that he was not referring to Dartmouth. But wiser folk had moved away from all that, for character "is too subtle to pin to a religious basis." The best attempts to associate it with the course of studies, however, had failed. He concludes that high character is, in any case, "contagious" (he offers no opinion whether this be equally true of low character). Men of high character are admittedly rare, but fortunately they abound among the teachers, administrators, and undergraduates in America's colleges. They are to be kept on the campuses "at all cost," but he does not suggest how that might become an explicit and operative concern in the appointment or admission processes. The faculty thereby went on record, in Hopkins's time, that the colleges now had as their chief purpose a service to the state, not the church. That duty was the exemplification and transmission of noble character. This would be too subtle an enterprise for religious sponsorship, but it was in any case assured by the quality of persons who spontaneously found their way to college.[94] Thus in 1924 the Dartmouth faculty understood fairly well that theirs was not a religious enterprise, at least as regarded its "chief purpose" and its academic work.

George Peterson has shown that character was already back in the mid–nineteenth century the accepted goal of college, as distinct from university, education. This accent on character replaced the original accent on piety, because religion was now seen to be only one element in the Whole Man, who was now understood as a paladin of civic virtues.

When this same Leon Richardson came some years later to write the conclusion to his college history, he asked himself the same question that Hopkins had posed. What if Eleazar Wheelock could return today to the college he founded? His answer was no different:

> His most pronounced feeling would surely be that of stupefaction and horror at the spirit prevailing in the institution which he had set upon its feet. His one aim in life was the saving of souls in strict accordance with the rules established by John Calvin and developed by the early divines of New England. In his college of today he would find no interest in the tenets of Calvin, except those of the antiquarian and investigator; he would find no anxiety for the souls of men, in that particular sense in which his anxiety was most keen. He would be content to return to his grave with a keen sense of relief that he did not have to do with a degenerate and a wicked generation and with a college in which scant attention was paid to the things which he held most dear.
>
> But if Wheelock were to be born again in the twentieth century, still imbued with those qualities of boldness, initiative and courage which were so marked in his active career, still inspired by that desire to benefit his fellow men which was the one purpose of all his activities while he was still upon the earth, but inspired with the modern point of view as to the direction in which those efforts might best be applied, we may be confident that he would look upon the activities of this college with a high degree of sympathy and satisfaction. Because, after all, the guiding purpose which he set for Dartmouth College has not changed in the lapse of years. What Wheelock had in mind was to arouse in those under his charge a respect for human knowledge, so far as the domain of human knowledge can extend, to inspire in them an intellectual curiosity wide in its range, to animate in them a spirit which would impel them to devote their talents and their acquirements to the service of their fellow men. Such is the aim of the college today.[95]

It requires stamina to study this cascade of discourse about religion, because its inclination toward elegant and earnest inanity, begun handsomely with William

Jewett Tucker, reached its term in the half-century that followed his arrival. This is a pattern we shall see often in these stories, for it was a rhetoric typically used to retain some reductivist impression of religious continuity when in fact all authentically Congregational or Christian conviction had evaporated and been replaced by bland commonplaces about class or country.

Dartmouth's Modern Religious Indices

The Dartmouth of today would be difficult to relate to what President Hopkins termed Wheelock's religious impulse. For one thing, the demography has changed. Dartmouth has become very reluctant to conduct religious surveys of its various constituencies. The current president is Jewish. The religious proclivities of the faculty remain steadfastly unexplored. Throughout its earlier years Dartmouth appears not to have conducted the surveys of religious preference that were customary elsewhere. During the past ten years the Christian chaplain has conducted such a survey, and the results show that Catholics have been the most numerous of those responding: they represent from 29 to 36 percent. Students reporting no religious preference emerge as the second-largest group; Jews are steadily in third place; and Episcopalians are usually fourth. Congregationalists disappeared from the charts several years ago, after appearing as 2 percent. The United Church of Christ, into which most Congregationalists merged in 1957, was most recently claimed by 1 percent.[96]

The incumbent of the college's premier chair endowed in 1789, the Phillips Professor of Theology, used his inaugural lecture to argue that human beings are not always to be accepted as persons and protected from injury and death; those in power must first determine whether their own interests and liberties might be jeopardized by such a commitment, before they make the "social decision" about who is to be gifted with the status of person.[97] The William Jewett Tucker Foundation, endowed by the college "to support and further the moral and spiritual work and influence" of Dartmouth, has devoted a large part of its energies to gay liberation and abortion rights. Without entering any judgment on any of these developments, one requires much imagination to relate this to Eleazar Wheelock's endeavor to Christianize the heathen.

Ernest Hopkins's successor in the presidency was John Sloan Dickey, who also saw long service — from 1945 to 1970. Dickey's continual theme was the twofold calling of American colleges: to liberate their students by enlarging both their conscience and their competence. What worried him was the evidence that the colleges were only weakly inclined toward this twofold institutional purpose, "a promising marriage between man's reluctant intellect and his faint conscience."

A democracy cannot remain healthy unless the power that resides in its members is inspired to action and guided by man's experience with good and evil. These

52

things must be taught in home, school, and church, but ultimately I believe such teaching will take its cue from the higher learning of a free society.

That, Dickey admitted, is unlikely to occur. "The dispersed and reduced position of formal religion in secular higher education is the most conspicuous and probably the most powerful negative factor in the progressive weakening in the college's sense of a dual purpose."[98]

That this abdication of a twofold purpose has continued rather than abated may be suggested in a recent autobiographical profile of Dartmouth's current president.

> Being Jewish means many things to me, but none more important to my identity than being part of a tradition of scholarship and learning. . . . Our home abounded with books and conversation about ideas: our pantheon was peopled with intellectuals — our rabbi, Freud, Brandeis, Einstein, and Salk — whom I admired as following in the footsteps of Isaiah, Hillel, Maimonides, Rashi, and Buber. And so, as I matured, my search for my most authentic self was ineluctably linked to my identity as an intellectual, and that identity was inextricably linked to my sense of myself as a Jew.[99]

If Dartmouth were to have an identity in which faith in the God of Abraham, Isaac, and Jacob were to play a magisterial part, then with the possible exception of the Freedmans' rabbi, those great sages of the past would find scant audience or continuation in the modern scholars mentioned.

The careers of William Jewett Tucker and many of his contemporaries exemplified a great upheaval that caught up Dartmouth College along with the entire Congregational movement. Such a dislocation had occurred before, and with a comparable outcome. The Great Awakening, which was in full cry in the 1740s, just a century and a half earlier, had released a geyser of fervor. It was an innovation fostered by the ministers who found that their preaching, if raised to a new pitch of intensity and immediacy, could release powerful energies for moral conversion, stimulated by awesome weeping, fainting, shouting, sleepless rejoicing, visions, and prophecy. It also aroused an appetite for more of the same. Resident ministers saw their congregations turning with deeper respect and expectation to the more headlong itinerant preachers, because they seemed more adept than the incumbents at blowing embers into flame. Even when the great and sweaty shouters moved on to the next town, clergy found that they could be overborne in this new discourse of emotional testimony by their own laity, especially those who were radical or demonstrative.

Theology went mute within this new idiom, and those who had mastered Calvinism's emphases and distinctions might still preside, but they were no longer expected to lead. William Youngs has shown how the ministers adjusted in order to reclaim the loyalty without which their profession would dissolve.

Being trained, ordained, and called had, in this brief and enthusiastic season of renewal, lost its power to make them valuable. Some — the New Lights — warmed to the new evangelical task, yet plied the enthusiasm as an enhancement, never a replacement, of their vocation to ministry. All — sober Old and ardent New — redefined their service as pastoral, not intellectual, and devoted themselves with energy and ardor to becoming the companionable counselors and sustainers of their flocks.[100]

There was a fair loss of membership to the more enthusiastic and less theological churches of the Baptists and Methodists. During the early nineteenth century the breakaway of so many Congregationalists into Unitarianism thinned out another zone of the Congregational spectrum. Each defection allowed Calvinist conservatives to restabilize their leadership by edging out various kinds of liberals. But they, too, were changing, and theology had something to do with it. Or, rather, the lack of theology. For the Calvinist corpus of belief, being essentially protestant, had developed as a corrective. To put a somewhat finer point on it, in the hands of Calvin himself — who was a very accomplished theologian with a capacious horizon of thought — and some of his close associates, it was a corrective to a known tradition. But in the compressed format wherein it was passed on afterward, it was treated as a self-standing creed that was repeated by generations unaware that to receive a tradition rightly one must appropriate it and renew it and recondition it as energetically as if it were a new creation. Calvinist divines were less responsive than they needed to be in the face of repeated pressures to repristinate and to renew their theology.

The struggle between Samuel Colcord Bartlett and his fellow conservatives and William Jewett Tucker and his fellow liberals was theological, in that the former proved incapable of restating those elements of Calvinist orthodoxy which were alleged most grievously to fall short of the gospel. What happened, however, was not that all the liberals departed, like many new sectaries did during the First and Second Great Awakenings. Instead, like the ministers threatened by the new enthusiasm that delegitimated the privileges of their professional learning, they kept their pulpits but lost their nerve — that is, their faith.

It was on Tucker's watch that the college determined to renounce what it called sectarian, that is, any faith with "distinctive tenets," in favor of "those fundamental obligations and incentives of religion in which we are all substantially agreed." Having moved, under Congregational auspices, away from a cramped orthodoxy and into a modernism that reduced faith to morals, and then having shifted its focus again from morals to manners, and its primary loyalties from church to class and country, it had become an enterprise unable to respond any longer to Christianity in any but a sentimental and trivial way.

THE CONGREGATIONAL EXPANSION

The heartland of Congregational churches was New England. It had been the established and tax-supported religion in the colonies that became Connecticut, Massachusetts (with its dependency that would become Maine), and New Hampshire. The early colleges there served as the model for all America once it pushed over the Alleghenies. New Englanders were prominent in that migration, and their colleges were among the earliest to spring up in Illinois and Ohio and the Upper Midwest (then still the "Northwest"). There had been Congregational influence in the drafting of the Northwest Ordinance of 1787, which made the new region "consecrated . . . irrevocably to human freedom, to religion, learning and free thought," preserving the Territory as free soil and proposing to fund religiously sponsored schools for the public benefit.[101] As the roster of Congregational-founded institutions shows, the movement spread to the plains, then to the West Coast, and back into the Rockies.

The founding impulse served a fourfold end. Schools were required to prepare a learned ministry to serve the rapidly proliferating churches in the West. They were also required for the education of the gentry, as in New England. There was, further, a pervading evangelical purpose in this great project, for the West was a morally hazardous environment for anyone seeking Christian salvation, and it housed a vast assortment of uprooted, unchurched migrants. The Congregationalists and the Presbyterians were as eager as the newer Baptists and Methodists to lead these people by the townful to salvation and to church. Special attention was given to those already in thrall to false, unevangelical religion, such as the Mormons in Utah and the Catholic Mexicans in New Mexico and Cubans in Florida. Also, the Congregationalists who had been such intrepid sponsors of abolition stepped forward after the Civil War to further the cause of emancipation by founding colleges for blacks in the South. And in an allied sense of empowerment they welcomed the founding of colleges for women.

To fund these variously intended institutions they established a tangle of societies and boards, whose saga of foundations and rivalries and amalgamations is indeed complex. Basically, there were two families of sponsorship. One was educational, beginning with the American Society for the Education of Pious Youth for the Gospel Ministry (1815), which eventually shook down into the American Education Society (AES). The other was evangelical, and mostly subsidized the preachers who served rough towns that could not yet support them or their families; it emerged as the American Home Missionary Society (AHMS).

The denomination engaged in a lengthy and ultimately frustrated struggle to continue its New England tradition of an educated ministry in the West. The Society for the Promotion of Collegiate and Theological Education at the West (SPCTEW) (conventionally called the Western College Society), a joint venture created by New England Congregationalists and Middle Atlantic Presbyterians in 1843, at a time when they were laying aside the prospect of an eventual merger, succeeded in collecting hefty donations up until the Civil War: to subsidize the tuition of ministerial candidates and to help struggling new colleges in the West.[102] After 1874, however, when the Congregationalists were doing this on their own, the income began to dwindle. In the 1890s their American College and Education Society (ACES) alerted the denomination that the net annual increase of ministers was then only one-eighteenth the number of new congregations established each year. By 1896 a quarter of all their churches were without ministers, while another 10 percent were served by clergy of other denominations. The Congregational ministers came in for criticism as too restless, without "staying power."[103] The continuing fact, however, was that many of these congregations were poor in both membership and treasury and could not pay a salary large enough to support a family, let alone attract competitive applications.[104] Also, most young men now studying for the ministry were coming from backward areas and uncultured churches, while students in the eastern colleges were showing a decreasing interest in the pulpit.

The leadership hastened to say that it was not turning up its nose at these backwoods candidates. For all their learning, the New England colleges were, by comparison, producing rather worldly candidates for ministry.

> Indeed, the colleges of the West are the direct outgrowth of the Home Missionary work; and the oldest of them are even yet not old enough to be unaffected by the characteristic spirit and influence of their missionary origin. In this respect they represent to-day what Williams and Amherst represented in their beginning and in their earlier history — distinctive and prolific centres of influence in the way of religious and ministerial life.
>
> On the other hand, the colleges of the East to-day are separated by long years, and in some instances by centuries, from the missionary influences of their founding. With the increase of their wealth they have widened their range of instruction and thus have grown more and more in assimilation to the methods, scope and scholastic character of the traditional university. . . .
>
> But so much being admitted as natural, and, perhaps, in a sense necessary, relative to the marked lessening of the number of ministerial students in our Eastern colleges, there yet exists, it is to be feared, especially in the older and larger institutions, an undue tendency to *secularization*. . . . The elements requisite to their distinctively Christian character are in danger of diminution and decay.[105]

There was no need for the New England establishment to look condescendingly at the West, however. The U.S. Commissioner of Education released a revealing report in the middle 1890s that less than 39 percent of New England ministers had received a full academic training.[106] Congregationalists reckoned that, whereas they had once proudly counted more than 94 percent of their ministers as fully educated (four years of college plus three years of divinity school), only half would pass muster as the nineteenth century was drawing to a close.[107]

Only the Lame and the Halt Remain

From the 1890s onward, Congregational efforts in higher education all seemed to be exercises in humiliation. The New England schools gathered strength unto themselves, but their western siblings had a faltering, uphill journey. The most marginal academies and colleges were sent just enough each year to pluck them back from annihilation. In the mid-1890s the CES was subsidizing only eight colleges with modest awards ranging from $1,500 to $4,000. Their combined enrollment was 975: only 121 were at the college level, and less than one-third were church members.[108] During the next quarter-century thirteen colleges received financial aid. Congregationalists were still less than one-third of the students, and each college typically graduated only twenty-seven students a year.[109] Among all twenty-five colleges which would then admit affiliation with the Congregationalists, only fifteen seemed to have reached the state of academic "adequacy." Tuition fees at the most costly of the colleges were still less than the lowest fees at typical state institutions. Less than 5 percent of the congregations canvassed were sending contributions for the educational effort.[110] Only the Methodists and the Catholics "gave evidence of having reached down to a large number of small givers."[111] Congregationally founded universities and colleges that had become academically successful and financially stable no longer acknowledged affiliation with the denomination. Middlebury was the only New England college left on the roster. Oberlin, Carleton, Beloit, Pomona, Grinnell: these were the few lights left in the Congregational firmament after nearly three centuries of educational endeavor. In a few years they, too, would disengage themselves from the denominational connection. The New England institutions were beginning to recruit both faculty and students in a way that steadily reduced the presence of Congregationalists on the campuses. Beyond New England, most of the colleges seem never to have enrolled a majority of students from the denomination.

The agencies back in Boston, for their purposes, would occasionally marshal with pride the names of their progeny, implying there was still an affiliation. The *Congregationalist Year-Book* for 1910 listed forty institutions, but with the immediate disclaimer: "Some of the colleges named below are undenominational, but are mentioned because of their Congregational origin and history."[112] The older foundations began to disappear from the lists, but by 1940 there they all were again: Harvard, Yale, Dartmouth, Smith, Bowdoin . . . always with the disclaimer that some "are mentioned because of their Congregational origin and history." In 1948 the Missions Council, an entirely different Congregational agency, published a list of church-related colleges, and gone were Amherst, Berea, Bowdoin, Colorado, Dartmouth, Harvard, Middlebury, Mount Holyoke, Oberlin, Pomona, Smith, Wellesley, Williams, Yale, all the black colleges, and a clutch of others. Then in 1960, of the thirty-three that had not closed in the meantime, all but two had risen to new life on the official lists.

In 1921 the denomination created a foundation authorized to gather "at least

$500,000 a year" and to create a great educational endowment. When the Association of Colleges of Congregational Affiliation (ACCA) was then called together, only a third of the presidents came; a third approved of the idea but stayed home, and the last third never even acknowledged the letter. The first year for fund-raising, the national yield was $35,000. The ACCA fell from sight.[113] On virtually the only occasion in this century when the Congregationalists asked the institutions they had founded to acknowledge in a minimal way that some bond between them still existed, only the lame and the halt complied.

Someone noticed in 1912 that Congregational youth were enrolling at state colleges and universities, possibly even 12,000 of them. The denomination therefore organized student pastorates at Illinois State, Wisconsin, Nebraska State, Kansas State, Kansas State Agricultural School, Michigan State, California State, Iowa State, and Iowa State Agricultural School.[114] It seemed as if Congregationalists were gaining a monopoly on engineering and agriculture. The enrollment on state campuses had multiplied fourteen times in the previous forty years, and the denomination realized that they were much easier to serve pastorally and to recruit for ministry than on their "own" campuses. On one state campus alone the census had revealed a thousand Congregationalists.[115]

In 1915 the education secretary wrote to all presidents and asked for their "account of the present movement of spiritual forces and purposes in the Christian Colleges." Their responses suggest that the spirit of Tucker lived on. Henry King of Oberlin thought that the Christian character of the campuses was on the decline, "due in no small part to lack of sufficient care in the choice of members of the faculty." What he would require of candidates, however, was nothing related to being Congregationalists. "The thing to be desired, of course, is to get men with what I call 'character-begetting power' . . . We try to make sure that our men are men whose influence we can count on for the best things in the entire college life." C. J. Bushnell at Pacific University said more money would help: his Baptist counterpart a few miles away at Linfield College was getting hefty annual grants from the Baptists, and a promise of $50,000 for the endowment. Stephen Penrose wrote from Whitman that students were not interested in ministry but in something more practical. The significant change in the past generation had been "the transfer of emphasis from religious services to religious service . . . helpfulness rather than piety is the characteristic quality of our religions right now." Alexander Meiklejohn at Amherst wrote somewhat archly that he was referring the inquiry to the general secretary of the campus YMCA.[116]

A Critique of Congregational Colleges

Five years later the Society had trebled its number of pastorates on state campuses, and the list of ministerial prospects being supported at "denominational" colleges had been drastically reduced.[117] A slow but inexorable mutual aloofness was estranging the denomination from the colleges. It awaited a nonacademic to bring the issue out fully into the open. Pastor Jay T. Stocking was an inveterate appointee to denominational committees and commissions. She addressed a seminar on the waning of Congregational investment in higher education:

> Our church-related colleges are craving a measure of support from our churches which they are not receiving. Our churches are craving from the colleges results that are more in harmony with the church's cherished aims. There is a wide-spread feeling among the church-affiliated colleges that the churches have forsaken their traditional interest in education, and perhaps an equally wide-spread feeling among our churches that the so-called Christian colleges have forsaken the purpose for which they were founded and that they fail to provide such an education as a competent citizen and a competent individual requires. . . .
>
> The ideals of the university have spread to the colleges. Even without the influence of the universities, the colleges could scarcely have remained unaffected by the growing secularization of life and the emphasis on the utilitarian. The desire for bigness and income has widened the gate and broadened the way that leads to the college and through the college. The presence in the student body of so many religious faiths or none has tended to modify traditional Christian practice and emphasis. . . . Not a few of our colleges with their eyes on enrollment and income seem . . . desirous of a public decision that they can not be called religious, and some are shy of the word "Christian." The colleges in large measure have succumbed to the secular spirit of the day. There is, in general, little to distinguish them, even our church-related ones, from our state universities, except that they are usually smaller and that because of lack of equipment and instructors, they often do not do their work so well.
>
> I recently wrote to the presidents of a dozen colleges, most of them Congregational in origin, asking whether they spoke of their respective colleges as Christian and their reason for the reply given. One replied that she had never spoken of her institution as a "Christian college." A second one replied that he rarely used the term "Christian college" as he rarely used the term "Christian gentleman." Seven replied positively that they do speak of their colleges as Christian. . . .
>
> Those who hesitate to apply the term Christian to their colleges may also reveal that they do not consider their work to be more Christian than that of tax-supported institutions. Indeed, one of them writes "I have always thought that the term 'Christian college' is a little unfortunate in its implications regarding state universities." One president who wrote that they had tried to keep the college Christian in accordance with the wishes of the founder added, "He used the term 'Christian' in a technical rather than a philosophical sense in order to indicate that the religious services of the college are Christian, that the meetings of the Board of Trustees are opened with prayer to God, and that all official assemblies are concluded with a benediction." I fail to find here anything that would differ-

entiate that college from certain state universities that I know, unless it be a pious recognition on the part of the Board of Trustees that they are "standing in the need of prayer."[118]

President Hopkins replies, "I always speak of Dartmouth as a Christian college because it was founded by Christians, and the religious motive in founding it was to advance the cause of Christianity. It has been under the administrative direction from the beginning of men who themselves believed that Christianity as a principle of life was the one highest motive which could actuate men, and it continues to be the belief of those responsible for the college of the present day that the ideals of Christianity represent the highest ideals which have been presented to the human race."

Though Hopkins's reply was taken by Stocking as positive, it reflects the operative notion at Dartmouth then that religious faith was to be a private, not a public, preoccupation on campus. Stocking went on:

The chief means on which a college must rely for the realization of its purposes are its teachers. It is Christian teachers who make a Christian college. They are not only the interpreters of facts; they are also the incarnation of interpretations. It is idle to expect men who are not Christians to help provide a Christian education.[119]

Stocking was not alone in her willingness to smell doublethink in the Congregational groves of academe, but she was singularly frank. And she was remarkably late: 1934. More than forty years earlier it had been noticed that the colonial foundations in New England had sloughed off the piety of their early years. For decades it had been known that all of the supportive energies of the denomination were being expended on institutions that managed to attract only one-third of their students from the Congregationalists. For twenty years it had been known, though perhaps not taken to heart, that state college and university campuses were better places to offer ministry and to recruit ministers. Ten years earlier the Congregationally founded institutions had made it explicit that they would not accept any public affiliation with the church. How then had devoted servants of the denomination in Boston and Chicago and New York managed, for so long a time, to preserve the fiction that the Puritan search for learning within the devout community was still dynamically at work in their progeny?

"Nonsectarian" Education in Santa Fe

A brief but intense Congregational venture in education manifests how ardently they defended beliefs that they could not say out loud. Toward the end of the nineteenth century the New West Education Commission in Boston was supporting an academy in Santa Fe. Every subsidized school had to guarantee that (1) it would be governed by a self-perpetuating board of trustees forever free of political or ecclesiastical control; (2) it would thereby remain and publicly present itself as nonsectarian; (3) a majority of the trustees would always be members in good and regular standing in Congregational churches; and (4) in order to maintain the characteristics of a vital Christian school, its president would always be an evangelical Christian.[120] Various distinguished citizens had been recruited for the board of the academy; the treasurer was now Mr. Lehman Spiegelberg, and the chairman of the executive committee was the Honorable Bernard Seligman. The Santa Fe board, under special restrictions, would have a majority of "Congregationalists of the Orthodox faith," and two-thirds would be members of evangelical churches; further, the teachers would all be Christians. The new trustees wanted to know how the academy was going to be nonsectarian with all that Christian and Congregational heft on the board. Mr. Spiegelberg said that if it was going to be sectarian, then let the Congregationalists come and build an academy themselves and not expect the board to do it. Mr. Seligman added that he took nonsectarian to mean "non-religious." Mr. Ritch, president of the board and a meek Congregationalist, thought that if a chapter from the Bible were read aloud and a prayer offered daily, that was surely enough to make it Christian — and probably the limit of what could rightly be done. The board agreed that the people back in Boston should disavow control on the part of the denomination.

Mr. Ladd, the principal, complained privately to Congregational House that the academy was "largely in the hands of irreligious and I may say infidel men" who refused to see the logic of a Christian school supported by Christians for Christian education . . . yet one in which Congregationalists would obviously retain a special standing. He went on to warn that the Presbyterians, the Methodists, the Baptists, and the Episcopalians were all waiting for the academy to falter so that they could come in and exploit the clamor for higher education in Santa Fe.

The board then reported difficulties in their attempts to raise funds. The certificate of incorporation said clearly that the academy should never come under ecclesiastical control, but potential donors were of the persuasion that it was obviously Congregational. Secretary Bliss replied by return mail from Boston that the academy could not possibly have come under sectarian control, for there was no ecclesiastical judicatory in New Mexico. This technicality of Congregational discipline was lost on the nonmembers on the board. Nor had any of the teachers been accused of giving the least sectarian "bias to the mind of any child, or sought to impress any moral or religious truth upon which all god-fearing men are not agreed."

The God-fearing trustees' misgivings were not laid to rest. They began to form a separate corporation which would build and own the new academy building. Its charter would then provide that whatever school leased the building must be "forever unsectarian: that is, while said schools, college, Academy (which it should be their purpose to form) accept the Bible generally, the teaching and curriculum thereof shall teach no creed, church, or denominational theology whatever." Ladd reported their thinking: "the recognition of the Bible is only like the recognition of a book on botany or history: no word, note or comment is ever to be made on its sayings. *Christianity* as such is in their view *sectarian.*"

The trustees provided in the draft of their schoolhouse charter that if any sectarian activity ever took place in the building, the school would have to pay rent retroactively from the date of first occupancy, and with interest! Bliss seems not to have noticed that the trustees were trumping the New West Commission with the same reversionary terms Boston imposed. Bliss was sure no Congregational churches could be asked to put up money for something grounded on such radically untraditional principles. He deplored what he saw as a Jewish boardroom plot: "The R.C.s could well call schools such as they contemplated in the new incorporation *atheistical.* They accept God no more than they do (if I can say it without irreverence) a burro, as a fact of existence. But they have no use for Him, and look down upon those who have." He was much distraught by Mr. Ritch, the spineless chairman, who explained that he was going along with the others to promote harmony, in order to found a school that "all friends of education" could join in supporting.

The New West Commission claimed the "right to have a *christian* school, limited only by the words non-sectarian and non-ecclesiastical. The interpretation of the words is left to us. Under that provision there is absolutely no instruction which we, as non-polemical, liberal-minded, practical Christians would wish to impart, which we would not have the right to impart." The word "Christian," Bliss noted, "is a term of very wide meaning and nothing which we shall wish to impart will violate either its letter or spirit." To the principal-in-waiting he wrote: "Of course you cannot insist on the Christian quality without offending Jews and infidels, and, while you have none to help you withstand their violence, your wisdom is to bide your time." Let them erect a building if they please: when the lease comes to be drawn, "the *power* is in our hands." Brother Ladd, meanwhile, was in parlay with local land developers and had obtained the promise of a grand plot of land for "Santa Fe University" if only the Commission would commit itself to spend $25,000 there within the first two years. Boston, which did not have that much money to spend on all their institutions combined, pleaded with him to realize that for Protestant interests to make any headway in as overwhelmingly Catholic a place as Santa Fe, they would have to make common cause and not alienate all of their friends.

The Santa Fe Academy vanished, leaving a handsome letterhead and a conflicted memory. Its delicious memoir, however, illustrates the dynamics then at work in the world of Congregational education. This all transpired in 1881. The Andover Trial was still five years off, but the faction to which Samuel Colcord Bartlett belonged was beginning to go down in defeat before the faction which William Jewett Tucker so handsomely embodied. The conservative Calvinists had a faith that was, though narrow in concern and scope, highly articulated. They were at pains to defend it, and their mistrust of fellow Congregationalists was hardly more severe than their judgment upon other, careless, Christians, and indeed the heathen. The liberals, as here displayed by the New West Commission, were soothed by their certitude that the requirements of their faith were sure to be honored by any ten Congregationalists that might assemble, and to be reliably taught by employees of any evangelical (i.e., decent) denomination. Brother Ladd's panicky sense out west of being a lonely disciple in an alien culture was the polar opposite of Mr. Bliss's assurance back east that the mass of right-minded citizens stood with him. The adversaries were so marginal to his culture as to be exotic: Jews, Mormons, Catholics. They could be managed by the prudent deployment of power (i.e., money) and by a shrewd use of equivocation.

In Santa Fe, men who considered themselves God-fearing were implicitly accusing the Boston establishment of duplicity. If the Congregationalists were so determined to retain control of their philanthropies by whatever Congregationalists were locally chosen, even those over whom Boston had no authoritative control, it must be because there were commitments and convictions that all Congregationalists dependably shared: commitments and convictions that obviously made a great deal of difference. Thus the critics were confirmed in their view that *"Christianity* as such is — *sectarian."*[121]

In 1881 these Congregationalists thought they shared with all other God-fearing people (i.e., Protestants) the crucial beliefs they meant securely to provide for the young. To do so they engaged in not-so-innocent wordplay, alleging that what they taught was nonsectarian. They claimed it was not specifically Congregational, yet for unspoken reasons only specifically Congregational people could be trusted to teach it. The hoax was meant to stymie not-very-God-fearing folks like the Jews, Catholics, and Mormons. But as time passed, it would turn out that the hoax was on them. They really did end up with teaching that was neither sectarian nor Christian. The commitments and convictions of Congregational House devolved into little more than any genteel American might assent to . . . without needing to be very God-fearing. Had Messrs. Seligman and Spiegelberg been more patient, they might have found much less to offend their sensibilities than either side supposed. Had they waited only a few decades, they would have seen a significant clarification in the Boston rules. The prohibition against "political or ecclesiastical control" was amended by adding "other than Congregational," and the pretense of nonsectarianism then obviously had to be deleted.[122] But by then the Congregationalists in control were finding it difficult to say what difference that was going to make. People like Brother Bliss, it turned out, had labored long and patiently so that people like Brother Ritch could be in charge.

BELOIT COLLEGE

When the Congregationalists joined with the Presbyterians in a Plan of Union in 1801, it encouraged them to coordinate the founding of churches and colleges and the training and support of ministers in the West. At that time the Congregationalists were the most numerous, affluent, and influential denomination in the United States: twice as large as any other. But when the nation crossed the Alleghenies, their partnership seemed to function in the Presbyterians' favor. The New Englanders abominated slavery, whereas their Middle Atlantic neighbors regarded it with ambivalence. Few Congregationalists therefore migrated on a southwesterly slant. Their settlements lay in a straight latitudinal band westward from Massachusetts and Connecticut. Any migrant congregations or individuals, whatever their original loyalty, that made their way into slaveholding territories inevitably ended up Presbyterian. Further, when the Democrats displaced the Federalists in the government, a chill wind blew in the faces of the New Englanders, who were, almost to a man, of the elder party. So strong was that loyalty that in western towns their preachers could seem more partisan than pastoral, and provocative to anyone inclined otherwise.

Also, there was an unresolved polity difference between Congregationalists from Massachusetts, who rigorously observed the independence of each congregation, and those from Connecticut, who through the networking of their ministers had woven an effective web of closer fellowship between congregations ("consociation," they called it). The Connecticut sort, who as we have seen were well represented in New Hampshire, were for most practical purposes functioning as Presbyterians. In the much less developed Northwest, Congregationalists were at a functional disadvantage, since the central authority which they had fundamentally rejected was what they would probably need in order to proliferate beyond the cultural palisade that had enclosed New England. As it turned out, the more durable "consociating" congregations found it easy to drift into Presbyterianism without much sense of change. Thus in the northern sector of the Western Reserve (Ohio), the Plan of Union's provision for mixed congregations worked in their favor. Most Congregationalists who settled there ended up as Presbyterians, and that trend continued westward through Indiana and Illinois (in the latter, strong pockets of proslavery sentiment brought outspoken abolitionist preachers' horsewhippings, and even death). Between 1800 and 1850, two thousand of their congregations from New York to Illinois became Presbyterian.[123]

But in Wisconsin it would be different. The Northwest Territory ran to the Mississippi, and Wisconsin, in its farthest corner, was the last commonwealth to be staked out. Indians in its southern marches had discouraged white immigration until the Black Hawk War, when U.S. troops (Captain Abraham Lincoln among them) captured this courageous chief and drove out the Sacs and the Foxes whom he had rallied. That was in 1832, and the white man then came in promptly and eagerly. Milwaukee was platted in 1835, and Wisconsin became a territory the next year. Immigrants poured in, especially from New England. By 1846 Wisconsin would be admitted as a state. In the 1840s the population soared from 31,000 to 300,000, the fastest rate of increase anywhere in the Union. In three decades it would exceed one million.[124]

For a while in the earliest territorial days Beloit, which sat adjacent to the Illinois border at the junction of the Rock River and Turtle Creek, was the largest of the new territorial settlements. Its residents had already secured a charter for their "seminary," or elementary school, in 1837. Meanwhile various companies of settlers were forming in New Hampshire, and one, organized in 1836 at Colebrook, quite near Dartmouth's northern landholdings, chose Beloit for its destination. In 1838 the First Congregational Church was formally organized there; that year the first four such congregations were established in the territory. First Congregational counted twenty-four founding members: considerable in a town of from 100 to 150 residents.[125] The town built itself a schoolhouse, which the various denominations used as their shared meetinghouse. Times were allotted according to the financial stake each denomination had in the building, and the Congregationalists had the first choice in scheduling.

The American Home Missionary Society (AHMS), jointly sponsored by Congregationalists and Presbyterians, was supporting various ministers in Wisconsin, and local reports said they functioned "like a single denomination." Their ministers were denominationally interchangeable. But in 1837 the national Plan of Union dissolved. The ascendancy of Presbyterians across the Northwest had provoked a new surge of sensitivity among their Congregational partners, who were finally noticing that whereas the Congregational churches in New England was contributing twice as much funding to the establishment of churches and schools in the West (by some accounts, three times as much), the Presbyterians had been the beneficiaries of twice as much funding. Already in 1840 when they founded the Presbyterian and Congregational Convention of Wisconsin (PCCW), the Congregationalists were determined this collaboration would not compromise their ability to maintain their own integrity, or to take a dominant role in the public affairs of the territory.[126]

A Presbyterian-Congregational College Meant to Be Congregational

A series of caucuses in 1844-45 that included ministers and laity from Illinois, Iowa, and Wisconsin agreed that "the interests of education are inseparably connected with the prosperity of religion in this territory."[127] They planned a regional network of colleges, female academies, and a theological school, and Wisconsin was assigned a college. Beloit was a leading village, and the Congregational church would put up more than half of the land and cash needed by the college. As one person explained it in Milwaukee, "Beloit was the only place then in Wisconsin where there was religion enough to have a college."[128] Perhaps more to the point,

Beloit College was financially grounded on a purposeful welcome by a village, rather than on a land grant from a state legislature (as in Dartmouth's case). Like many other western colleges such as Oberlin, Marietta, Knox, Olivet, Grinnell, Whitman, Carleton, Colorado, and Pomona, a community transplanted from New England saw it as needful to have a local church and school, plus a regional college. Beloit College opened in the basement of the simple stone church building in 1847, at which time Nathan Lord was presiding over a maturing Dartmouth College. Its initial board was composed equally of clergy and laity, Wisconsinites and Illinoisans, Congregationalists and Presbyterians.

It is remarkable how possible it was for these isolated and scantily financed new schools to secure well-educated faculty. The clerics on Beloit's board were predominantly Yale men, and so were the teachers they hired. They included Jackson J. Bushnell (brother to the more famous Horace) in mathematics and natural philosophy and his classmate Joseph Emerson (kinsman of Ralph Waldo) in languages. The college was open for two years before the board asked its chairman, Milwaukee Presbyterian pastor Aaron Chapin, also of Yale, to accept the presidency. All three would spend the rest of their lives at and for Beloit. Students came in abundance: 202 were enrolled within two years, though only 8 of them could yet study at the college level. Money was not so abundant, and the canvasses which kept the doors open in those early years drew about half their funds from missionaries in the region who were supported on miserable salaries by the AHMS, who sacrificially managed somehow to set aside enough each month to contribute $100 annually.

Though the college was a predominantly Congregational undertaking under the special patronage of the First Congregational Church, there was still some ambiguity about its staff, all of whom were clergy. When President Chapin, who was a Congregationalist in Beloit and a Presbyterian elsewhere, was asked how he wanted to be listed, he replied that he was "much of an Eclectic" and hated "all sorts of humbug," including questions of this sort. When left to its own course, he explained, the grace of God "will work through almost any channel through which truth flows. The mischief is that men dig and dike up some sort of canal and cry here and only here can saving grace flow." In 1849 this was a remarkably nondenominational statement.[129]

This was not Chapin's position when the college identity became a subject of dispute before the territorial legislature. The trustees sent up for incorporation a conventional draft charter modeled after that of Western Reserve College (Ohio). The bill had strong Yankee/Whig support in the upper house, but was unexpectedly subjected to amendment:

> Section 7. That no religious tenets or opinions shall be requisite to entitle any person to be admitted as a student in said college, and no such tenets or opinions shall be required as a qualification for any professor, tutor, or teacher of said college, and no student of said college shall be required to attend religious worship in any particular denomination.

The presumed motives of its proponent, Moses McCure Strong, provide the amendment with a context. Strong was a Vermont Yankee, educated at Middlebury and Dartmouth. His inclinations toward conviviality had helped him neither with his studies nor in his ability to live up to Congregationalism. He became a backslider, and after two letters of admonition from his congregation they publicly excommunicated him. He later became an Episcopalian, a devout man in church and at home, and a temperance activist after he came to terms with his own drinking habits. But he carried an abiding distaste for the Calvinism of the Congregationalists. Unlike many of the New Englanders come west, he was a Jeffersonian Democrat, which gave him a further cause for animosity toward Beloit as a likely center of antislavery advocacy.[130] He had become an advocate for the large Catholic population in Milwaukee, mostly Irish and German immigrants, in the face of the Know-Nothings and their Whig allies. To make matters worse, Milwaukee had been astir for the previous year after a Thanksgiving Day sermon in the First Congregational Church by John J. Miter, one of the incorporators of Beloit College. Miter had taken the occasion to warn his flock against Catholics: "*that class* of foreigners who have no just claim to the attributes of integrity and clear-sighted discretion" due to their obedience to a European despot.

The Wisconsin Catholics were looking to Strong to ensure that the forthcoming state constitution would make state schools nonsectarian. Older states with sizable Catholic populations were funding "common schools" which, to Horace Mann and his supporters, provided an unquestionably generic Christian tutelage. But to the Catholics they were, in effect, Protestant schools.[131] When the Beloit charter came before the Territorial Council, then, since its proponents would not openly claim it as a Congregational college, Strong decided to hold them to it. The trustees were much undone by this amended charter. Chapin, then only chairman, advised that they decline to accept it and await "a legislature that will have more sense than to knock all religious influence out of a charter." They prepared a resolution to refuse the charter because it would "seriously embarrass the Institution." But at the last moment they decided that the "obnoxious features" could all be sidestepped in the practical order.[132]

Chapin and his fellow incorporators apparently desired to found a college which would be consciously Congregational in its personnel and its instruction, and the nonsectarian requirement was taken to be an obstacle to that. On reconsideration, they determined among themselves that they could still carry on as planned, provided only that they not state their loyalties publicly. In later years Beloit would eventually try to make a virtue out of necessity and would brandish the originally obnoxious Section 7 as evidence of the college's authentic liberalism, much as Dartmouth had done for the nonsectarian clause imposed by Governor Wentworth in his charter. But at the beginning the trustees were not just relying on their capacity for finesse. They expected Beloit to offer a kind of Congregationalism that would seem familiar and unexceptional to all prospective comers, with the obvious exception of Unitarians and Catholics. When Chapin went into print a few months later to reassure the public of the college's broad catholicity, and spoke of the charter as essentially what the founders had requested all along, he was not likely to have been lying. But he was likely to have set aside the prospect that the faith they shared was in any significant way distinctive. Chapin had come a long way from New England.[133]

Beloit, Yale of the West

Much was made of Beloit as a replica of Yale. As already seen, the majority of the clerical incorporators were from Yale, as were Chapin, Bushnell, and Emerson, known in later years as the "Old Guard." They were all intertwined in the tradition. Bushnell and Emerson were classmates; Emerson was a Skull and Bones man; Emerson's father had taught Stephen Peet and Aratus Kent, two of the chief ministerial trustees; Chapin eventually reckoned that his New England connections had brought more than $70,000 to his college. At Chapin's inauguration Aratus Kent concluded his address thus:

> You and I are sons of Yale, and I know not how better to *magnetize* you to a high standard of excellence than to point to the portraiture of your old president and mine. As I sat musing in my study, anticipating the exercises of this day, my eye met the searching glance of the venerable ex-President [Jeremiah] Day and the sainted [Timothy] Dwight [the Elder]. They seemed to be looking down from the wall where they hung and come to my aid, just in time to administer the oath of office. Methinks I heard them say, "Young man, yours is a high destiny, an enviable station — yours is an awful responsibility, a delightful work. Take this charter and observe its provisions. Execute these laws with the firmness of Caesar — with the meekness of a christian. Make the impress of this seal the symbol of literary eminence, unrivalled between the oceans."[134]

They constructed a curriculum modeled on that of Yale, required the same preparatory grades for admission (and actually turned away applicants found wanting), and estimated that the quality of scholarship and "manly development" were on a par with those of New Haven. They were delighted when one of their first matriculants, after two years at Beloit, was accepted as a transfer student in Yale's junior class. Cyrus Northrup, president of the University of Minnesota, later told a commencement audience in New Haven: "The ideas of the founders of Beloit were the same old conservative Yale ideas which have so generally characterized Yale educators whether at home or abroad. . . . If I were seeking in the whole West for a young Yale, I should go at once to Beloit."[135]

Another essential link to their tradition was the religious identity of the college. The aim of the founders, notes Beloit's historian Robert Kimball Richardson, "was to make the Institution an instrument for the Puritanizing and New

Englandizing of what in their day was called the Northwest." An early circular to the college's contributors stated its ambition to be "the central fortress to represent and maintain the principles of Puritan, Calvinistic Protestantism."[136] James W. Strong, Beloit '58, founding president of Carleton College, chose his alma mater's twenty-fifth anniversary to rhapsodize on this:

> New England is the real mother of us all, and whether we look at our political theories, our educational systems, or our religious principles, we easily trace the features of the mother's face. This likeness in character and in aims makes it worth our while to call distinctly to mind to-day, that primal principle of the Pilgrims, . . . *individualism;* — freedom of the individual conscience and opinion, — the right of private judgment, without the dictate of Pope, bishop, priest, or king. . . . Beloit College is as truly a child of New England Puritanism as though its walls were standing on Plymouth Rock. . . . It could not be otherwise than that a college so founded and built up in prayer, so pervaded from its very beginning with religious ideas and aims, should ally itself most closely with that work which is the special care of the Christian church. . . . It has aimed to be distinctly and thoroughly Christian.[137]

Although this evocation of the Pilgrim/Puritan character often involved culture and class as well as religious fellowship, the close tie that bound Beloit College to the First Congregational Church was a tenacious and complex identifier with an institutional tradition. When the church built itself a new meetinghouse in 1862, directly adjacent to the college, its membership numbered 301, yet it was built for 1,200: to accommodate the college community. Commencements (none was held elsewhere until 1948), baccalaureate ceremonies, presidential inaugurals, rhetoricals and forensic competitions, lectures before the combined literary societies, concerts — all enjoyed the hospitality of the church. The congregation had contributed the largest part of the campus land cost and had given the college bell and books for the library. Indeed, by the end of the century the college reckoned it had received no less than $40,000 in gifts from the church. Members had lodged and boarded students. The two institutions had offered one another temporary accommodations, loans, revivals, and trustees. The college made the church the most aristocratic congregation for miles around, and the church served as pledge for the college's piety. Presidents and faculty often served in the pulpit, and pastors looked out upon as many as seventeen other ordained ministers from the college faculty sitting weekly in their congregation. If the college faculty were inclined to occasional mildness in reproving the high jinks of their juvenile students, there was always the sterner tradition of publicly maintained discipline within the church to hold them to their own standards. The church in early years had legislated against the sale or consumption of intoxicating liquor (extending that, after further experience, to "strong beer"); fornication; heresy; traveling, social visiting, worldly conversation, or reading on the Sabbath; and slavery (a condemnation in which they were not unanimous, and which elicited some negative response among the townsfolk). One member was excommunicated for denying the inspiration of the Scriptures and the divinity of Jesus, and another was refused a letter of dismission (vouching for his membership in good standing when moving to another town) because he was a doctor who had charged exorbitant fees. The church was probably given a good dose of patience and tolerance by the presence of so many students, while the young people were sobered by membership in this dominating community of their Calvinist elders.[138]

Abolitionist or Not?

Despite these symbols and securities for tradition, Beloit College was not at all a school committed to a truculent conservatism. From the outset its leaders were at pains to soften — sometimes even to compromise — any commitments that in this freer western air might give offense. We have seen, for instance, that the church and the college were both publicly identified as opposed to slavery: indeed, they were sympathetic to activism on behalf of abolition. But there was also a strong sentiment in the community against such moral advocacy, now that it had become so aggravated politically.[139] The first large benefaction received by the college, at a time when no other funds were available, was a parcel of real estate given by a wealthy Hudson Valley minister named Samuel Barber "upon the express condition that the said College shall forever allow students to enter and receive its entire benefits without distinction of color." Barber thought it "*a most unreasonable thing, that the free colored man should be reproached for his ignorance,* and at the same time be prevented from improving his mind, by being excluded from Seminaries of learning." He commended Stephen Peet (trustee and agent of the college): "I am accordingly pleased that public opinion in your growing State, is such as to warrant your Trustees to do justly & benevolently, without fear of ruining their institution. And I feel too, a great respect for *them,* for being willing to brave and meet any prejudice against their infant enterprise, which may lurk in any narrow minded individuals."

But the trustees were not all that anxious to do battle with local prejudice. Aaron Chapin, still more Presbyterian than Congregational, had himself undergone a change of conscience several years earlier and concluded that "slavery is the greatest evil against which our government has to contend." Peet stated in the *Herald of the Prairies* that he was "an abolitionist & should be ashamed not to be." But he added: "I have not allowed it to interfere with my business or injure my influence." Chapin and Peet were both opposed to aggressive and provocative tactics on a vexed issue that could split both the region and their new Convention. The brick walls of Middle College, the college's first building, had stood without floors, windows, or roof for many months because so many people in Beloit were withholding support from the "abolition college." The founders resolved not to

70

compromise their moral conviction, but to mute it in public, so as not to jeopardize their standing in a community where their Puritan identity no longer assured them of dominance.[140]

The Civil War would rally loyalties in the Union (though certainly not in all localities, such as New York City or Baltimore), and the service of Beloit men put the college's commitment to liberation in a context that gave it an unexceptionable dignity. In 1872 Joseph Emerson set forth the historical facts:

> Then came the war for country, law, and liberty, which are all watch-words in college thought and life; and every call was answered by alumni and by resident students, until, of less than eight hundred who could bear arms, more than four hundred were in the field. Nearly fifty did not return; and the Memorial Hall cherishes their memory, both as an honor to them and as a perpetual education to their successors.[141]

It was a moment when the college could well wrap itself in the nation's flag and justify itself by a standard no longer controversial. "Their service was in devotion to the principles which are the soul of the manhood which the college aims to train. . . . The enthusiasms of the time were so in accord with the spirit of the college that they could hardly be said to have interrupted its work."[142]

Before the war, and indeed through its early years, western Congregationalists were not entirely of one mind on the issue of slavery. A story was circulated in Beloit circles, however, of the privately expressed opinion of Lincoln that the Union owed the loyalty of the Northwest to the antislavery convictions of the AHMS missionaries in their churches and colleges.[143] In Beloit that loyalty was present, but prudently softened in its expression. Dexter Clary, however, who had been so central as minister of First Congregational Church and as a trustee of the college, had concluded a stressful decade in the local pulpit due in part to his insistence that slavery was not a closed issue and that the congregation should not position itself on the side of abolition. He stepped down in 1850, twelve years before Nathan Lord was obliged to resign at Dartmouth over the same issue.[144]

Congregational or Not?

There was a second issue which Beloit College was constrained to handle with discretion: its relationship, as a jointly sponsored yet Congregationally defined college, to the Presbyterians. Recall that the joint Convention was founded in 1840 with an eye toward permanent fellowship. The Presbyterian partners were New School Presbyterians, separated from the more orthodox Calvinist Old School by their evangelical adherence to the Second Great Awakening. Thus there was a special affinity between them and the Congregationalists. But Stephen Peet, chief founder of the college, who had ministered to the First Presbyterian Church of

Milwaukee and was serving as stated clerk to the PCCW, and also as the Wisconsin agent of the AHMS, was forced to resign this latter position because his work for the college was taken by some very partisan Congregationalists as favoring Presbyterians.[145] Feelings of mutual jealousy were not far below the surface between the two yokefellow denominations. Only four years after the college opened, and only seven years after the bipartite Convention reported itself to be "one denomination," the Presbyterians in nearby Illinois took Knox College as their own and founded a college in Galena and a university at Lake Forest, which would clearly rival Beloit on their understanding that the latter was now intended solely for a Congregational clientele. Thus it was not idle advice for Professor Ralph Emerson to write from Andover Seminary to his son Joseph "that the College ought best be quite conservative, sustaining the present order of things, yet in such a way as not to give offense to innovating Presbyterians."[146]

President Chapin deplored this, and was at pains to retain the patronage of the Presbyterians. The First Congregational Church pulpit just then came open, and Chapin supported a call to a Presbyterian minister who might not only minister to the congregation but also begin some theological teaching at the college. His purpose was to combine the two denominations more closely. The minister, however, did not accept. Chapin inveighed against aggressive Congregationalists who were trying to make Beloit all their own.[147] At the college's tenth anniversary in 1857 it was reported that Congregationalists and Presbyterians were "two kindred branches of the church of Christ," sharing at Beloit "an unsectional, unsectarian, catholic spirit . . . and the common faith of the gospel."[148] This was their wish, but not their accomplishment.

The demographics, however, were all in favor of the Congregationalists, and Chapin's coreligionists knew it. In 1851 several Presbyterian ministers broke away from the PCCW to form presbyteries, and in 1852 the collapse of joint home missionary efforts nationally made the local collaboration fairly hopeless. Thirty years later the Presbyterians were gone from the joint venture, and their name was dropped entirely.[149]

Accommodationist Rhetoric

This urgent need to construe the college's ecclesial loyalties in an emollient way became a central concern for Aaron Chapin. It led him to flatten out the profile of whatever their faith might have stood for. The more adroit Chapin and his colleagues grew, the more generic became the account of their Christianity. At one fund-raising meeting of the church, a discussion about the nature of Congregationalism was drawn out to some length. "Chapin's tall figure rose and was recognized. 'Congregationalism,' pronounced this erstwhile Presbyterian, 'is common sense.' "[150] Emerson, his colleague, was similarly inclined to quips which purveyed a tamed Puritanism. Asked once what "salvation by faith" meant, he defined it as acceptance of God's truth with the whole personality, "not only Bible truth but all truth." Robert H. Irrmann describes the Old Guard's Puritanism as of the liberal brand, an essential broad-mindedness, a "mild latitudinarianism."[151] His predecessor-historian, Robert Richardson, describes it as "kindly, liberal, open-minded, non-credal and magnanimous."[152]

Thus, though the Old Guard who founded Beloit College saw themselves as faithful heirs to the Puritan tradition, conservative sons of Yale come to reproduce in the West what they had been given in the East, they were at first dismayed by the unwelcome and "obnoxious" proviso in their charter which held them to forgo a sectarian community of faith and worship. But they easily overcame that frustration. Guided by the sense of compromise needed for peaceful coexistence with both their Convention and their state, and encouraged by their hope to achieve a dominant strength in both of those pluralist worlds, they began prudently to reconstruct the emphases of their faith, the agenda of their discipline, and the tenor of their worship, to make Beloit acceptable to just about anyone around. Thus Beloit remained Congregationalist, more and more accommodatingly defined.

This can easily be seen in the ethos of the college. The Calvinist tradition had not begotten an intense interest in doctrinal speculation. Morality was the focus of its message, directed as it was to original sin, consequent depravity, moral regeneration, and a publicly monitored code of behavior. It was natural, then, that Beloit's foundational interests were directed toward the will. Chapin, for example, in his very description of the intellectual task they faced, implied that the work of learning was primarily devoted to moral discipline:

> The process contemplated [for a liberal education] is a systematic, widely varied, and precise drilling of all the powers of the mind by actual exercise in the great leading departments of human thought and learning. The end sought is not so much to make great acquisitions of knowledge, as to gain facility in the manifold operations of which the mind is capable, so that all faculties shall be trained, brought under command, and made reliable for any purpose. . . . To make this training thorough and efficient, it must be carried on under a prescribed intellectual and moral regimen, close and severe.[153]

There were repeated explanations that Beloit offered the culture of the mind and the discipline of the moral faculties together (we have heard Aratus Kent on that at the laying of the cornerstone). As long as the culture of the mind inquired more into classical than into Christian wisdom, the college was not likely to alienate its regional constituency. The least controversial element in its program, the discipline of the moral faculties, devolved pretty much into the obvious pattern of behavior to be followed by those who wished to live in civilized fashion in the somewhat uncivilized West. Thus Professors Emerson and Whitney could explain that the college "was founded in order to provide for the young men of the Northwest an education *equal* to that given by *Eastern Colleges, near* to their own *homes,* and *within the means* of those whose *chief capital* is their *own manhood.*" It would be religious, "not in any narrow or sectarian sense, but upon the broad platform of *Evangelical Christianity.* The need of this feature in education lies in the fact that the foundation truths of religion are also the foundation of true science and of true manhood."[154]

Had that meant that there were challenging insights offered by Christianity which the culture urgently needed in order to be wholesome, Beloit would have been making a robust claim. But it seems to have been the other way around: the civilization (derived from New England, of course) which they emulated was what Christianity was all about. The desire and the need to serve the regional clientele identified faith with the preferred culture such that morals became indistinguishable from manners. Thus Professor Porter's famous remark about Jesus: "What a gentleman he was!" Thus, too, his (possibly contrary) comment on reading Cicero: "I sometimes think it is the last stage of grace when a man has as much respect for another's convictions as for his own."[155] Chapin and his colleagues were offering an initiation into a known culture. Its doctrinal beliefs were few and mainly free of intramural controversy. Its moral code was also beyond question, in that they saw it as the only ethos imaginable for cultivated people.[156] If such commonplaces as "positive Christian character" seemed to be without firm content, it was only because they were so availably embodied in the Whig, Calvinist, New England gentleman: generous, magnanimous, and in charge.

"It would seem," writes Beloit's chronicler Richardson, "that the faculty of the early days, certainly judged by Mr. Emerson, were men who, in modern parlance, steered a little to the right of middle." He also observes that "the dogmatic content" of what he deemed essential to education for life "was limited." It was also vague. The college should train people to be active in the political order, but the only Christian teaching offered to guide them is that "all men are created equal." The college "opposes error" and "enlarges its mind to welcome all truth," but there is little content to either. Richardson admits: "In these formulations of puritan education, it is the dogmatic element which, as compared with the liberal and progressive, appears to occupy the more precarious foothold, for what guarantees the plateau of the essentials against the erosion of the winds of the 'purer' and 'enlarging' truth? In any case, no doctrinal dispute has as yet marked the developing ideology of the college." Nor was it to be expected. These were men who held practically identical religious, political, economic, and social ideas, and who were trying to create an appealing social enclave in Wisconsin whose piety might be transmitted by example and by manners that would obviate dispute.[157]

Convinced that this orientation has been enduringly passed on by the founders to succeeding generations at Beloit (he himself had come to the campus just as the Old Guard was passing on), Richardson naturally asked, "Can Beloit still be a Christian college?" Their sense of the lineaments of Christianity, insofar as it was theological, lacked historical sophistication. But Christianity, Richardson would argue, "is not a set of doctrines *about* Jesus: it is Jesus' doctrines, divested of the cerements of his age and times and education, of God as Heavenly Father, and of men as God's sons, and, therefore, as each other's brothers." For verification he draws on a writer well known to the Old Guard: "To love Christ we must know him. But what must we know concerning him? Must we know his countenance and form? Must we know the manner in which he existed before his birth, or the manner in which he now exists? Must we know his precise rank in the universe, his precise power and influence? On all these points, indeed, just views would be gratifying and auxiliary to influence. But love to Christ may exist and grow strong without them." That was the view of William Ellery Channing, who most clearly stated the case for his fellow Unitarians, and it might not have pleased the reverend gentlemen of the Old Guard to have it suggested that their educational project was as intellectually flaccid as his.[158]

Aaron Chapin guided Beloit College for thirty-six years as its president. During his regime college piety, which Professor Emerson called "simply evangelical," was what would be ordinarily expected on most Protestant campuses. There were daily morning and evening prayers (with the faculty there on the platform, facing the students), and a Sabbath lecture, besides which each student was obliged to attend Sunday worship at any of the churches in the town. The daily prayers have left behind less trail of student rancor and disrespect than was common elsewhere; indeed, when in 1871 the students asked for Wednesday and Saturday afternoon prayers to be canceled due to the burden of their studies, the request was granted without ado. The students themselves took responsibility for most of the voluntary religious activities, including a weekly prayer meeting and volunteer teaching at Sabbath schools for local congregations. It was close to their hearts, for when the veterans returned from the Civil War they initiated a daily prayer meeting which was faithfully supported. It was led and maintained by the students for twenty years, and was generally thought to be the most potent religious element in the Beloit experience.[159] They had a mission society, and by the college's twenty-fifth anniversary the national mission board was sending out more missionaries from Beloit than from any two other colleges. During the first quarter-century 300 or 400 students were reckoned to have undergone conversion to a Christian life at Beloit, and nearly half its graduates had chosen the clerical profession. There were various calculations of the coming of the kingdom, but one report was that 135 of the first 175 graduates of the college had been avowedly Christian men.[160]

Among the reminiscences at the twenty-fifth anniversary, however, one by Professor James Joshua Blaisdell moves into a minor key. He senses that the college has become purposely understated in its Christian commitment.

> It may be thought best to shape the policy of the institution more nearly into conformity with general systems of education. In short, will you make it less a school for training young men to do telling Christian work? Will you cease to make Aeschylus and Plato a point of departure for opening up to the young the Desired of all Nations? There are some plausible reasons for this. There is a

prevailing drift towards the neutralizing of these Christian features. In certain circumstances it would ensure greater ostensible results. It would certainly disarm some prejudices. The change is not without noteworthy examples.

Here then, perhaps, is the most fitting place to say, that, according to the view taken by those who administer the college, in this distinctively Christian work the college has its essential significancy and value. Take out of the legend on its seal, *"Scientia vera cum fide pura,"* the last three words, and the college drops out of the peculiar desirableness of its mission and ceases to answer the profoundest wants of this great West.

Far be it from any of us to place a low estimate upon the public system of instruction, which, proceeding upon a compromise of religious preferences, leaves to other agencies the office of religious instruction. But is it not the alphabet of the responsibility of Christian men and women, that the youth whom they can influence should have their mental culture wrought out upon the revealed Christ as its informing principle, and that this cannot be done but by Christian teachers in Christian schools? How without a supply of men thus forged, can the truth be brought into effective operation in society? And has not the history of society taught this at least to those who medicine its ills, that without the inworking of Christ there can be for society no ultimate recovery? What other inference do we reach than this that there must be Christian colleges — colleges which are Christian — to furnish Christian workers?

The conclusion in regard to our future is plain. We must remain a Christian school. As such we must look to the friends of human good for pecuniary support and patronage. They must cherish it, defend it, furnish it to their sons. When you sent your sons to the war of liberty, it touched you to the quick if you found they were wanting for bread or arms or opportunity. *You have sent this college to the front; maintain it in the condition of effective battle.*161

This, in an 1897 public address to the alumni gathered in strength as never before, was a thunderclap on a cloudless day. Twenty-five years later, at an even more splendid gathering, one of the speakers was Thomas Crowder Chamberlin, Beloit alumnus, sometime professor, and trustee, a science professor at the University of Chicago and eventual president of the American Academy of Science. His topic was the intellectual attitudes at the college. The great challenge in the latter decades of the century had been the onrush of new truth, he said, much of it a stress on Christian faith. The college had had "to face the question of welcoming unwelcome truth." Beloit had been not very energetic in the production of new knowledge, but neither had it wasted its energies in an attempt to block what truth was being produced. Faith was a good reason for this attitude. "Faith best expresses itself in such a steadfast confidence in the universality of the divine imminence [*sic*] that it invites the most unhesitating search in all fields, confident that the outcome cannot be other than ultimate good." With that attitude, the most authentic kind of continuity would be not so much a consistent development of an intellectual tradition, but an "earnestness of moral endeavor," for "purity of faith is conditioned on sincerity and rectitude of intellectual action."[162] Chamberlin's remarks are significant as evidence that Blaisdell's appeal had not been taken to heart, for the prevailing attitude at Beloit had come to be that faith was a function of sincerity, not of a special sort of intellectual inquiry and synthesis. The establishment of that view was to occur under the new administration of another young man called to serve what would be a long term as president.

Eaton's Era

Edward Dwight Eaton, educated at Beloit, Yale, Leipzig, and Heidelberg, was serving as pastor of a leading Congregational church in Oak Park, Illinois, and as the youngest trustee of his alma mater when elected to replace Aaron Chapin in 1886, only fourteen years after his own graduation. He would serve for thirty-one years. His arrival brought an immediate onset of new energy: participatory decision making with the faculty, enlargement of the facilities, closer relations with the students. The curriculum began to be softened with electives and diversified by new disciplines, departments, and major sequences of study. Female students were admitted in 1895.

So innovating was the new administration that Aaron Chapin's son Robert, who succeeded him on the faculty, went out of his way at the semicentennial observances in 1897 to claim that "the changes of this period have been only the enlarged expression of the purpose of the founders." Eaton himself frequently spoke of his undertakings as part of a "steady, symmetrical development of the College from the beginning."[163] Richardson has offered a more disengaged estimate, worthy of extensive quotation because it could have been written about so many other colleges:

> By 1886 Beloit had "become herself" and the epithet "Yale of the West" was little but a pleasant phrase. Henceforth any Puritanizing mission and the aim of making the Middle West (in older times "the West") like old New England were quietly dropped, nor did the Institution longer find advantage in parading equality with "the best New England colleges." Revivals faded away, and spiritual concerns were increasingly pressed upon by more secular Campus interests. The Faculty, unlike the one familiar with the tutorial system described by Noah Porter, were increasingly laymen, specialists begotten of graduate schools, captivated with their respective subjects and, under an elective system, more tempted toward a competitive departmentalism — and at best, and in any case, forced to take account of clashes between their several branches of study on academic day and hour schedules. As the years rolled on they increasingly, and consciously, knew less of each other's fields and became ever less aware of the personalities, aims and spirits of the Founders.

The Fathers had always gloried in an evangelical undenominationalism. The undenominationalism survived, but obviously evangelicalism suffered. The non-sectarianism of the Charter, even at the beginning disliked by the Founders, became more and more esteemed, and the Faculty came increasingly to be recruited from communions other than Presbyterian or Congregationalist — not excepting those particularly distrusted by men like Stephen Peet, the Episcopalian and Roman Catholic. An Episcopalian was to be Dean of the College for many years and a Roman Catholic, Chairman of the Board of Trustees [after Eaton's death]. This latitudinarianism — legitimate, if unforeseen, offspring of the worship of the open mind of men like Joseph Emerson and Noah Porter — under Dr. Maurer found reflection in the interior, quite un-Puritan appointments of Eaton Chapel itself. Increasingly endowed — though never sufficiently so — and staffed by teachers with earned graduate degrees who viewed teaching less as "calling" and more as "profession" and with whom salary was something more than incidental, the College, of necessity, tended less to resemble the Yale of the Illinois Band and more the Yale and Harvard of Timothy Dwight the Younger, of Hadley and of Eliot and Lowell. With the disappearance of frontier conditions vanished occasion for Beloit's becoming, in her turn, a mother of colleges; and the replacement of an agricultural and simple-minded constituency by a sophisticated metropolitan one made more difficult the maintenance of the old interest in home and foreign missionary enterprise. The days of the College Missionary Society and of the daily prayer meeting were over. Biblical requirement was dropped in the Catalogue of 1917-18. The wonder is, not that there was noticeable change, but that so much of the old, and of the spirit of the old survived and still endures.[164]

Eaton had said at the outset that a unitary classical curriculum was shortsighted. Accordingly, professorships in astronomy, botany, astronomical physics, oratory, political economy, and biblical literature were created, and junior positions in biology, civil polity, history, music, geology, art, and physical culture were added. The instruction in classics immediately began to shrink. When Harvard's scheme of unlimited elective courses under Charles Eliot was modified by his successor Lawrence Lowell in 1909, the result proved to be pretty much what Beloit had already worked out.[165]

There was at the time of Eaton's accession a strong claim being made throughout New England for representation on the major university and college boards of alumni chosen by alumni. Once it became clear that the financial needs of development were quite beyond the expected yield from other philanthropic sources, institutions began to admit nominated alumni representatives into governance. Some, like Harvard, did so by keeping the overseers, all alumni representatives, separate from the much smaller and residually more powerful corporation. Beloit followed the other model and enlarged its board to receive alumni. The board did not at the time surrender its own prerogative to elect its own replacements, but by an informal process the recommended alumni now began to be chosen. Elections were changed from life to three-year terms, and the new trustees were younger, still in the upward climb of their careers, and they expected to become more actively involved in policy making. Later, in 1903, the alumni were invited to nominate formally three of their members for seats on the board. The advent of alumni members only accelerated a trend toward laicization on the Beloit board. The original sixteen incorporator-trustees, it will be recalled, comprised eight clergy and eight laity. In 1871 there began to be a lay majority, which stood at 14-9 during Chapin's last year and 24-5 by the end of the century.[166]

The Blessing and Curse of Wealth

Fortune kissed Beloit in the arrival of a remarkable benefactor. In 1889 the region was being suffocated by a depression and Beloit was gasping for resources. A wealthy Yankee physician who had invested well, and remembered visiting the campus briefly as a young man forty years earlier, sent this laconic letter in the mail in early May:

> Pres. Eaton:
> If I will give your college $100,000 can you raise $100,000 more before July 1st? I mean business.
>
> Truly, D. K. Pearsons

They did, and he did. Daniel Kimball Pearsons would live past the age of ninety and would give away all but a fragment of his fortune. He claimed to have given away five million dollars, used as the leverage to elicit ten million more from other sources. It was his firm policy to give grants only when matching funds were required. Another policy was to avoid the wealthier institutions. His first policy was adopted by the great philanthropists and foundations that appeared near the end of his life; his second was not. On the occasion of his ninetieth birthday the Beloit board adopted a resolution of gratitude, in which they praised Pearsons for "abhorring cant and religious pretense, but loving to discern a Providential guidance in the events of life," and for his "catholic spirit, superior to the claims of any sect or denomination." Of the forty-five colleges and seminaries he had endowed, twenty-seven were of Congregational origin and eight were Presbyterian. His catholic spirit was preferentially gracious to these two denominations, and especially to Beloit, which also discerned a Providence at work in these events of its life.[167]

Andrew Carnegie in 1904 gave $50,000 for a new library, on the condition that the college pledge to appropriate no less than $5,000 to its annual operations. This was followed shortly thereafter by the Carnegie Foundation's offer of endowment funds to finance faculty retirement. In the midst of these negotiations Eaton resigned abruptly from the presidency in mid-1905-6 and took a pastorate in Vermont. The public reason for this was a health problem, but he retained his seat on the board and after a year and a half of discussion, he accepted reelection after the trustees had agreed to work more aggressively in major fund-raising.

After the resignation the trustees unanimously adopted a resolution "embodying the convictions of the board as to the character of the man who should be chosen for President of the College":

> With the responsibility of securing a new President for Beloit College now resting upon them, the Trustees desire to put on record their deep appreciation of the fact that from the beginning Beloit has stood for Christian education, and that its greatest success has been the sending out of graduates with Christian ideals and Christian character, as well as with thorough mental equipment.
>
> The Board also records its earnest conviction that the broadest future success of the college depends upon its firm adherence to the Christian idea which has been the controlling principle of its past work.
>
> Therefore this Board hereby records its deliberate judgment that the man who shall now be chosen as President of Beloit College, whatever his other qualifications may be (and we want the best in all directions) *must be* one whose personal Christian life is definite and strong, one who will be in hearty sympathy with the idea of Christian education and therefore one who will be vigorous and aggressive in upholding and stimulating vital Christianity in all the varied relations of college life and activity.[168]

Several months later the president of the Carnegie Corporation brought to the college's attention their eligibility rule for beneficiaries. Applicant boards must certify that "no denominational test is imposed in the choice of Trustees, officers or teachers, nor in the admission of students; nor are any denominational tenets or doctrines taught to students." The secretary replied for the board and suggested that the nonsectarian Section 7 of the charter might suffice. Carnegie noted, however, that it did not apply to trustees. The Beloit board then adopted this resolution:

> RESOLVED, That no denominational test be imposed in the choice of trustees, officers or teachers, nor in the admission of students and that no denominational tenets or doctrines be taught to students.

Not only did the board thereby adopt a stricture upon its own freedom to elect its own successors, but it went beyond its charter in restricting the freedom of its faculty to teach. The Carnegie grant came through soon afterward. In response to a further request from Carnegie, the board also submitted a memorandum indicating the church affiliation of its own membership. Twenty-six names were listed. An apology was attached, because no such roster had previously existed, and they had not yet been able to query all of their members; four names remained without any affiliation identified. Of the other twenty-two, two belonged to no church, one was identified as "Union," one as Episcopalian, three as Presbyterian, and fifteen as Congregational. Four were identified as ministers. Beloit did not heed denomination enough to identify its trustees ecclesially, yet it cared enough to provide a board that was apparently more than three-quarters Congregationalist. This is but one more example of a preferential policy which could be as easily continued in the presence of a nondiscriminatory rule as in the absence of one.[169]

The General Education Board gave several hefty matching grants, and Carnegie followed up its earlier library and retirement fund awards with an endowed professorship. The secondary-level academy, after rendering sixty-five years of educational service, not least of which had been to deliver four-fifths of all the young college's students, closed its doors.

When Eaton had first come as president in 1886, he spoke mainly of two things: Christian education and "practical education." On the former topic, what he had to say was expressed, as Richardson puts it, "in the broadest terms."

> The education which Beloit College purposes giving, is to be a distinctly Christian education. We believe that man is more than an instrument for thinking; that convictions are essential to the integrity of manhood; that principles are higher than knowledge; that enlightened faith is the condition of national greatness and stability; that the ultimate kingdom is Christ's kingdom.
>
> This Christian education is not adequately given in forms of dogmatic assertion. The growing mind is sensitive and suspicious of mere authority. It dreads wearing a chain. If it submits itself for a time to the constraint of maturer minds, the reaction will be all the more pronounced when it emerges into the world of unbelief that is waiting to claim it. There is sometimes even an exalted feeling, as in the performance of high duty, when one abandons inherited convictions that seem to be invalidated by growth. . . . How great a thing it is, then, to save such souls from the tragic fate of becoming gallant leaders in a great rebellion; to keep them from fighting against God. The hope of accomplishing this lies in cherishing a spirit of fearless investigation, teachers and taught seeking the truth in the love of truth; not paddling in the still water of tradition, but pushing out into the rapids of present thought. Let the student feel the surge and quiver of the torrent, then he knows what stability is when he touches the Rock of Ages.[170]

There was, in fact, rarely any sense of the surge and quiver of the torrent when Edward Eaton spoke about matters religious. But when he turned his discourse to the social problems of the day, the vexed issues of drunkenness, crime, and poverty, and the Christian challenge to class and privilege, his voice picked up the vigor and the urgency of the social gospel. Like his contemporaries at Dartmouth during the administration of William Jewett Tucker, he sensed a need to disavow explicitly the anti-intellectual and bullying agenda of the aggressive conservatives who had only provoked students to fight against God, before he offered a flourish of commonplaces like character, conviction, and enlightenment that were hardly "distinctly Christian."

Beloit had never known much by way of serious religious inquiry until James Arnold Blaisdell, son of James Joshua, was brought back to teach biblical literature. The official description of these studies had in fact sounded pretty academic:

> BIBLE STUDIES: The first recitation on Monday morning of each week is in Bible studies. These are designed to bring into review the historical facts, the truths and principles of Christianity as they stand in the Original Scriptures, or are derived from them. In these exercises, the authority of God's word is recognized, the grand features of the scheme of redemption by Jesus Christ are contemplated, and the principles of pure morality and spiritual godliness therein embodied, are studied in their application to the life that now is and to that which is to come.[171]

That is a description which might apply in 1880 either to an omnium-gatherum course of religious catechesis or to a serious inquiry into the teachings of the biblical books in their contexts. In past years the texts had been studied in either Greek or German, thus allowing linguistic struggles to absorb most of the energy the students brought to the recitation room.[172] They were thus not very heavy in either biblical or in theological scholarship. Blaisdell set out to study the texts in the vernacular, and caused the president considerable apprehension when it became clear that he wanted to consider the various debates then current regarding historical criticism. Blaisdell was left free to proceed as he wished, but with presidential misgivings in the background.

Indices of Piety

What Eaton called the Christian life of the college required only half a page in his annual reports to the board. Religious activities, he stated, were wholesome and fruitful. The members of the Christian Associations had met the trains to welcome incoming students. The YMCA employment bureau found jobs. Student-directed courses on Bible and on missions, and weekly gatherings of men and women students separately, and of faculty with students, "were helpful centers of Christian thought and purpose." A Chicago pastor had given "an inspiring address" on the day of prayer, and students had collaborated with local churches in evangelistic work. The report does not suggest a religious program that turned away the students by its exhausting intensity. The centers of student religious activities were the YMCA and YWCA, and at Beloit they were principally looked to as a democratic counterforce to the fraternities that had divided the student body into antagonistic cliques.[173] The Christian agenda had at heart a strong social concern . . . exactly like President Eaton.

Evidence of the denominational complexion of the student body during the

Eaton years is not easily found. But there are some shifts in the rhetoric of the catalogues which express an intensified concern that students of all (imaginable) loyalties would find Beloit welcoming. In the traditional text the origins in a combined effort of Congregationalists and Presbyterians were retold, and then interpreted: "The union of different denominations in the plan marks its religious character as at once positive, evangelical and unsectarian." Beloit's descent from the New England colleges gave her the same purpose: "the thorough, liberal, Christian education of young men who are to be the leaders of opinion and influence in Society, in the Church, in the State." The college would go beyond the limits set on the state colleges, by offering *self-knowledge, self-possession, breadth of view,* "and a *moral and religious character* based on a love of truth for its own sake, and prompting the consecration of all powers of mind and all acquisitions gained to the good of men and the glory of God as the true end of being."[174]

After Eaton had been president for a few years the catalogue began to change (1892-93). The famous text of the Northwest Ordinance itself was now invoked as a civic authority that linked education to religion: "Religion, morality, and knowledge being necessary to good government and the happiness of mankind, schools and the means of education shall forever be encouraged." The gathering of Congregational and Presbyterian church leaders which led to Beloit's founding had now become a "gathering of the friends of Christian education to consider all the interests of the kingdom of Christ in the Mississippi valley." The native constituency was thereby converted in retrospect from a coalition of churches to the civil populace of a region. The two denominations are later mentioned as the "founders and most active friends of the College, but it has always had warm support from many branches of the Christian church."[175] In place of the rather fervent account of the college's advantages over state campuses, the catalogue simply asserts that a "strenuous endeavor is made to teach the heart as well as the mind."

Twenty years later catalogues would mention religion only mildly and in a historical way. Instead of any claim to offer an education that might be qualitatively different, the catalogue is left with the drier avowal that "it was established with the conviction that thoroughness in education was as good a thing for the West as for the East, and that a thorough and rounded education must combine learning, morality, and religion." Richardson observes that the tenor of the catalogues in this period "was hardly 'religious' in any direct sense and savored rather of the Academy and the Stoa than of Jerusalem or Paul of Tarsus."[176]

It was a time when some changes were under way in both the First Congregational Church and in the denomination nationally. The last of the "dogmatic preachers," George R. Leavitt, stepped down from the local pulpit and was replaced by Wilfrid A. Rowell, not much of a preacher but a warm and pastoral presence. Mr. Leavitt had displayed articulate concern about such matters as the virgin birth, the resurrection of Jesus, and the need for shedding of blood for the remission of sins. The shift from his wing collar to Mr. Rowell's turndown collar brought a milder message. He spoke often of the "Christian philosophy of life," at risk from alien philosophies like Bolshevism, Fascism, Nazism, and Catholicism.

> Christianity is a way of living. The idea of God, the person and work of Jesus Christ, the place of the individual, of freedom, sacrifice and faith are basic to the attainment of religious values for the individual and for the spread of the Christian religion. The people in our churches seeing the importance of a philosophy of life as illustrated in the conflicting ideologies in the world about them are ready to believe, to study, and to learn the basic teachings of the Christian way of life.

He confessed that this philosophy was not gripping many hearts, since half the Congregational churches in the country were reporting not a single new member that year.[177]

Rowell had been a sophomore at Beloit when Eaton came first as president, and there was a great deal of similarity in their outlooks. Eaton made the new minister a trustee when he came to town. Rowell had been a crack debater, but somehow when he spoke on religion there was a blur in what he had to say. Eaton suffered the same disadvantage. He had an unfathomable capacity for abstraction. Even granted the general disrepute of the baccalaureate genre, one can see this in the sermon he delivered at the end of Beloit's fiftieth year, 1897:

> Civilization depends on manhood for its permanence. The sudden downfall of civilizations has been the amazement of mankind. But when they totter and drop to pieces it is always and only when manhood has gone out of them. When self-indulgence rules, some hardy stock supplants the degenerate one. When a covetous and venal spirit prevails it shall heap up treasure in vain. Some new might will be disclosed, some tremendous gathering of moral indignation, some power that shall not regard silver nor delight in gold, and the rich accumulations are scattered like dust. There is absolutely no security except in an empowered manhood, clear-eyed, strong-hearted, loving God and loving men with profound and intelligent love. . . .
>
> Manhood is not self-creative. It is a divine gift. It . . . may be sought from God and he will not withhold the gift. Manhood may be fostered and trained by right surroundings, by worthy discipline. It is for the training of masterful manhood, and high-visioned womanhood without which the future will wait in vain for its men fitly trained and inspired, that Beloit College enters into the inheritance of the half-century, and girds itself for the years that are to be.[178]

Dr. Eaton considered himself evangelical, but his integrity and his educational vision were framed more by a sense of dignified and honest class than by an explicitly Christian vision. But there were limits to Beloit's and Eaton's nonsectarianism. From the time of the founders until Eaton's resignation in 1917, Beloit had been reminded repeatedly that if the Congregationalists were lax in their discipleship, the Catholics would prevail; no more awful prospect was held up as a threat. The archival history of the college is strewn from the very start with references to the Catholics as the menace.[179] But then Catholics began matriculating at Beloit.

Outsiders' Impressions

One early Catholic student was James L. Foley from Wauwatosa. He was already twenty-three years old and a veteran of three years' service in the war when he enrolled in the autumn of 1866 to pursue preparatory studies prior to college work. He kept a diary, in which he noted that he regularly took part in the chapel services and on Sundays acquitted his church obligation by going to mass at the Catholic church. If the priest was out on circuit he would worship elsewhere: with the Episcopalians, or at First Congregational. He records little displeasure at obligatory participation in worship and piety, except when the preaching went down badly. Thus on 18 November a chapel lecture by a missionary from India was recorded without comment, but on 25 November he attended a temperance lecture in the church. "It was very dry and of course affected me little." He joined a large crowd that went to hear Horace Greeley speak to the Sunday school. "As soon as the college bell began to toll about 100 of the College boys left the church much to the discomfiture of old H. Nevertheless out we went and were present at Col. Chapel and listened to a very dry lecture from Pres. Chapin." He went to Milwaukee and visited the Saint Gall's Fair. "I was talking to Father Lolimere there and he, the *'old cuss,'* abused me as well as he knew how, because I had the audacity to say that I thought Beloit College was a good school. He began to abuse all Protestant schools and in fact every thing that did not have Catholicity connected with [it]. Because I opposed him he said that I was no Christian and would warrant that before a year and a half I would be ashamed of the Catholic religion. I expressed my willingness to bet with him on that subject." Later that day he bought a somewhat expensive Bible as a gift for his father ($5.50, a good sum for a young man who was paid 15¢ an hour by faculty families to dig potatoes) and a less costly one ($2.50) for himself.

He went to a revival in the Presbyterian church. "The sermon by Potter was very good. He proved from the Scripture that there is a Hell. The way they urged persons 'to come forward to the mercy seat' was perfectly disgusting. The people here are half crazy on account of the present religious excitement." The next day: "The people are becoming more insane than before on religion. The way in which they act is enough to make a sensible person oppose the noble doctrine of Christ." Then, a fortnight later: "At the lecture this p.m. Pres. Chapin alluded very bitterly to the manners of the *'Romish Church.'* These last two lectures have *fairly* disgusted me with this institution. I believe that all men professing a religion are more aggravated by hearing it ridiculed than by most anything else. This great excess or extreme to which Protestants carry religion and the *various* forms used by Cath.

have at times filled my mind with thoughts of infidelity. Oh! *How earnestly* do I pray that God may keep me in the right path and lead me to his eternal home beyond the skies. Although professing to be a Christian, there are many things which appear very dark to me." The next day: "Old Fisk gave us a lecture this A.M. on deportment in Chapel. He says that all must bow their heads when 'Prex' is praying. I have resolved to do no such thing, and no man can make me do it. So we will see how his law will operate: if he is determined to enforce it he may count on one less in his school."

One week later there was more grief. "I attended the lecture delivered by Carl Shurz [*sic*] on 'the reconstruction of Germany.' He dwelt for a long time on the history of the country. Claiming that the backward condition of Austria was owing to Catholicity and the advanced state of affairs in Prussia was owing to the rule of Protestants! Such was, as he asserted, the effect of Catholic and Protestant rule generally. I came away heartily disgusted with the bigoted Dutchman." In April President Chapin's chapel talks had become no more agreeable. "Thank God I have but eleven of these miserable things to listen to." One Sunday in June the priest was away, so he went to First Congregational Church "and heard an excellent sermon by Bushnell." July 10: "Left Beloit on 12:15 train."[180]

The closest Catholic colleges available to young Foley then were in Dubuque, over the far border, in Iowa, or in Quincy in downstate Illinois. So it was natural that he would try Beloit, and find that the only disagreeable features were religious. One may easily reckon that for a Congregational student at Loras or Quincy the experience would have been similarly jarring. The avoidance of such experiences sent many students to the state campuses.

The Catholics began slowly to increase, and in 1915 they provoked a set-to which brought one of the first truly hostile encounters at Beloit College. In 1914 the Catholics had unsuccessfully asked for an exemption from the required freshman Bible course. The next autumn the local Catholic pastors requested that Catholic students be exempted from both chapel and Bible courses, and they, too, were turned down. The archbishop of Milwaukee then ordered Catholics to withdraw from the college if they continued to be forced to attend sectarian religious exercises and classes. The faculty met lengthily and continually, referred the issue to various committees, and privately told the president it would be best to make no public response. When that proved impossible a unanimous faculty and a suitably pensive president both refused to give in, on the ground that to do so would be to admit the college had somehow drifted into sectarianism. A later attempt to negotiate a quiet compromise without any public statement roused a chorus of criticism. The furor would require several years to cool down, and then without much publicity the Bible class was no longer required of anyone (1917) and Catholics were exempted from attendance at the vesper service (1922).[181]

The conflict was earnestly engaged, but with short perspective on either side. The faculty and administration saw Congregational piety and doctrine to be, simply, the normative form of Christianity. Since the Second Great Awakening had repressed theological interest and denominational animus, it was the understanding of American Congregationalists that only their polity was distinctive, and that polity never came into play at the college. They were conscious of no single doctrine in their repertoire which was distinctive; theirs was a gathering of free churches that were *simply Christian,* with no agenda but to hear Christ speak and to have him reign alone.[182] For Christians who thought, as Catholics and members of some other churches did, and as Congregationalists once had, that polity might have had a great deal to do with orthodoxy and right piety, the piety at Beloit was somewhat alien, distinctive, and certainly what "sectarian" should mean. They would have no way of knowing that it was becoming less and less sectarian by becoming less and less derivative of explicit faith.

Eaton had said in 1905 that, "although the intellectual life is important, the Christian life is the central thing at Beloit." When, with the coming of the war, he finally laid down his presidency, a pervasive alumni study made the same point.

> It is well for all to remember the College is a church college. If it is not so recognized it has no reason whatsoever for trying to exist. The constituency of the College is mainly a church constituency. The parents who send their children here to college do so because they desire to place them in a more restraining and a more religious atmosphere than is found at the state university.[183]

Eaton's leadership had increased both admissions and the endowment tenfold. A compound of four buildings had matured into a handsome campus of fourteen. Yet he also left Beloit substantively transformed in ways that were not yet evident. During his administration there had been no sense of any break with the Old Guard, no assertion of a liberal departure from outmoded tradition. In fact, there was some restlessness after thirty-six years of Chapin and thirty-one of Eaton, about Beloit's need of new venture. But it had changed withal. The change was not so much in an assertive innovation of new and liberalized views as in the depletion of the old views. It would require another regime for the results of that change to emerge.

The regime was, however, not to be that of Melvin Amos Brannon, who served for only five years. Pharaoh Akhenaton broke with the traditional polytheism of Egypt in the fourteenth century B.C. and worshiped only one god, the sun. His heresy did not survive him, however, and his successors ordered that the inscriptions on all of his state monuments should be meticulously defaced by a battalion of stone chiselers. The presidency of Dr. Brannon, who was neither a Congregationalist (he was a Presbyterian), nor a minister (though he had been an elder), nor a humanist (he was a biologist), nor a Beloit man or even a college man (he was trained at the University of Chicago and had already been president of the University of Idaho), has been effaced from the college history as a minor and aberrant interlude. His chief apostasy was to suggest that a purely liberal arts college could not draw enough students, and ought also to offer courses and departments that prepared them for professional careers.

When Eaton was recruiting him as a successor, Brannon raised the religion issue, since he was a Presbyterian, and in 1917 no one was going around saying that they were of one denomination. Eaton replied that "while Beloit is considerably under Congregational auspices, there is no denominational control and no ecclesiastical or dogmatic fetters but we love to think of Beloit as being a helper to the life of the spirit in this region and cooperating with the Christian forces of our generation." Eaton, as he often did, implied by disavowing any definition in the religion on campus that such a fear was normal among the uninitiated. Brannon replied in kind, stating that he was "more concerned with principles and correct living" than "with mere creeds." In 1920 he admitted a general decline of religious intensity at Beloit as elsewhere, and proposed to bring "virile" expressions of religion to the campus by stressing the principles of Christianity and accenting the importance of example as well as precept. This sounded vague to some alumni. He then pointed out that if students were slack in their religion, it reflected on their homes more than on their colleges. This sounded not vague enough to other alumni.[184] And Dr. Brannon left to become president of another state university.

The college he left was not notably strengthened in its Christian character during his time there. The YMCA and YWCA had flourished during the war, yet had taken on such a nationalistic temper that they largely disintegrated in the years that followed. The tenor of life at Beloit could not but be liberalized under a president who addressed his students as "Comrades," and with chapel services that took especially appreciative note of popular new regimes in Russia and elsewhere. Chapel talks were focused on social and personal concerns, with scant treatment of older religious themes. Humanism began to be a surrogate word for Christianity . . . or perhaps a residue. The student newspaper, the *Round Table,* acquired a lavish new feature: large cigarette advertisements. Dancing came to campus: indeed, dancing as it was done in the twenties. Moral concern was expressed about that. So there was the wherewithal for concern about the college's direction when Melvin Brannon went his way.[185]

Irving Maurer, Modernist

The third long-term president of Beloit, Washington Irving Maurer (he never used his first name), served from 1924 to 1942. He was a Beloit graduate, a humanist, and a Congregational minister. The college was again in familiar hands. He made sure that this was so, and seen to be so, by declining a unanimous invitation from the board of trustees until there was a concurrence by the faculty as well.

His previous pastorate was at the First Congregational Church of Columbus, where the venerable Washington Gladden, one of the leading lights in the Social Gospel movement, still lived as pastor emeritus. Much of the leverage for his election as president was managed by his friend Wilfrid Rowell, who had by then moved on from Beloit but remained active in the affairs of the college. Maurer shared with both preachers a high and explicit concern for social service and, if vagueness be any fair

88

evidence of it, a profound disinterest in matters of theology and, perhaps, of faith. With Edward Eaton, however, he shared an unconditional dedication to liberal education, as opposed (very opposed) to professional training. So he was perfectly able, as the one who was to come, to pick up where Eaton had left off.

Maurer was a modernist, more openly and perhaps more appealingly than Tucker and Hopkins were at Dartmouth. For instance, while still at Columbus he published several "Here I stand" sermons. In them, without a word of explicit rejection, he sets aside all of the central tenets of Calvinism that Aaron Chapin had said were the essential creed of a Congregationalist. He is cogent and even learned in his dismissal of the old doctrines. But what emerges instead is not a more critical and scholarly account of Christian belief, but a vapid feel-good sentiment. His faith in God, for example, is "faith that the spiritual side of life is a revelation of the ultimate reality. I feel less and less the importance of believers in a world which an enlarged man set up by divine fiat. I have less and less the sense of a throned Zeus beyond the clouds. . . . What does God mean to me? He means doing my duty, being good, allying myself with right things. And when I say that I believe, I mean that I believe in the moral make-up of life, I believe that goodness is the texture of life. . . . In this idea of the love of God my thought of a modern world has weakened the thought of a special providence. . . . There are no special favorites with God. . . ."[186]

> The faith which I have in Jesus does not rest upon the doctrine of the Virgin birth. When humanity lived in a dualistic world, the problem was as to how an infinite, limitless God could have anything to do with the world. I can see how Jesus' matchless character and the church's belief in his Messiahship created a tremendous question. How could anyone born of a woman be like him? The Virgin birth was the only answer, and that only a half-answer, for it still leaves open the problem as to how Jesus, born of Mary, escaped contamination from the blood which flowed in his mother's veins.
>
> I have no quarrel, save an intellectual one, with the Christians who believe in the Virgin birth, but I cannot submit to the notion that a modern man, who finds this faith a stumbling block, should be compelled to accept this doctrine. The oldest gospel has nothing to say about it.
>
> Nor does my faith in Jesus issue into a doctrine as to the essential difference between Jesus and mankind. I believe in the divinity of Jesus because I believe in the divinity of man. I believe that man and Christ have the moral characteristics of God. . . . he is the revelation of God, and helps me, as no other life helps me, to think of God.[187]

Likewise he sets aside classical doctrines as dear to Congregational hearts as bodily resurrection and atonement through blood sacrifice. He is as far from orthodox Calvinism as any Arminian or Unitarian. His original understanding of many of these doctrines — which were ancient before there were Congregationalists — is neither profound nor accurate. But this is not much to our point.

When he says that any quarrel he might have with orthodox believers would be merely intellectual, he conveys how little intellectual engagement there was for him, and for many comrades, between learning and faith. He is proceeding on sensibility, not intellectual inquiry. His sensibility is wonderfully healthy, his critique of his own tradition is so gracious and so hale that a generation of students and their seniors is carried by him into a new vista of faith. It was a faith that would no longer torment those who stood by the Calvinism of their past, not because he was challenging the biblical interpretation or the theological arguments they were used to, but because, without any notable capacity for either, he invited them away from their minds. This helps us to understand why he was found to be so nourishing in the pulpit, why his vesper sermons were never subject to student resistance. But it also helps us to understand why, without any religious revolt at Beloit, the possibility of vital engagement between religious inquiry and academic inquiry — which had gone flaccid during the Eaton years — was virtually extinguished during the long administration of Irving Maurer.

During his first year back at Beloit Maurer delivered an address which was a major attempt to show how religious faith and modern scholarship ought to make common cause. He begins with a litany of failure on the part of religion (he speaks only of Christianity):

> In mediaeval times, even during the period of the Renaissance, the fear of the Lord was not only the beginning, but the total content of wisdom. An established church dominated the thought of civilized Europe. Absorbed in the material concerns of government and control, religious institutions lost . . . the power to criticize and examine life. . . . At a time when the awakening of thought life was in need of a spiritual objective, the church buried herself with the attempt to torture men into conformity. . . . Taking to herself the right to dominate over private judgment, the church became a great economic, political, and intellectual tyranny. . . . The social status for various classes was fixed; man was taught to suffer and endure inescapable afflictions of existence, and for human inquiry was substituted the casuistry which attempted a Hellenistic interpretation of orthodoxy.

The result:

> The preaching of its pulpits is often weak because of the attempt to continue phrases and doctrines which have lost their meaning. . . . The church speaks hazy messages regarding war, regarding industrial strife, regarding partisanship.

And meanwhile:

> The basis (of science) was the freedom of the mind, the right to independent investigation, a detachedness of interest, so that prejudice and passion were

nullified. . . . Through the survey by man of his world, the human spirit was delivered — science was shown to be the true religion. . . . Our educational institutions are presenting a marvelously interesting account of life in a modern world. Their graduates are going out with a technical command of the material forces, such as no other generation had.

How, then, does he propose that religion and science, or academic learning, would find a new mutuality? Since learning consists in "an insatiable thirst for information" and "the acquiring of knowledge," religion would join to that disinterested quest for erudition a sense of "reverence and fear of God . . . a great vision of life." Religion must forfeit to scientific inquiry all responsibility for inquiry and knowledge, and in return be given leave to "ask science or education to help conserve or to promote great human values."

Somehow modern education must work through to an adequate thought of God. It is not an educational triumph to rid the world of God. No doubt the idea of God which religion brought to us is crude, based on superstition, is the reflection often of our own partial untutored selves. But humanity hungers for apprehension of the infinite mystery . . . Religion says to education — train men to recognize the moral reality of God, how life is still at its highest point in its striving after moral perfection, and how inescapable are the usual issues of our universe.[188]

It is remarkable how Maurer, who is so thoroughly distanced from Calvinism as he has known it, must in the end make the move of reducing religion to moral sentiment.[189] In the age of the Old Guard the clerical academics were more widely educated than he was, and in his time the various disciplines had advanced much further. Despite his liberal undergraduate education and his experience at Yale Divinity School, he was not a scholar, and was exceedingly naive about the nature and the preoccupations of science, not to mention the other families of academic learning. But most seriously, he was entirely unfamiliar with the corpus of theological and philosophical reflection which, in good times and in bad, had enabled bright and devout Christian scholars who were not intimidated by the empirical sciences as Maurer was to engage intellectually, not just morally, with their fellow academics.

When he set off on one of his moral pleadings he spoke with a different timbre, as in this 1923 sermon:

Folly, cries one, to ask the church to change the world. There is this talk of international good will. What right has the church to attempt to do away with war? How the church boasted of the coming peace, while all the time the world was arming to slay itself!

Let me tell you, that we may get tired of peace talks, of disarmament talks, and the like, but in the end the only religion which will satisfy us, will be the religion which preaches the end of war. When the dream of internationalism appears most impossible, and the peace talks most silly and futile, then is just the time for the large religion. And if at such a time your religion justifies your mounting hatred, supports the doctrine that the enemy is beyond the Pale, blesses the arms with which you are to strike, winks at the ties and the one-sided presentation of facts, winks at the sweeping away of civil liberties, declares that profiteering must be ended, if your religion lends itself to the pettiness of these things and never mounts beyond the ramparts of nationalism, then you have been betrayed. It isn't the religion of Jesus, whatever else it is.[190]

During the 1920s the Congregationalists suffered a steep and steady decline in membership and contributions, which after the 1931 merger to form the Congregational and Christian Churches declined even more steeply: 21 percent in only nine years. More serious was what historians call the "spiritual depression" of the period which afflicted this denomination with special virulence. Maurer observed then that the religious life at Beloit was marked by "the lack of initiative on the part of the men students in maintaining any religious activities." The YMCA had collapsed, but the YWCA had been reorganized and become a sponsor of various service and social activities. A number of students were active in churches in the town, he said, "but a majority of them depend upon compulsory chapel and vesper services for their culture in religious literature and worship." He concludes, mildly: "Coming out of a church history as it does, Beloit should keep warm the interest of the students in church matters." The only indices of religious vitality on campus he can think of are requests for organ concerts in Lent, annual collections for a mission in Turkey, and "a sense of worship" as manifested in the turnout for the Easter sunrise service. "Summing up, I may say that in the field of religion, the College is in a state of transition."[191]

It was — or, it had been — but Maurer seems not to have known whither. The problem of finding faculty who would support the college's commitments continued as one of his express concerns through the 1930s. Yet he swiveled, it would seem, in the nature of his concern. In a sermon given in 1932 he said there were "enough able men in the teaching profession" believing in God "to make it inexcusable for faculties to have in [their] membership non-believers." He then went on to say: "Jesus would welcome into his churches many who now would balk at signing the creeds which we lay down as conditions of membership." To the Kiwanis he put it otherwise: "The colleges must use a lot of care in the hiring of good teachers." Their responsibility "rests primarily within the field of the teacher's academic and professional qualifications. . . . Faculties in the colleges should be made up of men with a social spirit, men who love America, who are good citizens, who respect the American people. . . . Having that sort of man on our faculties, we should let him alone." Professor Burr, a veteran on the faculty, complained that the newcomers "didn't know how to pray." The faculty benches were taken off the platform in front of the chapel, and they were seated — those who came — down in the midst of the students. The president complained that the chapel exercises should not devolve upon him alone. Robert Richardson, the college historian, noted that "the emotional energy which the 'Old Guard' had expended on devotional exercises, occasional revivals and the encouragement of the quest for a quite distinctly individual salvation, the teachers of the first half of the Twentieth Century were inclined to divert to conscientious study and instruction, and to arousing in their pupils an intelligent interest in social welfare and in international justice, peace, understanding and security." He found consolation in what he thought both old and new colleagues agreed upon: "Neither group ever felt that sanctimoniousness could rightfully replace hard work, and both groups were, in general, sensitive to scholarship standards."[192]

In 1939 Maurer, in his report to the trustees, addressed the state of religion in the faculty:

> The interest of the members of the Faculty in religion does not reflect the intensity and definiteness of purpose which characterized Beloit College eighty years ago. At the same time, it is not possible to draw any lines and say that the younger members of the Faculty are less interested in religion than the older members of the Faculty. We have some members who do not work very hard at going to church, but this affects some of the oldest members as well as some of the younger ones. A recent appointee to the Faculty writes as follows in answer to the reminder I gave him that Beloit is interested in religion:
>
>> "Dear Dr. Maurer: Your letter was very encouraging. I am glad to learn of the ideals of those who make up Beloit College and you may be sure that you will have my active assistance as you have my deep sympathy with all that concerns the spirit."

We shall never know the spirit in which that remarkably ambiguous note was written.

The president had a fathomless ability to interpret the most dismaying turns of events as successful, however absurd he sounded. In this same report, he confessed disappointment that a collection for famine relief netted only forty-five dollars from the entire student body, an average of less than ten cents per student. One of the fraternities, made up of affluent students, contributed a total of one dollar. "I do not mean to infer," commented Maurer, "that the college student of today is more selfish."[193]

Maurer was an earnest churchman, and in his way utterly nonsectarian. Like Tucker, he spoke and wrote, not of Congregationalism, nor even of Christianity, but of "religion." And his discourse about religion was cast in such banalities that it would be difficult to imagine anyone caring enough to dissociate himself or herself from it. One last example: in a memo to his faculty at the outset of the 1939-40 academic year he exhorted his colleagues to "believe in" the liberal arts college.

93

It is also important for us to remember that Beloit College is not only a liberal arts college, but a Christian liberal arts college. Of course, the two terms are really synonymous. We are proud of the freedom of teaching which characterizes Beloit, nor has there been any effort ever to restrict or to define such freedom. At the same time, the source from which Beloit College has sprung should remind us all that our own individual doubts, our own intellectual difficulties, which ever recur, should have been resolved into positive affirmation and constructive attitude so that our classrooms are not so much hindrances as helps to a genuine religious faith, without which society would be meaningless and futile.[194]

Religion Wanes

Though the college seems rarely to have conducted a census of its students' religious affiliations, we do know that at the end of the 1930s only 21 percent of the students were identified as members of the Congregational and Christian Churches (merged in 1931). Presbyterians were slightly fewer (18 percent). The official statement of the college's aim, which emerged from long consultation among the faculty and with board approval, stated as its first principle: "A Christianity uncontrolled by nationalism or sectarianism."[195] A survey of religious attitudes, however, conducted in 1937 showed that the definition of religion most widely accepted was "a process of adjustment," meaning "the process, more or less rational, by which man so organizes his emotional life and its related activities as to give him a sense of security in dealing with the mysterious factors of his social situation." Nearly half of the respondents considered God "a symbol of the highest in man and the good in nature." Only 2.2 percent of the men and 4.7 percent of the women considered God a person. Immortality meant either "persistence of the spiritual life after death" or "survival of social values." Opinion ran strong against religious disapproval of drinking, lying, gambling, and other vices.

Historian Richardson, then a faculty member, notes that despite student complaints about the talks given at chapel and at vespers, which were still compulsory, people who knew what religious tenets were "were struck by their absence from College preaching." That preaching, we are told, was "basically of the prophetic as distinguished from the priestly order, and might be subsumed as the presentation of Jesus as the personal, social and governmental way, truth and light." We are assured that it was thoroughly theistic, and that dogmas were neither described, defended, nor attacked. Richardson characterizes the student mind of that day as "humanitarian and non-ascetic." Some observers were inclined to take student moralizing more lightly; one said their emphasis on peace was more passivism than pacifism.[196]

A century earlier, Stephen Peet had advised his Congregational brethren they would do well to edit the prickly specificities out of their faith so as not to antagonize their Presbyterian partners. It seems that with time his injunction came to be better and better heeded, though by then the Presbyterians need not have cared. Thus by 1942, when Irving Maurer died in office after long and faithful service, Beloit College's professed sense of its own religious concerns seems to have vaporized.

Today the board of trustees is a thoroughly lay group. One clergyman is remembered from 1949.[197] A query to the president's office as to whether there were any minister presently on the board was repeatedly interpreted as asking whether they had a chaplain.

The post-Maurer presidents make manifest that religious affiliation is no longer relevant. Carey Croneis (1944-53), a geologist by discipline, was a Baptist who became a Congregationalist. Miller Upton (1954-75), an economist, is a Presbyterian who once was an Episcopalian. Martha Peterson (1975-81), a mathematician, was descended from a family of Methodist missionaries in the prairies but attended various local churches only occasionally. Roger Hull (1981-90), a teacher of international law, is a Jew. Victor Ferrall, Jr. (1991-), a lawyer, was an Episcopalian but holds no membership in any local church.

The religious complexion of the faculty is evidently not a matter of record, and this, too, in the informal observation of campus veterans, has become increasingly diversified since World War II. Four members are said to be ministers. Perhaps more to the point of this inquiry, faculty involvement in or concern about a Christian identity of the college is nil.

Eighty years ago most of the student body came from small towns, villages, and rural homes. Less than 10 percent came from cities of more than 50,000 inhabitants. Ten years later, according to Richardson, most students were coming from urban homes. The modal student has been coming for decades from the suburbs of Chicago.[198] Religious preferences have been so rarely canvassed that it is difficult to track significant shifts in them. Forty years ago Congregational Christians constituted 18 percent of the student body, as did the Methodists; Lutherans were 17 percent; Catholics, 13 percent; and Presbyterians, 11 percent. Today, by informal estimate, Catholics form the largest cohort, amounting to perhaps one-third of the student body.[199]

The presidents no longer preside at such religious services as the college has decreasingly sponsored. Over the years a variety of deans of the chapel and chaplains have taken that role. Their different preoccupations have been described by a former Beloit historian and archivist who had been an undergraduate on campus:

> Beloit College has successively in twenty years suffered an ethical formulation of Congregational Christianity more akin to Unitarianism than to trinitarian doctrine; then a momentary return (under Dr. Rowell) to an older concept of religious expression. For a time we were immersed in expression of somewhat strict Calvinism that was more palatable to the Founders and the Old Guard than to the student body and to many of the Faculty in the years 1949-1952 (the chaplaincy of J. Rodman Williams). For a brief moment we had one of the most

attractive, personally and intellectually, of college Chaplains in the person of David Maitland, a young man who struck a strong note of student response to his intelligent understanding and effective campus ministry. Then, under the extended tenure of Dr. A. D. Beittel the formality of ceremony and ritual, elegantly coordinated with music, prayer and sermon, gave a heightened dignity to the traditional Vespers service, but the still-required weekday Chapels (or Convocations, if you will) degenerated, or at least fluctuated, in content and in student decorum. Mr. Beittel was preoccupied with concepts of social service, integration, and peace. His humanistic interests struck a responsive chord in certain students, but not in all. He was succeeded by a brilliant, sound Methodist scholar whose formal utterances as Dean of the Chapel suggested a rigidity of viewpoint that in personal confrontation seems largely absent from a kindly, generous and sensitive personality. We at the moment [1965] have as spokesman in the pulpit of the College Chapel a voice pronouncing the gospel according to William Graham Cole, with occasional overtones of Hugh Hefner. In truth we do reflect the macrocosm. But we do not reflect much continuity in the expression of a formalized or formula-ized Christian thought or pattern of generally accepted belief.[200]

The college discontinued appointing a full-time campus minister nearly three decades ago. A current catalogue entry, "Religious Life," begins: "Though not presuming to intrude upon any student's particular religious commitments, the College maintains an atmosphere of ecumenicity that encourages full expression of various religious heritages."[201]

In the early fifties there was a fairly full program of religious ministry at Beloit. Endorsed by the president because Beloit was "an institution whose roots are firmly embedded in the Christian tradition," and served by a full-time chaplain, the program still offered two chapels a week (they were for the most part nonreligious assemblies); Sunday vespers; an inter-Greek committee to plan the chaplaincy's program, monthly discussion groups; an annual Design for Living Conference with a distinguished theologian invited; a fellowship group offered for students considering lifework in the church; liaison with local congregations and denominational groups on campus; plus the Heretics Club (moderated by the head of the Religion Department), "not wholly in sympathy with the prevailing midwestern rationalism, and inclined rather to a serious view of classical Christianity." By way of contrast, the official college statement on religion speaks with the voice of Irving Maurer: "Beloit College aims to inspire her graduates with noble ideals. In the sense that religion is deeply involved in the organization of life into a whole and that many truths include not only factual content but great hopes and faith, Beloit College would have her students know religion."[202] In the early sixties there was still a program, but stiffer, with less student initiative and involvement. It emphasized that "the expression of religion may take many forms," and that many denominations were present on campus — not all of them Christian.[203]

By the later seventies Beloit's "concern for values" had been canonized as the sixth of its six goals (goal number one: "the ability to think clearly"). It was called the "whole person" goal, about being a person: "It has long been a tradition at Beloit that we are concerned with our students' values as well as with their test scores. This doesn't mean that we invade your privacy or try to impose our values on you. It does mean that we think values are important, that we do our best to live up to ours, and that we care what kind of person you turn out to be."[204] Several years later this goal underwent revision and emerged as: "Personal integrity, physical well-being, emotional maturity, aesthetic judgment, and a concern for others."[205] If the college was having difficulty at the policy level with the whole person, little fault should be found with its dwindling campus ministry.

The current introduction to the college discloses that Beloit was founded by an initiative of "seven New Englanders" who organized the Friends of Education. It was founded "to serve a society at its frontier by preparing persons who were capable of change and who valued learning for its own sake." There is no mention of Congregationalists, but the college history does recall with satisfaction that a course in evolution was offered as early as the 1890s. There is presently neither dean of chapel nor chapel services nor chapel (the Eaton Memorial Chapel now being an auditorium). Such campus ministry as exists is offered by the local churches. The pastor at First Congregational Church reports "a handful" who worship there. By his and other accounts, the most active ministry is being offered by the several Catholic parishes, especially that of Saint Thomas the Apostle, where James Foley had paid his pew rent in 1866.[206]

Beloit Knows It Is Gone

The consensus of older Beloit observers is that whatever religious ethos perdured from Chapin through Maurer began to disintegrate in the years after World War II. Already in 1945, when the Congregational and Christian Churches asked whether Beloit would agree even to be included on their list as "church-related," the board flinched, then replied that "while it is satisfactory to be regarded as a college related to the Congregational and Christian Churches, the College has greater opportunities by being regarded as a college ready to serve students of all denominations."[207] There was much to gain and, apparently, nothing to lose.

In 1965 President Miller Upton appointed a committee to work out an answer to the question: In what sense could Beloit College be called "Christian," in the past, present, or future? The Christian College Committee struggled with the question for three long years. Schools founded under religious auspices, they eventually agreed, have followed one of two paths. Some have devoted their main energies to their religious identity and have tended to protect it by required church membership, worship, religion courses, and a tendency to discourage dissent or unsettling questions. "A few of these schools manage to be academically excellent;

many are not. Their psychology is often defensive, and they face the modern world with fear and uncritical antipathy."

The other path has led, by purpose or by unplanned drift, into secularism. "Little by little the religious dimension fades out of the college community, leaving at most such vestiges as occasional chapel services and a course in 'Bible as literature.' The value-system of such a college is frankly indistinguishable from that of any school created under frankly secular auspices." Beloit had surely not followed the first path, said the committee, yet they did not wish to admit she had followed the second because "the 'feel' of the campus is not that of a completely secularized institution." This, they granted, was "a subtle nuance." So they stated with momentary bluntness: "Today, calling Beloit a Christian college contributes to neither clarity nor accuracy." That much bluntness was too much for the trustees, who removed the sentence. What they did claim to share was a "rich humanism." In describing their shared commitment the committee rose to a level of rhapsodic banality which none of Beloit's divines or presidents has ever surpassed. This richly humanistic higher education

> takes seriously those qualities and possibilities — intellectual, moral, spiritual — that give man a special place and destiny. It is not a romantically optimistic or pessimistic humanism; rather it recognizes both the heights and depths of human lives. Its emphasis is not on moral codes as such nor on anarchistic concepts of freedom, but upon individual and social responsibility. It recognizes the finitude of man and his tendency to view his own private or group interests as central. At the same time, it proclaims the freedom to take the world and history seriously, to accept responsibility for action while simultaneously accepting the ambiguity of the world and one's self.[208]

This fruit of three years' contemplation could put an entire campus to sleep more quickly than a compulsory chapel talk. Yet it caused a considerable ruckus on campus.

In 1973 the college accepted membership in the United Church of Christ's Council for Higher Education. But in the early 1980s the UCC revised the criteria for membership and required member institutions to accept a new formula if they wished to qualify for a share in the collections for higher education taken up in the churches.[209] The document, which had come forth after four years of strenuous discussion in the councils of the denomination, was framed in prose remarkable, even in UCC circles, for its generalities and for the absence of any area or issue wherein the colleges might feel the bite of any Christian imperatives. The church acknowledges that colleges are a liberating influence in society because they are single-mindedly devoted to the truth and, through self-criticism, ennoble their students and make them conscious of their lifelong calling to responsible citizenship. The college can thus help the church by being its stalwart critic. What the college has to gain from the church, except for modest annual financial contributions, is not clear, except for the church's service "as an ally which can help it to hold high the values of freedom, public service, and concern for persons and their development, and which can help interpret the role of education to American society."[210] The document repeatedly asserts that the church claims no authority or even influence which might impinge on the colleges' freedom. In fact, there is no hint, in a relationship wherein the church is so uniquely the suitor and the colleges so passive, of any possible critique of the academic world and its prepossessions. Nor is there any suggestion of a feature or element in the education offered which might be responsive to the Christian faith. It is said that the church's engagement in higher education is "essential because of the church's vision of what it means to be human and of a just and humane society." The only norm the colleges are to apply is "the human tradition of the liberal arts." It is difficult, therefore, to understand how that would justify the UCC in claiming this arrangement as a "ministry."[211]

Though this 1981 document was even less distinct than the previous text, President Roger Hull sensed it could arouse the same hostility the Christian College Committee Report did in the sixties, and did not even ask the trustees to act on the matter. Several other colleges also wished to avoid the embarrassing public process of signing on to the "covenant," yet wanted to remain on the UCC's list of affiliated institutions. The church agreed, but said that Beloit and other nonaffirming institutions would no longer qualify for their share in the annual collection taken up throughout the churches. Beloit has nevertheless been awarded program moneys since then.[212]

THE CONGREGATIONAL COLLEGES

The United Church of Christ today describes its relationship to Dartmouth College as merely historical, while listing Beloit College as related to the denomination. Neither college, for its part, claims any but historical ties — ties with no present efficacy. The colleges seem to be the more truthful parties.

The academic project was difficult for the Congregationalists. Their polity, from the late sixteenth century, has denied that it is acceptable or even possible for them to engage as a community in a defining exploration of their faith. In response to what they considered unsanctioned interference by human officers of church and state in the faith of the individual, they insisted that there is no human being who can claim authority over another in matters of faith. The local congregations are created by a gathering of saved individuals who themselves formulate a creed and a covenant upon which they must singly agree. That creed then carries the authority of each individual, and of the aggregate of individuals, but not of the church.

Congregationalists thereby accepted a restricted fellowship of the mind. The creeds of the various congregations, for example, are not lengthy; for in this process complexity, especially if it lusts after controversy, will inevitably compromise any text in its ability to unite a congregation. The congregations have thus had to state their creeds very sparingly, and to study them and enlarge upon them with Yankee restraint. There were exceptions to this, as in Boston at the time of the Mathers, but the disagreeable price of that was always tumult and schism.

Another result of this theological minimalism has been the Congregationalists' adoption of a ready-made theology which, over the course of the years, they never definitively appropriated. The Independents were originally a group of defiant English folks who rejected the religious establishment they knew: that of the Church of England. They had very little theology of their own, for their grievances were more in the area of discipline and style than in that of doctrine. In a sense, they were using all their energies to develop a doctrine of freedom from governance. They then adopted Calvinist doctrine and worship, but took little of the Calvinist polity which had made much room for authority and had yielded a considerable amount of its independence to civil authorities. This amalgam of Independent polity and Calvinist doctrine was always a restless one, for Congregationalists were pulled in two directions: to be very free, and to be very right. The yen to be free proved the stronger of the two. Put most simply: they were not a doctrinal people; they have had a very low appetite for inquiry or systematic reflection on their faith.

As the nineteenth century pursued its course the Congregational *depositum fidei* began to suffer: first by neglect, then by rejection, then by embarrassment. In a process that began around the 1840s with the beginnings of strong social conscience associated with abolitionism, and was settled in the minds of most congregations by the end of the Civil War, and was given its definitive justification in the events surrounding the Andover Trial, orthodox Calvinism was retired from active service in the Congregational fellowship. It is important to realize, however, that it was a desiccated relict of what Calvin himself had bequeathed.

The Congregational denomination, which had in early years summoned up massive energy to root out dissidence and deviation, was now prepared to accommodate an internal pluralism upon whose breadth no one could draw limits. In combination with the traditional and unweakened demand for individual freedom of belief, this led to considerable intellectual disunity. Schism and expulsion had in olden days torn great holes in the fabric of their unity. In latter days, though, the unity was no stronger since unlimited tolerance is, if anything, even less able to rally a fellowship into shared belief than are excommunication and hanging.

The community within colleges gathered by such a fellowship as this could be held together by no intellectual tradition; no fundament of revelation, witness, or contentious inquiry; no glutinous dialectic that might sustain and refresh a communal wisdom which they all might take to be an essential part in what made them a community.

The study of their religion was never central to their course of study: there was little tradition of that sort of thing. The threat from Darwin and Huxley was

100

never the problem, nor that from Strauss and Renan. They had little developed wisdom on the speculative subjects of biblical interpretation that could be threatened by these critics. The more ominous threat came in the moral sphere, where the issues of socialism, race, class, imperial economy, industrialization, and the rights of labor were being taken up. The Congregationalists had no substantial theological or philosophical tradition on which to base critical judgments that might vitalize them as a community. They were nevertheless a community in which there was a good deal of reciprocal influence, so for want of a faith-fed ideology they became the sponsors of an enlightened social movement of compassion for those exploited by slavery, industry, or political corruption. They were mostly educated liberals, upper-class reformers. Their faith and their denomination provided them with their force and their ardor . . . but not their direction.

The lively folks of Tucker's and Eaton's generation turned away in some impatience from the Calvinist fundament of their denomination. As the Congregationalists became actively committed to social responsibility, the new liaisons and projects of intellectual inquiry eventually made them awkward about their creed. Their sense of ease in the derring-do of national and international controversy made them regard those whose energies were devoted to traditional preaching and teaching, first as tiresome, then as misguided. Now that they were steaming in new oceans instead of sailing along familiar estuaries they needed much wisdom to verify their new inquiries and critical commitments. But it did not come from their own tradition, except insofar as they were bound in familiarity within a class or a party. They were free to be Americans through and through, because they were committed to no rival community — at least none with a mind of its own. It was thus that without noticing it they lost their independence, and any ethos or wisdom that fed on faith. It was their faith that began to take on the shape and texture and vocabulary of their other loyalties.

It is commonly said that Congregationalism slackened because it failed to engage the emotions as the Methodists and Baptists and other more vibrant and expressive, if even less cerebral, movements did so well. This was one observer's view of it in 1876:

> While our clergy were thus philosophizing about religion, and keeping watch over orthodoxy, and reading written essays to drowsy audiences, warm-hearted, zealous, soul-saving Baptists and Methodists, who, with Christian wisdom, took it as their apostolic mission to reach and convert the masses, came in and stole away the ears and hearts of the people, overran a large part of New England itself, and swept victoriously through the new settlements; using no manuscripts, dealing in no metaphysics, laying stress principally upon a personal experience of saving faith in Christ, and of the power of the Holy Spirit to renew and sanctify the soul, and allowing a privilege of preaching as broad as the language of Holy Writ: "Let him that heareth say come!" And the people came, by tens and hundreds of thousands![213]

On the contrary, as the story of Congregational colleges reveals, their drift away from a faith community was not because their orthodoxy was dry and dull. Actually the revival movement found considerable response throughout the denomination and on their campuses. The failure of the denomination was to engage the mind, not the heart. They had been so convinced and so determined to protect the independence of the individual believer that they had opposed any collegial responsibility for the mind's service to the gospel. Because of that, the early Congregationalist educators spoke both sincerely and accurately when they denied there would be anything distinctive about the content of their education.

After the great sea change in Congregationalism in the nineteenth century, the shift on their campuses was demonstrable. Much has been made of the fact that in sheerly academic terms, the faculties before the 1880s shared a common discourse. Despite their disciplinary specialties, each professor could be co-opted to teach most subjects in the curriculum, and all students studied that same basic curriculum. Twenty years later, after graduate studies and research and separate learned associations and their journals and departments and rivalry for resources, there was no longer a shared culture or discourse.

But in those same years another change took place, bearing more directly on the religious character of the Congregational campuses. In the earlier period the intellectual repertory of the denomination — Calvinist doctrine with its sharp focus on depravity and election and conversion — provided the matter for chapel and revivals, but not for the business of learning and of understanding what was learned. The fellowship of faith had not provided an ideology which the educators could take to work with them from the pulpit to the desk. After the great shift, however, the religiously committed educators did have a shared discourse. Since it was neither drawn from nor very attentively related to either the gospel (despite the fact that it was called "social gospel") or any Christian intellectual endeavor, it was as likely to induce coma as the recent Calvinism had been to cause hives. Tucker speaks earnestly about the order of moral advance — from commandments to ideals, and then to personal standards — after warning his audience that their faith no longer offers content, only tone. Davis, the seminary president, brushes away distracting and abstruse thoughts about God as too elementary, and invites reflection on the whole mighty movement of life. Maurer, another preacher-president, believes in the moral makeup of life, and believes in the divinity of Jesus because he believes in the divinity of man. Students covenant to observe clean living, and are told how much more advanced they are than when students debated whether gambling was wrong.

From that period when the Congregational fellowship provided their country with its most strident call to social justice, they also brought in an astoundingly thin harvest of religious discourse: mannered and stately, but without vitality.

A younger philosopher who was inclined to think of himself as an Elisha to William Jewett Tucker's Elijah observed that within ten years of the old president's retirement, Dartmouth liberalism had lost whatever religious sanctions had been

102

used to justify it. The ethical idealism born of the New England conscience had vanished with Tucker's passing. He went on to admit that in rejecting the stifling authority of orthodox Calvinism, Tucker had emerged a humanist, and one who gave a very thin account of how his emancipated faith could in any way gain force from the gospel or lend coherence to an integrated education. He was sure Tucker was a religious man. "I confess, however, that I have difficulty in determining the place of religion in Tucker's educational philosophy." This Elisha was John Moffatt Mecklin, who will figure significantly in the story of Lafayette College.

> The implications of his basic humanism for religion Tucker did not, perhaps dared not, draw. He still made use of the symbols of traditional religion. Whether he believed that these symbols were theological fictions, or whether he reified them and placed behind them transcendental religious realities that persist independent of the cultural and psychological reality of the way of life into which these symbols were woven in the loom of history, I cannot say. Tucker tactfully refrained from raising ultimate metaphysical questions.[214]

It was for want of any foundational, intellectual understanding of faith that Tucker at Dartmouth could beget offspring of his liberalism and humanism, but not of his Christian faith.

The chief parties to the transformation of Dartmouth were two triads of presidents, who were emblematic of three generations: Samuel Bartlett (1877-92), William Tucker (1893-1909), and Ernest Hopkins (1916-45) at Dartmouth, and Aaron Chapin (1849-86), Edward Eaton (1886-1917), and Irving Maurer (1924-42) at Beloit. Bartlett and Chapin were traditional, intrepid embodiments of a Congregational dignity that held fast to a minimal theological self-understanding, and with the passage of years showed itself loath to rethink and reconstrue their received tradition. Tucker and Eaton, grand gentlemen who dominate the histories of their colleges, had quietly withdrawn themselves from the sectarian orthodoxy of their past and embraced its modernist and probably its Unitarian revision. They were the engineers of radical transformation. But their era had no sense that a tradition was being repudiated. Tucker and Eaton were both gracious-spirited toward their colleagues and disinclined to emphasize discontinuity with the past. They both replaced an ecclesial vocabulary, not with a rival ecclesial vocabulary, but with one of generic secular ambiguity. They both continued in the traditional pieties and were admirable embodiments of the old morals of cultivated gentlemanliness. But by silencing the embarrassing Calvinist orthodoxy of their predecessors and replacing it, not with a renewed Christian vision but with a genteel, mannered Americanism, they uprooted Christianity, not just Congregationalism. Their successors, Hopkins and Maurer, inherited from them nothing but the manners, and an equivocal vocabulary which was allusive enough to the past pieties, and an affluence which offered so much promise for the future, that there could be not the slightest sense of loss. The work of the transformers was fully accomplished one generation before anyone could have noticed what they had done, by which time it would have been seriously impolite to discuss it.

Throughout the course of these years the Congregational colleges give the appearance of dissimulation, almost of duplicity, about their commitment. Recall that both Dartmouth and Beloit were unhappily presented with charters that obliged them to be nonsectarian, yet both later affected to be pleased with them.[215] Both have progressively retold their stories so that the religious motivation and support of their founders were increasingly obscured. At first both were known to be "Congregational." Then, to avoid the stigma of sectarianism, they began to be promoted as "Christian," though the unspoken intent was to remain as Congregational as before. This intention, however, was not realized. To avoid any compromise of academic freedom, they began to be promoted as "religious," though the unspoken intent was to remain as Christian as before. This intention, in its turn, was not realized. Today religion is a private pastime on these campuses, somewhat like camping and tutoring the poor. It is most literally extracurricular, indeed extramural.

Almost a century ago the sentiment was expressed in the Congregational Education Society that their schools were "Christian without creeds, religious but not denominational."[216] At that time, however, their colleges had already offered persuasive evidence that for want of creeds they had left off being "Christian," and for want of possession by a denomination they could not be stably "religious" either.

Today just about the only verifiable interest or influence by the United Church of Christ, the residuary heir of the Congregationalists, is an annual contribution of about $15,000 a year to each of its colleges, a grant which, adjusted for inflation, has been steadily decreasing by about 10 percent each year. The largest religiously identifiable group of students on their campuses is Catholics (though in one college approximately one-third of the students are Jewish). Members of the related United Church of Christ are assumed to constitute perhaps from 4 to 5 percent of their enrollment.[217] Yet, from the Congregational point of view, since these colleges were always meant to be self-defining and freestanding, and never subject to the authority of the church, this fact that the churches have no stake in their educational program does not raise the otherwise obvious question: Why continue to formalize a ligature that creates no dynamic unity?

Already in the 1960s Paul H. Sherry, the UCC executive for higher education, admitted publicly that with committed Christians no longer dominant among faculty, administrators, students, or benefactors, the related colleges had become "less and less 'Christian' in any meaningful sense of the word." In any case, he said, it might seem like an act of ideological imperialism for church-related colleges to sponsor any particular faith in an academic atmosphere meant to be free of coercion. The church should quit any pretense of an organic relationship, and work instead to produce certain specific results:

The Christian faith's concern for the uniqueness of every person needs to be heard by educators in an era when a mass man appears to be developing. Its concern for just social structures can influence the remodeling of those educational institutions which today deny justice to students and faculty. Its commitment to "the least of these" dictates special efforts on behalf of those to whom society has denied free access to equal opportunity. Its devotion to development of the "whole man" calls for support of efforts to develop the student's emotional and volitional life as well as his intellectual life. Its trust in a faithful God dictates taking risks in the midst of an educational establishment that likes to play it safe.

He concluded by endorsing the view that it was the business of UCC colleges, not to "make Christians," but to "help men become fully men."[218] Mr. Sherry is now the president of the United Church of Christ. The colleges related to Sherry's church are staffed by people without even minimal professional or personal concern for what his church thinks about justice or free access or who the "least of these" might be, or what elements of "the whole man" they might be missing.

NOTES TO CHAPTER I

1. In 1931 the Congregationalists joined with the General Convention of the Christian Church to become the Congregational and Christian Churches. The latter group brought along their two colleges: Defiance and Elon. Then in 1957 that body joined with the Evangelical and Reformed Churches to form the United Church of Christ. The latter group brought along their eight colleges: Catawba, Cedar Crest, Elmhurst, Franklin and Marshall, Heidelberg, Hood, Lakeland, and Ursinus. Once associated with the tradition but now defunct are Maunaolu, New, and Yankton.

2. Founded as Billings Polytechnic Institute and merged into another older institution which had had various names.

3. Several insightful studies of this struggle between continuity and adaptation are Perry Miller, *The New England Mind: From Colony to Province* (Cambridge: Harvard University Press, 1953); and J. William T. Youngs, *God's Messengers: Religious Leadership in Colonial New England, 1700-1750* (Baltimore: Johns Hopkins Press, 1976), esp. 121-41.

4. The early Wheelock and Dartmouth stories as given here are greatly in the debt of Frederick Chase, *A History of Dartmouth College and the Town of Hanover, New Hampshire,* ed. John K. Lord (Cambridge: John Wilson & Son, 1891), 1-6; also Leon Burr Richardson, *History of Dartmouth College,* vol. 1 (Hanover: Dartmouth College Publications, 1932), 1-27.

5. The entire charter is given in Chase, 639-49.

6. Chase, 311, 387.

7. L. B. Richardson, *History of Dartmouth College,* 1:190.

8. L. B. Richardson, *History of Dartmouth College,* 1:191.

9. L. B. Richardson, *History of Dartmouth College,* 1:257.

10. John King Lord, *A History of Dartmouth College, 1815-1909* (Concord, N.H.: Rumford Press, 1913), 118. Lord's volume is a continuation of Chase's *History* and will hereafter be cited as J. K. Lord.

11. Benoni Dewey, James Wheelock, and Ben. J. Gilbert, *A True and Concise Narrative, of the Origin and Progress of the Church Difficulties, in the Vicinity of Dartmouth College, in Hanover, the same being the Origin of President Wheelock's Disaffection to the Trustees and Professors of the College, with Documents relative thereto* (Hanover: Charles Spear, 1815).

12. J. K. Lord, 213-14.

13. J. K. Lord, 217.

14. J. K. Lord, 258; Wilder Dwight Quint, *The Story of Dartmouth* (Boston: Little, Brown, 1914), 140-41.

15. J. K. Lord, 332.

16. Leon Burr Richardson, *History of Dartmouth College,* vol. 2 (Hanover: Dartmouth College Publications, 1932), 441.

17. J. K. Lord, 240.

18. In 1854, 80 out of 264 undergraduates so identified themselves: *The Creed and Covenant of the Congregational Church at Dartmouth College, with a Catalogue of the Members* (Hanover: Dartmouth Press, 1855), 3. The original source is John Richards, "Statistics of the Church at Dartmouth College," 19 July 1854, the Congregational Library, Boston (hereafter cited as CLB).

19. J. K. Lord, 294.

20. J. K. Lord, 291.

21. They are here cited to their definitive publications.

[Nathan Lord], *A Letter of Inquiry to Ministers of the Gospel of all Denominations on Slavery by a Northern Presbyter* (1854)

Nathan Lord, *A Northern Presbyter's Second Letter to Ministers of the Gospel of All Denominations on Slavery* (Boston: Little, Brown, 1855)

Nathan Lord, *A Letter to J. M. Conrad, Esq., on Slavery* (Hanover: Dartmouth Press, 1860)

Rev. President Lord, *A True Picture of Abolition* (Boston: Daily Courier, 1863 [original publication: *Boston Daily Courier,* 22 November 1862])

22. Nathan Lord, *A True Picture of Abolition,* 15.

23. J K. Lord, 324.

24. *An Address delivered at the Inauguration of the Author as President of Dartmouth College, November 18, 1863, by Rev. Asa D. Smith, D.D., with the Introductory Address of His Excellency Joseph A. Gilmore, Governor of New Hampshire* (Hanover: Published by request of the Board of Trustees, 1863), 31-33, Dartmouth College Archives (hereafter cited as DCA).

25. J. K. Lord, 346.

26. W. D. Quint, 171.

27. Samuel Colcord Bartlett, "Relations to Religion," in *Centennial Celebration at Dartmouth College, July 21, 1869* (Hanover: B. Parker, 1870), 90-99, DCA.

28. "The Chief Elements of a Manly Culture," *Exercises at the Inauguration of Samuel Colcord Bartlett, D.D., as President of Dartmouth College, June 27, 1877* (Concord, N.H.: Republican Press Association, 1877), 38-39, DCA.

29. It should be noted that this was not a deficit peculiar to Dartmouth. Until literary societies went into decline in the latter decades of the nineteenth century, their debating agendas had often been more vital intellectually than the classical curriculum, and their private book collections were as large as or larger and incomparably more valuable than those of the colleges. It was commonly the case that a collegiate library would date its conversion to being a serious intellectual resource from the year when the campus societies handed over their holdings.

30. "Chief Elements," 33, 22.

31. Rev. Alonzo H. Quint, D.D., address, *Dedication of Rollins Chapel and Wilson Hall, Dartmouth College, June 24, 1885* (printed for the College, 1886), 4-17; *Christianity in the College: A Baccalaureate Sermon preached at Dartmouth College, by Samuel Colcord Bartlett, President of the College, June 20th, 1886* (Hanover: Dartmouth Press, 1886), 3-18, DCA.

32. See Bartlett's *Life and Death Eternal: A Refutation of the Theory of Annihilation* (Boston: American Tract Society, [1866]); *Future Punishment* (Boston: Congregational Publishing Society, 1875); "Responsibility for Religious Principles," baccalaureate sermon, June 23, 1878, in *Anniversary Addresses* (Boston and Chicago: Congregational Sunday-School and Publishing Society, 1894), 38-59; "Christianity in the Commonwealth," baccalaureate sermon, June 26, 1887, in *Anniversary Addresses,* 233-57, DCA. Bartlett, whose own discipline was Old Testament studies, was an ardent defender of the literal veracity of the earliest Scriptures, a position which he held with as much tenacity as Nathan Lord had devoted to his interpretation of Genesis on slavery; see his *The Veracity of the Hexateuch: A Defence of the Historic Character of the First Six Books of the Bible* (Chicago: Fleming H. Revell, 1897), DCA.

33. George E. Peterson, *The New England College in the Age of the University* (Amherst, Mass.: Amherst College Press, 1964), 123, 148. See also Richard Hofstadter, *The Age of Reform: From Bryan to F.D.R.* (New York: Knopf, 1955), 148-64.

34. Edwards A. Park, *The Associate Creed of Andover Theological Seminary* (Boston: Franklin Press, 1883), 23, CLB.

35. Henry K. Rowe, *History of Andover Theological Seminary* (Newton, Mass.: Thomas Todd, 1933), 1-22, 159-68.

36. Park, 3-5.

37. William Jewett Tucker, *My Generation: An Autobiographical Interpretation* (Boston and New York: Houghton Mifflin, 1919), 36, 54.

38. Stopford A. Brooke, *Life and Letters of Frederick W. Robertson,* 2 vols. in 1 (Boston: Fields, Osgood & Co., 1870), 2:147 (hereafter cited as Robertson, *Life and Letters*).

39. Robertson, *Life and Letters,* 2:148-49.

40. Robertson, *Life and Letters,* 1:329-34; 2:66-69, 341-54.

41. Robertson, *Life and Letters,* 1:302, 306.

42. Robertson, *Life and Letters,* 2:22-23, 55, 160.

43. Robertson, *Life and Letters,* 2:163.

44. Robertson, *Life and Letters,* 2:150.

45. Robertson, *Life and Letters,* 2:43.

46. Robertson, *Life and Letters,* 1:332, 337, 339; 2:42, 64-65.

47. Robertson, *Life and Letters,* 2:161-65. "It appears to me that Protestantism throws upon the intellect the work of healing which can only be performed by the heart. It comes with its parchment 'signed, sealed, and delivered,' making over heaven to you by a legal bond, gives its receipt in full, makes a debtor and creditor account, clears up the whole by a most business-like arrangement. And when this Shylock-like affair with the scales and weights is concluded, it bids you be sure that the most rigorous justice and savage cruelty can want no more" (1:299).

48. Robertson, *Life and Letters,* 1:56-57.

49. Tucker, *My Generation,* 54-62.

50. L. B. Richardson, *History of Dartmouth College,* 2:667. For the Andover group's own account of what they stood for, see *Progressive Orthodoxy, a contribution to the Christian interpretation of Christian doctrine* (Boston: n.p., 1892).

51. Andover, which had been founded in 1807 as a rejectionist haven against the liberalism which was taking Harvard into the Unitarian fold, now found itself as the new liberal outpost within American Congregationalism (Charles Eliot having long since assured that Harvard would have no meaningful entanglements with denominations of any sort). Yet the Andover Trial marked the beginning of a sharp decline. When Andover was celebrating its centennial as the oldest and at one time the most affluent seminary in America, it had more professors than students. The trustees went to court, pleaded that it was impossible in modern times for any respectable scholar to subscribe to the old Andover Creed, and had that legal requirement vacated. Henceforward it would be enough to be a trinitarian Congregationalist to qualify for a faculty appointment. After a brief morganatic affiliation with the Harvard Divinity School, it federated with the Baptist seminary in Newton, Massachusetts, and is extant today as the Andover-Newton Theological School. The seminary's historian noted with pleasure that the new faculty shared with their predecessors "the same high standards of scholarship, the same interest in interpreting religion in terms of present as well as future life. Both rested on faith in the ultimate spiritual reality as against the secular spirit of the age." H. K. Rowe, 204. But it was this disembodied "spiritual reality" with no recognizable Christian lineaments which eventually proved to be most congenial to the secular spirit of the age.

52. *The Historic College: Its Place in the Educational System,* an address delivered by William Jewett Tucker upon his inauguration as president of Dartmouth College, 28 June 1893, with the exercises attending upon the inauguration (Hanover: Printed for the College, 1894), 3-5, DCA.

Wilder Dwight Quint, who called Bartlett "the Man of Iron," describes his emeritus days:

The alert, sinewy figure of the rugged old man was familiar in Hanover for six years more. Often it was mounted on a bicycle, which the ex-president rode gallantly and well up to his eightieth year. Occasionally it was seen in the lecture-room, where the keen intellect, unclouded always, revelled in presenting to the students its orthodox conceptions of the relation of the Bible to science and history. Even in the mellower sunshine of the New Dartmouth this strong character was found fighting to the end with the ancient sword of Gideon for a faith that was wearing away. (p. 198)

When Bartlett died the trustees' brief resolution of condolence mentioned not a word about his astute financial determination that had brought the college out of deficit into the beginnings of its affluence. Explicit appreciation was expressed for the gallantry of his surrender: "retiring after fifteen years of successful service, he assumed the duties of the less exalted position with such good grace, such appreciation of changed relations, such cordial helpfulness, as illustrated his real greatness, his Christian nobility" (Dartmouth College, Records of the Board of Trustees, 5:254, 23 December 1898, DCA).

53. *The Historic College,* 18.

54. Robert French Leavens and Arthur Hardy Lord, *Dr. Tucker's Dartmouth* (Hanover: Dartmouth Publications, 1965), 261, 55, 141; slightly different statistics are provided in L. B. Richardson, *History of Dartmouth College,* 2:711. Tucker himself often pointed out that Dartmouth's disproportionate growth in these years was largely due to its choice to be a college rather than a university. See "Abstract of the Report of the President on the Relation of the Numerical Growth of the College to Its Educational Policy," ms. 906671, DCA.

55. L. B. Richardson, *History of Dartmouth College,* 2:685; Leavens and Lord, 43.

56. Leavens and Lord, 15; Records of the Board of Trustees, 5:200-201, 7 May 1897, DCA.

57. *The Report of President Tucker concerning His Administration, Issued to the Alumni* (Dartmouth College, 30 June 1909), 12-13, DCA.

58. Records of the Board of Trustees, 5:59, 4 May 1893, DCA.

59. L. B. Richardson, *History of Dartmouth College,* 2:714-15; Leavens and Lord, 214; Douglas Vanderhoof, "As the Century Turned," in *A Dartmouth Reader,* ed. Francis Brown (Hanover: Dartmouth Publications, 1969), 91.

60. Tucker, *My Generation,* 345-49; *Report of President Tucker,* 25-26.

61. *Dartmouth Alumni Magazine,* January 1909, 120-21; Leavens and Lord, 218.

62. Tucker, *The New Movement in Humanity: From Liberty to Unity,* oration delivered before the ΦBK Fraternity of Harvard University, 30 June 1892 (Boston and New York: Houghton Mifflin, 1892), 17, DCA.

63. Samuel Colcord Bartlett, *Christianity in the College: A Baccalaureate Sermon preached at Dartmouth College, June 20th, 1886* (Hanover: Dartmouth Press, 1886), 15, DCA.

64. Tucker, *The New Movement in Humanity,* 19, DCA.

65. Tucker, "The Religion of the Educator," in *Personal Power: Counsels to College Men* (Boston and New York: Houghton Mifflin, 1910), 270-73, 279-80, DCA.

66. Tucker, "Moral Maturity," in *Personal Power,* 144-45, 162. Francis Peabody extols Tucker's preaching, and this sermon, for its "sweep of thought and large conclusions . . . the heights of mature and prophetic vision. . . . Here is movement, lift, enlargement, surprise." "University Preaching," *Harvard Theological Review,* April 1916, quoted by Tucker, *My Generation,* 348-49. By contrast, when Tucker addressed social issues directly, he made little or no attempt to invoke his traditional religious principles or vocabulary, and wrote with an immediate, secular cogency. See his *The Conscience of the Nation, A Sermon on the Present Crisis Preached by President Tucker in the College Church, April seventeenth* [1898], DCA; also "The Progress of the Social Conscience," *Atlantic Monthly* 116, no. 3 (September 1915): 289-303.

67. Tucker, *The Function of the Church in Modern Society* (Boston and New York: Houghton Mifflin, 1911), 21-22.

68. Washington Gladden, *Recollections* (Boston: Houghton Mifflin, 1909), 206; quoted in J. William T. Youngs, *The Congregationalists* (New York: Greenwood Press, 1990), 173-74.

69. J. K. Lord, 491-93.

70. Frank E. Rowe, '91, to Henry Melville, '79, 11 December 1925: Chapel Collection, DA118, DCA.

71. *Dartmouth,* 9 March 1894.

72. *Dartmouth College Catalogue, 1904-05,* 168, "Religious Services."

73. DCA, Carnegie Foundation file: 1893-1909.

74. Ernest M. Hopkins, secretary of the college, to the Carnegie Foundation, 11 September 1905, DCA; Henry S. Pritchett, president of the Carnegie Foundation, to Tucker, 12 April 1907, "Carnegie Foundation, 1893-1909," DCA.

75. "College and the Sectarian Tie," *Congregationalist and Christian World,* 3 July 1909, 8-9.

76. L. B. Richardson, *History of Dartmouth College,* 2:697-98.

77. Charles H. Chandler, *A History of the Theological Society at Dartmouth College Read Before the Society,* 1 June 1868; Hanover: Chapin & Whitcomb, 1868. See also Robert W. Cook, "A History of Religion at Dartmouth College" (student thesis, Hanover, 1942, DCA).

78. Charles T. Brewster, "A History of the Dartmouth College Christian Association," 1927; R. B. Dwinell, "Facts about Dartmouth Christian Association 1909-1925," DCA.

79. L. B. Richardson, *History of Dartmouth College,* 2:750.

80. An editorial in the *Dartmouth,* 4 May 1894, which complains about compulsory church attendance, shows how very respectfully, even meekly, this was done under Tucker's presidency.

81. "Dartmouth Chapel Slimly Attended," *Boston Herald,* 17 January 1926.

82. These views on the abolition of compulsory chapel are to be found in ms. DA118, "Compulsory Chapel at Dartmouth College," DCA. Correspondents quoted are: Henry Melville, C. G. McDavitt, Henry Thayer, Lewis Parkhurst, Charles Albert Perkins, and President Hopkins.

83. "The Question of Prayers at Harvard," *Independent,* 23 April 1885, 16.

84. Melville to Hopkins, 9 February 1926, ms. DA118, DCA.

85. "Should Chapel Be Compulsory?" 5 December 1925, 31, publication unidentified, Chapel Collection, DA118, DCA.

86. "Yale Chapel Attack Wins Harvard's Help," *New York Times,* 16 February 1926.

87. *Daily Dartmouth,* 27 June 1910, 1.

88. *Daily Dartmouth,* 27 June 1910, 7.

89. Ozora Davis, "Sesqui-Centennial Sermon," in *150 Years of Dartmouth College,* ed. Homer Eaton Keyes and Eugene Francis Clark (Hanover: Dartmouth College Trustees, 1921), 106, 107, 110. At the same exercises President Marion Le Roy Burton of the University of Minnesota urged an "absolute, unqualified devotion to the truth" at institutions of higher learning, which must resist all interest groups and orthodoxies to protect the academic freedom of every professor, "so long as he lives in keeping with the normally accepted moral standards of the community and is a loyal defender of the constitution and government of the United States" (*150 Years of Dartmouth College,* 137). For Davis, country could claim a loyalty that class, color, and creed should not.

90. Hopkins, "Epilogue: Dartmouth College — an Attempt at Formal Interpretation," in *150 Years of Dartmouth College,* 143.

91. Hopkins, "The Faith of the Fathers," in *This Our Purpose* (Hanover: Dartmouth Publications, 1950), 45-46.

92. Hopkins, "Personal Responsibility," in *This Our Purpose,* 42.

93. Hopkins, "The Faith of the Fathers," 49.

94. Leon B. Richardson, *A Study of the Liberal College: A Report to the President of Dartmouth College* (Hanover, 1924), 21-22, DCA.

95. L. B. Richardson, *History of Dartmouth College,* 2:800.

96. Results of a survey of religious preference provided to the author by Rev. Gwendolyn King, the Christian chaplain to the college.

97. Ronald M. Green, "Toward a Copernican Revolution in Our Thinking about Life's Beginning and Life's Ending," *Soundings* 66, no. 2 (summer 1983): 152-73. Green notes, p. 171, that the "Nazi decision to declare Jews or Gypsies nonpersons is morally unacceptable," not because it was a "social decision" that it would be too burdensome to treat these humans as "persons," but because that decision was made by only one political community.

98. John Sloan Dickey, "Institutional Purpose in the Undergraduate College," address delivered at the inauguration of his Dartmouth classmate Robert Kenneth Carr as president of Oberlin College, *Dartmouth Alumni Magazine,* December 1960, 24-35. Dickey admitted that with the passing of preacher presidents, a curriculum strong in religion, and required worship, "the college's conscience was left without tangible, pervasive, and enduring witness." To that end he prevailed on the trustees to found the Tucker Foundation and to give its dean a campus-wide pastoral responsibility. He also asked the board to affirm formally that Dartmouth's "moral and spiritual purpose springs from a belief in the existence of good and evil, from faith in the ability of men to choose between them and a sense of duty to advance the good." Dickey, "Conscience and the Undergraduate," *Atlantic Monthly* 195, no. 4 (April 1955): 31-35. Nothing could have contradicted so directly the Congregational doctrines of depravity and atonement so earnestly sustained by Lord and Bartlett and their predecessors. Also, the text of this resolution, which Dickey thought likely "to remain resilient and meaningful under well-nigh any future circumstances," was cast in that flat new prose which Tucker had brought to Dartmouth, and which virtually assured that it would wither more rapidly than the discourse it had replaced.

99. James O. Freedman, "What Jewish Means to Me," advertisement of the American Jewish Committee, *New York Times,* 4 December 1994, E19.

100. Youngs, *God's Messengers,* 120-41.

101. The Ordinance provides: "Religion, morality, and knowledge being necessary to good government and the happiness of mankind, schools and the means of education shall forever be encouraged." See Edward Dwight Eaton, "The Inevitable Relation of Congregationalists to Education," in *Handbook of the Congregational Foundation for Education* ([Chicago], 1923), 13, CLB.

102. "Society for the Promotion of Collegiate and Theological Education at the West," report on annual meeting and activities, October 1859, CLB, Congregational Education Society (CES), Miscellaneous Materials, Box 23. Robert Lincoln Kelly notes a third reason for this shared venture: "to protect eastern donors from beggars who were seeking by hand-to-mouth feeding to keep their academic children alive." *Colleges and the Social Order* (New York: Macmillan, 1940), 34.

103. *22nd Annual Report of the Directors of the American Education Society,* 1896, 13-15 ([22/AES/1896]; hereafter other annual reports cited in similar abbreviated fashion). It should be appreciated, however, that the various denominations had long reported large numbers of their congregations without ministry. Sixty-five years earlier, for instance, the New England Congregationalists reported two hundred to three hundred "destitute churches." The German Reformed Church and the Evangelical Lutherans were reporting four times as many churches as ministers; the Associate Presbyterians and the Six Principle Baptists, more than twice as many. For denominations like the Congregationalists, whose clergy were often engaged in other services (including education), these figures understate the problem. See *Quarterly Register and Journal of the American Education Society* 1 (October 1828): 139; 1 (January 1829): 165; *Quarterly Register of the American Education Society* 6 (February 1834): 202, CLB.

104. A quarter-century later this was still the case: *Report of Congregational Education Commission to National Council* (Boston: CES, 1921), 27, CLB.

105. 18/ACES/1892, 10-12.

106. 20/AES/1894, 14-15.

107. 23/AES/1897, 16; Frederick Lewis Weis, *The Colonial Clergy and the Colonial Churches of New England* (Lancaster, Mass.: Society of the Descendants of the Colonial Clergy, 1936).

To assure a higher quality and reliability among their own candidates, the AES decided to withhold financial aid until after the successful completion of the freshman year in college, and to restrict it thereafter to students in the upper two-thirds of their class. For those in theological studies, preference was to be given to college graduates. 21/AES/1895, 13-14; 82/CES/1898, 13.

108. 20/AES/1894, "Tabular Report."

109. It is not easy to reconstruct the religious composition of nineteenth-century colleges, especially those in the Calvinist tradition. They were less concerned to classify students by denomination, since the most significant division for them was between those who had been converted and those who had not, and were therefore "confessedly strangers to the hopes of the Gospel." Thus for their reports they counted "professors of religion." And throughout the century they tended to include about one-third of their student bodies. For example, Dartmouth reported exactly one-third in 1826-27, when the New England colleges as a group reported 32 percent; Dartmouth reported 37 percent in 1827-28, 28 percent in 1828-29, 26 percent in 1829-30, 36 percent in 1830-31. But this cohort seems mostly to have been those who then went into the ministry. Commentaries speak of another category, never rendered statistically, of students who may not have undergone a proper conversion but practiced their religion with apparent sincerity: these were called "pious students." See *Quarterly Register and Journal of the American Eduction Society* 1 (October 1827): 26; 1 (April 1828): 75; 1 (October 1828): 137, 140; 1 (April 1829): 224; 2 (May 1830): 238; *Quarterly Register of the American Education Society* 3 (May 1831): 294, CLB. It was only after the Liberals had replaced the Calvinists in the Congregational ascendancy that the census changes to a roster of denominational membership.

These statistical reports of salvation, though customary, especially on campuses whose religion focused primarily upon experiential conversion, did not find universal approbation. One member of the Massachusetts legislature excoriated the practice at Amherst:

> I hold in my hand a sermon, purporting to have been preached by Heman Humphrey, President of Amherst College. It was published in 1826 and contains at its close, a list of the students in the classes of the College. The whole number is 126; and at the bottom are written these significant words, *"hopefully pious,* 98," — of the balance, 28, nothing is said, — no designation is given them. It needs no inspiration in these days of sectarian *watchfulness,* to understand, that those unfortunate 28 are *chaff,* — the "hopelessly damnable." Sir, has it come to this? Shall the government of a College, professing to rest upon the broad basis of public good, introduce such distinctions within their walls, and divide their students into two classes, the one *"hopeful"* and the other *"hopeless"* as to their spiritual concerns? Can any father have the cruelty to send his son to an institution where such a division will be made? Shall lads at 14 or 15 years of age be thus classified. . . ?

> Claude Moore Fuess, *Amherst: The Story of a New England College* (Boston: Little, Brown, 1935), 89.

110. 83/CES/1899, 45.

111. *Report of Congregational Education Commission to National Council,* 1921, 18, CLB, CES, Miscellaneous Materials, Box 15.

112. This disclaimer was almost certainly due, not simply to the informalities of Congregational polity, but to the ambiguity needed if many of the schools were to qualify for grants from the Carnegie Foundation, which was requiring freedom from denominational control.

113. *Handbook of the Congregational Foundation for Education* (Chicago, 1923), CLB; *Report of the Activities of the Congregational Foundation for Education, from the Time of Its Organization in July, 1921, to the Close of the Fiscal Year Ending June 30, 1924* (Chicago, 1924); *Annual Report of the Congregational Foundation for Education, July 1, 1924–June 30, 1925* (Chicago, 1925), CLB, CES, Miscellaneous Materials, Box 22.

114. 96/CES/1912, 30-32, 42; 97/CES/1913, 40. A minister was appointed to serve, or a student was paid to run the operation. On the earliest efforts see Clarence Prouty Shedd, *The Church Follows Its Students* (New Haven: Yale University Press, 1938), 17-18, 43-47.

115. 98/CES/1914, 10-12; 99/CES/1915, 12-13. The recently formed Council of Church Boards of Education had reached a near consensus that the ministry should follow the students

onto state campuses; see R. Watson Cooper, of the Board of Education of the Methodist Episcopal Church, to E. S. Tead, of the CES, 29 June 1916, CLB, CES, Miscellaneous Materials, Box 18.

116. Correspondence from the summer of 1915, in CLB, CES, Miscellaneous Materials, Box 8. The president of Wheaton (Illinois), Charles Blanchard, wrote in a startlingly different language and tenor, as much like Dartmouth's Bartlett as Meiklejohn resembled Tucker:

Fathers and brethren:

The Trustees and Faculty of our college send you greetings in the name of the Lord Jesus, our Saviour and King.

This institution began in prayer, as most colleges have begun. Before there was a brick or a stone placed in a building on our campus, the founders, a little group of poor men who loved Jesus Christ and hated the things that antagonize his work, met and knelt in the prairie grass where our buildings now stand. They dedicated the land and all the things that were to be placed upon it, to the service of God, the interests of the christian church. From that time to this present, this has been the key-note of our college life. Everything which has been done here has been done with reference to this dedication which lies at the foundation of all our college life. . . .

We do not appoint to positions in the college, teachers who are not confessed christians and while we do not require direct christian service, we expect it. Usually we are not disappointed. So far as our teachers are earnest and aggressive christians, they use what influence they have to bring our students into life and to light more abundant.

117. 103 and 104/CES/1920-21, 24-25, 30-31.

118. In 1921 the *Education Commission Report* had commented on the proclivity to use "Christian" as a preferred descriptor:

A test question which it is fair to apply to our colleges is to ask in how far is there definite planning to make themselves the bearers of the distinctively Christian elements in our civilization. Of course all of these schools claim to be Christian and most of them add "but not denominational." This addition the church accepts as having value largely for publicity purposes when the college is dealing with non-denominational groups. So long as it proves of value, the colleges are free to make use of it although one may question the wisdom of a college president advertising that he is president of a college which is "free from church and state," when it is perfectly well known that he is very much dependent upon the good-will of the church for students and funds.

> *Report of Congregational Education Commission to National Council, 1921,* 18, CLB.

But by 1921 neither students nor funds were being provided to colleges or universities by the Congregational churches or agencies. And the use of "Christian" instead of "Congregational" had an ideological as well as a marketing purpose.

119. Jay T. Stocking, *The Church and Higher Education* (Boston: CES, 1934), CLB, CES, Miscellaneous Materials, Box 22.

120. Over the years these requirements varied somewhat in their vocabulary. For instance, in earlier years the trustees had to be "Orthodox" Congregationalists; in later years, the "evangelical" specification for the president was dropped. These undertakings, however stated, were enforced. In 1882 Whitman Seminary in Walla Walla, Washington, was applying for financial help. The president explained that "the institution was started by Congregationalists, and has always been understood as theirs." But to qualify for aid from the ACES they had to rearrange their board of nine members: four Congregationalists, an Episcopalian, a Cumberland Presbyterian, a Methodist, a man who belonged to no church but whose wife and children attended Congregational Sunday school, and a former Methodist who had become a "backslider." The backslider was told to resign and be replaced by the new president, thus creating a Congregational majority.

The newly organized (and funded) institution then asserted in its new brochure: "Whitman College and Seminary will not be governed by any State or church authority whatever, but will be under the general control of a Board of Trustees who elect their own successors. It will aim to be, without sectarianism or fanaticism, distinctly Christian, inculcating complete loyalty to God and highest worthiness in man." The very deferential tone of the president's later correspondence with Boston implies a considerable dependence on the subsidy. CLB, CES, Miscellaneous Materials, Box 31.

121. Correspondence in CLB, CES, Miscellaneous Materials, Box 25. The insistence on freedom from ecclesiastical control and on a nonsectarian character dates back to the predecessor organization, the SPCTEW (much influenced by the expressed hope that Congregationalists and Presbyterians could collaborate closely toward the day when their denominations could merge), often called the Western College Society, a joint venture of Congregationalists and Presbyterians, both Calvinists and then moving toward a possible union. In its latter years, when denominational consciousness was ripening into rivalry, the traditional disclaimers of nondenominationalism continued, but they were accompanied by various covert tactics of control. See James Findlay, "The SPCTEW and Western Colleges: Religion and Higher Education in Mid-Nineteenth Century America," *History of Education Quarterly* 17 (spring 1977): 31-62.

122. See the "Rules of the Board of Directors" adopted in 1904, in 95/CES/1911, 55-57.

123. William Warren Sweet, *Religion on the American Frontier: 1780-1850,* vol. 3, *The Congregationalists* (Chicago: University of Chicago Press, 1939), 3-34; Youngs, *The Congregationalists,* 121-23. The Presbyterians, however, have evidence to support the view that the working of the Plan of Union in their favor has been exaggerated: Sweet, *Religion on the American Frontier: 1780-1850,* vol. 2, *The Presbyterians, 1783-1840* (New York: Harper & Brothers, 1936), 42-56, 99-101.

124. H[enry] M. Whitney, "Beloit College," in *The Columbian History of Education in Wisconsin,* ed. J[ohn] W. Stearns (Milwaukee: State Committee on Educational Exhibit for Wisconsin, 1893), 133-53; Aaron L. Chapin, "Beloit College: Its Origins and Its Aims," *New Englander* 31 (1872): 334-35; Edward Dwight Eaton, *Historical Sketches of Beloit College* (New York: A. S. Barnes, 1928), 2-6.

125. Lucius D. Mears, "Historical Address," in *Services at the Fiftieth Anniversary of the First Congregational Church, Beloit, Wis., December 23, 29 and 30, 1888: 1838-1888,* 31; First Congregational Church, Beloit (FCCB), courtesy of archivist Catherine Blakely.

126. *Annual Report of the SPCTEW,* 1859, 15, CLB; Robert Kimball Richardson, "How Beloit Won Its College," *Wisconsin Magazine of History* 28 (1945): 290-94; R. K. Richardson, "History of Beloit College, 1844-1942," ed. Helen Drew Richardson (Beloit College, 1980), chap. 1, pp. 5-10; chap. 3, pp. 1-11. R. K. Richardson, archivist-historian for the college and the church, was to have published a scholarly history of the college but died in 1952 with the manuscript incomplete and unpublishable. It is nevertheless a raw, voluminous, and invaluable compilation of materials and references. His widow labored over the text periodically until her own death in 1980. Both are held in typescript in the Beloit College Archives (BCA). His 1952 version will be cited as R. K. Richardson, *History* I; their 1980 version, as R. K. Richardson, *History* II.

127. R. K. Richardson, *History* II, chap. 1, p. 10.

128. D[exter] Clary, "On the Relation of Beloit College to the People of Beloit and Its Vicinity," in *Exercises at the Quarter-Centennial Anniversary of Beloit College. July 9, 1872* (Beloit: Garret Veeder, 1872), 13, BCA.

129. R. K. Richardson, *History* II, chap. 1, n. 7.

130. Fifteen years earlier Illinois College had encountered heavy weather in seeking its own charter, which finally was awarded with a nonsectarian proviso like the one Strong would propose for Beloit. Robert K. Richardson, "The Non-Sectarian Clause in the Charter of Beloit College," *Wisconsin Magazine of History* 22, no. 2 (December 1938): 151; Whitney, 25-29.

131. Charles Leslie Glenn, Jr., *The Myth of the Common School* (Amherst: University of Massachusetts Press, 1988). Merle Curti points out that the high incidence of illiteracy in the early

West helped foment a prejudice against intellectuals and against possible domination of government by church groups. This was easier to see in the southern states and territories. See Curti, *The Growth of American Thought* (New York: Harper, 1943); R. K. Richardson, "How Beloit Won Its College," 290.

132. R. K. Richardson, "The Non-Sectarian Clause," 127-55; R. K. Richardson, *History* II, chap. 2.

133. Ten years later the college publicly brushed aside the obnoxious amendments as "a few unimportant modifications." *Address of Professor J[oseph] Emerson, and Proceedings of Convention at the Tenth Anniversary of Beloit College, July 8, 1857* (Beloit: B. E. Hale, 1857), 21, BCA.

To appreciate the often strident contempt the Congregationalists and Presbyterians were directing toward the Catholics, one must know that in 1851 the former (united in the PCCW) were reporting a membership within Wisconsin of 5,038, while the latter were reporting a membership of "about" 85,000 (membership rolls were much more carefully kept by the former than the latter churches). In 1860 the respective figures were 16,000 and 190,000. See Stephen Peet, *History of the Presbyterian and Congregational Churches and Ministers in Wisconsin* (Milwaukee: Silas Chapman, 1851), 186; Dexter Clary, *History of the Churches and Ministers connected with the Presbyterian and Congregational Convention of Wisconsin* (Beloit: B. E. Hale, 1861), 128, BCA; and various volumes of the *American Catholic Almanac*. Catholic figures were provided by Timothy Cary, archivist of the Archdiocese of Milwaukee. Granted the aspiration of the educated New Englanders (Whigs then, we may assume) to a dominance in public affairs even faintly approaching what they had enjoyed at home, overtones of class and politics intensified their religious animus against these ostensibly uncultured Democrat immigrants.

134. Robert K. Richardson, "The Mindedness of the Early Faculty of Beloit College," *Wisconsin Magazine of History* 19, no. 1 (September 1935): 33-37.

135. "Report" from the faculty and board of trustees given in 1857, printed as an appendix in "1857 Report," 23; R. K. Richardson, "Mindedness," 49; R. K. Richardson, *History* I, 722, quoting *The Record of the Two Hundredth Anniversary of the Founding of Yale University*, [ed. Charlton M. Lewis] (New Haven: The University, 1902), 308-9.

136. R. K. Richardson, *History* I, 860, 727.

137. J[ames] W. Strong, "On the Relation of the College to the Church and Kingdom of Christ; and to Education," in *Exercises at the Quarter-Centennial*, 29-30, BCA.

138. Mears; R. K. Richardson, ed., *The Centenary: The First Congregational Church in Beloit, Wisconsin* (Beloit, 30 December 1938); R. K. Richardson, "The First Congregational Church in Beloit," sermon, 25 February 1951; Helen Drew Richardson, "The First Church and Beloit College," address at vesper service for the 100th anniversary of the dedication of the church edifice, 6 May 1962; Robert H[enry] Irrmann, "The Relationship of Beloit College to First Congregational Church of Beloit," 5 April 1986; all BCA or FCCB.

139. At this time there was a strong divide in the West between radical abolitionists and moderates; see Warford Malcolm Lyle, "Piety, Politics, and Pedagogy: An Evangelical Protestant Tradition in Higher Education at Lane, Oberlin, and Berea, 1834-1904" (Ed.D. diss., Columbia University, 1973).

140. R. K. Richardson, *History* II, chap. 12, pp. 1-4; J[ames] J[oshua] Blaisdell, "Reminiscences of Early Days and the Financial Affairs of the College," in *Exercises at the Quarter-Centennial*, 22-24.

141. Joseph Emerson, *Twenty-Five Years of Beloit College* (Milwaukee: Sentinel Printing Co., 1872), 9; also published in *Beloit College Monthly*, July 1872, 297-306. See also Emerson's 1869 address, "Our Martyrs," reprinted in Eaton, *Historical Sketches of Beloit College*, 66-71. President Eaton then appends a note of his own: "In a history of one of the prominent New England colleges, after the patriotic record of the institution in the Civil War is given, the statement is made that this record probably surpasses that of any other college. In view of the facts brought

out by Professor Emerson it may be questioned whether in this loyal service Beloit was surpassed by any other." He may well have had Dartmouth in mind.

142. Strong, *Exercises at the Quarter-Centennial,* 38.

143. R[obert] C[oit] Chapin, "Epochs in the History of the College," in *Semi-Centennial Anniversary, Beloit College, Commencement Week, June 20-23, 1897* (Beloit: Cham, Ingersoll, 1897), 49, BCA; Eaton, *Historical Sketches of Beloit College,* 73 n.

144. R. K. Richardson, *The Centenary,* 35-38.

145. Peet had for some time been wary of polarizing forces brought into Wisconsin by Old School Presbyterians and ultra-Congregationalists. Sweet, *The Congregationalists,* 396-99.

146. R. K. Richardson, "How Beloit Won Its College," 304-5; R. K. Richardson, *History* I, 730; R. K. Richardson, *History* II, chap. 3, pp. 6-12.

147. R. K. Richardson, *History* II, chap. 12, pp. 22-26, esp. n. 9.

148. Report of the Committee of the Friends of Christian Education, in appendix of *Address by Prof. J. Emerson,* 22, BCA.

149. John W. Wilson, "Development of the Wisconsin Congregational Conference," in *A Hundred Years of Congregational History in Wisconsin,* ed. Frank N. Dexter (n.p.: Wisconsin Congregational Conference, 1933), 83-84; Glenn T. Miller, *Piety and Intellect: The Aims and Purposes of Ante-Bellum Theological Education* (Atlanta: Scholars Press, 1990), 204.

150. Helen Drew Richardson, "First Church and Beloit College," 9.

151. Robert H[enry] Irrmann, "Beloit College: A Christian College. Its Historical Ethos" (December 1965), 27; BCA, Religion Box.

152. R. K. Richardson, "Can Beloit Still Be a Christian College?" *Alumnus,* January 1949, 5.

153. Aaron Chapin, "Beloit College," 334-35, in R. K. Richardson, *History* II, chap. 11, p. 16.

154. J. Emerson and H. M. Whitney, *Do You Want a Better Education?* 1877; R. K. Richardson, *History* I, 723-24.

155. Darwin A. Leavitt, "Our Colleges," in *A Hundred Years,* 151.

156. Thus, for example, Chapin speaking at the University Convocation of the State of New York:

> We have to notice one more distinctive particularity of the American college. It is the pervading presence through all its discipline and culture of a positive moral and religious influence. Historically the college was originated with Christian meaning for the interests of virtue and the Christian faith as essential to perfect and crown the development of rational faith — to be the sacred bands of order and purity and honor and integrity in human society, and to give security in a free republic to that government which is of the people, by the people and for the people. With very few exceptions, this characteristic of the college has been maintained in our country from the beginning until now. Accordingly its regimen enforces the rules of morality and provides for the participation of the college community as such in Christian worship. As a matter of fact too, its instruction and discipline are mainly in the hands of men of positive Christian character. It cannot be otherwise, to any great extent, if the college fulfills its function in the formation of moral character, well defined, stable and strong.
>
> Aaron Chapin, *The True Function of the American College,* 220-21; reprinted from *Proceedings of the University Convocation of the State of New York,* held 11-13 July 1882, BCA.

157. R. K. Richardson, "Mindedness."

158. R. K. Richardson, "Can Beloit?" 5-6.

159. Thus Professor George Lucius Collie, in R. K. Richardson, *History* I, 735; also Joseph Collie, "On the Inner Life of the College," in *Exercises at the Quarter-Centennial,* 19.

160. It should be remembered that few college-level students at Beloit or elsewhere at that time ever completed their course and earned a degree; among those who did, future ministers formed a high proportion. Eaton, *Historical Sketches of Beloit College,* 59, 114; Emerson, *Twenty-Five Years,* 8-9; see also J. Collie, 19; Strong, "On the Relation," 33-35.

161. J. J. Blaisdell, "On the Future of the College," in *Exercises at the Quarter-Centennial,* 48-49. Blaisdell, professor of philosophy, had been educated at Dartmouth and Andover, and would serve Beloit for thirty-eight years.

162. T[homas] C[rowder] Chamberlin, "A Glance at the Intellectual Attitudes of the College," in *Semi-Centennial Anniversary,* 91-92.

163. R. C. Chapin, 53; R. K. Richardson, *History* I, 10; "Commencement Program, 1916," *Beloit Alumnus* 7, no. 6 (July 1916): 9, BCA.

164. R. K. Richardson, *History* I, 737-38.

165. Eaton, *Historical Sketches of Beloit College,* 103.

166. R. K. Richardson, *History* I, 141-44; cp. Frederick H. Jackson, "Simeon E. Baldwin and the Clerical Control of Yale," *American Historical Review* 57 (1951-52): 909-18.

167. Edward F. Williams, *The Life of Dr. D. K. Pearsons, Friend of the Small College and of Missions* (New York: Pilgrim Press, 1911), esp. 235; BCA, Minute #353, Document File #353, Meeting of 19 April 1910, Beloit College, Record Book of the Board of Trustees, B: 252-4.

Pearson said he favored Beloit with his gifts because of the fidelity of the Old Guard. "They kept the curriculum up to the highest standard, never lowering it to catch the whims of others, less far-seeing than themselves. They nailed their colors to the mast, and keep them flying through long, discouraging years. The College has always taught a pure faith, and never diluted it with higher or lower criticism." This, Richardson later observed, "curiously missed the open-minded liberalism of the elder College statesmen." See Pearson, "Some Reasons for My Gifts to Beloit College," in *Glimpses of Beloit College as Seen by Representative Men,* BCA; R. K. Richardson, *History* I, 127.

168. BCA, Minute #152, Meeting of 8 November 1905, Beloit College, Record Book of the Board of Trustees, D: 17-28.

169. BCA, Document File #174, Minute #174, Meeting of 18 June 1906, Beloit College, Record Book of the Board of Trustees, B: 48-49. The General Education Board, which was actively engaged in making grants to institutions of higher education at the time, required only "that no part of the income from the fund so contributed by this Board shall ever be used for specifically theological instruction." BCA, Document File #272, Meeting of 11 February 1908, Beloit College, Record Book of the Board of Trustees, B: 162.

170. R. K. Richardson, *History* I, 48-49.

171. *Beloit College Catalogue, 1880-81,* 23.

172. R. K. Richardson, *History* I, 735.

173. BCA, President's Report, 1907-1908, 9-10; 1913-14, 17-18; *Beloit College Reports.*

174. *Beloit College Catalogue, 1884-85,* 14-16. This was in Chapin's penultimate year.

175. *Beloit College Catalogue, 1892-93,* 23-24.

176. *Beloit College Catalogue, 1912-13,* 22; R. K. Richardson, *History* I, 739b.

177. R. K. Richardson, *The Centenary,* 42-44, 48-52; R. K. Richardson, "First Congregational Church in Beloit," 7-8.

178. Eaton, "Baccalaureate Sermon," in *Semi-Centennial Anniversary,* 6-8.

179. The entire college-founding project in the West was much spurred on by fear that Catholics would get there first. Consider these warnings spoken in the councils of the SPCTEW:

There are those who are ready to take this business of providing seats of education at the West out of our hands entirely. . . . The Jesuits are willing, nay, longing, nay, plotting and toiling to become the educators of America. (1845)

It is a stirring thought that in the prosecution of our work we are fighting over the battles of the Reformation. . . . In our associate capacity, in conjunction with kindred organizations, we meet the Society of Jesus to decide the question, whether Protestant evangelical institutions or the institutions and influences of Rome shall cover that field, and mould the forming population. (1853)

> Paul Moyer Limbert, *Denominational Policies in the Support and Supervision of Higher Education* (New York: Teachers College, 1929), 11.

Catholics may have been the most motivating of rivals, but Baptists, Methodists, and Presbyterians were also much stirred by each other as educational competitors. See Albea Godbold, *The Church College of the Old South* (Durham: Duke University Press, 1944), 67-69.

180. The Diary of James L. Foley, transcript in BCA, microfilm copy in the Wisconsin State Historical Archives.

181. Memoranda and clippings, "The Catholic Problem," BCA, Religion Box; Dean's Report, 1915-16, 21-22, *Beloit College Reports*, BCA.

182. See, e.g., editorial, "Our Denominational Paradox," *Congregationalist* 109 (1924): 133.

183. R. K. Richardson, *History* I, 266, 250.

184. Lloyd V. Ballard, *Beloit College, 1917-1923: The Brannon Years* (n.p., The Brannon Family and Beloit College, n.d.), 16-17, 64-66, BCA.

185. Josh[uah G.] Reckord, "Beloit College 1917-1942: Changes in the Religious Character and Tradition of the College and General Trends toward a More Creative Expression of Theology," 1966?, 4-30, BCA, Religion Box. Some sense of how Brannon saw civic and religious issues fused with one another is to be got from the text of an oath he administered to the entire college body when first presented on campus in September 1917:

> Inasmuch as the greater part of the world is engaged in the most colossal, terrific, and destructive war ever waged, and inasmuch as my own Country and my own College are joined in this world struggle to make safe the life, liberty, and pursuit of happiness for all men for all time, I do hereby declare my devotion to the cause of liberty, and I do hereby anew pledge my loyalty to my Country and dedicate myself to the freedom of mankind.
>
> Furthermore, in appreciation of my own enlistment in educational preparedness during this year, I dedicate my choicest possession, my time, and my choicest heritage, my physical, mental and spiritual being, to the wisest procedure and activities offered by Beloit College, with all of her traditions, treasures, associations and opportunities.
>
> Furthermore, we covenant together to live normal, clean, and wholesome lives; to establish the best possible standards of academic relations in this, the college of our choice; and we do now, hereby, solemnly and sincerely pledge our example and our influence to make these ideals dominant in the American college.

> "Beloit's Pledge for 1917-18," *Round Table*, 6 October 1917, 1.

186. Irving Maurer, "My Belief in God," *My Christian Faith* (Columbus: First Church, 1922), 25-28, BCA, Maurer papers.

187. Maurer, "My Faith in Jesus," *My Christian Faith*, 34-35.

188. Maurer, "The American College and Religion," Founders' Day address, Knox College, 17 February 1925, BCA, Maurer papers.

189. This had been a theme in Maurer's inaugural lecture:

> Beloit College should insist that there is no dividing line between science and religion. There is no closing of doors which science may not open. There is, on the other hand, no freedom for the scientist from moral obligations. In this sense Beloit should be a religious

college, standing for a faith which invites intellectual freedom and for a culture which knows consecration to an unselfish order of life.

The order of knowledge and of culture, in this schema, is the responsibility of the scholar. *The warrant of religion is twofold: to speak to the moral conscience of the scholar, but to refrain from confronting his intellect.* (emphasis added)

R. K. Richardson, *History* I, 401-2.

190. Maurer, "The Value of a Large Religion," delivered at First Congregational Church, Columbus, 13 May 1923, BCA, Maurer papers.

191. President's Report, 1924-29, 3-4, 11-12; *Beloit College Reports.*

192. R. K. Richardson, *History* I, 422, 406, 456-57.

193. Maurer, Memorandum to the Board of Trustees, 3 June 1939, BCA.

194. Maurer, "Memo for Faculty." Maurer seems to have been aware that in his attempts to speak religiously to what he seems to have considered an intimidatingly rigorous academic audience, he was dithering:

> Many of those who no longer accept a Christian view of God may accept the Christian emphasis upon the morality of love. In so far as they do this we can keep company with them. But whether or not they agree with Christians in this latter particular, they would have us give up our faith in God. Let us at once admit that we Christians ourselves are neither very unified nor very satisfactory in our theories of God. Each of us is apt to idealize his own experiences and call it God. There is quite possible a statement of a modern theism which can stand on its own merits in the presence of all the bewildering knowledge of physical laws. We believe that this universe is more rationally described when we say that God is Father than it is in any other way.
>
> Irving Maurer, "An Apologetic for the Christian College," *Congregationalist and Herald of Gospel Liberty* 115, no. 36 (4 September 1930): 301.

195. This statement was carried in issues of the *Beloit College Catalogue* from 1939 until at least 1953.

196. R. K. Richardson, *History* I, 467-71.

197. R. K. Richardson, *History* I, 251.

198. Dean's Report, 1913-14, 18, BCA; *Beloit College Reports;* R. K. Richardson, *History* I, 466; *Beloit College Catalogue, 1964-65,* 209-19; *1993-95,* 237. The *Beloit College Catalogue, 1924-25* shows, however, that while students began to come from large cities (Chicago and Milwaukee), the retention rate was poorer for students with an urban background. Beloit was still a regional college.

199. Ruth Kolpack, director of religious education, Church of Saint Thomas the Apostle, interview with the author, 9 November 1994.

200. Irrmann, "Beloit College," 60-61. The last-characterized dean of the chapel, Anderson D. Clark, was present at a meeting of the board of trustees a few months after his colleague, Dr. Irrmann, had set down those observations.

> Mr. Sprague asked Dean Clark whether "God is dead on the campus." Dean Clark replied that "the dead God is dead," and that by traditional scales of measurement, interest in religion is indeed decreasing at Beloit as it is at most college campuses. To indicate the lessening of interest in traditional religious ceremony and organizations, the Dean noted the decrease in numbers attending Sunday Vespers during recent years; the fact that there is only one really active denominational group on campus at present [Catholic] and that this group is kept active by the intensive leadership given to it by the minister involved;

and that the general interest in religion aroused in the 1950's is now largely dissipated or at least taking different forms.

Using other norms, however, the Dean stated, Beloit has a very exciting religious life being carried on through an active student Chapel group including a Liturgy Committee and a Focus Committee; and through a growing intellectual interest in religion on the part of a good number of students and a greater questioning of the theological status quo on the part of students. Dean Clark noted particularly the uniqueness and vitality of many of the recent programs planned by student committees, including an Easter week series that included Maundy Thursday community dinners for students and faculty in faculty homes, a highly unusual Easter morning service of "expectation," and other programs designed to get interested students involved "for the right purpose." During discussion it was noted that across the country too many people continue to attend church for the wrong reasons and that present student disinterest and disrespect for traditional religious programs and procedures is partly an effort to break down this artificiality and to get to the heart of some genuine spiritual experience for the individual.

> Records of the Beloit College Board of Trustees, 23 April 1966 session, p. 12, BCA.

201. *Beloit College Catalogue, 1993-95,* 6-8, 199.

202. *Religious Life on the Campus* (Design for Living Council, Beloit College, ca. 1950-52), BCA.

203. *Beloit College Catalogue, 1960-61,* 34-35, 98-99; *1962-63,* 12.

204. *Beloit College Catalogue, 1978-79,* 8.

205. *Beloit College Catalogue, 1983-85,* 5.

206. Rev. Richard E. Hotchkin, interview with the author, 8 November 1994.

207. This information provided by Mr. David Mason, who is preparing a history of the college.

208. "The Shared Commitments of the College Community," a report of the Beloit Christian College Committee, with a preface, rationale, and covering memorandum from Miller Upton, 15 October 1968, BCA.

209. In 1934, after the merger which created the new denomination, a national conference defined the "college of Congregational and Christian background" (this was one of several terms meant to secure patronage without dependence). It is difficult to see what remained to attract the interest of the churches.

The college of such background was defined as an institution

> Where learning is supreme and where there exists a genuine search for truth at any and all costs. Where there is fostered an interpretation of life from a purposeful theistic point of view. Where the student is inspired to live a useful Christian life in a changing moral, social and economic order.
>
> The college must provide an adequate place in its curriculum for religion in general and the Christian religion in particular with the emphasis upon a theistic philosophy and a social gospel.

> "Oberlin Seminar on Christian Education," CLB, CES, Department of Education Institutions, *Bulletin* #23, 15 August 1934.

Religious leaders whose hearts failed to be enflamed by this prospect of subsidizing theism might not have read down to the final, apocalyptic flourish: "It would be suicidal for the church in these days of uncertainty and change in all phases of life to cast off or to become indifferent to its colleges."

In 1977 the UCC had proceeded further in portraying the Christian nature of its education. State, church, and school were intended as mutually autonomous within a single covenanted community. But "when the rule of reason [in the schools], and the rule of law [in the state], and the rule of faith [in the church] became separated from each other in a secularized society, the result is an arrogant, dehumanized rationalism, law without mercy or equal justice, and an isolated, fragmented esoteric sectarianism. For the reformers, separatism and extrication were necessary. For us, integration and synthesis are necessary." The terms used to describe a renewed Christian education, however, are not very integrated with faith. The conversion experience is a revelation by which "one is opened to the cosmic revelatory experience." A UCC education is "redemptive" because it includes "the transcendent as well as the secular." In any case, it would have to be a very indistinct synthesis that could bind the state, school, and church — each of them autonomous — into one covenanted community. See Wesley A. Hotchkiss, longtime general secretary of the UCC Division of Higher Education, "The Prophetic Academy: An Historical Perspective on UCC Related Colleges," *Journal of Social Issues* 14, no. 2 (spring 1977): 66-71; "The Case for Church-Related Higher Education," Statement of the UCC Council for Higher Education, *Journal of Social Issues* 14, no. 2 (spring 1977): 88-89.

210. "A Statement on Meaning, Purpose, and Standards of the Relationships among Colleges, Academies and the United Church of Christ," affirmed by the 13th General Synod of the United Church of Christ, 30 June 1981, Rochester, New York. This had been preceded by another policy document: "Pronouncement on Church-Related Higher Education," voted by the 12th General Synod of the United Church of Christ, 25 June 1979, Indianapolis, Indiana.

211. See also *The Educational Mission of the United Church of Christ* (New York: Division of Education and Publication, United Church Board for Homeland Ministries, 1988); *Plan of Work for the Educational Mission of the United Church of Christ* (New York: Division of Education and Publication, United Church Board for Homeland Ministries, 1990)

212. One recent grant supported a study into the feasibility of Beloit again having a campus chaplain, and offered a subsidy for such an appointment. The end result, however, is that Beloit, possibly alone among UCC-related colleges, has no chaplain at all.

213. William Patton, "The Last Century of Congregationalism; or, The Influence in Church and State of the Faith and Polity of the Pilgrim Fathers," *New Englander* 35 (1876): 645-46.

214. John M[offatt] Mecklin, *My Quest for Freedom* (New York: Scribner's, 1945), 215-59; quotation at p. 227.

215. It requires noticing that though the nondenominational provisions of the Dartmouth and Beloit charters were unsolicited and at first unwelcome by their respective founders, they were conventional in that they protected religious freedom among those teaching and those taught, but presumed a religiously homogeneous governance. A similar provision appeared in the Amherst College charter (1825): "that no Instructor in said College shall ever be required by the Trustees to profess any particular religious opinions, as a test of office; and no student shall be denied the privileges of said College on account of the religious opinions he may entertain" (Fuess, 72-73).

216. 87/CES/1903, 14.

217. Rev. James A. Smith, Jr., UCC Minister for Higher Education Relationships, interview with the author, 25 January 1995.

218. Paul H. Sherry, "Church or College: Either, but Not Both," *Christian Century,* 4 October 1967. See also the extensive correspondence in subsequent letters to the editor, esp. 7 February 1968, 168-69.

CHAPTER 2

The Presbyterians

The early colonization of North America was not undertaken by landless poor, as in the nineteenth and early twentieth centuries. There was a plentiful seventeenth- and eighteenth-century migration of middle-class religious dissenters who needed to escape state repression. Despite the fact that the early riparian colonies mostly reproduced the church patterns of Britain, some foundations were specifically hospitable to dissent (New England for Congregationalists, Rhode Island for Baptists, Maryland for all, Pennsylvania for Quakers). But even in the majority of colonies where the Church of England was established, Huguenots from France, Reformed from the Netherlands, Puritans from England, Covenanters from Scotland, Chapel people from Wales, and Presbyterians from Northern Ireland and Scotland peopled the estuaries. Their first ascendancy was in the middle colonies, and the form of Calvinism first organized there was Presbyterian.

The Presbyterians, who included experienced merchants, artisans, bankers, and professionals, were economically on their feet. Having struggled for their independence before setting sail to the West, and having adopted a form of church government that was representative and strenuous, they were not slow to initiate and then to dominate networks of political representation. They organized their first presbyteries in the region of New York, New Jersey, and Philadelphia, fanning out from the same land which had been New Netherland before the British wrested it from the Dutch. The early eighteenth century brought from Ulster an inundation of Scots (Saxon) Lowlanders who had been brought in to occupy Ulster only to find themselves economically crimped by British enforcement of the established church and crippled by pro-English laws which hindered them from exporting their crops either to England or to the American colonies. In the early 1700s they increased their numbers in Pennsylvania more than tenfold, becoming the dominant population there: an unsettling presence for the Penns. But they also quickly became

---

This essay was researched and written in 1995, and the statistics and facts it reports as current derive from the latest sources then available.

an effective church that reached down into the southern colonies. It is reckoned that one-third of the Scots brought into Ireland by the Stuarts and the House of Orange to dispossess and repress the unruly Catholics there later took their leave and came to America. They were as bourgeois and literate as their Congregational cousins to the north, and though literary institutions and colleges were first begun in New England, the Scotch-Irish (as they were called on this side of the Atlantic) brought with them a traditional fervor for the education of their children. With the coming of the Republic they were ready, and their pattern of "literary institutions" provides map markers for their westward migration. Unlike the New Englanders, their westward deployment gave them strength in both the South and the Upper Midwest, considerable presence later on the Pacific coast, and eventually in the plains and mountain regions. The Congregationalists had dominated the world of American higher education through the colonial and federal periods, but in the years precedent to the Civil War it was the Presbyterians who had the most expansive network of colleges.

Today the Presbyterian Church (U.S.A.) (PC[USA]) recognizes itself as related to sixty-four colleges and universities:

1776	Hampden-Sydney College	Hampden-Sydney, Va.
1794	Tusculum College	Greenville, Tenn.
1819	Centre College	Danville, Ky.
1819	Maryville College	Maryville, Tenn.
1826	Lafayette College	Easton, Pa.
1827	Hanover College	Hanover, Ind.
1827	Lindenwood College	Saint Charles, Mo.
1829	Illinois College	Jacksonville, Ill.
1834	University of the Ozarks	Clarksville, Ark.
1837	Blackburn College	Carlinville, Ill.
1837	Davidson College	Davidson, N.C.
1837	Muskingum College	New Concord, Ohio
1839	Erskine College	Due West, S.C.
1842	Mary Baldwin College	Staunton, Va.
1846	Carroll College	Waukesha, Wis.
1848	Rhodes College	Memphis, Tenn.
1849	Austin College	Sherman, Tex.
1849	Waynesburg College	Waynesburg, Pa.
1851	Coe College	Cedar Rapids, Iowa
1851	Westminster College	Fulton, Mo.
1852	University of Dubuque	Dubuque, Iowa
1852	Westminster College	New Wilmington, Pa.
1853	Beaver College	Glenside, Pa.
1853	Monmouth College	Monmouth, Ill.
1857	Queens College	Charlotte, N.C.

1857	Lake Forest College	Lake Forest, Ill.
1866	College of Wooster	Wooster, Ohio
1867	Barber-Scotia College	Concord, N.C.
1867	Johnson C. Smith University	Charlotte, N.C.
1867	King College	Bristol, Tenn.
1867	Lewis and Clark College	Portland, Oreg.
1868	Bloomfield College	Bloomfield, N.J.
1869	Trinity University	San Antonio, Tex.
1869	Wilson College	Chambersburg, Pa.
1872	Lyon College	Batesville, Ark.
1874	Macalester College	Saint Paul, Minn.
1875	Knoxville College	Knoxville, Tenn.
1875	Westminster College	Salt Lake City, Utah
1876	Grove City College	Grove City, Pa.
1876	Stillman College	Tuscaloosa, Ala.
1878	Rocky Mountain College	Billings, Mont.
1878	Sheldon Jackson College	Sitka, Alaska
1880	Presbyterian College	Clinton, S.C.
1882	Hastings College	Hastings, Nebr.
1883	Belhaven College	Jackson, Miss.
1884	Jamestown College	Jamestown, N.Dak.
1886	Alma College	Alma, Mich.
1887	Sterling College	Sterling, Kans.
1889	Missouri Valley College	Marshall, Mo.
1889	Agnes Scott College	Decatur, Ga.
1889	Pikeville College	Pikeville, Ky.
1890	Whitworth College	Spokane, Wash.
1891	Albertson College of Idaho	Caldwell, Idaho
1891	Buena Vista College	Storm Lake, Iowa
1894	University of Tulsa	Tulsa, Okla.
1894	Warren Wilson College	Swannanoa, N.C.
1900	Lees-McRae College	Banner Elk, N.C.
1901	Millikin University	Decatur, Ill.
1904	Davis and Elkins College	Elkins, W.Va.
1906	College of the Ozarks	Point Lookout, Mo.
1916	Montreat-Anderson College	Montreat, N.C.
1923	Schreiner College	Kerrville, Tex.
1958	Eckerd College	Saint Petersburg, Fla.
1958	Saint Andrews Presbyterian College	Laurinburg, N.C.[1]

The history of the Presbyterians in this country is riven by repeated schism and reunion. At one time in the mid–nineteenth century they were cloven in four by the issue of slavery and a chronic conservative-liberal division over evangelical piety. They have been reunited, in largest part, only since 1983. The northern churches were energetic in founding and sustaining schools on every level for the freedmen, and six of the schools presently related to the church were historically intended for the education of blacks. Those schools were founded in the teeth of resentment and harassment by Southern whites, including their coreligionists, and have had the slow and lean growth of desert plants. By far the greater portion of those schools perished for want of finances and the will to provide them: many as late as the time of the civil rights movement not long ago.[2]

The Presbyterians were socioeconomically well ahead of the Methodists who overtook and then exceeded them in college founding, yet not many of the Presbyterian foundations ripened into universities, as did many of the urban colleges of the Methodists. On the other hand, even the smaller schools of the Presbyterians proved sturdy, and their rate of survival is relatively high. The penchant of Presbyterians for organization, discipline, and unity (offset by a penchant for schism) gave them the stronger capability of marshaling their support for their colleges. And enrollment statistics suggest that the Protestants were able to maintain significant enrollments from their own church membership until after the Second World War.

The beginnings of Presbyterian education in America occurred during the Great Schism (1741-58) between the Old Sides (centered in the Synod of Philadelphia) and the New Sides (strong in the Synod of New York). The church had fallen out over divergent attitudes toward the Great Awakening. The New Sides considered accomplishment in piety to be a necessary element in any minister's competence, while the Old Sides stressed doctrinal orthodoxy and classical education. When William Tennent, Sr., opened an academy known as the "Log College" in Neshaminy, Pennsylvania, in the 1730s, the Presbyterians finally had a place to prepare young men for the ministry. The Old Sides, however, found its scholarship too rustic, and with their blessing Francis Alison moved on from there in 1744 to open a more rigorous classical academy in New London, Delaware. Meanwhile the seemingly reckless ebullience of the Great Awakening had caused the people of Philadelphia to open a Charity School in 1740, which grew into the College of Philadelphia, dominated by the Anglicans and frequented by the aristocracy. In 1755 Alison became the vice provost of the College of Philadelphia, and brought with him such Presbyterian patronage as the dwindling but genteel Synod of Philadelphia could provide. The numerous and now somewhat affluent but linguistically unamalgamated German Reformed were a desirable target population for this project, but they proved to be an aloof constituency. With the coming of the Revolution and the scattering of the mostly Anglican Tories, the college was expropriated by the state and converted into the University of Pennsylvania; it was designated as nonsectarian, but until 1810 Presbyterians would be its most influential constituency. The New Sides, meanwhile, had opened Nassau Hall, or the College of New Jersey, in 1746; it later settled in Princeton. And that, of course, is an entirely different story.

LAFAYETTE COLLEGE

The two factions, Old and New, reunited in 1758, and Princeton began to attract students from as far as Presbyterians could be found. The Revolution caused some weakening in their expectation that every minister should have a liberal education, but standards were again hoisted when the soldiers came home. A variety of academies sprang up within Philadelphia, but even more in the villages surrounding the city: Frankford, Germantown, Norristown, Montgomery Square, Abington. In the colonial and early federal periods Presbyterians, as individuals and as a church, were responsible for founding approximately one hundred schools in and around Pennsylvania. As they were spread farther out from Philadelphia, along the Delaware River, the town of Easton supported a series of small Presbyterian schools. Lafayette College was founded there, and after Princeton and Penn it is the eldest Presbyterian college foundation still extant in the old heartland of American Presbyterianism, the Delaware Valley.[3]

Easton had been laid out at the behest of the Penn family in 1750, on the far eastern border of Pennsylvania, where the Lehigh drains into the Delaware. The borough was affluent in the nineteenth century. The Lehigh River and its associated canals brought mountains of anthracite down from the coalfields in northeastern Pennsylvania; once in the Delaware system the coal could be conveyed on waterways up and down the coast. Alongside that cargo great forests of timber were rafted down to the Philadelphia shipyards. One of the country's more abundant cement deposits lay right behind Easton. The town also had one of the early steel plants, which would not be eclipsed by neighboring Bethlehem until the end of the century. One of the major roadways beckoning settlers westward to the Northwest Territory passed over Easton's bridge, and stages were deployed on roads in various directions. In addition to its water and highway connections to New York and Philadelphia, the town straddled four railroads. In a nation that was building its industrial base and its civil infrastructure, little Easton stood with sturdy shoulders.

A Lay Foundation, Not Priest-Ridden

The idea for a college there arose in 1824. It was a wobbly idea, for Easton had had a succession of schoolhouses since 1755, and had seen as many closings as openings. The elite of the town were English, or rather, English-speaking Scotch-Irish, but they seemed too few to support the school by themselves. The more numerous German population had previously seen little place for themselves under the English-language tutelage inevitably provided by the Presbyterian parsons-schoolmasters. The city fathers spent an evening together in the local taproom to discuss how to provide their children with something better, and they agreed that their more ambitious plan — for a college, not simply an academy — would need to assure full enrollment by also providing German studies. They had another, novel, marketing idea. Local militias were still required by federal law, though their function had become more social than martial. Easton's college would offer what almost none other then did: training in military science along with literary studies. A contingent of Easton's war veterans had recently turned out in their uniforms to welcome the old Marquis de La Fayette, who as a young soldier had gallantly embodied France's support during the Revolution, when he came to Philadelphia during a triumphant return visit in 1824. The suggestion to call their proposed school La Fayette College (as it would be written in early years) easily gathered a consensus around the fireplace that night.

The proposal they sent up to the legislature was in several respects exceptional. First, in governance. Thirty-nine leading citizens were named as charter trustees (most without their knowledge or consent). In a striking departure from custom, not a single clergyman was included. It was almost universal practice to give assurance to the segments of the population whose attendance was desired by reserving seats on school governing boards for their ministers. During Penn's decade of existence as a state university (1779-91), its board by charter had included the senior clergyman from each Christian denomination in the city: Episcopal, Presbyterian, Lutheran, German Reformed, and Catholic. (After the Presbyterian ascendancy this was no longer so.) Easton's erstwhile academy, in an effort to reach out to the Germans of the borough, had reserved board seats for the German Reformed and Lutheran pastors. But the organizers of Lafayette went out of their way to exclude clergy.

The second innovation appeared in the promised course of studies: Lafayette would deviate from the classical curriculum. There would be mathematics, as elsewhere, but its applications — for instance, in civil engineering — would be vigorously pursued. As everywhere else, the "dead languages" would be studied, but also the living, and especially that language studied nowhere else: English, with its Saxon and German antecedents.[4]

The sponsors required only three weeks to send their memorial up to the legislature, which then took an entire year before considering it. Lafayette would be the eighth college to win a charter in Pennsylvania, and though the proposal was briskly debated, the fact that its sponsors were Scotch-Irish was a clear mark in its favor, since they were at the time the dominant ethnic group, being abundantly augmented by fresh immigration.[5]

The legislature imposed a few provisions of its own. The applicants had planned to include the governor and several other state officers as trustees *ex officio,* but the legislature removed them lest they be used to wheedle appropriations from the state treasury. Another alteration may have come as a surprise to the burgesses of Easton, but it was becoming a common feature of college charters during this period:

Article VIII

That persons of every religious denomination shall be capable of being elected trustees, nor shall any person, either as principal, professor, tutor or pupil be refused admittance into said college, or denied any of the privileges, immunities or advantages thereof for or on account of his sentiments in matters of religion.

Lafayette's predecessors holding Pennsylvania charters included the University of Pennsylvania (1755), Dickinson (1783), Franklin (1787), Jefferson (1802), Washington (1806), Allegheny (1815), and Western University of Pennsylvania (1819; later the University of Pittsburgh). All had similar nondiscrimination articles in their charters. Apart from Franklin, which was jointly sponsored by Lutherans and German Reformed and functioned only as a secondary school until 1850 when it merged with Marshall College, all of these institutions had been under the dominant influence of Presbyterians (who had superseded the Episcopalians in that role at Penn in 1779). In 1833-34 the Presbyterians would default on their patronage of Dickinson and Allegheny, both of which were then adopted by the Methodists, but at the time when the burgesses of Easton were petitioning the state for a charter, in the eyes of the legislators who represented the Germans and others who were gaining in their presence and their aspirations in Pennsylvania, this was to be just one more Presbyterian college. And there was a long history in those parts of anti-Presbyterian animus. The eighteenth century had been theirs. When the Episcopalians in control of the College of Philadelphia had agreed to admit one or two Presbyterians onto their board in order to broaden its representation from the community, they were persuaded that if the Presbyterians were ever in power, they would never be reciprocally accommodating. In the event, that advice was correct.[6]

Besides this reluctance to extend the cultural clout of the Presbyterian elite, there was in the capital a well-represented disdain for higher education of any sort. Most legislators represented constituents who considered college education an extravagance for the wealthy. They strenuously resisted the multiplication of colleges which were all too likely to sup at the treasury table once they were established. One representative spoke for that sentiment when he derided the study of ancient languages as a useless waste of time: "The knowledge of all the dead languages, would not furnish a single idea, that could not be communicated in English . . . and [has] added no more to scientific knowledge than the croaking of frogs."[7]

Finally, after fifteen months of intermittent debate, Lafayette won its charter in 1826. And for a long while, a charter was all Lafayette College had. The first board meeting tallied seven trustees present, barely the necessary quorum. The president of the board, who would serve for twenty-six years, was James Madison Porter. His career is suggestive of the quality of people behind the new college. One of his brothers would be governor of Pennsylvania; another, of Michigan; a sister would be the mother of Mary Todd Lincoln. James, a lawyer, would serve as prosecutor in Easton, then as a legislator, then as judge, and president of the Lehigh Railroad. He would eventually be nominated Secretary of War. Several of his fellow trustees enjoyed comparable careers.

Porter took the lead in searching for an educator to run the college, and was frustrated to find that the few likely candidates were usually ministers. He explained a reluctance to choose any of them.

> In the original plan of our establishment we endeavored studiously to avoid the danger of the Institute being Priest-ridden. We deprecated the Clergy having it under their control, as being calculated to palsy its general usefulness by giving it the character of sectarianism; while, on the other hand, we would be equally alarmed at anything which would give it the reputation of infidelity.

The best candidate under consideration spoke to the subject in ways that relieved the founders' concerns:

> I sincerely rejoice at the pleasing discovery of gentlemen in America who, uninfected by religious party spirit and sectarianism and uninfluenced by Priest-craft and intolerance, have the courage to consider all human beings as children of one common father, and all Christians, whatever creed they may profess, as members of one brotherhood. Far from being averse, my dear Sir, to your wise resolution not to suffer your infant Institution to be blasted by the mildew of particular tenets and dogmas, I congratulate you for it with all my heart, may I have occasion of sharing your endeavors or not. For my part I confess to you openly, that as soon as I had discovered the jealousy and intolerance existing between the several religious parties in America, I made a sacred vow never to accept of a Clerical employment in this country, being well aware that I as a Clergyman would have to act diametrically contrary to the pure doctrine of our Saviour, whose will is not to divide and oppose, but to unite and befriend . . .[8]

They failed to agree upon his salary, and the candidate went instead to Princeton. Their efforts to erect a building for their college also failed: only twenty-five people in Easton contributed, and thirteen of the resident trustees gave nothing. Lafayette was too insolvent to hire either a bigot or a freethinker to educate its youth.

Six years would pass before George Junkin was hired to come to Easton and open the college. Junkin brought along a great deal of priestcraft. He was an ordained minister, bred of a Presbyterian family that included fifteen ministers and twenty-one ruling elders. Furthermore, he had no room in his mind for military science or civil engineering. When the Easton fathers found him, he was vigorously running an academy in Germantown (then a suburb of Philadelphia) based on the manual labor school in Hofwyl, Switzerland, according to the popular educational philosophy of Johann Heinrich Pestalozzi. His student body ranged in age from fifteen to twenty-eight. The trustees agreed to have their charter amended to remove all references to a military college, and Junkin agreed that if they provided a building rent-free he would carry full financial responsibility for operations, including the salaries of himself and all teaching staff. Junkin decamped from Germantown and came to Easton followed by most of his pupils, who provided the beginnings of a student body. Their age span now ranged from ten to forty years old. Events did not follow quite in logical order. The college opened in 1832, and the cornerstone of the college building was laid in 1833. Only a minority of the trustees contributed anything to the construction. The legislature responded to an appeal for funding and appropriated a modest but essential subsidy: $12,000, with a five-year payout.

Old School against New School

Despite the earnest concern of the founders not to associate their college with any particular denomination, they themselves were all to be found of a Sunday in the pews of the First Presbyterian Church of Easton. Their nonsectarian policy was obviously relied upon to protect their secondary German constituency, all Lutherans or Reformed, from any sense of estrangement. But religious tension came to Lafayette anyway — swiftly and forcefully. The surprise was that it would divide the Presbyterians, not from other denominations, but among themselves. The Presbyterian Church, which had since the Revolution increased more rapidly than any other in the United States, was being torn by two issues: slavery and the revival movement known as the Second Great Awakening. In Pennsylvania the hostilities divided Old School, who stood by Calvinist orthodoxy, from New School, who saw religious authenticity only when it had erupted in a conversion experience. Princeton Theological Seminary had been founded as an Old School redoubt in 1812; only twenty-five years later schism awaited. That party, strong in Philadelphia, would expel the New School, who were strong in the western counties. At the very time Lafayette was opening, animosities ran very high. For example, this from the seminary in 1835:

> (The Board of Education has the means) to do much in the way of stemming that impetuous torrent of sanctimonious barbarism [read: New School], which threatens, even within our church, to carry all before it. Its waves beat now against our colleges and schools, but the hour is coming when the flood, if not assuaged, will aim at the subversion of the pulpit and the press. Jesuitism without, and fanaticism within, uncongenial as they seem, are seeking the same centre — total darkness.[9]

By 1835 Lafayette College — and Dr. Junkin with it — notwithstanding their virtuous stance against barbarism, already faced financial collapse. First Junkin tried to mortgage the campus to Old School partisans in Philadelphia. No success. Then he turned to his Old School friends in New York, and framed the appeal in the most factional terms:

> Dear Sir, — A crisis has arrived in the Presbyterian Church, which requires decision in counsel and energy in action from all the friends of her ancient

131

orthodoxy. That efforts, long continued, systematic, persevering, and powerfully efficient, for changing essentially and practically her doctrinal standards, have been made, and are still in progress, we do conscientiously believe. Institutions not a few have been called into existence, and in some cases liberally patronized, through inadvertence, by sound Presbyterians; which, unless counteracted, must inevitably lead to a change in our doctrinal standards . . . unless *our friends* rival these brethren and their friends in *zeal* and *energy,* by getting up and sustaining one or more literary institutions, by whose preparatory training, men of the *right kind* — that is, real, pious, orthodox, and devoted Presbyterian youth, can be fitted for theological studies in the best manner, and on terms, as to *expense,* equally satisfactory with those in the other institutions; our cause must sink; our Theological Seminary must wane; and the Standards of our Church must, and will, in a few years, be modelled and moulded to suit the discoveries and improvements of a new theology. . . .

Why, Sir, the remedy is very simple; and under God it is perfectly within the power of the few friends to whom we severally address this epistle. It is merely the *establishment* of such a College, as we have alluded to. What! do you propose another College! No, Sir, not exactly that; but the *establishment* of one already chartered — its Faculty already (in part) selected with this very view and design . . . We mean La Fayette College . . . an institution in successful, though not in full operation . . . And now, dear Sir, we leave with you the question, "What share will you have in this scheme for mustering the hosts of the Lord?"[10]

The trustees back in Easton were not Old School; nor, it seems, were they truculently New. Witness President Porter's austerely Jeffersonian invocation at the blessing of the cornerstone: "And may the bounteous Author of nature bless this our undertaking . . ."[11] At the inauguration of the college Porter had defended Lafayette against the invidious charge of sectarianism brought by their opponents at the legislature. But the results of Junkin's energetic solicitations, though meager, brought to the college more than did the trustees, whose awareness of financial peril produced more resignations than cash.

Two years later came the schism, and also the financial Panic of 1837. Enrollment dropped to forty students, twenty-five of them in the preparatory department. Lafayette, like other colleges, was now receiving $1,000 from the state annually, but Junkin induced the trustees to solicit $28,000 more from the legislature. Howls of remonstrance were heard from taxpayers against Lafayette, which they insultingly called Junkin's "Church." The state gave not a penny; typhoid struck the campus; the manual labor scheme proved not to pay for itself, and was dropped; students began to indulge in violence, and with weapons. It was not a season of success for George Junkin. James Madison Porter by now was no patron of his. Porter's nephew, son of the governor of Pennsylvania, had been disciplined by the faculty for wounding a fellow student. The penalty was suspension and reinstatement if he apologize publicly, or expulsion if not. The family elders prevailed upon the boy to refuse apology, and so he was expelled. Junkin secured the presidency of Miami University (it reverted to College later) in Ohio, resigned from Lafayette, and reminded the board that they were in his debt for land he had purchased with his own funds on behalf of the college. It was then 1840, and Lafayette's first eight years had been a struggle — for everyone.

Numerous prospects refused the presidency, but finally another parson-schoolmaster managed to hold the office for four years, only to return finally to pastoral ministry. Junkin, in the meantime, had found a poor welcome for his Old School Presbyterianism at Miami, and was brought back to Lafayette in 1844 with fresh charges of sectarianism clinging to his coattails. He was received on remark-ably amicable terms, and the college began to gain in strength. But finances continued to be parlous. State subsidies had come to an end. Some modest grants were sent in by congregations in the region, to support the studies of candidates for the ministry. In 1846 the board tried to persuade the Presbyterian Synod of Philadelphia to award them $15,000 to endow a chair in ancient languages. The overture was refused, but it was a presage of patronage to come.

Enrollment continued to rise, but in his third year Junkin again found a way to foul relations with his board. Nearly all its leading members continued to be members — indeed, they occupied the posts of moderator, ruling elder, and trustee — of the First Presbyterian Church of Easton, as were the president and faculty. Junkin decided to offer a course of public lectures which he held, not in their own building, but in the local Baptist church. The line he took from that pulpit was that of traditional, Old School orthodoxy, and this began a divisive movement that issued in the creation of Second Presbyterian Church, clearly and assertively gathered around George Junkin. Once again intramural sectarianism wedged apart the president and the local aristocracy on his board. But in recent years the board had begun cultivating the church by electing clergy as trustees: eleven were seated the year Junkin provoked the local schism, and they tended to support his cause against the local lay faction. In this re-embittered atmosphere Junkin again laid claim to repayment of old, disputed debts, and after meeting with no success he intercepted a draft from the Presbyterian Board of Education in support of minis-terial students and garnisheed the payment for himself. He narrowly survived a termination vote, but in 1848 resigned to take up the presidency of Washington College (later Washington and Lee) in Virginia. This time student sentiment was manifestly in his favor . . . and tangibly so, for they vandalized the campus on commencement night, and a dozen or two left to follow him to Lexington.[12] Lafayette was left with a student body smaller than its board of trustees.

The Presbytery Takes Control

The college's total income was now barely enough to pay the salary of a president, period. The desperate trustees began negotiations with the (very Old School) Synod of Philadelphia, with a possible sponsorship by the General Assembly in prospect. Lafayette had a record which spoke well to the church authorities. She had, in the past fourteen years, graduated 128 students, of whom 62 had chosen to serve in the ministry. Twenty-two of her alumni were then enrolled in Princeton Theological Seminary (also very Old School). Instead of commending Lafayette to the national church, Philadelphia proposed terms for its own patronage. The synod would nominate all trustees, presidents, and faculty, and would send down its own Board of Visitors every six months with full powers of inspection and regulation. The synod, in return for this, would provide $1,000 a year, and would commend the college to Presbyterian congregations and individuals (of its choosing) for further support.[13] The resolution to extend patronage concluded grandly that "the Synod confides in the ability & fidelity of the Faculty of La Fayette College & recommends it to the patronage of our people, believing that the morality and minds of young men will there be formed in accordance with correct principles. They do this without wishing in the slightest degree to control individual liberty . . ."[14]

The board was forlorn enough to accept, but as the structure of their dependency began to unfold, it appeared that the entailments of being "under the Care and patronage of the Philadelphia Synod" were more onerous than they first appreciated. The synod stated that the college was now expected to provide tuition gratis to all ministerial candidates.[15] It also required enough seats on the board to be vacated immediately to allow a majority of its own nominees to assume control.[16] All funds accepted into the college endowment were to be accepted only on the condition that they never be spent "for purposes inconsistent with the views of Christian truth as now entertained by the Synod of Philadelphia in connection with the General Assembly of the Presbyterian Church in the United States." And henceforth all the students, not just the Presbyterians among them, would be obligated to attend Sabbath morning services at First Presbyterian Church down the hill in Easton.[17] An especially bitter sequela was a decision in Philadelphia, after representations from the Junkin family and other ill-wishers, to hold back all of the 1849 appropriation and to provide only a fraction thereof in the years to follow: $600 in 1850, $200 in 1851, $500 in 1852.[18] The concerns of the synod seem not to have been too intellectual. A general report form, apparently provided for all synodical schools, suggests considerable distraction from academic excellence. It grades students on piety, eloquence, talents, diligence, economy, prudence, zeal, health . . . and progress in knowledge.[19]

The college opened in the fall of 1850 with but thirteen students, and no freshman class. There was a new president, selected by the synod: Daniel Veech McLean, a Princeton Seminary graduate and pastor who had a few years earlier received an honorary degree of doctor of divinity at the Lafayette commencement. McLean determined to replenish the absolutely barren treasury by selling scholarship certificates, a gesture of desperation which bankrupted a number of nineteenth-century colleges and almost did the same to Lafayette. Tuition charges in 1850 were $40 per annum. Anyone who purchased a $100 certificate could claim free four-year tuition for all of his sons, or those of any one family he chose. The funds thus raised were intended for the endowment, but of course all ordinary revenues immediately dried up when these cut-rate certificates went on sale, and the new income was used simply to meet the more urgent current expenses. The present crisis of the college was somehow tided over, but immense financial obligations were created for a future when no other tuition revenue was likely to be realized for a generation. The college's only protection was the proviso that no pledge would be collected until after $100,000 was promised. Not nearly that sum had been pledged when the synod, imagining affluence in the offing, publicly urged all subscribers to withhold their funds unless and until the college board consisted entirely of synodical nominees. Seeing no alternative, the board secured a charter amendment in 1854 which enacted in law what had been established only by mutual agreement: the complete power of the synod over elections and appointments.

That year, with the end of the campaign in sight, President McLean himself purchased and then gave away the last $6,000 worth of scholarship certificates in order to reach the campaign goal. Of the $100,000 subscribed, one-quarter went immediately to pay the expenses of solicitation and the college's more clamorous debts. More than $30,000 of what was promised was never paid in the ten years it took for payments to dribble in. When the synod held its annual meeting in Easton that fall, there was only $26,000 on hand. But, of course, there was the wondrous fact that the college was open at all. When the synod manifested some exasperation at this fiscal evaporation, the trustees "showed for the first time resentment at the control the synod was attempting to exercise. The trustees opposed the requirement from the synod that all the details of the college finances be reported: 'Something must be confided to the wisdom and discretion of those having the immediate care of the Institution.' "[20]

This was a fissure of resentment that would widen. Operating deficits in succeeding years were handled by drawing down their hard-won endowment until in 1857, the twenty-fifth anniversary of the college's opening, the synod sent President McLean back to the pastorate, replaced him with a local minister, George Wilson McPhail, and turned down an urgent appeal to help cover the college's yearly deficit of $1,000.

On a quieter note, that same year Francis Andrew March, an early pupil at Noah Webster's Amherst who had arrived in Easton as a tutor in 1855, was promoted to be the first Professor of English Language and Comparative Philology: the first such at Lafayette, and in America, where English had not yet been considered a worthy academic discipline. March would serve the college for fifty-six years and reflect much glory, national and international, upon her. He would preside over the American Philological Society, succeed James Russell Lowell as president of the Modern Language Association, and be wreathed with honorary doctorates from Amherst, Princeton, Oxford, and Cambridge. Alongside those who anguished over the college's solvency, men of considerable gifts were laboring at her tasks of learning and teaching.

College life went on. As early as 1855 Lafayette students began secretly joining fraternities. Like many of the colleges in this study, Lafayette was very conscious of its part in the Civil War. In all, 247 Lafayette men served. Twenty of them fought for the Confederacy: patriotism, like sectarianism, also had its bloody schisms. Of those who had actually graduated (always a small proportion of matriculants in those days), 26 percent of those eligible served, which compares well with an average of 23 percent from all New England colleges, and even the highest among them, Yale, which claimed 25 percent.[21]

The period of the war saw some important religious innovations on campus. A new president was elected in 1863: William Cassaday Cattell, a popular pastor in Harrisburg who had earlier served as professor of Latin and Greek. He was the first "prexy" with a discipline of his own, instead of the traditional concurrent appointment as professor of mental and moral philosophy. Cattell introduced, for the first time, an integrated series of Bible courses. Previously students had studied the text in Greek, and the academic study of the Bible had been relegated to Sunday school; for those who would make it their career, of course, it awaited them in the seminary. But Cattell created a four-year sequence of biblical courses in the curriculum. A year after his arrival there was a student-initiated revival on campus, which was stabilized by ongoing voluntary prayer meetings. A religious scrutiny of the college in Cattell's early years by the not-entirely-sympathetic local newspaper reported that "in 1870 there are 187 on the rolls, of whom 95 are church members [an earlier expression for this was "pious"], *thirty-eight of them looking forward to the Christian ministry."* Somewhat less breathlessly it noted that in all their boarding clubs "grace" was said at meals, and of course, morning and evening prayers together in the chapel were required. Voluntary student-run prayer meetings occurred several times each week, and about 50 undergraduates helped teach Sabbath schools in the area. Lafayette had sent 140 students to Princeton Theological Seminary, and others to seminaries for Presbyterian, Reformed, Methodist, Lutheran, and Baptist ministry. The alumni office knew of 242 ministers (still the largest professional category).[22]

Wealth Pressed Down, Shaken Up, and Flowing Over

Financial realities never failed to loom large, and to overcloud the college's relations with the synod. After thirteen consecutive years during which the synod had regularly defaulted on its commitment to provide an annual subsidy of $1,000, in 1863 it finally complied, thus making it possible for the new president's salary to be paid. Three years later the synod convened on the campus. The faculty, student body, and buildings had all increased, but the classroom which served as a prayer hall had clearly been outgrown, so the synod pledged itself to build a fine new chapel. An urgent resolution was directed to the churches, but two years later only $640 had been gathered.[23] In 1870 Cattell chided the synod on the matter, and more resolutions were forthcoming, but no more money. When a chapel finally was dedicated seven years later, with $10,000 in assorted gifts and $20,000 in debt, there were no thanks due the synod.[24] On the road to solicit funds even before his inauguration, Cattell wrote of the difficulties he encountered: "All the clergy here are *sweet-spoken* — but not a solitary one will give me a *helping hand.*"[25] A coal mine owner did, however. One day in 1864, with only six students in the freshman class, no money in the budget to cover faculty salaries, and the prospect of closure the following June, Cattell was on the road as guest preacher in the Presbyterian church in Hazleton, and was hosted that day by a local mine owner who had hardly heard of the college but was so impressed by Cattell's pluck that he wrote him a note for $20,000 on the spot. Ario Pardee was a farm boy who had learned surveying as a rodman, then became wealthy building railroads, and was by now an affluent coal operator. "From this time on," writes the college historian, "the life of Lafayette was never seriously endangered." The first board of trustees had been local activist citizens; the synodical board which displaced them was mostly clergy, and not very capable. Under both of those bodies it was actually the faculty who had run the college. Pardee changed all that by beginning to assemble supporters of Lafayette who were affluent, influential, and effective.[26]

Pardee was naturally interested in science and technology, and Lafayette began to move in these directions after the Civil War. In the fall of 1865 the faculty proposed a new curriculum in science, with the innovation that there would be no classical languages included. Pardee then made over $100,000 to endow and house the program. The Bible courses which Cattell had designed were not, however, left behind. Pardee wanted Christian scholars teaching in every department of the college and "a systematic and thorough study of the Word of God" in the course-work.[27] Lafayette began for the first time to make good on the promise made by the charter trustees that it would offer education in technology, and not be merely a liberal arts school. Courses in engineering and mining were created as an option into which students studying for the bachelor of science degree could diverge in their final year. Later, with more courses offered such as applied mathematics, graphics, hygiene, metallurgy, civil and topographical and steam engineering, a degree in engineering became available. Lafayette was then one of the few colleges in the country that offered arts, science, and engineering.

Another major academic revision came in 1872. A New York financier, Benjamin Douglass, objected to the conventional instruction in Greek and Latin classics, arguing that a Christian college stood to offer better wisdom in those languages by studying Christian instead of pagan authors. The board was unprepared to take such an unprecedented (as they thought) step, but agreed that Douglass might fund and eventually endow an alternate track in the Christian classics. The nationally celebrated campus philologist, Professor March, began to assemble and publish texts, and to explain their advantage over the standard classics.

It is remarkable that no place has been given in the schools and colleges of England and America to the writings of the early Christians. For many centuries, and down to what is called the Pagan Renaissance, they were the common linguistic study of educated Christians. The stern piety of those times thought it wrong to dally with the sensual frivolities of heathen poets, and never imagined it possible that the best years of youth should be spent in mastering the refinements of a mythology and life which at first they feared and loathed, and which at last became as remote and unreal to them as the Veda is to us. . . .

It is the great fact of history that the sensualism of Rome and Greece, the best side of which Horace has so well sung, gave place to self-abnegation, to heroism, to a virtue which rejoiced in pain and suffering for the love of truth. To read the expression of this new character, when that expression was action, and a man put his life and death on each word, is high reading. The Latin hymns, too, have the right ring. There is no original poetry in the heathen Latin verses. The cultivation of the so-called classic age was but superficial. The meters were imported from Greece, and rehearsed to please the Greeklings. The repetition of these Greek prettinesses never roused the Roman. His character was stern, hard and fierce. His mind was bent on empire. Death did not daunt him. To suffer and die with rejoicing for truth suited men of the blood of Regulus and Curtius, and aroused their faculties at last to the height of song. The love of Christ melted them. They burst the shackles of the Greek meters, and shook off the stiffness of the Latin syntax, and sang the early Christian hymns. It is strange that our children should spend years on the faint Homeric echoes of Virgil, and commit to memory the graceful epicureanism of Horace, and never see the *Dies Irae*.[28]

This, from the president of the American Philological Association, must have prickled the ears of his colleagues elsewhere. It was an innovation singular in American higher education of the time, and might well have flourished at Lafayette, now in its new mood of creative change. But before Douglass could endow the program, he lost his speculative fortune in the Panic of 1873.[29]

Student Piety

The students who trudged up from Germantown with George Junkin to enroll in his new college brought with them a religious society they had already formed in their manual labor school. David Brainerd had been a young missionary to the Indians of the Delaware Valley from 1744 until his death three years later. The Brainerd Evangelical Society named in his honor was for forty years the only religious organization at Lafayette, hosting prayer meetings, community work among the Easton churches, and motivational study of foreign mission territories. It functioned in parallel with the literary societies; when they invited a notable as their annual orator at commencement, the Brainerd men invited a distinguished cleric to be their annual preacher the preceding evening. The religious revival of

1865 had warmed up the campus considerably. In 1870, after an atrocious outbreak of student vandalism, and then a student death from dreaded scarlet fever, the campus was ready for another revival. The Brainerd Society sent a delegation to a YMCA convention in nearby Scranton, and they came home aflame. A preacher by the charismatic name of Mutchmore was invited up from Philadelphia, and soon there were only thirty Lafayette holdouts who baulked at openly confessing their faith in Jesus as their Savior. At a final service before the end of the fall term, with the president, faculty, and clergy and elders of the local churches all present, the dedication of the students was brought solemnly and movingly into explicit form. All but two of the senior class made public profession of their religion. A temperance society was formed, and sixty-five students signed a pledge of total abstinence so long as they should remain at Lafayette.[30] In 1874 the old fervor returned, Mr. Mutchmore was recalled from Philadelphia to offer much more, and another generation of students (for in college a generation passes quickly) pledged their lives to Jesus.

President Cattell, on the ground that the Brainerd Society was devoted to mission work, founded a new group, the Christian Brotherhood. Brainerd men invited a merger, but Cattell was having none of it. Brainerd then secured the franchise as the local affiliate of the national YMCA, and the Brotherhood withered. Brainerd managed the service activities which were customary for the campus Y's. They issued an informational brochure called the *Freshman Bible,* and later managed an employment bureau.[31] Meanwhile the college required the students to partake of fifteen devotional exercises each week and a church service on Sundays. The Brainerd Society offered an after-supper prayer service nightly, and on Thursday evening there was a preaching service featuring the president. There was a moral expectation that "pious" students would be there for all of it. The faculty made the first voluntary concession in such a formidable uplifting of prayer by eliminating the Saturday afternoon service (just as sports began to emerge seriously on campus).

All of this vitality raised Lafayette's credit in the public eye. In 1872 she welcomed a freshman class of 115, larger than any but those at Harvard (200) and Yale (131). Four years later Lafayette was shown to have the largest faculty in the state save only for the University of Pennsylvania (College Department). A certain sobriety with regard to such statewide statistics is invited by the further disclosure that in size of student body Lafayette was surpassed by only Girard College, which later devolved into a secondary school. In total assets Lafayette was outdone by none except these two rivals. One other statistic exalts the college: in 1878 the American Academy of Medicine held its annual meeting on the campus, and among all its diplomates eleven were Lafayette men, more than from any other college. This is hardly compromised by the fact that its founding president, Dr. Traill Green, had first belonged to the Lafayette faculty in 1837.

Had it not been for this sharp rush of success, the Lafayette trustees would probably not have found the nerve to do what they did for the first time in 1871.[32]

The synod had been pathetically useless to the prosperity of the college, and its claim to control her affairs rang hollow. So the board took the step of electing two new members to its body without soliciting the usual nominations in advance. Instead, it sent up their names after the fact, "for confirmation or rejection." The synod was embarrassed enough to vote confirmation without rebuke, and this new precedent was followed thereafter. For the time being the board was satisfied to have made the change in practice; the matter of principle and of legal relationship could await another day. Another shift in board representation, one that was occurring generally throughout the country, was the claim by alumni for representation. Although seven years transpired between the formal request in 1881 and its acceptance (which was somewhat influenced by new financial clouds overhead), there was not nearly the resistance from within the board at Lafayette as on some other campuses. The board agreed to make over six places out of their thirty-nine for alumni nominees.

When Dr. Cattell completed his twenty years of service in 1883, he was the dean of the prominent college presidents in the country. Lafayette had become apparently stabilized, and with its energies now freed from the paralysis of insolvency, it had attracted a solid cadre of affluent supporters. The college had managed simultaneously to elaborate an academically serious and innovative curriculum and to rejuvenate what appears to have been a very well accepted religious program combining learning, piety, and service. Cattell was followed by another preacher, one trained in the German Reformed Church (he had pastored their church in Easton), who was at the time serving a Presbyterian congregation. James Hall Mason Knox was a man of quiet dignity who presided over the college for seven lean years.

At the same time, the college astutely withdrew itself some distance from the synod, whose policy had for so long been that it was more blessed to receive than to give. In 1885, after fourteen years of ignoring the legal requirement that the board seek prior nominations from the synod from which to elect trustees, presidents, and faculty, the time seemed ripe to amend the charter and regularize their practice. The synod (now of Pennsylvania instead of Philadelphia) could hardly muster any strong argument to the contrary, and acquiesced. Thereafter the board was legally required only to send down the names of their own already elected choices for confirmation. Other Presbyterian-related colleges "under the care of the Synod" had been wriggling their own way toward autonomy, so that in Knox's latter years the visitation committee would report: "This is the only college over which the Synod exercises any real ecclesiastical control. It has a veto power in the election of the Trustees and the Faculty, which makes its endowments safe — not liable to be perverted from the end for which they are given. Let our men of wealth, especially those in the eastern part of the Synod, see to it that our own college be not crippled for want of means."[33] The visitation committee ignored the fact that the endowment was in jeopardy, not because of the college's temptation to be religiously wayward, but for want of competent fiscal administration. Knox's own deficient gifts for either garnering or administering funds were partly responsible for the embarrassment when deficits drove Lafayette to accumulate mortgages that eventually equaled her endowment. He resigned.

A Very Presbyterian President, and a Not Very Presbyterian Student Body

Harvard, Columbia, and Pennsylvania were at the time being led by their first lay presidents. The Lafayette board, terrified of another insolvency, was persuaded that financial crisis required the force and talents of a layman, so they elected the president of Miami of Ohio, Ethelbert Dudley Warfield. He was then only thirty years old and was being concurrently courted by Pittsburgh, Parsons, Cincinnati, and Ohio State. He was a lawyer, educated at Princeton, Oxford, and Columbia, and was expected to bring a new professional sophistication to the presidency. Yet this first lay president came into office with a stridently strong statement of loyalty to the church and her colleges:

> The State universities in many instances, it is painful to observe, are inclined to repudiate the obligation of Christian instruction which rests upon them. I do not hesitate to say that they are a missionary field of first importance. There is nothing more ridiculous in a Christian land such as this than to say that it is contrary to the law to give religious instruction in State universities. . . .
>
> The Christian college is the peculiar target of contemporary criticism. . . . We are prone to shrink from this adjective, denominational. It is a thorn in the side of many of us, but it is an adjective of which I am not afraid, at least when applied to me. No, I am not afraid of being, or of being known, as a Presbyterian. I do object, as all right-minded people do, to being thought sectarian. . . .
>
> It has been claimed, indeed is constantly asserted, that the denominational school approaches everything from a prejudiced point of view and that thought and teaching have ceased to be free in them. This may once have been true. To-day it is not true, certainly in its broader aspect. The denominational character of most schools of this type is to be found chiefly in the influences that are thrown about the lives of the students, and the general direction which is given to their activities outside of classroom instruction proper.
>
> Of course, it is true, and it should be true, that the teaching force is in general selected from those who are affiliated to the denomination controlling the school. Of course, in accordance with the limitations of human nature, some teachers so selected are narrow-minded, but this is not because they belong to this or that denomination, but because they are men.[34]

The conventional way of reporting the religious standing of students was to indicate how many of them had been "credibly converted," or were "pious," or

141

"church members." Usually the proportion of the converted began rather low among the freshmen and increased over the four years. But just before Warfield arrived, the Brainerd Society (as the local YMCA affiliate) conducted a different sort of census, asking students first what church their parents belonged to, and then what church, if any, they belonged to. The result:

1888-89

Denomination	Family	Student
Presbyterian	50%	33%
Methodist	11%	5%
Lutheran	11%	6%
German Reformed	8%	6%
Episcopal	6%	1%
Evangelical Association	2%	2%
Baptist	2%	1%
Catholic	2%	1%
Other	9%	3%
None		42%

The tabulators made no note of it, but it was the students from Presbyterian and Reformed families who showed more disposition to declare themselves church-men than those from other homes. Reports from two Congregational campuses show how many students there were then reporting themselves as church members: 59 percent at Williams, 66 percent at Amherst.

Seventeen percent of the Lafayette student body said they were bound for the Christian ministry, and since most of those were seniors this is likely to underreport the true picture: like most career decisions, a decision for the ministry was often unripe among the underclassmen. Of all students who had matriculated at Lafayette since the beginning, 13 percent had gone into ministry (and another one percent into foreign missions), so there seems to have been no tapering off there. Those proportions rise sharply if one studies only the graduates. Reversing the earlier reports, lawyers now outnumber ministers as the largest vocational output: 17 percent. The survey notes demurely that in the past twenty years only 2 percent of Cornell grads had gone into the ministry.[35]

One stunning feature of this survey which went almost without comment was that in 1889 only half of the Lafayette students were coming from Presbyterian homes. This would turn out to be perhaps more significant than the recent curtailment of the synod's legal powers over the college.

Warfield, the lay president, manifested an abiding interest in the religious welfare of the college. He awarded so many tuition scholarships to ministerial and penurious students that the college had to raise its fees. He perked up chapel services by replacing faculty with outside speakers. He studied theology himself on the side, obtained a license to preach, and in 1899 had himself ordained to the ministry in the college chapel. Shortly after that he announced the Brainerd Society would have their own building; until then they had had the use of a meeting room, like the literary societies. But this building would also serve as the center for student activities. Thereby the Brainerd Society would be converted from an evangelical group oriented to piety and missions, to a school-spirit group responsible for recreation. That would somehow turn out to be a fatal swerve.

As Warfield's presidency moved through its second decade, it moved toward misfortune. There is no doubt that certain traits of his personality contributed greatly to it. But he confronted daunting difficulties. On the day of his inauguration the board had considered a motion to put a mortgage on the entire college property. Warfield had been recruited with the promise of a successful endowment campaign to bring in $100,000 before he arrived. It had foundered, due in part to the expectation that the campaign chairman would be chosen as president. Warfield took up the task with fair success. Second, he found the faculty divided, with the arts people usually overbearing the scientists and engineers by dint of their greater verbal fluency. But Warfield found, when he prompted them to consider a review of the various curricula, that the arts faculty were much the more difficult to deal with. Looming over that side of things was old Professor March, then seventy-five years old, a veteran of thirty-six years on the faculty with fifteen yet to serve. When Warfield remarked on how little modern language instruction was available, March explained that their students rightly were beginners in French and German, because it would be "unpatriotic" to teach those languages in high school. In any case, he said, the arts curriculum was entirely designed to culminate in his own senior course in comparative philology. When Warfield persisted in a discussion of curricular reform, March refused even to let it be considered. He had prepared the curriculum, he said, not for any particular time but for all time, and he could contemplate no improvement. March was perhaps the most obdurate among them, but the faculty as a whole were not used to presidential initiatives, except in fund-raising.[36] It seems to have been Dr. Warfield's singular handicap that in the swirl of people pursuing special interests with craft and sophistry, he lacked the sharpness of insight to see exactly what was going on. He also lacked the personal charm and adroitness to move people toward even wishing an accommodation.

Their tie to the Presbyterian Church offers a case in point. By the turn of the century the college was beginning to see its fortunes smile again. Enrollment, faculty salaries, endowment, breadth of program, buildings in prospect and under construction — all of these factors were beginning to mark out Lafayette as one of the strongest horses in the Presbyterian stable. Yet just when the likely source of significant funding was shifting from the synod (Pennsylvania was always the most affluent in the country) to the national church, its College Board imposed a policy that available moneys were to be withheld from the endowed colleges and parceled out to help the newer and weaker to survive. Warfield sent up letter after letter, pointing out that no Presbyterian college had sent so many of its men into ministry or missions or lay eldership, and urging that no other institution had offered free educations to sons of the church. But this only strengthened the College Board's decision to send money elsewhere. The race was to the lame and the victory to the halt. Warfield frazzled relations with these executives by his repeated and unanswerable appeals.

Carnegie Money and Carnegie Religion

The policy of the Carnegie Foundation for The Advancement of Teaching, which was then giving matching grants to fund retirement for faculty, was to exclude colleges and universities under denominational control. The Congregational schools, as we have seen, eased themselves around this rule because their denomination was founded precisely on the rejection of any but local control. But the Presbyterians could make no such claim, and for years they pled their case, alone and with other mainline Protestant groups, before an unyielding Foundation. The Carnegie position seemed simple and unambiguous. Mr. Carnegie himself, they were told, "does not think educational institutions should be sectarian and he hopes the day will soon come when Christianity will be one and not split into many differing sects quarreling about man-made theology." His president, Henry Pritchett, thought "that there is no necessary connection between religion and denominationalism."[37] As it actually turned out, Mr. Carnegie was simple but Dr. Pritchett was ambiguous.

The Carnegie policy merits some extended attention here because it elicited such intense efforts at astute self-definition among Christian educators, especially the Presbyterians. After the Foundation announced its second list of beneficiaries in 1907, Pritchett published a lengthy explanation which supplied some of the candor that had been missing from earlier explanations. Carnegie's first explanation of its exclusionary policy was that churches which claimed sponsorship ought to carry the full financial consequences of their patronage. Further, it would be unwise for a college to be controlled by any organization for which education was a secondary consideration (it was not explained how this might apply to state-controlled colleges and universities).

There had been considerable conviction — and contempt — involved in the Foundation policy. Carnegie, Pritchett now insisted, had no hostility toward denominations, nor bias against religion. He did doubt, however, that a denomination-related discrimination in the selection of trustees, officers, or students would really be "calculated to advance the larger interests of education." He then went on to make clear how hostile he was to church sponsorship of colleges.

The paper pivots on a distinction between "religion" and "denominations." Religion, Pritchett explains in a soaring excursus, is independent in both theory and practice from churches or denominations. It is "a life springing up in the soul which blossoms in forgetfulness of self and into service of God and of men." By contrast with that, denominations offer their own peculiar beliefs and worship. Education, and true religion as well, he associates with reason and the inquiring intellect, whereas denominations he associates with emotion, human hubris, the Sunday school, the shouting revival. What motives have impelled denominations to possess and control colleges? The desire to propagate their particular doctrines and to increase their influence, and their rivalry with competing denominations. This is all self-promotion, and a seeking after prestige and propaganda and power, even though "not consciously exprest or admitted." The reciprocal motives, according to Pritchett, which lead colleges to accept or even seek denominational sponsorship, are entirely pragmatic: to secure students and money.

The results, he claims, have been mostly negative: a proliferation of colleges with insufficient funds and enrollments, the total inadequacy of churches to offer significant subsidy, and the incapacity of their parochial clergy to have a discriminating understanding of higher education. Church colleges are miserably funded, and they make academic claims they cannot vindicate. In addition, the denominations have engaged in so much doublethink and double-talk that their purposes are confused, and to the public they appear dodgy. Their methods of teaching religion "contravene the intellectual ideals of trained students" and "fail to meet their honest inquiries." Even if one were to look to the churches for no more than a *moral* influence on campus, their apparent lack of educational integrity undermines their ability to offer it.

On the level of policy Pritchett narrows his concern to two issues. The first is control. The denominations ought indeed to wish to influence business, the state, the unions. But there is no prospect of their doing so through control. Instead, the denominations can and should see moral influence as their only rightful mode of presence there. Likewise in the professional world of education: moral influence, not legal power, is their legitimate way to serve.

His second concern is religion. The churches should look beyond their own peculiarities and self-interest and organizational partisanship, and advance religion instead.

Along the way he has some savage remarks about college catalogues, athletic admissions, professorial salaries at church colleges, clerical culture, and various other scams. Robert Hutchins would have more respect for the NCAA than Pritchett did for actively Protestant colleges. Basically, he says denominational control has been in inverse proportion to academic integrity and success. There was no contemporary critic of church colleges more ruthlessly eloquent than Henry Pritchett. His own concept of religion is terminally equivocal, yet he is devastating when he depicts and derides the ambiguities of church-college rhetoric.[38]

The official argument to Pritchett from the Presbyterian College Board was that minimal control was necessary simply to assure that funds settled on the colleges would always be used for their intended purposes, and to maintain the Christian character of the college. The church pledged that it would never want to affect the actual teaching and learning process.[39] Somehow, though they assuredly joined in Pritchett's hope that the day would come, history had not yet offered any examples of Christianity being sustained except by Christian churches. After Pritchett's article made it clear to Presbyterians that Carnegie was indulgent toward religion in general but not toward Christianity in particular, their mode of discourse softened into "making humanity Christlike in spirit," through the service of teachers that are "real Christians in mind, spirit and life." Far from wanting to recruit members, the Presbyterians spontaneously professed what "may fairly be called a horror of it."

The reality back at Lafayette, however, was still otherwise. The college was still chronically underfunded because the Presbyterians, who were still relatively affluent and relatively quite educated, had not been motivated to pay enough to provide Presbyterian colleges good enough for their children. Those whose children qualified were being sent to Columbia, Penn, Harvard, and Dartmouth. The subsidies that the church did provide were not nearly enough to justify serious control by Presbyterian judicatories. Their regular visitations were polite, but they had none of the bite of accreditation visits. The religious environment on campus was thoroughly Presbyterian in its piety, and though there was little overt attempt to recruit converts, it was in this period that the college dismissed a faculty member whose influence had led a Presbyterian student to become a Catholic. No one there had any notion about how to make possible a life springing up in the soul which blossoms in forgetfulness of self and into service of God and of men, except by discipleship of Jesus Christ.[40]

At the time of this controversy there was no need for any church to hold authority over, say, the Lafayette board in order to claim the college as Presbyterian. The board itself was as dedicated to the Presbyterian fellowship as was the synod, and the board had effective authority over the education offered there. But the day would come — soon — when the faculty would regard Presbyterianism as an irrelevance, even an intrusion. The board which had hired them would then find it had neither the nerve nor the power to interest them in either Presbyterian faith or life springing up in the soul.

In the same year that Pritchett made his apologia, some of the Lafayette trustees were beginning to think that the charter rights still belonging to the synod (the right to confirm or veto elections) might now be hindering the college by disqualifying her from Carnegie money. (Actually other Carnegie entities besides the Foundation's retirement scheme had begun to make generous grants to the college.) So conversations began, but no charter amendment was attempted. Trustees were worried about negative public interpretation of a legal break with the synod. Also, a series of generous benefactions, steered or given to the college by the College Board or the synod, began the endowments for professorial chairs. Some of these endowments came with reversionary clauses that would cause the endowments to be forfeited if Lafayette did not "adhere and remain under the control of the Synod of Pennsylvania."[41] The proposal to amend the charter vanished from sight. It was a distraction to focus so much attention on this one clause in the charter as if that were what provided a dynamic yet difficult bond with the church.

These were hefty issues, and their outcome would have much to do with Lafayette College's destiny. Ethelbert Dudley Warfield was ill prepared to appreciate all that was at stake. In another age he would have been Old School. His elder brother, Benjamin Breckenridge Warfield, was the formidable conservative theologian who dominated the faculty at Princeton Theological Seminary, and whose teaching was a lamp unto the feet of the orthodox. Since 1903 Ethelbert himself had been the president of the board at the seminary. Although his perception of where the faith was at stake was narrow, there were moments when he saw it his duty to foster and protect it. Such a moment was presented by the presence and performance of John Moffatt Mecklin.

Mecklin had been an exceptionally gifted Greek scholar who interrupted his early academic life to serve as a preacher in rural Georgia. There he quickly found he had no faith in Calvinism in either its orthodox or its revivalistic modes, though he admired his congregation for their warm and persuasive humanism: a Christianity in spirit. He returned to teaching and in 1905 was elected to the Chair in Mental and Moral Philosophy at Lafayette. He was a smash hit on campus. His negative experience with a constrictive Calvinism had left him convinced that all orthodox religion was a blindly submissive surrender to authority. Religion, he came to believe, must have no privileged place among loyalties, and surely no rightful place in the corporate consciousness of a good college. So he began to invite his students to think more freely, and he did it very winningly.

Warfield sensed something was amiss and began to sit in on Mecklin's teaching. He took it to be a problem of orthodoxy, since that was a category familiar to him. He seems not to have realized that the problem was more serious: Mecklin had no religious faith left at all, and had become evangelistic about his convictions. Warfield began to harass the young professor, who was much more nimble-minded and much more popular than he. When Warfield moved to force a resignation the board stood by him, and Mecklin agreed to leave, but a ferocious and tireless backlash of student anger made life on campus, and most particularly in chapel, an unceasing torment for the president. The American Philosophical Association and the American Psychological Association insisted on a public examination of the matter, and judged it a gross violation of academic freedom. The Mecklin case was the provocation that led to the organization of the nationwide American Association of University Professors (AAUP). Having taken enough heavy weather, the more liberal New York faction among the trustees took this occasion to ease past the conservative Philadelphians who had dominated the board, and Warfield left the college in 1914, one year after Mecklin did. Warfield's incumbency, no matter the manner of its ending, had been a time of considerable benefit to the college. Lafayette had more than doubled in its resources and operations (Engineering had trebled) during his incumbency. And no president before or after has served as long as his twenty-three-year term.

Mecklin saw Warfield as deeply perturbed that Lafayette, by becoming more liberal, was no longer going to be the premier supplier of students for Princeton Seminary; alumni were beginning to go up to New York, to the much more liberal Union Theological Seminary. Mecklin also claims that "the strange twist that ran through [Warfield's] nature often queered his best efforts, and made him many enemies and often made him the despair of his friends."[42] Be that so, Warfield was right in sensing that Mecklin was a subversive threat to faith in a Christian college. But his religious perspective seems not to have been fine enough to realize all that was under way. In that, he may have been emblematic of his Presbyterian contemporaries, for a great deal was then under way in their colleges that evaded their understanding. In any case, Warfield's faith was an equally subversive threat to Lafayette, *malgré lui.*

Presbyterian Money

John Henry MacCracken came to be the next president. He was a New York University graduate, with graduate education there, at Heidelberg, and at Halle. Apart from a term as president of Westminster College in Fulton, Missouri, he had spent his career in teaching and administration at his alma mater. He had recently been serving also as president of the Presbyterian College Board. With a father having long been chancellor of New York University and a brother as president of Vassar, he clearly came of strong academic stock. During his term (1915-26) Lafayette, as has been said, would benefit by large benefactions that went into the endowment, and some handsome new buildings, but also a chronic, worrying, annual operating deficit.

There were some quiet shifts with respect to the college's religious situation. The Presbyterians in the student body diminished from 42 to 34 percent during MacCracken's term, with Methodists, Episcopalians, and (an innovation) Catholics each comprising about 10 percent.[43] Granted the college's many affirmations of nonsectarianism, a census of religious affiliation among the faculty was something rarely done, at least openly. It would have seemed indecent. But two of the very rare instances of such information survive from 1919 and 1923. In 1919, 51 percent of the faculty were Presbyterian, 20 percent were Episcopalians, and 8 percent were Methodists.[44] Four years later there had been significant change, and with it had come a problem. The president wrote to the board:

> At the instigation of Mr. [William Jennings] Bryan, the General Assembly at its last meeting passed a resolution as follows: "That, in accordance with the declared policy of this church, no part of the educational fund of the Presbyterian Church in the United States of America shall be given to any school, college, university or theological seminary that employs any teacher in any grade who is

not a member in good standing of some branch of the Christian church and personally interested in the spiritual welfare of students."[45]

The President made an investigation of the church membership of members of the present faculty at Lafayette and found it to be as follows:

Presbyterian	25	34%
Methodist	12	16%
Methodist Protestant	1	1%
Protestant Episcopal	10	14%
Congregational	7	9%
Universalist	1	1%
Lutheran	3	4%
Reformed	3	4%
Dutch Reformed	1	1%
Evangelical	1	1%
Armenian Evangelical	1	1%
Baptist	1	1%
Roman Catholic	1	1%
Not members	7	9%
Total	74	

The Charter of Lafayette College provides: "That persons of every denomination shall be capable of being elected trustees, nor shall any person, either as principal, professor, tutor or pupil be refused admittance into said College, or denied any of the privileges, immunities or advantages thereof for or on account of his sentiments in matters of religion" (Article VIII). The President attended the Synod of Pennsylvania with a view to ascertain what the attitude of the Synod would be on this matter, and found neither the Board of Education nor the Synod were prepared to define their position.[46]

Obviously the General Assembly was defining its interests quite differently than its agency, the College Board, had done for Carnegie's benefit fifteen years earlier. If, as is likely, the General Assembly's resolution was motivated by concern for the religious membership of faculty in all related colleges, Lafayette's own situation would be a case in point. In only four years the Presbyterian cohort in the faculty seemed to have dropped from one-half to one-third. It was usual in mainline Protestant colleges through the late nineteenth century and early twentieth century that the decline of the sponsoring denomination amidst the faculty occurred more slowly than the decline among the students. At Lafayette the diversification of faculty came swift and early. The fact that the synodical authorities, confronted with this head-on collision of their resolution and the college charter, backed off suggests that the synod was not going to be a passionate, irredentist force jealously reclaiming its educational patrimony. MacCracken seems to have shared his trustees' restlessness regarding the synod, and had noted with some rancor that

Grove City College, a peer which had taken to advertising itself as "nonsectarian," was still being supported by the synod. He knew that if the synod wanted to enforce its resolution, Lafayette stood to lose $6,000 per annum. His mood at the time, privately expressed, was to forfeit the annual gift and think it a modest price to pay for freedom from vexation.[47]

One tiny datum from which one might infer that the board, at least, had not clothed itself in liberalism is buried in the president's report later that year. It speaks for itself, especially since it was spread on the written record:

> The College very nearly lost Professor Crawford, Professor of Latin, as he had been assured of an appointment at Hunter College, New York, at a salary of $6,000., increasing to $8,000., by the President. Owing to party politics the recommendation of the President was rejected and a Jew elected to the position.[48]

The tenor of the Pennsylvania Synod continued to be distinctly conservative, and that set up an almost inevitable dissonance from a college ambitiously seeking to restore its prestige and fortunes. Also, the long presidency of Dr. Warfield, who was remembered as intractable and conservative, left behind a lingering dyspepsia when the Presbyterian connection came to the fore. Yet the college endowment was swelling as the various capital gifts to sustain professorships appreciated, and the price of keeping them seemed to be a continued if unenthusiastic linkage with the synod.

Professor Albert Gendebien, author of the college's sesquicentennial history, believes that there was a decided shift in the religious stance at Lafayette in the 1920s:

> All early presidents had been clergymen. When searching for presidents in 1891, when Dr. Ethelbert D. Warfield was appointed, and again in 1915 when they chose Dr. MacCracken, the trustees had, it seems, deliberately sought laymen in an anticlerical, but not secularistic, mood. In 1926 the trustees advised the committee that if a candidate for the presidency were a clergyman, this should be considered neither an asset nor a liability in the assessment of his qualifications. This was not anticlericalism but secular indifference.[49]

Chapel, Bible, and Fervor Wane

Lafayette students seem to have abided chapel services and worship more amiably than their contemporaries elsewhere. But in the 1930s a rapid disintegration began under President William Mather Lewis (1927-45). Gendebien's chronicle deserves to be quoted intact, as a sort of time-motion study of what took decades to occur elsewhere:

> Sunday chapel was a more or less Presbyterian religious service from which non-Protestant students could be excused. It was attended not merely by the

captive students but by quite a few faculty families and people from the local community. After Mr. Yerger became organist and organized the choirs, there was excellent music. Preachers of national renown were selected and proudly announced each semester. They presented a significant educational experience for the attentive participant.

Daily chapel had lost its purely religious nature. The service was a time for announcements; for addresses by guest lecturers and performances by artists; for speakers from the faculty, administration, and students; and the Student Council or the honor societies to present issues, conduct polls, award prizes, and initiate members. Dr. Lewis defended the daily chapel:

> The chapel service gives an opportunity to touch all the students with educational matters of importance which cannot be stressed in the full schedule of the classroom: The observance of great anniversaries; the explanation of great events; as the recent eclipse of the sun (April 28, 1930); contact with fine music, appreciation of which added to any man's life; initiation of members of the honor societies of the college and other student ceremonies. . . .

Changes were taking place in daily chapel during the first years of the Lewis administration. Wednesdays were set aside for the freshman chapel as a continuation of orientation. Announcements were dropped, being replaced by a bulletin board in South College and the weekly calendar published in the *Lafayette*. In 1930 Saturday chapel, the remaining purely religious service, restricted to psalm reading, was dropped. The others, though still cloaked in hymn and prayer, were cultural rather than devotional events, when not concerned with college affairs. The daily sessions came to be called "convocations" rather than chapels. . . . It would be a long time before daily chapel exercises would disappear, but one can see the . . . general trend away from the religious.[50]

Years earlier old Professor March, whose convictions about tradition were lengthy in their derivation and stubborn in their expression, gave his thoughts on the chapel problem. It was back in 1888. He had reminisced about his own college days:

> We used to get up at Amherst in winter when it was black night, struggle through the snow waist deep sometimes, and hear prayers in a chapel without fire with the thermometer twenty degrees below zero, more or less, and then have a Greek recitation by the light of little oil lamps, before we went to breakfast before sun rise. . . .
>
> Lafayette was founded in prayer, and has been kept alive in prayer. It has always been a religious college. But there has been of late years an immense increase of religious life. It does not resemble the revivals of fifty years ago. It is not a revival of revivals, but a revival of religion. There is little of the old law

work. Confession of sin gives way to profession of faith and love. . . . yet we find a falling off in the number of college prayers and other religious services of the whole institution. . . .

Compulsory attendance on prayers and preaching is a special object of attack. But it is almost a misnomer to call the college discipline compulsion. It is nothing like so strong as the obligations of professional life, or the tyranny of fashion or social habits, or home influence. A college student is about the freest man there is. . . . It is certainly a pleasant thing to see our college now, bathed and break-fasted and ready for recitations, gathering at morning prayers.[51]

All that was long past.

Bible courses had traditionally been taught by faculty from various departments and therefore rarely at a level much beyond what they had learned as undergraduates. The Helen Manson Professorship (1916), brought to Lafayette at the recommendation of the College Board, occasioned the creation of a Department of Bible and Religious Education, and eventually all biblical instruction would be done by those trained in the discipline. Another innovation came with the new chair: its incumbent would be both professor of Bible and college pastor. In 1927 a new Manson Professor, Charles Harris, set out to make the department more professionally academic. Every year the synodical visitors would report back that religious instruction was being given as required by the church, and every year Harris was working to ensure that the courses would have as little bearing as possible on the Presbyterian tradition. Complaints of heresy began to come in, and the board soon realized that the department as constituted was not at all prepared to accept it as their duty to teach "according to the doctrine taught in the West-minster Confession," as required by the terms of the Manson deed of gift. Memories of the Mecklin incident were hauntingly fresh, and they were not at all prepared to initiate an investigation of the orthodoxy of the departmental faculty. A minister on the board suggested the solution: reduce the required courses in religion from three to two, and provide that only historical study of the Bible be offered. Without theology, there could be no objectionable theology. Thus was it done, very quietly, in 1938. But the board's concern to protect their financial and public-relations interests by excluding theological inquiry from the curriculum suggests that they sensed no appreciable loss to the college.[52]

Since being given their own building in 1902, the Brainerd Society had either created or been charged with the medley of social service programs on campus. The original focus on missionary work was still honored by their sponsorship of some of the campus worship, volunteer Sunday school teaching in local churches, and youth programs in poorer neighborhoods. In the late thirties they began a weeklong program of entertainment, films, and religious discussions. But between the two world wars the sociable elements of the program came to dominate their agenda. They sponsored tea dances and open houses, managed the bowling alleys and pool tables, the music practice rooms, the meeting rooms, and the student lounge. They arranged sports broadcasts, ran the lost-and-found bureau, a furniture exchange, a housing office, summer employment and then a placement office, and published the *Freshman Bible* (an orientation booklet). In 1940, when the military draft stirred up some discussion on campuses, and even some religious resistance, they sponsored a week of reflection. All of this programming required financing, and in 1928 a student activities fee was included in each student's bill, making every student thereby a member of the Brainerd Society, will he nill he. It also made every student a member of the YMCA, but this was quickly seen as inappropriate because Y membership was reserved to members of "evangelical Christian" churches, so the college relinquished its chapter of the YMCA. In the late 1940s — to move ahead in time somewhat — when a college church was formed, it took to itself all the religious activities sustained by Brainerd, which then became the Brainerd Student Union. Ten years later those activities, one by one, had been absorbed by other organizations: the Lafayette Press took the *Freshman Bible,* the chaplain took over the building, etc. When at last the Student Council intercepted the annual fees, Brainerd (est. 1833) was left without funding authority or much of a purpose, and expired (†1956).[53]

The student-run activities which replaced their religious initiatives were all eventually converted into institutional programs. The literary societies lost their weekend time to athletic matches; the arrival of history and the social sciences brought into the classroom the subjects so warmly debated in their chambers; and the college libraries absorbed their collections. Intramural sports eventually gave way to varsity. Teams acquired coaches who took leadership and selection away from elected captains, and then supervisory officers and boards began to govern the sports and collect the revenues. Prayer meetings were taken into the hands of chaplains, who then scheduled retreats and more prayer meetings. In every case, the student initiatives became routinized, professionalized, and absorbed by administration.

So also in the case of the Brainerd Society, as old as Lafayette College. A complex of piety and service and missionary activism, undertaken by generous students as the making and manifest of their faith, ended as a program of secular services that eventually had neither the need nor the possibility for religious motivation. It was one instance among many, of campus undertakings that became stifled when their founding spirit had to breathe the air of campus administration and governance.

The Moral Pattern Is Stressed

Between the wars Catholic and Jewish enrollment continued to rise, while Presbyterians declined to slightly less than one-fourth of the student body. After World War II the Jews and Catholics began to come in even higher numbers, until an unpublished but official limit was set: no more than 15 percent from either group were to be admitted. In the years to follow, both groups unwittingly and consistently pressed the ceiling. Such limits had been common throughout higher education (and usually much more restrictive); Lafayette was late, and not very severe, in its policy decision. As we shall see, the quotas did not long endure.

World War II produced a remarkable student mixture on campus. It being still an all-male college, Lafayette lost virtually all of its regular student body except students intending to go into the ministry, who were exempted from conscription. Engulfing them were young recruits being trained in five different military programs. There ought to have been little surprise in 1943, therefore, when President Lewis received notice of complaints circulating at high levels of the synod that there was some hard drinking on campus, and that every fraternity house had its own bar. These murmurs naturally enough stirred up the chronic problem: that the synod held a potentially martial authority over the college and was therefore the natural forum for any and all who saw reasons why they should withdraw their endorsement.

Presbyterians themselves had an awkward ambivalence about alcohol. They were heirs to a long tradition of temperance preaching. For instance, some years back the *Presbyterian* had expressed satisfaction that a polar expedition was relying on nothing stronger than tea and cocoa to keep their spirits stimulated. The church membership included large numbers of affluent people whose savoir-faire included social drinking. But within the same fellowship were people of lower social class who were indebted to the revivalist tradition and more inclined to agree with the Methodists and Baptists about liquor. The Pennsylvania Synod had plenty of conservatives who expected Lafayette to be bone-dry.

President Lewis replied that the campus was much more abstemious than most, and that even the 1,200 soldiers there were benefiting from the moral and spiritual influence of the college. But the ability of the synod to unnerve the college by its concern for adverse rumors remained remarkably high, despite the comparatively low number of Presbyterian students who might come there.[54]

Concern for Presbyterian-related colleges in the national offices began at this time to generate a series of new policy statements that tested Lafayette's ability and willingness to continue its "organic relationship" with the church. In 1943 the national Board of Christian Education defined its standards for affiliation. They were five in number, including academic accreditation, a certified annual audit, a published statement of purpose, a graduation requirement of at least one course in biblical studies, and a faculty employing only those "who are active members in good standing of some evangelical Christian church which affirms its loyalty to Jesus Christ as the Divine Lord and Savior." (Absent, now, was any requirement for obligatory worship.) That, at any rate, was what the original draft required. After the college presidents had made their comments it acquired an additional sentence: "The Board does not rule that this action is to affect faculty members already employed."[55] The trend in faculty hiring had clearly been toward more diversity and fewer Presbyterians, and now it seems to have yielded fewer Protestants. This requirement, then, if taken seriously, would bind the colleges to an increasingly strenuous recruiting process. Church officials were well aware that the Board of Christian Education had few financial incentives to offer to these colleges. Presbyterians contributed nationally about 25¢ a year per capita for the entire educational work of the church, and annual grants to colleges averaged less than $2,000. The general secretary of the Board admitted: "The college has not turned its back on the Church. The Church has turned from the college — leaving it to seek support where support could be found."[56]

At Lafayette there was little disposition to do that. A new president, Ralph Cooper Hutchison, was inaugurated in 1945. A Lafayette alumnus who had worked as a lay missionary in Iran after graduating, he held graduate degrees from Harvard and Penn and had served as dean overseas and as president at nearby Washington and Jefferson College. The new president needed no one's coaching to want Lafayette to be a through-and-through Presbyterian place. Most likely he was prepared to assent to the policy of the General Assembly that "evangelism should be at the center of the program of each Presbyterian college." The Assembly had immediately drawn a pragmatic conclusion: "A faculty on which each member is unreservedly committed to Christ and the Gospel is basic to this evangelistic effort."[57] But such specific measures were not as close to Hutchison's heart, at least in this troublesome matter.

As the Students Change, the College Must Change

The 1943 standards, especially the one regarding faculty, were evidently beyond what he considered possible. In an article prepared for publication in early 1948 he spoke of the relationship with the church as "fundamentally spiritual, a voluntary fellowship" to which the college would bring a consecration and loyalty which were more important than any legal ties. Hutchison claimed that the standard requiring evangelical Christian faculty was only a general norm, one that obviously allowed of exceptions. He added two significant comments. As everyone knew, the expression "evangelical Christian" was meant to exclude two groups: Catholics who were not evangelical, and Jews who were not Christian. Of course it would also stand in the way of Rosicrucians and Theravada Buddhists, but they were not queuing up at the gates of Lafayette, while Catholics and Jews were very much in evidence. Hutchison made it clear where he stood on that. "So far as we can discover, such a practice has always been the policy of Lafayette College, highlighted and emphasized by occasional exceptions of valued and honored men who may not have been members of any church. Nor has this policy now or at any time been interpreted to exclude active and interested members of the Roman Catholic Church. Some of our most cherished faculty members now are members of that church." Then, aware that the alumni and others might sense the entire restriction by the church as awkward and intrusive, he explained its real practical value: preventing infiltration by agents and dupes of America's totalitarian enemies (the year was 1948). One must infer that since President MacCracken's canvass of the faculty a quarter of a century earlier, Catholics and Jews were now becoming better represented in the ranks.[58]

But Hutchison was apparently not defaulting on what the Board of Christian Education really demanded. In the form to be filed by its member colleges were two questions about the faculty. Of those teaching in the Department of Bible (supported by a church trust), the query was whether they were in "good and regular standing in evangelical churches," and whether they were "in full sympathy and accord with the fundamental teachings of evangelical Christianity." Of the faculty in general, however, the questionnaire asked fuzzily whether they provided a "positive Christian influence." Hutchison replied with a blanket affirmative to both.[59]

The Hutchison presidency was a season of great change at Lafayette, yet most of it was beneath the surface. Hutchison, who would eventually be forced to resign, was nevertheless a man of his time and place. Though he eventually failed to rally the loyalty and affection any leader needs, he came back to Easton with the education, experience, and instincts of an efficient administrator. Yet so much of what he attempted or accomplished was eventually undermined by his tendency to envelop worthwhile but imperiled projects in a cloud of ambiguity.

He came to office when the veterans returned from war, and Lafayette had the joy of being packed to overflowing. There was no question but that the veterans — many of them now married — could never be expected or obliged to observe the traditional rules of student conduct. Lafayette's way of handling this was like that of most colleges and universities: the rules were left on the books to await the day when incoming freshmen were once again eighteen-year-olds, and meanwhile they were promulgated and enforced with much winking and blinking. One case in point, of symbolic importance, was the ban on alcohol. The fraternities continued to have open bars and the president continued to fume at them, but only that. Hutchison complained that those determined to drink should do so off campus, but since the rule forbade drinking anywhere, his sleight of mind over his own rule did nothing to make anyone convinced there was a principle at stake. Later, as the veterans passed from the scene and enforcement was again attempted, the students resisted and demanded the rule be abolished. The administration asked incoming students to sign pledges not to drink, but the voluntary scheme only brought more murkiness into the issue. Faculty began regularly to accept invitations to cocktail parties in the frat houses.

Alcohol was not really a central issue, but the wrangle over the rule may serve to illustrate a disorder that was becoming central. The rule was unclear since it implied that drinking was wrong, whereas the rule makers' concern was that intoxication was wrong. The enforcement was also unclear, because the senior generation was as unsettled in their convictions about temperance as was the junior generation in theirs about intemperance. As long as rules were enunciated but not enforced, the integrity of public moral discourse was subverted. The "real meaning" was never to be found in open policy statements.

The intractable controversy over Sunday worship is another example of this same ambiguity. Students were obliged to attend "the church of their choice" on Sunday, and by the time Hutchison arrived there was stiff resistance to this, on the ground that involuntary worship is false and abusive. At Washington and Jefferson Hutchison had created a college church, and he quietly arranged to so the same at Lafayette. Approval by the Lehigh Presbytery and the board of trustees was swiftly obtained, and in the fall of 1947 he announced it. It was officially a congregation of the Presbyterian church, with student elders and deacons and the usual church polity, yet any college person already a member of another denomination could apply and belong (that invitation implicitly being reserved to Protestants). The college chaplain thus became the college pastor as well. Simultaneously the obligation to attend Sunday (traditionally: Sabbath) worship was lifted. From then on it would all be voluntary. Membership, at first small, doubled and redoubled and attracted student spouses and some faculty families. But the College Church was founded astraddle a fault line. The pastor and the supervising judicatory were Presbyterian, but nearly half of the worshipers were not. Attendance and membership leveled off, and in a few years began slowly to wane. It was not an easy thing to nurture a congregation within a church and a gospel tradition, under the patronage of a college that registered only a small minority of that church and faith, and make it a peaceful communion of members whose deeper loyalties went in all directions. Apparently the ambiguity began to be felt by students; in 1954 Hutchison had to write to the nearby Methodist bishop to coax his communicants into signing up. (No success.) In the meantime the separate religious activities of the Jews, Catholics, Episcopalians, Lutherans, and evangelicals were quickened.[60]

Deeper still than the ambivalence of a church being at once denominational and interdenominational was that of a college population expected to worship the Lord on Sundays. Students who enrolled at Lafayette were expected to attend classes, accomplish assigned study exercises, write papers without plagiarism, and take exams without cheating. When the administration and faculty stated these requirements, they were never seen as imposing their preferences on an involuntary student body. If you went to college it was assumed that, though human weakness might often intervene (and for that reason the senior folks would monitor their juniors for faithful performance), you knew this was essential to the undertaking. Likewise, in early days when all students were expected to join in worship on Sundays, it was assumed that they would not have come to Lafayette were they not Christians and therefore committed to worship. No effort was expended in the admissions process to ensure that this would continue. When Protestants of other denominations did come, some felt at their ease joining the Presbyterians as guests, while others sought out nearby churches of their own. Catholics did not want to be guests at Presbyterian worship, nor were they expected or perhaps even welcome, and they went down the hill to their church. Nobody gave much thought to the Jews, especially since in early days there were classes on Saturdays. But as fewer Presbyterians came to Lafayette, the guests began to outnumber and then to swamp the "home team." Then the enrollment of all Protestants combined slipped downward. If one understands that for more than half a century the religious census was a survey, not of commitment but of (sometimes perfunctory) membership, or "preference," then the proportion of students who could meaningfully join in fellowship of faith and worship was small indeed. The same diversification had obviously been under way among the faculty.[61] Lafayette College could not possibly act as a church in the ways it had, say, up to the 1920s. To create a voluntary College Church could and did relieve a rankling hostility to compulsory worship. But as there was no college community available to people it, the well-intentioned effort, by its pretense, depleted the capacity of Lafayette leadership to know the truth of their circumstances.

Weekday chapel continued, but only on Wednesdays was it ostensibly religious. Other occasions were a variety show, oscillating between pep rallies and lectures by celebrities. When worship or prayer is made a normal part of life's events, it can either sanctify them or be profaned by them. The latter fortune befell Lafayette, as so many other similar campuses at the time.

If these initiatives were eventually to erode the Presbyterian character of the college, it was not because Ralph Cooper Hutchison was slack or passive-aggressive in his attitude toward his faith. It would be difficult to find a president, especially a layman, who at that time was more earnest in his desire to retain and restore the Christian orientation of his college. Nor was he always unsuccessful. It will be recalled that in 1938 the Department of Religion, in order to quell complaints within the synod, had had to cease and desist, at least in the required courses, from the teaching of religion. This bears out the observation of Longfield and Marsden, that "the price of having substantial theological traditions was that of having substantial theological controversies."[62] In a larger curriculum revision Hutchison decided that the Religion Department should take that risk once again, by offering courses on the sources and development of Christian faith (though more academically than in the past) and discontinuing courses on the Bible "as literature":

> It has been the conviction of the Administration that it is important academically that every student have a scholarly and accurate understanding of Christ and of the Christian religion regardless of his own religious faith. And particularly since Christianity has had a marked influence upon all phases of life and thought, it was felt that an understanding of Christian beliefs and thought should be basic in the academic preparation of any student regardless of his field of concentration.[63]

There were issues in which it was Hutchison who deplored double-talk. In 1954 the Presbyterian college presidents were working up a replacement for the 1943 standards. The new version called for consultation with the Board of Christian

158

Education before adopting institutional statements of purpose. Hutchison deplored "these effusive, elaborate codifications of baloney known as statements of purpose." (A few years later a visitation committee from the Presbyterian College Board, having perhaps come to the same conclusions, commended Lafayette for not having one in its catalogue.)[64] The new standard called for a religious counselor or chaplain who would be the witness for the church on campus (obviously relieving the president and faculty of that responsibility). To this requirement Hutchison objected that most of their colleges had not been able even to afford anyone full-time to guide Christian activities. The most significant change in the text was that faculty need not be Christian church members, but only "in full sympathy" with and give "loyal support" to the college's Christian purpose. He objected to this for three reasons: it was impracticably vague; it would not filter out those cunning radicals, Communists, rationalists, and other harmful elements who can look and sound as sympathetic as can be; and the General Assembly would indignantly turn it down.[65] The proposal eventually died. Hutchison was not sensitive or sophisticated in his perceptions, but he enjoyed a coarse and canny sense for the kind of wordwind that academics use to deceive others sometimes and themselves often.

The usual decennial rumbling from the synod geysered up in the latter years of Hutchison's tenure. Their desire, once again, was that their power of review be given more grip, and that no nomination be sent up for synodical approval so late that it could not realistically be vetoed. Lafayette trustees were once again ready to amend the charter to free their college of such bother, but Hutchison anticipated a public-relations disaster if they did, for it would be interpreted as a breach with the church. His voice prevailed, and after a quiet evening of cigars at the Union League Club the synod agreed to take a college trustee onto its Committee of Higher Education, while Lafayette agreed to take one of those committeemen onto its new Religious Program Council. And there was peace.[66]

In the meantime Hutchison had managed to stabilize the college's finances, at least by comparison with other colleges related to the church. Lafayette tended to be among the top two or three colleges for its professorial salary levels, and in the size of its annual grant from the Board of Christian Education (which had climbed toward $30,000 by the end of his administration); the grant from the synod was in addition to that, and the Synod of Pennsylvania had by far the most affluent budget in the entire church. It was not a time to be shaking fists.

When Ralph Hutchison was obliged by his trustees in 1957 to resign, there was much hostility in the air, directed toward the president's temperament and policies. Because of his advocacy of the Christian character of the college, there was a repeat of what had happened after Warfield's regime. The association of special religious interest with a dishonored president made religion an item of caution and distance for sophisticated academics on site during the next few years.

Roald Bergethon, a President of Principle

Kaare Roald Bergethon, educated at DePauw and Cornell, professor and dean at Brown, came in 1958 to be president for twenty years. His manner was gracious and dignified, and if President Cattell (1863-83) was the man most responsible for Lafayette's survival, it was Bergethon's years of service which witnessed its access to affluence and excellence. The new president was the son of a Baptist minister and was himself reported to be a Congregationalist-turned-Unitarian, but on arrival he transferred his membership to the Presbyterian church. As regards Lafayette's Presbyterian character, Bergethon probably worked more than any other to clarify · it, and he surely did more, eventually, to extinguish it.

He was not long in office when Dean Cole, also a newcomer, raised the question of the unpublished limit on the admission of Catholics and Jews. Because of the quota there were applicants with higher academic credentials being rejected in order to keep both cohorts near their set maxima of 15 percent each. This issue was addressed at the same time and in the same spirit as discrimination among the fraternities. Many of the campus chapters, whether by written or unwritten policy, had either excluded or severely limited Jews, blacks, and Catholics in their membership. There were not at the time significant numbers of black applicants, but Catholics and Jews together constituted almost a third of the student body. Jews were socially excluded and had organized a fraternity of their own, Pi Lambda Phi, which maintained an 85 percent Jewish membership. Bergethon thought both types of quota hindered the college and immediately moved to abolish them. Discrimination in the fraternities took years of very public pressure to eliminate. The limit on admissions, by contrast, could be handled by action of the administration and board, and was removed as noiselessly as it had been imposed.[67] Soon after the change the incoming freshman class arrived with a Jewish cohort of 28 percent, but that crest was never again reached. For about a decade there were no great changes, but in the sixties Presbyterians began again to decrease in numbers, and Catholics replaced them. By the middle of President Bergethon's term, Catholics outnumbered Presbyterians among the incoming class. By his last year, Catholics (38 percent) began to outnumber not just Presbyterians (9 percent) but all Protestants combined (37 percent); they have remained thus up to the present. Jews (18 percent), by 1972, outnumbered Presbyterians (11 percent) among matriculants, and most years since then they have retained second place behind Catholics. It is not clear that Roald Bergethon could have contemplated this outcome any more easily than George Junkin might have.[68]

Bergethon was a man who acted forthrightly to relieve chronic grievances on campus. His adjustments were typically in the direction of liberalization, and the unforeseen outcomes of some of them are still unfolding.

In his first year, after much serious discussion with student leaders, the ban on drinking was lifted for selected social events, and the Code of Conduct focused more on temperance than on abstinence. Thus another ancient aggravation was relieved, so it seemed.

That same year, Bergethon's first, the synod was back again, proposing that all faculty appointments be cleared in advance, not with the synod (which convened but once a year) but with its standing Committee on Higher Education, in order to verify that each candidate was qualified under the 1943 standards. It sweetened the request by voting to supplement the annual college grant from the Board of Christian Education such that their combined gifts would equal 10 percent of Lafayette's educational-and-general budget. The college briskly wrote back, said the proposed process would be unlawful, and told the synod that in any case it had no intention of abiding by the standard which required faculty even to be church members.[69]

In 1959 the college was visited by a team drawn from five other Presbyterian colleges, somewhat in the style of an informal peer accreditation. The visitation report devoted considerable attention to accounting procedures, plant maintenance, and the development office. The only comment bearing on the religious aspect of the college was a recommendation that it might be well to have a theologian or two on the board.[70] It had been several years since the last minister departed from the board.

If Methodists have led all other denominations in the transcendence of their discourse about church-related higher education, Presbyterians stand first in their capacity for major policy studies. The first of a series appeared in 1961: *The Church and Higher Education*.[71] "Has the time perhaps come when the church ought to recognize that it has no place in the college business?" it asked. The facts as recounted were sobering. The number of students seeking higher education would double in a decade. Three-quarters of them would be in state institutions, and an increasing proportion would want job-oriented training. National policy on education would be made at a distance from the campuses themselves. The intellectual climate of the academy would be prevailingly secularist. None of this held much promise for a collection of underfunded, Presbyterian church–related, liberal education colleges. Especially when, "to date, the United Presbyterian Church's financial support of its colleges has been woefully, almost ludicrously, inadequate."

Thus far the brass and timpani. After that came the strings. The report speaks repeatedly of the "openly avowed Christian purpose" of their colleges "intimately related" to the church, and of its "nourishing support." There is a clear Calvinist motif in its explanation of why their campuses would be especially welcoming to academic freedom: (1) "the greatest freedom is likely to be found where the critically theological and the truly secular are in conversation"; (2) "the man who is freed from guilt and anxiety by faith in Christ is free to serve God and pursue knowledge for his glory . . . in the scholar's perfect freedom." The campus is not a church, the report admits, but it is an institution of the church and should resemble one. Young scholars who come there will be eager, not just for teaching and research, but to be provided with "a sense of Christian community."

The College Is Impatient with the Church

The Church and Higher Education became a reference document through the sixties, but at Lafayette it could be only a fantasy. They were gradually finding the enjoyment of emulating the secular campuses, and hiring young faculty for teaching and research, period. Half the student body came from religious traditions that Lafayette had throughout its history considered foreign. How could this new faculty and this new student body form, under Presbyterian auspices, a Christian community? President Bergethon's expectation of the church was that it prove itself compatible with higher learning and make a better effort to cover at least 10 percent of the academic budget; the correlative duty of the college was simply to achieve academic excellence.[72] Obviously the relationship was, in his view, serving the college's concerns, not those of the church. And with Presbyterian church income then just beginning to falter, its contributions were going to get smaller, not larger. Furthermore, the church had finally realized that the great majority of its communicants were going elsewhere than to its sponsored colleges, and in recent years had shifted three-quarters of its higher education grant money to campus chaplaincies on state and independent campuses.[73]

There were small signs of a mild but darkening campus impatience with the church. A new restiveness about obligatory chapel had begotten renewed concern among the faculty that Lafayette was priest-ridden, and a lawyer on the board who had been serving as chairman of the Religious Program Council, Thomas Pomeroy, was chosen to allay those fears. He had high praise for the 1961 report, which he took to have repealed the 1943 Set of Standards (especially its odious requirement of a Christian faculty) and to have given robust assurances of academic freedom. The college was then receiving about $90,000 annually from the national and synodical levels of the church. More importantly, most of the large donors "were inspired by the aspirations of the Christian faith." But this, Pomeroy says, is surely not at the heart of Lafayette's tie to the church. "We are related because of the concern that we have for the things of the spirit." This, he admits, has become a rare concern in American higher education. "All the more important, therefore, is the preservation of a college which can openly avow a Christian motivation, a Christian purpose; where without fear of any law, the search for truth in all its aspects, spiritual and otherwise, can go forward in a free and open exchange among dedicated teachers and students, whether they be committed, doubting, or unbelievers."[74] This would have appealed to Henry Pritchett.

Meanwhile Bergethon, serving as president of the Presbyterian College Union, the presidents' roundtable, had presided over a rewrite of the old 1943 standards. The document is framed in smoother language and speaks of "active exchange between faith and the academic disciplines" but does not speak of how a faculty is to be assembled who would care to undertake this active exchange. The standards of 1943 were displaced by "Administrative Policies and Procedures," terms meant to convey that they are guidelines, not norms to gauge a college's fidelity. The two guidelines with some bite emerge very differently than before. Instead of requiring a Bible or religion course, now a college "shall require of each student a mature classroom encounter with the Judaic-Christian heritage." And — the point of it all, really — now there was a new guideline for hiring:

> The church-related college will seek to have well-qualified faculty members, administrative officers, and trustees who are dedicated to its declared institutional purpose and will faithfully serve the primary objective of academic excellence in a community that encourages true piety with integrity of thought and character.[75]

It was an excellent guideline, one that Penn State could as easily adopt. Of course, the declared institutional purpose of Lafayette was bound to be more explicitly Presbyterian, or at least Christian, than Penn State's. But this was not, "of course," quite the case. The most one could find, by way of published purpose, was a stated goal in the arts catalogue: "a sense of moral and spiritual values — a belief that such persistent problems as the difference between good and evil and the relationship between God and man cannot be evaded." That probably exceeded anything currently in vigor under Mount Nittany, but it was not going to send chills up most academics' — prospectively or actually in service at Easton — spines.

A reappraisal was mounted by the Board of Christian Education to evaluate compliance by the colleges with *The Church and Higher Education.* An elaborate questionnaire was circulated, and Lafayette had this to say about itself:

> Lafayette College has no statement which explicitly enunciates these convictions. However, in their words and actions, members of the faculty and administrative officers operationally represent the conviction that faith and learning are "unbreakably linked." Within a pluralistic context and in an area where "love of God" to many appears incompatible with "love of learning," the College presents a fully open learning and searching community in which *all* must consider the claims of religion and Biblical faith and in which a numerically significant [± 20 percent] and explicitly Christian congregation worships and witnesses. Here the College not only stands for the belief that students and faculty must "meet all truth fearlessly and freely" but also for the belief that the Church and the Christian must "meet all truth fearlessly and freely" in a truly competitive environment. The College cannot require all its faculty or its students to believe that "all truth is of God." It can in partnership with the Church incorporate the unafraid assumption that "love of learning is," whether known or denied, "firmly . . . [yoked with] love of God."[76]

The 1961 policy statement had expected faculty to be "dedicated to" its stated purpose; the college reply was that it expected them to be "sympathetic" to these purposes but no more than that. How assure even this much support? It was a matter taken up in unspecified ways at the recruitment interview with the president and dean. To what degree does this make the college "a Christian community"? "In general vital religion gets a fair and open consideration. It should not ask for more."

Bergethon explained to the local Presbyterian churches that any religious restriction on personnel was taken by students and faculty as "stacking the deck," by outsiders as bigotry, and by new legislation as possibly illegal. He concluded: the "ultimate tension is always to act in an imperfect world so as to reflect the conviction that the most essential element in human life is the Grace of Faith and the Redeeming Power of Love as most perfectly embodied in the figure of the Master."[77] He was assuring the churches that, even were this the disposition of the present administration and faculty (the evidence suggests it was not), they were not going to provide themselves with successors to abide that ultimate tension.

Sectarianism with a Vengeance

Meanwhile President Bergethon had cause to be alarmed by two legal matters. The first was the Pennsylvania Fair Educational Opportunities Act of 1961, which aimed to avert discrimination of all sorts (*Brown* v. *Board of Education* was slowly working its way into the nation's conscience). One provision forbade schools to inquire into applicants' religion before making their admission decisions. Exempt from that restriction were religious or denominational schools. At Bergethon's prompting the board approved an extensive certification that Lafayette was "a denominational institution . . . organically related to the Presbyterian Church . . . vitally interested in developing the spiritual and moral growth of each of its students." The college reported having received nearly $170,000 from the church during the two previous years. The state replied that Lafayette was now recognized as a bona fide religious or denominational institution.[78]

Before this transaction was even consummated Bergethon received advice that a denominational identity might disqualify the college as "sectarian" and make it ineligible to receive state or federal aid, which was just then beginning to be available. A court case in Maryland brought this issue before the public eye. At first Bergethon thought that having a college church would be the obstacle, and he considered using synodical or Presbyterian Board of Education funds to support it. But in 1965 the synod took the initiative. Since four of its six affiliated colleges had never required approval of their trustee elections or faculty appointments by the synod, Lafayette and Waynesburg were now permitted to amend their charters to regain the same autonomy. Lafayette promptly voted to do so. Since, however, there was a possible double jeopardy — being Presbyterian-related might preserve autonomy from some governmental control but might also lose eligibility for governmental support — the lawyers determined to move cautiously.[79]

These new legal circumstances spurred the college to inventory its personnel as it had neither wished nor done previously:

1966-67

Board of Trustees (26)

Presbyterians	13	50%
Episcopalians	4	15%
Methodists	2	8%
United Church of Christ	2	8%
Congregationalists	2	8%
Protestants (nondenominational)	2	8%
Lutheran	1	4%

Faculty (160)

Presbyterians	32	20%
Catholics	20	13%
Episcopalians	17	11%
Methodists	13	8%
Lutherans	7	4%
Baptists	6	4%
Unitarians	5	3%
Congregationalists	3	2%
United Church of Christ	3	2%
Society of Friends	3	2%
Evangelical and Reformed	2	1%
Jews	2	1%
Nondenominational	18	11%
Other	9	6%
No response	20	13%

Students (1,600)

Presbyterians	22%
All Protestants	39%
Catholics	14%
Jews	15%
Others, None, and No Response	10%

The college counsel studied these statistics, the chaplaincy, the College Church, the "rigorously academic" Department of Religion, the fact that the required daily gatherings were not "Chapel in the traditional sense," the fact that the church was then contributing 1.4 percent of the total operating budget, and the presence of religion elsewhere, e.g., in admissions, chaplaincy, alumni affairs, curriculum, extracurriculars, grants received. He then reviewed a recent study of

817 church-related institutions and estimated that "there are only a very few institutions in the entire list whose church-relationship could be considered 'looser' than that of Lafayette."[80]

After a long dithering that began in 1912, the college finally took the step in early 1967 and expunged all references to the synod from its charter.[81] Later that year, since a number of the endowments received from or through the church bound the college by their deeds of gift to certain measures of fidelity to Christian education, these too were renegotiated. Since the Board of Christian Education knew that all charter provisions could be amended at will by their respective college boards, the original purpose of these deeds was to bind the colleges by contract. The colleges had thereby committed themselves to submit elections for synodical approval, provide systematic instruction in Bible, maintain a teaching staff "for whose positive Christian influence the president . . . can vouch," and submit their records and performance to the church for visitation and approval. The "Amended Agreement" is much more sleek, and binds the trustees and officers to harbor "a continuing desire to relate the college to The United Presbyterian Church in the United States."[82] "A mature classroom encounter with the Judaic-Christian Heritage" would be required of every student. As for the faculty, they could be Nestorians, Confucians, or Fire Baptized.[83] In the immediate aftermath the college counsel privately described the church relationship of the college as "extremely tenuous." The Board of Christian Education, reflecting on similar changes in many related colleges, persevered in its highly detached discourse: "The college should evidence its concern for the education of young men and women in a Christian context. The college should recognize its responsibility to represent the concerns of the church in the councils of higher education. It should evidence its concern for the life and renewal of the church . . ." They had not heard the latch click.[84]

There was one aftershock. In 1970 the Board of Christian Education informed the colleges that the next annual appropriation would be their last. Money was tight. The presidents rose as one man to accuse the board of having "ignored the very real and substantial services which the church-related colleges perform in the total ministry of the Church." Then, the iron fist in the velvet glove: "The history of higher education in this country is replete with examples of where what was a condition of mutual support and cooperation has passed into one of merely historical and perhaps largely sentimental attachment on the part of a few. The transition from a church-related college to a secular one may proceed almost imperceptively [sic] at first, but as the distance widens it also accelerates and then becomes irreversible . . ." It would be a scandal, they earnestly intimated, if the board, by this withdrawal of funding, were to be responsible for snuffing out the "special awareness of the Church among the younger generation attending these colleges."[85]

By 1972 the board of trustees was once more fretting about its relationship to the church, and loath to send the president any longer to the Presbyterian College Union lest it jeopardize their chances for receiving federal funds. The Lafayette misgivings were taken to heart, and yet another policy document emerged, this time from an office with a more energized title: The Program Agency, UPC/USA. Entitled "The Church and Related Colleges and Universities: A Statement of Mutual Responsibilities," and going on for one-and-a-half pages, it succeeds in titrating all previous policy statements into a dilution that contains only trace elements of meaning floating in a sea of solvent. In a word: "the churches and colleges commit themselves to share with one another results of research, insights, and experiences that inform and reinforce the capacities of each to serve society with sensitivity and skill." To achieve this the educators will emphasize human values, will offer some religion courses, and will try somehow to express this relationship in their catalogues.[86]

The Chapel Has an Identity Crisis

This slow and hesitant alleviation of the encumbrance imposed by synodical sponsorship was not a matter of much public notice. It was carried on in boardrooms and in-trays. Throughout these same years the religious issue that was most vexed among the campus community was another perennial bother: obligatory chapel.

As Lafayette entered the 1960s its religious program was traditional, and stable. Six credit hours of religion were a graduation requirement, and were decently taught. The College Church had not continued to grow, but its membership was holding at about four hundred. And there was chapel. By 1960 the only remnant of that was a gathering every Wednesday at midday. The Wednesday service had at one time been the only clearly religious chapel event, with other weekday chapels being given over to various forms of civic whoopee. Now it was a happenstance half-breed. Since so many students insisted that enforced religious observance offended their freedom, the central element was a talk (no more than six minutes in length) on some neutral subject. Since elder traditionalists resisted the abolition of the college's oldest formal observance and the tie it represented to the Presbyterian past, the talk was showcased in the old format of introductory hymn, Scripture reading, choral anthem, and benediction. The entire service lasted only fifteen minutes, and since an earlier chapel fire had necessitated its transfer to a smaller hall, students were required to attend only every other week. This burden, however reduced, was nevertheless a chronic aggravation, being neither devout nor interesting, yet obligatory as if it were both. Lovers of tradition were stubborn in defending it as the one assertion of their Presbyterian heritage; students of the sixties were just as stubborn in assailing it as the one remaining nonvoluntary extracurricular.

In 1962 chapel absences were so flagrant (hundreds had gone delinquent by the end of the first month) that the dean's office announced it would enforce the rule and hold up their graduation. This easily converted indifference into hostility, and Jews and Catholics now stepped forward to say how chapel offended their religious convictions. The faculty council debated at length and showed by their vote how divided they were. The student council debated at exquisite length and showed by a series of consensus votes on contrary resolutions how united they were. The chaplain, whose lot in life it had been to deliver most of the addresses (cabinet ministers and Nobel laureates could not be brought in for six-minute exhortations), was a chaplain of the fifties, and complained that the variety show had profaned what was meant to be an event of reverence. The Religious Program Council canvassed other campuses: some Presbyterian colleges, like Macalester, Hanover, Wooster, and Millikin, required chapel while others, like Occidental, Trinity, Lewis and Clark, and Coe, did not. Most Lutheran colleges still required it, but most Ivy schools did not (Princeton required Sunday church but not weekday chapel).

Since the president, dean, and several leading trustees sat on the Religious Program Council along with faculty, alumni, and students (two students, much outnumbered in a group of fourteen), it was a group that tended to be conservative but possessed enough clout to make its policies take effect. They debated this endlessly. Bergethon was in the fore, guided by the need for authentic worship to be free. His suggestion was that chapel be restored as a service of worship — not in the style of a hodgepodge interfaith service, but in the Calvinist tradition — and that it continue to be obligatory. There would be only four per semester. For conscientious objectors, however, an intellectual alternative should be offered: a series of "theological confrontations" which would cogently expound some element of belief. Three per semester would be required. They would be followed by voluntary discussion, but would neither require nor presume any commitment by participants.

In effect, this meant that chapel was now made "voluntary," since there was an alternative. In the words of those who proposed it: "The College should protect the integrity of its church relationship; and the College should offer an alternative to required worship but not an escape from encounter."[87] The new arrangement was begun in September 1964. Few noticed that Bergethon had insisted on designating it "temporary." His misgivings emerged publicly in October. Beginning in the second semester chapel and confrontations would both be unconditionally voluntary. The college would now create a series of "assemblies" focused on college life itself, and these would be required.

How did these activities fare? That spring there were seventeen assemblies. Freshmen were summoned to eight of them, initiated into the college history and traditions and grading policy and regulations, and coached on study habits and social life. Seniors were required to come only three times, for advice on graduate school and placement, for Founders' Day, and for the senior dinner. Everybody was expected, and everybody came. Nobody prayed.

Chapel attendance dropped drastically. Lunch hour being an improbable time, chapel was shifted to 11:00 P.M., but still only an average of thirty attended. Again it was shifted, this time to 7:00 P.M., and participation became smaller still, so it was restored to 11:00 P.M., by which time less than twenty attended. It was now called the All College Chapel, but Jewish students generally didn't worship and Catholic students generally disliked worshiping with others, so the clientele was drawn from the now-shrinking Protestant pool.

The theological confrontations were the responsibility of a new chaplain, who was of the sixties, not the fifties. The chaplain was gratified at the generous budget provided by the college and reported that they "had covered a broad spectrum of subject areas." One year they included Theatre of Concern, Joseph Fletcher (the good soldier of situation ethics) on sexual morality, the Judson Love Workshop, a death-of-God talk by Thomas Altizer, and presentations by the founder of Students for a Democratic Society and a representative of the American Civil Liberties Union. The confrontation with theology was obviously not head-on, but at an angle, so to say. A faculty member asked, "How are we different as a Presbyterian Church-related college?" Other faculty on the Religious Program Council said that their response was "watchful waiting." Dr. Bergethon provided the answer: "We may not condition . . . we must expose."[88]

Meanwhile membership in the College Church had suddenly dropped ("stabilized" was the word used) to ninety, and many of these tended to have been freshmen who signed up in first-month enthusiasm but would not persevere. The chaplain, however, emphasized that "numbers are a poor index of commitment" (witness, he said, German Christianity under Hitler). He also insisted "on the right of the Church to be the Church," and on his own calling to the "prophetic imperative."

> It is true, of course, that *some* (rigidly conventional Christians, political conservatives) may have been deterred from active participation in religious programs. Insofar as hostility toward the Chaplain or the College Church reflects recognition of objective inadequacies in commitment to the Christian faith (the idolatries of ideology, tradition, denomination, race, and nation), it is analogous to a patient's hostility toward his therapist. . . . Concretely, the despised minority protesting war in Vietnam have a greater immediate claim on the visible presence and support of the church than the mob. The members of the mob, as individuals feeling confusion, guilt, hostility, have subsequent and equally valid claims. When a Pastor decides to become a full-time manipulator, political fence-maker, Church image-maker he is on the path to popularity and utter corruption.[89]

Thus the chaplain, prophetically. The chapel choir disbanded, Bible study was frightening away most students (a name change was being considered), Operation Crossroads Africa was dropped for want of enthusiasm, dialogue discussions of sermons petered out, volunteers for infirmary visitations kept failing to fulfill their commitments, there were no takers even for scholarships to try out a first year of seminary, the retreat program was discontinued, and seven out of every eight who signed up to tutor youngsters in town quit the project.[90]

The president spoke at the dedication of a new, small, Interfaith Chapel, accoutered with interchangeable Protestant, Catholic, and Jewish symbols. It is possible that few listened as closely as they should have.

We live at a time when old truths must be made fresh if they are not to be forgotten. It is a time when poets declaim the meaninglessness of meaning and none dare declare: "Thus saith the Lord." Our world is a Tower of Babel where wisdom is not preached in the confident absoluteness of proverbs, but is perceived situationally and obliquely in the small world of "Peanuts." . . .

We have come to a new time — a time when 'midst all the confusion of facts and numbers we hunger with ache and anguish for the sense of the personal in living. As mass production makes us everywhere more and more alike in appearance, there is increasing drive to feel distinct, to feel individually different. There is also the strong [need] for personal nearness to others, for the companionship of love. . . .

I believe this is why we have this room. It expresses a truth of the Biblical tradition. It states a position of the corporate entity of the College. It repeats and refreshes what has long been axiomatic. This room recognizes the fatherhood of the One and the brotherhood of all.[91]

As the sixties drew to a close, it was evident that Lafayette College did indeed hold in loose companionship a great diversity of religious difference and indifference. The only constituency — apart, perhaps, from that of the more generous donors — in which Presbyterian membership was significantly numerous was the board of trustees, and in their concerns for the church they seem to have regarded it primarily as a source of potential finance and embarrassment. The center was not holding. Roald Bergethon looked back, after his fifteenth year in office, with some sadness. The college founders had seen "education as a means of virtue" (thus, in their memorial to the Pennsylvania legislature). There was a belief then that educated persons were enlightened, but recent events seemed to have eroded that faith. The impulsive and disruptive events of the sixties, the degradation of educational standards, the faded expectations of probity in campus life . . . "the college experience is seen by many as a combination of sometimes dubious intellectual discipline and of sometimes egotistical individualistic experimentation rather than as education that is 'a means of virtue.' "[92]

The early seventies saw several more events that were markers in the descending religious history of the college. In 1970-71 a general review of the curriculum removed the last requirement that every student take one religion course. The department presumably still offered "a mature classroom encounter with the Judaic-Christian Heritage," but it was no longer going to be required of every student. As the president explained it to the Board of Christian Education, Lafayette believed "that very little good will be done educationally, or religiously, by forcing faculty and students to accord a College-Church agreement [signed three years earlier] which neither faculty nor student body would feel compatible with curricular conviction."[93]

170

The chaplaincy still strove to draw students into chapel. A booklet for new students assured all of a welcome, in the prose equivalent of a Dali painting:

> Far from indifferent toward the distinctive values in each religion, we affirm that by taking our own traditions seriously we meet on the deepest levels where aesthetics and human philosophies are overcome by the powerful love of the God who is Father of all mankind. And the religious dimension of life is not just there when we are consciously being religious. Thoughts and feelings, the deep searchings and struggles of our own life, are the very stuff of religion. No bland "religion in general" here! . . .
>
> Value and affirm whatever good gifts you have received from your home and church while taking the initiative to break free from stereotyped understandings and childish conceptions of religion. We offer to share with you a climate of freedom, growth, celebration, and commitment to the works of love and justice.[94]

Chapel services, which at the time were in an experimental mode, and were now known as the All College Chapel in order to accommodate the demographic shift, had been migrating through the weekly schedule in search of a popular day and hour. At this time they occurred at eleven o'clock at night on alternate Wednesdays. Sharing that time slot was Midnight Communion, a eucharistic celebration "with a strong New Testament basis." Attendance was varying between eighteen and forty-five. It was reported to have an unstable clientele: "strangers appear and disappear without even giving their names to the Chaplain or anyone else." But "Jews, Catholics and agnostics are participants."[95] No bland "religion in general" there.

Two years later, while the college was recruiting a new chaplain, a survey was made of his primary constituency, the Protestant students. Twelve percent of the student body were Protestants who went to church at least once a month, but attrition over the four years reduced that by more than half; another 12 percent went once a year. That was all. Almost three-fourths of the Protestant respondents were not aware of the Lafayette Church's denomination. When asked whether the presence of Protestant, Catholic, and Jewish worship, and of a full-time chaplain, were important for the campus, about a third responded positively. When asked if they were important for them personally, only about half as many said so. Was it important that the chaplain be Protestant? Only 3 percent thought so. The situation, as the interim chaplain described it, was that "the College Church is dealing with a nominally-Protestant constituency more than three-quarters of whom are hardly ever seen inside a church." The College Church was reporting a membership of 60, the Hillel counted 88 paid members; and the Catholics had 220 participating in Sunday Mass (not overwhelming in a population of nearly 2,000). The student assistant in the chaplaincy office put a brave face on it in reporting a very small turnout for the Wednesday night service: "the closeness of the final circle of worshipers shows the intenseness of the fellowship."[96] The man who was met with this ambivalent welcome as he arrived to fill the chaplaincy was Gary R. Miller. He arrived in the summer of 1973, and he survives to the present day.

Bergethon retired after twenty years and took satisfaction from changes in the church-college relationship which he had managed at Lafayette and influenced among the Presbyterian colleges nationally. It had been good for both parties, he said. The church had quit trying to control the colleges, and to require sectarian conformity. On their side, the colleges had grown in appreciation of that remarkable if opaque concept "human values," and its equally mysterious affiliate "the Judaeo-Christian heritage." The college was at last, and at least, and at most, free.

> In the realm of the church as in the colleges dogmatic rigidity and denominational self-service have for large numbers of people become suspect and self-defeating in religious outreach. When the church-college relationship began it was possible — even proper — for the church, crudely speaking, to use the colleges to reproduce its kind. When the church defined its educational mission in the nineteen-fifties and -sixties, the emphasis had to be more on serving the nation and its people than on perpetuating the Presbyterian way.[97]

This Henry Pritchett could have written. But it is difficult to take at face value. Dr. Bergethon's abiding concern regarding the church relationship as expressed throughout his presidency was the possibility that it might disqualify Lafayette for tax-supported grants. The church had indeed for more than a century referred to its "control" over the college, but not once between 1854 and 1967 did it exercise that power, its right to veto an appointment. It agreed to forfeit its legal prerogatives, step-by-step, whenever it was asked. The charter was a leash that was never yanked. The church attached to large capital endowments tightly written deeds of gift that would bind the college to certain religious elements in its program, and then without any motivation except that it was made to feel like an intruder, the church reduced those stipulations to a minimal few. When those last few were ignored, the church was silent. There had been grand talk of the colleges as an evangelical force in the intellectual life of the country and in the maturing life of the students, but the church over the years had always been daintily deferential to the autonomy of the educators. Apart from an occasional grumbling letter sent by way of complaint from some parent or pastor to the synod and passed on, the mailbag brought little from the church except money and soft talk.

Much Ado about Nothing in the Church

When David W. Ellis, a chemist and vice provost from the University of New Hampshire, came in 1978 to replace Bergethon, he specified nine educational objectives for his incumbency, and religion did not rank among them.[98]

Lest anyone see the college as having stiff-armed the church, let us scan yet another of the waves of major Presbyterian reports sent rolling in to dash itself on the rocks of the educational shoreline: *The Church's Mission in Higher Education* (known as the Peel Report, adopted 1981). It expressed dismay at a pattern of changes on the campuses, and each one of them was true of Lafayette:

1. an effort to retain liberal arts programs, but increasing pressures to provide vocationally oriented ones;
2. a greater dependency on state and federal funding, but a decreasing reliance on church support;
3. the retention of departments and/or offerings in the Judaeo-Christian religious tradition, but the diminution of required study in such subjects;
4. the maintenance of at least a part-time chaplain on the campuses, but the virtual elimination of all compulsory participation in community worship;
5. the decrease of assumption by the schools of an *in loco parentis* role, but the increase of supportive student services;
6. trends toward homogenization in programs and community life, as inflation/fiscal restraints may temper innovation and secular values of academe may replace theological values of the church-related institution;
7. an increase in attention to the needs and educational rights of minorities, but difficulties in attracting and retaining desired numbers;
8. a desire to provide education for all who qualify, but a drift toward economic elitism precipitated by spiraling tuition costs;
9. a desire to identify with a particular ecclesiastical past, but the need — in admissions — to appear as cosmopolitan as possible.

Across the Presbyterian-related campuses, 15 percent of all students declaring religious affiliations identified themselves as Presbyterians. This might make Lafayette's report of 12 percent look low, but had the two surveys calculated their base similarly the percentage of Presbyterians in the network would have been much lower than at Lafayette.[99] Since the 1961 policy statement, *The Church and Higher Education,* had loosened the earlier demand that all faculty be professing Christians, only 5 percent of the Presbyterian colleges still required that of all teaching staff; another 5 percent required it of the majority or said it was "a significant factor" in personnel decisions. Half the colleges reported an "expectation" that faculty would be Christian. The other colleges did not consider this a salient credential. Only seven campuses said they still had denominational worship.

The report recites at painful length the degree to which the colleges had effectively quit the church. Rather than following this with confrontation or complaint, the church then manifests once more a boundless capacity to adjust its rhetoric to avoid any sense of real loss. In the segment entitled "Affirmations," the document mentions that the colleges had little to say about what their relation-

173

ship to the church really meant. Little matter, the church would articulate it for them: "In purpose [obviously not in words, nor in deeds], they seek to insure that among all the perspectives contained in human thought, the Christian perspective will certainly have expression; that among all the values aired, Christian values will have advocacy, not preemptive, but effective and without apology."[100]

On the Lafayette campus this last issue had in recent years found various expressions when the Department of Religion needed defense against the charge of sectarianism. Intellectual integrity required that the religion taught on campus was "rigorously academic," which generally meant "educational, not evangelical." Bible courses were to be free of theology. No tenets of the church were to be expounded or taught. The department forbade "encroachment" by any outside religious bodies, and kept even the chaplain from "intruding." In a word, the academic teaching of religion was to be free of attempts at proselytization. Instruction there was to be exactly like it was in the other departments. No one saw any absurdity in that claim. Was no professor of English ever heard to expound why he thought the Metaphysical Poets were to be preferred over the Beat Poets? If literary critics could do that, why could critical thought in religion not do similarly? Surely there were instructors in civil engineering who offered arguments about the best modes of wastewater reclamation. Why were moral theologians then out of order if they saw certain courses of action as more ethically appropriate? Surely it was no more out of place for a theologian to display the merits of Presbyterian polity than for a political scientist to prefer the advantages of representative democracy. The Department of Philosophy harbored a strong tradition sympathetic to pragmatism. Why was that not as controversial as if someone across the corridor was beholden to Calvinism? Was a proselyte for expressionism or the theory of relativity or the new mathematics allowable? Surely they were gathered in every day, and if so, then why not proselytes for original sin? It is remarkable that the religion faculty were so anxious to swear such fierce oaths that they would never lead their students' minds through inference and intuition and analogy and simile to judgments of truth or falsity on the matter of their discipline. It was never made clear why the religion faculty were the only academics barred from examining and expounding the cogency of what they studied.

Yet the religion faculty seem not to have been activists on behalf of their own discipline. When Dr. Bergethon wrote in 1970 to inform the Board of Christian Education that Lafayette was going to ignore the "Amended Agreement" just made in 1967, by removing religion as a subject represented in the core curriculum every student would study, he mentioned specifically the conviction of the faculty "and with it the Religion Department in particular," that no special place should be made for religion in the intellectual horizon.[101]

We have been noting a miscellany of instances where the relationship with the church has been actively minimized in the 1960s and 1970s. There exists a remarkable contemporary document which attempted to decipher what it all meant, while it was happening. The observer was Peter Sabey, the very updated chaplain who tied Lafayette to the fast-moving social agenda of the sixties. The memorandum was written near the end of his tumultuous tenure. It displays a remarkable perspective:

The Relationship of Lafayette College to the United Presbyterian Church in the U.S.A.

Piecemeal dismantling of the traditional church-relationship of Lafayette may be detected in the abandonment of religious quotas in admissions policy and religious criteria in faculty selection; in the absence of Presbyterian clergy on the Board of Trustees; in the rigorous academic approach in the Religion Department with its stance of complete separation from the chaplaincy; in the abandonment of compulsory Chapel attendance beginning with the second semester of the 1964-5 academic year; in the refusal of the faculty, during the following year, to provide a meaningful time-slot in the mid-week class schedule for a voluntary chapel observance; in the removal of the requirement of two semesters of academic religion courses in the Spring of 1970; and in the discontinuation of Invocations at Faculty meetings in November of 1970. The increased freedom of social arrangements, the abandonment of the college's role *in loco parentis* might also be considered part of this picture.[102]

Sabey neglected to include the series of acts — some negotiated and others unilateral — whereby Lafayette accomplished its legal detachment from supervision by and loyalty to the church. He also may not have noticed that Lafayette had, quite late in life, begun to publish a statement of purpose. True to what had earlier been feared, no sooner was it in print than it had to be amended . . . repeatedly. These amendments were, of course, displays of what was happening, but they were in a way also among the causes. Historian Albert Gendebien has exhumed them from the catalogues.[103]

1890, under "General Information"

The aim of Lafayette College is distinctly religious. Under the general direction of the Synod of Pennsylvania of the Presbyterian Church its instruction is in full sympathy with the doctrines of that body. At the same time religious instruction is carried on with a view to a broad general development of Christian manhood within the lines of general acceptance among evangelical Christians, the points of agreement, rather than disagreement, being dwelt upon.

Between the World Wars, under "General Information"

Lafayette College aims to be distinctly Christian and is related to the Presbyterian Church not only historically and legally but by hearty accord in spirit and purpose. Religious instruction is carried on with a view to the development of Christian manhood and leadership in Christian service, not in any sectarian sense, but in full accord with essential truth as accepted by all evangelical Christians . . .

1950s, under "General Information"

Lafayette College is a private, church-related college, organically connected with the Presbyterian Church. The religious program on the campus is based on the belief that each student should enjoy complete freedom as he pursues religious truths and seeks a responsible religious expression.

1985, "Mission Statement" (Approved 28 May 1983)

Lafayette College seeks to promote the continued intellectual, imaginative, emotional, and spiritual growth of its students and faculty. The College sustains a concern with human meaning and values, a concern animated by its traditional — though now attenuated — ties with the Presbyterian Church. The College encourages recognition and respect for a wide variety of interests and opinions, and it draws strength from the diverse talents and backgrounds of its students and faculty. It asks them to work together to make Lafayette, from residences and playing fields to libraries and classrooms, an environment conducive to inquiry and discovery.

1989, within Introductory Statement

Since the 1840's Lafayette has had a lasting, though evolving, relationship with the Presbyterian Church, but its religious programs embrace all faiths.

1993, in a "Profile"

In 1854, the College formed a mutually supportive association with the Presbyterian Church . . . Today, Lafayette is an independent, coeducational, residential, undergraduate institution with a faculty of distinction . . .

Only Presbyterian Memories

President Bergethon has been followed by three successors. There is little to consider since his retirement in 1978 that would imply a vital relationship with the Presbyterian Church (U.S.A.). The Lafayette College Church membership dwindled to the point where they were too few to form a workable congregation. Thereafter they would simply meet and go together to worship at the College Hill Presbyterian Church. In April 1987, forty years after this unusual church was gathered, it was formally disbanded. The event passed without mention in the student newspaper. After the handsome Colton Chapel had remained locked for some time, the Catholics asked to use it and were welcomed, provided that between services they left it looking like a Presbyterian church. The notice board outside now announces the times of Sunday and weekday masses and confessions for the Catholics, and a weekly evening meeting of the Christian Fellowship, an evangelical group inclined somewhat toward fundamentalism, which in earlier years drew away part of the membership of the College Church, hastening its end.

The volunteer service activities of the sixties mostly died out in the seventies. A young Catholic chaplain organized an even larger outreach program in the later eighties, and a large proportion of the student body now works in myriad activities: AIDS education; environmental awareness; Caribbean and Kentucky work visits; a women's shelter; tutoring for prisoners, disadvantaged youth, and illiterate adults; hospital visiting; adopt-a-grandparent; single-parent respite; Big Brothers/Big Sisters; etc. The departure of the priest left the outreach in need of management. The Presbyterian Church (U.S.A.) could provide only $2,000 a year for this, but the American Council to Improve Our Neighborhoods provided a $47,000 three-year grant, and the service work is now orchestrated under the auspices of the federal government. The chaplain devotes about half of his time to working in it.

The chaplain also decided to refound the Brainerd Society for students interested in a program of piety, Bible study, and worship such as Protestant chaplaincies traditionally provide. But it fizzled out when attendance shrank to one or two persons. There is a Fellowship of Christian Athletes on campus, and a Muslim Students Association. Brown-bag luncheons continue, however, devoted to topics such as eating disorders, ethical issues in the Clinton health care proposal, and black women's concerns. The chaplaincy sponsors an annual musical (*Once upon a Mattress* this year), and Rev. Al Sharpton will speak in the chapel during Black History Month.

Catholics and Jews form the two largest cohorts in the student body. The chairman of the board and the president of the college are both Jews. The previous president proposed unilaterally to remove all references to the Presbyterian relationship from the catalogue but was strongly dissuaded.[104]

The college continues to respond to annual interrogatories by the synod. It has been decades since the synod asked whether there were any Presbyterians among the faculty or students, but it has been checking whether there were enough minorities, and enough disabled, and if the colleges had ROTC programs. The national office of the church has discontinued regular subsidies. The synod (now known as the Synod of the Trinity) presently contributes about $40,000 a year to Lafayette.[105] And this is perhaps the only residual reality which might make sense of the recognition today of the college as related to the Presbyterian Church (U.S.A.). Lafayette is related to the church by accepting its persistent and modest annual donations, but in no other discernible way.

Lafayette College's withdrawal from effective collaboration with the church is not untypical of what has befallen other colleges begotten of the Northern Presbyterians. A retrospective view of the college's story may help to focus our understanding of what did happen, and why.

There are two conventional stories of what happened. The sentimental story is that the college was faltering in its early struggles and turned to the synod for financial support. As the college matured, the understandable role of the synod in her governance became increasingly inappropriate, and by mutual consent that awkward tie was loosed. Today the synod and, to a lesser degree, the church

177

continue within their straitened means to sponsor Lafayette as a plucky, value-conscious liberal arts college sympathetic to the humane concerns of the PC(USA). The more tough-minded account is different. Poor administration obliged the trustees to put the college in the synod's control, and while that may have staved off catastrophe in the early years, the synod never had the competence or the nerve to do anything with its authority except to obstruct or to whine from time to time. The trustees finally reclaimed their independence, and the college has been on an upward vector ever since.

The actuality seems more ambivalent. The church-college union was enacted to obtain desperately needed money for Lafayette and an institutional resource for the synod. But in its most desperate years the college received virtually no support, and in the years when the investment might have matured for the synod and provided a confessional college, the churchmen did virtually nothing to claim it. After the first, rough purge of the board of trustees the synod never again bore down on the college. Its role as patsy might make sense in a traditionally anti-educational denomination, but that stereotype is faulty in all directions. The Baptists and Methodists were often more discriminating patrons, and the Presbyterians seem to have been as naive as a debutante at the blackjack table. Apart from seasonal (and seasonable) grumbling about minor academic and recreational misadventures on the campus, which usually took the form of letters not unlike those written by aggrieved parents of freshmen, the synodical officials never were a threat to the educators.

Yet we know that on several occasions the antipathy toward the synod's disused reserve powers provoked the trustees to prepare for secession, only to bide their time when significant financial grants and endowments began to be settled on the college. It took years of waiting, but the money did begin to flow, and the continued apportionment even now is not negligible. The church has been neither savior nor predator. And, in the recent times when the college did break off all other meaningful church roles except that of benefice holder, it was the church that laid down a smoke cover of apologetic rhetoric turgid enough to muddle public understanding of what was taking place.

Two Who Saw What Was Happening

The Lafayette story resembles others in that the cause of Presbyterian solidarity was close to the hearts of several presidents who were eventually repudiated by the college: Warfield and Hutchison. Both men were maladroit in the ways they carried authority; both aggravated the powerful patrons of the college; both earned the contempt of the college historian;[106] both were obliged to resign. Yet in the very Mecklin controversy which brought him down, Warfield was the only one who sensed the implacable hostility this very gifted and popular professor harbored, not just for the Old School Calvinist orthodoxy that had blighted his young years as a preacher, but for Christian faith itself. Mecklin had no religious grievance; he had become indifferent to it all. Despite Warfield's intellectual inferiority and political insensitivity, he somehow sensed that Mecklin could not be other than a subversionary colleague. Hutchison, in his time, was a temporizer: he quietly maintained the quotas that restrained Catholic and Jewish admissions, yet he worked to make Protestant worship voluntary (through the College Church), to allow Catholics to worship on campus (in the face of strong frowns from his board), and to make Jews feel more comfortable there. Hutchison was not perceptive enough to see that he was engaged in a losing struggle, but, like Warfield, he earnestly yet ineffectively was committed to the twofold goal of the college: that it be a community of both learning and faith. In fact, it was Mecklin who well described the tragic effort in which both of those discredited presidents were joined:

> The college was posing as an educational *Janus bifrons,* facing towards the early non-sectarian ideal of old Judge Porter on the one hand and towards the orthodox high Calvinism of Princeton Seminary on the other. The question at once arises, why was it necessary for the college to do this and lay itself open to a most serious charge of insincerity? The answer is found in the statistics given by the Synod's visiting committee as a result of a religious census of the student body. Over half of them were not of the Presbyterian persuasion. This non-Presbyterian majority included such sects as Methodists, Baptists, Friends, Moravians, Schwenkfeldters, Jews and Catholics. Our two-faced Janus said to the heretics, "We offer you a liberal and up-to-date education." To the minority of orthodox Presbyterians and so-called evangelicals this educational Janus said, "Behold, I give your boys a safe and sound Christian education." This may have been fine salesman's talk when seeking students. But the price paid was either a tragic lack of sincerity or an educational philosophy that was amusing in its naïveté.[107]

Mecklin saw what those who governed Lafayette did not choose to see: that you could not have a Presbyterian college without Presbyterians. For the longest time they had discounted the intrinsic conflict between Article VIII of the charter and the expectation of the Presbyterian synod, board, major donors, and parents that this would be a campus where they would find a home, not a hostel.

The man who would resolve this equivocation had no gene of Janus in him: Roald Bergethon. He arrived already determined to settle some of Lafayette's long-unresolved and conflicted compromises. In his first days on campus he let it be known that discrimination in the fraternities was doomed. Their exclusionary provisions had been framed to exclude or minimize Jews and Catholics. Now that blacks were beginning to arrive in significant numbers, they too had to be excluded, even if by simple blackballing. The fraternities, national and local, did not all respond readily, and to secure his end required much pushing and much patience, which only reinforced Bergethon's conviction that a great principle was at stake, one that touched on the integrity of the college.

The fraternities had given discrimination an odious face. It was inevitable that in these same months Bergethon would also regard the discriminatory limit on Catholic and Jewish admissions as similarly odious. Since the quotas had not been public his decision was not public, and therefore could be more discreet and unopposed. Even within the confidentiality of the trustees he spoke of it in professional, not moral, terms: the quotas had turned away from the college some applicants who were academically more qualified than some who were admitted.

The principle Bergethon obeyed, however, was not an academic one. Likewise its result. When Catholics and Jews flooded onto the campus and dominated the student population, only an inclination to fantasy could allow anyone to imagine (though for a long while many did imagine) that the college could be efficaciously related to the Presbyterian church. But it went further than that. Hutchison and the other temporizers had tried to honor both academic and religious values. Bergethon, whatever his conscience in the matter, effectively disvalued not only Presbyterianism, but also Christianity, as a sponsor of communities of learning. Bergethon had established that Lafayette could not unashamedly (to quote the adverb often used in denominational rhetoric) esteem, recruit, and attract scholars into a Presbyterian fellowship. The fraternity issue had narrowed the acceptable grounds for academic fellowship. Sectarianism was finally dead and Article VIII was finally being honored.

The president of Lafayette was following the lights of the young civil rights movement when he forbade the fraternities to treat race or religion as commonalties for their brotherhood (sisterhood would not come to campus for another eleven years). He must have been as discomfited as were WASP civil rights activists when they found a few years later that liberated "minorities" were happy to be able to take their proper place and proportion in hitherto restricted enterprises, but did not want to spend the rest of their lives in fellowships where they were doomed never to exceed their own 20 percent or 4 percent or 53 percent. Bergethon's nondiscrimination principle was much disdained when black students insisted on black residential units. By the light of that dawn one might have suspected that the fraternities had known something about fellowship that the college had missed.

Dr. Bergethon believed that there was but one appropriate criterion for fellowship at Lafayette: academic capability. He saw no injury done to unsuccessful applicants who did not make the cut on that ground. He seems never to have imagined that Lafayette could have claimed a twofold character, and admitted applicants because they were academically capable scholars and committed Presbyterians. There had never been within living memory enough Presbyterians interested in Lafayette to support it, and there had never been any display within living memory at Lafayette of an interesting synergism between Presbyterian faith and higher learning. The irony is that Bergethon came to office in perhaps the first era of the college's history when there was enough money and enough talent to attempt such a thing. All that was lacking was the imagination.

DAVIDSON COLLEGE

The Anglican Church, by law and tenacity established in the Carolinas, made those lands less welcoming to Presbyterian immigrants, but the Scotch-Irish nevertheless gathered there in such numbers that by the later seventeenth century they dominated most of the middle counties. They had brought with them a middle-class dedication to thrift and hard work, and they quickly began to thrive. Education, here as in the middle colonies, was close to their heart, and academies accordingly were wanted in their region. The only two, at New Bern and Edenton, were far away on the coast, so it was inevitable that they would seek one for themselves. The provincial legislature accordingly chartered the Queen's Museum, near Charlotte. The Crown swiftly canceled the charter, in the knowledge that this academy, unlike those along the Episcopal shore, would not appoint teachers of the established church. The Scotch-Irish simply went ahead with their unincorporated academy. Without proper patronage from the province, however, it failed to thrive, and the sons of the local burgesses made their way north for their higher studies, a few years younger than otherwise, to the College of New Jersey (Princeton).

As soon as the Carolinas made their break from Britain, however, their bent for education came to the fore. By Presbyterian initiative the North Carolina Constitution of 1776 committed the new government to found and fund schools and universities, and when the University of North Carolina opened its doors in 1789 there were Presbyterian parsons standing in those doorways as president and professors. It would be dominated by Presbyterians until forced to close after the Civil War. In 1777 their own college, now styled Liberty Hall, was incorporated, but it was given no further patronage by the state, so it, too, failed to thrive. In 1820 a gathering of influential gentlemen from the western region — mostly Presbyterians — met to discuss the disadvantage to their children at being so far distant from Chapel Hill, and petitioned the legislature for a charter for Western College. The state university had a strong and a jealous lobby, and the petitioners were sent home with nothing but their hats in their hands.

When the move for a college surged up again in 1835, it was an undertaking of the Concord Presbytery, and thus formally Presbyterian in its sponsorship. The organizers acted with dispatch and success: within a year they had a committee and, more importantly, pledges for $35,000. As their chairman put it, "We begged the College into existence." Within the second year they had acquired a large, well-situated tract of land, contracted to build eight buildings on it, and found a president (Rev. Robert H. Morrison, their committee chairman) and a professor (Robert Sparrow, who, despite never having gone to college himself, proved an able, self-taught teacher). The first of what would soon be many other presbyteries in North and South Carolina, Georgia, and Florida signed on as cosponsors. The doors opened in 1837, and a charter was enacted in 1838. As only $15,000 of the pledges were actually collected, Davidson College remained barely solvent; the treasurer at one point held only 42¢. The Chapel Hill faction at the capitol was no more anxious to anoint a competitor than in the previous decade, and the legislators were loath to establish a denominational college (the memories of Tory establishment had not yet entirely evaporated), but a committee which could throw up that many bricks in that little time was obviously on the move, and Morrison came home with the precious charter. The college seemed blessed at just the time when most colleges faltered.[108]

A Foundation of Churchmen

The first proposal to found the college had spoken of "securing the means of Education to young men within our bounds of hopeful talents and piety, preparatory to the Gospel ministry . . . in humble reliance upon the blessing of God." The earlier failure of Western College had been blamed on disunited sponsorship, but Davidson was going to be unified by being a church initiative: six of the twenty-four trustees were ministers, and all the others were elders. President Morrison had already gathered a Presbyterian congregation on his campus, to be known as the College Church. No surprise, then, that he would report legislative opposition to the charter "on the ground of its conflict with the University, its *religious character,* its *sectarian tendency,* its dreaded power and a long tirade about *Church and State* & the liberties of the Country." The charter, however, instead of carrying a strong antidiscrimination clause as most then did, merely stipulated that the college was "to educate youth of all classes without any regard to the distinction of religious denominations." The sponsoring presbyteries were awarded full authority, including the right to elect trustees, president, and professors. The presbyteries forthwith agreed on a constitution (they did not at the time use the term "bylaws"), which required that both trustees and professors be in full communion with the Presbyterian church, and that the president serve as pastor of the college. Faculty were to subscribe publicly to the following pledge, later known as the "vows":

> I do sincerely believe the Scriptures of the Old and New Testament to be the Word of God, the only infallible rule of faith and practice.
>
> I do sincerely receive and adopt the Constitution of the Presbyterian Church in the United States of America as faithfully exhibiting the doctrines taught in the Holy Scriptures.
>
> I do sincerely approve and adopt the form of government and discipline of the Presbyterian Church in these United States and I do solemnly engage not to teach anything that is opposed to any doctrines contained in the Confession of Faith, nor to oppose any of the fundamental principles of the Presbyterian Church government while I continue as Professor or teacher in this institution.

These were the equivalent of the undertakings made by those taking office in the church. Here was a Presbyterian enterprise, through and through. The sponsors were nothing if not publicly frank about their intentions.

We receive it as a settled truth, that no literary institution can long continue to flourish, where a direct religious influence does not prevail. . . . In an institution established by a State, and which is the common property of all, no exclusive privileges can be given. . . . Religion, and religious instructions, admitted into a literary institution by courtesy, must always be tame; and, in a great measure, inoperative in its effects. It will be endured only while it is regulated by the same courtesy by which it is admitted. . . . When religion sets up a distinctive claim to attention; when it demands a separation from the fashionable customs of the world, and administers unequivocal reproof for particular faults, then, it becomes an unwelcome intruder; and, if its rights are not made an inherent part of the institution, it will be ejected. . . .

The object of the founders of this institution was not merely to build up a Presbyterian College; but, to provide an institution, where religious instruction should not be left to the contingency of chance, or be dependent on courtesy for permission to be given; but should form a constituent part of a system of education; so that its influence should be brought to bear directly upon the mind, during the whole course of study. . . .

They regarded the prevalence of a religious influence, in a literary institution, as necessary, not only for giving a greater efficiency to discipline, but also for laying the foundation for a greater elevation of character; and for preparing young men to exert more salutary influence, when they go out to take a part in the concerns of society. . . . Another and prominent object with them, was, to provide a place, where young men, looking forward to the gospel ministry, might obtain an education, under an influence, and in connexion with circumstances, adapted to their contemplated profession.[109]

Within the vicinity of Davidson, Presbyterians constituted only from 8,000 to 9,000 of a population of 270,000: perhaps enough to need such a college, but probably not enough to sustain it on their own. "If conducted on liberal principles, the Presbyterian is not the only denomination that will patronize the institution." Such a liberality would of course preclude "that the Teacher, or institution, is to become the tool of a party, or sect; or that he is to cause every individual to learn the Shibboleths of his own party, or sect; but [the college's aim] is, to inculcate, by precept and example, the broad principles of revealed religion."[110]

There is a certain slickness in this claim to an ingratiating liberality which could hold its head high above sect and party. The Presbyterians themselves at that very time were being torn asunder by an ugly schism between Old School and New School, and this just after a General Assembly where slavery had been so bitterly at issue between North and South that it could not be discussed. What the founders did assume was that the only way for a college to be Christian was for it to be the work of a specific church, and for its educators to depend on that church for the soundness and unity of their faith, which they assumed was grounded on those broad principles of revealed religion and little else.

It is helpful to realize who the clientele actually were. In one of their early reports to the board of trustees (1848-49), the faculty noted an enrollment of seventy-six and sixty-eight students, respectively, in the two semesters. Only fourteen were "professors of religion," viz., active members in a church. The scanty records which do survive suggest that students from Presbyterian families were utterly dominant throughout the nineteenth century at Davidson, but in those earlier years only one-quarter of them had yet accepted church membership for themselves.[111] In 1859, however, it would be noted with pleasure that the graduating class of thirteen were all professors of religion.[112]

The program of piety varied in several respects from the national norm. There was, of course, a chapel service on weekday mornings (when students got to their breakfast two hours after rising) and late afternoons. On the Sabbath there was worship in the late morning and a "Bible recitation" (which sounds and was very much like the usual classroom format) in midafternoon. In addition, on Wednesday evening there was a longer devotional which was optional, replaced occasionally by the sacrament of the Lord's Supper, when approximately one-fourth "of the students of College, with the Professors and their families, and the little Church here sat down together at this feast of love." All these events were sponsored by the college and presided over by the president or a deputed faculty member. On their own initiative the students held a weekly prayer meeting on Sunday evenings with a heavy turnout, and they formed a Society of Inquiry for Foreign Missions whose meetings were regularly motivated by missionaries home on furlough.[113]

In the course of 1848-49 some students had defaulted badly in their studies. Various others had been drunk, had stolen the Bible from the chapel, had taken the college bell and destroyed it, and had fired pistols at neighbors and actually wounded one of them. Twelve students had variously been sent home in the course of the year. Student opinion mostly disapproved of the more serious misdemeanors: they took up a collection to replace the Bible (later happily recovered) and conducted their own inquiry into the fate of the bell. Those who refused to give evidence were suspended from the literary societies, which were the center of comradeship and social life on campus.[114] Good conduct provided the most unarguable evidence of piety — so thought the trustees:

> The Government of the College have relied chiefly as a means of securing propriety of demeanour and industry in study on an appeal to the higher views and generous impulses which should govern those engaged in literary pursuits. The mild, yet powerful, influence of religious pursuits is held to be the best means of governing paternally and of procuring the prompt and cheerful obedience which is indispensable in the maintenance of good order.[115]

The college was at its foundation organized as a manual-labor school, and this was expected to provide financial aid to capable students of modest means. As elsewhere the scheme soon proved counterproductive: the boys despised the farm-

184

work and could exert far more imagination in their malingering than in their studies. Successive stewards were blamed for repeated financial losses, and after a few years the trustees abandoned the work-study program. Having spent their relatively generous first funding on a relatively lavish plant, they were quickly mired in annual deficits. New funds solicited for endowment were used instead for operations. There was rapid turnover in both the presidency and the faculty, and the college's reputation was fraying. So in 1851 Davidson did what so many other colleges were doing. Scholarships were offered for sale: for an investment of $100 a family could acquire a scholarship voucher good for twenty years of tuition which, even without a raise in the going rate of $30 a year, would amount to a payback worth $600. Sales were brisk, in that more than four hundred were quickly sold, an endowment income began to be realized, and the enrollment increased. But by 1854 there were 101 students on campus, only 1 of whom was paying tuition. The Civil War would deflate much of the endowment's value, and students were still appearing in the 1870s, scholarship certificates in hand, for a free education.[116] To do that the college had to expend the endowment funds it had so laboriously gathered. But Davidson's historians render the same verdict on this potentially bankrupting scheme as other historians rendered on other campuses where it was tried: it did attract a faithful clientele — indeed, a dynastic one — that would bring generations of students to campus from many families. And though it did not augment the endowment as intended, it did keep the doors open during the bleakest years of the college's history.

Wealth, Too, for Davidson

Showers of blessing fell in 1855. Maxwell Chambers, an intense and frugal merchant in the town of Salisbury, astonished the region by leaving an estate believed to be in excess of $300,000, most of which was settled upon Davidson. Limitations in the charter blocked the college from clear title to the legacy, but after much horse-trading it came into nearly $250,000 (the emergent estate finally amounting to $460,000). Instead of investing this to guarantee a secure future, the trustees decided to erect an enormous brick, all-purpose building, eventually known as Old Chambers. It was intended to impose a newer, much more affluent style on the campus architecture. Indeed, for some years Davidson would be the most affluent college south of Princeton, albeit richer in plant than in liquid assets.[117]

The years immediately before the Civil War were a time of academic innovation. Many colleges would await the postbellum years to introduce a science course; Davidson was already about that task in 1857, about the same time she created a "Belles Lettres" chair with an earlier Chambers gift. There was room in the design of this professorship for the study of literature in the English language (just when Francis Andrew March was beginning his great work at Lafayette), but that undertaking at Davidson would remain dormant for decades.

A token of Davidson's solidarity with the Civil War may be seen in the fact that its first president, Robert Morrison, had three sons-in-law who would serve as major generals for the Confederacy: Stonewall Jackson, Rufus Barringer, and D. H. Hill. Hill, a West Point graduate who had served most bravely in Mexico and then taught mathematics at Washington College (later Washington and Lee), joined the Davidson faculty in 1854 and promptly dominated the college, especially in matters disciplinary, where his hand is seen in a volley of increasingly stern faculty resolutions, and on occasion was literally to be seen on the handle of his military sword in swift enforcement of the same. When war seemed certain he took command of the Charlotte Military Institute, and took the lead in training and then commanding floods of North Carolinians who went off to battle. He would later serve Davidson as a long-tenured trustee, and be buried from the College Church in the local graveyard.[118]

Even before Hill's arrival, student initiative created a military company in 1853, and they were allowed to arm themselves and drill on campus. And, as President Lincoln later put it, the war came. The faculty minutes are remarkable in that they avoided the term "war," preferring such euphemisms as "the existing troubles," "the present remarkable crisis," "the late unpleasantness."[119] A majority of the students streamed away from campus to take their part in what the faculty called "the political excitement pervading the country," despite strong faculty advice that this was precipitate and unnecessary. "Yet they could not say to young men who felt impelled to go to the defense of their Country in obedience to the call of its constituted authorities, that they ought not to do so." The college remained open, despite a noticed "decline in their attention to their studies."[120]

A President Who Was Also Pastor

The constitution of the college provided that the president was its pastor *ex officio,* and that all the professors were to take their turn leading prayers in chapel, while those who were in the ministry would also take their turns preaching (and, though not mentioned, teaching the Bible on the Sabbath). President John Lycan Kirkpatrick (1861-66) observed to the trustees that the "chaplaincy of the college," which was thus more widely construed than its pastorship, had in time all devolved back into the care and responsibility of the president. So burdensome had that become that he lodged a formal request for clarification: Was this really the intention of the board? But, if he is to be believed, his chief concern in writing was not his own job description but the rightful responsibility of faculty for the religious character of the college. What he wrote in 1861 would prove prophetic:

> There is a tendency in all literary institutions to eliminate by degrees the religious elements if any have been incorporated in their primary schemes. I am constrained to say that I fear that such a tendency has been developed in this; not, however,

through any deliberate purpose to that end, but in consequence of the desire, and a very natural one it is, on the part of the several instructors to obtain each more time for the special studies of his department.

When declaring that actual Church membership should be a condition of the occupancy of a professorial Chair, it seems to me that the founders of the College must have intended that the instructors should be something more than teachers of the languages and sciences, merely, however able and laborious in those functions.[121]

In the aftermath of the war the college mended itself and beheld the timely regathering of its people. The brave young men had been off killing and being killed (at least 82 out of the 302 in service [out of 1,039 eligible matriculants] were known to have perished).[122] Two years after Appomattox, after noting with due dismay that the scientific equipment had been "much damaged by wanton destruction from the party of Federal soldiers" who had ravaged the district, the faculty reported an enrollment large enough (twenty-four in 1866) to allow them to reject some egregiously unprepared applicants. Better, they were almost all members of the church, and a large proportion were candidates for the gospel ministry. There was a lively interest in prayer meetings and in volunteer assistance at Sabbath school in the area and in programs "for the spiritual welfare of the Colored people," assisted by the ladies of the village.

Before the war there had been some ambivalence toward the blacks. In 1853, for example, when students were teaching Sunday school and preaching a mission for blacks nearby, a near riot was begun and two Davidson students were eventually suspended when they demanded that some country servants take their hats off to them and, when refused, knocked them off instead. The racial ambivalence did not disappear during Reconstruction. The new president, George Wilson McPhail, a Virginian whom we have already met as president at Lafayette College (1857-63), forced the resignation of the beloved professor Alexander McIver, who had voted for General Grant in 1868 and whose continued presence on the faculty would therefore, McPhail feared, keep students away from Davidson. General Hill refused to administer Communion to his brother-in-law General Barringer after the latter had become a Republican. Blood is thicker than wine, more so when spilt.

But the faculty and trustees saw an ebullient postbellum religious revival as

the highest token of Divine approbation. An omen for good that at the re-organization of the Institution, this baptism of the Spirit should be given it which we trust may continue and make Davidson College a praise and a blessing in all the land. It is also a happy indication of God's good will to our suffering country, that He intends to build the walls of our Zion in troublous times. Let us humbly prostrate ourselves at His feet, and adore Him for His exceeding goodness and grace! Let us thank God and take courage.[123]

As has been noted, the faculty had already been composed largely of laymen before the war. It was natural that as laymen used to leading prayers in their homes but deferring to ministers when the prayers were offered in church, they came to regard the campus as no longer a domestic community, and themselves as not called to lead it to God. They were quite content to be teachers of the languages and sciences, merely. The trustees had begun, in 1854, to pass down to the faculty a large measure of the control they had thitherto held over discipline, textbooks, curriculum, etc. This was the beginning of a more intense professionalism among the faculty. Though they continued to be double-dipped Presbyterians, they were laymen and were regarding their calling less and less as pastoral, and more and more as scholarly.[124]

There were forces at work that would allow the character and thus the commitments of the board to change. In 1847 a proposal was made from within the Concord Presbytery to delete the constitutional requirement that trustees be members in full communion with the Presbyterian church. The proposal failed. A special committee of the sponsoring presbyteries in 1852 repeated this suggestion, but without effect. Then in 1869 the board itself petitioned the presbyteries "to strengthen the hold of Davidson College upon the country by connecting with its government men of wisdom and influence not of our denomination."[125] Though the proposal was again declined, its recurring defeats do not imply that the college's patronage was then shifting away from its orthodox Presbyterian footings. (It may be noted that in 1864 the Old School and New School factions in the South had reunited to form the Presbyterian Church in the United States [PCUS], thus consolidating the college's clientele.)

In 1871-72, eighty-five students out of ninety-five were "professors of religion" and thirty-one were candidates for the ministry. The faculty jubilated: "It is indeed a cause of devout thanksgiving to God that He has not only guided us in the paths of peace and harmony, and given us an entire year of undisturbed success in the discipline of the college, but has been pleased to pour out His Holy Spirit so abundantly upon us that most all our students have become professing Christians, and are living exemplary lives of devotion to their Divine Master."[126]

It was a sign, not of lukewarmness, but of good Scotch-Irish Presbyterian sagacity, when at the initiative of no-nonsense General Hill the board in 1875 moved to stave off freeloaders who were going through Davidson on ministerial scholarships and then riding off into the sunset. Hill's committee observed: "Past experience has taught us that the charity of the College has not always been a blessing to the Church of Christ. Some of the Beneficiaries have not the intellectual gifts to make them useful in ministry . . . some, after receiving the full benefit of the Charity of the College, have failed to enter the Ministry. Others have shown a want of Christian character, and brought reproach upon their high and holy vocation." The gist of their proposal was that the faculty "withhold the charity whenever satisfied that the Beneficiary is mentally incompetent, is incorrigibly idle, or is immoral." A minority report counseled moderation, for the issue was complex and the Presbyterian congregations in the South could be quite sensitive.[127]

In 1876 the board did decide to change the charter to allow the alumni association to elect four of its members for staggered terms. Eighteen of the forty-eight trustees elected by the presbyteries were already alumni (and all were ruling elders in the church as well), but eventually this new and self-selecting constituency would make a large difference in the affairs of the college. This move was made earlier at Davidson than at many other colleges.[128]

In 1885 the Davidson College Presbyterian Church finally built its own building and called its own minister: the president was at last relieved as official pastor of the college community. The trustees, however, were at that moment driven by a new resolve to make Davidson more dynamically Presbyterian than ever before. A new chair of Bible and Presbyterian History was endowed, and courses in Bible — no longer as a Greek text to be construed but now as an English text to be expounded — were made for the first time a part of the academic curriculum. This soon gave the students grounds for requesting an end to the Sunday school memorization-and-recitation sessions on the Bible.

Good Order, Pure Morality, and Evangelical Religion

The regional state colleges and universities, including those of both North and South Carolina, which had been shut since the first rigors of Reconstruction, finally reopened and took back much of the clientele who had in the meantime thickened the rolls on church college campuses. Davidson elected a new president, John Bunyan Shearer (1888-1900), who received but needed no instruction to revitalize Presbyterian patronage of the college. (He came from being pastor of the Presbyterian church in the seat of the adversary: Chapel Hill.) The intention was to stress to its public not only academic scholarship but Davidson's "good order, pure morality, and evangelical religion. Thus parents and guardians will be assured of its safety as a place for the education of their sons. The State colleges will excel us in pressing their claims, based on the principles and policy of patriotism and unsectarianism. Our safety lies in pressing our claims as an Institution based on Bible religion, and whose object is to give a liberal education regulated by Scripture principle." Shearer himself was seated in a new Bible chair, and announced that the Bible was now going to be a textbook. He let it be known publicly that the divorce of "secular learning and revealed truth" in Protestant schools had resulted in "the rationalistic tendencies of scholastic studies and the materialistic tendencies of scientific pursuits." The college's aim may still have been "to inculcate, by precept and example, the broad principles of revealed religion . . . without any regard to the distinction of religious denominations," but it was much clearer than ever before that they knew their prime constituency was Presbyterian . . . and Southern. Bunyan was warning them not to follow so many other Protestant schools

189

who were "afraid of being called sectarian."[129] A few years earlier the attempt had been made to attract some large donations from New York City and its (Presbyterian) wealth, but the utter failure of that expedition confirmed that Davidson's public was regional, not national. Yet in that region it was their own church people whose loyalty they would cultivate: perhaps even more easily with Presbyterians now a dominant population. That this was not mere public relations choral work is verified by decisions to pass over several otherwise excellent professorial prospects because they were not Presbyterian communicants.[130]

Shearer is remembered as forthrightly orthodox in matters of doctrine. One young man later recalled that as an old man in retirement, Shearer strode down the aisle to listen to "Sparehawk" Jones, a preacher invited by his successor. "The aged Doctor would laughingly say that his 'understanding' was weak. . . . When church was over, Dr. Jones stepped down from the pulpit to speak to Dr. Shearer. He said, 'Dr. Shearer, how are you feeling today?' The doctor replied, 'I am feeling very well, I thank you, and I hope you are feeling better since you got all that trash off your stomach.' "[131] Walter Lingle, who would succeed to the presidency four decades later, commented on Shearer's distaste for modern thought in biblical studies. "I am not sure that he knew that Higher Criticism is a method and not a result. He did not follow the method of Mark Hopkins in asking the student: 'What do *you* think?' At any rate, I cannot remember having done much thinking."[132] Lingle acclaims Shearer as the one who has promoted more interest in Christian education than any other Presbyterian. But he also recounts the story of Shearer offering the dedicatory prayer at an orphanage:

> To the amazement of everybody he prayed for twenty-seven minutes. In those days the brethren stood for prayer, but that day they sat down, one after another, until the last one, Dr. Peyton H. Hoge, went down. As Dr. Shearer always prayed with his eyes open he must have seen what was happening, but it did not shorten the prayer. I could not understand this until several years afterward, when he explained to me that Dr. W. P. Jacobs, of the Thornwell Orphanage, who made the address on that occasion, had promulgated some heresies about orphanages that needed to be corrected.[133]

Henry Louis Smith (1901-12), explicitly nominated by Shearer himself, would be Davidson's first lay president. Since the war enrollment had remained static and the enormous Old Chambers building was always much larger than needed to house and teach less than 150 young men. After the turn of the century, however, enrollment rose: during Smith's decade it more than trebled, and by the 1920s it would double that. Old Chambers was, *mirabile dictu,* crowded. With major matching grants from the Carnegie Foundation (for a library, not for a retirement fund) and John D. Rockefeller's General Education Board, those were good and timely years for building and fund-raising. There was uneasiness among the trustees about the Rockefeller grant, though, and objections that "Mature

Presbyterians are not easily stampeded." But mature southern Presbyterians were skittish about their numerous Methodist and Baptist neighbors who were funding colleges and universities more generously than they.[134] Smith kept his lines to the church open; the Presbyterian College Board was working nationally in a newly effective way and taking an interest in the southern Presbyterian colleges in a way that transcended the continuing breach between the PCUSA (North) and PCUS (South). Davidson was pleased to point out to New York that she enjoyed the largest enrollment in the regular college department of any Presbyterian college in America, and also the largest number of students on their way to the Presbyterian ministry.[135]

Smith tended to depict the religious profile of the college much more abstractly than his predecessor. "Davidson frankly avows her belief that *Character* is more important than Education, that Sincerity, Honor, and Purity are more valuable than Knowledge." But he was capable of saying out loud what he expected:

> The ideal College Professor is, first, a Man, second, a teacher, third, a scholar. Of the ten members of the Davidson faculty, not including Instructors and Assistants, each one is a Christian gentleman in the full meaning of these much abused words. No one is ever known to smoke a cigarette, use a profane or obscene word, or "take something" every now and then when away from home or off duty. Almost everyone of them is engaged in some form of active Christian work in Sabbath school or mission chapel.[136]

Smith would leave Davidson in 1912 to accept the presidency of Washington and Lee University: a move that was not obviously upward. The motive he gave was religious: "I feel that the religious atmosphere of Davidson is now practically assured for the future, as long as we retain the present Faculty, but there is no religious atmosphere at Washington — at least nothing to compare with that at Davidson."[137] A week before his letter of resignation was reluctantly accepted, he made this same point privately. Replying to a woman who was trying to decide between acceptances of her son by both Davidson and Washington and Lee, he wrote:

> At Washington & Lee the students are left very much more alone to do as they please than at Davidson College. The supervision of the individual student is far less constant, and it is much easier for a young man to deteriorate without the knowledge of the faculty than at Davidson. It is also the case that at Washington and Lee there is no regular daily religious exercise, nor compulsory attendance on any kind of religious exercise, and the Y.M.C.A. is a small and comparatively uninfluential body. Under all the circumstances, therefor considering just what you want for your boy and what you appreciate so highly, I would unhesitatingly advise that Davidson College is the better place for him. Should he afterward

decide to study law or anything of that kind he would then be mature enough in all probability to take the course at Washington and Lee without the disadvantages that you now fear with reference to his religious life.

Of course you won't understand me as claiming that the moral and religious atmosphere of any institution is ideal, or that no student even here can drift away from church interest and church work. All I mean is that the influences tending to increase his interest are here unusually powerful, backed by an admirable course in Biblical study which is worth a great deal for any man to take and which is not duplicated so far as I know anywhere else.[138]

Here, in a letter unlikely to find public circulation, President Smith leaves behind his valedictory to Davidson. The mother's letter had obviously framed her concern in terms of religious influence, and Smith's satisfaction with the college on that score is almost entirely moral, behavioral, tutelary. Except for its reference to the Bible course, there is little suggestion that Davidson has the edge religiously because its faculty and coursework offer the mind an intellectual enlightenment sharpened by its Presbyterian linkage. This stands foursquare on the college's satisfaction expressed back in 1856: that "the mild, yet powerful, influence of religious pursuits is held to be the best means of governing paternally and of procuring the prompt and cheerful obedience which is indispensable in the maintenance of good order."

There was concerted pressure upon the trustees to return to a clerical president. On the first ballot they elected a lay professor of chemistry: William Joseph Martin (1912-29). There was nothing secularizing about their lay choice, however. Martin was a ruling elder, and two years later he would hold the highest office in the PCUS: moderator of the General Assembly. Only one Davidson president had had that honor, Kirkpatrick in 1862, and only one other layman had ever been chosen. Martin's regime lasted seventeen years, the longest Davidson had yet had. It was marked by wave after wave of successful fund drives (reaping, successively, $281,000, $99,000, and $443,000), repeated and generous matching grants from the General Education Board, handsome new buildings, and a mounting endowment. The most luxuriant benefaction came in 1924. The Duke family, whose fortune had begun in tobacco and multiplied in electric power, created a permanent endowment with assigned beneficiaries representing various institutions in the region. Duke University was assigned 32 percent of the income, as were a group of hospitals; 6 percent was directed to the construction of rural Methodist churches and another 4 percent to their maintenance. Other regional colleges were given shares, and Davidson was awarded 5 percent. For Davidson's size and needs, that was a permanent annuity assuring that its days of financial worry were over, and would not long even be remembered.[139] Davidson was now comfortable.

The Fundamentalism Conflict

Martin's administration came during a period of intellectual challenge. His own view was that the Presbyterians (like the Episcopalians), because of their inveterate respect for learning, appealed to a class of people above the masses so enthusiastically recruited by the less educated Methodists and Baptists.[140] Nevertheless the silly season of debate over evolution in the 1920s did not spare Davidson. Martin, being a serious Presbyterian and a scientist, was naturally going to find that a topic for learned interest. In the midst of it all he was in correspondence with the Baptist president up the road at Wake Forest. William Louis Poteat (whom we shall meet later in these pages as the beloved "Doctor Billy") was a biologist and sat easily to evolution. Martin took up with him the question of simian ancestors:

> The question was asked me pointblank whether we taught that man was a descendant of the ape. I called in our Professors of Biology and Geology and the reply was that they did not, so that I could say no such theory was taught in the college. You know as well as I do that it is impossible to be dogmatic from a scientific viewpoint. Personally, in spite of the large number of statements of good people to the contrary, I believe I could be a real Christian man and still believe that God used the method of evolution from the lower forms of life to develop man, but as a scientist and in so far as my knowledge goes, I think I have always believed that the facts in support of that view are so meager and uncertain and inadequate that no definite conclusion nor ground of faith in that theory can be established. Personally, I believe we have got to discover not only one missing link but a large number of them before we can establish even to the satisfaction of a scientist that there is any connection.
>
> You are right in your assumption that whatever is taught in Davidson is taught from the Christian point of view. After all, is it not on the great cardinal fundamentals of Christianity? My faith in God as supreme, in Christ as his Son and the only Savior and Himself Divine, in the Holy Spirit as of the Godhead, in the heart of man teaching us the truths of Christ and energizing our wills to accepting him as our Savior? Belief in the inerrancy of the Scriptures as the very Word of God? With our faith founded on these fundamentals I do not believe we can be afraid to venture out into any of the avenues of scientific research.[141]

It was becoming more problematic to find excellent faculty who were also active Presbyterians. In 1921 Martin found a bright astronomer, but because the man was a Methodist he could offer him no more than a temporary appointment. Likewise with a Lutheran to teach German. He was much gratified to find a Presbyterian to teach Spanish. The president of his board (the trustees still took an active part in all such appointments) wrote him: "I like his age, his Spanish, and his religion." Most tricky of all, he located, wooed, and appointed a good Presbyterian biologist "with the right stamp on him from the Christian viewpoint," only to find that he was liberal on evolution. The man was swiftly shunted into geology. Despite Martin's assiduity in seeking out an all-Presbyterian faculty, he had misgivings: "Personally, I am much more concerned that a man shall be a positive Christian and exercise Christian influence over the young men, and that he shall be orthodox in the great fundamental truths of Scripture."[142] Martin's sensibilities about the religion needed to animate Davidson were not primarily denominational: religion at the college needed to be simple, and not cause controversy.

Simplicity, of course, came in several varieties. In 1919 a faculty member had described Davidson as "finer than ever, but not good enough." He looked to a Davidson that would be a much larger institution, no longer confining its clientele to the Southern Presbyterian Church. A graduating senior wrote more sharply (as seniors do). He saw the college as "narrow" and "blindly conservative."[143]

There was a shift of sorts in clientele on the board of trustees. South Carolina now had a Presbyterian college of its own to support (Clinton, later Presbyterian College), and it was natural for Georgia to agree to withdraw its patronage southward. That left just a few faraway presbyteries in Florida, plus those in North Carolina, as sponsors of Davidson. Rather than redistribute all the vacated board seats to the North Carolina presbyteries (thereby making them practically the lone patrons, and suzerains), the board diminished church representation by doubling alumni seats to twelve. Since the alumni were mostly North Carolina Presbyterians anyway, that did not make any obvious difference in the actual complexion of the governing body. But clergy were now coming to be elected less often, by the alumni and even by the presbyteries.[144]

In 1928 the requirement that tenured professors be members of the PCUS was amended: now they might be members of any branch of the Presbyterian church, which made room for alumni who were Northern Presbyterians, Cumberlanders, or communicants in the smaller fragments of the Presbyterian world. Untenured faculty must be members of "some evangelical church," which excluded Jews, Catholics, Unitarians, and Christian Scientists. This would not put the faculty out of kilter with the student population, which that year comprised 491 Presbyterians, 62 Methodists, 21 Baptists, 17 Episcopalians, 1 Lutheran, and apparently no Catholics or Jews. Presbyterians (mostly from North Carolina) continued to constitute four-fifths of the student body throughout the 1920s.

This homogeneity was noticed by Robert Lincoln Kelly, veteran college president and executive of the Association of American Colleges, who was asked to visit Davidson as a consultant and appraise its welfare and needs. His 1926 report noticed that 90 percent of the students were of Scotch-Irish descent, and practically to a man they were church members. One of every six or seven was a ministerial candidate. They belonged "to a race of men whose distinctive passions for centuries have been religion and education. The training of these men really began centuries before they were born." As for the faculty, their appointments had seemingly depended even more on their likelihood of providing a "positively Christian influence" than on their knowledge of their disciplines. "They are elders in the church, they superintend and teach in the Sunday School, they attend and participate in the prayer meetings, they are identified with student religious activities, they lead the chapel service and in general present a group demonstration, by precept and example, of the type of Christian life and doctrine approved by the College." Since it was policy that all faculty took a hand in teaching introductory courses, that influence was all the more pervasive.

Manners and Morals

Kelly also noted that ministerial students earned higher grades, predominated in elections to Phi Beta Kappa, and had won all of the Rhodes scholarships awarded to Davidsonians.[145] If future ministers furnished a larger number of intellectual leaders on campus than any other group, the far end of the spectrum was, by general consent, held by the fraternities. "There was no evidence discovered that the fraternities make any positive contribution to the religious life of the college."

The locus of religious vitality at Davidson, in Kelly's estimation, was not academic: it was the YMCA. All students were automatically enrolled (and billed for membership) when they came to Davidson, and more than a third of the student body was present at each weekly meeting. Their pattern of work was what obtained in other Y's: volunteer social and religious service in the neighborhood, evangelistic revivals, and leadership in student recreation. But the fact that it enjoyed high prestige among the students suggests that the YMCA was a focus for sociability, while the ministerial candidates harbored the highest interest in academics . . . and the fraternity crowd served as competition for them both.[146] Fraternity men, he said, were a dead loss in both studies and religious life. The YMCA's own general secretary admitted, however, that the nonfraternity men had practically no social life on campus, and most of their program — piety, voluntarism, and recreation — was intended to enliven student life. The ambition of the Y was to be "the organization that included every group on campus."[147] The handicap in their position was that religion so easily became a surrogate for recreation.

President Martin resigned to return to teaching, and the board elected as his successor the man who had long served as its president and was then chairman of the search committee itself: Walter Lee Lingle (1929-41). He later wrote, "President Hoover and I hit upon evil times." But, as often in the past, the college had a way of reaping affluence in the very times that left other campuses stricken. Davidson managed to enlarge its endowment and enrollment during the depression, while erecting and refitting several buildings.[148]

The depression was not Lingle's first trauma: it was a battle over ROTC. Davidson had long been a willing peacetime host to military training, having instituted such a program even before the Civil War became inevitable. A cadets program was resumed afterward, in the 1870s, and the college decided to retain a Reserve Officers Training Program after World War I came to a close. All students were obliged to participate unless excused on health grounds. Just after Lingle took office the Synod of North Carolina resolved to talk Davidson out of military training. Then in 1931 the General Assembly opposed compulsory military training in all PCUS colleges. Trustee opinion was disposed to comply, at least for students whose parents made conscientious objections. Lingle himself had been opposed to compulsory military training, but for reasons one might not expect. It simply seemed to him to have little to do with the purposes of higher education. Perhaps more strenuously, he objected because the military instructors had to be exempted from the academic and religious tests required of all other faculty. When the matter came to a vote after some years of strenuous debate, and military training was made optional, one minister on the board was so exercised by the result that he declined to offer grace at the next meal.[149]

The thirties brought this good president other tiresome controversies, e.g., drinking and dancing. On both subjects official Presbyterian discipline held for temperance, not abstinence. But popular sensibilities often range on a long tether from official policies. Lingle kept to hand an enchiridion of "Deliverances" (policy statements) on dancing issued by past PCUS General Assemblies. In 1865, admitting that the "lascivious dancing" deplored in Scripture was not what generally went on "in our best society," the General Assembly declared nevertheless that dancing of any sort was the sort of worldly amusement which, though not in its nature sinful, might still tempt people to sin. The Assembly of 1877 went into the subject at greater length, admitted that some forms of dance were more "mischievous" than others, but counseled great patience toward those who were ignorantly led astray by it. By 1883 the inclination to patience had clearly evaporated, and local church authorities were reminded to deliver the church from scandal by excommunicating offenders. In 1900 they clearly admitted that in dance, as in theater and card playing, there was a difference between moral and immoral behavior, but urged members "to abstain altogether from the amusements referred to as a matter of Christian proof, example, and out of the honor of Christ."[150]

Soon after Lingle's inauguration the trustees reaffirmed the college ban on dances. The students had for years simply held them in Charlotte, and when these events began receiving coverage in the press (not the Davidson student press, which was forbidden to print even the word "dance," just as the trustees also forbore to use the word in their ban), there was usually heavy weather from the presbyteries. The combined presidents of the student body, senior class, and YMCA asked for a reconsideration. The ban was reconsidered and reaffirmed, and the faculty were told that if the students were still dancing off campus it was up to them, the faculty, to minimize sinful outcomes. No chaperones were dispatched to the scene, however, for this would have seemed too overt an acquiescence. Lingle eventually concluded that students *would* dance, and the chaperones were once more mobilized. He would retire in 1941, and by then he was saying openly that they needed a new gymnasium for dances as well as sports. Eventually the trustees would hand the matter over to the faculty just when the Second World War had peopled the campus with an

196

entirely different crowd of students. The military officers recommended dancing as a needed recreation, and the faculty responded by making it obligatory that all dances take place *on* campus.[151]

What had made those dances objectionable was not their "lasciviousness" but the drinking. Here, too, Lingle sensed that there was no way to stop the flow. If supervision would not be possible, witness would. Davidson College had long been protected by a legal prohibition in the charter itself against sale of alcoholic beverages within three miles of the campus. This restrictive perimeter was reduced in 1933 to the tiny village of Davidson itself. Even to those without automobiles, drink was now going to be accessible. Lingle wrote the faculty and staff about it. Would it now be proper for them to serve wine and beer (nothing stronger was even mentioned) in their homes? "We are members," he wrote, "of a great Christian institution representing the Church and the Kingdom of God on earth. . . . we have placed upon us the responsibility of molding the lives, characters and habits of more than six hundred young men." Citing Paul, that some things may be lawful but not expedient, he ruled that it would not be proper to serve alcohol in their homes. "This is a Christian institution, and those of us who are connected with it should constantly strive in all things to reflect the highest ideals of the Christian religion." He granted that the college had no right to regulate the personal habits of its personnel, but added softly that "it always has the right to say what kind of individuals should hold places of responsibility in the College."[152] The record does not show whether the faculty abided the call of their president to bear witness to temperance by abstinence, but by making such an appeal in 1933 he assumed that, whatever their various responses, the faculty he knew so well would be prepared to understand self-denial as Christian witness.

In these matters of moral discipline the president always acted in the knowledge that the presbyteries were maintaining an admonitory vigilance over Davidson's doings. Closer to the bone (certainly to his, if not to theirs) were controversial ventures touching on orthodoxy. It was at about this same time that anxiety was arising in regard to the college's most admired scholar and cherished teacher, Kenneth J. Foreman, Sprunt Professor of Bible and Philosophy. Foreman had opined in print that the Pentateuch was the work of multiple writers, among whom Moses may or may not have been one. The factual historicity of many of those ancient narratives was also called into question, and he openly pointed out that the primitive state of biblical scholarship during the period when some of the normative Presbyterian documents, such as the *Large Catechism,* were published could not but have compromised their authority on subjects such as this.

Since the presbyteries elected most of the trustees, they had multiple avenues of expression for their concern, and their concern now was Foreman. Lingle admired Foreman as an honest colleague and a responsible scholar, and dealt closely with him as the complaints came in during 1933. Though Foreman was prepared to be obliged to resign, he stood his ground. "I think I begin to see why our Southern presbyterian brethren in the teaching profession never write anything," he wrote to Lingle. Lingle himself described the publications as no more than "indiscreet," and the trustees in 1934 found that the professor "does not seem to be seriously out of harmony with the fundamentals of our standards." The minority who had voted on the other side went home and exacerbated opinion in the presbyteries once more, and a year later their resolutions forced another review. Due principally to Lingle's own energetic efforts (the Davidson historian calls them "frantic"), the board interrogated Foreman and sent him out with their approval and appreciation.[153] Lingle's credibility in the matter was helped by his own previous career: eleven years as a pastor, fourteen years as a seminary professor, and six as chief of the General Assembly's Training School.

These various controversies show Lingle, his trustees, and his faculty as honest, intelligent, and faithful Presbyterians, and when they did not bend with the presbyterial wind it was discretion, not laxity, that moved them. Nor were the Davidson folks merely reactive. Lingle had some grievances of his own about the support given by the church. First of all, its financial support was not what it might be.

> Sometimes I think it would be a challenge to us if we would review the history of the College and see where her material resources have come from. Our largest annual income is from The Duke Endowment. Mr. Duke was not a Presbyterian, but a Methodist. When we look at the sources of our own Endowment we will discover that several hundred thousand dollars, at least one-third of the whole amount, came from the General Education Board. The funds for that Board were provided by members [really, only one member: John D. Rockefeller] of the Baptist Church. The same Board has $100,000 invested in this handsome new building [they were dedicating "New Chambers"]. Mr. Maxwell Chambers was the largest early benefactor of the College. It is stated in the History of Davidson College that he was not a member of the Presbyterian Church, but an attendant. . . . the Presbyterian Church has not done as much for the College as we had supposed.[154]

In 1940-41 Davidson received from the church a total of $4,119.55, slightly more than 1 percent of its annual budget, while that same year it had granted $2,920.00 in grants to ministerial candidates and $9,000.00 to the sons of ministers. His financial officer was continually reminding him that subsidies were running three-to-one in the church's direction.[155] But Lingle was a faithful churchman as well as a faithful president, and he preferred to pursue these issues diplomatically. Indeed, as the United States was being drawn into another world conflict, the relationship between Presbyterian colleges and their church was braced and refreshed by the patriotism in the air. There was an optimism then about their mission and its prospects that would never again be revived. Walter Lingle was the drafter for a 1940 statement by his fellow presidents: "Our dual system of education has always been one of our chief safeguards of civil and religious liberty." Not until well after the subsidence of the GI Bill would their successors realize that the church colleges had in the meantime somehow been put on the defensive.[156]

The YMCA had about as full a program in the prewar years as can be imagined. But Lingle decided in the late 1930s that Sunday morning worship had to become voluntary, and that it should be replaced by an evening service. The YMCA already had a voluntary vesper service, which the college expropriated. Lingle was persuaded that it was no loss to the young men in the Y, since interest in it "was sagging from year to year" and had "seemed almost to peter out." But the students were dissatisfied to have the responsibility for the event taken out of their hands. Davidson never had the acerbic resistance to obligatory chapel which we have encountered in most colleges, mostly because for a much longer time than most there was a strong religious commitment by the faculty. Over the years, however, the students managed to organize more heartfelt prayer occasions than their mentors, and this appropriation of vespers by the college was the first of a series of moves to edge the YMCA out of matters more directly religious, and to relocate it more fully in the area of student morale and recreation.[157]

An Outside Study

Lingle retired just as the Second World War was drawing America into its maw. His successor, John Rood Cunningham (1941-57), was another pastor, who had presided over the church's flagship seminary in Louisville. He promptly commissioned George A. Works of the University of Chicago to prepare a study of the college, much as Robert Kelly had done fifteen years earlier. The General Assembly had asked each of its affiliated colleges to have such a self-study conducted. Works noticed the healthy increase in enrollment through the depression years, but he pointed out what others had ignored: while the student body had increased by nearly 10 percent in fifteen years, the Presbyterians among them had actually decreased in total numbers, and their share in the enrollment had shrunk from 79 to 63 percent. Works called it a "slight" decrease, but both in numbers and proportion it was more serious than noticed. It would reoccur.

Professor Works enters, perhaps unguardedly, into the by-then ancient question of the relationship between the openly religious students and the fraternity men. The former are drenched in a shower of blessings, which he exhaustively recites: four semesters of required Bible courses ("largely factual in nature"), required chapel five days a week, required Sunday vespers, the campus church (where the Sunday morning service is optional, and only about one-seventh of the students attend), the YMCA with its panoply of services for and by the students, and the influence of the faculty members, most of them Presbyterians and all of them, perforce, Christians.

The study then delicately mentions several "tendencies which tend to work against the positive Christian influences on the campus." Some students appear to be indifferent, but Works is sure they are only concealing their real Christian convictions and religious enthusiasm: they are hesitant to express themselves. Some say they are hampered in their religious development "by the element of compulsion." Complaints are almost apologetic. Those who grumble about chapel say "that while they may resent it now, after they leave the institution their viewpoint may be somewhat different." The vesper service is dull, but it does get the students back to campus in time to begin their next week's work. There was much such faint praise.

Works also prepared a survey of the entire higher education network of the PCUS, in which he made some acerbic comments about anti-intellectual attitudes which are sharper than the report on Davidson itself. What many colleges meant by courses "taught from a Christian point of view" was that they excluded evidence or arguments from any but a conservative point of view. By doing this

> the colleges are failing to prepare their students for the kinds of problems and the kinds of thinking they will encounter when they leave college. One of the great opportunities, in fact, one of the primary reasons for the existence of the church-related colleges, is that they may so reinforce the beliefs and ideals of students that they may evaluate and interpret divergent and conflicting points of view in the light of established beliefs. In this respect most of the Presbyterian colleges fall short of realizing their full possibilities.[158]

After a long miscellany of vague compliments about faculty influence, prayer meetings, and the honor system ("indicating something of a Christian atmosphere"), Works delivers a very sobering criticism:

> It is frankly admitted by some of the faculty members, and by some of the students, that in many instances the actual evidences of the Christian influence of the institution are not much different from those that might be found in a state institution or in a private institution of some other type. It must also be noted in this connection that the religious life of the campus is pretty largely a continuation of the religious influences of the homes and the communities from which these students come. They are selected in part upon the basis of their already possessing the type of character and the attitudes which the institution is itself interested in developing.

The survey then notes that the college itself provides almost no social amenities or program. The dormitories have no staff except for physical maintenance. The college provides no commons, so on-campus students must all find their board elsewhere. Recreation is largely of their own making. Thus it is clear to any reader that the student faced only two alternatives for a social life: the fraternities and the YMCA. The YMCA was no longer succeeding in its ambition to be the integrated rallying point of a wholesome campus. The administration was meanwhile expropriating its religious initiatives one by one. The good times and fellowship were becoming the specialty of the fraternities.

The religious status of the faculty came in for comment. The full professors, who alone were tenured, were still obliged to take the "vows" at their inauguration. These were no longer cast in the original syntax: "I do sincerely believe . . . receive and adopt . . . approve . . . solemnly engage. . . ." A recent revision in 1938 required the professor-elect simply to give affirmative answers to questions put to him, but it had made the issues even more prolix. These vows were not, in fact, a local artifact; they were a variant of the "ordination vows" administered within the church:

> Do you believe the Scriptures of the Old and New Testament to be the Word of God, the only infallible rule of faith and practice?
>
> Do you sincerely receive and adopt the Confession of Faith and the Catechism of the Presbyterian Church in the United States as containing the system of doctrine taught in the Holy Scriptures?
>
> Do you accept the government and discipline of the Presbyterian Church in the United States?
>
> Do you solemnly engage not to teach anything contrary to the Holy Scriptures as interpreted by the Standards of the Presbyterian Church in the United States while you are connected with this institution?
>
> Do you promise in reliance upon the grace of God to live a becoming Christian life and to be faithful to the discharge of your duties in this College?
>
> Do you promise that if at any time you find yourself out of harmony with these solemn engagements which you have just made, you will notify the Trustees of the College?

The survey staff noted that the faculty included so many Davidson graduates as to raise the issue of inbreeding. And if it was credibly a college "where Christian education but not the Presbyterian creed is emphasized," then to require membership by the full professors in the Presbyterian church was open to question, especially when it was not required of faculty in the lower ranks. Works described a college where Presbyterian faith and piety were earnestly enough cultivated among the faculty, but somehow not dynamically integrated into either the academic or the social life on campus in a way that appealed to many students. His report was coolly received.[159]

Will the Faculty Be Presbyterian?

On the issue of the religious status of faculty, President Cunningham circularized the presidents of other PCUS colleges to learn their practices, which proved to be less restrictive. Some required that faculty be members of any evangelical, or

201

Protestant, church. Mary Baldwin stated what that meant: "We would not engage a person usually who is a member of the Roman Catholic Church, a Jew, a member of the Unitarian Church, or the Christian Science Church." Centre College formally required a Presbyterian majority. Others said that they informally assured that either the department heads or a majority of the faculty were Presbyterians. No other PCUS college had anything like the Davidson "vows"; one president thought they were appropriate for Davidson with its large contingent of ministerial students, but impractical otherwise; another called them "very unwise." The president of Hampden-Sydney was the most terse in his response: "We only require that anyone teaching should be a Christian. Davidson is still rather tight in some ways. Sincerely yours . . ."[160]

In 1945 Davidson liberalized its requirement: now a professor need only be a member of an evangelical church. No individual need be Presbyterian, but three-quarters of the professorate had to be, and all those in Bible and philosophy.[161] The inaugural vows were still a source of agitation. Well remembered was the comment of Kenneth Foreman: "The outsider, discovering this affirmation, is tempted to leap to the conclusion that professors here must be either bigots or hypocrites." Now that not all professors needed to be Presbyterians, there was a clear awkwardness in requiring them all to accept the government and discipline of that church, and that particular vow was duly removed.

An anomaly still remained: the professors, Presbyterian or not, had to abide by the doctrinal standards of the Presbyterian church. Agitation by the local chapter of the AAUP kept the issue alive. Perhaps unknown to them, the president had the same misgivings. He consulted with J. McDowell Richards, a Davidson man, Rhodes scholar, seminary president, and president of the Davidson trustees. Foreman had recently said publicly that the inaugural vows made the college sectarian. Richards was of two minds:

> I have come to think of sectarianism as being characterized by the spirit or attitude in which certain convictions are held, rather than by the convictions themselves. It is my personal hope that Davidson College will always stand for certain very definite convictions, yet in a spirit of the broadest charity and in an attitude of sympathy toward those with whom we differ. . . .
>
> I doubt very much whether any college will remain Christian which is not committed to the position of some Church and governed by that Church. If this be sectarianism, then I am willing for others to make the most of it, and perfectly willing for Davidson to be a sectarian college. I think the tragic history of the way in which the churches have lost college after college in America should be a clear warning to us against watering down the position held by any institution, or weakening the ties which bind it to the Church. . . .
>
> If we had some clear and unequivocal statement of the Christian faith which would be in accord with the convictions of the universal Church I would not be averse to substituting that for the Westminster Standards in so far as this vow is

concerned. I am afraid, however, that in the attempt to write such a statement we would probably run into more difficulties than we encounter at present.

Cunningham was agonized by the problem. He replied:

> I do believe that a Christian College which attempts to be such without particular relationship and responsibility to the Church — and under our conditions in America this is tantamount to saying a denomination — is paving the way for its loss of the distinctive Christian life and spirit. While I was in the pastorate I used to weary of meeting the response of persons who were approached about coming into the Church with the thought that they were so broad and tolerant that they just didn't belong to any Church, but believed in and loved all of them. I came to know that they were not worth much to any of them.[162]

Richards and Cunningham were clearly not walking the modernist road. They were uncommonly astute in seeing the nub of the issue: that there was no universal church comprising all Christians, only particular communions. They knew how to be Presbyterians; they had no knowledge of how to be Christians and float free of church. As the trustees slowly approached their decision, there was a wide diversity of opinion. One clerical trustee said he was concerned less with ecclesiastical control than about the "essential Presbyterian character in the teaching program." He would make concessions on all else, provided that professors in Bible and philosophy made the same confessional vow as teaching and ruling elders. Another trustee, a Davidson alumnus and that year's moderator of the PCUS, said that in order not to be unduly restrictive, his minimum requirement would be that professors confess their faith in Christ as Son of God and Savior.

An academic much recruited by Davidson declined the position because of the vow, even though he was himself an active churchman. Cunningham appealed to him:

> The Christian college stands always in danger of losing its Christian content and concern. As you know, many of the strongest institutions in the country today which have no church connection now, were really the children of the Christian church in earlier days. It is very easy, as I observe it, for a Christian college to slip, here a little and there a little and then perhaps with a great donation from some secular foundation or individual, it moves from under the Church's relation completely. I would cite Vanderbilt as an illustration. The vow seems to me to have a fine value not only in the life of the individual and in the corporate life of the faculty but in the understanding and observance of the public, the church included.[163]

In 1957 (Cunningham's final year in office), except for professors of Bible and philosophy, the vows were drastically simplified. No more Westminster:

Do you acknowledge Jesus Christ as Lord and Savior and do you believe in the fundamental teachings of evangelical Christianity?

Do you believe the scriptures of the Old and New Testaments to be the Word of God, the only infallible rule of faith and practice?

Do you promise so to live and teach as to give expression to the Christian faith?[164]

Also in the 1950s, the secretary of the YMCA was being gradually transmogrified into a college chaplain, thus furthering the seemingly inexorable process whereby autonomous student activities were absorbed into college programs. Chapel days were reduced to five (1941), to four (1954), and then three (1955).[165] Graduating students were surveyed about their campus memories, and their memories of chapel were often wan:

Yes, the chapel hour has been of value, but could be improved and made more interesting. Would like to see more business men come to lecture.

Devotional services have been helpful, interesting, and inspiring talks. Welcome break from classes, get to know more members of the Faculty better, promotes school spirit. . . . The devotional periods do not inspire worship, most of them.

The daily devotions are often meaningless, I confess, but Chapel develops a strong sense of unity in the student body.

The spirit of a school or any group depends upon getting together regularly, getting to know faces and names and have some fun and enjoy good entertainment together. No other means could be had to acquaint members of the student body and classes with each other.[166]

Cunningham saw the absence of faculty as a key factor in the degeneration of chapel. In 1950 he wrote to Kenneth Foreman:

When the War was over, we failed somehow to gather up again the concerted participation in religious life of the College which I believe we had previously. The result is that the large majority of men in the faculty do not attend the religious exercises of the College either in the week time or on Sunday evenings. . . . Meanwhile, the students have become somewhat more rowdy in chapel than formerly.[167]

Faculty, however, were finding what Cunningham called "somewhat more rowdy" to be repulsive. Even a loyalist like Clarence Pietenpohl, the veteran physicist who would be called in as acting president when Cunningham resigned, called it intolerable. "I feel that it will be physically impossible," he wrote the president, "for me to conduct even the devotional program under such conditions . . . I would become physically ill."[168]

There were other signs of a cooling fervor on the campus, or perhaps of a shrinking group for whom religion was a fervent concern. Presbyterians continued to be the largest cohort among the students, followed as always by the Methodists, Baptists, and Episcopalians. But by the early fifties those other groups had all established their own fellowship operations and several had part-time chaplains. The College Church now maintained a traditional Westminster Fellowship for the Presbyterians. It, rather than the YMCA, was now considered the link with the church. For the first time the Presbyterians were functioning like one among several denominations, rather than as the host.[169] But the Westminster Fellowship, with a potential membership of 479 Presbyterian undergraduates that year, was drawing only about 30 to its Sunday gatherings.

For years the YMCA had enrolled all students automatically when the college added a membership fee to everyone's bill. In the early fifties the YMCA program was replete with new programs, especially those in service of Negroes in the vicinity: several Boy Scout troops, a recreation center, a gift fund for "underdeveloped" children. But the leadership was concerned that automatic membership was religiously inauthentic. Besides, since the college had for three decades collected their fees, the Y, although technically free of day-to-day interference, had become answerable in subtler ways to the faculty, administration, and trustees, and now they wanted their student autonomy back. Another concern was that they might be drawn into the national trend in other chapters and become a merely social do-good association. In 1954-55 membership was made voluntary, but at the same time the general secretary was put in charge of the religious program and of the chaplaincy (which was finally being officially divested by the presidency). The co-optation of the YMCA into campus ministry was inevitable from that day onward.[170]

The Synod Endorses Christian Theism

It was at this time that the Synod of North Carolina decided to examine its investment in higher education. The examination consisted of three senior colleges (Davidson, Flora McDonald, and Queens) and three junior colleges. Much of the report is a hymn to the need for "Christian theism," to provide "spiritual values" that will combat agnosticism, materialism, and (most particularly) Communism. Looking round the country the investigators noticed that "some colleges known as 'openly and urgently' religious have difficulty in reconciling faith with critical inquiry. In their zeal for faith they sometimes confuse fervor with erudition. Often they do not follow truth to its logical conclusions. In their zeal they tie their students to traditions through authoritarian edicts" and thus encourage anti-intellectualism. On the other hand, it is equally derelict to employ professors "solely

205

on the strength of their academic attainments," as if they were to be strictly neutral on all issues.

But then the report warms to its more pragmatic concerns. Presbyterians were twice as likely as Baptists to send their children to college. But while the overwhelming majority of students in Baptist colleges were Baptists, Presbyterian colleges enrolled only 52 percent Presbyterians. "These comparisons indicate that Presbyterians believe in higher education and pursue an education in institutions of higher learning," but nearly three-fourths of them avoid their own colleges. If all Presbyterian students were enrolled in Presbyterian colleges, all the campuses would be at their minimal optimum capacity. If, as the report ominously concluded, they remained elsewhere, then the synod would be wise to withdraw much of its financial stake from the church colleges and spend it instead in chaplaincies on other campuses. It had to be clear now that Davidson's main worry about the synod was no longer doctrinal but financial. And since per capita college giving in the synod was then $2.88 annually (from about 130,000 communicants), it was a good thing that Davidson was getting on as well as it was with the Ford Foundation and the Reynolds family and the Duke Endowment.[171]

Under Cunningham's presidency Davidson College had survived handsomely and militarily during World War II, had burgeoned when the veterans returned, and devoted the fifties to serious fund-raising, building, and consolidation of the academic program. It was not much noticed that although the number of Presbyterian students increased modestly after the war, they did not keep pace with the growth of the college. When Cunningham stepped down they formed but three-fifths of the enrollment.

Before his resignation, however, John Cunningham was beginning to encounter a constituency problem without precedent. The YMCA leadership had been urging the admission of black students since 1951-52. After intense debate Davidson agreed to admit two young men sent by the missions in the Congo in 1963, and two American blacks the following year. Even in its end stages it was a slow deliberation. What draws our attention, however, is the framework in which it was debated. The possibility was mooted already in the midfifties, and the president began to endure a vehement stream of opinion from alumni. The following are examples.

From an attorney in 1954:

I notice by the press that our General Assembly has declared the practice of segregation a sin. . . .

The Christian procedure in this matter has already been decided for me. The source of Christianity and the source of the difference in the races is one and the same, to wit: God. "What God has joined let no man set asunder" is the foundation of our home. "What God has set asunder let no man join together" is just as true. . . .

In this blind movement I see no help for the negro race but only destruction

206

of his and my race alike, by an integration of the two and the loss of the identity
of both. If God had intended this, why has he in his wisdom allowed the races
to remain separate and apart down through the ages? He in his wisdom has
continued the difference as one of his divine laws of nature. If we break his law
we are doomed. . . .

I still do not desire my sons to go to a negro school and one having a mixed
student body cannot be designated as white.

From an insurance executive in 1955:

I was greatly surprised and disappointed that you feel as you do about the
amalgamation of the white and Negro races. To be sure, however, you are entitled
to your opinion and I have only commendation for your frankness in expressing
it. My views are diametrically opposite from yours, and I will fight to the death,
and pledge myself and my every faculty and every resource in their behalf. Nor
am I alone, for the great masses of humanity, who are down on the level of the
problem day by day, are resentful over efforts to deliver them and their children
into race mongrelization. . . .

A former member of the Communist Party testified under oath that a part of
the Communist approach was through the Negro race, trying to foment discord
between the two races. . . .

Ministers and churches are losing the respect of their members. . . . You . . .
gave me the opinions expressed by the group which attended the World Council
of Churches that there is no theological or Biblical support for the separation of
races. I assure you I have no respect whatever for that evil organization . . . it is
openly working for the integration of the races, the abolition of capitalism and
the system of free enterprise. . . .

Cunningham was not an open advocate of integration at Davidson. He repeatedly used subsidiary arguments to defend the eventual possibility that it might
occur. To the attorney quoted above he wrote that it would be a decision made by
the presbyteries which would guide the trustees. To a man who refused to send his
son to a racially mixed campus he replied that he would send his own son. To a
constituent angry that some blacks might be included in a large international
seminar on campus, he argued that tens of millions of people around the world
were of dark skin, and such conferences were intended to save the world from a
war with Communism that might extinguish all life on the planet. In any case, he
reassured the man, the visitors would live in quarters entirely separated from the
summer school students, with their own kitchen and dining facilities, and they
would do their own cleaning. The correspondence does not manifest a president
arguing as a Presbyterian minister-educator, to Presbyterians, about a gospel-based
solidarity with potential students who would include in their numbers a good
proportion of Presbyterians. Also, despite having argued in this direction whenever

207

challenged, he never made a move during his administration to integrate the college. He said openly that this would have to be a gradual matter, and that the time was not yet ripe. The segregationist insurance executive challenged his gradualism. "If it is a sin, shouldn't one who believes it is such do all he can to correct it? And wouldn't that include immediate and vigorous action to remedy the wrong which has been done for all these years, which was done by our fathers?"[172]

John Cunningham resigned in the middle of the academic year to direct the Presbyterian Foundation in nearby Charlotte. After two consecutive theologian presidents Davidson turned to its financial officer, David Grier Martin (1958-68). His presidency would be a time of the most unremitting controversy and significant changes in the college's religious texture.

Abolish Chapel or Abolish Prayer?

His college chaplain warned Martin at the start that student behavior at daily chapel had become an embarrassment. Their gross conduct seemed now to be worse than at any known campus with obligatory religious exercises. The chaplain's recommendation was to make two of the gatherings secular in nature (a convocation and a student body meeting) and three devotional; to require attendance twice a week; and to have the college authorities insist on courtesy and consideration.[173] The response took two years. The dean of students issued a no-nonsense directive to the student body, with a copy to their parents, notifying them that the trustees had just reaffirmed their conviction that obligatory religious exercises were a vital part of the life of Davidson, and that radical improvement in student behavior was expected. He concluded with a promise of appropriate disciplinary procedures, "up to and including required withdrawal from the College." A statement from the executive committee of the faculty was attached, and it, too, had doom writ across it. The college, it stated, had no requirement whatever concerning students' religious beliefs, but their attendance was nevertheless required at the Sunday vesper service and at three of the five weekly services. Just as in the required Bible courses, their acceptance or rejection of what was presented to them was immaterial to their academic progress. What was required was their presence, and comportment which would allow those who were interested to participate. The statement undoubtedly captured their attention with this sentence: "It is our judgment that any student who has strong conscientious objections or intellectual objections, or both, to required attendance at religious services should exercise his freedom of choice by choosing to attend a college which does not have such requirements as a clearly stated part of its program."

The college chapel policy, however, proved to have a marshmallow center. In reviewing the advantages of participation in these "religious" events, the faculty statement did not dwell on the need for or meaning of communal worship. It spoke instead of contact with important personalities . . . distinguished visitors . . . the president's only opportunity to speak to the students . . . a feeling of unity . . . an opportunity for student body business. Instead of "chapel," it spoke of "assemblies." Any careful reader could see just how little was at stake religiously in these religious services.[174] And, the students quickly found, most of what took place in chapel thenceforward could as easily have transpired in the gym. There were five meetings weekly: three were required (a student body meeting on Monday, an assembly on Tuesday, and chapel on Thursday) and two were optional (chapels on Wednesday and Friday). Student conduct the first year was reported to have improved.[175]

When the issue next raised its aggravated head, it would be clergy, not students, who were concerned. Five years later, at a discussion group for local clergy, the wisdom of required religious activity came up. Students' rights of conscience seemed to be abused when they were obliged to act against their theological convictions, or lack thereof. The college was claiming that students were obliged to do no more than listen; the clergy were now saying that compulsory listening somehow constituted coercion — if only in matters theological.[176]

Harold Viehman, higher education executive for the Northern Presbyterians (with whom the Southerners would not reunite until 1983), was invited to give an address to the faculty on "The Place of Worship in the Program of the Christian College." Both Puritanism and Pietism, their spiritual forebears, had "held that the Holy Spirit was stultified and held in chains by systematic forms of worship — and sanctioned undirected worship — with the exaltation of free prayer and almost complete license in the ordering of the parts of the service of worship." Viehman's church, the UPCUSA, had moved away from that tradition when it recently issued a new order of worship. It was now considered a communal response to the gospel, not a surge of emotion. Whenever Christians gather to worship, he said, they do so "as a portion of the church of Jesus Christ."

Viehman expressed grave doubts about using the adjective "Christian" about any cultural institution except the confessional church. Colleges thus are not in themselves Christian, but may be related to a church by common purpose and covenant. A college as such could not worship, because it was not a church. Indeed, Viehman believed no college any longer required church membership as a condition of admission or appointment. Therefore: no compulsory worship, though plenty of provision for worship was appropriate.[177]

What the faculty thought of the radical from the North we cannot know, but after a two-year study the Religious Life Committee asked in 1965 that the college vesper service be no longer obligatory. Two reasons were advanced: vespers did not have the support of students, and therefore could not be an adequate expression of the corporate community's worship; and sister PCUS institutions had already eliminated required Sunday worship.[178] The Student Union hosted a debate wherein mostly religious-minded faculty faced a sizable student group who were apparently just then learning what it was to be in the sixties. The students thought there was entirely too much Christian commitment at the college, and that it was downright tiresome: "the

College's posture produced an over-homogeneous faculty; the cross-fertilization of religious exotics and nay-sayers was lacking. There were several who castigated what they called Christian moralism, as manifested by the College's opposition to drinking, gambling, and promiscuity."[179] So Students for Religious Freedom determined to "end the whitewash and hypocrisy of compulsory vespers" by turning from quiet acquiescence and grumbling to "ACTION (petitions and committees are not enough)." They decided to boycott vespers in March of 1966, apparently with the counsel of the local Episcopal rector.[180] The college chaplain admitted failure.

> Early in the year we did our music to the accompaniment of stringed instruments — banjo, guitar, etc., offering a little contemporary flavor to it. We have done a play. We have had the film from the New York World's Fair — The Parable. We have had a musical program. None of them seems to have really in any way been a good apology for Vespers, as was their intent. Our Vesper preachers have been some of the best "names" in the country. This year, for the first time, the preachers themselves have said that they were of the conviction that students were polite and sat there, but did not really hear and did not listen. . . . Vespers no longer has any enthusiastic support from the most solid members of the faculty here. They have come to the conclusion sooner than I that it was a mode of our expression of Christian commitment that one time was valid, but no longer is.[181]

The college responded by suspending vespers, revoking the obligation to attend chapel, and, of course, appointing a committee: this time the Special Committee on Religion. It met frequently throughout the fall and affirmed that religious life at Davidson, undiminished by the unpleasantness of the past spring, was "active, vigorous and vital." It recommended the creation of two permanent committees. It also suggested, in a new ecumenical mood, that the Presbyterians had taken the heat long enough, and a new, voluntary service on Sunday evenings ought to be jointly planned by the chaplain; the Episcopal, Methodist, and Presbyterian pastors; and the students from the YMCA. The service should be very brief and use experimental techniques (art, music, drama).[182] The trustees were assured at the end of the year that there was "a marked decrease in antagonism and hostility to Christian commitment," that there was faith and hope about the future, and also that added personnel were needed in the Psychology Department to provide more clinical assistance to the students.[183] Thus came to an end, in 1967, corporate worship at and by the college. The place was changing. At least, the students were changing.

A Fog Bank of Religious Discourse

The Martin administration was also a time for redefinition of the college's purpose. In 1962 Davidson discovered that it had never really crafted a formal statement of purpose. So the president wrote round to sister colleges to ask what they had by way of self-definition. The responses were wildly diverse. Wabash spoke of "education for citizenship and leadership in a free society." It also aimed "to encourage traits of character and spiritual attitudes in accord with the ideals of Western civilization," but apparently did not look to any religious — let alone Christian or Presbyterian — source, commentary, or critique for those ideals. Occidental did make mention of its "Presbyterian relationship and fellowship," which offered "respect for the Lordship of God over the individual conscience." That Lordship did not have much apparent mediation through Christianity, which was now a needle in a rhetorical haystack: "Any real awareness of facts and values must take into account our vast and rich Christian and other spiritual heritages, the religious and cultural frameworks within which man sought facts and values in the past and in which he still seeks them. We especially prize the Christian heritage, and we seek Christian values; but they, too, like all else, are subject to inquiry, analysis, reflection, and redefinition. While we believe we know what Christian values are, we cannot know fully what they may mean in our day and in the future except as they are seen in the dimensions of modern thought." In the end, the only Christian value of unarguable worth at Occidental seems to have been "Christian concern for each student." On the other end of the spectrum was the statement in the bylaws of Southwestern at Memphis (Rhodes) which said the college was "founded for the glory of God and is dedicated to the service of the Lord Jesus Christ." Christianity was to be "not only a welcome guest, but the ruling spirit within its walls." And it was "essential that the members of both the Board of Directors and of the Faculty be in manifest sympathy with the religious spirit and aim in which the college was founded." Agnes Scott College spoke in the same voice: "This confrontation of a student with Christian truth in an atmosphere where academic excellence is cherished and where intellectual interests are dominant is so integral to Agnes Scott's purposes that those who know the college can scarcely conceive of a valid reason for its existence if this should ever cease to be important." In between was a welter of various proses, such as at Florida Presbyterian (Eckerd): "We believe in the sanctity of the home and the need to preserve it as the basic unit of civilization."[184]

The production of Davidson's statement of purpose took only slightly less than two years — slow by local standards — and the final text was adopted by faculty and board without dissent. The college was late in developing such a policy statement; most institutions had been working and reworking theirs for many years. What everyone easily agreed upon in 1964 began by asserting that the "ties which bind the college to the Presbyterian Church have remained close and strong." It then went on immediately to say that Davidson's primary loyalty now reached "beyond the bonds of denomination to the Christian Community as a whole." Passing swiftly to the perennial Presbyterian doctrine of "God as the source of all truth," the statement said the college would "set no limits to the adventures of the mind." For this task the teachers would have to be "men of genuine spirituality," the curriculum would design "men of humane instincts . . . and of Christian character," and thus the college "must be a worshipping as well as a studying community, if it is to nurture the whole man and if it is to be genuinely Christian."[185] This commitment to be a worshiping community came just three years before all corporate worship at the college would be terminated. The 1964 statement is a historical marker for Davidson. Had these goals been claimed by an effectively Presbyterian community, say, twenty years earlier, they would mark a high point of sophistication. But at this point they are vague generalities by a college that wants to be better than Presbyterian, and is beginning to slip its moorings.

What Davidson thought of itself would be worn smoother still under the weather of change. The college was compromised by several internal contradictions. This was the very last year, 1963-64, when Presbyterians would constitute a majority (51 percent) of the student body. Even if nothing more distinctively ecclesial than "genuine spirituality" was now required of the mentors on this campus, the sixties had many competing forms of spirituality ready to cast their shadows over Presbyterian faith. Further, if the college promised the freedom to look all truth in the face because it is of God, it said nothing about any Christian gift for discernment between truth and its counterfeits. There was no confidence expressed that orthodox faith could sit at table with disciplined scholarship as an arbiter in the marketplace of intellectual hucksterism. So the purpose, as stated, certainly did not protest o'ermuch. More was diminishing than the college's hereditary constituency.

The National Review *Exposé*

Just at this time Davidson loyalists received a jolt from Bill Buckley's *National Review*. The *Harvard Crimson* had published a survey of religious and political attitudes held by students at Harvard and Radcliffe, and the same questionnaire was then administered to undergraduates from twelve campuses: Sarah Lawrence, Williams, Reed, Davidson, Yale, Marquette, Boston, Indiana, Brandeis, South Carolina, Howard, and Stanford. Davidson students achieved some notoriety by their replies. They stood high in reporting that religion had influenced their upbringing, and that they had spent the longest years in Sunday school and even helped teach there, and that in college they did the most reading about religion. But they also reported that later they had reacted against their faith, and that their religion courses in college had done the most to provoke that change. They reported the least membership of any college in religious fellowship on campus. They were also the most negatively disposed toward Catholics, Jews, and agnostics. Half of the Davidson students believed that God had taken flesh in Jesus; a third of them said their notion of Christ was that he should be regarded as a great prophet or teacher, much as Moslems accept Mohammed. Answers from some other schools were, on the whole, less orthodox: nevertheless, this publicity cannot have gone down too well in the North Carolina presbyteries.[186]

At this same time the trustees were responding to renewed faculty restiveness about the "vows." They returned to the matter meeting after meeting and eventually, in the fall of 1964, the board was proposing to modify the questions only slightly. There would be a new question whether incoming faculty approved of the newly stated "Purpose"; they would be asked what evangelical church they belonged to; and the Scriptures would now be "the revelation of God's will, the final guide" instead of "the Word of God, the only infallible guide."[187]

There was really no new astringency in the affirmations. Nevertheless, when the issue reached a wider public through the horrified reportage of the *New York Times,* Davidson was very embarrassed. Most impressive among the letters of indignation visited upon the president and trustees were those from alumni who were professional divines. Thomas A. Langford, '51, who was teaching religion at Duke (and would one day serve there as provost), wrote:

> Surely we cannot hope to preserve a viable Christian education by insulating the minds of our young men from the alternatives which challenge them. . . . The college is strongest when it comprises a microcosm of the cultural context.[188]

This was a wish on its way to fulfillment. Dwight Moody Smith, '54, urged that it was not necessary or desirable for every faculty member to believe in "the fundamental teachings of evangelical Christianity." Catholic, Jewish, and even non-religious viewpoints were desirable within the mix. Any "loyalty oath" would betray "a fear and lack of confidence in one's own religious convictions," and make it "more difficult if not completely impossible" to recruit or train competent faculty persons.[189] Donald W. Shriver, Jr., '51, later president of Union Theological Seminary in New York, thought explicit theological standards and affirmations were counterproductive. Better, he thought, for a diligent administration to vet candidates unobtrusively. "There is a whole series of moral, social, and other personal graces which I would like to see in any faculty member brought to Davidson," and they should be verified by the personal appraisal of the dean and the president.[190]

The administration had been thoroughly spooked by these and more strident reactions. The dean's view, which he thought was shared by many faculty, now objected "to any sort of catechizing and formal ecclesiastical standards to which subscription must be made when these standards are put in other people's words."[191] The president and the dean addressed a letter to the trustees admitting that they had been wrong to support the earlier proposal, which would cost Davidson some of her best teachers and fend off many promising young scholars by requiring of them "anachronistic" vows that subscribe to "words that often carry theological connotations which are not the same to all men."[192] No one seems to have asked where, in these extraordinarily lean and generic affirmations, lay the invitations to cunning and quibbles.

The trustees yielded once more and abolished all explicit need for commitment by faculty. Instead the administrators, using whatever wit, candor, or craft they wished, were thereafter obliged to "certify" to the trustees that any candidate for permanent appointment "1) Is committed to the Christian faith and is a member of a Christian church; 2) Comprehends the Statement of Purpose of Davidson College and intends to promote this purpose." These were matters best spoken of in private. All faculty were still required to be members of a Christian church ("evangelical" was removed during the negotiations), and a majority of them all, and of those of professorial rank, had to be Presbyterians. Present faculty would have to answer in writing the questions originally meant for public presentation to those receiving tenure. The president explained to them that this was no "inquisition," but reflected the board's belief that "the relationship of all faculty members to the college should be the same." The members of the Departments of Bible and Philosophy now needed "evidence of strong Christian convictions and character"; if not ministers or officers of the Presbyterian church, they should be people who had given equivalent evidence of their "general agreement" with the Reformed (i.e., PCUS) view of Scripture. The president must, as always, be a member of the PCUS.

In a separate action the trustees expected of their own successors substantially the same slackened affirmations they had prepared earlier for the professors. The president of the board gave the customary assurance that these relaxations in their practice "in no way lessened the college's commitment to Christian purpose."[193] While these deliberations were under way a national newsletter informed educators that the Public Health Service and National Institutes of Health would henceforth require an oath of allegiance to the United States by all recipients of their fellowships and traineeships. President Martin's copy is annotated: "Shades of the VOW!"[194]

A Turning Point

The year 1965-66 was, by all signs, a turning point in Davidson's history. The dominance of Presbyterians in the student body had come to an end, and the college detached itself from the Presbyterian church in two of its most traditional roles: as a community able to define the true terms of its discipleship, and as a community in whose worship the college joined. Davidson did not renounce its belief that the authority to discern doctrine and to call to prayer was needful. The essence of the change was that these responsibilities would thereafter be exercised by the college itself as an autonomous community, and they would be done privately instead of publicly. More, naturally, would follow. Much more.

There were other, subtle signs of a cultural shift. The board had always managed its affairs in a genteel style. Retirements and deaths of central figures in the life of the college had been observed by formal resolutions, traditionally couched in the language of faith. To illustrate: in 1871 Angus Bethune Gillis had died after several painful weeks of illness. The minutes honor his passing:

> Mr. Gillis was one of the most promising members of the Freshman Class. He was a child of the Covenant, having made a public profession of his Faith in Christ more than two years before entering College. He had lived the life of the righteous, and though dying early, he has left to his friends the sweet hope that he has gone early to Glory.[195]

A 1962 graduate, son of the college physician and member of the Davidson College Church, was killed in action in Vietnam. The tenor of the board's condolence was not much different from what it had been a century earlier, save that it is the nation, not the church, with which the trustees join in giving honor:

> Young Jimmy has made the supreme sacrifice for us all. In obedience to his country's call he laid down his life for freedom, for justice, and — we trust — for the establishment and maintenance of a more lasting peace. . . .
>
> Therefore, be it resolved by the Trustees of Davidson College that:
>
> 1. We bow in submission before our Heavenly Father, in whose inscrutable wisdom this life of promise was completed so soon.
>
> 2. That we express to Dr. and Mrs. J. B. Woods, Jr., and to Mrs. J. B. Woods, III, our heartfelt sympathy for them in the loss which they have suffered.
>
> 3. That we inscribe in the Minutes of the Trustees not only our own sense of loss, but our pride in this gallant young alumnus of Davidson.
>
> 4. That we declare our determination to do all within our power to see that James Woods shall not have died in vain.[196]

By 1975, something had changed:

> WHEREAS, this Board of Trustees wishes to express its sorrow in the loss of one so dedicated to Davidson College, and also to extend its sincere sympathy to his family,
>
> NOW THEREFORE, we, the Board of Trustees of Davidson College, do hereby adopt the following statement as a memorial of his life and service.
>
> ANDREW HEATH WHITTLE, who coached Davidson College track teams for 42 years until his retirement in 1972, died suddenly on August 16, 1975, in Huntsville, Alabama, while visiting his daughter. He is survived by his wife, Daisy Southerland Whittle; two daughters, Mrs. Newton Vaughan and Mrs. Perrin Wright; one son, A. H. Whittle, Jr.; six grandchildren; and three sisters. . . .
>
> [There followed three pages of affectionate biography.]
>
> When, upon his retirement in 1972, a special night was held during Alumni Weekend to recognize and honor him, he responded with a sentence which has for us more meaning than he knew. "It has been a wonderful life," he said.

Indeed, it has been a wonderful life for all who knew him, and it was wonderful for Davidson College as well.[197]

Resolutions and notices have become more plentiful, but they are rarely more than expressions of sympathy to the survivors. As the college's sense of its own history is modified, so is its retrospect on those who have shared in it, and on what has been shared.

There was another change to come in 1967-68, when a curriculum review eliminated all required courses (except, for the time being, military science), including Bible. Like other disciplines considered basic, Bible could be chosen from among a range of options, but it was now possible to graduate without ever having studied it. Military science would be required for several more years because of the special relationship with the Department of Defense: more special, apparently, than that with the Presbyterian church.

Yet a third change, less subtle and more public, although hardly ever mentioned in public, affected the complexion of the student body. In 1964-65, as mentioned, Presbyterians first became a minority: 47 percent. They had reached their all-time maximum in numbers, 546, only three years earlier, and now were proportionately diminishing. Methodists, Baptists, and Episcopalians were still in their traditional rank order: 18 percent, 11 percent, and 10 percent, respectively. By 1970 Presbyterians had been further reduced to 36 percent. In 1995 they number 403, exactly the same as in 1934; but in a student body that has meanwhile grown they have dropped from 65 percent in 1934 to 25 percent. It would appear that they are going to decline further.[198]

There was an understandable unwillingness to notice. For instance, in 1967 the administration reminded the board that since Davidson was an academic institution, academic potential was the first consideration in the admission process. "Interested prospects and their parents are told that Davidson is a church-related college with a total program which has a Christian orientation. . . . no denominational quotas are set. The Committee has a general goal of seeing that at least fifty percent of the student body is Presbyterian. The Committee would choose a church member over a non-church member if the applicants were otherwise equal."[199] That spring the committee had just admitted a freshman class in which only 39 percent were Presbyterians.[200]

In recent years two cohorts, the Episcopalians and the Catholics, have dramatically risen in number and proportion. Since 1964-65, when Presbyterians became a minority, Episcopalians have doubled their numbers and now compose 12 percent of the student body. They passed the Methodists as the second-largest cohort in the early 1980s but since then have slightly declined. The Catholics, in that same period, have increased their numbers tenfold to pass the Methodists into third place with 11 percent, and they will soon outnumber all but the Presbyterians. Jewish students constitute only 0.6 percent of the student body.

At a college which still draws the preponderance of its students from a region where Catholics used to be thinner on the ground than in China, this suggests that rather than drawing its students merely by geography, it may also be drawing them by class. As Davidson has grown more affluent, its clientele may have made the same shift. Becoming more religiously disparate has strained its ability to maintain a dynamic relationship with the Presbyterian church. As we shall see, that trend continues.

Martin was succeeded by Samuel Reid Spencer, Jr. (1968-83), then president of Mary Baldwin College. He was no stranger to Davidson, where he had been student body president and history professor. Back in 1954, when serving as dean of students, he had written a revealing essay entitled "Why Choose a Church College?" which the PCUS Board of Higher Education published as a brochure. After clearing away two misconceptions — that a church college is for training preachers, or for serving the church — he made it clear that democracy, not Christianity, was the keynote of its program. What, the reader might then ask, makes a church college different? It offers training "not only in the intellectual disciplines, but in something beyond that, . . . certain things that lie beyond the concern of the secular institution." The certain things were not specified, but he did insist that in order to offer them "at the church college every teacher must be, at least ideally, a Christian."[201] All that one could infer about Spencer's views on church colleges was that they were an ideal.

Davidson Studies Itself

Spencer quickly appointed a study commission on church relationship. The removal of vows two years earlier was still a sore issue, and the commission's work was attended by lively speculation. A series of articles in the *Davidsonian* noted that, though the alumni elected none of their clerical members to the board, the presbyteries (who filled thirty-seven out of fifty-one seats) were choosing clergy about half of the time. How, the article implied, could the college be well governed by a board so unrepresentative? And why was the church, whose annual contribution was only $66,529.51, less than 2 percent of Davidson's income, empowered in return to elect the great majority of its trustees? Some comfort was taken from the remark of one church-elected trustee, that ministers on the board were "extremely flexible and liberal" on issues of social change and discipline. And in any case, the president regularly cued the presbyteries on likely candidates for the office.

The campus chaplain was asked to comment on the general student lack of concern for the college's Presbyterian ties. His, he said, was "a ministry of presence. I am involved where students are, and I am interested in what students are thinking and doing." Were they interested in what he was thinking and doing? "Students," he observed, "are looking for what's authentic," not dogma or denominationalism. Religion at Davidson, he said, offered three major advantages: Christian faith would be "a viable option," there would be a great deal of concern about values, and it brought some financial support. As reported, religion seemed to enjoy an importance among options and values commensurate with its contribution to the annual income: less than 2 percent.[202]

The issue of admissions came before the Commission on Church Relationship. Members met with the admissions staff and committee and reinforced their apparent conviction that religion should not play much of a part in an applicant's decision to choose Davidson. Academics should be decisive. There was clear discomfort at one report that "inside the Southeast, the church had more influence than basketball in interesting students in Davidson," and that recommendations from ministers were among the most effective. The Commission suggested revising the application form by removing the request for a letter from one's minister or church youth advisor (which might be off-putting) and replacing it with a reference from "a non-academic person who knows you well." And it recommended deleting the irrelevant request: "Include an indication of the frequency of the applicant's attendance at church services and the degree of participation."[203]

The Commission, whose concern for church relationship was focused upon minimizing it, also recommended restructuring the board of trustees. It should consist of forty-two members: twenty-four elected by twelve presbyteries; eight by the Alumni Association (to be chosen from nominee panels provided by the board); four by and from the recent graduating classes; two by but not from the faculty; and four by the board at large. This would effectively end oversight by the church.

The issue addressed by the Commission with most vehemence was that of religious qualifications for faculty, considered to be a negative factor in recruiting the best qualified scholars and teachers. Other colleges reported no such restrictions. A survey revealed that a majority of students and faculty disagreed with the policy of seeking only committed Christians. Alumni under the age of thirty also disagreed, while those over thirty supported the policy. No constituency saw any need for a majority of the faculty to be Presbyterians. Asked whether the president need be a Presbyterian and the dean a "loyal and active churchman," the alumni over thirty were once again the only ones who agreed. The Commission acknowledged the problem: How to maintain a Christian commitment without commitment by the faculty? But the only advice it had on how to address the problem was to replace formal requirements with "informal methods": delete all religious requirements for faculty and administrators; have the dean interview faculty, and the board interview presidential candidates, with the statement of purpose in hand, to ascertain informally if they are "willing, conscientiously and wholeheartedly" to work in a community with these aims. The Commission "felt" that those who emerged from this process would likely be Christians. There seems to have been no discussion of the anomaly in their proposal. The college was to maintain some explicitly Christian aims; the faculty members would all affirm that they were happy the college had such aims; yet no teacher need be expected to share them.[204]

One family has given Davidson three generations of trustees, all of them named W. Taliaferro Thompson. W. T. T., Jr., expressed in 1970 the negative reaction by many of the college's older loyalists:

> If membership in a Protestant church and the oath requirements are done away with, Davidson College as we know it will cease to be. Perhaps this is inevitable anyway, but I am confident that if such basic changes are made at the ultimate source of authority for any college, these changes are reflected in the character of the college. Davidson may well become a more outstanding educational institution, achieving the standards of the ivy league and more prestigious New England colleges. It will not be a Presbyterian college, and will not even be a Protestant church-related college.[205]

The deliberations that ensued took several years; indeed, one begins to think that taking time is the principal function of such deliberations. The Commission was not a cluster of Jacobins: its eleven members included a minister from the board, the college chaplain, and the minister of the College Church, with a professor of religion in the chair. These same clerics dominated the board's own Committee on Religious Life and Community Church Relations, and while the deliberations were still under way that committee reported on the religious state of the campus, freed as it now was from church, chapel, and Bible. The student body had unfortunately "written off the organized church as irrelevant" to their concerns. Only a small number attended services or religion classes, which was partly to be explained by their general weekend absence, and by the unreformed state of local religious expression. But despite all that, the religious welfare of Davidson was, by the unanimous testimony of the clergy, wondrously authentic. "The students were showing by their quality of life a genuine concern for the well-being of the community in works of various types." Its proper measure was "the quality of life that unfolds by reason of the relationship of a committed faculty to the student body and its community." And the committee itself made this manifest by that best of all possible reactions to ambiguity: "deep concern." The board seems not to have acknowledged that in this report they had beheld one of the purest manifestations of works righteousness since it had been anathematized by the sixteenth-century Reformers.[206]

In October 1971 the board again amended its bylaws. It was significant that they retained Article I, the statement of purpose, without any change. Davidson's manner of radical but largely unconscious transformation was to modify various elements in succession, always relying on those left untouched in each particular round of devolution to certify that the college was retaining its essential character intact and only adjusting various collaterals to the needs of changing circumstance. The statement of purpose, when written, was a self-description of a traditional community which derived its character from the church. There was no problem that it was couched in terms that were indistinct, generic, even casual, for it was descriptive, not prescriptive. That was in 1964. Now, eight years later, it was being treated as if it were a constitutional document, enacting what it took to make Davidson faithful to its original mission.

The changes in the bylaws were designed to assure change, not continuity. The process for electing the board followed the Commission's suggestions, though with moderation. The various constituencies would be free to elect whom they wished, without being restricted by panels of nominees. There was clearly going to be more diversity, though all trustees were to be "active members of a Christian Church." The inaugural interrogation, nevertheless, was much slimmed down:

1966 Version	1972 Version
a. Do you approve the purpose of Davidson College as stated by the Trustees?	a. Do you approve of the purpose of Davidson College as stated in Article I of the By-Laws?
b. Do you acknowledge Jesus Christ as Lord and Saviour and do you believe in the fundamental teachings of evangelical Christianity?	b. In accepting the office of Trustee, do you undertake to be faithful in promoting the purpose of the College and in seeking to increase its effectiveness as an institution of Christian learning?
c. Do you accept the Scriptures of the Old and New Testaments as the revelation of God's will, the final guide in matters of faith and practice?	
d. In accepting the office of trustee do you undertake to be faithful in promoting the purpose of the College and in seeking to increase its effectiveness as an institution of Christian learning?	

The president was still required to be a "loyal and active churchman, giving evidence by his life of the strength of his Christian faith and commitment." That meant he must be a member of the PCUS and also (this is new) an active participant in the life of the College Church. All tenured faculty had to be active members of some Christian church, and all faculty of whatever status must be aware of the college's purpose and "prepared conscientiously to uphold and seek to increase its effectiveness as an institution of Christian learning." But no longer did they need to be committed to the Christian faith and to teaching consistently with that faith. No longer did any specified proportion of their whole number need to be Presbyterian. The faculty members in the Religion and Philosophy Departments no longer needed to conform to the doctrine on Scripture of the Presbyterian church; they must, however, "give evidence of Christian conviction and character and be persons of vital Christian faith and unusual teaching gifts." There was no provision for any inaugural commitments by president or faculty, even one as abbreviated as what was provided for trustees.

The college had, in a short ambit of time, executed a great turn. Originally Davidson tied its identity to the Presbyterian church and required that the church serve as the guarantor of the college's fidelity. When that became outdated the college undertook to vouch for its own fidelity. With the 1972 bylaws it fairly well disengaged itself from any norm or authority for faithful discipleship — Calvinist fundamentals, church, Westminster, Scriptures, or Jesus. The president and twenty-two of the forty voting trustees had to be members of the PCUS. No one else at Davidson College, including the educators, had to be in communion with that church. The only entity binding them together was a statement of purpose, which both Clarence Darrow and H. L. Mencken could perhaps have found their way to embrace. At this very time the moderator of the General Assembly was lecturing the church on their need to learn to live with the new onset of pluralism within their fellowship.[207] Davidson had, to the extent that Presbyterian interest still lingered, inevitably confronted that same stress on unity. Yet the situation there was much aggravated, since the college no longer acknowledged any church as its home and lacked the loyalty to a common faith which enables a church to negotiate its disputes.

Religion Professors Find Christianity a Suffocating Environment

The members of the Department of Bible and Religion had exercised intrepid leadership among the faculty in dissolving these religious restrictions, and only a year after these new bylaws were published they were again militating for further change. Alexander J. McKelway, a member since 1965, was joined by four of his five departmental colleagues and the minister of the College Church, among others, in claiming there was increasing dissatisfaction on the campus and proposing to remove every requirement that faculty members need be Christian or even religious in any way. This is the argument given by McKelway:

> Many students have expressed to me the feeling that religious requirements for faculty are a direct contradiction of our public espousal of an open and unlimited search for truth. And I suspect that many more feel it than have expressed such a view. The pressures which this policy have [*sic*] put upon many individuals on the faculty are well known, and lead one to ask whether or not this requirement of religious conformity may not actually undermine the very quality of life it intends to uphold. The temptation to toss in the pinch of incense to protect one's future is a strong one. That a faculty member must satisfy administrators as to his religious convictions to secure his career cannot, in my opinion, withstand

ethical examination. Finally, the administration itself is placed in a position where an uneven application of this requirement is a constant danger. . . .

I believe, however, that the most compelling argument lies in a quite different direction. That is, it is precisely in a Christian college where one ought to find both an openness for and cordiality to instruction from a non-Christian perspective. The Christian man is not called to a life of pious isolation, but is both freed and challenged to participate in the world of men and ideas openly and fearlessly. Nor does the Church exist in the world as a fortress, protecting itself from disbelief. Rather, it opens itself to criticism, engages in free and honest dialogue with its antagonists, and joyfully embraces those who reject its creed but share its concern for men.[208]

Much Sturm und Drang ensued, but the trustees had been uprooting bylaws with singular regularity, and they outwaited the faculty. In the spring of 1973 they expressed a strong consensus that it was "vital to the Christian commitment of Davidson College to have a Christian faculty and administration."[209] It occurred to them that the point at issue was the college's professional reputation, and that concern might be minimized if the religious requirement were removed from public exposure in the bylaws and stashed away in a more discreet policy statement.[210] Joint meetings were held for a year, but the faculty eventually refused. The board pursued the matter and finally adopted a bylaw amendment that would permit what the faculty wanted but only as a supposedly "rare exception":

> In view of the fact that the Christian community has always had a place for the reverent seeker, the Trustees may in special circumstances grant tenure to a person who respects the Christian tradition without commitment to all its tenets. Within the general policy stated above, such cases will necessarily be rare. The President shall be responsible to the Trustees for being certain that each person employed as a member of the Faculty and Staff, at the time of his or her appointment, is fully aware of and supports the purpose of the college as set forth in the preamble of the Davidson College Constitution and is prepared conscientiously to uphold and seek to increase its effectiveness as a church-related college.[211]

The support given by the faculty was not one of satisfaction, but of new ground gained and further horizons eagerly in sight. The trustees were inattentive to the dynamics of "rare exceptions" in such an environment. A pertinent example is instructive. Since the demise of inaugural vows in 1966, the specifying qualification for tenured faculty had been that they be members of a Christian church. The removal of the restrictive code word "evangelical" now meant that Catholics were eligible. This was a new access to be opened only gingerly. Sometime later a faculty recruit reported to be a Catholic came under special discussion. In defense of his candidacy reassurance was given that he was no longer a Catholic and was in the process of choosing some new church in the area, that his wife was a

Presbyterian, and that the recommending department strongly wanted him. Eventually the appointment was made. Three years later the new appointees included one Presbyterian, one Catholic (this time without comment), one Baptist, one Lutheran, and one member of a community church. These were not the kind of appointments by which a Presbyterian majority is rebuilt. More than a decade later the promotions list would include three Catholics, two Presbyterians, two Episcopalians, two Methodists, one from the United Church of Christ, and one unchurched. Thus the course of rare exceptions.[212]

Also, Davidson was in a period when certain downward factors were disagreeable to the board, and tended to be ignored. In the early 1970s when this tug-of-war was under way, the board received "enthusiastic" reports that new staff at the College Church had given rise to a "significant accomplishment": a new Tuesday evening worship service of high quality. Attendance, including students, faculty, and administrators, was reported as "stabilized" (the term then being used to report downward trends) at about two hundred. The local clergy were taking their turns leading them, so although worship had for some time become balkanized into various churches and denominations, it was plausible that this service drew more than Presbyterians (then about one-third of the student body). An attendance that was then drawing about 15 percent of the students was perhaps good, but "enthusiasm" was perhaps unmerited in those down times.[213]

In October of 1974, when the exception for the "reverent seeker" was first offered as a gesture of compromise, the college released the usual self-study report required before its ten-year visitation leading to renewal of accreditation. Though meant to rouse the institution itself to self-scrutiny, such compilations are primarily directed to the evaluators as evidence of a house in good order. At Davidson the faculty seems to have shared in its preparation, and they used the document to put new pressure on the trustees. The requisite introductory essay on "history and purpose" observed rather poutingly: "It can hardly be denied that tradition has hung heavy at Davidson College, and that memories are long." They then proceeded to call for deletion of all religious requirements for either the president or faculty of any status, and regular access for non-Christians. This, of course, was intentionally provocative and was meant to solicit added leverage for their cause from the presumably sympathetic visitors from the Southern Association.[214]

The Linden Affair

Nothing much came of it. The trustees and faculty were at an impasse until they were jumped by events that at first looked as if they might move both sides beyond their respective equivocations. In 1976-77, the year following the major revision of the bylaws, a position available in political science attracted 190 applicants. The department's first choice was Ronald Linden — Ph.D., Princeton — then lecturing at Swarthmore. Linden was a Jew, and Spencer went on at some length in their

223

interview about the terms under which non-Christians could be appointed. He gave him the statement of purpose and explained that if he were offered an appointment it would be conditional on his being "prepared conscientiously to uphold and seek to increase the college's effectiveness as a church college." When the letter of appointment went out, the same point was made in writing. Linden's acceptance came after a six-week delay, with this reservation:

> With respect to the college by-laws which mandate or encourage hiring and promotion practices, I should make clear my strong opposition to such policies as morally repugnant, socially anachronistic, and scholastically unwise. During my time at Davidson, I will strongly support any movement to eliminate such laws and practices.

The lawyers who looked at his letter doubted that Linden was a reverent seeker. They told the president that the bylaws would not allow him to consider it an acceptance of the key terms of the appointment, so it was withdrawn and soon Davidson was being howled at in the academic and secular press. The *Davidsonian* itself was in full cry: "The assertion that others who hold divergent religious beliefs cannot teach virtue is absurd. Their minds are not polluted with philistinism; their bodies have not been Satanized by an alternative ethical theory. . . . From a moral point of view this is contemptible. From a legal point of view, controversial. In essence, a Jewish teacher had been offered a contract on the condition that he deny his faith and integrity."[215] The chairman of the Philosophy Department, a politically active Presbyterian, raged in print that Linden had been set up to be denied his freedom of speech: were he to speak his mind he would forgo all possibility of reappointment or tenure. "It would be better to insure the presence of Christian faith in the campus through a strong religion department, through a strong campus ministry, and through Christian behavior (the love and respect of other persons including a respect for their freedom of expression)."[216] A committee chaired by a religion professor presented a resolution to the faculty demanding an end to all religious requirements: they had only hurt recruitment, caused embarrassment, and created a misleading impression of Davidson's character.[217]

President Spencer, who had seemed to see the issue decisively with lawyers to the right and to the left, explained himself later. The college had surely acted within its rights, he insisted, but perhaps not wisely. Davidson had been founded on the conviction "that a group of persons who share a common commitment to Jesus Christ as Lord can together form an academic community distinctive in its approach to higher education." That could hardly obstruct its access to the "best" teachers, for Davidson's "best" is one "who combines to the highest degree academic competence with Christian commitment."[218] Spencer might then have gone on the offensive and said that Davidson was meant to be a community where Linden would not understand a good deal of what was being said. To the professors of religion and philosophy, who had ostensibly been chosen for their manifestly "strong Christian convictions and character" since they dealt "with matters which are particularly important in the life of the Church," Spencer might have expressed some astonishment at their presumption that a gathering of Christian intellectuals would be stifling. But Spencer had before him considerable evidence that his campus no longer mustered "a group of persons who share a common commitment to Jesus Christ" or, in any case, who could manage such a commitment in a way that made them a community capable of profitable intramural debate. Spencer kept repeating that the college was meant to be "distinctive," and was being shouted down by a faculty who were affronted by such a notion.

The trustees huddled and then issued an expression of regret for the misunderstanding that had arisen — indeed, a misunderstanding they had caused. It was now obvious to them that their "reverent seeker" exception was discriminatory, and that Davidson needed the freedom to "seek out the best qualified to further the goals of the College as defined in its Statement of Purpose." They proposed to replace the old language with this:

> The President is also authorized to recommend for appointment as officers and Faculty members non-Christian persons of genuine spirituality, who can work with respect for the Christian tradition even if they cannot conscientiously join it, and who can live in harmony with the purpose and policies of the College as set forth in the Davidson College Constitution.

Before the amendment came up for final adoption, faculty shame caused deletion of "of genuine spirituality."[219] But in a counterpoising move the board slipped in an unexpected resolution to the effect that at least "a preponderant majority of the teaching faculty and administrative staff should continue to be professing and practicing Christians. In the implementation of this policy it is appropriate to inquire as to the religious faith and practice of those who are to join the faculty or staff of the college."[220] Someone asked afterward if the new rule would exclude an atheist or a Communist. The chairman, a Presbyterian clergyman who had directed the Presbyterian Foundation, replied: "I would be astonished if a good Marxist would find this a congenial situation in which to work." He then explained that they had changed nothing but the tone of the document. "This says it positively, while the other one said it negatively."[221]

The trustees were visited at their next meeting by a student delegation, the Subcommittee on Religious Life. These students exhibited strong support for the Christian faith as the *raison d'être* of Davidson, but admitted they were a very small minority of the student body. Most students, they said, came to the college for its academic or social benefits and feared that Christian commitment might obstruct the pursuits closest to their hearts. What the subcommittee asked of the trustees was a more cogent explanation of why a Christian college offers advantages.[222] None was forthcoming.

As a quiet background to this drama on campus, the Presbyterian Church in the United States was shrinking. Representatives of higher education from all synods were called together in 1976 and told that the church's available funds in real dollars were less than a third of what they had been ten years earlier. One result: an inability to do anything more for Presbyterian colleges.[223] One effect of this penury was a newly critical concern within the church for the authenticity of their sponsored colleges. There seemed to be a pervasive sense of drift and double-talk on the campuses. The suggestion was being floated that this was due to the legal nature of their relations: Synods or presbyteries might elect trustees, but once elected they were independent and unilaterally controlled their own charters. Therefore the church should no longer leave the relationships with colleges entirely in the hands of their relational "partners." The proposal was that every collegiate relationship should be anchored by a bilateral contract, or covenant.

To the presidents this bilateralism was gall. One administrator was untypically candid:

> Writing a contract or covenant between the Synods and institutions does *not* make the institutions "church-related," and it is insufficient grounds for Synods to call the contracting colleges "our institutions." I cannot think of one case where the new contract or covenant agreements were intended to *strengthen* the relationship between the institution and the Synod, in spite of pious phrasing and frantic arm-waving to the contrary! The "progressive" colleges admit privately that they have been afraid of losing federal funds and consequently have gone to self-perpetuating Boards and "visiting teams" that come around every four years in an expensive four-day foray of public relations. On the other hand, the "conservative" institutions admit privately that they have come up with contracts or covenants so they can carry water on both shoulders; that is, they write these marvelous contracts with both the PCUS and the withdrawn Presbyterians at the same time! For anti-ecumenists this is an unprecedented flurry of ecumenical activity very akin to sleeping around![224]

There seemed to be a dispute brewing that belonged in a domestic relations court. President Spencer, though less flamboyant in expression, saw this new requirement for "eligibility" for church relationship as a severe threat to the autonomy of the colleges, which would no longer be free simply to declare themselves "church-related," receive their annual subsidies (shrinking though they be), and make of it what they would. As the proponents put it: "There are some colleges which call themselves Presbyterian, or which are Presbyterian in origin and tradition, but do not choose to be church-related." That was the kind of accusation which could be turned on Davidson. The president engaged in an energetic lobbying effort to head off the proposal at the 1982 synod, but failed.[225]

Sam Spencer announced his resignation that year (1982-83). Faculty opinions expressed were that the college should be willing to forgo academic credentials in his successor, provided he be compassionate, someone with vision, and . . . a strong churchman. "Get another Sam Spencer!" "Get a very able academician who is a minister who can raise lots of money."[226] Somehow the relationship to the church had a way of being a convertible debenture, not an intellectual resource. Taking office in 1984, and inheriting a college that by then had become more than stable financially, was John Wells Kuykendall, a Davidson alumnus who had worked in both alumni affairs and the dean of students' office before going into the ministry.

The Presbyterian element in Davidson's identity, which was such a vexed issue during Samuel Spencer's administration, has flared up less often under President Kuykendall. In the decennial self-study report for accreditation in 1985, the statement of purpose was reproduced in full, but with the admission that some were made uneasy by the theological language of the second paragraph (which mentions God). It is unlikely to have caused major heartburn. The one place it might have emerged as a matter of significance is in the tenuring procedure, but the elaborate description of that process makes not the slightest mention of religion or faith, let alone the God sojourning in paragraph two. The evaluation process does refer to Davidson as a church-related college, with the consequent expectation that its faculty will manifest "the highest ethical ideals" and "a life of service." What this amounts to is "concern for students, service to the institution, and service to the wider community." Reduced to this tame minimum, it was hardly in danger of dissuading competitive young academics from pursuing careers at Davidson.[227]

There have been a few minor mopping-up operations to cleanse the campus of earlier causes for embarrassment. For example, in 1987 the bylaws were amended to remove the Philosophy Department from the paragraph where it had once shared with the Department of Religion the need for strong Christian convictions and vital Christian faith in its faculty. The deletion, as the campus was inevitably reminded, was "in no way intended to undermine the commitment of the College to the Christian faith." Indeed, that commitment was becoming unsubvertible.[228] At the same time the trustees gave a carefully hedged assent to a new bilateral instrument affirming its relationship with the church. The vote was to accept "the spirit of the resolution . . . subject to refinement of the wording from a legal standpoint in order to guarantee the College is in control." The sentence continues, but perhaps in a misprint: "and to eliminate any ambiguity."[229] The next year the board formally adopted a brief "Philosophy of Service." "Its strong, historic tie to the Presbyterian Church causes Davidson to place service at the center of its religious identity and calling." Then, ignoring the risk of uneasiness in the godless, the college adopted a helpful working definition of love that could be understood only in a faith- (and fog-) filled community: "Davidson College is committed to the cultivation of outgoing of self into the lives of others which is love — a love that is willing to change and to grow, to share time, resources, and abilities with others, even as it recognizes the tentativeness of its own perceptions and seeks to engage the server with the served in a relationship of mutual learning and empowerment."[230]

Finally: the inevitable. The statement of purpose had been the polestar in a wheeling galaxy since first crafted and adopted in 1963-64: always reaffirmed, never amended. It had, by its very insubstantial yet classical presence allowed so much around it to be first changed, then eliminated, always with the assurance that this was neither intended nor destined to deplete the religious character of the college. In 1994 the statement itself was finally altered. The emergent text is not much more than half the length of the original. Brevity is thus one obvious goal. The other is to convert the religious references strewn across the text, which had originally all referred to the college community as bound in fellowship by the church, into centrifugal references. Let one excerpt suffice.

Old Text	New Text
Davidson recognizes God as the source of all truth. As a college committed to the historic Christian faith, it sees Jesus Christ as the central fact of history, giving purpose, order, and value to the whole life. . . . The primary loyalty of the college extends beyond the bounds of the denomination to the Christian Community as a whole, through which medium it would seek to serve the world.	Davidson commits itself to a Christian tradition that recognizes God as the source of all truth, and finds in Jesus Christ the revelation of that God, a God bound by no church or creed. The loyalty of the college thus extends beyond the Christian community to the whole human community and necessarily includes an openness to and respect for the world's various religious traditions.

The earlier Davidson, remembered even as late as 1963-64, would never have imagined God known in Jesus as bound by church or creed. And it believed that there would be a considerable difference intellectually between a primary loyalty to the Christian community and one to the world at large, which it would not have called a community. That is all clearly renounced by the later text.

To make 1994 an even fuller year, both the faculty and the students were urging yet another bylaws revision, this time to eliminate the requirement of active membership in a Christian church for board membership. Indeed, it was no small wonder how that board had continued so long in its parochial homogeneity while presiding over the college's rich, humane amalgam of students and faculty.

To give voice to these proposals, which were as anticipatable as Halley's comet, though at briefer intervals, Professor McKelway of the Religion Department made another of his public appearances to give what the Puritans used to call an "Election Day Sermon." It requires a somewhat lengthy excerpt (though this is only an excerpt) in order to appreciate that the line of discrete alterations wrought over the years had indeed formed a purposeful, rational trajectory. Those who voted on the amendments had claimed at every ballot that each one changed nothing of significance. But those whose voices clamored up from the public *Platz* for these periodic acts of relief knew and intended that their very significant purpose was precisely to change the character of the place and its people — though not in that order. The literary conceit of McKelway's explanation is to be found in the wonderful way in which it continues, tongue in cheek, to disclose how everything at Davidson is the very opposite of what it is said to be. It is a private joke, played on a surely-by-now-knowing public. McElway declaimed thus to the assembled trustees:

> I now speak more in my capacity as a theologian than as Vice Chairman pro tem of the faculty . . . Can Davidson continue to be a church-related college? . . . Can we maintain it in face of the changes we have made over the last quarter century? In the sixties we eliminated the faculty oath as well as required chapel and vespers. In the seventies we opened faculty tenure to non-Christians. In the eighties we committed ourselves to diversity of all kinds [the reader has been spared this], now in the nineties we are considering a Statement of Purpose more welcoming to other faiths.
>
> For many these developments signal an irreversible course toward divestment of our religious heritage — and they regret or applaud it in perhaps equal numbers. For others of us, however, these decisions have been made precisely in order to *maintain* a relation with the church which otherwise would already be lost.
>
> The troubled history of church-related colleges provides useful illustrations. Of the great colleges and universities with denominational origins, many maintained rather wooden and sectarian expressions of Christian commitment until the gulf between what they claimed and what they actually were and wanted to be became so great that they had to abandon their religious affiliations as mere relics of the past. Other and perhaps less distinguished schools have fiercely maintained an exclusive religious identity, and in doing so have prejudiced their ability to recruit talented students or faculty. Yet again, we have discovered that many colleges with the same history as Davidson continue to advertize themselves as in some sense church related, but in their statements of purpose make no mention of deity, much less of Christ, and thereby assure one and all that their religious heritage will cause no embarrassment or offense.
>
> Typically, Davidson has chosen a road less travelled. We will not repudiate our heritage, nor will we retreat into a narrow sectarianism. More to the point, we will not engage in what seems to me a rather contemptible desire to obscure the confessional implications of our relation to Christian faith. Against much well-meant and insistent advice we will not be embarrassed by the name of God or of his Son. At the same time, and again against the opinion of both friend and foe, we must make it clear that Christian faith implies no intellectual limitation or condemnation of other faith. That, I think, was the intention of our older Statement of Purpose, and the new one simply sharpens the point. And we *have* to sharpen the point, for we are confronted by an academic environment which

increasingly rejects the very possibility of openness in a self-consciously church-related college. . . .

But while this is a necessary condition for our survival, it is not a sufficient condition. Just as important is that our common life exhibit the influence of Jesus Christ and that we maintain a critical mass of faculty, staff and trustees committed to our heritage. . . .[231]

The McKelway "Purpose" speaks without evident embarrassment of the deity — indeed, even of God, and of Jesus Christ. The God in question, however, is clearly not the God of Abraham, Isaac, and Jacob, nor is Jesus identified as this God's only begotten Son. That is because Davidson College still admits it was established by Presbyterians and commits itself to a Christian tradition, but does not commit itself to being a Christian community, much less a Presbyterian one. This is, as Professor McKelway says, a welcoming statement of purpose yet a vacant one, since it denies that there is any host present at Davidson to welcome guests.

His guiding assumption is that no community of settled conviction, no matter how open to continuous critical inquiry, could be trusted to be open-minded. But no Christian community, and surely no Presbyterian community, could claim to hold a faith as devoid of confessional affirmation as would satisfy the McKelway vision. No Christian community could be so uncritical toward other religious claims as to have formulated no judgment whatever in their regard. In fact, McKelway himself makes some very critical judgments about the college's erstwhile sponsors, the Presbyterians. Fair enough, because critical inquiry is sterile without its natural issue, judgment. But since judgments about other religions, we are told, involve "intellectual limitation," he allows himself negative judgments only about Presbyterians. Only the religion of Davidson's own tradition is fair game for "condemnation."[232]

This was logically followed by an initiative by the religion faculty. While the proposal to remove the requirement that trustees be active members of some Christian church was still under consideration, the Student Government Association (SGA) president, Eric Rosenbach, noted that only Christians could be appointed to the religion faculty, and he denounced the requirement as discriminatory. The chairman of that department said the issue had never come up among them, but now that it had been raised by the students, well, yes, he would like to see the requirement removed. "In the process of redefinition, sometimes an institution outgrows its documents." A resolution to that effect was quickly passed by the faculty with minimal dissent.[233]

A Wrangle with Nothing at Stake

The logical and inevitable sequel to this successive renunciation of Presbyterian relationship would target the last single requirement that anyone at all on the

Davidson campus be a Presbyterian: it concerned the presidency. President Kuy-kendall took office in 1984, and in the expectation that he might retire before long, SGA president Rosenbach said in November 1994 that there was something "in-herently wrong" with the bylaw requiring that his successor be, not only a Pres-byterian, but a loyal and active one. There being now only 1.5 million confirmed Presbyterians in the country, the candidate pool was so limited as to cripple Davidson's presidential search.[234] Rosenbach assured his constituents, in any case, that the president "feels strongly that his Presbyterian title does not affect his job one way or another." Others noted that since only 0.6 percent of Presbyterians were African Americans, Davidson's ethnic options were also severely cramped. Student senators researched the issue and discovered that only about one-fourth of the student body were Presbyterians. Roughly $20,000 per year was being contributed directly by the church, though eight of the ten major donors to the college were Presbyterians.

The Ecumenical Council, a student group associated with the chaplaincy, then mounted what was the most overt resistance to any of the many initiatives to deinstitutionalize Christianity on campus. "We feel that the effort to change this requirement is an example of inclusiveness carried too far. . . . Davidson should be tolerant and respectful of all traditions but it should be proud and unapologetic of the tradition it grew upon and stands for today and, we pray, will continue in the future." They secured two hundred signatures on a petition to "affirm the school's relationship with the Presbyterian Church and support these significant ties in the future." Since the principal signatories were representatives of the Presbyterian, Catholic, Episcopal, and Methodist fellowships, as well as the Inter-Varsity Christian Fellowship and the Fellowship of Christian Athletes, taking sides against the veteran movement captained by the Presbyterian faculty of religion, those who followed these matters on campus from an indifferent distance might have been puzzled. Among administrators who spoke out, the Reverend Will Terry, newly retired dean of students (we have seen him earlier as college chaplain and as minister at the College Church), expressed the uncharacteristic worry that David-son might be sacrificing something that made it distinctive. "If we become like everyone else, I'm not sure we can compete. The Ivy League is sexier than we are. Our ace in the hole is our distinctiveness." The new dean of students said forthrightly: "We should ask ourselves how much of the importance is due to [Davidson's] guiding principles, such as the affiliation with the church, our Pres-byterian alumni, and people who are not even necessarily Presbyterian but believe in Christian values. There is a certain timeless quality about all that — we must at least pause before changing."[235] Stern talk.

What of the president himself, who must sometimes have been tempted to feel like a Spanish Habsburg governing the Netherlands? In 1987, after three years in office, he addressed the question: "Is it possible that we are 'losing our faith'?" Not so. The trustees had just affirmed their determination to seek the majority of board members from the ranks of the Presbyterian church. He pointed as well to the

Department of Religion, the chaplaincy, and the YMCA Student Service Corps as signs of "a vital attentiveness to the things of the spirit." Thus the president in 1987. The Y is now gone. The religion faculty is, it must fairly be said, ambivalent on the matter at issue. The chaplain's office is indeed vitally active in pastoral counseling, volunteer services, and retreats. But with only a few dozen students taking part in the worship services there, and from fifty to seventy-five worshiping at the Davidson College Presbyterian Church, one is talking about a remnant, not a renewal. Kuykendall himself must have felt that even in 1987, for he went on to say, with perhaps a note of desperation: "Our commitment to service, our commitment to truth, our commitment to accessibility, even our commitment to academic excellence — all can be understood as expressions of our special commitment to serve God with the life of the mind." But if one must point to wheelchair ramps in order to find evidence of faith on campus, what is this faith? How are these signs of "vital ties to the Church"?[236]

The three open issues — whether the trustees and the religion professors need be active Christians, and the president need be an active Presbyterian — lay on the table before the board for three years.[237] In the spring of 1996 they decided to open the religion faculty to non-Christians. Several current members said they had not been aware of the requirement when they were hired. In any case, the religion faculty reassured all concerned that their faith never jostled their scholarship, or vice versa. The trustees decided that their board should include only Christians, and that the president give "evidence of strong Christian faith and commitment," and at least agree to participate actively in the campus church.[238]

This extensive chronicle of the uninterrupted 150-year struggle to remove Presbyterian or evangelical or Christian piety, and then Presbyterian or evangelical or Christian persons, from Davidson is very tedious. But it is also very revealing — doubly so. First, it seems clear that though the decisions to remove these qualifications came late in the day, Davidson had been a community substantially uninterested in being Presbyterian even before the wrangle began. Second, during these last thirty years the arguments on behalf of change offer a relatively pure example of the poker-faced artifice we behold in more helter-skelter form in other narratives. It has often been said that academics are wanting in humor. But if even a few of the advocates of Davidson's flight from "narrow sectarianism" were, beneath it all, capable of true merriment in their extravagances, then perhaps this story is redeemed.

THE PRESBYTERIAN EXPERIENCE

George Marsden and Bradley Longfield, in the keynote paragraph of their very perceptive study of Presbyterian higher education, had originally rendered this severe judgment:

> In the course of the twentieth century the Christian character of many Presbyterian colleges has become so diluted that it is difficult to determine what, if anything,

distinguishes them from their avowedly secular counterparts. Though decreasing church support for the colleges might account for some of this change, the key factor in the secularization of church-related colleges seems to lie in the realm of ideas. In an effort to retain their respectability in an age dominated by increasingly naturalistic ideas, the schools embraced, first, the general tenets of liberal Christianity, and then effectively abandoned Christianity as a determinative perspective. Curiously, the church largely failed to protest this gradual secularization and has, often with the best of intentions, aided in this drift away from Christian influences.[239]

Little in the record would gainsay that observation. The Presbyterian churches, which for a long and formative period in the nation's history gathered communicants who were cultivated and affluent, never provided for themselves colleges or universities of academic quality suitable enough for their own children. Church executives have repeatedly scorched the pages of the General Assembly minutes, rebuking their coreligionists for being such pinchpennies toward their schools. It is difficult to know whether it was more the halting academic progress of their colleges that failed to secure the confidence of their intramural clientele, or the stinginess of the Presbyterians which stunted their schools' capacity to ripen. But to the extent the church was at fault as an educational sponsor, its sin was surely one of omission, not commission.

But the default was surely more intellectual than fiscal.

The two case studies offered here show that Lafayette's synod and Davidson's presbyteries were exceptionally meager financial providers: so much so that when the boards of the respective schools — then still dominated by the church's selectmen among the trustees — made their progressive moves toward disengagement, there was hardly any ground for indignation. The church's judicatories had the legal authority but meager moral standing to refuse these overtures. This would justify Marsden and Longfield in their published observation: "the Presbyterian Church (U.S.A.) seems to show little interest in its colleges, most of which in turn seldom display substantive Christian identity."[240] Their remark has a wider than fiscal application: the church, even when silver and gold were lacking, might have given what it had to give, like Peter on the temple steps. The church might have preached to its colleges.

A certain amount of criticism was served on the colleges from time to time by their sponsoring courts. Much of it, of course, was uneducated gossip or disgruntled carping. But some criticism was on the mark, a real challenge to the trustees' consciences, for it poked into the pathologies of the schools. When grievances did come their way, educators would usually finesse them with church officials, who would then sympathetically affirm their own appreciation of professional realities in the academic world. A grievance thus tamed became only a minor public relations task. But often the churchmen were unable to discriminate between the normal static of grumbling and real prophetic insight. What little there was of the latter was easily dismissed as more of the former. The institutional histories do not really report many meddlesome clerics. Indeed, the presbyteries were too inclined to praise their colleges. In retrospect, the church may have been more grudging with its discerning religious judgment than with its cash.

At the turn of the century the two Presbyterian churches, North and South, became more energetic about higher education on a national level. This might have given the Presbyterians a more professional voice because, unlike the churchmen at local levels, the national staff would usually be peers of the educators. The educational offices of the church have tried to serve their two constituencies — ecclesial and educational — in a professional manner. But what they have lacked in depth they have made up for in breadth. For instance: the 1981 UPCUSA Task Force on the Church and Higher Education filed a report with eleven affirmations and 76 recommendations; the 1982 PCUS Task Force on Higher Education filed a report with 46 recommendations. When North and South merged, it was as if they compounded the problem: the 1991 PC(USA) study of the Committee on Higher Education filed a much longer document with 110 recommendations.[241] "Prophetic" is not the word which comes to mind after reading all — or any — of it.

Today the Presbyterian Church (U.S.A.) has few people and no money — at least money for colleges. But its lack of realism may be a more critical loss. The rhetoric currently in use is very pulpous. Let one example suffice.

> The church-related college has some new opportunities — one of which is to be a center for reflection on moral and religious values in a pluralistic world. Its task is not to make people Christian or Presbyterian. To be church-related is, in the most important sense, to be humanity-related. What does it mean to be humanity-oriented? I am not altogether sure but the new age dawning requires of us new sensibilities. Today the task is to hold up visions — of what it means to be morally committed as individuals, to find coherence of life and meaning, to be responsible to self and to the larger community.[242]

Behind this bewildered public discourse is another, one more cynical. The experienced executives of the church soberly regard the colleges as long lost. The colleges, they know, are uninterested in the church except for its meager funding potential. Said one church executive: "If it's money you want, we haven't got any; if it's not money then why in the world do you want to be related to the church?"[243] The colleges and universities allow the church no voice in their policies, little preferment in their financial aid, and no assured presence in their faculties. Some of these Presbyterian executives are vexed with the church for continuing to be intimidated by educators, and for continuing to spin out policy statements that lack all clout.[244]

There seems to be a problem in the bloodstream of the Presbyterians that has affected their colleges. The church was, from the beginning, largely composed of an industrious bourgeoisie. They were already well educated, and their Calvinist

234

consciousness of public polity had from the beginning made Presbyterians instinctively supportive of the American civil authorities (as distinct from the British authorities, who had awarded them a hedged citizenship). Over here the Presbyterians were culture-friendly, and from the beginning they marketed their colleges openly: not simply to attract students and income, but because they saw the nation as a divinely blessed commonwealth. In this mood their educators were wholly undisposed to see their colleges as intellectually set apart. For moral purposes they were prepared to make their campuses defensive havens against a threatening environment, but not for intellectual purposes.[245] Marsden and Longfield see this:

> In 1935 H. Richard Niebuhr had warned that "if the church has no other plan of salvation . . . than one of deliverance by force, education, idealism or planned economy, it really has no existence as a church and needs to resolve itself into a political party or a school." By the latter half of the twentieth century most mainline Protestant church schools had resolved themselves into being simply schools. . . . Twentieth-century mainline Presbyterians, assuming that they were part of the cultural establishment, have seldom seen American culture as a threat and so have trusted in education.[246]

Old School to New School to No School

To understand this comment, though, one must appreciate that it is primarily a New School Presbyterianism they are describing. Over the years something effectively disabled the suspicious Old Calvinist orthodoxy.

The stories told here appear to narrate a gradual transformation of the colleges from one loyalty to the other. Both colleges were founded and patronized by predominantly Old School judicatories. Quite independently of the timing of national schism and reunion, they were eventually taken over by the New School, Pietism's progeny. The entire project of Presbyterian higher education, one might suggest, eventually became infused with the New School sensibility, which seemed continually willing to soften any truth claim if it obstructed fellowship *ad extra*. But it was not that simple.

This is the hope David Schaff explained to that remarkably polymorphous audience, the Parliament of Religions in 1893, in Chicago:

> A pressing necessity is felt of institutions managed by denominational control vouching for the Christian character of the influences brought to bear upon our students. This does not mean that the control should be clerical or sectarian, but generously Christian and religious. . . . Too close a denominational control will inevitably limit the sphere of an institution's usefulness in our country, while all lack of church control is apt to be attended with a total disregard of religious observance, if not of religious principles. A growing constituency is demanding

that at our colleges something beyond mere respect be had for religion. . . . While as little compulsion as possible should be employed in the matter of religious observance, a definite regard for Christianity should be had in outward exercises, and definite courses of instruction be given on religious subjects.[247]

This was no new idea of the late nineteenth century. Back in 1829 the Reverend Philip Lindsley, a Presbyterian college president, was hostile to his colleagues who wanted state funding, unrestricted recruitment, but a covertly sectarian governance.

I am aware that as soon as any sect succeeds in obtaining a charter for a *something* called a college, they become, all of a sudden, wondrously liberal and catholic. They forthwith proclaim to the public that their college is the best in the world — and withal, perfectly free from the odious taint of sectarianism. The youth of all religions may come to it without the slightest risk of being converted to the faith of the governing sect. This is very modest and very specious, and very hollow, and very hypocritical. They hold out false colours to allure and to deceive the incautious. Their college *is* sectarian, and they know it. Else why is it under the absolute and perpetual management and control of a party?[248]

Lindsley was a New School Presbyterian (as, obviously, was Schaff), and he was speaking here in a consciously partisan way against the Old School educators, whom he saw as duplicitous.

The instinctual Old/New division had shown itself already in the early 1700s.[249] The Great Awakening, with its tumultuous breakthrough of revivalist enthusiasm, caused many Presbyterians to worry lest their church be destabilized. The authority of the ministry, and even of the presbyteries, was being ignored by those who were reborn to a more fervent (fevered, said the Old Sides) faith. Wandering preachers were not only competing with established pastors but were pointing the finger at their coldness and venality. Basic Calvinist doctrines were being replaced with popular but unorthodox sloganeering. The primary community for the Old Sides was their church, and the Awakening threatened disorder with its new preaching and converting that so easily crossed denominational lines. The New Sides, by contrast, thought of the new civic commonwealth as their basic community. They seemed always ready to cast a critical eye on their clergy, and able to recognize a spirit-filled preacher when he came along. As for orthodoxy, they were content with loose agreements about the essentials, for written creeds always tended to divide folks. Theology they preferred in lighter doses, lest good Christian consciences be violated. They wanted good room for the individual conscience.

To the Old Sides, who tended to hold office, the New Sides had abandoned the authority that held the church together, and in 1741 they expelled most of them. But pacifiers almost immediately began the negotiations which soothed tempers and brought about reconciliation. The terms of reunion favored the New Sides, in that the traditionalists finally conceded that authority was to be invoked only on matters where there was true consensus, not a mere voting majority, and that their communion was grounded on the essentials of their faith, not the finer points of theology.

Civil resistance and then revolution elicited a new, united loyalty from the colonists, and this gave the New Sides an even stronger dedication to their new republic as the organic community they considered to be their primary home. That this threw them into fellowship with Quakers, Congregationalists, Baptists, Methodists, and even some Anglicans and Catholics caused little of the uneasiness it might have earlier. Even the Old Sides found contentment in the new and generous spirit that this new citizenship afforded them.

But then, just as the eighteenth century was ending, two things happened. The young nation itself began to be unsettled again by political conflict, and the unifying altruism that had come with the Revolution was wearing off, in the rough struggles of land-grabbing and profiteering. That was all destabilizing the Republic. The church simultaneously encountered heavy weather in the Second Great Awakening, an even more raucous revival than its predecessor. The General Assembly first issued annual misgivings and then snorts of dismay, as reports of wild and hysterical carryings-on came in from the West. Sessions were insisting on the right to reject or pick their ministers. Universal salvation (dreaded Arminianism) and Jesus as a mere man (Socinianism) were being preached to congregations that seemed no longer to know the difference. Ministers were being ordained with no education or presbyterial examination simply because they were seen as Jesus-filled. And the New School (as they were newly called) were disavowing their own church colleges as "sectarian" if they did not recognize an equality and solidarity with the Methodists and Baptists and Congregationalists who had shared the same drenching in the blood of the Lamb. The Old School was appalled that their brethren had rejected the need for a church led by an unquestioned and divinely sanctioned authority, defining its belief as needed, and holding itself apart from the civil society. The revivalists were enjoying solidarity with any who manifested spiritual rebirth, and when expelled by their sessions or presbyteries or even synods they did not regard it as schism simply to create rival judicatories.[250]

In the aftermath of this second schism (in 1837), the Old School had little of the compunction that followed their expulsion of the liberals a century earlier. They set about reinforcing the structures of authority at every level: the creed was more explicitly defined and tended; every single member of the denomination was obligated to hold formal membership in the hierarchical matrix, colleges were reformed and seminaries were founded that would be absolutely responsive to the official ministry. Guy Howard Miller reports this as the cause for a movement of disciplinary repression in the Presbyterian colleges, accompanied by the subordination of science to religion. The outcome, in the early decades of the nineteenth century, was a rough orthodoxy. The primary, organic community of the Old School was the church, which now saw itself as a competitor, no longer a partner, with other Christian fellowships. This, Miller says, was in contrast with the broadly based, cosmopolitan Christianity of the New Sides (at their best in early Princeton) and now the New School, who preferred an easygoing, consensual Christianity resiliently tolerant of dogmatic differences.

If one can take these two partisan stances not as contraries but as coexistent counterparts, one will see them wrangling under the surface in all periods. The Old and New were again reunited (1864 in the South, 1870 in the North). Since then there have been further crises that affected them characteristically: Reconstruction, the biblical controversy in the 1920s, and the social awakening of the 1960s. In the first two crises, an initial stiffening by the Old School soon provoked and gave way to a resurgence of the New School, and recent years have seen a clean sweep for their New descendants.[251]

The Presbyterians were unsuccessful, and perhaps diffident, in providing themselves with a theology. Though they suffered repeated conflict and reconciliation between Old Sides, Old School, and their New counterparts, over their long and unresolved quarrel about whether authentic faith resided in assent or affect — for this is what it was all about — they had never established in their midst as stark a theology as had their Congregational cousins. Likewise, by repeatedly reuniting they never produced a radical abreaction in the way the Congregationalists begot the Unitarians or the Catholics and Anglicans begot the Deists. On the other hand, their foundational protest had been so centered upon polity that denominational morale and character eventually took the civic virtues to be the embodiment of the gospel. So, though they experienced little embarrassed recoil from a discredited Calvinism during the fundamentalist hubbub of the 1920s, there was enough of a theological vacuum in their community for it to be filled by the various messages of social salvation that revealed themselves in the 1930s. They not only embraced social compassion and service (thus providing the New Deal with some of its strong impetus), but went further and accepted the usually inconspicuous philosophy which quickened those movements as a surrogate for theological understanding. This was affect without any required assent. And it was repeated, in spades, in the 1960s and thereafter.

The spokesmen for the Old conservatives have, on each occasion, fastened their attention more on the authorized procedure for resolving conflicts than on the merits of what was being argued (even though they were not above sidestepping a chancy vote or rigging an occasional election). They have trusted the clergy more than the laity. If the liberals were cosmopolitan, the conservatives were separatist. Yet, after any season when the conservatives have been in power, there were institutions to be reformed and invigorated. After a season of liberal, New hegemony, by contrast, the institutions were no longer there, or no longer theirs, and certainly no longer within reach of the church were it disposed to renewal.

The Presbyterian colleges have witnessed this same gradual predominance of the New School.[252] Davidson lagged behind Lafayette by about twenty years in the dissolution of its Christian identity, because of its more conservative Presbyterian environment. Each college and its sponsors had assumed that with enough deft doctrinal modulation, joined to generous civic cooperation and sobriety of campus manners, they would maintain both religious fidelity and rightful liberty. The liberty survived; the fidelity did not. The outcome on both campuses has been similar: there is no longer either a community of sponsorship (a providing church) or a community of mentorship (a believing faculty) or a community of discipleship (a faithful student body).

The ostensible story line of the Presbyterians and their colleges is muddled by paradox. Whenever the academics arose to ward off the ecclesiastics, there was defensive talk about narrow and forbidding doctrines, backwardness, and a threat to academic freedom and inquiry. When one looks closely, though, this proves to have been mostly spookery. The advocates of Presbyterianism at Lafayette and Davidson who were drawing down complaints about their frowning Calvinism were anything but bigots. Throughout the years of most intense conflict, when the two institutions were dissolving their formal requirements that the educators be Presbyterian, or Christian, the practitioners of religious discourse on campus were purveying a creed, code, and cult that revealed only trace elements of the Presbyterian tradition. Latter-day New educators have been at pains to disavow any narrow, restrictive, inhospitable doctrine — the kind one would expect from rigorous Old divines. As they did so, there was hardly anyone living who could recall that Old kind of theology anyway. It was just at that time that the financial means and the scholarly training and the enlightened clientele opened the possibility for the colleges to make good on their Old promise: to offer sound scholarship infused by faith. Yet then — just then — is when the colleges came into the hands of academics who not only did not believe that integration of faith and scholarship to be possible, but found it an unattractive ideal.

NOTES TO CHAPTER 2

1. Not all of these began as Presbyterian. Rhodes College in Memphis, for instance, was founded in Clarksburg by the Grand Masonic Lodge as Montgomery University of Tennessee, and only when the Masons failed to support it did the Presbyterians assume its patronage (first as Stewart College, then as Southwestern at Memphis). Scores of colleges and universities that were once sponsored by congregations or presbyteries or synods or the General Assembly have not survived to the present, including such schools as Emporia, Lenox, Flora McDonald, Stonewall Jackson, Silliman, and Tarkio Colleges, which closed or merged. Others, like Lincoln University, have become state schools. There was enough involvement by Presbyterians, especially clergy, in the foundations of some state universities, and of continued dominance in their early years, for Presbyterians to remember them as effectively their own establishments; this might include Delaware, North Carolina, Miami of Ohio, Ohio (at Athens), Indiana, SUNY at Buffalo, Kentucky, Georgia, Tennessee, and South Carolina. Presbyterian Academy became the University of Pittsburgh, Transylvania shifted its affiliation to the Disciples of Christ, Allegheny and Dickinson Colleges transferred to Methodist sponsorship, Cedarville College now counts itself as Baptist related, while Parsons College has become the Maharishi International University, and Huron University is now a proprietary school.

One estimate published in 1940 listed forty-one colleges founded by the PCUSA (Presbyterian Church in the United States of America), and sixty-eight "dead colleges": C. Harve Geiger, *The Program of Higher Education of the Presbyterian Church in the United States of America: An Historical Analysis of Its Growth in the United States* (Cedar Rapids, Iowa: Laurance Press, 1940), 80. Princeton, the first Presbyterian college (and then university) in the country (1746), has severed all ties with the church, as have other Presbyterian foundations: Washington and Lee, Cumberland (Tennessee), Elmira, Hamilton, Park, Wabash, Washington and Jefferson, Occidental, Bellevue, and New York University.

Other colleges report affiliation with one of the smaller Presbyterian churches not part of PC(USA): Erskine (South Carolina: Associate Reformed Presbyterian Church); Bethel (Tennessee: Cumberland Presbyterian Church); and Geneva (Pennsylvania: Reformed Presbyterian Church of North America).

Several of these colleges are more confessionally evangelical and belong to the Coalition for Christian Colleges and Universities, and are separately studied in chapter 7: Belhaven, Erskine, King, Montreat-Anderson, Sterling, and Whitworth.

2. Inez Moore Parker, *The Rise and Decline of the Program of Education for Black Presbyterians of the United Presbyterian Church U.S.A., 1865-1970* (San Antonio: Trinity University Press, 1977).

3. Margaret Adair Hunter, *Education in Pennsylvania Promoted by the Presbyterian Church, 1726-1837* (Philadelphia: Temple University, 1937).

4. David Bishop Skillman, *The Biography of a College, Being the History of the First Century of the Life of Lafayette College,* vol. 1 (Easton: Lafayette College, 1932), 1-33; vol. 2, 295-303. The pages that follow are heavily indebted to this history, and to the eventual third volume by Professor Gendebien.

5. After invading and subduing Ireland the British government expropriated large estates in the Northeast, in and around Ulster, and awarded land grants to thousands of lowland Scots and their retainers, all Presbyterians. When successor governments, in order to protect the English agricultural market, obstructed Irish trade with both England and the American colonies, the resulting depression drove massive numbers of these now-Irish Protestants to emigrate to America,

where they were the most numerous group to arrive in the later eighteenth century. It was in America that they became known as Scotch-Irish. See William Warren Sweet, *Religion on the American Frontier,* vol. 2, *The Presbyterians, 1783-1840* (New York: Harper & Bros., 1936).

6. Ann D. Gordon, *The College of Philadelphia, 1749-1779: Impact of an Institution* (New York: Garland, 1989), 96-98. In New York it had been otherwise: the Presbyterians pressed King's College (later Columbia) to relax its exclusive bonds to the established church and give representation to dissenters. The board gave way and admitted the pastors of four denominations in the city.

7. Skillman, 1:35.

8. Skillman, 1:45.

9. Review of *The Annual of the Board of Education of the Presbyterian Church in the United States: A New Year's Offering for 1835,* ed. John Breckenridge (Philadelphia, 1835), in *Biblical Repertory and Princeton Theological Review* 7 (1835): 273.

10. Untitled letter of solicitation, New York, 13 November 1835, in the name of Joseph McElroy et al., Lafayette College Special Collections and Archives (LCSCA)/II. Presidents' Papers/35; Religious Affairs/Box 1.

11. Skillman, 1:84.

12. Skillman, 1:172-87.

13. Skillman, 1:192-93. The precise arrangement was that the synod would usually send down one or more names for the various posts, to be elected by the board; if none of the nominees were to accept election, or if a replacement were urgent (as in the case of a faculty resignation), then the board would undertake to propose names for the synod to confirm. Minutes of the Synod of Philadelphia, 16-22 October 1850, LCSCA/Skillman Files/1850/#60.

14. Committee report (1850), LCSCA/Skillman Files/1849/#21, p. 3.

15. Minutes of the Synod of Philadelphia, 22 October 1850.

16. James Madison Porter to William Porter(?), 24 November 1849, LCSCA/Skillman Files/1849/#63. This was not accomplished without some expressions of rage within the board. Porter writes in the aftermath: "We do believe that Dr. Junkin's removal [from his board seat, on grounds of remote residence] was absolutely necessary for the good, not only of the College, but of this community. He was fierce and malevolent in his denunciation of all who refused to permit him to domineer over them."

17. "The Second Annual Report of the Board of Trustees of La Fayette College to the Synod of Philadelphia" (1850), LCSCA/Skillman Files/1850/#8.

18. James Madison Porter to William Porter(?), LCSCA/Skillman Files/1849/#63, writes: "I care infinitely less for the loss of the appropriation of $1,000 a year from the Board of Education than I feel hurt at the idea that the Ex. Committee of that board should even appear to indorse the charges of our accusers by listening to them for a moment."

19. "Form of a Report," 4 February 1851, LCSCA/Skillman Files/1851/#48. An examiner during the next semester ignored all grading categories except "talents" and "progress."

20. Skillman, 1:214.

21. Skillman, 1:223, 245.

22. Selden J. Coffin, "Lafayette College, and Daily Prayer Meetings," February 1869, LCSCA/Skillman Files/1869/#54.

23. A flyer was printed and sent round to all the congregations:

Cannot some scheme be devised by which the entire Synod will unite in erecting, among the new buildings now crowning College Hill, a "Memorial Chapel"? There are scores of congregations within our bounds who could each furnish the necessary funds, but let the honor be shared among all. What ever views may have been entertained with reference to the College, in any previous part of its history, surely all can now heartily unite in providing a suitable place of prayer for the young men of the College, and this, we have no doubt, will be done most cheerfully by those who were not called upon to contribute to the noble endowment of $200,000 just secured.

LCSCA/Skillman Files/1866/#75.

It appears that memories in the synod were long, and intra-Presbyterian animus continued to affect the college's fortunes. Imagined affluence had brought Lafayette a double fortune within the synod: respectability, and the assurance that it could delve for further funds without help. At the same time in Easton itself, some of the old strains between the college and First Presbyterian Church reoccurred, so that commencement ceremonies had to be held in other churches. Skillman, 1:299.

24. Skillman, 1:292-93, 327-28, 355-56.

25. Skillman, 1:260.

26. Skillman, 1:271-73.

27. Skillman, 1:281.

28. The first paragraph is from the publisher's notice of the text series, almost certainly written by March; the remainder is excerpted from his 1874 presidential address to the American Philological Association. See W[illiam] B[axter] Owen, *Historical Sketches of Lafayette College, with an account of its present organization and courses of study,* prepared at the request of the U.S. Bureau of Education (Easton: n.p., 1876), 51-52, bound together with Selden J. Coffin, *Record of the Men of Lafayette: Biographical Sketches of the Alumni of Lafayette College, from its organization to the present time* (Easton: Skinner & Finch, 1879).

29. Skillman, 1:348-49. There is a sorrowful correspondence wherein Douglass explains that he will not be able to fulfill his pledge, and why. LCSCA/Skillman Files/1877/##1-5.

30. Skillman, 1:333-34.

31. "Brainerd Society; Records, 1833-1992," in LCSCA/Brainerd Society/Records/Boxes 1 and 2.

32. An important contextual note: in this immediate postbellum period Presbyterian investment in higher education across the country was much surpassed by that of Baptists, Methodists, and Congregationalists. Presbyterian-related colleges as a group ranked fourth in enrollment, endowment, real property, and income. D[aniel] S[eely] Gregory, *The Presbyterian Church in its Relation to Higher Education and the Ministry* (Lake Forest, Ill.: Presbyterian Ministerial Association, 1882).

33. *Report of the Committee of the Synod of Pennsylvania appointed to visit Lafayette College, 1889* [written by Selden J. Coffin], January 1889, LCSCA/Skillman Files/1889/#25.

34. "Christian Education," in *Addresses on the Occasion of the Inauguration of Ethelbert Dudley Warfield, LL.D., as President of Lafayette College* (Easton: Lafayette College, 1891), 27-29, 37.

35. [Selden J. Coffin, registrar], "Lafayette Statistics," January 1889, LCSCA/Skillman Files/1889/#25. This survey is remarkable: it is a transition from earlier inquiries into students' own professed adherence to faith and (later) church, to later inquiries into affiliation or (later) preference, which latter might refer either to professed adherence or to an inertial and inactive identification with the religion of one's family. Synod's visitation report one year later notes that of 319 students, 206 (65 percent) are "members of the Church," but then goes on to report that seventeen "denominations are represented," and that their total membership amounts to 311, practically the entire student body. The census: Presbyterians, 52 percent; Lutherans, 11 percent; Methodists, 11 percent; Reformed, 8 percent; Episcopalians, 6 percent; evangelicals, 3 percent; Baptists, 2 percent; Catholics, 1 percent; others, 3 percent. Here, then, we see two successive and very different manners of reporting: one of "active," "practicing," "observant" Christians, and another including those identified by mere "affiliation." *Annual Report on Lafayette College to the Synod of Pennsylvania* (Philadelphia: American Printing House), 14-15, LCSCA/Bp/Reports to Synod/1890.

36. See three communications from Warfield, 10, 18, and 30 March 1931, to Skillman, who was engaged in writing the college's centennial history, LCSCA/Skillman Files/1891/##51, 53, 55. The Lafayette faculty by custom held full authority for many matters which elsewhere had already begun to devolve upon the president and other administrators. The 1913 Faculty Rules, IV, 382, provided that in emergencies when the faculty was not in session the president could act as their representative, but at their next meeting they would have the power to set his action aside.

37. James Bertram, Andrew Carnegie's private secretary, to [James S.] Dickson, secretary of the Presbyterian College Board, 3 December 1908; Pritchett, president of the Carnegie Foundation for The Advancement of Teaching, to Lewis E. Holden, president of the College of Wooster, 6 November 1909, PCUSA College Board, RG 32-41-18-9/Carnegie Materials, Presbyterian Church (U.S.A.), Department of History and Records Management Services (Philadelphia) (hereafter cited as DOHP). Also "Carnegie Policy Decried," *New York Times,* 8 February 1912, 3.

38. Henry S. Pritchett, "The Relations of Christian Denominations to Colleges," *Educational Review* 36 (October 1908): 217-41.

39. Presbyterians have not been consistent in their aspirations to control their colleges. For example, the Board of Aid for Colleges (1883) said that the colleges it founded should be "under denominational control." After it had become the College Board (1904) it asserted: "The Board will seek neither to dominate the colleges nor to carry them. It will cooperate with them. . . ." It usually had something to do with how much funding was involved. Geiger, 84, 107.

40. See Carnegie Materials, loc. cit.; also RG 32-15-17/Lafayette College, DOHP.

41. Minutes of the Board of Trustees, Lafayette College, 2 May 1912, 12 June 1916, 3 May 1917; Edward J. Fox to the Board of Trustees, 8 February 1912, and David Bennett King to John Welles Hollenback, 1 May 1912, LCSCA/Skillman Files/1912/##23, 29; "The Lafayette Alumni Meeting," *Presbyterian* 11 (March 1914): 8.

42. John M[offatt] Mecklin, *My Quest for Freedom* (New York: Scribners, 1945); also Mecklin letters in 1931 to Skillman, who had asked for background materials as he prepared the college's centennial history, LCSCA/Skillman Files. Lafayette at the time abounded in students who planned to enter the ministry. In 1910, 24 were reported; within the church only the College of Wooster had more. Some nearby colleges had few: Princeton, 9; New York University, 1; Washington and Jefferson, 3; Franklin and Marshall, 1. *Annual Report of the Board of Christian Education to the General Assembly of the Presbyterian Church in the United States of America, 1910,* 24-26 ([GA/BCE1910/PCUSA]; hereafter such reports are cited in similar abbreviated fashion).

43. In 1930 an informal survey of the PCUSA-related colleges showed that about 41 percent of their students were Presbyterians, 21 percent Methodists, 3 percent Catholics, with no Jews appearing in the tabulation. This suggests that the diminution of Presbyterians and the augmentation of Catholics and Jews were several decades further along at Lafayette than in other Presbyterian colleges. GA/BCE1930/PCUSA, 85.

44. MacCracken, Report to the Board of Trustees, February 1919, 4, LCSCA/CF14/Annual Reports/1918-19. The president also noted that clergy on the board were now reduced to four, only two of whom were active pastors.

45. William Jennings Bryan (with the Scopes trial still two years off), then a member of the General Assembly's Standing Committee on Education, had stirred considerable debate at the 1923 meeting. The mind of the Assembly was that "church offerings for education are essentially missionary offerings," and Bryan provoked them to begin exercising "careful oversight" and to withhold subsidy from schools offering a "materialistic evolutionary philosophy of life, or otherwise discrediting the Christian faith." Minutes of the 1923 General Assembly, Presbyterian Church in the United States of America, 209-12 ([PCUSA/GA/M1923]; hereafter proceedings of General Assemblies are cited in similar abbreviated fashion). In 1930 the issue had not died down; if

anything, the Board of Christian Education was pressing harder. Trustees and faculty of cooperating colleges were asked to declare:

1. that the primary purpose of the institution in all its educational procedures is so to interpret life to its students that they may experience that growing fellowship with God through Jesus our Lord and Saviour which will be increasingly controlling in the whole range of conduct.

2. that they are seeking to achieve this primary Christian aim in the experience of its students "completely in accord with the purposes and principles of the Presbyterian Church in the U.S.A."

GA/BCE1930/PCUSA, 88.

46. MacCracken, Report to the Board of Trustees, 31 October 1923, 2-3, LCSCA/CF14/Annual Reports/1923-24.

47. MacCracken to James E. Clarke, 10 June 1919, LCSCA/II. Presidents' Papers/35, Reports/4/Religious Affairs. MacCracken had received a query from the chairman of the synodical committee appointed to visit Lafayette that year, asking the college to purge itself of suspicion of infidelity. The letter contained indirect references to an undercurrent of innuendo and suspicion (not unusual in the tense days of the early 1920s, when liberals and conservatives in the Protestant churches were at daggers drawn). He immediately wrote to Israel Pardee, president of his board, with some apprehension that if pressed, this issue might sever the college from the synod. He does not seem to have been averse. He wrote: "Of the men not members of churches in the present faculty, Prentice and Tupper are our two most valuable men. Their high moral character and essential Christian spirit are unquestioned. To dismiss them in order to conform to the resolution would, in my judgment, not only be illegal, but a case of throwing away the substance for the sake of the form." G. E. Hawes to MacCracken, 12 October 1923, and MacCracken to Pardee, 13 October 1923, LCSCA/II. Presidents' Papers/35, Reports/4/Religious Affairs. See also Hawes's earlier letter to Judge John Fox (who would serve more than half a century on the Lafayette board, and was chairman of the board of the congregation Hawes served as pastor), 1 November 1922.

48. MacCracken, Report to the Board of Trustees, 1 May 1924, 2. LCSCA/II. Presidents' Papers/1. Reports/4. Presidents' Reports to Board.

49. Albert W. Gendebien, *The Biography of a College, Being the History of the Third Half-Century of Lafayette College* (Easton: Lafayette College, 1986), 23.

50. Gendebien, *Biography,* 63-64.

51. Francis A. March, *The Growth of Lafayette: A Post-Prandial Address* (Philadelphia Alumni Association of Lafayette College, 1888), 13-15, LCSCA.

52. Gendebien, *Biography,* 97-99, 126-28.

53. Gendebien, *Biography,* 52-55, 152, 169, 206, 322-28; LCSCA/Brainerd Society/Records/Boxes 1 and 2.

54. Dr. George Johnson to Lewis, 27 December 1943; Lewis to Johnson, 30 December, LCSCA/II. Presidents' Papers/35. Religious Affairs/Box 1.

55. Draft: "Set of Standards for Colleges Affiliated with the Presbyterian Church, Adopted by the Board of Christian Education, Presbyterian Church, USA, 28 April 1943." Cp. PCUSA/GA/M1943, 188. These standards are the descendants of five "marks," or "chief characteristics," of a Christian college published by the Board of Christian Education in 1925:

1. The professors and instructors professing Christians and members of some evangelical church.

2. Teaching of the Bible organized into the regular curriculum with a professor ranking as a faculty member.

3. Regular services of public worship in which student attendance and faculty participation are expected.

4. Positive Christian point of view in the teaching of all subjects laid down in the curriculum.

5. The development and culture of Christian character as the supreme end of all academic influences. (PCUSA/GA/BCE1925, 7-8, 56-67)

To see these "marks" in context one must realize that in 1925 the PCUSA still held either direct or indirect power of control over three-quarters of its related colleges, and expected that its policy in so central a matter would elicit compliance. Paul M. Limbert, *Denominational Policies in the Support and Supervision of Higher Education* (New York: Teachers College, 1929), 57. Much more importantly, in 1925 a large proportion of the educators in those colleges were observant Presbyterians and apparently accepted, with varying degrees of activist conviction, the evangelical purpose of the institutions. Thus the board could say explicitly that its relationship had been "one of coöperation and not control," and that it claimed no right to interfere with management or curriculum. The formulation of the "marks" was intended to guide the synods, not in governing, but in "accrediting" the colleges they chose to sponsor.

56. Paul Calvin Payne, PCUSA/GA/BCE1943, 16. After the war the grants rose to $5,000 per college, PCUSA/GA/BCE1946, 49. By 1947 Presbyterians were giving less to benevolence per capita than in 1930, PCUSA/GA/BCE1947, 72. A further note: in 1943 the board's annual report listed the percentage of Presbyterians in the student bodies of its affiliated colleges. At Lafayette it was 23 percent. This would be the last time the religious composition of their student bodies was reported to the church at large.

57. PCUSA/GA/1946, 119-20. The context for this assertion was the report that the churches were flaccid in their work of drawing in new members. Nearly a third of the congregations had not received a single new convert in the course of a year.

58. This essay was prepared in February 1948 for the "President's Page," a regular feature in the *Lafayette Alumnus,* but the president must have had second thoughts because it evidently did not appear. LCSCA/II. Presidents' Papers/35. Religious Affairs/Box 1.

59. "Report of Department of Bible Partly Supported by a Trust Fund Held and Administered by the Board of Education of the Presbyterian Church in the U.S.A.," as submitted by Lafayette College for 1947-48 and 1948-49. In the latter year, to the query about "exceptions," Hutchison replied: "One Jewish instructor, in Chemistry on temporary appointment, a man of excellent character." LCSCA/II. Presidents' Papers/35. Religious Affairs/Box 1.

60. "Charter Members of the Lafayette College Church" lists eighty-six, of whom at least thirty-four are Methodists, Congregationalists, Lutherans, or Reformed. Hutchison to Rt. Rev. Fred Corson, Methodist bishop of Philadelphia, 29 September 1954. See also "The Church at Lafayette" (brochure, n.d.); Mark Thompson, "The New College Church," *Lafayette Alumnus,* March 1948, 8-9; Lois C. Moon, "Lafayette's Campus Church," *Presbyterian Life,* 19 January 1952, 16ff. LCSCA/II. Presidents' Papers/35. Religious Affairs/Box 1.

61. Membership in an evangelical church was evidently not required at this time, though candidates were said to have been asked if they belonged to a church. Gendebien, *Biography,* 257.

62. Bradley J. Longfield and George M. Marsden, "Presbyterian Colleges in Twentieth-Century America," in *The Pluralist Vision: Presbyterians and Mainstream Protestant Education and Leadership,* ed. Milton J. Coalter, John M. Mulder, and Louis B. Weeks (Louisville: Westminster/John Knox, 1992), 100.

63. Gendebien, *Biography,* 247.

64. Report of Inter-College Visitation Committee, 6-8 May 1959, 2, LCSCA/II. Presidents' Papers/35. Religious Affairs/Box 1.

65. Morgan S. Odell to Hutchison, 6 November 1954, enclosing draft of new standards; Hutchison to Odell, 12 November 1954, LCSCA/II. Presidents' Papers/35. Religious Affairs/Box 1.

66. Hutchison to Cyrus S. Fleck (trustee), 27 September 1956; "Reflections on the Meeting

with Trustees of Lafayette, 9 October 1956," LCSCA/II. Presidents' Papers/35. Religious Affairs/Box 1.

67. Albert W. Gendebien, interview with the author, 17 February 1995; Minutes of the Board of Trustees, 8 June 1962, 3, LCSCA.

68. This is not untypical of the other colleges in this vicinity. Moravian College, for instance, now has about 60 percent Catholics in its student body (and about 2 percent Moravians); Catholics are the largest cohort at Lehigh University; and at Muhlenberg Catholics outnumber Lutherans three-to-one and Jews outnumber Lutherans two-to-one.

69. Lloyd M. Felmly, president of the board of trustees, to the Synod of Pennsylvania (draft), 2 February 1958, LCSCA/II. Presidents' Papers/35. Religious Affairs/Box 1.

70. Report of Inter-College Visitation Committee, 6-8 May 1959, 3, LCSCA/II. Presidents' Papers/35. Religious Affairs/Box 1.

71. Drafted for the Board of Christian Education. This policy document was published with the authority of the General Assembly of what had since 1958 become the United Presbyterian Church in the United States of America (UPCUSA) through a merger with another Presbyterian body.

72. Bergethon to Richard R. Johnson, 31 May 1962; Johnson, a doctoral candidate at Teachers College, was studying campus responses to the 1961 report. LCSCA/II. Presidents' Papers/35. Religious Affairs/Box 1. See also "Church Lags on College Support," *Christian Education News,* UPCUSA/BCE, 1962.

73. Statement of the Board of Christian Education to the Long Range Planning Committee, September 1962, LCSCA/II. Presidents' Papers/35. Religious Affairs/Box 1.

74. Thomas W. Pomeroy, [Jr.], "The Status of Lafayette College as a Church Related Institution," *Lafayette Alumnus,* February 1963, 3-6.

75. "Administrative Guidelines for Colleges Related to the United Presbyterian Church in the U.S.A.," adopted by the Board of Christian Education, 18 April 1963. On 25 October 1963 the Lafayette board resolved it to be the declared purpose of the college to conform to both *The Church and Higher Education* (1961) and the "Administrative Guidelines" (1963). Their purpose was to free themselves from the 1943 standards. As matters later turned out, accepting even these attenuated policies of the sixties would soon make the administration nervous.

76. *The Reappraisal Study: Answers to Questionnaire Submitted by Lafayette College,* 31 July 1963, LCSCA/II. Presidents' Papers/35. Religious Affairs/Box 1.

77. Bergethon, notes for presentation to the Lehigh Presbytery Meeting, 23 January 1962, LCSCA/II. Presidents' Papers/35. Religious Affairs/Box 1.

78. Minutes of the Board of Trustees, 20 October 1961, LCSCA; Elliott M. Shirk, Pennsylvania Human Relations Commission, to George C. Laub, counsel and trustee, 11 September 1962, LCSCA/II. Presidents' Papers/35. Religious Affairs/Box 1.

79. Bergethon, Reports to the Board of Trustees, 4 May and 8 June 1962, LCSCA/II. Presidents' Papers/1. Reports/4. Presidents' Reports to Board. Bergethon to Pomeroy, 11 March 1965; Charles E. Terry, stated clerk of the Synod of Pennsylvania, to Bergethon, 6 July 1965; Bergethon to Terry, 10 July 1965; Minutes of the Board of Trustees, 22 October 1965; Laub to Bergethon, 19 December 1966; Bergethon to Laub, 10 January 1967, LCSCA.

80. Laub to Bergethon, 19 December 1966, enclosure, "Lafayette College Facts."

81. 6 February 1967.

82. A year later Bergethon explained privately that this desire to relate the college to the church was required of the actual trustees and officers who had signed the "Amended Agreement," but it did not compel them to provide successors who shared the same desire. Minutes of the Religious Program Council, 2 March 1968, 2, LCSCA/II. Presidents' Papers/35. Religious Affairs/Box 1.

83. "Indenture between the General Board of Education of the Presbyterian Church in the United States of America and Lafayette College, concerning the Challenge Fund Endowment,"

30 November 1921; "Amended Agreement between the Board of Christian Education of the United Presbyterian Church in the U.S.A. and Lafayette College," 16 March 1968, LCSCA.

84. Recommendations of 1968 in respect to Church-College Relations in the Synods of the United Presbyterian Church in the USA.

85. Memorandum from the Presbyterian College Union to the Board of Christian Education, circulated 11 February 1971.

86. Minutes of the Board of Trustees, 16 September 1972, 18 November 1972; the Lafayette faculty voted their acceptance of the statement, and the board followed suit on 20 October 1973. It is difficult to imagine any further step in this sequence of successive discommitments. The church itself later acknowledged that the "Mutual Responsibilities" document of 1973 was shifty where the "Administrative Guidelines" of 1963 had been forthright. The earlier document, for example, spoke of Christian tradition, witness, and wisdom as what the colleges should be offering, while the later text associated it only with the colleges' founding fathers. See *The Church's Mission in Higher Education: A Report and Recommendations* (New York: UPC[USA], 1981), 21-22.

87. "Proposed Changes in the Religious Program at Lafayette," appendix to "A Report to the Religious Program Council from its Drafting Committee on the Problem of the Required Convocation or Chapel Service at the College," 16 December 1963, LCSCA/II. Presidents' Papers/35. Religious Affairs/Box 1.

88. Minutes of the Religious Program Council, 11 March 1966, LCSCA/II. Presidents' Papers/35. Religious Affairs/Box 1.

89. [Rev. F. Peter Sabey], Annual Report, Chaplain of the College and Pastor of The Lafayette College Church, 1966-67, LCSCA/X. 1. Chaplain's Office/Files.

90. [Sabey], Annual Report of the Chaplain, 1968-69, LCSCA.

91. Bergethon, Presentation Statement at the Dedication of the Interfaith Chapel–Hogg Hall–11 March 1966, LCSCA/II. Presidents' Papers/35. Religious Affairs/Box 1.

92. Bergethon, Reports of the President to the Board of Trustees, 1972-73, and 1958-73, 1: 4-5. LCSCA/II. Presidents' Papers/1. Reports/4. Presidents' Reports to the Board.

93. Bergethon to Harold H. Viehman, secretary of the General Division of Higher Education, UPCUSA/BCE, 24 April 1970, LCSCA/II. Presidents' Papers/35. Religious Affairs/Box 1.

94. *Religion at Lafayette,* a booklet produced in 1971 by the chaplain's office; it replaced an earlier *The Church at Lafayette,* LCSCA.

95. Minutes of the Religious Program Council, 7 November 1970, 3, LCSCA/II. Presidents' Papers/35. Religious Affairs/Box 1.

96. Richard S. Hays, Religious Attitudes Survey, February 1973, Office of the Chaplain, Minutes of the Religious Program Council, 17 February 1973, LCSCA.

97. Bergethon, president emeritus, "Background Remarks for General Session of the Presbyterian College Union with the National Task Force on the United Presbyterian Church and Higher Education," 4 February 1979.

98. Gendebien, *Biography,* 623-24.

99. The national report calculated the number of Presbyterians divided by all religiously active students; the report at Lafayette calculated the number of Presbyterians divided by all respondents.

100. *The Church's Mission in Higher Education: A Report and Recommendations* (New York: UPC[USA], 1981), 19-20; see UPC(USA)/GA/1981, 51, 378-84.

101. Bergethon to Viehman, 24 April 1970.

102. Draft submitted to the Religious Program Council, 7 November 1970, LCSCA/II. Presidents' Papers/35. Religious Affairs/Box 2. Sabey's essay was apparently given a hasty discussion: Minutes of the Religious Program Council, 7 November 1970, LCSCA/II. Presidents' Papers/35. Religious Affairs/Box 1.

103. Gendebien, "The College Presidency," an address on the occasion of the inauguration of Arthur J. Rothkopf as president of Lafayette College (1994), ms. courtesy of the author.

104. Dr. Gary R. Miller, chaplain of the college, interview with the author, 1 March 1995;

Dr. Albert W. Gendebien, professor emeritus of history and archivist emeritus of the college, interview with the author, 1 March 1995; Rev. Thomas Hagan, O.S.F.S., former chaplain to the Catholic students at Lafayette and Moravian Colleges, interview with the author, 7 March 1995.

105. Information provided by Linda H. Thomson, assistant to the vice president for development and college relations, 23 March 1995.

106. David Skillman was a member of the class of 1913, which had stood up for Mecklin and launched public insult at Warfield during the year after Mecklin's resignation; he later served in the administration, and under Hutchison enjoyed the confidence of the board while they were determining to sack the president.

107. Mecklin, *My Quest for Freedom,* 134.

108. Cornelia Rebekah Shaw, *Davidson College* (New York: Fleming H. Revell, 1923), 1-49; Mary D. Beaty, *A History of Davidson College* (Davidson: Briarpatch Press, 1988), 3-28. What follows is much beholden to these two institutional histories.

109. *A Report of a Committee of the Presbytery of Fayetteville, on the Condition and Prospects of Davidson College* (Fayetteville, N.C.: Edward J. Hale, 1845), 11-13, Davidson College Archives (DCA).

110. *Report of a Committee,* 19.

111. Minutes of the Board of Trustees, 8 August 1849; vol. 1 (transcript), 130-31. Demographics could vary widely from year to year (and within any year depending on when the count was made). The proportion of church members to student body was 22:66 in 1849-50; 18:52 in 1850-51; 22:61 in 1851-52; and 23:80 in 1852-53 (in this last year "a considerable number of the others, probably between fifteen and twenty, are believed to be hopefully pious"). Minutes of the Board of Trustees, 7 August 1860, 142; 12 August 1851, 156; 11 August 1852, 166; 10 August 1853, 184, DCA.

112. When the *North Carolina Presbyterian* brandished this fact throughout the constituency as "unprecedented in the history of colleges," a partisan admirer of Hanover College in Indiana wrote to point out that in 1837 their graduating class of 15 was comprised of "fifteen young gentlemen, all professors of religion, and thirteen of the number became ministers of the Gospel." A further statistic was proudly cited: from 1834 to 1859, 136 of Hanover's 225 graduates were in or studying for ministry. Minutes of the Board of Trustees, 8 October 1859, DCA. Beaty, 92, reports that about 20 percent of Davidson graduates, 1837-60, went into the ministry. These were, to the churches that gave their patronage, significant — and competitive — statistics.

113. Minutes of the Board of Trustees, 24 June 1856, 1:245; 14 July 1857, 270, DCA.

114. Minutes of the Board of Trustees, 8 August 1849, 1:131, DCA.

115. Minutes of the Board of Trustees, 24 June 1856, 1:245, DCA. Though the first six faculty at Davidson were Presbyterian ministers, subsequent appointments were predominantly given to laity, whose sponsorship of student piety was, at least in these years, no less purposeful. Beaty, 102.

116. Beaty, 53-54.

117. Beaty, 60-69.

118. Shaw, 72-81. Hill's patriotism as a Southern man, telltale of the college at this time, is on exhibit in a mathematics textbook he published at the time:

> A planter, who knows that his negro-man can do a piece of work in 5 days, when the days are 12 hours long, asks how long it will take him when the days are 15 hours long.
>
> *Ans.* 4 days.

> In the year 1637, all the Pequod Indians that survived the slaughter on the Mystic River were either banished from Connecticut, or sold into slavery. The square root of twice the number of survivors is equal to 1/10th that number. What was the number?
>
> *Ans.* 200

> Major D. H. Hill, *Elements of Algebra* (Philadelphia: J. B. Lippincott & Co., 1857), 106, 318.

119. Beaty, 109.

120. Minutes of the Board of Trustees, 9 July 1861, 1:340-41, DCA.

121. Incorporated into the Minutes of the Board of Trustees, 9 July 1861, 1:348, DCA.

122. Shaw, 109-10, 297.

123. Minutes of the Board of Trustees, 16 July 1867, 1:425-32, DCA; Shaw, 69; Beaty, 113.

124. Beaty, 102-3, 118-19. At the same time the power to appoint the faculty and to exercise plenary governance over the college had devolved from the presbyteries to the trustees. Beaty, 94.

125. Shaw, 66-67; Minutes of the Board of Trustees, 16 February 1869, 1:452, DCA.

126. These proportions held fairly constant from year to year. Minutes of the Board of Trustees, 27 June 1871, 2:494-95; 25 June 1872, 525; 24 June 1873, 572; 23 June 1874, 602, DCA.

127. Minutes of the Board of Trustees, 22 June 1875, 2:607-11, DCA; Beaty, 130. It seems, however, that ecclesial sensitivity eventually prevailed, and the measure was never taken off the table. Minutes of the Board of Trustees, 27 June 1876, 2:629.

128. Beaty, 142.

129. John Bunyan Shearer, "Bible Study in College," *Davidson Monthly,* May 1889, 7-9.

130. Beaty, 149-52, 164-66, 170-72; Shearer, 7. Geiger points out that through most of the nineteenth century the Presbyterian argument on behalf of their own colleges was that they were a haven from the state universities and their irreligious influences and godless teaching. As the century aged, the hostility softened into emulation. Now the church schools were portrayed as like unto the state schools, except that they could be explicit about their religion and fuller in their inquiry. Geiger, 52-55 (see n. 1 above).

131. F[rank] L[ee] Jackson, longtime business manager and treasurer of Davidson College and mayor of Davidson, "Memories of Davidson College," 1970-71, 42, DCA.

132. Walter L[ee] Lingle, *Memories of Davidson College* (Richmond: John Knox Press, 1947), 30.

133. W. L. Lingle, *Memories of Davidson College,* 30-31.

134. Beaty, 215.

135. Thomas W. Lingle, fund-raising officer and brother of Walter L., to Robert Mackenzie, 28 November 1910, RG 32-7-15, DOHP. At its fiftieth anniversary the college had noted that there were more ministers among its graduates (181 out of 579, or 31 percent) than any other occupation (though ministers accounted for only 8 percent of those who had matriculated without graduating). *The Semi-Centennial Catalogue of Davidson College, 1837-1887* (Raleigh: E. M. Uzzell, 1891), 168. Smith estimated that since then about 25 percent of Davidson's incoming students intended a life of ministry, while 35 to 40 percent of those graduating had that intention: Smith to A. R. Shaw, 18 May 1912, DCA/Presidents' Papers/H(enry) L(ouis) Smith/"Davidson College (General)."

136. [Smith], "The Work and Aims of Davidson College," *Davidson College Bulletin,* October 1904, 4-5, 8.

137. Smith to J. H. Wearn, March 1912, quoted in Beaty, 227 n.

138. Smith to Mrs. J. E. Hampton, Fordyce, Arkansas, 20 May 1912, DCA/Presidents' Papers/H. L. Smith/"Davidson College (General)."

139. W. L. Lingle, *Memories of Davidson College,* 99-119.

140. See J. W. Lafferty to Martin, 7 February 1913; Martin to Lafferty, 10 February 1913, DCA: Presidents' Papers/W[illiam] J[oseph] Martin/"Presbyterianism-Growth."

141. Martin to Poteat, 10 November 1922, DCA/Presidents' Papers/W. J. Martin/"Evolution." Poteat, for whom the code word "fundamentals" in 1922 would have had chilling overtones, replied brusquely: "I am not aware that any scientists teach that man is descended from an ape. I am not quite sure that I can agree with you in the statement that there is little support for any

definite conclusion about the theory of Evolution. I incline to the view that practically all we know about natural processes is in harmony with it." Poteat to Martin, 15 November 1922, DCA/Presidents' Papers/W. J. Martin/"Evolution."

142. Beaty, 243-48.

143. Beaty, 269-70.

144. Beaty, 279-80, 306.

145. The report did observe, however, that whereas farming, medicine, and law were the major claimants of alumni in early years, business established itself as the leading vocation by 1855. The ministry had thereafter held second place except for a brief postbellum period when more went into the clergy than into business.

146. Robert L[incoln] Kelly, "Davidson College: A Diagnosis and Prescription," *Christian Education* 9, no. 8 (May 1926): 297-354, esp. 325ff. Kelly edited this journal from 1917 to 1935.

147. M. Camper O'Neal, "A Report of the Work of the Y.M.C.A. of Davidson College for the Year 1929-30"; O'Neal to W. L. Lingle, 30 May 1930, DCA/Presidents' Papers/W[alter] L[ee] Lingle/"YMCA."

148. W. L. Lingle, *Memories of Davidson College,* 126; Beaty, 293.

149. W. L. Lingle, *Memories of Davidson College,* 131-33. Davidson did not make military training completely voluntary until 1960, three decades after the General Assembly had made its request.

150. "Some Deliverances of the General Assembly on Dancing," DCA/Presidents' Papers/ W. L. Lingle/"Dancing."

151. Beaty, 310-12, 324; W. L. Lingle, *Memories of Davidson College,* 133-35.

152. W. L. Lingle, "To the Members of the Faculty and Staff of Davidson College," 6 May 1933, DCA/Presidents' Papers/W. L. Lingle/"Drinking."

153. Beaty, 314-16.

154. W. L. Lingle, "Report of the President of Davidson College to the Trustees," 15 February 1933, DCA/Presidents' Papers/W. L. Lingle/"Presbyterian Church in U.S."

155. Beaty, 326.

156. See *Source Book on Christian Education, as Related to the Colleges and Theological Seminaries of the Church,* ed. Henry H. Sweets (Louisville: Executive Committee of Christian Education of the PCUS, 1942), 48, 157-67.

157. W. L. Lingle, "Report of the President of Davidson College to the Trustees," 30 May 1936, 7-9, DCA/Presidents' Papers/W. L. Lingle/"Presbyterian Church in U.S."; W. L. Lingle to W. T. Thompson, 21 February 1938, DCA/Presidents' Papers/W. L. Lingle/"YMCA."

158. George A. Works, *Report of a Survey of the Colleges and Theological Seminaries of the Presbyterian Church in the United States* (Louisville: PCUS, 1941-42), 122.

159. George A. Works, "Survey of Davidson College," 1942, 8, 24, 43-46, Appendix 4; see cover letter of J. R. Cunningham, 1943(?), DCA/Presidents' Papers/J[ohn] R[ood] Cunningham/"Works-Survey."

160. Correspondence (September-October 1943) in DCA/Presidents' Papers/J[ohn] R[ood] Cunningham/"Faculty-Inaugural Vows."

161. Cunningham was at the time content with this. "It seems to me that in order to maintain the doctrinal and ecclesiastical connections . . . it is well to guarantee the continuance of a good proportion of persons who belong to our branch of the Church. On the other hand, to limit an institution in its choice of men to those who hold our particular denominational tenets seems to be doubtful." Cunningham to P. E. Monroe, president of Lenoir-Rhyne College, 19 April 1946, DCA/Presidents' Papers/J. R. Cunningham/"Faculty-Inaugural Vows."

162. Cunningham to Richards, 7 July 1953; Richards to Cunningham, 10 July 1953; Cunningham to Richards, 11 July 1953, DCA/Presidents' Papers/J. R. Cunningham/"Faculty-Inaugural Vows." See also Cunningham, "What Is a Christian College?" in *Church and Campus,* ed. DeWitt C. Reddick (Richmond: John Knox Press, 1956), 71-87.

163. Wayne Fulton to Richards, 27 April 1956; W. Taliaferro Thompson to Cunningham, 11 January 1957; Cunningham to Jay H. Ostwalt, 25 May 1957, DCA/Presidents' Papers/J. R. Cunningham/"Faculty-Inaugural Vows."

164. Beaty, 352-54.

165. Beaty, 357-59.

166. Student comments on chapel, in DCA/Presidents' Papers/J. R. Cunningham/"Chapel, Etc."

167. Cunningham to Foreman (since 1947 teaching at the Louisville Theological Seminary), 3 March 1950, DCA/Presidents' Papers/J. R. Cunningham/"Religious Life-Campus."

168. Pietenpohl to Cunningham, 20 February 1952, DCA/Presidents' Papers/J. R. Cunningham/"Chapel, Etc."

169. Alan G. Gripe, "The Chaplain's Job at Davidson College," 20 February 1952, DCA/Presidents' Papers/J. R. Cunningham/"YMCA." Gripe, who was both secretary of the YMCA and incumbent of the new chaplaincy, after reporting on these fellowship initiatives, writes: "At the same time the Roman Catholic Church has asked us if we would like to have a Newman Club on the campus. The Catholics were informed that since we have no Catholic students at present there seems to be no need for such an organization." There was not a single Catholic in the student body, and only one Jew. The only other group of notable size were the Lutherans, who numbered fifteen.

170. Alan G. Gripe, "Report of Joint Meeting of the Y.M.C.A. Board of Directors and Cabinet," 23 October 1951; Gripe, "Y.M.C.A. Program at Davidson College 1951-1952," 20 February 1952, DCA/Presidents' Papers/J. R. Cunningham/"YMCA"; Beaty, 357-58.

171. "Report in the Educational Institutions Survey by the Committee on Educational Institutions to the Synod of North Carolina, Presbyterian Church in the United States, May 1955," DCA. The report observed, in a slightly envious footnote, that the new Wake Forest College campus being built in Winston-Salem would cost more than the combined value of the endowments and property of all PCUS Presbyterian colleges.

172. Correspondence, DCA/Presidents' Papers/J. R. Cunningham/"Integration."

173. George Staples to Martin, 6 June 1958, with "Report of the College Chaplain 1957-58," DCA/Presidents' Papers/D. G. Martin/"Religious Life."

174. John C. Bailey, Jr., dean of students, memorandum to students on chapel and vespers at Davidson College, 1 September 1960, with "A Statement concerning the Program of Week-Day Assemblies and Sunday Vesper Services at Davidson College," DCA/Presidents' Papers/D. G. Martin/"Religious Life."

175. George Staples, "Report of the College Chaplain 1960-61," 1-2, DCA/Presidents' Papers/D. G. Martin/"Religious Life."

176. William C. Morris, Jr., Saint Alban's Church (Davidson), to Martin, 19 July 1965, DCA/Presidents' Papers/D. G. Martin/"Religious Life."

177. Harold H. Viehman, "The Place of Worship in the Program of the Christian College," DCA/Presidents' Papers/D. G. Martin/"Faculty Committee on Religious Life."

178. "Report of the Religious Life Committee to the Faculty," 5 April 1965, DCA/Presidents' Papers/D. G. Martin/"Religious Life."

179. C[harles] E. Lloyd to Martin, 11 March 1966, DCA/Presidents' Papers/D. G. Martin/"Religious Life."

180. Morris to Martin, 17 March 1966, DCA/Presidents' Papers/D. G. Martin/"Religious Life."

181. Will H. Terry, chaplain, to James McDowell Richards, president of the board of trustees, 25 April 1966; Richards to Terry, 28 April 1966, DCA/Presidents' Papers/D. G. Martin/"Religious Life."

182. "Report of the Special Committee on Religion," [fall 1966], DCA/Presidents' Papers/D. G. Martin/"Religious Life."

183. Excerpts from the Report of the Committee on Religious Life and Community Church Relations, in Minutes of the Board of Trustees, 5 May 1967, 13, DCA.

184. Responses to an inquiry by President Martin, June 1962, DCA/Presidents' Papers/D. G. Martin/"Purpose, Statement of."

185. "Davidson College — A Statement of Purpose," adopted 19 February 1964.

186. Educational Reviewer, Inc. [Russell Kirk, Ernest Van den Haag, et al.], "A Survey of the Political and Religious Attitudes of American College Students," *National Review,* 8 October 1963, 279-302.

187. Minutes of the Board of Trustees, 16 October 1964, 4, DCA.

188. Langford to Richards, president of the board of trustees, 17 November 1964, DCA/Presidents' Papers/D. G. Martin/"Faculty Vow."

189. Smith to Martin, 26 October 1964, DCA/Presidents' Papers/D. G. Martin/"Faculty Vow."

190. Shriver to Martin, 25 January 1965, DCA/Presidents' Papers/D. G. Martin/"Faculty Vow."

191. Frontis W. Johnson, dean of the faculty, to Shriver, 18 February 1965, DCA/Presidents' Papers/D. G. Martin/"Faculty Vow."

192. Martin and Johnson to Richards, 9 March 1965, DCA/Presidents' Papers/D. G. Martin/"Faculty Vow." This complaint, though perhaps overheated at Davidson, echoes a discussion in the church at large about the bearing of the ordination vows, from which the Davidson inaugural vows were derived. See "The Meaning of 'Doctrinal Loyalty' in the Ordination Vows," "Report of the Standing Theological Committee," Minutes of the 112th General Assembly of the Presbyterian Church in the United States, 1972, *Journal,* pp. 196-200, PCUS/GA/M1972, 196-200.

193. These amendments were voted on preliminarily in the spring of 1965, Minutes of the Board of Trustees, 30 April 1965, 11-12; news release, Davidson College, 1 May 1965; Martin, memorandum to the faculty, 3 May 1965, DCA. They were definitively approved at the next meeting: Minutes, 22 October 1965, 6-7; 5 May 1966, 4-5. It was just three years short of a century since the board had petitioned the presbyteries to relax the requirement that all trustees need be Presbyterians.

194. DCA/Presidents' Papers/D. G. Martin/"Faculty Vow."

195. Minutes of the Board of Trustees, 27 June 1871, 2:494-95, DCA.

196. Minutes of the Board of Trustees, 5 May 1966, 10-11, DCA. It should be noted that Davidson retained obligatory training in military science until 1969, when the trustees very reluctantly agreed to make it voluntary. Beaty, 377 n.

197. Minutes of the Board of Trustees, 17 October 1975, Appendix, DCA.

198. Denominational statistics for earlier years at Davidson are scattered throughout many kinds of sources. For information on the last several decades, the author is grateful to Ms. Chloe Myers of the office of the registrar.

199. Report of the Dean of the Faculty, May 1967, in "Report of the President and Administrative Officers to the Trustees of Davidson College, 5 May 1967," 15-16, DCA.

200. The 1969 edition of *Barron's Profiles of American Colleges* reports — not too accurately — that 50 percent of Davidson's students are Presbyterians.

201. Samuel R[eid] Spencer, Jr., *Why Choose a Church College?* (Richmond: Board of Higher Education, PCUS, [1954?]).

202. Charles McEwen, "College-Church Relationship: 'Not a Balance Sheet,' " "Church-'Relatedness': Add Faith, Pinch of Learning," and "College and Church: 'You'd Like to Believe and Don't,' " *Davidsonian,* 17, 24, and 31 January 1969.

203. Report of the Subcommittee on Admissions, in "Report of the President's Study Commission on Davidson College's Church Relation," 1969, DCA/Presidents' Papers/J. R. Spencer/"Church/College Relationship."

204. List of Recommendations, 2, "Report of the President's Study Commission," DCA.

The Commission took encouragement from a proposal then circulating in the Presbyterian College Union, formed of all the college presidents: "An assurance that no confessional test shall be exacted of students, faculty, and other employees of the college beyond sympathy with its stated purpose." Appendix 1, "Report of the President's Study Commission."

205. Thompson, Jr., to Spencer, 24 February 1970, DCA/Presidents' Papers/J. R. Spencer/ "Church/College Relationship."

206. Minutes of the Board of Trustees, 16 October 1970, 10-11, DCA.

207. Ben Lacy Rose, moderator, PCUS/GA/M1972, 204.

208. Alexander J. McElway et al., Circular to the Faculty, 4 October 1972, DCA/Presidents' Papers/J. R. Spencer/"Religion and Davidson College."

209. Spencer, Memorandum to All Members of the Trustees, Faculty and Staff, announcing retreat, 4 April 1973, DCA/Presidents' Papers/J. R. Spencer/"Religion and Davidson College"; Minutes of the Board of Trustees, 4 May 1973, 4, DCA.

210. Memorandum of the Educational Policy Committee to the Faculty, on Proposed Resolution regarding the Christian Commitment of Davidson College, 24 May 1973, DCA/Presidents' Papers/J. R. Spencer/"Religion and Davidson College."

211. Warner L. Hall, chairman of the board of trustees, Letter to the Faculty, soliciting comment on draft of bylaw amendment, 20 August 1974; Minutes of the Board of Trustees, 25 October 1974, 3; 21 February 1975, 3-4, DCA. The revision of the bylaws continued into 1976: Minutes, 27 February 1976.

212. Minutes of the Executive Committee of the Board of Trustees, various years, DCA.

213. Report of the Religious Program and Policy Committee, Minutes of the Board of Trustees, 26 October 1973, 4, DCA.

214. *Davidson College Self-Study Report for the Southern Association of Colleges and Schools* (SACS), October 1974, 15, 59-60, DCA. By the time the accreditation visit had been completed, the faculty vows had been eliminated and the "reverent seeker" exception had been enacted. The response by the SACS visitation team was ambivalent. On the statement of purpose, they wrote:

> The statement composed by the personnel of the College is truly distinctive. The institution is to be commended for its forthright dedication to its Christian commitment. This reassertion of its fundamental purpose denies the view of many, however, including some educators, who frequently declare that a church college can not survive with a high level of quality. . . . at least a minority of academicians will continue to object to the necessity for a "permanent member of the faculty" to be "committed to the Christian faith and is a member of a Christian church." (pp. 5-6)

On possibly negative implications for academic freedom:

> The removal of the vow requirement has, of course, been well received in general, although this sentiment is not universal. . . . some promotions have been withheld on account of the vow, and some possibly withheld or deferred because of the unpopularity or controversial nature of opinions held in the spheres of economics and politics. (p. 20)

215. "Christian Tenure Inconsistent with College's Ideals," *Davidsonian,* 22 April 1977, 4.

216. Earl R. MacCormac, "Two Views of Davidson: Non-Christians Are Denied Free Speech," *Charlotte Observer,* 1 May 1977, 30.

217. R[obert] D[avid] Kaylor et al., Letter to the Faculty of Davidson College, 29 April 1977, DCA/Faculty-Christian Commitment, Linden.

218. Spencer, memorandum to all members of the college community, 26 April 1977, enclosing his statement made at the alumni luncheon, 23 April 1977, DCA/Faculty-Christian Commitment, Linden. See also Earl Lawrimore, "Christian Tenure Issue: Background and Main Events of Controversy," *Davidson Update,* May 1977, 3.

219. Minutes of the Board of Trustees, 6 May 1977, 5-7, attachments 1-2, DCA.

220. Minutes of the Board of Trustees, 7 October 1977, DCA.

221. Harold Warren, "Davidson Faculty Plan OKd," *Charlotte Observer,* n.d., 1, 20A, DCA/Faculty-Christian Commitment, Linden.

222. Minutes of the Board of Trustees, 5 May 1978, 3-4, DCA.

223. George Telford, higher education executive for the General Assembly, PCUS, "The Immediate Context of This Consultation," 4, in papers of PCUS Consultation on Church and Higher Education, Charlotte, 26-28 January 1976, DCA/Presidents' Papers/J. R. Spencer/"PCUS Task Force."

224. James H. Daughdrill, Jr., president of Southwestern University at Memphis, "What Next for Church-Related Colleges?" DCA/Presidents' Papers/J. R. Spencer/"PCUS Task Force."

225. Spencer to J. Randolph Taylor, 13 April 1982, and attachments; "Task Force on Higher Education: Final Report to the 122nd General Assembly (1982)"; Memorandum to those interested in the Report of the Task Force on Higher Education and its implications, DCA/Presidents' Papers/J. R. Spencer/"PCUS Task Force"; Minutes of the Board of Trustees, 9 October 1982, 2-3, DCA.

226. Minutes of the Board of Trustees, 7 January 1983, 5, DCA.

227. "Davidson College Self-Study Report for the Southern Association of Colleges and Schools, September 1986," 12, Appendix 2, DCA.

228. Minutes of the Board of Trustees, 20 February 1987, 5-6, DCA. The Department of Philosophy wished at the time to appoint a non-Christian: see David Kaylor, *Davidsonian,* 5 December 1994, 4.

229. Minutes of the Board of Trustees, 20 February 1987, 9, DCA.

230. Minutes of the Board of Trustees, 7 October 1988, attachment, DCA.

231. Minutes of the Board of Trustees, 4 February 1994, 9; attachment I, "Proposed Statement of Purpose for Davidson College"; attachment II, A[lexander] J. McElway, Report to the Trustees; Minutes of the Board of Trustees, 22 April 1994, 2, DCA.

232. There is a deep paradox here. When Davidson was founded, it was the contention of the Old School that their New School coreligionists, in their fascination with popular religious developments and social activism, had drifted away from the discipline of serious scholarship and were degrading the church's good standing. "This retrograde movement . . . impairs our respectability. While society at large continues to respect real learning and refinement, no religious body which undervalues either, can expect to hold a commanding station in the public eye. . . . Loss of respect must involve a loss of influence. . . ." The liberal faculty, in their determination to protect Davidson's reputation in the eyes of the academic guild, were reproducing the argument of the very conservative Old School against unseemly piety 130 years earlier. Review of Breckenridge, *Annual of the Board of Education, 1835,* 276.

233. Meg Wolff, "Debate Continues about the Role of Religion at Davidson," *Davidsonian,* 5 December 1994, 4.

234. There were actually about twice this many confirmed Presbyterians in the country.

235. Courtauld McBryde, "Rosenbach Challenges Requirement That College President Be 'Active Churchman,'" *Davidsonian,* 24 October 1994, 4; Meg Wolff, "SGA Discussion on Presidential Requirements Continues," *Davidsonian,* 7 November 1994, 5; Matthew Eirich, "Must President Be Presbyterian?" *Davidsonian,* 14 November 1994, 3; Mary Clare Jalonick, "Ecumenical Council Starts Petition to Reaffirm Presidential Ties to Presbyterian Church," *Davidsonian,* 28 November 1994, 2; Wolff, "Debate Continues," 3; Ecumenical Council minutes, 27 October, 7 November, 1 December 1994; Letter of the Ecumenical Council to Craig Wall, chairman of the board, and John Kuykendall, president, 1 December 1994, DCA.

236. John W[ells] Kuykendall, "The Church-Related College: A Partnership between Faith and Learning," *Davidson Journal* 2 (fall/winter 1987): 3-5.

237. Sarah Teachworth, "Trustees Debate Religion," *Davidsonian,* 24 April 1995, 5.

238. Kit Lively, "Davidson Tries to Keep Presbyterian Heritage While Welcoming Students of Other Faiths," *Chronicle of Higher Education,* 12 July 1996, A15-16.

239. Longfield and Marsden, unpublished draft, 1 (see n. 62).

240. Longfield and Marsden, 100.

241. Very little cogent comment is offered on the startling demographics. In 1992 Presbyterians constituted only 12 percent of the enrollment in colleges claimed by the PC(USA). The highest proportion in any college was 43 percent. No other college enrolled more than one-third Presbyterians, and there are colleges which had only 2 or 1 percent. "Loving God with Our Minds: The Mission of the Presbyterian Church (U.S.A.) in Higher Education within the Global Community," approved GA/1991 (Louisville: Committee on Higher Education/PC[USA], 1992), 30.

242. Wade Clark Roof, "The Changing Patterns of Denominationalism: To Whom or What Do Colleges Relate," in *A Point of View,* [PC(USA) Committee on Higher Education and Association of Presbyterian Colleges and Universities] #1 (18 May 1990), 7. Roof, with John McKinney, is author of *American Mainline Religion: Its Changing Shape and Future* (New Brunswick, N.J.: Rutgers University Press, 1987), which has more substance than this quotation might imply.

243. Victor Stoltzfus, *Church-Affiliated Higher Education* (Goshen, Ind.: Pinchpenny Press, 1992), 60.

244. James E. Andrews, stated clerk (chief executive officer) of the PC(USA), memorandum to Duncan Ferguson, director of the Committee on Higher Education, 27 June 1990; Richard Rodman, international education specialist in the Office of Global Ministries, PC(USA), memorandum to Ferguson, 26 April 1990, DOHP.

245. There was a time, especially in the later nineteenth century, when Presbyterian educators did oppose state colleges and universities as worldly campuses hostile to Christian teaching. But this was because, after the Morrill Acts, the church-related colleges, which had originally cost less than their state counterparts, were at a disadvantage financially. It was the price, more than the permissiveness, that rankled. In the early twentieth century this critique would revert to competition, then emulation. Geiger, 52-55.

246. Longfield and Marsden, 123.

247. David S. Schaff, "Presbyterianism and Education," *Reformed Quarterly Review* 41 (1894): 78-79.

248. "Baccalaureate Address, delivered on the Fourth Anniversary Commencement of the University of Nashville, October 7, 1829," in *The Works of Philip Lindsley,* ed. Le Roy J. Halsey, vol. 1 (Philadelphia: J. B. Lippincott, 1866), 254-55. Lindsley, a graduate of and later professor at Princeton, had been offered presidencies at many colleges and universities: Transylvania, Washington (later Washington and Lee), Princeton, Dickinson, Ohio, Pennsylvania, Louisiana, and South Alabama. He accepted only one, at Cumberland College (1824-50), which the next year was rechristened the University of Nashville (still later to become George Peabody College, which was in turn merged into Vanderbilt University). Along the way Lindsley served as moderator of the PCUS. His own institution, Lindsley said, was neither sectarian nor dependent upon ecclesiastical patronage, but "perfectly catholic and perfectly impartial," all trustees, faculty, and students being merely "Christians and patriots." He does, however, make derogatory references to one or another church not his own: *Works,* 1:88-94, 164-68, 254-58, 273-75, 306-15, 349, 366-67, 377-78.

249. Much of what follows is guided by a remarkable study of Guy Howard Miller, "A Contracting Community: American Presbyterians, Social Conflict, and Higher Education 1730-1820," 2 vols. (Ph.D. diss., University of Michigan, 1970).

250. See also David W. Robson, *Educating Republicans: The College in the Era of the American Revolution, 1750-1800* (Westport, Conn.: Greenwood, 1985).

251. John M. Mulder and Lee A. Wyatt, "The Predicament of Pluralism: The Study of Theology in Presbyterian Seminaries Since the 1920s," in *The Pluralistic Vision,* 37-70.

252. Little in our two case studies varies significantly from what has been reported in

various research surveys, including Douglas G. Trout, "The Changing Character of Ten United Presbyterian Church-Related Colleges, 1914-1964" (Ph.D. diss., University of Michigan, 1965); John Irwin Page, "A Study of Secularistic Trends and Their Effect upon Seven Protestant Colleges of Kansas" (Ph.D. diss., Kansas State University, 1989), 63-71; William Bryan Adrian, Jr., "Changes in Christian Emphasis among Selected Church-Related Colleges in Illinois" (Ph.D. diss., Denver University, 1967), 193-214; Kenneth Eugene Gowdy, "The Decline of Religious Characteristics in the Pursuit of Academic Excellence: A Study of Minnesota Private Liberal Arts Colleges" (Ph.D. diss., Fordham University, 1979), 112-31.

CHAPTER 3

The Methodists

John Wesley himself — who, without intending it to be more than a reform movement, became the founder of the Methodist church — was ambivalent on the matter
of learning. He instructed his preachers "to preach expressly on education. . . . Gift
or no gift, you are to do it, else you are not called to be a Methodist preacher."
Yet he also wrote in *The Book of Discipline:* "Gaining Knowledge is a good thing,
but saving Souls is a better . . . If you can do but one, let your Studies alone. I
would rather throw by all the Libraries in the World rather than be guilty of the
Loss of one Soul."[1]

The ambivalence continued. Francis Asbury and Thomas Coke, the two
preachers sent by Wesley to found Methodism in America, were divided in their
respective emphases on elementary and higher education. Asbury wanted elementary schools and Coke, the LL.D. from Oxford and indeed the only participant at
the founding conference in 1784 with a formal university education, wanted colleges. When their first, joint namesake, college, Cokesbury (in Virginia), burned
to the ground a year after it was incorporated in 1794, Asbury wrote in his journal:
"Would any man give me ten thousand pounds a year to do and suffer again what
I have done for that house, I would not do it. The Lord called not Mr. Whitefield
(the preacher who had stirred up the Great Awakening) or the Methodists to build
colleges." The next year their second venture also went up in flames, and Asbury
wrote: "I conclude God loveth the people of Baltimore, and will keep them poor
in order to keep them pure." A third attempt, also in Baltimore, perished for other
reasons: shortage of funds and "a mongrel religion" (few of its teachers were
Methodists).[2]

The membership of the early Methodist movement, largely rural and poor
and therefore indifferent toward education of any but the most rustic sort, provided
neither clientele nor patronage for academies and colleges.[3] William Capers, a

---

This essay was researched and written in 1993-94, and the statistics and facts it reports as current
derive from the latest sources then available.

college-educated minister who served in South Carolina, was told: "If you are called to preach, and sinners are falling daily into hell, take care lest the blood of some of them be found on your skirts."[4]

Consequently the Methodist enterprise in American higher education got off to a late start:

> . . . 15 years after Roman Catholicism, 57 years after the German Reformed Church, 65 years after the Baptist denomination, 74 years after the Dutch Reformed Church, 84 years after Presbyterianism, 137 years after the Protestant Episcopal Church, and 194 years after Congregationalism. Harvard, Yale, William and Mary, Princeton, and Brown were recognized institutions of higher learning before Methodism was even organized into a church.[5]

Eventually Methodist sympathy for education grew, and in 1820 (significantly, after Asbury's death) the General Conference recommended that each of the local annual (regional) conferences sponsor or cosponsor a "literary institution" in its territory. The oldest college originally and still affiliated with the Methodists is Lycoming, founded as a secondary school in 1812. Randolph-Macon has been a Methodist institution of higher education longer than any other.[6] From 1820 onward, a spate of Methodist colleges were founded. The old ambivalence continued, however. It was well embodied in the Reverend Peter Cartwright, successively an exhorter, preacher, and presiding elder in the roughest parts of Kentucky, where he was known to thrash anyone who disturbed his revival meetings. Uncle Peter's view was not untypical:

> Methodism in Europe this day would have been a thousand to one, if the Wesleyans had stood by the old land-marks of John Wesley: but no; they must introduce pews, literary institutions and theological institutes, till a plain, old-fashioned preacher, such as one of Mr. Wesley's "lay preachers," would be scouted, and not allowed to occupy one of their pulpits. . . .
>
> The Presbyterians, and other Calvinistic branches of the Protestant Church, used to contend for an educated ministry, for pews, for instrumental music, for a congregational or stated salaried ministry. The Methodists universally opposed these ideas; and the illiterate Methodist preachers actually set the world on fire, [the American world at least,] while they were lighting their matches! . . . I do not wish to undervalue education, but really I have seen so many of these educated preachers who forcibly reminded me of lettuce growing under the shade of a peach tree . . . that I turn away sick and faint
>
> Is it not manifest to every candid observer that very few of those young men who believe they are called of God to preach the Gospel, and are persuaded to go to a college or a Biblical Institute, the better to qualify them for the great work of the ministry, ever go into the regular traveling ministry? The reason is plainly this: having quieted their consciences with the flattering unction of ob-

taining a sanctified education, while they have neglected the duty of regularly preaching Jesus to dying sinners, their moral sensibilities are blunted, and they see an opening prospect of getting better pay as teachers in high schools or other institutions of learning, and from the prospect of gain they are easily persuaded that they can meet their moral obligations in disseminating sanctified learning.[7]

Yet this same Cartwright, D.D. *honoris causa,* was one of the foremost organizers of Illinois Wesleyan University and McKendree College, and actively involved in MacMurray College for Women and the Garrett Biblical Institute.[8] Many of the farmers who had been converted by the rugged itinerant preachers sent their sons (and some, their daughters) to these literary institutions, and that generation began to find the itinerant preachers ignorant and unsympathetic. They began to drift away from Methodism, until canny ministers like Cartwright began to yield to this new imperative of educated (and therefore residential) preachers for educated people. But not until 1846 would the Methodists establish a theological seminary. Sweet remarks that "every leading denomination in the United States had established at least one theological seminary before the Methodists . . . the Episcopalians, the Congregationalists, the Unitarians, the Baptists, the German Reformed, the Dutch Reformed, the Lutherans, the Free Will Baptists, and the Catholics, while the Presbyterians had no less than nine."[9]

Colleges for Laity, Not Ministers

In a departure from the older Episcopal, Congregational, and Presbyterian educational precedents, Methodists created their "literary institutions" for the laity, not their clergy. No college course was required or presumed for those on their way to the pulpit. Their ministers were trained by the Course of Study, a correspondence course followed by board examinations. Not until a half-century ago was seminary training recognized as the equivalent of the Course of Study, whose curriculum underwent continual revision. The academies and colleges were from the start intended for the laity — a devout and Pietist laity — and they grew in accord with their people's social, economic, and cultural aspirations. Evangelism, not education, was seen as the foundation of faith. What Methodists meant by their "faith" was the gospel powerfully seized, and not any intellectual reflections upon it or arguments over it. Thus academic training was not considered a professional requirement for the ministry.[10]

As the Second Great Awakening spread across the country, the Methodist membership swelled enormously. The evangelical, relatively unecclesiastical format of that movement, which sent untrained but intensely motivated preachers across the vast areas of the South and the West that were just then opening up to national expansion and settlement, and which offered a theology that was not complex and a worship that was spontaneous and a piety and a morality that befitted those rough circumstances, ignited a prairie fire of conversions that favored primarily the Methodists and the Baptists. The people called Methodists were on their way to becoming for a while the most numerous church in the country. Theirs was what came to be called "Christianity in earnest."[11]

Response to the exhortation to found and sponsor schools locally was slow . . . at first. But as their membership and wherewithal swelled, the American Methodists embarked with unexpected energy on the path of education. From 1829 to 1850 they founded nearly 400 schools and colleges. They are reckoned to have established more than 1,200 schools. Though nearly 90 percent of them have closed, merged, or disaffiliated, the Methodists have founded and sponsored more colleges than any other Protestant denomination and, for a while, more than the Catholics.[12] Today their list of related institutions includes 87 universities and four-year colleges:[13]

1773	Dickinson College	Carlisle, Pa.
1812	Lycoming College	Williamsport, Pa.
1815	Allegheny College	Meadville, Pa.
1825	Centenary College of Louisiana	Shreveport, La.
1828	McKendree College	Lebanon, Ill.
1830	Randolph-Macon College	Ashland, Va.
1831	LaGrange College	LaGrange, Ga.
1835	Albion College	Albion, Mich.
1836	Emory University	Atlanta, Ga.
1836	Emory and Henry College	Emory, Va.
1836	Wesleyan College	Macon, Ga.
1837	DePauw University	Greencastle, Ind.
1838	Duke University	Durham, N.C.
1838	Greensboro College	Greensboro, N.C.
1839	Boston University	Boston, Mass.
1840	Southwestern University	Georgetown, Tex.
1842	Iowa Wesleyan College	Mount Pleasant, Iowa
1842	Ohio Wesleyan University	Delaware, Ohio
1842	Willamette University	Salem, Oreg.
1843	Lambuth University	Jackson, Tenn.
1845	Baldwin-Wallace College	Berea, Ohio
1846	MacMurray College	Jacksonville, Ill.
1846	Mount Union College	Alliance, Ohio
1847	Otterbein College	Westerville, Ohio
1850	Illinois Wesleyan University	Bloomington, Ill.
1851	University of the Pacific	Stockton, Calif.
1853	Cornell College	Mount Vernon, Iowa
1854	Central Methodist College	Fayette, Mo.
1854	Columbia College	Columbia, S.C.

1854	Hamline University	Saint Paul, Minn.
1854	Huntingdon College	Montgomery, Ala.
1854	University of Evansville	Evansville, Ind.
1854	Wofford College	Spartanburg, S.C.
1856	Albright College	Reading, Pa.
1856	Birmingham-Southern College	Birmingham, Ala.
1857	Tennessee Wesleyan College	Athens, Tenn.
1858	Baker University	Baldwin City, Kans.
1858	Kentucky Wesleyan College	Owensboro, Ky.
1859	Adrian College	Adrian, Mich.
1860	Simpson College	Indianola, Iowa
1861	North Central College	Naperville, Ill.
1864	University of Denver	Denver, Colo.
1865	Clark Atlanta University	Atlanta, Ga.
1866	Lebanon Valley College	Annville, Pa.
1866	Rust College	Holly Springs, Miss.
1867	Centenary College	Hackettstown, N.J.
1867	Drew University	Madison, N.J.
1869	Claflin College	Orangeburg, S.C.
1869	Dillard University	New Orleans, La.
1870	Syracuse University	Syracuse, N.Y.
1871	Ohio Northern University	Ada, Ohio
1872	Bethune-Cookman College	Daytona Beach, Fla.
1873	Bennett College	Greensboro, N.C.
1873	Wesley College	Dover, Del.
1873	Wiley College	Marshall, Tex.
1875	Huston-Tillotson College	Austin, Tex.
1875	Shenandoah University	Winchester, Va.
1876	Hendrix College	Conway, Ark.
1877	Philander Smith College	Little Rock, Ark.
1878	Rocky Mountain College	Billings, Mont.
1879	Union College	Barbourville, Ky.
1882	Paine College	Augusta, Ga.
1883	Dakota Wesleyan University	Mitchell, S.Dak.
1885	Florida Southern College	Lakeland, Fla.
1885	Pfeiffer University	Misenheimer, N.C.
1885	Southwestern College	Winfield, Kans.
1886	Kansas Wesleyan University	Salina, Kans.
1887	Nebraska Wesleyan University	Lincoln, Nebr.
1888	University of Puget Sound	Tacoma, Wash.
1890	Millsaps College	Jackson, Miss.
1890	Texas Wesleyan University	Fort Worth, Tex.
1890	West Virginia Wesleyan College	Buckhannon, W.Va.

1891	Randolph-Macon Woman's College	Lynchburg, Va.
1893	American University	Washington, D.C.
1894	Morningside College	Sioux City, Iowa
1902	University of Indianapolis	Indianapolis, Ind.
1903	Lindsey Wilson College	Columbia, Ky.
1904	Oklahoma City University	Oklahoma City, Okla.
1911	Southern Methodist University	Dallas, Tex.
1913	Ferrum College	Ferrum, Va.
1923	McMurry University	Abilene, Tex.
1924	High Point University	High Point, N.C.
1934	Kendall College	Evanston, Ill.
1956	Methodist College	Fayetteville, N.C.
1956	North Carolina Wesleyan College	Rocky Mount, N.C.
1957	Alaska Pacific University	Anchorage, Alaska
1961	Virginia Wesleyan College	Norfolk, Va.

Eleven of these colleges are predominantly for blacks,[14] and four (out of hundreds previously sponsored by Methodists) are still exclusively for women.[15]

Institutions that were once in the Methodist network but have disaffiliated include Southern California, Vanderbilt, Northwestern, Lawrence, and Wesleyan Universities, and Green Mountain, Asbury, Dickinson, Goucher, and Wheaton Colleges. Along the way, various Methodist schools were converted (generally through land grants) to state institutions, such as Henderson State, Maryland Eastern Shore, Tennessee at Chattanooga, Morgan State, Kansas State, Valdosta State, Marshall, Wilberforce, and Auburn Universities.

The present investment of the United Methodist Church (UMC) in higher education is in several respects remarkable. The bulk of the enterprise itself is amazing: 87 universities and four-year colleges; Meharry Medical College; 12 junior colleges; 9 preparatory schools; and 13 denominational schools of theology (the numbers, however, go on shrinking). These 122 schools dispose of total assets of more than $10 billion and combined annual operating budgets of more than $4 billion; the total enrollment is more than 190,000 students, and faculties number more than 15,000. Obviously in an establishment of this size the institutions move mostly on their own steam, yet annual contributions through the church peaked a few years ago at about $60 million: not much when compared to the annual revenues, but far more than any other church or denomination claims to offer as a direct subsidy to its higher education establishment.

The United Methodist relationship with all these institutions is managed by a sophisticated Division of Higher Education (DHE) within a general Board of Higher Education and Ministry (BHEM). The DHE drafts and administers constantly revised policy statements for the church; awards scholarships and loans (with the lowest default rate in the nation) to UMC students; manages an educational foundation; lobbies federal and state governments on matters of public policy; raises and allots special subsidies for traditionally black colleges; conducts conferences for Methodist-affiliated institutions and their executives; supplies professional consultative services; publishes a sheaf of specialized newsletters for campus presidents, attorneys, ministers, and foreign studies officers; orchestrates relations between its institutions and their Methodist peers abroad; and manages an elaborate interactive database linking all of its affiliates. The Methodists also have their own cost-efficient insurance plans for life, health, property, casualty, and student coverage. Among all the centralized denominational establishments of higher education, the Methodists stand out as the most professional and the best resourced.

Another UMC agency, founded more than a century ago and still unique among the churches, is the University Senate, an elected body of educational professionals — many of them affiliate presidents — which has the authority to visit and evaluate campuses; assess their financial stability, academic integrity, and church-relatedness; and determine whether they deserve to be listed as affiliates of the church and thereby qualified for financial and other assistance. The Senate thus functions as an ecclesial accrediting agency.[16]

A Disintegrating Network?

The unofficial motto for higher learning among Methodists is provided by the much-cited quatrain from one of Charles Wesley's hymns:

> Unite the pair so long disjoin'd,
> Knowledge and vital piety;
> Learning and holiness combined,
> And truth and love let all men see.[17]

Within this proficient establishment, however, there are some signs that not all this ado may be about knowledge and vital piety. Methodist assurance that its affiliates remain vitally connected to the church has increasingly relied on those in governance. The church has said that it means to support its colleges and universities, not control them, but the expectation lingers that Methodist interests should be represented by Methodist membership on the boards of trustees. At one time two-thirds of any board's membership were expected to be members of the church, and a good portion of them nominated or elected by the annual conferences (the regional church bodies presided over by bishops). One suggestion in the early 1970s called for a reversal of policy: to remove all evidence of "sectarianism," affiliated colleges should rescind any bylaws requiring that a majority of their trustees be determined by the church or approved by the University Senate.[18] But today it is still customary for some Methodist-related colleges or universities to include on their boards the bishop(s) of the sponsoring local annual conference(s), and sometimes to have a set number (typically about one-fourth to one-third) of the board seats occupied by clergy and laity elected by those conferences. This continues even at institutions which give every other sign of secularization, and there seems to be little boardroom dissonance between church representatives and other trustees.

Another traditional though informal expectation among Methodists is that their colleges and universities depend on the churches for student enrollment and for an annual subsidy. The churches, in turn, count on preferential admission and financial aid for their members, and special aid in the training of those intending ministry.

In stark figures it would seem that these expectations are poorly met. As we have seen, church contributions amount to less than 2 percent of college budgets, on average (curiously, this is not one of the correlations included in the DHE database).[19] United Methodists constitute only 18 percent of the students enrolled in their own institutions. The Methodist enrollment is usually in inverse proportion to the academic maturity of the institutions, running from 24 percent in the junior colleges down to 7 percent in the universities. In individual institutions it ranges from 54 to 0 percent, and has been sinking annually.[20] When one considers that the number of young people in the United Methodist Church fell by the 1980s to one-third of what it was in the 1960s, it is difficult to imagine how these colleges and universities will see themselves serving a Methodist clientele.[21]

But there are a good number of smaller colleges where this mutual traffic is still a tangible and effective adhesive. At Oklahoma City University, which advertises itself as "for UMC students," 34 percent of the student body are Methodists. The school awards dozens of scholarships annually to ministerial candidates. Local Methodist families volunteer to befriend students from abroad and host them in their homes, especially at holiday times. The annual conference meets on the campus and the university spreads out a complimentary barbecue for them all. A majority of honorary degree recipients are recognizably Methodists. Similarly, in Fayetteville, North Carolina, during the course of an average year the annual conference holds nearly a hundred events on the campus of Methodist College. The president and vice president both take their turns in local pulpits about twice a month. Pastors in the conference are each given $1,000 vouchers redeemable for tuition by any church member who enrolls. A few years back the United Methodist Women sent in 83,000 Campbell Soup labels, which were redeemed for new audiovisual and library equipment. Fifty-three ministers within the conference are alumni of the college. Clearly there is a mutual interest and service there.

At Central Methodist College a cash flow crisis in the summer of 1988 prompted an appeal to each Methodist church in Missouri to hold one fund-raiser for the college. After a welter of ham and bean dinners, talent shows, and ice cream socials, the college realized $140,000. Now the college has persuaded 300 of the 1,000 United Methodist churches in Missouri to assemble endowments of $25,000 each to fund scholarships for their members at Central.

These are tangible evidences of loyalty. But they seem to be stronger as the educational institutions are weaker. As they mature academically and flourish financially, they no longer look to the church for their better students or their larger benefactions.

No Eagerness to Be Identified as Methodist

The church has expressed a continual expectation that the Methodist relationship be canonized in mission statements and other public literature. Compliance is desultory. DePauw University, in a "Purposes and Aims" statement approved by the faculty, typically makes no mention of a Methodist connection, but offers this blathery self-description:

> DePauw University stands today as a prime example of the independent liberal arts college which has served its state and nation in the best traditions of American educational institutions. . . . It does so in a context of an intentional commitment to an examination of values, a pursuit of heightened aptitude in critical thinking and the establishment of a sufficiently broad base of general learning to constitute a foundation for living with meaning as well as making a living . . .
>
> The University would nurture a lively acquaintance with the expressions of self-understanding which inform the religious traditions and be a setting for the thoughtful observance of religious belief and practice. There are various opportunities for worship and participation in volunteer service-learning projects.[22]

Boston University, "coeducational and nonsectarian," notes it was founded by a group of Methodist lay leaders. No further reference to the church is made. "Today the University retains its dual character: Yankee independence combined with a cosmopolitan outlook."[23] The only reference to a church relationship in the *Dickinson College Catalogue* is a note that, though founded by Presbyterians, the college "came under the sponsorship of Methodists" in 1834.[24] Morningside College continues to subscribe to foundational statements of 1894: "To unite the two so long divided, knowledge and vital piety, holiness and learning combined . . . The purpose of this school shall be to train leadership for the Church and State."[25] Willamette University publishes its "values" statement:

> While Willamette, as a modern university in a pluralistic setting cannot (and should not) admit students or hire faculty according to a doctrinal test, it can (and should) inculcate those basic Christian values which lead to individual and social wholeness. Willamette can teach theology and ethics without falling afoul of church-state separation; and it can support projects that, for example, put students in touch with community needs or that give them the opportunity to consider Christian vocation. The university motto, "Not unto ourselves alone are

we born,'' suggests we are here to serve God and neighbor, as well as to realize our own potential as individuals.[26]

Pfeiffer College, acknowledging church sponsorship, affirms that

[We] commit ourselves to the concept that educational achievement can best be realized within a community that fosters collegiality, Judeo-Christian values, and shared responsibility for learning. This mission addresses the human need for a sense of purposeful longing, shared values, and the responsibility for self and others. . . .

In the United Methodist tradition, we provide an environment for the development of intellectual, moral, and spiritual growth while recognizing a diversity of backgrounds and faiths.[27]

Pfeiffer is not the only Methodist-related college to make the bewildering profession that it simultaneously seeks both diversity of background and faith, and shared values. Southwestern University, in a lengthy mission statement, makes a similar profession:

Diversity: There is . . . a diversity of personal values, ethnic backgrounds, culture, and religious traditions. Southwestern affirms this diversity and reflects it in its life. The search for and expression of individual identity is valued, and the worth of each person respected. All forms of racism, sexism, religious intolerance, and group prejudice are consciously opposed. Ethnic and cultural self-awareness is supported. . . .

Community: Community is the discovery of what differing persons learn from one another and how distinctive ways of thinking inform one another, and the way what is learned manifests itself in what is done together. There is a shared purpose and mutuality in the academic life at Southwestern that distinguishes it from a secular institution.[28]

The mission statements of these institutions never seem to characterize the church-college link in terms native to Methodism or Christianity. Instead they tend to designate some academic or societal quality as what typifies Methodism: sometimes patriotism, sometimes liberal education, and most recently a commitment to diversity. One might imagine John Wesley to have invented affirmative action.[29]

Among the approved universities and colleges, all of which constitute the National Association of Schools and Colleges of the Methodist Church, some apparently blench at drawing public notice to their Methodist connection. In their own catalogues, and in their prepared notices for directories such as the American Council on Education's *American Universities and Colleges,* or *The College Blue Book,* or *Peterson's Register of Higher Education* or *Guide to*

266

Four-Year Colleges, while most do list themselves as "affiliated with the United Methodist Church," some do not. Dickinson College, Boston University, the University of Denver, Centenary College, and Syracuse University, e.g., usually make no mention of a Methodist linkage. The University of the Pacific states that it was "formerly affiliated." Others, like Duke, are uneven in their self-descriptions, or depict the relationship in merely historical terms: e.g., the college was "founded" by plucky Methodists in yesteryear. Methodist-related institutions often advertise for personnel, including presidents, without any mention of their relation to the church. Invariably, however (except for some black colleges), the institution declares itself as an "affirmative action/equal opportunity educator/employer."

What Is a Methodist College?

The question was put to the University Senate at its very beginnings, in 1893: What is a Methodist college? Their answer was that such a college must (1) observe academic standards required for granting baccalaureate degrees, and (2) accept the church's sponsorship. Some thought that was not much of an answer. After labored drafting the Senate finally adopted this statement in 1912:

> We do not think that the time has come to give any formal hard-and-fast definition of a Methodist Episcopal institution. We offer now only the suggestions given by our present methods and the regular provisions of the Discipline. We would present a tentative statement as follows:
>
> A Methodist Episcopal institution is one which, frankly declaring it is under the auspices of the church and distinctly claiming that it aims to plan and conduct its work so as to serve the Kingdom of Christ as represented by the life of the Methodist Episcopal Church, shall have the recognition and endorsement of the Board of Education, and official classification by the University Senate.[30]

The question, of course, had not been about a "definition," but about the indices or evidences of an institution as effectively Methodist. The response implies some impatience that the question was even asked. But the question persisted, and in 1928 received this astonishing response:

> Educational institutions now appearing on the approved list of the Board of Education shall be recognized under the auspices of the Methodist Episcopal Church. Such institutions are requested to file annually with the Board of Education a complete financial statement properly audited.[31]

This was a return to the first policy: that a college which said it was Methodist was a Methodist college. In 1931 the Board of Education became more subtle and said that institutions could decide for themselves whether they were Christian (not "Methodist") by answering two questions:

> 1. What goes on in the way of fellowship, or the lack of it, in the classroom? To be Christian in the human relationships involving students and teachers there must be reality, honesty, fairness, and all such everyday virtues.
> 2. What about the relations of the college as employer to employee?[32]

By the time of World War II Methodist students had become a minority on their own campuses, and the church's higher education executive claimed that though educational work had once been regarded as a ministry of equal urgency with evangelism, one now had to admit "that there has been some relinquishing of interest by the church and its institutions and that some of the institutions have wanted to be free from strict institutional control." There never had been any strict institutional control. The colleges then received only 3 percent of their income from the church. There was no wavering, however, in the voice of G. Bromley Oxnam, once a Methodist university president and then a Methodist bishop, who had this to say to the presidents at their meeting in 1942:

> The Church desires that the actual contribution of the campus in terms of religion shall be more than chapel, more or less successful, and a few courses in Bible or religion; it shall be of such a nature religiously as to justify support. I am frank to say that very few schools have realized in practice that being a first-rate educational institution is not enough. The question of the religious life of the student is not faced with the same concern with which the educational life of that student is faced. The Church must be convinced that we stand deliberately for something in the field of religion and in practices that religion demands. There is a Christian world-view, a Christian way of life, a Christian commitment to the Christian leader. One is your leader, even Christ. The effort of our colleges must be, in addition to our educational service, evangelistic in the proper sense of that term. Our schools must be Christian without apology, and Methodist with pride. Our faculties must be Christian. Our efforts should be to make the student Christian just as truly as we teach him to think. We must seek to graduate Christians as certainly as we graduate doctors, lawyers, and musicians.[33]

During the 1950s the topic of religious life on the campuses ceased to appear in the Senate's minutes, but the Division of Higher Education occasionally chided colleges for not "standing deliberately for something in the field of religion." Anything.

The Methodist Church declared Christian higher education its special emphasis during the 1956 quadrennium, and this brought to the surface a sharp division of opinion. Some educators argued for a more confessional purpose of "church-related colleges." One seminary professor had this to say:

The church-related college is nothing less than a Church in education. . . . It is the Church communicating its faith. . . . Faith should co-ordinate as well as motivate inquiry. . . .

It is failing its distinctive task unless it has an administration definitely aware of its nature and committed firmly to its task, and unless a large group of the instructors are actively and intelligently concerned with the primary purpose of the college. A church-related college without a Christian faculty fellowship is a misnomer. . . .

The administration ought to select faculty with the double function of the church-related college in mind. Competence and integrity in one's subject are definitely not enough to qualify for such teaching, nor is it enough to add to these requirements a good character. Faith is of the essence, not only of the good essence, of the Christian college. This fact makes staffing a most troublesome task. . . .

Certainly regular worship by the whole college is part and parcel of the reason for the college's existence, and to be apologetic about required chapel services, required convocations, and required courses in religion is to call into question the very ground on which the college is built. These are required in the same sense in which any course requires attendance: if the students are not interested in pursuing such a line, they ought not to be in such a college.[34]

More typical by far, but somewhat more gaseous, were the remarks of a university president:

Only when we believe in law above power, righteousness in the nature of the universe, and persons of infinite worth, capable of understanding and using all resources for human good, can we emerge from our pessimism, our frustration, and our greed.

Reason, conviction, and faith, which have often been bartered for the pottage of power, are coming into their rightful place. Our chief problem is not how to produce more supersonic planes, but how to develop more superior people who will be wise, good, and mature citizens at home and abroad. This is the point at which our pioneer forefathers entered the scene. They believed in enlightenment, not for self-inflation, but for self-discovery. . . .

Methodism seeks a clear idea of what Christian higher education is . . . The *kind* of education the church provides will be much more important than the *amount* of education it underwrites. As the Carnegie Foundation report says, "The objective of liberal arts education is to develop mature, good, and wise men and women." This is not a sectarian aim. It is a universal concern. It is the underpinning of freedom. It rests on the creation of an atmosphere in which intellectual curiosity is encouraged, independent thinking stimulated, values articulated, convictions strengthened, and intelligent religious faith vitalized.[35]

In 1965 "Twelve Marks of a Church College" were set forth sixtyishly by the higher education staff, including the following:

> (1) a climate of decision making in which trustees, administrators, and faculty members understand and accept the ethical implications of the Christian heritage.
>
> (2) development of genuine Christian community in which persons feel accepted and valued *as persons*. The principles of acceptance and reconciliation should be apparent in all human relationships which center in the life of the college . . .
>
> (5) a campus-wide concern to face the persistent questions of life, death, and purpose to which the great religions speak, and which are implicit in the work of an academic community.[36]

One senses an onset of sensitivity training.

In 1966 the Board of Education created a Council on the Church-Related College to articulate the church's rationale for being in education. The Council labored for five years and declared that it had taken a "hard-headed, critical stance" on this perpetual topic. These affirmations presented by the General Secretary of the Division of Higher Education give some feel for how hardheaded that stance was (interminable emphasis is original):

> *When church-related colleges take seriously the problem of the student as an individual — seriously, not sentimentally — they meet a tremendously vital need in the American scene.*
>
> *When church-related colleges work hard at the enlistment of broad-gauged, stimulating teachers and, finding such, give them every encouragement as teachers, the colleges fulfill the most vital of educational needs by bringing together sound students and fine teachers in a community of learning.*
>
> *When the church-related college takes the curriculum with utmost seriousness as a plan to achieve the ends of literacy, sensitivity, and competence, it is meeting a tremendous need in American higher education.*
>
> *When a church-related college is aware in a sophisticated way of the total impact of the campus, and is dedicated to the honoring of those qualities and activities which mark the thoughtful, responsible man, it is filling a need of utmost importance.*[37]

Another Council member deplored the "quest for uniqueness." Church-related colleges, he argued, try to justify their existence — indeed their indispensability — by claiming some plus-value over secular education. It may be instruction in religion, character building, education with a heart, or openness to Christian values. (Some educators would not think any of this was "unique.") "Christian faith, I am convinced, leads the church-related college not to seek for an isolated uniqueness of function but rather to move toward solidarity with man and society, raising such questions as: what is the common good? and how can we contribute to it? . . . Such a change of view, from pride to servanthood, from uniqueness to solidarity, from the pursuit of isolation to pursuit of the common good, may lead to greater freedom and pioneering . . . The way toward deeper faithfulness to our Christian heritage is to move beyond the images of the sectarian past with its seeking for unique functions and seek ways toward greater solidarity with the society around and within the campus community."[38]

It was in the context of that inquiry that the suggestion was strongly made that the Methodist church make over its colleges and universities to state sponsorship. If the essays quoted here typify widespread Methodist views of the time, such a change in sponsorship might have gone unnoticed.

Methodists Neither Control Nor Define

In 1976 the National Commission on United Methodist Higher Education asserted that the colleges of the church were not auxiliaries or properties, but colleague and partner institutions.[39] The church's mission was therefore to support, not to control, these institutions. Thomas Trotter, the higher education executive at the time, explained why this was a step forward:

> It should be clear that the college is not a church. Among educators, there has been an interesting discussion about the proper term to be used in describing the college in the church family. Is it a *Christian* college? a *church* college? or is it a *church-related* college? To some, this progression of terms is a regression, a weakening of the specificity of the relationship. But, this terminological progression may represent a maturing of the vision of learning and faith that is consistent with the best interests of the church. Often the college has been expected by its church constituency to be more involved in indoctrination than in learning. Big issues of debate in the recent generations have not generally been those of predestination or Arminianism or Gospel holiness, but parietal rules and required chapel. No wonder many young people find college years a time of alienation from the church. The term *church-related* college at least suggests a relationship of mutuality and respect, an acknowledgment of a common history and a possibility for dialogue and trust.[40]

In 1980 the Senate said that since church-relatedness is so hard to standardize or define, each institution must define it for itself, and be judged by its own standard.[41] Since the Senate's entire purpose for existence was to appraise Methodist-related institutions by common standards, this was a position awkward to maintain, so several years later the Senate published some new guidelines for its visitation teams.

> 1. How is church relatedness presented in the institution's Charter, Bylaws, catalog, and other published documents? Does the institution identify itself as United Methodist-related in directories of higher education?

271

2. What is the manner in which the school regards itself as related to The United Methodist Church and what is the evidence that the purported relationship exists in fact?

3. What are the perceptions of the bishop, the chair of the annual conference Board of Higher Education and Campus Ministry, and other appropriate officials of the church toward the college?

4. How, if at all, does church relatedness reflect itself in the life of the institution (curriculum, student life, research, and publications)?

5. What is the extent of the religious program and how is it staffed?

6. How does the college relate to other United Methodist structures?

7. How is church relatedness reflected in the processes of governance?[42]

Roger Ireson, the general secretary of the BHEM/UMC, later presented what he saw as the six "strong expectations" the church had for its own institutions:

1. Intellectual challenge and nurture, with a strong humanities program.

2. A community of faith, focused in strong philosophy and religion departments and strong nurture for students.

3. Integrity in management.

4. Partnership for the church's intellectual life.

5. An indwelling presence of vision for our society.

6. Mutual recognition and shared identity.[43]

The surreal tone of these hopes is stunning. Everyone who heard them expressed was aware that many — perhaps most — of these philosophy and religion departments now functioned under an obedience quite aloof to faith (if Christian faith was what was meant), and that only a small remnant of the students on these campuses could realistically be expected to look to the largely non-Methodist faculty for enlightenment about what college might have to do with eternity. Several of the dicta in this document are positively wistful: "Religion is not a stranger or an intruder on the campus of a church-related institution . . . There is an intentionality in providing opportunity for perspective and introspection at a church-related school that is not always provided in other settings. . . . Perhaps our church relatedness protects us from the euphoria of misplaced goals and shallow victories." Here were no shallow victories.

In 1989 a special handbook was issued to clear up these matters for Methodists at the local level. The sempiternal question, What is a United Methodist school or college? was specifically addressed . . . sort of. Some colleges had been founded by local churches, and others had been steadily supported by them at great sacrifice. Whatever close bonds may have forged between college and church, the book explains, are not conclusive, because only the University Senate can certify real affiliation.

What does the Senate base its judgment on? The *Discipline* charges the Senate to review institutions to make certain they have "intellectual integrity, well-structured programs, sound management, and clearly defined [*sic*] Church relationships" (par. 1519.3). In addition, the Senate must ascertain that the institutions "maintain appropriate academic accreditation" (par. 1519.4) and must "support the development of institutions whose aims are to address and whose programs reflect significant educational, cultural, social, and human issues in a manner reflecting the values held in common by the institutions and the Church." (par. 1518.2)[44]

This deserves, though it does not invite, a second reading. The handbook goes on to describe the requisite fidelity in more casual terms:

> The church wants students at its colleges to challenge and enhance their faith. It wants the scholarly study of religion, and wishes it as rigorous as good scholarship demands. But it also wants to know that the college nests itself and its programs in its affection for the church. To feel that a college is destructive of or indifferent to the Christian faith is to lose faith in the college.
> A college is intellectually faithful to the church when its scholarship is intact and first rate, and when it provides an environment in which the Christian faith is honored and supported. That can be done through student religious groups, through interdisciplinary courses that deal with questions of ethics, through programs for preseminary students, through some courses of service to the church (such as Christian Education), and through attention to the faculty of the college (not that all must be either United Methodist or Christian, but that all deal respectfully with the religious traditions and beliefs of the students).[45]

It would seem clear from this that while the faith of the students is relevant, the faith of the faculty is not: their only task is to be respectful. Thus no more is required of the faculty at Illinois Wesleyan than of the faculty at Illinois State.

In 1992 a DHE task force appointed to do "visioning" reported that higher education had been adrift amid the priorities of the United Methodist Church, and now it required a new definition of what "church-related" means.

> A belief in God at the center of all creation and therefore of all knowledge and learning evokes several theological affirmations from which our vision evolves.
> Basic to the church's higher education enterprise is the presupposition that God has created us with minds and the responsibility to think critically and act justly with love and compassion for others, following the life and teachings of Jesus Christ. With John Wesley we celebrate the integration of faith and reason, and we affirm the pursuit of both in the college and university community.[46]

This is bland enough, save for the mention of the life and teachings of Jesus Christ, which is a strident shout amid current Methodist educational literature. When the task force began to convert this into policy, however, the first goal for the twenty-first century was "to embody value-centered teaching and learning."[47] The national office forthwith rewrote its documentation and instructed board members of the DHE in a new mission statement that the way "to foster a renewed commitment between The United Methodist Church" and its educational institutions was

> To ensure that United Methodist students have access to quality value-centered higher education
> To enhance value-centered education at all United Methodist-related institutions of higher education.[48]

"Value-Centered": Which Values? and Whose?

This lengthy process of self-definition began with the stipulation that any decent college which wanted to call itself Methodist was Methodist. That, one might say, was the purest of procedural definitions. The latest dictum states that any college which is Methodist-related will be value-centered. That may not represent much gain for a century's work. The U.S. Coast Guard Academy has a distinctive value-centered education. So, too, Cal Tech and the Rhode Island School of Design. Value-centered education is everywhere, but the values at the center can differ from institution to institution . . . and from professor to professor.[49] If a college or university is to have Methodist values at its center, the task force is not forthcoming about what those might be. When Pfeiffer College pledges in its mission statement to foster "examination of one's [own] value system," that may be nearer the theory and practice of many schools. Yet one is not told why Methodists claim any gift for this self-inquiry, and there is no intimation at all of what value system they might commend.

It might seem that nothing more vapid or insubstantial could be claimed as the justification for one's lifework in higher education than that it be value-centered. One Methodist president recently offered a norm of even coarser grain. In his appeal for scholarship funds from the churches, he characterized the college's work by one freshman course description:

> The term "values" is broadly interpreted secularly and spiritually as follows: Secularly, the course interprets in the best light of evolutionary history the Jeffersonian ideals made clear in the Constitution, our laws, and our system of education. Spiritually, the course interprets the best of Christian tradition in terms of the Golden Rule and the highest of the Pauline virtues. By "love" we intend for our students to "care" beyond all borders of human enterprise and political organization.[50]

The Methodists have demonstrated a prodigious capacity to ask themselves

274

what they are about, and to reply to their own query in a vocabulary as indistinct as possible. "Value-centered nurture" seems to provide just the right response to Bishop Oxnam's forceful appeal "to stand for something in the field of religion." There is an elusive consistency in these attempts at self-definition: the text strains and the voice is raised, but there is no message. It brings to mind an anecdote that Tom Trotter, the well-respected UMC higher education executive from 1972 to 1984, used to tell. Asked by interviewer David Frost to describe God, the Archbishop of Canterbury replied: "Something within one and beyond one that fills one with awe, and reverence, and gives one a sense of supreme obligation . . ." Frost murmured, "That could be the Inland Revenue [income tax] Office."[51]

One of the critical norms that might have been assessed — the religious commitments or affiliations of the faculty — is naturally nowhere included in the extensive database which the church assembles, nor does it ever seem to have been itemized as an appropriate issue for an institution's claim to be authentically committed to amalgamating knowledge with vital piety.[52]

A recent and thorough survey of the presidents of UMC-related colleges and universities inquired into what factors they thought most contributed to optimal relations between the church and the colleges. The three factors to which they ascribed highest importance were, in order:

1. Historical ties with the UMC.
2. Supportive attitude among UMC constituency,
3. Denominational affiliation of the president.

The three factors at the bottom of their long list were:

18. Percentage of the institutional budget coming from the UMC.
19. Religion or Bible courses as curricular requirements.
20. Percentage of faculty and administration who are UMC members.[53]

It is remarkable that the presidents would think their own churchmanship so much more efficacious than that of their colleagues who do the educating. They also ranked the presence of a chaplain and/or church-relations officer as more likely to create an optimal relationship with the church than would a large proportion of Methodists among the student body. These survey results seem to imply that the presidents are moved more by perfunctory realities than by efficacious ones.

It is assumable that when the Senate began its work a century ago, most of the personnel at Methodist colleges were Methodist. They had an understood communal identity and task, and it was provided for them by the church. The college, whatever the legalities of relationship, was a branch of the church's vine. In those days one did not really need to define a Methodist college; one had only to point to one. But in days to come, two ominous changes would take place. First, an incremental dilution of Methodist personnel at every level would take place, unnoticed except when it occurred on the board of trustees and required an amendment to the charter or bylaws. Second, when the colleges claimed and the church granted their claim to define and cultivate their own character, they seem never to have inherited from the church a self-consciousness adequate to create and develop a tradition of pious scholarship. The Senate in 1893 was correct: There may be little more required to be a Methodist-related college — and little more involved — than consenting to the name.

Millsaps College[54]

The white newcomers who settled Mississippi included a fair representation of cultured families that were immediately concerned to have education available for their children. The early students were obliged to journey northward, to Princeton or Virginia or Washington and Lee, or to Methodist institutions such as Southern (Alabama), Augusta (Kentucky), LaGrange (Georgia), or Asbury (Indiana), or to go locally to Mississippi College (1826, taken over by Baptists in 1853) at Jackson.[55] The preaching of Methodism in the territory, begun by the Reverend Tobias Gibson working out of Natchez in 1799 and consolidated by creation of the Mississippi Conference in 1813, eventually summoned enough Methodist congregations into existence for them to want colleges of their own. Gibson founded Madison Academy near (and later in) Port Gibson as early as 1809. Elizabeth Female Academy emerged in 1818. Many other institutions were to follow, most of which soon evaporated: Hernando, Emery, Gallatin, Lane, Vicksburg Female and Sharon Female, Eudocia/Black Hawk, Marshall Female, Byhalia, Wilmarth, Kosciusko, and dozens of others. Only two of those early foundations are extant: Centenary College of Louisiana, which began in Brandon Springs in 1839 (later merging with the College of Louisiana, founded 1825) and emigrated to Shreveport in 1908; and Rust College, founded in 1866 for newly freed Negroes.[56]

It was not until 1888 that a proposal was made by two Conferences of Mississippi Methodism to endorse a college for young men. A leading citizen of Jackson, Major Reuben Webster Millsaps, offered $50,000 for endowment (to be evenly matched by other contributions), a charter was secured in 1890, and the faculty and students arrived in 1892.[57] Jackson at the time had a population of only nine thousand; one index of its slow development is the fact that the post office, granted in 1882, would distribute mail there by rural free delivery until 1903. Millsaps was himself an educated Mississippian who had had to journey up to Hanover College (a Presbyterian school in Indiana) for his first three undergraduate years, and eventually earned his degree at Asbury, later DePauw University.[58]

Bishop Charles Betts Galloway would preside over the board of the new college. An ardent advocate of advancement for blacks, he would be the 1904 commencement speaker at Tuskegee, in the heat of the Jim Crow period. One local politician called him "a greater traitor to the South than Benedict Arnold was to the Colonies."[59] The founding president was William Belton Murrah (1890-1910). He was, as well, dean, registrar, and professor of religion, philosophy, and psychology.

Millsaps College was to be for "poor boys." Its first prospectus advertised no tuition charges and inexpensive board. It attracted 116 students the first day and 149 by the end of the year. Twenty-one were sons of ministers, and 14 were "potential ministers."[60] Ministerial students continued to represent a notable segment of the student body in those early years, rising through the nineties to 36 percent, then subsiding to 21 percent in 1905-6.[61] Most colleges begun with so little income in prospect would have spent their first fifty years or so in financial stress, subordinating all other decisions to the imperatives of survival. But this little college in Mississippi had remarkable financial success from the start. By the end of its first year the college could boast of an endowment of nearly $100,000, due largely to statewide solicitations by Bishop Galloway and Rev. A. F. Watkins. By 1908 that had doubled, by 1910 it reached $300,000, and by 1917 it exceeded a half-million dollars. Indeed, before Emory had been refounded as a university, and before Southern Methodist was founded, Millsaps would rank second to Trinity (later Duke) among southern Methodist colleges in the size of its endowment.[62] In 1905 Andrew Carnegie, whose large foundation would have rejected any Millsaps request to fund faculty pensions because it was too sectarian, reached into another pocket and offered half the cost of a library building. Major Millsaps promptly matched that gift. Two years later John D. Rockefeller's General Education Board awarded $25,000 to match thrice that amount if raised by the college; it was raised. In 1913 Major Millsaps donated another college building — the largest. By 1898 a modest tuition charge had had to be levied, but ministerial students were exempted from even that. In 1902-3 the board felt financially secure enough to extend its offer of free tuition not only to the children of Methodist ministers and to candidates for Methodist ministry, but to potential ministers in any Christian denomination. These are all evidences of a generous and apparently stable financial base for the young college.[63]

Millsaps succeeded in gaining various kinds of official recognition, often without either seeking or sometimes even appreciating it. The college was given accreditation by the Southern Association in 1912, ahead of five older institutions in the state.[64] A series of investigative reports to the Association of American Universities, the Southern Association, and the General Board were uniformly complimentary. The O'Shea Report commissioned by the Mississippi Department of Education in 1927 stated: "It is practically certain that the freshmen students at Millsaps stand out distinctly ahead of the students in the other colleges and in the University. It appears that Millsaps has secured a reputation for high scholarship and thorough training and the effect of this is to attract students of superior ability to do college work of a literary, linguistic and mathematical type. . . . Millsaps students are distinctly in the lead in educational achievement, as well as in intellectual ability."[65]

Despite its late beginnings and its ambition to educate young men of little means, Millsaps took itself seriously from the start. Murrah, the factotum president, had previously served both as a pastor and as an academic administrator. Four of his first nine faculty members had the Ph.D. degree, and he deployed his teachers for graduate work to Chicago, Rome, Athens, Johns Hopkins, and Vanderbilt.[66] The curriculum, however, began in the strictly classical mode with hardly an elective course in sight. As a reminder of the infinite suppleness of academic language, however, Murrah could say spaciously in his inaugural address that the college would offer its students the "widest range of investigation and research and the fullest recognition of the truth wherever found."[67]

An Easy Religious Common Life

Baptists, Presbyterians, and Episcopalians had registered at the college in its earliest years. More unusual was the presence, almost from the start, of some Jewish and Catholic students. Notwithstanding this somewhat pluralist enrollment the president was required to be a Methodist, and preferably a minister. No such restriction controlled faculty appointments, yet in the early days there was an easy collegial participation in common worship which reflected a close religious fellowship.

> Chapel exercises were held each morning before classes began and were conducted by all members of the faculty in order of seniority. Exercises were opened with the singing of a hymn, followed by a reading from the Bible and prayer. Sometimes the teacher commented upon the Scripture that had been read or delivered a short talk on a moral or religious subject. Those members of the faculty that were unable to pray extemporaneously made use of the Lord's prayer. Since the faculty was small and all lived on or near the campus, it was our custom to gather in the President's office fifteen minutes before the chapel exercises and go into the chapel in a body, where we occupied a semi-circle of chairs upon the platform. These pre-chapel meetings were pleasant little "get-togethers" and moreover served as informal faculty meetings in that we were frequently able to dispose of business that required little or no discussion but which was often of enough importance to justify a called meeting of the faculty if it had not been settled at such a time. . . . So far as my experience goes, this was a unique academic procedure, serving many useful purposes.[68]

A YMCA was organized on campus less than two weeks after the college opened. As was customary, it functioned largely as a student initiative. Membership was voluntary. This likened it to the literary societies, fraternities, and early varsity sports of the nineteenth century, all of which operated under the rather loose patronage of the administration and faculty, but with very little of their supervision. The Y accommodated well the denominational mixture of the student body, while providing some of the evangelical enthusiasm and the occasional revivalist energies of a Methodist institution. The Millsaps unit was said to be "dominated by the double purpose of leading men to accept Christ and to form such associations as will guard them against the temptations of College life."[69] The temptations at Millsaps in those early days were, it would seem, mild. President Murrah was described as a strict disciplinarian, famous for his threats that student misdemeanors would not be tolerated. Yet the record of his administration offers little evidence of ferocity or of any need for it. In fact, the college literature gives very sparing rosters of rules regarding student behavior until the late 1960s, and even then they were at pains to distinguish what was "not helpful," "not approved," and "forbidden." When intercollegiate sports were banned for a while in 1895, the student reaction was to intensify intramural contests rather than to kick against the goad. The manners and morality of faculty and students seem to have been in remarkable harmony throughout the college's formative years.

Academic developments were timely. As was usual even in the 1890s, the college began with a Preparatory Department which offered remedial studies. In the first year, two-thirds of the students were enrolled in this "Sub-Collegiate Program." It would be phased out after thirty years.[70] A Law School was opened in the college's fourth year of operation with a number of distinguished Mississippi jurists on its faculty, and the number of its graduates soon equaled that of the college. By 1918 the college closed the Law School, however, and formed a lasting conviction that its future lay in consolidation, not proliferation.[71]

Female students entered Millsaps *de facto* well before they were admitted *de jure*. The very first year, a well-connected young lady enrolled as a "special student"; the first full-time female earned her B.A. in 1901; and in 1906 the college was officially made coeducational. Women had to wait twenty-two years longer for boarding accommodations, however.[72] In the late 1930s two Methodist institutions for females, Whitworth and Grenada Colleges, were merged into Millsaps, increasing its assets and its female complement.

In 1921 a Department of Religious Education was established, and with a handsome benefaction it became the first separately endowed department. In 1924 the library building had to be replaced, and the Carnegie Corporation was again forthcoming with an even larger gift to rebuild it.[73]

But Then, Conflict

Adversity seems to have stricken Millsaps only after several decades of stable establishment and growth. One national paroxysm which might have affected the college was the fundamentalist/secularist controversy over evolution and the interpretation of Genesis, which had its symbolic flash point at the 1925 Scopes trial in Tennessee. In 1926 the Mississippi legislature passed a bill forbidding state-supported institutions from offering courses or textbooks which would "teach that mankind ascended or descended from a lower order of animals." Chancellor Hume of the University of Mississippi protested against this as "intellectual bondage," but the governor signed the bill into law. Ole Miss was forthwith censured by the American Association of University Professors, the American Association of Civil Engineers, the American Chemical Society, and the American Association of Medical Schools. Several years later Governor Theodore Bilbo returned to office and had the chancellor removed. Mississippi Methodists were inclined to support the law, but David M. Key (1923-38), Millsaps' first lay president, was joined by Methodists from other states at the Methodist Educational Association meeting in Nashville in a resolution opposing "all legislation that would interfere with the proper teaching of science in American schools and colleges." For his opponents at home Key had this to say: "Their opinions have only such insight as their scholarship and character give them." Looking back on the controversy in 1941, the college could report: "Not in spite of, but because of its relation to the church, the college's policies have been determined by a faith in the unity of truth wherever and however tested." This, however, was to put too good a face on the spat over evolution, for there were many Methodists in Mississippi whose loyalty to the college was loosened by what Key had defended.[74]

Several years later another dispute arose, and it, too, displayed the college as more liberal than its constituents could allow and still remain comfortable. In the latter 1930s Mississippi led the nation in lynchings: 574 in 1937 alone, and 534 of the victims were blacks. When an antilynching bill was introduced in the Congress that year, the Millsaps International Relations Club sent telegrams to Mississippi legislators in Washington, urging their support. One such lawmaker was Theodore Bilbo, who had been elected to the Senate. Bilbo immediately proposed to hold local hearings and called for "a complete overhaul of the teaching force of any college that will persist in permitting this secret spread of communist doctrine among the student body." President Key, still on duty, retorted:

A College worthy of the name is an educational institution and not an organ of propaganda. Its function is to teach how to think and not what to think. Millsaps College does not propose to control the views of its students other than by the free exchange of ideas, facts, and opinions, and by the inescapable compulsion of truth and of wise and sympathetic counsel.[75]

He had the support of his board, and Bilbo backed off. But it is noteworthy that Key did not take a stand on the issue of lynching itself, nor did he invoke the gospel. The student initiative was defended exclusively on procedural grounds. And there were plenty of Methodists in Mississippi who could not have regarded this with sympathy in 1937.

Ten years earlier when evolution was again the aggravation, Key dealt with it in his annual report to the church:

From the day when a university was defined as Mark Hopkins on one end of a log and a student on the other, it has been recognized that the personnel and personality of the faculty is the most determinative element in the character shaping effectiveness of the college.

Measured by this test, Millsaps College has been peculiarly fortunate, and is so today. . . . There are now twenty-five people on the teaching and administrative staff of the college. Four are ministers of the gospel in the Methodist Church. Seventeen are active participants in the work of the church, either as ministers, officers of the Conference, district or local congregation, or teachers in the Sunday school. Five are or have been qualified instructors in Sunday School Teacher Training Institutes. Six are members of the board of stewards of the local church. Seventeen are or have recently been teachers of Sunday school classes. . . .

I do not hesitate to say that in many essential characteristics of a live, vital Christian community the college [student body] excells the most pious community in the Conference. Ninety-eight per cent belong to the church, ninety-nine per cent attend church regularly. A great majority live a life of self denial, consecration and self sacrifice. Recently in answering a questionnaire of Dr. Anderson, Secretary of Education, in which he asked me to state the elements that make for Christian character in our colleges, I cited the physical hardships and self denial in our present day students as one of the most significant forces for character building. These young people have seen a vision. Over sixty per cent are earning part of their expenses. Students work all night in the express offices. They rush from the class room to the store and the warehouse. They dress well and make a brave show with their loud ties and socks but there is the iron of self denial and self sacrifice in their hearts. The other day our college physician called for some boys for transfusion of blood in the hospitals, and over forty boys clamored for the opportunity. Do you think that young men who will buy life training with their very life blood are frivolous?[76]

To put this portrait of the morally wholesome student in context, one must know that throughout the twenties Key and the faculty had been steadily upgrading the academic requirements for the college, to the increasing distress of the athletic coaches (varsity sports had quietly found their way onto campus). Students with lagging grades were obliged to reduce their registration loads; grade minimums for retention and graduation were established and then raised; tuition reductions were awarded to students with the highest performance (tuition was $125 for those with averages below 75 percent, but $75 for those above 90 percent); absences were penalized. After this hoisting of standards, enrollment had more than doubled.[77]

Methodist Support Begins to Falter

It was in this otherwise self-assured era at Millsaps, however, that the Mississippi Methodist support showed a first sign of faltering. In 1928 a $650,000 statewide

281

campaign was conducted, to enlarge the physical plant. Only $328,000 was pledged, half of that from Jackson itself, especially its affluent and traditionally supportive families. The construction went forward nevertheless, and the campus soon boasted of a new science building, gymnasium, and female residence hall. Much of even the little pledged was never paid, however, and the college staggered under a debt it could service only by reducing salaries 25 percent and drawing down its endowment. After World War II the Millsaps endowment stood at only 88 percent of its value in 1932. There had been days at the beginning of the century when Millsaps knew it was losing some of its faculty because of higher salaries available elsewhere, but the financial crisis of the thirties, caused by the depression but compounded by its decision to build and the failure of its appeal for support, was a more stunning experience. President Key resigned in 1938 to become dean.[78] Nevertheless, when the Methodist Episcopal Church, South, whose colleges had seen their new income decrease by 60 percent from 1925 to 1935, drew up a triage list of the institutions "which, because of their high academic rating, their distinctive religious objectives, their strategic locations, and their reasonable assurance of financial security merit the vigorous and unqualified support of the Church," Millsaps College was on that list.[79]

But support from the constituency was not all that solid. In 1932 the two Methodist annual conferences took note of the fact that the four state colleges in Mississippi were enrolling almost three times as many of their church membership as were the three Methodist colleges. "After making reasonable allowance for professional or pre-professional work offered by the state which is not provided by church colleges, it is clear that Methodist institutions as at present organized are not holding Methodist patronage in this state."[80] The remedy adopted was to merge the two small women's colleges into Millsaps. The result was an overall further decline in Methodists on the Millsaps campus.

Enrollment totals over the years are one indicator of the financial (and often the academic) health of an institution; the religious census is usually suggestive of a college's ability to serve its denominational public. Enrollment in Millsaps College had grown steadily with few reversals, to the point where, on its thirty-fifth anniversary in 1927, the undergraduates numbered 453, about nine times the number of collegians who came in 1892-93.[81] Much of that growth had occurred in the twenties. Net gains in the thirties were nil. Enrollments during the postwar years shot up to nearly twice the 1927 high, subsided a bit in the early fifties, but then began again to climb: 882 in 1960; 772 in 1965; 938 in 1970; 1,240 at present.[82] Clearly, with the student body increasing by less than half during the past forty years of growth, Millsaps' academic progress has been supported more by an increase of finances than by one of students.

How many of these students have been Methodists? Back in 1927 when President Key was reporting near-optimal levels of religious piety, 69 percent of that observant student body identified themselves as Methodists. That declined soon afterward to 50 percent (1932), and after a surge upward in the later thirties it declined to 45 percent during the war years. Thereafter it gradually increased again to a high of 61 percent in 1954, and has been declining ever since. Today Methodists constitute 27 percent of the student body. There are numerically fewer Methodist students at Millsaps than there were in 1927.[83]

It is more difficult to ascertain the Methodist representation among the faculty. In 1927 they accounted for twenty of the twenty-one faculty members (Key's report cited above combined faculty and administrators). Two years later they were twenty-five out of twenty-eight: 89 percent. In the 1950s and 1960s the annual intake of new faculty members showed that a shift was under way.

In 1954: two Methodists and one Presbyterian

In 1957: five Methodists, two Presbyterians, and two Episcopalians

In 1958: two Methodists, two Episcopalians, and one Presbyterian

In 1962: three Methodists, three Presbyterians, one Baptist, and one Episcopalian

In 1963: five Methodists, one Catholic, and one Baptist

By 1970, though no Jew had ever been appointed and no Catholic had ever been awarded tenure, and though twelve denominations were represented among the faculty, only 43 percent of them were Methodists (exactly the same proportion as Methodists then in the student body). Today no one knows the religious complexion of the faculty because no one asks.[84]

Another component of the college whose Methodist membership would be an important factor is the board of trustees, but to understand how that became an agitated issue at Millsaps one must first view the financial stake the college has had over recent years in the church. Church support for annual operations in 1952 amounted to only $10,000. When President Finger arrived in 1957 the churches were giving $100,000 annually. Capital contributions from the churches for plant and endowment were for a while a significant source of income for the college. In the Million for Millsaps campaign in the late fifties, 93 percent of the revenues came through the Methodist churches of Mississippi, with alumni and friends giving only 7 percent of the total. Obviously many alumni were giving through their churches, but in so doing they were signaling to their alma mater how they were to be identified as a constituency. Since the coming of George Harmon as president in 1978, however, the situation has reversed. Gifts from alumni and other lay benefactors have, since 1980, greatly outweighed gifts through the church. There is no longer any capital income from the churches, and the apportionment given by the Mississippi Annual Conference most recently totaled $318,000, amounting to only 1.3 percent of the $24.5 million Millsaps received as gifts and grants during the year, and less than 1 percent of total revenues, down from nearly 10 percent in the midsixties. The church is no longer even separately noted as a source of revenue in the *Annual Report* of the college. Of course, many Mississippi Methodists give capital gifts and Annual Fund donations as alumni, but in so doing they are signaling to their conference-related college how they are now to be identified: as primarily patronizing Millsaps College, rather than the Methodist Church.[85]

The Finger Regime

President Homer Ellis Finger, Jr., an alumnus who had come back to Millsaps as its very young sixth president (1952-64), was a minister whose only academic credential was one year served as a high school mathematics teacher right after graduation. Finger's primary perspective was pastoral. There is in his files a very moving correspondence that affords a sense of the Millsaps ethos in 1952. A colleague of his, a pastor in the north of the state, wrote Finger out of concern for a girl from his church who, after only a few months as a freshman, was having an unhappy time at Millsaps. She had received no bid to a good sorority. "And then, for another thing, she is disappointed in some student attitudes she has found there. She says that Millsaps isn't like a church college, that the girls smoke much and that the conversation among the girls is too much taken up with the subject of boys." By return mail Finger reported that the young woman had already withdrawn from college, but that he would be glad to make the journey to her town and talk over the whole matter with her parents. He had already interviewed several of her friends to learn what he could about her unhappiness. He then observed: "I am also concerned about the lack of high values among some of our students. It is a problem which I think all of us share. These young men and women come from our local churches. They are all members of the church but somehow we fail to get over to them a seriousness of purpose, a sense of high values, and a desirable refinement about life." The minister replied with appreciation, and pressed Finger to come to his church to preach, especially since the college had a fund-raising campaign under way. This exchange embodies well the easy rapport between college and church in the early fifties.[86] The college was continuing to see itself as a unit of the pastoral mission of the church.

Finger's administration, nevertheless, was to be disturbed by a scarring brawl more damaging to college-church relations than any his predecessor, David Key, had undergone with Theodore Bilbo. The U.S. Supreme Court's 1954 integration decision had made no more impression on the Millsaps campus than on that of Ole Miss. But three years later a white professor at nearby Tougaloo College (a postbellum school for Negroes founded by the Congregationalists) was given the use of a Millsaps classroom to teach German to a group of students from both institutions: it was a small venture of cautious, nondemonstrative, and unofficial integration. In 1958 the chairman of the Department of Sociology invited students from both campuses to meet at Millsaps for a series of discussions that would give the white students some acquaintance with the black viewpoint on race relations. This triggered fierce criticisms from the Jackson press. When

Ellis Finger defended the campus activities, he followed David Key's precedent and did so on grounds of academic freedom.[87] Ronald Goodbread describes the vehemence of the rebuttal:

> The extent to which Millsaps had always been pressured to submit to the majority's concept of educational philosophy was exhibited by a resolution passed about this time by the official board of a Methodist Church in a small community only a few miles from Jackson. The resolution sent to Dr. Finger was in response to his suggestion that every issue had two sides and that the college ought to expose the students to divergent opinions in their best educational interest.
>
> Expressing what they termed their "firm Christian convictions," the board members volunteered that their opinions had been gratefully formed "far removed from the teachings and practices of Millsaps . . . and Emory." They realized, they said, "that two sides of most questions do exist. One being the right side and the other being the wrong. We do not take our children and carry them from the church to the houses of evil and have them exposed to the evil forces to show them that it is wrong," they illustrated by way of philosophical example. "Neither do we invite the thief, the bootlegger, the drunkard, and others into our churches to lecture on their side of the existing question. . . . Therefore we feel that it is wrong for our church colleges to practice or teach by such methods . . ."
>
> The *Clarion Ledger* predictably agreed. "Citizens Council officials and legislators want to know," it reported objectively, "if the students should have some prisoners down from Parchman to give the other side, or perhaps some prostitutes or what have you?" One letter to President Finger lectured him, "I have no patience with this position. You do not endorse a little whiskey for a few drunks to learn both sides about whiskey. . . ."
>
> Others were simply at a total loss as to what to think. "It was with a great deal of disappointment that I learned you wanted to do away with segregation," one former supporter plaintively wrote to Dr. Finger. "The several times that I have met you, you always seemed to be such a high class fellow."[88]

The board of trustees supported the president but made it clear that it was academic freedom they were defending, not racial justice or gospel imperatives. Millsaps' trustees stated explicitly that they still supported segregation, and that the college policy had not changed in that matter.[89] The student senate invoked "all that America and the State of Mississippi have historically stood for." They also invoked Scripture: "We do not intend to be deprived by any person, group, or organization of our belief in the Scriptural admonition, 'Ye shall know the truth, and the truth shall make you free.' " The point at issue, they said, was not race but whether they might explore the question of race.[90] The student editors fretted about the inquiry becoming too intense: "We are not saying that the study of the problem of integration should be considered a vice; but to bring out the point that, viewed too closely, and with the resultant non-objectivity, integration will first be accepted as inevitable, then condoned, then advocated."[91]

Integration at Millsaps had to await the Civil Rights Act of 1964, with its threat to cut off all federal funds. The trustees decided in 1965 to admit colored students. Millsaps would be the first all-white college in Mississippi to do so "voluntarily." It had been a costly battle. Some reckoned that Millsaps had forfeited two million dollars in contributions.[92]

The college had sacrificed considerable goodwill within the Methodist community in Mississippi. In a fierce conflict that engaged evangelical Christians on both sides, the only scriptural mandate or Methodist principle invoked by the college was freedom. But, of course, it was not freedom for blacks in their lives, but freedom for whites in their studies. Still, though the public terms of the debate had not engaged the academics explicitly on behalf of racial integration, that was the grievance of their antagonists, and withstanding their hostility surely drew the Millsaps people subliminally in a liberal direction, so that the choice to integrate later came more naturally. It is significant that when that decision was made, after six years of open rancor, the college defended it publicly on three grounds: American democracy, Christian liberality, and academic excellence — in that order:

As an American institution and one dedicated to the fundamental concept of majority rule in a democracy, Millsaps believes that it has an obligation to abide by the laws of this nation. This it believes even though there may be substantial disagreement among its constituency on the merit of a particular set of laws. Law and order must be maintained if there is to be peace, tranquility and progress in our beloved nation and state.

As an institution of the Methodist Church, Millsaps has throughout its history attempted to express in its policies and actions, and in the atmosphere on its campus, the highest ideals of the Christian faith. In this tradition, the college cannot remain unresponsive to the call of the church for an end to discrimination and for the opening of its facilities to qualified persons in a spirit of Christian concern for all men.

As an institution of higher learning, Millsaps cannot cut itself off from the mainstream of American life and thought in the mid-twentieth century. Any restriction on the free exchange of ideas among men raises serious questions about the academic integrity of a college or university. From its founding, Millsaps College has emphasized excellence in Christian higher education. This standard of excellence has been recognized in this state and throughout the nation. The reputation of the college and its ability to attract outstanding young men and women to its faculty can be maintained only if a condition of unbiased search for truth and a concern for individual men is preserved.[93]

The Board Takes Effective Control from the Methodist Conferences

It was this pastorally oriented president, Ellis Finger, in whose early tenancy church contributions had so abruptly increased, who later foresaw (in his season of rancor) that they would never be reliable or plentiful enough. He began to suggest that the statutory limitation of college trusteeship to Mississippi Methodists ought to be relaxed, but he was not to prevail. An amendment to provide for eight new trustees on the board, to be elected by regular trustees instead of by the annual conferences, was simply ignored.[94] When Finger resigned in 1964 he expressed his regrets to the trustees that, even though Methodists now constituted only half of the Millsaps student body, the board had never approved his proposal to diversify their own membership.[95] The very next year his successor, Benjamin Barnes Graves (1965-70), was chiding the churches for their delinquency and eventual default in paying off their pledges to the college in its seventy-fifth anniversary campaign, and for contributing less than a dollar per person in annual giving.[96] In 1966, when church giving was clearly on the wane, the board considered a revision of the charter to permit the sixteen regularly elected members to elect eight further, "special" trustees. A motion to require these special trustees to be Methodists died without a second.[97]

In 1969 the board finally made the change, and in a measure well beyond what had earlier been asked for. The sixteen regular trustees would nominate fourteen further, special, trustees who would then be elected by the conferences. The conferences, "after considerable discussion," acquiesced, but with the request that clergy be given consideration by the board in drawing up its slate of nominees. As it turned out, twelve of the fourteen nominees were laity.[98]

The charter underwent a further change in 1985. The trustees would henceforth number up to forty voting members, all but the resident bishop to be nominated by the board itself and then elected by the two conferences. A majority must be Methodists, including four clergy and four laity from each of the conferences.[99] Resistance to this change was anticipated, and a rhetorical blitz was directed at the Methodist constituency to secure their vote. "Q. Does the proposed change in Charter in any way diminish the ties between The United Methodist Church in Mississippi and Millsaps College? A. The answer is an emphatic No. . . . Millsaps College is one of the most 'owned' colleges of The United Methodist Church anywhere in this country."[100] A theological memorandum submitted with the charter amendments provides a remarkable background note to the proceedings, and significant evidence that more was at stake than just the procedures for electing trustees:

The Nature of the United Methodist Church and its institutions is characterized by AN OPEN AND PLURALISTIC THEOLOGICAL STANCE. Against the backdrop of our Wesleyan orientation, there is an array of doctrinal diversity in the United Methodist Church and Millsaps College. The college's purpose and mission does not include teaching doctrine or demanding conformity, but rather operates from a core of truth which is affirmed with all Christian people. We affirm our willingness to be open, to think and let think, as long as those beliefs are tested by the Wesley Quadrilateral, viz., experience, Scripture, reason and tradition. . . . Millsaps College has established itself as an institution that is open, reflective, and truth-seeking. As such, its main characteristics can be described as: (1) an emphasis on excellent education, (2) an emphasis on the individual, and (3) an emphasis on serving the Church even as the college receives mutual support from that constituency.

The exposition of the latter two emphases deals mostly in academic platitudes ("dignity and respect, trust and mutual support, sense of national heritage and global consciousness, affecting the state with the best of Church and higher education values"). But the exposition of "excellent education" rewards close attention:

Excellent education begins with good critical scholarship, that is, an unceasing search for truth; a probing analysis of all questions, and a process of critical inquiry into all areas of life. The issue of academic freedom is uppermost in United Methodist Church-related education.

Good critical scholarship of necessity begins with a supportive constituency, that is, a sponsoring body whose very existence is built upon an open system of critical reflection. The United Methodist Church because of its theological roots provides this initial ingredient.

Another vital ingredient is a supportive faculty well grounded in their own fields and capable of engaging the student in a dynamic process of learning. They see good education as enabling students to develop ways of thinking and relating to the world. Not only should they be experts in their disciplines and masters in the art of teaching, but they should themselves be persons who are at home in the universe, persons who themselves are already the kinds of persons we want our students to become.

The two vital ingredients, good critical scholarship and a supportive faculty, enable an educational philosophy to develop which sees learning as more than acquiring job skills and gaining good information. It means helping individuals learn how to think analytically, synthetically, and relationally. It means enabling persons to develop a broad framework within which they are able to make crucial value judgments and solid moral decisions. It challenges individuals to be "thinking" persons, to appreciate the universe, and to discover the implications of an ever-changing and complex culture for their lives and for their future.[101]

This is the sort of oratory which academics usually impose only on their own kind, and it is the more remarkable in having been prepared for the voting members of a church conference. The clergy and activist laity from largely rural Mississippi might have wanted more assurance than that Wesley had left them a formless faith to hand on to their children, and the puzzling revelation that the Millsaps faculty felt themselves at home in the universe. But lest one imagine that this was a putsch imposed on the church by its subsidized intellectuals, one must consider that the charter change reducing church initiative in trustee selection was proposed by a committee chaired by the resident bishop.[102]

The Millsaps board, at the time of this study, contained twenty-three Methodists (including seven clergy), eight Episcopalians, four Presbyterians, and two Baptists.[103] From the beginning, the president (later chairman) of the board was the resident Methodist bishop. When the board was converted to a less church-oriented group, that position devolved upon a layperson, but the vice chairmanship is still reserved for the resident bishop.

An Increasingly Ambiguous Relationship to the Church

Millsaps recently celebrated its hundredth anniversary. Its relationship to the Methodist church is, at best, ambiguous. Traditionally the college has looked on the church as its basic constituency. Pragmatically that meant students and money. By those indices, the constituency is no longer very forthcoming. The apportionment — the church's annual contribution to the college's operating fund — is at its highest: nearly a third of a million dollars. But as we have seen, it represents only a sliver of the total benefactions the college takes in. As for students, Millsaps enrolls no more Methodists today than it did nearly seventy years ago when President Key was admiring their virtues of industry and self-denial.

When one contemplates this relative recession in patronage by the church, and the self-description of the college which reduces Methodism to a willingness to be open to whatever scholars choose to commend, it is impossible to ignore that over the years there has been an estrangement: sometimes quiet, occasionally rancorous.

On the part of the college, there has also been a recession in its commitment to being an overtly Methodist institution. Key in 1927 and Finger in 1952 had pointed with satisfaction to the piety of both the faculty and the student body as evidences of the college's health. A straightforward expression of this self-understanding was reprinted year after year in the *Catalog:*

> Millsaps College is a church related college under the care and control of the Mississippi and North Mississippi Conferences of the Methodist Church. The college is non-sectarian but devoutly Christian. During the 1948-49 session it numbered in its student body members of thirteen denominations [54 percent were Methodists that year] and in its faculty members of four denominations.[104]

That conventional self-description already displayed how the college acknowledged sponsorship by the church, but not a sponsorship that might infuse its educational endeavor with any specifically Methodist convictions.

In 1955 the faculty labored mightily together to elaborate a more formal and consensual statement of purpose, which the trustees then adopted. It would be reprinted in the *Catalog* for thirty consecutive years:

Millsaps College has as its primary aim the development of men and women for responsible leadership and well-rounded lives of useful service to their fellow men, their country, and their God. It seeks to function as a community of learners where faculty and students together seek that truth that frees the minds of men.

As an institution of the Methodist Church, Millsaps College is dedicated to the idea that religion is a vital part of education; that education is an integral part of the Christian religion; and that church-related colleges, providing a sound academic program in a Christian environment, afford a kind of discipline and influence which no other type of institution can offer. The College provides a congenial atmosphere where persons of all faiths may study and work together for the development of their physical, intellectual, and spiritual capacities. . . .

As an institution of higher learning, Millsaps College fosters an attitude of continuing intellectual awareness, of tolerance, and of unbiased inquiry, without which true education cannot exist. It does not seek to indoctrinate, but to inform and inspire. It does not shape the student in a common mold of thought and ideas, but rather attempts to search out his often deeply held aptitudes, capacities, and aspirations and to provide opportunities for his maximum possible development. . . .[105]

The *Catalog* quickly conformed to the new statement. Instead of saying "The college is non-sectarian but devoutly Christian," it now stated simply: "The college strives to be devoutly Christian."[106] To take the statement of purpose at face value, that Christian character would reside, not in the learning itself, but in an environment, a discipline, an influence. And by being an atmosphere in which non-Methodists would be as at home as Methodists, it might not be too different from the campuses sponsored by the State of Mississippi.

But beginning in the 1960s, an alternate doctrine slowly began to emerge from within the academic fellowship. As Millsaps prepared for its regular accreditation visit by the Southern Association in 1959-60, its self-study report bespoke a campus consensus that Methodism and scholarship were mutually beneficial, and that their amalgamation at the college was not problematic.

The trustees, administration, and faculty believe deeply that a combination of liberal arts education and Christian Higher Education constitutes the best possible service to the state and region. It is further believed that a firm commitment to Christian Higher Education may in fact constitute the strongest motivation for a vigorous pursuit of truth disclosed through study of the arts and sciences.

Some special aspects of our acknowledged task may be mentioned. To serve the state and region Millsaps College desires to produce graduates who will supply enlightened, intelligent and bold leadership in the Church, in community affairs, and in political action. The College wishes to place well-disciplined teachers in the classroom and competent preachers in the pulpits. The faculty and administration join with the trustees in an effort to furnish imaginative business and professional leaders.

Although generously supported by the Methodist Church, the college has no policy of giving any kind of priority to Methodist students. An analysis of the denominational preference of the students shows about 60 per cent [actually 55-56 percent] of the students indicating a preference for the Methodist Church.[107]

The accreditation team praised the college for its statement of purpose and suggested only that at some future time the faculty review and revise it so as to make it their own, and not merely a hand-me-down from the past.[108] Ten years later, with another accreditation visit in the offing, the consensus of the Millsaps faculty was that the statement of purpose should be left intact. The preaccreditation self-study disclosed, however, "a growing concern among both faculty and students over the attrition experienced in the area of religious life. The College has neglected the stated concern for the spiritual development of our students." At the same time, however, the report commended Millsaps' nonsectarian tradition, which "made room for 'all faiths.' " It noted that Methodists had become a minority in the student body, and that the "diverse religious activities tend to be of an ecumenical nature."[109] There was a difficulty, however. If the relationship to the church was best left indistinct, and if Methodist presence on campus was diminishing, any initiative toward religious revival would depend for its vitality on the college, not the church, and the college was on record as avoiding any denominational focus. Thus it should have been no surprise that spiritual development had become somewhat blurry. Sure enough, that same year the *Catalog* dropped its statement about Millsaps being devoutly Christian in favor of something impenetrable: "The College adheres to the view that one of the fundamental bases of a church-related institution is Christian in the sense that knowledge of truth is a part of its work. Millsaps College, therefore, is not narrow in its outlook."[110]

In 1980 the statement of purpose was twenty-five years old, and despite a call for "cautious revision," campus opinion was still either complacent or indifferent and the text was not touched.[111] In 1985 the board of trustees reaffirmed their adoption of it. But in 1990, with another accreditation visit impending, the self-study said it was "dated and reminiscent of a time characterized by institutions which served a more limited and homogeneous student body than is now the case." The stress between a church relationship and freedom from church specificities was being felt. The faculty labored for the better part of a year and sent to the trustees a new statement, "The Millsaps Purpose," which began thus:

Millsaps College is a community founded on trust in disciplined learning as a key to a rewarding life.

In keeping with its character as a liberal arts college and its historic role in the mission of the United Methodist Church, Millsaps seeks to provide a learning environment which increases knowledge, deepens understanding of faith, and inspires the development of mature citizens with the intellectual capacities, ethical principles, and sense of responsibility that are needed for leadership in all sectors of society.

The programs of the college are designed to promote independent and critical thinking; individual and collaborative problem solving; creativity, sensitivity, and tolerance; the power to inform and challenge others; and an expanded appreciation of humanity and the universe.[112]

Apart from the reference to the college's role in the church, now filed as an item of history, and a later call to foster a mutually supportive relationship with the Mississippi Conference, there is no allusion to a Methodist identity. Even the visitors on the accreditation team observed that the college's role within the church had been passed over.[113]

By virtually all indices, Millsaps has in recent years achieved a distinct betterment in its academic credentials. As late as 1967 the dean reported to the board that only one-third of the faculty possessed the terminal degree in their respective fields, foolishly adding that this was "a high percentage for any college." The president reported, at the same time, that eight departmental chairmen lacked their terminal degrees. Today nineteen out of twenty chairmen hold terminal degrees; the sole exception is a veteran in the fine arts. Among the ninety-six active faculty, all but nine possess the terminal degree, and those exceptions are either young faculty still working on their dissertations or senior faculty appointed before 1970.[114]

There are as well some signs of a continuing and sympathetic tie between Methodism and Millsaps. For example, the ministry still includes numerous Millsaps graduates. Six Methodist bishops are alumni, more than any other university or college in the country can boast of. And one of Millsaps' strongest ties to its Methodist constituency has been the presence of so many of its alumni in Methodist manses around the state. In 1967, for instance, 300 ministers, 56 percent of all those in Mississippi, were Millsaps graduates (200 others served churches beyond the state borders). But intra-Methodist struggles during the civil rights period of the sixties led 50 or 60 of the more liberal Millsaps alumni in the ministry to leave Mississippi, and this has deprived the college of many of its most effective advocates in the conference.[115]

Though the scope of financial links between church and college is greatly reduced, mutualities remain in place. When church contributions to Millsaps were rising to record highs during President Finger's administration, the board of trustees made a move to reciprocate. The college would invest 20 percent of its capital fund contributions from Mississippi churches in the various churches' extension programs, provided that they were guaranteed and bore interest at current rates. This, in addition to the continued practice of educating ministerial students with generous tuition remissions, was a tangible sign of reciprocal goodwill.[116]

But the indices of a growing indifference were also there to be seen. Down at the Mississippi Conference, annual subsidies to Millsaps were beginning to shrink, even during her centennial celebration, and each year there has been an increasing interest in and financial support for campus ministry to Methodists on state college and university campuses.[117]

When H. Ellis Finger resigned in 1964 after twelve years as president, the chairman of the board proposed four qualifications for his successor: "(1) A true Christian; (2) Educationally strong; (3) Proven record of administrative ability; and (4) A good mixer with public relations talent, tact and courage."[118] In some contexts the stipulation "a true Christian" might be vague and/or ambivalent. But Finger, the incumbent, had come to the presidency with only pastoral qualifications, and was leaving to become a bishop. In that context, "a true Christian" would be the equivalent of "an enlightened Methodist." And a Methodist is what they chose. By way of contrast, when George Harmon (1978-) succeeded to the presidency he left the Episcopal Church to become a Methodist. Some on the faculty regarded him as a Methodist of convenience. As one senior professor put it unkindly, if the University of Kuwait had called Harmon to its presidency he would be a Moslem.

One matter of custom, minor in itself, also marks the shift in religious sensibilities among the faculty. Years ago a faculty meeting would begin with a Methodist "devotion." This gradually became simplified to a single prayer. Most recently, since the late 1980s, faculty meetings have begun with a period of silence. More than a century separates this apophatic faculty from those who took it in turn to lead the college in worship under Murrah.

A Universal Chaplaincy

One service which might be expected to labor under ambiguity in a college as religiously disparate as Millsaps is campus ministry. Its fortunes are an interesting variant of church-college relations. By the end of the sixties it had become a marginal enterprise at the college. Communal worship on campus had been discontinued since 1964. The rancor of the civil rights movement had injected bitterness into student-faculty relations, and between factions within the faculty. There was no operative campus ministry organization among the students, or faculty involvement in such ministry. The only religious organization on campus was the InterVarsity Fellowship, which met off campus.[119] It was from the faculty — indeed, from the leader of the local chapter of the American Association of University Professors — that a complaint was finally raised in 1968:

> I think we need a College Chaplain, a Preacher to the college. My good neighbor Jack Woodward is an administrator of awards, government grants, loans, and

heaven knows what else. He does not have time to be the Chaplain. The religion department professors are all ordained Methodist clerics, but I suspect they have neither the training, the time, nor the inclination to be the college Preacher. We need one.[120]

A young new chaplain, Don Fortenberry, was brought back to his alma mater in 1973, and he is still the Millsaps chaplain today. Fortenberry found a student body that was affluent, white, deprived of community on the campus, and, in the words of the college's own self-study report, "dedicated to the status quo."[121] Perhaps most difficult, they were fragmented religiously. The 60 percent or more of the student body who were not Methodists now included members of other Protestant denominations, significant numbers of Catholics, and increasing numbers of Jews, Moslems, and other non-Christians.

He set out to bind this conflicted miscellany into a community. "Although worship had been part of the campus ministry program from its early days, the priorities of the chaplain were education about issues of injustice and exploitation in the society and experiences aimed at the personal liberation of individuals from prejudices and stereotypes (racial, sexual, gender, national, religious)."[122] Fortenberry found little support in traditional Christianity, which understood faith as a form of knowing and understanding God in an objective and detached manner. This fixation on the cognitive, he found, was what had fragmented the church. He turned instead to a revisionist Christianity, rooted in subjective experience. Refusing to be beguiled by the dominant culture with its covert exploitation and repression (a culture from which Millsaps students came and within which they would otherwise aspire to succeed), Fortenberry invited his flock to follow Jesus in his solidarity with the marginal and his involvement with the brokenness and suffering of the downtrodden and his struggle for a global community.

Those who pursued this call to radical social involvement would find their faith universalized. They would transcend particular loyalties such as churches or denominations, in the interest of a "total trust in and loyalty to the principle of being." A rereading of the Millsaps story showed Fortenberry that the college had all along been groping its way to this revolutionary social activism: the concern of the founders to educate the poorer classes, the commitment to academic freedom in the evolution controversy, the pacifism among the students during World War II, the civil rights movement in the sixties, the antiwar protests during Vietnam, the sexual liberation among the student body . . . all this has been a providential movement, nurtured always by the "Christian orientation" of the college, toward "affirmation of the worth of individuals apart from social definitions."[123]

The protracted faculty wrangles over a new mission statement for Millsaps, which occupied much of the 1980s, provoked Fortenberry to formulate his own mission more explicitly and publicly. While the faculty was talking about "critical thinking," he was calling for empathetic experience. The faculty was exalting the "diverse social ethnic, geographical, and age backgrounds" of the student body, and he reminded them of its homogeneity: they were teaching fewer than 6 percent African Americans in a state where they constituted 36 percent, and in a city where they constituted 56 percent, of the population.

There was one inclination of the faculty with which he and his chapel-oriented students did concur: their objections to any reference to church relationship, or even to God, which "would suggest partisanship toward Christian faith or compromise of intellectual integrity." This same instinct surfaced in his campus ministry discussions when students strenuously insisted on affirming all the religious traditions as offering comparable access to ultimate truth.[124] Fortenberry pressed on to formulate his own religious vision for the college, one held out to skeptical academics unhappy about any denominational claims and to undetermined students who wanted to defer to them all. His product merits generous quotation, for it says much about the religious status of Millsaps as a (non-)Methodist-related school.

Mission Statement: Office of the Chaplain, Millsaps College

The program of the Chaplain's Office at Millsaps College aims fundamentally at encouraging members of the Millsaps community to participate in the creation of a global community that is characterized by justice, compassion and mutual appreciation. This goal is to be understood as a vocation that can be realized through the various personal and professional endeavors of students, faculty, staff, alumni and supporters of the college.

In order to achieve the vision of a global community, members of the Millsaps community must be able to identify with the humanity of members of the global family, especially those who are different. To this end, barriers of race, nation, creed, gender or ideology must be transcended. The greatest promise for doing this resides in opening members of the community to the experience of pain among fellow human beings. Such experience invites empathy, provides concrete experience of the common humanity of individuals, encourages solidarity with those who suffer, and motivates persons to involvement in improving the quality of life for all people.

Education for this task of creating such a global community necessitates information and understanding, communities that share this vision and nurture their members in it, and experience through which ideas and perceptions can be shaped, refined and energized. To the degree that all three of these elements can be incorporated into the ministry of the Chaplain's Office, the possibility of such a global vision will be enhanced. The fullest realization of this vision depends on the college and the campus ministry program's ability to combine the life of the mind, with its emphasis on information, critical evaluation and synthesis, and the life of the heart, with its qualities of affection, empathy and passion. . . .

Furthermore, emphasis on a global community does not preclude affirmation of the particular traditions and histories that individuals bring to the college community. The campus ministry program at Millsaps rejoices in diversity. Yet even with that diversity, the campus ministry program is grounded in the Christian witness and directs special attention to the nurture of the Christian community within the college. This witness grows out of the biblical record of God's action in the world that calls people to partnership with God in the interest of justice and love. . . .

Students enter Millsaps College at various stages of moral, intellectual and faith development. The largest segment of traditional-age students is characterized by dualistic thinking that renders impossible the integration of conflicting truths, by moral reasoning that focuses on the interests of persons with whom one has significant relationships and by faith development that is not yet able to articulate one's own beliefs adequately in dialogue with persons operating out of different faith traditions or with different theological presuppositions. A fundamental task of campus ministry is to provide structures and relationships that enable persons and groups to make transitions to more comprehensive ways of thinking about their faith and acting out of it.

The ecumenical and interfaith campus ministry program at Millsaps acknowledges that morally-grounded action is the concern of all religious traditions and can be the vehicle for common ministries of healing in the world. Nevertheless, it is also acknowledged that special sustenance is drawn from the United Methodist Church and there exists a peculiar responsibility to participate in the wider campus ministry program of that denomination.[125]

Despite its prolix and emollient doses of "nurture," the policy claims responsibility for something that would be very ambitious on any college campus: to combine the life of the mind with the life of the heart, somehow to correlate the academic experience with the religious experience. But if that were to be done, it would surely require commitment and coordination from within the academic enterprise. The signs are that neither the academic administration nor the faculty has manifested any disposition to join in this very moral enterprise. Absent that willingness, any chaplain is audacious to claim either the authority or the leverage to marshal the campus in an integrated assault on suffering and alienation in the cosmos.

Apart from the vague and somewhat apologetic concluding sentence, there is no tie-in with the church. Indeed, despite the indistinct reference to Christian witness, the campus ministry would seem not to be the ministry of or within any church, but of a college. There are unresolved obstacles to social and moral programs sponsored by an undifferentiated coalition of "religious" people. For there are some religious communities for whom race or nation or ideology is not a matter of indifference. And although "morally-grounded action is the concern of all religious traditions," the religions, churches, and denominations have principled reasons to differ among themselves about what actions are unjust, what remedies are just, who are victims, and who are exploiters. Those are issues on which a moral community must expend much energy and goodwill and grace in order to reach a workable consensus. The United Methodist Church might aspire to that task, but for the ephemeral student body of Millsaps College it would be a much more daunting ambition.

At present neither the Mississippi Conference nor Millsaps College seems restive under the public affirmation that they are related. But it would be difficult to imagine how the college could, especially in its academic function, demonstrate any more unconcern for the United Methodist Church, or how the Mississippi Methodists could invest even fewer of their resources in Millsaps. In the absence of an antagonizing crisis, the lines that still tether the college and the church together are under no particular strain, and they draw neither entity much out of its way in the other's behalf.

OHIO WESLEYAN UNIVERSITY

As early America gradually absorbed immigrant populations into its seaboard colonies, it was in the South, for several reasons, that the new Methodism found the most hospitable situation. Despite their legal establishment in southern colonies, Anglicans were numerically predominant in only a few regions. Thus their actual social dominance was not as strong as their legal precedence. The Church of England provided a natural host environment for Methodists. Wesley's movement was, to begin with, a reformist piety within that church in which he was an ordained minister, and his followers found more familiarity there than in the more doctrinally focused Calvinist climate to the north. Furthermore, any disposition the Anglicans might have had to repress the Methodists as nonconformists was neutralized by their own growing unpopularity as Tories. Thus, when the Revolution succeeded, Methodists found themselves situated nine-to-one below what would someday become the Mason-Dixon line. Baltimore was their natural center. And from that staging ground their usage of lay preachers, circuit riders, and localized authority made them especially mobilized to march west with the migrants who were pouring through the Appalachians toward the Mississippi Valley. Once out there they were similarly advantaged in recruiting converts who, for want of clergy or because of the rough mores of the frontier, had become unchurched. One of the new territories where Methodists most quickly gained the ascendancy was Ohio, which contained the old Western Reserve of Connecticut.[126]

The General Conference of 1820, as we have seen, had enjoined each annual conference (region) to provide itself with a school. The first response to that call was Augusta College, organized in 1822 and built in 1825 as a joint endeavor of the Conferences of Ohio and Kentucky. The school was situated on the Kentucky bank of the Ohio River, so from the very start the Ohioans considered it not quite theirs. When their inclinations to abolition began to chill relations with their slave-owning coreligionists in Kentucky, the estrangement from Augusta was only intensified. Norwalk Seminary was Ohio's own, but it was inconveniently distant from the population centers and, in any case, only a lower school. Ohio University itself might have provided for their needs, but the Presbyterians were in firm charge there. Adam Poe, minister to a Methodist congregation in the town of Delaware just to the north of Columbus, rallied a group of his townspeople in 1841 to purchase an unsuccessful spa-hotel beside a sulfur spring nearby and offer it to the Ohio conferences for a college. The Methodists responded, and only months later they secured a charter for Ohio Wesleyan University which provided that it "is forever to be conducted on the most liberal principles, accessible to all religious denominations and designed for the benefit of our citizens in general."[127] Delaware had at the time hardly a thousand inhabitants, and Poe himself had to supply the last $500 to clinch the purchase. The trustees brought in an ex-governor of Ohio as their chairman (in those days called president), and they brought down Edward Thomson, principal of Norwalk Seminary, as their first university president. They forthwith enacted a rule that "none but professors of religion" be employed on the faculty. The academy opened with only four boys but it grew, and collegiate studies were begun in 1844.[128] By the end of that year the student body included two juniors, two sophomores, fourteen freshmen, and ninety-two in preparatory courses. Thomson held an M.D. and was a powerful preacher and a dedicated abolitionist. Said he: "I will not obey the fugitive slave law, but will suffer the extreme penalty in case of need." He would be the first of three Ohio Wesleyan presidents to serve later as bishops.[129]

Thomson's inaugural address, which must have required several hours for its delivery, was a classic. He addressed himself to his constituency, which was clearly more municipal than ecclesiastical. As their client he had to present a college education as something well worth their investment; but as a Wesleyan minister he had to describe its benefits as an enhancement of God's gifts rather than a mere gateway to affluence.

Delaware, said Thomson, was obviously not a Methodist stronghold, but so much the better: "It is a matter of joy to me that the University is located in a community divided in political and religious opinions; the friction of a mixed society prevents dogmatism and develops energy." In a word: all were welcome. Yet Delaware did well to invite in the Methodists as its educators. It could easily be seen "that a college, to be permanent, must be endowed, and to be useful, must be patronized; and that to secure both endowment and patronage, it must be placed under the fostering care of some religious denomination. Now to which of the sects in Ohio were the People of Delaware to look for the aid indispensable to the establishment of a literary institution? . . . lo! the Methodists, with a membership of 150,000, had no literary institution of a higher grade than the academy. To them, therefore, it was natural that our citizens should turn." Great was to be their reward.

In the region of the college, there is a gradual elevation of the whole platform of society. Industry is stimulated, intelligence diffused, improvements introduced, the public taste refined, enterprise provoked, acquaintance extended, and correspondence with distant points established: cabins become villas, swamps parterres, the forest is fragrant with the lily and the rose, and the whole land seems to be moving upward to the sun and the bosom of the clouds.

Whence come earth's great ones — the Jeffersons, the Erskines, the Websters; the founders of constitutions, the expounders of law, the ambassadors of nations? As a general rule, from the college. Hither come the bench, the bar, the senate chamber, the pulpit, the throne, to fill their vacant seats. Place the names of your children upon the college catalogue, and, as a general rule, you enroll them upon the scroll of respectability, if not of fame. Graduate them, and they are fair candidates for the highest honors and emoluments of the government. How great, then, the advantages you possess over the people of many neighboring towns!
. . .

When I hear the Methodist preachers of former days accused of opposing education, I repel the charge (unless it be qualified) as a base calumny. 'Tis pseudo-Methodism, not genuine, that sneers at learning. Some of *her* preachers, I know, did underrate knowledge, and there are a few now among us, both old and young, of the same character. They will have nothing to do with science, because it is not the smooth stone from the brook; they won't use Goliath's sword, even to cut off Goliath's head. They tell us, God has no need of human *learning;* but they seem to think he has great need of human *ignorance.* We believe he *can* carry on his work without either. The question is, whether he *will.*

Thomson was in no hurry that day, as he advanced six duties Methodists would fulfill through their colleges. The first duty: to hold on to her best minds. "Methodist youths may be sent to Presbyterian, or other colleges. That *has* been done, and what, generally, is the result? They are Methodists no longer, but give their talents to the church which has educated them. There are, probably, one hundred Methodist youths in the other denominational colleges of this state." Second: to provide teachers for the republic. Third: to train her members in the literary arts to compete against the godless for control of the press. Fourth: to allow religion to advance step-by-step with learning. "Brethren may say, let other Churches attend to science — be it ours, like our fathers, to preach salvation. Our fathers did not merely do this. Witness Clarke, and Watson, and Benson, and Bunting. Circumstances, too, have changed since the days of our American fathers. Methodism can no longer, like the wild ass free, scorn the multitudes of the city, while she makes the wilderness her house, and the barren land her dwelling." Fifth: "It is the duty of the Church to resist the encroachments of Romanism. . . . That she is striving for the ascendancy, there can be no doubt, and that she aims to compass this end by becoming the presiding genius of American education, seems equally clear. When once she allures the youth to her halls, *'Religioni et artibus sacrum,'* she begins to spread her vail over his eyes. And this is easy; for she directs his studies, closes up his communication with the world, wins his confidence by kind attentions, enchants him with her imposing ceremonies, and alarms him by gradually pressing upon his immature mind her favorite dogma, 'Salvation in the arms of the *Church* only.' We blame her not for this: her principles demand it. But *shame* on the Protestantism which says those principles are from hell, yet stirs not to counterwork them." Sixth: to prepare missionaries, and not just with piety and a call. "As the Bible must be translated, stupid millions aroused and enlightened, the rising generation trained and educated, the captious Brahmin met and confounded, and the hollowness of a venerable and gorgeous philosophy exposed, surely, in a world, and under a dispensation, where God works according to immutable laws, a disciplined understanding, a taste for study, and a knowledge of the principles of language, and the laws of the human mind, are indispensable. If, therefore, the Church needs missionaries of such qualifications, she is bound to erect colleges, where they may be obtained: not that she may make missionaries, but that she may make *men,* whom God may make missionaries."

To stave off any venal misunderstanding Thomson promised that a college education would actually be a barrier to avarice, by furnishing the understanding, the taste, and the perspective that direct us to life's higher purposes. It would serve political tranquillity, both by accrediting the truly apt candidates for office and by creating a citizenry astutely able to assert its liberty against any government's tendency to encroach. But let no one imagine that the educators who will accomplish all this have any selfish interests to be served:

> The post of instructor in college is, by no means, an enviable one. The compensation, small; the honors, after death; the labors, arduous and incessant. I know of no employment more heart-trying, spirit-wasting, health-destroying. . . . Why, then, do men of God leave the word of God to serve college tables? Men, called to preach, have qualifications to influence mind that others have not, and surely the highest abilities for operating upon the human soul are needed in the college.[130]

Thomson's inaugural was an oratorical extravaganza. He commended the disciplined study of classical Latin and Greek to the farmers and artisans of a small town in a state without railroads, where neither streets nor walkways were surfaced, where the stagecoach passed by only three times a week and took an entire day to labor up the twenty miles from Columbus, and where the campus served as pasturage for the browsing cattle and swine of nearby farmyards. In return for hefty tuition payments now he hinted to the parents what affluence awaited their children after graduation, while assuring them not a hard-earned dollar would be wasted by overpaying the teachers. And after describing the opportunity Methodists had to sponsor a community college for a religiously diverse population, "forever to be conducted on the most liberal principles, accessible to all religious denominations and designed for the benefit of our citizens in general," he went on to commend it almost exclusively to Methodists.

Soon the Largest College of the Church

Ohio Wesleyan's beginnings were typical for an evangelical antebellum college: local clientele, clerical faculty, and marginal finances. During the course of her first half-century, most developments were similar to what sister institutions were experiencing, yet some suggested a sharper rate of climb. All of the OWU presidents were Methodist ministers: the first lay president would not be appointed for more than a century. Three of the first four presidents had earned doctorates. The faculty were increasingly well trained, with earned master's degrees plus honorary doctorates in the early years, and earned doctorates from Yale, Ohio State, Halle, and Johns Hopkins beginning to appear in the postbellum period. Of the twenty-three male professors who served during the first half-century, sixteen were Methodist ministers and the other seven were OWU graduates.[131] Ministers on the faculty would frequently begin in their first disciplines — chemistry or mathematics or physics or civil engineering — and would eventually migrate back to moral philosophy or English Bible.[132] They all obviously enjoyed a shared intellectual foundation.

In its first fifty years the university conferred degrees on 2,186 of its students, one-seventh of all who had matriculated.[133] Of the graduates, 277 (17 percent) entered the ministry (only one-third of those ministers, however, had gone on to theological schools), 64 had served as missionaries, 140 had become professors, and 60 had become presidents. There were significant numbers who had gone on to the bar, to medicine, and to various advanced degrees.[134] Ohio Wesleyan at that time was acknowledged as "the largest and most successful school in the Methodist Episcopal Church."[135] Just before the semicentennial the president reported to his board that more than one-tenth of all (Northern) Methodists lived within a radius of 150 miles of the OWU campus, and they had more undergraduates (531) and more students at all levels (1,217) than any other Methodist college or university in the world.[136] About three-fourths of them were reported to be "professing Christians," in a year when the average rate in Northern Methodist schools was reported to be about 50 percent.[137]

After a respectable courtship the university merged with the nearby Ohio Wesleyan Female College in 1877. Monnett Hall, as the women's school was called, had itself been the residual beneficiary of three nearby female institutions that had closed. Ohio Wesleyan therewith claims authorship of the term "coed." The practice of educating both genders together was widely accepted in the region: at Antioch, DePauw, and Oberlin, for instance. Methodist mores prevailed on the campus, though not without some resistance. When Greek-letter fraternities were being established at colleges across the nation in the early 1870s, they were prohibited at Ohio Wesleyan by Frederick Merrick, M.D. (1860-73), the second president. They survived in a clandestine existence, but the ban lasted only two years. His successor was himself a fraternity man. Sororities eventually came to join them. Alcohol was, of course, not allowed, and those interactions between the sexes curiously called "fraternization" were closely monitored. In 1884 the faculty

301

passed a rule forbidding attendance at the local theater, the "Opera House," and nine seniors were suspended the next year for attending a Shakespearean play. The Wabash student paper spoke of OWU as a "monastery from which students escaped and went to DePauw."[138] A poll revealed that there were nearly three times as many Prohibitionists as Democrats in the student body, but a majority of Republicans. As the important issue of the day in 1893, 133 chose the tariff dispute; 96, the liquor traffic; 21, the economy; 4, Romanism; 3, capital and labor.[139] The burghers of Delaware were evidently getting what Thomson had so largely promised, and then some.

Chapel services numbered thirteen per week in the earliest years: morning and evening except on Sunday when students trooped off to a church in town. They only occasionally had Bible lectures besides. Tutelage in speech was a strong discipline on the campus, and one of its intended outcomes was occasional devotional addresses by students in chapel. Revivals were a regular feature of college life, and the president's account of the revival of 1891 shows they had not abated by that date:

At the opening of our revival services, two hundred and forty two unconverted students and about seven hundred Christian students were on the grounds. Nearly a year ago the Faculty invited Rev. S. A. Keen, D.D., a graduate of the University, a man of beautiful Christian spirit, of large faith in God, and with a genius for evangelistic work, to take charge of the revival services. . . . Three weeks before Dr. Keen came, the churches commenced Union Services; and some thirty began the Christian life previous to his arrival. In the meantime the Christian students were not idle. Every class was carefully canvassed and persons were appointed to see every unconverted student and engage in personal conversation upon the subject of religion. The Day of Prayer for colleges proved a red-letter day in our history. A large number of students began the Christian life in the college chapel during the forenoon and afternoon services. At night the Union Services proper began in William St. Church. Dr. Keen invited three classes to come to the altar: those desiring to make a fuller consecration and to reach a higher Christian life; those who had wandered away from God and desired to return to Him; and those desiring conversion. Nearly fifty were at the altar the first evening. The work increased in interest from the beginning, and requests for prayer multiplied at the daily chapel services, at the Pentecostal services held by Dr. Keen at the church each afternoon, and at the evening services.

The city was stirred as it had not been for years. Wednesday of the second week was observed as a mid-week Sabbath by the churches and the college. Business was suspended. The revival was upon everybody's lips. Students and citizens packed the largest auditorium in Delaware. It was a day of glorious victories. The interest in religion became so deep that the college appointed a special service in the chapel on Saturday. While this service was entirely voluntary, the chapel was crowded with students; and the Holy Spirit's presence was marvelously manifested in convicting, converting and sanctifying power. It seemed as if another day of such victories would bring all the students to Christ; and Monday was named as a third day of prayer; and many more began the Christian life. . . . Upon the whole over two hundred students and over four hundred citizens have been converted in Delaware the present winter, and a multitude of Christians have been led to a higher plane of privilege and of usefulness.[140]

Methodists Find They Like Learning

As the university drew to its fiftieth birthday, the theologian president James Bashford (1889-1904) described it as presidents often do: "Rising infinitely above all financial considerations, rising above all material interests, of the University in buildings and appliances, far exceeding even the daily instruction in importance, is the growth of manhood and womanhood, the development of character among our students." Its first historian, no minister but a scientist, and clearly on Reverend Thomson's wavelength more than Reverend Bashford's, spoke of prosperity, not character:

> Methodism in Ohio has not always seemed to appreciate (the University's) needs and its services, and possibilities of good to the Church. But it has had a steady growth in popular favor, resources, students and influences. It enters upon its second half century with a reputation, equipments and consecration of great promise. The place of the denominational college in the work of the Church is better understood. Wealthy laymen are coming to adopt it as their heir. Loyal alumni are planning to place their *Alma Mater* above want. People of all faiths and no faiths are learning, as never before, that the Christian college is the best educational center for their sons and daughters. The monument of fifty years of successful history is a prophecy of the greater prosperity that will be realized in the future.[141]

The university's growth had been extraordinarily steady, across years that for many campuses were destructive. And now she would indeed take prosperity to her bosom.

James Whitford Bashford was only forty years old when he came to OWU as its fourth president. The university began to change. New faculty were recruited, virtually all with earned doctorates. Specialization fledged out the classical curriculum: more natural sciences, new social sciences. Funding swelled, and the campus acquired a series of new buildings. Bashford said it was time for this university to live up to its name and cease being just a college. OWU opened a medical school and began to offer master's degrees and the Ph.D. Meanwhile Ohio Wesleyan graduates were found to outnumber alumni of any other school among those doing graduate studies at Harvard. Two seniors were appointed Rhodes scholars in the space of three years. A chapter of Phi Beta Kappa was awarded. Evolution was taught without let or hindrance in both biology and philosophy courses, and Walter Rauschenbusch came to lecture about the new Social Gospel. Turned down by Carnegie for a pension fund grant because most of the trustees were elected by the sponsoring Methodist conferences, the university succeeded in winning a $400,000 grant from the General Education Board, followed later by further awards amounting to $375,000.[142]

When Bashford concluded fifteen years of leadership to become a bishop in China, the prophecy of a greater prosperity seemed to have been fulfilled. And it was not as if Ohio Wesleyan had bent the knee to Baal. The university's centennial historian observed: "In a spirit of great optimism horizons widened, late nineteenth century Christian liberalism became enthroned in classroom, laboratory and chapel, and the new experimental and Darwinian science came in, all this intellectual advance, however, being cast in a frame of zealous evangelistic religion."[143] Nor did all this innovation seem discontinuous with this university's past. This was, after all, the place where the faculty had voted to introduce electives into the curriculum in 1866, three years before Charles Eliot even went back to Harvard. In 1872, when anti-Darwinian rage was running fresh and high, an OWU professor gave a chapel lecture reconciling Genesis with the theory of evolution. When, near the turn of the century, Bashford was interviewing Edward Rice for a faculty position in zoology, and Rice warned him he would feel obliged to teach evolution, the president replied: "I wouldn't want you if you didn't." Several decades later Rice would be called as an expert witness in the Scopes trial. There was a continuity here of easy and responsible liberalism. And in the full flourish of all that academic endeavor, there were hundreds of students enrolled in extracurricular Bible study in the YMCA, and hundreds more in their mission study classes. So all of this movement had the feel of authentic development, and of an integration of "the pair so long disjoin'd, knowledge and vital piety."[144]

Some of it was overdone. Though the momentum Bashford had generated ran on strongly, they came to realize that the expansion went well beyond what they could maintain. The medical school was given away to Western Reserve University; the Ph.D. program was dropped and the master's degree programs greatly constricted; the academy (which at times had enjoyed a much larger enrollment than the undergraduate program) was closed, along with the School of Business. OWU decided it should be a liberal arts college and nothing else.

Religious Factors in Decline

In the early twenties, however, other developments began to dissociate the academic vigor of the university from its Methodist attachments. Sunday church attendance was no longer required. When the decline in voluntary attendance became disturbing, the Sabbath lecture was transmogrified into a weekly convocation on campus at the same hour, with big-name speakers. Students began to come to these, for a time. The daily "devotions" held in the chapel began to alternate with other programs — civic, "inspirational," entertaining, oratorical. In the late thirties a large gift was solicited to refurbish the chapel (an all-purpose auditorium), and the daily devotional period was reinstated but quickly receded into an occasional event.[145]

The revivals went into decline. Evidently there had been misgivings about them all along. In 1888 one writer objected to outside speakers as "slangy and sacrilegious, an abomination." In 1896 the complaint was lodged that revivals created a division among the students — between saved and unsaved — of which they were never otherwise conscious. One professor whose recollections went back to Bashford days published this retrospective comment in 1939: "Many of us looked forward to the time (of the revival) with dread, and looked upon its final passing with relief." A colleague described the meetings as "emotional spasms."[146] Uneasiness must have had some part in effecting a change of style. One student had this recollection of a revival after the Bashford presidency:

> The great majority of students were encouraged to talk about personal problems of relationships, about their general sense of inadequacy, and their hopes and ambitions. . . . We had many interviews with the faculty and gained results which in our day a student might get from talking freely with a consulting psychologist. . . . Many of the students looked forward to the meetings as a time when they could be most truly themselves and not be fearful or ashamed of this kind of self-revelation.[147]

This was in 1915, not 1965. The sawdust trail had pretty much reached its end, and in the late 1920s the revivals — or their therapeutic progeny — were discontinued.[148]

There seems to be no record of concern about it, but the religious complexion of the student body began to change in the 1920s. Recall that in 1891 President Bashford had reported to his trustees that 75 percent of the student body were "professing Christians." In 1923 more than 70 percent were reported as Methodists, but by 1930 that had diminished to 56 percent, a sharp decline. By the midthirties it would descend below 50 percent.[149] On campus this seems to have been lost amid other, possibly more noteworthy, trends: "In recent years an increase in the number chosen from the upper third of the high school class has occurred and an interesting trend has been the enrollment growth from the city of Delaware. Graduates have gone into business in very large numbers, and the decline in the attendance at theological schools has been very marked."[150]

Ohio Wesleyan was successful too in attracting a more cosmopolitan student. Before World War I the president could still report that farm families contributed the largest socioeconomic segment of the student body, but in the twenties the rural rootage of students rapidly gave way to the urban: freshmen by then were most likely to come from the homes of businessmen.[151] But after the war the faculty and administration became concerned that the fraternities were too discriminatory in their recruitment, and were shutting out the more "straight" students from the center of social life. So they founded para-fraternities: the Union before 1920, the Commons in the early 1920s, and the Brotherhood in the later 1920s. These were successive unsuccessful attempts to create nonfraternities that could enjoy staid fun. They were said to be a gesture of "democratic idealism." When one student actually left his fraternity and joined the Brotherhood, he was praised for his "deep social interest." But most students focused their deep social interest on the fraternities and sororities, and these faculty-sponsored groups quickly collapsed, one after the other.[152] Sororities, several times suppressed in former years, were reintroduced in 1922, just as the old literary and debating societies, which had probably been the most intellectually and socially vital activities on campus for the past seventy-five years, were about to go extinct.[153] In 1931 the honor system, which had existed for twenty years, was abandoned because students disapproved of "spying" on one another.[154] And dancing began in earnest.[155] Ohio Wesleyan was becoming a fun place.

Faculty used to be identified, upon their appointment, by their religious affiliations. Thus in 1928, ten new faculty included four Methodists, four Presbyterians, and two Lutherans.[156] Yet by 1929, when a presidential search was being mounted, after ninety-seven years of presidency by Methodist ministers (three of whom had become bishops), a questionnaire circulated among faculty and staff recommended no more than that the nominee be "preferably a Methodist."[157] Was there distance developing between college and church?

If so, it left few outward traces in those days. The 1920s, with their fierce antagonism between fundamentalists and agnostics, left few Methodist presidents unscathed. But in Delaware few spent shell casings were to be found on the ground after that controversy. The OWU board continued to be elected mostly by the Ohio conferences, and there was no open stress such as so many campuses experienced. The archives do tell of one person with a growing concern: Edmund D. Soper, who presided over OWU from 1928 to 1938.

The Church Could Lose Ohio Wesleyan

In his inaugural address Soper offered a revisionist notion of academic freedom. The faculty's right to teach freely, with no restraints, he said, has allowed some teachers to undermine the purpose and faith of their students. But the Christian character of a church college is its highest concern, and the college has both the right and the duty to control its teaching. He did not propose, however, that this duty is fulfilled by monitoring the content and conduct of what is taught. It is accomplished by the way the college hires its faculty.

The men and women who join the faculty should accept heartily and without reserve the purposes for which the school stands. This does not mean accepting a creed or signing a statement as a guarantee of orthodoxy. It does not mean being a member of the Methodist Episcopal Church, though I can see how probable and even desirable it is that a good proportion of the faculty should be Methodists. What I have in mind penetrates deeper than church membership, which so frequently is merely a formal relation and conveys little or no information as to the inner meaning of one's life and its significant attitudes. . . .

There is no hint that men will be asked to change their opinions, or to do violence to their convictions. No one will be asked to live a life of intellectual restraint. What is desired is to discover those who have come to their permanent life attitudes and find themselves in accord with the Christian principles on which the college rests, who know they can be truest to themselves and will be under the least restraint when they enter the fellowship of a faculty whose guiding principles are determined by their loyalty to Christ and his teaching. . . . When a member of the faculty has thus been secured, he is to be trusted. . . . When his fundamental attitude to Christ is assured I can see no limit to his freedom.[158]

In 1930 he set forth before his board how the university was being pulled between two opposite poles.

There is a strong tendency in some quarters for a college to draw away from the Church and to feel that it is a little below the dignity of an institution of higher learning to be known as having denominational affiliations. . . . I am afraid sometimes that Methodist colleges are acknowledged to be such only when they run out of funds. I am also afraid that there are those who are graduates of church colleges who are ashamed of the fact and belittle the relationship their Alma Mater has with the Church. They seem to want to be free, . . . free from church control, which is scorned by those who come from the independent schools. . . . I am convinced there is a great future for the Christian college which can only be achieved by intelligent cooperation with the Church. Ohio Wesleyan would find it very difficult to discover a reason for its existence and a valid appeal for support except on the basis that it stands for Christian character as well as for high intellectual standards. . . .

If the Church were reactionary, superstitious, and timid, if it were fearful of scientific investigation and were held down by antiquated traditions which cramped its thinking and allowed no free study of industrial and social problems, we should certainly be in a difficult situation. Without doubt the Methodist Church has its share of just such folks as I have described and representatives are to be found in the ministry; but I have been led to believe that the leadership of the Church in Ohio is in very different hands.[159]

The board, from all the record shows, was not disposed to differ with him. To appreciate the university's situation at this time one must be aware that of all four-year liberal arts colleges then sponsored by the Methodist Episcopal Church, Ohio Wesleyan ranked first in enrollment (3.5 times the size of the average northern Methodist college; OWU also ranked third in student retention), second in invested funds (six times the average), first in educational income per student (close to five times the average), first in student aid available (seven times the average), and first in admissions requirements. At the same time, Ohio Wesleyan was enrolling more students in religion-related courses and sending proportionately more men into ministry than its Methodist-related peers.[160]

But several years later Soper was telling them of a significant drought in the church's patronage. He spoke in the depths of the Great Depression, but he perceived the problem to be more than economic.

> The church gave birth to Ohio Wesleyan and has continued through the years to give nurture to her child. Just now the financial support is practically nil. Over $20,000 a year came by direct gift through the Board of Education when I came to Ohio Wesleyan seven years ago; now it is down to less than $200 and no one can tell whether there will be any marked increase in the years to come. . . . If control goes with financial support, as so frequently it does, then it would seem that it is passing out of the hands of the church. I am putting it very bluntly on purpose. In doing so I am not forgetful of another fact which in many ways is quite as significant as the financial, namely, that even now, despite the financial failure, the church is an invaluable supporting influence back of Ohio Wesleyan. The other of course is the alumni, who are increasing rapidly in numbers and influence. It is not only conceivable but probable that influence will within a short time be more powerful than it is at present. At the present, however, the church and the alumni are so intermingled that it is hard to separate them in attempting to gage their influence. . . .
>
> The Methodist Church constituency in Ohio is not college-minded as it once was. . . . Many Methodist families are so situated financially that they cannot send their children to Ohio Wesleyan. They must place them in state schools. This is true, very unfortunately, of many ministers and of many alumni. The inevitable result is that their interest is turned in another direction . . . Another cause is that many Methodists feel that Ohio Wesleyan has departed from the old ways and has become so much like the world that there is little or no distinction between their college and other colleges which make no claim to be religious. . . .
>
> I am fully convinced that Ohio Wesleyan has not receded from its former position any farther than the church with which it is connected. Whether it be the theater, the card table, the dance, or use of tobacco, we are where the Methodist Church now is, or a part of it at least. That is one of our chief difficulties. What one group in the church desires another repudiates. . . .

Much of the criticism would cease were it recognized that in the nature of the case a college cannot be operated like a church. There are at least two important differences. One is that in a college the students come from all the Christian denominations and a few from none. They do not come as guests but become in a full sense members of the family. While the majority of our students are Methodists [in the academic year to begin three months later, Methodists would account for only 47 percent of the enrollment], they are only a little more than a majority and I cannot see that the ratio is likely to change in the near future. But there is an even greater difference between a college and a church. A church exercises direct control over the activities of its young people, particularly its social activities, only a few hours each week, that is, if it exercises control over social activities at all. On the other hand, the college is asked to assume such responsibility seven days in the week and twenty-four hours in the day. . . .

Ohio Wesleyan cannot long remain in any real relation with a church if the ministers and the laymen on the Board cannot get together in deciding how a college should be run under the actual conditions which exist out in the churches from which the students come, as well as in the college itself. There is danger that the laymen will feel that the ministers regard them as less loyal to the church and even less Christian than they might be.[161]

The Reductionist Rhetoric of Vague Methodism

This is as candid a presentation as one finds in the minutes of college boards. In public, however, OWU was in the course of developing a different rhetoric. The rhetoric of academics would be inconsequential were it not for their uncritical tendency to believe that they believe what they say so earnestly. It is a literary genre to be ingested with caution. Nevertheless, at Ohio Wesleyan a school of rhetoric was developing whose words themselves would become an interesting trail of facts.

The archives disclose two somewhat different corpora of rhetorical literature. The first, though not unique, is nevertheless more florid and ebullient at Ohio Wesleyan than at many other colleges. Its purpose seems to be to construe the university's mission in the most diffuse terms available.

We might begin with some remarks of Herbert Welch (1905-18), who succeeded Bashford as president and followed him later into the office of bishop. In 1916 he had this to say about "The Christian College":

The term "Christian College" is surely not to be limited to those colleges whose name or charter or denominational control gives outward evidence of a religious motive — "by their fruits ye shall know them." It is doubtless true that, just as the church is the chief pattern and instrument of the kingdom of God, so the denominational college is the typical form of the Christian ideal operating in education. But any college founded and conducted for a Christian purpose is obviously to be included among Christian colleges, whatever its formal relation to a Christian body. The Christian college, in short, is one whose ideals and aims are determined by the great conceptions of life which we count distinctively Christian.

The first of such aims is *culture*. The ideal of a liberal education is really a Christian ideal, since it is based on the Christian conception of personality. It has spread far beyond the institutions which by title and organization claim to represent the Christian Church and the Christian cause, but in its origin and essence it is Christian. . . . Moreover, this Christian ideal of a full-orbed education must include *character* as well as culture. If the entire nature of man is the proper subject of education, then conscience, loyalty, aspiration, reverence — all that enters into the moral and religious life — must receive adequate recognition in our educational plan.[162]

This is an early example of the reductive motif: Christian education defined so broadly and blandly that any decent college might claim it if so disposed. In 1930 the church's Commission on Survey of Educational Institutions paid its regular accreditation visit to OWU and left behind an impressively detailed appraisal of the welfare of the university. There is very little in their study that refers directly to its relationship to the church. But they did have comment to make upon the draft of an aims statement that the trustees had approved, though the faculty had not acted on it. Here are some excerpts from that draft:

We believe that Ohio Wesleyan should do its part in sending out men and women who are trained to lead in the solving of the problems which in each generation face mankind. They should feel the responsibility and be fitted to take their part in furthering the beneficent ends of human life. They should be ready to accept the opportunity to promote health, uphold high ideals of citizenship and economic life, enrich the meaning of recreation and the use of leisure, foster an appreciation of beauty, truth, and goodness, and promote true religion by precept and example. Anything less than the full acceptance of this purpose can only mean neglect of our responsibility at one point or another. . . .

What then are the more specific objectives in the lives of our students to which our attention must be directed?

They should have healthy, well-trained bodies, able to resist disease, with strength sufficient to meet the demands of an active, wholesome life.

They should have the sense of the power and joy of efficient thinking and living, having attained attitudes towards life and its problems which will call out the best that is in them and send them out with the desire to serve. . . .

They should develop deep respect for human personality and a sense of their obligation towards society. . . .

They should be men and women with a genuine religious experience, with faith in God and loyal devotion to Jesus Christ, and issuing in a life of personal rectitude and love of their fellow-men. On this foundation they should build a working philosophy of life giving them a satisfying interpretation of the universe and human life, providing them with a high purpose, and making them broadly tolerant and sympathetic with all that is noble and true wherever it is found. . . .

We fully recognize the great difficulties confronting us in carrying out these high purposes. It gives us pause and causes us the deepest concern. We have set our aim high; are we equal to the task?[163]

The survey staff evidently thought that they were not — or at least not yet — equal to it, and implied that their "Aim" was poor. The text was too broad and general, and they recommended further editing. It seems never to have been published. The point, though, is not that beauty, truth, and goodness might be a skewed purpose for educators at OWU. The drafters suffered from the same affliction as President Welch: a stupor-inducing vagueness. It was, apparently, an enduring handicap. In 1968 the Ohio Wesleyan Commission to Study Student Life outside the Classroom released its report on the ideal college. What, they asked, are the criteria for an ideal Christian liberal arts college, criteria that would apply especially to OWU? They proposed four:

Perception is both humanistic and factual. As a humanism, perception draws no limits upon human possibilities. It invites both the arts and the sciences to speak. Even the unschooled visionary can find a hearing among those who value perception. The humanism of perception is an ecumenicity befitting the belief that man is made in the image of God. It is a humanism which rises above the sectarianism of schools which seek to perpetuate stereotypes. . . .

Critical judgment is the necessity to choose at those points where choice must be lonely and irrevocable. . . . The University serves its students by exposing the deceptions and evasions which tempt us to stop short of responsibility before God. . . .

Enjoyment . . . Certainly a religious institution can entertain joy without a sense of guilt. Perhaps the temptation to despair is so great that only a religious institution can believe in joy, for enjoyment is first of all a matter of belief, which expresses itself in the doing of enjoyable things. . . .

Active responsibility for the problems of society . . . A socially concerned individual who had no capacity for enjoyment, who exercised glib and trite rather than critical judgment, and who had no perception of reality would be a public menace. Perhaps this is the meaning of "do-gooder." On the other hand, the absence of active responsibility for social problems might degenerate into obsession with self, and that perception might become dilettantism.[164]

After long labors, OWU published a new aims statement in 1979, which we must also consider later on. It recommended that the university educate in a context

311

of values, but omitted to suggest whether there were any values that might be more appropriate than others. President Thomas E. Wenzlau (1969-84) took the occasion of an annual trustees dinner to enumerate the specific values he recommended. Of his ten, here are two.

> First and foremost is the fundamental significance of human kind. To state this as a value may appear redundant but I believe it needs to be stated because it is the point of origin for many related values we transmit. It encompasses both the importance of the individual and of society (all individuals). It means that human rights have priority, at least initially, over other rights. It means, too, that an action whether taken by an individual or by a social organization would be evaluated by its affects [sic] not only on the initiator of the action but also by its affects [sic] on other members of the society. The very existence of Ohio Wesleyan with its liberal arts emphasis conveys its commitment to the preeminence of human beings. . . .
>
> Nine, Tolerance. Values and value systems are not alike nor are they equally valid and defensible. The University stands for certain values as do individuals who are part of the University. The University encourages exposure to and understanding of values outside of its own cultural heritage. No student or other individual is required to adopt or accept the University's set of values of any particular value or value system. However, the person must be responsible for actions taken based on whatever values or value system the person employs especially when those values are not consistent with those of the University.[165]

One gasps for air after reading texts as anoxic as this. Lastly, consider an example of this fulsome mission rhetoric from the recent president, David Liles Warren (1984-93), at his inauguration:

> If there is one phrase which I believe best characterizes our Wesleyan education, it is: "Here I Stand." Within these three words of Martin Luther — "Here I stand" — is compressed the whole of our historical endeavor. . . .
>
> Said (Henry David Thoreau): "I did not wish, when I came to die, to discover that I had not lived." That, it seems to me, is the point, the purpose, and the program of Ohio Wesleyan University. We want our young men and women to know *what* they believe and *why* they believe it, where they stand, and *why* they stand there, so that when finally they come to die, they will know that indeed, they have lived!
>
> And therefore, at Ohio Wesleyan, we shall commit the resources of this institution to an educational process which helps our young people to "architect" their lives, and which allows them to build on a scaffolding of values, and of knowledge, and of skills. Ohio Wesleyan shall provide them with the capacities to remodel their lives as they grow in experience, and yes, even to repair their lives when life grows difficult and sometimes breaks down. And most impor-

tantly, we shall enable them to make their lives creative and productive and responsible to their families, their friends, their communities, their nations, and to this imperiled earth. . . . We need to graduate young men and women who know their own hearts, and who know that to which they will be faithful.[166]

The reason why we should make the effort to read such discourse is not just that it is obscure, but that it is abject. It appears to imply that everyone easily knows what distinctive and wholesome things a Methodist fellowship would want to teach, yet as portrayed here these attempts to propound them are so empty of anything worth saying. What is taught will inevitably be supplied, not by any venerable (thus criticizable) tradition, but by whatever cut-rate doctrine is contemporarily available.

The Apologetic Rhetoric of "Unabashed" Methodism

Another rhetorical motif, more traditional at Ohio Wesleyan, might be called the "unabashed." In this line of rhetoric the university unselfconsciously identifies itself in official utterances with its church. Let us see whether these statements offer any traceable itinerary of purpose over the years. Long ago, under the heading of "Government," the early pages of the *Catalog* used to carry this statement:

> The Ohio Wesleyan University was founded, and is largely maintained, by the gifts of Christian men and women for the purpose of developing scholarship and Christian character. Out of the gifts thus generously made, more than half of the cost of educating every student attending the University is paid. These funds are committed to the University in trust, to be wisely and conscientiously invested in the education of young men and women whose life and work prove they are worthy of the benefit.

One clearly stated purpose of this sponsorship was to lead students freely "to accept Jesus as Savior and Lord." This statement was standard fare for many years, and then in 1925 a buffering insert was added:

> Although the Ohio Wesleyan University was established by the Methodist Episcopal Church and has been continuously under the patronage of that denomination, it is in no sense sectarian and makes no denominational requirements of its students, faculty, or trustees.[167] As its charter declares, the "University is forever to be conducted on the most liberal principles, accessible to all denominations, and designed for the benefit of our citizens in general." But, in accordance with the ideals and purposes of the founders, it seeks to be positively Christian in spirit and policy. To this end daily devotional services are held during the academic week in Gray Chapel, at which the attendance of students is required.[168]

313

The avowal of denominational attachment remains clear. It is only its effects that are compromised. A "positive Christian spirit and policy" is not quite what people had meant by "accepting Jesus as Savior and Lord." As OWU edged into the parlous thirties the caption was again altered to fit the new picture:

> Although established by the Methodist Episcopal Church and conducted under its continued patronage, Ohio Wesleyan is in no sense sectarian and makes no denominational requirement of its trustees, faculty or students. A majority of its students are Methodists [the precise figure then was 59 percent] but several hundred members of other denominations are always included in the student body and other Protestant churches are represented upon the faculty.
>
> From the beginning of its history Ohio Wesleyan has been administered in the belief that higher education and character building are the inseparable functions of the Christian college. As President Edmund Soper has expressed it in a recent statement, "The unique thing about Ohio Wesleyan is that she has combined an emphasis on high scholastic standing with an equal emphasis on moral ideals and religion." As unmistakable evidence of the continued pursuance and success of this principle, stand the thousands of the University's graduates who have rendered valued service to society as Christian citizens.[169]

The overture to a new emphasis is wholly contained in the initial *"Although."* Once the church's sponsorship begins to be an "although" factor in public relations, what is unique must now be described in generic terms, such as "moral ideals and religion." From what we have seen of Soper's views *in camera,* his terms would have intended a more distinctive sense than they were taken to mean here.

By 1940 a new vocabulary has emerged. Ohio Wesleyan is "a liberal arts college for men and women." Now "many" of its students are Methodists and "many churches" are represented among its faculty. "This is consistent, nevertheless, with its aim to function as a Christian institution for higher education. In accordance with its traditional policy, Ohio Wesleyan seeks to provide a proper environment for its students by selecting carefully those admitted to the university and by requiring a high type of life of all who remain." The "distinctive chapel" is now a daily assembly, no longer "devotional," and it "is addressed frequently by outstanding scholars and men of affairs" and is "cherished by many of the university's alumni [though only after their graduation] as the most valuable experience of their college days."[170] The nature of that assembly was, of course, a floating one, as is the nature of the institution.

In 1944 the "Aims of Ohio Wesleyan University" were significantly recast. The aim now was to provide "those educational disciplines and experiences which are fundamental to enduring personal satisfaction, social usefulness, and occupational competence." The seven habits to be acquired are listed and described, including bodily skills; competent use of English; awareness of the humane heritage of Western culture; knowledge of the scientific method and the laws of natural and human existence; an active concern for democracy and social justice; and an insightful taste for the arts. Seventh, and last, OWU intends "that through an examination of the concepts in the major philosophical and religious traditions and especially of the impact and vitality of Christian faith [the student] shall be able to arrive at a scheme of values which not only is confident and rational, but also finds its ultimate issue in human conduct."[171]

One notes that in this new scheme the university positively endorses and inculcates democracy over all of its political alternatives, but it cannot offer any similar endorsement to Christian faith over its alternatives. It states only that, within a thoughtful consideration of them all, the Christian faith is commended for special attention. There is no mention whatever of the Methodist Church and its faith. It is of note that the first six attainments are described as communal endeavors, into which the senior scholars as a group induct their students. By contrast the seventh and, ostensibly, the climactic attainment, the formulation of a scheme of values and disciplined conduct, sounds like a solo flight, with plenty of people watching supportively from the ground but no instructor aboard.

Twenty years later that was superseded by another statement of aims. This drafting committee announced that they had followed an Emersonian inspiration, with freedom of inquiry and the pursuit of excellence as guiding principles. Their third principle was as follows:

> The Christian religion has always been at the heart of Ohio Wesleyan's educational principles. Although the University is naturally infused with the spirit of its own denomination, it seeks to impose upon its students neither Methodism nor any specific set of convictions about the nature of godhead, reality, or man. But although Ohio Wesleyan is not narrowly sectarian, neither is it religiously or ethically neutral. It does deliberately encourage conscious concern over religious and ethical issues, and it attempts to stimulate its students constantly to re-examine their own views on such matters. The best evidence of Ohio Wesleyan's continuing affirmation of the genuine spirit of Methodism lies in the opportunity it affords to all students, of whatever race or creed, freely to pursue a liberal education and the cultivation of excellence.[172]

The report was very meticulously drafted and deserves to be read with close care. This statement of principle is clearly at pains to disavow any doctrinaire coercion. When it states what the Methodist character of the university offers, it can speak only of "concern" about religious issues, not about any reliable wisdom or enlightenment. The best embodiment of the genuine spirit of Methodism is a campus which has worked hard to be very concerned about the race of its students and very unconcerned about their religion. There is no suggestion that the intellectual ferment which the campus wants to cultivate might be stimulated or guided or instructed by Christian faith; only the assurance that it would not — as many might evidently fear because of the "although" — intrude itself into academics.

This document moved slowly through the various echelons of approval, and when it was finally adopted by the trustees in 1963 they did demand that the "godhead" be identified as "God." In an associated provision they insisted on restoring at least one required religion course, which had been dropped from the curriculum. Meanwhile the Religion Department had sequestered most of its Christianity-related courses within the biblical studies area.[173]

In 1979 the effort was repeated, and an entirely new statement emerged. Now the reference to religion had seemingly become less apologetic.

> Since its founding, Ohio Wesleyan University has maintained its connection with the Methodist Church, offering a quality of scholarship, leadership, and service that has enriched both Church and Society. Its Charter provided that "the University is forever to be conducted on the most liberal principles, accessible to all religious denominations, and designed for the benefit of our citizens in general." In the spirit of this heritage, the University defines itself as a community of teachers and students devoted to the free pursuit of truth.[174]

At its conclusion the statement adds only this: "Consistent with our Methodist tradition, Ohio Wesleyan encourages concern for all religious and ethical issues and stimulates its students to examine their own views in light of these issues." How one profitably examines one's own views in light of all religious and moral issues is not made clear. The drafters had been told to produce something "more flexible, general, and open," and they could hardly be faulted. It would be difficult to craft a more minimalist account of what the church meant to the university. The only thing said is that their connection has enriched the church, even if it seems to have offered no advantage to the university, save perhaps to keep the church out of its way while the university freely pursues the truth. The statement has been dismissed by some on campus as "so much rhetoric," which seems to be an unkind thing to say about rhetoric.[175]

President Warren soon found that the planning process at OWU was "doing everything backwards" for want of any overall plan or priorities, and initiated the creation of a "Five-Year Plan," which required three years just to write. Near the end of this plan, between passages affirming "hands-on experience" and a "friendly and caring environment," it had this to say about "Church-Relatedness":

> Another mark of distinction is the University's relationship with the United Methodist Church. Indeed, the University's nickname, the "Battling Bishops" [who had replaced the "Methodists" on the playing fields in the early twenties], is derived from the large number of ministers and bishops who matriculated at Ohio Wesleyan. The East and West Ohio Conference(s) are represented by clergy and lay trustees, and the bishops of the two conferences are ex officio members of the Board of Trustees. The Beeghly Library includes a rare collection of books devoted to Methodist history in Ohio. A University Chaplain is responsible for

316

coordinating the religious life of the campus community. Worship on campus and in nearby churches, personal counseling, small group meetings, and service projects aimed at alleviating serious social needs at home and abroad are available to all. Most of the major world religions are represented by an increasing international student body, thereby enriching the total community.

Reference has previously been made to education in the context of values. Neither the church nor the college forces students to accept ready-made answers to life's most searching questions: what do I believe? To what or whom am I committed? But they do provide the setting in which each person is challenged to seek his/her own answers. That ultimately is the most important mission of a church-related community.[176]

Thus Methodist books and bishops, battling or presiding, enhance Ohio Wesleyan, but not Methodist faculty or students. Buddhists and Baptists enrich the total community, but not Methodists.

Elsewhere the plan speaks of "study in depth," and describes the university's mission thus: "It must provide for the kind of focused, sequential inquiry that should lead to some degree of mastery of — and the thrill of moving forward in — a formal body of knowledge. It should also teach the lesson that no matter how deeply and widely students dig, no matter how much they know, they cannot know enough." This conventional description of education as a disciplined initiation of apprentice pupils by master scholars into a cumulative corpus of knowledge and insight, which will then empower them as journeymen of the mind to think more critically and rightly, stands in remarkable contrast to the repeated depictions of religious inquiry, which seem to offer only two alternatives: doctrinaire impositions by the church or individualist preferences by the students. Throughout the years, almost every time Ohio Wesleyan has adverted to its Methodist sponsorship it has felt the need to offer immediate reassurance that religion would offer neither threat nor contribution to the mainstream intellectual work on campus.

It is not often that a sequential study of any college's public rhetoric could reveal much of its real development, but Ohio Wesleyan has been both more effusive and more disclosive in these statements than many peer schools. They can serve as a sort of *obbligato* accompanying the changes of the past fifty years, between OWU's centennial and her recent sesquicentennial.

Relations with the Church Wither

In 1942 the university's governance was in the hands of a board upon which the church's presence was still supposedly assured by a majority of trustees provided by the conferences. Among the students Methodists held a similarly slim majority: 51 percent, up from a low of 37 percent in 1938. After the centennial year there would never be another Methodist majority in the student body. That year the

317

combined gifts from the Methodist Church, nationally and in Ohio, amounted to $3,753. Not until 1947 would church contributions return to the dollar level they had last reached in 1920.[177]

Much of the ministry on campus was provided by local pastors, and by faculty across the campus. Despite a resolve by the president and board that OWU should finally have a full-time director of religious life on campus, the incumbent taught religion as a part-time instructor, ran the YMCA (which was a salient force on the campus sports scene), and was responsible for liaison with the various student religious organizations. He had a female colleague who served as assistant director and held corresponding responsibility for the YWCA. The range of religious activities was traditional: all-college communion services, religious emphasis week, international week, social service projects, missionary work, weekend and summer training conferences.[178]

There were Departments of English Bible and Applied Christianity/Social Ethics, as well as History of Religion (the descendant of the old missions department). With the dean of the college himself a professor of religious education, and most of the philosophy faculty with theological training, the religionists had allies on all sides. Every student was required to take one Bible course and one other in the area of philosophy and religion. Chapel, which for several years had been called daily assembly instead of daily devotional services, was held five times a week and students were obliged to attend, though they were allowed twenty-five cuts a year. Even military trainees during the war were required to go. The programs were a medley of religion, announcements, school spirit, outside speakers on public affairs, and entertainment. There were misgivings at the time: on the part of the students, about how to be free of the obligation; on the part of the faculty, about how secular it was becoming.[179] The university historian allowed himself this ambivalent comment:

> A restoration of the five-day-a-week, more purely devotional chapel would no doubt bring objection from the student; his interest today is primarily directed toward the social features of the daily assembly, toward the musical or other entertainment numbers. Nevertheless, the not infrequent masterly presentation of a case by an outside speaker is always well received, and the occasional striking of a deep religious note is still perhaps the chief glory of this historic service. The pertinent question is often asked, however, whether, to obtain these moments of higher value, it is not expensive of time and money to include so many programs of other kinds.[180]

When one listens to the audio of the 1942 aims statement while watching the video of these activities, one suspects that the campus was still pretty much at ease with the older ways of their Methodist practice, as these were undergoing progressive annual modification. The university was perhaps not as diffident about sharing faith with the students as the faculty and trustees professed to be.

By the time the next aims statement was issued in 1963, there were significant differences. The board of trustees was now composed of forty-one members; the church retained a slim majority of twenty-one.[181] But church giving was way up: the Ohio Methodists had contributed nearly 9 percent of the gifts to OWU that year. There was evidence, however, that this was not an unqualified sign of support. First of all, the alumni contributions amounted to nearly three times that much, a presage of things yet to come.[182] Secondly: though more, the church gift may not have been enough, at least enough to signify hearty support. The chairman of the board had recently said as much:

We seem to have a super-abundance of critics and not enough cheer-leaders. Many of these critics, I hate to say, are among our own Methodist constituency. I have been both amazed and dismayed by this fact. It has appeared to me that we have more lifting of eyebrows than of muscles. If those who profess an interest in us were to emphasize our strong points and become genuine salesmen for Ohio Wesleyan — our weaknesses would be less obvious to them. . . .

Methodists cannot expect to keep a firm hold on this institution by reason of its critics, well meaning as they believe themselves to be. I bring up this subject because from the very sources that we are criticized for not getting our share of students from Methodist families, we are usually getting the least assistance. There are localities in Ohio from which we are getting many more students from churches other than Methodist. . . .

During the 1958-59 period, scholarships given to Methodist students totaled $175,690.00. From Ohio Methodist Churches, we received $92,017.77, in other words we received from the churches $83,673.00 less than we allowed to Methodist students.[183] [Most Methodist-related colleges and universities spent more on scholarships for United Methodists than they received from their sponsoring churches.][184]

Methodists among the student body had meanwhile declined to 45 percent. The church was giving more money but fewer students. Earl McGrath, who had been brought in at the head of a team of consultants to appraise the health and prospects of the university, chided them about the waning presence of their native clientele:

This is a church-related institution. It receives financial support directly and indirectly from a Methodist constituency. A large proportion of its alumni are members of this faith, among them some of the leaders of the church. [One out of every five Methodist ministers in Ohio at that time was an OWU alumnus.] A practical question must be raised, therefore, as to whether the admissions policies should disregard the fact that the University does have a special constituency. Conceivably the standards could be raised to so high a level that many worthy students of Methodist affiliation could not gain admission. Aside from

319

the religious factors involved there is also the matter of social selection. Emphasis on academic ability, combined with relatively high tuition, will reduce the numbers from the middle and lower income groups unless prohibitively large scholarship appropriations are made.[185]

Religious Life on Campus

The decennial survey prepared for OWU's accreditation by the Methodist University Senate had reported already in 1960 that there was "something to be desired in terms of working rapport between the religious life staff and the full-time teaching staff. There is not even general agreement that religious activities can be educationally important . . ."[186] Usually that might signal Luddites in the natural sciences departments, but at Ohio Wesleyan the chill was being administered by the newly named Religion Department. There was a special irony in the fact that the university had, for the first time, recruited a Ph.D. as its director of religious life, only to find that the department now believed its academic legitimacy required it to sever relations with anything ministerial. In fact, the leading religion professor refused even to borrow books from the Methodist seminary down the street.[187] They were no longer disposed to extend a part-time courtesy appointment to the chaplain (as he now began to be called).

The survey had a great deal to say about the religious situation on campus. Though the weight of Wesleyan faculty opinion was favorable toward the Methodist relationship, the visiting committee said, some were suspicious or fearful about what this might mean in fact. (One small but always significant milestone had been reached back in 1951 when the *Catalog* changed its reference to the university from a "Christian institution" to a "church-related institution.")[188] The church's stand on alcoholic beverages, for instance, provided a point at issue, and seemed to put the church in the position of a scold. But the evaluators had misgivings about another issue: compulsory chapel. The services themselves would be hard to improve upon. "There is no chapel anywhere which offers the student a more frequent opportunity to hear the great voices of contemporary Protestantism." There were only three gatherings a week now, and students were permitted three absences a semester (one entire semester of their eight was relieved of any chapel obligation). But extra cuts incurred the penalty of added academic credits required to graduate. Objections to this sanction were coming more strongly from the Protestant students than from the non-Protestants (who were now becoming numerous enough to be noticed). In the accreditors' opinion this compulsory worship was "bad practice."

Their recommendation: get a real house of worship, and reserve the term "chapel" for specifically religious services conducted there. "Individual services sometimes become a hodge-podge of prayers, announcements, and either pep sessions or addresses upon miscellaneous topics. On the day the survey committee was present a hillbilly quartet of students preceded the worship service. There seems to be at the present time no central theme guiding the selection of chapel topics and little discernible relationship to the remainder of the educational program of the institution."

By 1963 the Office of Religious Life was getting more heavily involved in counseling work. There were new student organizations, like the Christian Science Club and the Canterbury Club, which gave more public standing to other denominational cohorts among the student body. The new chaplain reported strong interest in social justice (the growing movement for racial integration, and recruitment for the Peace Corps) and in ecumenism (seders with the Jews, retreats with the Catholics). He had also quickly moved to mitigate the sanctions for nonattendance at chapel (the previous year, when chapel credits required for graduation had failed to rally the troops, a five-dollar fine for absences had been imposed).[189]

Only a few years earlier the former dean of the college had reported: "In the appointment of faculty members the university makes a persistent effort to select persons who, in addition to the principles of Christianity, are genuinely concerned about helping students to develop Christian attitudes."[190] At the time he said this, core courses in disciplines such as philosophy and history had components that were religiously focused. The chairmen of the Psychology, Sociology, and History Departments were at the time ordained ministers, and 12 percent of the faculty at large had theological training.[191] Members of the Religion Department itself, however, were at pains to demonstrate that they addressed their subject with the same detachment they assumed to control other disciplines. The fact that they were all ordained ministers perhaps intensified their professions of aloofness. Their exposure to the student body had been greatly reduced from the traditional two required courses to inclusion with other departments in a distribution scheme; had it not been for the initiative of the board of trustees in reinstating one required course in religion (which might be taken, however, in either the History, Humanities, Philosophy, or Religion Departments), they might not have had the opportunity to demonstrate the new objectivity to most students.

The 1963 aims statement claimed that the university was naturally infused with the spirit of its own denomination. But the Methodist survey, shortly before that year, was uneasy about that. It was not clear, the visitors said, "that within this excellent context most students become aware that the Christian faith is a living, growing, intellectual, spiritual concern, or that the faith is a live option which is relevant to the deepest problems of our age."

The size and composition of the board of trustees have been altered repeatedly since 1960. The proportion of their membership provided by the Ohio Methodist conferences has continued to shrink. Originally they composed the entire board, and in modern times a legally required majority, but step-by-step members from the Ohio conferences have been reduced to somewhat less than one-fourth of the voting membership.[192] The church could still speak with a loud voice in the councils of the university, but it could no longer deliver the vote. Methodist presence in the student body had plummeted from 45 to 16 percent.

Contributions from the two sponsoring Methodist conferences at the end of the seventies accounted for 11 percent of OWU gifts from all sources. The annual contributions from the church rose to a peak of $280,000, then fell to $65,000, less than 3 percent of the university's annual giving. The church's direct contributions to the Campaign for Ohio Wesleyan, a larger fund-raising effort recently concluded, amounted to less than 1 percent.[193]

The mode of chaplaincy had become even more intensely identified with social service. What resulted was a change in motivation as well as one of method. One faculty member looks back:

> The 1960s witnessed a heightening of moral concern and social awareness in areas such as race relations, economic inequality, peace concerns, and governmental disregard of individual liberties. In all those areas, the Chaplain's office as well as the YWCA were involved in attempting to fulfill former president Arthur Flemming's hope of bringing "the kingdom of God to this earth." What was difficult, or perhaps impossible, to maintain was an underlying sense of religious mission and theological meaning. During the sixties, at Ohio Wesleyan and throughout American society, questions of justice and fairness and of human dignity ceased to be perceived as religious concerns and became fully secularized.[194]

In 1966 chapel attendance had become voluntary. It was the end of an era; some said, the end of an error. Student interest rapidly sought its own level, which was as low as low could be. The chaplain offered a worship service as weekly "chapel," and then began the first of a series of thematic programs. His were called Convocations, replaced soon by a faculty-led Forum, a generously funded lecture-series-cum-seminar available for attendance or for credit. The Forum treated such issues as "The Family — American Style," "Technology and Human Values," and "The New Iconoclasm: Revolt and Secularity." Though created as a substitute for the chapel experience, it was mostly blind to religious insight. Speakers included folks like Allen Ginsberg and Jack Anderson.[195]

The Department of Religion was well and respectably staffed, but religion was no longer a discipline that anyone need study.

The one thing religion at OWU could not have been accused of in those days was being intrusive. Indeed, while students had been combating racism and injustice all around them, some new problems emerged in their midst. Alcohol was now on sale in the Memorial Union Building, and in 1979 President Thomas E. Wenzlau said that "the drinking situation here is getting to the point that it's severely affecting the reputation of the college." The academic qualifications of applicants headed downward, and freshmen began to come less from rigorous high schools and more from prep schools. Enrollment began to drop: by 20 percent in one year. Earl McGrath's politely worded warning seemed to be borne out: Ohio Wesleyan was becoming a party school. On campus, however, this was usually referred to as

OWU's party school "image," or its "reputation" for drinking.[196] Religion professor Blake Michael had this comment:

> The campus ethos of the late seventies . . . was less concerned with piety than with partying, with gender than with sex. All the good efforts of [campus chaplain] Dr. Leslie and the Y directors could not reverse the University's slide from social conscience past social contract into social chaos. The lofty ideals of a dedicated few — staff and students — could not be successfully integrated into the overall life of the University, and it temporarily lost purpose, direction, and a coherent rationale for its existence.[197]

That year the university had declared itself a community of teachers and students devoted to the free pursuit of truth, in a way that would enrich both church and society. At that point Methodists may have had some cause to wonder whether the only enrichment in progress was being processed by the university comptroller, while OWU was really devoted to the pursuit of freedom. It was a bleak time, and the aims statement seems to have served more as sedative than stimulant.

The Religion Department has survived several traumas. Its senior faculty were reduced from five to three due to budgetary stress, and for seven years it was merged into a single department with Philosophy before being released. Very few students are likely to register in religion courses to fulfill their humanities requirements, which are marketed by a group of ten departments. On the other hand, no department has more courses than the Religion Department whereby to fulfill the "diversity requirement."[198]

Another Universal Chaplaincy

The chaplain became involved as the affirmative action officer of the university, and his female associate took over the Women's Resource Center, in which post she continued after the YWCA sank from sight. In 1988 Chaplain Jon Powers came to campus and under him the twin emphases manifest under Chaplain Leslie came to full bloom: interreligious amity and social activism. Interfaith activity is a signature item. Muslims worship regularly in the new Norman Vincent Peale Chapel; Quakers and Unitarians have Sunday services and Catholics occasionally have mass there. There was a rosary service and a Holocaust memorial. Last year some Druids held a service there. There is a student Imam, an Episcopalian chaplain, a B'nai B'rith Hillel director two days a week, a part-time director for the Coalition for Christian Outreach and the Fellowship of Christian Athletes, a Catholic chaplain who also teaches modern languages, and Jon Powers "for Methodists in particular but for all." In the winter the chaplaincy sponsored a shared event inquiring into Passover, Lent, and Ramadan. Books by Rushdie and Kazantzakis were assigned for discussion, with a Jewish moderator. Several dozen clergy from local churches serve as ministry adjuncts and supervisors. Thirty-one different group activities are sponsored, from the Buddhist Association to Bible studies, from Students for Choice to Big Pal/Little Pal. There is a frontal assault on the ills and injustices of the world, with Habitat for Humanity, a Caribbean Seminar, Amnesty International, a hunger project and a literacy project and a peace project, and a mentoring and tutoring initiative in local schools funded by a $435,000 grant.

Ohio Wesleyan, Chaplain Powers explains, epitomizes the missional aspect of Methodism, since the church appears here as a service source. At the turn of the century it was called the "West Point of Methodism" because of the large numbers of graduates who went forth as missionaries. Later OWU boasted the highest proportion of its graduates in the Peace Corps. Today from 85 to 90 percent of the students are engaged in voluntary service of some sort.

With the continuing diminution of Methodist presence among the student body, and presumably among the faculty and administration as well, what will become of this operation when there are no longer enough Methodists in place to make it in any meaningful sense a Methodist-related endeavor? The chaplain's reply: "The United Methodist Church proudly claims OWU as a place where good things happen in faith." One of the newest student groups organized under the chaplaincy's aegis is the Methodist Student Movement. The largest religious representation on campus today belongs to the Catholics, who for the past twenty years have outnumbered Methodists and are now reported as approximately 28 percent of the student body, while Methodists are 18 percent.[199]

The Forum, which rose out of the ashes of compulsory chapel, suffered in its turn from student indifference, and was replaced by a more advanced model, the National Colloquium. Begun by President Warren soon after his arrival, it was soon beefed up by a half-million-dollar grant from the Pew Memorial Trusts. It has thus been able to bring in big-ticket, high-draw speakers such as Paul Ehrlich, Ellie Smeal, and Terry Anderson. Dedicated annually to topics such as "Population, Environment and Human Values," "Personal Choice and Public Interest," and "Waging War/Waging Peace," the Colloquium has managed to draw in strong participation from faculty members offering spot seminars in their respective specialties. But it is clear that there is no thread of continuity, other than historical coincidence, with OWU's earlier, foundering attempts to worship as a community.[200]

There are some very vital survivals of religion on the campus, however. President Warren, shortly before leaving office, celebrated it before his fellow Methodists:

> Visiting the top floor of the Campus Center, you find boxes upon boxes, containing more than 5,000 books donated by Ohio Wesleyan's faculty and students. These books, collected in honor of our sesquicentennial and soon to be shipped by way of UMCOR to Rural Nigeria, will help establish the St. John Bosco Memorial Library in Agbani, an African village where no library previously

existed. Approach the Campus Center's Peale Chapel and you may hear the chantings of an Islamic prayer service, or a Hebrew folk-song service, or a Catholic Mass prayed in Spanish, or a Methodist Student Movement communion service for the World Day of Prayer.

In a conference room across the hall, you hear the lively report of two students who represented Ohio Wesleyan at last summer's World Conference on the Environment, sponsored by the United Nations and held in Brazil in the home-town of one of our students.

The Chaplain's Office nearby bustles with creative chaos as supplies are readied for shipment to Otmutninsk, Delaware's sister city in the former USSR; schedules are organized for students to work at Global Village, a university/com-munity/Third World venture to sell hand-crafted goods with all profit returning to the native artisans; vans are reserved for a trip to the Toledo Mosque; a Swedish prayer service for one student's grandmother begins, at the same time a eulogy begins back home in Stockholm; colored candles are readied for a Buddhist Diwali celebration; an evangelism conference is planned for 60 Ohio Wesleyan students; and planning begins for another spring break week in the Dominican Republic village of Paso Bajito, building school houses and latrines.

Catch your breath outside the chaplain's Office, and hear the pulsating rhythms of African drums. Looking over the balcony to the Campus Center lobby, you see the intricate choreography of six African women students demonstrating their native tribal dance. Each month, a different national heritage is celebrated in the Campus Center. Today is their day.

Across campus in the Department of Religion, a dean, who is also a United Methodist minister, teaches a course on John Wesley [which was not, however, in the *Catalog*]. An internationally acclaimed German scholar, the son of an Ohio Methodist bishop, teaches the intricacies of the Gospel of John. An exiled Epis-copal priest from Uganda, Africa, teaches the Social Principles of the United Methodist Church. Another United Methodist minister teaches Hebrew. A black pastor teaches professional ethics. And a Hassidic (Jewish) mystic teaches Islamic studies.[201]

Much Religious Life, Though Not Christian or Methodist

What of the university's relationship to the United Methodist Church? From the church's side it would seem to be a vital alliance. The most recent Academic Senate accreditation visit in 1990 yielded astonishing praise: "The University has a strong sense of its church identity, an admirable commitment to values and service, a growing tie to the institutional church and a vigorous and well-directed chaplaincy." Blake Michael, the professor of religion who wrote the overview of religious life on campus in the most recent OWU history, reads the same events differently: "There were also signs of revitalization in the realm of religious life and church relationship, although it was clear that in no foreseeable future would Ohio Wesleyan redefine itself as a Christian college, enjoy the uncritical support of Ohio Methodists, or become again anything like the 'West Point of Missions.' "202

The repeated assurances that this college is not a doctrinaire serf of Methodism now have a strange ring to them. The church never did have much of an ideological agenda, but somehow Methodist educators have felt intimidated by the expectation that it would. The record does not show that the church grieved or murmured or raged much about deviancy or infidelity in Delaware. The Methodist churches have lost interest in the school, but their disaffection has not followed sharp rebukes or threats. They have simply withdrawn. About 325 Methodist students and an annual subsidy of $65,000 are not evidence of significant support from two annual conferences with combined resources of 2,162 congregations (double the number of fifty years ago),203 496,805 members, and annual budgets of $187,487,540.204 In its personnel, its resources, and its students, Ohio Wesleyan is not a symbiotic intimate of the United Methodist Church.

The Department of Religion seems to display an ambivalence about theology. Though its manifesto is strewn with the usual religious-studies talk about "the careful study of religious phenomena and history" and "looking objectively at the faith and devotion of other religious persons," the courses themselves seem primarily to offer a studious understanding of the Christian Scriptures and tradition. (The *Catalog* lists courses dealing with Hinduism, Zionism, liberation theologies, Roman religions, and ancient Mediterranean religions, though none that treats specifically of Methodism.) A sober prognosis for both of these enterprises, however, is that they stand, not on a vital community of belief in place today, so much as on the inertial force of yesterday's church, and they are not likely to continue indefinitely, since Ohio Wesleyan has no strategy or will to recruit believers, let alone Methodists, for the task.

President Warren himself spoke lyrically to this issue on the occasion of the sesquicentennial:

Q. Do you think Ohio Wesleyan lost a lot when it gave up its religious identity?

A. I don't think it has lost its religious identity altogether. It is true that liberal arts colleges are no longer in the business of moral philosophy, as they were when they were under direct religious auspices. But we still carry many elements of the Methodist tradition; that ethos still influences a belief in the democratic process, a concern for the disadvantaged, a commitment to the education of all persons.

Q. Do you favor strong ties with the Methodist Church?

A. Our relationship with the United Methodist Church is a very positive one. . . . I am certainly comfortable with it, and I believe the faculty is comfortable with it. But, I don't think anything more needs to be done.205

326

If there is any constant refrain that links the many stanzas of Ohio Wesleyan's narrative into one saga, it is the disclaimer that the university will be neither narrow nor sectarian. It promised from the first to be accessible to all denominations, and it kept that promise. It should be obvious, however, that its pioneer leaders could not have anticipated the diversity of which its recent leaders boast. Indeed, when the founders and their near successors threw the doors open, they neither anticipated nor desired many — nearly most — of the students who are now matriculated. President Thomson was explicit enough in his remarks about Catholics. His notion of a student body of "professing Christians" did not include them. A century later, President Herbert J. Burgstahler (1939-47) felt no need to be more explicit in his admissions policy than to say that the school was seeking "students of good moral character and in so far as possible from Christian homes." But by this time, whatever their moral character, students were now identifying themselves as Jews, Jehovah's Witnesses, Mormons, Unitarians, and Christian Scientists.[206] This cannot have come easily. It had been a practice to list as "denominations" only mainline Protestants, and then to follow them with a separate list of Catholics, Christian Scientists, Quakers, Jews, and the unchurched.[207] President Soper had reported in 1929, after listing Protestant student totals: "It is interesting to note that there are 19 Roman Catholics, 1 Greek Orthodox and 1 Jew, while 134 students stated no church preference. I should say that our student body remains a homogeneous Protestant group of American lineage."[208] In 1946 the religious affiliation report indicated that Methodists, while still clearly the most numerous group in the student body (then 48 percent), had declined considerably over the previous twenty years, while Catholics had increased (from 0.6 to 3.5 percent). The administration offered this observation to the trustees: "The large Catholic enrollment is due largely to returning Navy V-5 and V-13 enrollees. Non-Protestant enrollment makes maintaining our traditions and former standards somewhat difficult."[209]

So, although the early OWU leaders sowed their invitations broadcast, and for half the university's history their own kind came, in the second half of this history the response has been increasingly diverse, to the point where Methodists compose an insignificant proportion of the enrollment. Truth to tell, those who presided over these years have held true to the charter and taken all who came. But that is not the main point of comparison. What marks the early presidents off from the latter presidents is that now they don't care. Earl McGrath's admonition that they should recognize the Methodists as their primary clientele and make that an admissions priority was not accepted. In Edmund Soper's day, he could ignore the clear evidence of diversification among both students and faculty and reaffirm the hope that OWU would continue to draw in its traditional constituencies to assure that their homogeneity would be preserved. In his case it was a delusion. But thirty years later when McGrath raised the question, homogeneity was no longer either expected, desired, or striven for.

The early records of the university do not speak about religious freedom nearly as much as the recent ones. As long as the campus gathered in and sustained a community of belief, and both students and faculty hoped to find and renew their salvation together, it would have seemed strange to make assurances that no ideology would be imposed. Methodism had very little to impose anyway, since it was grounded on few theological footings and held to a moral code that was fairly malleable. But when the promises begin to sound, that people need not fear they will be pressured to conform to any normative faith or morals, and when they are instead encouraged — even obliged — to work that out for themselves individually, it is so for two reasons. First, the administration and faculty no longer hold any ideology in common. Second, the university is no longer a community in which the younger members come to be guided by their elders in a religious tradition. So the students are not asking, and the faculty are not offering.

Were the scholars at Ohio Wesleyan as united in loyalty and purpose as, say, the African National Congress or a lodge of Alcoholics Anonymous, they might be stirred to wrath by the vagaries of Herbert Welch's musings on character and culture, and the never-published call in 1930 to develop deep respect for human personality, or President Wenzlau's confession that the university had no values it urgently wished to convey, or President Warren's reformulation of Polonius's advice to Laërtes, his freshman son, that students do best to know their own hearts and need not look to their mentors for any help toward salvation. Communities that live and strive and even die together in shared faith tend to be intolerant of platitudes. Those whose ties are transient and instrumental, by contrast, submit to them with seemingly endless absorptive composure. If this be so, there is little shared religious purpose at Ohio Wesleyan.

METHODIST PATTERNS

Despite its British origins and associations, American Methodism has been American. For example, English Methodists reacted against Anglican episcopacy and made their rejection of bishops a signature item in their new church, whereas American Methodists got bishops as soon as Francis Asbury could arrange it. Its roots were not in the Continental Reformation, but in the latter stages of the Pietism of the seventeenth century: a reform of a reform. John Wesley saw his work as that of a revivalist. But when his disciples proved too enlivened for the Church of England, he found himself a church founder anyway. As the immigrant Methodist movement cast about over here for the equipage of a church, its elements tended to be more adaptive than creative, and carried less of the Wesleyan charism. Preaching they already had; worship, polity, piety, ministry, theology they needed. And they grew these limbs of ecclesial community without enduring much conflict or enjoying much originality.

Their theology and the intellectual life it would need to beget were mostly on the lite side, which had the effect of making the Methodists uninterested in but also unusually uncritical of ideologies. They were thus especially vulnerable to the

Enlightenment, whose scientific swagger, philosophical skepticism, and antipathy for theological inquiry drew the Methodists into a codependent relationship. It was not that they became converts or adepts in the new learning, but that they were intimidated, and were persuaded to develop a religious community which forwent intellectual work, which they felt to be a rival of religious sincerity. But they forwent it because of ennui, not enmity.

Thus they were unprepared to be the sponsors and professionals of a system of higher education. And indeed they never did imagine themselves to be creating an establishment where they would offer a traditional learning affected by their conversion-faith. The Methodist campuses would be a variant on the campgrounds: places where young (and prospectively influential) men and women could be gathered as an audience for the heralding of the gospel. The colleges were not an intellectual project; they were, in effect, a labor-intensive surrogate for the ancient sacrament of confirmation. Education, for the Methodists, was a special, hopeful venue for evangelism. That it would associate itself with the best and the brightest of the public culture was their naive evangelical hope, and this would be the entrée for liberalism, which it lacked the theological resources to identify or to fear. Theology they associated with the unattractive dogmatisms of the Catholics, Lutherans, and Calvinists (in their pre-Pietist forms), and they made a point — honest and tragic — of presenting their education as innocent of any such agenda.

Meanwhile ordinary congregational life also encountered serious problems, since as a church founded upon adult conversion they discovered, after several generations, that they were not very successful in handing on their experience or their faith to their children. The vulnerability of their educational institutions to secularization was only a specialized instance of this general problem within the church that had not been meant to be a church. In the twentieth century, when Methodists did engender cadres of intellectuals, they, too, tended to adapt to — or simply to adopt — personalism, existentialism, process thought, etc. By the time some serious internal challenge was raised, along with a scholarly reconsideration of the Wesleyan sources, there was not much of an academic home to harbor it, in colleges, universities, or even seminaries.

Thus, the Methodist educational story is doubly difficult to understand, because the educators themselves were not reflectively clear about what they were doing. Just as Wesley's evangelism was meant as a reform but became a foundation, the Methodist colleges were designed for evangelism but were swept up (half-heartedly at first) into the culture and purposes of the American academy.[210]

Liberals Embarrassed by a Conservative Reputation

This helps one understand the chronic misgivings about the academic integrity of Methodist higher education, lest it be run too closely by the church. Methodist educators have been persistent in avowing that they really do engage in free inquiry.

Vanderbilt pledged "a broad and thorough education," one that "knows no denominational distinctions." Millsaps pledges that "it does not seek to indoctrinate, but to inform and inspire." Ohio Wesleyan solemnly promises that "it seeks to impose upon its students neither Methodism nor any specific set of convictions." But these implicitly defensive claims themselves can reinforce the suspicion that they must have some sort of proselytizing or coercive reputation to live down. The record suggests the contrary: that there was considerable intellectual freedom on these campuses, even in the early years. The Methodist educators wanted their students' souls, not their minds.

This has remained true despite the sustained presence of Methodists among their trustees and presidents. The universities and colleges continue typically to provide for seats on their boards to be filled by the bishops and elected members of the sponsoring conferences. Though the proportion of those seats has diminished, the church is usually given a significant representation. Furthermore, even though religion is rarely mentioned as a qualification for presidential office, about four-fifths of the those who preside on these campuses are Methodists. So strong a Methodist presence at the highest level of governance would lead one to expect overt tension between them and their diversified faculties, yet there is very little evidence of the kind of confessional witness from the top which might provoke such a stress. The clerical trustees, at least, might have been expected to dig in their heels on occasion. In 1935 President Soper of Ohio Wesleyan expressed dismay that the clergy on his board had voted as a bloc (unsuccessfully) against a proposal to liberalize the student rules.[211] But the burden of evidence suggests that the trustees provided by the church have been either compliant or unaware as their institutions distanced themselves from Methodist identity. It was the local bishop himself who chaired the Millsaps committee in 1985 that transferred the actual selection of trustees from the church to the board itself. So the fact that Methodist institutions continue to have a relatively visible presence of church members in positions of authority may still have given the church an inaudible voice, because it does not have much of a message for the educational enterprise.

But what of the generally right-wing expectations of the Methodist laity who were to provide finances and students? If the academics provided broad room for liberal thought and liberal teaching, then surely a lay constituency as uneducated and conservative as the Methodists would have had repeated cause to bring their pressure to bear. But the record shows a remarkably low level of explicit congregational hostility toward academic liberalism. The flare-up over interracial discussion at Millsaps was indeed a heated dispute, but it arose from sectional prejudice, not sectarian belief. The college, in any case, was hardly proposing to desegregate at that time, and the fracas was untypical in its public intensity. When one takes note of the fact that church support for Methodist colleges and universities came primarily from their neighbors in the sponsoring annual conferences, the church-people were remarkably tolerant of the free-mindedness of their campuses.

It is the very stereotype of Methodists as inclined to be prudish and conservative which is rebuked by these stories of their venture in higher education. One reason the Methodist constituency has not exhibited overt offense at the gradual secularization of the colleges it sponsors is that Methodism itself has been liberalizing, though perhaps less openly, all the while. Even in the early years when they were founding their colleges, Methodists realized they were going to serve a sector of the church that was becoming bourgeois enough to care about President Murrah's offers of upward mobility. When larger benefactions began to come their way, much of the largesse was provided by Methodists whose new affluence made them more liberal, not more conservative. Edmund Soper could point out to grumbling critics that his student population were no libertines: they were simply following the manners and morals of a large and liberalized sector of the church population — in a word, their parents. Today the Women's Division of the United Methodist Church brandishes a liberal agenda that makes the mores of Methodist-related campuses seem prudish by comparison.

Methodism in America has been gently polarizing for a long while. The original program of resistance to the crudities of morals and manners in the American West has continued to form the official norm for the church through eras when other, urgent moral issues might have replaced the foundational injunctions to temperance and simplicity. For many years the conservative wing continued to express its traditional convictions aloud, whereas those who adapted quietly to the mores of their socioeconomic neighbors did not press much for a public revision of the church's moral message. But their piety and their preaching did go its own way. This is the constituency with which the colleges and universities made common cause, and it supported the academics as they transformed their institutions resolutely, though without adverting to the radical changes they were effecting.

Methodists Never Were Very Exclusivist

For want of intensive self-consciousness the Methodist story has been one in which considerable change could be effected while the descriptors and symbols remained constant. As examples of that, one may examine two very similar claims: that the Methodist-related colleges did not restrict faculty appointments to their own church members, and that they were not sectarian.

One of the earliest and most persistent continuities in Methodist higher education has been a public refusal to stipulate that the staff need be Methodist. At their very first foundation, Cokesbury College in 1787, the first teacher was a Quaker. At the historic Conference of 1820, the proposal to found and support literary institutions in every region was the subject of an amendment requiring trustees, principals, and teachers to be members of the Methodist Episcopal Church. The amendment was voted down.[212]

It is not quite as if the Wesleyans saw all Protestants, or even all evangelicals, as one undifferentiated fellowship. The eighteenth century had seen two harsh theological controversies which left the Wesleyan Methodists conscious of not being on entirely easy terms with their neighbors. Wesley himself had disagreed openly with George Whitefield, a chief excitator of the Great Awakening. Whitefield followed the Calvinist doctrine that some accept the gospel and others refuse its call because God has from the first decreed which individuals will be graced by salvation and which will be rejected. Wesley, in disagreement, insisted that God efficaciously offers salvation to every living soul, and that those who refuse are lost by their own refusal, not his prior reprobation. This put his Methodists fundamentally at odds with the Puritans and Congregationalists to the north, and most Presbyterians in the middle colonies. Wesley later dissented from another Reformation tenet, more Lutheran than Calvinist, that human depravity rendered everyone incapable of good action, and therefore salvation involved a decision by God to treat people as righteous even though they remained sinners. That, said Wesley, might be true of the first onset of salvation, but thereafter God provided transformative grace which made a life of integrity and holiness incumbent on the Christian. This doctrine of moral sanctification put Methodists at a distance from both Calvinists and Lutherans. The Methodists' readiness to baptize children, and preferably by sprinkling instead of immersion, was a point of fundamental disagreement with the Baptists. So there were the rudiments of a sense of singularity among these people called Methodists.

But as we have seen, the Wesleyans did not for the most part settle within those unwelcoming geographic spheres of influence. They established their first beachheads among the Episcopalians in the Southern colonies. Their most salient differences from that establishment were more liturgical than doctrinal: even the brothers Wesley, during their sojourns in America, had become *personae non gratae* among their own following by their insistence on following an enriched Anglican horarium of formal worship and prayer. By the time of the 1820 Conference the Methodist movement was pouring through the Cumberland Gap and enlarging its membership in wide areas of the West, where the sense of ecclesial separatism had little to sustain it. So out in those new settlements there was little ideological incentive to restrict their educational staffs to their own church.

There were, in addition, sound pragmatic reasons not to be exclusivist. For one thing, there were simply not going to be that many Methodists capable of the educational task. Unlike their English counterparts whose leadership was notably peopled by Oxford and Cambridge men, the American Methodists were simple folk. Wilbur Fisk, who had graduated from Brown only five years before the 1820 Conference, was one of the first of their people ever to graduate from college. When Methodist establishments in the Midwest later found their applications for collegiate charters rebuffed by the legislatures, it was because their church was so widely disdained by both educators and educated.[213] In 1835, when Methodists complained that there was not a single member of their church on the board or even the professorate of Indiana University, the snooty response was: "The Methodist Church has only one man in the country fit to fill a professor's chair."[214]

332

Further, the action by the Conference in calling for local schools effectively established the calling of the educator as technically equivalent to that of the itinerant minister. With those preaching ministries still clamoring for more incumbents, there was a natural resistance to creating a competitor vocation that would draw many of the most able brethren from the service of the word. Since, by contrast with the itinerancy, these academic posts were to be residential appointments with assured salaries, they would naturally invite invidious feelings from the horseback preachers who labored so hard for the gospel. It made sense, then, to leave room for capable teaching candidates from other churches.

One should not infer, however, that the early Methodist faculties were richly diverse. Recall that Edward Thomson welcomed all fee-paying young men to enroll at Ohio Wesleyan in 1846, but on the other hand he wanted no Methodist scholars to fall under the spell of Presbyterian or Catholic tutelage. A Protestant who had not undergone a vigorous conversion to Jesus and forsworn the coarse vices of the frontier (and who would therefore hardly be accounted a "professing Christian") would have had no more entrée in their colleges than a Mormon or a Jew. The faculties were mostly Methodists, indeed mostly ministers. The nondiscrimination policy regarding faculty in the early years was a sign of their homogeneity, not their diversity. At this stage the education was characterized as generically Christian because they regarded a Methodist education as the Christian ideal.

The diversity came later. A half-century later at Vanderbilt University, flagship of the Methodist fleet, James Kirkland went to the wall with his trustees precisely over the policy that the faculty and administrators need not be Methodists. His goal was to ensure that they would not be an ecclesially homogeneous group. Vanderbilt would offer an education which would be Methodist in sponsorship but not in substance, except in an ambiguously liberal meaning of the term. "To serve the trust given to Vanderbilt he sought those most suited to the task. Who, when ill, would choose a physician because he was a Methodist? Why was the teaching of young men different?" By Kirkland's day (he was chancellor from 1893 to 1937) the Methodist educational project had grown prodigiously, and there was an abundance of his coreligionists trained as academics. But the universities had meanwhile abandoned the uniform classical curriculum in favor of distinct subjects and departments and advanced research and publication. It was as difficult to find a competitive Methodist candidate in that more specialized market as it had been fifty years earlier to find one who stood out as a generalist. Thus Kirkland's academic ambitions for Vanderbilt moved him to assemble a faculty that was not very Methodist at all, for Kirkland "did not wish it to be the exponent of any sect or creed, save such as belongs to our common Christianity."[215]

Today the nondiscrimination language continues in use. "While Willamette, as a modern university in a pluralistic setting, cannot (and should not) admit students or hire faculty according to a doctrinal test, it can (and should) inculcate those basic Christian values which lead to individual and social wholeness." Here the inclusivist claim justifies a faculty where Methodists are thin on the ground,

333

not that they are difficult to recruit, but that a faculty member's religion is considered irrelevant to his or her professional task. Even to inquire about it is an affront. There is no consciousness that being Methodist would carry transmissible intellectual implications.

Yet, a Radical Discontinuity

One perduring formula has created an illusion of continuity and obscures a radical change within the enterprise. In Thomson's time a thoroughly Methodist team offered a generically Christian education, because what they shared so easily in common was not just a culture or a theology or an intellectual synthesis, but a piety, an ethos. When Millsaps was young and Ohio Wesleyan was beginning its own transition from classical to modern, a Vanderbilt that was no longer very Methodist but still rather Christian was offering an education that was no longer very Christian. Today Methodist-related institutions may have reached the point where, regardless of whether they admit or reject Methodist sponsorship, the education they offer is neither Methodist nor Christian nor religious. In the early nineteenth century a nonsectarian Methodist college was a place where Methodists presided over a Methodist-style community in an agreeable way that would not offend other Protestants. In the late twentieth century a nonsectarian Methodist-related college is a place where faculty of no known religious sentiments preside over a secular aggregation of students in a way that would not offend Muslims, Druids, or atheists.

In these days when diversity is such an issue in personnel offices, the United Methodist Church itself is looking at this issue quite openly. The Board of Higher Education and Ministry has its own Affirmative Action Plan, first adopted in 1974. The fact that twenty years later it is undergoing a sixth revision verifies "a high degree of sensitivity and responsiveness to the peculiar needs and aspirations of minority groups." Or the instability of the educators' sense of purpose. Yet while the policy specifically disavows discrimination on grounds of race, color, sex, age, and national origin, it does reserve the right to make religion an admissible credential. While this is a legal right of any religious entity, one naturally wonders how a church agency that has so long countenanced an ever declining desire in its sponsored institutions to appoint Methodists would speak to that question intramurally. The Equal Employment Opportunity Policy begins in the literary genre often found in Methodist policy statements:

Theological Perspective

The Board of Higher Education and Ministry affirms the several statements and policies of the United Methodist Church regarding the church's intention to be inclusive. The board believes that it is a representative community of persons in the church with a dual accountability. It is accountable, as all Christian communities are, to the intention of God that all may be one. This suggests a community that intentionally seeks to include persons of various ethnic backgrounds, both sexes, age and special conditions, as directors and staff. Furthermore, the board is accountable to lead the denomination in modeling such unity within diversity. This is an evangelical responsibility. The board believes that persons are brought into relationship with Jesus Christ ultimately through communities of believers. It is God's intention that those communities reflect the wholeness of Creation and the unity of humankind.[216]

Thus the sponsoring agency continues to profess its belief in the church as its source of unity that can sustain every other kind of diversity, but it proffers its witness to a host of educational institutions which no longer pursue that belief.

Another descriptor which has remained constant throughout institutional change is the claim to be "nonsectarian." When Millsaps asserted, in its early days, that it would not offer a narrowly sectarian education, what it meant was that a predominantly Methodist faculty would repress those articles of faith which students from other Protestant mainline denominations might find controversial or repugnant. Despite the several theological quarrels whereby Wesleyans had staked their claim in the open country of Pietist Protestantism, Methodists preferred to accent devotion and morals over creed.[217] Indeed, one may ask to what extent Wesley's original understanding of Methodism being a movement instead of a church was explicitly reversed when he and his American disciples made their break and set off on their own. They considered themselves advantaged over the more doctrinally aggressive denominations in being able to present a Christianity which dwelt only upon matters of salvific importance. But their difficulty in expressing and disciplining an ecclesial self-understanding may have compromised their ability to maintain stable sponsorship of institutions of inquiry like colleges and universities.

Thus in early days Methodists were deemed the right people to hand on a Christianity that was generic enough to be pan-Protestant (or, at the beginning, perhaps pan-evangelical). It became difficult to fend off the idea that a Christianity which appealed to any Protestant might as well be presented by any Protestant. That grew into policy, and the faculties diversified. No one noticed — at least for a while — that the faculty who no longer professed Methodism presently ceased to profess any Christianity.

The signature descriptor, "nonsectarian," began by meaning that mostly Methodist educators would offer an education that was not noticeably or consciously Methodist. Now "nonsectarian" has come to mean that educators whose religious status is irrelevant offer an education that is consciously not Christian. Quite counter to that is the advice given by moral philosopher Alasdair MacIntyre to the educational executives of Methodist-related higher education:

No one can educate students into an Augustinian sense of history, and of their place in history, or into a Platonic or Augustinian view of the place of the virtues, and of the relationship of the community to virtues and of virtues to rules, who does not him or herself share the Platonic and Augustinian commitment. If you entrust the teaching of young people to people who believe in the tenets of modern liberalism, you make this impossible. This does not imply that we should impose narrow doctrinal tests upon our faculty. Nonetheless it is important that faculty members are in fact committed to these tasks and that in our appointments we do not look for that diversity of views so characteristic of the liberal university.

In a liberal society Christians have too often paid too much deference to the values of liberal society. This has indeed been one of the errors of many Christian colleges. We have to be sufficiently illiberal to insist that questions of moral character and of the relationship of the intellectual life to the moral virtues in a person are relevant to academic appointments, something which will put us very much at odds with the dominant trends in American higher education.[218]

It is only after Methodism was first muted in, and then purged from, their institutions that Methodists began with singular intensity to write and repeatedly to revise statements of purpose, aim, identity, vision, etc., which by a sort of titration repeatedly halved the strength of the previous commitment. The emergent surrogates for Christian faith have been social activism, "character," and "values." Bishop Oxnam's injunction to "stand for something," and President Warren's call for his students to take a stand and know why, no matter what that stand might be, both imply that there is no shared or articulated understanding of what those "values" need be, and that to call them "Judaeo-Christian" adds no clarity at all.

Warren had gone on to disclaim that his university offered any "ready-made answers to life's most searching questions: what do I believe? To what or whom am I committed? But they do provide the setting in which each person is challenged to seek his/her own answers. That ultimately is the most important mission of a church-related community."

Edward Thomson and William Murrah would both probably have flinched at the phrase "ready-made answers," but they were likely to have thought that in chemistry and Greek and natural philosophy it was the professors, not the students, who were expected to have worthwhile answers. That might be even more the case in religion, where revelation had offered even more accessible answers (at least to the few, most basic, questions) — as they thought. Yet in the institutions they founded religion seems to have become the one discipline in which no reliable wisdom is on offer. In the Methodist connection religion has not found its way into the intellectual agenda of the colleges, and has ended up being eased aside in the piety and the morals and the manners of the campuses as well. It is worth considering that the ease with which the founders, surrounded by Methodists, disavowed any intention to act as an inculcating community began a process which simply awaited later scholars who would take the traditional words at their face value.[219]

F. Thomas Trotter, Methodist professor, dean, president, and sometime first general secretary of the Board of Higher Education and Ministry, admits that

"Our colleges have become mirror images of other public and independent schools and have viewed increasingly 'church-relatedness' as a liability rather than as part of institutional self-understanding."[220] Elsewhere he says: "It comes as a surprise, if not a shock, for students in some of our institutions to discover that the college has an identifiable, albeit remote, connection to the church. It is incumbent upon us to think what we mean by this relationship."[221] This is obviously a devolution from what was originally intended. Wilbur Fisk, one of the great early Methodist educators, who built Wesleyan University, had believed that higher education was an integral part of the gospel ministry, and said that "when the ministers and the members of the M.E. Church can satisfy themselves that the education of the young is not appropriately a religious work, then let them as a Church, engage in it no farther."[222] As a result, the preponderance of institutions listed as UMC-related may today have only trace elements of effective interest in what the church is supposed to be interested in.[223] William R. Cannon, church historian, has remarked that "Methodism, in its concern to be broad-minded and inclusive, has had a genius for establishing institutions which others have later come to control."[224]

Larger Change within the Church

Throughout our survey of Methodist higher education, we have encountered an abundance of discourse intended to stabilize an essentially uncontrolled relationship between church and universities and colleges. On a national level and on the several campuses, as the tether between them has been paid out further and further, Methodist educators have been at pains constantly to redescribe what it was that made a school distinctive for being Methodist. It stands to reason that as the campus constituencies contained a more and more dilute Methodist presence, the church constituencies would restate their commonalty in broader and broader terms to keep it plausible. But eventually one is obliged to consider a further explanation: that the relationship is shifting, not only because of changes in the academic term in the equation, but also — and possibly even more so — because of changes in the ecclesial term.

In 1958 the Methodist Board of Education circulated this question, provoked by the fact that Christian schools seemed to be not too different from others:

> What then makes a Christian college distinctive? We can set up external criteria — church relationship, declaration of purpose, proportion of professing Christians, chapel and church attendance, religious programs and activities and Bible classes — but the end of it all would seem to lie in the constant conversion of the ordinary matters of a school to the great purposes of God, and a fellowship of consecrated lives in which the Spirit of God is at work to reveal that Will in terms appropriate to a college community.[225]

337

This sounds like an authentic outcry of the old Pietism: it is the rectitude of heart which counts, more than any ecclesial conformity. It is, like most Pietism, an agnostic confession that the church may not be very central to God's work — not just in the world, but among Christians. It is a reassertion of the end over the means, of spirit over letter, of God's invisible intervention through the Spirit over visible intervention through the Son and his church.

In 1978 the central staff proposed a four-year churchwide emphasis on higher education. Like many reductive texts, it etherealizes a single notion, "evangelism," in order to make it applicable to contemporary Methodist undertakings despite their radical discontinuity with those of the traditional past.

THE CHURCH AND CAMPUS — AN ESSENTIAL EVANGELISM

United Methodists, by history and theological stance, are committed to evangelical Christianity. Although evangelism has been deeply misunderstood and frequently defiled, it remains the core of United Methodist commitment to institutions. United Methodist educational expressions have been created to "do" a theology of enlightenment and caring.

Therefore, The United Methodist Church, with the institutions and ministries in its care, should confirm partnership in an *essential* evangelism that would continue to

(1) Sensitize The United Methodist Church to intellectual, moral and value-centered issues;

(2) Search for means and methods to liberate further the church and the learning arts for vital Christian witness;

(3) Serve the world through those who have been set free in this renewed understanding;

to the end that this partnership will continue to affirm a universal gospel for a universal community.[226]

This is a remarkable account of Methodist tradition: that evangelism would consist essentially in the *intellectuals* liberating the bearers of the gospel and rousing the conscience of the *church* to value-centered issues. This "essential evangelism" is not just a reduction to its most abstract elements. It is a radical reversal . . . and one wrought not by academics but by Methodist church leaders. If the text is telling us that "value-centered issues," which are offered here as some sort of puffed-rice confection, are the present medium of God's saving Word, then what has most drastically changed is their view of salvation, not just education.

Does official relationship with the United Methodist Church make much difference? In 1914 Vanderbilt University and the Methodist Episcopal Church, South, severed formal ties. Vanderbilt administrators imagined that freedom from episcopal intrusion would allow the university to settle into a more authentic kind of Methodist identity. It was not to be. There has been a slow entropy of Christianity on the campus. In the early 1960s the cooling process may have been halted momentarily when the chancellor, himself a former divinity school dean, erected a chapel suitable for university functions, and dominated by a large cross. But in 1992 the university chaplain and director of religious affairs, a Methodist cleric, presented a strong argument for removing the cross, to allow non-Christian groups to feel equally at home there. His own responsibility, as he saw it, was to "defend the importance of the university as a secular culture against all forms of orthodoxy . . . to offer a vision of a universal culture and to promote the rational discussion to which a university is dedicated." This would obviously leave behind the Protestant hegemony of the past. He then mused about the kind of chaplain needed for that all-embracing task:

It would be someone so deeply rooted in religion, that she or he would see the vital importance of the university as a secular culture devoted to rational discourse, to the health and future of religion, and to the health and the future of the nation. It would be someone who knows in his or her gut as well as in the head that culture is universal but that it expresses itself in a variety of modes. The chaplain would know and embrace the conviction that each particular cultural mode of religion, Protestantism, Catholicism, Judaism, Islam, defines itself in distinction to every other. So, the chaplain would know that it is the particularistic modes themselves that give birth to culture war — the holy nation against the nations of the world, the holy faith against the infidels, the believers against the unbelievers, the orthodox against the progressives.

"At what we might call their best," he said, all these faith traditions have affirmed secular culture by abandoning their old claims to offer a revelation really different from any of the others.[227] By a reversal of the old Wesleyan verse, knowledge had fairly well buried vital piety alive. If Chaplain Asbury is even close to the truth, then the energetic professional sophistication of the Methodists' General Board of Higher Education and Ministry, empowered by still-abundant annual subsidies in tens of millions of dollars and engaged in more workshops and institutes and inquiries than any other Christian church bureaucracy, would have to be cast in the role of the Sorcerer's Apprentice.

Asbury's position seems leagues apart from the church-sponsored social ministries of the Millsaps chaplaincy and the celebratory pan-religious program at Ohio Wesleyan. The question arises, however: Is the complete secularity of the chaplain at Vanderbilt, which officially severed ties with the church eighty years ago, different in kind, or only in degree, from the establishments at Millsaps and Ohio Wesleyan, which admit happily to an amorphous relationship with the United Methodist Church? Is legal severance the critical point of disengagement, or is it only a punctuation in a lengthy process?

NOTES TO CHAPTER 3

1. See Beth Adams Bowser, *Living the Vision: The University Senate of the Methodist Episcopal Church, the Methodist Church, and the United Methodist Church, 1892-1991* (Nashville: Board of Higher Education and Ministry/United Methodist Church [BHEM/UMC], 1992), v, vii.

2. William Warren Sweet, *Methodism in American History,* rev. ed. (Nashville: Abingdon, 1954), 208-10.

3. Donald G. Tewksbury, *The Founding of American Colleges and Universities before the Civil War* (New York: Columbia University, 1932), 103-11.

4. Sweet, 222.

5. William R. Cannon, "Education, Publication, Benevolent Work, and Missions," in *The History of American Methodism,* ed. Emory Stevens Bucke, vol. 1 (New York: Abingdon, 1964), 549.

6. Dickinson College, Allegheny College, and Centenary College of Louisiana (originally in Jackson) were not in Methodist hands during their earliest years. Louisburg College was founded early, in 1787, but it is a two-year college. McKendree College in Lebanon, Illinois, founded in 1828, presents itself as the oldest with "continuous ties" to the United Methodist Church.

7. *Autobiography of Peter Cartwright,* ed. Charles L. Wallis (New York: Abingdon, 1964), 64-65.

8. Elmo Scott Watson, *The Illinois Wesleyan Story* (Bloomington: Illinois Wesleyan University Press, 1950), 13-15.

9. Sweet, 225.

10. I am grateful to Thomas A. Langford, emeritus professor and provost at Duke University, for this clarification.

11. The Evangelical United Brethren, now merged into the United Methodist Church, had also had a strong antieducation tradition. One of its constituents, the Evangelical Association, voted down a proposed institution for the training of preachers in 1848. One preacher recalled that, during his student days in 1868-70,

> when he returned to his Conference in Michigan and took a front seat at the Session, none of the preachers sat in the same seat with him. And when he got up and attempted to sit in the same bench with them, the whole bench full of them got up and promptly left that bench and moved ahead where he had been seated. They didn't want to be contaminated by sitting in the same seat with one who had been at "that preacher-factory" in Plainfield.
>
> > Armin Charles Hoesch, "Factors Affecting the Denominational Relationship of Church-Related Colleges" (Ph.D. diss., University of Chicago, 1964), 60.

12. Robert H. Conn and Michael Nickerson, *United Methodists and Their Colleges: Themes in the History of a College-Related Church* (Nashville: BHEM/UMC, 1989), 1-5. Though the figure of 1,200 has been in circulation for years, a systematic attempt to reconstruct the full history unearthed 839 colleges and universities that at one time were related to the Methodist church: National Commission on United Methodist Higher Education, *To Give the Key of Knowledge: United Methodists and Education, 1784-1976* (Nashville: BHEM/UMC, 1976).

13. This roster results from the confluence of the Methodist Episcopal Church and the Methodist Episcopal Church, South (divided in 1844 and reunited in 1939), who formed the Methodist Church, and the Evangelical United Brethren (themselves an earlier amalgam of the

United Brethren in Christ, the United Brethren in Christ [Old Constitution], and the Evangelical Association), who joined in 1968 to form the United Methodist Church.

14. See James P. Brawley, *Two Centuries of Methodist Concern: Bondage, Freedom, and Education of Black People* (New York: Vantage, 1974).

15. In the first three-quarters of the nineteenth century, Methodists founded more than two hundred colleges and academies for women: Conn and Nickerson, 18. Theirs was the first denomination to offer women a liberal arts education.

16. Bowser; Conn and Nickerson, 57-69. There has been an inveterate ambiguity of relationship between the Board of Higher Education, composed of church administrators, and the University Senate, composed of college and university professionals. The *Discipline* actually charges both of them with the authority and the responsibility to set and apply norms that authenticate institutions as Methodist related (*The Book of Discipline of the United Methodist Church, 1992,* §1505, 21-22; §1515, 1; §1517, 1; §1518, 1; §1519, 1).

17. "Come, Father, Son, and Holy Ghost."

18. This was one expression of a new concern that the church had better protect itself from legal and financial liability for its educational institutions. The expression "Methodist-related," which had long been used by colleges to distance themselves from the church, now became a canonical expression preferred by the church to disclaim liability for the colleges. Dr. Ken Yamada, associate general secretary, DHE/BHEM/UMC, interview with the author, 6 July 1993.

19. UMC colleges sometimes report to their church constituency how their gift income from the annual conferences compares to the scholarship money awarded to United Methodist students. Illinois Wesleyan (Bloomington) reported income of $120,000 and outgo of $400,000 (plus another $200,000 for the chaplaincy, the religion department, and the sacred music program): Chaplain's Newsletter #25, January 1986. Methodist College (Fayetteville, North Carolina) reported income of $430,000 and outgo of $626,166: "Methodist College for United Methodist Youth," flier (1992), in *Connections: Church Relations Programs at United Methodist-Related Schools, Colleges, and Universities* (DHE/BHEM/UMC, 1993).

20. Methodist institutions, like most others, have had a remarkable influx of Catholic students. Boston University, e.g., reports 45 percent Catholics, 14 percent Jews, and only 18 percent Protestants (no figure is given for Methodists): *Boston University Viewbook, 1993.* Baldwin-Wallace (Berea, Ohio) reports that about half of its students are Catholics: "Religious Life at Baldwin-Wallace College," Chaplain's Office, 1993. Even in the South, Southwestern University (Georgetown, Texas) reports one-fourth Methodists and nearly one-fifth Catholics: "The Distinction of Southwestern University within United Methodist Higher Education," Mission Statement revised 28 October 1992, in *Connections.*

21. "Comparative Data on United Methodist-Related Colleges and Universities, June 1992," DHE/BHEM/UMC; see also Conn and Nickerson, 98, 156. The total enrollment of UMC institutions of higher education is itself in question. In 1950, as the wave of war veterans was filling campuses to and beyond their capacity, the Board of Education appealed for financial help; total enrollment stood at 250,000 students, 10 percent of the total in the United States, and church members were contributing only 31¢ per capita each year. In 1955 enrollment had dropped to 237,000, but demographic figures persuaded the church that it would have to more than double its higher education capacity. Ten years later the university and college enrollment had dropped to 182,000 (while Methodist campus ministers were serving 245,000 Methodist students at non-Methodist institutions). Today the enrollment at Methodist-related universities and colleges is 183,000, with an annually falling proportion of UMC students within that number. See "Methodist Responsibility for Higher Education," a Statement from the General Board of Education, Methodist Church (1950); Paul Neff Garber, "A Call to Action," in *A Perspective on Methodist Higher Education,* ed. Woodrow A. Geier (Nashville: Commission on Christian Higher Education/The Methodist Church, 1960), 9-11; "Statistical Summary for Educational Institutions Related

to the Methodist Church 1965-66," *President's Bulletin Board* insert, June 1967 (Nashville: DHE/Board of Education, the Methodist Church); "Comparative Data, June 1992," 25, 27.

22. *DePauw University Catalog, 1992-94*, 7-8. In its historical précis it states that DePauw "has religious roots" by dint of being founded by frontier Methodists. The usual disclaimer immediately follows: "But even at its conception the school was meant to be an ecumenical institution of national stature; in fact, the college [originally Indiana Asbury University] was 'forever to be conducted on the most liberal principles, accessible to all religious denominations, and designed for the benefit of our citizens in general.' " "Religion" is included as one of the categories which cannot "provide a legitimate basis for institutional decisions." There are thus certain appointments on campus for which sex and age can be bona fide occupational qualifications, but none for which religion would be significant (pp. 8-9).

23. *Boston University Undergraduate Programs, 1993/94*, 5. The university states that "spiritual development is as vital to its community as academic, cultural, physical, and social development," and announces campus ministry for Christians, Jews, Catholics, Episcopalians, Lutherans, and evangelicals, but nothing specifically for Methodists. In its Department of Religion, Islamic Studies and South and East Asian Studies offer more courses that deal with Christianity, and Judaic Studies offers twice as many (pp. 32-33, 207-8).

In 1966 Boston University, all of whose presidents had been ordained Methodist ministers, asserted formally that except for the School of Theology its relations with the church had been historic, informal, and oral. "The University is free from ecclesiastical control, and even from significant sectarian influence in program or policies." It agreed to continue its relationship, but stated pointedly that it expected the church to begin covering the annual deficits of the School of Theology. Minutes of Boston University Board of Trustees Meeting, 20 October 1966, pp. 26-27, Records of the General Board of Higher Education and Ministry, General Commission on Archives and History, the United Methodist Church, Madison, N.J. (hereafter cited as UMCA)/1987-047/2634-5-3-24.

24. *Dickinson College Catalogue, 1993-1994*, 3. In 1907 the Board of Trustees of Dickinson College, anxious to qualify for a grant from the Carnegie Foundation for the Advancement of Teaching, declared the college to be "non-sectarian," though under the friendly auspices of the Methodist Episcopal Church. The Board of Education has continued to list it as its firstborn institution.

25. Arnold Herbst, assistant to the president for church relations, in a memorandum to the DHE, in *Connections*.

26. Bulletin insert by campus ministry for Willamette Sunday 1993, in *Connections*. The same document included this quotation from Oregon senator Mark O. Hatfield, who has been a student, professor, dean of students, and trustee at Willamette: "There have been periods when institutions founded by people of faith have considered loosening their church ties and their moorings in faith because this is, after all, a great secular age. If that happens at Willamette, even with the magnificence of our buildings and the dedication of our faculty and students, the University cannot compete with the quality of public education. Together, we must reaffirm our distinctive Christian commitment because that is the quality that maintains the role of our institution."

27. "The Mission and Philosophy of Pfeiffer College," adopted by the board of trustees 19 April 1988, in *Connections*.

28. "The Distinction of Southwestern University," mission statement, in *Connections*.

29. Yet in this network of higher education white men preside over seventy out of seventy-four integrated, coeducational schools and over two of the three integrated women's schools; black men preside over all eight coeducational schools serving African Americans. Almost without exception all are married, and a recent survey showed that four-fifths of them are Methodists (two-thirds, at the universities). The nine seminaries, twelve junior colleges, and nine college preparatory schools all have white male presidents. *1993 Directory of Chief Executive Officers,*

United Methodist–Related Schools, Colleges, Universities, and Theological Schools (Nashville: BHEM, 1993); Roger D. Wessel, "Profiles and Career Patterns of Private College Presidents," *Presidential Papers* (DHE/BHEM) 9, no. 3 (December 1993); Betty W. Masters Alexander, "College-Church Relations: Perceptions of United Methodist College and University Presidents" (Ed.D. diss., Peabody College of Vanderbilt University, 1990), 99.

30. Bowser, 40.

31. Bowser, 40.

32. Bowser, 41. In 1972, when a number of related institutions were engaging in passive-aggressive resistance prior to severance of ties to the church, it was still the case that "throughout its history the senate had always avoided establishing specific criteria." Minutes of the University Senate, 6 February 1971, 10, UMCA/1987-047/2448-6-2:17.

33. Board of Education of the Methodist Church, *Second Annual Report* (John O. Gross, secretary), 20-22 May 1942, 49-53.

34. Nels F. S. Ferré, professor at Andover Newton Theological School, "The Church-Related College and a Mature Faith," in *Perspective on Methodist Higher Education,* 56-65.

35. Harold C. Case, president of Boston University, "The Christian College and the Concourse of History," in *Perspective on Methodist Higher Education,* 72-73.

36. Richard N. Bender, "Marks of the Christian College," 19,2 *Trustee* (March 1965): 3-4.

37. Myron F. Wicke, "Reflection on Higher Education and the Role of the Church-Related College," in *The Church Related College Today: Anachronism or Opportunity? A Symposium of Papers Produced by the Council on the Church-Related College,* ed. Richard N. Bender (Nashville: BHEM/UMC, 1971), 24-26.

38. Charles S. McCoy, professor of religion in higher education at Pacific School of Religion, "A Christian Theological Perspective," in *The Church Related College Today,* 36-39.

39. National Commission on United Methodist Higher Education, *The College-Related Church: United Methodist Perspectives* (Nashville: BHEM, 1976).

40. F. Thomas Trotter, *Loving God with One's Mind: Essays, Articles, and Speeches,* ed. Robert H. Conn (Nashville: BHEM, 1987), 135.

41. *The Book of Discipline* now incorporates this policy: "Inasmuch as declarations of church relationships are expected to differ one from another, and because of the diversity of heritage and other aspects of institutional life, declarations of church relationship will necessarily be of institutional design" (§1519, 5).

42. *The United Methodist Church, the University Senate: Structure and Guidelines* (Nashville, [1988]), 13.

43. Roger W. Ireson, "What Does the Church Expect of Institutions of Higher Education?" *Occasional Papers* (BHEM/UMC), no. 77, 10 October 1988.

44. Robert H. Conn, *A Handbook for Higher Education and Campus Ministry in the Annual Conference* (Nashville: DHE/BHEM, the United Methodist Church, 1989), 17.

45. Conn, *Handbook,* 29.

46. *Vision and Reality: The Mission of the Division of Higher Education for the 1990s and Beyond* (DHE, 1992), 18.

47. *Vision and Reality,* 21.

48. *Handbook, 1993-1996,* DHE/BHEM, 5.

49. "No institution of higher education teaches facts without some values (even if it is only the value of value relativity). No institution of higher education teaches fragmentary specializations without some integrating philosophy of life, data without some ethical principles, or techniques without some convictions concerning life's ultimate meanings. The issue is whether Christian, or some other, faith and values will provide the norms for the life and educational activities of the college." John H. Westerhoff, "In Search of a Future: The Church-Related College," in *The Church's Ministry in Higher Education,* ed. Westerhoff (New York: United Ministries in Higher Education Communication Office, 1978), 203.

50. Joe A. Howell, "The United Methodist Connection: A Plan for All Seasons," transcript of an address given at Central Methodist College, 30 October 1990, in *Connections*.

For those who would search for some definition of Methodist values beyond the notion of "caring," this president does give it some concrete feel which, though it may have no direct bearing on Methodism, is one of the more chewy evocations of purpose in the literature:

I become worried when I read that one of the most prestigious universities in America has adopted a housing plan which states that any two students — regardless of their sex — may live together in college housing as if they were married.

I become concerned when I read the results of the *Civic Progress Study for Higher Education* in St. Louis which states that only five percent of college graduates who applied for a job can write at an acceptable level, that only twenty-four percent converse well enough to sell an idea, and that only thirty-five percent can get along with their fellow workers.

I was alarmed when I heard of two recent graduates from a major university who never had an academic advisor. I was amazed when I learned there are freshmen in universities in this state being taught by graduate assistants who cannot speak English well enough to be understood. Finally, when I read a national report that says nearly 50% of entering freshmen this past fall said they would lie, steal, or cheat in order to make a better grade to get into a better school to make more money, I felt angry — as should you.

51. Trotter, "Theology and Imagination," in *Loving God with One's Mind,* 59.

52. See Bowser, 39-43, 75-79, 108-11. Although questionnaires distributed to institutions by the University Senate have, over the years, asked for reports on the Methodist presence or religious affiliations of faculty or student body, they have rarely included these entries in their published tables. For many years this usage was in contrast with the Wesley Foundation reports that have stated how many "Methodist or Methodist-preference" students were enrolled at the various state colleges they served in campus ministry. The Senate's "Working Rules of the Commission on Theological Education" do not discuss the need even for seminaries to have a Methodist staff, though they do require them to meet standards of inclusiveness in race, gender, and national origin. *The United Methodist Church, the University Senate: Structure and Guidelines,* 21-25.

53. B. W. M. Alexander, 123. The responses of two-year college presidents have been ignored, since the present study is examining only four-year institutions.

54. Any study of this college is handicapped by its lack of a published history. As long ago as 1969 a history of Millsaps was said to be in preparation, but its centennial has come and gone without that hope being realized. Over the years various historical essays have been published, however. Comparable statistics whereby to track the college's development are also difficult to assemble, and those reported here have been collated from multiple sources.

55. Marguerite Watkins Goodman, "History of Millsaps College" (1972), 2-4, typescript in the J. B. Cain Archives of Mississippi Methodism and Millsaps College Archives (MCA).

56. Leona Polson, "Methodist Schools and Colleges in Mississippi before 1890: A Testament of Commitment" (1983), typescript in the MCA, briefly accounts for forty-one early Methodist educational ventures.

57. These two dates have at various times been identified as Millsaps' year of foundation. The college seal has been altered to reflect the current claim: 1890. Reuben Millsaps was a generous benefactor to many Methodist institutions, as well as to Belhaven College, a Presbyterian school in Jackson, and Piney Woods School for blacks. Goodman, 17.

58. Goodman, 5-17; Boyd Campbell, "The First Hundred Thousand," *Millsaps College Bulletin* 27, no. 4 (April 1944): 3-15. One can track the discussions and initiatives that led to the creation of a college robust from its birth: see *Methodism in the Mississippi Conference,* ed. W. B.

Jones (Jackson: The Hawkins Foundation [Mississippi Annual Conference], 1951), 252, 360-62, 379, 386-87, 408-10, 421-22, 437-38, 454-57.

59. W. L. Duren, *Charles Betts Galloway* (Atlanta: Banner Press/Emory University, 1932), 270.

60. Goodman, 27-34, 159. L. E. Alford, the first Millsaps graduate to become a Methodist minister, gave this account of the attrition experienced by the young institution:

> There were fifty of us taken into the Freshman Class in English and Mathematics. But most of us had to start from the beginning in Latin and Greek. Of that fifty that started in the Freshman Class, half were unable to pass the Mid-Term Examination, hence were left behind. Almost half of that half failed in the final examination. Only fifteen were eligible for the Sophomore Class. A number of these failed and one or two did not return. Only eight entered the Junior Class. One died, I dropped out on account of sickness for one year. Two others failed to return for the Senior year. So in the graduating class of 1896 only three of the boys who started in the first freshman class of fifty finished the course, the 4th of the boys coming into the Sophomore year. I returned and finished with the Class of '97. (Goodman, 31)

61. Goodman, 163-73. Statistics on "ministerial" students for this period vary. First of all, record keeping was less formal at the time; secondly, the term sometimes referred to the children of ministers, sometimes to prospective ministers, and sometimes to both. Cp. *Methodism in the Mississippi Conference,* 422, 438, 454.

62. Edward Nelson Akin, "Mississippi," in *Encyclopedia of Religion in the South,* ed. Samuel S. Hill (Macon, Ga.: Mercer University Press, 1984), 493.

63. David M. Key, "Historical Sketch of Millsaps College," *Millsaps College Bulletin* 30, no. 4 (December 1946): 18-19; Campbell, 3-15; Goodman, 141-42, 169, 56, 116-17, 179; G. L. Harrell, "History of Millsaps College," *Millsaps College Bulletin* 26, no. 6 (September 1943): 10-16.

64. Theodore G. Bilbo, second-term governor of Mississippi from 1928 to 1932, decided to make the boards of the state educational institutions a venue of new patronage. His new appointees began to dismiss president after president, until the Southern Association reacted by withdrawing accreditation from every state university and college in Mississippi. As a result, Millsaps today rightly boasts of being the oldest continuously accredited college in Mississippi. Rust College, founded for Negroes in 1866, had to wait until 1970 for its accreditation. Ronald A. Goodbread, "In Search of the Historical Millsaps: An Address on the Occasion of Founders Day at Millsaps College February 18, 1983, and the Sesquicentennial of the Birth of Reuben Webster Millsaps," typescript in the MCA, 2-7.

65. Key, "Historical Sketch of Millsaps College," 14-16; Key, "Report of Millsaps College to the Board of Education, North Mississippi Conference, Grenada, October 4th [1927]," MCA, Key presidential papers, 2-3. Dr. M. V. O'Shea, who chaired the commission of inquiry, was from the University of Minnesota.

66. Key, "Historical Sketch of Millsaps College," 8-9.

67. Goodbread, 1-2.

68. A. A. Kern, who joined the faculty in 1904, in Goodman, 35. Chapel exercises at Millsaps seem to have generated less antipathy among both students and faculty than on many other Protestant campuses. Indeed, chapel can be said to have been cherished in the early days. It was the day's only event where the faculty were humbled, and the students were exalted, to the status of worshipers.

69. *Register of Millsaps College, 1907-1908,* 81.

70. Goodman, 27; Harrell, 17.

71. Harrell, 11-16.

72. Goodman, 115, 135; Harrell, 19.

73. Harrell, 17-18.

74. Goodbread, 7-13.

75. Goodbread, 16.

76. Key, "Report of Millsaps College [1927]," 1-4. Key also gave findings from a survey of recent graduates: "34% have been young preachers . . . 98% are church members . . . 66% attend church regularly; 13% irregularly; no report 19% . . . 81% take communion . . . 99% are considered a good moral influence in the community."

77. Key, "Historical Sketch of Millsaps College," 11-13; Harrell, 20.

78. Key, "Historical Sketch of Millsaps College," 21-24; Goodman, 170-73; Harrell, 21.

79. "Report of the General Commission on College Policy, to the General Board of Christian Education, April 26, 1938," in MCA, Key Papers, Box 36. Key himself was on the "Commission of Five" which ranked the institutions.

80. B. Warren Brown, "The Educational Situation in the Mississippi and North Mississippi Conferences, Methodist Episcopal Church, South, March 1932," MCA, Key Papers, Box 35.

81. Key, "Report of Millsaps College [1927]," 5; Goodman, 159-73.

82. Attrition from first to second semesters has been a problem over these years, so these figures are averages of fall and spring reports.

83. In this last figure, the percentage is reckoned upon all students who responded to the question about religious affiliation. There are some periods in Millsaps' history when the student body lost proportionately more Methodists than non-Methodists through ordinary attrition.

Baptists always constituted the second-largest cohort, followed by Presbyterians and Episcopalians. Recently Catholics have moved into third place. It is surprising that at this Mississippi school where Catholic students composed about one-tenth of the student body in the 1920s, and then declined to 2-3 percent in the 1950s, they now account for 17 percent. Thus Methodists are proportionately fewer at Millsaps than in the Mississippi population, and Catholics are proportionately more numerous.

84. These figures are found in the Minutes of Meetings of the Millsaps College Board of Trustees, MCA; also Key Papers, Box 35; also "Self-Study Report, Millsaps College, Jackson Mississippi, 1969-70," 13; *Millsaps College Catalog, 1969-70,* 8. In the earlier reports the religious affiliations of incoming faculty spouses were also noted.

85. Minutes of the Board of Trustees, 3 June 1957, MCA; Kay Barksdale, executive director of alumni and church relations, Millsaps College, interview with the author, 2 February 1994; "Self-Study Report, 1980-81," 122; "Millsaps College: A Report to Mississippi Methodists," fall 1966, 4; Millsaps College, *Annual Report, 1992-1993.* Millsaps assigns its total apportionment proceeds to its scholarship fund, and even as a percentage of these expenditures it has been shrinking: 7 percent in 1988-89; 6 percent in 1989-90; 5 percent in 1990-91. *Journal, 1990: Mississippi Conference of the United Methodist Church,* 374-55; *Journal, 1991,* 336; *Journal, 1992,* 93.

86. Finger Papers, December 1952, MCA. Finger had had this to say in his inaugural address:

We are concerned here with the Christian faith. . . . The greatest need of our day is a training in integrity, in character, in the discipline of prayer and worship and service. We need to know what other men have said, we need to know much more what God now says! We need doctors, nurses, engineers, farmers, teachers — but we need Christian physicians, Christian farmers, Christian business men, and Christian all-the-rest! The Christian College must give light; it must also give power. We can enlighten. We can also invigorate. We can erase ignorance. We must also destroy despair and cynicism. We can give feelings of appreciation. We must also give conviction and courage. . . .

To accomplish this . . . task, we have here a well-qualified faculty, who know their own fields, but who know there are others besides their own. We have instructors who study to learn and study that they might better teach. Here we have teachers who combine their wisdom with a dedication. Committed themselves to a Christian philosophy, they are intent upon leading other people to the same. We recognize that there is no such thing as Christian mathematics or Christian chemistry or Christian political science. We do note that there can be Christian mathematicians, Christian chemists, Christian politicians. Not only can there be — there must be, if ultimately there is to be any kind at all. We believe that if a man is a committed believer in the Christian faith, he will be a good teacher. He will be an active participant in society, attempting to improve it where it is weak by being himself improved.

Millsaps College Bulletin 37, no. 4 (December 1952).

87. The college statement reported that a white Tougaloo professor had spoken at Millsaps on race relations "as he understands that the Negro sees it." The college's conclusion: "It is exceedingly regrettable that this invitation was issued." Another white speaker, who favored nonviolent resistance to racial segregation, had been scheduled to speak at Millsaps. "It is also exceedingly regrettable that this invitation was extended." A Millsaps professor had spoken at a monthly Social Seminar Forum on the Tougaloo campus, and when some of his own students asked to come he arranged for segregated seating for them in the audience. "The administration of Millsaps College will urge all staff members to be discriminating in accepting speaking engagements and be always mindful of their responsibilities to the college." The statement does refer to the issue as a religious one, but only with regard to freedom: "The Christian tradition maintains steadfastly that we are ultimately governed by Christ. This is . . . a plea for the freedom we treasure and for which our forefathers died." "Millsaps President Issues Statement of Policies," *Purple and White* (Millsaps' student newspaper), 15 March 1958. Thus it was the freedom of blacks that its critics deplored and the freedom of whites that the college defended.

88. Goodbread, 18-19.

89. Said the board: "The purpose of a college is not to tell people what to think but to teach them how to think. [This is a direct excerpt from President Key's defense in 1937, quoted above.] Our purpose at Millsaps College is to create an atmosphere in which Christian convictions may grow and mature. Neither segregation nor integration is an issue at Millsaps College. Segregation always has been, and is now, the policy at Millsaps College. There is no thought, purpose, or intention on the part of those in charge of its affairs to change this policy." "To the Friends of Millsaps College," *Mississippi Methodist Advocate,* 26 March 1958.

90. "Millsaps Student Senate Supports Administration," *Mississippi Methodist Advocate,* 26 March 1958.

91. Editorial, "Pope's Lines Apply Here," *Purple and White,* 6 March 1958.

92. "A Profile of Millsaps College, 1956 to 1976" (1966), 4 n. 1.

93. "Self-Study Report," 1969-70, 16-17, MCA.

94. Minutes of the Board of Trustees, 24 May 1961, MCA.

95. Minutes of the Board of Trustees, 21 January and 24 July 1964, MCA.

96. *The North Mississippi Conference Journal, 1965,* 101 (hereafter cited as *North Mississippi,* followed by the year); "Millsaps College: A Report to Mississippi Methodists," Fall 1966, 4; Minutes of the Board of Trustees, Finance Committee, 5 May 1965, MCA. Income from the church, after a decade of growth, had begun a steady decline.

97. Minutes of the Board of Trustees, 28 May 1966, MCA.

98. *Journal: 1969 Session, Mississippi Conference,* 74, 135 (hereafter cited as *Mississippi,* followed by the year). These same minutes record the delight provided to Millsaps by its anticipation of $1.5 million as its share of a forthcoming campaign within the conference: *Mississippi/1969,* 174.

99. *Mississippi/1985,* 257-63; *North Mississippi/1985,* 247-58.

100. *North Mississippi/1985,* 251-52.

101. *North Mississippi*/1985, 256-57; *Mississippi*/1985, 262-63.

102. Indeed, the custom of reducing its mission to generic terms was already well established at this time. It is illustrated by W. M. Alexander, secretary of the Department of Schools and Colleges, General Board of Christian Education, Methodist Episcopal Church, South, in 1936.

[P]ractically all of the earliest colleges in America were established and maintained by the Church. In a unique sense the Church has always considered its major function to spread *light* and *truth* and *righteousness* throughout the earth. The Church, therefore, has never been greatly concerned about distinguishing between learning and evangelism and religious culture. A few words taken from the printed aims of the first American colleges will show how religion and general culture were interwoven in the thinking of their founders. These early colleges were established "to fit youth for public employment in Church and State" (Yale), "to see that the Churches be protected from an illiterate ministry" (Harvard), and "to teach and engage children (students) to Know God in Jesus Christ" (King's College [now Columbia University]).

The ultimate question was not whether these goals be harmonious, but whether the Methodist religious agenda was an independent ensemble of convictions and commitments by which the academic enterprise was to be motivated and critiqued, or a title by which everything undertaken at Methodist institutions was legitimated as Methodist. Later the author appears to imply that the relationship to the Methodist Church was one of loyalty, rather than anything controlled by the church's authenticity: "While narrow sectarianism is never to be defended, we are nevertheless organized along denominational lines, and for that reason we need to be intelligent and loyal with reference to our own denominational programs." See W. M. Alexander, "The Church College in the Field of Higher Education" (1936), radio broadcast manuscript, in Key Papers, Box 35; MCA.

103. Barksdale interview.

104. *Catalog of Millsaps College, 1949-50,* 8.

105. Adopted by the faculty and board of trustees of Millsaps College, 1955-56; *Catalog of Millsaps College, 1956-57,* 4. There had been a predecessor statement: "Aims and Purposes of Millsaps College: A Faculty Consensus, 1934-35." See Key Papers, MCA; also "Self-Study Report," 1969-70, 3.

106. *Catalog of Millsaps College, 1957-58,* 8.

107. "Self-Study Report," Millsaps College, Session 1959-60, 14. While the college gave no priority to the admission of Methodist students, it was then admitting about nine out of every ten applicants, whatever their religious preference. MCA/A-2-4-2.

108. "The Report of the Visiting Committee to Millsaps College, Jackson, Mississippi, November 13-16, 1960," W. Hugh McEniry, chairman, 2-3. MCA/A-2-2-8.

109. "Self-Study Report," 1969-70, 8, 25, 12, MCA.

110. *Catalog of Millsaps College, 1969-70,* 8.

111. "Self-Study Report," Millsaps College, 1980-81, 8-9, MCA.

112. *Catalog of Millsaps College, 1992-93,* 4-5.

113. Commission on Colleges, Southern Association of Colleges and Schools, "Report of the Reaffirmation Committee," Millsaps College, Jackson, Mississippi, 17-20 February 1992, 3, MCA.

114. Minutes of the Board of Trustees, 22 and 24 February 1967; *Millsaps College Catalog, 1993-94.*

115. *Campus Ministry at Millsaps: A Major Opportunity* (1993); "Millsaps College: A Report to Mississippi Methodists," Fall 1966, 2; Minutes of the Board of Trustees, 3 June 1967, MCA; Barksdale interview. Only three years later, however, another source reckoned that "over 1/3" of the Methodist clergy in Mississippi were Millsaps alumni: Robert E. Bergmark et al.,

statement of the Committee on the Statement for the Case for Support of Millsaps College [1970], MCA.

116. Minutes of the Board of Trustees, 24 May 1961, MCA.

117. *Journal, 1990: Mississippi Conference of the United Methodist Church,* 186, 332-34, 373-75, 548, S-334. The Mississippi and Northern Mississippi Conferences had merged in 1988. *Journal, 1991,* 334-36, S-334; *Journal, 1992,* 91-93, S-334.

118. Minutes of the Board of Trustees, 17 June 1964, MCA.

119. What follows on campus ministry at Millsaps is indebted to Donald Fortenberry, chaplain of Millsaps College, interview with the author, 3 February 1994; also Donald Peyton Fortenberry, "A Vision for Campus Ministry at Millsaps College" (D.Min. diss., Emory University, 1993).

120. George W. Boyd, "The State of the College: 1968-1969," the American Association of University Professors' presidential address, delivered on October 3, 1968, 8; Graves Papers, F-15-2; MCA.

121. "Self-Study Report," 1969-70, 21.

122. Fortenberry, "Vision," 129.

123. Fortenberry, "Vision," 99.

124. Fortenberry, "Vision," 117, 194.

125. Fortenberry, "Vision," 210-11.

126. Sweet, 66, 99.

127. Henry Clyde Hubbart, *Ohio Wesleyan's First Hundred Years* (Delaware, Ohio: Ohio Wesleyan University, 1943), 14.

128. Ohio Methodists would later come to sponsor four other colleges that continue today: Baldwin-Wallace in Berea, Mount Union in Alliance, Otterbein in Westerville, and Ohio Northern in Ada.

129. Hubbart, 14, 19, 31-32.

130. Edward Thomson, D.D., *Inaugural Address, delivered at the Ohio Wesleyan University, Delaware, Ohio, at its Annual Commencement, Aug. 5, 1846* (Cincinnati: Methodist Book Concern, 1846). Copy in the Ohio Wesleyan Historical Collection, Beeghly Library, Ohio Wesleyan University (hereafter cited as OWCA).

131. E[dward]. T. Nelson, *Fifty Years of History of the Ohio Wesleyan University, Delaware, Ohio: 1844-1894* (Cleveland: Cleveland Printing and Publishing Co., 1895), 257-66.

132. Hubbart, 203, 235-38, 252-54.

133. Lest this seem to be an unacceptable ratio between matriculants and graduates, one may compare it with Illinois Wesleyan University, which in its first half-century awarded 1,121 degrees but had matriculated from 25,000 to 30,000 students. Watson, 133.

134. Nelson, 113-15; Hubbart, 100-101.

135. William G. Williams, "Ohio Wesleyan University," in *The Early Schools of Methodism,* ed. A. W. Cummings (New York: Phillips & Hunt, 1886), 336.

136. James Whitford Bashford, Annual Report of the President, 1891-92, 4-5, OWCA. See also John Marshall Barker, *History of Ohio Methodism: A Study in Social Science* (Cincinnati: Curts & Jennings, 1898), 258. The *Quadrennial Report of the Board of Education of the Methodist Episcopal Church to the General Conference of 1892,* 32-33, indicates that Boston University that year had more undergraduates than Ohio Wesleyan but a lesser total enrollment for want of any subcollegiate instruction, while Northwestern University had fewer undergraduates but more total students because of a larger subcollegiate enrollment. Thus the OWU claim, artfully presented, was to be the largest if both totals were calculated.

Williams, however, reports that OWU had been outstandingly successful in selling four thousand cheap but permanent family scholarships in the early years. This provided it with a onetime infusion of capital but a never-ending influx of students who could claim free education.

In the 1880s its large enrollment was both a boast and a burden, since almost none of the students paid tuition. In *The Early Schools of Methodism,* 337, 346.

137. *Quadrennial Report, 1892,* 29-30.

138. Hubbart, 49-58, 78-80; William Roy Diem and Rollin Clarence Hunter, *The Story of Speech at Ohio Wesleyan* (Columbus: F. J. Heer Printing Co., 1964), give a slightly different account. In 1905 an OWU Shakespeare class presented *As You Like It* in a glen near the campus.

139. Hubbart, 335.

140. Bashford, Report of the President, 1891-92, 26-27.

141. Bashford, Report of the President, 1891-92, 26; Nelson, 115.

142. Hubbart, 87-127, 145.

143. Hubbart, 87.

144. Hubbart, 330, 332, 336; Loyd D. Easton, "The Curriculum: Patterns of Learning," in *Noble Achievements: The History of Ohio Wesleyan University from 1942 to 1992,* ed. Bernard Murchland (Delaware, Ohio: Ohio Wesleyan University, 1991), 125.

145. Hubbart, 163-64, 222-23, 309-14, 177.

146. Hubbart, 317-18.

147. Hubbart, 115.

148. Kay (Catherine N.) Schlichting, "OWU and Methodism," typescript in the OWCA, 3.

149. Information about the religious makeup of the student body at OWU is hard to come by, and the statistics reported here have had to be gleaned from a variety of sources.

150. Hubbart, 175.

151. Herbert Welch, Report of the President, 29 December 1910, 2; John W. Hoffman, Report of the President, 9 December 1924, 21, OWCA.

152. Hubbart, 156-58.

153. Hubbart, 153-56, 255-62.

154. Hubbart, 165-67.

155. "Report of the Special Committee on Dancing," Minutes of the Board of Trustees, 9 December 1924, 17, OWCA. Dancing was allowed, "on trial," under numerous regulations. Women could attend only if written parental permission were on file, and sororities could sponsor dances only once a year, compared with fraternities, who could do so once a semester. In 1924 this was very liberal for a Methodist institution.

156. Minutes of the Board of Trustees, 11 December 1928, 6, OWCA. Throughout OWU's history up to this point, Presbyterians had represented the second-largest cohort in the student body.

157. Hubbart, 175.

158. *Academic Freedom in a Christian College: An Address Delivered by Edmund Davison Soper on the Occasion of His Inauguration as President of Ohio Wesleyan University, Friday, February Fifteenth, Nineteen Hundred and Twenty-Nine,* OWCA. It is significant that Soper, having treated church membership as no reliable indicator of doctrinal fellowship, falls back upon an account of what a Christian stands for that is fuzzy even for a Wesleyan: "A Christian is a man of deeply reverent spirit whose God is the one personal creative Spirit at the center of the universe, a God who can be in significant contact with things through prayer. He is one who has caught the meaning of Jesus Christ and who sees in Him and His way of life the hope of social righteousness and the assurance of personal emancipation" (p. 10). Two years earlier Clarence E. Ficken had produced an extensive protocol for faculty development which omitted all consideration of religion: "Building a Faculty," 1926, OWCA. Ficken would serve lengthy years as dean, and also acting president and interim president.

159. Edmund D. Soper, Report of the President, 11 December 1930, 11-12, OWCA.

160. Floyd W. Reeves et al., *The Liberal Arts College: Based upon Surveys of Thirty-Five Colleges Related to the Methodist Episcopal Church* (Chicago: University of Chicago Press, 1932),

39, 53, 554, 513, 659, 360, 196, 418, 57. Reeves, professor of education at the University of Chicago, headed a survey team of education specialists from various universities.

161. Soper, Report of the President, 7 June 1935, 11-15, OWCA. At the same meeting Soper reminded the board that the faculty payroll that year had had to be cut by 38 percent, yet they continued on. Soper returned to the troubled relations between college and church: see Minutes of the Board of Trustees, 10 December 1935, 15-16; 5 June 1936, 12-14; 30 November 1936, 5-7, OWCA. To put this in context, however: it was generally the case that the northern Methodist colleges received relatively little from their church constituencies (local, conference, and national), and that the smaller, more marginal colleges tended to receive the larger grants. Ohio Wesleyan in the early years of the depression received no appreciable funding from the local conference, and there was only one college related to the church which received less from the national Board of Education. See Reeves et al., 513-23.

162. Herbert Welch, "The Ideals and Aims of the Christian College," in Herbert Welch, Henry Churchill King, and Thomas Nicholson, *The Christian College* (Cincinnati: Methodist Book Concern, 1916), 11-17.

163. "The Aims of the Ohio Wesleyan University" (draft), in "Report of a Survey of Ohio Wesleyan University, under the Auspices of the Commission on Survey of Educational Institutions of the Methodist Episcopal Church," February 1931, 3-5, in OWCA.

164. "A Study-Recommendation Report on Student Life outside the Classroom for the Student Affairs Committee, the Faculty and Administration, the Board of Trustees," by the Commission to Study Student Life outside the Classroom, May 1968, in OWCA.

165. *Values at Ohio Wesleyan: An Address by Dr. Thomas E. Wenzlau, President, Ohio Wesleyan University, at the Ninth Annual Board of Trustees President's Dinner, 20 June 1980,* OWCA.

166. David Liles Warren, "The Greatest Calling," *Ohio Wesleyan Magazine,* November 1984, 12.

167. This is not quite accurate. At this time a majority of the OWU board of trustees were elected by the church.

168. *Ohio Wesleyan University Catalog, 1926-27,* 41-42.

169. *Ohio Wesleyan University Catalog, 1932-33,* 37.

170. *Ohio Wesleyan University Catalog, 1940-41,* 18.

171. Herbert J. Burgstahler, Report of the President, 29 May 1942, 67, OWCA; *Ohio Wesleyan University Catalog, 1944-45,* 7-8.

172. "Report and Recommendations of the Committee of Nine," 1 May 1962, OWCA. The university had gone through most of the 1950s with a largely absentee president, one result being an increase in faculty autonomy; his successor quickly clashed with the faculty over personnel issues, and the mention of diversity offers some resonance from that struggle. See Easton, 136.

173. Minutes of the Board of Trustees, 7 June 1963, 10:190-91, OWCA; *Ohio Wesleyan University Catalog, 1978-79,* 69-70.

174. "Statement of Aims," *Ohio Wesleyan Magazine* 54, no. 2 (December 1979): 4.

175. Easton, 147-49.

176. "Ohio-Wesleyan University Five-Year Plan: May, 1987," 6, OWCA.

177. Burgstahler, Report of the Chancellor, 25 May 1948, OWCA. The 1932 survey had reported, however, that although church bodies still usually held the right of election or confirmation of a majority of board positions on Methodist campuses, the nominations and suggestions of the local boards were generally honored. Reeves et al., 70-72.

178. Burgstahler, Report of the President, 6 June 1941, 16-19; Burgstahler, Report of the Chancellor, 25 May 1948, 9, OWCA; Blake Michael, "Religious Life: The Promises and Perils of Piety," in *Noble Achievements,* 184.

179. Hubbart, 177-80, 308, 313.

180. Hubbart, 314.

181. Code of Regulations adopted by the board of trustees, 27 October 1961, OWCA.

182. Minutes of the Board of Trustees, 9 February 1962, 10:162; 1 June 1962, 10:168, OWCA. Church support was rising: in 1960 they had given 7.7 percent of all gifts, yet alumni contributions that year were only about half again as much as the church's, so their rise was on an even steeper curve; W. Noel Johnston, vice president for university relations, Report, Minutes of the Board of Trustees, June 1961; 10:130, OWCA.

183. C. B. Mills, Report of the Chairman of the Board, 3 June 1960, 1, OWCA. At this time church contributions amounted to about 2.4 percent of the budget, and 7.7 percent of all gift income: Johnston, Report, OWCA.

184. Conn, *Handbook,* 28.

185. Earl J. McGrath, "A Report to the Trustees and Faculty of Ohio Wesleyan University," 25 October 1961, 9-10, OWCA.

186. University Senate and Board of Education of the Methodist Church, "Survey Report: Ohio Wesleyan University," 1960, 141, OWCA.

187. Michael, 185-86.

188. *Ohio Wesleyan University Catalog, 1951-52,* 22.

189. James S. Leslie, Report of the University Chaplain, Minutes of the Board of Trustees, 4 June 1963, OWCA.

190. This might be compared with a policy statement drafted at Illinois Wesleyan University (IWU) in 1963 by the president. It is as vague in its aspirations, but more specific in its strategy:

> Church-relatedness implies a dedicated devotion to the truth and an obligation to keep humbly searching for the truth, realizing that truth is always growing, never complete, and that no man ever has all the truth, even about his own special field of study. Moreover, after one has satisfied himself as to *what* is true, he still needs to deal with the question as to *why* it is true, and who the ultimate author of truth is. Every academic discipline, indeed every course, is taught from the "faith perspective" of the professor. It is, in our opinion, essential that most teachers in a Christian university teach from the perspective of the Judeo-Christian faith. Therefore, as a Christian university we are seeking to have a faculty that shares essentially the kind of faith — about the universe, and God, and man, and human history — that is expressed in the Bible, particularly the New Testament. "A university is a comradeship of faith" (Buttrick).
>
> A prospective member of the Illinois Wesleyan faculty or administrative staff should therefore ask himself or herself: "Can I warmly support such an attitude, and do I desire to contribute to the enhancement of such an atmosphere?"
>
> We assume that nearly everyone who answers the above questions in the affirmative will be an active member of some church. Most will belong to Protestant churches, but membership in a non-Protestant church will not disqualify a candidate. We are more interested in basic religious presuppositions and convictions than affiliation with any particular denomination. (Revised form, 1965)

When released in draft form the policy statement was buried beneath an avalanche of criticism and was never adopted. Methodists at the time constituted from 40 to 50 percent of the IWU student body. Lloyd M. Bertholf, *A Personal Memoir of the Bertholf Years at Illinois Wesleyan University, 1958-68* (Bloomington: Illinois Wesleyan University, 1984), 70-71; see also 58, 61-63, 68-69, 81; Bertholf, communication to the author, 30 May 1994.

191. Harold J. and (Alma S.) Sheridan, "Religion in the Program of Ohio Wesleyan University," Minutes of the Board of Trustees, 28 October 1955; Michael, 182, OWCA.

192. In 1960 the Ohio conferences chose 20 of 46 voting members; in 1970, 14 of 40; in 1980, 13 of 45; in 1993, 14 of 50. Statistics provided by Susan J. Cohen, curator of the OWCA.

193. Information provided by Ms. Jeanette Kraus, of the office of public relations. See also

Ohio Wesleyan University: Report of the President, 1991-92, 13; Jennifer Hamlin Church, "Ambitious Goals and Historic Success: Five Years of Remarkable Achievement," *Ohio Wesleyan Magazine,* summer 1993, does not specify the amount given by the church.

194. Michael, 190.

195. Michael, 189; in the same volume, *Noble Achievements,* see 32-33, 41, 139.

196. Earl Warner, "The Presidents: Fifty Years of Administration," in *Noble Achievements,* 40-41; Amy McClure, "Student Life: Generation upon Generation," in *Noble Achievements,* 193.

197. Michael, 193.

198. This consists in a course with a substantial focus on non-Euro-American topics. Such courses will deal with the people and cultures of Africa, Asia (including the Middle East), Latin America, Native North America (Amerindians), and Oceania or with American ethnic minorities who trace their ancestry to one of these regions. New Testament courses and those dealing with Christianity are not presently listed as fulfilling this requirement.

199. Jon R. Powers, university chaplain, interview with the author, 21 January 1994; Annual Report of the University Chaplain, 1991-92; Donald C. Bishop, dean for enrollment management and dean of admission, communication to the author, 1 July 1994. The annual Cooperative Institutional Research Program (CIRP), in which OWU participated until 1989, suggested that incoming students were then only 12 percent Methodists and 24 percent Catholics.

200. Murchland, *Noble Achievements,* 45-46, 149-53, 194-95, 259.

201. Warren, in *West Ohio Annual Conference, 1993,* 364-65.

202. Michael, 194-95.

203. Minutes of the Board of Trustees, 2 December 1941, 24, OWCA.

204. The low proportion of Methodist students at OWU cannot be ascribed to too selective an enrollment policy, as Earl McGrath had feared, for the university has been admitting a very high percentage of students who apply. Sources for the church statistics (1992) are *Twenty-Fourth Session, West Ohio Annual Conference, United Methodist Church, 1993,* 1:S-76, 2:249; *1993 Journal, the East Ohio Conference, United Methodist Church,* 1:171, 2:140.

205. Bernard Murchland, "The Sesquicentennial President: An Interview with David Liles Warren," in *Noble Achievements,* 262.

206. Burgstahler, Report of the President, 2 December 1940, 4; 6 January 1941, 17, OWCA.

207. See, e.g., Soper, Report of the President, 14 December 1933, 4, OWCA.

208. Soper, Report of the President, 10 December 1929, 2, OWCA.

209. Burgstahler, Report of the President, 2 December 1946, 4, OWCA.

210. Thomas A. Langford has been helpful to the author in clarifying these issues.

211. Minutes of the Board of Trustees, 7 June 1935, 14-15, OWCA.

212. Sweet, 209; Cannon, 552.

213. Leland Scott, "The Message of American Methodism," in *The History of American Methodism,* 1:552-59.

214. Irene Martin, "Asbury College of De Pauw University," in *The Early Schools of Methodism,* 254-55. The reference was evidently to John McLean of Ohio, an associate justice of the U.S. Supreme Court.

215. James Tunstead Burtchaell, C.S.C., "The Alienation of Christian Higher Education in America: Diagnosis and Prognosis," in *Schooling Christians: "Holy Experiments" in American Education,* ed. Stanley Hauerwas and John H. Westerhoff (Grand Rapids: William B. Eerdmans Publishing Co., 1992), 129-83.

216. "Affirmative Action Plan," *1991 Yearbook,* BHEM/UMC, 29-30.

217. It should be remembered, however, that Wesley himself had in early days assigned only one condition of membership in his societies: desiring to flee from the wrath to come. Methodists, he said, do not impose any opinions. "Let them hold particular or general redemption, absolute or conditional decrees; let them be churchmen, or dissenters, Presbyterians or Independents, it is no obstacle. Let them choose one mode of baptism or another, it is no bar to their

admission. The Presbyterian may be a Presbyterian still; the Independent and Anabaptist use his own mode of worship. So may the Quaker; and none will contend with him about it. They think and let think. One condition, and one only, is required — a real desire to save the soul. Where this is, it is enough; they desire no more; they lay stress upon nothing else; they only ask, 'Is thy heart herein as my heart? If it be, give me thy hand.'" Sweet, 41-42.

218. Alasdair MacIntyre, "Values and Distinctive Characteristics of Teaching and Learning in Church-Related Colleges," in *Institutional Integrity and Values: Perspectives on United Methodist Higher Education* (Nashville: DHE/BHEM, 1989), 19-20.

219. One small index of the declining status of religion in United Methodist institutions of higher education was provided fifteen years ago in a dissertation that canvassed administrators and faculty for their respective judgments about goals for their schools: goals as they would prefer them ranked, and goals as they perceived them to be implicitly ranked in the way their schools were then functioning. Out of twenty possible goals, such as "vocational preparation," "off-campus learning," "meeting local needs," "cultural/aesthetic awareness," "public service," "social egalitarianism," "social criticism/activism," "academic development," and "democratic governance," faculty thought that "traditional religiousness" should rank in sixteenth place, although they thought it was actually ranked in eleventh place. Administrators would place it in thirteenth place, but saw it actually in twelfth place. More interesting, perhaps, than the low estate to which both study groups would assign religion is the fact that only one of eight groups surveyed would have given religion more emphasis, rather than less, than it presently had. See Robert Michael O'Brien, "Goal Congruence in Four Church-Related Colleges" (Ed.D. diss, University of Tennessee, 1979).

220. Trotter, "The Staff and the Intellectual Life of the Church," in *Loving God with One's Mind,* 234.

221. Trotter, "United Methodist Higher Education: The Next Decade," in *Loving God with One's Mind,* 103-4.

222. Wilbur Fisk, in *Minutes of the New England Conference of the Methodist Episcopal Church* (Boston: David H. Ela, 1835), 11; quoted by Douglas J. Williamson, "Wilbur Fisk (1792-1839)," in *Something More Than Human: Biographies of Leaders in American Methodist Higher Education,* ed. Charles E. Cole (Nashville: BHEM/UMC, 1986), 106.

223. The records of the University Senate show that during the past half-century when various universities and colleges such as Boston, Wesleyan, Albion, Allegheny, Southern California, Northwestern, Lawrence, and Westminster began publicly to present themselves as "private and non-sectarian" and to refuse requests for annual information, the Committee on Church Membership pled that since the notion of church relationship was so undefined they could do no more than request a "conversation" with the respective presidents and hope for a reply. One bishop on such a board counseled a passive approach: "The relationship between the college and the church is improving gradually all the time, and if we are patient things will work out all right. I do not expect that the Charter of the college will ever be changed to the old status but I do believe that the influence and interest of The Methodist Church in the college and its influence upon college policies will be maintained." Six months later the Senate minutes noted that the college "has severed all legal relationships to the Methodist Church and has repeatedly suggested that it has 'moved beyond the confines of active connection with Methodism.'" The expressed attitude of the church bodies appears repeatedly as timid. UMCA/1987-047: 2634-5-2:39, pp. 31-34; 2634-5-3:05; 2632-5-3:20, pp. 14-15; 2634-5-3:24, pp. 26-27; 2448 6 2:17, pp. 9 11; 2630-6-1:37, pp. 12-13.

224. Cannon, 552-53. There is an irony that Fisk's Wesleyan is one of the institutions that Cannon gave as an example.

225. Quoted from Asia Colleges Newsletter, in *President's Bulletin Board,* Division of Educational Institutions, Board of Education, the Methodist Church, January 1958, UMCA/1987-047/2634-5-3-01.

226. "Board of Higher Education and Ministry Proposes a Quadrennial Emphasis on Higher Education, 1981-1984: The Church and Campus — An Essential Evangelism" (draft), November 1978, UMCA/1987-047/2630-6-1:38.

227. Beverly A. Asbury, "Campus Life in a Time of Culture War," *Soundings* 75, no. 4 (winter 1992): 473-75. In a reply to Stanley Hauerwas's "A Non-Violent Proposal for Christian Participation in the Culture Wars," pp. 477-92, in the same issue of *Soundings,* Asbury concludes: "If all forms of faith are partial windows on the truth and not the 'Thing Itself,' my job ought to be one of joining with others in making the university a safe and hospitable place for teachers and learners to try out ideas, to form and re-form communities, and to get a *moral* education if not a particularistic religious one." "A Reply to Hauerwas," *Soundings* 75, no. 4 (winter 1992): 497.

CHAPTER 4

The Baptists

A signature item in Baptist belief and discipline, from the days of their beginnings in the Pietist reform, has been "antipedobaptism": an insistence that to be capable of baptism someone must be mature enough to sin and undergo conversion and make an act of personal faith. Thus child baptism is rejected, and adults who have undergone these rites must be rebaptized. There is another belief of effectively equal force: that the only authentic "church" is the local congregation. While congregations are free to make common cause with others, say, to coordinate mission efforts or educational institutions, these collaborative networks are not churches and have no authority over their members. Thus Baptists at large form a "denomination," not a church. A third foundational tenet is that each believer has the capacity to understand and construe the Scriptures for himself or herself, and does not depend upon church or denomination for this. It is inevitable that this "soul sufficiency" and congregationalism coexist awkwardly, because the sovereignty of any congregation composed of sovereign individuals is an uneasy sovereignty. But from this and several other stresses has come forth the seismic history of the Baptists in America.

The usual motive for the early foundation of academies and of colleges was the education of clergy. Baptists had customarily not sought learning in their preachers; indeed, they had distrusted it as one of the abiding sources of corruption. Nevertheless a venerable faction within the Baptists disagreed with that tradition, and the Baptists, both by their early start and by the wide scatter and eventual abundance of their foundations, were to join the Christian communities that most energetically sponsored higher education in America.[1]

After the Civil War Baptist colleges enjoyed a larger combined endowment than those of the Congregationalists and the Presbyterians, the two denominations that placed high value on education, especially for ministry. It also exceeded that

---

This essay was researched and written in 1993, and the statistics and facts it reports as current derive from the latest sources then available.

of the Methodists, who were on their way to establishing themselves as the most numerous Christian communion in America. At that time the Baptists had more students enrolled in their seminaries than either of the two "educated" denominations had in theirs, and more — many more — in their colleges and academies than the Congregationalists, Presbyterians, and Methodists.[2] This period immediately after the Civil War was a time of both membership growth and emphasis on education for Baptists. The Methodists would gradually come to sponsor a larger roster of colleges and universities, but the immediate postbellum period is an unnoticed season of Baptist prominence in higher education. Today, however, many of their most prestigious foundations would not be widely remembered as originally Baptist related: Brown, George Washington, Richmond, Chicago, Rochester, Colgate, Temple, Bucknell, Alfred, and Jackson State Universities, and Bates, Vassar, Morehouse, Spelman, and Hillsdale Colleges. How came such a drastic defection?

It is related to the difficulties Baptists have encountered in keeping themselves together. Despite the fact that Baptists take it as creed that there is no defining creed — or perhaps because of that — their internal alliances have been fragile and fluctuating. The great majority of congregations were tied by membership to regional associations and to state conventions, and thence to a Triennial Convention which managed to unite Baptists across the country for joint efforts to support missions foreign and domestic (mostly in the South and West) and higher education. This one national link came apart in 1845 over the issue of slavery and abolition. The Southern Baptist Convention (SBC) was founded that year, leaving the American Baptist Convention with only a northern constituency. Needless to say, the black Baptists in the South found the SBC an increasingly inhospitable communion, and they eventually formed their own convention which, though fragmented, today constitutes the second-largest Baptist sector. Unlike the Methodists and the Presbyterians, who also split apart over the peculiar institution of human bondage, the Baptists have never reunited. Thus we must examine their respective ventures in higher education through their denominational families, the Southern Baptist Convention and the American Baptist Churches in the USA (ABC/USA).

THE SOUTHERN BAPTISTS

Almost all Baptist colleges and universities in the South (and indeed many of the seminaries) were founded by local initiative. But eventually it fell out that the SBC has become the patron of the seminaries, and the state conventions have become the sponsors of the colleges and universities. The presently affiliated colleges and universities include the following:

1823	Union University	Jackson, Tenn.
1826	Furman University	Greenville, S.C.
1826	Mississippi College	Clinton, Miss.

358

1829	Georgetown College	Georgetown, Ky.
1830	University of Richmond	Richmond, Va.
1833	Mercer University	Macon, Ga.
1834	Wake Forest University	Winston-Salem, N.C.
1838	Judson College	Marion, Ala.
1841	Samford University	Birmingham, Ala.
1845	Baylor University	Waco, Tex.
1845	University of Mary Hardin–Baylor	Belton, Tex.
1848	Chowan College	Murfreesboro, N.C.
1849	William Jewell College	Liberty, Mo.[3]
1851	Carson-Newman College	Jefferson City, Tenn.
1856	Mars Hill College	Mars Hill, N.C.
1858	Hannibal-LaGrange College	Hannibal, Mo.
1859	Averett College	Danville, Va.
1873	Blue Mountain College	Blue Mountain, Miss.
1873	Shorter College	Rome, Ga.
1878	Southwest Baptist University	Bolivar, Mo.
1883	Stetson University	De Land, Fla.
1884	Virginia Intermont College	Bristol, Va.
1886	Ouachita Baptist College	Arkadelphia, Ark.
1887	Campbell University	Buies Creek, N.C.
1889	Cumberland College	Williamsburg, Ky.
1889	Howard Payne University	Brownwood, Tex.
1891	Hardin-Simmons College	Abilene, Tex.
1891	Meredith College	Raleigh, N.C.
1896	Wingate University	Wingate, N.C.
1904	Brewton-Parker College	Mount Vernon, Ga.
1905	Gardner-Webb College	Boiling Springs, N.C.
1906	Campbellsville College	Campbellsville, Ky.
1906	Louisiana College	Pineville, La.
1908	Wayland Baptist University	Plainview, Tex.
1910	Oklahoma Baptist University	Shawnee, Okla.
1911	William Carey College	Hattiesburg, Miss.
1911	Anderson College	Anderson, S.C.
1912	East Texas Baptist University	Marshall, Tex.
1922	Bluefield College	Bluefield, Va.
1941	Williams Baptist College	Walnut Ridge, Ark.
1943	Florida Baptist Theological College	Graceland, Fla.
1949	Grand Canyon University	Phoenix, Ariz.
1950	California Baptist College	Riverside, Calif.
1951	Belmont University	Nashville, Tenn.
1960	Houston Baptist University	Houston, Tex.
1961	Mobile College	Mobile, Ala.

1964	Charleston Southern University	Charleston, S.C.
1964	Missouri Baptist College	Saint Louis, Mo.[4]
1968	Dallas Baptist University	Dallas, Tex.
1968	Palm Beach Atlantic College	West Palm Beach, Fla.

To illustrate something of the experience of the Southern Baptist four-year colleges, fifty of which survived over the years and retained recognition by the Southern Baptist Convention, we offer a case study of Wake Forest University (WFU). At the time of the case study WFU had recently removed itself from official sponsorship by the Baptist State Convention of North Carolina, but claimed a continuity in its Baptist allegiance. Since that time a number of SBC-related institutions have withdrawn in various degrees from the control of their State Conventions, including Wake Forest, Richmond, Baylor, Samford, Ouachita Baptist, Furman, Mercer, Stetson, and Meredith. The SBC determined to dissolve all centralized sponsorship of higher education in 1997.

WAKE FOREST UNIVERSITY

In 1830 the census for North Carolina counted 668,439 persons, categorized as 403,295 whites, 19,543 free Negroes, and 245,601 slaves. The fact that no town in the state yet held five thousand inhabitants implies how scattered and rural that population was. There were no state schools anywhere and none would appear until 1841, when some of the counties established the first free elementary schools. There were private secondary schools in some localities where population clustered. Their teachers were often itinerants, and none too reliable. Even so, those schools were affordable only by the affluent.

When North Carolina Baptists began to desire education for their ministers, Furman Academy and Theological Institution, in South Carolina since 1826, seemed to stand at a forbidding distance, transportation being then so primitive. The state university, founded in Chapel Hill in 1795, though by 1840 it served a hefty enrollment of 189 students, was no place for Baptists, what with drinking, cockfighting, and dancing among the students and Enlightenment ideas inclining the faculty to infidelity.[5]

Earlier Baptists in England and New England had expected education for their clergy much as other Dissenters did. By the time they began to outnumber other denominations in New England, even though their strength was mostly in rural areas, they provided academies for themselves. When they began to migrate southward, the special inclination of Baptists for schism was beginning to manifest itself, from which a bewildering variety of sectarian variants would emerge: General, Particular, Landmark, New Connection, Old Lights, New Lights, Separate, General Six Principle, Strict Particular, Primitive, Free Will, Two-Seed-in-the-Spirit Predestinatarian, Seventh Day, General Conference, and Missionary Baptists. The

Baptist story in North Carolina from approximately the 1760s until the 1830s shows them dividing into two main groups. The General, Regular, and Particular Baptists were overwhelmingly surpassed by the Separates, who believed in a Pentecostal conversion experience as prior in importance to baptism; in the direct and tumultuous illumination of individuals by the Holy Spirit as eclipsing all attempts to formulate confessions of faith or altercations between Arminians and Calvinists; and in the missionary spread of their belief by uncultured preachers rather than the creation of a caste of educated and ordained resident pastors. The Second Great Awakening, which had a secular accompaniment in Jacksonian populism discrediting the old New England and Virginia aristocracies, placed the Separates in the ascendant, leaving the conservative heirs of the older traditions chagrined, angry, and contemptuous of their short-of-breath brethren.

The older North Carolina Baptists were strong enough, when the various local associations united into a statewide effort, to include an educated ministry in their explicit purposes. In the northern states most Baptist colleges were sponsored and governed by independent societies. In the South, they would be creatures of the state conventions, whose charter rights were assured by their prerogative of choosing the trustees. The abiding persistence of antieducational convictions among North Carolina Baptists, although it did not block such establishments, has continued to the present day to assure that their patronage and supervision would always speak with two voices, one quite distrustful. The first Baptist State Convention of North Carolina met in 1830, and the Separates were obliged to contain their deep seated and enduring suspicion of educated ministers so that the convention could find a way to provide the residential clergy with a classical education, and thus attract a better sort of incumbent. A second object in their federation was the support of foreign missionaries, also a subject of continual contention between various Baptist groups.[6]

Since they had no resources or authority to impose a levy on the congregations strewn across the tidewater, piedmont, and mountains of North Carolina, the delegates recruited one of their number as general agent to canvass for funds. Samuel Wait, a preacher with some postsecondary education, accepted that call in the face of many handicaps. In a South already touchy about the contempt for slavery coming down from the North, he was a Yankee; for many of the rough-hewn Baptists among whom the colonial tax for the established Episcopal Church was still a hated memory, he was a "money-coveting priest" engaged in an unscriptural begging tour; and the backcountry farmers whose cash he solicited could see no benefit in a college for their own sons, and much mischief for their churches if they were served by effete preachers.[7] Two hundred sixty-eight sermons and collections later, Wait met with the education committee, and they resolved to buy a farm in Wake Forest on the convention's behalf.

An Institute to Educate Preachers

The state legislature, which could issue the needed charter, proved to be as dry and rocky a field to till as the state Baptists had been, mainly because "antimissionary Baptists" (who rejected joint efforts to sponsor salaried missionaries and teachers, and the higher organizational entanglements that entailed) carried their remonstrance to Raleigh, arguing that religious schooling was "the first step to a rich church and a proud and pompous ministry," since "school priests" had always preyed upon the wealth of the faithful. Statutory incorporation by the state, they insisted, would be "a trespassing on the Kingdom of God . . . the supporting and sustaining of a Christian ministry."[8] Even with the support of legislators who were themselves educated, the bill to grant a charter drew a tie vote, which had to be broken by the aye of the speaker of the senate.

Wake Forest Institute opened in 1834, with Samuel Wait himself as its principal (1834-45). From the start it was foreseen that this school founded to educate preachers would have to attract a majority of lay students to be viable. From sixteen boys, some as young as twelve years old, who appeared on opening day, the enrollment swelled to seventy-two by year's end. Only four of them aspired to be preachers; indeed, only eighteen professed any religion at all.[9]

Like many of the schools begun in this period, it combined manual labor with studies: for teachers no less than students. A working farm would allow the students to work off some of their fees and make the school self-sustaining; and farmers might be more disposed to see schooling as useful for their sons if it offered them an apprenticeship in advanced methods in agriculture. But the arrangement lasted only five years. There never was any skilled agricultural direction, and the boys' three hours of hated daily farmwork led by the indefatigable Samuel Wait and supervised by a farm manager never turned a profit.

When the farm closed down, the institute secured legislation making it Wake Forest College and empowering it to grant degrees (generally after five years of post-elementary study). Even in its early, hardscrabble period the students had to face a board of external examiners that included the governor and a (Catholic) supreme court justice, to be questioned on geography, English, grammar, orthography, rhetoric, declamation, natural philosophy, biblical history, U.S. history, Caesar, Cicero, Virgil, Sallust, French, Italian, Spanish, the Greek New Testament, arithmetic, and algebra — all taught by only two teachers and a tutor or two. Despite this prodigious curriculum, the intellectual vitality of the place, as was often the case in colleges of the time, was found in the literary societies. As elsewhere, there were two, and they were sharp rivals: the Philomathesian and the Euzelian. Conducted entirely by students, they held debates on large geopolitical and ethical questions, alternately sponsored the annual commencement ceremonies and invited the main speaker, and somehow acquired book collections which far surpassed what the college library could buy. Eventually they ceded their collections to the college and provided the nucleus of a much enriched library.[10]

Already in 1835 the issue arose of how the original incorporators were to be succeeded as trustees. The convention sent down its nominations, but the trustees insisted on two names for each position to be filled. Thus from earliest days the school's board kept some deft distance from denominational control.

It was not uncommon for the teachers to be ordained by the Wake Forest Baptist Church after they had joined the faculty. But this was not nearly enough to appease the resentment of those who took offense that they were almost all from New England — which was where most educated Baptists were then to be found. Some were explicit disciples of Francis Wayland, the Baptist president at Brown whose textbook *Moral Science* was banned by the Wake Forest trustees because of its forceful condemnation of slavery.

A more theoretical resentment was harbored by the antimissionary Baptists — not confined to the Separate Baptist ranks — who were opposed to the very notion of a state convention because they thought no body beyond the local congregation was even licit. Having this convention-sponsored school approved by the State of North Carolina was contrary to the doctrinaire Baptist rejection of church-state entanglements, in addition to its being staffed by abolitionists, which made it all the more odious. Hostility was especially strong in the western mountain areas.[11]

Wait was frequently on the road, preaching, baptizing, and soliciting funds for the college. It was no easy task, for the college was not very popular. Even with these subsidies, impecunious Baptists grumbled that the tuition should be free, or within reach of any church member.[12] It did not appease them to know that, as was usually the case then, the costs at Wake Forest were considerably less than those at the University of North Carolina. Since taxpayers were even less disposed than Baptists to subsidize the education of the affluent, paradoxically their denial of funds to the state university in the early nineteenth century assured that only the affluent could go to Chapel Hill.[13]

Baptist grievances were only augmented when the trustees obtained tax-exempt status in 1839. The next year Wake Forest's finances were in such ruin that the property was about to be sold off to pay its debts, and the college made an urgent appeal to the legislature for a loan, which was granted. This was the state which had its own constitutional ban on giving tax moneys to religious institutions, and which had held the federal Constitution hostage until it was similarly amended.

The beginnings of an educational network were forming. Though Baptists were then the second-largest denomination in North Carolina, they were poorly represented among the academy teachers who influenced their pupils' college choices. Eventually some local Baptist associations created secondary schools which allowed Wake Forest to close its own preparatory department, previously necessary as its only dependable feeder school. Wake Forest delayed long in establishing its own Department of Bible, or Religion, since its candidates for the ministry could move on after graduation to Furman for that, while by reciprocity South Carolina Baptists could and did send some of their sons up to Wake Forest for collegiate studies.

Sectional resistance flared up and drove out John Brown White, third president. Though himself a slaveholder, he had made the proposal (unanimously accepted) in 1849 that Negroes be admitted to the Lord's Supper in the Wake Forest Baptist Church.[14] The Baptists and the Methodists had already divided, North and South, in 1845 over their aggravated dispute about slavery and abolition.

The college was effectively closed down by the Civil War, and commandeered as a Confederate hospital. Its small but remarkable endowment, the fruit of bequests and legacies and of tireless canvassing from church to church by its presidents and faculty, was loyally liquidated and invested in Confederate States bonds. After the surrender its value shrank from about $100,000 to $11,000. But Wake Forest fared well enough among the dozen Southern Baptist colleges founded before the war: most were closed, and some never reopened. Up to the Civil War, Wake Forest had matriculated 1,087 students, of whom only 119 had received degrees. About 100 of the matriculates had gone on to the ministry, 49 of them with degrees; a similar number had become physicians; 71 had become lawyers; and 67 perished in the war.[15]

Postbellum Survival

Survival was not easy for Wake Forest. Though she reopened in 1866, by the start of her third year — amidst severe depression — only 42 students had appeared. But things were far worse in Chapel Hill, where the state university had become a spoil of Reconstruction, with president and faculty sent packing, the campus left pretty much as a ghost town, and its refugee students boosting Wake Forest's enrollment that year to 98. Her neighbors, Trinity (later to become Duke), a Methodist college, and Davidson, which was Presbyterian, saw their student bodies grow thereby even more plentifully. Since the faculty and trustees at Chapel Hill had been almost exclusively Episcopalian and Presbyterian, Baptists and Methodists had understandably seen it as a state-funded sectarian competitor and an emblem of the social exclusion they had suffered in state politics. Nevertheless, Wake Forest would support the reopening of UNC in 1875.

There were 204,000 Baptists in North Carolina and only 6,000 Episcopalians. Yet the Chapel Hill president, a majority of the board, and also of the faculty were Episcopalians, while but one faculty member was a Baptist; for seventy years there had been none. The Methodists, with 150,000 citizens and one faculty member, were similarly aggrieved. A further complaint was that by functionally remaining only an undergraduate college and not yet adding the professional schools of a true university, Chapel Hill was the adversary, not the collaborator, of the denominational colleges. In 1881 the state proposed to pass on its land grant income ($7,500 annually) to Chapel Hill as its first annual subsidy, with the proviso that it award free tuition to two students from each of the state's ninety-four counties. That was roughly equivalent to the combined student bodies of Wake Forest, Trinity, and Davidson, and would more than triple the university student body. Great was the lament heard in Raleigh from Baptist, Methodist, and Presbyterian throats. The compromise reached was that the university would receive only $5,000 annually, and would award only one scholarship per county.[16]

By 1891 Chapel Hill managed to offer more scholarships and in three years practically doubled its student body, mostly by defections from the three denominational colleges. Chapel Hill enjoyed several other advantages besides funding. The state's system of secondary schools was practically an adjunct of the university since its graduates dominated the staffing of both administrative and teaching positions in local high schools, and were thus well able to steer their pupils to their alma mater. The argument from Wake Forest, by President Charles Elisha Taylor (1884-1905), was that North Carolina should not be subsidizing the university's ambition to eliminate the Christian colleges. Instead, the state should leave to the independent sector what it was already capable of doing on the college level and use tax moneys to build up the elementary and secondary schools, which were too few and in lamentable condition. For any further development the university should depend on the same resources that the colleges had to rely upon: private philanthropy.

Then the Wake Forest argument took a turn. Though the state university had in fact been permeated with Christianity in its obligatory chapel and church services, its rules of conduct, and its teaching, this, Taylor insisted, was in violation of the constitutions of both North Carolina and the United States. Legally only independent colleges and universities were free to offer an integral education, one that incorporated Christianity.[17] Like Caiaphas, the truth he spoke was greater than he knew.

What was under way was a reversal of the traditional class distinction between state and independent colleges. Throughout the nineteenth century it was the state campuses that levied the higher fees and educated the children of the affluent, and the church campuses that educated the middle class and even some poor students. In 1891 63 percent of the Chapel Hill students were from cities and towns, whereas at Wake Forest only 20 percent were urban, the rest being from villages and the countryside.[18] In the latter years of the nineteenth century it would become the ambition of state universities to provide a highly subsidized education for all who were academically qualified, while paying more attractive salaries to their faculties. The church schools, unless they had substantial endowments, were tuition-driven and obliged to recruit more and more from the economic elite. That shift was going to be a very uphill climb for the Southern Baptists, whose membership was still heavily rural, agricultural, and economically marginal.

By the Civil War three-quarters of the North Carolina preachers were Wake Forest alumni. Later ministerial students tended to be limited in their numbers to those whose expenses the convention's Board of Education could pay: by 1870 they numbered only a dozen annually.[19] In the postbellum years Wake Forest continued to have a very high wastage rate, in that less than 15 percent of its students persevered until graduation. But of those who did, about 30 percent became preachers; of those who did not graduate, at one point it was reckoned that 26 percent — a far greater net number — entered the ministry.[20]

In the late nineteenth century it was reckoned that half the North Carolina Baptists were illiterate (more than three-quarters of all children in the state had no schooling). The pockets of Baptist animus toward Wake Forest were slow to dissipate; the great divide over godly learning and human study seemed to linger.[21] It is thus all the more remarkable that persisting efforts by the college to solicit funds among fellow Baptists had what success they did. The fund drive in 1870-73 was a failure, but so were most enterprises at that time of national economic collapse. Yet from 1876 onward the endowment no longer had to be used to cover annual deficits in the operating fund, and by the 1880s it was yielding more income than the student tuition fees. Between 1862 and 1915 the Board of Education would garner enough funds to give tuition assistance to 660 students who aspired to the ministry.

Another sign of growing appreciation of education among the constituency was the proliferation of local high schools under Baptist auspices. Throughout America the numbers of pupils enrolled in secondary schools leapt more than fourfold between 1870 and 1900. In that period Southern Baptists built perhaps six hundred academies to provide their children with secondary education, twenty-nine of them in North Carolina. Baptists began to feel more loyal toward their college, and more of them were becoming convinced that their preachers should be educated.[22]

Then came the first hints of new stress between the denomination and its educators: criticism of the college, not for its learning, but for its defections from Baptist ideals.

Charles E. Taylor, a Latin professor, was the president who saw Wake Forest into the twentieth century. He was an ordained minister, like his predecessors, but the first who did not serve simultaneously as pastor to the Wake Forest church, though he did preside at the weekday chapel services. Those services were, of course, obligatory for students, as everything for students was obligatory. The trustees took their first occasion in 1888 to nudge the faculty "in the most earnest terms" about their need to be there as well, and again two years later to signal their awareness that "nearly all" present was not good enough — they wanted them all at chapel. Taylor was on published record that the work at Wake Forest "be done by consistent men under distinctively Christian and Baptist influences, and that it shall never be forgotten that the College sustains to the Baptist State Convention and through it to the Kingdom of Christ on earth a close and vital relation." That use of "Christian" might sound generic, but thus far in the college's history there is no sign of faculty or administrators who were other than Baptists, and for all practical purposes Baptists so predominated that "Christian" functioned as a synonym. There were, however, some un-Baptist goings-on noticed among the students. It was reported near the end of the Taylor regime that "there is an unusual amount of drinking among the students — more than at any other college in the State."[23]

366

Doctor Billy

Taylor's successor, William Louis Poteat, known fondly as "Doctor Billy," was Wake Forest's first lay president (1905-27), a teacher of biology and natural history at the college since 1878. His brother was president at Furman, and William had just been elected president of Mercer University in Georgia and had to back out of that post to accept his alma mater's offer. He was a veteran song director at the Wake Forest chapel and church, and had always been a Sunday school teacher.

The college biographer, with one sweeping paragraph, narrates the deprecia-tion of chapel that began with Poteat's presidency.

> Gradually the change came about so that after a few years the chapel services were less reverent and worshipful. The members of the faculty no longer sitting on the platform facing the students but finding their places with them where they could on the benches, no longer exercised much influence even when they were present, and many of them left off attendance altogether. Complaint was sometimes made at faculty meetings and sometimes by the Trustees, but there was no improvement in attendance. Even before the loss of the Chapel by fire the service had become largely administrative, especially after the creation of the office of dean in 1912. The other members of the faculty [who had previously taken their turns in reading, commen-tating, or leading prayers], having no part in the services, left them to the president and the dean. There was no improvement after the services were put in charge of the college chaplain in 1932; since that time it often happens that neither president nor dean is present, and no member of the faculty except the one asked by the chaplain to speak at the service for that day. The neglect of the chapel services by the faculty has not been without deleterious effect on student attendance; why should they have greater interest than their teachers? Once, as if in mockery, the students kept a record of the attendance of faculty members and published it in the *Wake Forest Student.* This expedient made the members of the faculty squirm but it did not quicken them to reform. In fact, the character of the chapel services has been changed. At times only the semblance of worship is maintained. A fruitless effort has been made to increase interest by discussions of scientific, literary, political, historical, educational and social concern, to the minimizing of time for scripture-reading and prayer. Not infrequently the chapel periods are given over to musical programs and student meetings of various kinds. Thus the services have become largely secularized, and have remained so, even since they were put in charge of the college chaplain . . .[24]

The change was both unobtrusive and gradual. Another event of Poteat's administration was neither. Poteat was a forthright believer in evolution: a divinely guided enhancement found in all of creation. In the 1920s trench warfare was well under way between philosophically unequipped scientists who understood geology to have made creation intellectually untenable and theologically unequipped

367

preachers whose reading of Genesis 1–3 had God making light on Sunday and the sun on Thursday. Fierce attacks on Poteat were circulated through the state, and eventually he was put up to defend himself at the Baptist State Convention. Without even mentioning the word "evolution," he stood his ground as a doctrinally conservative Baptist, a scholarly biologist, and a devout man of the church. It was his acknowledged personal integrity that eventually put him in the clear. And it was an occasion for Wake Forest to make the exemplary amalgamation of learning and belief a point of honor among North Carolina Baptists.[25]

Since Wake Forest's founding ninety years earlier, its trustees had elected their successors from nominees approved by the state convention. From the Civil War onward this nominating process had been in abeyance. In 1912, with Columbian College and Brown, Colgate, and Rochester Universities all slipping out of their denominational ties, and the Methodists losing Vanderbilt and Randolph-Macon, the convention saw its "property . . . being caught up in the sweep of liberalism and materialism" and had the charters of its three colleges (Wake Forest now joined by Meredith [for women] and Thomasville) amended to provide that boards would continue to elect their successors, but that each election would now require confirmation by the state convention. The trustees were not entirely trusted.

In 1924 the issue arose again, under "Doctor Billy" Poteat. The Southern Baptist Convention had launched a denominational fund drive in the early 1920s, the 75 Million Campaign, from which Wake Forest was promised a stout portion. The fund was overpledged, but there were massive defaults when it came time to send in the dollars. This threw Wake Forest's financial stability awry and made the college more sensitive of its need to cultivate amiable relations with the state convention, especially when the evolution controversy was lending momentum to the notion that liberal colleges like Wake Forest ought to be cut off from all funding. It was in this atmosphere that a proposal was made to change the trustee election procedure. The convention took to itself the power both to nominate and to elect (or remove) all trustees. The boards could make any prior suggestions for their own successors that they wished. Wake Forest acquiesced in this new proposed amendment of its charter in the hope that a strengthened sense of ownership would make the North Carolina Baptists less carping patrons. Though the convention in fact settled into electing the candidates proposed by the colleges, the day would come when this legal move would bring much vexation upon the college.[26]

Religious Drift

The 1930s, however, were a season of religious drift for Wake Forest, though not one which set off alarms among North Carolina Baptists the way Poteat's stubborn acceptance of evolution had. There was also a drift of Baptists to other campuses. A survey in 1930-31 reported that while there were 435 North Carolina (male)

Baptists at Wake Forest that year, and 182 more at its little sister, Mars Hill College, there were 543 Baptists at Chapel Hill, 244 at North Carolina State, and 104 at Duke.[27]

In the midthirties the chaplain grieved that chapel was but twice a week and now voluntary, and "the student body as a whole has not generally participated."[28] It was not the same kind of student body as in the remembered past. Baptists numbered only two-thirds now, and although the next-largest cohorts were Methodists and Presbyterians, who, in the South especially, would be at home with the evangelism of the Baptists, now there were significant numbers of Catholics, Episcopalians, and Lutherans to whom it would be foreign.

From its earliest years the religious life at Wake Forest, college and town alike, had its artesian moments most years during the preaching of a revival, usually by an invited and charismatic pastor. There were years when classes would be suspended for two weeks if the revival began to work up strong momentum, and often one or two dozen converts, mostly students, would make their professions of faith and be baptized, giving a "revival" of joy to the entire congregation. But the revival in 1934 would be the last. Despite record attendance, the final three revivals had yielded a cumulative total of only four students baptized. In the nine years following, not more than a half-dozen students would be baptized. The flame flickered.

Historian George Washington Paschal, trying to unpuzzle this waning of evangelistic religion by hindsight a few years later, observed that even among students who "are regular in their attendance on Sunday school classes, little concern is manifested for the winning of their fellow students to Christ, while the idea is sometimes expressed that it is bigotry to have fixed religious beliefs, and that one man's religion is about as good as another's. The great majority of the students are doubtless true to the faith of the churches from which they come, but they have lost their aggressiveness; they no longer have what the students of the early days had, 'little Bethels,' where they retire to pray for the salvation of their fellow students."[29]

He identifies several causes. Weekends away, either at home or for varsity sports matches or even (for ministerial students) in service to country churches, deprived the college of its weekly worship as a congregation. A surge of interest in the foreign missions had been quenched when the failure of the 75 Million Campaign forced the Foreign Mission Board to recall many of its recent envoys for want of funds. The chief cause for evangelism's decline, however, was the new theology that had drawn people's attention to racial discrimination, unjust poverty, and warfare. Instead of revivals to convert individuals, they held conferences to convert governments.

One last cause for decline, according to Paschal, but surely the one which drew the most fire from the Baptist constituency, was a shift in recreational habits. This brings up the "Dancing Debacle." The first underground fraternity was discovered at Wake Forest in 1882. The reactions, in chronological order, were severe prohibition, then severe regulation, then supervision by the faculty, whose capacity for words without deeds eventually forced the president and trustees to approve fraternities formally. But, as Paschal notes, "Occupying chief place in the fraternity social life is the dance." Arrangements for dances in the early 1930s were exceedingly awkward. The college avoided taking responsibility for the dances by exiling them from the campus, yet implicitly claimed responsibility for them by requiring faculty supervision. The trustees in 1932 sought to finesse this by forbidding any publicity that could imply collegiate approval and give offense to the Baptists of the state who were opposed to dancing. There were many of them, and they were very opposed. The very mention in 1935 that the students had submitted a petition to use a new gymnasium for dancing brought the issue into the *Biblical Recorder,* the official journal for North Carolina Baptists. When the petition, said to have the support of 97 percent of the students and a majority of the faculty, was granted by the board, the *Biblical Recorder* reminded Wake Forest that those who had built up the school with their financial generosity "had on their hearts that the primary purpose of Wake Forest College from the first day until now has been to give our Baptist people an educated ministry for their churches . . . all else is secondary." They foresaw a year of turmoil in the convention. A storm of letters fell upon them, the annual collection for the budget was stalled, and the Baptist State Convention's secretary-treasurer quickly negotiated a compromise: the *Biblical Recorder* would stop publishing letters on the subject, and the Wake Forest trustees would reconsider their resolution. The issue was kept from the floor of the 1937 convention, but the report of the Committee on Social Service and Civil Righteousness included a stiff condemnation of dancing, "a custom so clearly calculated to injure and demoralize character," and resolved it should never be allowed at any Baptist institution in the state.

The students were parties to no compromise, however, and they became pointedly aggressive in publicizing their dances, always with the prohibited mention of the college name. In 1941 a new student move to hold a dance on campus was met by a board resolution threatening expulsion, which was awarded many "Amens" at the 1941 convention. The trustees reaffirmed the college's emphasis on spiritual values (always an ominous phrase) and rededicated themselves to the major purposes of the college.[30] During the war the president was still obliged to repeat the story that Wake Forest permitted no dancing whatever, but added that they could not, as a Baptist institution committed to individual freedom, dictate behavior by students when they were off campus.[31]

To move forward in time: the trustees in 1957 finally approved of dancing on campus when "properly chaperoned and properly supervised," and pastors rose in wrath across the state. The trustees, said the president of the Baptist State Convention, were "waving a red flag in a bull's face." Yet there were a few voices raised with a different timbre. A Wake Forest faculty member wrote: "We should confront the fact that man has the material power to destroy life on this planet, and the voice of Christian conscience is almost unheard; we should realize that the dark-skinned peoples in the world are toiling in revolt and we largely ignore the Golden Rule. In the light of these challenging problems our debate over dancing makes us appear ridiculous.'' But the next session of the convention, by a proportion of about five-to-one, reaffirmed the 1937 ban, and that persuaded the trustees to suspend their resolution.[32]

Other indices of Baptist character at Wake Forest were mixed. As mentioned previously, unlike Furman to the south, the college in its early years did not teach religion academically. Shortly after a Department of Bible was begun in 1896 the trustees forbade any of its courses to be required in the curriculum. In the early 1920s a faculty member was added to the department, and six credit hours in that subject were required; for ministerial students, further coursework was required.[33] Just at that time, however, an official faculty study named the Department of Bible and the Law School as those which had bent standards most to satisfy "our constituency." This stray datum suggests that the ministerial students may have been less academically equipped on average than the student body.[34]

Harold Tribble, a Determined Man

A pivotal administration would come to Wake Forest with the inauguration of Harold Wayland Tribble as president (1950-67). He was both preacher and academic, then serving as president of Andover-Newton Seminary in Massachusetts. Some trustees apparently thought that with a new and organized wave of fundamentalist sentiment washing over the Baptist State Convention and the prospect of a conservative takeover there, their new president might be an effective liaison with that sector of the North Carolina Baptists. It was not to be. Not at all.[35]

Wake Forest College in the early forties had been a conservative institution very stable in its clientele and development. Four out of five students were natives of North Carolina; one-third were the children of alumni. And the tuition and fees had not been raised in forty years. In 1946 an overture was made by the Reynolds family, of the R. J. Reynolds Tobacco Company, that would draw Wake Forest in a new direction, quite literally. Just as the Duke family had settled considerable wealth upon Trinity College, which then ripened into Duke University, the Reynolds family wished to take Wake Forest under its considerable patronage.[36] The first offer was for a family foundation to commit itself to an annual subsidy (representing roughly the income on $7 million) if the college would move to Winston-Salem, the Reynolds family's city, and if the Baptist State Convention would guarantee a continuance of its sponsorship and subsidies. A new campus would have to be built from footings to roof peaks, but there were hints of significant benefactions to follow, and thus it came to pass. There was, the trustees noticed, significant advantage in moving about one hundred miles westward, since the population toward that end of the state was much more white and Baptist than around Wake Forest.

The editor of the *Biblical Recorder,* in pondering such a benefaction, was put in mind of the line from *Julius Caesar:*

> There is a tide in the affairs of men,
> Which, taken at the flood, leads on to fortune.

It is unlikely he was aware that it was Brutus's wisdom. The trustees resolved without delay to accept the gift. The Baptist State Convention heard strong criticism from some of its pastors. One from Raleigh said that "our greatest need is not more education but a return to the spirit of Christ." Another asked whether Baptists were to be ruled by the New Testament or a package of Camels. Others said it boded badly for Baptists to be so beholden to the tobacco interests. The offer was then accepted by a vote reckoned to be 95 percent or more in favor.[37]

As the massive fund drive required by a new campus was well under way, President Tribble noted with chagrin that two-thirds of the Baptist congregations in the state had not contributed. Indeed, now the preponderance of financial support for the college was coming from beyond its Baptist constituency.

Criticism of Wake Forest as a liberal, heavy-drinking, godless school, which became more shrill as the temper of the denomination in North Carolina became more conservative, finally found a hearing among the trustees themselves. A committee began to hold hearings on President Tribble's performance in office. Questionnaires were circulated. A leak to the press finally embarrassed the trustees who were behind the harassment, and the inquiry was dropped.

The move to a new campus in 1956 put the college into greater prominence, which seemed to make it regionally and then nationally attractive . . . in proportion as it became exposed to more reproach from North Carolina Baptists. President Tribble had the intrepid capacity to antagonize groups in all directions. He dismissed several coaches who enjoyed great popularity, and he refused to assign the cafeteria and bookstore profits to the athletic department. Thence the ire of sports fans. But then he sustained mordant criticism for allowing the baseball team to play on a Sunday in the NCAA playoffs (a complaint somewhat softened by their championship). The school decided to allow dancing finally, and then backed off in the face of a strong rebuke by the convention (as already mentioned). His public relations director published a novel, *The Education of Jonathan Beam,* taken to be autobiographical, which depicted the harassment of a Baptist college at the hands of backward churchmen. Pastors throughout the state deplored it as "smut" and "indescribable filth," though some hailed it as "chocked full of truth about us Baptists." The campus magazine spoofed prayers at athletic events ("Prayers for All Athletic Occasions") and a Billy Graham crusade on campus ("W.F. to Forsake Sin"). After years of strong advocacy by student journalists and politicians and the Wake Forest Baptist Church, the trustees eliminated segregation in 1962 and black students began to be admitted. A subsequent poll revealed that the move had the support of less than half of the student body. Wake Forest was nevertheless the first major independent college in the South to abandon segregation. The Tribble era ran on much nervous energy.

In prospect of an expensive move to introduce graduate studies (projected to cost $69 million), the trustees voted to allow a minority of their own number to be exempt from the requirement to be North Carolinian and Baptist.[38] All of this provoked repeated carping by conservative pastors that Wake Forest was flouting convention directives and condoning lax morality. When one large group of pastors released a public statement to that effect just before the Baptist State Convention was due to meet, and Tribble complained it was not fair play, the reply was that they were just engaging in "good Baptist politics."[39]

Wake Forest was then put somewhat on the defensive. A report to the 1963 convention admitted that Baptists constituted 62 percent of the faculty and only 44 percent of the student body. The college gave ardent assurances that it continued to canvass North Carolina as its prime venue for students. It had obliged the student newspaper to remove liquor advertisements picturing students mixing drinks in a dormitory room. It described the *Jonathan Beam* problem as "painful" and "complicated," and apologized for whatever had been offensive to North Carolina Baptists, but it defended the decision not to dismiss the author. This "tensions report" only elicited a cannonade from 286 North Carolina churchmen, which in turn prompted statements of support from faculty and students, and from two thousand North Carolina Baptists.

The Wake Forest proposal to diversify its board membership achieved a majority vote at the convention but not the requisite two-thirds. Tribble went home defeated by the convention, but welcomed as never before by the college. At the next session in 1964 the same proposal was defeated even more soundly, as also a college request to accept federal building grants (in virtue of an abiding [though intermittent] Baptist aversion to accepting tax moneys and the resultant church-state entanglements). Sentiments on the Wake Forest board toward the convention were bitter and unforgetting, and there was quiet talk about taking the "millstone" from around their neck.[40]

Aggravated by the Convention

Tribble retired in 1967, leaving Wake Forest enormously advanced academically and financially. The trustees chose that as the moment to upgrade the college's status: henceforth it would be Wake Forest University. Years later Tribble identified the opposition to Wake Forest's hopes to be a great liberal institution: first, the board of trustees, and later, the Baptist State Convention. Opposition from the trustees had been neutralized when the conservative cohort within their membership had been eased aside. Tribble looked to no such political shift in the Baptist State Convention, and from the time of his retirement had quietly suggested that the trustees should somehow reclaim the autonomy they had once enjoyed before Doctor Billy Poteat had signed over ultimate control to the convention.[41]

It was an idea that was already gaining some momentum. Two years earlier the Council on Christian Higher Education of the Baptist State Convention (of which Tribble was a member *ex officio*) suggested a changed and very liberal relationship with colleges: a covenant between independent parties rather than authority by one over the other. Though the Baptist colleges had been called into being by their denominational parent, and owed the state convention deference, that presupposed they were free agents, not subordinates of the church. "It is not the denomination's responsibility to hover protectively over its colleges," but to respect that the "church-related college" (new phraseology for Southern Baptists) has its own work to do which complements but does not duplicate that of the church. In a long discussion of the "Christian teacher," the study noted that since Baptists constituted less than 10 percent of all registered teachers, Baptist colleges were going to be hard put to maintain their academic excellence if obliged to draw only on Baptists for teachers. "A college with an inbred faculty and a provincial outlook can afford only a stultifying environment which encourages prejudice and divisiveness. The presence of highly qualified Christian teachers of other Christian faiths is healthful and enriching to the faculties of Baptist colleges. Such teachers should have an informed appreciation of Baptist doctrines and should be in harmony with the aims of the colleges in which they teach." Likewise, though the colleges would give preference to Baptist applicants, their admissions policy would have to consider competitive academic qualifications as well. In a word, the colleges should be freed of denominational control and trusted to remain Baptist in both their teaching staff and their student bodies.[42]

Yet Wake Forest's record in this matter of Baptist personnel was one matter to which Tribble had not drawn public attention. In its earlier years, because the college had been founded and supported for the explicit purpose of educating young Southern Baptists for the ministry, the statistic that served as a quick index of fidelity to its calling was the percentage of students declared as ministers (in Baptist parlance they were already ministers, and so designated). This figure would vary, usually in the range of 20-25 percent. Another index was the number of students who were members of the Wake Forest Baptist Church. Since, however, the tendency among Baptist students was to retain official membership in their home congregations, this statistic also tended to be about what was normal in Southern Baptist colleges: 10-25 percent.[43]

It was only late in the college's history that any interest was evinced in how many students actually identified themselves as Baptist. In the earlier years their numbers were so predominant as not to require notice. It was only in 1927-28 that President Francis Pendleton Gaines (1927-30), in the course of his regular report to the trustees that 92 percent of the students were from North Carolina, 24 percent from within a radius of fifty miles, 30 percent from farm households, 17 percent the sons of merchants, and 5 percent the sons of ministers, also announced almost as an *obiter dictum* that 79 percent of them were Baptists.[44]

The percentage fluctuated for decades, but never very far. In 1930-31 it fell to 65 percent, rallied to 71 percent in 1933-34, then hit a valley of 58 percent in 1941-42 when the men went off to war. It bounded back to 70 percent in 1946-47 when the veterans came back to find the coeds there, and then it undulated through the low seventies and high sixties until the move to Winston-Salem in 1956. That year there were 70 percent Baptists at Wake Forest, but thereafter their presence began to wane yearly: 67, 66, and 62 percent, respectively. In 1959-60 this factor disappeared from the annual *Report of the President* and seems never again to have been systematically reported. A reconstruction of the unpublished data reveals, however, that it continued inexorably to descend: 44 percent in 1963-64, 41 percent in 1965-66, 39 percent in 1966-67 (Tribble's last year; Baptists had constituted 67 percent when he came). In the first year of James Ralph Scales's presidency there were 38 percent Baptists, and 25 percent in 1983 when he was succeeded by Thomas K. Hearn, Jr. In 1992-93 there were 18 percent. Baptists were sparser on the ground at Wake Forest than they were in North Carolina.[45] That figure continues to decline, as it has without exception since the move in 1956, so that in 1993-94 there would be more Catholics than Baptists in the Wake Forest student body, as the author and the WFU registrar were surprised to discover together one afternoon.[46]

Faculty are asked to declare their religious affiliation, but their responses are not, according to the office of the provost, entered into the university database, and one is unaware of their having been reported publicly for three decades.

But these facts about the Baptist depletion at Wake Forest may serve as a bass accompaniment to the melodic line that ensued between the university and the convention, for there was much that happened.

Open Hostilities

The obvious prosperity of the university continued to alienate some elements within the denomination. In 1970, for instance, Baptists United for Spiritual Survival called for a cutoff of convention aid to Wake Forest, since the school was now so dependent on the Z. Smith Reynolds Foundation and the federal government. The annual convention subsidy, which at the time was $400,000, was in any case a small fragment of the annual operating budget.[47] At the 1974 convention Rev. Cecil Sherman rose to move a one percent reduction of annual grants to their colleges, and reallocation of that amount to more biblical missions. He was not willing "to subsidize the education of young people who must be somewhat prosperous, else they would not be at Wake . . . I do not accuse the university of teaching heresy. I do say that the school is not a mission and has little claim to lay upon mission money."[48]

Wake Forest stirred itself to flourish the breadth of its Baptist commitment in a handsome brochure: "A Partnership of Faith and Learning." The Department of Religion, with nine full-time and two part-time faculty, most of whom were Baptist college or seminary graduates, was showcased with their credentials and interests. The continuing education program offered Baptist ministers preaching workshops and Sunday school preparation workshops. Campus ministry, with a university chaplain, was augmented by denominational chaplains (Baptists were now on a par with the Methodists and Presbyterians in that their chaplain no longer claimed to serve the university) and took an active part in freshman orientation. Voluntary chapel worship on Thursday mornings was regularly led by students. The big worship event of the year, the Moravian Lovefest (complete with candles, coffee, and Moravian buns), prepared a congregation of eight hundred for Christmas. There were various fellowship programs, outreach to the community, and Bible study, along with vocational discernment groups. With nearby Belmont Abbey College (Catholic) the Ecumenical Institute sponsored a full annual program. The brochure was highlighted by a quotation from Harold T. P. Hayes, a trustee:

> Twice a year at board meetings, I have listened with awe as faculty and administration have struggled, without a whit of self-consciousness, to define that special quality a Wake Forest education should provide for its students. Always this tension — the imperatives of faith against the imperatives of scholarship — underlies the dialogue. I hope we never lose it. It sends us out into the world with perhaps a little more guilt than our contemporaries, but guilt is a concomitant of responsibility, and that's all right, too.[49]

Alas, shortly after the appearance of this brochure another untoward event would jangle the nerves of North Carolina Baptists. The president of the Men's Residence Council decided to sponsor a campus debate on pornography and invited Larry Flynt, publisher of *Hustler* magazine, and Pastor Coy Privette, president of the Baptist State Convention of North Carolina, to speak to either side of the issue. Practically on the day of the debate, Privette sent word that he could not appear, but promised to speak separately two nights later. Flynt appeared before a packed house and was somehow acclaimed "Man of the Year" by the sponsors. Privette later gave a quiet talk to a small audience. The press, of course, simply carried a story about Wake Forest exalting the publisher of America's hindmost hard-porn magazine, and a wildfire burnt across North Carolina.[50] President Scales, privately furious at the convention president for having ducked out of the encounter and publicly furious at the students for having made it appear that Flynt had been officially honored, chose to defend the event as consonant with the Baptist tradition of freedom and Wake Forest's reputation, dating back to Joe McCarthy days, of denying its speaker's platform to no one. The college had at one time been on record as ready to receive any speaker banned at Chapel Hill (Duke having made the same offer).[51]

It would probably have been better to tell the constituency what had really happened. As it was, the next year Wake Forest was presented with the prestigious

Alexander Meiklejohn Award by the American Association of University Professors for its valorous defense of academic freedom. The administration claimed it was for a long history of open discourse, but the preachers in the western mountain towns saw it as confirmation of all that was shameful in Winston-Salem. President Scales' only consolation, and not much of one, would come at the hands of Ruth Carter Stapleton, Jimmy Carter's evangelist sister, who announced about six months later that Flynt had been born again as her Christian convert. He continued, nevertheless, to Hustle.[52]

In November 1977, vexed by what they considered a passive trustee response to the Flynt affair, the Baptist State Convention forbade the university to accept part of a federal research grant. The convention had a standing policy since 1959 that federal funding could be accepted by its colleges and hospitals only for services rendered, never as an outright grant. This $300,000 National Science Foundation curriculum grant to the Biology Department passed muster, except for one $85,000 line item to construct a greenhouse. The convention, whose pique had been aroused by the fact that Wake Forest had snubbed its committee charged with advance clearance of federal grants and had signed the contract, instructed the university to refuse that portion of the grant. The trustees went back to Winston-Salem and defied the convention by accepting it. "We desire no conflict with our Convention. Wake Forest is unashamedly a Christian institution and seeks to shape its goals, policies and practices by Christian ideals."[53]

Events hastened unashamedly toward divorce. The executive committee of the general board of the convention decided to press the issue of governance. Surely it had a claim on the university's compliance. And how authentically Baptist was Wake Forest, anyway? they asked. Chapel had not been compulsory since 1968; now only three credits in religion were required; one hundred out of a student body of three thousand attended Thursday chapel, and only six hundred to eight hundred, town and gown combined, joined at the Sunday service.

The convention's executive committee reminded the trustees that in 1950 they had rejected an entire $700,000 federal grant to Baptist Hospital by a vote of 3,000 to 100. It was pointed out in return that recently the hospital had become free to accept building grants, and the denominational office admitted it was inconsistent to hold hospitals and universities to different standards.[54]

Pastors began to be heard, as is their nature. Rev. Frank Ellis of Greenville: "We as a Convention do not give enough support financially to really stick our nose into its affairs as much as we do." In that year Wake Forest had received $800,000 from the convention and $820,000 from Reynolds toward its $52 million operating budget.[55] Another pastor (and WFU alumnus), Rev. W. W. Findlater of Raleigh, wrote that the Baptist preachers themselves were the problem. Like all clergy, he observed, they see "their possession of 'the whole truth' being challenged, feel threatened and discomfited and move to restrain and control the institution by raising questions of ownership and direction."[56] Four past presidents of the convention wrote a circular to all pastors in the state and urged them to show their concern by attending the General Board meeting (the sitting president quickly suggested letters or calls instead). Fifty ministers did crowd into the meeting room as a show of concern.[57] When President Scales pointed out that 93 of Wake Forest's 4,500 students were heading for ministry and church-related vocations, a minister replied that this 2 percent figure was not that awesome, when at Southwest Baptist College in Bolivar, Missouri, 632 students out of 1,700 were studying to be preachers, and 69 to be foreign missionaries.[58]

In the end: compromise. The trustees transferred $85,000 in supplemental operating funds to the Biology Department and at the same time accepted the same amount in federal funds to build a greenhouse. Thus any interested party could satisfy himself or herself by thinking that the facility was built with university or with government funds.[59] Yet this was not truly the end.

The First Break

Only nine months later in 1978, after a November convention meeting that the trustees again found frustrating, they came back to campus and decided to rewrite the Wake Forest charter, deleting the provision that described the university as an agency of the Baptist State Convention and — as was within their power — withdrawing the convention's power to elect trustees and the requirement that all trustees be North Carolina Baptists. The president of the convention forthwith cut off the annual subsidy and put the funds in escrow: "It is no longer a Baptist institution. It is a private institution that wants to work closely with Baptists."[60]

But within the year a new compromise had been reached. The convention and the university decided in 1979 to enact a covenant, effective 1 January 1981. The convention would discontinue subsidizing the university, but congregations could earmark special contributions they would send through the convention office. One-third of the trustees need not be North Carolina residents or Baptists. At the very last minute, an amendment from the floor altered this heavily brokered compromise by adding the requirement that all trustees be members of an "evangelical Christian denomination," the obvious intention being to exclude Catholics and Jews. This last proviso caused considerable gnashing of teeth at Wake Forest, but the trustees eventually consented to the covenant.[61] The covenant itself was a fulsome document, with abundant accounts of how much the convention and the university meant to one another, now that the latter was only "church-related." The convention would assure its support, both tangible and intangible, while the university would "express clearly [its] commitment to Christian objectives and to Baptist principles" by open declaration of its relationship, by "making the values of the church clearly recognizable" in campus life, and by endeavoring "to bring to its learning community faculty and administrators who are committed to the purposes of the University as an institution that shapes its goals, policies, and practices by Christian ideals; who understand that the Christian faith is part of the institution's common life; and who are committed to excellence in scholarship and teaching and to the intellectual and spiritual development of students."[62]

The dynamics of progressive estrangement between convention and university were being driven by authorities at the top of each institution. In the convention, that meant Rev. Mark Corts, the elected president that year, and Rev. Cecil A. Ray, the executive secretary. In the university it meant James Mason, Esq., president of the board of trustees. One level down, there was less animus and ego. James Ralph Scales, Wake Forest president, and Rev. T. Robert Mullinax, executive secretary of the convention's council on Christian higher education, were less inclined to confrontation and separation.

The various recollections in Wake Forest's Oral History Project portray this. Secretary Ray is depicted as an outsider from Texas where Baptist schools are "owned and operated" by the denomination, who came to his post determined to lessen the denomination's heavy financial outlay to its colleges and to shift some of that funding to evangelism operations. His custom of inquiring how many of the faculty or the students were Baptists was considered an insulting manifestation of an intrusive, "managerial" style.[63] His own account of the situation is that the negotiations came thirty years too late, and were futile. The covenant was like a divorce in a family, but the estrangement had been progressive and thorough, and the more recent imbroglios like the Larry Flynt affair had been symptoms of a long-standing loss of Baptist character.[64] Presiding trustee Mason, on his side, had become impatient with the too-congenial Scales and pushed him from the center of the negotiations in ways that some found demeaning. Convinced that the denomination would never leave the university free to be a scholarly place, he had determined well before the covenant that Wake Forest had to be free of Baptist control.[65]

Mullinax showed his own capacity for mediation in *On Mission: The Church/College Alliance, the Purpose and Role of North Carolina Baptist Colleges and Universities*. North Carolina Baptists, "once a largely uneducated people," had nevertheless been pioneers in education. Sometimes their motivation was no different from that of one association in 1889:

> Education is power. Proper education is power for good, a power which cannot be overestimated . . . This will apply to denominations as well as individuals. We, as Baptists, must not ignore the education of our people if we would expect the greatest power in uplifting the masses and aggressively prosecute the work assigned to us.

It is not proper, Mullinax wrote, to ask how Baptist colleges are "different," since at every educational level it was the churches which had led the way in founding schools and the states which followed. Church colleges were the norm setters, not the followers. "A Baptist college is a community of faith and learning . . . blended so that faith can give direction and meaning to learning, and so learning can give enlightenment to faith." A "Christian" college is not going to be perfect, any more than a Christian home or a Christian denomination is going to be. (This by way of answer to those who said "Christian college" was an unreachable ideal.) But like them it sets out to be of service to God and one's fellows, with a good capacity for forgiveness, reconciliation, and renewal along the way. Trustees are chosen by the convention, because "Baptists have agreed that it is neither possible nor wise to direct the affairs of institutions from the floor of the annual session of the Convention." As for faculty:

> Baptist colleges seek to enlist faculty members who are well prepared to teach in their respective fields and whose personal qualifications are compatible with the heritage and purpose of the schools. During the employment interview, prospective faculty are acquainted with the church relatedness of the college and the purpose of the institution. Great care is given to seek Christian faculty, persons who are comfortable teaching on a Baptist college campus, and those whose personal beliefs and lifestyles are not in conflict with the basic purposes of Christian higher education.

As for students, "It is the strong desire of the Baptist colleges to enroll an increasing number of young people from Baptist churches." Why should Baptist people support their colleges? Because "the moral and ethical climate in the society, the enforced secularity of state-supported higher education, and the condition of man — make mandatory the idea of Christian higher education."[66]

Mullinax writes mostly in the optative mood. What history had actually shown was that some North Carolina Baptists had fostered schools, while many others had been suspicious of them. There was still many a North Carolina Baptist who, if he were a careful reader, would snag on Mullinax's statement that learning could give enlightenment to faith, because his belief was that it worked just the other way around. Others would notice the special pleading in the "we're not perfect" passage, but would simply have responded that it was the duty, then, of the responsible college officers to be openly accountable to the denomination and sometimes to get roughed up by "messengers" to the convention, as Baptist delegates are called. A really shrewd reader would quickly observe what soft, passive language was used to define the faculty: Christian but not Baptist; required to be compatible and comfortable but not protagonists; "not opposed," instead of actively witnessing. An attentive Baptist would have fastened on the plea for more Baptist students if he was aware that this very year the downward sag of Baptist enrollment approached the one-quarter mark. As for moral and ethical climate, a discerning Baptist would grumble that this was the very issue: Wake Forest was managing to fade into the landscape of secularity, and doing so without even the enforced norms the law imposed on Chapel Hill. The only difficulty was that most Baptists canny and astute enough to critique Mullinax's proacademic prose were likely to be educated, and therefore uncritical readers. Those who intuited that this was propaganda — the worst kind, which even its purveyors believed — were likely to be ill-mannered rustics from the hinterlands.

For those who watched Wake Forest on the move there would have been only light curiosity when the trustees issued "Wake Forest University: 2000 Study" in 1983, a document intended to define the university's hopes for future development. "The Baptist Relationship" is not blended into the Mission and Goals statement, but finally makes its way onstage at page 22. Keynoting with a cheerleading "We are and we ought to remain the finest Baptist-related university in the world," the document ambiguously commits itself "to universal Biblical religion through its Baptist expression." "Wake Forest can remain broadly ecumenical in its purposes while retaining its specific Baptist identity." The covenant "insures that the University will not become an instrument for merely sectarian purposes." "The University has a need to maintain a solid contingent of Baptist administrators, faculty, and students; a sizable company of other scholars who are sympathetic with the religious character of the University; and a significant number of critics who insure our honesty by challenging our basic assumptions and traditions." The critical Baptist reader would note that this last policy statement was a sharp departure from earlier aspirations that all faculty might at the very least find Wake Forest's Baptist heritage compatible. One would also observe that these three cohorts were listed in descending order of the university's need but ascending order of its efforts.[67]

The Baptist congregations did not take up the financial slack after the state convention discontinued its direct funding of Wake Forest. The convention's last direct subsidy, in 1980, amounted to $987,000. In 1981 only one church in every seven had earmarked a contribution for Wake Forest, for a total congregational subsidy of about $300,000. The Z. Smith Reynolds Foundation loyally increased its annual gift.[68]

In 1983 Cecil Ray stepped down as executive secretary at the state convention. President Scales was asked to resign at Wake Forest, and was replaced with Thomas K. Hearn, Jr., a Baptist minister who had become a philosopher and a Presbyterian (out of frustration with the denomination's attitudes on the race issue, it was said). After a while at Wake Forest, however, he and his family formally joined the Wake Forest Baptist Church. It was just about time to give the covenant its formal review before its five-year term expired.[69] The Wake Forest representatives came to those meetings in a restless mood, since the nominations committee at the convention had not been perfunctorily sending the board's own nominations for trustee elections to the convention floor. Instead, there had been queries, and requests for fuller documentation. This could only remind Wake Foresters of the days when, at Ray's initiative, the nominations committee had undertaken to replace the board's nominees with faithful but uneducated missionaries returned from years of service abroad, or faithful Sunday school teachers, or deacons.[70]

They negotiated a new covenant, providing that the trustees would be given final say in electing that one-third of their number who might be non–North Carolinians or non-Baptists. Approved successively by the Board of Christian

Higher Education, the Executive Committee, and the General Board, the covenant was turned down by the 1985 convention for want of a two-thirds affirmation. Once again the trustees took their leave and grimly gathered in Winston-Salem. Days later they voted themselves the power to elect all their successors without any convention approval. The trustees assured the convention that their action was "a reaffirmation of Wake Forest University's basic commitment to God and to the Baptist State Convention of North Carolina." They promised *ex officio* seats on the board to the executive secretaries of both the convention and its Board of Christian Higher Education, and the election of not less than four ministers.[71]

The Final Break

In the year that followed anger rose and fell, and partisans at either end of the argument for quite opposite reasons agreed it was time for the two institutions to go their separate ways. So at the 1986 convention the denomination yielded all claim to governance and Wake Forest yielded all claim to funding. The earlier offer of board seats to convention executives had evaporated during the intervening months. Wake Forest's public relations officer, author of the troublesome *Jonathan Beam,* did his best to turn water into wine: "At the same time, Baptist beliefs and traditions, and a relationship with the Convention which provides an opportunity for sharing in those beliefs and traditions, will continue to give Wake Forest University a unique perspective and unique opportunities in Christian higher education."[72] Once again, an attentive reader would have asked how Wake Forest, by simply providing an "opportunity" to share in Baptist beliefs and traditions, would differ from the University of North Carolina or even nearby Belmont Abbey College, where such opportunity also existed.

Reactions to this final severance were understandably varied. Two days later the *Winston-Salem Journal,* which had been so supportive of the university during its wrangles with Raleigh, ran its editorial under the headline "Wake Forest Goes Secular." The message was much more ambivalent than on previous occasions:

> The trustees will pick their own successors. The university will face no great threat to academic freedom, save perhaps the threat that comes from the surprising complacency that exists on many campuses.
>
> If there is a practical down side to the freeing of Wake Forest, this is it. While the lectern has been saved from the intrusion of moral majoritarians and the will to power that even the self proclaimed pure of heart seem obsessed by these days, something of the love for deeper questions has also been lost. As higher education becomes wholly secularized it may also become trivial. . . . How to preserve a sense of the perennial questions, the higher law and the common good on campuses given over not only to the secular but the current? To progress? To growth? To vocational, even lifestyle facilitation?[73]

From the campus came more affirmative comments. Barry G. Maine, assistant professor of English (B.A., Virginia; Ph.D., Chapel Hill): "Wake Forest is clearly in transition from a small Baptist college to becoming one of the more prestigious colleges in the Southeast." The breakup with the Baptist State Convention will help that transition. "It means the university can now define ourselves any way we want to. We don't have to look over our shoulders any more."[74]

President Hearn, in his Founder's Day address in February, said this:

Baptists are a worthy people. They deserve a university representative of their best and noblest contributions to the culture. Wake Forest has a unique and special opportunity to be that institution. To be a Baptist university in this sense is not to be narrowly sectarian. It is to be open, waiting and expectant. To be a Baptist university is to celebrate the diversity that results from a tradition grounded in freedom, autonomy and independence in the context of a community of faith and service. . . . "Diversity in all things" is all but the Baptist motto. Let it ever be so at Wake Forest.[75]

The current bylaws speak of Wake Forest's "Baptist and Christian heritage" in a lengthy prose excursus:

Far from being exclusive and parochial, this religious tradition gives the University roots that ensure its lasting identity and branches that provide a supportive environment for a wide variety of faiths. The Baptist insistence on both the separation of church and state and local autonomy has helped to protect the University from interference and domination by outside interests, whether these be commercial, governmental, or ecclesiastical. The Baptist stress upon an uncoerced conscience in matters of religious freedom has been translated into a concern for academic freedom. The Baptist emphasis upon revealed truth enables a strong religious critique of human reason, even as the claims of revelation are put under the scrutiny of reason. The character of intellectual life at Wake Forest encourages open and frank dialogue and provides assurance that the University will be ecumenical and not provincial in scope, and that it must encompass perspectives other than the Christian. Wake Forest thus seeks to maintain and invigorate what is noblest in its religious heritage.[76]

The bylaws require that the Baptist constituencies be "fully and appropriately represented," and that "the membership of the Board consists of persons who will honor the University's commitment to services to Baptist causes," but no actual Baptists are now required for such compliance.[77]

What happened in 1986? President Hearn has repeatedly and publicly affirmed that this "voluntary and fraternal" relationship will free the university to enhance its Baptist commitment in ways even more appropriate to its intellectual calling.[78] His tendency, however, to drift into reductive terminology, and to constrict the Baptist faith to autonomy and diversity, makes one wish for further clues as to his purposes. His quieter afterthoughts about the North Carolina Baptist State Convention may be of help:

> This particular tie to a particular denomination and a specific state through an organization that meets two and a half or three days a year in the midst of boredom and bedlam — I have never believed that this particular association had very much to do with whatever was this larger institutional heritage.[79]

There may be in prospect, then, a more spacious vision of the Baptist heritage than can be entertained within the cramped atmosphere of the North Carolina Baptist perspective. This might be a summoning of the Wake Forest community to a higher cubit of faith. He goes on:

> I would hasten to say that much will depend on what happens in Baptist life, and Wake Forest will have nothing to do with a heritage or with a specific denominational tie to an organization that has no commitment to freedom of thought, and no respect for diversity and the tolerance of the views of others, which are, in our view, historic Baptist commitments. . . .
>
> There is a new orthodoxy developing among Southern Baptists with which Wake Forest has nothing in common. Therefore, our Baptist heritage, what this institution stands for, may in the future have less and less to do with the specific denominational organizations through which we have had that heritage transmitted to us.[80]

It is understandable that Dr. Hearn would hold some of the more cantankerous elements among the North Carolina Baptists at arm's length. They were the heirs of the old adversaries, the Separate, revivalist, Spirit-assured, and antimissionary Baptists who had never trusted the sincerity of higher learning. The story is told of his first public appearance on campus after word of his election had been published. He had driven up in the hot summertime to meet the faculty and others, and a good number of preachers decided that they would come to the reception and have a look at the new president for themselves. When Hearn got tired of shaking hands, he said he was exhausted and left. His wife got up and said she would be glad to answer any questions, but some saw it as a first glimmer of contempt for the preachers come down from the hills.

An Oral History Project at Wake Forest has gathered some perspectives on the "voluntary and fraternal relationship" that marked the end of a Baptist identity at Wake Forest. Dr. Warren Carr, who served as pastor of the Wake Forest Baptist Church from 1964 to 1985, states in his interview that he had been a supporter of change.

> It began to be apparent to me that the Convention no longer had the wisdom, nor the right attitude. They did not even have sufficient integrity to run an

educational institution like Wake Forest. I had been, throughout the years, against a separation, but I was convinced that separation was inevitable, or the change of governance. And, in fact, wrote Dr. Hearn to that effect.

I . . . did so in light of Dr. Hearn's statements, public and to me privately, that once the governance issue was settled, he intended Wake Forest to have an even stronger relationship with Baptists than it had had at any previous time.[81]

But with a later hindsight Carr takes another view:

I think Wake Forest has gone the way of all the flesh, educationally speaking, and I do not think it has kept faith with its promise. I see no evidence since the time of that separation that Wake Forest is in the slightest inclined to strengthen ties with Baptist people and Baptist churches in North Carolina or anywhere else. There is simply indifference, if not a growing contempt for things Baptist on the part of this University.[82]

Asked later to enlarge upon this, Carr remembered contacting the president after the charter change. This was the tenor of Carr's message: "Now that we're free, I presume to make some suggestions about strengthening the [Baptist] ties. I've never been much to believe in what is called 'Christian atmosphere' on an academic campus. Anything you believe in is worth programming. If and when you should leave here in any foreseeable future, then your attitude is not likely to carry over to the next president." Hearn's response was: "I've resolved not to think about it," by which Carr understood he had resolved to ignore the matter, not just for the time being, but for good.[83]

A Repugnance for the Preachers

It would seem that in turning aside from the Baptist State Convention, Wake Forest did not do so to retain and enhance any more compelling account of Christian faith. Rather than taking the preachers' crabbed faith as a distortion and turning to some other Baptist fellowship, they seem to have turned away from the Baptist enterprise entirely. This faith is insubstantial enough never to be invoked except in perfunctory ways, as is implied in the increasing disposition to speak of the faith on campus as Christian, rather than Baptist.

Hearn's repugnance to what the preachers are and stand for was widespread — indeed, it is standard — among the educational elite. Edgar Christman, Wake Forest's chaplain since 1954, first reacted to the severance with disappointment: "I recognize the potential problem that could come with the Convention telling us how to run the school. But aren't we prepared to take a little criticism without calling it a violation of academic freedom?"[84] Now he thinks otherwise: "I've been proved wrong because it's clear the present leadership in the Southern Baptist Convention, however long it lasts, is destructive of education. It's destructive of religion. . . . So, Wake Forest's freedom is an absolute necessity."[85] Russell Brantley, now retired as Wake Forest's director of communications, says: "The Baptist State Convention of North Carolina is not as conservative as the Southern Baptist Convention. Nevertheless, it's conservative enough for me. A crowd of 30 poets frightens me and 3,000 religious fanatics scare the hell out of me."[86]

Rev. Mark Corts, who had been president of the convention in 1977-78 when the covenant was being negotiated, describes what he perceived as "anti-clerical bias": "There were constant references, 'We're not going to let you dumb preachers run Wake Forest.' And I got that cloaked in many phrases. And, again, that was uniquely Wake Forest bias, . . . that saw this as a handful of white socks, polyester-suited clergymen, uneducated, using poor grammar, without an understanding of the nuances of academic freedom, et cetera, et cetera, who were trying to foist their philosophies upon Wake Forest."[87] James Ralph Scales describes how James Mason, the board chairman, came by his animus toward the denomination's official authorities: "I believe (he got this conviction) at the Dancing Convention in '57. He had spoken to me of the unfairness of the way the convention was constituted. They bussed in all of the Aunt Minnies and Uncle Toms. Several associational missionaries filled their cars with children. They had seven-, and nine-, and eleven-year-old children standing, voting, on the great issues affecting higher education. . . . At that point I think Mason thought, 'This is no way to run an institution of higher learning, from the floor of a Convention.' "[88]

Corts has this recollection of dealing with Scales as convention president to university president:

> I remember being in the boardroom, next to his office there at the University one day, and I made this statement: "Just please convey, if you're going, for instance, to hire professors who are not professing Christians, at least hire those with respect for the Christian religion, as Davidson College did." When Davidson College eliminated its Confession of Faith that had to be signed by faculty — being a confessional church they had one — at least they made the requirement that all faculty members would have profound respect for the Christian religion. Don't hire somebody on the faculty, as was related to me, who was in profound disagreement, and had taken a confrontational stance against Christianity.
>
> Then your charter says, "This shall be an institution of Christian higher education." I can remember saying to Dr. Scales, "Please convey back to us how you intend to fulfill that charter." And he would roll his eyes in characteristic fashion, and say, "We don't need to defend ourselves to anyone."

Warren Carr, who served as pastor throughout Scales's presidency, recalls some quite different attitudes toward churchmen:

So long as the university was in a sense intellectually faulting the Baptists, Scales knew what was going on. When that kind of challenge began to dissipate, then of course the university's mission began to merge with the mission of any university, and he didn't know what to do with that. He also always welcomed the criticism of Baptists. He would chuckle when a moderately well-educated Baptist preacher would criticize the university or take issue with a professor — not out of any intellectual knowledge, but on the basis of what he considered revelation. Scales thought there was something to that. He and I were on a panel here on the campus and someone . . . asked me what did I think was the primary justification for the presence of the church on the campus. I said if we do no more than laugh at the pretense of the university we have fulfilled our mission. Scales said he thought this was right.[89]

The old Separate Baptists of the eighteenth century live on among the Southern Baptists today, and their confidence in the Spirit lives on in the rural preachers whom Wake Forest regards as arrogant and ignorant. In recent years the Separate tradition has surfaced in a newly powerful movement that has taken over the SBC and some of the state conventions. Those in authority at Wake Forest found it tiresome and impertinent for officials of the convention to hold them accountable for the fulfillment of duties they themselves publicly acknowledged: nominating trustees with some demonstrated devotion to the denomination; appointing faculty with active Baptist membership or sympathies; gathering a student body who would want and help the university to be tangibly Baptist. They bridled at the questions because these were tasks they were not accomplishing. The presidents were embarrassed to admit to academics that it was their duty, and embarrassed to admit to Baptists that they were defaulting on it.

Consider one typical rednecked, white-socks, polyester-suited North Carolina Baptist, writing just after the Wake Forest trustees had said they were going their own way:

Sir:

In the January 4 issue of the *Biblical Recorder,* I believe the question raised why the decline in baptisms in our churches was answered in two other articles.

First the controversy of Wake Forest University. Was it not Wake Forest that was one of the first to demand dancing be allowed on college campuses? Then the demands got larger and more bold until the tail now wags the dog instead of the dog wagging the tail in my opinion.

How many raised on the dance floor are now involved in the trustee takeover?

Second you featured the story of a church having a cornshucking, pot pie supper, and dancing. I believe dancing is a form of sexual stimulation. The Bible tells us he that soweth to the flesh shall of the flesh reap corruption, but he that soweth to the Spirit shall of the Spirit reap life everlasting.

Also the damsel danced before the king and he promised to give her up to

387

half of his Kingdom. Her request upon advice of her mother was the head of John the Baptist.

I believe the world is winning the church instead of the church winning the world. I believe this is why baptisms are down.

I thank God for a Christian mother who stopped a dance before it really got started at our first cornshucking and pot pie supper. At the next one she had a gospel singing.

Today my brother and I practice wagon train, barbecue supper, and gospel singing. Jesus Christ said, if I be lifted up I will draw all men unto me. I doubt if Jesus is lifted up on a dance floor. I believe when we again lift up Jesus Christ instead of another's wife or husband, we shall see baptisms go up.

Charles J. Wagner
Hickory, N.C.[90]

It is doubtful that one such as Charles Wagner would ever find his way to Wake Forest and enroll as a student. If he did, one can only imagine what might follow from such a synergistic collision. There would, of course, be a collision of manners, and Charles might come to see that dancing, while often engaged in precisely because it is sexually stimulating, also allows of chaste and gracious usage. He might. His fraternity brothers and instructors might come to see that there are some other forms of social intercourse that are truly delightful and even more liable to encourage friendship than those which involve substance abuse or erotic pursuit. They might. It would be much more likely to come to pass if they and he shared a Baptist faith and allegiance. It would be as chancy for him to see they are not all libertines as for them to see he is not all clodhopper.

But the deeper encounter between Charles and the campus would be one of morals, not manners. Charles might come to a twofold realization: that there are things a lot more morally significant at Wake Forest (and in the world) than dancing; and that he has exhausted his moral energy in identifying what he must avoid, and saved too little to search out what things he must pursue. His buddies and mentors might, in their turn, be helped by his presence to come to a twofold realization of their own: that this *simplicissimus* could be a lot more open to discovery than they are, and that the moral disorder of their life might be a drag on their mind's work.

And this collision of hick and hip might have another yield: of the mind and of the spirit. Charles might learn that his knowledge of Jesus' call has suffered much from his backwardness, and he might realize especially that to venerate the prophets and apostles whose writings are handed on to him he must make the effort to put them in context and find what they meant to say to their addressees. His Wake Forest companions might realize that any wisdom of theirs which they cannot put to the test of Charles's mind, imagination, and conscience might, no matter what its currency in the *Chronicle of Higher Education,* be culture-bound and biased.

But, of course, Charles Wagner will neither seek nor be welcomed at Wake Forest. He and his will go one way; they and theirs, another. And each group will thereby justify the worst that their antagonists think of them.

Indeed, were Charles Wagner to leaf through the student newspaper just a few years later, it might be hard to persuade him that Wake Forest was anything his fellow Baptists might want to sponsor or join. In the final issue of the 1992-93 academic year, for instance, items such as this would be spread on the page:

> A spokesman for the delegation from the Gay, Lesbian and Bisexual issues Awareness Group just back from the gay rights march in Washington said the march left him virtually paralyzed with emotion. "It was the most spiritually charged thing I ever felt. It was like a catapult whose cord had been cut. (Our spirits) were vaulted into the air and we kept rising and rising."
>
> Local taverns placed large ads advertising Thursday as "Free-Draft Night," or "Ladies with Wake ID in FREE" for Friday night specials.
>
> Students enrolled in the Gay and Lesbian Literature and Theory course held a public symposium on "Queer Theory." One student who presented her paper on homosexuality and Christianity, "Why God Is on Our Side," explained, "I'm looking at the liberating side of God in that God is on the side of the oppressed and wants them to be free."
>
> A graduating senior offered his valedictory interpretation of the campus architecture: "The chapel, in all its phallic glory, seems to represent the faculty and administration's uncanny ability to screw the students whenever they see fit to. . . . The students, being the sperm of the phallic symbol, are ejaculated into the world after this orgasm of graduation. The dorms around the Quad are the testicles of the school where the sperm are housed until they are ready for ejaculation. . . . The feminine Reynolda Hall eternally beckons the chapel in all its enormity. Reynolda beckons in the hopes that some of the sperm will circulate back into the system so that the system will perpetuate itself . . ."
>
> An art student, joined by more than a dozen volunteers, created a gathering place for women on campus by carving eight sandstone blocks left over from a new school of law and management into female figures, mostly goddesses.[91]

In the old days that would have brought the preachers down from the hills.

The claim made by those presiding at Wake Forest was that there are other vital relationships possible with the Baptist State Convention of North Carolina than submission, and that the university's Baptist character stood to be enhanced by the dissolution of the legal bond. "Wake Forest thus seeks to maintain and invigorate what is noblest in its religious heritage," say the new bylaws. "The recent action does not, then, mark a 'secularization' of the University as some reporters opined. We remain determined to serve the Baptists of North Carolina and the denomination at large in all those ways in which we have in the past sought to advance our common aims," asserted President Hearn.[92]

The facts, however, suggest that termination of the convention's supervisory powers was only a punctuation mark within a lengthy and unrelieved process of shucking a Baptist tradition that had been an embarrassment and was now becoming a threat.

Other Baptist Universities Go Independent

Severance of educational institutions from Southern Baptist control has become more common of late. In 1990 three major breaches took place. The first affected Baylor University in Texas, the largest Southern Baptist university. Already in 1984, students representing the fundamentalist ascendancy among Texas Baptists had been asserting that "Baylor blasphemes the name of Christ." A manifesto demanded the dismissal of any faculty members who refused to provide "a written account of their salvation experience" or failed to give active support to the pro-life movement.[93] In September Baylor University took back control over regent selection from the Baptist General Convention of Texas, which promptly suspended disbursements of its annual $6 million subsidy. President Herbert H. Reynolds explained: "We are, and we will remain a Texas Baptist institution, as we have been since 1845. We are not Baptists because of the Convention or because of the funds we receive from the Convention, but rather because of our commitment to Christ, to historic Baptist principles, to the mission and goals of Texas Baptists, and to what once were the mission and goals of a now much changed Southern Baptist Convention."[94]

Baylor promptly incurred a $6 million deficit in its annual operating fund. Strenuous negotiations between the two parties ensued, and in the summer of 1991 a compromise was struck. Baylor would elect three-quarters of the new regents, and the convention would elect one-quarter; the president would be Baptist; the charter and bylaws would require that all regents be Baptist, "that Baylor will continue to be operated within Christian-oriented aims and ideals of Baptists"; and the convention would receive the university's assets should it be liquidated.[95] The convention then resumed payments on its $6 million subsidy.[96]

In October 1990, Furman University in South Carolina took back control over trustee election from the South Carolina Baptist Convention and declared itself an "independent" institution, but one that would remain faithful to Baptist values. President John E. Johns explained that this insured "Furman's academic freedom and accreditation by preventing possible outside interference in Furman's internal affairs." Two years later the convention withdrew its legal claims and took all moneys withheld since then from Furman and made them available to its three remaining Baptist colleges. Furman's in-house comment: "Since the separation, some fundamentalists have predicted that Furman will become a secular university, that without the Baptist influence the school will forget its Christian mission. In response, Johns points out that the board of trustees has adopted a statement of character and values for the university that defines and supports the concept of Christian higher education."[97]

One month later Stetson College in Florida took control over trustee selection from the Florida Baptist Convention and forfeited its annual subsidy. H. Douglas Lee, Stetson president, has said: "We remain a Christian university with a Baptist relationship. We have just redefined that relationship in a mutually supportive way."[98] Richmond, Mercer, Samford, Mississippi, and Meredith have also declared their autonomy from state conventions.

In enrollments and finances, Southern Baptist higher education has been burgeoning. In the past three decades their students increased from 72,000 to 230,000, and their endowments and real property increased in value from $349,055,000 to $3,611,557,000.[99]

Intensifying hostilities among Southern Baptists rapidly render these accounts out of date. It seems reasonable to observe, however, that the animus between Wake Forest and its constituency, especially some North Carolina preachers, antedated the aggressive efforts of the fundamentalist, neo-Separate party to seize control of the state and general conventions. The preachers were not that much more obnoxious and obtuse after Wake Forest moved into the Big Time (after 1956) than beforehand, but they were regarded as much more tiresome and obstructionist, the more academically excellent the college and then the university became, at least by its lights.[100]

Wake Forest went through the usual era of elaborating "mission statements" and writing press releases that declared its loyalty to the Baptist denomination. The other universities that have moved beyond the denomination's effective reach have done the same, and this seems to be enough to persuade the Southern Baptist Convention's Education Commission to list them as their own.

Arthur L. Walker, Jr., recently retired executive secretary of the Education Commission of the Southern Baptist Convention, explained in his final statement to college and university administrators how it was that schools with no operative links to the denomination, such as governance or subsidy or church membership by the educators, could still be carried on the Southern Baptist roster. Their association's bylaws had just been rewritten, he said, so that a bare assertion of identity would keep a school Southern Baptist. "The determining factor for an institution must be its 'heritage,' its mission/purpose statement." It is too early to determine, however, whether schools which have so definitively shrugged off any institutional unity with the churches can be expected to share Walker's expectation: "The future of Baptist institutions is premised on the truth, 'God was in Christ.' The identity of Baptist institutions must be the commitment to this truth, even if new relationships and structures develop in our midst."[101]

The rhetoric of those mutual assurances reminds one of what Ben Fisher, Walker's beloved and respected predecessor, had to say a decade earlier:

> I sometimes say facetiously that I hope I shall never be asked again to sit down with a college committee to help write out a statement of Christian purpose. Actually we have known for years the purpose of our schools. The most beautifully worded and theologically sound statement of purpose, the most carefully articulated covenant, the reaffirmation of doctrinal principles, and binding statement of intent in the charters, the constitution and bylaws of our sponsoring bodies all have little or no force apart from the Christian commitment of the administration and faculty.[102]

As the ethos and faith of the sponsoring Baptists became more and more repugnant to the Baptists responsible for Wake Forest University, the only action which would have given credibility to their public claims of fidelity would have been an intensified and, to use their own frequently used term, unashamed recruitment of Baptists — as administrators, teachers, and students — who satisfied them as being both devout and scholarly. There was a clear and strong tradition among the early Baptists of England and New England, of Baptists who were completely at their ease with higher learning, and that tradition might have been invoked. If faith and learning could not be exemplified in the Baptist State Convention of North Carolina, it could at least have shone forth as a city set on a hill in Winston-Salem. But this never was an energetic pursuit, and the campus community had lost its nerve to stand apart from the academic ethos as found in other learned campuses.

THE AMERICAN BAPTISTS

When the Southerners broke away in 1845, the Northern Baptists continued alone to sponsor the existing cooperative societies for missions and education, and then in 1907 formed the Northern Baptist Convention (NBC), succeeded in 1950 by the American Baptist Convention (ABC), and in 1972 by the American Baptist Churches in the USA (ABC/USA). The Northerners already had about a dozen colleges that are still extant today, and would found another dozen before the end of the Civil War.

In the South most colleges and universities have been dependent upon their state conventions but independent of the SBC, whose role was always consultative. In the North the institutions themselves always had legal autonomy, but came under strong central influence by the ABC as a founder and sometime funder and supervisor of its institutions. Thus a narrative of denominational policy and outcome is more constructible for the Northern Baptists.

There is also a difference of scale. While the Southern Baptist membership today is roughly ten times that of the American Baptists, the Southern Baptists founded only about twice as many colleges as their Northern cousins (200 to 96), most of the latter now being either defunct or secularized. The following are presently listed by the ABC/USA as Baptist related:

1833	Kalamazoo College	Kalamazoo, Mich.
1834	Franklin College	Franklin, Ind.
1849	William Jewell College	Liberty, Mo.
1857	Linfield College	McMinnville, Oreg.
1865	Ottawa University*	Ottawa, Kans.
1865	Shaw University**	Raleigh, N.C.
1865	Virginia Union University**	Richmond, Va.
1870	Benedict College**	Columbia, S.C.
1871	Alderson-Broaddus College	Philippi, W.Va.
1879	Florida Memorial College**	Maimi, Fla.
1880	Bacone College*	Bacone, Okla.
1883	University of Sioux Falls	Sioux Falls, S.Dak.
1890	Keuka College	Keuka Park, N.Y.
1907	University of Redlands	Redlands, Calif.
1952	Eastern College	Saint Davids, Pa.
1963	Judson College	Elgin, Ill.

*Colleges founded to serve Native Americans.
**Colleges founded to serve African Americans.

The first record of Baptist educational activity in the North is in 1756. Isaac Eaton, a preacher in Hopewell, New Jersey, began to take in students with patronage from the Philadelphia Association of churches. Eaton's pupils went on to pastor churches throughout the region, and this success encouraged talk of a college. But there was resistance. "Many of the Baptists themselves discouraged the design (prophesying evil to the churches in case it should take place) and from an unhappy prejudice against learning; and threatened (not only non-concurrence but) opposition."[103]

Frank Padelford, longtime executive of the ABC Board of Education, explains:

As was natural, these groups which gradually became known as Baptists as a term of contempt, were composed almost entirely of very humble folk. There were few educated people, or people of "high estate" among them. It was commonly said that "none but ignorant and illiterate men have embraced Baptist sentiments." They were, therefore, not much concerned about the education of their ministers; in fact, they were opposed to educated ministers, because from their observation they were convinced that educated ministers could not be spiritually minded. It is not strange therefore that one hundred years after the first church was established there were only two Baptist ministers with college education in New England, and very few elsewhere. . . . This attitude manifests itself also, even today, in the large number of our churches which prefer uneducated or partly educated ministers to those who are well trained. In some sections of our country this is developing into an alarming situation for our denomination. Unless it can be checked, we shall soon be a denomination without influence in American life.[104]

Though the Baptists were a very small body in 1750, by 1790 they had become the third-largest denomination in America, outnumbered only by the Congregationalists and the Presbyterians. They were the religious group that would benefit most from the Second Great Awakening. Revolutionary sentiment had weakened the status of the established churches, and the lay immediacy of the Baptist ministry and its readiness to sponsor itinerant preachers reached out to the tens of thousands of settlers in the rural townships — especially in the South and West (beyond the Alleghenies) — who had become unchurched for want of clergy.[105]

Rhode Island College (1760, later Brown), their first, had promised more liberty than Baptists had enjoyed in the surrounding colonies:

And furthermore, it is hereby enacted and declared,

That into this liberal and catholic Institution shall never be admitted any religious tests:

But on the contrary, all the members hereof shall forever enjoy full, free, absolute, and uninterrupted liberty of conscience:

And that the places of Professors, Tutors, and all other officers, the President alone excepted, shall be free and open for all denominations of Protestants:

And that youth of all religious denominations shall and may be freely admitted to the equal advantages, emoluments, and honors of the College or University; and shall receive a like fair, generous and equal treatment, during their residence therein, they conducting themselves peaceably, and conforming to the laws and statutes thereof.

And that the public teaching shall, in general, respect the sciences; and that the sectarian differences of opinions shall not make any part of the public and classical instruction:

Although all religious controversies may be studied freely, examined, and explained by the President, Professors, and Tutors, in a personal, separate, and distinct manner, to the youth of any or each denomination:

And above all, a constant regard be paid to, and effectual care taken of the morals of the College.[106]

A Mighty Educational Establishment

No other Baptist college would be founded for more than fifty years, but Northern Baptists had enough supporters of education to have founded twenty-three colleges and universities and sixty-four preparatory schools in the early nineteenth century. The colleges extended from Maine (where Baptists, despite imprisonment and other impositions by the Massachusetts legislature, had become the largest denomination by 1810)[107] to Oregon, with a concentration of foundations in the Midwest: Ohio, Indiana, Michigan, Wisconsin, Illinois, Iowa, Missouri. This was not to every Baptist's taste. Colgate was sneered at as the "minister factory" by local critics of ministerial education. One observer in the Midwest said there were more than 250 ministers there and no schools at all. "Some of them were as much afraid of a dictionary as they were of a missionary."[108] Many of the preachers in the Midwest had come up from the Deep South, and carried with them a resentment against the itinerant missionaries whose mandate from national or regional societies threatened their local autonomy, and whose education evoked unfavorable comparisons.[109] Also, the common folk tended to think of the educators as uppity. Even in the antebellum years various colleges were rumored to be soft in their Baptist loyalties, and denominational committees sometimes visited campuses to check on this.[110]

The end of the Civil War unleashed a twofold burst of new energy for higher education. During the war the Northern Baptist Home Mission Society began to plan missionary and educational efforts to the four million blacks about to be freed.[111] Spurred by the Emancipation Proclamation, the board resolved to send "assistants to our missionaries in the South, to engage in such *instruction of the colored people* as will enable them to read the Bible and to become self-supporting and self-directing churches."[112]

A first priority was the training of black preachers, and ministers and deacons institutes were held throughout the South: nonacademic, weekend gatherings for hasty initiation. They were superseded by educational institutions, most of which had perforce to begin at the very threshold of literacy (some of the early student bodies had an average age in the forties) and then slowly to upgrade their levels of instruction to the point where a few came into their own as colleges. By the end of the century there were twenty-seven such foundations: most founded from the North, but some founded by blacks and then adopted by the Northern Baptists. Expenditures were large, rising from $40,000 in 1869-70 to $105,000 in 1876-77. During Reconstruction, though their program collaborated in some ways with the Freedmen's Bureau, they encountered indifference from the government and open hostility from the local white populations. White teachers working with Negroes in the South risked violence. Southern Baptists did not take their work kindly. And there was internal polarization among the American Baptists over fund-raising and sponsorship.[113]

Coupled with this zeal and generosity the Northerners brought a sense of patronizing professionalism that in time would begin to aggravate relations with their beneficiaries. The schools for blacks were managed by the American Baptist Home Mission Society (ABHMS), which reserved to itself the final say in appointments of all teachers, professors, and presidents. The Northern subsidy brought white overlordship, which became more galling as years went on.[114] Nevertheless, the educational effort of Northern churches and denominations in the postbellum South was critically important to the black people there.

> If the black churches had left the South with the Union Army or with the Freedmen's Bureau, the institutions established up to that time for the education of the Negro inevitably would have collapsed and the chief teacher training field for Negro teachers from that time to the present time, 1930, would have been lost to the South.[115]

On the other hand, in the two decades following the war it was the blacks, who represented only one-eighth of the national population, that provided 40 percent of all new Baptist members.[116]

A second major expansion took place under the auspices of the American Baptist Educational Commission ([ABEC], founded 1868). An 1887 report lists 173 schools at every level.[117] There was a conviction in the highest councils of the American Baptists that education was essential to their calling, expressed in this 1873 policy statement:

> The establishment of schools of higher education is an indispensable supplement of all evangelical work. Every period of successful evangelical activity, from the Christian era down, has blossomed into such schools, and these schools have been the conservators of all achievements gained, and the essential preparation for all further and greater conquests. The schools of Alexandria, of the period of the Reformation, and of the rise of New England, were alike fruits of Christian activity, and instruments of Christian progress. The characteristic difference of the fruits of Protestant missions from those of the Roman Catholic Church, and of the permanency and beneficence of the influence of Protestant missions, is found in the superior place given by those missions to education. The history of the Baptist denomination in the United States is most significant in illustration of this question. We have had a surprising growth in the period which has elapsed since the Declaration of Independence. But where are we strongest for the service of our Lord to-day? We are strongest in those States, without an exception, where the most and best work has been done by us in the department of Christian education. OUR EDUCATIONAL CENTRES ARE OUR CENTRES OF INFLUENCE AND POWER. . . . With the general advance of education in the country, educated minds pass to the higher spheres of control in every department of life, and any denomination of Christians which fails to push forward its educational in an even ratio with its evangelical work, will sink more and more to inferiority, and ought to sink.[118]

But Baptists suffered from overfounding. The zeal of the policy makers and founders was not matched by the support of the membership who had to fund them. For example, out of sixteen schools founded by Missouri Baptists, by 1906 only seven remained "more or less alive."[119] The Educational Commission had heavy words to say about Missouri.

> True, there are 80,000 Baptists in Missouri, but not more than one-fourth, others say less than one-eighth, of these can be counted among the friends of liberal education; and of the ministry of all this mass of professing Baptists there are not more than twenty-five or thirty who, according to the information given, are educated men.[120]

When the ABEC was made a permanent institution in 1872, its purposes were ordered thus: "the promotion of Education and the Increase of the ministry, of the Baptist denomination."[121] But neither goal was ever broadly enough adopted by the Baptist people. The educational endeavor had emphatically undertaken the preparation of Baptist laity to take their influential places in American society. But there were many Baptists then who had no such aspirations for their children. And within a few years only about one in ten male students in their colleges was heading toward the ministry.[122]

The University of Chicago, Nonpareil

The Baptist educational venture was sent soaring by the University of Chicago, which would yield a sobering denouement. Augustus Hopkins Strong, president of Rochester Seminary, had been arguing that the Baptist network required a hub: a super-university with a vital graduate school, preferably in New York. The low level of Baptist culture and the growing religious indifference on Baptist college campuses required a venture both more sophisticated and more confessional than was the Baptist custom. At the very same time, Thomas Wakefield Goodspeed joined other Baptists in lamenting the closure of the (first) University of Chicago (1858-86) and was soliciting funds to refound it. He appealed to John D. Rockefeller, the nation's wealthiest Baptist, and in 1889 Rockefeller concurred. From the very beginning it was clear that the university would be Baptist in cause and control, but not in its education. The first announcement said:

> The new University is to be a Christian institution. It is to be forever under the auspices of the Baptist denomination. It is to be conducted in a spirit of the widest liberality, seeking thus to deserve the sympathy and co-operation of all public-spirited men, and inviting to its halls the largest possible number of students from every class of the community that it may give to them a true Christian culture.

397

The president and two-thirds of the board had to be Baptists, and the ABES was to elect the first trustees. All major gifts would be given to the ABES, which would then transfer them to the university, subject to a reversionary clause if the university were later judged to default on its Baptist commitments. The Baptist seminary in Chicago, the sole remaining fragment of what was now to be known as the Old University, would be annexed as the divinity school, with its own independent board and endowment. The first president was Strong's nominee, William Rainey Harper, a young and liberal Hebrew professor at Yale.[123] The year before his inauguration, president-elect Harper set forth to the ABES convention what the new university would be.

> Its President and two thirds of its Trustees will be Baptists. The theological instruction given will be that of a Baptist Divinity School. Could any Baptist ask for more? On the other hand, it is clear, that in all departments, save the theological, there can be no such thing as denominational spirit or instruction. It is everywhere recognized that when we speak of an institution as for example, Baptist, we mean that such an institution is the contribution of the Baptists toward that great cause of higher education in which all alike are interested. . . .
>
> In all and above all and under all, the University of Chicago, whatever else it may be, by the grace of God shall be Christian in tone, in influence and in work. The provisions of this charter, and the close connection of a theological department, are pledges to you that this shall always remain true.[124]

During the next twenty years Rockefeller would contribute more than $20 million to the ABES for the university, which, practically from its birth, was richer in plant and endowment than all other Baptist colleges and seminaries combined. Rockefeller's sentiments toward the university, wherein the original "Christianity" is replaced by his even more indirect "religion," are perceivable in his letter accompanying a gift of $1.5 million for a chapel:

> As the spirit of religion should penetrate and control the University, so that building which represents religion ought to be the central and dominant feature of the University group . . . so that all the other buildings on the campus will seem to have caught their inspiration from the Chapel, and in turn will seem to be contributing their worthiest to the Chapel . . . (to) proclaim that the University, in its ideal, is dominated by the spirit of religion, all its departments are inspired by the religious feeling, and all its work is directed to the highest ends.[125]

In 1894, only two years after the university had opened, the student newspaper carried this observation: "This is no denominational college. It is not a Baptist university. The only thing Baptist about the university is the divinity school. It may not be agreeable to the Baptists to think so, but this university is broader than the Baptist denomination can ever expect to be." Henry Morehouse, who that year became secretary of the ABES as well as of the ABHMS, roared into print:

Who were the originators of the University of Chicago? Baptists. Who composed the society that first formally determined in 1888 to found it? Baptists. Who was the first great donor that made success possible? A Baptist. Who were the two heroic men that devoted their undivided energies for a year or more to securing the amount required by the conditions of the first gift? Baptists. Who paid their salaries and the expenses of the effort? Baptists. Who composed the meeting in Boston in 1889 to whom the first great pledge was announced? Baptists. Who composed the vast assemblage in a Baptist church and in the Auditorium, in Chicago, in 1890, at which thousands of dollars were pledged and where the grand jubilation occurred? Baptists. To what society was the university site originally conveyed? The American Baptist Education Society. By its charter who must forever be president of the university? A Baptist. Who must forever compose two-thirds of the trustees? Baptists. And who has added more than three million dollars to his original gift? A Baptist. Really, it looks something like a Baptist institution, if there ever was one. . . .

What, in the common acceptance of the term, is a "denominational" college? Not one where denominational tests for admission are applied, or denominational tenets are taught, but an institution originated, founded, fostered, and conspicuously represented in its faculty and its board of trustees by a particular denomination of Christians. In this usual meaning of the word, the University of Chicago is emphatically a Baptist institution, just as Lake Forest University is a Presbyterian institution; just as the Northwestern University is a Methodist institution; and Yale University, an institution under Congregational auspices.[126]

From the outset, then, the University of Chicago was to be Baptist in cause but not in effect. And so it was. To present religion as the shared and unifying commitment of the entire academic community, Harper construed it in terms so generic that it floated above any possible affiliation or conviction. The religion he proposed was "the essence" of the teachings of Jesus and Israel's inspired prophets and sages. That essence was "fear of the Lord": "belief in and acceptance of One who has power to help." This was obviously not related to any actual believing community. "The dividing line runs, not between this and that form of religious faith, but through all forms. The name is insignificant; the serious thing is the character of your religion." Jesus was the exemplar for anyone's belief. With a theology this gelatinous, Harper hardly needed to insist that the university required "absolute freedom from interference of any kind, civic or ecclesiastical."

The second handicap afflicting Harper's religious vision for the university was his unwillingness or inability to assemble a community of colleagues who shared his concern.

Harper seems never to have pressed his faculty to grapple with his full vision. In fact, colleagues felt free to participate in it selectively, appropriating only what meshed with their own wishes and dreams. Thus J. W. Montcrief assumed he was hired to teach at a "Baptist University" while his colleague William C. Hale chafed when he heard the term and was concerned that Chicago's non-religious character be maintained. Clarence Luther Herrick . . . saw in Harper's university the opportunity to do a Christian version of field-encompassing science. Charles Whitman, on the other hand, came to Chicago to devote a career to studying the evolution of pigeons. Each found aspects of Harper's vision to be compatible with basic private goals and beliefs; although many . . . thought they understood him, few if any of his colleagues seemed fully aware of what he was up to.[127]

In 1902 John D. Rockefeller terminated his abundant philanthropy to the American Baptist Education Society. In those twelve years he had contributed more than $20 million for the University of Chicago, and another $1.3 million for Baptist higher education in general. His benefactions had amounted to 99.97 percent of all Baptist contributions during that period: total receipts from all other sources amounted to $6,000. It was clear as a lightning flash to the university that it had been a Baptist, not Baptists, that had created her, and that she need not look to the Education Society for further help. Rockefeller had come suddenly into the midst of the Baptists in 1889 and suddenly departed in 1912. When he transferred his funds to the secular General Education Board, the American Baptist Education Society (ABES) instantly went out of operation, lacking funds even to rent an office.[128]

Within two years there ensued a restiveness on the Midway about the relationship, and the first suggestions that the governance ties be relaxed.[129] In 1923 the university requested approval to reduce the Baptists on the board from two-thirds to three-fifths, and to remove the requirement that the president needed to be Baptist. After two hours of "lively discussion" the request was approved by the Northern Baptist Convention.[130] By 1930 the three-fifths of the board had only to be members of "Christian churches." Robert Hutchins, the new young president, was emphatic, and he was vague: "Whatever changes in outward forms may ensue, the University of Chicago will never forget that it was founded by religious people whose work was carried on here in a religious spirit. That spirit will dominate this University to the end."[131] In 1944 he unilaterally announced that the university had matured into independence from the Baptists, and that it was discontinuing all ties except that the Baptist Theological Union should always have one member on the university board. The convention accepted. The ABES had negotiated binding restrictions on the university, but on three separate occasions it had agreed to attenuate and then to eliminate them.[132] Twenty years later the American Baptist Convention was still listing the University of Chicago as one of its institutions, and its educational historian observed that the university "remains a splendid illustration of the educational concern which has moved many American Baptists through the years."[133]

The Colleges Divorce the Churches, or Vice Versa?

The Baptist educational establishment, North and South, in 1902 was, by one way of calculating it, grand: thirty-six colleges and universities, seven seminaries, twenty-nine colleges (at various levels) for women, thirty-three schools for southern blacks and western Indians, and sixty-four secondary schools, with a total enrollment of 54,000 students.[134] But the University of Chicago accounted for about 60 percent of the students (collegiate and graduate) in NBC higher education, half the income, more than half the real assets, and nearly two-thirds of the endowment. Add to that Brown, Vassar, and Rochester, which were moving away from the denomination with all deliberate speed, and together they accounted for 78 percent of the NBC students, 74 percent of the income, 79 percent of the physical plant assets, and 78 percent of the endowment. The race was to the swift, and the battle to the strong.[135]

The grand statistical array of Northern Baptist investment in higher education was suddenly bankrupt. Or, truth to tell, it had never really been taken to heart by the Baptist people. Baptists still had a manifest corporate apathy toward learning. In the states where their denomination functioned, Congregationalists had 1 out of every 69 of their members in college; Presbyterians, 1 in 70; Methodists, 1 in 143; while Baptists had 1 in 176. Baptists had decent enrollments in their schools, but many of those students were not Baptists,[136] and if Chicago and Vassar were removed from the lists the average enrollment would shrink to the point of embarrassment. The academic quality of the schools, as ranked by the U.S. Bureau of Education, put most Baptist colleges in lower categories. In the West, where more than twice as many Baptists were enrolled in state colleges as in their own, the situation was especially deplorable. Frank Padelford, their educational officer, confronted the denomination:

> We Baptists have assumed a strange attitude toward these State schools. We have failed to provide adequate denominational colleges, and have forced our children into the State universities. We have demanded that the State schools shall not teach religion. Then we have utterly failed to throw religious influences about our children while within their walls, and then we have loudly condemned them because they have not trained and developed the religious character of the children we sent them. This is a strange attitude for Baptists to take.
>
> The Baptist situation at many university centers [chaplaincies] is deplorable. In many cases the church buildings are small, unattractive, inadequate, while all about them other denominations have established fine plants. In several cases the churches themselves have assumed a jealous or hostile attitude toward the university community. . . . While we were the first to introduce the university pastor, we have now only three men engaged in this work . . .

"The only excuse," he argued, "for maintaining a denominational college where the State is ready to furnish the highest intellectual training without cost is that the Christian school can furnish a clearer moral and religious atmosphere for the student."[137]

But atmosphere was not enough. In 1914 the Board of Education reported surprise at how little distinctive religious instruction was being offered in Baptist colleges and universities.

> These schools are supposedly Christian, were founded and maintained to give a distinctively Christian education. Without doubt most of them have a Christian atmosphere, and their professors exert a Christian influence, but it seems to the Board that their curricula should contain ample courses of instruction in the Bible, Christian ethics, and Christian history. . . . We know of few Baptist colleges that have such distinctive departments.[138]

The NBC announced an unprecedented fund appeal modeled on the recent Liberty Bond drives: the New World Movement, with a goal of $100 million. Almost a third was earmarked for schools and colleges. It was just then, in 1920, that conservatives, aggravated in part by the Social Gospel movement initiated by Walter Rauschenbusch, a professor at Rochester Seminary, called for an investigation of all Baptist schools:

> to give special attention to the question of whether these schools and individual teachers are still loyal to the great fundamental Baptist truths as held by the denomination in the past, with particular reference to the inspiration of the Word of God, the Deity of Christ, the atonement, the resurrection, the return of the Lord, the spiritual nature of the church, the necessity for a regenerated, baptized church-membership, the unchanged nature of the obligation of the ordinances of baptism and the Lord's Supper, and the imperative responsibility of carrying out the great commission.[139]

The Board of Education at first headed in the opposite direction, and began to ululate in the most indistinct terms: "We are in serious danger of raising up a generation of men and women who know nothing of the ideals or the sanctions of religion. . . . The church cannot afford for one moment to abate its efforts to permeate the whole educational system with the spirit and power of Christianity."[140] Others trafficked in enthusiasm, like one preacher: "Probably if I had discussed theories of [Christ's] divinity I might easily confuse them. When I speak of the atonement wrought on the cross I can see they understand its spiritual meaning, but I fear if I tried to rationalize the cross by running it into a theory there might again be 'darkness over the land.' "[141] The implication was that bad theology was best avoided on campuses by avoiding religious inquiry altogether.

Some criticism of the Baptist colleges came from the educators themselves, like Kenneth Scott Latourette at Denison:

One finds it hard to face with anything but disappointment and a conviction that there has been a betrayal of trust, the increasingly non-Christian atmosphere of its classrooms and campus. . . . Many presidents and faculties, in a misdirected eagerness not to appear sectarian, minimize or completely ignore a candidate's religious life, supposing falsely that that feature of the institution can be maintained by a strong chair of biblical literature or philosophy, or by an aggressive college church.

The difficulty is enhanced by the fact that as an institution grows older and wealthier, a position on its teaching staff attracts not only men who, as was the case in the days of its youth, view a professorship as a call to sacrificial service, but also those who are lured by the social position which the chair carries and the opportunity for a sufficiently even if moderately salaried scholarly career.[142]

A Committee of Nine was appointed to investigate the "fundamentals" on the campuses and filed their report at the next convention.[143] Most accusations, they reported, had been vague. No proof having been offered, the Nine declined to delve into it. Their conclusion was that the schools were providing an education that was wholesome and of which Baptists could be proud. Indeed, "most of the replies that came were from eminent pastors scattered widely over the country, who at some time had been students of the University of Chicago or its Divinity School. They told of the new-born Christian faith that came to them while they were students in Chicago, usually as a result of contact with certain teachers."[144]

The fundamentalist accusations effectively repressed self-criticism throughout the 1920s. But by 1935 Frank Padelford was able once more to be blunt with his constituency:

There can be no question but that vital religious education has become an almost neglected factor in the program of all our colleges. It is no longer at the heart of even our Christian colleges. One has to confess that so far as effective religious influences are concerned they are almost as completely negligent upon the campuses of our Christian colleges as a whole, as upon those of the state universities. There are exceptions of course, but in most cases the college administrations are bewildered and helpless, and have surrendered to the present zeitgeist.[145]

While total college enrollments across the country had increased 500 percent in the previous twenty-five years, the number of Protestant colleges had decreased.[146] The greater cause for concern, however, was qualitative.

It would require a rather discriminating statement to reveal very much difference today between the colleges that call themselves Christian and those that do not use this title. In other words, some of our colleges seem to be losing their distinctively Christian characteristics. There still remain, to be sure, the occasional religious services of the chapel and advertised courses in religious education. But those strongly Christian aspects of education that marked colleges of the nineteenth century have in some of them largely disappeared in the twentieth. It was doubtless well for some of them to go, but whether we have a right to pretend to any lingering superiority of influence is a serious question. If that superiority no longer exists then we ought not to pretend that it does. I have the conviction that many of our so-called Christian colleges need to face very honestly the question as to what constitutes their right to this distinctive title. . . .

These colleges of ours were founded by men and women who believed profoundly in a Christian education. They have been supported and endowed for the distinct purpose of giving such an education. It is a question whether many of them are faithful to their trust.[147]

A sudden alarm about secularization now swept the college circuit. A spate of articles appeared, asking "When is a church college Christian?"[148] How much did all this matter to the Baptist constituency? In Baptist colleges in the mid-1930s, only 32 percent of their student bodies were Baptists.[149] Out of the convention's entire unified budget, only 2.6 percent was allotted to educational needs (including academies, colleges, and seminaries). By 1940 Baptists appeared to constitute only 17 percent of their own collegiate student bodies. A study of the college system that year repeated one president's comment:

The faculty does not quite understand why the denomination cannot help its colleges, but it seems to prefer to remain a church-related college. The trustees also seem to prefer such an affiliation, while the students do not care. The donors do not seem to take the denomination into account.[150]

What the Preachers Thought

The most ominous element in the report may have been a survey of Baptist preachers, whose attitudes would surely be reflected in the readiness of their church memberships to contribute to education. The convention did not know how many ministers it had, since many were not registered. Of those on their books, two-thirds had spent some time in a Baptist college, and three-fifths in a Baptist seminary. But the study commission admitted they had received a response to their inquiry from only 5 percent of the preachers, "the smallest number of replies ever received to an important questionnaire." Their attitudes were scattered, but some of the negative ones were bitter:

I am a Baptist by conviction, but all three of my children have been educated in other than Baptist schools. They have all finished colleges and had it not been for the very liberal help from these non-Baptist schools, they would be in some C.C.C. camp or living on charity.

Since you have asked for my opinion I will give it. I do not cherish any delusion that it will make any impression on the policy of your Board. I am a graduate of a Baptist academy and seminary. I trust I am not unmindful nor unappreciative of what my schools did for me. But as I look back over the years spent in these institutions I can, outside of one teacher, remember nothing taught me of importance to the Baptist denomination. I am probably as much to blame as the institutions for the impressions I got, but the fact is I came out of school with a lurking sneer that Baptists had nothing distinctive to add to the world.

The Baptist as well as all other colleges are useless as far as building God's kingdom is concerned . . . Better for God's people and godly parents if the greater part of the schools ceased to function since they tend only to educate, not to give spiritual help. They rather wreck the faith students may have had when they entered.[151]

As always, there seemed to be "a small number of wise, far-seeing men who have known that no group can have influence unless it has a trained leadership and an educated constituency, while on the other hand we have had large groups who have been suspicious of education."[152] That small group now appeared quite small indeed, while the large groups had never seemed so large.

One notes, however, that the proposed benefit from education was public influence, not any better capacity to understand or enlarge upon the Christian faith.[153] Such reminiscences as were favorable tended to say that one's faith was enkindled at college, yet not by the education itself. There was something in the Baptist tradition, distinct even from the tendency to depreciate sophistication, that did not easily envision faith itself as susceptible of learned cultivation.

In the 1940s the more established Baptist colleges and universities began to admit publicly that they no longer considered themselves related to the denomination. Temple, Des Moines, Vassar, Rochester, Colgate, Brown, and Chicago; Colby, Bates, and Ricker in Maine; Denison and Rio Grande in Ohio; Stephens in Missouri; Hillsdale in Michigan; Bucknell and Keystone in Pennsylvania; Morehouse and Spelman in Georgia; Selma in Alabama; and Carleton in Minnesota — all sent word that they had severed their relationship. Nevertheless the Board of Education persisted in retaining their names on its roster for years, for decades, until the institutions complained that it was an embarrassment. It is safe to say that every formal separation of a college from American Baptist sponsorship came at the college's initiative, and usually its repeated insistence.[154]

There were various in-house explanations for this shakeout. Baptist social concern was intimidating in its moral claims; or the increasing sophistication of their youth was drawing them to Episcopal and Presbyterian campuses; or the Baptist people could not come up with the money needed for a system of higher education; or, as the student bodies in Baptist colleges attracted a more religiously diversified student body, the colleges naturally altered their identifications to accommodate their clientele.[155]

There were other reasons less cited. The Baptist pastorate was still not an educated one. A major 1945 study found that only 36 percent of all their ministers had received an education that included four years of college and three years of postgraduate seminary, then the recommended standard. Ten percent of their ministers had only a high school education or less, and another 22 percent lacked any college experience but had studied at a Bible college or seminary. Nineteen percent had no theological training at all. Of those who had college or university experience, only one-fifth had received it from Baptist institutions. The study concluded that "ordination standards among Northern Baptists cannot be spoken of, with any sense of realism, as requirements."[156] As historian Robert Torbet has observed, progress in Baptist-sponsored education has been gradual owing to the fact that "the churches have been dependent to so large a degree upon ministers whose own limited and inadequate training has made them unenthusiastic about education."[157]

A Virtue out of Necessity

As its membership began to diminish and its education office had less money — and then no money — to subsidize its affiliated schools, and as more than half of these schools either disappeared or severed their relationship to the denomination, the American Baptists began elaborating surreal, detailed postmortem policy statements about what it might mean to be a Baptist college.[158] In the 1940s they spoke of Baptist educators, and sound worship, but then they began to drift off into "Christian social idealism" and "the highest respect for personality." By the 1950s the Baptist rhetoric had become odorless, colorless, and lethal:

> Christian higher education is person-centered. Its every process is focused on the welfare and the development of the student, as an individual and a member of society. All its striving begins and ends here where Jesus placed the emphasis. All Christian educational philosophy and practice rest on a single premise: Every man should strive to realize his fullest potential as the supreme creation. . . .
>
> Christian higher education seeks the impingement of the Christian presuppositions upon the student through his distinctly academic experiences — through the curriculum. This aim assumes the curricular objectives that are universally valid and appends these distinctive objectives:
>
> 1. Comprehensiveness in the search for truth. Welcome all questions and utilize all ways of seeking and testing truth.
> 2. The discovery of meanings. Seek depth, not just specifically religious meaning.
> 3. The discovery and appreciation of values, especially moral and spiritual values.

4. The integration of learning experiences and of their content.
5. A functional relationship to life. Strive to meet student needs and to achieve life-related consequences.
6. The development of the inner qualities and attitudes sometimes called character.
7. A Christian intellectual perspective — the acknowledgement of a bias founded on religious concepts and a theistic world view. Created world. Transcendent creator. Truth has unity and personal identity.
8. A knowledge of church teachings.
9. Student recognition of his life work as a vocation — a work in which God leads, guides, blesses.[159]

The stark reality darkening all this idealism was the fact that for a quarter of a century at least three-quarters of all Baptist students had been enrolled in state colleges and universities, and recently that had risen to 90 percent.[160]

The years moved on, with little following. In 1982 the denomination made another effort to clarify and renew its relationships with colleges. Three years of collaborative debate yielded a complex covenant that could be offered to the college presidents.

Affirming that all truth is from God, the churches also acknowledge the crucial role of the colleges in discovering and conveying truth in its several disciplines and vocations, and in promoting liberal arts education. Affirming the Lordship of Jesus Christ, the churches also acknowledge the role of the colleges in developing commitment to values, and in seeking to make men and women integral and whole in conscience as well as knowledge. Affirming the Church as an expression of God's Kingdom, the churches also acknowledge the role of the colleges in building communities of those who seek to know and serve the truth, and in developing intelligent and committed leadership, both lay and professional, for the ongoing ministry of the churches in the world.[161]

One imagines that a covenant drawn in terms this bland might have gone down easily, but shortly after it had been signed several of the signatory presidents and boards began to have misgivings.[162] It is difficult to appreciate how a college able to subscribe to this prose could ever become restive within it. All it lacks is the memorable 1947 injunction to "manifest at all times and in all circumstances the highest possible respect for personality."

As the years have passed the membership of the ABC has declined, so that its census is now about what it was in 1930. In 1989 a severe funding shortfall led to the termination of the entire Division of Christian Higher Education. The college presidents meet, but they prefer their Baptist relationship to be quiet and inexplicit. Some presidents are "more Baptist than Christian," and are content with their Baptist identity. Others are "more Christian than Baptist," and their evangelical faith carries them more easily. Most of the rest see their mission as sponsoring "free inquiry," which should prevent the intrusion of any normative convictions. These presidents tend to see the covenant as neither describing nor governing their relationship with the denomination. One of them calls it "hypocritical."

One president openly described the ambiguity of the present situation in his annual report:

> Franklin College was born American Baptist. That voluntary association has served as the college's window to the larger Judeo-Christian tradition. Throughout our history, the college has striven to shape and sharpen the spirit as well as the body and mind. As recently as the college's sesquicentennial, the founders' commitment to ethical insight, religious inspiration, and honest intellectual endeavor was reaffirmed.
>
> In this scientific, technological, information age, when the college has more Catholic and Methodist students than American Baptists, more "un-churched" than "churched" students, and at least 24 students from non-Christian religions, what does it mean to be a values-focused, church-related college? How can Franklin College live out its heritage and ideals in ways that are appropriate, relevant, and honest?[163]

It is now two-and-a-quarter centuries since Baptists founded Brown University, and as things now stand the American Baptists of the North play little role in the lives of the colleges that still allow themselves to be called Baptist-related. Perhaps only three of the sixteen listed today are purposeful in professing that identity.

VIRGINIA UNION UNIVERSITY

Between 1865 and 1910, 259 institutions were founded under Christian auspices for the education of the freed black slaves of the South. Northern Baptists founded and/or supported at least 27 of them.[164] One example of this initiative, in Richmond, Virginia, amalgamates the resources and histories of five distinct institutions that were begun in Washington, Richmond, and Harpers Ferry.

Even before Isaac Eaton had founded the first Baptist academy in Hopewell, George Whitefield, the preacher who aroused the countryside in the Great Awakening, himself a slaveholder, disclosed to a friend in 1740 his desire to open a school in Pennsylvania for blacks. In 1774 a Presbyterian minister in Newport, Rhode Island, enrolled two young Negroes from his congregation at the College of New Jersey (later Princeton), with the intention of preparing them as missionaries to the Gold Coast, their homeland. These were the first blacks known to be given an entrée into higher education in America.

It was abolition sentiment, however, which originated first among the Congregationalists and the Quakers and later grew hot among Northern Baptists in the early nineteenth century, that would raise the prospect of educating African Americans once their bondage had been lifted. The American Missionary Association, a radical abolitionist venture of the Congregationalists that sponsored Oberlin and Berea Colleges before the Civil War and Howard and Fisk afterward, meant to train black missionaries for work both in America and in the African homeland.[165]

Baptist enterprise was not far behind. Their initial motivation was to train blacks in the basic skills needed for preaching; later it would include and then emphasize educational advantages for all blacks. As one black Baptist later put it, "Patriotic Christian philanthropy of the North came down to us with the spelling book in one hand and the Bible in the other."[166] Even before the outcome of the war began to emerge, the severity of such a task was clear. Literacy was reported of 60 percent of free blacks in the country; in the South it was reckoned to be 50 percent. But 95 percent of all American blacks were enslaved, and it had been a crime to teach them the skills of literacy. Of those four million, only 5 percent had somehow learned to read.[167]

As vagrant slaves began helplessly to trudge after the Union troops in their campaigns through the South, the American Baptist Home Mission Society (ABHMS) resolved to evangelize them. Already in 1862 it voted to send missionaries south, and to subsidize the building of churches and schools for the former slaves. By 1865 it knew better the enormity of its undertaking:

> They are houseless, penniless, without business experience, without capital or credit, their social, civil, and religious condition chaotic. How to evolve order; how out of the mire of servile degradation to produce the lilies of the Christian virtues; how to displace superstition with truth; how to educate them to read and think for themselves; how to provide them with meeting-houses, of which they have but few; how to train the ministers, most of whom cannot read a sentence in the Scriptures; — these are some of the problems confronting the American Baptists . . .
>
> To the close of the war, the common school system is unknown in the South. The door of no schoolhouse opens to the children of these emancipated millions. They need the schoolhouse and the schoolmaster, the meeting-house and the missionary, in a thousand places.[168]

Southern whites, to whom these incursions from the North were all elements of the odious Reconstruction, visited hostility and violence upon some of the missionaries, especially if they brought a menacing educational program in their carpetbags.[169] Jeremiah Jeter, a leading Virginia Baptist, explained why the white Baptist General Association of Virginia rejected an overture of fellowship from the black Virginia Baptist State Convention:

> God has made two races widely different; not only in complexion, but in their instincts and social qualities. We take it for granted that it was not the purpose

409

of the creator that they should be blended. . . . Nature abhors the union. . . . Suppose we admit colored delegates to seats in our association, we must, of course, allow them to sit where they choose, in juxtaposition with our wives and daughters . . .[170]

John Hart argued before the Baptist General Association that slavery, whatever its faults, had brought Virginia Negroes along faster and farther in two hundred years than the Saxons and Normans had progressed from 1066 to 1266. Rev. A. Broaddus clearly expressed what they called "the Negro problem":

I believe in education, the widest, most thorough and perfect education. I advocate the education of brutes because education will make them useful . . .

But education must be adapted to the capacities and endowments of the beings who are to be trained. No effort or skill can draw out intellectual powers which never existed. . . . [The Negro] ought to be trained for the place for which God endowed him. He cannot be a judge, a professor in a college, a legislator; he *can* be a laborer, a teamster, a stevedore. . . . God never intended all men to be alike.[171]

In 1867 the SBC invited the ABHMS to keep its missionary educators at home but to send down their funds, and they, the Southerners, would provide for the needs of the freedmen. The offer was ignored.[172] The Northern educators had a powerful friend, however, and in light of traditional Baptist repugnance to entanglements with the government, a surprising one, in the Freedmen's Bureau, headed by General O. O. Howard. The Bureau made bountiful grants for the purchase of land and the construction of buildings; for instance, two of the eventual constituents of Virginia Union — Wayland Seminary and the National Theological Institute in the District of Columbia — purchased their properties with federal grants.[173]

The nomenclature of the Baptist schools requires some explanation. Whatever the title or ambition of their educational establishments, the early ABHMS efforts for the freed African Americans had to recruit most of their students at the entry level. Thus for years even universities had "preparatory departments" which offered elementary courses from the lowest level to pupils who included adults entering at middle age. At the secondary level there were "academic" (or sometimes "preparatory") and "industrial" departments, offering scholastic studies or practical training. Academic studies at this level were commonly included in the designation of "higher education." The "collegiate" departments offered what were called "literary" studies. There were two kinds of theological schools or institutes, and they functioned either below or above the collegiate level: most were what today would be called "Bible schools," and offered religious training for the ministry to those who might have received some secondary schooling but would never enroll in college; a very few of these theological schools offered ministerial training to college graduates. Virtually all postbellum schools for blacks were built upward from their preparatory departments — slowly.

The religious denominations quickly became aware that their institutional engagements had far outstripped their resources. As the Southern states began to open schools for blacks — grudgingly and stingily — the academic departments in Christian schools began to have their Northern funding withdrawn, and they were closed. The fate of the industrial departments was more controversial, because of a division of sentiment among Southern Negroes (about which more below). Some argued that these programs were effective and direct avenues to employment and the ability to raise a family for many — perhaps most — emancipated blacks. Others strenuously resented the growing inclination of Northern philanthropy to favor industrial programs because of the imputed assumption that most blacks were incapable of anything more demanding.[174]

A group of Boston Baptists who had stimulated foundations for blacks in Nashville, New Orleans, Raleigh, and elsewhere decided to do the same in Richmond, the old Confederate capital. J. B. Binney, erstwhile president of Columbian University in Washington, founded a night preachers school for blacks in 1865. Next came Nathaniel Colver in 1867, erstwhile professor at the (old) University of Chicago, who leased a former slave stockade and opened a full-time school. A year later he was succeeded by Charles Henry Corey, erstwhile president of the Theological Institute in Augusta (later Morehouse College in Atlanta), who stayed for thirty years. In 1869 the school was taken under the patronage of the ABHMS.[175] In the latter 1880s Corey and his board (including several local black Baptists) resolved with the ABHMS to upgrade their school to a higher status: it would discontinue college courses and become Richmond Theological Seminary, an exclusively ministerial school for black Baptists, rechartered to grant degrees.

This move was gratifying to African Americans, who saw it as a new reach of academic accomplishment available to them. But another sensibility was on the rise. The decision to close down the college department seemed to ABHMS executives to be an act of sensible stewardship, but to local blacks it meant that only ministers would now be educated in Richmond. The Educational Committee of the Virginia blacks supported an educated ministry, but what they wanted was a coeducational college with a theological department.

Fellowship or Paternalism?

There was more at stake in this conflict than the sensible deployment of resources. In the twenty-five years since the war, black Baptists in the South had contributed to their educational network funds which, when counted in New York, seemed to be not even token amounts. Meanwhile the ABHMS had spent $2 million. As Henry Morehouse, the corresponding secretary, put it:

From the first the Society has been the steadfast friend and helper of the colored people. Though in several States the colored people have contributed generously to the support of this work, yet, as frequent failures prove, they are unable of themselves to sustain such Institutions as they need. Upon the Society, therefore, still rests the great burden and responsibility for the efficient maintenance of these Institutions.[176]

Smoldering resentment at white paternalism made this sort of Northern prose repugnant to many Southern blacks. After a quarter-century their colleges all carried the names of white people: Roger Williams, Bishop, Wayland, Benedict, Hartshorn, Shaw, Spelman. Their presidents and principals were all white, their trustees were mostly white, their faculties were still mostly white. Black leaders admitted that their efforts at fund-raising had been unsuccessful, but their explanation was the reverse of the white one: black hesitation to give was the effect, rather than the cause, of their exclusion from educational policy-making.[177]

When the Virginia blacks had offered to pay for a new building on the Richmond campus (to make it more suitable for a coed student body), and had asked that they might name the building and nominate some more blacks to the board of trustees, Morehouse had turned their offer aside. They had no money to offer at the time, and the ABHMS could not reasonably advance the funds in hope of reimbursement because the blacks had never yet redeemed a monetary pledge.

The Virginia Baptist State Convention decided to found its own college in Lynchburg, with black leadership and funding. Its young president, Gregory Hayes, an Oberlin graduate and Baptist convert, became one of the most ardent spokesmen for black self-reliance. Unfortunately for the cause, the new school, Virginia Seminary, ran short of funds after its first year and had to go to the ABHMS for help. They reluctantly agreed to pay the president's salary and several other expenses, on the condition that they be sent monthly financial statements. Morehouse understandably thought this responsible, and Hayes understandably found it insulting.

Eventually the Home Mission Society presented a further plan, to create a university — its first in the South — in Richmond. It would incorporate a men's college then in Washington,[178] the recently established Hartshorn Memorial College for women, a new men's college, and eventually law and medical schools. Spiller Academy in Hampton and Virginia Seminary in Lynchburg would become feeder schools (thus reducing an unhappy Hayes's title from president to principal). Virginia black Baptists found themselves rent into two parties: cooperationists and separatists (who sometimes called themselves "race people"). Morehouse defended the ambitious plan of reorganization with the argument that the most gifted blacks, whom he called "the talented tenth," must have an institution for the highest learning.

Hayes's role as principal antagonist finally provoked the ABHMS to demand his ouster. But at the Virginia Baptist State Convention in 1899, known afterward as "The Battle of Lexington," Hayes's party was in the ascendant, and they cut all ties with the ABHMS and restricted their financial commitments to Lynchburg. The cooperationists, convinced that there was more word than deed in the doctrine of self-reliance, seceded and founded their own Baptist General Association of Virginia, and retained their loyalties to the Richmond venture.[179]

When they were finally left entirely to themselves, the Lynchburg rebels did harrow their constituency effectively enough to survive financially. And when faced with the counterexample of capable blacks in positions of responsibility, the Home Mission Society began to be much more proactive in filling the board and faculty in Richmond with blacks.[180]

But progress in Richmond still came slowly. Virginia blacks could not produce significant contributions to the new university. The Home Mission Society finally decided to close Wayland Seminary in Washington, liquidate its appreciated properties there, and use those funds to build a men's college on a new campus beside Hartshorn. There would be a theological school, a college department, an academy (with manual training as well), a preparatory department, and the girls' college next door. Virginia Union University (VUU) thus emerged in 1899. When President Corey retired, the ABHMS brought down veteran Malcolm MacVicar (1899-1904), who had been the founding president of what would be McMaster University in Toronto, to lead the new flagship campus.

Two years later the campus newspaper reported with chagrin that the colored Baptists of Virginia had promised to construct and equip a building for industrial education on campus but were stalled in the latter stages of their fund drive; the dedicatory stone attesting to their gift would have to await full payment.[181] General Morgan, corresponding secretary, reported that ABHMS expenditures in their direction had now reached $3 million, and that Negroes were being appointed to positions of trust.

> In the whole matter of administration of its educational and missionary work for the Negroes the Society has had before it the one great object of doing what it thought best for them; its schools were built and maintained exclusively for them; its missionary work was done for them; all its appointments of agents and teachers have been with a view to the highest benefit to the Negroes. Its whole administration has been unselfish and altruistic. . . . The society has not been able to accomplish for them all that was desirable, partly for lack of funds and partly for the lack of hearty cooperation and even from opposition on the part of some of the Negroes themselves, but it looks back upon nearly forty years of history without self-reproach, but with pride and satisfaction . . .[182]

Blacks were at this time engaged in strenuous debate about their education. Booker T. Washington, president of Tuskegee Institute, was arguing that "industrial education" of a practical sort would give them a broad base of skills and ready employment. W. E. B. DuBois at Harvard contended that in order for them to claim the political, social, and professional standing required to free their people from

413

white domination, their best people had to have access to an elite education. Ironically, it was Henry Morehouse who had coined the phrase DuBois would use: the overall welfare of all Negroes would depend on the excellence of the "talented tenth" of their number. Blacks at Virginia Union were being led by the American Baptists to cast their vote with DuBois, while still giving Washington full honor for all that he had done on their behalf.[183]

The university struggled to recruit students to enroll in its programs. They noted that in the surrounding region where it was the only institution of higher education available for Negroes, there were 1.25 million blacks, about half of whom were likely to be Baptists.[184] So there seemed to be a sizable pool to draw from. But by their reckoning only one in five hundred colored people advanced beyond the elementary level, and one in fifty thousand graduated from college.[185] There were then four black institutions in Virginia listed at college grade, yet most of their students were still enrolled at the secondary or elementary levels. In 1904, in the entire state of Virginia, Negro institutions graduated 240 students at all levels, yet only 12 of those were at the college level. The previous year, when Virginia Union had awarded its first four baccalaureate degrees, only 16 of its entire student body of 218 were even in the college department.[186]

There was a formidable financial obstacle which helps explain this. The auditor of public accounts calculated in 1904 that black residents of Virginia possessed more than $19 million worth of real and personal property; but divided among nearly 700,000 Negroes, that yields less than twenty-eight dollars of real property per person. In that context, a tuition of seventy-eight dollars per year at Virginia Union was an extravagant expense.[187] It was an arduous time to be preaching self-reliance to blacks.

Slowly, slowly, the situation was bettered. Literacy began to increase. By 1890 43 percent of American blacks could read and write; twenty years later 70 percent were literate.[188] By that time Virginia Union had 240 students enrolled, not many more than when it had opened its doors eleven years earlier. But now 35 of them were in the college program. By 1920 the preparatory (elementary) department was gone; total enrollment had more than doubled to 462, of whom 169 were now at college level; and students were coming in good numbers from the West Indies, Maryland, North and South Carolina, Pennsylvania, New Jersey, and New York.[189] In 1924 the State Board of Education gave its accreditation, and in 1930 and 1935 the Southern Association gave Class B and then Class A regional accreditation. In 1920 John D. Rockefeller's General Education Board began a series of annual $10,000 grants (which VUU duly matched with $5,000 from other sources), and in 1923 it replaced this annual subvention with a gift of $200,000 to its endowment. By then college enrollment had risen to 236.[190] Law school classes began in 1922, the same year the School of Education began, and the academy (high school) was discontinued in 1929. Hartshorn Memorial College for women was absorbed by the university in 1932.

A Black President

Dr. John Marcus Ellison, who held degrees from Virginia Union, Oberlin, and Drew, was elected VUU's first black president (1941-55). This moment, perhaps more than any other, marks the university's emancipation as a black endeavor. In general, the colleges and universities for blacks which have matured to greatest strength are those which were founded by the Christian denominations from the North. They took longer, however, to be put into the hands of black educators and trustees. Both the state institutions which depended on white supervision, and the independent schools which avoided all white involvement, had for opposite reasons been long starved of resources.

Our question, however, is not whether Virginia Union is a black endeavor but whether it is a Baptist endeavor.

In 1935 the ABHMS concluded seventy years of sponsorship by handing over its responsibilities to the NBC's Board of Education, and by distributing a further $100,000 of Rockefeller money to each institution's endowment. This was intended to wean the colleges founded for blacks (and Native Americans) from continued annual subsidies. The transfer put the educational institutions, finally, under the purview of educators, not missionaries. But the Board of Education was a much less generously funded operation than the home and foreign mission societies. It managed to pay the fire insurance premiums on the black campuses, and to fund occasional small projects, but the days of regular subsidy were over. In one last act of patronage the ABC gave Virginia Union in 1964 a good share in the liquidated assets of Storer College in Harpers Ferry, its onetime feeder school which had had to close its doors in 1955.[191]

From about the time of World War II onward, the Southern Baptists began to take a patronal interest in this university that was once an incubus in its midst. The SBC Home Mission Board began to finance some scholarships, and the First Baptist Church of Richmond has been a regular annual contributor, as are scattered ABC congregations. Yet, without any prospect of participating in policy making for these independent-minded beneficiaries, the SBC has retained only a modest monetary interest in their welfare.

In recent years the contributions of black churches have dramatically increased. After World War II they totaled from $10,000 to $15,000 annually. By the end of the 1950s they had mounted to nearly $40,000, nearly four times what the ABC and SBC together were then able to contribute. At the present time the churches of the black Baptist General Convention of Virginia contribute upwards of $300,000 a year. The United Negro College Fund (UNCF), which Virginia Union joined as a charter member in 1944, was in its early years providing annual grants about as large as those from the black Baptists. Today, however, the UNCF gives over $1 million a year.[192] This embodies a more general fact: that the largest provision of subsidy and development, since the ABHMS disengaged itself from its educational mission to the freedmen, is no longer coming from Baptist institutions, North or South, white or black.

As one reads through the documentation of the Richmond Institute and Wayland Seminary and then Virginia Union University, one is struck by differences from the other Baptist narratives of the SBC and the ABC. There is little mention of concern for the Baptist character of the institution: its orthodoxy, its faculty and student body, its worship, its piety. For those who are responsible, there seem to be two concerns which put all others in near total eclipse. The abiding and urgent concern was survival. The school-become-university spent its first century hovering on the precipice of desolation. Only by consolidating institutions too feeble to survive alone and by wheedling credit and living in relative poverty could this institution survive to open its doors each autumn.

While at various periods white Baptists were critically judgmental of the religious fidelity of their colleges, black Baptists' enduring concern was that their institution assume the manners and the dignity of, and receive the acknowledgment that they were the peers of, their white counterparts. Wayland Seminary and Richmond Institute were founded just when Reconstruction was beginning; blacks were freed legally but in hardly any other sense. Virginia Union University was chartered just when the Virginia legislature was about to fashion the Jim Crow laws that would again disenfranchise and segregate Negroes without hope of equal dignity. Any young man or woman who was enrolled in these institutions, with the possible exception of those in the preparatory department, was likely to be the intellectual and cultural superior of more than nine-tenths of the whites he or she met . . . and to whom he or she was forced to be deferential and from whom he or she was bound to accept daily disdain. What the Baptist denomination offered these long-suffering, capable young African Americans was the hope somehow to win their due honor through education and certification.

Their Baptist identity was never in question. The ability of those who became preachers to serve better in ministry was hardly affected by their education; for many years they would serve congregations that required little or none of that. Their piety was not protected and reinforced against a hostile world in an enclosed Baptist environment, for their entire lives were forcibly estranged from those who dominated the national culture, and most of their comrades within that social enclosure then were either Baptists or Methodists. Thus the black churches of the South and the white churches of the North agreed in their explicit expectations of Virginia Union: not that it would enhance the piety and belief of its students as Baptists, but that it would cultivate in them a mannerly excellence which might neutralize, if not eliminate, the odium of racism.

Being Black and Being Baptist

The evidence shows clearly that the university moved through a shift of sensibilities that involved no aggressive moves toward secularization . . . but which nevertheless carried it in that direction.

416

When Virginia Union was dedicated, the Reverend Dr. H. B. Gross warned those assembled that the Bible and modernity did not agree on what the new university had to offer. "Where the Bible says, 'Seek ye first the kingdom of God and his righteousness, and all these things shall be added unto you,' the Age-spirit says, 'Seek ye first the riches of this world, without being too particular as to righteousness.' " He delivered a cultivated sermon, warning them of the danger in thinking that money meant advancement. "For true civilization, for a regenerate nature as the only hope of man, white or black, for manhood reaching unto the stature of Jesus Christ, this University shall stand." Their race needed Negro pastors of culture, consecration, ability, and masterful leadership, and teachers of high ability and character in the common (state) schools.[193]

In Washington about one-third of the students in the various levels were studying for the ministry; in Richmond it was between a quarter and a half. Many of the other students — sometimes the majority — were taking a normal course to be teachers. VUU graduates were prominent in organizing the National Baptist Convention, the first great association of black Baptist churches, and they have dominated the Baptist General Association of Virginia.[194]

Revivals were held from year to year and exuberant results were described. Yet one does not find the intensity of interest in conversions that marked so many SBC and ABC campuses, possibly because there were few infidels in the student body to begin with.[195]

Yet in its self-presentation over the years, there is a steady diminution in Baptist-oriented prose. For example, the 1910-11 *Catalogue* contains this:

Purpose and Discipline of the University

The University is a Christian school. It was established and is in large part sustained by the American Baptist Home Mission Society. Unlike a State school, it definitely aims to develop religious character no less than intellectual ability and culture. By teaching the Bible, by personal example and influence, by the presentation of high ideals, and also by definite rules and regulations, the Faculty attempts to carry out the purpose of the founders of the school — that it prepare men for Christian living and service. Conduct has been said to be three-fourths of life. The formation of right habits of conduct is, therefore, the most important part of all education. This school expects the conduct of its students to be in harmony with the Golden Rule, and the behavior of gentlemen.[196]

All students attended regular courses on the Bible, and weekly prayer and devotional meetings were "strongly encouraged" by the faculty, to impress on each student the value of making this undertaking:

"During my lifetime, I promise to seek the will of God in the care of my body and in the keeping of my thoughts, the nature of my conversation and the character of my conduct in private and in public, and this I will do, following the example of the perfect Christ, and relying upon the Holy Spirit for guidance and strength."[197]

The next year, however, the *Catalogue,* after stating that VUU was a Christian school founded and sustained by the ABC, went on to state: "It is Christian rather than denominational, and welcomes teachers and students from many denominations." There is no longer any promise-formula, but church on Sunday morning and afternoon and chapel daily were now "required."[198]

Twenty years later this remained mostly the same, except that the University's "Aim" received added specification. VUU would follow the best traditions of liberal scholarship, would develop intelligent Christian leadership trained not only in theology but also in understanding current social problems, and would encourage its students to go on to postgraduate schools.[199]

There is evidence of a piety on campus during the 1950s that was unstrained. Of those who responded to a query about their religion, 85 percent reported themselves as Baptist. Campus worship was dignified, devout, and evidently uncontentious.[200]

By 1961 the university had its first lay (and third Negro) president. The *Catalogue* took a mellower view of itself as religious:

What Kind of College Is Virginia Union?

Virginia Union University is an accredited, coeducational, liberal arts college and graduate school of religion which resulted from the merger of two institutions which had been founded by the American Baptist Home Mission Societies. It is independent of governmental support, deriving its church support from Baptists and other support from alumni, philanthropists, and the United Negro College Fund, a fund-raising federation of more than thirty accredited private institutions.

The focus of the University is on the development of strong religious convictions and commitment but insists on rigorous intellectual discipline. The basic rule of the University is that students must deport themselves at all times as ladies or gentlemen and Christian citizens. As a Christian institution, the University family includes alumni, students, and teachers from many denominations, both sexes, and several countries and racial or ethnic groups.[201]

By now the rhetoric had changed: VUU is Baptist "but" intellectual; previously it had been Baptist "and" intellectual.

But by 1972 something drastic had obviously occurred:

Purpose of the University

Virginia Union University is a community committed to the liberation of the human mind and to the understanding of man's role in this world. In pursuit of

418

specific goals and through their implementation, the University is a vital contributor to American life. We pledge:

To foster an environment which would enhance an appreciation of Negro heritage and identity, thus uniting the relevance of education for the students' challenges in life.

To keep alive the best of liberal scholarship through which the initiative, interests and integrity of the student is developed.

To offer a program of education broad enough to inspire a range of interests, a depth of appreciation and an ability of thought to provide for effective citizenship and responsible leadership.

To present programs of specialization in more than one area of concentration to increase inquiry of the student and provoke extended study.

To provide a variety of personal and group counseling experiences designed to expand the personality of the student, to help him take full advantage of his opportunities.

To serve those disadvantaged by environment and/or educational resources through a special program prior to college entrance. This program develops the skills necessary for college proficiency.

To recruit actively superior students throughout the country as well as such students who, despite cultural deprivation and limited finances, show the potential necessary for the realization of the University's objectives.

To provide for students and other adults continuing education which will enable them to invest their abilities in solving the problems of our world.[202]

Even through this dense prose for which academics have a special gift, it is clear that religion, whether Christian, Baptist, or otherwise, is nowhere to be found amidst the university's "purpose." At that time the university benefited from a $2 million gift from Sydney Lewis to open a business school named after him. Some people at Virginia Union believe this was a turning point in (or from) its religious character.

The present mission statement is as brief and bland as any:

Virginia Union University was founded in 1865 to give to the newly emancipated an opportunity for freeing the mind in a Christian, humanistic environment. Good teaching and enlightened guidance were, and still are, the institution's primary concerns. That the student will develop the knowledge, skills, and attitudes for enriching his own life and that of the community in which he will serve remains the generating force of the total academic endeavor. A foundation in the liberal arts and sciences is designed to acquaint all students with the traditions of Western culture and African-American heritage. The University encourages scholarly inquiry and freedom of discussion in the search for professional excellence, stable values, and a sense of personal worth. Opportunity for growth at Virginia Union University is open to all, regardless of race or creed.

As an urban university, Virginia Union seeks to make its resources of locale, staff, and graduates, assets to metropolitan Richmond and the nation.[203]

Neither here, nor in the longer exposition of "goals," is there any mention of Baptists. Notable too is the sole reference to African American heritage on what is still an overwhelmingly black campus.

The university's needs far exceed the means of the black churches (though there are nine hundred black Baptist congregations in Virginia), and thus the presence of corporate executives on the board of trustees has apparently replaced all Baptist ministers except the executive minister of the Baptist General Association of Virginia, which has its headquarters beside the campus.[204]

The ABC, of course, now appears only in a historical role, in the past tense, in the university's narratives. The president reports that it "does not participate in the affairs" of Virginia Union, though there is a relationship between them. The bond to the black National Baptist Convention is different: VUU is a "member" of the convention; it also enjoys a relationship with the black Progressive National Baptist Convention, Inc.[205] It is important to realize that the combined memberships of the various nationwide black Baptist conventions today are about equal to that of the Southern Baptist Convention itself.

Black but Not Baptist

The Articles of Incorporation of the University, in their successive amendments, provide a chronicle of the shift in the institution's self-understanding:

1876: The oldest incorporation creates "a literary institution or college, to be called the Richmond Institute." There is no mention of either race or religion. The incorporators, however, included three men from the ABHMS and five from Richmond, of whom three were black.

1886: The school becomes Richmond Theological Seminary, empowered to grant degrees in divinity, and every trustee is required to be "a member in good standing of a regular Baptist church." Still no reference to race, though the board is still biracial.

1896: A first charter for the new Virginia Union University is enacted, and its board is to include one-third "Afro-American" membership, mostly nominated by the black Baptist State Convention.

1900: This charter is quickly swallowed up in the turmoil between Lynchburg and Richmond, and succeeded by another which, though it honors the tradition of biracial incorporators, no longer requires that there be any specific proportion of blacks among the trustees. They must all be "members in good standing in evangelical churches, and not less than three-fourths of them and the president of the university and the officers of the board of trustees shall be members of churches now known as regular Baptists." The ABHMS is given a portfolio of supervisory rights: to nominate two-thirds of the trustees; to approve all alienations of property, and appointments, dismissals, and salaries of employees; and to inspect the university. These rights are awarded as long as the university is maintained, "in whole or in part," by the society.

1960: With a stable black administration ready to install its third black president, the board takes back the right of the ABHMS to nominate two-thirds of its members and reduces the religious stipulations on its own membership. Trustees must be members of "Protestant Christian" churches, not evangelical, and Baptists must constitute only a majority instead of three-fourths of the membership. Of the board officers, only the president must be Baptist.

1974: The ABHMS is stripped of all rights of visitation and approval. All religious credentials for all offices are removed. In one less noted but equally significant amendment, the description of Hartshorn College is modified. Since its merger into the university in 1932, it was "an institution of christian learning of collegiate grade for the education of young women . . . in science, literature and arts, and especially in biblical and christian learning." Both references to Christian learning are deleted, though "ethics and religion" are included as subjects of study.[206]

By the 1970s, without any remaining reference to race in the legal instruments, Virginia Union was more than ever a university by and for African Americans. The provisions for oversight by the Northern Baptists were eventually removed as their role as funders and bankers faded. Yet in law and — by a slower schedule — in fact, Union was also revoking its commitment to being Baptist.

Faculty are not asked nowadays about their religious affiliations, hence the university has no knowledge of what they might be. Of students who responded to a registration questionnaire, 55 percent said they were Baptists, 28 percent said they were "undeclared," and 5 percent, the next largest percentage, said they were Catholics.[207]

There is still a weekly convocation in chapel on Thursdays. Attendance has not been mandatory since the late 1960s, but every student must attend eighty "cultural events" in four years, and chapel services qualify as "cultural events."

The Graduate School of Theology, however, despite its long-standing claim to be interdenominational, is thought to have a vital relationship with the Baptist denomination. It is said that 90 percent of the black Baptist preachers in Virginia who have the M.Div. degree received it from Virginia Union. Also, the Department of Philosophy and Religion is traditionally chaired by a local pastor who serves as informal liaison with the churches.

In 1960 two other ABC-founded colleges — Morehouse and Spelman, both in Atlanta — had expressed their preference to be called "independent, private colleges." Benjamin Mays, president of Morehouse, commented:

> I hardly know what to say as a reason Morehouse College has continued to exist as a Baptist or Church-related College. The main reason is we are Baptist in origin and we have never had any desire to deny our heritage. Although we are now a private institution, we are happy to remain Baptist in the tradition of the founders.[208]

In that same year Fred Brownlee, after a career devoted to black colleges, gave his valedictory look to their tendency to become unmoored from their churches.

> In the early days the teachers carried a spelling book in one hand and the Bible in the other. In reporting the number of students who had been in attendance the presidents also told how many of them had given their hearts to Christ during the year. This still is true of some of the colleges, but most of them have come to breathe the atmosphere of the call issued in 1846 by several abolitionist societies which united in forming The American Missionary Association:
>
> > The time has come when those who would sustain a free and pure Christianity must not only abstain themselves from the practice of all sins of caste, but also seek at all times and in all places to eliminate those sins from American culture.
>
> Nevertheless most of the greater universities which [had] Christian foundations and not a few of the lesser ones are sensitive about calling their colleges Christian, evangelical or church-related. This is particularly true when they are after money and students. The late president Faunce of Brown University, a Baptist foundation, is reported to have said facetiously (no doubt apocryphal): "When I speak in Baptist churches and their mission boards, Brown is a church-related university. When I speak to the officers of the educational foundations, Brown is a *university*."
>
> The chronicler of Harvard's Tercentenary . . . said this about Harvard:
>
> > Harvard was a religious foundation. Christianity was its inspiration and the unifying force of all its studies. . . . But the spirit of religion in the university has been ebbing during the last century. Instead of learning by and for religion, we are fortunate if we can make a religion of learning. It could hardly be otherwise; for the Puritan creed was too illogical for the human intellect, and too severe for human nature.
>
> By keeping clear of sectarian reefs, Harvard finally floated off Christianity entirely and it is a little lonely on the high seas of philosophy. Fifty years ago the logical step was taken of abolishing compulsory chapel and making Chris-

tianity, as it were, a free elective. The loss is part of the price we paid to become a university.[209]

If the contemporary mission statement of Virginia Union quoted above is to be credited, the university is being assimilated smoothly into the moral and doctrinal imperatives of American higher education. If so, then a great deal has happened there in its century and a quarter of history.

Despite the fact that senior African Americans who threw in their lot with VUU adhered to the cooperationist party in a sharply divided black Baptist community, their experiences and their responses were not all that different from those of their more polarized separatist brethren. Throughout the postbellum days of Richmond Institute and Wayland Seminary, and afterward in the university, black students found there one of the few places in America where black people and white people lived and worked together in a relatively relaxed community. Both cohorts brought to the campus unusual, and unusually high, motivations.[210] As the years wore on, however, it was inevitable that the sentiments toward the Baptist denomination would be strained. In the experience of the black students and faculty, the white Southerners of Richmond treated them to daily, unselfconscious disdain. There appears to have been little or no difference in what they encountered from white Southern Baptists, who seemed to deal with them as whites with blacks, rather than as Baptists with Baptists. As long as the American Baptists stood by them with their financial support and their personal presence and dedication, their identity in the face of the world could be both black and Baptist. But as things fell out, in time the missionary project from the North failed to do what missionaries claim to do: to raise up peers in the faith and, in their case, in the academy. No matter whether they were strident or silent in their chagrin, Southern Negroes began to feel that the Northern Baptists were patronizing them. So they seemed to be, after all, just like the Southern Baptists . . . or possibly worse. This estrangement would inevitably weaken the identity of the university's constituency as a Baptist community, for their salient identity before the outside world was black, not Baptist.

If, in the progressively changing climate of Virginia and academia, VUU students and graduates are more and more dealt with on their merits, then it could be that the black identity of the institution, in its turn, would be weakened.

Virginia Union University has a considerably higher proportion of Baptists in its student body than either of the predominantly white Baptist institutions we studied, and a piety and worship on campus that remain more unselfconsciously Baptist than on many other SBC or ABC campuses. This alone would slow down the drift away from the denomination, but not prevent it.

It would also appear that while there was an antieducation resistance among the untutored black clerical establishment in the earliest days of the ABHMS outreach to Southern blacks, the attitudes of the black Baptist laity toward education — even college education — were more uniformly positive than those of white Baptist laity. The predominant attitude toward education was that whoever could get it, should. There seems little evidence of any conviction among Negroes that learning was likely to suffocate spirituality. In the long run it could turn out that they were wrong.

LINFIELD COLLEGE

To study a school which the American Baptists founded for their own membership, one can scan across the continent to the Far West. From 1818 until 1846 the Oregon territory, previously a buffer zone between the early Spanish to the south and Russians to the north, was jointly occupied by the United States and Great Britain. Thus any Americans who settled there did so with uncertainty as to their civil future. In 1844 Baptists were thin on the ground, but five of them founded the West Union Church near Portland, without meetinghouse or minister. They were the first Baptist congregation to gather west of the riverine states along the Mississippi, and only two of the five congregants lived within twenty-five miles of their gathering place.[211]

> In spite of inevitable discouragement, the organization survived, and during territorial days not only sought to prepare its members for the Hereafter but exercised a rigid and somewhat detailed supervision of their behavior on earth. The church minutes are well spiced with specific references to the specific sins of designated members and with descriptions of the remedies being applied to the erring ones.[212]

The ABHMS forthwith sent out two paid missionaries with educational experience: Ezra Fisher, an Amherst graduate, had helped found Franklin College in Indiana, and Hezekiah Johnson had been an early supporter of Denison University in Ohio. By 1848 there were five Oregon churches with a total of eighty-seven members, banded together into the Willamette Association. Fisher started a school in the meetinghouse at Oregon City (then the end of the Oregon Trail) in 1848, and Johnson founded the Oregon Baptist Education Society in 1849. Some money was collected, but more was contributed by the two zealous missionaries themselves (Fisher had had a successful time in the California gold rush), and much came from non-Baptists.[213] At this time Baptists constituted less than 1 percent of the very sparse population of Oregon.[214] Seeing there were no funds, the local supporters changed the school's name from Oregon City College to Oregon City University, but somehow this did not budge destiny, and in 1859 the doors were closed.[215]

A homesteader in the Yamhill Valley, a tributary of the Willamette, disliked farming, so he platted his land instead for a town, called it McMinnville, and set out to persuade some church to start a school there in order to make the lots more salable. The Disciples of Christ turned him down; they already had two schools in the region. The Central Association of Baptists then struck a deal to open a school, with one proviso: that the title would revert to the local school district if alcohol were ever sold or served there. It seemed at the time a redundant restriction on Baptists. By 1858 Baptist College at McMinnville enjoyed incorporation by the legislature and forty-four pupils, virtually all at the elementary level.

Quite in neglect of Baptist polity, the school simultaneously served as the local common school through the 1860s and 1870s and thus received a subsidy from the government. There were limits to this church-state liaison, however. "A precaution against dissension on dangerous doctrines was the prohibition of the use of the building for any political presentation by anyone whatsoever."[216]

A College Poor and Small

Thus was a mighty acorn planted. In the 1860s there were 1,100 Baptists in Oregon (a tenfold increase within a decade), 300 inhabitants of McMinnville, and 104 pupils in the school. Its president would go on to become the first president of the University of Oregon. Interest in the school remained quite local, though, since more than 90 percent of the pupils were from the immediate area (thus one infers that not many of them can have been Baptists), and an appeal to all Baptist churches in Oregon and Washington to assume responsibility for the college was a failure. The teachers went without their pay for a while. When two other Baptist schools were founded in Washington in the late 1870s, it made no difference to enrollments at McMinnville.

The Baptist College in McMinnville (later McMinnville College) waxed, and classes at the secondary and collegiate levels slowly emerged. This tiny lyceum amid remote farmsteads, under the tutelage of a Yale man, nevertheless followed the formidable curriculum of the time:

> In the first year of the preparatory department, English, Latin and Greek Grammar, natural philosophy, Latin reader, Caesar, and arithmetic was enough. During the next year, arithmetic, Cicero's orations, Xenophon's Anabasis, Latin and Greek grammars, elementary algebra, Cicero and Virgil, Homer's Iliad and Virgil's Aeneid were studied, if not mastered. The ambitious student who entered the collegiate department confronted university algebra, Livy, Herodotus, Roman history, Horace, The Odyssey, Grecian history, geometry, De Senectute, Memorabilia, and modern history. If he passed that assortment successfully he would not be abashed by the sophomore course including geometry and trigonometry, Tacitus, Greek Testament, modern history, surveying, rhetoric, principles of linguistic science, French, analytical geometry, and philosophy of history. In the junior year calculus, elements of criticism, philosophy of history, German, mechanics, chemistry, acoustics, mental science, metaphysics, and botany were intended to afford mental stimulation and growth. For the seniors the elements necessary to round out their collegiate training and make them competent to carry

on the serious work of the world were found in optics, moral science, logic, geology, astronomy, political economy, science of government, Greek Testament, Butler's Analogy, and evidences of Christianity.[217]

How were they going to keep them down on the farm, after they'd seen Xenophon?

But the college was poor. There were no laboratories or equipment, and the president said the library contained enough books to "fill the apron of a generous old maid." A new state high school, which was coeducational and enrolled twice the college's numbers, came as an inevitable threat. The awarding of the first B.A. degree came only in 1884, a quarter-century after the college was founded.[218]

In 1878 the first theology course was added, for the needs of three ministerial students. But despite the Home Mission Society's insistence that the training of ministers was a prime purpose of the college (it was a prime motive for contributions from member churches back east), it was difficult to mount a program in the Northwest to educate men for the ministry, for ministerial students generally received their education tuition-free, and the finances at McMinnville would not allow much of that.[219]

The college's first substantial philanthropist appeared: Henry Failing, a prosperous importer and banker from Portland, and a staunch Baptist trustee. His first challenge grant of $5,000 for endowment was successfully matched two-to-one by other donors. In its thirtieth year the college had only ninety-six students, seven in the collegiate department. But by then the three Baptist schools in Oregon and the five in Washington had begun to draw away students, as did nearby schools of other denominations in nearby Lafayette and Newberg, and state colleges in Monmouth and Corvallis. The Oregon Baptists seemed indifferent to both higher education in general and McMinnville College in particular. Of those few Oregon Baptists who were going to college, five-sixths went elsewhere than to McMinnville.[220]

They inched forward. Women were admitted, and the elementary level was eventually eliminated. A Bible course was added as a requirement in 1895, lectures by local pastors were scheduled for prospective ministers in 1897, and theological studies began again in 1901. Yet by 1905 there were still no more than six students in the college course,[221] there was a large debt, and the trustees in Portland recommended closure.

President Harry L. Boardman's candid and glum reports to his trustees convey the strain of those days. In 1897-98 he presided over six faculty members and an unstable enrollment of ninety, only 57 of whom attended throughout the year. And this represented a 50 percent increase over the previous year. College students constituted less than half of the student body (this would remain so until the First World War). Ministerial students at all levels totaled seven.

His own duties are staggering to read. His classroom responsibilities for that year included beginning Latin, beginning Greek, Caesar, Virgil, Homer, Xenophon, Demosthenes, New Testament Greek, and biblical literature.[222] He traveled widely to visit the churches and recruit students. Indifference among the churches, however, was stolid. Most Baptist churches in the state refused to observe a "College Day" to promote McMinnville. The next year he reported giving sixty sermons and addresses in a public relations effort, but had to admit that "The beneficences from the churches have not been large." In 1900 the ABES offered a grant of $5,000 if McMinnville could raise $20,000 to match it. Boardman failed to raise more than one-fifth of that. "Our men of means" in Portland, he said, were not interested, and the reaction in McMinnville itself was "apathetic."

He was equally lugubrious about the religious situation on campus. The YMCA and YWCA showed "vigorous workings," but religious interest was down. The special lectures arranged for prospective ministers drew such little interest he was embarrassed to ask any more pastors to campus. Enrollment in a ministerial course dipped down to two students. One year he says diffidently that "a number of conversions are to be reported," but in 1899-1900 he reported:

> The religious life of the college seems to have been at low ebb during the entire year. The Christian associations have maintained vigorous organizations and have done faithful work; but the results on the unconverted part of the student body have been inconsiderable as far as visible results are concerned. This fact of the seeming lack of revival interest among the students, and the dearth of spiritual results for the year, are matters of profoundest regret.[223]

A Whirlwind President

The Lord raised up a captain for his people in the person of Leonard W. Riley, who in four years as pastor in tiny Lebanon, Oregon, had closed down every one of its ten saloons and was now the pastor of the McMinnville church (218 members) and also the General Missionary for Oregon appointed and paid by the ABHMS. He moved into the presidency in 1906 and remained for twenty-five years. His was to be the leading initiative in the organization of the American Baptist Board of Education in 1910.

Shortly after Riley took over, John D. Rockefeller's General Education Board refused grants to any of the schools in the Willamette Valley, explaining that there were too many of them. Reporting this rebuff and another from Carnegie, the new president assured his board: "There are funds enough in the Northwest in Baptist hands to do all we have planned for McMinnville College."[224] Who could believe it? But Riley immediately put on a drive for $100,000 followed by another, for endowment, for $300,000, and both succeeded.[225] He began to work on his constituent churches; proceeds fell far short of assigned goals, but still began to rise. For instance, fifty-nine churches contributed $1,930 in 1911-12, though their goals totaled $8,000.[226] The New World Movement campaign of the early 1920s never paid what it had promised, but the $148,000 they did receive (of the expected yield of $700,000) was still welcome at the college, which had just taken the name of Linfield to honor a legacy from a wealthy minister's widow.[227]

The General Education Board, now satisfied that the college was on the move, in 1921 pledged an endowment gift of $200,000, which the college matched with another $400,000.[228] In 1927 four state conventions pledged more than $50,000 to the building fund. By 1928 endowment income ($47,000) had become the largest single source of revenue, followed by student fees ($30,000) and the ABES ($3,500). In 1930 the Linfield endowment reached $1.5 million, compared with such other West Coast Baptist institutions as the University of Redlands ($5 million plus) and the Berkeley Divinity School ($1.25 million). But more than two-thirds of all these funds had come from three individuals, one of them a Congregationalist. Riley observed: "The day is past when colleges like Linfield can secure adequate funds from a rank and file canvass of our churches."[229] This was not quite true: that day had never dawned.

The student body had meanwhile become quite predominantly Baptist, as its territorial draw reached across the Northwest. The first religious census (1917) showed that 86 percent were Baptists. Seven percent were listed as "not reporting," but Riley commented that "The larger portion of the latter during the school year were led to profess faith in Christ, so that less than half a dozen reached the end of the year outside the fold of Jesus Christ."[230]

There is no doubt that Riley intended the college to be devoutly Baptist.[231] He had hardly taken office in 1906 when he reported: "Thus far I have not been able to find for [the Commercial] Department a competent man who is a Baptist. I have found a man who seems to possess every qualification save this one."[232] In his last report he identified the religious status of each incoming faculty member: Jonasson (who would write the college history) was Baptist; Dillin (who would seven years later become president) was Baptist and was shortly to marry a Baptist girl; Bolton was a Congregationalist "and a devout Christian man."[233]

During the struggle by fundamentalists against the liberalism of the Social Gospel movement Riley took note that "inasmuch as so many of our institutions upon attaining financial independence have drifted away from their original purpose, it would seem wise at this time [1921] to endeavor to ascertain by what means the future of this institution may be safeguarded." His recommendation: careful selection of trustees and of faculty. "We must elect as trustees only such men and women as are devoutly interested in and sacrificially committed to the attainment of this purpose." He recommended more thorough investigation of the ideas, ideals, and habits of life of possible nominees. As for faculty, if their mission was to send forth men and women to serve in the spirit of the Lord Jesus Christ, the conclusion was obvious. "Like produces like. Such well-trained graduates cannot be produced except they are molded and inspired by teachers who know Jesus Christ and whose great desire is to do His will. . . . In view of certain subtle tendencies of our times, it would seem the part of wisdom to scrutinize more carefully the Christian character and the religious and theological views held by those whom we put in charge of our classrooms."[234]

During the fundamentalist hubbub of the 1920s the college became a target of investigation by the Oregon State Convention. An investigatory Committee of Five reported that Linfield was managed by sound Baptists and that no deviant doctrine could be found, but noted that its having a self-perpetuating board carried risks. "Grave fears are expressed that the college may, in time, be a Baptist college nominally only, such as BROWN AND VASSAR, which were founded through the sacrifice of our Baptist forebears, and no longer adhere to the principles of their founders."[235]

To strengthen a sense of patronage among Baptist leadership Riley had suggested already in 1909 that each of the state conventions in the Northwest be entitled to fill two or three seats on the board. No action had then been taken.[236] In 1922 the college was not prepared to put itself entirely in the hands of a constituency that was still ambivalent about the value of higher education. In 1926, when the Baptist constituencies were demanding full control of the college, the Linfield board quietly filed amendments to its Articles of Incorporation that represented a compromise. Of the twenty-eight trustees, one (the president) would serve *ex officio;* three would be elected by the Alumni Association; nine would be nominated and elected by the board; and candidates for fifteen would be nominated by the various Baptist conventions in the Northwest states (three nominations for each seat) but elected by the board. This arrangement, which gave the constituency some part in governance but not control, was presented at the Oregon Baptist State Convention in 1927 "in the interest of harmony, and especially for the sake of the College dear to us all," and, after much soothing speech, accepted without dissent.[237]

Leonard Riley swept all before him, and was singularly successful in his long presidency at Linfield. Two of his more difficult and stubborn stands demonstrate his willingness to risk unpopularity. He was an unflinching critic of varsity football because of its brawling and brutal style and because of the risk of incapacitating injuries. In 1906, when the sport had established itself on campus as rather successful and very popular, he persuaded the trustees to ban it. Year after year the students and often the alumni petitioned to have it reinstated. Riley's advocacy (and the similar decision at Reed College) at one point influenced the Association of Independent Colleges of Oregon to recommend the abolition of intercollegiate football. Unlike Riley, the other presidents flinched at putting their resolution into practice. Eventually the Linfield trustees were worn down by the growing national enthusiasm for the sport. But instead of reversing their own original vote they decided to lay the issue on Riley's desk, and in 1922 he finally gave in. He had held out for sixteen very determined years. On another matter of moral conviction, he had the use of tobacco banned in 1916 — not just in certain places on campus, but wherever students were. The rule was enforced, at times by dismissal. And on this matter he never backed down.[238]

Riley had all along been explicitly concerned about student piety on campus. In one of his early years he noted that a revival had resulted in many conversions, "so that about nine-tenths of the entire student body were professed followers of Jesus Christ during the major portion of the year."[239] In 1911: "I do not hesitate to say that we have had the finest, manliest, strongest company of students we have ever known. All are professing Christians with the exception of four or five."[240] In 1913 when boasting of the statement by the secretary of the NBC Home Mission Society that McMinnville was "the most Christian college we have today," ahead of even Denison and Colgate, he ratified the accolade by reporting that as a result of twenty-four students being led to surrender themselves to the Lord that year, "with one exception every student leaves the institution a professed follower of the Master."[241] In 1926 he reported with pride that student teams from the Linfield religious education program were going out to churches to revitalize their Sunday schools, music, missionary programs, etc. Students ran revivals, and directed worship in smaller rural churches.[242]

On a somewhat dissonant note he admits, in response to an accreditation evaluator's earlier suggestion that the college should separate the preparatory program from that of the college, that in the eyes of some of their clientele the campus was offering an education that was more moral than intellectual:

> We have hitherto maintained our Preparatory Department for the benefit of young people beyond the usual high school age and the young people whose parents desire to have them under the same influences during the high school period which they have maintained for them in their own homes. There is still sufficient reason to maintain an Academy for these two classes of young people. We have, however, received not only these two classes but also many young people who have passed beyond the control of their parents and who have been sent to our Preparatory Department for the same reason some are sent to reform schools.[243]

As he looked back over a presidency notably successful for its fund-raising, Riley admitted there was a terrible irony in it all. People of means who gave the large gifts that allowed Christian colleges to survive and to thrive were explicit and emphatic that they wanted these schools to remain servants of the church. Yet almost in direct proportion to their enlarged resources and affluence, those colleges had drawn away from the church.[244]

Baptists Go Elsewhere to College

After Riley retired from the presidency in 1931, a medley of factors began to suggest a cooling in the Baptist momentum at Linfield. The census reports showed that although enrollment resolutely climbed, the Baptist proportion of the student body declined. The middle years of the Riley administration had seen the Baptist percentile of enrollment standing in the high eighties, but by 1927 it had slipped to 75 percent. It would continue to diminish inexorably to 24 percent in 1970.[245]

In half a century the Baptist presence had continually diminished from 90 percent to less than one-quarter of the student body. Obviously other shifts would be likely to accompany such a turnabout. They show in various ways. The widely distributed annual brochure *Concise Information concerning Linfield College* carries in 1924 a section called "A Baptist College," which discloses that all but two members of the board were then members of Baptist churches; that the college enjoyed the support of the Northern Baptist Convention and those of all the Northwest states; and that "The members of the faculty are all devoted Christians and take an aggressive part in the work of the churches in the community and nearby fields."[246] The *Catalogue, 1931-1932* begins its presentation thus: "Linfield College was founded in 1857 through the foresight and faith of our Baptist pioneers. Their leaders recognized the need of education under Christian influences as a means of strengthening and multiplying the work to which they gave themselves with absolute abandon." Under "College Life," Christian influences are the first activities described, though with a lean toward vagueness and a yaw from Baptist to Christian:

> The ideals of Linfield College are based upon Christian principles. Its supreme aim is to give young men and women a thorough preparation for life under conditions favorable to the development of Christian character. For this reason it encourages everything that aids in the realization of this purpose; on the other hand, it seeks to suppress any tendency not consistent with its ideals. Because the Bible is the most important book in the world and because a knowledge of its contents is essential to an education in the truest sense, opportunity is given to all students to take courses in Religious Education in which the Bible itself is used as the principal text-book. The instruction given in these courses, however, is not sectarian in any invidious sense of that word. It is needless to say that only Christian men and women are employed as teachers in the college.[247]

By 1960 the same document states in a more detached way that "Linfield College is a Liberal Arts co-educational institution, emphasizing higher education under conditions of Christian leadership." It was "founded by Baptists," who are no longer referred to in the first person. The Linfield objectives have become considerably more demure, and Ezra Fisher and Hezekiah Johnson now emerge as libertarian sages:

> Training for Christian democracy, an objective conceived by the founders of the College, has been the guiding principle during Linfield's growth through the years. The student is encouraged to discover the resources furnished by the Christian faith in accordance with his own pattern, as an inescapable part of his education, and is given freest opportunity for renewed understanding of the

Christian democratic tradition at its best, as applied to the intellectual and social problems of contemporary life.[248]

A decade later Linfield, though maintaining "strong ties to Baptist churches in the Northwest," is staffed by faculty "with a strong Christian commitment. The college, however, is not sectarian. The student body, faculty, and trustees are drawn from many religious traditions, and no creedal requirements or practices are imposed." The old paragraph from the thirties, "The ideals of Linfield College . . . ," continues to be reprinted, save that its second half has now vanished. The educational philosophy is centered around the liberal arts, with no mention of Baptist or Christian perspective. Those are now viewed as matters of private concern: "The issues raised by religious faith are fundamental to man's understanding of himself and the world, and the College consequently expects that each member of the college community will concern himself with his own response to questions of ultimate values in his belief and behavior."[249] One notices it is just at this point, when religious faith had been transformed from a collegial to an individual undertaking, that Linfield documents began paradoxically to speak of a "college community."

Another decade passed, and once again the intentions of the founders and their successors were updated: "The untrammeled pioneer spirit, the commitment to quality learning, the significant church relationship, and the caring attitude of the past continue to influence the Linfield experience in 1979-80."[250] The current catalogue presents "Linfield College: A World of Difference," as a diverse place where students "prepare for world citizenship." Its mission from the pioneers onward "has remained constant — to teach undergraduates in an atmosphere of academic freedom that fosters intellectual rigor, creativity and a sense of personal and social responsibility."[251]

Concurrent with this metamorphosis in Linfield's self-understanding was a rolling sequence of descriptions of the theological enterprise at Linfield. In the early years all instruction in Bible or religion was given by faculty of any department, as an extracurricular offering. In 1906 President Riley noted to the board that they had long required Bible courses of all students. Hitherto this had consisted in lectures by "various brethren and has involved little actual study of the Word." In a word, they had been preached at. He said he planned to teach it himself, and presented a four-year curriculum: freshmen, Old Testament books; sophomores, New Testament books; juniors, Bible as history, Bible as literature; seniors, life of Christ, life of Paul, Christian evidences.[252] The course in apologetics — Christian evidences — had been in the curriculum since 1872, but it was for seniors; and since the first student completed a degree course only in 1884, and very few since then, it may not have been a constant offering.

By 1910 there was one faculty member designated as professor of both Bible and public speaking. This was the first explicit faculty assignment in religion. Not until 1922 did Linfield appoint its first full-time professor in the new Department of Sacred Literature and Religious Education. Some of the curricular teaching was also done on invitation by various Baptist pastors in the vicinity.[253] Throughout this second fifty years the classroom enterprise was seen as Baptists teaching Baptists a more sophisticated understanding of the Bible. The course offerings in the early thirties, for instance, seem to have future teachers as their clientele.[254] By 1960, although the courses themselves seem in continuity with the past, the stated aims of the department had taken a shift:

> The aims of the Department of Religion are: (1) to give to the student an awareness of the place, the nature and the function of religion in human life; (2) to assist the student in the adjustment of his religious outlook while he is advancing in his understanding of other fields of knowledge; (3) to provide pre-theological training and guidance for persons planning to do graduate work in religion; (4) to direct the student in the acquisition of such data and skills as will qualify him for intelligent non-professional leadership in the program of the Christian churches of the regular denominations. The endeavor is to promote a spirit of unity rather than divisiveness in the face of the world's need.[255]

There is no longer any suggestion of the apologetic or the catechetical. The department is clearly getting down to business, and the business is academic and preprofessional theology. The audience is now mostly non-Baptist, but assumed to be evangelical Protestant. The last sentence is a very refurbished form of the older disclaimer that the instruction will not be "sectarian in any invidious sense of that word."

By 1970 the department presents the same statement of aims, but it has a new name, Religious Studies; and it invites cross-registration at other nearby colleges (two Catholic, one Congregational, and one Presbyterian, but not including their Quaker and Methodist neighbors). The hands are the hands of Jacob, but the voice is the voice of Esau. By the end of the seventies the department really has become a "religious studies" endeavor:

> From the beginning, men and women have sought answers to questions of ultimate significance. This most personal of human drives has long been associated with the process of education, and while the various academic disciplines add much to an understanding of the infinite, many of the questions are couched in religious terms. Drawing upon more than 3,000 years of revelation and religious experience, the religion department is dedicated to helping students in their personal search for a deeper understanding of religious truths.[256]

At the present time the department has ostensibly completed its journey. The study of religion is no longer a communal initiation but an individual search. The method is inductive, aligned somewhat with the social sciences. The department is unified by its subject matter only, and that subject matter is generic religion. The prose breathes heavily.

Religion is a complex and variegated phenomenon which has had a profound effect upon human culture. Religion has appeared as a dramatic and fearful encounter with the holy, as laboriously acquired spiritual discipline, as exemplary story and ritual, and as intimate communal interdependence. Religion has evoked both trust and terror, bliss and rage, peace and war, and hope and despair. In its various cultural and historical manifestations, the experience of religion has called forth the best and the worst in human conduct.

By learning to ask appropriate and productive questions about religion, one develops the capacity to know one's own way and the ways of others as well. The academic study of religion is indeed an integral part of a liberal arts education which can create mutual respect and support within the world community.

Objectives of the department are: to provide an awareness of the place, nature and function of religion in human life and culture; to study the history and sacred texts of a variety of world religions; and to aid students who desire to increase their knowledge and understanding of religion. Assistance is also given by the department to students preparing for the seminary and for graduate work in religious studies.[257]

A Tradition, Not a Commitment

In recent years there have been other indicia of a discomfort with any explicit religious assertion on the part of the institution. There has been no ugly incident, no rough power play by denominational executives, no academic chief executive determined to secularize the campus. Just a growing discomfort with manners and mandates that had been expressive of a Baptist character in the institution.

In 1972 the *Faculty Handbook* stated, within its "Statement of Purpose and Organization": "The College affirms its own Baptist traditions and the Christian commitment of a large part of its constituency . . ." Four years later: "The College affirms the Christian commitment of a large part of its constituency and its asso- ciation with the American Baptist Churches in the U.S.A." The older text proffers the Baptist traditions as "its own"; the later one speaks only of an association with the ABC.[258] The current mission statement begins by asserting that "Linfield College is a four-year, non-profit, coeducational, liberal arts institution historically and currently affiliated with the American Baptist Churches" and declares that the college supports the Christian commitment of a large part of its students. Otherwise the Linfield mission, extensively stated, does not explicitly concern itself with religion.[259]

Despite the casual belief and occasional statement that the faculty still includes a large number of Baptists, not to mention Christians, the college does not ask and does not know what their affiliations might be. The former president used to ask prospective personnel, "in an unthreatening way," whether they would be com- fortable at a college with Linfield's historic affiliation, and whether they would be open to a request by the chaplain to take a leading role in a religious activity. The present view is that it would be unlawful even to ask a candidate's religious status.

The older requirement that the president and three-quarters of the trustees must be Baptists has been amended to require only that Baptists must be in the majority on the board.[260] The president, a Methodist (her predecessor came as a Methodist but became a Baptist), has explained that although the religious affiliations of trustees are not a matter of the public record, she doubts that Linfield is in compliance with the bylaw requiring a Baptist majority. Some at Linfield have expressed misgivings about restoring a Baptist majority on the board, because of its ability to vote as a bloc. But recently the board was discussing an administration plan to install condom machines as a health measure in the residence halls. Some trustees began to object, saying that it also involved a moral issue. The clergy on the board turned out to be the most enthusiastic supporters of the proposal, thus allaying fears of an unenlightened Baptist hegemony.[261]

The college chaplain, who also serves as professor of religion, is an ordained Methodist minister who worships at First Baptist Church in McMinnville and has been at Linfield for nearly two decades. Throughout that period Catholics have been the largest constituency among the students, about twice as numerous as Baptists. One reason for this, he says, might be Linfield's active athletic program (highly successful in football, thus disturbing the posthumous peace of President Riley). Whereas the president speaks of the campus community as "highly churched," the chaplain sees it as "largely unchurched." He worries that in the near future they may no longer have a "critical mass." Granted the likelihood that a strong majority of the students are now religiously inert, one wonders what amount of mass it would take to be critical.[262]

The college seems on its way to stable finances. With an endowment of $22 million, it has just concluded a $34 million campaign with an overrun of $4.5 million. Contributions from Baptist churches, by contrast, are much less significant, amounting to slightly less than $20,000 a year,[263] and the denominational budget has no funds available for subsidies. There would seem to be no financial interest in the Baptist connection.

There is one final and chiastic sign of where Linfield now stands in respect of its Baptist founders. Recall that the original deed for its land was conditioned by a reversionary clause that would strip the college of its title if ever alcohol were sold or consumed on the campus. The wine writer of the *New York Times* recently paid a visit:

> McMinnville is Oregon's unofficial wine capital. There are some 50 wineries in the Willamette Valley, most of them less than an hour from here. McMinnville is also the home of Linfield College, which is so All-American that it could have been ordered by Louis B. Mayer for an Andy Hardy movie. Since it began in 1987, the [International] Pinot Noir Celebration has been held on the Linfield campus.[264]

THE BAPTIST STORY

The three institutional stories we have recounted describe a gradual movement away from any vital synergism between the denomination and the campuses. This is true of both Southern and Northern Baptists. Among the case studies, Virginia Union is the institution still the least resourced and academically developed, yet in some ways still the most Baptist. Yet even in Richmond the trend is the same; only the velocity is different. What can one understand, in retrospect, about the almost relentless drift of those nearly three hundred Baptist collegiate foundations away from the denomination?

The original purpose put forth by those who founded Baptist colleges was to educate those set aside for ministry. Yet this expressed resolve was befouled by three realities. Throughout the denomination there was an irrepressible, though never consensual, conviction that learning compromised the straightforward sincerity needed to preach the gospel, and higher education was sure to corrupt it. In the South this conviction was manifest in an irascible, down-from-the-mountains hostility; in the North it was more likely to take the form of passive indifference. But in both regions the hope of a learned clergy was pursued by an elite in the teeth of (usually) low-intensity resistance.[265] Second, since the ministers to be educated were never numerous enough to constitute collegiate student bodies (as distinct from peopling a seminary), the concept required from the first a much larger lay clientele who, even if they could be motivated to enroll, would by their numbers require a different program and curriculum from the ministerial students.[266] Third, though ministerial students were usually not expected to pay — or to be able to pay — the costs of their own education, the burden of their support would have to derive either from scholarships funded by the churches or from a surplus created by a surcharge on the tuition payments levied on the lay students. Neither alternative was workable. Thus, from the very start, the Baptist colleges were not going to be able to fulfill the primary objective given for their existence.

The same difficulties, compounded, bedeviled the possibility that these schools would exist to educate Baptist laypeople. By their class, their geographic dispersion, and their religious ideals Baptists were not inclined to seek higher learning in the numbers required to make so many foundations financially viable. Thus from the outset the survival of Baptist colleges required the recruitment of non-Baptist students to such an extent as to make it difficult to sustain a Baptist ethos on the campus.

Yet these internal contrarieties which so handicapped the Baptist educational endeavors were not at all peculiar to their experience. Most other denominations, especially those of an evangelical inclination, had to cope with the same realities.

There was a further problem, from the start. Baptist academics customarily made explicit avowals that the education they offered was not "sectarian." Some think this claim was an act of deference to liberal cant. It might also be understood as an act of modesty by Baptists who, despite their having suffered as a despised and persecuted sect, and imagining that the shape of their piety and belief was no more than biblical, really did not consider that they had much by way of distinctive doctrine to offer. The Baptists also shared with other "believers' churches" (e.g., Mennonites, Brethren, Quakers, Disciples of Christ) the conviction that to be responsive to the governance of the Holy Spirit they might have to be as wary of denominational authorities as of civil governments.[267] What Baptist educators meant effectively by "nonsectarian" was that their schools required a faculty that was necessarily "Christian" but not necessarily Baptist. If we define "Christian" as used here, it cannot include Catholics or Orthodox or confessing Lutherans or (perhaps) Episcopalians. It means evangelical Protestants.

What then does "sectarian" mean? The notion was begotten of the Pietist reform, which called believers away from the secondary theological controversies that were distracting them from the "one thing necessary": pure and undefiled devotion to the gospel. It encouraged the view that the Christian faith included few essential and simple components, and it discouraged an overzealous inquiry into their meaning. What the Baptist founders meant by their disavowal of "sectarian" education was to exclude any fixation on theological accidentals that would concentrate on the differences that separated Baptists from other evangelicals, so as to make their schools inhospitable to the Methodists, Presbyterians, Disciples, Moravians, Congregationalists, and others who were essential to their survival.

In practice, however, "nonsectarian" came to mean "nondenominational," and by an inexorable inner logic, not necessarily Christian, or even religious. This devolution was not apparently intended. But so much in life is never intended.

The Baptist doctrine of church held that Christian conversion was what the individual, converted believer brought to the church rather than what he or she was invited into the church to share. And if the church did not beget faith at its onset, then it would not be seen as the necessary community wherein faith would seek further understanding. It could not be obvious, then, that to be Christian their schools would have to represent a functioning church actively seeking to develop its faith. There was little conviction that they might need to be functionally Baptist, not just Baptist-founded, Baptist-sponsored, Baptist-related. Like the first two difficulties mentioned above, this was not an impairment that handicapped only the Baptists. It afflicted many traditions of Christian higher education.

Baptist Difficulties

Baptist higher education did, however, labor under some ideological limitations of its own. They relate to three enduring Baptist doctrines: (1) The Scriptures are the ultimate and sufficient authority for Christian faith. (2) The individual believer, with "soul sufficiency," is empowered to resolve the right meaning of the Scriptures and derive faith from them. (3) No traditional creedal formula may be used to test others' faith, for that would make the living subject to the dead.

Notwithstanding the first doctrine, that Scripture is the supreme, sufficient, and only norm for faith, Baptists have not produced many outstanding biblical academicians. They have generally lacked the scholarly ability to disengage from rationalist usage the historical and literary methods whereby to discern what the inspired authors, in context, truly meant to convey. The result has not been that Baptists had no shared communal understanding of the Scriptures, for they do. What it has meant is that their exegesis has been undisciplined. The result is that the Bible, instead of governing private and public discourse within the denomination, has been vulnerable to a conventional and often undebatable (and thus un-self-conscious, uncritical) interpretation which becomes the effectively ultimate authority. Except for an educated elite, the Bible has thus become subject, not supreme. And that educated elite has often been so permeated by religious indifference that some of them do not much care what the Bible has to say.

As regards the second doctrine, that the individual is the sovereign, or at least autonomous, interpreter of Scripture, one might expect that Baptists as solo practitioners of interpretation would generate more internal diversity than the churches which consider the reading and exposition of Scripture and its elaboration into doctrine to be a communal activity, energized by those endowed with the charisms of prophet and sage. To the contrary, Baptists have displayed a fellowship of belief and expression which suggests that they do in fact engage in a communal (though less self-conscious) process of discernment with effectively authoritative boundaries. That the belief has been carried in two or three traditions (which often interact disagreeably), and not just a single one, does not mean there is no community of discourse; it means that the denomination shelters several. The difficulty is that, not realizing or even admitting that the elaboration of faith is a shared intellectual task, they must do it covertly, and thus it escapes a fuller inspection and critique.

As regards the third doctrine, that the contemporary generation is sovereign and not accountable to any persons or texts between the New Testament and the present: if accepted unthoughtfully it would lead one to imagine that Baptists have no tradition. Yet Baptist teaching is very traditional. It bears the marks and prints of the various controversies that have made Baptists march to battle.[268] A clandestine tradition, however, does not permit enough open and conscious deliberation for it to be adequately cultivated as every generation has need.

If Baptists have been unsuccessful in creating an intellectual field of Scripture-animated discourse that enlivens and integrates their minds' work in their colleges and universities, it may be due in part to this impeded self-consciousness. Baptists have been slow to admit and to develop a shared tradition of inquiry and discourse that would bring the light of their faith to bear in a critical yet distinctively Christian fashion upon the public culture and the various intellectual disciplines. Often, when pressed to defend the existence of denominational colleges, Baptist educators have replied with the commonplace that "All truth is of God." It is not much of an answer, for it is the business of a house of learning to detect in an inspired way how much of what is purveyed in the culture is repugnant to God, and not truth. Perhaps because of an impeded tradition of exegesis, and a diffidence about being a community of shared faith and shared inquiry into and application of the faith, and little success in building up the mediating educational understructure that would cantilever the faith out into the humanities and the natural and social sciences and the professions, Baptist intellectuals were slow to create a truly integrated educational enterprise on the campuses that were once theirs.

By distancing themselves from the internal communion of wise reflection and dialogue and renewal, and from the external, rambunctious intercourse between the churches and the cultures, disciplines, and persuasions that are the nourishment and provocation of higher education, Baptists have exposed themselves to the risk of becoming dull intellectuals.

Because of these particular inhibitions on doctrinal proficiency, Baptist educators have often described the Christian element in their colleges as "moral." Yet here, too, for want of enough historical perspective and theological dialectic, Baptists have often engaged in manners rather than morals. There has been a twofold result: they have failed to take an eager or influential enough part in public disputes on Christian moral duty, while treating manners with the deference due to morals. When they have taken a firm moral position, for want of theological footings they have sometimes uncritically adopted practices or programs that were essentially secular, like Walter Rauschenbusch's social gospel, which was much more social than gospel.[269]

Baptists would have been more animated and successful sponsors of higher education if they could have developed and honored the exegetical, historical, philosophical, and theological proficiency which is part of the software that faith requires to engage publicly, and if they could have questioned the doctrinaire conviction that believers make their way to God only as isolated individuals.

Sandford Fleming, in his loving and indefatigable manuscript chronicle of these scores and scores of academies, colleges, universities, and seminaries that were once Baptist, and then so persistently were not, often concludes his vignettes with a coda like this one: "Although ———— University does not appear in the present list of Baptist institutions, a situation regretted by many, Baptists can take satisfaction in this institution which was born and reared in their fellowship." Surely, though, regret can yield to satisfaction only if one believes that what a university thereby lost was of only nominal value, not a light giving insight without which learning goes dark.

NOTES TO CHAPTER 4

1. A major point of policy change might have occurred at the Triennial Convention of 1820, when the influence of Luther Rice persuaded the body to bring educational operations under central direction. Without financial support, the policy failed of effect. Robert Lincoln Kelly, *The American Colleges and the Social Order* (New York: Macmillan, 1940), 32-33.

2. D[aniel] S[eely] Gregory, *The Presbyterian Church in its Relation to Higher Education and the Ministry* (Lake Forest, Ill.: Presbyterian Ministerial Association, 1882).

3. This college is related to both the SBC and the ABC/USA.

4. Besides these institutions which award the bachelor's degree, the various Southern Baptist state conventions sponsor two junior colleges and five Bible colleges which are not included in this study.

5. George Washington Paschal, *History of Wake Forest College I, 1834-1865* (Wake Forest: Wake Forest College, 1935), 1-13.

6. I have been much assisted in understanding these matters by Dr. Michael Beaty. William L. Lumpkin, *Baptist Foundations in the South: Tracing through the Separates the Influence of the Great Awakening, 1754-1787* (Nashville: Broadman, 1961); George Washington Paschal, *History of North Carolina Baptists* (Raleigh: General Board, North Carolina Baptist State Convention, 1930); H. Leon McBeth, *The Baptist Heritage* (Nashville: Broadman, 1987); McBeth, "Southern Baptist Higher Education," in *The Lord's Free People in a Free Land,* ed. William R. Estep (Fort Worth: Evans, 1976), 11-26; David F. D'Amico, "Piety and Intellect: Baptist Educational Efforts after the Great Awakening," in *Free People,* 39-53; Donald G. Tewksbury, *The Founding of American Colleges and Universities before the Civil War* (New York: Columbia University, 1932), 111; Paschal, *History of Wake Forest,* 1:16-29.

7. Paschal, *History of Wake Forest,* 1:30-39; Nancy Tatom Ammerman, *Baptist Battles* (New Brunswick, N.J.: Rutgers University Press, 1990), 27; Rubun L. Brantley, ed., *Baptist Education Study Task [BEST]* (Nashville: Education Commission of the Southern Baptist Convention, 1967), 3.

8. Paschal, *History of Wake Forest,* 1:57.

9. Paschal, *History of Wake Forest,* 1:76-89; *Wake Forest College Bulletin, 1951,* 30; Charles D. Johnson, *Higher Education of Southern Baptists: An Institutional History, 1826-1954* (Waco: Baylor University Press, 1955), 10-12. Though ministerial students were only a small number amid the total student body, they were more likely to see the curriculum through, and to earn degrees; e.g., in 1839 all four graduates were preachers; Paschal, *History of Wake Forest,* 1:357. The Society for Promoting Manual Labor in Literary Institutions had been founded three years earlier, in 1831, and reflected a widespread hope for such schools as wholesome and, in particular, congruent with the evangelical revival movement.

10. The literary societies forbade the discussion of controverted religious questions, though this restriction was not seen to apply to matters dealing with Catholics, Mormons, or atheists. Paschal, *History of Wake Forest,* 1:539.

11. Paschal, *History of Wake Forest,* 1:175-81; Ammerman, 28-30.

12. Though the trustees were on record early that they wished to offer tuition free to ministerial students and the sons of ministers, this became financially possible only in 1859. Paschal, *History of Wake Forest,* 1:350-51.

13. One Wake Forest alumnus gave voice in 1855 to a sharp class consciousness between the denominational and the state institutions:

Here [at the state college] are collected from every distinction of sect or political party the sons of our great men, who are generally so free with their fathers' purses (as much as with their reputations), and the sons, worse still, of our overgrown rich men — these having little to do in the ordinary drudgeries of life, and their fathers having reputation or money enough to last some two or three generations of spoiled and petted children, conclude to spend their time as becomes their birth or wealth; and then follows upon those wise deductions a round of wild, reckless extravagance, that one would scarcely believe, were he not an eye witness. But of what force is this to the argument? Just this: The young man who would mingle with a large company of these, without going their rounds of smoking, eating, drinking and dressing, would be treated by these young lords with a haughty superciliousness and cool effrontery, which would drive away one of ordinary nerve.

Paschal, *History of Wake Forest*, 1:465-66.

14. Slavery, a continual topic of debate in the literary societies, was regularly affirmed not to be a moral evil. Paschal, *History of Wake Forest*, 1:547.

15. Paschal, *History of Wake Forest*, 1:605-56.

16. Paschal, *History of Wake Forest College II, 1865-1905* (Wake Forest: Wake Forest College, 1943), 2:190-202, 65 n.

17. Paschal, *History of Wake Forest*, 2:293-308.

18. Paschal, *History of Wake Forest*, 2:295.

19. At Davidson College, by contrast, ministerial students numbered between thirty and forty. Paschal, *History of Wake Forest*, 2:15, 23.

20. Paschal, *History of Wake Forest*, 2:335, 140, 181, 211.

21. Paschal, *History of Wake Forest*, 2:103, 135-40.

22. Paschal, *History of Wake Forest*, 2:226, 262, 454-89, 419; Johnson, 421; Rubun L. Brantley, 4. The resolve of the state, as of 1905, to build a system of 155 public high schools quickly closed down the Baptist high school network. Paschal, *History of Wake Forest College III, 1905-1943* (Wake Forest: Wake Forest College, 1943), 293-300.

23. Paschal, *History of Wake Forest*, 2:217, 326-27, 353.

24. Paschal, *History of Wake Forest*, 3:13. The "Report of the Dean" in 1923-24 finds otherwise: "Practically all members of the faculty have participated and their regular attendance explains the lack of difficulty sometimes felt in enforcing chapel regulations." Yet during this time faculty were asked to include chapel attendance as a factor in the calculation of grades in courses and honors at graduation, and the attendance at church on Sunday is said to have included only one-fourth of the student body. Paschal, *History of Wake Forest*, 3:16, 15.

In the "Report of the Dean" for 1916-17, one reads this awesome observation: "My opinion is that there has been less drinking, gambling, and immorality than before."

25. Paschal, *History of Wake Forest*, 3:119-34. Poteat also harbored unconventional views on warfare (pp. 89-90). It is of note that in 1925-26 Poteat could disclose in his annual report that 42 percent of the faculty at Wake Forest then had the doctorate, a rate higher than at Duke, Richmond, Davidson, Washington and Lee, and even Chapel Hill (37 percent). In 1948 Wake Forest reported 39 percent with the doctorate, and in 1955, 42 percent. Johnson, 428-29.

26. Paschal, *History of Wake Forest*, 3:225-42.

27. "Report of the Registrar," in *Report of the President, Wake Forest College, 1930-1931*. What made these figures more disagreeable was the knowledge that very few North Carolinians went to college to begin with: 1 of every 250 residents, compared to 1 of 167 nationally. *Report of the President, 1926-1927*.

28. "Report of the Chaplain," in *Report of the President, Wake Forest College, 1935-1936*.

29. Paschal, *History of Wake Forest*, 3:439. His discussion of Wake Forest religion in the thirties is at 436-51.

30. Paschal, *History of Wake Forest*, 3:444-51.

31. Bynum Shaw, *The History of Wake Forest College IV:1943-1967* (Wake Forest: Wake Forest University, 1988), 13-14.

32. Shaw, 4:118-27.

33. Paschal, *History of Wake Forest*, 3:48-49, 139.

34. A statement drafted by the Centennial Committee and approved by the faculty, incorporated in the *Report of the President, Wake Forest College, 1923-1924*, 8-10.

35. Shaw, 4:65-74.

36. Reynolds, it was believed, had made earlier overtures to Baylor University, but a revolt among Texas Baptists had kept Baylor from accepting and moving to Cameron Park from downtown Waco. See the recollections of Dr. Fred Bentley, then president of Mars Hill College, and a close participant in negotiations between the convention and the university: "The Wake Forest/Baptist State Convention Relationship, 1979-1986, An Oral History Project, Commissioned and Owned by the Council on Christian Higher Education, Deposited with and Administered by the Baptist Historical Collection, Z. Smith Reynolds Library, Wake Forest University" ([WFU/BSC/2/Bentley]; subsequent references to the Oral History Project hereafter cited in similar fashion), Dr. Percival Perry, interviewer: BSCRG 12.1, 1/2, 7.

37. Shaw, 4:25-44.

38. Shaw, 4:92-145. While most Southern Baptist colleges in the midsixties did not have self-perpetuating boards, and their trustees had to be Baptists from their home states, Richmond, Mercer, and Stetson Universities and William Jewell College were exceptions. Ben C. Fisher, *A Manual for College Trustees* (Council on Christian Education of the North Carolina Baptist State Convention, 1968 [1st ed. 1965]), 10.

At about this time, due to a failed fund drive by the convention, annual subsidies to the colleges were beginning to taper off. Ben C. Fisher, "An Analysis of Cooperative Program Support and Current Financial Problems of the North Carolina State Colleges," Council on Christian Education, July 1963.

39. Shaw, 4:141.

40. Shaw, 4:135-59.

41. Shaw, 4:346-57.

42. *Council Self-Study* (Preliminary Report), Council on Christian Higher Education, Baptist State Convention of North Carolina (1965), 2, 11.

43. H. I. Hester, *Southern Baptists in Higher Education* (Murfreesboro, N.C.: Privately Printed, 1968), 15. At Wake Forest the reported ministerial students fell in 1936-37 to 8 percent of the enrollment.

44. *Report of the President, Wake Forest College, 1927-1928*. Except where otherwise noted, the data that follow are drawn from the annual presidential reports. Also, they include the undergraduates and (later) the graduate students from the Reynolda campus, but not students from the professional schools, where the Baptist presence is presumed to be much less.

45. In 1990 Southern Baptists constituted 21.8 percent of North Carolina's population: Martin B. Bradley et al., *Churches and Church Membership in the United States, 1990* (Atlanta: Glenmary Research Center, 1992).

46. The author owes special gratitude to Mrs. Margaret Perry, veteran registrar of Wake Forest University, for her patience and perseverance in unearthing these statistics.

47. "Baptist Group Seeks to Cut WFU Support," *Winston-Salem Journal*, 9 July 1970.

48. "Baptist Still Fighting Support of Colleges," *Winston-Salem Journal and Sentinel*, 10 November 1974. The North Carolina Baptist Convention continued to honor its agreement with the Z. Smith Reynolds Foundation that it would allot 7.5 percent of its distributable annual funds to Wake Forest; the foundation was going well beyond its commitment to match that amount. "Convention Asked to Consider Commitment to Wake Forest," *Winston-Salem Journal and Sentinel*, 11 November 1975.

49. The brochure was drawn from a self-study report published in 1975 and issued in

January 1977. Hayes, a 1948 Wake Forest graduate, had been a candidate for student body president of the IDGAD (I Don't Give a Damn) Party, and editor of the student magazine; during his years on the board of trustees he was editor of *Esquire*. See also "WFU Plan Aims at Stronger Baptist Ties," *Winston-Salem Sentinel,* 9 November 1976. The changes included a full-time administrator for church relations, enlargement of the church music program, resumption of a medical missions conference at the medical school, more continuing education for clergy, more student volunteer services through area churches, closer collaboration with pastoral care at Baptist Hospital, larger tuition concessions for ministerial students, and new concessions for North Carolina pastors, their spouses, and their children. This announcement came just as the Baptist State Convention was about to have its annual meeting.

50. See, e.g., "Cut WFU Ties, Baptists Told," *Winston-Salem Sentinel,* 8 April 1977.

51. What is probably the most reliable account of the entire Flynt debacle is available in an interview given years later by Dr. James Ralph Scales, president emeritus: WFU/BSC/22/Scales, 19-23.

52. From his retirement, Tribble railed at Baptist critics. "It has often been said that Dr. Billy Poteat won the battle, but lost the war with the Baptists and unfortunately the lure was money. In all the years since, Wake Forest has not received enough money to justify that fatal mistake" (surrendering control over the board to the convention). "Tribble Lashes Out at Wake Forest's Baptist Foes," *Winston-Salem Sentinel,* 26 July 1977.

53. "Wake Forest — The Tie That Binds?" *Charlotte Observer,* 25 December 1977. Baylor University in Waco, the largest of Baptist educational institutions, backed away in 1943 from an offer to incorporate its College of Medicine in a large new medical complex in Dallas, because it would have had to surrender governance. A later invitation to a similar complex in Houston was accepted, with Baylor retaining control. In 1968, in the space of only four weeks the College of Medicine persuaded the Baylor trustees and the Baptist General Convention of Texas (which approved almost without dissent) to allow it to incorporate independently of them in order to be free to seek state and federal funding (the Baptists were at the time providing less than 1 percent of the college's annual budget). Said the *(Baptist) Standard:* "Texas Baptists do not need to apologize for giving the College of Medicine birth nor for their efforts to nurture it from infancy to maturity. Neither do we need to apologize nor grieve over turning it loose." In 1971 the College of Dentistry in Dallas was similarly detached. Eugene W. Baker, *To Light the Ways of Time: An Illustrated History of Baylor University, 1845-1986* (Waco: Baylor University, 1987).

54. "Convention-WFU Relationship at Serious Stage," *Biblical Recorder,* 24 December 1977; "Baptist Official Wants WFU Accord," *Winston-Salem Sentinel,* 27 December 1977.

55. "Ministers Favor Redefining Wake Forest U. Role," *Greenville Daily Reflector,* 1 January 1978.

56. Rev. W. W. Findlater, "Dear Old Wake Forest!" *Winston-Salem Sentinel,* 19 February 1978.

57. "Baptist Pastors Invited to Discussion of Wake," *Winston-Salem Sentinel,* 17 January 1978; "Baptists Make 56 Resolutions on WF 'Crisis,'" *Winston-Salem Journal,* 24 January 1978.

58. "Scales, Minister Dispute 'Mission,'" *Winston-Salem Journal,* 24 January 1978.

59. "Compromise Eases Wake Forest University Controversy," *Winston-Salem Journal,* 11 March 1978.

60. "Corts to Push for Holding Baptist Money from Wake Forest University," *Winston-Salem Journal,* 12 December 1978; "Committee to Propose Cutoff of Wake Forest University Funds," *Winston-Salem Sentinel,* 23 January 1979. About the same time fundamentalists in the Virginia Baptist General Association lost a vote to sever ties with the University of Richmond. Their grievances included drinking, dormitory visitation, and a liberal religion professor. "Virginia Baptists Argue over Support for University," *Winston-Salem Sentinel,* 21 November 1978.

The press was generally sympathetic to the university. For instance, the *Charlotte Observer:* "As it has grown in size and national status, Wake Forest's need for greater freedom has grown more apparent. It cannot attract gifted faculty and promising students under restraints the convention might impose. (For instance, the convention would like to require that all Wake Forest faculty be professing Christians, a move that would offend many scholars.) Wake Forest probably would be happy to be Baptist in the same way that Davidson is Presbyterian and Duke is Methodist." "Wake Forest: More Self-Rule Is Needed," 20 November 1978.

61. "Wake Forest Begins Quest for Financing," *Raleigh News and Observer,* 15 November 1979; "Wake Forest Trustees Say Covenant OK," *Raleigh News and Observer,* 16 December 1979. These events were given bitter comment by Paige Patterson and Paul Pressler, leaders of the eventually successful fundamentalist drive to take control of the Southern Baptist Convention: "The saddest part about our denomination is there is no shame that we've lost Wake Forest University completely. There's no shame that we have virtually lost the University of Richmond; no shame that in the institutions and even the pulpits of our Land the Word of God is not honored and magnified, but rather, we talk about sociology and psychology and the events of the day." "We've Lost Wake Forest Completely," *Winston-Salem Sentinel,* 27 September 1980. The *Sentinel* itself commended the university as worthy of church support. "Baptists' Board: Wake Deserves Our Support," 1 October 1980.

62. "The Covenant between the Baptist State Convention of North Carolina and Wake Forest University," effective 1 January 1981 and distributed to the faculty in 1982-83. Any inclination to criticize the substance of this covenant should be tempered by its ethereal antecedent, the "Reaffirmations" endorsed by nine hundred Southern Baptist educators at a conference in Willamsburg in July 1976. H. I. Hester, *Partners in Purpose and Progress: A Brief History of The Education Commission of The Southern Baptist Convention* (N.P.: The Education Commission of the Southern Baptist Conventon, 1977), 79-82.

63. WFU/BSC/22/Scales, 15-16, 23; WFU/BSC/2/Bentley, 17-33. Rev. Warren Carr, then pastor of the Wake Forest Baptist Church, had considered Ray hostile: "Minister Tags Official as WFU Adversary," *Winston-Salem Sentinel,* 1 March 1978; see also WFU/BSC/7/Bentley, 12-19. See also Rev. Edgar D. Christman, longtime Wake Forest chaplain, WFU/BSC/8/Christman, 19-22; Weston P. Hatfield, Esq., chairman of the Wake Forest board during its final severance, WFU/BSC/11/Hatfield, 12. It is significant that, according to President Scales, whenever the denomination looked ready to ignore the names recommended by Wake Forest for election to its board, his intervention always sufficed to have the original roster reinstated.

64. Dr. Cecil A. Ray, WFU/BSC/20/Ray, 24, 55-56.

65. WFU/BSC/2/Bentley, 31; WFU/BSC/22/Scales, 30-31.

66. *On Mission: The Church/College Alliance, the Purpose and Role of North Carolina Baptist Colleges and Universities* (Raleigh: Council on Christian Higher Education of the Baptist State Convention of North Carolina, 1981), vii-viii, 1, 3, 4, 6, 7, 24.

67. "Wake Forest University: 2000 Study," May 1983: a report prepared for and discussed by the board of trustees, revised by a joint trustee/university committee, and submitted for acceptance and release.

68. "He Made Them Hopping Mad," *Winston-Salem Sentinel,* 4 March 1982; "Given a Choice, Churches Donate Less to Wake Forest," *Raleigh News and Observer,* 14 March 1982.

69. "The Covenant," *Winston-Salem Sentinel,* 3 January 1984.

70. WFU/BSC/22/Scales, 31; WFU/BSC/2/Bentley, 24. The record shows that denominational officials never actually elected trustees other than those put forward by the university.

71. "December Actions Affect University Governance," news release circulated by President Hearn in February 1986.

72. *Annual of the 156th Annual Session of the Baptist State Convention of North Carolina,* Greensboro, 10-12 November 1986, 100-102; Russell Brantley, "Wake Forest, Baptist Convention Begin New Relationship," *Wake Forest University Magazine,* January 1977, 2-3.

73. Editorial, "Wake Forest Goes Secular," *Winston-Salem Journal,* 13 November 1986.

74. Quoted in Zoë Ingalls, "Balancing a Baptist Tradition and the Liberal Arts," *Chronicle of Higher Education,* 7 January 1987.

75. *Annual of the 157th Annual Session of the Baptist State Convention of North Carolina,* Greensboro, 9-11 November 1987, 151-52; Thomas K. Hearn, Jr., *Heritage and Prospect: Excerpts from Essays and Addresses* (prepared by the Wake Forest Office of University Relations in 1989), 3-4, 19.

76. Bylaws of Wake Forest University, I: "Mission and Purpose."

77. Bylaws of Wake Forest University, IV:A,6: "Qualifications (of Trustees)."

78. Hearn also said he was confident that "with direct contributions from churches and other friends, we will replace the Cooperative Program funding that we relinquished in the new agreement." Russell Brantley, 3. Whatever the "other friends" gave (and the Reynolds family remained most friendly), the churches were not forthcoming. Earmarked contributions by congregations through the convention had begun to rise to about $500,000 per annum. But their direct contributions after the severance totaled only $89,000 in 1988. *Biblical Recorder,* 14 January 1989, 1.

79. WFU/BSC/12/Hearn, 22.

80. WFU/BSC/12/Hearn, 23.

81. WFU/BSC/7/Carr, 30.

82. WFU/BSC/7/Carr, 35.

83. Carr, interview with the author, 7 May 1993.

84. "Courts May Have to Settle Dispute between Wake Forest and Baptists," *High Point Enterprise,* 1 February 1986.

85. WFU/BSC/8/Christman, 59-60.

86. "Courts May Have to Settle."

87. WFU/BSC/9/Corts, 10-11.

88. WFU/BSC/22/Scales, 30.

89. Interview with the author, 7 May 1993. Carr went on to make it clear that this was his own position:

> But I thought that it was a lot of fun in the University, scolding the preachers and the church for embracing unexamined concepts. And I thought it was also a lot of fun hearing some preacher from the mountains out here come down to this sophisticated place and take on the learned professors, only because in his own judgment he was speaking the Word of God! It was great! I don't know what your experience has been, Doctor, but it seems to me that it is the university which hasn't been able to stand the heat in the kitchen, and it has run from the criticism of the church rather than the opposite. These institutions that are supposed to be such open places of inquiry are scared to death of honest criticism.

90. *Biblical Recorder,* 25 January 1986, 2.

91. These items come from Wake Forest's *Old Gold and Black,* 29 April 1993: "Gay Rights Advocates Show Support for Civil Rights by Marching upon Capitol," 1; advertisements, 4; "Students Present Papers on Gay Studies," 2; letter to the editor from Brian Thacker, 8; "Student Makes Controversial Art," 3.

92. Hearn, *Heritage and Prospect,* 4.

93. "Fundamentalist Students Assail Baylor U. Policies," *Chronicle of Higher Education,* 9 January 1985, 3.

94. "Conversation with the President," *Baylor Line,* November 1990, 47.

95. News release jointly issued by the Baptist General Convention of Texas and Baylor University, 24 July 1991, 2.

96. "State Baptist Panel Recommends BU Funds Release," *Waco Tribune-Herald,* 14 August 1991, 1A. The appraisal of Baylor's future prospects continues to be a subject of speculation: William E. Hull, provost of Samford University, "The Crisis in Baptist Higher Education:

An Historical Perspective," *Journal of the South Carolina Baptist Historical Society* 18 (November 1992): 2-11; James Parker III, "The Secularization of Our Colleges and Universities," *Texas Baptist,* October 1993, 14-15.

97. "Trustees Limit Baptist Control over University," *New York Times,* 21 October 1990, 49; Religious News Service Release #13295, 22 November 1990 (hereafter cited as RNS); "Baptists Sever Ties with Furman U.," *Chronicle of Higher Education,* 27 May 1992; *Chronicle of Higher Education,* 8 July 1992; Jim Stewart, "A New Beginning," *Furman Magazine,* summer 1992, 12-19. In an aside, President Johns said, "Everything started over the issue of power, but it ended over the issue of money." Stewart, 13.

98. "A Peaceful Way of Easing Control by the Baptists," *New York Times,* 18 November 1990, 52. The Religious News Service reports: "Some members of the Florida Baptist Convention have suggested that the state body take some of the money away from Stetson and spend it on evangelism and fighting abortion. On the other hand, the school's refusal to bar abortion-rights advocates from speaking on campus has also upset some pro-life activists in the state convention" (RNS #13476, 20 November 1990). See also "More Baptist Colleges Hope to Loosen Ties to Church Leaders," *Chronicle of Higher Education,* 5 December 1990, A15.

99. These figures, from 1960 to 1990, include all institutions of higher education, not just four-year colleges and universities. See "1961 Southern Baptist Handbook," *Quarterly Review* 21, no. 3 (July-September 1961): 46-49; *Southern Baptist Handbook: 1991* (Nashville: Sunday School Board of the Southern Baptist Convention, 1991), 101-6.

100. In 1997 the Meredith College board revised its charter to eliminate the need for approval of trustee elections by the North Carolina Baptist State Convention, with the assurance that "Meredith has been a Baptist College for 106 years. We will continue to be a Baptist College." "Meredith College Severs Its Ties to N.C. Baptists," *Chronicle of Higher Education,* 14 March 1997, A34.

101. Arthur L. Walker, [Jr.], "The Future of the Association of Southern Baptist Colleges and Schools," 22 June 1993, 4, 5. Just a few months earlier Secretary Walker had written: "Church-related educational institutions developed because of the conviction that they were a part of the mission of the church to affect change in both the life of the individual and in society. Some institutions have lost sight of the significance of this mission." "Christian Education Requires Renewed Emphasis," *Southern Baptist Educator* 57, no. 6 (April 1993): 15.

102. Benjamin Coleman Fisher, *The Challenge of Secularism to Christian Higher Education,* the 1982 Hester Lectures (Nashville: Education Commission of the Southern Baptist Convention, [1982]), 19. This is reprinted in *Integrating Faith and Academic Discipline,* selected H. I. Hester Lectures, ed. Arthur L. Walker, Jr. (Nashville: Education Commission of the Southern Baptist Convention, 1992), 129.

103. Morgan Edwards, a pastor in Philadelphia, quoted in Frank William Padelford, "The Story of Baptist Education," *Colgate-Rochester Divinity School Bulletin* 11, no. 1 (October 1938): 7.

104. Padelford, "The Story of Baptist Education," 5-6, 13. For comparisons with the experience, attitudes, and educational endeavors of another Anabaptist group, the Mennonites, see Harold Ernest Bauman, "The Believers' Church and the Church College" (Ed.D. diss., Columbia University, 1972), 83-93.

105. William Warren Sweet, *Religion on the American Frontier: The Baptists, 1783-1830* (New York: Henry Holt, 1931), 1-57; Lumpkin (see n. 6 above); Eugene Eli DuBois, "The Secularization of Selected Church Related Institutions of Higher Education in New York State" (Ed.D. diss., Wayne State University, 1966), 21-22; Robert G. Torbet, *A History of the Baptists,* 3rd ed. (Valley Forge, Pa.: Judson, 1973), 224-34.

106. Sandford Fleming, "American Baptists and Higher Education in the Area of the American (Northern) Baptist Convention" (unpublished typescript, © The American Baptist Board of Education and Publication, 1965), 27-28; this typescript exists in three copies, one of which is kept in the American Baptist Archives Center, Valley Forge, Pennsylvania (hereafter cited as

ABCA). "No college in America, no university in England stood upon such a platform," said William MacDonald. *Exercises Commemorating the Restoration of the University* (Providence: Brown University, 1905), 32.

George P. Schmidt explains this charter in its Baptist context:

> The Baptist church in the late eighteenth century was by no means the large powerful body it has since grown to be. A group of dissenters, whose history was one long struggle against hostile and disintegrating forces, it was but natural that they should jealously safeguard their corporate integrity by exercising close control over their institutions. At the same time their very existence had depended upon the recognition of the principle of toleration, and it would have been inconsistent to demand toleration for themselves while denying it to others.

> *The Old-Time College President* (New York: Columbia University Press, 1930), 30.

107. Fleming, 37-42.

108. Fleming, 46, 80.

109. The resident ministers, many of them illiterate, mostly served without pay. "They considered it unfair and wicked for the traveling agents of the newly organized missionary and educational causes to take collections from their people." Frank Padelford, "When an Educated Minister Was an Insult," *Missions* 27, no. 6 (June 1936): 350-51.

110. See, e.g., Fleming, 87-88, on the vicissitudes of Shurtleff College's relationship to the Baptists.

111. "The Baptists are by no means uniform in their opinions of slavery. Many let it alone, some remonstrate against it in general terms, others oppose it vehemently, while far the greater part of them hold slaves." David Benedict, *A History of the Baptists* (Boston: Lincoln & Edmands, 1813), 2:207; quoted in Ullin Whitney Leavell, *Philanthropy in Negro Education* (Nashville: Peabody College for Teachers, 1930), 21. The Southern Baptists, after their schism in 1845, took little initiative to educate blacks in their midst. By contrast, the Southern Methodists were active in evangelical and educational work among Negroes. "They had separated from the northern division to retain their slaves. Now they redoubled their efforts to better the condition of the slaves." Leavell, 19.

112. Fleming, 366-68.

113. Fleming, 370-78. The *American Baptist Quarterly* 11, no. 4-12, no. 1 (December 1992 and March 1993), devoted two consecutive issues to this enterprise: "Pursuit of the Promise: American Baptists and Black Higher Education," associate editor Ralph Reavis, Sr. See Beverly Clark Carlson, "Pursuit of the Promise: An Overview," *American Baptist Quarterly* 11, no. 4 (December 1992): 282-89.

114. See, e.g., Mamie O. Oliver, "The Lord's Work in the Mississippi Minefield: Baptist Home Missions and Jackson College," *American Baptist Quarterly* 11, no. 4 (December 1992): 340..

115. Leavell, 154.

116. The report claims that 600,000 freed blacks had become Baptists since the Emancipation. "The Educational Work of the American Baptist Home Mission Society," originally published in the *Home Mission Monthly* (August 1889), reproduced in the *American Baptist Quarterly* 11, no. 4 (December 1992): 44.

117. "Baptist Educational Institutions in United States and Canada," American Baptist Educational Committee, circular no. 2 (June 1887); copy in the archives of Linfield College.

118. *Centennial*, no. 1 (July 1873): 3-4, ABCA.

119. Fleming, 138.

120. *Centennial*, no. 1, p. 2. One motive proposed to the membership was the prospect that Catholics were actively founding schools of their own. See Augustus Hopkins Strong, 1889,

quoted in *Colgate-Rochester Divinity School Bulletin* 11, no. 3 (February 1939): 126-27; Evelyn Brooks Higginbotham, "En-Gendering Leadership in the Home Mission Schools," *American Baptist Quarterly* 12, no. 1 (March 1993): 19. As Catholics later moved into a numerical and (sometimes) proportional dominance in higher education, the relevant statistics were often used as a goad for Baptist motivation: J. Hillis Miller, president of Keuka College in New York, "A Tragic Drift," *Watchman-Examiner* 26, no. 22 (2 June 1938): 609. See also Miller, "The Possible Black-Out for Baptist Schools and Colleges," *Annual of the Northern Baptist Convention, 1940,* 187, where he reports (though without identifying the institution) that the University of Chicago was enrolling 10 percent Catholics and 4 percent Baptists (and 13 percent "Hebrews"). An earlier census — allegedly the first, in 1922 — reported that 11 percent of 4,970 postgraduate students reporting identified their religious preference as Methodist, 9 percent as Presbyterian, 6 percent as Jewish, 6 percent as Baptist ("only fourth"), 5 percent as Catholic, 5 percent as Episcopalian, 5 percent as Congregationalist, 4 percent as Lutheran, 3 percent as Disciples. "Men and Things," *Watchman-Examiner* 10, no. 8 (23 February 1922): 226.

121. Fleming, 455-56. It was also noted that the Educational Commission discontinued activity in 1876, four years after being made permanent. Fleming, 468.

122. By 1889 the Home Mission Society's twenty colleges in the South and in the Indian territories reported that only 10 percent of their students were studying for the ministry. Reckoning that about half of those enrolled were females, one would conclude that 20 percent of the male students were seeking the ministry. By 1908 the ministry students amounted to 5 percent of a total enrollment that has become three-fifths female: thus only 8 percent of the males. "The Educational Work of the American Baptist Home Mission Society," 43, 64; William C. Turner, "African-American Education in Eastern North Carolina: American Baptist Mission Work," *American Baptist Quarterly* 11, no. 4 (December 1992): 306.

Among the ABC colleges, William Jewell College in Missouri might serve here as a case in point. Through the 1870s and 1880s the ministerial students regularly amounted to one-third of the enrollment, secondary and collegiate. Forty years later it had leveled off at about 10 percent. James G. Clark, *History of William Jewell College, Liberty, Clay County, Missouri* (Saint Louis: Central Baptist Printery, 1893), 277-78; "Report of the (NBC) Board of Education, 1922," 10-15, ABCA.

In 1888, all Baptist colleges and universities, ABC and SBC and Free Baptists combined, reported 17 percent ministry students, which would probably represent 35 percent of the males. By 1902 that had shifted to 6 percent of total enrollment, and perhaps 13 percent of the males. *Annual of the Northern Baptist Convention, 1914,* 67.

123. Conrad Henry Moehlman, "How the Baptist Super-University Planned for New York City Was Built in Chicago," *Colgate-Rochester Divinity School Bulletin* 11, no. 3 (February 1939): 119-34.

124. W. R. Harper, "Some Features of an Ideal University," *Third Annual Meeting of the American Baptist Education Society,* held with the Southern Baptist Convention, 1891, 49, 59-60. It is of note that in contrast to Morehouse, quoted below, Harper mentions no need for the faculty or their academic work to be Baptist.

125. Thomas Wakefield Goodspeed, *A History of the University of Chicago, Founded by John D. Rockefeller* (Chicago: University of Chicago Press, 1916), 292-93.

126. H. L. Morehouse, "The University of Chicago: Is It a Baptist Institution?" *Standard* 41, no. 27 (1894): 4. On the same page President Harper explains at length how he had been misunderstood in his statement that the Cain and Abel narrative bears a formal resemblance to ancient myths.

127. James P. Wind, *The Bible and the University: The Messianic Vision of William Rainey Harper* (Atlanta: Scholars Press, 1987), 168. See also 33, 35, 109, 114, 125, 135, 136, 162, 178.

128. Padelford, "The Story of Baptist Education," 16; "Report of the Board of Education, Table Number One," *Annual of the Northern Baptist Convention, 1914,* 66.

129. Fleming, 665-66. The initiative for loosened ties is ascribed to Fred T. Gates, the founding secretary of the ABES, who had finally negotiated with Rockefeller his decision to make the University of Chicago a major object of his philanthropy, and who in the midnineties then went to work for Rockefeller as his philanthropic agent. The Chicago board seemingly instructed the president to approach the denomination to suggest that the Baptists surrender their reversionary rights and the control they conferred. Frank Padelford, Gates's successor, was enormously distressed by the proposal. He wrote to Ernest Burton, head of the Department of New Testament at Chicago and also chairman of the Board of Education of the NBC (successor to the ABES), to protest: "I feel sure that if we were to be a party to changing conditions of pledges, which were drawn as strongly as those made in Chicago, it would be utterly useless for us to appeal to Baptist men to make contributions for Baptist institutions." The issue became the subject of repeated and inconclusive negotiations until 1923. Fleming, 878-85.

130. "Education and Social Service," *Watchman-Examiner* 11, no. 23 (7 June 1923): 712-13.

131. *Annual of the Northern Baptist Convention, 1930*, 98-105.

132. In December of 1912 a staff member of the (Northern) Presbyterian College Board wrote to Ernest Burton, the new chairman of the NBC Education Board, to share with him a tactic which the Presbyterians thought effective to "hold a college to definite Christian principals [*sic*] and policy." He enclosed an elaborate deed of gift drafted to accompany all church subsidies. If the beneficiary college should fail to have a board elected or at least approved by church authorities, a determined number of required Bible courses, or a teaching staff comprising "only professors for whose positive Christian influence the president" can vouch, or if it failed to submit annual reports and receive visitations and annual approval from the church, then the gift would be forfeited and would revert to the church. Burton would himself play a central role in dismantling a much less pervasive reversionary deed at Chicago. George Rutger Brauer to Burton, 18 December 1912, ABCA.

133. *Church-Related Boards Responsible for Higher Education,* ed. James C. Messersmith (Washington: Departmen of Health, Education, and Welfare, Office of Education, 1964), 92. The University of Chicago's entry is thus annotated: "founded by and historically related to American Baptists, where the question of official policy concerning relationship is open for continuing consideration." The university was by that time giving the question very little continuing consideration indeed; Fleming, 666.

134. Torbet, 325.

135. "Report of the Board of Education, Table Number Three," *Annual of the Northern Baptist Convention, 1914*, 68.

136. One estimate was that already in 1913 Baptist students were a minority at Baptist colleges: E. A. Hanley, president of Franklin College, "What's the Good of Denominational Schools? Ten College Presidents Answer the Question," *Standard* 60, no. 49 (9 August 1913): 1442.

137. "Report of the Education Board," *Annual of the Northern Baptist Convention, 1913*, 38-42. Padelford here summarizes Baptist rankings in the government study: "Our position in this classification is far from satisfactory." A year later he discusses the same findings in a more popular publication and observes that "as compared with others, the standing of the Baptists is gratifying." "Classification of Baptist Colleges," *Pacific Baptist* 20, no. 31 (10 January 1914): 8-9.

In a subsequent article Padelford disclosed that there were three times as many Baptist students on state campuses as on their own. "The New Educational Force, the Board of Education," *Standard* 60, no. 44 (5 July 1913): 1320-21.

138. "Report of the Board of Education," *Annual of the Northern Baptist Convention, 1914*, 62.

139. *Annual of the Northern Baptist Convention, 1920*, 48.

140. "Report of the Board of Education: 'The Christian Element in Education,' " *Annual of the Northern Baptist Convention, 1921,* 107.

141. Allyn K. Foster, "The Pulse of the Colleges," *Baptist* 2, no. 6 (12 March 1921): 173.

142. Kenneth S. Latourette, "How Can We Keep Our Colleges Christian?" *Baptist* 1, no. 40 (3 October 1920): 1355-57. Latourette was the grandson of Ezra Fisher, who shared in the founding of Franklin and Linfield Colleges, of whom more below.

143. *Report of the Committee on Denominational Schools, 1921.* Besides this brochure, the complete text appears in the *Annual of the Northern Baptist Convention, 1921,* 49-98. References are to the freestanding publication, held by the ABCA.

144. *Report of the Committee,* 13.

145. January 1935; Padelford, "Semi-Annual Report to the Board of Education," 2 January 1935, 8, in Fleming, 976.

146. Padelford, "Twenty-Five Years in the Colleges," *Christian Education* 19, no. 3 (February 1936): 210-11. The decrease from 1910 to 1930, from 403 to 395, he ascribed to colleges breaking relations with their churches. Padelford opined that had the statistics been extended through 1935 they would have displayed an even greater reduction due to closures during the depression. The figure which he noted for Catholics in the same period was a twofold increase: from 63 to 126 institutions. It is worthy of note that in this article and to this audience Padelford uses the expression "church-related college," which had not been part of his vocabulary previously.

147. Padelford, "Twenty-Five Years," 217. A decade earlier, in the teeth of fundamentalist critique, he had been saying to his fellow Baptists: "Our colleges are Christian. They are exerting a Christian influence on their students. They are building the best type of manhood and womanhood. . . . When the facts are known, they are the glory of the Christian church." "Report of the Board of Education," *Annual of the Northern Baptist Convention, 1921,* 109.

148. Fleming, 977-79.

149. Floyd C. Wilcox, "The Churches and Higher Education," *Christian Education* 19, no. 5 (June 1936): 361-69. Other studies, however, reported that Baptist enrollment in 1937-38 was 14 percent at Bucknell, 29 percent at Denison, 23 percent at Kalamazoo, 12 percent at Colgate, 11 percent at the College for Women at the University of Rochester, 26 percent at Keuka, 2 percent at Vassar.

150. Report of the Committee on Baptist Higher Education, J. H. Miller, chairman, *Annual of the Northern Baptist Convention 1940,* 194.

151. "Report of the Committee on Baptist Higher Education," *Annual of the Northern Baptist Convention, 1940,* 157-230.

152. Padelford, "The Story of Baptist Education," 13.

153. This had been evident also in Padelford, "Education in the Christian Program," *Baptist,* 21 July 1923, 782-88.

154. Shimer, Storer, Shurtleff, Colorado Women's, Wayland, and Bishop Colleges either merged, devolved to the status of academy, or closed their doors.

155. Elmer G. Million to DuBois, 15 July 1965, in DuBois, "Secularization," 53-54.

156. The Ministers Council had proposed a "standard" and a "minimum standard" of education for ordination in 1938. However, the standards were not uniformly adopted by the state conventions, and local churches could in any case invoke Baptist polity to ignore them, and only half the number required to serve the churches was emerging from Baptist seminaries (who had educated only 38 percent of Baptist clergy). Hugh Hartshorne and Milton C. Froyd, *Theological Education in the Northern Baptist Convention: A Survey* (Philadelphia: Judson, 1945), 99-105.

157. Torbet, 448-50.

158. Association of American (Northern) Baptist Educational Institutions, *Criteria of Membership* (16 June 1947), ABCA. The document then goes on to itemize evidences of educational soundness in curriculum, finance, and diverse intangibles. The financial criteria were likely to be beyond the reach of most members at the time.

159. M. C. Ballenger, director of the ABC Department of Schools and Colleges, "Memorandum on the Nature of the Christian College," 7 May 1953, ABCA. For a similar reductive approach, see Andrew B. Martin, "Invitation to Christian Learning," *Baptist Leader* 12, no. 8 (November 1950): 9. Martin was president of Ottawa University. Also: Ballenger to staff of the ABC Board of Education and Publication, June 1955, ABCA; Ballenger, "The Next Step in American Baptist Collegiate Education," discussion paper circulated in June 1955, ABCA; *What Is a Baptist College Related to the American Baptist Convention?* adopted January 1957 by the Association of School and College Administrators of the ABC and the Board of Managers of the Board of Education and Publication of the ABC; reprinted in DuBois, "Secularization," Appendix XX.

160. Ronald V. Wells of the ABC Board of Education and Publication to Harry L. Dillin, president of Linfield College, 15 April 1953, ABCA.

161. "ABC Church and College Covenant," 1982, ABCA. The American Baptist Association of Colleges and Universities then proceeded to broker a number of joint arrangements which some of its members have entered: student and faculty exchanges, mutual tuition remission for faculty and administrative dependents, and shared visiting scholars.

162. Frank T. Hoadley, "American Baptist Christian Higher Education, 1960-1989" (unpublished typescript, © The American Baptist Board of Education and Publication, 1989), 56. This volume is an extension of Sandford Fleming's great six-volume manuscript, ABCA.

163. William Bryan Martin, president of Franklin College, "Annual Report for 1990-1991," 3.

164. W. H. Hartshorn, *An Era of Progress and Promise, 1863-1910* (Boston: Priscilla Publishing Co., 1910).

165. Horace Mann Bond, "The Origin and Development of the Negro Church-Related College," *Journal of Negro Education* 29, no. 3 (summer 1960): 218-23. "The first religious bodies to interest themselves in the education of the slaves were the Puritans, the Quakers, and the French and Spanish Catholics. Later in the period these were joined by the 'Baptists and Methodists who, thanks to the spirit of toleration incident to the Revolution, were allowed access to Negroes, bond and free.' The Puritans established separate schools for the Negroes. The Quakers and Catholics gave to the Negroes the opportunity of learning and worshipping along with themselves." Leavell, 5.

166. G. B. Howard, "What of the Night?" *University Journal* (Virginia Union University — Hartshorn Memorial College) 3, no. 6 (March 1903): 5.

167. Leroy Fitts, *A History of Black Baptists* (Nashville: Broadman, 1985), 175; Latta R. Thomas, "The American Baptist Churches' Contribution to Black Education in Southern America: Testimony from a Beneficiary," *American Baptist Quarterly* 11, no. 4 (December 1992): 345.

168. Report to the 1865 meeting of the ABHMS; Fitts, 181.

169. Fitts, 176.

170. Ralph Reavis, Sr., *Virginia Seminary: A Journey of Black Independence* (Bedford, Va.: The Print Shop, 1989), 7.

171. Reavis, *Virginia Seminary*, 31-33. An 1892 report to the Home Mission Board of the Southern Baptist Convention stated, in Reavis, 75:

> Nothing is plainer to anyone who knows this race than its perfect willingness to accept a subordinate place, provided there be confidence that in the position of subordination it will receive justice and kindness. That is the condition it prefers above all others, and this is the condition in which it attains the highest development of every attribute of manhood. Whenever it shall understandingly and cheerfully accept this condition, the race problem is settled forever.

172. McBeth, *The Baptist Heritage,* 404-5.

173. "A Century of Service to Education and Religion," *Virginia Union Bulletin* 65, no. 5 (June 1965): 5-6; Bond, 221-22. In its brief existence from 1865 to 1870, the Bureau of Refugees,

Freedmen, and Abandoned Lands expended more than $3.5 million (Leavell, 48-50). General Howard's erstwhile colleague, General Thomas J. Morgan, had been Commissioner of Indian Affairs before serving the ABHMS as corresponding secretary, and was much praised for having followed Baptist church-state principles by terminating federal funding to Catholic schools on Indian reservations. It is instructive to note that in addition to Morgan's conviction that Catholics were the "insidious foe" of Baptists, their schools were "sectarian" whereas the Baptist schools were obviously not. This gives some insight into the late nineteenth-century use of that epithet. Obituary, "General T. J. Morgan," *University Journal* 3, no. 2 (November 1902): 2-4; Higginbotham, 19.

174. Bond, 224; Fitts, 179-80.

175. Fleming, 370-78.

176. [Henry L. Morehouse], "Some Boiled Down Facts about the Society's Work for the Colored People, from 1862 to 1889," in "The Educational Work of the American Baptist Home Mission Society" (1889), 46.

177. Reavis, *Virginia Seminary,* 38.

178. In 1865 Wayland Seminary, a joint effort of the ABHMS and the Freedmen's Bureau, named after the abolitionist president of Brown University, opened in Washington to train black men as preachers and teachers. G. F. Richings, *Evidences of Progress among Colored People,* 10th ed. (Philadelphia: George Ferguson, 1903), 25-26; "Wayland Seminary," in "The Educational Work of the American Baptist Home Mission Society," 62-63.

179. For the story and interpretation of this bitter controversy, see Reavis, *Virginia Seminary;* Reavis, "Black Higher Education among American Baptists in Virginia: From Slave Pen to University," *American Baptist Quarterly* 11, no. 4 (December 1992): 357-74; Adolph H. Grundman, "Northern Baptists and the Founding of Virginia Union University: The Perils of Paternalism," *Journal of Negro History* 63, no. 1 (January 1978): 26-41. The division among black Baptists in Virginia continues to be institutionalized in two statewide organizations. The Baptist General Convention (much the larger) is the successor of the Richmond cooperationists, and the Virginia Baptist Convention is the successor of the Lynchburg separatists.

180. The Virginia confrontation had two phases. In the first, the North-sponsored educational foundations were a threat to the established but entirely uneducated black ministers, and were supported by black progressives. In the later phase, the opposition came from the ranks of the old progressives, who wanted help from the Northern Baptists, but by way of incentive, not control. And it is ironic that it was the intransigence of both parties, provoking the separatists to isolate themselves from both the American Baptists and the black Virginia cooperationists, that provoked fruitful change. Grundman, 38.

181. *(Virginia Union) University Journal* 1, no. 2 (February 1901): 3. Later that same year the editor grieved about another limping appeal: "WHY SHOULD NOT THE COLORED PEOPLE WHO APPRECIATE THE BENEFITS WHICH THEY HAVE RECEIVED FROM HARTSHORN PROVIDE ONE THOUSAND DOLLARS TOWARD A NEW BUILDING WHICH SHALL COST TWENTY FIVE THOUSAND DOLLARS? HOW EASILY THIS COULD BE DONE!" *University Journal* 2, no. 3 (December 1901): 12.

182. General T. J. Morgan, "The American Baptist Home Mission Society and the Negroes," *University Journal* 1, no. 2 (February 1901): 8.

183. See Washington, "Industrial Education for the Negro," and DuBois, "The Talented Tenth," in Booker T. Washington et al., *The Negro Problem: A Series of Articles by Representative Negroes of Today* (New York: James Pott, 1903), 9-29, 33-75; Washington, *Up from Slavery: An Autobiography* (New York: Doubleday, Page, 1903); Dubois, *The College Bred Negro American* (Atlanta: Atlanta University Press, 1911). For early elitist exhortations at VUU, see *University Journal* 1, no. 4 (April 1901): 2-3; 2, no. 3 (December 1901): 2-3, 13-14; 2, no. 4 (January 1902): 1-3 (Morgan); 2, no. 7 (April 1902): 3-6.

184. *University Journal* 2, no. 3 (December 1901): 8.

185. *University Journal* 2, no. 7 (April 1902): 5; *Union-Hartshorn Journal* 7, no. 2 (February 1907): 17.

186. *Union-Hartshorn Journal* 7, no. 2 (February 1907): 11-15; *University Journal* 5, no. 2 (December 1904): 1; 2, no. 7 (April 1902): 2-3. In 1904 a survey of twenty-two Negro universities found that only 12 percent of their students were in college departments: W. T. B. Williams, *The Place of the Negro College, An Address at the Dedication of Huntley Hall* (Richmond: Virginia Union University, 1913), 7.

187. *University Journal* 5, no. 7 (May 1905): 103; 2, no. 3 (December 1901): 8; 2, no. 8 (May 1902): 3.

188. Fitts, 211.

189. *Virginia Union University Catalogue, 1910-1911,* 60; *1920-1921,* 62-63.

190. Rockefeller, through his General Education Board (GEB), gave the ABHMS colleges for Negroes and Indians nearly $2.5 million between 1908 and 1928; Torbet, 410. Total GEB grants to improve state education for Negroes, 1914-28, equaled $3,336,000. Leavell, 175, 179. See also Miles Mark Fisher, *Virginia Union University and Some of Her Achievements* (Richmond: Virginia Union University, 1924), 52-53.

191. "A Century of Service," 31, 35; Carlson, 285-86; Fitts, 185.

192. "A Century of Service," 60, 96-97; John M. Ellison, "Policies and Rationale Underlying the Support of Colleges Maintained by the Baptist Denomination," *Journal of Negro Education* 29, no. 3 (summer 1960): 332-35; Col. Anthony E. Manning, vice president for development at Virginia Union University, interview with the author, 15 July 1993.

193. H. B. Gross, "The Essential Factors of Race Education," *University Journal* 1, no. 1 (January 1901): 5-7.

194. M. M. Fisher, 77-89.

195. M. M. Fisher, 54, gives one preacher's account of an intense revival in 1918:

At Union we went over the top in everything. All work was suspended and the faculty and entire student body, led by the President, entered into a hearty co-operation with our program. The response exceeded anything the team had met with heretofore, and we were compelled to telegraph to New York for a special edition of cards both for life purpose and dedication work. At times the interest was so high, especially for interviews, that meals were forgotten, and on two occasions my wife and myself were up until two o'clock holding interviews, with students. Not a moment did we have for anything else during the entire time the team was there.

In all, 290 men signed Life Purpose cards, and 152 interviews were recorded.

196. *Virginia Union University Catalogue, 1910-1911,* 10.

197. *Virginia Union University Catalogue, 1910-1911,* 16.

198. *Virginia Union University Catalogue, 1911-1912,* 15-16.

199. *Virginia Union University Catalogue, 1934-1935,* 13.

200. A "Freshman Consecration Service," led by the dean of the chapel and presided over by the president, opened the 1954-55 academic year and was unself-consciously devout. An Annual Week of Prayer the next spring seemed to involve most of the student body, and disclosed that as underclassmen students tended to attend Sunday worship nearly every Sunday, but as seniors they were there only about half of the time. VUU was becoming mainstream.

201. *Virginia Union University Catalogue, 1961-1962,* 9.

202. *Virginia Union University Catalogue, 1972-1974,* 16.

203. *Virginia Union University Catalogue, 1993-1995,* 19.

204. Rev. Cessar L. Scott, executive minister of the Baptist General Convention of Virginia and trustee of Virginia Union University, interview with the author, 23 September 1993; W. Weldon Hill, chairman of the division of humanities, VUU, interview with the author, 15 July 1993.

205. Dr. S. Dallas Simmons, president of VUU, correspondence with the author, 20 August 1993.

206. Articles of Incorporation, Amendment, or Restatement have been enacted in 1876, 1886, 1890, 1896, 1900, 1932, 1959, 1960, 1974, and 1981.

207. Office of the Registrar, Virginia Union University, communication to the author, fall 1993.

208. Ellison, 333-34. In the same year, Mays was writing of the Christian spirit "permeating" the private and church-related colleges: Benjamin E. Mays, "The Significance of the Negro Private and Church-Related College," *Journal of Negro Education* 29, no. 3 (summer 1960): 249.

209. Fred L. Brownlee, retired educational director of the American Missionary Association (Congregational), "Heritage and Opportunity: The Negro Church-Related College: A Critical Summary," *Journal of Negro Education* 29, no. 3 (summer 1960): 402-3.

210. Robert C. Weaver, "The Negro Private and Church-Related College: A Critical Summary," *Journal of Negro Education* 29, no. 3 (summer 1960): 395.

211. C[harles] H[iram] Mattoon, *Baptist Annals of Oregon, 1844 to 1900* (McMinnville: Telephone Register Publishing, 1905), 1:1. Mattoon, a Baptist preacher, was the first professor of mathematics and science at the Baptist College in McMinnville. For his account of its beginnings see 36-38, 152-59, 232-34, 389-406.

212. Jonas A. Jonasson, *Bricks without Straw: The Story of Linfield College* (Caldwell, Idaho: Caxton Printers, 1938), 15.

213. The missionaries were moved to found a school against such stern odds by the prior efforts of the "Romanists." Fisher wrote in 1846: "I am informed by indubitable authority that there is not a place in the whole Territory where the higher branches can be acquired except by a private teacher or in a Catholic school." Mattoon, 1:30.

214. Mattoon, 1:20.

215. Jonasson, 13-22.

216. Jonasson, 31.

217. Jonasson, 42.

218. The college today gives 1849 as its foundation date; that was when the Oregon Baptist Education Society was begun, back in the Oregon City days. The college in McMinnville was chartered in 1858.

219. Jonasson, 59-60. In one survey the college ascertained that of 216 graduates in 1925-29, only 3 were in ministry; "Annual and Semi-Annual Reports of Leonard W. Riley to the Board of Trustees of Linfield (McMinnville) College, March 1, 1906–May 26, 1931," unnumbered page near the end; Archives of Linfield College (LCA). For a fair appreciation of why Baptist clergy were the least educated and trained in America, and why they were so well received in the West, see Clifford R. Miller, "Ministers of Reconciliation," *Baptists and the Oregon Frontier* (Ashland: Southern Oregon College, 1967), 109-27.

220. Jonasson, 70-71.

221. Not until 1916 did college enrollment reach 100 students; Jonasson, 123.

222. The next year he would teach logic, rhetoric, political economy, general history, history of civilization, sociology, psychology, Old Testament history, Christian evidences, and homiletics. In 1901-2 he would teach history of education, history of civilization, history of modern Europe, critical period of American history, history of American politics, sociology, psychology, political economics, pedagogics, logic, ethics, English Bible, Christian evidences, and homiletics.

223. Harry L. Boardman, "President's Reports to the Board," 1897-1902; LCA.

224. "Reports of Leonard W. Riley," 1:35.

225. Jonasson, 81-99.

226. "Reports of Leonard W. Riley," 1:99.

227. "Reports of Leonard W. Riley," 2:6-7; Jonasson, 110.

228. *Linfield College Bulletin* 21, no. 2 (March 1924): 5. The college's *Annual Catalogue*

has traditionally been published as one issue of a more general publication, the *Linfield College Bulletin*.

229. "Reports of Leonard W. Riley," 2:145.

230. "Reports of Leonard W. Riley," 2:197. Other census reports (which were irregularly reported) listed the Baptist proportion of total enrollment as 85 percent (1917), 89 percent (1919), 88 percent (1921), 81 percent (1925), 75 percent (1927), 61 percent (1931).

231. Here is a typical introduction to one of his reports to the board:

Brethren:

As heretofore in beginning these reports I desire to first of all ascribe a word of praise and thanksgiving to Almighty God for the great measure of His grace and wisdom and blessing which he has vouch-safed during the past months since our Annual meeting. McMinnville College is a vine of His planting. Its interests are all in His hands and inasmuch as hitherto He has blessed us, it is ours to acknowledge His good hand upon us and ask Him still for more prosperity, spiritual and material. In building us such an institution as this we need a faith that is unwavering and growing.

"Reports of Leonard W. Riley," 1:41; 19 January 1909.

232. "Reports of Leonard W. Riley," 1:5.

233. "Reports of Leonard W. Riley," 2:161.

234. "Reports of Leonard W. Riley," 1:263-64. This was no new concern of Riley's. In 1920, just after the appointment by the NBC of the Committee of Nine, the college went on record as welcoming its investigation of the loyalty of Baptist schools: "McMinnville College and the Committee of Nine," *McMinnville College Bulletin* 17, no. 4 (September 1920): 2-3.

In 1912 Riley had lectured the trustees at length about the character of the professors as the chief factor in building good character in the students:

It goes without saying that these teachers must have real ability and scholarship and know how to teach. All institutions look carefully after these points. But the policy followed by McMinnville College recognizes this as only the beginning of the work of selecting a properly qualified teacher. A Professor may have all the strong points mentioned and still be utterly unfit for contact with young people in a college classroom. In addition to these qualifications we have inquired concerning the one we are about to employ: Is he a genuine Christian who will take an active part in all the religious services and exercises of the College, the Church and the Prayermeeting. More than this, is he free from all objectionable habits, one whose whole life and influence will tend to inspire young people to seek the truest ideals in life? Is he positive in his teaching, both in the classroom and outside of it, and not negative; is he constructive in all and destructive of naught save that which is evil and injurious? There are many institutions in our land which require these things theoretically, but very few which have strictly adhered to such a policy. Personally I am far more anxious concerning the permanence of this policy in the future of McMinnville College than I am of anything else or all else combined. The things that money can buy for an educational institution are valuable, but the things which money cannot buy are absolutely invaluable!

"Reports of Leonard W. Riley," 1:90.

235. "Proceedings of the Thirty-Ninth Annual Session of the Oregon Baptist State Convention," *Oregon Baptist Annual, 1924,* 24 ([OBSC/1924]; proceedings hereafter cited in similar fashion).

236. "Reports of Leonard W. Riley," 1:43.

237. OBSC/1922, 9-13; OBSC/1923, 16; OBSC/1924, 24-27; OBSC/1925, 23; OBSC/1926, 19-22. See also Jonasson, 128-35; "Reports of Leonard W. Riley," 2:36. It was already

required that three-fourths of the trustees be members of Baptist churches, and that the president be a Baptist; see "Reports of Leonard W. Riley," 1:395, 405, 429.

The local controversy arose somewhat before the national one, with the arrival of a new pastor at McMinnville Baptist Church, who in 1917 began accusing specific faculty members of deviant teaching. Several of those faculty had left McMinnville before the issue broke out at the state convention held at Columbia City in 1922, giving rise to the popular reference to the entire controversy as the "Columbia City Episode." For Riley on this see "Reports of Leonard W. Riley," 1:263-64, 359. He concludes:

> One of the considerations which led me to accept the presidency of this institution was to see whether in the twentieth century a real Christian college could be maintained and developed. I have sought always teachers who have been genuine Christian men and women, holding the generally accepted views of the Baptist denomination. I have never swerved from this purpose and am not ready yet to yield to any man in my devotion to this great Christian ideal. I have endeavored to so conduct the affairs of our college that I might win the approval and cooperation, not only of our Baptist constituency, but of all those who love our Lord sincerely and seek the advancement of His kingdom.

238. Jonasson, 144-50.

239. "Reports of Leonard W. Riley," 1:33.

240. "Reports of Leonard W. Riley," 1:81.

241. "Reports of Leonard W. Riley," 1:113.

242. "Reports of Leonard W. Riley," 2:41-42. All things are relative. In the latter 1920s, when the struggle between fundamentalists and modernists was at its bitterest, the Baptist Bible Union took control of Des Moines University and began to purge it of all elements destructive of the faith. These more conservative Baptists had looked over the array of colleges sponsored by the American Baptists in the North and found most of them leavened with "the leaven of the Sadducees." *Gospel Witness* (Toronto), 16 June 1927, 11; R[obert] J. Leonard, E. S. Evenden, and F. B. O'Rear, *Survey of Higher Education for the United Lutheran Church in America* 3 (New York: Teachers College, 1929), 213.

243. "Reports of Leonard W. Riley," 1:257-58.

244. "Reports of Leonard W. Riley," 2:145-46.

245. Baptists constituted 61 percent in 1931, 58 percent in 1932, 51 percent in 1941, 44 percent in 1963, 34 percent in 1966, 28 percent in 1968. The early statistics are from the *Linfield College Bulletin;* those from 1963 onward were provided by the registrar's office.

246. *Linfield College Bulletin* 21, no. 2 (March 1924): 4-5.

247. *Linfield College Bulletin* 29, no. 3 (March 1932): 9, 12-13.

248. *Linfield College Bulletin* 57, no. 9 (July 1960): 5, 7.

249. *Linfield College Bulletin* 67, no. 5 (May 1970): 1, 3, 9, 16.

250. *Linfield College Bulletin* 77, no. 1 (September 1979): 5.

251. *Linfield College Bulletin* 90, no. 1 (July/August 1992): 1, 7.

252. "Reports of Leonard W. Riley," 1:5.

253. J. Hybert Pollard, "Religion at Linfield," in *Linfield's Hundred Years: A Centennial History of Linfield College, McMinnville, Oregon,* ed. Kenneth L. Holmes (Portland: Binfords & Mort, 1956), 168-72.

254. During this period it was located in a rather large Department of Education, Psychology, Philosophy and Religion, which clearly directed its attentions to undergraduates intending to go on to normal school. *Linfield College Bulletin* 29, no. 3 (March 1932): 42-43, 48-49.

255. *Linfield College Bulletin* 57, no. 9 (July 1960): 87.

256. *Linfield College Bulletin* 75, no. 1 (September 1977): 98.

257. *Linfield College Bulletin* 90, no. 1 (July/August 1993): 85.

258. The prior text is from the *Linfield College Faculty Handbook, 1972,* 2. The latter text

is excerpted from a text adopted by the board of trustees, 21 February 1976, and carried in subsequent faculty handbooks.

259. Adopted by the faculty, 1983; published in the *Linfield College Faculty Handbook, 1972,* I-2.

260. *Bylaws of Linfield College* (as amended 31 May 1986), art. V, sec. 1. Three regional Baptist Conventions still present nominations for fifteen of the now fifty-one seats, and their three executives sit on the board *ex officio.*

261. President Vivian A. Bull, interview with the author, 28 July 1993.

262. Rev. William D. Apel, chaplain and professor of religion, interview with the author, 20 August 1993.

263. Elisabeth Holden, director of planned giving, interview with the author, 31 August 1993.

264. Frank J. Prial, "Wine Talk," *New York Times,* 4 August 1993.

265. Walter Shurden has characterized the two Southern Baptist traditions as expressive of "ardor" and "order." The Separate Baptists elaborated theologically careful confessions of faith and maintained a liturgical tradition and an educated ministry, while the Regular Baptists opposed attempts to formulate creeds out of the Bible, preferred revivalist spontaneity in worship, and considered preaching as a calling, never a profession. This cleavage, with some modifications, replicated itself in the North. Walter B. Shurden, "The Southern Baptist Synthesis: Is It Cracking?" *Baptist History and Heritage,* April 1981, 2-11; McBeth, *The Baptist Heritage,* 234-35. In both sectors of the denomination the educational endeavor was conducted by the latter group, with constant skepticism and occasional intrusion by the former. Sloan and D'Amico have pointed out that while the Second Great Awakening had a strong antieducational effect, though mostly in the South and West, the revivalism of the First Great Awakening in the colonial era looked to education as a means of implanting its convictions in the culture. Douglas Sloan, *The Great Awakening and American Education* (New York: Teachers College Press, 1973), 19; D'Amico, "Piety and Intellect."

266. David B. Potts, in a study of antebellum Baptist colleges, has argued convincingly that until the 1860s the primarily local character of these schools which provided their constituency, students, governing board, and financial support proved a stronger identifier than denominational ties: "colleges were closely tied with the local, cultural, and economic ambitions of citizens, parents, and students; special religious interests became of major significance only in the unusual cases where these ties were weak or absent." It was in the latter half of the century that the denominational ties became strengthened. Thus, until perhaps the 1920s, the drift of the Baptist colleges was toward denominationalism rather than secularism. "American Colleges in the Nineteenth Century: From Localism to Denominationalism," *History of Education Quarterly* 11 (1971): 363-80; Potts, "Baptist Colleges in the Development of American Society, 1812-1861" (Ph.D. diss., Harvard University, 1967).

267. Harold Ernest Bauman, "The Believers' Church and the Church College" (Ed.D. diss., Columbia University, 1972), 127-34.

268. In the midst of the controversy between fundamentalism and the Social Gospel, and the more recent one between professing Christians and Enlightenment liberals, Baptists have been caught in a bind. It is settled Baptist doctrine that there may be no creedal formulae to which Baptists are obliged to subscribe. On the other hand, in a time of backsliding faith, how else can a true believer be discerned from a modernist? Eastern College, founded in the backwash of the fundamentalist struggle, has braved that prohibition and formulated a doctrinal statement which is not untypical of other formulae or of the unwritten particulars of what Baptists have tended to agree upon. Trustees, administrators, and faculty were all obliged to subscribe to it or resign. Let it be offered as an example:

457

We believe that the Bible, composed of the Old and New Testaments, is inspired of God, and is of supreme and final authority in faith and life.

We believe in the supernatural as the vital element in the revelation and operation of the Christian faith.

We believe in one God eternally existing in three Persons — Father, Son, and Holy Spirit.

We believe that Jesus Christ was begotten of the Holy Spirit and born of the virgin Mary, and that He is true God and true man, and is the only and sufficient Mediator between God and man.

We believe in the personality of the Holy Spirit and that His ministry is to reveal Christ to men in the regeneration and sanctification of their souls.

We believe that man was created in the image of God, and that he sinned and thereby incurred spiritual death.

We believe in the vicarious death of the Lord Jesus Christ for our sins, in the resurrection of His body, His ascension into Heaven, and His personal and visible future return to the earth; and that salvation is received only through personal faith in Him.

We believe that baptism is immersion of a believer in water, in the name of the Father, and of the Son, and of the Holy Spirit; setting forth the essential facts in redemption — the death and resurrection of Christ; also essential facts in the experience of the believer — death to sin and resurrection to newness of life; and the Lord's Supper is a commemoration of the Lord's death until He comes.

We believe that a New Testament church is a body of believers thus baptized, associated for worship, service, the spread of the Gospel, and the establishing of the Kingdom in all the world.

Published version, 1965; DuBois, "Secularization," 35-36.

This creed, like those of the "apostles" or of Nicaea, has many dead people speaking through it, for its assertions and phrases were wrought in various controversies over the years. It is a witness to the fact that Baptists, like all Christians, do indeed nurture a developing faith that is beholden to those who have argued for its coherence with Scripture and who have passed it on.

269. See Walter Rauschenbusch, professor of New Testament (1897-1902) and church history (1902-18) at Rochester Theological Seminary, *Christianity and the Social Crisis* (New York: Macmillan, 1907); Shailer Mathews, dean of the Divinity School at the University of Chicago (1908-33), *The Faith of Modernism* (New York: Macmillan, 1924).

CHAPTER 5

The Lutherans

Lutherans migrated to America from their relatively limited ambit in Europe: mostly the German and Scandinavian states. Though they came from churches that were unified nationally, they have never formed a single communion in this country. They have shared a common devotion to Martin Luther as their reforming founder and a doctrinal reverence for the Augsburg Confession and other early consensus statements of Lutheran orthodoxy. But their geographical scatter and their ethnic and linguistic separatism, compounded by a sober determination to define and police right doctrine and draw membership lines accordingly, have combined to make functional unity among Lutherans thus far unattainable.[1]

Lutheran polity in America has been for the most part congregational. The first Lutheran immigrants, being neither closely directed from their homeland churches nor yet networked among themselves, understandably accustomed themselves to managing their own religious affairs locally. Yet despite this claim that each local community is autonomous and will not defer to any higher authority except by voluntary agreement, the history of the denomination has been more synodical than congregational, with scores of realignments through amalgamation and secession. Another paradox in the Lutheran story — though by no means peculiar to them — is the fact that although synodical and congregational governance has been formally democratic, at critical moments it has been strong-minded, charismatically forceful pastors whose voices have carried most authority.

Although at present there are sixteen Lutheran churches in the United States, the enormous majority of their 8.3 million members belong to two churches: the Evangelical Lutheran Church in America (ELCA) and the Lutheran Church–Missouri Synod (LCMS). Historically, there have been three major (and endlessly shifting) confluences. The Eastern colonial branch, Pietistic and German "Americanist Lutherans," once gathered into the Lutheran Church in America (LCA), and

---

This essay was researched and written in 1992-93, and the statistics and facts it reports as current derive from the latest sources then available.

459

the Upper Midwest Scandinavians and Germans, or "Confessing Lutherans," gathered into the American Lutheran Church (ALC), amalgamated in 1987 to form the ELCA. The third group were dissident German Lutherans who left behind them hostile rulers and compromising coreligionists and created a large cluster in Illinois and Missouri. These three traditions — LCA, ALC, and LCMS — tell three different tales of the church, and also of church-related higher education.

The very first Lutheran immigrants, arriving early in the seventeenth century, included a settlement of Swedes in the Delaware Valley (where they were served by the state church of Sweden) and a small band of Lutherans in New Netherland (where, despite the Dutch willingness to harbor dissidents from other countries, they were pressured by the Dutch West Indian Company regime to conform to the polity and piety of the Dutch Reformed Church). Later in the colonial period, however, Lutherans in far greater numbers flowed across from Germany, especially the Rhineland, to settle in Pennsylvania, New York, Maryland, Virginia, the Carolinas, and Georgia. Most were farmers and artisans. They seem to have migrated as families, not congregations. Their Lutheranism was heavily indebted to the Pietist reform that had called both Lutherans and Calvinists back to spontaneous lay devotion. As the two groups favored the same evangelical practices of prayer and populism, the two denominations were drawn more sympathetically to one other. This first influx of Lutheran settlers we shall refer to as "Americanist Lutherans" (hoping not to confuse them with the ALC), to connote their ease with (some) other churches and their positive disposition to the new culture of their new civic home.

For many years these Lutheran immigrants had their clergy provided from Halle, an active center of German Pietism. One of those early pastors, Henry Melchior Muhlenberg, would within six years of his arrival lead to the formation of the first union of scattered congregations: the Ministerium of Pennsylvania (1748). These congregations were located mostly in smaller towns strewn along the original coastal colonies. A lively, ongoing dispute persistently divided them into those who felt more free to draw on the practices of their neighbors, whether secular or religious, and to modify their own Lutheran belief and practice accordingly, and those who saw the early corpus of sixteenth-century confessional documents as the only reliable norms and resisted compromises in their Lutheran identity. The disposition to adopt English as a primary language, or to preserve German, served as a reliable indicator of whither a congregation or synod leaned: toward assimilation or toward keeping their own counsel.

When the great waves of new immigration began in the 1830s, the Lutheran census in America began to be swelled by arrivals from Norway, Denmark, Sweden, Finland, and Iceland. Bypassing the East, they settled in the Upper Midwest: in Illinois, Wisconsin, Iowa, Minnesota, and the Dakotas. The diversity of faith and language and leadership brought in by these immigrants elicited wrangles between lay evangelism and clerical tradition, congregationalism versus synodalism, social reform (e.g., abolition and temperance) over against personal piety, spiritual conversion versus liturgical expression. Synods were founded almost immediately, but they were easily fractured to the point where at any moment there might be three or four competing judicatories within a single national group. Gradually predominating, however, was a bias against Pietism and Rationalism and for a return to authentic Lutheran origins. These we call the "Confessing Lutherans," who found some allies among German "Old Lutherans" who were resisting conformity to the American ethos.

The third cohort of immigrants came, not merely for the main chance of land and economic promise, but precisely to preserve their faith from an inimical environment. A large band of Lutherans from Saxony, dissatisfied with the rationalist compromises of their native church, came to Missouri to settle in the early 1840s and soon called a young pastor, C. F. W. Walther, to lead them. At the same time a governmentally enforced union of Lutheran and Reformed churches in Prussia drove other Lutherans across the Atlantic, where many settled in Buffalo. Other dissidents from Franconia would find their way to Michigan and Iowa. This wave of German immigrants was of decidedly conservative disposition. The Missouri Synod, their strongest embodiment, was from the start critical of the assimilationist Lutherans they encountered in America.

The "Missouri Lutherans" found it was not only the Old World Pietism, nor the rationalism that followed on its heels, which threatened their communicants with indifference and compromise. The Second Great Awakening, an evangelical movement that swept America in the early nineteenth century, easily drew most of the Protestant churches away from their peculiar moorings and their confessional beliefs, toward a more generic form of piety. As historian Abdel Ross Wentz observes: "Many now began to manifest intense fervor and zeal in the evangelical movement, with a resultant degree of confessional laxity that for a time threatened to obliterate the historic traits that had for centuries marked their individuality among Protestants. The insidious danger of unionism and loss of confessional standards soon called upon Lutheran leaders for decisive measures of education and conservation."[2] Faced with new threats after having fled from older ones, the Missouri Lutherans understandably drew their language and ethnicity about them as one effective barrier to assimilation with other Christians and "unionism" with other Lutherans. Not until the threshold of World War I did the predominant language for worship in their congregations shift from German to English.

The array of major Lutheran groupings in America, then, presented the "Americanist Lutherans" (eventually represented by the LCA) on the liberal side, the "Confessing Lutherans" (eventually represented by the ALC) in the center, and the LCMS on the conservative side. The terms of the disputes that divided them were, in a way, set by two great events that had affected the churches in Europe sometime before.

Pietism and Rationalism

The Pietist reform of the late seventeenth and early eighteenth centuries was an intramural critique of almost every feature of Christian life, and it was directed simultaneously at both Lutheran and Reformed churches. (Another variant of Pietism was working for renewal within the Catholic Church.) The scholasticism which solidified the insights of the sixteenth-century Reformation had been distracted from the central vision of faith and become snarled in quirky, quibbling questions that led no one nearer salvation: so said the Pietists. Church polity had again become paralyzed in the hands of a clerical hierarchy. Moral teaching had once again forgotten the gospel. Worship was a sterile performance of ritual rather than an encounter with the living God. The Pietist reformers called, accordingly, for a return to Scripture as the all-sufficient norm for both belief and behavior. They insisted that the laity not be subject to the clergy, but that as the active people of God they should summon and dismiss and direct their clergy. And beside a liturgy that was simple and spontaneous and intelligible to the most unlettered congregations, they promoted a repertoire of devotional practices which did not require the presence or leadership of clergy.

What followed directly from this critique was sometimes fraught with difficulty. By turning from the cumulative tradition of biblical commentaries, symbolic definitions, and theological disputation, and by drawing upon Scripture alone as a basis for doctrine and morality, the adherents of the reform did not successfully set aside the thoughts of man in favor of the thoughts of God. Too easily they simply exchanged the agenda of the sages of the past for the agenda of the preachers of the present. By replacing an ordained hierarchy with elective assemblies, they sometimes turned from unresponsive and remote clerics to demagogues. And what they devised by way of worship often proved to be either vapid or rabid. Had their call to purity of heart been taken to heart by the "establishments" of the several churches, perhaps instead of dividing into hardened, adversarial parties that inclined to stiff observance or simpleton innovation, they would have enacted a shared renewal that married wisdom to sincerity. Yet this is often the way of reforms. In the dialectical to-and-fro of church development, every leaf of springtime becomes mulch for the following autumn. As things emerged, by fixing their attention upon individual devotion but largely ignoring the task of the faith community to beat its bounds and define its understanding, they caused some of the essential functions of the church to atrophy. The Protestant reformers had founded a clutch of new churches. The Pietist reformers invented the denomination, a looser aggregation of believers.

But something else ensued, and quickly. For fast on the tracks of Pietism came rationalism. The two movements might seem to have been adversarial to one another; surely their originators would have despised each other's programs had they lived beside one another in time. But there is a fascinating way in which the Pietists' intramural critique of dogmatism, clericalism, legalism, and formalism seemed to open the way for the rationalists' critique that was clearly an assault from the outside.

There was, it seems, a middle stage. The Pietists directed Christians' attention back to the simplicities of Scripture, over the heads of the scholars and their analogies and casuistic applications of ancient texts to later issues and disputes. Some who listened looked for simplicities that were banal instead of radical. They began to sieve out from the Bible its most derivative and generic truths: clean ore, as they thought, freed from the mystifying slag of inspiration, revelation, or incarnation. For governance they chose, not a polity that might best respect and defer to the authority of the Spirit, but a representative form of management that counted on no divine governance but only on sensible procedure. Moral wisdom would be conflated into norms of justice and peace that required no Cross, no sanctity, no yet-more-perfect way. As for worship, they required only that it be mannered and tasteful. These direct disciples of the Pietists were the liberals, whose reductive pieties were a midway stage between Pietism and Rationalism.

Luther's doctrine of the two kingdoms taught that in the social and political order, for example in matters concerned with property, legal contracts, or marriage, Christians could not expect the norms for society to be set by the gospel, i.e., by grace and forgiveness. In that realm the law set the standards by which communal life would be governed. The Pietists evaded this doctrine, in order to charge Christians with a higher responsibility for the structural and social integrity of the public order. There was no intrinsic follow-through from this Pietist maneuver to the liberal expectation that if Christians enter the public forum as activists, they must do so on only such moral grounds as are agreed to by nonbelievers. But the one did follow the other. The hope for a kingdom of heaven that could be established on earth could kindle a later, lesser hope that there could be no heaven but what we create on earth. There is no logical reason why, having accepted the Pietists' preference for irenic regard toward others' beliefs, one should then carry the idea so far as to be indifferent toward religious debate. Indeed, if Lutherans chose to take to themselves some of "the vigor of Presbyterianism and the warmth of Methodism,"[3] that need not have disposed them later to seek their inspiration from Whigs, Unitarians, and Deists. If one found a new energy and commitment in open discourse among one's fellow believers without regard to rank or privilege, one need not then have denied that any members of the community could be commissioned by divine sanction to preside.[4] Yet, somehow, some Lutherans — among many others — did accept tutelage from Pietism first, and then passed from that through liberalism to rationalism.

Pietism was surely not an early, soft variant of the heathen gentility of the later rationalism which followed close upon it, but there was a kinship between them. Both deplored the confessional particularities of the churches, referring to them contemptuously as "sectarian," yet had quite different meanings in their accusation. Their "sectarian" opponents clung all the more tenaciously (though perhaps not always more wisely) to their denominational identities — with particular emphasis on their differences from other believers, more than those which held all Christians apart from an unbelieving world.

Whatever the relationship between the two ideologies, there is some mystery entangled in the fact that from Halle there came to the Lutherans in America, in possibly inexorable succession, Pietism, liberal indifferentism, and rationalism.

And in America this strange sequence of friendly reform leading to destructive subversion seems to have repeated itself in a later generation. For the Second Great Awakening, the evangelical reform of the early nineteenth century which called the churches (not just their members) to judgment, was in many respects a reprise of the Pietist movement, and the secularism that followed it later in the nineteenth century appears to be a lineal descendant of rationalism.

The characteristic stances of the several cohorts of Lutherans in this country would seem to have replicated the same interest in or repugnance toward rationalists that they had manifested a century or so earlier toward Pietists. And the story of their efforts in higher education may be better exegeted if one keeps this in mind.[5]

THE "AMERICANIST LUTHERANS"

Sixteen presently existing[6] four-year institutions of higher education came through the confluence of the LCA into the present ELCA.

1832	Gettysburg College	Gettysburg, Pa.
1842	Roanoke College	Salem, Va.
1845	Wittenberg University	Springfield, Ohio
1847	Carthage College	Kenosha, Wis.
1848	Muhlenberg College	Allentown, Pa.
1856	Newberry College	Newberry, S.C.
1858	Susquehanna University	Selinsgrove, Pa.
1860	Augustana College	Rock Island, Ill.
1862	Gustavus Adolphus College	Saint Peter, Minn.
1866	Thiel College	Greenville, Pa.
1881	Bethany College	Lindsborg, Kans.
1883	Midland Lutheran College	Fremont, Nebr.
1883	Wagner College	Staten Island, N.Y.
1891	Lenoir-Rhyne College	Hickory, N.C.
1893	Upsala College	East Orange, N.J.
1959	California Lutheran University	Thousand Oaks, Calif.[7]

Virtually all these institutions are nineteenth-century foundations, and only three are located in urban areas. They do not tend to be large. The average full-time enrollment (FTE) is about 1,500 students; the largest (Wittenberg) enrolls just over 2,300 students, and five have less than 1,000 each. Two of the colleges have significant graduate programs in education and business, mostly for part-time urban students; otherwise the clientele is almost all undergraduate; whatever their nomenclature, they are colleges, not universities. Only one institution has a majority of Lutheran students (Gustavus Adolphus, with 59 percent); in all other schools Lutherans represent a minority, the average being 23 percent. Five colleges have only 10 percent Lutherans or less, with one as low as 4 percent. Seven colleges have more Catholics than Lutherans (often several times as many); one has half again as many Jewish students as Lutherans; another has more Baptists.

But as an avenue toward considering these "Americanist Lutheran" colleges in their contemporary stance, let us consider the history of one of them, Gettysburg College.

GETTYSBURG COLLEGE[8]

The early organization of the Ministerium of Pennsylvania as the first Lutheran synod in America reflects a concentration of German Lutherans in that state. The original colonists included the English and Welsh Quakers under John Penn, followed by other "plain people" like the Mennonites and the Amish. Then came the "church people," especially German Calvinists, Lutherans, Moravian Brethren, Catholics, and the Scotch-Irish Presbyterians. By 1784 Benjamin Franklin could complain that the Scotch-Irish had taken over the commonwealth, both in ownership of land and control of the legislature.[9]

When Dr. Benjamin Rush, another of the signers of the Declaration of Independence, was founding Dickinson College in Carlisle in 1783 to supply the educational needs of those Scotch-Irish Presbyterians then in the ascendant, he strove to involve the sizable German constituency by including four of their pastors and four laymen on its board of trustees, and by urging the appointment of a German faculty member. Rush quickly found that the Germans were unlikely to take much part in this new foundation, where their language and religious affiliations would be disadvantaged. So he proposed that the Germans establish a college of their own. Franklin College was duly chartered and opened at Lancaster in 1787, with a third of its trustees Reformed and a third Lutheran. But so meager was the response that from then until 1850 it never granted a single degree, functioning really as a secondary school. The German immigrants, mostly poor and rural, had little aspiration and felt little need for collegiate education.[10]

But in the early nineteenth century many of the Scotch-Irish Presbyterians moved on and were replaced by new German arrivals, greatly increasing the German presence in central Pennsylvania. They began to prosper. As the supply of new pastors sent from Germany thinned out, indigenous candidates were being trained under the tutelage of older pastors, though without any exposure to college education. But the establishment of seminaries changed this. Hartwick Seminary near Cooperstown, which served mostly New Yorkers, was founded in 1797, the first Protestant seminary in America.[11] In 1826 Samuel Simon Schmucker, trained and ordained by his father, led in the establishment of Gettysburg Seminary, meant to serve candidates from New York to Virginia.

Before the seminary even opened, it was clear that many interests had a stake in the institution. The board of directors solicited and received tenders from three towns which offered land, buildings, and cash to attract the enterprise to their locale; thus was Gettysburg selected. This civic patronage was essential, since no money was provided directly by the Lutheran General Synod. This brought the seminary to a town where the Reformed and the Lutheran congregations had built and shared a single church building, known as the "German Church."[12] The inaugural ceremonies took place in this shared church, marshaled by leading citizens, joined by the local Presbyterian synod then sitting in town, and addressed by its moderator, Ashbel Green, erstwhile president of the College of New Jersey (later Princeton). Clearly this Lutheran institution bore no signs of old antagonisms toward the Calvinist persuasion.[13]

The new seminary was hardly open in 1826 before it was clear that most candidates lacked the basic educational skills needed for this study. A Classical School was opened in 1827, and in 1829 it became the Gettysburg Gymnasium, replicating the German experience that ordinands would study first at the gymnasium and then at a seminary. Typically for the times, the single teacher engaged to run the school was declared qualified in Latin, Greek, English, grammar, arithmetic, mathematics, geography, astronomy, history, composition, elocution, political economy, chemistry, and philosophy (natural, political, and moral). To give the little endeavor a chance to survive, enrollments were limited neither to those intending the ministry, nor even to Lutherans. By 1830 the pupils were said to include thirty-three who intended to go on to seminary and fifty in the classical and mathematical sequences.

Schmucker then proposed an institution at the collegiate level. To support the plan he gathered the local citizens whose financial interests were tied to economic development. Though the college would be put forward as Lutheran and German (perhaps not in that order), the patrons included important members who belonged to neither community. Schmucker told them in advance that "the college he aimed at was to be un-sectarian in its instruction, but at the same time to be prevailingly under Lutheran influence and control."[14] The bill to charter the new college encountered some resistance in the legislature, since the commonwealth had made substantial financial grants to its early colleges, and the citizenry, most of whom foresaw no benefit to their own families, had begun to frown on continuing such largesse. Pennsylvanians had long been known not to be prodigal with their tax moneys. So Schmucker journeyed to Harrisburg and lobbied with the legislators for a college to serve the "Anglicized descendants" of the Germans in Pennsylvania. He got his charter approved and some crucial subsidies granted. The charter provided:

> At elections for patrons, or trustees, or teachers, or other officers, and in the reception of pupils, no person shall be rejected on account of his conscientious

persuasion in matters of religion, provided he shall demean himself in a sober manner, and conform to the rules and regulations of the College.[15]

Far from intending this as deceptive rhetoric, Schmucker in fact tried to recruit a Congregationalist as first president (he himself would dedicate his career to teaching in the seminary). Non-Lutherans were included among the patrons and trustees. The college's first published advertisement makes no mention of Lutheran identity. Schmucker was not incapable of finesse. To the legislature he appealed for his college on behalf of the politically significant German population, while quietly admitting that it was the English-speaking German constituency they would be serving.

There was no subsidy from Lutheran bodies at the start, and several appeals sent out in early years yielded no appreciable income. Apparently the German Lutherans, most of whom expected no benefit to accrue to their children, felt the same as Pennsylvanians in general (who cut off a helpful annual state subsidy at this same time).

Gettysburg College lived on. Most of the faculty were Lutheran ministers, who took it in turn each Sunday to preach at church. The board of trustees tended to be about two-thirds to three-quarters Lutherans. The students in those days were about three-quarters Lutherans; indeed, 56 percent of the graduates went on for the ministry during the first sixty years. The piety of the campus tended to be generically evangelical more than specifically Lutheran. Shortly after the Civil War paid its tragic visit to campus, the YMCA was organized as the salient spiritual force at the college, with students holding the chief role of leadership, as they already did in daily and weekly prayer meetings. The early years saw college religion roused by a series of revivals. Milton Valentine (1868-84), who held the presidency when the college was in its fiftieth year, remembered:

> These occasions were marked by a decided quickening of the religious life of the Christian students, by earnest and faithful preaching of the word in the Church, daily meetings for prayer and fellowship in the College, and personal effort of students among their fellow-students. Sometimes the interest reached nearly all the students, many connecting themselves with the Church, some of them here, some of them at their homes. In the religious awakening of 1875, only two of the students of the College proper, it is said, were left that did not confess the Saviour.[16]

A College for the Public or for the Church?

By this time, however, the German Lutherans were not at all of one mind about the amiably broad-minded atmosphere of the college and of the church. In mid-century the sons of Schmucker and his liberalizing contemporaries rose up to ask

467

"whether a college could be considered Lutheran that did not teach Lutheranism."[17] The controversy was powerful enough to cleave the General Synod, with the more "confessional" Lutherans forming a new federation. A rival and more "denominational" seminary was opened in Philadelphia to draw the conservative candidates away from Gettysburg Seminary.

Valentine — no conformist he — was of the view that the college's Lutheran character was largely a matter of campus piety, which by a remarkably straight route he related to civic life.

> The conception of education which underlies the foundation of the institution is that the young can be rightly trained for the work and responsibilities of life, for their place and duties in both society and the State, only when their intellect is educated under the light and quickening force of Christian truth and principles. It holds that the highest end of the educational process is character, that the true manhood is Christian manhood, and that education fails of its noblest function if carried on in neglect of the moral and spiritual nature, or the truth given for it. . . . This conception accepts all the truths of nature and science, of human experience and history, as divine, to be studied and used under the special illumination that comes from revelation.[18]

The dispute at this time was whether Lutheran schools should be their denomination's contribution to a general Christian educational endeavor or a ministry intended to cultivate the Lutheran faith of their own members. In 1873 the trustees of the college turned to their constituency to raise $100,000 for endowment. The great colleges in the land were the endowed colleges. Harvard, with more than $2.5 million invested, had added nearly $120,000 the previous year. Yale, Princeton, Cornell, Williams, Amherst, Wittenberg, Lafayette, Franklin and Marshall (here they were getting closer to home) — all were successful because they had endowments.

To allay a growing murmur of dissatisfaction in the church, President Valentine and the endowment committee of the board published a brochure, *Pennsylvania College and the Lutheran Church*.[19] With a wide sweep of the arm the educational ministry was traced forward from "the Saviour's tuition of the twelve" through the great Christian academies of Alexandria and Rome, the monastic schools, and the University of Wittenberg itself. They argued that never before had higher education offered more power to the church than it now did in America.

> Though these colleges are unsectarian, Christianity, in its essential doctrines, is fully and constantly taught. Its truths are made to pervade and mould all the teaching. . . .
> The Colleges confer incalculable blessings on secular life. . . . Without these brain shops, where would be the world's boasted progress? . . . Can any man over-estimate the importance of thus Christianizing the higher education of the country?

With an appreciative glance at the older Congregational and Presbyterian foundations that had suckled the nation's establishment, the authors prophesied: "The denomination which educates the most and best, will outrank others, and, other advantages being equal, become the most successful and powerful." Pointing out how many pastors and synodical leaders the college had provided to the church, they looked beyond to the influence and success in the press, the legal and medical professions, government, and commerce that the church might thus influence. "Has the money given by it in any other direction, in equal amount, been more fruitful?" Anticipating the criticisms of those who would see this as a less-than-devout ambition, the brochure rose to its crescendo: "The Christian Church has given the Colleges to our land, and cannot, without treachery to the cause of religion and truth, surrender the control of them to merely secular aims. The infidelity and false liberalism that are ready to give up the Bible in Common Schools education, are urging a separation of scientific culture from the control of Christianity."

But in 1873 the forces that looked to intrude upon Gettysburg College's governance were not secular. They were Lutheran. The growing conservative, "confessional" mood in the regional synods that were crucial to any serious fund-raising was of a mind that the college ought somehow to be under the church's control.[20] There was the old grievance that German studies were not adequately cultivated, at least to the degree required for a reliable center of Lutheranism. Muhlenberg College in Allentown and Susquehanna College in Selinsgrove were regional competitors that were more closely sponsored by synods. Even the Presbyterians had recently reclaimed control over Lafayette College. Perhaps any fund drive commenced in the financially disastrous year of 1873 was doomed to fail, but the reserve of the surrounding synods was in any case enough to chill the college's efforts.

Twenty years later, during the presidency of Harvey McKnight (1884-1904), the issue broke out again. Articles critical of the college's orthodoxy began to appear, calling for seats on its self-perpetuating board of trustees to be filled by representatives of the surrounding synods. A caucus of conservative faculty, including H. Louis Baugher, Charles Porterfield Krauth, and Henry Eyster Jacobs, all sons of distinguished Lutheran leaders of the founding generation, began to encourage outside critics. In 1892 a new endowed chair in "English Bible" was established with unusual provisions. The incumbent was also to serve as college chaplain, and his courses in the Bible were to be required of all students. It was further stipulated that "the Teaching in the department shall be positively Christian, according to the accepted standards of Evangelical Christendom, but in no sense denominational."[21] This caused much grumbling through the church.

McKnight quickly issued a defense, cosigned by the chairman of the board and retired president Valentine: *The Lutheran Status of Pennsylvania College.*[22] The brochure argued that the college was, of course, Lutheran. Lutherans had founded it. Thirty-two of its trustees were Lutherans, and the other four were alumni. Every faculty member save one was Lutheran. Why then was denominational theology excluded (from required courses, not electives)? They wanted "positive Christian teaching, without sectarian particularity."

> An institution necessarily surrenders its best chance of strength and prominence as an educational center by cutting itself off, by sectarian teaching, from the patronage of the great general public, and drawing only from a particular denomination or a section of its territory . . . The policy of exclusion mortgages it to littleness and comparative inefficiency. . . . A denomination could take no surer way than this to insure a perpetual stampede of the talented, ambitious and wealthy sons of its own fold to the great educational centers under other auspices. . . .

> Moreover, even as a matter of dutiful work for Christ, the College ought to adhere to the plan that gathers under its training the largest possible number of the young men from "the *world*," and shapes their thinking and character in the moulds of a Christian education, for leadership in the high places of life. The policy by which the Church's institutions obtain the largest patronage and grow into the most commanding strength is thus, at the same time, the policy by which it accomplishes most for Christ and for the denomination conducting it.

The authors explained that 10 percent of non-Lutherans in the student body spelled the difference "between a flourishing and a failing college." They then cited letters of endorsement from presidents of other colleges: Lutheran, Methodist, Baptist, Brethren, Reformed, Presbyterian, Quaker. All denied that their colleges engaged in denominational teaching, or "propaganda." This, testified President McKnight, was typical of upwards of three hundred colleges which "teach religion without interfering with any one's conscience . . . You might attend such colleges for months without discovering what denominations patronize them." And this, President McKnight would not have realized, was what Pietism was all about.

Lutheran in Atmosphere

The Lutheranism at Gettysburg, the brochure explained, was a matter of atmosphere, general direction, influence. "Indirectly and unconsciously it becomes formative. . . . By the rule of the institution the instruction in each and every department is to be thoroughly Christian, so that truth in all its branches may be seen and understood in the light and illumination of Christianity." If the individual views of the various faculty were given public expression on denominational controversies, party rancor and polemic would poison the entire college.

The synods were not persuaded, and in 1894 the Gettysburg trustees endeavored to appease them by an amendment to the charter specifying that no less than three-fourths of their members must be members of the Lutheran church. Professor Baugher, the gadfly, was dismissed.

It is difficult to know how to assess the claims being made by President McKnight and his associates. Comparison is helpful with a speech given a few years later, in 1898, at a conference in Philadelphia. Two of the speakers belonged to the same tradition as their contemporaries in Gettysburg: Professor F. V. N. Painter, of Roanoke College in Salem, Virginia, and President S. A. Ort of Wittenberg College and Seminary in Springfield, Ohio.[23]

Together they speak to the same themes as McKnight. The Reformation has made Lutherans the mother of popular education and Germany the schoolmistress of the world. In the atmosphere of intellectual freedom in America, where all power must devolve upon persuasion, influence and progress belong to whoever masters education, and the Lutherans are best able to do that: not narrow like the Calvinists, nor foreshortened in their perspective like the secularists, nor authoritarian like the Catholics. The Lutheran colleges offer religious culture before all else. This they describe in the by-now familiar terms: suffused with the Christian spirit, broad enough (i.e., free of sectarian imposition) to commend itself to the public at large. But just as surely, their schools are "ministers of good to the State." They offer education at a lower cost than the state colleges (this was still the case). And they give the church the capacity to educate "the leaders and chief actors of the coming generation."

Thus far their calling. But the results had been disappointing. First of all, the Lutherans were late: the Revolutionary War had interrupted their first foundations. By 1800 they had perhaps 100,000 members in America, yet it would be thirty years before they had their first college. Second, they now had far too many colleges. Whereas the Methodists had one college for every 55,000 members; the Baptists, one for every 80,000; and the Episcopalians, one for every 90,000, the Lutherans had much smaller constituencies: only 30,000 members per college. Other systems had much larger endowments: $108,000 for the average Methodist college, $267,000 for the Baptists, $315,000 for the Episcopalians, $330,000 for the Congregationalists, and $582,000 for nonsectarians, while the average Lutheran college had an endowment of $18,000. Their standards of admission and graduation were abysmally low. In most cases the preparatory department school had more students than the college itself. Only five of their fifty colleges had an enrollment of more than a hundred students.[24] "It is a humiliating fact, and from this time on we should insist on greater things; and instead of multiplying weak and struggling colleges, we should henceforth strive, in our higher education, at least to approximate the average standard in our country."

Why so many colleges? ask Painter and Ort. Many Lutherans resisted adopting English, and their colleges were taught in four or five languages. Their constituencies were divided into more than two dozen small synods. "Questions of anise and cumin" and similar doctrinal squabbles have divided and subdivided the various partisans of belief. The result was that very few, even of Lutheran students, were enrolled in their own colleges. From this report it seems clear that while they were probably educating their church's future clergy, neither Gettysburg

471

nor its sister Lutheran colleges were likely to be educating leaders for other sectors of public life. And the efforts to make their institutions inoffensive to other Protestants, especially in the English-speaking colleges, had yielded only a 10 percent increase in enrollment.

The situation at Gettysburg was on the high end of the Lutheran scale. The endowment stood at about $200,000, but tuition income had to cover 70 percent of the annual budget, whereas at Columbia it paid only one-third, and at Harvard one-fifth. The college charged students only $50 a year, one of the lowest rates in Pennsylvania, whereas peer schools asked for from $75 to $200. In the years that followed, however, change began to set in. Faculty attendance at daily chapel became voluntary, and they would begin to attend less, then much less, regularly. Young men heading toward the Lutheran ministry, who at the turn of the century tended to represent half of a graduating class, would begin to go elsewhere on their way to ministry. Lutheran clergy, who represented 42 percent of the board of trustees, would begin to be replaced by laymen.

Samuel G. Hefelbower (1904-10), who replaced McKnight as president, determined not to work with a "preacher-dominated board." He castigated the college for its acquiescence in low standards, raised the admissions requirements, and announced that only university-trained candidates would be appointed to the faculty. "Up to this time, with a few exceptions, professorships in the college were filled from the Lutheran Ministry and were regarded, to some extent at least, as rewards for supposed successful work in this field."[25] When Andrew Carnegie offered matching endowment funds to support faculty pensions but disqualified colleges that required a majority of their trustees to belong to any "sect," the Gettysburg faculty asked the trustees to remove the charter amendment which required three-quarters of their number to be Lutherans. The board demurred (though taking four years to do so), lest the college's loyalty or the church's confidence be disturbed.

His successor, William A. Granville (1910-23), Gettysburg's first lay president, found that one thing clergymen were good for was soliciting funds from congregations. His inaugural address predictably deplored the national "moral decay" and claimed that only denominational colleges could restore America as a "Christian nation." A denominational college, however, was one which looked to a church for most of its funding and students while remaining nonsectarian: "the students entering or graduating, are not subject to any theological test, nor does the college curriculum include sectarian doctrine as part of the required work."[26] He turned to the church for financial help in the college's struggle to raise enough endowment to qualify for a matching grant from John D. Rockefeller's General Education Board. The United Lutheran Church in America gave him its endorsement, but not much more than that. Many congregations pledged much but then defaulted in their payments, leading to a disastrous shortfall in the fund drive.[27]

In 1918 three Lutheran synods combined to form the United Lutheran Church in America (ULCA). In 1921, when the college was in the midst of a large fund drive and looked to the church for direct support, the trustees amended the charter to require that no less than three-quarters of their number must be, not merely Lutherans, but members of the ULCA. While this was under discussion the faculty registered their misgivings. If the change in any way implied control of the college by the synod or the church, "We should regard the adoption of this suggestion as tending toward a narrowing parochialism out of all harmony with the democratic spirit of our American institutions."[28]

President Hanson's Cloud of Convictions

Then came President Henry W. A. Hanson (1923-52). It was on his watch that relations between the college and the church seem to have shifted, in ways that claim our scrutiny. He was a graduate of Roanoke College, the second-oldest "Americanist Lutheran" college in America, and had studied for the ministry at Gettysburg Seminary. After twenty years of parochial ministry and the presidency of the East Pennsylvania Synod, he was chosen to lead Gettysburg College. He had been a churchman, not an academic. In his inaugural address he stated a position that would see him through the twenty-nine years of his administration: "An education for leadership which is not Christian is for the needs of our day no education at all. . . . Religion is the root; ideals are the blossoms; service is the fruit." What did this Christian education produce? "A virile, rugged, red-blooded manhood, which is passionately loyal to the worthwhile ideals."[29]

During the Hanson presidency undergraduate enrollment doubled: from 567 to 1,164.[30] The Lutheran proportion among them, however, seems meanwhile to have declined from 97 to 43 percent; with almost a 10 percent decline in the actual number of Lutherans.[31] The faculty were also doubled in that period,[32] while the Lutheran representation among them slumped from 94 to 51 percent.[33] The endowment fund fell from $781,000[34] to just over a half-million dollars.[35] These indicia do not by themselves seem so significant if one contemplates how they have developed since Hanson's time. In 1991 Gettysburg College had an endowment fund worth $52,453,430.[36] Its student body numbered 2,118 full-time, of whom only 10 percent were Lutheran.[37] Its faculty numbered 161, of whom perhaps 12 percent were Lutheran.[38] Yet there are reasons to identify the Hanson regime, 1923-52, as the time when the college settled into a new direction.

There was already strong concern afoot in the 1920s that colleges like Gettysburg were being lost to their churches.[39] But explanations differed. In 1928 the director of education at Teachers College concluded a commissioned four-year study of ULCA colleges. In a brusque report to the biennial convention, he depicted the problem as a loss of nerve: by both the colleges and their sponsoring churches.

For twenty years or more the church colleges have occupied a competitive position, somewhat of a defensive character. By the process of upgrading they have tried to hold their own and become as well regarded academically as the state universities or the endowed colleges. Perforce, the standards of the state institutions have been copied, and each year the church college has become more like them in educational program, athletics and sports, social life and general objectives. To retain their place in the educational world they have tended to sacrifice the very thing for which they were established, and the only reason for their claim upon church support.

Such is the general situation among Christian colleges in the United States, and such is true of the Lutheran situation in broad, general outline. The problem is not only to make and keep the colleges of high grade as to scholarship, but to bring to the front conspicuously the one purpose which differentiates them from state and private institutions — religion. . . .

No Lutheran college now maintains a religious program adequate for the great ends of the church, in terms of leadership, or facilities for worship, activities or instruction! It is not because of the lack of desire, but for the lack of funds . . .[40]

Included in the report itself was the further observation that the Lutheran colleges were in danger of becoming too tame:

Presidents have been successful in recruiting faculty members who hold conservative views and who therefore are assured of the necessary freedom to teach in accordance with them because such views are apparently acceptable to the Church. It is implicit in the organization of the Lutheran colleges what views in accordance with scriptural teaching and church doctrines will be entertained by instructors. Restriction in teaching comes by the process of selection. It is entirely proper to achieve restriction in this manner. Yet this principle, pressed unduly, results in a type of institution which is not likely to foster (to a marked degree) scientific inquiry, nor to entertain or encourage wide differences of opinion in religion and science. Such institutions, in turn, naturally attract and hold students who are at home in such an educational environment and lose those who wish the freer intellectual life. The type of belief and intellectual reaction most valued by the majority of these institutions may be summarized by quoting from one of the presidents: "Religious education, along sound lines; philosophy, a Christian point of view; history, no destructive theory; biology, evolution allowed from a theistic point of view and psychology, materialistic theories not encouraged."[41]

The church's own educational executive expressed uneasiness in 1930: "It is common knowledge that when a church college becomes successful it tries to withdraw from the mother who gave it birth and fostered it during the dangerous period of childhood and youth. . . . the cry of thirty years ago, 'away with the small college,' became 'away with the liberal arts college,' and it is now heard as 'away with the church college.' "[42] What the one observer attributed to poverty, the other ascribed to prosperity. But they both saw the estrangement between colleges and church.

474

At Gettysburg, which was neither bankrupt nor affluent, other forces were in play. Historians have already noticed that Hanson was "fully in sympathy with the tradition stressing the Christian over the Lutheran character" of the college.[43]

The Hanson style clearly shaped the college emphasis in religious matters during this period. Hanson was not particularly interested in strong Lutheran identification but rather in evangelical commitment. He had a taste for evangelical theology, an optimistic world view, and a preference for nonliturgical practice. Some of this attitude was developed, no doubt, by his "American Lutheran" background and by his graduate theological study in Germany at a time when liberal theology was at its zenith there.[44]

A gifted orator, Hanson inveterately spoke of the college's religious task in generic Christian terms without reference to the Lutheran faith. In his 1926 report to the East Pennsylvania Synod he claimed that Gettysburg had "on its staff of teachers only men of Christian convictions."[45] On closer notice, however, one sees that President Hanson, besides reducing Lutheranism to generic Christianity, further tended to characterize Christianity as an amalgam of heartiness and patriotism. In his periodic reports to the trustees he was accustomed to offer a homiletic preface which expressed his central aspirations for the college. The following excerpts convey the drift of his homiletic thought.

Upon approaching each class [Louis Agassiz], the venerable scientist, said to his students, "Before entering upon a study of creation, let us seek wisdom from the creator." In this, we have the Christian philosophy of education. We must somehow link the seeking mind with the all embracing presence of God which gives significance and unity to the universe.

Americanism is a matter of the soul. It gathers up and expresses idealism, comradeship, and good will. American traditions have always placed a premium on justice, fair dealing, and individual initiative.[46]

The thing I covet for Gettysburg College more than anything else is steady growth of a truly great ideal of what it seeks to do for successive academic generations. *There are human values.* The student is, first of all, a human being. Within him must be developed attitudes, appreciations, loyalty to obligations. He must be made to walk understandingly through the immensities of life with a head erect; with a heart that is sensitive! *There are social values.* Each individual born into this world is born with obligations; with debts of honor to others. It is only when these debts have been frankly faced and honestly met that there can be either self-respect or personal happiness. *There are spiritual values.* Religion enables an individual to draw on a wisdom, strength, perspective, and patience which is not his own. It is no more possible to teach a student music without sound, art without color, than to teach one to live without religion. Gettysburg College is not groping in the dark nor grovelling in the dirt to open up channels upon which those about to live may draw — Gettysburg College is a religious institution.[47]

Our warrant in drawing excerpts at such great length is President Hanson's uncommon capacity to embody the religious mission of the college in the very vagueness he disavows. He could never be accused of a tendentious, sectarian Lutheranism. There is nothing here to give offense to Mennonites, Baptists, or Episcopalians. Nor to Catholics or Orthodox. Nor, for that matter, to Mormons, Christian Scientists, Jews, or Moral Re-Armamentarians.

Lest Hanson be thought to be setting his own standard in the matter, one ought to consult a contemporaneous policy statement of the ULCA's Board of Education on "The Purposes of the Church in a Church-Related College." The general purpose is vaguely said to be "to help discover and apply truth, and to develop Christian personality under the best educational standards and procedures." These are the means:

1. *The policy* of the church will be positively Christian, in business administration, in academic standards, and in the supervision of Christian life.
2. *The activities of the students* will correspond to the principles of Christian culture and will be planned to develop Christian personality in the students.
3. *The teachers* will be Christians. Such teachers, having Christian consciousness, Christian convictions, and Christian courage, are essential to the development of Christian personality. Their example and their varied activities, apart from their teaching, will be instruments to that end.
4. *The correlated curriculum,* in the hands of these Christian teachers, will afford the student a comprehensive knowledge of the Bible, an adequate understanding of Christian truth, and right techniques of Christian living.[48]

Suddenly a Worry

At the church convention of 1948 the staff of the Board of Education, in an alarmed report on secularism in higher education (as well as materialism, mechanism, humanism, and totalitarianism), grieved: "Many schools are more interested in scientific progress than in moral development. Students are required to study the teachings of Karl Marx, but no courses are offered in the teachings of Jesus." By contrast: "The Christian college exists to educate Christians, to challenge youth to a personal dedication to the eternal God, revealed in Jesus Christ, and to develop a larger appreciation of human values in all relations." The convention went on to address this with the following resolution: "That the United Lutheran Church in America urge the colleges to develop the Christian emphasis in larger degree in classroom and campus activity and to counteract the trend of secularism in American life."[49]

In 1972 the LCA Board of College Education and Church Vocations reported that "the central crisis of our society is a crisis in meaning. The integrity of the nation has been questioned; the validity of traditions has been undermined; the limit of material abundance in providing satisfaction has been discovered; and the future is threatened by pollution, population and nuclear power proliferation. . . . In an unexpected way the validity of the church-related liberal arts college is renewed." At this same meeting an assertive statement claiming the rightful place of Lutheran colleges as beneficiaries of governmental support ended in a series of "Affirmations," the first of which read: "Lutherans sponsor colleges and universities because they believe that the educational programs of these institutions are a proper and important expression of their commitment to the gospel." One delegate moved to amend this by adding "and that these institutions be instructed to study very carefully how they can more effectively carry out their commitment to the Gospel." The amendment was defeated.[50]

Church executives were understandably concerned that so few Lutherans were enrolling in Lutheran colleges. A 1937 survey reported at least 38,339 Lutherans in college: 20,945 in state institutions,[51] 9,795 in other independent colleges, and only 7,599 in Lutheran colleges.[52] When a later survey suggested that students at their own Lutheran colleges did not give as their primary reason for enrollment "the fact that it was a Christian college," the LCA Board asked: "Is it possible that 'the principles and ideals around which Christian education is organized have not been effectively integrated into the total educational program as they should be'? Are the principles of Christianity 'hidden behind a screen of evasion or subterfuge,' or are they made explicit at every opportunity?"[53] President Hanson's vagueness may not have been evasion and subterfuge, but the effect was the same.

During the Hanson regime there is little evidence that the actual study of religion was emphasized. In 1920 the newly formed ULCA had accused its affiliated colleges of a "distressing lack of attention" to the study of the Bible and Christian religion. Henceforth, it decided, every college that received subsidies from the church was obliged in conscience to spend the funds "definitely promoting a Christian mind in the students." A graduation requirement of twenty-four semester hours in religious courses was considered a minimum.[54] When Dr. Hanson arrived in 1923, the curriculum required but two semester hours of religious study. During his regime that was increased to four semester hours, and in 1941 Bible was approved as a major field of study.[55] But by the end of his presidency Gettysburg still reported only one required course in Bible (their departmental title for religion).[56]

Worship at Gettysburg was problematic. All students were required to attend Christ Church on Sunday, or (if they were not Lutherans) another church in town designated by their parents. In 1931 Hanson noted that so many students who lived in the region and had access to transport were spending weekends at home and taking friends with them, it would be best to make Sunday worship voluntary. He admitted to the trustees that it had become a rule impossible to enforce.[57]

Daily chapel attendance was a more vexed point at Gettysburg, as it was on most campuses. When Hanson assumed office, students were suspended for excessive absences. Hanson imposed further required credits for graduation as a progressive penalty for cuts. Students arranged for others to sit in their seats, or went but studied, slept, or read through the service, or distracted themselves by riotous assembly. The college historian recalls: "There is some evidence that at least a few accepted the chapel requirement, went out of conviction or ignorance, and could testify to certain benefits from the experience." Resisting student appeals for voluntary chapel, Hanson instead changed what it was they were compelled to attend. To please the faculty, who mostly stayed away, he tried changing the scheduled hour of prayer. They still stayed away. Then he eliminated Saturday chapel. Then he let the students organize the services two days a week, converted the service on the third day to class meetings, presided himself on the fourth day with one of his inspirational talks, and on the fifth day invited outside speakers, who as time went on devolved from nearby pastors to public personalities in government, church, or industry.[58] A rare instance of renewed interest in chapel was noted privately to the trustees in 1944 by the board member who served as rapporteur on campus religious affairs:

> Faculty and students have repeatedly observed that the daily chapel exercises have been "different" this year. A new interest and a new reverence has permeated these services. It should be a matter of considerable gratification that by the almost unanimous vote of the students themselves, several chapel periods each week have been made more formal by the use of the altar and a simple liturgy. This was not an idea which originated with the faculty or administration; it sprang spontaneously from the felt needs of the boys and girls.[59]

Though Hanson had previously been synodical president, as college president he preferred to keep church authorities at arm's length, lest they intrude upon the college's autonomy. Though he made regular reports to the various synodical conventions, he preferred to solicit funds from congregations directly. In 1935 the charter was revised to reduce the statutory presence of ULCA church members from three-fourths to two-thirds of the board of trustees. The nearby supporting synods tried repeatedly but unsuccessfully to have the right of appointment to several board seats each.[60]

Hanson Rhetoric Continues

Several themes of Henry Hanson's long period of service have been repeated since then. Walter Langsam (1952-55) articulated the "immutable" principles of Christian education thus:

> That higher education is right which emphasizes the dignity of the individual as one who is created in the image of God; which teaches the student that spiritual

values are superior to and more lasting than material values; which develops stable men and women who can hold fast to basic values even in times of stress; which makes it clear that giving, based on love, is far more rewarding than any kind of taking; which teaches young people how men and women throughout the ages have lived together, have made a living, and have interpreted the universe around them; which, in short, helped produce effective Christian citizens and leaders for tomorrow.[61]

C. Arnold Hanson (1961-77) on the same theme:

> Stripped of all secondary adjectives, [Gettysburg] is a Christian college in the liberal tradition which seeks to provide an education the distinctive quality of which resides in common pursuit of academic and religious insight. . . . We commit ourselves to the task . . . , convinced that in the determination of that which is "salutary" we may draw on the integrity which the tradition of scholarship provides and on the faith which is ever a part of man's search for ultimate understanding.[62]

This strand of rhetoric was perhaps drawn out to its finest in the inaugural remarks of Gettysburg's first non-Lutheran president, Charles Glassick (1977-90), a Methodist:

> We will not require the students to adopt any particular set of values and beliefs; in other words, there is no *doctrine* required to graduate from Gettysburg College. But in the close church/college atmosphere we enjoy here, I believe they will be more inclined to examine their own *personal* values and hopefully come to an ethical framework that they can use as a benchmark in the years ahead for their behavior and decision-making. It is that relationship with the Lutheran Church which rounds out the education, that takes it from just an academic enterprise to an education of the whole person. I'm very much committed to that.[63]

It is rhetoric of this sort which must have occasioned Alexander Miller's observation that "a scrutiny of the catalogues of Christian colleges now turns up with monotonous frequency what Joseph Sittler calls 'the melancholy statement' that the aim of the college is the cultivation of 'moral and spiritual values.' "[64] One might be led to wonder how an educational institution whose public self-presentation is so tenaciously enveloped in clouds of banality could long retain any identity. Charles Glatfelter, the college historian, has noted that anyone who inquired about the specific purposes of Gettysburg would find the institution reluctant to answer. As a campus steering committee told the Middle States accreditation team in 1973, "We must be aware that one characteristic of the style of Gettysburg College, as manifested by many members of the faculty in recent years, is a reluctance to develop detailed statements of purposes and then secure adherence to them. The purposes are to be seen rather in the way in which the institution in practice behaves."[65]

The ULCA Wants Accountability

This was to change. When the ULCA joined with several Scandinavian synods in 1962 to form the Lutheran Church in America, the LCA began an incessant inquiry into why it was involved in higher education. In the years of negotiation before the merger a strong consensus had formed among church leaders:

> In the new Church all of the colleges will be *church-colleges* in the best sense of the word — colleges whose faculties, administrations, and boards seek to provide a quality education within the framework of the Gospel of Jesus Christ. Such institutions are avowed champions of the Christian point of view.

The church should "set standards, both of academic excellence and of church participation in their government and life," for continued recognition of the colleges. That was to be perhaps the strongest account in this century of the bond between "Americanist Lutherans" and their colleges.[66] As far as the educators were concerned, however, there was no good sense of the word "church-colleges." They needed church money, not church scrutiny.

Gettysburg and its peers were founded to provide preliminary education for ministerial candidates. To ensure their Lutheran subsidies they developed an ecclesial rhetoric. But to be viable they had to recruit many more students who wanted a postsecondary education but were indifferent to the Lutheran faith.[67] From this a double-tongued promotional rhetoric was born. Long-term executive secretary of the ULCA Board of Higher Education Gould Wickey said in 1962 that if a college or university claims to be Lutheran, then it ought to welcome "consultative and supervisory relationships" with the educational board of the national church, and to accept a sort of accreditation process according to published standards. *"Lutheran education is an education permeated by the thought and life of the Lutheran church."*[68] Yet he would disown church authority as strongly as state authority:

> They are the servants of the church for the sake of the Kingdom of God, and consequently the church will not allow them to become subservient to any group within or without the church. They should be left free to search for and to witness to the truth of God. . . . The education institutions of the church are under the control only of the Head of the church, who is "the way, and the truth, and the life."[69]

The issue in 1962, however, was that the faculties and student bodies of these colleges, both now about 60 percent non-Lutheran, were using their freedom, not to search for and witness to the truth of God in deviant ways, but to ignore it as a distraction.

Theologian Martin Heinecken spoke in both directions even more strongly. For the benefit of the Lutheran constituency, he put it clearly: "A school that is related to the *Lutheran* church should stand squarely and unashamedly in the Lutheran tradition among the family of churches." But being Lutheran did not imply any involvement by the church: "The first task of a college is to be a first-rate educational institution. Its task is not redemption, but education." There should no more be Lutheran fire departments, labor unions, or political parties, than Lutheran colleges. The Word is to be proclaimed and the sacraments administered and lives transformed, but this is the ministry of the church upon individuals, not institutions. The redeemed may then explore the relevance of their faith to all areas of learning. But "this can and should be done by the creative minority of Christians in the public, tax-supported schools of the land where education properly belongs. This is where Martin Luther put it when he called not upon the prelates of the church but upon the princes of the land to establish public schools open to all."[70]

Prompted by the new church's Board of College Education and Church Vocations, the Central Pennsylvania Synod examined Gettysburg College and Susquehanna University, the two institutions assigned to its regional patronage. The synod found that worship and chaplaincy were available; their life and curricula showed that academic integrity and Christian witness were compatible; they had significant numbers of Lutheran personnel; they had a manifest desire to relate amiably to the synod; and they maintained standards of conduct higher than those in society as a whole. Therefore the synod voted official recognition. A local state college might have qualified on these same grounds.[71]

In that same year, 1964, the new LCA made its first statement about its seventeen four-year colleges. It was on those campuses that the church acted as a "transformer of culture" and helped "shape the minds of tomorrow's leaders in congregation and community." To support this resource the church's total contributions amounted to 7 percent of total expenditures, representing an average contribution of only $1.05 by each confirmed member ($3.00 per capita was thought to be a realistic minimum to ask for). The church also categorized four models of church-college relationship. This would include (in descending order of relationship) vocational schools for church professionals, colleges for Lutherans, colleges run in a Lutheran "cultural pattern" for a general clientele, and colleges of "ecumenical Christian witness" without any Lutheran features "in evidence." Yet all four modes of education were deemed "to provide an effective Christian witness," without differentiation.[72] For $1.05 it is not clear how much cultural transformation one had a right to expect.

A Series of Reports, All Critical

Edgar M. Carlson, president of Gustavus Adolphus College, chaired a large policy study some years later. The report explained that the colleges associated with the church — which it avoids calling "Lutheran colleges" — do not exist for the church's benefit, nor are they agencies of the church. They are a vehicle of service by the church in the world. (It was clear that the Carlson group was leaving no room for the first and second of the above LCA models . . . or perhaps the third.)

> The most appropriate form within which to conceive this common undertaking may be the form of "covenant." Unless the administration and faculty of the church college consciously share the commitment to Christ as Lord and voluntarily adopt a Christian point of view toward major issues, no legal relationships will assure that an effective Christian witness is being made. . . .
>
> A church college will seek teachers who are highly competent in their disciplines and who are dedicated to the aims and purposes of the institution. While this may not exclude persons of other faiths or of no faith from teaching roles, for longer or shorter periods, the readiness of such persons to work within the declared purposes of the institution should be ascertained in advance of their employment.[73]

To maintain its "atmosphere or ethos" (the ethereal metaphor perdures here), to give proper nurture to Christian faith and life on campus, the colleges must offer vital worship, instruction of high quality in Christianity, pastoral counseling, and programs of service that unite faculty and students. The report concedes that worship had caused "uneasiness" in the past and suggests chapel-for-credit as a remedy: since it had not worked well as worship, it should be redesigned to have "genuine educational value" and be awarded credits toward graduation.[74]

The function of the church was to provide money. And that very year, though the writers of this document could not then have known it, LCA subsidies for its colleges reached a peak from which they would immediately recede. The average per capita contribution from the church was $1.42.[75] Responses to the Carlson study were so conflicted that it was never accepted as an LCA policy statement. The convention called for more conferences, self-examination, continuing dialogue, etc. It was, after all, 1968.[76]

The Carlson report had noted a recent study at the University of Michigan. The primary sources of most world religions were being studied there, but the study found it strange that the Talmud and the New Testament, the sources of most direct significance to the student body, were given only the "most cursory" treatment. "This inverted provincialism severely limits the University's capacity to provide for its own students an understanding of their own civilization." But the Lutherans believed that most secular institutions were now going to follow their lead and remedy that deficiency, so that "Christianity as a social and historical phenomenon" would find new acceptance in their curricula.[77] Quite the contrary, Christian institutions would follow the trend they deplored at Michigan. They would replace their studies of Christianity as the belief of the community to which both students and their educators belonged with courses in religious studies that treated it as a phenomenon, a curiosity similar to Islam and shamanism.

In any case, the idea was spreading that secularization might be beneficial for church-related colleges. Lutheran theologian William Jennings, taking his writ from Dietrich Bonhoeffer that now "everything gets along without 'God,' and just as well as before," and from Harvey Cox that "Christian" institutions have not been possible since the Middle Ages, was arguing that both the idea and the term "Christian college" (or "church college") were out of step with the needs of twentieth-century, secular America and must be abandoned. The only legitimate reason for a church to support colleges (without, of course, interfering in any way with their autonomy) is service to society at large. Why colleges instead of soup kitchens or refugee agencies? "It would do well to keep its fingers where the action is, and the action is increasingly on college campuses." Atheism would be a welcome feature on these campuses. "A church-related college needs honest atheists, for in a secular age atheism is for some the most tenable position. A church cannot expect her colleges to be homogeneous in theism while claiming to be a full part of a society which is pluralistic in outlook."[78]

The Carlson report was followed by another effort: "A Statement": *The Mission of LCA Colleges and Universities.* The Board of College Education and Church Vocations formally adopted it as its official policy in 1970, and called it "definitive." It closely resembles the Carlson document. What it asked of its collegiate covenant partners was a campus atmosphere where religious debate was possible. Church-related colleges were valuable simply for being an alternative to state institutions. This was clearly a political point: governmental funding was becoming available to independent colleges and universities, and the capacity of religiously affiliated schools to receive any of it was being constitutionally challenged.[79]

That very year, however, a gust of impatience toward its colleges ruffled the church. Benevolence gifts had been diminishing for several years now. In the Central Pennsylvania Synod, note was taken that at Susquehanna the Lutherans now constituted only a third of the enrollment, and at Gettysburg they were less than a fifth. With the Lutheran educators insisting that what they offered was essentially a secular activity suffused by a religious "atmosphere," the synodical delegates became increasingly aware of how many more young Lutherans were enrolled at other colleges and universities in their region, yet provided with only part-time pastoral care. Their needs had received no mention in the recent LCA mission statement. If it really was the LCA colleges' ambition to make Christian witness no more than "possible" on their campuses, was it not just as possible on other campuses, and to better effect? So the convention voted to reduce its subsidy to their two related colleges and to award an equal sum to campus ministry on nonrelated campuses.[80] This was the harbinger of a gradual decline in synodical support of the two colleges. In 1965 its subsidy had amounted to 10.2 percent of their budgets; twenty years later it would amount to less than 2.5 percent.[81]

Francis Gamelin, former educational executive for the church, lectured Lutherans of all churches on the realities of their situation. Despite the enormous range of institutional models — from the Missouri Synod colleges meant to educate church professionals to the highly independent and secularized LCA schools — they all had a shared, dual purpose: "public service and church service." But many of them had constituencies too small to give them a Lutheran student body. "The churches have diluted the strength of their college effort. They now have about 20 colleges more than they probably would erect today if they could start over, cooperate, and locate their institutions strategically."[82]

Gamelin's data displayed how different were the educational involvements of the three Lutheran families. Their respective enrollments of Lutheran students differed greatly: LCMS colleges, almost 100 percent; ALC colleges, all over 50 percent, with half over 75 percent; and LCA colleges, mostly under 50 percent, all the way down to 13 percent. Reports showed the faculties were about 57 percent Lutheran. These too varied greatly: LCMS, nearly 100 percent; ALC, 63 percent; LCA, 35 percent. But these figures were unreliable since half the colleges seemed not to know the religious preferences of their faculty. Per capita annual contributions from the churches also differed: LCMS, $3.22; ALC, $1.24; LCA, $1.11. Gamelin's data argue that the Lutherans had founded and sponsored far more colleges than they now needed or used. His mild conclusion: cooperation between the colleges.[83]

Covenants That Commit Nothing

Meanwhile covenant negotiations between churches and colleges were under way, and already in 1971 Gettysburg College and the Maryland Synod had concluded their pact. The document was actually called a "Background Statement," and during floor debate at the synodical convention it was remarked that it smacked of description, not of commitment. But it was referred to ever after as a covenant.[84] The language of the document implies how desultory the synod was about Gettysburg. It deals heavily in general statements, such as: "Gettysburg College . . . is a community for learning committed to discovery, exploration, and evaluation of the ideas and actions of man, and to the creative extension of that developing heritage. Gettysburg's Lutheran affiliation, as well as its intention to perpetuate that church-relatedness, makes evident the fact that it proceeds 'under God.' "[85] It is not evident whether this has anything to do with academics. "The College considers its purpose fulfilled if its graduates continue to be informed, humane, creative, and constructively critical individuals, well prepared to act responsibly in the complex world of the future."

"The church related college with a company of persons of common commitment possesses an enhanced possibility of dealing creatively and openly with questions of meaning, purpose and personal destiny." How persons of common commitment were to be assembled is handled with finesse. Lutherans were to be given preference in admissions, all else being equal. Since few Lutherans wanted to enroll, this was no point of contention. For faculty it was more delicate.

> Thus a person under consideration for appointment to the staff of the College is made aware of the College's purpose and program as a church related institution and is asked to decide whether his beliefs are congenial to the purposes and policies of the College as a church related institution. Relying on the intellectual honesty of the candidate the College is willing to accept an affirmative answer from the prospective staff member as sufficient evidence of his loyalty to the nature of the College.

It is not said how the candidate would know what if anything was involved in being church-related. A copy of this Background Statement would certainly not be very disclosive. It sounded like a subject no one was anxious to discuss.

The discussions between the Central Pennsylvania Synod and its two institutions, Gettysburg and Susquehanna, were lengthier. The college noted distantly that it had "proceeded under Lutheran influence." Despite the declining presence of Lutherans among its student body, it affirmed that "the opportunity for corporate worship and for witness is unabashedly available for all who comprise the community." It will continue to help prepare students for future leadership, lay and clerical, in the church. It makes available its "traffic of ideas" for the benefit of the church. It promises to acquaint new staff with the character and purpose of the college, and expects compliance. The synod, for its part, affirms that if its colleges became completely secular "they might easily lose contact with the virtues and goals which it is the obligations of Christians to foster." Thus it wishes to retain its position of influence with higher education. It expects the college to offer religion courses that deal with the values and traditions of the Christian church, and the experience of the Lutheran community. It honors the college's right and need to hire staff without regard for their religious affiliation. And it promises to offer the college its advice and support.[86] The draft of the covenant was much debated by the college faculty, who fretted over passages which (perhaps to them alone) might seem to yield too much entrée to the synod.[87]

In essence the 1973 covenant reiterated the old formula: the synod promised students and support, and the college promised a relationship. How substantial these commitments were is open to question. Faculty recollection is that while the subject of religion had been brought up in faculty hiring interviews through the early sixties, by 1973 it was no longer mentioned. With a Lutheran presence on the faculty of less than a quarter and steadily shrinking, the religious intentionality of the campus would be the work of a few, obliged to move upstream against

485

indifference and resistance. As for the synod, it really had no way of persuading more of its members to enroll at Gettysburg. The Lutheran contingent there stood at 20 percent and would continue to diminish. The proposed annual subsidy of $123,380, amounting to 2 percent of the college's budget, had to survive two attempts on the floor of the convention to reduce it to less than half of that. There were evidently some delegates who did not see the relationship as productive.[88] The only reason to be abashed was that they treated it as worthy of discussion.

The next year the Gettysburg board abolished the charter requirement that two-thirds of its membership must be members of the LCA. One enthusiastic faculty commentator remarked that the proviso had become "superfluous" now that the covenants were in place. He may have been correct, but in a sense opposite to what he intended.[89]

More Critical Reports

In 1975 Francis Gamelin produced a more extensive study of Lutheran colleges. He offered a typology that ranked them by their relationship to the church. The group most tenuously related, he called "Church-Related Colleges,"[90]

> which recognize an historic relationship and affiliation with the Lutheran Church but do not proclaim a Christian stance. In their catalog statements of purpose, at least, they are not affirming colleges. Instead they refer to their religious or Christian heritage, they identify themselves as "in the Christian tradition," they help students "examine conflicting value systems" and "make judgements consistent with the Christian faith." They may even provide students "a Christian-oriented environment." But they make no ringing affirmations of Christian intent. One neglects to mention its church-relatedness in its statement of purpose, another takes pains to emphasize that its church relationship does not affect its essential functions.

All seven colleges which he categorizes as "church-related" are of the LCA, and they include Gettysburg, whose catalogue entry then read as follows:

> Gettysburg College maintains a relationship with the religious tradition from which its founders came. The first Lutheran College in America is still associated with the Lutheran Church. But it is equally aware of the injunction of its founders that it remain "unsectarian in its instruction," and that it set no barriers of race or belief in the hiring of faculty or the admission of students.[91]

Gamelin then studies the covenants that had been enacted recently within the LCA and finds them consistent in their insignificance. Church members took a much more sharply profiled view of the matter. By large majorities, especially among youth, Lutherans expected their colleges to be distinctive, to offer and require Christian religion courses, and to have selective faith requirements for faculty. In particular, he sees many covenants, especially in the "church-related" category, to be at odds with expectations in the church, in which laity seemed to be more demanding than clergy.

> No measure of presidential eloquence or chapel emphasis can compensate for faculty ignorance of Christian experience, indifference to it, or sequestration of it in a religion department.
>
> There appears to be some faith in LCA, according to covenant data, that a Christian president is the essential factor in maintaining a Christian college. That faith may be naive. Although a president at the heart of a college may continually refresh its lifeblood, he simply makes it possible for the faculty to function efficiently. Faculty direction and teaching are really determined by each one's network of values and convictions. Only a Christian faculty member can be expected to implement a President's or his own vision of a Christian College . . .[92]

Charles Bruning, also commissioned by the church to report on the state of its colleges, deplores the way in which its college educators had turned away from their original purpose. "On the one hand there is a widespread tendency to repudiate the sectarian past, often without trying to salvage what may be worth retaining. . . . on the other hand, there is a furious effort to catch up with the rapidly changing order, as if relevance to society were alone sufficient. One can almost hear the pathetic cry from churchmen, 'please stop the world — we want to get on.' "[93]

By 1976 twenty-four covenants had been negotiated and approved by various synods, and the church thought it time for another policy statement, only six years after its last definitive one. The text, "The Basis for Partnership between Church and College," does show there has been a shift in conviction, a shift toward acknowledging that they are indeed two diverse ventures. Indeed, the statement says,

> it is both unbiblical and misleading to speak of "Christian" higher education or a "Christian" college. People, needing salvation, are baptized into Christ; institutions, entrusted with a secular task, do not need to be baptized to be faithful servants of God the Creator. Thus, the term "church-related" is to be preferred.[94]

This document canonizes the theological dictum that had been a-building for some years, based on the Lutheran doctrine of two kingdoms. Education, even when church-related, prepares one for responsible citizenship, not for a life of faith, and is still God's work even though it is assigned to the state, not the church. "This association is God-given; this cooperation in the secular is God-pleasing. For the term secular means non-redemptive; it does not mean God-forsaken."[95] As the education executive explained it to the convention, "The distinctiveness of the church-related college lies not in some unique mission, different from all other institutions of higher learning, but rather in the motivation that inspires its educational tasks."[96]

After clearly admitting that partnership with the church will not intrinsically affect the shape or texture of a college's academic project, the document claims that sponsorship gives the church "access" to the settings where the large issues of social welfare are debated, and allows the church to manifest its "prophetic concern that the structures of society become wiser, more just and more compassionate."[97]

At this point the church shows the symptoms of a detached retina. If those charged with responsibility for the colleges related to the Lutheran church were now no longer predominantly Lutherans, and if the imposing norms of academic custom now inhibited them from letting their faith impinge upon their academic work, then what play would the church's prophetic concern have on those campuses, save in the bleatings of marginalized campus ministers? If the Lutheran community had some gospel-rooted notions of its own about "responsible citizenship," how could they reach the minds and consciences of students at colleges where Lutherans no longer gathered?

In a fascinating study of the LCA at exactly this time, sociologist Merton Strommen found significant division between the Lutheran and the non-Lutheran educators on their campuses. A minority of the non-Lutheran faculty reported themselves as religiously active (versus 85 percent of the Lutherans), and were much more indifferent to any religious emphasis in the colleges. With exquisite subtlety he notes: "Inasmuch as non-Lutheran faculty comprise two-thirds of the teaching force, one becomes aware of the potential erosion of faculty interest in a church relationship."

Faculty dysfunction was broader than imagined. "The presence of significant numbers of teachers who actually profess indifference to so fundamental a dimension of human culture as religion [not just Lutheran religion, but any religion] may constitute as much of a threat to liberal education as to Christian witness." But while reporting that 85 percent of pastors, synod board members, and trustees think most faculty should be professing Christians, Strommen discloses that only a minority of the dominant non-Lutheran faculty agrees with this view, and only one-third of the students.[98]

Trustees rank highest among all constituency groups in wanting their college to be religiously distinctive, yet they confess they have defaulted and been passive toward the mission of their institutions. "Their admitted lack of understanding and perception is reflected in an over-romanticized perception of their school. On a number of evaluative measures, they are as unrealistic in their perception of campus realities as the parents of freshmen."[99] Meanwhile the Central Pennsylvania Synod's subsidy to Gettysburg declined by 20 percent in one year.[100]

The Gettysburg faculty had never showed a disposition to adopt detailed statements of purpose. But by 1981, with the LCA's skyline aflurry with official policy statements, the campus people decided the time had come for them to speak as well. As of 1911 the catalogue had carried their founders' laconic statement that

Gettysburg "promises to exert a salutary influence in advancing the cause of liberal education." The Statement of Purpose of 1981 had said very little about its Lutheran identity, save that it cherished its rank as eldest of the colleges affiliated with the LCA and "intends to continue that church relatedness." It outlined three features in its program: academics, student life, and religious life. The asymmetry between academics and religion is suggested by the statement that the college "nurtures" intellectual values, whereas it only gives "opportunities for the examination of spiritual and moral values."[101]

Less Meaningful Partnerships

It was just at this moment that the college's two synodical compacts came up for renewal. This time they were only "statements of partnership." The Central Pennsylvania Synod negotiated a common text for its partnership with both Gettysburg and Susquehanna, and it was approved by all three parties in 1981. The text contains some uncommonly sonorous yet pointless assertions of what the colleges meant to the church.

> Although some of the circumstances have changed since the founding of these colleges, there are compelling reasons — both traditional and contemporary — for continuing these relationships. Throughout their histories the church and the colleges have worked to provide avenues for discussion and debate on the goals of society and to develop leadership in nurturing values which enhance the sacredness of life.
>
> Within the context of American higher education, it is on the campus of the church-related institution where the church has the greatest freedom to foster visibly the virtues and goals it espouses. The church must not cut itself off from the historic and contemporary intellectual and spiritual challenges which a church relationship poses. It is therefore imperative that the church continue its close contact with specific colleges.
>
> In addition, Gettysburg College and Susquehanna University acknowledge the vital importance of close contact with the church. Traditionally and presently these colleges have maintained, and do maintain, that for them liberal arts education needs to occur in a setting where the Christian faith is presented as a living option. Such a setting can best be sustained where the college and church work together in close partnership to support the free exploration of ideas, the pursuit of high academic standards, the growth of concern for others, and the building of one's faith within a community guided by Judeo-Christian values.[102]

The absurdity in these passages is that they characterize the relationship as close, compelling, vital, imperative, yet they describe a religious program indistinguishable from what was offered members of the synod at nearby Shippensburg or Millersville State Colleges: free exploration of ideas, pastoral care, worship, religion courses, all "in a setting where the Christian faith is a living option." The dwindling Lutheran enrollment and subsidy, however, were being matched by the marginalization of religious practice and theological inquiry. Neither party in this partnership was going to deliver.

One item in the partnership statement which touched on the capacity of the colleges ever to consider the church as a vital co-agent, was the paragraph dealing with faculty hiring. Objection was raised subsequently within the Susquehanna board by a non-Christian trustee: it sounded as if the synod were being invited to meddle in faculty appointments, and the text was correspondingly redrafted:

Original Draft	Revised Text
The colleges will acquaint each present and prospective member of the faculty and staff with the nature of the church-college relationship and make every effort to employ persons who are supportive of this relationship. The synod upholds the colleges' need for and right to employ the best qualified persons. The synod will assist in the search by offering for consideration qualified candidates who have Christian commitment.	The synod supports the university's commitment to build and maintain a faculty of outstanding teachers and scholars congenial to the full mission of the university. Central to that mission is an education in which the quest for values, wisdom, and religious understanding enlivens and deepens the search for knowledge and the formation of character. As partners, both the university and the synod stand firmly for academic freedom and religious pluralism in the university's life. The university, with the assistance, support, and encouragement of the synod, welcomes needed and qualified faculty and staff of any religious view who agree to join in this education endeavor at a Lutheran Church in America–related university whose ideals and aspirations are rooted in, sustained, and challenged by the Judeo-Christian tradition.

The Gettysburg faculty, which had debated the fine points of the 1973 covenant at great length, had given this draft a more cursory treatment and, in the memory of one member closely involved, swiftly approved it because it was "not offensive." When Susquehanna wanted it amended, Gettysburg said it preferred to let stand what they had already agreed upon. Susquehanna, however, pressed the synod to agree to the revision, which had been drawn up by a distinguished national Jewish-Christian committee. It would be difficult for the synod not to honor this initiative. It had been raised by one of Susquehanna's greatest trustee benefactors, and the synod's own contribution to its colleges had now become insignificant in their annual budgets. But the synod, despite recommendations from its own Church-College Relations Committee, its Commission on Higher Education, and its Executive Board, remarkably voted the amendment down.[103]

490

The constitution of the Maryland Synod specifically included among its duties the "provision of Christian higher education for the youth of the synod and others through Gettysburg College." Yet when the synod and the college sat down together in 1983 to renew their agreement, they began by invoking a very nay-saying notion of what Christian higher education might be:

> Occasionally, church members view church-related colleges as "Christian insti-tutions" which teach religious orthodoxy and ethical certitude. . . . The church should not expect its schools to become "Christian colleges" which provide insulation from the world. This particular image of a "Christian" college may be attractive in the midst of what some people consider to be moral permissive-ness and confusion, but this idea runs counter to the Lutheran understanding of faith and the world. No matter how much discipline colleges may attempt to impose, they cannot create safe havens for their students.

That said, it was a simple matter to identify worship, pastoral counseling, community service, and Christian witness as what the church would have a stake in, with the rest — academics, for instance — left unrelated to faith.[104]

In 1990 the LCA united with the American Lutheran Church (ALC) to form the new Evangelical Lutheran Church in America (ELCA), the largest Lutheran church in American history. According to current policy in the ELCA, bilateral covenants or statements are no longer sought; now they "function in an experiential mode." The church simply enunciates a policy and the colleges need not react to it . . . or notice it. The 1991 "ELCA Mission Statement for Colleges and Univer-sities" uses a more assertive vernacular than its LCA predecessors:

> The colleges and universities of the ELCA endeavor to continue the values of rigorous academic life and religious commitment in an intentional, explicit, and critical fashion. They find in the church their historical foundation, a rich con-fessional tradition, the source of their life, and their reason for being.
>
> The educational enterprise to which this church gives life is rooted in the Gospel. While sin means separation, God in Christ brings reconciliation to a broken and divided world, an action compassing the created order and every human enterprise. In the colleges and universities of the church the integrating element is the assurance that in Christ all things hold together.
>
> This assurance gives distinctive coherence to the educational enterprise of the colleges and universities of the church. The gospel also accounts for their com-mitment to develop in students and faculty a sense of vocation and responsible discipleship.

It is likely that the intensification of religious language is owing partly to the fact that this is not a text that needs to pass muster with academics. But it is surely due, as well, to the amalgamation of the LCA with the former ALC, which has always been more affirming and confessional about its educational interests, and has argued theologically (as we shall see) that they were intended, not as a secular contribution to civic society, but as a formational ministry to younger church members. The term "church-related," for instance, appears nowhere in the document; these are now colleges "of the church."

One notes, however, that when the church specifies what it expects of the colleges and universities in return, it mentions that they "carry a special responsibility for educating the sons and daughters of this church," yet there is no word about the sons and daughters of the church doing the educating.[105] At the time, Lutherans constituted only 35 percent of the enrollment in all twenty-nine ELCA colleges and universities. In the former LCA schools, however, they composed 23 percent. At Gettysburg they amounted to about 10 percent. Benevolence support from the church in 1991-92 amounted to two-tenths of one percent of the Gettysburg College budget; the four sponsoring synods contributed less than half of that.[106]

Lutheran Indicia at Gettysburg

How, at the end of these years of development, does Gettysburg College embody the LCA sector of the Lutheran experience?

As Painter had argued in 1898 and Gamelin in 1971, the LCA Lutherans had overbuilt . . . both for ministerial candidates and for Lutherans. Candidates had formed a good portion of the student body well into this century, but now their numbers are no longer even reported in church statistics. Gettysburg, intended especially for the needs of the Lutherans in Pennsylvania, soon found itself competing with nearby Muhlenberg (founded in 1848 to be more directly accountable to the church), Susquehanna (founded in 1858 as the Missionary Institute when Gettysburg declined to offer a less rigorous alternative curriculum for those intending to work in the missions), and Thiel (1866, located at the far end of the state), and later with Wagner (1883) and Upsala (1892) in nearby New York and New Jersey. With 98 percent of its students traditionally coming from the Middle Atlantic and New England areas, regional competition has made a difference. When Lutherans noticeably declined among the student body, admissions preference in their favor was quietly tried.[107] The assignment of financial aid was also somewhat in their favor.[108] Nevertheless, the proportion of Lutherans has ceaselessly declined. But enrollments have not. Indeed, during the period 1979-80 to 1991-92 the number of eighteen-year-olds in America dropped 28.4 percent, but the enrollment at Lutheran colleges and universities increased 2 percent;[109] at Gettysburg it increased 12 percent. Meanwhile the proportion of Lutherans at Gettysburg declined from 17 to 10 percent, and in actual numbers there were one-third less.[110]

In recent years, the college has forgone what few options it had to recruit more Lutherans. In formulating the nondiscrimination policy published in its catalogue, as a Christian college it retains the legal right to exclude "creed" from the categories it promises not to consider in decisions on admissions, financial aid, appointments, and promotions. But Gettysburg has chosen not to reserve that right.[111] Two years after concluding its 1983 statement of partnership with the Maryland Synod, it successfully petitioned the synod for an amendment that would specifically authorize the college vigorously to recruit more minority students (who now number nearly half as many as Lutherans on campus).[112] By contrast with its successful affirmative action to attract more students "of color and language" (whose numbers doubled in five years), the college's acquiescence in ever smaller numbers of Lutherans stands out the more clearly.[113]

Gettysburg College, like most early foundations, was founded by clergymen who had basic learning and preferred (or accepted) the scholarly work of the classroom to the pastoral work of the congregation as a way to earn their living.

In 1916 a brochure stated that "for a man to be eligible for election on the teaching staff of Gettysburg College an absolute requirement is that he shall be a Christian gentleman of the highest type, the sort of man with whom parents would like to have their sons come in the closest personal and confidential relations."[114] Nothing was said about his being a Lutheran, because those who came to be appointed were mostly Lutherans. By the time that concern might have wanted stating, a contrary trend was already under way. In 1950, for instance, it was reported to the LCA convention that at Wagner College active church membership was required of each faculty member, and that at Wittenberg "the most distinctive part of the program lies in the choice of the faculty on the grounds of Christian faith as well as scholastic ability." That year Lutherans composed only 56 percent of each college's faculty.[115]

Gettysburg had in various ways articulated its policy that only professing Christians could hold faculty positions. But in 1959 a faculty committee proposed a new formulation: that the college "assumes that each faculty member entertains some sincere religious conviction."[116] That did not pass muster with the president and board. Phraseology for this issue in the church was tending to be increasingly viscous: "professing Christian faith not inconsistent with the church relationship," "definitely committed to the Christian cause," "clear perception of personal and social aims and ideals," "a sincere commitment to some religious tradition," "a sense of personal responsibility for the religious character of the college."[117]

A present LCA-style understanding of the matter can be found in the *Faculty Handbook* of Muhlenberg College, Gettysburg's neighbor in Allentown.

3.3   Evaluation of Faculty
3.3.4 Commitment to the Goals of the College

Each faculty member is expected to exhibit values consistent with the traditions of Muhlenberg College as a church-related liberal arts institution. This does not mean a uniform subscription to any particular belief, pattern of worship, or lifestyle. It does mean a respect for persons who differ, a readiness to engage open-mindedly in a corporate search for truth, and attentiveness to the role of values in the educational task. The professional behavior of each faculty member should evidence a demonstrated concern for the growth of students as whole persons, as social, moral and religious as well as intellectual beings. Included is a willingness and capacity, at times and in ways appropriate to an academic community, to treat fairly the Christian point of view and the values inherent in it.[118]

Gould Wickey, former educational executive for Lutherans of all allegiances, had said that faculty recruitment was not all that decisive: "The number of Lutheran students, the number of Lutheran faculty members, and even the ownership of a school by the Lutheran Church do not guarantee a Lutheran education. *Lutheran education is an education permeated by the thought and life of the Lutheran Church.*" But it is difficult to imagine who would see to the Lutheran permeation with a faculty that includes possibly 12 percent Lutherans.

It is worthy of note that in the cascade of documents that bespoke the mutualities between college and church, it was usually said that the college allowed the church to be critical of itself, while the church allowed the college to nurture the students and order their lives. It is never said that the church might prompt the academic enterprise to criticize itself. Indeed, there is hardly a thought that the church could seriously affect the intellectual life of the campus.

Gettysburg's history does not record that the Religion Department (assigned so many titles over the years) has been truly central to the educational process. Perhaps this derives from the days when a preponderance of the undergraduates were bound for the seminary, and might require little theology on their way there.[119] As late as 1953, among the 115 periodicals received by the library, only 3 were in the field of religion (Bible). Physical Education received 6.[120] The two required religion courses in the classical curriculum at the end of the last century have for most of the intervening years been reduced to only one.[121] Today the department presents itself very much in the "religious studies" mode, in which students are invited to study the "phenomenon" of religion as outsiders, rather than as believers (like the difference between studying comparative languages and studying English). The catalogue explains:

> Essential to an understanding of the past and the present is a study of the varied religious experiences and traditions of humankind. The department offers courses in sacred texts, historical traditions, and religious thought and institutions, all of which investigate the complex phenomenon of religion.[122]

There is accordingly a course on Martin Luther King, Jr., but none on Martin Luther.[123]

Campus piety seems on the upswing since the debacle of student resistance to chapel services. Throughout most of Gettysburg's history religious activities, save for Sunday services, tended to be entrusted to voluntary student organizations. From 1867 onward, as on many evangelical campuses, this was the YMCA.[124] In 1935 the Y was in decline, and it was superseded by the Student Christian Association (SCA). The degree to which it was a "voluntary" success is unclear. From 1953 to 1962, to block competition the college forbade any denominational group, even a Lutheran one, to meet on college premises. But even with that strong-arm ban on its rivals, the SCA did not enjoy unqualified success. In 1960 the board was told that its committee work was strong but that its programs were weak. Only 9 percent of the students were active members.[125] Campus piety seems generally to have been improved by the eventual appointment of full-time chaplains.[126] But at present one has the impression that it is marginalized. Henry Hanson (1923-52) was the last president of the college to preside at college worship, which, to his preference, was evangelistic in the revival tradition.

From a secular point of view Gettysburg College stands sound and successful. It stands at or near the top of all Lutheran colleges and universities in many of the common indicia of academic prosperity: faculty salaries, student fees, development income, alumni giving, applicant test scores, endowment, and annual budget.[127] About this achievement the college is modest, even demure, in its self-presentation. But as the indicia of vital relationship with the Lutheran church have waned, there has been an uncommon capacity to mollify this embarrassment with inordinate optimism. Some speak of the college as an instance of "reversing the trend toward secularism," believing that despite the reduction of Lutheran presence among their teachers and students to trace levels, the official covenants of the 1970s and 1980s had finally forged a bond between college and church that allows for "hopeful indications."

> As a matter of fact this pluralistic setting offers a number of opportunities not before available. It presents an opportunity to spell out and give greater understanding of Lutheran doctrine and practice to the non-Lutheran majority. It gives Lutheran students the opportunity during their college career to experience and adapt to the pluralistic community which will face them in future life while at the same time getting a deeper awareness of their own faith through academic courses and chaplain's counsel. It challenges to a greater commitment and witness on the part of the Lutheran faculty, administrators and student leaders in a setting of free and open investigation unrestricted by certain regulations that exist in the state college and university systems. The gospel calls attention to the potentiality of "a little leaven." It reminds the church of its need to encourage "the faithful remnant" in the pluralistic setting with hope and confidence that such a faithful minority may not be ashamed of their gospel witness.[128]

The "Americanist Lutheran" Colleges: An Appraisal

In some respects the emergence of Gettysburg College and its LCA peers has followed a course common to Christian colleges of many church affiliations. For the earliest and the longest portion of its history most of its students, faculty, administrators, and trustees were Lutherans. The church bodies in whose patronage Gettysburg and its sisters lay provided modest support and expressed only mild and formal concern for the service their colleges rendered. It was a place where Lutherans knew themselves to be at home. They needed and wanted others to feel at home there as well, and in the congenial fellowship of American evangelical Protestantism they saw this to require no great effort on their part. There was therefore no ideology generated to vouch for the authenticity of their Lutheran identity.

With time, and increased regional populations, and slowly evolving academic sophistication they saw a slow but mounting increment of non-Lutherans on campus. As this happened, the educators initiated a shift in their presentation. They spoke of their colleges as Christian. Though this was done to identify with their diversifying clientele, it was a rhetoric used amiably toward their Lutheran constituency, too.

In a second phase, as the colleges grew in age and scholarship and resources, students of any allegiance sought them out, no longer primarily as a local convenience but as an educational preference. Educators sought appointments there for reasons having nothing to do with anything religious. In this changed environment "religious" soon became the identifier, for some Catholics and Jews did come to stay, and were found congenial to the undertaking. But "religious" is an exceedingly unstable identity, and in most recent years the colleges have tended to identify themselves by a bouquet of reductive items thought to bespeak their distinctive heritage: character, liberal studies, free inquiry.

Thus far, the story line is a familiar one. Throughout the period, the Lutheran church bodies have provided direct funding that was always modest, and more often merely token. Most of the time they showed no more disposition to sponsor an educational system for their young than the taxpayers of Pennsylvania in the Jacksonian period wanted to pay for colleges. The colleges were never taken to be crucial to the churches' welfare, at least compared with their seminaries. In return, apart from a few flare-ups of discontent, the "Americanist Lutheran" churches have never demanded a very "affirming" or intentional stance from their educators. And as the years passed, Lutherans became an ever lesser component, first of the students, then of the faculty, then of the administration. And after a certain level of insignificance, when the "leaven," or "remnant," was too scant, it no longer mattered much whether the trustees were Lutheran.

Throughout this process of gradual dissociation from the church, what account did Gettysburg College give of its Lutheran character? Before the college yet existed, Samuel Simon Schmucker stated his intentions to his prospective patrons, several local notables of various denominations: "He informed them that the college he aimed at was to be un-sectarian in its instruction, but at the same time to be prevailingly under Lutheran influence and control."[129] Schmucker, as was said earlier, was much under the influence of the Pietist movement and of one of its later progeny, the Second Great Awakening. The Pietists had rebuked the various Protestant churches for having smothered the outburst of the Reform in their scholasticism and their quarrelsome fixation on the niceties of orthodoxy. To Schmucker in the 1830s, this rebuke continued to be deserved by Lutherans who excommunicated or seceded from one another repeatedly because of varying estimates of baptismal regeneration or the divine origin of the Christian Sabbath or the authoritative status of the Book of Concord. For Schmucker and his college in its youth, "sectarian" teaching meant a preoccupation with those matters of domestic dispute that put Lutherans at odds with one another, were of no interest to most other Protestants, and in any case were a distraction from the simple verities of the gospel. To be sure, the religion taught from the pulpit and in the classroom at Gettysburg was thoroughly Lutheran, but it steered clear of the overheated issues of the day. To be "un-sectarian" meant to be very settled in one's Lutheran belief. And in the days when the college was presided over and taught by men who were virtually all Lutheran pastors and took their turns leading the campus community at prayer; when the largest cohort among the student body was preparing to be trained for the ministry; and when the small proportion of non-Lutheran students and faculty nicely melded into the Lutheran preponderance — no one needed to explain whether or how the place was Lutheran. How could it be anything else?[130]

When the college encountered criticism in the 1870s under Valentine and in the 1890s under McKnight, it was caught up in a domestic quarrel between Lutherans. Valentine was honest in saying, "Though these colleges are unsectarian, Christianity, in its essential doctrines, is fully and constantly taught. Its truths are made to pervade and mould all the teaching."[131] But the "Confessing," or Old Lutheran, critics were correct in noticing that Gettysburg and other colleges were sidling away from the church. By forgoing any share in the church's work of discerning and defining the faith, Gettysburg was reducing the "essential doctrines" to what would pass muster before a now increasingly disparate campus population. This trend would find its most neutered expression in the prose of Henry Hanson, who guided the college in the critical period from the 1920s to the 1950s. By the time the convulsion of concern about the church-college relationship was stirred up in the sixties, Gettysburg was no longer peopled by the same kind of folks.

When Gould Wickey claimed in 1962 that they were offering an education "permeated by the life and thought of the Lutheran Church," and Edgar Carlson spoke about the Lutheran "atmosphere," it was several generations too late for that to be true. By then three-fifths of the campus was not Lutheran. Saul Alinsky was claiming at that time that he could give an urban neighborhood power over its own destiny if only 2 percent of its residents became organized activists. But no one was telling the Lutherans at Gettysburg in 1962 that they needed to become activists. Wickey and Carlson may have carried the transmitted memory of the days when the campuses were permeated with Lutheran life. But when the most that Gettysburg's 1973 covenant with the church could affirm was that "the opportunity for corporate worship and for witness is unabashedly available" on campus, four-fifths of the people there were no longer able to join in corporate Lutheran worship or witness. And when the ELCA was unabashedly proclaiming that on campus "the integrating element is the assurance that in Christ all things hold together," only 10 percent of the students left were Lutheran and might understand how that was meant.

The only way for a college to be effectively Lutheran by "suffusion," or "atmosphere," would be to admit and appoint students and faculty who were as prepared for solidarity in faith as for solidarity in scholarship. In the earliest days this had received no attention because it seemed unnecessary: the clientele was predominantly Lutheran, and the annual rate of Lutheran diminution seemed negligible. By the time it was clear that Lutheran members — the only resource that could make the college a meaningful beneficiary of the Lutheran community of faith — would have to be recruited purposefully, there was no one with the gumption to make that effort. The college had shown itself capable of competent and professional fund-raising whereas before it had not; it had shown itself capable of educating women whereas before it had not; it had shown itself capable of recruiting minorities of color and tongue; it had shown itself capable of replacing an amateur faculty with a highly professional one. But it had not shown itself capable of admitting it wanted to be purposefully Lutheran.[132]

The "Americanist Lutheran" church bodies have not shown except in symbolic ways that they had much of a stake in their colleges. When they were very poor immigrants they had little wealth to give for colleges. As they gained in prosperity and the wider prospect of sending their children to college, they never acted as if their own colleges were essential to their welfare. In recent years about one in every nineteen young Lutherans of college age has matriculated at a Lutheran-related college.[133] By this reckoning one might discount the traditional claim that the Lutheran colleges are training Lutheran church members for leadership, in the church or in society at large. On the other hand, 77 percent of all ELCA bishops spent their undergraduate years on Lutheran-related campuses; this was traditionally so for a large proportion of the pastors, though the word from the seminaries today is that it is no longer the case.[134] Whether or not they be that "dedicated and vital Christian leadership" the literature often speaks of, is difficult to determine.

In the 1960s when LCA colleges wanted to accept federal regulation as the price of federal dollars, the doctrine of the two kingdoms was invoked: education is an "order of society" entrusted to the state to be run under the law. Likewise the other elements of the welfare state: hospitals, child welfare programs, neighborhood reconstruction initiatives, homes for the elderly, and other institutional endeavors which the church was anxious to hand over to civil patronage.[135] The argument has historical problems, since Luther's educational writings presumed that schooling belongs to the family, and even when delegated to the burghers it was a Christian project. But the second problem is greater. These state-sponsored services are primarily dominated, not by the government, but by professional interest groups: the professorate, the social work guild, the medical guild, the various cults of social management, each with its own ideology and interests. Lutherans had at times been handicapped in their capacity to challenge state policy and actions from the perspective of the gospel because of their doctrine that the state was an element of creation that needed no redemption. That habit of deference to the civil power would make "Americanist Lutherans" passive when the academic guild in recent years began to exert an inveterate repugnance toward Christian belief and doctrine. Having deferred already to one secular establishment, Lutherans were going to find it hard to challenge another.

THE "CONFESSING LUTHERANS"

The Lutherans in the Upper Midwest, whom we shall call the "Confessing Lutherans," were mostly Scandinavian immigrants, who formed common cause with many regional Germans as well. They arrived later — near the middle of the nineteenth century — and so began their colleges later than the German Lutherans who had come to the eastern coastal regions during colonial times. These are their foundations.

1850	Capital University	Columbus, Ohio
1852	Wartburg College	Waverly, Iowa
1860	Augustana College	Sioux Falls, S Dak.
1861	Luther College	Decorah, Iowa
1869	Augsburg College	Minneapolis, Minn.
1874	St. Olaf College	Northfield, Minn.
1884	Dana College	Blair, Nebr.
1890	Pacific Lutheran University	Tacoma, Wash.
1891	Concordia College	Moorhead, Minn.
1891	Texas Lutheran College	Seguin, Tex.
1959	California Lutheran University	Thousand Oaks, Calif.[136]

The Lutherans in the student bodies of these colleges, which at one time were gathered under the American Lutheran Convention, later re-formed into the American Lutheran Church (ALC), presently equal about 46 percent of their enrollments (ranging from 68 to 18 percent), compared with 23 percent in the former LCA colleges (ranging from 59 to 4 percent). Lutheran presence in ALC colleges has all along been proportionately double that at LCA campuses.

The relationship between these colleges and their church had a closeness from the start which can still be heard in their self-presentations today, quite unlike the mission statements usual among the "Americanist Lutheran" colleges. The *Augustana College Catalogue,* for instance, states:

As a college of the Church, Augustana

— provides programs designed to establish and strengthen Christian faith and ideals as the foundation of personal and social integrity, and as a stimulus to integrate all learning to make it more meaningful,

— assists students in understanding theological concepts and the important elements of the Christian life — faith, hope, love, compassion, forgiveness and reconciliation,

— prepares persons for Christian witness and leadership in congregations and society,

— serves the church through continuing education programs for lay and clergy, and as a resource for congregations and the Church in the modern world,

— welcomes those with diverse viewpoints to explore together in academic freedom questions of truth and meaning,

— provides a setting where regular worship is encouraged and faculty and staff members offer Christian witness through their lives and teaching.[137]

By contrast, one considers this from the East: "Susquehanna is strengthened by its relationship to the Lutheran Church, and there is respect here for the values and beliefs of the Lutheran tradition. However, this tradition is a diverse and accepting one: individuals of all religious backgrounds and those with no religious commitments are welcomed. The free exploration of ideas is central to Susquehanna's mission."[138]

It is instructive to study the refashioning of this identity rhetoric over the years. St. Olaf, in the first catalogue after it added a "college department" to the original secondary school, stated:

To impart knowledge is not the ultimate aim of St. Olaf's School. Knowledge is a means and not the end of man. A man who cannot use his knowledge to his own happiness is like a man who has collected a library of books but cannot himself read. The student must, however, acquire knowledge before he can be taught to use it, and the aim of this institution is to impart knowledge and to teach the student to use it [so] as to enable him to reach the ultimate end of man — eternal bliss. It is noble work to lead man to truth, but it is more noble to lead him beyond it to its source — the God of truth; for God is love, and a man is blessed only when in communion with God, his Creator.[139]

By 1935-36, what the catalogue had to say is slightly more indirect:

As a standard and recognized liberal arts college St. Olaf aims to provide an academic training, which shall be fully abreast of the best scholarship of today, and to furnish the facilities and the equipment for teaching, study, and research, which will make possible an efficient and progressive academic life.

In the conviction that character and personality are equally important with

500

scholarship in the making of ideal manhood and womanhood, it strives, through careful selection of its teaching staff, through its form of government and rules of conduct, and through the guiding and dominant spirit of the institution, to develop in its students high ideals of character and well rounded, unselfish, and public spirited personalities.

As a college of the Lutheran Church, it is loyal to the beliefs and practices of this church. In its religious teaching it lays special stress on [changed in 1937 to *emphasizes*] specific Lutheran doctrines and traditions [in 1937, *doctrines and* is omitted], and seeks to give an insight into and training for the tasks and opportunities for constructive service in many important lines of church activity within the church [added in 1937: *as well as in the world at large*]. It carries on no propaganda with respect to those who may belong to other denominations beyond the general Christian spirit and influence of the college.[140]

By 1992-93 the catalogue was still relatively up front about its religious character:

St. Olaf, a four-year college of the Evangelical Lutheran Church in America, provides an education committed to the liberal arts, rooted in the Christian Gospel, and incorporating a global perspective. In the conviction that life is more than a livelihood, it focuses on what is ultimately worthwhile and fosters the development of the whole person in mind, body, and spirit.

Now in its second century, St. Olaf College remains dedicated to the high standards set by its Norwegian immigrant founders. In the spirit of free inquiry and free expression, it offers a distinctive environment that integrates teaching, scholarship, creative activity, and opportunities for encounter with the Christian Gospel and God's call to faith. The college intends that its graduates combine academic excellence and theological literacy with a commitment to lifelong learning.

St. Olaf College strives to be an inclusive community, respecting those of differing backgrounds and beliefs. Through its curriculum, campus life, and off-campus programs, it stimulates students' critical thinking and heightens their moral sensitivity; it encourages them to be seekers of truth, leading lives of unselfish service to others, and it challenges them to be responsible and knowledgeable citizens of the world.[141]

The financial contribution of the "Confessing Lutherans" to their colleges was at one time quite substantial. In the early 1920s, for example, St. Olaf received appropriations that amounted to about 40 percent of its annual budget.[142] Its recent subsidy from the ELCA, however, amounts to 0.4 percent of its annual budget.[143]

Closer to the Church

The ALC tradition located college governance much more within the church. The colleges were all chartered as membership corporations. Half of them had the members of the General Convention as their corporate members, and the delegates would adjourn during their proceedings and then sit as the governing corporations of the several colleges, electing regents or trustees, and officers, and even granting tenure to faculty. The other half had a similar arrangement with a local synod or district. In early years the local regents had to be drawn from the trustees of the church and the members of its board of education, but in 1934 the Norwegian Lutheran Church of America relaxed this and required only that they be members of the church. By the later 1960s the rule was further relaxed: at least 51 percent had to be church members, with the remaining trustees to be from other Lutheran churches or non-Lutherans, neither group to exceed 25 percent.[144] At its most relaxed, this was a tradition of much closer ecclesiastical governance than anything experienced among the "Americanist Lutherans" out east. And since half the delegates at church conventions were clergy, and approximately three-quarters of the ALC clergy had been graduates of Lutheran colleges, they were well disposed to their colleges.[145]

One other form of nurture which the "Confessing Lutherans" visited upon their colleges has been strident criticism of perceived deviations from the church. The *Lutheran Commentator,* a vigilante newsletter of Lutherans for Religious and Political Freedom, recently grieved:

> During the past school year, St. Olaf College in Northfield, Minnesota completed its revision of its curriculum. We are sad to report that the religion requirement has been reduced in the new curriculum from *three courses to two.* . . .
>
> As might be expected, the college spin doctors were out in force, having concocted the story that the religion requirement *has not been weakened but strengthened* by the new decision. Here's one of the spins: The third course in religion has been replaced by a new one that draws on the strengths of the faculty at large, not just on those of the religion department. The official description is as follows:
>
>> *An upper level course that addresses issues of current moral concern and examines perspectives providing norms of justice and well-being that guide moral reasoning. Issues may be considered from the standpoint of: (a) major ethical perspectives; (b) current theological perspectives; (c) other normative perspectives prominent in contemporary culture; (d) a combination of these. The course will include dialogue with normative aspects of the Christian tradition, though the disciplinary basis of the course need not be theological.*
>
> Oh boy . . . isn't this the perfect vehicle for the Politically Correct Thought Police to hammer their way into the tender minds of Lutheran youth? "Peace,"

social engineering, and the bottomless rage of self-defined minorities could take center stage. . . . Keep in mind that the faculty that will probably teach this new course has changed in recent years, notably in two ways:

1) It has almost entirely abandoned the college's daily chapel service. There are around two hundred and fifty full-time faculty members at the school. Only about *fifteen* of them attend chapel regularly.

2) There are few if any academic departments in which confessing Lutherans form at least a "critical mass" or are a majority. An example: in one of its larger departments, with around twenty faculty members, there are but three full-time faculty members who are confessing Lutherans.[146]

The grievance is significant, not for its accuracy (which is defective), but for its ardor. Ardor abounded among the "Confessing Lutherans," and their story runs differently from that we have seen in the East . . . for a while.

St. Olaf College

The development of St. Olaf College in Northfield, Minnesota, provides an instructive contrast with Gettysburg, as a "Confessing Lutheran" college. It was founded in 1874 by Bernt Julius Muus, a Norwegian American pastor. Like Schmucker in Gettysburg, he had previously run an academic program in his own home, but on the secondary level, not the seminary level. In postbellum America, the Midwest Scandinavians were sending their ministerial candidates down to the Missouri German seminary. But many of them distrusted the state-run "common schools," and so a network of academies was established. Unlike the Pennsylvania situation, Muus could establish a school for Norse Americans without needing the patronage of any other church or denomination.

The instruction was very emphatically to be in English, so as to ease the new immigrants into their new culture. Though they required a learned ministry, the Norwegian immigrants were neither affluent nor educated. And coming to America had affected their religion. Whereas under the state church in Norway church membership was obligatory and formalized, in the new land their Lutheran faith was the strongest bond of their ethnic identity, especially since they had determined so early to adopt English as their language. And so at the college, from the inaugural address to the diploma, all was in English.[147]

Unlike Luther College, its elder sister founded thirteen years earlier in Iowa to prepare young Norwegian American men for seminary, and unlike Gettysburg College, which waited more than a century to begin collegiate coeducation,[148] St. Olaf admitted female students from the outset, and made much of it. By 1889 St. Olaf officially added a collegiate program to its secondary school. The college was explicitly intended neither to prepare candidates for the seminary (as was done in many Lutheran colleges of the time) nor to offer career training (as colleges and universities had ardently begun to do since the Morrill Act of 1862), but from the first to give a liberal arts education.[149]

> The place of religion in the original conception of St. Olaf's School was prominent but not conventional. The primary intention was that a Christian view of life should permeate the entire work of the School. The goal, wrote [founding] Principal Mohn, was "to give young men and women a practical education on the foundation of Christianity." Religion was included in the curriculum but did not dominate it. According to Mohn, "Our school is not what is called a 'school of religion,' yet it is for the sake of religion that this school was founded. . . ."
>
> Muus and Mohn held that genuine religion is specific and confessional at its core, and at the same time broad and universal in its application. Muus, loyal Lutheran that he was, had no time for schools which allegedly upheld "Christian principles" but denied allegiance to any "Christian sect." The document of incorporation included in its statement of general purpose this clause: "preserve the pupils in the true Christian faith, as taught by the Evangelical Lutheran Church and nothing taught in contravention with the Symbolum Apostolicum, Nicenum & Athanasianum; the Unaltered Confession delivered to the Emperor Charles the Fifth at Augsburg in Germany in the year of our Lord 1530 and the small Catechism of Luther." Revisions of the Articles mercifully reduced the statement to read: "the Christian faith as taught in the Evangelical Lutheran Church."[150]

Controversy was a part of vigorous midwestern Lutheran life in those days, and it often affected the young college's fortunes. When Pastor Muus founded the academy, the Norwegian Lutherans were divided over whether they should have schools of their own. Many argued in favor of the common schools, not only because they were economical but also because they were, as they thought, thoroughly American. To resort to a network of parochial schools was, they argued, close to treason. Religious instruction could well be offered by the congregations in summer schools. But Muus sided with those who found that the common schools were poorly run and, what is more, provided neither religious instruction nor the freedom to relate other subjects to the students' faith.[151]

A more embittered controversy arose about whether the preaching of the gospel was of any avail to listeners not destined to respond in faith, and the Norwegians were divided into those who said it was, the "Missourians" (mostly clergy, they inclined to the view of their German coreligionists to the south), and the "Anti-Missourians" who said it was not. One side of the Election Controversy stressed God's sovereign choice of those to be saved, while the other side (strongly lay in its membership) stressed the causality of human response. Muus and his colleagues at St. Olaf took their stand with the Anti-Missourians, and found themselves outside their church as a result. St. Olaf learned that doctrine had its costs. But when they coalesced with several other Lutheran synods to form the

United Norwegian Lutheran Church (UNLC) in 1890, St. Olaf offered itself as the college of that church and was given its patronage and promised its support.[152] The formal relationship with the church, then, came to St. Olaf some years after its founding.

The president of the college might well have recalled what he had written to a prospective trustee only the year before:

> Not being under the direct control of a religious denomination nor erected with the sole aim of educating ministers of the gospel, the college is removed from church politics and not exposed to the religious cyclones that seem occasionally to visit our people.
>
> There is, I believe, a strong tendency among our countrymen to get away from German influence and to blend more with the Americans and at the same time to erect an institution of learning in this country worthy of our record as a nation.[153]

St. Olaf graduates could now go to Augsburg Seminary in Minneapolis, also under UNLC sponsorship, for ministerial training. Augsburg already had a college department and an academy, and its supporters understandably lobbied on behalf of a total educational program on the one campus. St. Olaf's separate program, they insisted, had a dangerously humanistic view of the world. The result of this contention with Augsburg was that St. Olaf was dropped from church sponsorship by referendum in 1893, only three years after it had been accepted. The results on enrollment and income were catastrophic. This was a painful way of being freed from church politics and religious cyclones. But then Augsburg and its coterie seceded in 1897 to form yet another new church, and in 1899 St. Olaf was welcomed back into the fold. Twelve years later, apprehensive that the college's growing endowment might be lost to the church if the school ever became secularized, the UNLC actually purchased St. Olaf for one gold dollar.

These vicissitudes were foreign to the more placid experience of Gettysburg, which was never this entangled in partisan struggles within the church (not that the "Americanist Lutherans" never had any). Still, once St. Olaf belonged to the church securely, it turned out to be a mutually peaceful and even prosperous relationship.

Since then, as synodical groupings have repeatedly shifted, St. Olaf has been, successively, a college of the UNLC, Norwegian Lutheran Church, ALC, and ELCA. Legally it is the church itself in which ultimate governance is vested, yet over the years the college has moved easily and freely in its own effective independence. Unlike most colleges and universities in this study, St. Olaf has never since seceded from the governing authority of its church.

With Stability and Success, Change

On its fiftieth anniversary the acknowledged indicia of Lutheran fidelity were certainly all in place. All faculty members were active members of the Lutheran church, as were 97 percent of the students. The Department of Religious Instruction offered a three-year sequence of required courses, somewhat more theological and less evangelical than the fare then at Gettysburg. Faculty and students alike were expected to attend daily chapel, as well as Sunday services in the town churches, though the latter was not subject to sanction. Students themselves managed special Bible and mission study classes (one-third of the student body was claimed to attend), besides men's and women's prayer circles and an active chapter of the mission-oriented Student Volunteer Movement. Half of those enrolled at Luther Seminary in Saint Paul were St. Olaf graduates; indeed, 29 percent of the men who had gone forth from the college had gone into ministry. But, one early historian reminds his readers, "There is a broader field in the many Christian lay activities, which we expect every capable and active church member to engage in the Church of the future and in the leadership which we expect from those who have enjoyed the advantages of a higher education."[154]

Not that the Norsemen of Minnesota took anyone's faith for granted. Back in 1890 President Mohn had turned down an application by Thorstein Veblen, who would become one of Norway's most eminent scholarly émigrés, for a faculty position because he seemed somewhat skeptical in his religious expression. A year later when Mohn was reporting to the church convention, a criticism arose: "Mohn failed to mention religious commitment as a goal of St. Olaf's Program; apparently he assumed that this was implicit." A fair assumption in 1891.[155]

Very slowly but inexorably the socioeconomic standing of the college clientele began to change. In 1924-25, after fifty years of existence, a third of St. Olaf's students were coming from farm families and another 12 percent from clergy or missionary families.[156] President Lars W. Boe (1918-42) could remind his students that Carleton College, on the other side of Northfield, "appeals to an economic stratum to which we do not belong."[157] At the end of World War II parents of students included 23 percent farmers and 9 percent clergy, 6 percent semiskilled labor, and only 4 percent executives.[158] By 1970 freshman families were 6-8 percent working class, 50 percent middle class, and 40 percent upper middle class (there never seems to be an upper class, anywhere).[159] At the hundred-year point, 1974, when Lutherans constituted less than 60 percent of the student body, the *Centennial Study* asserted: "Thus while religious diversity has increased, socioeconomic diversity has decreased, so that by 1969 St. Olaf had become one of the two most homogeneously middle and upper-middle class institutions in the Associated Colleges of the Midwest."[160]

It is notable (and the *Centennial Study* did note it)[161] that Lutheran enrollment began to slide during the 1960s, coinciding with the rise in socioeconomic status of students:

1960	90%
1965	80%
1970	65%
1975	59%
1980	60%
1985	59%
1990	55%
1991	52%

Thus there was a dramatic slide in the sixties and early seventies, and now another slide under way since the latter eighties. It is currently believed in the administration that this represents not a withdrawal of Lutherans, but the addition of many others, yet thirty years ago there were numerically more Lutheran students at the college than there are now. This is a close parallel with the enrollment reports from other ALC colleges.[162]

The college is not at one in its view of this change. The president is greatly concerned to increase the financial aid available, because many Lutheran families are not affluent. On the other hand, some faculty are affronted when the *College Catalog* announces that "preference may be given to Lutherans."[163]

The early policy of appointing only active Lutherans to the permanent faculty, still in force in the midtwenties,[164] has since then receded before other priorities. By the centennial year of the college things were quite different, as shown in a revised set of standards for faculty evaluation adopted in 1974. The appropriate section of the *Faculty Manual* began thus:

St. Olaf College seeks to attract and retain a distinctive and competent faculty expert in the liberal disciplines and committed to undergraduate teaching in a Christian context. While the college gives primary emphasis to effective under-graduate instruction, it holds that high quality teaching is inseparable from scholarly and creative effort, and it expects that members of its faculty will ground their teaching in research, scholarship, and creative activity. It further expects that members of its faculty will be concerned with the religious and moral dimensions of life and learning. While there are no sectarian requirements for tenure nor sectarian limits on what can be expressed or taught, it is basic to the identity of the college that its faculty consist of persons who take seriously questions concerning the relation of religion to learning and who consider their work and the work of the college in the light of such questions.

One notices immediately the rhetorical shift in the middle of the paragraph. Faculty are expected to be not only committed to teaching but competent and effective. Not only are they to make scholarly and creative efforts; they are to be actively productive scholars. But regarding the unspecified role of an unspecified religion on campus, they are required to be concerned about it, but not to be involved; to take seriously questions concerning it, but not to share in any collegial response to these questions; and to consider their own performance in the light of these questions, whatever be the answers. This dissociation of religious solidarity from the usual professional criteria of accomplishment for faculty appointment is made clearer by what follows. Effective teaching, significant professional activity, and other contributions to the college are all provided with more or less specific criteria for evaluation to be used by those responsible for the personnel decision. By contrast, for a faculty member's potential contribution to St. Olaf as a college of the church, there is no standard for judgment. Faith, it becomes clear, is to supply the context but not the content of the educational process.

Different People, Different Education

Identity and Mission in a Changing Context: A Centennial Publication of St. Olaf College, published that same year, notes two recent changes in the context: a decline in students who come from families "of Lutheran background," and a similar decline in Lutheran faculty. The change in the student body shows that St. Olaf has begun to attract students "who see the distinctive character of the college not in its religious affiliation but in its innovative educational features, academic reputation, and unusual musical heritage." The new faculty are said not to differ markedly in their educational philosophy from their more Lutheran elders. In any case, the variable religious stance of students and teachers does not, the *Centennial Study* insists, affect the definition of St. Olaf. It represents, however, a serious break with the previous self-understandings, which take their religious commitments far more seriously.[165]

In its less circulated explanatory volume, the study does "affirm that if St. Olaf is to fulfill its purpose as a college of the Church, a sizable proportion of the faculty and administration must consist of persons who locate themselves within the community of Christian faith and understanding."[166] Statistics on the religious commitments of St. Olaf faculty have not been collected for many years. In 1968 Lutherans were reported as constituting 73 percent; this is only 1 percent less than the Lutherans in the student body that year. But it is likely that the proportion of Lutherans in the faculty has declined more rapidly than in the student body. One very oblique indicator would be the fact that 42 percent of the present faculty received their baccalaureate degrees from Lutheran or Lutheran-related institutions. It is the estimate of some administrators, however, that only a quarter of the faculty are actively Lutheran.

One index of shift may be seen in the Religion Department. Thirty years ago a faculty group called "the Old Norwegians" were in the ascendant, and they determined that their successors should be younger scholars who had had more access to graduate study. This they accomplished. The measure of the accomplishment might be sensed by comparing the paragraphs which describe the department's work in the *College Catalog*s for 1961-62 and 1992-93. The former says this:

> St. Olaf College gives opportunity in the curriculum for a systematic study of the sources, history, and teachings of Christianity and the application of its principles to modern conditions and problems. It is natural also that the history and principles of Lutheranism should receive attention.

The latter:

> The study of religion is an integral part of the liberal arts curriculum and attends to the religious elements of culture — scriptures, rituals, symbols, traditions, beliefs, worship practices, values, and theologies. At St. Olaf the study of religion emphasizes study of the Christian tradition, its history, practice and contemporary expression.[167]

Beginning in the latter 1970s a succession of appointments converted a Lutheran unanimity in the department into a minority.[168] It was a Baptist who recommended recently (and unsuccessfully) that a Lutheran-oriented religion course should be required in the curriculum. And it was a Catholic who pled (also unsuccessfully) that the religion requirement be maximized, and that it involve courses with theological content.[169]

Morality and Worship

The college had always had a ban on social dancing, and after years of low-level grumbling it came to issue and was abolished in 1961. This departure from conservative decorum was attended by much formality. After the board of regents had worked its way to a decision, it was forwarded for higher review by the Board of College Education of the church, which pondered it for months and then returned it with the comment that they thought it was a matter for decision by the regents. After a year and a half of this infinitely discursive process, the college chaplain was deputed to explain it all to the students, which he did in a four-page, single-spaced, labored apologia. He embodies much of the gravity that went into the decision, and the sense of its involving the nature of the college as Lutheran.

> The college, as an institution of the church, carries on a vital program of Christian education, yet it is not the church. While the church, in itself, is responsible for the preaching of the Word and the administration of the sacraments as its primary function, it is not responsible for providing the entire ethos in which the Christian

lives. That is not to say that the so-called "secular" involvements of the Christian outside the Church are out of harmony with the Christian message. Indeed he becomes involved in these as a Christian; and because he is one, his involvement is distinctive and quite different from the involvement of the non-Christian engaged in the same activity.[170]

An entirely different note is struck near the end of the sixties after successful student agitation for free intervisitation in the dormitories, and a few years later for coeducational housing. The change lay not so much in the relaxation of rules as in a new consensus that students should behave as they wished, without control by a collegiate ethos for which the senior members of the college had enduring responsibility. Joseph Shaw, participant and historian, put it this way:

> This development did not spell the end of Christian morality at St. Olaf, but it marked the end of a consensus about the kind of responsibility the College should assume regarding the relationships between men and women students. While the College had never aimed to control those relationships, it had taken the view that since the Christian ethic disapproved of premarital sexual intercourse, a Christian institution gave public witness to its identity and to its sense of care for students by both moral instruction and appropriate regulations.[171]

More than simply seven years had intervened since Pastor Swanson's discourse to the students. What had diminished was a shared sense that the college was answerable for the church's moral wisdom.

In the matter of worship things seem to have gone much better at St. Olaf than at Gettysburg, at least until recently. The college appointed its first full-time pastor in 1951, two years before Gettysburg did the same. Forthwith a student congregation was organized, which brought Sunday worship onto campus from local churches. With a daily chapel attendance of 60 percent and Sunday participation of 80 percent, plus another eight hundred who came to a Sunday evening Communion service, any chaplain might be gratified. Much of this was perhaps due to the constant and tasteful provision of liturgical prayer and worship, different from the revivalist evangelicalism that governed chapel and church life at Gettysburg.

When Pastor Clifford Swanson, second to serve as chaplain, presented his regular report to the board of regents in 1963, the religious program was, if anything, more articulated than ever. The accent was on worship, which he claimed to be the one thing that distinguished a church campus from all others. The students, he reported, "are more responsive to services of Holy Communion on campus than any other single activity offered by the congregation apart from the Sunday morning worship services." Since preaching was his highest task, he kept his own pulpit on most occasions, rather than showcasing outside personalities. Daily chapels (136 of them in the academic year) were worship events, not assemblies or entertainments. In fact, when visitors did occupy the pulpit he refused to publish their names in advance: "One comes to participate in a brief worship and not just to hear a particular speaker."

The student congregation, he reported, took up regular collections to fund its own social projects. It also sponsored freshmen religious orientation, weekends of spiritual reflection, coffeehouse religious discussions on the fine arts, ecumenical services and an annual retreat with neighboring Carleton College, in-depth seminars with invited speakers, a premarital seminar, a lecture series on contemporary social issues, visitation at the local state mental hospital, a chaplain to participate in the annual Political Emphasis Week on campus, religious instruction at a school for delinquent teenagers and visiting at a home for the elderly, summer service projects, and pastoral counseling. Obviously the chaplaincy was not in the doldrums.[172]

Seven years later, in 1970, Pastor Swanson begins to report otherwise. Students are disenchanted with the church. "Many, perhaps most of them, are not very regular in chapel or church attendance on campus." And some who come "couldn't care less about the world around them."[173] A year later he sees a "rather drastic change in the attitude of the majority of the students." When they stay away from worship it is no longer an act of developmental rebellion, as before. Now they are simply ignoring the church with no sense of guilt. The Sunday turnout includes 800-1,200 students, and the Wednesday evening Communion service draws only 75-100 (out of a student body of 2,674, 1,743 of whom were Lutherans). He concludes, somewhat forlornly, that worship should probably go on whatever the attendance. "Simply the fact that we pause for worship continues to say something about the unique stance of the college from the standpoint of its declared purpose as an institution of the church and we all need to be reminded of that purpose by such disciplines as regularly scheduled worship periods offer."[174]

By 1973 the pastor is feeling clearly beleaguered, and the readiness of the forthcoming *Centennial Study* to welcome religious pluralism on campus aggravates him. "As never before we need to discover a kind of corporate solidarity within the context of that body of people committed to Jesus Christ as Lord. I studiously and intentionally avoid the use of the term 'church' at this point because of negative connotations attached to its institutional usage." He thinks it a good thing that St. Olaf has worked to rise above "sectarian religiosity." But to get and retain the "essentially Christian and Biblical perspective" on campus which the *Centennial Study* claims, they need a program, not just a philosophy. Not loyalty oaths or doctrinal uniformity, but some way of demonstrating commitment. "I deem the visible evidence of the presence of the body of Christ through its worship life on campus to be of utmost importance." Affirmation of the Christian faith at St. Olaf has to be, not an additive, but "a permeating and integral part of the whole. . . . Only the spirit of Christ's presence will enliven the consciences of its students and thus keep competence civilized."

The chaplain had been roused as a confessing Lutheran. Yet paradoxically he had begun to use the same language of diffidence toward the church which he took to be a threat to the church on campus.[175] Today, two decades later, chapel attendance is at an all-time low. When the author visited the campus the featured preacher at the morning chapel was Senator John Danforth, an Episcopal priest. The attendance, said to be high, equaled slightly less than 10 percent of the student body, with a somewhat lesser proportion of the faculty.

Boe and Granskou, the Great Years

The 1963-64 catalogue stated, under "Aims and Objectives":

> In the spirit of free inquiry and free expression, St. Olaf aims to offer an education that prepares for self-understanding, vocational usefulness, and responsible citizenship. Indispensable to this program is a confrontation with the Christian Gospel, hopefully leading to a mature faith in God. . . . The College takes the position that men and women are called by God to faith and service. Accordingly, it provides the opportunity for worship and seeks to graduate students who are morally sensitive and theologically literate.[176]

The 1987-88 catalogue stated, under "Mission":

> In the spirit of free inquiry and free expression, it offers a distinctive environment that integrates teaching, scholarship, creative activity, and opportunities for encounter with the Christian Gospel and God's call to faith. The College intends that its graduates combine academic excellence and theological literacy with a commitment to life-long learning. St. Olaf College strives to be an inclusive community, respecting those of differing backgrounds and beliefs.[177]

Something has been changing at St. Olaf. In 1963-64 the college took the position that all are called to faith and service. By 1987-88 the college was disinclined to declare itself a community of faith which the student was invited, even expected, to join. Obviously the conservative manners of the place have been liberalized. The faculty has become more professionalized. The student body has increased while the selectivity of its admissions process has been enhanced. The religious change has as its telltale indicia, not simply a decline in the Lutheran proportion in all constituencies on campus (except perhaps the regents); or in corporate worship; or in required religion courses and their theological content; or in oversight, subsidy, and influence by the church, but also the specific shift one can see in these two statements.

It is often possible to study the archaeology of such a change in the discourse of presidents. The college had an extended experience of growth under two long-serving presidents: Lars Boe (1918-42) and Clemens M. Granskou (1943-63).

Boe, somewhat like his contemporary Henry Hanson at Gettysburg, was an orator, but his style was more folksy than grand. "In an institution like St. Olaf," Boe wrote, "no amount of piety will make up for poor scholarship, and no amount of scholarship and culture will make up for a lack of real Christian life and faith."[178] In one of his numerous chapel talks he mused:

> What is St. Olaf? It is a few acres of land, a few buildings, some books, some tools, and so on. It is a faculty, a student body. Still there is something we feel back of it all, and that is a personality that has grown up, certain ideals and ideas. I don't think we are of the type here who have any contribution to make on being men of advanced thinking, because we have our eyes fastened on bigger things than that. Times change and I tell you it isn't an easy matter for those who have tried to get a hold on the unchanging ideas and hold on to them. Then I have seen many institutions which have hung onto their ideals until they become something to hang in a museum. They have encased them. They are not standing for them as living realities; they stand for them antagonistically. We are frankly a Lutheran college. We have, thank God, many who do not belong to the Lutheran Church. If you want to come to St. Olaf, take St. Olaf as it is. We make no pretense of being anything but a Christian college. It isn't a type of Christianity that is a series of dogmatic statements. We want to stand for Christianity as something that functions, something that is lived, not merely in the religion class but on the baseball ground, the football field, in your amusements, as a living reality.[179]

Clemens Granskou was the president who most significantly served the college toward academic and intellectual excellence. He was not himself an intellectual — few presidents are — but he articulated and administered the ideal of the liberal arts college.[180] His concerns for St. Olaf as Lutheran mostly concerned an appropriate ambit of independence from church executives and financial subsidy from them. His convictions about the place as Christian are frequently expressed, and confident. "Christianity is no little 'plus' which is added to the curriculum. Christianity is more than one of the extra-curricular activities of the campus life. St. Olaf is avowedly and purposely dedicated to make Christ more real to the thinking youth of our day, and to demonstrate that Christianity is infinitely more than a theory of life. It is the essence of life. In the words of Professor Clarke of Earlham, *St. Olaf does not 'have a religious program. It is a religious program.'*"[181]

In Granskou's time one could still depict Lutheran piety and thought as "permeating" the St. Olaf education; it was still an undertaking predominantly and intently staffed by Lutherans. His extramural worry was to keep professionally inept church officials from meddling with it.[182] Granskou's efforts to upgrade the college academically seem not to have required serious trade-offs with its being a confessing Lutheran college. But with the advent of Sidney A. Rand (1963-80), who followed Granskou, a change was under way.

The Blahs

Rand had served the churches as education executive: first for the Evangelical Lutheran Church (ELC) (1956-60) and then for the new ALC (1960-63). In negotiations for the merger of three churches into one, his had been the decisive voice in ensuring the autonomy of the church colleges.[183] And he would then preside at St. Olaf for seventeen transitional years.

There are several thematic emphases which appear with regularity in Rand's presidential statements. For instance, in his first address to the faculty he acknowledges that colleges like St. Olaf are seriously questioned in contemporary society. They are said to be propaganda tools for their churches and therefore prejudiced participants in the public culture. As "private" institutions — doubly private, by their church affiliation — they are increasingly outbid by tax-supported institutions. Rand replied:

> A chorus of voices well-informed or simply hopeful keeps saying in our time that the moral and spiritual element is part and parcel of education, that no man is truly himself apart from an understanding of his own existence in relation to a God who both transcends and is very really present in life and history. . . . It seems to me that we live in a time which needs as much as did any generation this perspective, this discussion of depth, this quality of eternal meaning, which comes from the gospel of Jesus Christ. It is my conviction that the college of the Church works to satisfy that need.[184]

This is the kind of utterance which can cause the listener to forget the beginning of the paragraph before the speaker has reached the end.

When Rand identifies the character of a Lutheran education, he reviews a roster of familiar doctrinal axioms. "At St. Olaf we are committed to what we believe is a realistic view of man, one which reckons with his possibilities and his limitations, his corruption as well as his integrity, his capability for evil as well as good. . . . And we say that life becomes infinitely more realistic, rewarding and useful if it is seen as the object of the love of a creating, redeeming and sustaining God."[185]

When his audience is the church and not the college, his tone alters (thus was it ever). To the Board of College Education of his church he described the early Lutheran colleges as basically conservative theologically and politically and socially, "somewhat separated from the mainstream of American education."[186] The same note of Lutheran self-criticism emerges when he speaks to his fellow Lutheran educational administrators:

> We in the private, church-connected liberal arts colleges may say we are less directly enmeshed than are other colleges in the society of which we are a part . . . Church colleges are in some ways more committed to do this than certain

other social institutions, for they are committed to basic purposes rooted in what we have considered the unchanging values: God, redemption, the dignity of man, personal responsibility, *et al.*

To be a college in this time is to be involved in entangling alliances with social movements, with the world of business and of course with the Church. . . . [Yet] we are living in a time when the ties between Church and college continue to loosen. . . . If our day calls for anything, it calls for a clear voice from the Lutheran college speaking from a set of principles and convictions that lie much deeper than the simple observation of the known problems of society.

There is a known catalogue of undergirding principles which can be effective guides to the life of a college: God's presence in human life, human fallibility and educability, the sure conviction that progress is not automatic, the danger of self-interest to individuals and to social institutions.[187]

At the same time he was telling people on his own campus:

It remains to be seen whether we will continue to be a true college of the church. There are outward signs of a weakening of that tie. Chapel attendance is much smaller than in former years. Many persons we interview for teaching positions have no background in our kind of institution and profess no interest in a relationship between college teaching and the Christian faith. Students not infrequently confess that they have lost interest in religion. . . . We need a conscience awakened to the seriousness of life, the implications of the decisions we make, and, above all, the God-relatedness of all we do.[188]

Rand is distressed that the "Confessing Lutherans" might be backward in their colleges, holding back from the vitality of the public culture. Yet when he comes to describe what benefits Lutherans bring to their educational work, he repeatedly itemizes "principles" that seem to be platitudes.

These commonplaces which he offers as the Lutheran repertoire for higher learning would hardly gain the ALC a reputation as either a recluse or a daredevil. Boe had portrayed a Lutheranism that was more concrete: "We make no pretense of being anything but a Christian college. It isn't a type of Christianity that is a series of dogmatic statements. We want to stand for Christianity as something that functions, something that is lived." Boe is of course less explicit than Rand, in that he fails to disclose what Lutherans stand for. But he is more articulate than Rand because he is pointing to a specific community with its specific history and practices, and such a community still exists on his campus. This Rand could not do.

Rand's rhetoric is suggestive of what Henry Hanson had employed at Gettysburg. It is not his expressions; Lars Boe, Hanson's contemporary, was much more given to folksy talk of virile character. It is his reticence to display any real pride or enthusiasm in what Norwegian American Lutherans might have to offer that would enliven their colleges.

515

It was during Rand's presidency that Lutherans fell from 84 to 60 percent of the student body. Had anyone had the nerve to keep track of the religious commitments among the faculty during those years, the decline might have been seen as drastic.

A Faculty Indifferent

But perhaps the situation in the Rand period is conveyed best in two statements by veteran religion professor Harold H. Ditmanson. He served on several presidential search committees and was a close confidant of Sidney Rand, who chose him to deliver the address at his own presidential inauguration and to chair the Steering Committee of the Centennial Study. Joseph Shaw, St. Olaf's historian, describes him as "the genial, trusted spokesman who could marshal from his extensive reading and clear thinking the ideas and felicitous expressions which reflected the best aspirations of the community."[189] He had other, more candid thoughts that did not find their way into the public domain.

In 1974, *Identity and Mission in a Changing Context,* the Centennial Study which Ditmanson drafted, had this to say about the St. Olaf faculty:

> Whereas Lutheran graduates of Lutheran colleges once comprised the vast majority of the faculty, they now comprise a bare majority. The younger members of the faculty represent a broader mix of educational and religious backgrounds. Despite this difference, these two groups do not differ markedly in their educational philosophy and they feel a common concern for the moral and emotional growth of students as well as for their intellectual development.[190]

But at this same time Ditmanson wrote privately, and differently, to a faculty colleague:

> . . . just between you and me, it is my considered judgment that IF the present faculty were to be tenured, St. Olaf could forget about being a Christian college. I simply can't understand why some teachers who say openly that they have no sympathy with the aims and objectives of St. Olaf want to stay here and wreck the tradition that has made this the kind of place at which you and I are willing to spend our lives.[191]

In latter times at St. Olaf, the prerequisite to being a college of the church — that it have a faculty of the church — has caused much public debate. When the *St. Olaf Magazine* sponsored an essay contest in 1979 (Rand's last year in office) on "The Distinctiveness of a College of the Church," there were two winners. The senior award went to William Narum, a '43 alumnus and professor of philosophy. He dislikes the St. Olaf phrase "education in a Christian context" for being as ambiguous as the older "atmospheric" metaphors. It is, he writes, a spiritual objective which makes a church college distinctive. The college has a wisdom to pass on: *the* liberal art because it is the art of being, not mere doing. But who is competent to develop and share this wisdom? Here he quotes Quaker educator Elton Trueblood: "The selection of faculty becomes important, for the Christian character of an institution 'is attested by the mood and conviction of the major teaching of the institution.'" Narum's conclusion? "If not all the teachers of a church college are Christian, at least they should understand Christian thought and be reverent in the face of its great historic convictions."[192]

In 1987 the magazine published a faculty forum on "St. Olaf: A College of the Church." One faculty member thinks St. Olaf would need a substantial number (20-100 percent) of faculty who know what the church tradition is and are not indifferent or antagonistic to it. Another admits to anxiety because she fears "the church connection will mean interference with faculty freedom. . . . What is required is that faculty approach the task of knowledge meditatively, admit the possibility that other languages than that of their own discipline can also be used in describing reality, and realize that among these other languages religious language operates on an equal footing." Another writes: "I don't propose religious tests nor suggest quotas, but I do believe that we and the college should appoint faculty who see the religious nature of St. Olaf as an asset in its liberal arts education. . . . We should not appoint faculty who look upon its church affiliation as similar to the Minnesota winter — i.e., something one must tolerate in order to teach at St. Olaf." A Catholic contributor argues that Christians should expect their college to be a sign of contradiction before the academic world, as Jesus crucified was. He regrets the decline in prayer at chapel services and the absence of an academic major in the Lutheran tradition. The last faculty essayist discloses that St. Olaf all along has had a little-known bylaw on the subject:

> As a general rule the qualifications for teaching at St. Olaf College shall include membership in the Lutheran Church. In all cases faculty members and personnel shall be persons of moral integrity and Christian character.[193]

She fears that to apply this bylaw would risk replacing conscience with conformity and expression with repression. "Any reputation for sectarian limits, whether deserved or not, imposes an unnecessary handicap in recruiting faculty and attracting students."[194]

All but one of these faculty seem unsettled about the effect (or, more often, the perceived effect) of an active share in Christianity (no one mentions Lutheranism) as a qualification to teach at a college of the Lutheran church. One is drawn to speculate how they might have reacted to a proposal that St. Olaf needs at least 20 percent of its faculty to know the Western tradition and not be indifferent or antagonistic to it; or to a plea for history to be treated on an equal footing with other disciplines; or to fears that English as a teaching language might impose an unnecessary handicap in recruitment.

Clearly a Lutheran identity was more purposefully claimed, a lamination of scholarship with piety and theology more bindingly achieved, an institutional integrity with responsiveness to the church more amiably combined, and secularization much longer staved off, at St. Olaf than at Gettysburg. To take but one index, the proportional Lutheran presence in the St. Olaf student body today, 52 percent, is what Gettysburg had seventy years ago. Also, whereas Gettysburg legally commits itself not to consider religion in decisions about employment, admission, or financial aid, St. Olaf has pointedly declined to exclude religion as a significant qualification in its nondiscrimination policy.[195]

Yet by other indicia the Midwest college is entering into a divestiture of its Lutheran identity that, though much longer in coming, could be swifter in its eventual accomplishment. As a foil for them both it behooves us to study the Missouri Synod experience in higher education: so different from either of those we have observed, so much more apparently confessional, yet possibly more fragile than one would imagine.

THE "MISSOURI LUTHERANS"

The waves of German Lutheran immigrants who came to America in the mid–nineteenth century were, as already noted, motivated to come not only for economic opportunity but also, for the religious freedom it offered. They were bound to be more self-consciously wary about their independence, even from other Lutherans. Their core group was the band of Saxons who came up the river to Missouri in 1839 and found strong leadership in their chosen pastor, Carl Ferdinand Wilhelm Walther.

In the very year of their arrival they opened in the town of Altenburg their first "college," a primitive attempt to replicate the *Gymnasium,* the secondary school from which educated Germans traditionally went to either the university or the seminary. Supported by its "mother" congregation in Saint Louis, its curriculum was at first that of a traditional secondary school, but in a few years it was specifically redesigned for future pastors and church teachers. This meant heavy emphasis on German, Greek, and Latin, and on theology. Part of the plan was to provide teaching assignments for graduates while they awaited their calls to serve congregations.[196]

When this school moved from its rural log cabin to Saint Louis in 1847 (the year the Missouri Synod was organized) and was conveyed from congregational to synodical ownership and support two years later (the first "collegiate" institution to be formally sponsored by a Lutheran synod in North America), there were strong provisos attached to the transfer, stipulating that pastoral candidates would always be the premier student population.[197]

518

These Missouri Synod pioneers had from the start obligated every congregation to maintain its own parochial elementary school. In a short while they had begun to generate a network of regional "colleges," or *Gymnasia,* and theological seminaries, the antecedents of the church's higher education establishment today.

1864	Concordia University	River Forest, Ill.
1881	Concordia College	Bronxville, N.Y.
1881	Concordia University, Wisconsin	Mequon, Wis.
1893	Concordia College	Saint Paul, Minn.
1894	Concordia Teachers College	Seward, Nebr.
1905	Concordia College	Portland, Oreg.
1922	Concordia College	Selma, Ala.
1926	Concordia Lutheran College	Austin, Tex.
1962	Concordia College	Ann Arbor, Mich.
1976	Christ College Irvine	Irvine, Calif.
1925	Valparaiso University	Valparaiso, Ind.[198]

A Closely Held Educational Network

For most of the Missouri Synod's history the *Gymnasium* has been the basic unit of the LCMS educational network. In time the original four-year program added on a fifth and then a sixth year at the American junior college level. Candidates for the pastoral ministry would then go directly to one of the two seminaries: one the "theoretical" seminary (in Saint Louis, with the mandate to have a more rigorously academic program); the other the "practical" seminary (now in Fort Wayne, with the mandate to accentuate pastoral training). When seminary accreditation standards eventually required the baccalaureate degree for admission, the synod created one senior college to provide the last two years of study and the degree for those on their way to the seminary. Candidates for the teaching ministry, for whom four years of secondary school had once sufficed, were required by successive increases in licensure requirements to go to one of the teachers colleges for first two, and later four, years of college.[199] The network grew in strict conformity with these professional needs.

When local Lutheran enterprise in the wake of World War II abruptly created a vast network of about seventy "community" high schools, sponsored at the district or congregational level, the high school departments of the synodical schools began to atrophy, and most of them transformed their upper divisions into freestanding junior colleges, in emulation of the community schools being established under state sponsorship in so many locales. Then, when synod supervision slackened, and when federal grants and loans became liberally available, most of these were upgraded into four-year degree-granting colleges.

The advantage of this scheme was that the geographically compact population of the LCMS was served by a network of elementary, secondary, and postsecondary education that enrolled nearly 200,000 pupils. Students were directed easily through the levels in the system. Also, since the primary objective of the system to train church workers — pastors, teachers, musicians, etc. — has been an unflagging priority for the governing body of the church, the system's vocational mission has been closely honored, at least until recently. Further, since the central authority of the church has owned and operated these institutions, and for most of their history has provided a substantial portion of their operating funds (for years future church workers paid little or no tuition),[200] its authority and ability to monitor ideological unity has never been effectively challenged.

The countervailing weaknesses have been significant, however. The seminary level was the only one at which the church has maintained a sensible number of institutions — two — and sustained an effective enrollment. At the college level enrollments have been chronically meager. In 1930 only two of the colleges had enrollments of more than 300 students, including four years of high school and two years of college.[201] Even in 1960, a time of great enrollment increase around the country, the average LCMS college had an enrollment of 450 students and a teaching staff of thirty-five.[202] In 1986, when the synodical configuration stood at two seminaries, ten colleges, and two junior colleges, and average enrollments stood respectively at only 482, 535, and 232, the decision to close the two least viable colleges encountered great resistance.[203] It has been exceedingly difficult for these colleges to attain or even aspire to a level of academic accomplishment that would make them attractive on intellectual grounds.

A second weakness is that while the system has been under a highly central-ized authority, that authority has rarely taken an initiative for change. The absence of determined policy or strategy plans has not rendered the system unchangeable. On the contrary, the Missouri colleges have undergone changes so rapid and unforeseen as to render the system unstable. But the forces for change have always been from without. It is an instructive instance of a closely held central governance which, for want of initiative, has lost the power to control or even to withstand many of the system's changes.[204]

Much of this is embodied in the story of Concordia University in River Forest, the Missouri Synod's seniormost and now second-largest college.

CONCORDIA UNIVERSITY

The founder of the Missouri Synod, C. F. W. Walther, bade every congregation provide itself with a parochial school; if they could not afford a teacher, then the pastor himself must teach. Synodical rules accordingly required every congregation, as a condition of its membership in the church, to provide a Christian education for its children, and obligated all children of the church to attend.[205] Though the classes were mostly conducted in German, English was obviously required, and the teachers who came over from Germany proved themselves quite deficient in that tongue. Also, Missouri leaders smelled the taint of rationalism in the training of these imported schoolmasters. Eventually the Americans came to the consensus that they had to recruit and train their own teachers.

After muddled early efforts, the congregation in Addison, Illinois, near Chicago, made an offer of land and cash for a training school to be built in their town, and in 1864 a vacant tavern served as the temporary quarters for the first arrivals: forty-three men and boys of every age and condition. The place would be called Concordia Teachers Seminary. Their curriculum was said to include Bible, Bible history, catechism, memory work, the Augsburg Confession, Luther's *Large Catechism*, music, violin, piano, organ, and singing. The president's own formal training above secondary school amounted to only one year and four months.

At First, a Gymnasium

A fifth year of study was added in 1868, and by 1908 the addition of the sixth year completed the classical *Gymnasium.* Completion of the four-year segment was forthwith made the prerequisite for admission to the two-year college program at Concordia, the very year that high school graduation became the national requirement for admission to normal schools. In its twenty-fifth year Concordia had an enrollment of 203 students; by its fiftieth year they were reduced to 188.

During the 1880s English gradually replaced German as the language of instruction in all subjects except religion. One index of the gradual indigenization of the Missouri Synod is provided by the educational journal which River Forest's self-made president, Pastor Johann C. W. Lindemann (1864-79), also founded. In 1865 it began as the *Evangelisch-Lutherisches Schulblatt.* Four years later the synod made it its official educational journal. Its first English article appeared in 1879. In 1921 its name was changed to *Lutheran School Journal,* and its last German article appeared in 1935.[206]

Against stubborn opposition from the faculty the synod decided to move the institution from Addison to River Forest, just north of Chicago, and a large set of buildings was dedicated there in 1913 as Concordia Teachers College before a crowd estimated at 30,000-45,000. Even more interesting statistics for that time were that the Missouri Synod had 934,199 members, 70,000 of whom resided in Chicago, and it maintained 2,216 schools that hired 2,487 teachers. In 1919 the Illinois Board of Education recognized Concordia as a normal school. The baccalaureate would not be required for teaching licensure in Illinois until 1964.

The third college year was added in 1933, but tentatively, as an optional year for students who could not find a placement. The high school program was finally accredited in 1935 and 1936 by the state and regional agencies. In 1938 female students were admitted to both high school and college departments, and in 1939 the fourth college year was added, and the college prepared to begin awarding the degree of bachelor of science in education. River Forest thus became the Missouri Synod's first four-year college, exactly 100 years after its educational endeavors began. In that year, his last of 26 as president, William C. Kohn (1913-39) counted among his duties "spiritual counseling and supervision of the student body, representing the school, being chief editor of the *Lutheran School Journal,* supervising at mealtimes and in study periods, counseling with faculty members, and acting as school doctor and nurse, besides handling correspondence and attending innumerable meetings. He was urged by the Board of Control not to overexert himself as they provided secretarial help in 1929."[207]

Arthur W. Klinck (1939-53) was the first president with an earned doctorate, and apparently the first with an earned degree of any sort. His predecessors had been awarded honorary doctorates by LCMS institutions as a conventional courtesy. After the war Concordia began to lose its high school students to the newer, nonsynodical Lutheran high schools. In 1946, for the first time, the college student body at Concordia was slightly more numerous than that of the high school, and by 1950 the high school department was closed down. Also in 1950, negotiations begun back in 1939 resulted in accreditation of the college by the North Central Association, followed in 1952 by a high rating for teacher education by the University of Illinois. Concordia then had 557 students, all of whom were there to qualify for professional service to the church and had signed a "Declaration of Intention" to assure the synod that its subsidy to the college was not misspent.[208]

Jesus Up Front

At the conclusion of a long study commissioned by the synod, the Concordia faculty published these objectives in 1958, which give some sense of the uncommon character the college then had:

1. A firm faith in Jesus Christ as the only Savior from sin, a ready consent to the will of God in every life situation and a sense of wonder and appreciation for all the work of God.
2. A sincere acceptance of the Holy Scriptures as the revealed truth of God, an assent to the Lutheran Confessions as the correct expression of that truth, a growing ability to evaluate human learning and conduct in the light of God's Word.
3. A grateful consecration to the ministry of the Word and to the extension of the Kingdom of God, an active cooperation in promoting the purposes of The Lutheran Church–Missouri Synod, and a high standard of ethics in the professional life of a Christian teacher.
4. A respect for the dignity and worth of the individual as a redeemed child of God, an understanding and development of the resources of the human

personality, and an effective practice of personal and professional stewardship of God-given talents. . . .

These are the assumptions they made about each of their graduates:

1. They will teach in a Lutheran elementary school or a Lutheran high school.
2. They will ordinarily be expected to teach religion in addition to the common subjects of learning.
3. They will teach all subjects in the framework of Christianity and in accordance with the doctrines and beliefs of The Lutheran Church–Missouri Synod.
4. In nearly all instances they will teach in self-contained classrooms if assigned to elementary school positions.
5. They will begin their teaching careers in grades 7-10 if assigned to high school positions.
6. They will need at least minimal skills in music, particularly sacred music, for their classroom teaching.
7. They will in most cases be expected to assist in the work of the various religious education agencies in addition to their classroom teaching.
8. They will make teaching a life-time career and will regard their positions as part of the educational ministry of the Lutheran Church–Missouri Synod.[209]

That was in 1958. At the same time that this forthright set of assertions issued from the college, it began to be clear that Concordia could not find enough qualified candidates who were products of the LCMS system to staff its own faculty. By 1960 one-third of all new faculty had not been trained in the synodical schools or seminaries.[210] This was to be a turning point of sorts, and as so often happens, the rhetoric was becoming more assertive just as the reality was becoming more ambiguous. Concordia at this time was graduating more elementary teachers than any other institution of higher learning in the state of Illinois. This new situation was a tiny cloud, no larger than a small fist lifted above the horizon, but it would grow to overshadow the synod.[211]

Market Forces Prevail

A series of changes had begun to occur: changes which befell the Missouri Synod's educational *Apparat,* not changes it initiated. The most obvious — though most changes were recognized after the fact rather than before — were demographic. At the end of the war, for instance, when there were twelve synodically sponsored high schools in existence, there were only a handful of community (locally sponsored) high schools. By 1955 the community schools had increased to twelve; and by 1985, to seventy. During that same short time eleven of the twelve synodical high schools had been shut down.[212] The convenience of a local day school over a regional boarding school (and the attractiveness of one with modest language requirements over another whose curriculum and faculty seemed half dedicated to ancient and foreign languages) was considerable. What this did was to take away from the synodical colleges like River Forest one stream of easily recruitable freshmen. In their recruitment efforts to make up for the loss, they were naturally inclined to appeal to LCMS youngsters who might not have a church vocation in mind.

That was one change which began in the sixties and enlarged in the seventies. Another was initiated by the "practical seminary," then in Springfield, Illinois. Concerned to free itself from its reputation as the "slower" of the two institutions, it began to recruit more actively and attracted LCMS candidates who had eluded the synodical system and earned their baccalaureates elsewhere. Concordia, Saint Louis, followed that example, and it became abruptly clear to young men and women who felt a calling to serve the church that they might find another route than through colleges like Concordia, River Forest.[213] The junior colleges, being deprived of their own feeder high schools and their monopoly on pastoral candidates, began to petition the church to enlarge their program to that of a four-year college, and soon all but two of them were competing alongside River Forest for the professional and the pastoral as well as the general students.[214]

As this was happening, the Missouri Synod was able for a while in the 1960s and early 1970s to augment its annual subsidies to the colleges and seminaries, but eventually the numbers and proportion of undergraduates who did not intend professional church work expanded the colleges and their budgets, and a long decline in the percentage of the budget covered by the church set in. For instance, in 1950 the church was able to provide 70 percent of River Forest's total income; in two great reductions the subsidy has fallen to only 5 percent.[215] When the church saw that increasing numbers of general students were replacing the church-work students the system was primarily intended for, it modified the subsidy to a make it more proportionate to the numbers of the latter group. This only served to decrease the total subsidy in colleges with large numbers of general students, which in turn made them more tuition-dependent and obliged them to recruit still more vigorously for nonchurch professionals. In 1960 virtually all of the River Forest students intended church careers,[216] but by 1992 only 23 percent pursued that calling. Throughout the LCMS system, in twenty years the actual number of students choosing the pastoral profession has been halved; those choosing teaching have diminished by two-thirds.[217] And as church-work students declined, even the proportion of LCMS church members in the student bodies has diminished: they became a minority as of 1990, and fell to 41 percent in 1992.[218]

These changes have set up a spiraling vortex of unintended change for Concordia and for the rest of its synodical peer schools, whose statistics follow hers rather closely. The LCMS has throughout its existence heavily subsidized and closely controlled its higher education system, not for the children of its members, but for ministerial candidates who would staff the pastoral and educational ranks of the church. Yet in the space of three — or perhaps two — decades, it has seen the student bodies of those schools lose 70 percent of their intended clientele. It is clear that the church governed only certain features of the system, and made decisions that were often stymied by unanticipated market forces. Of all the denominational education networks, this one is ostensibly the most closely "owned and operated" by the church, yet it is not and cannot be controlled.

Tumult in the Missouri Synod

As this head-over-heels tumble proceeded, another complex of changes was affecting the qualitative atmosphere on campus. In the 1960s the Missouri Synod was rent by an antagonized and vehement conflict over right doctrine. The disagreement, which by all accounts was mortal, arose over two of the inmost doctrines of the church: whether some of the newer modes of interpreting Scripture were acceptable and, if not, whether the church could offer comity or communion to those who engaged or acquiesced in such teaching. The *Proceedings* of the 1965 convention are heavy with denunciations of various scholars of the church, calling for them to be disciplined for teaching that David lived too early to be a monotheist, or that resurrection would not reassemble the actual fleshly remains of one's body, or that the literary genre of the book of Jonah is not historical. These grievances were followed by an immensely long commission report on guarding their fellowship from Satan's disruption by heresy, schism, backsliding on the Lutheran Confessions, etc.: thirty large pages of fine print.[219]

A new president was elected by the LCMS in 1969, with a clear mandate to bring the conflict to a resolution: Pastor Jacob A. O. Preus. The faculty of the Saint Louis seminary eventually seceded, and various academics were removed from their positions during his incumbency. In a lengthy and articulate account of what was at stake, President Preus described the point at issue:

> We have determined that no philosophy of writing history and no literary critic using hypothetical theories regarding the origin of the Bible will take away from us our childlike faith in the clear and inerrant Word which testifies to and connects us with our Lord Jesus Christ.[220]

If to be truly dependent upon the Bible for faith imposes on the reading community the responsibility to acquaint itself with the conventions and developmental background and controversial environment that would allow them to discern who is reading his or her notions into the text from who is deferring to the authors' intent and nuances and implications, then a truly Bible-reverencing church would have to develop a school of painstaking and scholarly cultivation of the text. In the management of this intense and divisive controversy, the LCMS authorities have not developed such an essential resource in their academic network. As a result, the effective norm for the church, especially in the hurly-burly of controversy and discipline, has tended to be the sixteenth-century confessions (or selective excerpts from them), not the Scriptures. In 1975 Dr. Preus traced the quarrel back to the fifties: "It is evident that for the past two decades at least we have had two opposing theologies, particularly with reference to the doctrine of Holy Scripture. No church body can long support two theologies which are in conflict."[221]

One study of Concordia, River Forest, noted in the midsixties that the students were by then a thoroughly urban group, no longer rural as Missouri Lutherans had once been. They were also becoming more affluent.[222] The researcher noticed two trends among these students. Interviews showed that while administrators, faculty, and students alike affirmed the religious purpose of the college, the students were preparing themselves less to be servants of the church than to serve the world through the church, to be servants of a wider community. As one teacher put it:

> I would say that the change of direction has taken place in a greater openness to the world . . . I suppose there has been a tendency in the past for the college to be concerned with serving the church and to be somewhat turned inwardly. I think that there is a different mood that has come over both faculty and students and that is a greater consciousness that the church and this institution related to the church exists really for the sake of people on the outside.

Another trend was initiated by the theology faculty. Their official mandate was to provide "a broader knowledge of the Holy Scriptures; a firmer conviction of their verbal inspiration, inerrancy, and authority." "This objective," the researcher observed, "was not openly challenged by the faculty, but the emphasis within the [Theology] Division was away from the traditional view of the Bible. The crux of the problem seemed to be whether the Bible was verbally inspired by God or the vessel by which God is made known through the writings of ordinary men who might have made mistakes or exaggerated."[223]

The word around campus was that Concordia was more liberal theologically than its sister, Concordia Teachers College in Seward, Nebraska. Because religion was such a pervasive conversation topic on these campuses, the faculty were ardently discussing biblical interpretation, and the student body were eagerly eavesdropping on their colloquies. On a campus like Concordia, where chapel had been voluntary since the early fifties for the opposite reason from why it was finally made voluntary at Gettysburg, and where there was typically about a 60 percent daily attendance, and where there were three years of required theology courses, it was not difficult for word to get around.[224]

Grace Church, which sits directly across the street from Concordia, had a liberal clergy and congregation, and in the turmoil it would sever itself from the Missouri Synod. Synod discipline then required all faculty and administrators to dissociate themselves from the congregation as deviant, or be disqualified to serve at an LCMS college.

In 1973 the church eventually visited its official annoyance upon the college itself. After a yearlong search for a new president who would "clean house," a former assistant to Pastor Preus was appointed. The liberals were in the ascendant on campus, but concerned less to control the college than to change the synod in alliance with the faculty members being ousted from the seminary. The new president was confronted by the faculty and urged to resign, but declined. Eventually, near the latter years of his decade of service, the purge subsided.

Faculty recollection is that this president, Paul Zimmerman, was so concerned about the orthodoxy of teacher candidates that he appointed a number of mediocre faculty simply because they passed theological muster. The current administration operates under a synodical regulation which allows up to 10 percent of a college faculty to be non-LCMS persons, though only after extensive exploration of their theological compatibility. River Forest has used this proviso to appoint some teachers of other allegiances.[225]

The campus is quieter now, as is the Lutheran Church–Missouri Synod. The brushfire of dispute has been beaten out. While the church lost many of its intellectuals, Concordia has not. Yet to a faculty most of whom (whatever their academic discipline and degrees) have practically the equivalent of a master's degree in theology as a prerequisite to their appointment to an LCMS college, the matters that were so loudly disputed remain issues of abiding interest. The costs of open inquiry, however, are heavy. Both the bylaws of the Missouri Synod and its policy on academic freedom allow dissent on any matter of church tradition, but such dissent must be submitted privately within the church, from one's faculty peers, to the Commission on Theology and Church Relations, to the Synodical Convention, and in the meantime it is not to be publicly aired or brought into the classroom.[226] The result has been a campus (and perhaps a church) where theological discourse and inquiry have in large part been sedated.

The Concordia Paradox

The shift and slide of the Missouri Synod educational endeavor brings to light a double paradox. On the one hand, in the field of higher education the church has long seen itself as governing an organically interrelated complex of educational institutions, generously subsidized and centrally directed by the church[227] as the recruitment and training apparatus for its many learned ministries. The facts are otherwise:

1. The church's educational executives, who believe that the synodical schools "face serious problems, most of which are financial in nature," confess that only five of their thirteen seminaries, colleges, and high schools are meeting their own (not very rigorous) minimal standards for fiscal viability. Meanwhile the church has been advancing millions of dollars to failing schools in order to cover their large annual operating deficits.[228]

2. The ability of the church to subsidize its schools has been steadily compromised. In the 1950s it managed to supply about 40 percent of the annual budgets; now it cannot manage one-quarter of the costs. Indeed, it has been almost two decades since the Board of Higher Education discontinued publishing these figures.[229]

3. The recruitment system has broken down. At a time when the national college-age population has just declined 30 percent, after a long period when hardly more than half of those baptized as Missouri Synod Lutherans have sought confirmation (half of the church's congregations were reporting only one confirmation a year, or none), only 4 percent of them are matriculating at a Lutheran college of any kind, LCMS or ELCA.[230] Less than a quarter of the college students now intend to be church workers. Indeed, the number of graduating teachers placed in church schools has fallen to less than half of what it was five years earlier. Far less than half of the student population — 41 percent — are Missouri Synod Lutherans. And less than half of those in training for pastoral ministry graduated from synodical colleges before entering the seminary.[231]

4. Studies in the liberal arts have been edged aside by newer career-oriented programs. And academically, no college in the system has had the wherewithal to achieve distinction, least of all in the premier subject for the church and the system, theology.

5. The apparatus of central direction is still in place, yet for years the dynamic forces dictating change have never been from the center. They have been the independent preferences of students and the autonomous, competitive energies of the presidents.

From the floor of the New Orleans Convention back in 1973 came sober complaint that something was awry in the LCMS educational effort:

> Without seeking to find fault or to place the blame at anyone's doorstep, it appears that the Synod's educational system has departed from the concept of "system" . . . In order to meet enrollment goals, greater emphasis has been placed on general education, because all schools cannot hope to enroll that large a number of church-worker students. In order to enroll the stated number of students, several schools face major expansion needs that cannot be supported with current income and synodical subsidy.[232]

What has been the reaction within the church to this major inability to achieve its educational goals? We have pointed out that in other Lutheran venues an emollient form of rhetoric has been created so as to give some cosmetic protection to the steady marginalization of Christian faith from campuses that are still nominally invested with Lutheran identity. In the Missouri Synod, where smooth talk is not nearly so palatable in matters of doctrine, there is nevertheless a rhetoric that is flamboyant in its understatement used to describe this systemic breakdown.

In 1975 a Task Force to Consider Restructuring Synod's System of Higher Education handed in its report. Noting that over the course of years when virtually every single factor had gone negative the church's colleges had begun a variety of programs that "appeared at times to be contrary to the basic philosophy of the institution of the Synod but have been found to be necessary and desirable for institutional survival," the task force acknowledged that there were far more colleges than the church needed, but that it would be "extremely complex" to close any of them. "Change has not always come easy in the church. Traditions are long-lived and difficult to alter. However, in spite of any difficulties that may have occurred from time to time, the operation of The Lutheran Church–Missouri Synod's colleges and seminaries has been the envy of nearly every church denomination in this country."[233]

Also, in 1975 the Board for Higher Education, after noting that only one out of every sixty-seven high school graduates in the church had entered an LCMS college to become a church worker, compared with one out of twenty-nine a decade earlier,[234] and after displaying enrollment and funding graphs that looked like ski runs down Mont Blanc, was able to conclude: "On the other hand, the board definitely looks forward to its work with joy and anticipation. It sees the number and nature of the problems as opportunities. Changes and problems are inevitable. . . . The board realizes that the Lord will keep heaping far more blessings and opportunities on our Synod and its educational system than we will be able and willing to use. He will lead us forward as He always has in the past."[235]

Jacob Preus, after ten years of presidency, reported in 1979: "The philosophy and structure called 'the System' has undergone little change . . . I think we should try to retain all of our schools, allowing them if possible to attain four-year status. We should talk of closing them only when the local constituents fail to use them."[236]

Studies to No Avail

The Concordia system became the subject of a remarkable succession of special investigations, whose outcomes may be more instructive in retrospect, perhaps, than they were at the time.

> 1971: The convention denies an overture for a special study of the synod's higher education system.[237]
>
> 1973: Admitting that the "continuous feed" arrangement uniting the higher education system has been broken down by redundancy and rivalry, the convention commissions a task force to recommend the elimination of wasteful duplication in schools and programs.[238]
>
> 1975: A task force reports: for decades there have been too many colleges

and junior colleges, and they are inefficiently small; now an oversupply of ministers reduces the need still more; many of those who are bound for the seminary now go elsewhere for college; and a drastic decline in teacher education has greatly reduced their presence. The results: junior and senior colleges have recruited student bodies largely composed of general and non-LCMS students; candidates for the various church ministries, who since 1850 were supposed to receive an LCMS education free, now receive little aid, and the subsidies the synod can afford are simply keeping the schools open, not serving the church's needs, because reallocations are so politically painful. The task force recommends many reforms, admitting that "drastic action may not prove to be in the best interest of the Synod." The sentiment is sound, because they were not accepted.[239]

1979: The Board of Higher Education proposes "Planning Principles," such as: to devote the synodical institutions primarily to professional church workers and secondarily to consecrated laity; to give high priority to special financial aid for church-work students; *not* to "turn schools loose" to pursue their independent interests; to close or consolidate schools when appropriate. Though formally adopted at the convention, the principles soon succumb to stronger forces.[240]

1986: A President's Commission on Synodical Higher Education, with a budget of $200,000, is told to look at the same old problems and report. "The old 'system' of synodical higher education had started to come apart," the commission admits. The answer: to reestablish the system and hold the institutions accountable. All the ski-run graphs plotted in 1975 are here again, in updated form. Their slopes have now descended from the alpine meadows to the piedmont, yet their rates of incline never seem to level out. The commission repeatedly stipulates that the primary population for their colleges are those destined for church work. General education students must pay their own way without church subsidy. The synod should commit itself to supplying 25 percent of educational-and-general expenditures, and assume responsibility for capital costs. No new programs for general education clientele, undergraduate or graduate. All programs to be submitted to the Synod Board for prior approval. Enunciating tables of standards for fiscal viability and academic excellence, the commission says with a sharp tone in its voice that straggler colleges would simply have to be left behind. In a word, local enterprise by the institutions has to knuckle under to management from Saint Louis. "The time is past for synodical resolutions that are not put into action." All recommendations are passed; none is put into effect. The synod opens a line of credit for the colleges to service their continuing deficits.[241]

1992: A new task force, chaired by Jacob Preus himself, accepts the presence of lay students in the church's colleges. "Without them," it began, "some of the institutions would have had difficulty continuing to operate." Since they now amount to more than two-thirds of the total enrollment, the "difficulty" is not difficult to imagine. The task force, without rehearsing the list of difficulties that continued to burden the higher education system, recommends a reorganization of all the colleges and universities into a new corporate entity, the Concordia University System, Inc., confident that a new echelon of central supervision will help the institutions of higher education achieve their full potential.[242]

The theory is that the Lutheran Church–Missouri Synod owns and operates a close-knit system of two seminaries, ten colleges or universities, and one residential high school: all governed, coordinated with the vocational needs of the church, and purposefully related to one another by the central authority of the church.[243] The synod, so leonine in disciplining doctrine, is feline in supervising its colleges. The reason they have survived is not their unified governance, but the modest (and uncooperative) entrepreneurial resourcefulness of the individual campuses, their administrators, and their supporters. In working for that survival they have found in Saint Louis neither autocrats nor benefactors, but distant bureaucrats. At no point have the common good or the needs of the church been strongly pled or imposed. Study after study, ignoring and ignored, leads one to infer that the understanding which the church has of its higher education enterprise is at least thirty years off true.

Since World War II the governing power of the synod, in the supervision of its higher education system, despite its reputation for tight discipline, has so repeatedly deferred to the preferences and interests of each school's local constituencies, and so passively responded to contextual realities and outside forces, as to have virtually forfeited real control and allowed the "system" to dissolve. In striking contrast with this diffidence, the events of the doctrinal struggle centering on the Preus regime, despite the synod's profession not to be a definer of faith and to welcome dissent, display its resolute capacity to suppress all manner of open dissent in favor of a centralized definition of acceptable belief.

The paradox is that both these performances — so flaccid in the governance of teaching institutions and so adamantine in the governance of teaching — have simultaneously weakened the capacity of the synodical colleges like Concordia University, River Forest, to fulfill their mission.

On the other hand, the one gift which a church so assiduously devoted to its colleges had to give, and could well protect by assuring that the faculty and administration had special training and loyalties so as to make it possible, was an education in which the study of theology was a central and enlivening inquiry. The ability of the LCMS to preserve the domestic identity of its colleges — from the regents down to the choral coaches — gave it an unusual capacity to afford that old word "permeate" a stable home. Instead, theological inquiry is one of the more muted academic disciplines in the system. When biblical studies came into new strength in this century, and allowed fresh inquiry and enhanced understanding if

531

practiced by devout and learned believers, the Missouri Synod leadership was so traumatized by the abuse of this scholarship at the hands of the descendants of their old nemesis, rationalism, that their response was to shun virtually all scholarly inquiry into Scripture. Also, since the new buds and branches of understanding that came from scriptural inquiry challenged some earlier understandings that were venerable but not, as it turned out, all that authentically scriptural (much as had happened in the days of Erasmus and Luther), they easily seemed to be so much cockle and tares. The aftermath of the dispersal of the Concordia Seminary faculty, which had been the only scholarly working group sponsored by the church, has imposed an informal but effective cloture on open theological renewal and inquiry in the colleges, where it has perhaps the readiest audience the church could provide. As a result, the one specialty that could have given these modest colleges an educational specialty, a pearl of great value but modest price, remains buried in the field.

Meanwhile River Forest, which in 1979 changed from Concordia Teachers College to Concordia College, changed again in 1990 to Concordia University. Both new nomenclatures were intended to open the door more invitingly to general students in the vicinity. The internal reason for the last change was not simply that several professional programs were now in place. As it was explained then to the board of regents: "It is *not* structure that makes a university, but diversity of *programs, faculties,* and *students.* In that light, Concordia achieved — and earned — University status much earlier in this decade." Arts and sciences, by becoming a college with a dean, would no longer be considered a "poor cousin" of teacher education. In a word, Concordia has now made the general education student its primary client, and will welcome the church worker student if room can be made.[244] Thus the long-standing mandate has been stood on its head.

What Governance Cannot Control

In admissions, although for many years Concordia honored an informal *entente cordiale* whereby the LCMS colleges pretty much left each other's region alone, now it competes vigorously for students out of anybody's backyard. Concordia offers preferential financial aid to Lutheran pastors' children, graduates of Lutheran high schools, and highest scoring applicants, but not to church worker students, the one group that the synod has most insistently said it wanted to receive a direct tuition break.[245] LCMS students constitute 41 percent of the total enrollment and other Lutherans add another 5 percent, leaving all Lutherans still a minority of 46 percent. Among undergraduates alone, the respective figures are 50 + 6 = 56 percent. These proportions have been diminishing annually. Nursing may have only about 10 percent Lutherans, and there are more Catholics than Lutherans in the graduate programs.[246]

River Forest, by exception, and contrary to the synod's own policy, accepts "creed" as a category not to be considered in personnel and educational decisions.[247] This divergence from church policy is given a say-nothing explanation: "It would not be appropriate to infer that the change in wording was made because the institution intended to move away from its Lutheran roots or was determined to change its mission. . . . At the present, it is still the posture of the University to serve the synod and to use its resources to assist the synod in the achievement of its mission when this is possible."[248]

Donald Ray Just, in a perceptive 1981 study of the great enrollment shift in LCMS colleges from church workers to general education students, concluded that this unintended change of clientele, drastic though it was, did not seem to be the factor which enervated the institutions' capacity to be dynamically Lutheran. The two pivotal elements in secularization were the chief administrators and faculty:

> Style of institutional leadership and constituent perception of that leadership appeared to be the key variables in the degree to which the institutions declared a Lutheran/Christian stance. Teaching styles and personal integration of faith and learning by individual instructors appeared to be the critical factor in determining the degree to which a Christian point of view was expressed in the educational process.[249]

But that was more than a decade ago, and the proportion of church workers and — more importantly — of Lutherans in the student body at River Forest has surely provoked a change in the way the university understands and presents itself.

The 1988 mission statement is attractive to just about all categories of prospective students, staff, and contributors.

> Concordia offers Christian education at the collegiate level as its way of sharing the Gospel of Jesus Christ, aiding students to develop a sense of vocation and preparing them for leadership in a variety of fields and endeavors. As a university of The Lutheran Church–Missouri Synod, Concordia aspires to the highest standards of excellence, blending a confessional Lutheran perspective with a liberal arts foundation for the free pursuit of knowledge and understanding. The spiritual elements of collegiate life and worship provide a focus for growth, renewal and personal expressions of faith.
>
> Concordia University challenges itself
>> to become an institution which intentionally serves as a locus for Christian higher education, sharing the Gospel from a confessional Lutheran perspective;
>> to provide undergraduate programs in academic disciplines, church work and other professions, rooting them in the liberal arts to prepare persons well-educated for ministry in the church and the world . . .[250]

It is only when one looks at its predecessor, drawn up in 1981, that one gains a sense of the distance traveled:

> Under the grace of God, Concordia College is a community directed by God's Word, motivated by the Gospel of Jesus Christ, and dedicated to Christian scholarship.
>
> As an institution owned and maintained by the Lutheran Church–Missouri Synod, Concordia is committed to the mission of the church to bring the Good News of Jesus Christ to the world. This commitment is met by (a) offering programs providing for the education of dedicated people who desire to serve the Church in full-time positions of public ministry, (b) offering programs providing for the education of dedicated people who will serve the church as Christian laypeople, and (c) serving as a model of Christian character and living for all who come in contact with it. . . .
>
> While respecting the Christian prohibition against violating the sanctity of the individual conscience, Concordia seeks to affirm faith in Jesus Christ as the only Savior from sin, sincere acceptance of the Holy Scriptures as the revealed truth of God, a sense of wonder and appreciation for all the works of God, a growing ability to evaluate human learning and conduct in light of God's Word, and ready consent to the will of God in every life situation . . .[251]

In the 1992 draft of the "Strategic Planning Committee Goals and Objectives" there is no reference to the Lutheran character of the university. Things change.

Most of the former LCA colleges have religion departments that follow the "religious studies" model: religion as a universal phenomenon to be examined anthropologically. Most of the former ALC colleges follow the "theology" model: the Christian religion critically and comparatively studied by its disciples. Concordia joins the other LCMS colleges in having a Theology Department. The members of that department, all pastors (as are sixteen other faculty across the university), take their turns in presiding at campus worship, besides which many of them make themselves regularly available for pastoral counseling. There is some talk of a full-time chaplain, but at present the assignment of dean of chapel is carried by a regular Theology Department member, a recent Harvard Ph.D., along with his virtually full teaching load. He describes a high level of spontaneous faith expression by the students: devotions, Lutherans for Life, youth ministry, work teams in the ghetto, etc. Meanwhile the Music Department, which in days past played a major role in training teachers to double as choirmaster/musicians in their congregations, retains a faculty as large as the Theology Department, even though only 9 out of 432 freshmen have declared their intention to major in music.

It is difficult to believe that the people in charge at River Forest would be very prompt to conform to policy statements from the convention or from the church staff. Nor would they be prompt to contradict them openly. Their ingenuity is mostly

534

devoted to making the university work. And since the synod does not officially want to sponsor the way they are doing it, it is both polite and politic not to make an issue of it. Under such conditions of mutual distraction, it is imaginable that the university may be subject to very swift and thorough transformation which, considering its conservative background, most observers would never expect.

The Lutheran Experiences

The "Americanist Lutherans," who took a good while before beginning to build colleges, expected at the outset that to survive they would require a larger clientele than they could themselves provide. Since their Pietism made similarly influenced evangelical Protestants seem on all fours with them in what was essential, their educational establishment began with little self-consciousness about being Lutheran. They were more conscious of being German, yet just when the colleges were opening these Lutherans were leaving their old language aside. So there was no sense or need of being distinctive.

Their colleges were small and poor at first. Nothing unusual in that. And they were quite regional, for why would a family send its son over long and costly distance simply to find another small and poor college? In the early days a college education was attractive to those who wanted to be pastors, or those who wanted to be lawyers or doctors, or those who would be gentlemen. The curriculum was accordingly strait and narrow. Most Lutherans saw no value in such expense and endeavor. In this century, when many more Lutherans had the fancy and the finances for higher education, the brighter among them were drawn to the greater schools at long distance, while the less ambitious now found the Lutheran campuses too far from home.

In any case, the church had not engendered in its faithful much of a proprietary sense about its colleges. Indeed, the foundations had often been the initiative of scholarly pastors who created their own academic vocations. The synods and churches had not invested much of their meager wealth in the early years or their more ample wealth in later times.

Their churchmanship had never favored theology much, for it could be so querulous and divisive. Nor had they fostered ordered worship, for it could be so hollow. So over the years the "Americanist Lutheran" colleges accommodated more and more of their non-Lutheran neighbors as students and teachers and trustees and donors. The founders had so expected that their own kind would naturally gravitate to their own schools, to be joined there by like-minded others, that they forbade their successors to make others feel less authentic in their membership. And so, little by little, the Lutheran designation became more and more nominal. After World War II even the old observances which were the heirlooms and furniture of the insouciant Lutheran days became awkward and were removed one by one to the attic.

535

Today, when the former LCA colleges and universities are more settled financially and secure academically, their Lutheran character is, like the lovely old antebellum building that serves as the Gettysburg logo, attractive, respected, and of yesteryear. There were, in the course of this gentle transition, only a few bitter recriminations, and they leave almost no residual sense of diminishment. What was Lutheran at Gettysburg had never become very scholarly, never very aware of being needful for Lutherans.

The Missouri Lutherans seemed at first sight to be so different. They arrived all feisty about their faith and anything but neighborly to other churches. Indeed, suspicion and dispute divided them among themselves as much as from others. Unlike their eastern cousins they made their colleges the church's own undertaking. Unfortunately, they were for a long time not really colleges, and there were too many of them for the church to manage. Beguiled by the myth that they all marched to the same melody, they never noticed that their "unified system" was in fact a scattering of outposts left pretty much to their own initiatives. As regards right doctrine, conformity was traded off heavily against energetic articulation or exploration, so although theology was the premier discipline at the colleges, it was not particularly biblical in its development or scholarly in its outcome.

The Concordia system, which was by explicit design intended only for those who would serve the church professionally, was barely justified in the numbers of its campuses by years of population growth in the church. Eventually they faced corporate collapse and survived as small colleges catering to a mixed, local clientele . . . but only by dint of this never being officially countenanced or condoned. The result is a chain of campuses that cannot do what the church continues to say is their chief task: to educate church-work students in a distinctive environment and curriculum. They presently have faculties that are nearly all Missouri Synod Lutherans, but student bodies that are only about one-third church workers and only about one-half church members. This is in curious contrast with the one institution that claims affiliation with the LCMS but has never submitted to its control: Valparaiso. It has never had official church endorsement, and it is one of the most recent of Lutheran foundations, yet it is the Lutheran campus that is maturing the fastest into a university. It has a faculty that is about half Lutheran, yet its student body contains a higher proportion of Lutheran lay students than most others.

The present situation of the LCMS colleges is unstable, for the church has once again asserted its determination to restore the "system" to its original purpose, yet seems to dispose of neither the finances nor the clout to bring this about. Under cover of this effort, further dispersal of energy seems possible.

The "Confessing Lutherans" of the Upper Midwest, largely Scandinavian, would seem to be the happy medium. Though their foundations were many, they enjoyed the loyalty and the custom of enough ethnic sponsors and feeder regions to grow at a healthy pace. Their theology has been less truculent than that of the LCMS, and it has enjoyed a stronger appetite than in the LCA. Their population wanted higher education for their children sooner after arrival, and sent them in numbers plenteous enough to spare the campuses from needing to recruit heavily beyond their own membership. They have remained closely gathered in their ethnicity (or ethnicities) much longer than their eastern cousins, who Americanized more eagerly.

As for faculty, the ALC campuses seem to have enjoyed what the LCA campuses may have wanted but were denied: a length of years when mostly loyal Lutherans applied and were hired, without anyone needing to put a fine point on it.

The result is that of all Lutheran cohorts, the former ALC colleges seem to have retained their Lutheran character in the most stable fashion while achieving early and continually improving academic excellence. But at present this may be more in jeopardy than anyone likes to notice, for the ethos of the campuses is being carried in inertial fashion by the recollections of the veterans and the usages of the past, but does not seem to be reproducing itself in the younger members — faculty or students — such that they are likely to continue or even to remember it two generations hence. Make that one generation.

Thus, if one were to designate as the apogee in a Lutheran college's development that era when its growth energies are most vitalized, its intellectual pursuits most enlivened by the faith community, and its satisfaction in service to the church at its warmest, the LCA colleges may have reached their high point in the interim between the two world wars; the LCMS colleges may have crested in the 1960s and 1970s, and the ALC colleges are coasting into their *diminuendo* now. The LCA schools do not miss anything they have lost. The LCMS colleges do not notice what they never had. And the ALC colleges cannot imagine losing what they remember so well having.

Richard Baepler's sense of certitude in 1977 about Lutheran higher education is surely shared by many:

> It may be that the church will finally give up its involvement in hospital work and other institutional forms in which she pioneered and which the welfare state has taken over. But the education of the young is another matter. The church cannot abandon this wholly to the State. **There have to be strong church-related colleges where the young who bear the future can collaborate with an older generation in freely and amply probing cultural memory, current realities and future prospects for man even when a majority of men may have forgotten their roots and lost their hope.** (emphasis in original)[252]

The present facts and, more importantly, the present flow of facts, would not offer much comfort to that hope.

However the differences of stress, priority, and achievement may have led the three companies of Lutherans on distinctive journeys since their origins on this continent, a closer commonalty of situation may now be drawing them closer together. In forecasting the program of the Lutheran Educational Conference of North America for the near future, the college presidents of all three traditions agreed emphatically that they should no longer direct their concern to the falling numbers of Lutherans in their membership. One officer explained it thus:

> What is happening, I believe, is that the presidents feel that there has been enough discussion of "critical mass" issues and no longer feel that counting putative Lutherans in the student body or nominal Lutherans in the faculty and staff is a real measure of the strength of the college's commitment to being a church college nor a good indication of the vigor of the relationship between the church and the college. . . . Admittedly, issues of the kind of faculty we have and the nature of the student body will become important, but it seems to many of us that they are secondary to this broader question and are derivative from the way in which the mission of the college is related to and strategic to the mission of the church.[253]

There is a valedictory ring in this view, however earnest. For although it is the vocation and mission of the Lutheran venture in higher education that most counts, Lutherans are likely to be the only people who could be committed to it enough to dedicate their careers and their very lives to it. And such Lutherans would seem to be the critical resource which the Lutheran colleges and universities have lost.

NOTES TO CHAPTER 5

1. See Abdel Ross Wentz, *A Basic History of Lutheranism in America* (Philadelphia: Muhlenberg, 1955).

2. Wentz, 67.

3. Wentz, 137.

4. Paul P. Kuenning, *The Rise and Fall of American Lutheran Pietism* (Macon, Ga.: Mercer University Press, 1988), 1-31.

5. Wentz, 73-77, has interesting observations on this. We consider this peculiar descendancy here because of its immediate bearing on the Pietist Lutherans of the first immigrations, but since Pietism was in the bloodstream of many of the denominations and churches considered here, we must return to it at the end of these stories.

6. In 1969 Hartwick, by unilateral action of its board of trustees, dissociated itself from the church in order to participate in new funding made available by the State of New York to colleges that were not "sectarian." The president indicated to the church's education office "that its basic program and emphasis will not change and that it still considers itself historically related to the Lutheran Church." Minutes of the 1969 meeting of the Lutheran Educational Conference of North America, 87 ([LECNA/1969]; similar proceedings hereafter cited as LECNA followed by the year of meeting). Wagner College (LCA, Staten Island) and Concordia College (LCMS, in Bronxville) retained their church affiliation and have participated in state funding.

7. California Lutheran University was cosponsored by the ALC from the time of its founding. The LCA also had two affiliated two-year colleges which are not directly examined in this study: Grand View in Des Moines, Iowa, and Suomi in Hancock, Michigan.

8. This was founded as the Pennsylvania College and changed its name in 1921 to Gettysburg College. It is designated throughout by its latter name.

9. Charles H. Glatfelter, *A Salutary Influence: Gettysburg College, 1832-1985* (Gettysburg: Gettysburg College, 1987), 5, 7.

10. Glatfelter, 7-13. Samuel Gring Hefelbower, *The History of Gettysburg College, 1832-1932* (Gettysburg: Gettysburg College, 1932), 8-9. Hefelbower was president of the college from 1904 to 1910. The political need of these new colleges to curry favor with various constituencies is shown also by the fact that they were named after John Dickinson and Benjamin Franklin, both presidents of the Supreme Executive Council of Pennsylvania and both Quakers. The Franklin College Board, furthermore, was by charter divided: one-third Reformed, one-third Lutheran, and one-third of other denominations. The Reformed, however, informally dominated the undertaking.

11. Gould Wickey, *The Lutheran Venture in Higher Education* (Philadelphia: Muhlenberg Press, 1962), 24.

12. Only in 1832 would English-speaking Lutherans build Christ Church in Gettysburg, to which the Gettysburg College community joined itself for worship. It was called "the English Church."

13. Milton Valentine, who was then president, "History of Pennsylvania College," in *The Pennsylvania College Book, 1832-1882*, ed. E. S. Breidenbaugh (Philadelphia: Lutheran Publication Society, 1882), 8.

14. Glatfelter, 32. This is Schmucker's own account of his presentation.

15. Valentine, "History of Pennsylvania College," 4. Valentine explained fifty years later: "The institution is, therefore, non-sectarian, as are most American colleges established under church auspices, the denominational relation expressing only the fact that the College has been

organized and is carried on under the special patronage of the Lutheran Church, and for the purpose of bearing part in the work of the higher Christian education."

16. Valentine, "History of Pennsylvania College," 54, 63.

17. Hefelbower, 273. See also Wentz, 73ff., 137ff.

18. Valentine, "History of Pennsylvania College," 61.

19. It would be another half-century before its official name would be changed to Gettysburg College.

20. Glatfelter, 383ff.; Harold A. Dunkelberger, "Gettysburg College and the Lutheran Connection: An Open-Ended Story of a Proud Relationship," *Gettysburg Bulletin* 66, no. 5 (December 1975): 6.

21. Glatfelter, 392.

22. Published as a brochure by the board of trustees, 1892.

23. F. V. N. Painter and S. A. Ort, "Our Educational Institutions," in *The First General Conference of Lutherans in America, held in Philadelphia, December 27-29, 1898: Proceedings, Essays, and Debates* (Philadelphia: General Council Publication Board and Lutheran Publication Society, 1899), 94-104, 105-15. Of the two, Professor Painter is considerably more sober about current realities than his administrative colleague President Ort.

24. Nearly half of the Lutheran colleges had less than 50 students, and some enrolled less than 25. That year Gettysburg had 185 degree-seeking students, and it conferred thirty-three degrees.

25. Joseph Eugene Rowe, "The Administration of Dr. Hefelbower, 1904-1910," in Hefelbower, 285. Ex-president Hefelbower, the author of the college's centennial history, invited Rowe to contribute the chapter on his own incumbency.

26. Glatfelter, 467-68.

27. Glatfelter, 431-37. Nearby Dickinson College, which had begun as Presbyterian in 1783 and then converted to Methodism in 1833, reported itself as nonsectarian in order to qualify for the Carnegie funds (1907): Hefelbower, 45; Glatfelter, 448.

28. "A Report by the Religious Activities Committee," 2-3. The Religious Activities Committee was a faculty group which filed their report in May 1959; it is now found in the Gettysburg College Archives (GCA) as an appendix to the Minutes of the 12 December 1961 meeting of the Board of Trustees. The report, 4-5, offers a survey of contemporary theological opinion on church-college relations, framed entirely within the polarities of control or autonomy:

> It seems fair to say that the principal emphasis in their thinking and in their recommendations has been upon the necessity that the Christian interests within colleges and universities exert their influence through the framework of free inquiry and scientific spirit that is the basis of the academic enterprise. Although there is agreement that religion should play a larger role in the academic life, it is thought that this role should be realized in terms of increased freedom and sympathy among faculty and between faculty and student and that it must not take the form of increased official sanction or preferment. There seems to be a general recognition — probably part of the impact of "tension" theology upon Christian thought — that truth can best be served, in the academic context, by allowing full play to the diversity of thought which invariably marks such a community. It is believed that theology has insights that can be of value to the academic disciplines and that it should, in turn, make use of those findings, but that this interchange should not involve the imposing of presuppositions, methods, or conclusions.
>
> In summary, an objective view of the materials in this area discloses that the burden of purposes has been to argue for the autonomy of academic institutions, disciplines, and workers, and to find the distinguishing feature of a Christian college in the spirit of the community which constitutes it. There are a few voices which maintain the conservative

tradition that revealed religion possesses determinative jurisdiction in the methods and the content of the academic disciplines. But their influence does not seem significant.

29. Glatfelter, 476-78.

30. *Minutes of the Fourth Biennial Convention of the United Lutheran Church in America* (1924), 306 ([ULCA/1924]; proceedings of conventions hereafter cited in similar fashion); Glatfelter, 490 and 585, reports 628 students; Glatfelter, 908; ULCA/1952, 711, reports 1,231 in 1950-51; and ULCA/1954, 922, reports 1,171 in 1952-53.

31. R[obert]. J. Leonard, E. S. Evenden, and F. B. O'Rear, *Survey of Higher Education for the United Lutheran Church in America* (New York: Teachers College, 1929), 1:303.

32. Glatfelter, 490, reports forty faculty when Hanson arrived; this includes only those in the four regular ranks. He reports sixty-two at the end of his term of service, p. 807, but ULCA/1952, 711, and ULCA/1954, 922, conflated, report slightly more than ninety.

33. Leonard, Evenden, and O'Rear, 1:267; ULCA/1952, 711, and ULCA/1954, 922. Included in his study of the ULCA colleges in 1929 was the repeated recommendation by Leonard that "Attention should be called to the dangers incident to the process of inbreeding, due to the tendency to appoint to the faculty too large a proportion of Lutherans and graduates of Lutheran colleges." Leonard, Evenden, and O'Rear, 2:35.

34. Glatfelter, 438. The story of Gettysburg College's endowment during Henry Hanson's tenure is indeed strange. The first review of the college's books by an external auditor in 1924 reported an endowment of $751,467.44, while the 1952 audit reported the endowment at only $472,847.00. Throughout the Hanson presidency the college regularly covered its arrears by borrowing, though at the end of his presidency Hanson himself was earning a substantial salary.

35. Thus Glatfelter, 759. ULCA/1952, 710, and ULCA/1954, 920, report $487,000 in 1951 and $522,000 in 1953.

36. 1992 Higher Education Trends Analysis: Colleges and Universities, Division for Higher Education and Schools, Evangelical Lutheran Church in America, V:K.3 (hereafter cited as ELCA/1992).

37. ELCA/1992, I:B, E. In 1992-93 this had declined to 8.6 percent.

38. *Gettysburg College Catalog, 1992-93;* ELCA/1992, I:L.2, reports 155 full-time faculty. Though the proportion of females and various minorities of color and language is annually reported, the representation of Lutheran or other religious preference has not been reported, or perhaps recorded, since the formation of the Lutheran Church in America in 1962, at which time Lutherans were declining to one-third of the Gettysburg faculty. This present estimate is an extrapolation from the fact that in the catalogue, 20 of the 161 faculty (12 percent) are identified as graduates of a Lutheran college.

39. In 1920 the church had directed its colleges, especially those like Gettysburg with self-perpetuating boards of trustees, to put themselves under the control of their sponsoring synods by amending their bylaws to allow the synods to elect their boards. Gettysburg's trustees declined to make any change. ULCA/1920, 74; Leonard, Evenden, and O'Rear, 3:198.

40. Robert J. Leonard, ULCA/1928, 399-400.

41. Leonard, Evenden, and O'Rear, 2:26-27.

42. "The Position of the Church College," ULCA/1930, 382-85.

43. Glatfelter, 710.

44. Dunkelberger, "Gettysburg College," 24.

45. Glatfelter, 710 n. 421. Glatfelter notes the apparent breach of the 1832 charter's prohibition of any religious test for faculty. The Minutes of the 6 June 1959 meeting of the Board of Trustees, 3, GCA, report intensifying resistance to compulsory chapel services on campus. After a faculty committee made an extensive presentation on the subject, Henry Hanson, who had remained a trustee after retiring from the presidency, wanly "expressed the hope that the basic ideology of Gettysburg College remains Protestant Christian."

46. Hanson, "Preface to Report to the Board of Trustees," 3 December 1934, with Board Minutes, 2, 4, 5, GCA. Elisions are not indicated.

47. Hanson, Board Minutes, 1 December 1936, 3-5, GCA. Dunkelberger, "Gettysburg College," 25, describing Hanson's oratorical propensities and magnetism, has said that he "rarely dealt with specific matters of financing, campus housekeeping, faculty and student problems, and the like, concentrating instead on macroideas and ideals." There are however two contraries to *specific: large* and *vague*. The passages cited here, which are typical, could not be said to present macro-ideas.

48. ULCA/1936, 205. In its next report the board saw its mission to "witness the reality of the living personal God," indicating "the reality of the spiritual," and teaching an ethic "that meets human needs." ULCA/1938, 258-59.

49. ULCA/1948, 469, 478.

50. *Proceedings of the Sixth Biennial Convention of the Lutheran Church in America* (1972), 600-601, 604, 609 ([LCA/1972]; convention proceedings hereafter cited in similar fashion).

51. This was understated, since one-fifth of these institutions did not respond to the survey.

52. ULCA/1938, 313-16. An earlier survey had shown that (1) less than half the students in the church's colleges were Lutheran, and (2) the enormous majority of Lutherans in college were in state or other independent institutions. This raised the question of purpose. A church executive observed that if the church wanted colleges to serve the church, it ought to move them to centers of Lutheran population. If, on the contrary, they had a primarily missionary purpose, then they ought to be moved as far as possible from Lutheran concentrations. As it was, they seemed to serve no religious purpose: the church was simply functioning as a civic servant. ULCA/1932, 108.

53. ULCA/1942, 364-65.

54. ULCA/1920, 260, 264. A modest annual subsidy from the General Synod to Gettysburg ($3,000) had been begun during President Hefelbower's administration. By 1918 when the General Synod was merged into the new ULCA, those subsidies had amounted to $38,700. The religion requirement seems never to have been enacted in the church's colleges.

55. Glatfelter, 545, 548, 549, 866. For years, religion courses at Gettysburg were entitled "English Bible."

56. *Minutes of the Sixteenth Annual Convention of the Central Pennsylvania Synod* (1953), 159 ([CPenn/1953]; proceedings of such conventions hereafter cited in similar fashion). See also Dunkelberger, "Lutheran Higher Education in the 1980's: Heritage and Challenge," *Papers and Proceedings of the 66th Annual Convention of the Lutheran Educational Conference of North America,* 1980, 26.

57. Board Minutes, 8 December 1931, 246-47, GCA. Glatfelter, 612, says the administration had already stopped enforcing the rule about two years earlier.

58. Glatfelter, 613-14.

59. Board Minutes, 20 May 1944, 161, GCA.

60. Dunkelberger, "Gettysburg College," 25; Glatfelter, 712; Dunkelberger, "Lutheran Higher Education," 26.

61. Glatfelter, 776.

62. Glatfelter, 795. Hanson's reference is to the original charter, which committed the college to be "a salutary influence in advancing the cause of liberal education."

63. Charles E. Glassick, quoted in "Wide Range of Goals Is Offered by New President," ed. Dan Mangan, *Gettysburg* 68, no. 2 (October 1977): 5.

64. Alexander Miller, *Faith and Learning* (New York: Association Press, 1960), 171.

65. Glatfelter, 861.

66. Johannes Knudsen, *The Formation of the Lutheran Church in America* (Philadelphia: Fortress, 1978), 74-77.

67. What Charles McCoy said of the colonial foundations was true of these nineteenth-

century colleges: they "were the product of a societal effort to serve the welfare of the whole community." "The Church-Related College in American Society," in *The Contribution of the Church-Related College to the Public Good,* ed. Samuel H. Magill (Washington: Association of American Colleges, 1970), 50.

68. Wickey, 72, 4. Wickey had been a college professor, president of ULCA's Carthage College, denominational executive from 1929 to 1958, then executive director of the National Lutheran Educational Conference (later the Lutheran Educational Conference of North America [LECNA]), a joint agency serving all the Lutheran churches.

69. Wickey, 130-32.

70. Martin J. Heinecken, *Christ and Culture in the Process of Education* (pamphlet) (Oneonta, N.Y.: Hartwick College, 1962).

71. CPenn/1964, 214-17.

72. LCA/1964, 506-11.

73. Edgar M. Carlson, *Church Sponsored Higher Education and the Lutheran Church in America* (New York: Board of College Education and Church Vocations, Lutheran Church in America, 1967), 57-58.

74. The idea of "chapel for credit" is not exclusive to Gettysburg. In the early 1950s the practice was begun at Aurora College in Illinois: William Bryan Adrian, Jr., "Changes in Christian Emphasis among Selected Church-Related Colleges in Illinois" (Ph.D. diss., University of Denver, 1967), 111.

75. Carlson, 16-17; Dunkelberger, "Gettysburg College," 30, spreads the figures for this as a peak year for Gettysburg College as an individual case; LCA/1968, 475.

76. LCA/1968, 476.

77. Carlson, 49.

78. William H. Jennings, "Some Observations on the Church-Related College in a Secular Society," *Liberal Education* 54 (1968): 513-20.

79. *The Mission of LCA Colleges and Universities: A Statement Prepared by the Council on the Mission of LCA Colleges and Universities* (New York: Lutheran Church in America, 1970). See also LCA/1970, 465ff.

80. CPenn/1970, 312-13.

81. CPenn/1985, 305. See also Dunkelberger, "Gettysburg College," 29.

82. Francis C. Gamelin, "Toward a Master Plan," LECNA/1971, 19.

83. Gamelin, "Toward a Master Plan," 40, 47, 65. Gamelin reports that he had once proposed to the LCA presidents that their colleges form a consortium, "but the most telling criticism was that the common characteristic linking these particular colleges would be Lutheranism, a sectarian identity in an ecumenical time" (p. 66). Gettysburg since 1969 was a member of the Central Pennsylvania Consortium, along with Dickinson, Franklin and Marshall, and Wilson Colleges, which had been effectively disaffiliated from their respective churches: Methodist, Reformed, and Presbyterian.

84. Minutes of the Annual Convention of the Maryland Synod, 1971, 138-41 ([MD/1971]; such conventions hereafter cited in similar fashion); MD/1972, 95.

85. MD/1971, 139.

86. CPenn/1973, 207-17.

87. Dunkelberger, "Gettysburg College," 31.

88. CPenn/1973, 226-27.

89. Dunkelberger, "Gettysburg College," 31. The constitution adopted at the creation of the LCA did not require, as some of its constituent synods did, that the boards of its colleges be composed exclusively of Lutherans: Adrian, 81.

90. Francis C. Gamelin, *Church-Related Identity of Lutheran Colleges, A Report to the Commission on the Future of the Lutheran Educational Conference of North America* (Washington: LECNA, 1975), 3. The other styles were: "Church Vocations Colleges," "Church Colleges," "Bible-Centered Colleges," and "Christian Colleges."

91. Gamelin, *Church-Related Identity,* 14-15.

92. Gamelin, *Church-Related Identity,* 45. Gamelin's conclusion, p. 49, was grim for LCA schools:

> A large majority of both Lutheran church members and college leaders expect Lutheran colleges to serve primarily the church's educational needs ("Church Colleges") or broader constituencies from an open Christian stance ("Christian Colleges"). The fate of non-affirming "Church-Related Colleges" appears dim with respect to church support, financial or psychological.

93. Charles R. Bruning, *A Review of the Literature: Relationships between Church-Related Colleges and Their Constituencies* (New York: Department for Higher Education/Division for Mission in North America/Lutheran Church in America, 1975), 23-24. He quotes Charles S. McCoy, *The Responsible Campus: Toward a New Identity for the Church-Related College* (Nashville: Board of Education of the United Methodist Church, 1972).

94. *A Statement of the Lutheran Church in America: The Basis for Partnership between Church and College* (New York: Division for Mission in North America/Lutheran Church in America, 1976), 5. The chair of the drafting committee was Rev. Franklin D. Fry (not to be confused with his father, Franklin Clark Fry, who served the church as bishop). The committee included C. Arnold Hanson, Gettysburg's president and the only link with the committee that had written the 1970 "Mission" statement.

95. *The Basis for Partnership,* 4.

96. LCA/1976, 458. Thus one scholar, in his assessment of how an LCA-related college had maintained its identity through several crises of abrupt change, could admit that he had left aside any consideration of its church relationship. William Albert Rowen, "The Emerging Identity of Wagner College" (Ed.D. diss., Indiana University, 1972), 109-10. In a recent bid to retain its character, in 1971 Wagner would remove all curricular requirements from its curriculum save that no more than 60 out of 128 credits be required in one's major subject (75 credits in science). "It remains to be seen just how strong an identity [the religion] department will retain. . . . This curriculum is open in that a student can now graduate from the college without ever completing a required course outside his major area" (p. 86). Walter Langsam had been Wagner's president before succeeding Henry Hanson at Gettysburg in 1952.

97. *The Basis for Partnership,* 6.

98. Richard W. Solberg and Merton P. Strommen, *How Church-Related Are Church-Related Colleges?* (New York: Board of Publication, Lutheran Church in America, 1980), 57. This is the final report on the study first reported above.

99. Merton P. Strommen, "Images and Expectations of LCA Colleges," LECNA/1977, 8-19. His own conclusion is wholly sentimental: "In spite of these warning signs that ought not be ignored, I find the study encouraging because it clearly shows an overwhelming desire to establish closer ties between college and church."

100. CPenn/1977, 273.

101. Glatfelter, 861-65.

102. "Statement of Partnership between the Central Pennsylvania Synod of the Lutheran Church in America and the Institutions of Higher Education Related to It: Gettysburg College and Susquehanna University," CPenn/1981, 232ff., 343, 351.

103. CPenn/1982, 351-52; CPenn/1983, 257, 327-30, 333-37, 344, 346-47, 367-77. That year Susquehanna University, in its report to the synod on its institutional purpose, functions, and programs, stated:

> As a church-related college, Susquehanna plays an important role in values development, life-style choices and career decisions for young people. What makes the church-related college unique is not the articulation of these tasks, for all colleges face them, but the

climate and community that is created at a college founded and informed by the Judeo-Christian tradition.

CPenn/1983, 343.

104. MD/1983, 158-64, 269. The statement is specifically characterized as a "description," not a commitment. Two years later Gettysburg successfully negotiated an amendment which enjoined church and college to strive for more ethnic and racial diversity on campus. MD/1985, 238.

105. "ELCA Mission Statement for Colleges and Universities," April 1991, text provided by the Division for Higher Education and Schools, ELCA. In 1990 the ELCA also began to elaborate a more general "Mission Statement for Education" at all academic levels.

106. Statistics provided by the Gettysburg College Business Office. Of this contribution, 23 percent came from the four sponsoring synods (Allegheny, Delaware-Maryland, Lower Susquehanna, Upper Susquehanna) and 77 percent from the ELCA.

107. See,e.g., CPenn/1966, 243.

108. The two large national insurance companies, the Aid Association for Lutherans and the Lutheran Brotherhood, have regularly offered grants to the dependents of their policyholders enrolled at Lutheran colleges.

109. ELCA/1992, III.2.

110. *The Lutheran Status of Pennsylvania College,* 8; Dunkelberger, "Gettysburg College," 8; Glatfelter, 900-904.

111. As have many of the previously LCA colleges in their catalogues. This right to consider religious factors was also enjoyed in the face of a Pennsylvania state law governing college admissions; Board Minutes, 12 December 1961, 4, GCA.

112. Glatfelter, 985.

113. ELCA/1992, III:G; CPenn/1972, 206; CPenn/1985, 308.

114. Glatfelter, 493.

115. LCA/1950, 766.

116. Board Minutes, 12 December 1961, Appendix, 8, GCA; Glatfelter, 808-9.

117. C. A. Hanson, Board Minutes, 12 December 1961, 5, GCA; Gould Wickey, ULCA/1956, 995. In 1962, when Wickey had moved from ULCA to LECNA, which served all Lutheran churches, his view was of sterner stuff: "Faculty Members, all of whom should be Christian, have a prior commitment to Jesus Christ, and have a duty to witness for him through all their activities and human relations." Wickey, *Lutheran Venture,* 81; *Gettysburg College Faculty Handbook,* CPenn/1963, 228; Edgar D. Ziegler, Gettysburg synodical trustee, CPenn/1963, 229.

The emergent situation at Gettysburg, in which an association with a specific church is replaced by vague emotive "values," resembles what a research visitation team reported about its LCA peer, Lenoir-Rhyne College in Hickory, North Carolina:

> Religious roots manifest themselves in faculty acceptance of the fact that the spiritual is important at Lenoir-Rhyne. The lack of having to conform to a dominant religious posture is viewed as positive. Faculty enjoy and respect the freedom that is associated with the opportunity to demonstrate or profess one's belief in accordance with their own personal faith. Although many referred to the tie to the Lutheran Church, the team did not really find that it was a specific denominational tie narrowly defined that sustained the sense of mission present, particularly among the younger faculty. However, the church relationship does provide the general values of caring and concern that appear to permeate the entire college. This shared sense of values allows faculty to focus on teaching in a secure environment, one in which they are comfortable.

> Ann E. Austin et al., *A Good Place to Work: Sourcebook for the Academic Workplace* (Washington: Council of Independent Colleges, 1991), 108.

118. This provision in the *Faculty Handbook* is pursuant to the similarly unusual "Preamble to the Bylaws," *Muhlenberg College Charter and Bylaws*, 7-8, now current but published without date. The tenor of the *Handbook* is congruent with the comment made several years ago by the college's director of church relations, that the Lutheran church is present more by "a vital faith than formal religion." Michael John McGovern, "The Significant Survival of Private Liberal Arts Colleges: A Case History Analysis of Resistance to Conditions of Decline" (Ed.D. diss., Lehigh University, 1986), 148.

119. Milton Valentine et al., Committee of the Board of Trustees, *Pennsylvania College and the Lutheran Church* (composed 1872, published 1879), 9, e.g., report that 56 percent of its students had proceeded thence to the seminary, but there is no mention of religious studies being important at the college.

120. Board Minutes, 6 June 1953, 6, GCA.

121. Glatfelter, 281-85, 548-49.

122. Gettysburg College *Catalogue 1992-1993*, 137. Some former LCA colleges present their religion departments as theological; others, as religious studies. But in some of the latter, despite the department's self-description, most of the courses offer critical exposition of the Christian religion.

123. One faculty veteran opines that in the Department of Religion there are now only one or two "in the Lutheran tradition."

124. Glatfelter, 334-38.

125. Board Minutes, 6 December 1960, Appendix: "Report of the Religious Program Committee," 11, GCA.

126. Glatfelter, 924-27, 970.

127. See ELCA/1992, passim.

128. Dunkelberger, "Lutheran Higher Education," 27. In 1955 one speaker at the annual LECNA meeting spoke of the fact that 2 percent of the students in Lutheran colleges were reporting no church affiliation as a "missionary opportunity": LECNA/1955, 9. But in those days the Lutherans who might do this missionary work constituted 40 percent of the students at LCA colleges, 75 percent at ALC, and 90 percent at LCMS.

129. Glatfelter, 32.

130. This notion of a Christian college that is not sectarian was not uncommon, especially in the slipstream of Pietism and rationalism. To illustrate: "Aurora College [Illinois] was founded [1893] and is supported by the Advent Christian Church and by other friends of young people to provide a Christian environment for a college education. Without being sectarian the college is concerned to maintain the best in Christian attitudes and practice on the campus" (*1947 Aurora College Catalog*, 10). Millikin University (Illinois) was founded (1901) by a philanthropist who stipulated that it must, to qualify for income from his trust, remain "Christian but not sectarian." Olivet Nazarene College (Illinois, 1909) stated in its *1947-1948 Catalog* that "While [it] is an institution of the Church of the Nazarene, it is not strictly sectarian." Two decades later, however, in the midst of an effort by the church to reclaim its colleges, a very different formulation emerged: "Nazarene colleges are sectarian and denominational in a healthy sense that the colleges must be uniquely Nazarene if they deserve their existence. Nazarene colleges are not community colleges with Christian overtones." Adrian, 105, 193, 59.

131. Valentine, *Pennsylvania College and the Lutheran Church*, 4.

132. An example of ardent optimism may be seen in Robert Benne, "Recovering a Christian College: From Suspicious Tension toward Christian Presence," *Lutheran Forum* 27, no. 2 (May 1993): 58-61. Presenting his own Roanoke College as a possible instance of reversibility in the trend to secularization, he instances determined administrators, a new requirement of "institutional fit" in faculty hiring, an increase in Lutheran staff, a thoroughly Lutheran religion/philosophy department, a central curricular requirement entitled "Values and the Responsible Life" (which "examines the major religious, moral and intellectual values of the West"), and strong chaplaincy

and choral music programs. Optimism must surely be dimmed, however, by the admission that the proportion of Lutheran students is quite low — 12 percent — "and probably always will be because of our location." And the faculty, hired in other times, "are disturbed by and suspicious of recent developments. They understandably resist them since they have been here under a different set of understandings. Most department heads still believe that religious considerations are and ought to be an irrelevant factor in faculty recruitment. There is no public faculty consensus that we should move in the direction we have been. Many are apathetic; a few hostile and alarmed." It may be an understatement to depict these latter facts as "challenges." Interestingly, a letter of encouragement from the chairman of the board of trustees was sent to all student applicants to the college for 1993. Among all Roanoke's attractive features that he itemizes, there is no word about its being Lutheran.

133. Solberg and Strommen, 89; James M. Unglaube, "The Church and Its Students: A Resource for the Colleges," LECNA/1981, 56-62. ELCA education executives now reckon, however, that while Lutheran colleges enroll only 5 percent of their church members who are of college age, they enroll 15 percent of those who actually go to college: James M. Unglaube, director, Colleges and Universities, Division for Higher Education and Schools, ELCA, to author, 18 March 1993; interview with the author, 11 September 1992.

134. *Reports and Records,* 1991 Churchwide Assembly, Evangelical Lutheran Church in America, 88 (hereafter cited as ELCA/1991). Also, e.g., MD/1971, 49. At its 1960 convention the ULCA membership was alerted to the fact that whereas in 1900 the enrollment in U.S. higher education was divided into 39 percent in state institutions and 61 percent in independent institutions, by 1959 the percentages had been reversed, to 58/42 percent, and would likely stand at 65/35 percent by 1970; LCA/1960, 989. As it turned out this warning was too optimistic: Elmer D. West and Charles J. Anderson, "Changing Public/Private Ratios in Higher Education," *Educational Record* (fall 1970): 347-50.

135. German Pietism had laid a heavy emphasis upon ethical activism instead of controvertible theology. In this it was a forerunner of the "Americanist Lutherans." Luther's doctrine of the two kingdoms, however, which by awarding public life to the governance of the state had closed it off as a theater of operations for transformative moral endeavor under the aegis of the gospel, was largely ignored by the Pietists. This raises a question whether this doctrine, lifted up to prominence in the 1960s, actually meant much to the founders of the LCA colleges in the nineteenth century. See Kuenning, 13-31.

136. California Lutheran University was cosponsored by the LCA. The ALC also has one affiliated two-year college which is not directly examined in this study: Waldorf (1903) in Forest City, Iowa.

137. Augustana College (South Dakota) *Catalogue, 1992-1994,* 9. The Texas Lutheran College *Bulletin, 1992-1993,* 4, states:

> Texas Lutheran College is a community of learning and a community of faith.
> As a community of learning, the college stresses the liberating potential of the disciplined pursuit of academic excellence within the context of academic freedom. . . .
> As a community of faith, the college celebrates the liberating power of gospel as applied to the whole of human life. . . .
> As an institution of the church, the college provides an education in the arts and sciences which is given perspective by the Christian faith. . . .
> In working to bring learning and faith into intimate relationship, Texas Lutheran College is discovering afresh that each can strengthen, clarify and enrich the other. . . .
> Adopted by the faculty in 1967; revised in 1979.

138. Susquehanna University *General Catalogue, 1992-1993,* 3.

139. St. Olaf's School *Catalogue 1887-1888,* quoted in *Integration in Christian Higher*

Education, by the St. Olaf College Self-Study Committee, ed. Howard Hong ([Northfield]: St. Olaf College Press, 1955), 2 (Appendices): 4, St. Olaf College Archives (SOCA).

140. Hong, *Integration in Christian Higher Education,* 2 (Appendices): 6, SOCA.

141. St. Olaf *College Catalog, 1992-1993,* 3. The text bears this rubric: *"(Approved by the St. Olaf faculty in 1987 and the opening paragraph adopted, as a shorter version, by the Board of Regents that same year)"* (one hundred years after college instruction had begun).

142. C. A. Mellby, *St. Olaf College through Fifty Years: 1874-1924* (Northfield: n.p., 1925), 79. This was reduced to only 20 percent at the end of World War II, but as recently as two decades ago the ALC still contributed more than $5 million, or 35 percent of its gift income (though only 3 percent of its budget), to its colleges: Norman Dale Fintel, "The Attitudes of Lutherans toward Church Colleges" (Ph.D. diss., University of Minnesota, 1972), 3, 34.

143. Interview with President Melvin D. George of St. Olaf College, 22 October 1992.

144. Joseph M. Shaw, *History of St. Olaf College: 1874-1974* (Northfield: St. Olaf College Press, 1974), 349; Fintel, 20; Board of Regents Minutes, 20-22 August 1969, "Report of the President," 2, SOCA. The college story which follows is much indebted to the Shaw and Mellby histories.

145. Fintel, 6. Also, ALC clergy had tended to more liberal attitudes than their laity (p. 109).

146. "Bad News from St. Olaf," *Lutheran Commentator* 5, no. 2 (September/October 1991): 1. See also "Back to School: Are Lutheran Colleges Lutheran?" *Lutheran Commentator* 6, no. 2 (September/October 1992): 1. This view of the curricular change is disputed by many faculty who are solicitous for St. Olaf's Lutheran identity.

147. Mellby, 11-15; Shaw, 19, 79, 92. College publications advertised from the first that St. Olaf was designed to serve young Norwegians. Then in this century the emphasis shifted to Scandinavians; later to Scandinavians and those of North European ancestry; later, simply to those of North European ancestry (1937-53). Today it "remains dedicated to the high standards set by its Norwegian immigrant founders." See various editions of the *College Catalog.*

148. Gettysburg had allowed women to enroll and graduate as of 1881, but their status was never regularized and female students disappeared until a women's division on (more or less) equal terms with men was opened in 1935. Glatfelter, 302-4, 537-38, 586-94.

149. On the liberal arts curriculum see Shaw, 13, 16-20. Throughout the early decades of the twentieth century, however, the *College Catalog* stated: "The chief and special object of this school is to prepare young men for taking up the study of theology, in order that they may become ministers or missionaries of the Church." Hong, *Integration in Christian Higher Education,* 2 — Appendices: 5, SOCA.

150. Shaw, 17.

151. Shaw, 32-42; Richard W. Solberg, *Lutheran Higher Education in North America* (Minneapolis: Augsburg, 1985), 225-28.

152. Mellby, 28; Shaw, 68-71. See E. Clifford Nelson and Eugene L. Fevold, *The Lutheran Church among Norwegian Americans,* 2 vols. (Minneapolis: Augsburg, 1960).

153. Thorbjörn Mohn to Knute Nelson (later governor and senator), Shaw, 88.

154. Mellby, 46-50.

155. Shaw, 229. The detractor was a partisan of Augsburg Seminary.

156. William C. Benson, *High on Manitou: A History of St. Olaf College, 1874-1949* (Northfield: St. Olaf College Press, 1949), 229.

157. Erik Hetle, *Lars Wilhelm Boe: A Biography* (Minneapolis: Augsburg, 1949), 99.

158. *St. Olaf College Catalog, 1944-1945.*

159. Shaw, 584.

160. *The Identity, Aims, and Objectives of St. Olaf College: Report of the Steering Committee of the Centennial Study* (hereafter cited as *Centennial Study*), Harold Ditmanson, chairman, Part III: Explanations, Appendices (4 September 1973), 3, SOCA. In Part I, 4, the study claims that approximately two-thirds of the students come from middle- and upper-middle-class families,

an abrupt drop from the 90 percent reported only four years earlier. Possibly the norms for such class assignment were fluid.

When reporting the drop in Lutheran student numbers, and claiming that this was not one of the forms of diversity and heterogeneity which the college sought, the study asserts:

> Religious tests or quotas for students are not recommended and we should find abhorrent a situation in which persons did not challenge religious and moral assumptions or did not examine critically their ultimate values. But serious dialogue about the religious and moral dimensions of life and learning is difficult to sustain in institutions with too great diversity. We have urged, moreover, that St. Olaf see its relationship to the Church as a primary factor in defining its task in higher education. The relationship of church and college requires that we not serve only persons from the church constituency. Nevertheless, the College should sustain a special relationship to its constituency, in particular by seeing the education of its ablest youth as a special responsibility and opportunity. (pp. 1-2)

While expressing concern about the decline in Lutheran enrollment, the committee clearly recommends that the college leave the matter to market forces, in the desire that St. Olaf will nevertheless be chosen by the "ablest" young Lutherans, who will inevitably be the children of those who can afford it. Anent the remark that St. Olaf served the most affluent clientele among the Associated Colleges of the Midwest group, Shaw, 442-43, also reports that among those colleges St. Olaf was manifestly the most "church type" institution.

161. *Centennial Study,* III:16.

162. Alarmed at the drop in Lutheran attendance at its own colleges, the 1978 ALC General Convention mandated a serious discussion at its next biennial meeting. The result, submitted by its Division for College and University Services, can be found in two wan documents: "Church, College and Student: A Partnership for the 1980s" and "Life in Relationship: Colleges and the Church," Exhibits C and D, *Reports and Actions of the Tenth General Convention of the American Lutheran Church,* 1980 ([ALC/1980]; convention proceedings hereafter cited in similar fashion). Nothing produced by the LCA in this period exceeds the rhetorical vacancy of these statements.

163. *College Catalog, 1992-1993,* 11. A consultant's report submitted years earlier had recommended that the college recruit more aggressively for students among Lutherans beyond the local region, but the report was seen by neither the faculty nor the president, having been quashed by the administrator whose area was being criticized.

164. Benson, 231.

165. *Centennial Study,* 4-5; introduction by President Sidney A. Rand. The tone of the *Centennial Study* is a new one for St. Olaf. The church, despite loyal acknowledgment, is regarded as potentially intrusive though valuable as a supplier of students. It is warily and patronizingly described. Nowhere is there a comparable critique or wariness about the academic establishment, or worry about its inclinations to censorship or ideology.

166. *Centennial Study,* III:22-23. Here can be found the statement cited above, which the *Faculty Manual* adopted as the keynote of its standards for faculty evaluation.

167. *Centennial Study,* III:43-45, meanwhile had suggested that since the religious aspects of every discipline ought to be investigated, it should be done in all departments of the college whose offerings could be alternative means to fulfilling the religion requirement.

168. In 1973 the visitation team for North Central accreditation made this arch observation: "The presence of three required courses in religion listed among the general requirements led the team to question students about this requirement and found to our surprise, at least among the students queried, that students view these religion courses as being enlightened and enjoyable." Board Minutes, 23 August 1973, Exhibit A, p. 15, SOCA.

169. Edmund N. Santurri, "Theological Literacy at St. Olaf," address delivered to the St. Olaf faculty, spring 1990; also a memorandum to faculty colleagues under the same title, outlining the four components of theological literacy, dated 9 April 1990, SOCA. He notes that the college's

extensive admissions requirements (e.g., from three to four years of mathematics, four years of English and also of a foreign language, electives such as computer science, music, and geography) neither require nor apparently expect any preparation in theology, and that students are as ill prepared to study it as at any time in the college's history.

> The problem is also that they often harbor deeply entrenched convictions and attitudes about religion that impede serious theological study. Students typically come to St. Olaf with the view, encouraged by the secularity of our public realm, that religion is a private matter, a matter of undisciplined feeling or choice, a matter of mere opinion, a matter that does not admit of reasoned reflection. Religion in this view should not be talked about, thought about, at all outside of church and family, and many students resent having to face a variety of unsettling questions about their most cherished "theological" assumptions. . . . Imagine that in teaching college chemistry one were dealing with students who believed in and were existentially committed to the truth of alchemy.

Opponents, who had heard no theological sounds from the department for decades and noticed that most faculty recently appointed were in the "religious studies" mode, saw it simply as a bid for a larger department.

170. He ends with injunctions against temptation and against helping the news media sensationalize this as a lurid item. Clifford J. Swanson, "Report of the College Pastor," Board Minutes, 17 April 1961, 19-22. See also Shaw, 407.

171. Shaw, 572. Not all struggles over public morality ended so consensually. About the same time female students on campus mounted a persistent and enduring campaign on behalf of their freedom to smoke. Finally the desired rule change was issued. But then the sale of cigarettes in the bookstore was discontinued because of their danger to health. Shaw, 569.

172. Swanson, "Report of the College Pastor," Board Minutes, 26 August 1963, 15-23.

173. Swanson, "Report of the College Pastor," Board Minutes, 21 August 1970, Exhibit A, 11-12.

174. Swanson, "Report of the College Pastor," Board Minutes, 20 August 1971, Exhibit D, 15-18.

175. Swanson, "Report of the College Pastor," Board Minutes, 23 August 1973, Exhibit B, 18-20. A faculty member who had ongoing conversations with Pastor Swanson about these preoccupations of his noted that he was not one to show this dismay publicly, though he would express it fully to the president and board. He told the professor he thought it inappropriate to deplore the erosion of Christian life within the hearing of students. "When you hang up that much crêpe, they will begin to smell the corpse."

176. *College Catalog, 1963-64,* 6. This text was entirely new that year.

177. *College Catalog, 1987-88,* 4. This text was said to have approval by the faculty and board of regents.

178. Shaw, 359. On the growth of the college during his presidency, see Benson, 228ff.

179. Hetle, 101. This is the sort of chapel talk that inclines one to imagine the speaker with a cigar.

180. Granskou cultivated the Ford Foundation effectively and sponsored the Hong committee and its self-study publication, *Integration in the Liberal Arts College,* which was to enjoy national influence. See Russell Thomas, "Will the Liberal Arts Colleges Return to Liberal Education? II. Integration and the Liberal Arts Curriculum," *Journal of General Education* 10, no. 1 (January 1957): 30-36. This was said in tribute to Granskou at his retirement banquet:

> We shall remember, in gratitude, and shall seek to carry forward, for one, your stalwart defense of the intellectual freedom of a church college. You are a man unafraid of ideas, and while some may point with pride to the buildings erected during your presidency, I think your lasting contribution will be that in the history of the college you will be remembered as the builder of that other side of the college — the intellectual side. . . . A

spirit of intellectual freedom prevails, the attitude that a Christian college is completely unafraid of truth from any quarter. . . . It led a Harvard president to say in your presence at a meeting with many other college and university presidents that he had never in his experience encountered a college that was both a strong church institution and strong academically — with one exception: St. Olaf College.

Board Minutes, 26 August 1963, R/4-7.

181. Granskou, "Christian Higher Education — A Major Missionary Enterprise" [1954?], Granskou Papers, SOCA.

182. See also by Granskou, "The Place of Christian Higher Education in the Church, an Occasional Paper of the Department of Christian Education of the Evangelical Lutheran Church" (Minneapolis, 1957); "The Purpose and Character of Christian Education," 1962; Granskou Papers, SOCA.

183. Shaw, 510-11. As president he would speak up strongly against moves by his successor in the church to use its subsidy as a lever of influence over the colleges. See Rand, "Some Comments regarding the Addendum of the Staff Report to the Board of College Education for October 25-27, 1965," Rand Papers, SOCA.

184. Draft for address to the faculty, September 1963, 3-4, Rand Papers, SOCA.

185. Draft for address to the faculty, 1966, 9, Rand Papers, SOCA. Compare his later remarks:

St. Olaf is a college of the Church. Its objectives are aligned with those of the Church. We believe in life as the gift of God. We believe human life is understood best when it is viewed as the object of the concern of a God whose love has led him to redeem a straying mankind through the life and death of one who is called His Son, Jesus Christ. We work here in an educational climate given a special quality by this view of man and the world.

Draft for address to the faculty, 1968, 12.

What can a church-related college in a little town in Minnesota possibly have to do with the world and its problems? Nothing — unless that college finds a way to immerse itself in the tragedies and the triumphs that beset man in our time and to bring to the full consciousness of those who study here that this is God's world, not ours, and that we have a divinely appointed role to make this a better place to live.

Draft for address to the faculty, 1969, 14.

In this college the goals and purposes, at least in their basic principles, hold firm. I refer here to the view of man as a creature of God, imperfect yet improvable, and of the surpassing goodness of God, known to us daily in blessings large and small, and summed up for us in the creative, redemptive presence we know as Jesus Christ. . . . We would offer, not paternalistically or pontifically, but simply out of a concern for the truth as it is in the human condition, that education is a sacred business which cannot be separated from man's concern for the ultimate meaning of man and his existence.

Draft for address to the faculty, 1970, 17.

186. Memorandum for the ALC Board of College Education, 1969, 1, Rand Papers, SOCA. In 1965 he put it this way to a Lutheran audience: "Theologically we live in a day of emphasis on the 'secularizing of the faith.' We are being told that the Church has too long been apart from life, a secluded haven for those who would escape a full involvement with the world. And we are astonished to live our Christian lives in the world through 'involvement' rather than 'withdrawal.' . . . Perhaps we have also seen the Church only as opposition [to the state] and have succeeded in alienating from the church large segments of our people so that finally religion is rejected and only a general cultural spirit is embraced." "Ways through the Wall," first of four lectures on church and state at the Luther Academy in Dubuque, 24 July 1967, 4-5, Rand Papers, SOCA.

187. Rand, "Educational Strategies for Social Change," Lina R. Meyer Lecture, delivered at LECNA, January 1970, Board Minutes, 20 March 1970, Exhibit A, 1, 2, 4, 5.

188. Rand, Draft of remarks prepared for delivery on campus: Board Minutes, 20 March 1970, Exhibit B, 17.

189. Shaw, 515.

190. *Centennial Study,* 4. In 1968, four to five years earlier than this was drafted, 73 percent of the St. Olaf faculty had been reported to be Lutheran.

191. Ditmanson was accustomed to speaking of the "new faculty" as the "swelling tribe of new barbarians."

192. William H. K. Narum, "The Distinctiveness of a College of the Church," *St. Olaf Magazine,* fall 1979, 2-4. A junior essayist, a St. Olaf honors undergraduate, took the more direct route: "A college with a relationship to the Christian church finds its meaning and motivation in its willful dedication to the task of preparing people for lives of active discipleship in the name of Jesus the Christ." Mark W. Gonnerman, "The Distinctiveness of a College of the Church," *St. Olaf Magazine,* winter 1980, 2-3. There was no need, after that, for him to discuss faculty appointments as a problem.

193. By-laws of St. Olaf College, revised July 1959, sec. 4.01. This same text was repeated in a revised version published in April 1987. The corresponding passage in the May 1930 revision had simply stated: "The teachers shall be elected or appointed from the membership of the Lutheran Church." Sec. 20.

194. Harold Ditmanson, Constance Gengenback, Lowell Johnson, James May, and Lynn Steen, "St. Olaf: A College of the Church," *St. Olaf Magazine,* March 1987, 1-7.

195. There is no uniformity throughout the former ALC colleges. Capital University, however, the easternmost and perhaps the most secularized of the campuses, takes the position "that it does not discriminate against anyone on the basis of religion, but that it regards its Lutheran affiliation as an important factor which may properly inform personnel as well as programmatic and policy decisions." J. Victor Hahn, vice president for legal affairs, Capital University, to the author, 2 February 1993. Capital no longer requires its president to be a member of the ELCA, and the present incumbent is not Lutheran. Capital is not the only institution to make this arguable claim: that it can use religion as a positive factor of appraisal but never as a negative factor.

196. Solberg, 119.

197. Solberg, 142-43.

198. Valparaiso University, the most academically successful foundation, is "related" to the church but not governed by it. Paradoxically, unlike the sponsored institutions it is given one Sunday each year for a special collection in all LCMS churches on its behalf. In the 1950s a seminary president speaking to the ELC convention is remembered to have grieved less that the colleges were moving away from the churches than that the churches were moving away from the colleges. "On one Sunday the Missouri Synod collects more money for Valparaiso University than our Church provides in a year for *all* of our colleges."

199. In 1947 the LCMS found itself the last major Protestant denomination to require college graduation for admission to its seminaries: Lutheran Church–Missouri Synod, Fifty-Second Regular Convention, 1975, *Workbook,* 283 ([LCMS/1975W]; references to conventions hereafter cited in similar fashion; references to workbooks include "W"). Twenty years later the "practical seminary" (then in Springfield) was still accepting high percentages of students without college degrees. LCMS/1975W, 294.

200. Solberg, 144.

201. Solberg, 292.

202. *LCMS Statistical Yearbook, 1960,* 219.

203. LCMS/1986W, 287-92.

204. This is powerfully argued by William Lehmann, Jr., "New Directions for Lutheran

Higher Education: Response to David Berger," *Lutheran Education* 127, no. 2 (November/December 1992): 88-95. See below, note 213.

205. Alfred J. Freitag, *College with a Cause: A History of Concordia Teachers College* (River Forest: Concordia Teachers College, 1964), 14-15. The story that follows is indebted to the Freitag history.

206. Today it is published at the university as *Lutheran Education* (as of 1947), now in its 128th volume, and is thought to be the oldest continuously published educational journal in the country. Freitag, 46-47.

207. Freitag, 80-87, 112-15, 152-53, 136, 162-63, 139-40.

208. Freitag, 33-34, 170-71, 190. This required declaration was abolished in 1981, by which time nearly 40 percent of the synodical college students were no longer intending church work: LCMS/1981, 194.

209. Freitag, 209-10.

210. Freitag, 217. Ninety-eight percent of the faculty that year were Lutherans.

211. Only shortly before, Albert Huegli, who had been teaching at River Forest since 1940 and had been dean of students and then academic dean (and would go on to become president of Valparaiso University), published a much-noticed article, "The Big Change and Its Challenge to the Church." Reviewing how drastically the church's environment and its own demographics had recently been altered, he urged that adaptation by the LCMS educational system would surely be necessary. "It is hard for any of us to accept the inevitability of change. We like to have the course of our lives continue in accustomed paths. The more rapid the changes in our environment, the more anxiously we cling to the known and the familiar. The Church, insofar as it is made up of human beings, resists change in much the same way." *Lutheran Education,* February 1957, 20.

212. Ross Stueber, office of parish services, LCMS headquarters, telephone interview with the author, December 1992. Another drastic change, but with less immediate bearing on the destiny of synodical colleges, has been the early childhood education movement, which brought preschoolers and kindergarten pupils in droves to Lutheran elementary schools, typically constituting 40 percent or more of their total enrollments and also diluting the LCMS representation among the teaching staff. Today hardly one-half of the elementary school pupils are from Lutheran homes.

213. In 1982 66 percent of the new students at Concordia Seminary in Saint Louis came from synodical schools; by 1991 the number had declined to 44 percent; a majority of students in both seminaries are state college graduates. David O. Berger, "Whither Higher Education in Missouri?" *Lutheran Education* 127, no. 3 (January/February 1992): 141; LCMS/1992, 118.

214. See Solberg, 344.

215. Paul G. Bunjes and Merle L. Radke, eds., *Changeless Change: Concordia College 125 Years, 1864-1989* (River Forest: Concordia College, 1989), 95, 111. Richard Walstra, CU controller, interview with the author, 14 May 1993.

216. Reports for the LCMS system stated that the general students had been declining in the college population since World War II, and in 1958-59 amounted to only 5 percent (and 20 percent in the synodical high schools); *Reports and Memorials:* Forty-Fourth Regular Convention, the Lutheran Church–Missouri Synod, 1959, 107-9 ([LCMS/1959RM]; reports and memorials to synodical conventions hereafter cited in similar fashion).

217. Berger, 125. See also the very astute comments by Lehmann, 91ff., who notes that whereas in earlier times a church vocation might have provided the only available educational subsidy for an LCMS youngster from a lower-income family, the advent of federal grants and loans now opened up a variety of subsidized career-training options.

218. Already in the early 1950s, although church worker enrollments were annually increasing ever so slightly, general education enrollments were increasing more rapidly and thus depressing their share of the student body: LCMS/1956RM, 139. Also, because the LCMS system has been sponsored for the sake of church workers, as well as because the church has not been in communion with other major Lutheran denominations, their reports on church membership

tend to be for their church separately, and then a separate statistic for "Other Lutherans." "Other Lutherans" have tended to compose about 5 percent of the student body. Statistics on the religious affiliation of students at LCMS institutions seem not to be available for the years when their decline set in, ostensibly because it came as something of a gradual surprise.

219. LCMS/1965, 212-21, 264-95.

220. J. A. O. Preus, "President's Report," LCMS/1975, 57-63 at 61; Preus, LCMS/1971, 51-61.

221. Preus, "President's Report," LCMS/1975, 58.

222. Adrian, 48. Today the LCMS membership is three-fourths urban, with little variation in the various districts. *Statistical Yearbook, 1990.*

223. Adrian, 35-37. The study also reports that down the road in Rock Island, students and faculty at Augustana, the Swedish LCA college there, were also challenging Lutheran traditions. Various faculty accounts: "The newer people, by and large, are much more open and ecumenical partly as a result of a deliberate recruiting policy of the president. He wants good scholars with inquiring minds who are open and ecumenical." "The faculty are more mobile, I think that more of them have been going to different kinds of universities for their own graduate work, they've rubbed shoulders with others of different backgrounds and traditions so that they are more flexible, pliable, or plastic." Adrian, 89-90.

224. Adrian, 39, 44-45, 41, 47.

225. "Non-LCMS Christians on Faculties," resolution passed by the LCMS Board of Higher Education Services, July 1987. This permission does not apply to theology appointments, and it does not authorize tenured contracts, though it permits repeating, "rollover" appointments in some cases.

226. By-Laws of the LCMS, II, F, 2.39.c, *Handbook of the Lutheran Church–Missouri Synod,* 1992 ed.; "Limitation on Academic Freedom," policy statement adopted by the Board of Higher Education, 8-9 March 1974.

227. The current subsidy for colleges requires about 10 percent of total annual synodical revenues: LCMS/1992W, 122, reports 10.33 percent in 1991-92, 9.71 percent in 1992-93. The subsidy for seminaries in those years amounted to 9.35 percent and 9.71 percent, respectively. Twenty years earlier 39 percent of the synodical budget had gone to higher education. LCMS/1975W, 292.

228. LCMS/1992W, 116-17.

229. LCMS/1992W, 270. A resolution adopted by the 1981 convention, noting the drop in subsidy from 45 percent to 25 percent of the colleges' budgets, wanly enjoined the church not to let the subsidy fall any further but declined to authorize the synod to borrow funds for that purpose: LCMS/1981, 191.

230. LCMS/1975, 60, 62; LCMS/1983, 80; LCMS/1989W, 124.

231. LCMS/1992W, 270, 118.

232. LCMS/1973, 185-86.

233. LCMS/1975W, 294-95.

234. LCMS/1975W, 271. The task force report issued the same year, using slightly different comparisons, reported the proportion had dropped "rather dramatically" in ten years from 1:107 to 1:300. LCMS/1975W, 286. In the decade after World War II this ratio had improved from 1:48 to 1:30. LCMS/1959RM, 105.

235. LCMS/1975W, 276.

236. LCMS/1979, 62.

237. LCMS/1971, 173-74.

238. LCMS/1973, 185-86.

239. LCMS/1975W, 280-302; LCMS/1975, 144-47.

240. LCMS/1979, 139-40.

241. LCMS/1983, 90-91; LCMS/1986W, 336-41, 419-40; LCMS/1986, 189-90.

242. LCMS/1992W, 265-68.

243. There is still widespread belief that this is so. Retired LCMS educator Albert Huegli notes: "While other denominations have permitted their colleges to drift away with only a minimal relationship to the church body or none at all, the Lutheran Church–Missouri Synod can take justifiable pride in its institutions as an integral part of its mission." But the LCMS colleges have been subject to a different kind of centrifugal force than, say, the LCA and ALC colleges. Huegli's prescription for the future is tighter central governance: "Their mission for the church can probably best be fulfilled at this time by drawing them closer together in a single clearly identifiable system." Lehmann, 86-87. See also President Emeritus Paul A. Zimmerman, writing anonymously: "A Climate for Change," in *Changeless Change,* 106-8.

244. Agenda, Board Meeting, 17 October 1989, I.A.5. Recommendation re: Change of Status and Structure from "College" to "University," Concordia University Archives (CUA).

245. Sara Kiske Dahms, director of undergraduate admission, interview with the author, 18 November 1992.

246. Registrar's statistical report, 20 October 1992, based on fall census. These figures somewhat overstate the Lutheran proportions, since they do not include winter and spring transfers and the adult degree-completion program, all of which tend to include heavy non-Lutheran majorities. Dahms to the author, 22 April 1993.

247. The category of "creed" begins to be restored in some versions of the nondiscrimination statement in 1978-79, and as of 1981-82 it is consistently included. The synodical policy statement appears in *LCMS Reporter,* 9 November 1992, 7; 14 December 1992, 8.

248. President Eugene L. Krentz to the author, 29 December 1992.

249. Donald Ray Just, "The Purposes and Performances of Lutheran Church–Missouri Synod Colleges: A Study of Four Cases" (Ph.D. diss., Claremont School of Theology, 1981), 199; see also 186.

250. "Concordia University Mission Statement," adopted by the Plenary Faculty and the Board of Regents, 1988 (while it was still a college), CUA.

251. "The Purpose, Mission and Scope of Concordia College," adopted by the Plenary Faculty and the Board of Regents, 1981, CUA. This document is approximately five times as long as the 1988 version.

252. Richard Baepler, "Nourishing the Saga," in Baepler et al., *The Quest for a Visible Saga* (Valparaiso, Ind.: Association of Lutheran College Faculties, 1977), 132-33.

253. Melvin D. George, president of St. Olaf College and vice president of LECNA, to the author, 15 April 1993.

CHAPTER 6

The Catholics

Catholics were slow to enter seriously into higher education, but they have come
to be the sponsors of the largest array of colleges and universities in the country.

1789	Georgetown University	Washington, D.C.
1808	Mount Saint Mary's College*	Emmitsburg, Md.
1814	Spalding University	Louisville, Ky.
1818	Saint Louis University	Saint Louis, Mo.
1830	Spring Hill College	Mobile, Ala.
1831	Xavier University	Cincinnati, Ohio
1839	Loras College*	Dubuque, Iowa
1840	Saint Mary-of-the-Woods College	Saint Mary-of-the-Woods, Ind.
1841	Fordham University	Bronx, N.Y.
1842	University of Notre Dame	Notre Dame, Ind.
1842	Villanova University	Villanova, Pa.
1843	College of the Holy Cross	Worcester, Mass.
1843	Clarke College	Dubuque, Iowa
1844	Saint Mary's College	Notre Dame, Ind.
1846	Saint Vincent College	Latrobe, Pa.
1847	College of Mount Saint Vincent	Riverdale, N.Y.
1847	Saint Francis College	Loretto, Pa.
1848	Rosary College	River Forest, Ill.
1850	University of Dayton	Dayton, Ohio
1851	College of Notre Dame	Belmont, Calif.
1851	Marian College	Indianapolis, Ind.

*Institutions sponsored by the See of Rome or the local see.

This essay was researched and written in 1995-96, and the statistics and facts it reports as current
derive from the latest sources then available.

1851	Saint Joseph's University	Philadelphia, Pa.
1851	Santa Clara University	Santa Clara, Calif.
1852	Loyola College in Maryland	Baltimore, Md.
1852	Saint Mary's University	San Antonio, Tex.
1853	Manhattan College	Riverdale, N.Y.
1855	University of San Francisco	San Francisco, Calif.
1856	Niagara University	Niagara University, N.Y.
1856	Seton Hall University*	South Orange, N.J.
1857	Saint John's University	Collegeville, Minn.
1858	Barat College	Lake Forest, Ill.
1858	Saint Bonaventure University	Saint Bonaventure, N.Y.
1859	Benedictine College	Atchison, Kans.
1860	Quincy University	Quincy, Ill.
1863	Boston College	Chestnut Hill, Mass.
1863	La Salle University	Philadelphia, Pa.
1863	Saint Mary's College of California	Moraga, Calif.
1868	Holy Names College	Oakland, Calif.
1870	Canisius College	Buffalo, N.Y.
1870	Loyola University of Chicago	Chicago, Ill.
1870	Saint John's University	Jamaica, N.Y.
1871	Chestnut Hill College	Philadelphia, Pa.
1871	Christian Brothers University	Memphis, Tenn.
1871	Ursuline College	Pepper Pike, Ohio
1872	Saint Peter's College	Jersey City, N.J.
1873	College of Notre Dame of Maryland	Baltimore, Md.
1877	Mount Mary College	Milwaukee, Wis.
1877	Regis University	Denver, Colo.
1877	University of Detroit Mercy	Detroit, Mich.
1878	Creighton University	Omaha, Nebr.
1880	U. del Sagrado Corazon	Santurce, P.R.
1881	Incarnate Word University	San Antonio, Tex.
1881	Marquette University	Milwaukee, Wis.
1882	Saint Ambrose University*	Davenport, Iowa
1883	Seton Hill College	Greensburg, Pa.
1884	Saint Francis College	Brooklyn Heights, N.Y.
1885	Saint Edward's University	Austin, Tex.
1885	Saint Mary's College*	Orchard Lake, Mich.
1885	University of Saint Thomas*	Saint Paul, Minn.
1886	John Carroll University	University Heights, Ohio
1887	Alverno College	Milwaukee, Wis.
1887	Benedictine University	Lisle, Ill.
1887	Catholic University of America*	Washington, D.C.
1887	Gonzaga University	Spokane, Wash.

1888	University of Scranton	Scranton, Pa.
1889	Saint Anselm College	Manchester, N.H.
1889	Saint Joseph's College	Rensselaer, Ind.
1889	Saint Leo College	Saint Leo, Fla.
1890	Dominican College of San Rafael	San Rafael, Calif.
1890	Saint Francis College	Fort Wayne, Ind.
1890	Viterbo College	La Crosse, Wis.
1891	Seattle University	Seattle, Wash.
1895	Mount Saint Clare College	Clinton, Iowa
1895	Our Lady of the Lake University	San Antonio, Tex.
1895	Saint Martin's College	Lacey, Wash.
1897	Trinity College	Washington, D.C.
1898	DePaul University	Chicago, Ill.
1898	Saint Norbert College	De Pere, Wis.
1899	College of Saint Elizabeth	Morristown, N.J.
1901	University of Portland	Portland, Oreg.
1903	Mount Carmel College of Nursing	Columbus, Ohio
1904	Assumption College	Worcester, Mass.
1904	College of New Rochelle	New Rochelle, N.Y.
1904	Saint Michael's College	Colchester, Vt.
1905	College of Saint Catherine	Saint Paul, Minn.
1907	Marymount College	Tarrytown, N.Y.
1908	Georgian Court College	Lakewood, N.J.
1909	Carroll College*	Helena, Mont.
1910	Rockhurst College	Kansas City, Mo.
1911	Loyola Marymount University	Los Angeles, Calif.
1911	Ohio Dominican College	Columbus, Ohio
1912	College of Saint Scholastica	Duluth, Minn.
1912	Divine Word College	Epworth, Iowa
1912	Loyola University, New Orleans	New Orleans, La.
1912	Saint Joseph's College	Standish, Maine
1912	Saint Mary's University of Minnesota	Winona, Minn.
1913	College of Saint Benedict	Saint Joseph, Minn.
1915	Marywood College	Scranton, Pa.
1915	Xavier University of Louisiana	New Orleans, La.
1916	Avila College	Kansas City, Mo.
1916	Our Lady of Holy Cross College	New Orleans, La.
1917	Fontbonne College	Saint Louis, Mo.
1917	Providence College	Providence, R.I.
1919	Emmanuel College	Boston, Mass.
1919	Siena Heights College	Adrian, Mich.
1920	College of Mount Saint Joseph	Mount Saint Joseph, Ohio
1920	College of Saint Rose	Albany, N.Y.

1920	Immaculata College	Immaculata, Pa.
1921	Rosemont College	Rosemont, Pa.
1921	Thomas More College*	Crestview Hills, Ky.
1922	Notre Dame College of Ohio	Cleveland, Ohio
1923	College of Saint Mary	Omaha, Nebr.
1923	Saint Mary College	Leavenworth, Kans.
1924	C. Misericordia	Dallas, Pa.
1924	Nazareth College of Rochester	Rochester, N.Y.
1925	Albertus Magnus College	New Haven, Conn.
1925	Gannon University*	Erie, Pa.
1925	Mount Saint Mary's College	Los Angeles, Calif.
1925	Trinity College of Vermont	Burlington, Vt.
1926	Mercyhurst College	Erie, Pa.
1927	Edgewood College	Madison, Wis.
1927	Regis College	Weston, Mass.
1928	College of Our Lady of the Elms	Chicopee, Mass.
1928	Mount Mercy College	Cedar Rapids, Iowa
1929	Carlow College	Pittsburgh, Pa.
1929	Marist College	Poughkeepsie, N.Y.
1930	Briar Cliff College	Sioux City, Iowa
1930	Lewis University	Romeoville, Ill.
1930	Mount Saint Mary College	Newburgh, N.Y.
1932	Saint Joseph College	West Hartford, Conn.
1932	University of Great Falls	Great Falls, Mont.
1933	Kansas Newman College	Wichita, Kans.
1933	Rivier College	Nashua, N.H.
1934	Salve Regina University	Newport, R.I.
1935	Silver Lake College	Manitowoc, Wis.
1936	Marian College of Fond du Lac	Fond du Lac, Wis.
1936	Marymount Manhattan College	New York, N.Y.
1936	Mount Marty College	Yankton, S.Dak.
1937	Cardinal Stritch College	Milwaukee, Wis.
1937	Madonna University	Livonia, Mich.
1937	Siena College	Loudonville, N.Y.
1939	Caldwell College	Caldwell, N.J.
1940	Barry University	Miami Shores, Fla.
1940	Iona College	New Rochelle, N.Y.
1942	Fairfield University	Fairfield, Conn.
1942	Felician College	Lodi, N.J.
1946	Anna Maria College	Paxton, Mass.
1946	Franciscan University of Steubenville	Steubenville, Ohio
1946	King's College	Wilkes-Barre, Pa.
1946	Le Moyne College	Syracuse, N.Y.

1947	College of Santa Fe	Santa Fe, N.Mex.
1947	Merrimack College	North Andover, Mass.
1947	University of Saint Thomas	Houston, Tex.
1948	Gwynedd-Mercy College	Gwynedd Valley, Pa.
1948	Catholic University of Puerto Rico*	Ponce, P.R.
1948	Saint John Fisher College	Rochester, N.Y.
1948	Stonehill College	North Easton, Mass.
1949	University of San Diego	San Diego, Calif.
1950	Bellarmine College	Louisville, Ky.
1950	Brescia College	Owensboro, Ky.
1950	Marymount University	Arlington, Va.
1950	Notre Dame College	Manchester, N.H.
1951	Calumet College	Whiting, Ind.
1951	Presentation College	Aberdeen, S.Dak.
1952	Dominican College	Orangeburg, N.Y.
1952	Saint Thomas Aquinas College	Sparkill, N.Y.
1954	College of St. Joseph	Rutland, Vt.
1954	Holy Family College	Philadelphia, Pa.
1954	Wheeling Jesuit College	Wheeling, W.Va.
1955	Chaminade University of Honolulu	Honolulu, Hawaii
1955	Molloy College	Rockville Centre, N.Y.
1956	University of Dallas*	Dallas, Tex.
1957	Cabrini College	Radnor, Pa.
1958	Alvernia College	Reading, Pa.
1958	Lourdes College	Sylvania, Ohio
1958	Walsh University	Canton, Ohio
1959	University of Mary	Bismarck, N.Dak.
1961	Saint Thomas University*	Miami, Fla.
1961	U. Central de Bayamon	Bayamon, P.R.
1963	La Roche College	Pittsburgh, Pa.
1963	Sacred Heart University*	Fairfield, Conn.
1964	Allentown College of Saint Francis de Sales	Center Valley, Pa.
1965	Neumann College	Aston, Pa.

This list includes the current domestic membership of the Association of Catholic Colleges and Universities (ACCU).[1] The mortality rate, especially in recent years, of Catholic colleges for women has left behind more institutions than some denominations have ever founded.[2]

The demography of Catholic higher education is in many respects unusual. First, the institutions listed above are more numerous than the roster of any other denomination. The Catholics can also still count a plethora of institutions that have failed, or seceded: many in the early years, and others still fresh in memory. But the Catholics have remained as active founders well into this century. Between 1920 and 1970 the Catholics founded seventy-six institutions that are still extant and belong to the ACCU. This was a time when all the mainline Protestant denominations we have studied opened only thirty-two. But then came the sharp reversal. One Catholic observer recalls that in the early 1970s the mortality rate (through closing or merger) was about one per week.[3]

Second, the Catholics began early. Because their numerical ascendancy came late, one neglects the fact that thirty-eight of the extant Catholic institutions were antebellum foundations; only the Methodists count that many that old. As we have seen and shall presently review, the early spread of Catholic educational institutions was one of the most vigorous incentives for their Protestant contemporaries in the nineteenth century.

Third, the Catholics were very late to accept coeducation.[4] Though most high schools sponsored by large parishes or dioceses were coeducational, Catholic fee-paying high schools sponsored by religious congregations were mostly single-sex until recently, and that pattern was the more easily continued in Catholic postsecondary schools because most of them were sponsored by religious congregations. Since the course of studies in most American women's colleges was not academically on a par with that on men's campuses (and could not have been until the 1890s), serious women began to realize that they would need to matriculate in the men's colleges to obtain the education they required. Female members of religious orders were the first to be admitted, to special summer sessions devised for them after Marquette offered one on the undergraduate level in 1909 and Notre Dame did so on the graduate level in 1918. Catholic University created a separately incorporated and located Sisters College and was offering instruction on both undergraduate and graduate levels in 1911. Laywomen saw no reason why they could not also be accommodated, nor could the male educators propose any, so they, too, came along. DePaul admitted women on a par with men in 1914, but only after World War II did men's colleges generally begin to become coeducational. By the 1970s virtually all the men's campuses had been integrated. Thus for a while there were more Catholic women's colleges than men's, though the latter enrolled more than four times the total number of students than the former, which were almost all quite small institutions. Economic necessity persuaded the women's colleges to follow suit, and they began to admit men. Yet today there are nearly twenty colleges which still pursue the calling — now more articulately and intentionally — of offering an education specifically for women.

Fourth, and perhaps least obvious, the Catholic colleges and universities have always been more independent from church authorities in their governance, finance, and intellectual initiative than any of the other traditions we have studied, including even the Congregationalists. Only fourteen of these schools are now sponsored by bishops or local dioceses. The presence of representatives from the dioceses on governing boards is rare and minimal. Direct contributions from

Catholic parishes or dioceses, except in those few instances of direct patronage, are mostly unheard of. The ties to the religious orders that have begotten and nurtured all but sixteen of these schools have — at least until recently — been strong, and although they have entailed variable accountability to the orders, the presidents have over the years enjoyed more autonomy, and more freedom from supervision, than their counterparts in Protestant institutions. We shall have occasion to notice that, until the last quarter-century, the role of governing boards has been virtually moot.

The case studies which follow deal with institutions sponsored by three of the most experienced Catholic teaching congregations: the Jesuits, the Ursulines, and the Brothers of the Christian Schools. They are drawn from three distinctive types: one is a major urban university; one was and in part is still a college for women; and one is a residential college in the countryside. All three began in the classical mode, offering academic training in the humanities and sciences, and all three ended up with a wide array of professional departments and schools.

More to the point at hand, all three fulfilled their mission to provide a Catholic education by Catholic teachers for Catholic young men and women. But all three — at practically the same time — suffered a drastic trauma in the late 1960s and almost without warning faced collapse. Their sponsoring orders suddenly proved unable to provide plentiful leadership or scholarship. Their traditional clientele began to go elsewhere. And their treasuries, after a brief and harried period of annual deficits, came within the touch of bankruptcy. Those are the tangible facts which explain the stubborn, energetic, and innovative struggles on each of the three campuses to survive, struggles which succeeded to the point where the schools can truly be said now to thrive. More significant and more interesting is the failure of nerve, the deviance of purpose, and the degradation of public discourse which have drawn these schools, severally, to abandon their calling to be ministries of the Catholic Church. The *who, what, when, where, why* of these stories are there to be seen, and will be spread upon the page. The *whether* — Might it might have happened otherwise? — each reader will have to ponder afterward. In doing so he or she will perhaps be drawn to wonder whether — and in what sense — the drive for self-survival is, as the anthropologists tell us, our most basic instinct, if the *who* or the *what* threatened is not the *who* or the *what* that survives.

BOSTON COLLEGE

Catholics have begotten a relatively large number of universities — as distinguished from colleges — which have succeeded in retaining their solidarity with the church even through modern times. The most impressive subset of these larger institutions is the work of the Society of Jesus, and it is all the more appropriate that we examine the Jesuit accomplishment as a most remarkable instance of Catholic higher education. The roster itself is impressive:

1789	Georgetown University	Washington, D.C.
1818	Saint Louis University	Saint Louis, Mo.
1830	Spring Hill College	Mobile, Ala.
1841	Fordham University	Bronx, N.Y.
1841	Xavier University	Cincinnati, Ohio
1843	College of the Holy Cross	Worcester, Mass.
1851	Saint Joseph's University	Philadelphia, Pa.
1851	Santa Clara University	Santa Clara, Calif.
1852	Loyola College in Maryland	Baltimore, Md.
1855	University of San Francisco	San Francisco, Calif.
1863	Boston College	Chestnut Hill, Mass.
1870	Canisius College	Buffalo, N.Y.
1870	Loyola University of Chicago	Chicago, Ill.
1872	Saint Peter's College	Jersey City, N.J.
1877	Regis University	Denver, Colo.
1877	University of Detroit Mercy	Detroit, Mich.
1878	Creighton University	Omaha, Nebr.
1881	Marquette University	Milwaukee, Wis.
1886	John Carroll University	University Heights, Ohio
1887	Gonzaga University	Spokane, Wash.
1888	University of Scranton	Scranton, Pa.
1891	Seattle University	Seattle, Wash.
1910	Rockhurst College	Kansas City, Mo.
1912	Loyola University, New Orleans	New Orleans, La.
1914	Loyola Marymount University	Los Angeles, Calif.
1942	Fairfield University	Fairfield, Conn.
1946	Le Moyne College	Syracuse, N.Y.
1954	Wheeling Jesuit College	Wheeling, W.Va.

In numbers of institutions, and even more in their endowments, enrollments, and faculty resources, the Jesuit colleges and universities would rank ahead of all but perhaps three denominations. One illustration of their singularity: whereas about 80 percent of American Protestants lived in rural locales, 80 percent of the Catholics were urban. The location of their respective colleges and universities reflects that geography. The Jesuits have been especially notable in founding schools in or near large metropolitan centers, thus allowing for large enrollments. By the end of the 1980s, there were more than a million alumni of American Jesuit higher education.[5]

The Catholic gentry in Maryland, encouraged by the numerous Jesuits who served them in the colony, often sent their sons (as did some English Catholics of the time) to the Jesuit school at Saint-Omer, in French Flanders. As the ebb and flow of penal laws permitted, they had opened a few academies of their own, as early as 1634 and throughout the eighteenth century. These schools drew on a pattern quite distinct historically from the antecedents of most of American higher education, which would be modeled after the English colleges, the Scottish universities, and later the German universities. Ignatius of Loyola had founded the Society of Jesus in order to convert the Turks to Christianity. But all ten of his first comrades were masters of arts of the University of Paris. Their educational ministry began in 1547 when Ignatius sent a large cadre of Jesuits to Messina in Sicily, where the city fathers had asked them to open a college. During his lifetime (d. 1556) they would found 37 schools in Sicily, Italy, Spain, Portugal, Germany, France, Bohemia, and Austria. Fifty years after Messina they were administering 245 educational institutions that reached to India, Japan, Cuba, Mexico, and the Philippines. Since their purpose was not only to enhance but also to share the Catholic faith, their pedagogy traveled without trauma from Europe to areas where non-Catholic students would matriculate. Also, it was their rule that all their schools had to be endowed or funded by the local community. Therefore Jesuit education was able to be offered without tuition charges, to accept students on merit rather than affluence, and thus to offer a unique forum for social integration.[6]

The colleges or universities took pupils after their elementary studies (including Latin and arithmetic), at about the age of ten, and gave them four years of preparatory schooling (first in grammar and then in rhetoric, poetry, and history). Three years of philosophy and mathematics followed, with the degree of bachelor of arts and then, after the writing and defense of a masterpiece, the degree of master of arts. Those proceeding to professional studies in divinity, law, or medicine might follow with four to seven more years of study before earning their respective doctorates. The Jesuits would typically — and, in America until this century, invariably — begin with a seven-year "college" comprising secondary and baccalaureate studies. As it turned out, this was nearly what the earliest American foundations, from Harvard onward, were doing at first, save that the Jesuit pattern came from their own Continental experience.[7]

The oldest permanent Catholic foundation in the United States was a Jesuit undertaking, though at the time of its founding there were no Jesuits in America. Clement XIV gave in to intense pressure from the largely Bourbon governments in Europe and suppressed the Society in 1773. The Jesuit system had been large, disciplined, and endowed, and thus able to dominate the educational scene in France, Spain, Portugal, and Austria. Its college and university buildings were confiscated, as well as the income-bearing properties that had allowed rich and poor to be educated together. In Maryland the former Jesuits jointly retained and administered their extensive properties until under the leadership of John Carroll they managed to incorporate under the State of Maryland as the Corporation of Catholic Clergymen. It was formerly Jesuit land which paid for the construction of an academy at "George-Town on the Potowmack." It was the sixteenth-century Jesuit *Ratio Studiorum* that would be the pattern for its studies. Former Jesuits served as its rectors until the restoration, with one exception: a French Sulpician who was eventually eased out.

Thus Catholic higher (or prospectively higher) education was established in the United States in 1789, the same year which saw the founding of the federal Republic, on a Jesuit plot of Maryland land whose sovereignty would be ceded to the District of Columbia.[8] One great difference which separated this new establishment from the great tradition of pre-1773 Jesuit higher education was financial. Georgetown was not endowed. Located in the midst of a Catholic population whose gentry were wealthy enough to send their sons there (Charles Carroll of Carrollton, John's cousin and a signer of the Declaration of Independence, was thought at the time to be the wealthiest man in the country), Georgetown could not offer much education to any but the gentry.

A recent survey of Jesuit education, to which the largest vowed religious community in the Catholic Church has traditionally committed a third of its manpower, counts more than 430 secondary schools in fifty-five countries, 36 professional schools, 24 colleges affiliated with state universities and 27 university residences, 59 universities and colleges, and 37 professional schools of philosophy or theology.[9] A galaxy that dense ought have a considerable gravity field, strong enough to bind its members more tightly among themselves than competing systems would be to attract them in other directions. Whether or not that be so will be a question to consider as we study one of the older and more developed Jesuit universities: Boston College.

Foundation

Whatever may be the case in later years, Catholics were not significant in Massachusetts in its early days. When the colonies claimed their independence, less than 1 percent of its inhabitants were Catholics. They were denied domicile itself in the Bay State until 1780, and public office until 1821, and they were taxed for Protestant schools until 1833. In 1847 John McElroy came to town. As a young immigrant he had joined a clandestine group of Jesuits at Georgetown.[10] Born in Ulster when it was a crime to admit Catholics to schools at any level, he was only slightly educated, and served nine years as a lay brother. When the decision was made to call him to the priesthood, his studies occupied a hasty two years. He went on to notable service as pastor, preacher, retreat director, theologian at a national gathering of bishops, and army chaplain. Sent, after the Mexican War, to start a college in Philadelphia, he failed there but moved on to Boston and tried again. It required ten years of struggle, involving repeated denials of a permit by the committee on public lands, for him to acquire a plot of land in the south end of Boston. Hostility to a Jesuit college was inevitable. Yale's Noah Porter had warned a few years earlier:

> To those who, like ourselves, look upon the Romish system as a system of dangerous and fatal error, as a monstrous incubus, stifling and oppressing the Gospel of Christ, no place can be so dangerous to the young as a Jesuit college, every exercise of which is made to assume a religious aspect, and to exert a religious influence.[11]

McElroy first built a large parish church, whose congregation, along with another he had served as pastor, produced an amazing amount of money from Irish pauper families to erect a large college for boys next door. Thus was Boston College (BC) chartered in 1863. The charter warranted John McElroy and his colleagues to "promote virtue and piety and learning," and bade that "No student in said college shall be refused admission to or denied any of the privileges, honors or degrees of said college on account of the religious opinions he may entertain."[12]

Harsh were the beginnings of the little school. Fr. McElroy was already in his eighties when he won the charter, and John Bapst, a Jesuit missionary who had been tarred, feathered, and almost burned alive by Know-Nothing stalwarts while serving in Maine, was responsible for actually getting the college open. Bapst was Swiss; his successors (by Jesuit custom the title of "rector," or religious superior of the local community, prevailed over that of "president" of a college, both being held concurrently) would hail from Virginia, Maryland, Ireland, New York, West Virginia, Italy, New Brunswick, and England (not until 1914 would Boston College have a Bostonian at the helm) — testifying to the international character of the Society of Jesus, but also to the helter-skelter way in which professional tasks were assigned. After incumbencies of only one, two, three, or four years, these early rectors might be sent off as parish priests, high school teachers, provincial superiors, or missionaries in the wilderness.

On opening day twenty-two boys came to enroll: not much of a consolation for those who were working to amortize a debt of $150,000. Others followed, but they brought little money and little talent.[13] Nevertheless, on prize day sixty-four prizes were awarded to forty-eight pupils. Saint Mary's parish, which helped finance the school's beginnings, had promised an annual subsidy of $3,000 but promptly withdrew the promise. That might have seemed a husky burden to carry, unless one realizes that this one congregation numbered twenty thousand souls.[14]

The Sodality of the Immaculate Conception, the Society of Saint Cecilia with its interest in sacred music, the Debating Society, and the Athletic Association all served the same interests as the missionary, arts, sporting, and literary societies on Protestant campuses of the time. There was a YMCA, and to be sure the "C" stood for Catholic. Unlike its counterparts at Protestant colleges, the Y sponsored by BC was organized by the Jesuits as a fraternal, literary, and recreational club for not-so-young Catholic professionals and working men throughout Boston and its suburbs: few had gone to Catholic schools, and very few to BC.[15] Enrollment at the college grew handily: those 22 pioneers had grown to 140 by 1870. But at one point in the early 1870s BC was unable to continue expanding its offerings and fill out its curriculum. Advanced coursework in philosophy could not be staffed, and the reaction on the part of the student body was a sizable exodus. Due largely to the strict standards of Robert Fulton, S.J., once dean and twice rector, the college waited thirteen years before it judged the curriculum and the standard of student performance strong enough to begin awarding degrees.

It is not clear how many non-Catholics took advantage of the welcome provided for them in the charter. The *Catalogue* promised they would "not be required to participate in any distinctively Catholic exercise, nor will any undue influence be exerted to induce a change of religious belief. But though no evidence of creed will be a bar to admission, evidence will be demanded of the candidate to prove a good moral character."[16] Fr. Bapst recorded that many non-Catholics had given generously to help reduce the debt.

Though Boston College followed the classical Jesuit curriculum and offered none but a humanistic education, in 1889 it changed from the Continental seven-year college to what was becoming the normal American "4 + 4" arrangement of a high school and college distinct from one another.[17] The secondary school was then free to highlight a two-track option, with a commercial course to attract pupils who would not be intending college afterward. Yet after the turn of the century it would be the Boston College High School with its strictly academic program that grew to be the largest classical high school in America.

BC Asserts Itself

The latter years of the century saw an increasingly crowded campus. Enrollment and finances improved steadily.[18] It was a thriving time, and BC benefited by having two successive rectors of special character: Timothy Brosnahan, S.J. (1894-98), and W. G. Read Mullan, S.J. (1898-1903).

Brosnahan was an articulate defender of the classical education which, as we shall later see more fully, sent every graduate out with a major concentration in philosophy. While the typical Protestant college followed the English tradition and placed Greek and Latin classics at the center of the B.A. curriculum, the Jesuits spent virtually all of the fourth year and part of the third on almost nothing but philosophy. The 1894 *Catalogue* carried a policy statement written by Brosnahan himself while still a philosophy teacher:

The System of Education

Education is understood by the Fathers of the Society, in its completest sense, as the full and harmonious development of all the faculties that are distinctive of man. It is not, therefore, mere instruction or the communication of knowledge. In fact, the acquisition of knowledge, though it necessarily accompanies any right system of education, is a secondary result of education. Learning is an instrument of education, not its end. The end is culture, and mental and moral development. . . .

Such studies, sciences or languages are chosen as will most effectively further that end. These studies are chosen, moreover, only in proportion as, and in such numbers as, are sufficient and required. A student who is to be educated will not be forced, in the short period of his college course, and with his immature faculties, to study a multiplicity of the languages and the sciences into which the vast world of modern knowledge has been scientifically divided. If two or more sciences, for instance, give similar training to some mental faculty, that one is chosen which combines the most effective training with the largest and most fundamental knowledge. . . .

The Jesuit system of education, then, aims at developing, side by side, the moral and intellectual faculties of the student, and sending forth to the world men of sound judgment, of acute and rounded intellect, of upright and manly conscience. And since men are not made better citizens by mere accumulation of knowledge, without a guiding and controlling force, the principal faculties to be developed are the moral faculties. Moreover, morality is to be taught continuously; it must be the underlying base, the vital force supporting and animating the whole organic structure of education. It must be the atmosphere the student breathes; it must suffuse with its light all that he reads, illumining what is noble and exposing what is base; giving to the true and the false their relative light and shade.[19]

What the Jesuits took for granted, however, was by no means an unchallenged vision in the latter years of the nineteenth century. Across the Charles River lay BC's venerable cousin, Harvard University ("sister" is too intimate a term for that relationship). She had been presided over for nearly thirty years by Charles W. Eliot, for whom the above disquisition would represent all that he had been leading Harvard away from. The Harvard Law School issued a list of approved colleges whose graduates (and no others) would qualify for admission as of 1896. Only one of the then twenty-two Jesuit colleges was on the list: Georgetown. Boston College and the College of the Holy Cross in Worcester both objected that their curricula were quite the same as at Georgetown. Harvard reconsidered and added them to its list. Then came Saint John's College (later Fordham) to complain, making the same argument. Harvard reconsidered once again in 1898, but this time decided to reject Fordham and to remove both BC and Holy Cross from the list they had so briefly graced.

Eliot's criticism emerged in more public and explicit form in the *Atlantic Monthly*. Harvard had dismantled the traditional matrix of required courses in favor of free electives. Having succeeded there (though not easily), Eliot expounded his theory with evangelical fervor to the nation's educators, and in 1899 thought it time to urge it upon high schools as well. The "supreme object" of education from first grade to university, he insisted, was "to implant an intellectual longing that will continue to demand some satisfaction long after school days or college days are over." Custom had obliged any pupil bright enough to aspire to college to confine himself or herself to the classical course in high school, thus stunting the imagination and zest for learning of youngsters whose minds would be more enlivened, say, by science or technology. Eliot deplored this system that treated certain subjects as obligatory: any subject well and thoroughly taught "in a way to inspire interest and train mental power, ought to count toward admission to college." Then, perhaps with a glance across the river to the teeming South End, he added:

> There are those who say that there should be no election of studies in secondary schools — that the school committee, or the superintendent, or the neighboring college, or a consensus of university opinion, should lay down the right course of study for the secondary school, and that every child should be obliged to follow it. This is precisely the method followed in Moslem countries, where the Koran prescribes the perfect education, to be administered to all children alike. . . . almost the only mental power cultivated is the memory. Another instance of uniform prescribed education may be found in the curriculum of the Jesuit colleges, which has remained almost unchanged for four hundred years, disregarding some trifling concessions made to natural science. That these examples are both ecclesiastical is not without significance. . . . Direct revelation from on high would be the only satisfactory basis for a uniform, prescribed school curriculum.[20]

The *Atlantic* rejected a response from Brosnahan: the magazine "did not encourage controversy." Instead, it published a tart rebuke to Eliot from Princeton. Brosnahan, knowing his place, as Boston Irish were wont to say (though he came from a gentle Virginia background), went into print in a Catholic magazine. The Jesuit pattern of studies, he admitted, was an old one — though precisely 300 years old, not the 400 casually assigned. In the present it could be found alike in Germany, China, the Philippines, Hungary, Syria, and England. But as new disciplines developed over time, they had been merged into the curriculum so that at Georgetown, for instance, half of the coursework was assigned to the more modern subjects. More time was being given to the natural sciences than was required at most colleges. "Every one knows that a young man may graduate and receive a college degree from Harvard without having given any time whatsoever during his four years to the study of natural sciences. And it would seem that in such cases Harvard has made no concession at all, either trifling or important, to natural sciences."

Without a basic curriculum a university might offer a broad array of studies, but if none be required of any individual, the education gained might be exceedingly narrow. Actually, Brosnahan wrote, if the Jesuits were out of date, it was not by 400 years or 300, but by 15, for it was only that long since President Eliot had persuaded his colleagues at Harvard that studies must be entirely elective. The Jesuit tradition offered a patterned education to accommodate both shared intellectual needs and differing individual interests. As for "direct revelation from on high," it would seem required to justify an education which imposed either total uniformity or total individuality, not one which followed a middle course. It was the latter extreme, Brosnahan noted, that Eliot had been expounding "with such dogmatic intensity."

The young man applying for an education is told to look out on the whole realm of learning, to him unknown and untrodden, and to elect his path. To do thus with judgment and discrimination, he must know the end he wishes to reach; he must moreover know himself — his mental and moral characteristics, his aptitudes, his temperament, his tastes; and finally, he must know which of the numberless paths will lead him to the goal of his ambition . . . He is "strongly urged to choose his studies with the utmost caution and under the best advice." But these provisions do not modify the general character of the system. He must distinctly understand that it is no longer the province of his Alma Mater to act as earthly providence for him. Circumstances have obliged her to become a caterer. Each student is free to choose his intellectual *pabulum* [nourishment], and must assume in the main the direction of his own studies. If he solve the problem wisely, to him the profit; if unwisely, this same *Alma Noverca* [Stepmother] disclaims the responsibility.

The university, Brosnahan continued, especially at the level of graduate studies, presumes a liberal culture in its student and rightly offers an array of electives. By contrast, "the college undertakes to mould the character of the boy or half-man to habits of patient industry, of mental and moral temperance, and of wide intelligent interests. Its supervision over his moral life is as systematic as that over his mental life. . . . between the ages of fourteen and twenty the average boy will work, like electricity, along the line of least resistance. . . . To apply to their education, therefore, university methods applicable only to men of intellectual and moral maturity, before they are able to feel judiciously the relations of their studies to their life's purpose, must necessarily put to some extent the standard of education under their control, and almost wholly commit to them the character of their own formation."[21]

At just that time Brosnahan was handing on the BC presidency to Mullan, and the latter engaged in a politely persistent but unsuccessful correspondence with Eliot, who offered in defense of the law faculty decision some generally disparaging remarks about the inferiority of Jesuit education.[22] Mullan engaged Eliot in a contentious private correspondence (which he later published), but he did not pursue the conflict. He seems to have had some educational reforms of his own in mind. The *(Boston) Pilot* had carried a report — only one month before BC had been snubbed by Harvard Law School — of a speech made by Mullan to the first national gathering of Catholic college and university presidents. Their clientele, he warned his colleagues, were drifting away to non-Catholic colleges, where scholarships and grants for room and board were more plentiful. They were also drawn in that direction "by the wide scope possible in the selections of courses of study by which they can study only what they like, or what helps most for further professional study . . . also, by the reputation of non-Catholic colleges, and by the larger chances of the most refining intercourse with men and women students." Catholic colleges, Mullan insisted, should modify the severity of their residential discipline, separate their colleges from their preparatory schools, and raise the intellectual level of their courses and thus the value of their degrees.[23]

Catholic Colleges and Protestant Rivalry

A historical note may provide some background for the Harvard–Boston College altercation. Of all the manifestations of Catholics' presence in the nineteenth century, it was their schools that most easily aroused antagonism. Those of the Jesuits provided special anxiety to some Protestant groups. The joint Congregational-Presbyterian venture to sustain colleges west of the Appalachians had this entry in its annual report:

> The great battle for American institutions is to be fought in the Valley of the Mississippi . . . never was the Roman Catholic movement toward the region so vigorous and so sagacious. Here colleges and Theological schools have quadrupled in eight years.[24]

The Presbyterian Board of Education saw in the "eager ambition of the Jesuits to obtain possession of the educational resources of the Great Valley, an additional plea for Presbyterian activity. . . . We must be on the alert." That was in 1848. Thirty years later the Presbyterians were no less disturbed: "Rome in America has nearly 10,000 young men in colleges and seminaries today . . . (and) the gigantic marching of the Society of Jesus is getting under way at this moment." And in 1882: "Romanism . . . has her colleges . . . and she does not fail to educate the Jesuits. . . . She knows the best educated, and the best trained minds will always be the leaders."[25]

When the academy that would become Saint Louis University was offered to the Jesuits in 1828, local Protestants had joined the Catholics to support it. In the 1830s, however, radical journalist Elijah Lovejoy was successful in stirring up nativist attacks on the Jesuits in Illinois. The Know-Nothings did the same in the 1850s. The College of Medicine in Saint Louis was trashed by vandals, despite the fact that all but one of its faculty were Protestants, and Presbyterian and Methodist congregations had been worshiping on the premises.[26]

Back in the motherland of American Calvinism, Catholics were more numerous but were not considered so worrisome. In 1830 the *Quarterly Review,* for instance, in the course of lengthy investigation of the numbers and circumstances of the adherents of the "Church of Rome," usurpers of the title "Catholic," had expressed astonishment at the notion that Boston, the capital of the Puritans, could be a bishopric subject to Rome. The author gave an especially sharp eye to the resuscitation of the Jesuits, whose very name was "synonymous with all of ambition, craft, and treachery, duplicity and talent, to be conceived by the human mind." Their efforts, however, were "not to be despised." In surveying the Catholics in

Boston he counted seven thousand, "mostly poor, ignorant foreigners." The Jesuits, the Ursulines ("female Jesuits"), and their schools remained a true cause for worry. Otherwise, the account concluded, "the Papists around us have no great occasion for mutual gratulation, at the favorable prospects of converting New England."[27] By Mr. Eliot's time all the converting had been done by the Unitarians, and there was hardly a Congregationalist left at Harvard. But the earlier contempt, perhaps more ethnic and socioeconomic than religious, had hardly dissipated. Thus could Brosnahan end his remonstrance with these sharp words:

> President Eliot's whole career heretofore forbids us to put any interpretation on it which would imply that he was even subconsciously motived by unreasonable hostility. What inspired this criticism of Jesuit schools, therefore, we can not even conjecture. We can only await further enlightenment, assuring the President of Harvard that if he give reasons for his dislike of our method they will always get that respectful consideration due them because of his position and personal worth.[28]

All parties to the dispute were well aware of the old anti-Jesuit feeling. What the Jesuits may not have known was that Mr. Eliot harbored disdain for almost all orthodox Christians. But it was an incendiary moment for the fellowship of a Society which had striven earnestly to gain a hearing from those whose opinion counted in the academic world.[29]

The differing responses of these two Jesuits to the disdain of Charles Eliot, who had presided at Harvard since both of them were grade-school boys, are paradigms of two modes of advocacy. Brosnahan, the more cultivated of the two, viewed the conflict in large, theoretical terms, saw Eliot as a bully sponsored by a hostile culture, and gave him a truculent reply, cogently argued and cleverly set forth. Mullan, more pragmatic, was blistered by the humiliation of his college, but turned by instinct to see what needed to be done to get past it. It was not his way to cast his Society as an opponent of the land's most distinguished university and president. The two men were both proud of the venerable tradition of Jesuit education they represented, but Mullan was the more capable of seeing that its particular embodiment in Boston was still primitive. During the years of greatness before the suppression, when every school had been endowed, the Society had not acquired the different knack — to be required of them after restoration — of providing for a clientele that could pay the costs of their own education. But more significantly, Mullan carried more easily within himself a conviction that whatever the hostility for Catholics (especially if they were Irish, and deprived) in the area, in the academic profession, and in the country, the Society of Jesus was called to put the best face on its faith and to emulate, not to despise, those in influence. It was the style of Mullan, not of Brosnahan, that most Jesuit educators would be more inclined to follow. Their courting of academic respectability would prove fateful for Boston College, as we shall see.

Boston College Greatly Enlarged

Boston College went busily on. Mullan separated secondary classes from the college proper, and then divided the college into two tracks: the A.B., still centered on the classics, and the "English" track where one studied English, modern languages, and sciences, without classics. Under him the school reached the maximum size that could be served on its premises: 460 students, only half of whom paid tuition. In 1900 Boston College, hardly more than three decades old, boasted the largest enrollment of any Jesuit college, and of any Jesuit high school, in the United States.

A move was in order, so in 1909 the Jesuits began to build a new campus, splendid in its prominence and new structures, atop Chestnut Hill. From the restrained Georgian elegance of Cambridge one was meant to see assertive Tudor Gothic towers in the skyline. Before the new campus was even ready for occupancy the school had more than doubled its enrollment. Boston College was now the second-largest classical college in the country (behind the Jesuits' College of the Holy Cross in Worcester), and BC High School was the largest classical high school. By the time they moved in 1913 there was a freshman class of 400, and the High School, having swelled to 1,100, immediately expanded to fill the entire establishment it had shared with the college.

The first half of the twentieth century was a time when the campus and its programs on Chestnut Hill grew sturdily. There were several large developments which we must study — developments which would make Boston College a different place, though only gradually.

The unchallenged centrality of the arts degree — an A.B. that required intensive study of both the Latin and Greek classics — had established Boston College as a seat of liberal education. But Boston, and the larger recruitment basin of New England, produced numerous young men who had neither the knack nor the appetite for this curriculum. Mullan's decision back in 1898 to create a parallel track, the "English" department for nonclassical studies, was the first compromise made in BC's classical commitment. Bewilderingly, the enrollment had fallen by 30 percent in six years. But the move to Chestnut Hill had brought new vitality and dignity to the school, and a series of other programmatic enlargements would follow.

In 1919 a School of Education was begun, which offered master's degrees to men needed in the public school system. BC began to offer extension courses to the sisters teaching in the Catholic schools, and this quickly grew into a regular program for credit leading to the degree. But bringing females to the new campus, however vowed and garbed, was a grave matter, and that program was kept down in the lowlands for some years. With the permission of the Jesuit superior general in Rome, who appointed every college rector and reviewed every change of program, the first female students were admitted in 1924: 230 of them to begin with.

In 1927 the Jesuit novitiate and houses of studies in philosophy and in theology, all located nearby in Massachusetts, were affiliated to BC as professional schools. The Law School was opened downtown in 1929 and became a quick success in enrollment and accreditation. The Intown Center then attracted a congeries of evening and weekend lectures, and then courses, and at one time seemed on the way to becoming a junior college. A program and then a graduate School of Social Work, a Jesuit specialty grounded on Catholic social principles which had been expounded and discussed since the time of Leo XIII, was opened in 1936. The popularity of electives in accounting led to a parallel undergraduate College of Business Administration. It was quite unlike others of the same nomenclature, in that the students were required to take the full sequence of philosophy courses (thirty credits in the junior and senior years), which exceeded any college major, plus the arts requirements, and then the full array of business courses for their major. The college opened in 1938 and was located in the Intown complex, until it was beckoned up the hill during the war. Every one of these new programs was proposed by a Jesuit, who then became its founding dean. Every one of them was incorporated into the college complex, which thereby gained a serious investment in professional education at undergraduate and postgraduate levels. Though BC persisted as a liberal arts school, its professional enrollments and faculty membership had in the span of two decades made it a diversified, small university. It would have been timely for Boston College to become Boston University, but that title was not available; her name was now so fond a possession that BC decided, as a university, simply to remain BC.

In 1935 a joint team from Holy Cross and Boston College, working in a clandestine mode as hush-hush as the future Manhattan Project, emerged with a proposal to grant the A.B. degree without requiring Greek (Latin, of course, remained). Honors students, however, could still be named only from the honest-to-goodness A.B. candidates. This was another, and a grave, breach in the classical tradition.

The tidal wave of veterans who came to Boston College on the GI Bill after World War II put pressures on the curriculum, but the required theology and philosophy courses were left untouched when other variances were introduced for their temporary benefit. The postwar disorientation persuaded the department heads to vote 13-2 to allow the study of classics in translation instead of in the Greek and Latin originals, but a newly arrived president threw that out as an ill-begotten suggestion.

In 1947 a School of Nursing was inaugurated. With permission of the Jesuit curia in Rome, women were now to be admitted as undergraduates (the coeducational School of Education had operated only on the graduate level). Also, for the first time a dean was appointed who was not a member of the Society of Jesus. Instead, a Jesuit was appointed to the new school in the office of regent: a commissar who would insure that the administrative linkage was shadowed by an informal governance connection with the religious order.

575

Could the Jesuit Curriculum Hold?

In 1951 Joseph R. N. Maxwell, S.J., arrived as the new rector (still also called president). After four years as dean of arts and sciences at BC, he had served a term as president at the College of the Holy Cross, and also at the exclusive Cranwell Preparatory School. Maxwell would be president of the Classical Society of New England and of the Association of American Colleges. He brought added professional stature to the campus. One of his first brisk moves was to secure permission from Jesuit headquarters to make the School of Education coeducational on both undergraduate and graduate levels. Now that there were four undergraduate tracks, there was strong sentiment to open a Graduate School of Arts and Sciences. Back in the 1920s a few doctoral degrees had been awarded in the School of Education, but outside accreditors had growled at this move and insisted that the college was still not well enough resourced to grant the Ph.D. In the 1950s, however, Maxwell, the first president possessed of that degree (in English, from Fordham), went about it very deliberately, and in 1952 the graduate school opened to preside over twelve master's degree programs and three doctoral programs.[30]

The ramification of all these professional and graduate units, degrees, and curricula was not untypical of other institutions with comparable resources. But at Boston College it had special consequences. The ethos of the school had been single-mindedly one of liberal education in the most classical mode, and now BC was a large combine with many professional students and schools. At the start of this evolution Jesuits had been there as the academic magistrates of every unit, binding them all together into a complex operation that was as unified intellectually and religiously as it was administratively and financially. In Maxwell's time Jesuits were firmly in place at the head of the School of Arts and Sciences, the graduate school, and the college itself. Twelve of the academic deans were Jesuits, and two were laypeople (in nursing and graduate business administration).[31] Thereafter, in all but the "central" deanships Jesuits would have only an occasional presence. Thus Jesuit dominance was quietly, inadvertently, giving way to Jesuit leverage. Leveraged influence, naturally, functioned differently.

In 1958 the decision was finally made to remove the course of studies in Latin as a central requirement for the A.B. degree. All twenty-seven Jesuit colleges and universities had stood fast by that requirement; not until 1955 did the provincial superiors petition the superior general for permission to eliminate it in any institution which thought it best.[32] Thus perished the last vestige of the classical tradition that defined the BC experience (Greek had perished earlier), as it had the *Ratio Studiorum* in the Jesuit tradition of liberal education. This modification concluded a slow process of change that had begun exactly sixty years earlier, when Read Mullan had created a separate "English" department free of the classics requirements. The change had proceeded by gentle stages, each one thought to have sufficed. It occurred synergistically with the simultaneous change already noted: as the serious study of the classics was being gradually unloaded from the curriculum for the baccalaureate in arts, the College of Arts and Sciences itself was gradually receding: not in the imagination of the Jesuits who since Ignatius had all been educated in that mode, but in the day-to-day traffic of the growing university where it was on its way to becoming a smaller precinct.

What bearing has this proliferation of professional schools around the original, humanistic arts and sciences core of the college on the story of BC's religious character? While each innovation seems to have been timely, even shrewd, what came of it all was unforeseen and unintended. BC was no longer a liberal arts college. As each new innovation was achieved, BC simply beheld what it had created and saw that it was good. In retrospect there have been few that love the college who thought of the developments as anything but gain and growth. They were most likely correct, but that is not the only point. Not all growth is gain, and this growth is an example of a succession of academic decisions which were each made with a canny sense of the moment but little forethought about how they might combine to transform the texture and purpose of the school. It was thus an analogy for other, greater, change.

The undergraduate curriculum at Boston College was stamped with another Jesuit hallmark, one borne by the professional programs as well. This was the intensive study of scholastic philosophy. Philip Gleason has shown persuasively how neo-Thomist philosophy served as the sturdy armature on which American Catholic higher education found its distinctive intellectual shape in the first half of this century.[33] On most campuses it took the form of basic curricular requirements, similar to those in mathematics and literature. At BC the Jesuit tradition required much more. Philosophy provided the finishing of one's collegiate education, the worldview which allowed and goaded each undergraduate — in nursing and business and education just as in arts and sciences — to organize all that he or she had learned, and to meld it into a coherent understanding that allowed the various disciplines and their respective avenues of insight to become more interactive within the integrative way of thinking that was provided by Thomist philosophy . . . not theology.

In the 1950s a student would still take ten courses for a whopping twenty-eight credits in philosophy during his or her last two years: logic, epistemology, metaphysics, cosmology, fundamental psychology, empirical psychology, rational psychology, natural theology, general ethics, and special ethics. To students on other campuses this would seem like a massive intrusion upon their chosen major, yet by Jesuit graduates it was often remembered as a time to make sense of all they had learned. It was the signature item in Jesuit education, and a definitive denial of both the Continental single-discipline university education and Charles Eliot's unpatterned electivism.

Boston College, along with the other Jesuit colleges and universities and Frank Sinatra, did it her way. But this formidably liberal curriculum began to be easier for the colleges than for the universities, where both the humanists and the professional students found it an increasing frustration. To aggravate matters further, these courses were customarily taught by the Jesuit fathers. In the immediate postwar years the Jesuit faculty members still held the Ph.D. in higher proportion than their lay colleagues.[34] But the massive teaching assignments in philosophy depended on many Jesuits who had not really been trained as academics; their seminary training in philosophy was their only credential. That made the stiff load of philosophy more burdensome, particularly for the brighter students who were more demanding and more articulate. So changes gradually began to be made. In 1957 the requirements were spread over all four years, and could no longer pretend to serve as a capstone experience. Phi Beta Kappa considered the university for membership in 1962 (at which time they were still notoriously biased against Catholic applications), and gave the disproportionate place of philosophy, which effectively eliminated electives, as one ground for turning down BC. The fact that the national honor fraternity objected to that much philosophy as a deficiency in liberal education added insult to injury. Then came the collapse. A general revamping of the curriculum in the centennial year, 1963-64, reduced the requirement to five courses for fifteen credit hours, effectively halving what it had been. By 1971 it was further reduced to two courses for six credits. At just this time, the Department of Philosophy was improving the academic repertoire of its faculty and was offering as many as sixty-four different electives. It is unlikely anyone noticed that BC was now in the embarrassing position of doing what Brosnahan reproached Harvard for: offering a wide array of courses but doing little to require that any student enroll in any particular ones.[35]

Thus the undergraduate experience at Boston College was evacuated of the presence of philosophy as its dominant discipline and integrative finale. This removed one of the most purposeful Jesuit singularities in the BC program, and it depreciated the role of all those Jesuits who were not front-runners in academic achievement as now defined by disciplinary excellence instead of integrative (though sometimes amateur) philosophical wisdom. This part of the complex process of change took fourteen years instead of sixty, and was completed at the threshold of the 1970s.

The Jesuits Must Diminish

Throughout this period the demographics atop Chestnut Hill had remained very stable in some constituencies; less so, in others. The proportion of Catholics in the student body was relatively high, even compared with Jesuit peers. For instance, just before World War II, BC was reporting 95 percent Catholics.[36] That was outdone by Holy Cross, with 99 percent, but stood well ahead of other urban universities such as Loyola of Chicago (83 percent), Loyola of Los Angeles (81 percent), Saint Louis (71 percent), and Marquette (65 percent). In 1949-50, as the GI Bill was nearing the end of its power to bring economically disadvantaged groups to the colleges of their choice, the BC Catholics were more than holding at 97 percent. In 1964-65, when other federal grants and loans were beginning to flow, BC could still report a very high proportion of 95 percent Catholics when most Jesuit schools were in the 75-80 percent range.

Just before World War II, Jesuits had constituted 41 percent of the BC faculty, and laity 59 percent (these were the two categories in which Jesuit schools were then asked to report). But 93 percent of those lay faculty members were Catholics, thus yielding a faculty comprising 96 percent Catholics in its entirety. By comparison, Jesuits then made up 76 percent of the faculty at Gonzaga, 54 percent at Loyola of Los Angeles, 37 percent at Saint Louis, and only 18 percent at Seattle. After the war, in 1949-50, even after the BC faculty had abruptly increased to accommodate the veterans, the Jesuits had also increased their presence to an amazing 43 percent, and among the lay faculty 96 percent were Catholics.

Only in 1964-65 does a downward shift begin to appear. The Jesuit presence in the faculty tumbled to 21 percent, only half of what it had been. Perhaps even more significantly, there was no notion of how many of the lay faculty were Catholics because the university had ceased to ask faculty about their religious commitments.[37] It is likely that such non-Catholics as there were among the laity in those days increased proportionately as their discipline was "distant" from the humanities. For example, a survey taken among twenty-three Jesuit colleges and universities in 1947-48 found that in selected departments non-Catholics averaged 14 percent of the laity; but whereas in history, English, and modern languages they were 7 percent, 8 percent, and 10 percent respectively, in biology, economics, and mathematics they were 15 percent, 23 percent, and 26 percent.[38] In the midsixties the presence of Catholics and Jesuits in the faculty had already become a critical issue.

Jesuits in the United States were aware that in other countries their confreres staffed educational institutions in much lesser proportions. For example, there were only eighteen Jesuits maintaining their college in Rio de Janeiro with an enrollment of 3,859; eighteen in Buenos Aires with 4,392; twenty-one in Caracas with 4,688.[39] Some years earlier Flemish father John Baptist Janssens, the Jesuit superior general (1946-64), had called for a concerted effort to reduce the proportion of lay teachers in Jesuit schools, echoing Ignatius' conviction that for Jesuit schools to be effective, practically all the teachers needed to be from the Society. American Jesuits breathed easier when told he had been roused by a French *collège* with a faculty of seventy-one laymen and only two Jesuits.[40] Back in the 1950s the Jesuit Educational Association (JEA) had privately calculated that the Catholic proportion (including Jesuits) of the Jesuit college and university faculties in the United States amounted to about 70 percent. Boston College by 1967 had a total enrollment approaching 10,000 students. With a Jesuit complement of thirty-one administrators, fifty full-time faculty, and twenty-six part-time faculty, it could feel well supplied . . . unless it was looking at the trends, for both Jesuits and Catholics were on the wane among the faculty.[41] From then onward, they could only guess at how many Catholic faculty they had. There seems to have been little desire to know.

Obviously the twentieth century had been good to Boston College by most measures one chose to use. Long years of financial stringency had given way to stability and then to working surplus. Students had gathered unto the campus faster than BC could open and staff colleges, schools, and programs to serve their increasingly various requirements. The competence of the faculty and the qualifications of their students and the intellectual seriousness of the education had maintained a steady rise. Boston College stood tall among its Jesuit peers, had assumed a leading position among Catholic campuses, and began to receive a respect from its geographical neighbors which Boston, so richly provided in colleges and universities, thought never to see. The ghost of Charles Eliot, it may be supposed, was now ready to give a tip of his hat to this Jesuit enterprise. More importantly, BC had earned the appreciative and energetic support of its primary constituency: Catholics in Boston, in New England, and now throughout America.

But in the 1960s, beginning almost exactly at the time BC was celebrating its centennial year, signs of stress began to show. The developments we have just reviewed probably had something to do with it, though the slow ascendancy of professional over liberal studies and the evaporation of the primacy of philosophy in the undergraduate curriculum, which together weakened the College of Arts and Sciences as BC's powerful intellectual center, would have caused major heartburn perhaps only in the hearts of elder and dyspeptic Jesuits. But there was considerable significance, recognized or not, in the fact that now the programs which engaged large numbers of Boston College's students were offered in colleges and schools in which Jesuits were not at home, and could be found only as stray individuals. An unpredictably large part of the BC enterprise was not grounded on Jesuit tradition or personnel, but was cantilevered out on all sides.

The Walsh Era

It was just in the 1960s that a series of other factors caused concern, even insecurity, among the Jesuits who had given their lives to BC and to the Jesuit mission. From this point onward the story of Boston College becomes so thoroughly enmeshed in the ventures of American Jesuit higher education that the two must be recounted as one. Father Michael P. Walsh, S.J., who served as rector-president of Boston College and was a leading figure in national and international Catholic education, was responsible during the decade when gratification gave way to concern: 1958 to 1968.

The first great concern really began early in Walsh's presidency. Robert Harvanek, S.J., a philosophy teacher who had served as the province prefect (regional coordinator for higher education), declared in print in 1961 that the Jesuit universities had expanded beyond their ability to offer a characteristically Jesuit education. In some academic units 40-50 percent of the faculty were now non-Catholics.

Harvanek saw three possibilities. The first would be to acknowledge that unforeseen demographics had already changed the character of their universities irreversibly. The Society might acknowledge them as trusts owed to their local clientele, and simply continue to staff them as best it could. The second would be for Jesuits simply to declare the changeover from liberal arts colleges to comprehensive institutions a success. Making a virtue out of necessity, Jesuits should then affirm that laypeople would do a better job of it than they could, that clerical domination was a handicap, that moralizing by members of religious orders had led to mediocre scholarship, and that however haphazard had been the replacement of Jesuits by laypeople, it was providential. On this view of the matter the obvious outcome would be a staged withdrawal by the Society. The third possibility would be retrenchment. Jesuits would concentrate themselves in colleges few enough for them to staff and cede the others to lay sponsorship. The program on their own campuses would be authentically Jesuit, the faculty actively collaborative without exception, the pastoral activity pervasive, and the result distinctive even among Catholic campuses. Harvanek admitted that events might have gone so far that one or both of the first two options were simply unavoidable. But Ignatius' mandate — that the pursuit of learning must be for the double goal of the knowledge and the service of God — could be fulfilled only by aggressively choosing the third, rejecting the ambitions and standards of even the "best" universities as too narrowly conceived.[42]

In the end the choice was made by no choice being made. And it was not what Ignatius had chosen. Harvanek's historic essay was one of the first prophetic statements, but not the last, which the Society   and especially the presidents — found too disagreeable to accept. The presidents dismissed Harvanek and others of similar perception as Chickens Little, in order to support a braver attitude toward their uncertain future. Their determination sometimes suggested the bravura of Willy Loman: "First thing in the morning, everything'll be all right."

The Harvanek essay, meant to catch the imagination of the younger Jesuits, received a no-go reply from Michael Walsh.[43] Rather than imagine they could improve on the American educational model, he argued, the Jesuits should master it and try to deploy their manpower where it could be most influential, not off in a corner. That meant a sizable network of first-class universities, not a chain of small, eccentric liberal arts colleges. Harvanek, Walsh thought, was both mistaken and unrealistic to think that an institution is more Jesuit simply by having more Jesuits. "I will not concede that Marquette, Saint Louis or Georgetown, with their relatively small percentage of Jesuit faculty members, have been engaged in a less genuinely Jesuit enterprise or one that has contributed less to the furtherance of Catholic ideals and interests than have European schools with all-Jesuit faculties." (Harvanek had pointed to no Continental examples, and had not called for exclusively Jesuit faculties.) Walsh denied that there was any set minimum of Jesuits to assure Jesuitness (Harvanek had not suggested one); he could imagine fifteen good Jesuit *scholar*-teachers managing the task in a faculty of a hundred. "With a few outstanding Jesuit administrators, one very competent, scholarly Jesuit in each department of Arts & Sciences, one in each professional school, and with more, though equally well-trained, Jesuits in Philosophy and Theology, we could have a stronger *Jesuit* university," better than at present. The Jesuit reputation depends on accomplishments, not upon numbers. Their task is to be a "leaven" among the lay members of the faculty. "We have not yet tested how much more broadly Catholic or Jesuit a college or university can be when select laymen are welcomed as partners in the pursuit of the total objectives of our education."[44] As Richard Freeland reads this claim by Walsh, it allowed him to "celebrate the secularization of B.C. without ambivalence or irony."[45]

As events unfolded, the shortage of Jesuits available for this ministry was just then about to become aggravated. In 1960 the number of novices entering the Society in the American Assistancy (the worldwide Society is administratively divided into cultural "assistancies") began to decline from an all-time high. Shortly after Walsh's response was published in 1964, the rate of entries went into free-fall descent: by 1972 it shrank to less than 25 percent of those in 1960. The total census rose for a few years as the bounty of the past emerged from the long Jesuit training period, but crested in 1965. By the later 1970s the overall net decline would show with stark clarity. A second source of numerical decline was just beginning to be apparent when Father Walsh's ill-timed forecast was made. Jesuits were starting to resign from the Society in unprecedented numbers: by the end of the decade the number of departures by young Jesuits in training had tripled, and the departures by ordained priests had increased nineteenfold.[46] Each week throughout the world, six new members entered the Society of Jesus, seven members died, and twenty members departed. Today there are fewer than half as many Jesuits in the United States as when the Harvanek-Walsh exchange took place, and that number is expected to be halved again within another fifteen years.[47] Jesuits a few years ago represented only 4 percent of their college and university faculties.[48] At Fordham today, for instance, they are only a third as many as when Harvanek and Walsh argued.[49]

How fared Boston College? Not long after his statement Walsh asked for a statistical survey on the Jesuits in his Boston College community, and expressed some surprise to learn that those involved in teaching numbered only seventy-five. Though he was rector of the community, he had somehow thought they were more numerous, and had been concerned by what he thought was their poor showing at faculty meetings. He confided to the provincial superior that he was more than ever "convinced that the burden of Jesuit influence in the university must fall upon a few well-trained and most competent individuals." Apropos of competence, Walsh faced two concerns. There were still some older Jesuits at BC whose training and abilities were inferior to those of the new breed of lay faculty being recruited, and that generated a feeling in some quarters that unqualified Jesuits were being thrust upon the university. Walsh was also worried that in even their priestly ministry the campus Jesuits might not deserve high praise. He had noticed that few were directly involved pastorally with students, and confessed that many of those younger than fifty, whose age would make them more adapted to this ministry, did not possess the personality or the interest necessary for such involvement.[50]

Granted the enormity of this demographic projection and the radical threat it posed to the Jesuit ministry which, despite having received an allotment of the Society's manpower that exceeded in numbers and credentials what any other ministry did, was already unable to hold its own in their expanding colleges and universities, it is remarkable how soberly and swiftly the Jesuit educators did finally accept it as valid, and began to consider the great policy changes it imposed on them.

It was at just this time that Vatican II, and the energetic imagination fostered in the Society by Pedro Arrupe, the Basque superior general (1965-83), began to persuade some of the brighter young Jesuits that direct ministry to the deprived was a more evangelical work ("apostolic" would have been their word) than scholarship and teaching. Since the presidents had been urging them to emulate the standards and accomplishments of their secular competitors, they were some-what compromised in their ability to convince even this shrinking number of gifted men in the Society to look upon the academy as an ideal venue for prophetic service. These young men were critically important to the future of Boston College, Gonzaga, Xavier, and the other Jesuit campuses, and were they to prefer Brazil or the Bronx or retreat preaching as the bliss to be followed, no one would be more frustrated than the presidents who, paradoxically, had for some time been promoting the "principle of attraction," i.e., that superiors should assign young Jesuits where they preferred and would therefore be most likely to excel, rather than where they seemed to be most needed.

A New Kind of Jesuit President

Already in the 1950s a cadre of men had begun to move up through the ranks of faculty — member, chairman, dean, vice president — with the prospect of appointment as president of one of their twenty-eight institutions. The first academies had all been ministries of a residential community, and the man appointed to preside over the community was *ex officio* the chief of the ministry as well. Church law forbade any individual from exercising that authority over the same community (and ministry) for more than six consecutive years. The superior general, who appointed them all, could and did occasionally extend a superior's service, but tradition and expectation made those exceptions rare. The men just then reaching the crest, e.g., Paul Reinert, Michael Walsh, John Raynor, Leo McLaughlin, Robert Henle, Timothy Healy, and their contemporaries, were more thoroughly defined as academics than their predecessors. A typical president might have served a three-year stint as a scholastic teaching in a Jesuit high school, later emerged with a "Jesuit" M.A., taught philosophy to seminarians, served as chaplain on a small college campus, been called to be superior of a theologate, then been appointed a college president. Six years later, he might find himself a missionary in Jamaica (the assignment Father Maxwell received after his term as president of BC), or could pass the rest of his years in the Montana Indian reservations. The generation then maturing in the 1950s and 1960s had been sent out to earn their doctorates, and since their first academic appointments they had seen higher education as their life's work. Their superiors had also quietly shifted their attitude: instead of being all-purpose Jesuits ready under obedience to walk away from any assignment to another, these men were accorded an informal immunity from sudden removal. They were, in an entirely new sense, professional academics. They shared a comradeship that led them as a generational cohort to want the Jesuit schools to become more professional, and to surmount the barrier which had caused Jesuits to regard "indifference" to professional aspirations as a signature virtue of their Society.[51] And they shared the view that the Jesuit regime had inhibited the growth of professionalism among its college administrators.[52]

This was the decade in which the role of the Jesuit presidents underwent a remarkable transformation. In 1960 the presidents were men who were usually but not invariably credentialed as academics. Their task was to govern the local Jesuit community, preside over the college or university for a short span of years, answer for their performance to their religious superiors, and then move on to another assignment. By the end of the decade, the presidents were specifically trained as academics and more likely to have come up through ascending academic responsibilities; they looked to hold office for an indefinite period (preferably until retirement); they had willingly handed over responsibility for the religious integrity of their local Jesuit communities; they now accounted for their stewardship to their lay boards; they had become adept at actively soliciting very large capital gifts; and they expected to spend the rest of their careers (just to consider their mission/apostolate/vocation as a career was itself new) in higher education. They had been transformed into educational executives, and every step of that metamorphosis was accomplished by dint of their presidential initiative and by the not always eager relaxation of the Society's oversight. Another factor in all this change was their slow-burn impatience with traditional authority within the Society of Jesus itself. The presidents said, and perhaps thought, that the sixties were the season of emancipation for their colleges and universities. But prior to that, both in intention and in effect, it was the decade when the presidents were emancipated, and when their professional self-understanding became more precise, and also more constricted.

It did not take the presidents long to notice that a major barrier to academic excellence was the Jesuit tradition of strong central authority. They noticed how many ways it frustrated their work. Every province had the responsibility for two or more campuses, and no province would easily allow one of its own qualified men to leave the province and help out on another's campus. This made things especially difficult for a smaller province when new presidents had to be found every six years. Another vexation was the need to secure authorization for campus decisions through so many layers of approval: the province prefect, the provincial himself, the general assistant in Rome, and the general himself. Until 1967 approval from higher authorities in the Society had to be secured for such matters as the creation of a new school or college within an institution; the introduction of coeducation; creation of new major offices and appointments to them; the introduction or closure of a summer, extension, or evening program; honorary degrees; admissions policy; tuition changes; athletic policies; curricular requirements for any degree; introduction of a new major or minor; attendance by Jesuit faculty at scholarly meetings requiring overnight absence, etc. For the older Jesuit administrators whose social world was mostly Jesuit, this was a tradition with which one had learned to be comfortable. But as the presidents' comradeship and sense of peerage threw them together with educational professionals elsewhere, and as their responsibilities became more professionalized and required a more decisive style, this Jesuit structure of supervision, often by men with little or no experience in the academy, felt like an indignity and a vexation.[53]

There was another potentially threatening entity within the Society which had all the presidents worried as the 1960s were passing by. It is no distraction from the Boston College story to attend to it, for it was to have profound effects upon the entire Jesuit educational effort.[54] In 1920 a group of Jesuit college presidents had suggested an Inter-Province Committee (IPC), to discuss and perhaps collaborate on the raising of academic standards. The American provincials were skeptical: by forming a united front the presidents might compromise their supervisory authority. The general administration in Rome thought it even more ominous, since it might serve to intensify criticism of their institutional independence by American bishops. The IPC was given reluctant approval, and specifically denied any authority to publish its minutes or proposals. Nonetheless, it was the beginning of a lobby for the college presidents.

The general might have used some such intermediary in 1927, when presented with allegations from Rome that the Jesuit universities in the United States were not truly Catholic: it was being said the faculty were mostly non-Catholics, Jews, and atheists, the rectors were not truly academics, and Jesuit spiritual influence was nil. The Jesuit defense was vigorous: only 7 percent of the combined faculties were non-Catholics (though that rose to more than 50 percent in graduate and professional programs). Father Wlodomir Ledochowski, the Polish superior general (1915-42), now wanted concerted action, and he turned, neither to the presidents' IPC nor to the provincials. In 1934 he appointed a midwestern man, Daniel O'Connell, to visit all of the campuses. His authority was plenipotentiary, exceeding even that of the provincials. The American Council on Education had recently published its list of approved doctoral degree programs. Among Catholic schools, Catholic University had five on the list and Notre Dame had one. Not a single Jesuit graduate program was listed. Had O'Connell's authority lacked anything, this academic humiliation supplied all the urgency he required. He determined that to sponsor competitively excellent programs, disciplined resource priorities were necessary, and he proposed and then imposed them, interfering with the free-enterprise approach previously used by both colleges and provinces. He followed the guiding principles of the pacesetting Association of American Colleges, and great was the grief on most campuses after his reformatory visits. He was brought down after only two years, but he had given Jesuit education its most industrious moment.

O'Connell had proposed a Jesuit Educational Association controlled by a board of governors (all the American provincials) and managed by an executive committee (all of the province prefects). This would subject the presidents to a two-layered supervisory *Apparat*. Edward Rooney, S.J., was installed as secretary in 1937, and remained for twenty-nine years. He would become the most important single person in American Jesuit education. The educators usually found it a strenuous experience to secure agreement to their proposals from their provincials, for though they were acting here *en banc* as governors of the JEA, each superior still remained sovereign within his own province over its own colleges and universities. One example: the presidents tried in vain to put the education of their Jesuit trainees in philosophy and theology under the control of academics, rather than of provincial aides. As an accolade for serious research they drew up a list of scholarly publications by members of the Society, but when another list — of acknowledged "Jesuit scholars" — was drafted, it was heatedly opposed as an incitement to vanity and rivalry. The new general, Father Janssens, used the JEA to restrain any overexpansion that might dilute the Jesuit mission and educational quality of a university. Janssens also criticized the American tendency, in the 1950s, to give mounting attention to career training and professional schools.

The JEA eventually proved to be a collision point for the judgments and ambitions of the general, the provincials, the province prefects, and the presidents. Rooney usually tried to stand off to one side . . . though not too far. A milestone essential to our concerns was passed in 1958 when the presidents, sensing that there was strength in unity, finally formed their own conference under the JEA umbrella and began to speak (when a consensus or common enemy permitted) with one voice.

At Fr. Ledochowski's instructions in 1934, some campuses had experimented with dual leadership: a rector for the Jesuit community and a president for the college or university. The intent was that the rector answer for the overall welfare of the combined enterprise, but when it was first tried at Fordham the president treated the rector as his third-level assistant. By the 1950s a pattern emerged: the rectorship and presidency remained united in one man, but a "superior" would, under his authority, handle the day-to-day affairs of the resident Jesuits and leave all matters of state to the chief. Freed of this daily responsibility for the religious, personal, and professional lives of the local Jesuit community, the presidency thus took a step further toward a more narrowly profiled professional identity.

Historian John Tracy Ellis's celebrated address in 1955, which jolted the American Catholic community about their academic mediocrity, provided another occasion for the Jesuit presidents to draw back from the control of their superiors. Ellis said the Catholic educational establishments were as indifferent as their most ill-willed critics said they were. Worse still: their aspirations were no better.[55] Jesuit responses to this call to excellence were divided. The presidents saw excellence in expansion; the general administration saw it in consolidation and inter-institutional collaboration. Janssens sent round a team of inspectors, and their mostly favorable report did not settle his worries about the growing number of educators on their campuses who did not share their Catholic faith. Rooney, however, persuaded him that any public admonition might now be taken as a threat to academic freedom. The provincials commissioned a report, and what emerged was the Harvanek statement we have already seen, countered vehemently by Walsh on behalf of the presidents. The presidents had no intention of doing anything collaboratively except to resist inroads on their individual autonomy by any national authority.

Michael Walsh was one Jesuit who had been deeply impressed by the Ellis lament. He had also taken a lesson from the dispatch of his predecessor Maxwell to the missions, that the Jesuit regimen offered little encouragement for professional presidents with minds of their own. Robert Gannon, whose earlier tour of duty as president at Fordham had ended in some disappointment for him, had warned Walsh that the authority tradition in the Society instinctively stifled academic excellence.[56]

By the end of Vatican II in the middle 1960s, the twenty-eight presidents were persuaded that professional ministries of the church to the world had to be freed from ecclesiastical control: not their own own control, but that of their superiors. Pedro Arrupe, the new Basque general, encouraged them. During the 1960s, which were such a season of adjustment for Boston College, the presidents came to regard Edward Rooney, who had longer experience than any of them, who enjoyed the confidence of the provincials and, much more importantly, an annual *tête-à-tête* with the general, as their last serious obstacle. The authority incumbent in an officer elected for an indefinite period rather than for a set term was something the presidents knew was rare in the Jesuit experience, yet desirable for their own responsibilities, and highly undesirable in anyone like Rooney who could obstruct them.[57] Rooney was a target for the presidents' annoyance with the JEA, whereby the provincials wielded a corporate restraint upon their educational initiatives.

Does Catholic Mean Answerable to Rome?

While the presidents were chafing under the traditional oversight by their superiors in the Society, several incidents occurred which gave cause for alarm that the Vatican (possibly under the provocation of quiet grievances sent in by American bishops) might be planning to step in. The incidents provided another serious reason for the presidents to form a common resolve that they needed a new autonomy.

The Vatican had created an International Association of Catholic Universities and called for its first meeting in 1949, but had limited membership to "pontifical"

587

institutions: those chartered or recognized by and under the authority of the Holy See. That severely limited the scope of the organization, but when the educator-delegates drafted statutes to include civilly chartered Catholic institutions (more than 95 percent of all the Catholic universities and colleges in this country),[58] Giuseppe Cardinal Pizzardo of the Sacred Congregation of Seminaries and Universities said that other institutions might be admitted but only after individual Roman scrutiny to verify their Catholic credentials. A sixteen-year wrangle ensued. Knowledgeable observers were aware that the cardinal's own intellectual gifts were not such as would have gained him admission to any of their institutions had he applied. Pizzardo rejected suggestions that the status of "Catholic" might be assured by local bishops or a peer accreditation process. New York's Cardinal Spellman (who knew Pizzardo from their days together in the curia) was drawn in through Fordham University. Governmental moneys, Spellman wrote, were now beginning to become available for higher education, and assertions of ecclesiastical jurisdiction would be very compromising for the American universities. Pizzardo stood fast, and told the American educators (who outnumbered all other national cohorts combined) that they should apply for pontifical charters. He also expressed his disdain for administrators who were in constant communication with Jesuit authorities in Rome, but never with the *Catholic* authorities (the emphasis was his). In 1959 Pizzardo had evidently persuaded John XXIII to agree that all Catholic universities operated by clergy or religious orders, even if they had no papal charter, were subject to supervision by Pizzardo's office. Using that alleged papal decision as his warrant, Pizzardo later insisted (when the pope was but a few days from death in 1963) that no honorary degrees be conferred henceforth from any Catholic college or university without his approval. (Saint Louis had just caused apoplexy in Rome by honoring Hans Küng.) Letters went back and forth; Spellman's were often drafted for him by Rooney, and copies duly flowed through the Jesuit circulatory system.

The educators in the Association (now renamed the International Federation of Catholic Universities [IFCU]) decided to force Pizzardo's hand and proceeded to elect Fr. Theodore Hesburgh, C.S.C., of the civilly chartered University of Notre Dame, as their president. Rome refused to recognize the election. That issue had been eclipsed in any case by Pizzardo's claim of eminent domain. The Rooney-Spellman letters, couched in courtly grace, pressed the issue ever more severely. The argument which Rome finally accepted was that these honorary degrees were civil degrees, and in the American tradition it would be anathema for the trustees of any civil corporation to require church approval before performing a civil act. Giving Pizzardo's elbow a discreet twist was the papal secretary of state, Amleto Cardinal Cicognani, veteran of a quarter-century as the papal delegate in Washington. In 1965, after sixteen years of altercation, all was forgiven: the Americans were admitted, the elected officers were recognized, Pizzardo was thanked, and presumably Spellman had responded to Pizzardo's closing personal request for a modest contribution to help him repair some fire damage in his own local seminary.[59] But a traumatic double lesson had been learned: Roman authorities of manifest incompetence meant to assert and to use a newly claimed right to supervise all colleges and universities which used the name "Catholic"; and only by invoking American civil jurisprudence had they been disabled.[60]

Another spate of concern regarding church authorities came in 1967, just when the Jesuit presidents were lobbying to reduce the long list of academic decisions that required permission from higher authorities in the order. This, too, was a matter the presidents would keep strictly confidential, though it received heated discussion among themselves. Augustin Cardinal Bea, himself a Jesuit, a venerable scriptural scholar, and an ecumenical hero in Vatican II, had raised an alarm to Fr. Arrupe when a non-Catholic had been hired to teach Old Testament in one of their American universities. The general asked the Americans to justify such a move, and the provincials undertook to draft a policy that would pass muster in Rome. They took the view that competent scholars "who do not share in the fullness of our Faith" can give independent witness to scriptural truth and thus reinforce a student's faith. Since, as Jesuits, they were "striving to prepare our students for an effective witness in a pluralistic society," it was only right that students explore that faith with non-Catholic mentors, since it would be "within the context of a Catholic institution." They agreed that a careful screening process was in order before such an appointment. "The candidate should be fully informed regarding the aims and ideals of the institution and of the theology department. No one should be hired who is not in sympathy with, and willing to contribute to, the achievement of these goals."[61] The matter was kept confidential between the provincials and the presidents, but for the latter it was another event, mild yet alarming, where their better instincts were being held to account by authorities who wanted evidence of their prudence and fidelity. As long as they were accountable to provincials and bishops, men nearby whom they could meet face-to-face as responsible pastoral executives, they could usually secure appropriate respect for their own judgments. But when policies, directives, inquiries, or supervision came from beyond the perimeter of personal encounter, they seemed degrading . . . and uncontrollable.

These new and vexing challenges to the presidents' freedom to act on their own campuses all came upon them in a short season, so that the animus Edward Rooney felt in the *Putsch* that drove him from office in 1966 was really a compressed reaction to a storm front of interference that had swept through in a period of only two years. What galvanized all this frustration into unprecedented action seemed a different sort of threat. The presidents were fearful that litigation under way might disqualify their colleges and universities from receiving federal or state funds for building construction, student aid, and noncategorical grants. Two major lawsuits touched them closely, for they involved states where Jesuit colleges were at risk: the *Maryland* case and the *Connecticut* case.[62] In its final outcome (in 1976) the litigation would vindicate the capacity of most religiously affiliated colleges and universities to receive public funds because they were not so "pervasively sectarian" that such appropriations would constitute the establishment of religion forbidden by the First Amendment. But in 1966 that outcome was far from clear. The Jesuit presidents were intensely aware that if ultimate control by outside religious authorities were to block their access to needed funding, the schools to which they had dedicated their ministries were liable to be destroyed. The stakes had been raised from excellence to survival.

The Presidents Persuade the Society to Relinquish Their Institutions

Jesuit institutions were destabilized by a complex threat to their colleges' and universities' hopes for academic excellence and recognition, and this created a crisis that called forth new initiative from the presidents. The elements of the crisis included:

1. the dissolution of the distinctively Jesuit curriculum as the dominant intellectual experience;
2. the demographics of the Society which promised a drastic shrinkage in their academic manpower;
3. the anti-intellectual disposition of some bright young Jesuits to consider academic work inferior to social activism;
4. the inhibiting submission of their institutions to the system of Jesuit obedience;
5. a newly intrusive attempt by an uncomprehending Vatican;
6. and, most urgent of all, the threat of being denied federal or state funding because of church control.

The first of these problems seems to have preoccupied the presidents very little. It was surely a problem — it involved an abandonment of what had been considered a central load-bearing element in the distinctively Jesuit educational tradition — but their concerns at this time were less turned toward the texture of the education they were offering. It was the competitive need to enhance the resources of their institutions that claimed their energies.

All the other problems they hoped to resolve by a single stroke: the Society of Jesus should divest itself of juridical control and management of its American colleges and universities, freeing them to take their rightful place as fully acknowledged peers of other leading independent institutions. And what the Society formally discharged, the presidents would then informally take into their own charge.

Between the two sessions of the Thirty-First General Congregation ([GC31] 1965-66), called to elect a successor to Janssens and to review large policy issues, the JEA quickly drew up a promotional report on its work. Besides reports on growing endowment and new construction, the high sociopolitical status and influence of alumni and board members, and *curricula vitae* of their more cosmopolitan presidents, the report included brief essays such as "Influential Americans of Every Faith Ally Themselves with American Jesuit Higher Education" and "American Jesuit Institutions of Higher Education Continue to Make Jesuit Education Available for the Children from Low and Middle Income Families."[63] The presidents were concerned that younger men in training had begun to shift their vocational hopes from university work to mission work in poor areas, and they urgently wanted an endorsement of their ministry by the highest authority in the Society.

They received it. Education, asserted GC31, is a chief instrument of the church's salutary influence in the contemporary, and especially the intellectual, world. It is the place where atheism and agnosticism are to be confronted, where non-Christians can be provided with a humanistic formation and be brought "by degrees to the knowledge and love of God or at least the acceptance of moral, and even religious, values."[64] They should be formed through ethics courses in sound moral judgment even if they have no Christian faith. Students should be selected with an eye to their eventual cultural influence. Then, under Saint Louis University president Paul Reinert's guiding hand, the Congregation advised a greater role for the laity, "the natural interpreters for us of the modern world, and . . . effective help in this apostolate. Therefore, we should consider handing over to them the roles they are prepared to assume in the work of education, whether these be in teaching, in academic and business administration, and even on the board of directors." The decree mooted that it might be wise "to establish in some of our own institutions of higher education a board of trustees which is composed partly of Jesuits and partly of lay people; the responsibility both of ownership and of direction would pertain to this board." Lest anyone think that pure research could not serve Christ, "Jesuits should have a high regard for scholarly activity, especially scientific research properly so called, and they are to view this as one of the most necessary works of the Society. [Men assigned to that work] are to be on guard against the illusion that they will serve God better in other occupations which can seem more pastoral, and they are to offer their whole life as a holocaust to God." This provision, however, followed: "they are enlisted in the cause of Christian truth and are serving the people of God either by showing forth the presence of the Church among the men of the scientific community or by enriching the understanding of revelation itself through the progress of human understanding."[65]

The presidents set about their work. Father Rooney was removed from the JEA and sent to the missions. Paul Reinert of Saint Louis, then the most seasoned of the Jesuit presidents, took over the JEA. He remained at the helm in Saint Louis, transferred the office from New York to Washington to be near the national educational *omphalos* there, and posted a full-time deputy to run it.

Arrupe, the new and admired general, came to address the JEA meeting and strengthened the members' resolve by commending the American Jesuit ministry of higher education for having won the confidence of secular educators on secular terms: "They consider us as peers and colleagues . . ." When he did allude to the character of their education, he did so in vague terms: "America will always need a parallel educational system that can speak with positive conviction and teach with authority of absolute values, a system where morality and virtue can be explicitly and formally cultivated."[66] His message brought the presidents no anxiety.

Reinert — now firmly in the chair, with the presidents as the initiative takers and the provincials and prefects trailing behind — suggested to the provincials what he thought the universities and colleges should do. He began with an issue that was very much to the fore on American campuses, but which had not figured in the agenda of the presidents: the need and the right of lay faculty to have an active voice in academic policies. This, he said, required a more general change in structures. The Society should decide that the civil incorporation of their universities and colleges made them civil trusts, and that the community whose interests they were thereby obligated to serve was neither the Society of Jesus nor the Catholic Church, but the American civil public. They must take necessary steps to establish that they were not (and really had never been) canonical, ecclesiastical establishments. The Jesuits must confide their governance to predominantly lay boards of trustees and acknowledge that academic officers, rather than Jesuit superiors, should rightly appoint Jesuits to their institutions. Superiors must relieve the presidents of all vestiges of the role as Jesuit rectors, for the colleges and universities themselves were not apostolates of the Society; they were good works which the Society had founded and wished to sustain. Thus the presidents would be elected by boards, and not appointed by the Jesuit superior general. Divestiture, Reinert argued, was in the spirit of Vatican II (sharing responsibility with the laity and moving out of the ghetto into the world), in the spirit of the participatory decision making so ardently claimed on campuses, and in the spirit of their own vow of poverty which made them stewards, not possessors.[67]

Webster College Goes First: 1967

It is unlikely that Reinert or any of those who heard him out that day could anticipate all that would have to change if a Jesuit university were primarily a creature of the civil state, thus subject ultimately to the authority and priorities of the civil government.

That was in May 1966. In June the presidents and chief academic officers all sat down with Reinert to devise the best ways to introduce laymen to their boards of trustees. To convey ownership of their institutions would require permission from the Holy See, which by canon law had to authorize the alienation of large properties. Their discussions were about how to do this without involvement by the Vatican, and their legal advice was either (1) to retain a Jesuit majority on their boards, or (2) to retain ownership but create a second board to manage operations, or (3) to pass a special bylaw requiring lay trustees to obligate themselves to obey canon law as well as civil law. The consensus was to make the change but to have each institution proceed on its own. Throughout this process the presidents almost never agreed on a common policy, except for their unanimity on whatever augmented their individual authority.

In January 1967 the presidents conferred with the attorney handling the *Maryland* case *(Roemer),* and his advice was to eliminate even the appearance of Jesuit domination of their campuses. Reinert's own advice, it was now disclosed, had not been speculative. Despite his presence in Rome for more than three months at GC31, and at so many national meetings, his own school, Saint Louis University, was ready to announce in two weeks a change in governance.[68]

This was somewhat dislocated by the news which broke while the presidents were still together. Sister Jacqueline Grennan, the vigorous president of Webster College, located only a few miles from Saint Louis University, announced that her college would become a lay institution, no longer owned or conducted by the Sisters of Loretto. Higher education, she insisted, was incompatible with juridical control by a church, and it would embarrass the college to have the hierarchy either endorsing or vetoing anything done on campus (there was no suggestion that endorsing or vetoing had been going on). Webster would now be "a legally secular institution in which the power of Christian presence is an important force." The sisters could now scatter and work effectively on state campuses, or apply to Webster and be considered competitively on their merits. She had rejected a mixed board of lay and religious members, for, with a religious congregation involved, "the final responsibility and authority still remains with the Church."

The president simultaneously announced that she, too, would be laicized, by leaving the Sisters of Loretto. She became Miss Jacqueline Grennan, and thereafter Mrs. Jacqueline Grennan Wexler, a prominent national interreligious leader. Tiny Webster College has become Webster University with an enrollment of nearly ten thousand, 90 percent of whom are "non-traditional" students; 28 percent are Catholics. Twenty-one Sisters of Loretto worked at Webster at the time; three continue to teach and administer there today. Ms. Grennan and others were vexed by the use of "secular" and "secularized" in news stories. Journalists at the time may have been confused by ambiguous descriptions of the college's religious status. The formal articles enacting the change spoke of "a spirit of inquiry in both secular and sacro-secular concerns. . . . The college, founded as a denominational Roman Catholic institution, will incorporate Judeo-Christian tradition with her Roman Catholic heritage in the ecumenical future." Ms. Grennan may have been confused. What she said she would do was to laicize the college; what she did do was to secularize it.

L'Affaire Grennan laid bare the thoughts of many. Father Leo McLaughlin, S.J., president of Fordham University, said that the Webster shift "could be the beginning of a trend." His Jesuit peers, however, could take little comfort from her view that no one with a vow of obedience had any business being a college president. One editorial writer in the Jesuit magazine, *America,* wondered about "her unremitting campaign to secularize Webster College, always with the proviso that she, and no other, be the president of the new Webster." He noted that her powerful drive was "marked not only by inflexibility of purpose but by brilliance in maneuver." The academic vice president of Boston College took public offense at another Jesuit's editorial comment that Webster might thus become a truly professional Catholic college "where your credentials are your competence, not your collar or your coif."[69]

As events swirled about them, the presidents made an attempt to write a clear and shareable statement on "The Objectives of a Catholic University." Walsh of Boston College was the drafter, and they spent considerable time together in March of 1967 kneading it into shape. A Catholic university, like every other, they said, aims at the "civilization of intelligence." Insofar as it is Catholic, it has a further, quite compatible objective. But that Catholic objective concerns only the Catholic community. The university provides Catholics with an "intellectual and humanistic environment," "atmosphere," "situations," "setting," where people of the church can gather and think reflectively about its belief. But the Catholic university would be only the scene and not the subject of this ecclesial reflection. When the presidents say that this kind of institution must "bring together the sacral and secular orders," they no longer see them both inhabiting the same institution. The sacral activity, the "faith in search of further understanding," is done by the church *at* the newly secular university; in the past it had been the university that was the gathering of believers for all manner of reflection, sacred and secular. In the presidents' imaginations, the church was now a sojourner on their campuses, not the host.[70]

In June 1967 Saint Louis University's new board met: eighteen lay members and ten Jesuits. The Jesuit community was separately incorporated, with no rights over the university corporation. Father Arrupe had given the necessary approval, noting how congenial the change was with GC31's call (secured by Reinert) for such mixed boards. Shortly afterward the presidents dug in their newly cleated heels and refused to accept a solution brokered by the provincials about the hiring of non-Catholics to teach Scripture. These appointments, the presidents decided, should be treated no differently from any other appointment in whatever department.

It was this announcement which first snagged Arrupe's concern. He had authorized the change of governance without imagining what it would mean for Saint Louis University to be the only Jesuit entity in the world over which he now had responsibility but no authority. "Why," he now asked in some bewilderment, "should the Society of Jesus permit its name to be identified with an institution in which the responsible superiors of the Society can exercise no authority?" The matrix of authority was so central to the Jesuit experience that he had simply not considered how radical was the departure from tradition he had approved. The answer offered to his question was to the effect that nomenclature is not that important if there is a commitment. What, then, he rejoined, would embody the commitment? The reply was turgid: "It would be, in American terminology, a private, independent, church-related institution sponsored by the Society of Jesus on behalf of that segment of the American public that wishes to perpetuate . . . a style of education that emphasizes traditionally Jesuit values."[71]

One month later twenty-six educators met at Land O'Lakes, Wisconsin, to prepare a position paper for a forthcoming IFCU gathering. Jesuit personnel and institutions were dominant at the gathering, including Walsh and Charles Donovan from Boston College and others from Georgetown, Saint Louis, Fordham, the Catholic University of Peru, and the Jesuit curia in Rome. Their brief product, *The Idea of the Catholic University,* would become the classic doctrine on how modern Catholic universities were to be defined primarily by their membership in the modern educational establishment, sharing the same autonomy, academic freedom, functions, services, disciplines, public, and norms of academic excellence. Because of their being Catholic they would have added modifications: theological studies, Christian public service, a variety of worship, and a distinctive lifestyle. Their primary public would be the civil society and culture, but there would also be a bond with the church. The relationship, however, is asymmetrical: *to* the church the university offers the "benefit of continual counsel"; *from* the church the university asks only to be left alone. In the words that were to become classical: "To perform its teaching and research functions effectively the Catholic university must have a true autonomy and academic freedom in the face of authority of whatever kind, lay or clerical, external to the academic community itself." Beyond that the document mentions nothing that the university needs from the church. This protection from outside interference thus placed both the church and the state at a distance from the university, though not quite the same distance. At the time little notice was given to the full scope of this particular claim. The sovereign "academic community" would be, not the individual Catholic university, but the educational establishment. The conferees, who had meticulously emancipated their institutions from the church, though somewhat less from the state (whose rights to incorporate and regulate were left unchallenged), were unreservedly prepared to confide their universities to the canons, dogmas, and authority internal to academia. In 1967 they harbored no misgivings about how confining that obedience could prove to be.

"Catholicism," the Land O'Lakes document emphasized, must be *"perceptibly present* and *effectively active"* on these campuses. The means mentioned was the theology department: the Catholic university must acknowledge theology as a legitimate discipline; the department must explore Christianity and religion "appreciatively." Catholicism, by contrast, would need to be explored "critically"; theology must engage other disciplines (with the explicit caution to show them honor and respect, and never to deal with them imperialistically). Apart from that wary welcome to theology, no other means to make Catholicism perceptibly present and effectively active is mentioned. In one passage that foreshadowed numerous Jesuit statements destined to follow, it describes the "special social characteristics" of such a place, such as liturgy and Christian service, but describes no concern that a community interested in such things ought to be recruited.[72]

Boston College Claims Its Freedom

Walsh returned to Boston and gathered his trustees. They were ten in number: Walsh as rector of the Jesuit community, president of the university, and chairman of the board, plus the four Jesuit vice presidents and five other Jesuits in the inner circle: all named by Jesuit superiors. The board ordinarily met every September to legalize all the appointments, resignations, salaries, financial aid, real estate transactions, and other arrangements made for the fiscal year by the administration; and every December to approve honorary degrees. In 1967 they would follow a different schedule. They held a special November meeting to discuss the proposal to create a second body, a board of directors, to include themselves and about twenty-five laypeople (most of them already associated with BC in advisory and contributory capacities). The trustees, all still Jesuits but now self-perpetuating rather than appointed by the order, would continue to hold the university in trust, to elect the board of directors, and to elect or remove the president (some around the table wanted to pass this prerogative over to the directors, but they could muster only two votes). At the December meeting they moved from discussion to decision. They were in unanimous agreement by the end of the meeting (as had been their usual custom), and it was also decided to add a preamble to the draft bylaws to define "the purpose and objectives of this Catholic university." It was also thought timely to tell the provincial about their decisions.[73]

In January they discussed separate incorporation for the Jesuit community, to eliminate all possible overlap of governance. A Jesuit attorney persuaded them to render the incorporation still more religiously neutral by eliminating the explicit requirement that the BC trustees be Jesuits. They were also advised to forget the preamble expressing a Catholic commitment, since the church-state issue was festering and they might embarrass some of their sister institutions which had purposely omitted any such "sectarian" identification. The discussion which ensued was very earnest, and was recorded more attentively than usual in the minutes. Would the absence of identification as a religiously affiliated institution in the foundational documents inhibit BC's ability to take stands on religious issues when dealing with faculty? That, they were advised, could be taken care of more discreetly in faculty contracts. Without such a preamble, how would candidates for high administrative responsibility be advised of the strong religious commitment of the institution? The answer: presumably BC would select only candidates who were already cognizant of and sympathetic to the aims and purposes of Jesuit education. If the religious objective and commitment of Boston College were not contained in the bylaws, where would they be stated? The student handbook and its faculty counterpart were indicated as the appropriate place. So the board voted unanimously to make the articles of incorporation and bylaws silent about the religious character ("Jesuit" was no longer used in the discussion) of Boston College.[74]

Walsh meanwhile had announced his intended retirement at the end of the academic year. Previously his superiors would have decided such a matter. All the juridical documents were drawn up and agreed to during the latter months of his tenure, ready to be enacted in the fall under the new president. Walsh admitted privately that there were misgivings about "rushing this whole matter," for two reasons. The change in governance was entirely grounded on a controversial theory that the original civil incorporation, issued to a group of five men and their successors without any reference to their being Jesuits, created an independent civil trust over which the Jesuits could have no proprietary rights, and which lacked all customary legal standing as a Catholic institution before canon law. There was a strongly argued countertheory that the purposes and the history of Boston College demonstrated that it had always been a Jesuit, Catholic institution, just as much as the Archdiocese of Boston, which was also civilly incorporated. The second reason why caution might have been preferred was that the church-state controversy which impelled the process was not yet mature, and their hasty move was possibly giving away more than was prudent.[75] But the process hastened on. Permission from the provincial came in March, and from the general in May. Father W. Seavey Joyce, S.J., former dean of the College of Business Administration and then vice president for community affairs, succeeded Walsh. By October the new dual board structure was operational. Four years later the documents were again rewritten and the two boards were conflated into a single board of trustees, mostly lay in membership and no longer chaired by the college president.

The proprietary relationship between the Society of Jesus and Boston College was ended, and replaced by a contractual arrangement devoted to their respective financial obligations. As the joint "Foundational Statements" now put it, any Jesuit working at BC was related to his superiors no differently from a "Jesuit assigned to the faculty of, e.g., Brandeis, Harvard or Notre Dame." The Jesuit community, not the trustees or officers or faculty of Boston College, was to be the group that "makes Boston College a Catholic and a Jesuit University," and its sole remaining means of accomplishing this, as a sponsor, was to provide personnel.[76]

Fordham Follows

Just before Boston College actually executed all these changes, Arrupe asked representatives of Jesuit higher education from the Americas, Europe, Asia, and India to meet with his staff in Rome on their way to the IFCU meeting in Kinshasa. He presented them with his misgivings about the new autonomy, especially in the United States:

> On the broad question of secularization . . . are there any limits which, as Jesuits, we will put to this process? . . . What is being done to ensure that the Jesuit spirit still will be present? . . . What of our ability to continue . . . We know that many young Jesuits are not too favorable to work in a Jesuit university.

Jesuit institutions elsewhere offered broad differences in governance (most without external boards of trustees, some with internal councils that included no Jesuits, others entirely controlled by Jesuits), in proportion of Jesuits teaching (from 2 to 10 percent), and in the Catholic representation among the students (from 5 percent upward). But it was the North Americans Arrupe was fretting about. Robert Henle, then dean at Saint Louis, explained the changes in light of Vatican II. The Catholic education system had been designed to preserve the faith of the Catholics studying in it, but the new ecumenical climate was reducing that emphasis. Some favored the conversion of all Catholic and Jesuit schools to secular status, and Jesuits could then "make their impact in the university world as individuals or members of small groups." The new bylaws at Saint Louis, Henle assured them, stated clearly that it was a Catholic and Jesuit institution, and the new Protestant and Jewish trustees "are extremely anxious to know what they should do to maintain the Catholic character." John P. Leary of Gonzaga University said that Jesuit influence would now come through their living, active presence rather than legal structures and formalities, and he grieved that the Jesuit curia in Rome was responding so sluggishly to requests for approval of governance changes in the States. Leo McLaughlin, president of Fordham, pointed out that for 127 years Fordham had been considered a Jesuit university without the Society of Jesus having been mentioned in its charter.

But the Jesuits in Rome kept insisting that whoever has responsibility must also have authority. Henle somehow failed to reassure them by invoking "the substantive nature of the institution as an educational, philosophical and ideological organization internally committed to maintaining itself as such." Said Fordham's McLaughlin: "When the decision was made, consciously or unconsciously, to allow our universities in the United States to become many in number and large with many different schools, I think that effectively at that time control by the Society was abdicated." Paolo Dezza, spokesman for the curia, countered that, for instance, although the current Saint Louis board had committed itself to maintaining the university as Catholic and Jesuit, there was no sufficient guarantee that their successors would not later rescind the commitment. If Jesuits cede juridical authority, i.e., the right to make ultimate decisions, then they must make it clear that all they have left is personal influence, and that the institution as such is no longer Jesuit. Henle insisted that it was the Catholic and Jesuit sympathies of their academic colleagues, not those of overseers, which counted, and that this could be guaranteed only by their "living Jesuit presence." The minutes of the meeting do not record any meeting of minds.[77]

The Kinshasa conference proved somewhat disappointing to the Americans. There was insufficient support for the Land O'Lakes doctrine of complete autonomy for it to be adopted as IFCU policy. Kinshasa was remembered for having stressed the (lowercase) "'catholicity' of the academic community." The presidents gathered at the winter JEA meeting to hear Father Henle's account of his dispute with Father Dezza. Henle explained that their respective positions distinguished a university which is "substantially" Catholic or Jesuit from one which is "legally" so. What would assure the former, if not the latter? The reply: a statement of commitment by the board of trustees. This, of course, ignored Leo McLaughlin's confession in Rome that once the universities had become so large and diversified that the internal personnel were people largely indifferent to religion, no external, legal authority — the Vatican, the Society of Jesus, or a board of trustees — could make it "substantially" Catholic or Jesuit.

McLaughlin was obliged to resign during the Christmas vacation of 1968, and within months of having stepped down from the Boston College presidency Michael Walsh, chairman of the Fordham board of trustees throughout the transitional years, was asked to serve there as president for three years. It was he, therefore, who briefed the JEA in January on the pending change of governance there. The Fordham story provides an illuminating companion narrative to that of Boston College, especially since Walsh was simultaneously a leader at both.

New York, like many states, had had a "Blaine Amendment" added to its constitution in the backwash of Know-Nothing anti-Catholicism. New York had originally funded common schools managed by a variety of religious groups, but when immigration began to produce Catholic groups who claimed the same subsidy for their schools, all funding was thereafter reserved to state-run schools. A new constitutional amendment explicitly forbade any grants to educational organizations under "sectarian" control. As the three great state systems, SUNY, CUNY, and the state colleges, began to draw New Yorkers into their highly funded and low-priced campuses, the state's church-related colleges and universities were afflicted by severe deficits. Governor Nelson Rockefeller, seeing that it would be much more economical for the state to provide a modest subsidy to make it possible for some of these students to continue attending church-related colleges of their choice rather than to support their total expense at New York's state campuses (then among the most highly funded in the country), appointed a blue-ribbon commission under McGeorge Bundy to find some way to provide such subsidies without falling afoul of the Blaine Amendment. The Bundy Report said that the qualifying institutions (mostly Catholic) should simply find a way to certify that they were not under sectarian control.

Fordham had its own consultants, Walter Gellhorn and R. Kent Greenawalt of the Columbia University Law School. Gellhorn was a known ally of Leo Pfeffer, the usual plaintiff's attorney in major anti-Catholic litigation, and so was thought to be the right man for this job. The Gellhorn Report, "An Independent Fordham? A Choice for Catholic Higher Education," was causing a stir in New York. The *New York Times* had caused much heartburn on the Rose Hill Campus with its headline: "End of Jesuit Rule."[78] Walsh reviewed its recommendations for his colleagues. To qualify for state aid Fordham had not only to become "*completely* independent," but somehow to "change certain characteristics" while not changing its "fundamental 'character.' " These were the changes Gellhorn and Greenawalt recommended:

1. Terminate affiliation with the Jesuit seminary.
2. Terminate ties with Fordham Prep.
3. Withdraw Fordham's certification as a religious institution under New York's antidiscrimination laws.
4. Give title over the Jesuits' summer villa to their separate corporation.
5. Separately incorporate the Jesuit community.
6. Expand the board of trustees to include a significant number of laymen answerable to no outside authority. Do not restrict the presidency to Jesuits.
7. Continue to give no preference to Catholics or Jesuits in recruiting faculty and administrators.
8. Continue Fordham's nondiscrimination policy in admissions and financial aid, giving no preference to lay or religious Catholics.
9. Assure that all philosophy and theology courses are academic and not indoctrinational. Graduate studies in theology were queried because they trained teachers for Catholic schools.
10. Create new institutes, centers, programs with a non-Catholic or secular emphasis.
11. Expand the usage of Fordham's facilities to make it "a *great* community Center."
12. Diversify the publications of the university press.
13. No compulsory religious exercises. Sell the campus church to the Jesuit community or province.
14. No compulsory classroom prayer.
15. No religious symbols in the buildings; optional garb for religious personnel.
16. Consider withdrawal from Catholic educational associations. (They "give the wrong impression.")
17. Update catalogs, handbooks, etc., to stress that Fordham "provides an opportunity not only for mastery of secular disciplines but the possibility of studying them in an environment where religious values have a coordinate presence on the campus."

Walsh stressed that the Blaine Amendment (unlike the Gellhorn advice) focused its attention on governance more than atmosphere or image.[79] Fordham adopted most of the recommendations. It meant a drastic change for Fordham, to annul her statutory determination to be a place where "scholars, informed with a spirit of Christianity, may be enabled through enlightened intelligence and cooperative effort to form a center of Catholic culture."[80] In 1948 Fordham had filed a certificate with the New York Education Department stating that it was a denominational institution with specifically religious aims, and had accordingly been exempted from the law forbidding the consideration of religion in hiring or admissions. Now that certificate was returned, and the price of qualifying for state aid was the forfeiture of the university's freedom to create a distinctive Catholic faculty. Even Gellhorn and Greenawalt drew attention to what Jencks and Riesman said in 1968:

Academic professionals want their colleagues chosen on the basis of professional accomplishments, and they want them chosen by fellow professionals. An institution that refuses to follow these rules is unlikely to attract appreciable numbers of distinguished scholars over the years, for they will not regard it as a "real university." Yet we find it very hard to see how an institution that accepts these rules can long remain Catholic in any important sense.[81]

Fordham simultaneously announced that it would continue as a Catholic and Jesuit university, albeit an independent one, while admitting that it did not yet know what that might mean in the practical order. A shower of public statements now identified its religious identity in terms of "auspices," "origins," "traditions," "opportunities," "ideas," "perspectives," "values," "a loving and respectful openness" — all of which, without "people," became abstractions. Since the Catholic undergraduate population was then and has continued to be extremely high in its Catholic cohort (often 95 percent or higher) without any effort by the admissions office, it is possible that Walsh and his colleagues simply imagined that the Catholic component in the faculty would also be assured through self-selection. Fordham was cleared to receive state funds, though education officials in Albany quietly expressed surprise that their dissociative measures went well beyond what seemed necessary.[82]

Gellhorn and McLaughlin did not quite sweep all before them. An exceptionally sharp rebuke came from Charles Whelan, a Jesuit constitutional lawyer on the Fordham Law School faculty:

> I do not see how any university that honestly executed the Gellhorn recommendations could seriously call itself Catholic. Gellhorn and Greenawalt, understandably misled by the questions they were asked to answer, lost sight of the real problem at Fordham: not how to change it into another Columbia, but how to develop it into a first-rate Catholic university. In scratching the word "Catholic" from their answer, Gellhorn and Greenawalt have mutilated the problem as well as the university.[83]

This somewhat missed the point that Fordham was now willing not to call itself Catholic. Though this program had no direct bearing on the Boston College experience, the doings in New York were attracting enormous attention from Jesuit educators, partly because of Fordham's prestige and partly because of their respect for Walsh, who had picked up the reins. It was not widely known then that McLaughlin, who had enthusiastically initiated the changes because of Fordham's dire need for public financial aid, had helped to exacerbate that crisis by financial management that had almost bankrupted the school.[84]

Other Jesuit hands at Fordham were energetic in supporting the official divestiture. Ladislas Örsy, S.J., a canonist and chairman of the thenceforth nonindoctrinational Department of Theology, explained that Jesuit universities were civic institutions, existing by state action within state laws and regulations. Nothing, he went on to say, can be "Catholic" except the church or a baptized individual. No university can have faith, hope, or love, or can expect the assistance of the Holy Spirit. One can therefore speak only of a "Catholic presence," not a Catholic university. That presence could be augmented by requiring that Catholics be chosen as trustees or teachers or students, but if such provisions have to be imposed upon the university community, "the gentle inspiration of the gospel would be transformed into subtle coercion."[85]

Changes beyond Governance

In 1969 Fordham's lay dean, sociologist Paul Reiss, explained to a Jesuit educators workshop in Denver some social trends which persuaded him that "Jesuit administrators and trustees are presiding over institutions which are largely secular in character." Throughout all Jesuit colleges and universities, he reported, a steady-state Jesuit faculty now represented a shrinking proportion of the growing total faculty. From 31 percent in 1948, Jesuits provided only 16 percent of the faculty in 1968, and were projected to provide only 5 percent by 1978. The present range among Jesuit institutions was from 32 to 5 percent: highest at the smaller colleges and lowest at the large universities. This represented a substantial change, he concluded, and if there were any surviving truth in their claim to offer students a Jesuit education, it could not depend on their being taught by Jesuits. As for the lay colleagues, they largely resembled faculty on any American campus.

> With the Jesuit-founded institutions maintaining an image as "Catholic," naturally they have attracted Catholic lay faculty. This appears to be more by accident than by conscious design. In fact, a non-Catholic professor being recruited for the college will usually be assured that his faith or lack thereof will not present an obstacle to his appointment, nor to his being able to carry out his scholarly work and teaching. So long as he is not a militant atheist or anti-Catholic (and that eliminates only a few, since most would not be interested in an appointment at a Catholic college anyway), he will find no difficulty in this respect in joining the faculty.

But the Jesuits themselves "on the whole do not exert an impact which is significantly different, either in degree or in type, from that of lay teachers." To their credit, the Jesuits have insisted that their members meet the ordinary standards, but in the process they have "largely adopted secular faculty roles." But this, says Reiss, shows that they belong to a more unified faculty than ever before. The unity has obviously come by the assimilation of the Jesuits into the academy, not by any assimilation of their lay colleagues into the "gentle inspiration of the gospel."

Reiss also reported how diminished were the Jesuits in higher education administration. From 45 percent in 1958 they had become 27 percent in 1968, and were projected to be only 15 percent in 1978: not vanishing as quickly as Jesuits among the faculty, but vanishing. The new lay administrators, recruited for their skilled competence, had brought increased bureaucratization and professionalism. But their Jesuit peers have tended to adapt to this style and have dropped their paternalism, so that in the recruitment and appointment process clerical status was now deemed to be irrelevant, if not a hindrance, for an administrator. And so, Reis believed, Jesuits and laity in this work had also moved on to a higher form of community. With the development of this community, by which Reiss means an assimilation which will make Jesuit identity an irrelevant and nonprofessional consideration, there is no reason to anticipate any reversal of trends. However, if the faculty and administration contain few Jesuits, then it becomes "a very danger-ous situation" to have a board of trustees that comprises 100 percent Jesuits, so that might need downward adjustment also.

Jesuits could consolidate and maintain three or four Jesuit colleges. Or they could continue (on their own initiative, for they would have no guarantee or preference in the appointments process) to serve all twenty-eight campuses and provide whatever influence their numbers allow. "Such a college or university could hardly be called a 'Jesuit' college or university; it may not be called a 'Catholic' college or university." Reiss then concluded with a judgment that is most amazing precisely because no one registered amazement in Denver in 1969: "It should not, however, be viewed by Jesuits as a failure."[86] This was Harvanek a decade later, sugarcoated.

Is Jesuit Education Distinctive?

If the Land O'Lakes Statement made "autonomy" the byword for 1967, within only two years many Jesuit educators were drawing the conclusion that they had nothing "distinctive" to contribute to their colleges and universities.

Edmund Ryan, S.J., of Saint Peter's College showed how it should change their recruitment process: "The Jesuit campus heeds the contemporary call of the Catholic Church in the name of ecumenism and religious freedom to encourage religious pluralism in the composition of faculty, administration, and the student body." This statement, wherein Ryan spoke for many Catholics and Jesuits, implies a very significant turn of mind. The pluralism would thus be within the college instead of the college being within the pluralism. Rather than being an enlightened, identifiable participant in a diversified society, a Jesuit school would now reproduce all that diversity within itself and claim no peculiar enlightenment or perspective, let alone convictions. For several years now Catholics had been berating themselves for maintaining a "ghetto": the penitential term is as ubiq-uitous in the educational literature as mosquitoes at a June picnic. The preferred way to emerge from this "isolation," this "ghetto," this "backwater," was not to be a more self-defined, articulate, effective party to the general academic enterprise, but to assimilate into its own system the full Babel of American education. Ryan's hope was that within this newly diversified campus community the Jesuits would offer an effective communal witness of their faith. If the college could no longer have an identity, at least the Jesuits could have an identity within the college. He expresses no sense of loss that the college would (indeed, "should") no longer be susceptible of a shared faith, and thus could no longer be a distinctive protagonist within society.[87]

With the future of Jesuit education suddenly so problematic, Michael Walsh himself seemed confused even about the identity of Catholic education as they had reconfigured it, much as Pedro Arrupe had been confused in retrospect by what he had permitted. "Should we acknowledge that there is no distinctiveness; that Boston College is no different than Harvard or the University of Massachusetts? I hope that we can focus upon something at least in the word Catholic. Is there anything distinctive? I myself cannot see it."[88] Charles Donovan, who had worked with Walsh as chief academic officer at BC and would see a further decade of service under two other presidents, recalled that their own faculty recruitment process had already been changing:

> I find myself talking less explicitly about religion with prospective faculty members than I did five or six years ago. I simply ask them if they feel they would be comfortable in this institution, and then we talk about whether or not this situation would be relevant to them. People realize that we are a church-related school, and we are drawing people of many faiths who are turned off by the mechanical philosophy of some of the other institutions.[89]

As their sense of distinctive identity is blurred, so are their requirements for participation. In their consensus statement the Jesuits at Denver said:

> Thus, a school may be designated "Catholic" because most of those who gather there to teach or to learn consider Christianity in the Roman Catholic tradition vitally important in our history and our present world. Some will be personally committed to it in a free and mature faith; others will recognize it as a worthy partner in dialogue and community.[90]

Descartes and Voltaire, those notable Jesuit alumni, might now qualify for faculty status.

That fall the provincials acknowledged the obvious anachronism of their sitting as a board of governors over the Jesuit Educational Association when as individual superiors they had lost or would shortly lose their authority over the colleges and universities. The presidents effectively walked away from the JEA and founded the Association of Jesuit Colleges and Universities, to be run by, and very much for, the presidents. Laboring to make a virtue out of necessity, the provincials told the presidents they would support the AJCU, but then enormously annoyed them by a gratuitous suggestion:

> We also see it as somewhat analogous to a voluntary accrediting association, with the accreditation being the right to use the Jesuit name. We would prefer that the criteria or norms for judging the "Jesuitness" of our Colleges be both written and enforced by the members of the Association. However, we think that initial approval of the criteria would have to come from Father General and from the U.S. Provincials. To carry the analogy further, we would consider the Jesuit Provincials as analogous to the Directors of a Foundation or of a Governmental Agency, i.e., the Provincials would offer additional Jesuit manpower to a "Jesuit" institution only as long as it continued to maintain "accreditation" by the Association of Jesuit Colleges and Universities. Similarly, local Jesuit communities would continue to return part of their earnings to the institution they serve only as long as it maintains "Jesuit accreditation."[91]

In an act of uncharacteristic and belated *Realpolitik,* the provincials then took the quiet precautionary measure of registering "Jesuit" as a trademark.[92]

The match ended in a seeming draw. The provincials accepted that they were now to be excluded from any responsibility toward the Jesuit colleges and universities, except to provide their best men, equipped with fifteen years or so of higher education at Jesuit expense, for the service of the schools, and then to rebate most of their salaries to the schools. But as a farewell gesture they charged the presidents with a task so vexatious that they cannot have seriously believed it would be accepted. The presidents had stood with arms linked on only one issue: autonomy for each institution. The JEA had been a strategic forum for these efforts. But on repeated occasions they had backed away from any policy setting that might have made them severally accountable even to their own roundtable. The provincials' delicate threat, to use their remaining powers to grant or withhold personnel and their annual rebate, made their proposal both difficult to ignore and difficult to accept.

The presidents were agreed that no criteria of "Jesuitness," as they called them, should actually be written into the bylaws of their AJCU. Perhaps they could be put in a codicil or a side letter to the provincials. But their criteria for institutional membership in the AJCU made it clear how minimalist they wished to be:

1. An official commitment on the part of the institution to being a Jesuit college or university (e.g., by a statement in its by-laws or by the tradition of its published statements);
2. A community of Jesuits visible as a corporate body whose major apostolate is higher education in this institution;
3. An institutional arrangement which declares, displays, and perpetuates the Jesuit character of the institution (e.g., substantial representation of Jesuits on the Board of Trustees);

4. An acceptance and realization of the educational ideals and spirit of the Society of Jesus.[93]

The presidents had excluded both provincials and possible future lay presidents from membership on the AJCU board of directors, after sharp debate among themselves. To put the provincials even further out of the way, they voted to make the policy-making AJCU meetings closed to all but themselves.[94]

The AJCU was formally activated in the summer of 1970, and the presidents were aware that their provincials were not entirely reconciled to dowager status. In 1971 the presidents addressed a public letter to them. It abounded in positive affect — "appreciate the interest . . . their concerns and ours are, for the most part, identical" — and promised better scholarship, religious influence, and Jesuit community life on the campuses. After having stripped the provincials of their right to supervise Jesuit higher education, and to direct, belong to, or even attend the meetings of the Jesuit higher education roundtable, the presidents urged the "need for closer cooperation between institutional leadership and Society leadership."

Behind the document were two concerns. First, the young Jesuits were now taking the presidents at their word — that a Jesuit assigned to BC or Georgetown or Saint Louis was considered no differently than were he on the faculty of Brandeis, Harvard, or Notre Dame. So the young Jesuits were getting more interested in solo appointments at Brandeis, Harvard, and Notre Dame. So much for the presidents' appeal to stick together: "Designation of any apostolate as 'Jesuit' will involve a corporate engagement and witness. We believe that, in general, more efficacious apostolates will be effected through corporate or institutional means." A second presidential vexation was the hard-nosed way in which the provincials had bargained for pension rights, medical insurance, residential space, and other considerations when the contracts between Jesuit communities and the educational institutions were being drawn up. Thus their message ended on the moral high ground: "The concerns over finances, comfortable living, and the loss of control over institutions are harmful to creative sharing of our Jesuit spirit with faculty and students."[95]

Before returning our attention to Boston College, whose denizens had watched as their destiny had been debated and decided over their heads, one thing must be noted. The radical removal of the Society of Jesus from its chartered position as overseer of its colleges and universities was the result of a mounting anxiety on the part of the presidents. It did not begin as a contest with the provincials. It was directed first against the province prefects of education, then Rooney, then the provincials, then the federal government, then Rome, both Jesuit and papal. But its directing spirit all along was an entrepreneurial autonomy that resisted deferring to any agenda larger than that of each president's campus. The presidents ultimately wanted institutional independence, to be free to increase the heartbeat of their respective schools. But as the dust settled, it was the presidents, not their schools, that emerged in possession of almost unchallengeable power.

Tilton v. *Richardson* in 1971 was a first presage that they were going to qualify for a share in governmental funding. Rome, in the persons of both its White Pope and its Black Pope, had been put on notice that U.S. civil law had wrapped a new palisade of nonintervention around the Jesuit campuses. The presidents said they were now formally subject to new plenipotentiaries: boards over which they no longer presided, and which could make and unmake presidents. But these presidents and their next successors were the clear masters of their boards, provided only that they avoid the unforgivable sin of financial folly, one which the worldly boardfolk were equipped to recognize and to punish.[96] It was, from the presidents' point of view, a providentially right time to come into that much power, since these very years were the season when faculty were claiming their share in deliberative policy making, and forming unions, and striking, and students were resorting to their own threatening tactics to get a share of the say-so. A president whose campus constituencies were climbing over the outer defenses could always tell them that their issue was indeed large, and had to be referred to the board. And boards could outwait the students and outwit the faculty, at least a good deal of the time. At least for the present, the changes yielded all power to the prexy.

A Strong Jesuit President, a Weakening Jesuit Community

At Boston College the president needed all the power he could get. Father Seavey Joyce served four devastatingly difficult years as president, 1968-72. The change in governance had to be seen through some of its last stages: the Jesuit superior became rector in his own right; Weston College, the Jesuit seminary, became disaffiliated; required credits in undergraduate theology were reduced from twelve to nine to six. Joyce's campus became an arena of wild new events beyond his control. Student resistance to the Vietnam hostilities led to the closure of the ROTC program. Blacks came to the campus in suddenly greater numbers, and there were touchy feelings on all sides. Bill Baird, Boston's notorious abortion clinic entrepreneur, came to lecture against the pope. Mary Daly, then in only her youthful stages as the Patty Hearst of Catholic theology, was denied tenure on recommendation of the department and then after student demonstrations was given it by the president. Walsh had left Joyce an institution whose claim to academic greatness was grounded on greatly expanded expenditures but not a greatly consolidated income base.[97] A series of harsh deficits had already begun during Walsh's last year, but had been obscured then by draining scholarship reserves. An abrupt series of tuition raises led to a student strike, back-and-forth negotiations, and a revision in the charges. The student newspaper bugged the board of trustees (in the electronic sense), and its editors received criminal convictions.

But more deeply than the usual student disturbances and faculty self-assertion, Seavey Joyce's presidency was swimming against the current financially, and developing cramps. The university had a considerable amount of building restoration

607

and expansion to do, and engaged in new construction. Endowment was very modest. But in 1968 BC was receiving contributions to the Annual Fund from only 6 percent of her alumni, and the average annual gift was only $2.13. Up the road in Worcester, Holy Cross was receiving an average gift of $34.16 from 23 percent of its alums. In four of the previous five years Holy Cross, with one-third as many alumni, had raised more actual dollars than BC. Despite its dominating size, BC ranked eighth among the ten Jesuit universities in total gifts received, and was outdone by four of the smaller colleges as well. She was spending 70¢ of every dollar raised to pay the costs of fund-raising (compared with the University of Detroit, which spent only 7¢).[98] In one year alone, Boston College faced a shortfall of $4.2 million in its Current Fund.[99] The year was 1970, and none of the crucial litigation had yet been resolved in favor of BC's or her peers' capacity to receive government assistance. Joyce commissioned an opinion survey which reported disapproval of "the financial situation, 'administrative permissiveness,' and the decline in Catholicity and 'Jesuit presence.'" It was nevertheless his view that, "If B.C. should cease to be Jesuit, there is no reason for its continued existence."[100]

By the time Joyce handed on the baton in 1972, Jesuit demography on the BC campus had shifted considerably since Father Walsh took over in 1958. At the start of that era, nine of eleven deans were Jesuits; at the end, they were six out of twelve. The Jesuits had constituted 24 percent of the faculty, and now they were only 12 percent. Jesuits were now fewer in numbers, proportion, and credentials, and the ambit of their work was increasingly restricted to the College of Arts and Sciences, and indeed to only certain departments there.[101]

The provincials had for some time been following the lead of the presidents. They had formed their own agency for common endeavor, the Jesuit Conference, and like the presidents they were at pains to assure that whatever they did in common never encroached upon the autonomy of the member provincials. In this respect they were somewhat like the central agencies of congregational churches. They chose for their first joint project a Carnegie-like study of their apostolate of education, and called it *Project 1*. It began with a quantitative survey that arrayed such nontheological facts as the total number of Jesuits involved in Jesuit schools (1,849: 19 percent of their manpower) and on other campuses (120); the average amount of earned salaries they had returned to their institutions that year ($201,692); the average number of "programs per year to acquaint non-Jesuits with Jesuit educational aims and ideals" (3.4); the attendance rate of academic Jesuits at community liturgies (33 percent); the percentage of Jesuit academics, besides those in campus ministry, who were active in student religious life (28 percent); the number of Jesuit campus communities who looked to their rector, instead of the president, for leadership in their ministry (twelve out of twenty-eight); the average proportion of Jesuits among teachers and administrators (13 percent and 21 percent) — all this while high schools had doubled in number and college enrollments had quadrupled.[102] Whatever their specific and subconscious finality, these were depressing data.

Subsequent volumes which emerged every few months explored various options. Thirteen years after Robert Harvanek's sober and unwelcome proposals, the facts had become even more ominous, but proposed responses were much the same. The Society could retain sponsorship of all campuses and continue to serve them as local communities; or withdraw Jesuit manpower and resources to the number of campuses they could thoroughly manage; or confine themselves to certain functions; or simply serve as individual freelancers on their present campuses; or form the twenty-eight schools into a centrally managed system, as some large state universities were beginning to do; or sponsor residential Jesuit "colleges" on large campuses; or prepare for some newer and more radical departure from the past. An opinion poll of American Jesuits showed an awareness of difficulties stymieing their educational apostolate, but massive preference for doing nothing.

A Jesuit College without Jesuits?

At best, the Society soon would have neither the freehold nor the manpower to maintain their establishment as Jesuit. So various Jesuit groups, and the twenty-eight universities and colleges themselves, fell to speculating about how their patrimony might somehow be preserved.[103] Countless manifestoes tried to describe what a "Jesuit institution" would look like, but were silent about how to assure that it happened — or, more to the point, how to people these campuses with people who would want it to happen.[104]

Their imaginations went in many directions. The present father general, Peter-Hans Kolvenbach, once said extravagantly that "one Jesuit who is truly a Jesuit can be all that is needed to guarantee the authority or the Jesuitness of the university."[105] No one has wanted to take that literally. Fordham in 1977 soberly confessed, late in the day, that "the goals of the University and the goals of the Jesuit Community no longer coincide." So, along with Saint Louis (1977), Fordham proposed that Jesuits should no longer speak of their universities as their apostolates, but of "the Jesuit apostolate at (or 'in') the University."

Some think the laity will pick up the task as the Jesuits lay it down. "Even a tiny minority of lay partners, provided they have unimpeachable academic credibility, . . . who have publicly promised themselves to God and to service to others," could be an adequate force for renewal on traditionally Jesuit campuses.[106] How could lay colleagues be prepared to take up such a tradition? Some argued that the "Ignatian vision," a "decisive, religiously humanistic vision," is transmissible through his *Spiritual Exercises*.[107] Followed in the classical way, this requires a thirty-day retreat. Would many of their colleagues undergo such an initiation? At the University of Detroit, seven hundred staff and faculty were invited to a series of one-day seminars on the *Spiritual Exercises* and the "Jesuit Vision in Higher Education," and forty-three came.[108] Others saw the *Ratio Studiorum* as the template laymen could use. A Jesuit educator in India scoffed: "The average Jesuit's attitude to the *Ratio* parallels that of the average Catholic to the Bible: most have a vague reverence for the *Ratio* (even this is doubtful), but neither read it nor are familiar with it."[109]

There were plenty who ridiculed the notion of a Jesuit institution animated by laypeople, however trained. Says Robert S. Miola, a layman who teaches English at Loyola College: "What makes a Jesuit college different is Jesuits — their spirituality, rigor, ideals, learning — in a word, their presence."[110] His colleagues agreed that Jesuit education needed Jesuits:

> There is something specific and valuable and quite different that a Jesuit can and should contribute to an institution. This something is unsubstitutable by lay people, no matter how holy, no matter how well trained. To deny this is to say that the 15-year-long Jesuit course, the Ignatian training that should be in the marrows of a Jesuit, the singularity of aim *(Ad maiorem Dei gloriam)* that gives the Jesuit apostolate its extra thrust — are all really nothing.[111]

Some chose to interpret the passing away of the Jesuits as a blessing in disguise. The president of the AJCU wrote of a "psychological possessiveness and resistance to change" on the part of the religious orders in the bad old days. In Omaha the Jesuit community (1975) was anxious to deny "that Jesuits hold a superior or sheltered position at Creighton." Santa Clara's avowal (1979) that it was "a community opposed to narrow indoctrination or proselytizing of any kind" seems to imply that some must think otherwise.

The Jesuit evacuation, on the other hand, could be a welcome turn to diversity, a matter for celebration. Many statements describe their campus population as diversified in race, gender, and religion, leaving one to wonder whether all three diversities could really mean the same to a Jesuit university. At Fordham's Graduate School of Religion and Religious Education (1984), since Catholic belief and theology no longer unite its scholars and students or provide a common, intelligible faith language, "all share a vision of a society enriched by human accomplishment but also suffused with religious-ethical ideas." Yes, but the Society for Ethical Culture did it first. At newly pluralist Loyola, New Orleans (1977) "all are bound together by a common search for knowledge." But the same might be said of everyone in the reading room of the New Orleans Public Library.

Some statements went further, from description to prescription, and said that religious pluralism was a purposeful choice for a religious college. Loyola, New Orleans claims that the search for wisdom "will best be accomplished in our day by a community drawn from many religious, ethnic, and cultural backgrounds." This is not stating a fact but favoring a fact. Santa Clara devotes a section of its *Guidelines for Policy* to "Catholicism and Diversity" (1977):

> Santa Clara is committed to retaining its Catholic character. It is also committed to religious diversity and freedom of expression. Are these goals incompatible?

We believe not. While valuing its Catholic and Jesuit tradition, Santa Clara does not seek conformity. [The 1984 version adds defensively:] for by its very nature a university is pluralistic.

Santa Clara in the same section affirms the vigorous recruitment of people from various social, economic, and racial backgrounds. One must suppose that they are being welcomed, not as guests by hosts, but as members by members, so that their social, economic, and racial differences present no obstacle to their full membership in the Santa Clara community. But to claim that religious diversity is similarly "an essential for a lively educational environment," implies that Catholics are no longer hosts warmly welcoming guests from many religious commitments or none, for such religious differences must, on this view of things, now be inconsequential at Santa Clara. How then can Santa Clara have a Catholic or Jesuit character, if it disavows a special affinity for Catholics as its host population?

If the answer could not be in personnel, some imagined a formula for Jesuitness. " 'Jesuitness,' " insisted Creighton, "is by no means restricted to members of a single religious order." There were many who identified it as the affirmation of the goodness of creation, of nature, of culture. "The world of nature and of persons is good" is the assurance given by Wheeling. To many ears this would seem not very contentious, but it is a central doctrine for the sons of Ignatius, who wrote that "all things in the world are gifts of God, presented to us so that we can know him more easily." Thus Loyola, New Orleans claims "a reverence for creation," and Saint Louis follows through with a "commitment to the secular," "an affirmation of all things created." "Finding God in all things" is a refrain heard all round. Georgetown's bard-president Timothy Healy said it his way: "All of creation is touched with the laboring presence of God."[112] He quotes Teilhard de Chardin, who carries the point further: "Nothing secular is less than secular."

In 1975 Pedro Arrupe convoked an unusual General Congregation (GC32), rarely summoned except for the election of a new father general. The centerpiece of its legislation, which enlarged upon Arrupe's own call for ministry to those rendered helpless by systemic misery, was Decree 4: "Our Mission Today." Every single Jesuit ministry was enjoined to enlarge its agenda. "The mission of the Society of Jesus today is the service of faith, of which the promotion of justice is an absolute requirement."[113] Since too many Jesuits labored in isolation from oppression, solidarity with victims and social activism against systemic injustice was henceforth to be, not a specialized work, but an essential aspect of any legitimate Jesuit ministry. This call to serve justice was more welcome to the presidents than much of what they had had to listen to. It was much used as a public examination of conscience (not always one's own). A hunger and thirst for justice seemed valid evidence that a campus was either Catholic or Jesuit. Justice was a reality that could be pursued energetically in a respectable university. It could reassure the Jesuit and Catholic constituencies without sounding sectarian to the *Chronicle of Higher Education.*

It had always been the presidents' preference to define their work as Jesuit education, not Catholic. The former was understood as one variant within the latter: possibly the best.[114] But after 1967 and All That, Jesuits were pressed to defend even the Catholic character of their campuses. Michael Walsh, we have seen, despite — or perhaps because of — having drafted "The Objectives of a Catholic University" for his fellow presidents in 1967, confessed two years later that he was at a loss to describe what was "distinctive" even about Catholic universities. He returned to "Jesuit" as a less tendentious identity, and one that might more easily be finessed. By 1971 it was clear that he did not mind functional descriptions which specified what was required for a university to be Jesuit. But a newer prose nevertheless arose, which he called "philosophical," and which analyzed at some length what should be the distinctive benefits and outcomes of a Jesuit university . . . if there were one.[115] At the time, the attempts to describe a Jesuit university seemed more distracting than helpful.

BC Defines Itself

What did Boston College say during that period to define itself? The question was addressed in its self-study for reaccreditation in 1975. It was therefore addressed to the academy, but to be overheard by the church, and it deftly wove together various literary genres, including editorial prose, marketing copy, and fictional story line.

> In an age of growing secularism and intellectual pluralism institutions of higher learning with a strong religious tradition find the struggle to locate their identity, to proclaim their distinctiveness, and to set their goals a special challenge. Boston College is no exception. . . .
>
> Its Jesuit faculty, so closely associated with the religious and humanistic aspects of the university from the beginning but now proportionately smaller than it was ten or fifteen years ago, must remain a strong center of influence both in and out of the classroom. Their presence, along with that of other religious and laity who are part of the community, is essential, and the administration will lose no opportunity to attract such committed and professional scholar-teachers as will manifest in their lives the ideal of learning, questioning, and religious dedication so central to their tradition. . . .
>
> There are no written university procedures on the recruiting and selection of faculty other than the mandatory requirements that all hiring be done in strict compliance with the university's published Affirmative Action Guidelines. . . .
>
> Boston College, as a community of learners and teachers, both religious and lay, nevertheless holds to a distinctive purpose. We take a certain pride and satisfaction in affirming that our institution is different. Rooted in the Judaeo-Christian and classical traditions, the university of 1974 and of the years ahead

subscribes to a fundamentally religious vision, not narrow or restrictive, but generous and open. It reaffirms a belief in God as Creator and Redeemer, as the model of love and wisdom Whose life and teachings proclaimed a higher goal of thought and action. As a contemporary university it conceives of this ideal not as an abstraction but as a living reality which should pervade every aspect of university life and should express itself in the sense of common purpose we all share as colleagues, in our concern for the person and his or her ideas, in a spirit of inquiry and a sensitivity to values as they touch our many studies. . . .

The university is concerned with having a diverse student body, including people with differing racial, religious, cultural, economic and geographical backgrounds.[116]

This statement manages to round up all the usual themes. Boston College says it stands with an identity of its own against a secularizing and fractured society, grounded on belief which, though portrayed here in nearly Unitarian terms, is locally understood as relating to Jesus. It owes much of this to the Jesuits, who gave BC a religious and humanistic foundation. It calls its teachers and students a community. They are joined in this distinctive purpose, and there is a need for like-minded professional scholar-teachers to join them.

Using that most elusive of terms, BC also says it is rooted in the Judaeo-Christian tradition. "Rooted" suggests a commitment of the past (when, one may infer, BC may possibly have been narrow and restrictive, not generous and open as it now is), contrasted with a refreshingly indefinite present. "Judaeo-Christian" is a friendly term because it has no existing membership, and abstract "tradition" can easily occupy the space where existential "church" once might have stood. Thus the sum of the college's religious profession is this: that it wants to bring together a student body as random as society at large, and a faculty whose amiable religious beliefs it will welcome but not recruit, or prefer, or gaze upon too rudely. After such a modest proposal the statement wisely declines to forecast what good that would accomplish.

It was probably not a good time to ask Americans to articulate what was required to have a Jesuit or Catholic institution without Jesuits or Catholics. Jesuit academics were becoming very few. Catholic academics were becoming very many, but those determined to hire them had become very few. The only parties to this crisis that manifested impatience were in Rome. In 1973 the Vatican itself, worn down by repeated refusals of American educators to come to terms on that matter, announced that its demands were reduced to two. Educators should forthwith draft policies:

1. on the necessity for each Catholic university to set out formally and without equivocation, either in its Statutes or in some other internal document, its character and commitment as "Catholic"; and
2. on the necessity for every Catholic university to create within itself appro-

priate and efficacious instruments so as to be able to put into effect proper self-regulation in the sectors of faith, morality and discipline.[117]

John Donohue, S.J., chief education writer for *America,* the Jesuit weekly, winced out loud. The expression "without equivocation," he grieved, was one of several expressions whereby the communiqué was "darkened by an outdated tone of suspicion."[118] But much equivocation would nevertheless survive this hurtful Vatican remark.

Another expression of impatience came from the Jesuit headquarters. In 1975 Pedro Arrupe summoned to Rome all the presidents of Jesuit colleges and universities in the world, and seventy came. What he had to say was not welcome. Were they and their lay colleagues distinguishable from their peers in the academy? he asked. "Has a 'dominant secularism' become our native air, so that God is effectively absent from our world?" Their proper world, he said, was that of scholarship, and their task was to incarnate into that culture Christian faith and service, and to offer the reflection and transcendental values whereby our faith transforms research into a life-giving work. "Let us not be too easily persuaded that students are developing this spirit of reflectiveness and synthesis merely because they study at our institutions." Jesuits were fewer and older on their campuses, and lay professors were now anywhere from two to forty times more numerous. Do those lay colleagues regard the Jesuit project as theirs too? he asked. Does their selection process purposefully look for those whose interests and preferences will strengthen Jesuit priorities? Were the presidents actively using their campuses to educate and influence those who would be opinion makers: in the media and the arts? Jesuit educators, as individuals and as communities, he said to them, should be prophets.

The Arrupe who had signed over the Jesuit system in America had evidently suffered a bad aftertaste in the intervening decade.[119] Two days later he lectured them again. Their universities, he reminded them, are Jesuit universities, because they either belong to the Society or are still considered by public opinion to be Jesuit, even though it is now by way of influence, not control. And even if they are elected by a board, the Jesuit presidents serve because the Society has released them for that work, and has given them a formal mission. Their work is thereby an extension of the mission of Jesus. And precisely because their work is so secularized externally, they require an even more determined spirit to preserve a religious state of mind.

It could have been a direct evocation of those Jesuits who had once moved at their ease in royal courts, with their hair shirts constantly to remind them of another loyalty. But Arrupe was worried that the opposite was now happening. "As one succeeds in hiding his own identity and kind of life," he argued, "there is no difference externally from the life of lay presidents of secular universities." Thus their need to abide by a spirit of simplicity and personal austerity. They were no longer rectors of their communities, but they still owed the witness of their own obedience and discretion and simple faith to their fellow Jesuits, and a humble submission to their provincials.[120] From later exchanges between the Americans, it would appear that the second discourse was even more disturbing than the first, for it looked them more personally in the eye. In particular — more even than by the injunctions to humility — several resented Arrupe's stubborn insistence that the Society still thought of them as answerable for their presidency.

Ten years later Arrupe's successor, Father Kolvenbach, summoned the Jesuit presidents back again. He repeated the principal Arrupe themes: no matter who actually elected them, these presidents were on a mission from the Society, which still claimed to be the "principal author" of the institutions it still considered "Ours."[121] He warmed to his point. If a college or university were not just a place where some Jesuits happen to be working, but a "Jesuit institution," then it had to be an apostolic endeavor with an apostolic leader. And "it cannot be Catholic and at the same time completely autonomous!" Then, curiously, he backed off: "I am not using that word in any juridical sense, but only insisting that there has to be a close relationship with the Church."[122]

One of Kolvenbach's deputies pursued the challenge. "Recourse to the laity in order to compensate for a lack of Jesuit personnel is a wrong idea . . . A common sense of purpose and a common commitment in an apostolic community can only flow from a common spirit among all those who make up this community. Certainly the origin and purpose of this common spirit can only be the Gospel of Jesus, the faith of the Church of Christ," which, on a Jesuit campus, would be enhanced by the spirituality of Ignatius.[123]

But for the harried presidents there was a balm in Gilead. From across the river Charles came some good comment from David Riesman, Harvard's learned observer of social realities in American education. He had regularly shown an interest in Catholic schools (to the point where he had a passage at arms with his own president, James Bryant Conant, who favored a single obligatory system of state education in early years). Riesman had some appreciative things to say about the Jesuit campuses, especially their diversity. "The Jesuit order has its own ecumenicity which transcends, in large measure, the ethnic and provincial Catholicisms of the various nation-states." From that point of view Boston College, with a student body so comprehensively Boston-Irish, would find blessing in direction by priests who had received portions of their Jesuit formation in England, Germany, India, France, or the Philippines, and were governed successively by a Pole, a Fleming, a Basque who had spent his life working in Japan, and a Dutchman whose ministry had been in Beirut. Secondly, Riesman observed that their student bodies were religiously variegated. He cited approvingly the University of Detroit, where only 44 percent of the students were Catholics, and Georgetown with its 40 percent. Thirdly, in their philosophy and theology courses the students were exposed to a wide latitude of dissent, even among Catholics.[124]

Far better even than Riesman's own Harvard, Jesuit colleges had maintained an ethos which allowed a measure of "formation" among their lay students. Their religion was not claustrophobic, and their low rates of attrition were enviable. Thus he commended Boston College for carrying 82 percent of its students to graduation. (Some conservative Protestant schools were suffering wastage rates of 25 percent, 30 percent, 40 percent, even 60 percent; the national rate was 50 percent.) The Jesuits, he thought, were wise to require liberal education of all students, and formal religious practices from none. Thus they were initiated into a strong tradition with intellectual and historical continuity, yet not exposed to proselytism. He complimented the Jesuits for being able to provide all of their campuses with a Jesuit president "without having the candidate go through a screen like that of a political campaign." And he regretted that "the children of many of the Catholic parents who themselves had excellent Jesuit education are now inclined to seek out, for reasons not only of status," institutions like Oberlin, Yale, or Chicago.[125] Riesman, sympathetic and fair-minded, seems to have had no premonition of a different morrow already dawning.

The Last of the Imperial Presidents

As the Jesuit establishment underwent all this turmoil, there were struggles for survival and authenticity on Chestnut Hill, where a new president in 1972 was trying to save one of the Society's leading institutions that most of the faculty and even most of the Jesuits on campus did not realize was near collapse.

J. Donald Monan would preside more than twice as long as any predecessor, four times longer than most. He was the first president to be elected by the trustees and not appointed by the father general. Shortly after his arrival he guided the proprietary Jesuit board through the legal process of eliminating their body in favor of a single, mostly lay, board with ultimate powers. His recruitment, as a Jesuit who had joined and served in the New York Province, showed how suddenly the old provincial frontiers had been breached by what was now virtually an open market where every Jesuit college and university competed for Jesuit personnel all across the country.

Monan's stewardship has been effective. The competence and scholarship of the faculty, the maturity of many graduate programs, the lodging and gear of the departments and schools, the growth of the endowment — all have burgeoned. A few random exhibits suggest the scale of this development. In 1982 Monan was awarded an honorary doctorate from Harvard, symbolically reversing the old animosity between Mullan and Eliot.[126] More graduates of BC now go on to earn doctorates than from any other Jesuit university.[127] The endowment stands at a half-billion dollars, ranking thirty-fourth in the nation, and BC was very pleased recently when its three-year growth outpaced that of other Boston-area universities, including Harvard and MIT.[128] Monan had begun his presidency with an endowment of $5 million (barely enough then to balance outstanding current debt), smaller than fourteen other Jesuit endowments. Twenty-five percent of the alumni now contribute each year, and last year they sent in $9.4 million. Research contracts bring in $16.5 million annually: trebled in the last decade. Faculty compensation stands well above the national averages in institutions of the same category; in 1993-94, the last reported year, the median professorial compensation was $96,400 for a nine-month year. Applications for the freshman class have been running at about 15,000, very generous for a class one-seventh that size. BC announces with satisfaction that its applicants are also candidates for Harvard, Yale, Brown, Cornell, Princeton, and the like (if there be any). The BC enrollment has for decades now been the largest, in full-time students, of all twenty-eight Jesuit campuses. And Doug Flutie lives (albeit in the CFL).

Factors less noticed include these: Jesuits on the faculty, who in the 1950s still had higher credentials than their lay colleagues, have fallen behind. Slightly less than half the students are now enrolled in the College of Arts and Sciences, whereas in yesteryear that school was much more dominant. The Jesuit demographics are iffy. There are 9 Jesuits among the 44 trustees; 48 Jesuits work on the campus, including 18 administrators and 30 full-time faculty. More than half are over the age of sixty.[129] The Jesuits continue to maintain a very large campus community: 130 in residence, the largest such community of Jesuits in the United States. But most of these men are not presently staffing the college.

Michael Walsh had reckoned that "15 good *scholar*-teacher" Jesuits were leaven enough for any hundred lay faculty. Leaving aside all appraisals of how good they be, it would be a daunting task for these Jesuit scholar-teachers (including some active emeriti) and administrators to leaven the mass of a regular faculty who now number 623. All the more so if only about 35 percent of the faculty, by one veteran estimate, or 30 percent or even 20 percent as others reckon, are Catholics.[130] Only in the Departments of Philosophy and Theology are Jesuits present in significant numbers (one-fourth of each department). Elsewhere they appear in ones and twos; most academic units in the university have none. Outside the College of Arts and Sciences Jesuits constitute only 1.5 percent of the regular faculty.[131] Prospects of further supply are poor. American Jesuits, who were more than nine thousand in 1965, now number less than half that. Their novices now number one-fourth of what they once were, and in the year 2010 the Society in the United States is projecting its total membership to be one-fourth of what it had been.

Student demographics are in flux as well. Despite the biblical hundredfold increase in endowment during the Monan administration, BC still relies heavily on tuition income, and it is becoming an expensive school. The total annual charges amount to approximately $25,000, with actual costs raising that to perhaps $30,000 per student. Financial aid has not kept up with those costs, so, with the exception of a few favored beneficiaries, students can find it difficult to come to Chestnut Hill unless they are affluent. This may have contributed to the slow annual decrease in Catholics among the student body.[132] From their former predominance at 97 percent, they have been slowly decreasing and now represent perhaps 79 percent of the student body.[133]

Throughout most of its history Boston College had served the educational aspirations and needs of Boston Catholics. Now it was identifying with the much less identifiable interests of the Judaeo-Christian tradition. Michael Walsh was given a nudge about this when he accompanied his successor on a visit to the Mellon Foundation, whose president was Nathan Pusey, previously president at Harvard. They were seeking funds from a program for urban universities. Pusey told them BC had no hope for a grant, since Northeastern was the university that was most actively involved in the life of the city.[134] This interview, plus the latter-day accession of Boston Catholics to affluence, may have influenced Father Monan to pay more attention to BC's native constituency, geographical and ecclesiastical.

Boston College has ostensibly been thriving, and no small part in that has been played for twenty-four years by Monan, known admiringly among his colleagues as the "Last of the Imperial Presidents." It was, at least as far as Jesuits were concerned, an unstable period, though no more so than on any other traditionally Jesuit campus.

In 1986 the University Planning Council prepared for the regular reaccreditation visit with an introductory policy statement, "Goals for the Nineties." The Catholic and Jesuit identity of the university received heavy attention. Enrolling the largest full-time student body of any Catholic university in the country, BC promised a "reassertion" of its religious character, in order to be "a visibly Catholic and Jesuit university and . . . a preeminent center of Catholic intellectual activity." In prose unusually lush for the times, the statement admits that since the college has opened its doors to pluralism, it needs to appraise its several concentric identities: the church, the society, and the college. It lists the essential characteristics of Catholicism: "an international community pervaded by a sense of peoplehood, a respect for tradition, a conviction that God's presence is mediated by sacramental signs, a sense of charity, and a prizing of reason."[135] The Jesuit tradition "has linked humanism with devotion to God; the Jesuit call to holiness meant a commitment to a life of learning as a way of service." The qualities claimed by BC itself are "a sense of Christian hope, a recognition of the dignity of the individuals, a supportive personal environment." Boston College alumni would "ideally" carry away rich benefits from this tutelage, e.g., "a mature and tested commitment to values, . . . a sacramental view of the world so that they can see in their own lives and in the world signs of transcendence, as well as an awareness of sin and the capacity to do evil."

A Catholic College without Catholic Faculty

By 1986, however, BC's challenge was not to determine the Catholic and Jesuit characteristics it would reductively describe and claim. The challenge was to find a faculty of Catholics and Jesuits actively willing to share such a claim. BC acknowledged that its "faculty are the primary bearers of its values and traditions," yet after this rhapsody about goals, the statement seemed to expect very little from them:

> A critical mass of the faculty should be familiar with the Catholic intellectual tradition, and all should regard spiritual as well as moral questions as worthy of serious exploration. . . .
>
> [Its foremost expectation is] that the faculty will be faithful to the Jesuit tradition of excellent teaching, . . . will go beyond the desire to stimulate intellectual growth to a concern for the personal development of students, both spiritually and morally . . . [and will] have a broad perspective in liberal education.[136]

If an indeterminate cadre of faculty were expected to be no more than "familiar" with the Catholic intellectual tradition — not "committed," not even "sympathetic," but merely "familiar" — how would they ever begin to take up the task seemingly made in heaven?

A Jesuit-dominated subcommittee on "Jesuit and Catholic identity" had previously debated the ways and means of securing needed faculty support. Disavowing any policy to "hire Catholics" as an "inappropriate resolution of this complex matter," the subcommittee urged that being "interested in some of the activities related to the Catholic and Jesuit identity" might describe the needed credential.[137] It is difficult to imagine that a faculty of such minimal commitment would even take the time to read over a goals statement this extravagant.

In diverse ways and sundry manners Jesuits at BC have spoken to this issue of faculty participation. The year following BC's reaccreditation Father William Neenan, S.J., the academic vice president, spoke to the faculty convocation. What, he asked, were the odds of Boston College remaining Catholic and Jesuit? So many Protestant institutions like Harvard, Yale, Boston University, and Amherst College had lost their religious identification once their campus life was no longer controlled by a code of personal behavior. By contrast with that dark Protestant view of fallen humankind and evil permeating human structures and institutions, Neenan said the Catholic and Ignatian tradition was sacramental and thus "finds God in all things." By virtue of that tradition BC could boast of certain "essential characteristics":

> Free and open inquiry;
> Learning and artistic creation valued for their own sakes;
> Educational achievement held in stewardship for the service of others;
> Assurance that reality transcends what we see; and
> Sympathetic attention to the Catholic tradition.[138]

The point at issue, however, was not whether God be in all things, but whether the human inclination to search and find and understand God in all things is enlivened or served by the Catholic Church and its communal faith in any especially helpful way. If so, what need be the dynamics between the scholars of Boston College and the church? If so, what goals for the nineties had Boston College already chosen by promising to "hire scholars" but not "Catholic scholars"? None of this was considered in the Neenan address.

One of BC campus's most articulate Jesuits (also rector of the Jesuit community on campus), Joseph Appleyard of the English Department, asked how the "Thin, Black Line" of Jesuits could preserve the character of their colleges. The Society had considered binding agreements and accreditation and other devices of *Realpolitik* to hold their schools faithful to the tradition, but diminishing Jesuit numbers had diminished the order's ability to enforce such measures. In any case, they would still be exercises in control; and control, it went without saying, was ignoble. Appleyard then drew on Tocqueville's observations that voluntary associations abounded in America, and proposed that activist Catholics create voluntary programs and projects on Jesuit campuses. These might be Jesuit think tanks, or service projects for the deprived, or chaplaincies. It was already unrealistic to believe that Jesuit ideals could touch or affect most of their students, but this array of Jesuit-Catholic activities would affect at least some of them.[139] What this "strategic hamlet" model assumes is that the apostolate would no longer *be* the university, but be *at* the university.

The idea was promoted locally by Appleyard's colleague Judith Wilt, whose sympathetic advocacy of abortion choice and ardent feminism was already a witness to the desired diversity on campus. She, too, was keen on the idea of volunteer efforts that would associate Catholic endeavors on campus, not with the university and its policies, but with scattered groups of individuals. Indeed, she thought, their prophetic integrity would be better protected at the edge of campus life than near its power center.

A Vatican directive that non-Catholic teachers should not outnumber the Catholics was deplored by Wilt as "an impossible and not particularly desirable goal." It were a far, far better thing to hire faculty by offering them all the mainstream perquisites — "excellence, freedom, diversity and personal or social value" — and after they arrive to let them see and savor BC's "special identity" in these voluntary outposts. In a word, sever the Catholic/Jesuit missionary endeavors from patronage by the university itself.[140]

The Jesuit community on campus has had its own say — several times. In 1974 they looked regretfully at the failure of the university to take a critical, Christian stand and said:

> The society we live in is deeply influenced by values which we do not share as Jesuits, as Christians or even as inheritors of a tradition of human learning. The purely academic ideals of the secular university tradition in America are not reliable enough guides for our purposes. Too often the universities seem to mirror the values of the society in which they exist: they train specialists to fit into the

slots prescribed by the power structure of that society, and leave unexamined the large scale inequities of the system around them. . . .

What is perhaps more serious, our students, we ourselves and the very structure of our institution, often seem to operate by self-centered, competitive, and materialistic notions of what constitutes success, praiseworthy behavior, and a life well lived. . . . There may be more authentic religious belief and moral passion around than appears on the surface, but if so it is muted, problematic, not what we talk openly about, not what anyone would call our strong point.

With the philosophical heart torn out of the curriculum, which was now being dominated by supposedly value-free specialty courses, the Jesuits asked: How could BC transmit a critical culture? Then, as if another hand had snatched the pen, the Jesuit community seemingly acquiesced in the undoing of the original endeavor. BC was obliged somehow to reproduce in its membership the same chaos of divergence and dispute as found in the national public. The university was somehow forbidden to be distinctive and united in either its personnel or its philosophy:

> The first additions to the Jesuit faculty were committed Catholic men and women. But it was apparent as the college grew to true university status that a pluralist society requires institutions which are effectively pluralist in outlook, and that education for life in this society has to be conceived as broadly as the full range of responsible options in the society is broad. A diversity of viewpoints contributes to the intellectual and spiritual health of the university, and it is inconceivable now that it be entirely or even mainly staffed by men who are members of the religious order or even by Catholics alone.[141]

This was not a policy statement by some rump group trying to subvert the university. It was the considered view of the Jesuit community on the BC campus. The Jesuits, whose march through history had been unified not merely by command and collaboration, but by a community of belief, here make the astonishing claim that their university had wisely (or unavoidably) abandoned its determination to function as a committed, scholarly fellowship. What is more, they were gratified that their fractious and irreconcilable society could be served by a Boston College that was comparably fragmented. At least this relieved BC of the problem of finding Catholics and Jesuits.

Two decades later (1994) the Jesuit community would take an even more elegant and upbeat tone. They still believed that what one found at Boston College was pretty much what one would find in the national culture, a culture no less disintegrated than the last time they had looked.

> Some would say that [the colleges founded by the Jesuits] have adapted too thoroughly to the standards of secular academic life . . . In the 1990s, the argument would go, these institutions offer upper middle-class students a vaguely

621

liberal education colored by a rhetoric of spiritual values . . . Particularly in graduate programs and in the research agendas of faculty these institutions take most of their values from mainstream American academic life, offer curriculums not notably different from what is available elsewhere, and work to advance the same kinds of knowledge as do secular institutions.

Indeed, some would say this. But the updated Jesuit judgment in 1994 was no counsel of despair.

Unlike religious traditions that have distrusted or fled the world Ignatian spirituality sees the world of nature and culture in and around us as graced at its core by God's self-giving, therefore worth our work and our study. This point of view discloses God to the discerning eye and discloses God drawing all that is of our world and all that is human into God's own life. Our very yearning for fulfillment directs our search Godwards and will be satisfied only in the possession of God for which we have been made.[142]

Twenty years earlier the Jesuits had despaired of consensus at BC. The faculty in 1994 is even less likely to manifest an interest, let alone a dynamic and consensual interest, in Ignatian spirituality. Yet the Ignatian insight that the Jesuits hope will draw such a faculty together is this: that those "values which we do not share as Jesuits, as Christians or even as inheritors of a tradition of human learning" are nevertheless graced at the core. If even the moral dystrophy of the culture somehow discloses God to the discerning eye; if the "self-centered, competitive, and materialistic notions of what constitutes success" are an early surge of our yearning for God, then BC's future can probably be declared a success in advance.

This document was circulated by the Jesuit community as a working paper for discussion, but some campus Jesuits had wearied of the prolonged discussion and came up with a rival document. They, too, believed the Society should provide BC with a distinctive unity. In fact, they went out of their way to say that it was as *Jesuit,* not as *Catholic,* that the college should present itself. "For many the former term connotes intellectual inquiry, liberal attitudes, flexibility, while the latter seems to suggest moral restrictions, dogmatic control, and oppressive institutional structures, for example, in regard to women." (The authors had evidently gone through the system after Pascal, Voltaire, and Madison and their unkind views on Jesuits had been eliminated from the curriculum, and they retained no memory of the ill-willed Bostonians for whom "Jesuit" had been "synonymous with all of ambition, craft, and treachery, duplicity and talent, to be conceived by the human mind.")

The alternative policy paper wanted massive expenditures for religion on campus. One instance: since worship was celebrated in scattered fashion around the campus, with students joining in the mass as residential groups, the report asked for a large university church with spacious quarters for the chaplaincy: a visible center to showcase religion. "We pride ourselves on first-class libraries, laboratories, and sports facilities. We should not be indifferent to the symbolism and practical utility of a central chapel for expressing the religious identity of the university." The text does not discuss attendance at worship. One veteran Jesuit observed: "There may be 200 at Mass, or even a maximum of 400, but that is not so impressive in a university with 6,500 resident students."

Since the statement sees Jesuit influence mostly in the nonacademic sectors of the campus, in ministry and in social activism, a distinctive faculty is less important.

> People of different faiths and non-believers have important roles to play in a university community and even in the dialogue of religion and culture, for two reasons. First, the concerns about human dignity, a just community, students' personal development, and so forth, that attract these men and women to B.C. converge with the concerns of those who have an articulated Christian perspective on these issues and a commitment to addressing them. Furthermore, the differences in viewpoint that they bring are educational; they help focus and clarify what is central and what is marginal in these questions; they can open up new perspectives and directions for thinking about the issues.[143]

These two Jesuit manifestoes — apparently different, yet so much in agreement — proclaim that Jesuits no longer offer a Catholic wisdom cogent enough to nucleate a faculty intellectually and lead it in a critical judgment of cultures near and far. Traditionally one came to a university like BC to become knowledgeable and critical under the mentorship of a community of scholars who would expound and refine an interpretive wisdom developed by the Society of Jesus in the Catholic Church. One Jesuit proposal wants to put away all the old polemics and appreciate how wholesome are all culture's artifacts. Another would be willing instead to withdraw into traditional priestly ministry and contemporary social advocacy on campus. Thus would they both relieve the university of the need to recruit a Catholic faculty that might make the academic endeavor itself Catholic.

The Jesuit Institute

Boston College has one Jesuit on campus who has at times spoken quite differently. Jesuits do not debate one another much in public, but Michael Buckley has taken public exception to the late Timothy Healy's doctrine that the Catholic Church and the Catholic university are two distinct, though interconnected, entities. Healy had said: "How does the Church live within a university? . . . First, it leads its own life on our grounds; secondly, the Church joins in, shares and influences the life and the work of the university itself." Replied Buckley: the same could be said of the church in New York City. The respected Jesuit canonist Ladislas Örsy had insisted that a university itself could not technically be Catholic, though it could have Catholics active on campus: "A human institution is not transformed into a supernatural one; it simply offers an opportunity to persons with religious belief to share the life and the work of a university community in freedom and sympathy that supports them." Buckley's critical reply: that also describes a secular campus with an influential Newman Club.

At Boston College now, Buckley directs the classiest of strategic hamlets, the Jesuit Institute. With a multimillion-dollar endowment, it is a focus of Jesuit imagination and initiative on the BC campus, sponsoring conferences and occasional publications that give a venue to the untiring Jesuit energy for self-study. It brings Jesuit researchers and lecturers annually to campus. One scholar came for a year of inquiry into the structure of matter in light of Ignatian spirituality; another used recent feminist critique to reappraise quantum mechanics' description of nature. The Institute also sponsors invitational faculty seminars (involving more than eighty participants) on such subjects as "AIDS and the Church," "Alienation of Intellectuals from Religion within American Culture," and "God and the World of the Sciences."

Buckley, the gray eminence behind much recent BC policy, has his own distinctive way of arguing how the religious and the academic are intrinsically related. "Any movement towards meaning and truth is inchoatively religious. For the dynamism inherent in knowledge is towards that completion given only in the self-disclosure of God — the truth of the finite." If left to their own honest instincts, intellectual inquiry and religious commitment pursue related goals. The former pursues its interests and questions toward ever deeper explanations, the deepest of which turns out to be God; the latter pursues its convictions toward ever wiser understanding and wider application, which turn out to require ever more disciplined knowledge. But when Buckley comes to describe the university that would sponsor this mutual inquiry, he enters into great ambiguity. The Catholic university, he says, is sponsored by the church; indeed, it is a "sub-community of the Church," a Christian, religious community (and if Jesuit, a residence of the Society). It is, he says, a community of faith, and of sacramental culture. Yet it is not a church, not a group of believers gathered in Christ. It is a privileged enclave where the doctrinal discipline of the church is not free to enter, and where "the vast pluralism of persons and persuasions representative of 'all human culture' " is assimilated. It is therefore a truly strange "Catholic community," where the members need not share the Catholic faith or sacraments, but simply "be willing to enter into the conversations." He sees no need for those who guide students through these conversations to be able to speak of the self-disclosure of God to honest scholars, from personal experience.[144]

Father Buckley's sense of BC as the place where Catholics are at home in the world, rather than to the world, seems handicapped by his inclination to the theoretical. His confrere, Father Neenan, the academic vice president, is not at all theoretical, yet his message is equivalent as regards the need for a Catholic faculty in a Catholic university. Neenan explains for the administration why there has been no attempt to hire Catholic faculty. "It's inappropriate to ask a job candidate their religion. When we're hiring an economist, we're interested in hiring the best economist." He says he has no idea how many of his faculty consider themselves committed Catholics.[145] As an index of the university's Catholicity, Neenan points instead to the students, though not to what they do as students. "These kids volunteer; they do service over Christmas. This is part of the Jesuit education. BC has a very vibrant Catholicism."[146] The equation of authentic Catholicism and social service seems to have reminded no one of the comparable turn by New England Congregational progressivism nearly a century earlier.

In 1994-95 John Mahoney, who has taught English at BC for thirty-nine years, hosted monthly luncheons at the Jesuit Institute for invited faculty. He is reluctant to accept the campus criticism that they attract "the same people" who come to most gatherings of this sort, or that the Institute is "preaching to the converted." Their agenda was to the point: "How important to you are the origins of Boston College as a Jesuit University? Are you aware of the declining numbers of Jesuits on our faculty? Will Boston College end up secularized like Boston University?" The moment of truth came when participants agreed on three findings: (1) they wanted BC to be Catholic, (2) only a determined effort to recruit Catholic faculty could bring that about, and (3) they were solidly against such an effort.[147] The series concluded in lively optimism which found lush expressions such as: "Boston College will be strongest when the combination of *Eruditio* and *Religio* is alive and well, when there is that unique openness to the sacred and the secular, and commitment to the academic intelligibility of faith." But faculty who sit down to lunch together to avow a shared and vital hope, and then admit it is a hope they dare not invite others to share, only confirm the saying that there is no such thing as a free lunch.

Theology and Philosophy

The Theology Department is commonly mentioned as a factor in the university's Catholic identity. As recently as the 1960s it was still teaching simplified versions of the old seminary tracts in dogmatic theology, but it became much more professional in the 1970s, and then entered something of a modest golden age: a unified and productive faculty, dedicated both to the Catholic consensus and to critical scholarship. Under new leadership it is now mutating into a religious studies program, primarily responsible to the secular consensus within the field . . . though not without resistance from some senior scholars.

Senior BC theologian Thomas Wangler remembers that, according to the early BC statements of purpose, "the chief aim of the College is to educate the pupils in the principles and practices of the Catholic faith."[148] The 1887-88 catalogue insisted that "the moral and religious part of education is to be considered the more important." By 1894 the claim had become more explicit in Timothy Brosnahan's formulation. Education was not "mere instruction or the communication of knowledge. . . . Learning is an instrument of education, not its end. The end is culture, and mental and moral development." The Jesuits put their accent on *éducation,* training, not on *enseignement,* instruction.

Religion did not even appear in the curriculum during BC's first three decades. It involved "duties," not classes. One "recited" at the daily catechetical instruction and "attended" the weekly lecture on church doctrine. One was initiated into religious sensibilities and values by the Jesuit example, the iconography of the campus, the cycle of prayer and sacraments, the liturgical year and the college's own feasts, the extracurriculars of debate and service and music and vocational coaching, the honors and awards. One of the grammar textbooks studied the syntax and structures of a catechism, and another course in the English curriculum used biblical history as its text. The Thomistic philosophy was framed in its order and its goals by theological understanding. BC was a community into whose piety and self-understanding the students were inducted. One strong index of success was the fact that 54 percent of all living graduates in 1894 were either priests or seminarians.

But 1894, says Wangler, was the year when all this shifted. The "religious duties" were superseded by a new curricular unit called "Christian doctrine." The old catechism, which had been largely biblical and historical in scope and pastoral in tone, a manual of piety, was replaced by a series of new books that were apologetic and polemical and aimed to refute the threats to religion from critical-historical research and modernist doctrines. The weekly recitations and lecture were now transmogrified into a "course," and religion courses received two credits for three hours of class, due to their less dense format. Religion became Theology in 1949, but for more than a decade its courses were still given discounted credit. Theology, once established as a full member of the curriculum, went out of its way to be *enseignement* instead of *éducation.* But it was the college, not just its curriculum, that had laid aside that amalgam of witness, symbol, discipline, history, Scripture, piety, philosophy, and lore that had once been acknowledged as the premier element in the BC experience. Wangler explains: "The original aim of educating in the principles and practices of the Catholic faith is no longer a central and affective institutional goal. . . . The general retreat from its founding chief aim of educating in the faith by way of training, symbols and religious education, is the most fundamental shift of Boston College history to date."[149] It would surely make the issue of a Catholic faculty unimportant.

A study of secularization in Catholic theology departments offers further perspective on the discipline at BC, which served as one of its subject campuses. All course descriptions from 1955 to 1985 were examined. Some courses studied elements of Catholic faith — Scripture, doctrine, moral theology, church history, worship, etc. — and appraised them from its own principles (these courses were classed as "Catholic-perspective"). Others studied elements of various religions from a viewpoint that accorded no authority to Catholic doctrine ("secular-perspective"). There was an intermediate category, which studied Catholic faith and practice, but with some comparison to other religions, and used secular disciplines to corroborate or improve a critical Catholic viewpoint ("mixed-perspective"). The study found there had been a landslide shift from the "Catholic-perspective" type to the "secular-perspective" type.

It is quite possible to treat the study of world religions and secular disciplines in one's religious curricula from within a perspective of inherent authority based *solely* within one's integrative sacred order. At the point at which such reliance upon inherent authority gives way to sole reliance upon the authority of a secular discipline in one's arguments, however, secularization becomes a documentable possibility within the religious curricula.

It seems plausible that, as reported, the "mixed-perspective" type of course represented an academic improvement on the confined perspective used previously, but that it somehow led to an abandonment of Catholic perspectives. The table below shows how the respective percentages of *Catholic-, mixed-,* and *secular-*perspectived courses shifted during the three decades.

	1955-65	1965-75	1975-85
Catholic University	89/10/01	32/33/35	09/36/55
Saint John's University	79/13/08	18/44/38	05/45/50
Boston College	90/07/03	10/43/47	06/44/50[150]

In this schematization BC shifted in twenty years from offering 90 percent "Catholic-perspective" courses to 6 percent, and from 3 percent "secular-perspective" courses to 50 percent.[151] But there is something even more interesting here. As the faculty was gaining in its competence and field of vision during this short period, and became better able to deal critically with both the Catholic and other Christian traditions and their critics, it became more versatile within the perspective of orthodoxy. But when the theology faculty was undergoing its quantum jump in competence, it aimed at the second, "mixed-perspective," kind of teaching but somehow initiated a momentum that carried the department, not further, but in another direction. What seemed like a gain in professionalism turned out to be a radical detachment from what was intended: the scholarly appropriation of a tradition planted in divine revelation and developed within a privileged people (as the scriptural documents themselves had been in their time). What began with a finer sense of discrimination between unreflective and reflective faith unintentionally became undiscriminating about where its own intellectual trust was directed. What began as loyal reform somehow deviated.[152]

The Department of Philosophy is, of course, no longer the intellectual center of the BC education. But it is perhaps more retentive of the older orientation than

627

its theological sister department. Philosophy is traditional, classical, somewhat conservative. The great books are read there. There is little Enlightenment philosophy, and very little linguistic analysis. The theology faculty, by contrast, sees its task as liberating students from narrow, provincial Catholicism.

A recent faculty discussion in the department turned to the subject of religion at BC. Most faculty present were not Catholic, and most of them say they like BC the way it is. A majority at the meeting, however, strongly rejected the prospect of BC itself being Catholic; it was rejected as off-putting to students. In the course of the discussion the pope was referred to as fascist. Some spoke of even a "Christian" identity as repugnant, too redolent of Jerry Falwell and right-wing extremists. They were comfortable with a "Jesuit identity," however, since the Jesuits connote social outreach and academic freedom.

Most faculty members on campus have no Jesuit colleague in their department, and some have yet to become acquainted with a Jesuit. For an increasing proportion of them these activities operate beyond the range of either experience or interest. In addition to the usual constriction of knowledge and interest among academics, BC has its own distancing factors. A fair number of the emeriti and other veteran faculty have experience in Catholic colleges, often Jesuit, as undergraduates. But the more numerous, more recently arrived faculty lack that background. For instance, the political science faculty had their undergraduate experiences at Dartmouth, Oberlin, Brandeis, Cornell, Johns Hopkins, Reed, Michigan, Brooklyn, UCLA, Chicago, and Kalamazoo. None did graduate studies on a Catholic campus. Therefore no one in the department has ever experienced what BC claims to offer. Ignatius had insisted that the two purposes of Jesuit schooling — truth and moral character — were not to be balkanized lest staff divide up the two concerns; it was to be an amalgamated endeavor.[153] The situation at BC, with so few academics that have Catholic faith or experience, appears to isolate overtly Catholic activities from the primary educators. Many of them could and perhaps do serve as mentors in "the search for higher meaning," but Ignatius probably had something more specific in mind.

Senior faculty who were interviewed reported a professorate that is neither actively disaffected by nor actively interested in the Jesuit or Catholic destiny of Boston College. It is a comfortable place to work these days, and the high salaries and perquisites are appreciated. As one professor put it: Boston College is Catholic enough for him to feel at home and pagan enough for him to consider it a mission field. But another teacher describes it as an ominously indifferent neutrality. "The line has been crossed. BC is not retrievable as a recognizable Catholic institution. . . . It's gone." His reason: the university has been recruiting "the best possible faculty" and intentionally omitting religious faith from the criteria of what makes for the "best." Several of the most experienced Jesuits say it is "all over." There is a shared opinion that the Jesuits are as a group still remote from the rest of the campus, and that they seem to dwell overmuch upon their own past. As one professor put it: "The Jesuits are as obsessed with their own situation as the Vatican was about the loss of the Papal States."

President Monan appears to believe that Catholic faith is not essential to the faculty task at Boston College. Since all of human culture is an artifact of God's unceasing activity, he explains (borrowing a phrase from Pedro Arrupe), the mature Catholic university will always be at its ease in the public culture, and its collegial search for truth will provide "an institutional expression of the redemptive mission of the Incarnation and its transforming consequences on our human vocation and on human culture." He readily grants that faculty who do not share that faith cannot do much to promote or even appreciate this mission, but at least their Catholic colleagues will appreciate the "apparently secular endeavors" of their non-Catholic colleagues. What Monan seems not to contemplate is the likelihood that the transforming consequences appear to be working in reverse.[154]

Critical Voices

But there are other voices being heard. David O'Brien, a layman whose career has been spent teaching history at the College of the Holy Cross, is one of those who see an inner contradiction in the current desultory Jesuit concerns.

> While they can justify affirmative action for "qualified Jesuits," they could not show their heads at a meeting of the Association of Jesuit Colleges and Universities if it became known that they fought disciplinary autonomy, were urging the faculty to reshape the curriculum in light of the changing mission of the Church and the Society, or were giving preference in hiring to men and women who were sympathetic to those ideals. Deep down, out of their own life experience, they may doubt that academic excellence, as it is generally understood, is really compatible with religious commitment or even commitment to "a humanism defined first of all by the responsibility of each person toward his brothers and toward society." Only such a loss of faith can account for the remark of one Jesuit academic vice president that "if sympathy with the Catholic objectives were the primary determinant in faculty selection, you might well end up with a second-rate faculty." Such a loss of faith could account, too, for the interview that is intended merely to determine whether candidates are "comfortable" with college objectives as set forth in the catalogue . . .[155]

Martin Tripole, a Jesuit at Saint Joseph's in Philadelphia, has offered a general critique of the Society's recent educational policies, insofar as their results can be seen in this country. The recent emphasis on justice — a follow-up to the older interpretation of Catholic education as primarily moral in purpose — that has been given such new voice since GC32, he argues, has done unintentional harm by distracting Jesuits from the sweeping change in their institutions. Most students on Jesuit campuses today, in his observation, are middle class, inclined to selfishness, and ambitious for the wealth and comfort and power that education can offer. They

THE DYING OF THE LIGHT

are offered programs of benevolence: car-wash day, soup kitchen, visiting the handicapped, etc. These service programs beget a superficial idea of what it is to be a Christian. "We do not succeed in transforming the self-identity of our students, so that they define themselves as children of God, redeemed by the death and resurrection of Christ, committed to him personally and motivated by his values, so that they accept the spirit of the Beatitudes as the acceptable form of Christian and human living. . . . Such a task demands far more of us than the promotion of justice. To promote justice is to seek to establish equitable relations among people individually and collectively. To seek to establish Christian and human culture is to seek to transform the inner lives of people, the precondition for the establishment of a stable society of structural justice." The problem today is not the lack of justice but the lack of fully human beings.[156] If the Jesuit colleges and universities are at fault, Tripole says it is more for their failure to serve faith than for their failure to promote justice.[157]

Philosopher Joseph Flanagan, S.J., has observed the scene on the BC campus even more tartly. If he is correct, hopeful observers are whistling in the dark. Most BC students, he points out, are considerably formed and educated before ever coming to the university. They already have a philosophy and a theology, and there is nothing Catholic about either of them. The young students are bred into rampant individualism, which makes them largely immune to Christianity. "An authentic American tends to think of himself or herself as a sovereign while a true Christian thinks of self as a servant. . . ." Even if they do have an ethical conversion and turn their lives toward the needs of others, their hearts have not been converted. "They are actually living as servants of other people but they talk the language of sovereigns."[158]

He Who Is to Come

Marquette University was the subject of a study ten years after it, like BC, had undergone a decade of autonomy. Gregory Lucey narrates how the university was at first simply "Jesuit," then became "an independent private corporate entity of the State of Wisconsin, conducted under the auspices, and consonant with the educational principles, of the Society of Jesus." The "auspices" in question, we are assured, meant "kindly patronage and guidance," not any kind of direction by Jesuit superiors. Later the constitutional documents spoke only of its "Christian and Catholic foundations." "Catholic" began to be edged aside by "Christian" in university publications. Catholicity was neither "flaunted" nor "strident" in the revised texts. There then ensued years of documentation rivaling the Pentagon Papers in volume, about unfettered inquiry, the religious dimension of human existence, and the intrinsic value of humankind. Outsiders began to sense a change under way, and President John Raynor, S.J., hastened to reassure them. "This University is Catholic to its marrow . . . Marquette is a corporate Christian witness in the specific context of the university world." He spoke of "750 faculty members who breathe a common atmosphere, philosophy and set of intentions."

After ten years of this shared atmosphere the study found that the majority of the trustees were not Catholics, and they could not recall ever having deliberated about the Catholic or Jesuit character of the place. Those interviewed saw their task as financial. The new regimen which actively aspired to a faculty "of differing religious convictions" was quickly taking hold. The faculty, who had included about 65 percent Catholics in 1970,[159] was being replenished in 1977 by faculty of whom 44 percent claimed to be Catholics. The administration allayed concern by articulating its market-driven principle of Catholic survival: "Catholics will seek us, and others who do not value our character will tend to opt away from us." As for the Jesuits, there was not a single associate professor then to succeed the eight professors. By contrast, 82 percent of the students said they were Catholics, and 60 percent of them said that Marquette's being a Catholic, and a Jesuit, school formed part of their reason for enrolling.[160]

Boston College's choice to succeed Fr. Monan as president in 1996 is Marquette's executive vice president, William P. Leahy, S.J. Leahy has already faced the difficult issue of a Catholic university staffed by non-Catholics. Enough, he wrote then, to have "trustees and at least a solid core of administrators and faculty who are sympathetic with Catholicism and who want greatly to enhance the Catholic character of their schools."[161] When asked about the pluralism of the BC faculty, he observed that many faculty at Marquette were ignorant of Catholicism, but fortunately some who were Presbyterian, Jewish, or Lutheran "very much believe in the importance of an education that takes religion seriously [and] are very much committed to it."[162] His is the familiar theory of the small "core" who are "sympathetic" and "very much want to enhance the Catholic character of their schools," and who "very much believe in the importance of an education that takes religion seriously" and can therefore sustain BC as a Catholic university. One can only speculate whether he would be confident in BC's academic future if he had to rely on a small core of faculty who were sympathetic with original scholarship but were not scholars; who were committed to effective teaching but not themselves master teachers; who very much believed in graduate studies but were not qualified to direct dissertations; who took spoken English seriously but had never mastered it. Leahy has already written that Catholic education's need today is not for people. The urgent need is for "a coherent, convincing theory of education and articulate, persuasive proponents of it."[163] This is most improbable. Theory they already have. Conviction will cost him more.

At his previous posting, the undergraduate student body has continued to be largely Catholic. The board has been both laicized and secularized; that is, neither are they mostly Jesuits or Catholics, nor have they made Marquette's Jesuit or Catholic character a primary concern. The faculty, long since lay, is moving toward becoming non-Catholic, and perhaps secularized. At the Boston College which awaits him the undergraduates are still mostly Catholics; the board is still heavily

Catholic, mostly lay, and apparently secularized (though in an acquiescent rather than an aggressive mode); and the faculty is lay, heavily non-Catholic, and rapidly secularizing. It would seem that both may be following the path of Webster College, which imagined it was becoming lay while in fact it was becoming secular.

BC has been a boat borne along on the currents of American academic life by the winds of Jesuit ministry. As the Jesuits purposely moved out of the tributary into the mainstream, the currents easily outpowered the winds. The great power shift of the late 1960s took the tiller from the hands of the Jesuit order and confided it to the Jesuit president, who for one or two incumbencies was master of the craft. In time, however, a confluence of the massive cross-interests of the faculty, the board, and the students-as-consumers put the future at issue. The surest likelihood is that the faculty will emerge as the strongest of these forces. The previously Jesuit colleges may then be carried on a stream that finds its wisdom, not in the Ignatian *Exercises* or *Constitutions,* but in the *Chronicle of Higher Education . . .* indeed, in the current issue. Then those who fretted over all that Jesuit talk may experience what a true ideology is.

Those who do believe that a Catholic/Jesuit university requires Catholic and Jesuit academics are distressed that these two cohorts are diminishing on the BC campus and not being replenished. One repeatedly hears the master metaphor of the "critical mass." A critical mass is the amount of fissile material — U^{233}, U^{235}, Pu^{239} — needed to sustain a nuclear chain reaction. Some materials in some circumstances require hundreds of tons to ignite a chain reaction, but the mind's eye has thought of the kilogram, or less, as potent enough to blow up an atoll or a metropolis. That image of the tiny but incredibly potent mass ready to go critical was what encouraged the thought that a few, a brave few, a band of Jesuit brothers, could fuel a great university with Jesuitness. It would be an Einsteinian conversion of a tiny mass into irresistible energy. Faced with the deplorable image of their own massive membership swiftly decomposing, the Jesuits found it helpful to imagine the diminutive surviving mass bursting with energy that in swiftly successive generations might engulf all around it. The problem is that instead of a critical mass they have a landfill, and an apparently endless supply of its natural product, methane gas.

The critical mass was the metaphor of the liberals. They had a conscientious revulsion for the sorts of power that came with trusteeship, governance, and control (though not for presidency). They berated the foot-dragging Jesuits who agonized at the forfeiture of their institutions. There was no merit, the innovators said, in clinging to the status quo. But the evidence of the years suggests that clinging in name and imagination to all twenty-eight universities and colleges as "Jesuit" is the greater act of possessiveness. The possessiveness, however, turns out to be not for power, only for nostalgia and familiar turf.

A recent General Congregation, GC34, held in 1995, has a statement on education that has attracted a great deal of attention. For a college or university "to call itself a Jesuit institution it will be necessary to evaluate and give an account

632

of itself to the Society periodically in order to see whether its dynamics are being developed in line with the Jesuit mission." The prospect of Jesuit "accreditation" is no less toxic to Jesuit educators than when it was first proposed, and ignored, in the 1960s.[164] An opinion expressed at Georgetown, the seniormost Jesuit foundation in America, might represent many at Chestnut Hill:

> So, it would hardly be an unmitigated calamity if Georgetown were to become "just" another distinguished center of research. Indeed, it would be an accomplishment of the first magnitude. And it would be an important sign, too, of the "coming of age" of Catholicism in this country. What better evidence could there be of the assumption of full responsibility for the fate of the American "experiment" by Catholics than to attract the very ablest minds, Catholic and non-Catholic alike?[165]

This contemporary myth supporting the colleges and universities "come of age" brightens the present by disfiguring the past. That was recently exemplified in the commencement address by the president of Fordham University, commemorating the 150th anniversary of the Jesuits' arrival there. The achievement to be celebrated most, however, was Fordham's more modern "assimilation into American culture," "full participation in the higher education community in the United States," and new readiness to "collaborate with men and women of other traditions in common human projects that reflected our common aspiration." This open venture of the present has freed Fordham from an awful threat: "ecclesiastical control," "juridical control," "sanctions," "a sometimes insular and parochial outlook," "the suppression of competing ideas," voices "who substitute accusation for analysis, who seek not to disagree with their adversaries but to excommunicate them." The newly independent Catholic university "is not the place to impose religious tests on faculty or students, engage in narrow proselytizing or rigid indoctrination." What, after this close escape from totalitarianism, is the nature of this yet more perfect way by which Fordham found its freedom? "Consistent with the post-Vatican II Church, Fordham University welcomes to our faculty and to our student body men and women of all religious faiths and none. . . . We are a community that can come together in worship."[166] But this does raise a question or two. And who are the Jesuits who had threatened Fordham with such oppression? Whom is it that people of all religious faiths and none worship together?

When Mike Walsh was an older man, two years away from death, he reminisced about the troubles he had encountered from his fellow Jesuits. Stifled by the obligation to apply for permission before even minor decisions such as textbook choices, class assignments of Jesuit faculty, and any expenditure above $10,000, he led BC away from religious accountability and was criticized by fellow Jesuits for, as he put it, "kicking Christ out of the place." In his early years as president he had had misgivings:

I said to myself, "Oh, God, what have I done with this university? Here I've led it to great academic strength. [But] I've laicized it, and I've turned it against my own crowd."

He admitted that the direction he was taking inevitably jeopardized their view of what Catholic higher education should be all about, and that at the end "all the Jesuits were glad to see me leave BC."[167]

His interviewer, Richard Freeland, later the president of nearby Northeastern University, drew on the Walsh materials for his own study of how BC, like several of its neighbor institutions, had been led by competition for prestige and resources to forfeit its institutional commitments and distinctiveness, and thereby joined a general trend away from a desirable diversity. The process, as Freeland sees it, "turned BC more nearly into a Catholic Brandeis: a university broadly reflective of Catholic and Jesuit culture where teaching and scholarship mainly expressed secular academic concerns." Walsh, however, was so convinced that emancipation from Jesuit and Catholic control was necessary for academic excellence that he could "celebrate the secularization of BC without ambivalence or irony."[168] Subsequent celebrations seem to have gone even further, preferring equivocation to ambivalence.

THE COLLEGE OF NEW ROCHELLE

Angela Merici was a contemporary of Ignatius of Loyola. Orphaned as a girl and raised by relatives, she lived in Brescia as a young woman, worked in a hospice for the terminally ill, and was associated with various movements of lay piety. In 1535 she gathered a group of like-minded young unmarried women into the Company of Saint Ursula. They joined in private promises to remain virgins and to work together as a community of faith under the supervision of some respectable matrons and town notables. They were not a religious order, took no ecclesiastical vows, wore no distinguishing garb, and lived with their own families. They would go out to care for young girls and women in orphanages and hostels. Even when some of them resided in these institutions they observed no cloister. By 1539 (one year after Ignatius had gathered his company) the Ursulines numbered 150 women.

At her death in 1540 Angela would leave behind a rule, and some explicit advice to her Ursuline Sisters on how to be effective educators. Her educational philosophy was as radically creative as the lay institute she had founded. It was notable by ignoring conventional pedagogical doctrines about the depravity of human nature, and counseling her sisters to be assiduously positive in their manner and discipline. She enjoined on them the need to know and cultivate each of their girls as individually as a mother would. She stressed personal integration and understanding over memorization as the best way to learn. And her community was adaptable to many classes and circumstances: in orphanages, asylums for delinquent girls, and schools for the affluent. Indeed, the very membership of the first Company united women of the servant, merchant, and affluent classes. Just as Ignatius' educational counsels in his *Constitutions* were later codified and expanded by his order into the *Ratio Studiorum* in the later years of the sixteenth century, so were Angela's in the *Règlements des Ursulines*.

The community life Angela had created for her sisters was soon deranged. The Council of Trent, as part of its reform legislation, insisted on an enclosed, monastic life for all religious orders of women, and Saint Charles Borromeo, the reforming archbishop of Milan, presided over that drastic change in their fellowship and ministry. Thenceforth they would be able to care only for those young women who lived or studied within their cloistered convents. Angela's own rule was lost for centuries, and although Ursuline houses were founded throughout Europe and in missionary lands, they were not bound to one another in the fellowship of a single order.[169]

Angela Merici's daughters currently sponsor three colleges in the United States:

1872	Ursuline College	Pepper Pike, Ohio
1904	College of New Rochelle	New Rochelle, N.Y.
1925	Brescia College	Owensboro, Ky.

French Ursulines came to live and work in Quebec in 1639, followed in 1727 by others in New Orleans, where their convent opened the first Catholic academy for women in what would be the United States. An Irish group arrived in 1812 but returned after an unsuccessful attempt to establish themselves in Manhattan. A convent was established in the Charlestown neighborhood of Boston until it was ransacked and burnt by an anti-Catholic mob in 1834. Ursulines also worked with Bishop John England in Charleston.

A band from Hungary and Bavaria was invited to serve the German Catholics in Saint Louis in 1852, and three years later they deployed some of their nuns to New York, where they settled in the Bronx and lower Manhattan. After the Germans in the latter neighborhood were displaced by incoming Irish, the convent attracted a good number of these girls to join it; they were then persuaded by their parish priest to separate themselves from their largely Bavarian community and found an independent house for Irish Ursulines. They took the name of the parish: the Community of Saint Teresa. They staffed both the parochial elementary school, with an enrollment of more than a thousand children, and an upscale, fee-based academy for girls.

The Irish were the only immigrant population at that time who spoke English as their native tongue, and this made the teaching profession especially attractive to Irish women. The breakaway Ursuline Community of Saint Teresa therefore took on a third educational challenge: an after-school program of adult education to train women for the New York teachers examinations. They were soon running the only accredited normal school in the city, and the only Catholic one. In 1893 Mother Irene Gill was the superior of this complex educational establishment, and when the Board of Education finally opened its own mandatory training school, her students were the only New York residents already qualified to enter. Twenty years after Saint Teresa became the first Catholic high school approved in the state of New York, Mother Irene's advanced teacher-training operation received its charter from the New York Board of Regents.

Irene's Folly

This success persuaded her to open a college for young women, and since the Irish were now moving uptown she began looking for property. In 1897 she opened a secondary school for girls, the Ursuline Seminary in New Rochelle, just beyond the Bronx in Westchester County. She acquired a faux castle gutted by fire, swiftly secured a college charter, and incorporated the College of Saint Angela in 1904. Among the skeptical clergy it was known as "Irene's Folly." In addition, the Ursulines staffed the nearby parish school. Several years later when she got word that another educational group was looking to found a college nearby, she initiated a preemptive change of title, and now she presided over the College of New Rochelle (CNR).[170]

Her advertisement in the *New York Times* gave notice: "Members of all denominations received."[171] This, of course, was to make a virtue out of necessity. The first *Bulletin* explained: *"The college ideal of its graduates is that of a woman of culture, of efficiency and of power —* a woman capable of upholding the noblest ideals of the home and of the Church and possessed of the training that shall make her an efficient worker in society and in the professional world."

There were at the time more than 52,000 Catholic sisters in the United States, and nearly seven hundred Catholic academies conducted by them for young women; the Ursuline academy in New Orleans remained the eldest of them all.[172] But now some of these academies were beginning to mature into colleges. Saint Mary-of-the-Woods (1841) had begun postsecondary instruction in 1845; Saint Mary's, also in Indiana (1844), had awarded its first baccalaureate degree in 1898; Notre Dame of Maryland (1863), chartered in 1896, granted the first degree as a college in 1899; Trinity, in the District of Columbia, was the first to be founded as a college without first being an academy, in 1897. All these were awarding degrees by 1904 when the Ursulines chartered and opened their college in New Rochelle. There was already one sister institution in Ohio: Ursuline College for Women. Later, Ursulines would found Brescia College in Kentucky.

The College of New Rochelle grew in wisdom, age, and grace. After a quarter-century of operation its enrollment had risen from the original 12 to 802: the largest Catholic women's college in the country. It was, in many respects, not untypical of other young colleges founded and maintained by Catholic religious orders, yet the New Rochelle story, and that of the Ursuline women who were its main characters, has rarely corresponded to the expectations and commonplace prejudices which often amused Americans at their expense. Various strong-minded convent school alumnae such as George Sand, Kate Chopin, Agnes Repplier, and Mary McCarthy have in their memoirs created a resentful stereotype that deserves some balancing.

Irene Gill's aspiration to educate women "of culture, of efficiency and of power" was not at the time widely shared. Cynthia Farr Brown, in an interesting historical comparison of Bryn Mawr, Wellesley, Trinity, and New Rochelle, has observed that the prototypical secular women's colleges, which were in their second generation when the Catholics got into the business, were then led by women of less confidence than their own founding generation. The indisputable academic superiority of the men's colleges and universities had inspired a failure of nerve, and they began to share the belief that men were better suited to leadership. It began to be the fashion for some of them to replace their female presidents with males. The Catholic schools, by contrast, exalted female leadership, and requires and prepared women for careers.

At New Rochelle, the archbishop of New York would appoint (not without Ursuline advice) a succession of diocesan monsignori as presidents until 1950. These honorary gentlemen, somewhat in the Continental tradition of absentee chancellors, would come to campus for state occasions only. The college was actually administered by a dynasty of deans that saw CNR through its first forty-five years: Mothers Irene Gill, Ignatius Wallace, and Thomas Aquinas O'Reilly. Behind them were Irene's blood sister, Mother Augustine Gill, and Mother Xavier Fitzgerald, both on duty through those decades in a variety of offices. The board of trustees, chaired by the clerical president, was composed entirely of men until the first Ursuline was elected in 1942. The early trustees were all handpicked by Irene, and included state and city educational executives. The college was fifty years old before the nuns held the presidency and the majority of seats on the board. Yet through all that time it was the Ursuline women who provided the initiative, the imagination, and the responsibility. The glass ceiling had not really held them down.

Despite their withdrawn way of life (the Ursulines at CNR still observed the Tridentine cloister, though in mitigated form), the Ursuline deans and their Catholic peers were out actively cultivating the patronage of state educational officials and leaders in the financial, legal, and social worlds. Throughout an era when secular female educators suffered obloquy in the academic world for being naive spinsters, the nuns were regarded as credible mentors for their students as they encouraged them toward both family and professional lives.[173]

A second area in which the CNR history would surprise expectations is that of the early faculty. The first CNR *Bulletin* lists twenty-six faculty. Five, including Mother Irene, were Ursulines who had not a single academic degree among them. At the time, nuns were neither admitted to any of the all-male Catholic universities (until 1911) nor permitted to enroll in the secular ones (though a rare few began as early as 1904). Their lay colleagues, however, bore credentials from Georgetown, Paris, Harvard, Columbia, Western Reserve, Pratt, Saint Lawrence, and Bellevue. In years to follow, their qualifications would become better still. The first professor of pedagogy was also the first non-Catholic to join the faculty.

The college announced that since it meant to train young women

> according to ideals and methods characteristic of the Ursuline Order, . . . certain departments will be headed by representative Ursulines [who held the chairs in mathematics and instrumental music]. In the three thousand Ursuline houses, widely distributed throughout the world, there are many young Sisters who are steadily preparing themselves, through the attainment of college and university degrees, to enter the most advanced educational work. From this number, professors, judged by the triple standard of native ability, educational equipment and nobility of character, shall be chosen to preside over other departments.[174]

Mother Xavier had to eke out her baccalaureate at the age of thirty-eight in 1909 through extension and summer courses, and then went on to earn her M.A. in social science at Columbia. Mother Thomas Aquinas would earn her Ph.D. in English at Fordham. Others would follow. At length the Community of Saint Teresa acquired the educational wherewithal to staff their school. By 1929 the ten Ursulines among a total faculty of forty-one held proportionately higher graduate degrees than their lay associates. A 1959-60 survey of all Catholic women's colleges (which then constituted more than half of all Catholic institutions of higher education) would disclose that 63 percent of their combined faculties were nuns. Seventy percent of all nuns at the rank of professor, 22 percent of the associates, 13 percent of the assistants, and 7 percent of the instructors held earned doctorates, a higher proportion than their colleagues.[175]

New Rochelle: A Classical College for Serious Women

The curriculum was from the beginning centered upon the liberal arts, and included Greek, Latin, French, German, English, mathematics, physics, chemistry, biology, economics, history, philosophy, and religion, plus music, drawing, painting, art history, education, domestic economy, and law. Courses required for teaching certification were also available, and an extension program prepared active teachers for higher certification. Extension lecturers included deans and professors from Barnard, NYU, Teachers College, and the Armour Institute; superintendents and principals and school commissioners; and an archbishop and a chief justice besides. A 1929 survey showed that about half (641) of the CNR alumnae were going into teaching, 105 into business, 14 into social service, 12 into journalism, and 69 to graduate school, while 46 had entered religious orders. Vocational programs such as secretarial studies (1916), social work (1918), home economics (1929), and commerce (1937) were opened but eventually discontinued. Mother Irene's women of power were encouraged to aim high.

New Rochelle met with early recognition. In 1917 the Department of Education rated all colleges in the state, and CNR was placed in the first of three ranks. In 1919 Columbia University ranked it high on the list of its feeder schools. In 1921 CNR became a founding member of the Middle States Association by accreditation, and in 1926 was listed by the Association of American Colleges and Universities. When the latter agency suggested the propriety of having female representation on the college's board, New Rochelle invited one of its own alumnae, a professor at Hunter College, to become a trustee.

Not until 1956, when the Ford Foundation awarded a grant of $280,000 for faculty salaries and endowment, was CNR successful in efforts at major fundraising. Essential to the college's financial survival was the commitment of the Ursulines to serve without compensation. In addition, nuns teaching at nearby schools or in the city resided at New Rochelle and augmented the residential staff. As a result, even without the aid of major benefactors the college was able slowly to augment its campus and the granite buildings it added, one by one. Each new construction effort would put the college into major debt, but frugal management allowed it to retire each debt after several years. If the Ursulines were the financial mainstay for the college, they also found benefit in it. In 1943 Ursulines throughout the United States determined that their younger members in training should have access to a college education, and they established an interprovincial house of studies at New Rochelle.

After its first fifty years the College of New Rochelle had a settled existence. It had taken its place alongside the other leading colleges of its type: Trinity, Manhattanville, and Saint Mary's. It had a good name with the Board of Regents and the New York State Department of Education. It had cleared away some opportunistic vocational programs and successful extension offerings and had restored its basically liberal-arts curriculum. It had managed, despite modest finances, to gather a respectable and very dedicated faculty. It had constructed a handsome campus in a strategic location for its clientele, both residential and commuting, drawing from the city and the Westchester area, but by the 1950s it was also beginning to attract a majority of its students from beyond New York State. Its enrollment, which blended the children of suburban affluence with young women who had to work their way through college, had grown steadily toward a total of one thousand students. And it was served by a large Ursuline community now thickly populated with women who had entered the convent from their own student days at CNR, and had acquired their own graduate education at increasingly good universities. Its only clear failure had been in what was called "advancement." New Rochelle had never succeeded in attracting large financial gifts or grants, and nurtured an endowment of only $400,000 (1956).[176]

Then came change. During the 1950s the college came under the more purposeful and independent influence of an activist Ursuline community and emerged with a more sophisticated and explicitly Catholic character. Then during the 1960s New Rochelle abruptly encountered deficits in enrollment, finance, purpose, and morale and was exposed to discouragement and even a threat of closure. During the 1970s, under purposeful and determined leadership, the college would undertake major changes of program, clientele, and self-understanding which promised a stable future, though at the cost of an unexpected transformation of identity. This sequential experience was not untypical of other Catholic colleges for women. We must study New Rochelle in those various stages of later development.

In 1942 the board had elected first one, then seven, Ursulines as trustees and assigned them a controlling role on its practically plenipotentiary executive committee. By the early 1950s Ursulines constituted two-thirds of the board. When the last monsignor-president resigned in 1949, instead of turning to the cardinal for his successor the Ursuline provincial simply promoted one of their own: the dean, Mother Dorothea Dunkerley.

The Ursulines had already taken advantage of their large local membership (swelled by younger nuns in training, and others teaching in nearby schools) to put nuns in all student-advisory positions. Nuns were responsible for dormitories and student organizations. A number of the more sagacious religious were designated "spiritual mothers," and each student was encouraged to pick one as mentor and confidante. Alumnae recollections suggest that these overtures and personal services were taken to heart by the young women. As World War II approached, with a student body that was 95 percent Catholic and a faculty that was endogenous to nearly the same extent (one-third were Ursulines), it was timely yet surprising that the nuns would become even more purposeful in assuring the college's religious authenticity. Joseph Brennan, then a young teacher, remembered that shift.

> In the early days of my tenure at New Rochelle, the Ursulines had been careful not to interfere with the teaching of the lay faculty, philosophy included. Since most of my teaching concerned formal logic, there seemed little danger of that. The nuns knew my taste for General Franco was less than enthusiastic. They paid no attention to the complaint of an odious little instructor who tried in vain to get me and others of the junior faculty to sign a petition supporting the disgraceful blocking of Bertrand Russell's appointment to City College in 1940. They avoided any show of concern in the personal affairs and private devotions (or lack of them) of their young faculty. Late in my stay at the college a change occurred. There came a definite shift in the winds of orthodoxy — why, I don't know.[177]

The Ursulines encouraged the faculty to integrate religious perspective into their instruction, and since their inclinations were conservative and those of the faculty, like Brennan's, were inclined in a liberal direction, there was strain. To some on the faculty it seemed that an educational community so Catholic in its membership hardly needed to be preoccupied with its religious interests. The nuns took the view that students preparing "chiefly for Catholic cultural and intellectual leadership" in an anti-Christian society deserved a more explicit religious program. The 1944-45 *Bulletin* described it. The syntax was descriptive, but the meaning was clearly prescriptive.

> The College is conducted under Catholic auspices and provision is made to live a Christian life according to the ideals of Jesus Christ, the Founder of The Church. All students irrespective of creeds must take courses in religion for four years.
>
> The daily sacrifice of the Mass is offered at seven thirty o'clock and though attendance is not compulsory, the chapel is always well filled with devout young girls dedicating the studies and activities of the day to the service of Almighty God.
>
> The advantages of all the traditional devotions of the Church may be enjoyed at New Rochelle. A yearly retreat of three days is provided for all students. Every student is a member of the Society for the Propagation of the Faith. Interest in missionary activity is high and finds a splendid culmination in the annual Mission Day held in May.
>
> The New Rochelle student is outstanding in the field of Catholic Action and exercises her zeal in charitable work for the poor and the outcast, for the crippled and the shut-in, by lecture work in secondary schools, by radio-broadcasting, by catechetical instruction in the neighboring churches and by press correction.[178]

Assertively Catholic

As New Rochelle moved into the 1950s, it seemed to be standing far apart from the mainstream. The college faculty assembled one day in 1951 and listened to Allys Vergara, a lifelong lay colleague, review for them the educational aims of the better-known women's liberal arts colleges: Radcliffe, Sarah Lawrence, Mount Holyoke, Barnard, Vassar, Wellesley, Smith, and Goucher. All of them used similar language: of growth, citizenship, intellectual resourcefulness, and women's equality. Most of them also offered education about religion and "an opportunity for participation in common worship as a fundamental part of their life at College." One spoke of "faithful honesty and honest faith." But the colleges themselves were not identified with church or faith. Smith College's statement was typical: "While the fundamentally religious interest of the founder is stressed, the college is kept clear of entanglement with institutional Christianity, and the only prescription is the pervading of instruction by the spirit of the gospel of Jesus Christ." To the Ursulines in 1951 that had to be a sad evolution: for a women's college to put away its religious inspiration. It was beyond imagination that their New Rochelle could step aside from its founding purpose, in pursuit of growth, citizenship, intellectual resourcefulness, and women's equality.

The dean, Mother Mary Peter Carthy, made it clear at the time that New Rochelle doubted that the spirit of Christ's gospel was likely to pervade under that kind of detached sponsorship. She quoted Pius XI on Christian education: "The ultimate aim of education is to secure the Supreme Good — that is, God — for the souls of those who are being educated. . . . Christian education takes in the whole aggregate of human life, physical and spiritual, intellectual and moral, individual, domestic and social, not with a view of reducing it in any way, but in order to elevate, regulate and perfect it in accordance with the example and teaching of Christ."[179]

That, of course, was spoken to an internal audience. It may be compared with the self-study report filed by CNR with the Middle States Association prior to the reaccreditation visit in 1955-56. The rhetoric is utterly unabashed.

As a Catholic college, it seeks to illuminate all teaching with Christian principles and to train its students to serve Christ by the full development of their natural powers of intelligence, conscience, and taste.

As a Catholic institution, New Rochelle's religious objectives emphasize the importance of religion in the life of the individual and of Christian morality as the animating principle of sound citizenship. While non-Catholic students who meet entrance requirements are welcomed into the student body, the latter is almost exclusively made up of members of the Roman Catholic Church, about sixty per cent of whom receive their secondary school training in Catholic institutions and are, therefore, prepared to benefit to the full by the College's educational plan. . . .[180]

In wholesome support of this unshaded Catholic assertiveness, the college did maintain a theology program that was, for the time, academically ambitious. For years CNR had housed a Labor School (1950), run by the Association of Catholic Trade Unionists, and the Westchester Management Forum, intended to challenge both labor and management with Catholic social doctrine about industrial relations. Also, the Catholic Family Institute (1947) and Marriage Counseling Service (1954) dealt with domestic relations and child behavior problems. The campus was a meeting point for the Christian Family Movement. The CNR students had long been involved in diverse community service programs. At the same time CNR was nationally showcased for the intensity and integrity of its active liturgical practice.[181]

Had the Middle States Association of Colleges and Schools team members read the self-study carefully, though, they would have felt the breath of thought control on the New Rochelle campus.

Every member of the faculty is encouraged fully to explore and explain the area of his professional field that lies within the courses assigned to him, guided by the intention of showing its central truths as such, of indicating its relationships with other areas, and of inculcating its proper methodology. He is free to present hypotheses, theories, and his personal opinions, provided that they are labeled as such. But he can never teach anything contrary to the truths made known by God through revelation and interpreted by the Catholic Church. He is likewise required to uphold American principles as embodied in the Declaration of Independence and the Constitution of the United States.[182]

Twenty years earlier this might have gone without much notice. But in the 1950s a new spirit of independent thought and expression was abroad, and it was already present enough on the New Rochelle campus for these restrictions to chafe. One year later a number of priests in the Department of Theology took strong exception to liberal views being expressed by certain colleagues. They dealt with papal authority, birth control, academic freedom, and ecumenism. This eventually led to meticulously precise formal statements of accusation confidentially submitted to the superior of the Ursulines. Three colleagues — Eugene Fontinell and John Bannon in philosophy, and Joseph Cunneen in English — eventually quit the faculty. The whispered report and the steel-handed response were keeping the College of New Rochelle doctrinally pure and loyal. The price of orthodoxy is a vigilance seemingly more eternal than that of freedom.[183] These men were an embarrassment. But not many years afterward, the college leadership would consider the purge as the embarrassment.

The 1960s brought Pope John XXIII and *aggiornamento;* and the windows of the church and of the college were thrown open by Vatican II. The first effects of that renewal were visible in the Ursulines themselves. In 1960 a young historian, Mother Dorothy Ann Kelly, spoke to her sisters at a Nuns' Study Day. After citing the Ursuline *Règlements,* she highlighted her text with borrowings from several avant-garde Jesuits — anthropologist Pierre Teilhard de Chardin, political theorist John Courtney Murray, theologian Henri de Lubac — plus community organizer Father Jack Egan of Chicago and George Meany from the AFL-CIO. These were men who four years earlier might have triggered cautionary concern within the New Rochelle theology faculty, as some of them had already elicited from Rome itself. Mother Dorothy Ann went on to remind her sisters of Angela Merici's injunction: to encourage their young women to think, more than to repeat. There was a traditional call to follow the church . . . but now it was an ostensibly untraditional church to be followed. "To some degree the girls must be able to see in us this thoroughly Catholic mind — alert to the present state of the question in biblical studies, in the liturgical and ecumenical movements . . . aware of the current direction being taken in the perennial 'Church-State' problem (so as not to handicap the church with outmoded positions . . .)."[184] At this juncture 59 percent of the New Rochelle women were reporting that they participated in Mass daily, and only 3 percent said they never went, except on Sundays.[185]

John Kennedy's election offered the Catholics at CNR another motivation to sing with the contemporary choir. The class of 1961 was addressed at commencement by the president of Hunter College, who put it to them that the final appraisal of Kennedy's presidency would depend on Catholics like them. "We now have a chance to demonstrate that American Catholics are not the ignorant immigrants of song and story, that they are not a priest-ridden, unthinking mob prepared to follow orders on all subjects emanating from the parish rectory, that, above all, they are thinking, intelligent Americans with the welfare of the country they love at heart." How should they give evidence of such fulsome citizenship? By stifling any social criticism that might make Catholics sound strident or separatist. By an intelligent willingness to compromise, by viewing policy issues as civically acceptable, rather than religiously repugnant. He called them to "intellectual excellence," which seemed to involve Catholics blending as inoffensively into the American culture as Kennedy himself had done.[186] And he was heard.

The Sixties: Time to Turn from an Embarrassing Past

When New Rochelle presented itself for reaccreditation in 1966, there was an astonishing change from the confessional explicitness of its statement ten years earlier. Its public prose had begun to shift. For years the college had been "a four year Catholic liberal arts college for women." In 1965-66 it had become slightly more diffident: "a liberal arts college for women administered under Catholic auspices." The submission to Middle States now rang with a new vitality, mostly of dissociation from the past. From the start, "the challenge of the students was to be presented within a framework of attitudes and values with their deeply Christian principles and yet, wholly relevant to their own times. . . . Tradition can be a stultifying matter if it is adhered to blindly or indiscriminately." There were allusions to the "dynamic quality" of CNR's "educational heritage." The college purpose? "The education of its students toward their complete development as persons, committed to the creative and disciplined use of their intellects and the courageous and constructive use of their freedom." No more mention of Pius XI's "in accordance with the example and teaching of Christ."

The statement about theology is muted and somewhat apologetic: "Committed to the Christian tradition in its uniqueness and complexity, the College provides a full program of theology. It holds firmly that theological and philosophical studies open up dimensions of reality which are necessary to genuine educational growth, and that the Christian faith is relevant to learning and to life." When the report goes on to tell that the campus has been torn in two by a student editors' feud over the Vietnam War (this is only 1966) and names Mary Calderone, the sex education activist, at the head of its list of campus lecturers, any reader could know that something new and inoffensive was stirring. New Rochelle was not going to be strident or divisive, nor to embarrass the memory of President Kennedy. The word "Catholic" never appears in the document except in cases of dire necessity; it is replaced by "deeply Christian." "Christ" is gone altogether.[187] This is not for the priest-ridden or the unthinking.

The shift in institutional prose is stark and abrupt, yet so were many elements of campus life in the late 1960s, even at New Rochelle. Beneath the surface the college was in the grip of a new and biting worry. The report to Middle States asserts several times that the college had purposely held enrollment down so as to preserve the close personal style of CNR education.[188] This was not quite true. Applications had been declining steadily since 1960, and the college had been accepting a higher and higher proportion of applicants each year in order to keep enrollment stable. The catchment basin for students had shrunk back to consist mainly of New York and Connecticut.[189] New Rochelle was suffering from competition. By the late 1960s there were a dozen other Catholic colleges for women in their vicinity, and there was the wisp of a suspicion that some of the nearby men's colleges might decide to become coeducational. It was still too early for the fear to follow: that their peer colleges might begin admitting men. A much more ominous threat, however, was posed by Governor Nelson Rockefeller's success in founding and funding multiple campuses of the three systems of state universities and colleges, where the highest-paid faculties in the country were available for very modest tuition charges.

Without newly imaginative efforts to increase applications, CNR was going to lack the students it needed to meet the payroll. Somehow the college would have to appeal not just to a wider geography, but to a larger definitional base. The question of admitting men began to be discussed, but few on campus could bring themselves to consider that. It would so radically transform the self-understanding of the school. New Rochelle's past success and satisfaction as a women's college simply did not permit imaginations to consider a coeducational future. Several top-level committees were appointed in the next few years to study the possibility of coeducation, but somehow they never seemed to bring in reports. With that kind of diversity beyond imagination, an alternative was to attract more non-Catholics. New Rochelle already had the experience of the congenial presence of a few Protestants and Jews. One young woman at the time used to sign "BLOC" after her name, for "Big Lutheran on Campus."[190] But the experience was mutually warmhearted, and it was easy to imagine that even a few hundred Protestants and Jews would not seriously change the atmosphere, especially when their tuition payments might salvage the atmosphere for everyone. What several hundred Catholic men might do was a much more troublesome thought. In one early effort to draw upon this wider clientele, in 1967 the college took out a snappy full-page ad in *Time,* pointedly describing its student body as "girls from East, West, North and South, Catholic and non-Catholic," receiving "many-faceted training for the pluralistic, ecumenical, post-Vatican II life today's girl will live."[191] But still the numbers declined.

The college found itself suddenly at pains to loosen up what it perceived as an unattractive, straitened style of Catholicism. Internally, the faculty had been engaged in an effort of nearly two years to prepare a policy statement on academic freedom, but was stymied by the widely shared expectation that such a policy had to take due regard of the college's being "committed to the Catholic Faith." Should an otherwise free faculty member be expected to sustain established Catholic teaching, or not to contradict it, or to give it sympathetic treatment, or at least to identify his dissent as private opinion? The gravamen of this extended wrangle was not which measure of obligation to accept, but whether any such public expression of religious commitment was expedient. In the end the policy simply called for unconditional freedom to teach as one wished, within the ambit of one's discipline and of one's course.[192]

Bundy versus Bankruptcy

The Ursulines were having recruitment and retention problems of their own. No sooner had Vatican II encouraged an update of authority and lifestyle in religious communities than their membership began to shrink rapidly. The order modified its sixteenth-century habit, eased the rules of cloister, and eliminated everything that might be redolent of quaintness. Mothers downgraded to sisters; many discarded the new names (often from male saints) they had been given when they entered the order and resumed their baptismal names; then they began to omit the use of any title. But still the numbers declined. It became clear to the Ursulines, as it had to the Jesuits, that they were not going to be able to sustain their personnel at the college. The need to begin replacing them with salaried laypeople aggravated a worsening financial situation. The college began to go into deficit in 1965. A public appeal for $16 million was launched, and failed. Properties were sold off, but those gains were immediately annulled by sudden new expenses. By 1971 there would be a deficit almost large enough to wipe out the very small endowment. The College of New Rochelle would then be looking at bankruptcy.[193]

In 1967 a possible rescue came into sight. That year would prove to be as critical for the future identity of the College of New Rochelle as it was for Boston College, though the changes took place in different ways. For it was in 1967 that Governor Rockefeller appointed the Select Committee on the Future of Private and Independent Higher Education in New York State, commonly known as the Bundy Committee, whose work, as we have seen, fired imaginations even up north in Chestnut Hill. Independent four-year institutions then enrolled exactly one-third of the New York students in higher education. The eighty-four church-related institutions, sixty-five of which were Catholic, accounted for 80,500 students: 13 percent of the total enrollment and 20 percent of the graduate enrollment in the state . . . and a hefty political influence. All the independents were then in financial difficulty, and an unrestricted capitation grant large enough to allow them to survive would also relieve New York State of the much larger cost — perhaps ten to twenty times larger — it would incur if they continued to transfer to state schools.[194]

The Bundy Committee recommended such a grant program, and intended it for all colleges and universities except those which functioned as theological schools for the training of clergy. The plan was easily enacted into law. The New York Constitution's "Blaine Amendment," however, forbade public appropriations to schools "wholly or in part under the control or direction of any religious denomination, or in which any denominational tenet or doctrine is taught." To clear the way for these grants, known as "Bundy money," to be recommended, a constitutional convention agreed to adopt a proposal to delete that provision, but when the new constitution was (for varied reasons) overwhelmingly voted down, there was great angst in both Albany and New Rochelle.[195]

There then ensued a wide variety of interpretations of what kind of institution the Constitution frowned upon. The Select Committee had received legal advice that a recipient would have to be "essentially secular."[196] New Rochelle's harried president, Sister Mary Robert Falls, turned the issue around: "Can public funds be denied an institution which is competently and conscientiously carrying out the objectives of the State, promoting its welfare and that of its citizenry, making possible an educated and dedicated people?"[197]

The Bundy Committee, while stating unanimous objection to the New York constitutional ban, wrestled with a variety of wordings to express its own sense of what degree of religious commitment ought to disqualify colleges from receiving unconditional grants from the state. An institution "whose central purpose is the teaching of religious belief," or which is "primarily a religious institution" and therefore not "primarily an institution of higher education," or one "mainly concerned with the indoctrination" of its own faithful, or that "discriminates in its admissions on religious grounds" should be excluded. If a school were "primarily a religious institution," so that any subsidy it received would primarily serve "the advancement of religion," and if its "secular ends" were only derivative from its religious effectiveness, then such a school ought to be denied Bundy money.[198]

The committee then went on to observe how the majority of private colleges and universities in America had moved away from their original "religious connection," first by replacing clerical control with lay control, then by shifting from denominational to nondenominational "but equally explicitly 'Christian' " identity, until finally becoming "plainly secular." They noted with satisfaction that Catholic colleges were now moving rapidly through this same "evolutionary" process: from a "narrow" to a "broader" self-understanding, like Harvard, Columbia, and Cornell before them. "We believe that this movement is greatly in the interest of all."[199] Sister Mary Robert strongly doubted that it was.

The legislation enacted to carry out the Bundy Committee's recommendations would later be described as "crudely drawn and excessively vague," because instead of customary statutory terminology it expressed academic aspirations.[200] More likely the vagueness was generated by the fog of equivocation which surrounded the effort to circumvent the New York Constitution. The State Education Department, however, moved quickly to formulate criteria of eligibility. The first issue, which attracted much less public notice, was the academic quality of programs at independent schools. Education officials remembered that the Bundy Report had recommended they be more energetic in either weeding out or upgrading inferior institutions: "public funds must not be used to sustain at a subsistence level institutions which would better be dissolved or merged."[201] Consequently applicants were being asked to show evidence of continual improvement of their educational offerings. In her reply to this query, Sister Mary Robert vented New Rochelle's frustration. The Education Department already knew, and she may have known, that of the ten Catholic institutions suffering from enrollment decreases, eight were women's colleges, and New Rochelle was one of them.[202] The greatest threat to her college's academic excellence, she wrote, was financial, and it was all she could presently do to maintain, let alone strengthen, its program. The Bundy money was desperately needed. The risk in her plea was that CNR's need for money might itself mark the college as marginal and persuade the state not to waste its money.[203]

The constitutional question pivoted on two issues: church control and church doctrine. The commissioner of education sent out a lengthy questionnaire on eligibility. On the issue of control, he asked about the religious census of governing boards, administrations, and faculties, and whether creed was a qualification for their selection, or for admissions or scholarships. Sister Mary Robert was irked by these questions. She doubted that the state had any right to ask what the denomination of her board members was, and she turned the question around by charging that the only existing violation of every citizen's immunity from religious tests was the questionnaire itself.[204]

But control was actually the issue which showed off New Rochelle to best advantage. Sister Mary Robert could report that for the first thirty-eight years of CNR's existence there had never been an Ursuline on the board of trustees, and for the first forty-five years all its presidents had been men. What she would not need to report was that from the first moment of the college's existence none of that made any difference: undiluted control over the college was held by Ursuline women picked by the Ursuline Order. The various archbishops of New York and the various men and women they picked to sit on the New Rochelle board knew that they were assisting the women whose lifework it was. Only one year earlier the board had again changed under the press of financial exigency, and it now had a chairman and a strong majority of lay members. But none of those shifts, in the mind of Sister Mary Robert or her colleagues, had changed the college's real governance. This opportunity of successfully presenting an aspect of the college which was effectively Ursuline as if it were really lay, was an important rehearsal for later opportunities to present aspects that were effectively Catholic as if they were really secular. Later still, this rhetoric would be reversed.

The other issue, that of denominational teaching, was much more difficult. Mother Irene had set out to educate "a woman of culture, of efficiency and of power — a woman capable of upholding the noblest ideals of the home and of the

Church." A convent full of Ursulines, backed up by a cemetery rowed with sisters who had worked there before them, shared the conviction of Sister Dorothy Ann (now serving as dean) that "the girls must be able to see in us this thoroughly Catholic mind — alert to the present state of the question" in every inquiry and wrangle being undertaken to enliven the church's faith. The Ursulines and their colleagues were committed, not simply to teaching "denominational doctrine," but to educating women who would take an active part in developing and expounding that doctrine. New Rochelle took particular pride in the integrated way in which its students were taught to combine religious insight and critical scholarship. Historian Sister Alice Gallin recalled:

> A particular course that was taught in this period — and required of all students — was entitled "Christian Tradition and Culture." . . . The students read their way through the Apostolic Fathers, the Benedictine monks, the art and culture of medieval Europe, and finally the entrance of the Church into modern times. The students were exposed to the writings of modern popes from Leo XIII to Pius XII and became familiar with the Church as a significant institution in the development of Western Civilization. This course was a good example of how the tools of a discipline — in this case, historical analysis of institutional growth — were combined with a basic attempt to integrate the knowledge gained here with the truth of faith as taught in the theology courses. It was, I would maintain, a symbol of the whole curriculum and was designed by those in charge as a central integrating experience for the student. It is also symbolic, perhaps, that the course was dropped in the late 60's because a State examiner said that while it was an excellent course it could not be considered "history" because it centered on the church.[205]

"New Rochelle Is Not Catholic"

The presidents of the New York Catholic colleges and universities had been holding emergency meetings to share information and counsel about this crisis they were facing, and the minutes make clear that it was their lawyers who now came to the fore. The lawyers' advice was that the institutions undertake a thorough revision of their public self-presentation and purge it of any elements that implied the institutions were Catholic in purpose and effect.

The Bundy legislation had already given them a clue how this might be done when it stated that the "standards of quality" in New York education should be set by the state institutions. The spokesman for the independent schools took understandable offense. "Over the years it has been the good private colleges and universities which have set the goals of quality the public colleges and universities have striven to reach. I have suggested that the regulations currently being drafted should not be phrased to give the impression that it is the private sector which has to aspire to reach the level of 'comparable public institutions.' "[206] It was soon clear that any ideal or norm would serve, provided only that it be secular. Even then, a Jesuit objected when the Education Department hired a Protestant theologian from Chicago to inspect a made-over Fordham to verify whether the philosophy and theology departments were still "doctrinally shackled." "One can imagine the outcry," he wrote, "that the presence of a Jesuit on the Columbia University campus, with the same investigative, not to say inquisitorial, mandate would have aroused."[207] Holding their wet fingers to the wind, the lawyers urged their clients not to eliminate religion from their campuses, but simply to adjust its status to what it presently enjoyed on state campuses. Religion might be a revered memory from the founding past, an academic discipline, a pastoral activity allowed to function on campus, a private preference of many individuals. What it must not appear to be was a local chapter of some community of faith wide as the world and primeval as Palestine, claiming to have an enlightenment of its own.

Thus the College of New Rochelle:

1. handed back to the state its 1948 certification as a religious institution and its exemption from a statute that outlawed any consideration of religion in personnel decisions;
2. assured separate incorporation and property for the Ursuline community and the college;
3. abolished reserved seats for Ursulines on the board or its executive committee;
4. rewrote the *Bulletin* to show that religious studies (not theology) courses were not to be taught from a Catholic point of view. The departmental course descriptions now bloomed with readings from Schleiermacher, Barth, Berger, Bellah, Buber, Maslow, Keen, Tillich, Gandhi, Confucius, Santayana, Dewey, Tolstoy, Niebuhr, Bonhoeffer, Otto, James, Kierkegaard, Tennessee Williams, and Truman Capote;
5. reduced the requirement in religious studies to three credits (from a one-time high of sixteen), to put it on par with other disciplines;
6. arranged that campus ministry would now respond to individual student interest rather than presume it in the student body. Religious services would now be available for individuals rather than part of the educational program;
7. removed from admissions applications any request for information "of a prejudicial nature";
8. assured that state holidays, not church holy days, punctuate the calendar;
9. examined the college seal for religious elements (the symbols were left, but their interpretations muted). Before: "The burning torch, symbol of the faith which illumines and guides, plunges deep below this symbol of learning and towers high above it, indicating that the learning is deeply rooted in Christian origins and is made brilliant by their light." After: "The burning torch

illumines and guides the learning that is deeply rooted in Judeo-Christian origins"; and

10. rewrote the "Aims and Objectives of the College":

1963: "The College of New Rochelle, a Catholic liberal arts college for women, proposes to educate its students to be thoroughly formed, truly Christian members of the Church and of Society, distinguished by minds trained to think correctly and by wills formed to respond to true values. . . . As a Catholic college, the College of New Rochelle assumes as its own the world-view and penetrating analysis of man and his relations to God and to other men which theology alone can provide."

1965: "Committed to the Christian tradition in its uniqueness and complexity, New Rochelle provides a full program of theology. Far from compromising academic freedom or excellence, such commitment bears witness to the liberating role of Christ and to God's revelation in Him. The college holds firmly that theological and philosophical studies open up dimensions of reality which are necessary to genuine educational growth, and that faith is relevant to learning and to life."

1971: "The College strives to articulate its academic tradition and religious heritage in ways that are consonant with the best contemporary understandings of both. It provides opportunities for spiritual growth in a context of freedom and ecumenism."

In 1972 that austere statement was garlanded with new phrases: "values which motivated the founding . . . openness to the shape of the future . . . quest for meaning in life . . . sensitivity to human dignity . . . growth in self acceptance."

Essential to each institution's request for the new funding was an elaborate response to the interrogatory circulated by the commissioner of education in 1968.[208] New Rochelle was occupied in remaking itself in secular image and likeness, and applied a year late. Sister Mary Robert and her counsel were told by the attorneys advising all the Catholic applicants to make it clear the college "would willingly accept any condition imposed by the State Education Department."[209]

Sister Robert went to her task after being warned by the Admissions Task Force that applications were about to fall beneath the level needed for survival. Virtually all applicants were Catholics who preferred Catholic women's colleges but not Catholic worship, discipline, or much theology.[210] Her treasurer made her aware that the Ursuline rebate to the college from their salaries had shrunk from 10 percent of the budget to 5 percent since she had become president.[211] It was urgent that the Bundy money come to New Rochelle.

The college application stated repeatedly that faith had no part in admitting or funding students, or in choosing and promoting faculty, or in qualifying anyone to sit on the board of trustees. What place did religion have in the institution? Passing quickly beyond religion in the "narrow sense" (prayer and worship, which were available but not essential), the response bravely spoke up for religion as a civic condiment:

> If there is one conviction which predominates concerning the nature and role of religion it is the conviction that wholly secularistic society is a denial of the American concept of pluralism and a betrayal of our role in American society. Hence, a sustaining effort is made to help students achieve both conviction and balance in the matter of personal commitment and a value system which takes into account the religious as well as the social and political heritage of man. . . .
>
> As a Catholic college, the College of New Rochelle tries to provide a situation in which Christianity is a vital reality.

The application concluded with a complaint that most of the questions asked were irrelevant and distracting. As New Rochelle saw it, the only thing the commissioner should ask is: "What is it that this institution is accomplishing? In what way does this promote the welfare of the citizens of the state and the very objectives for which the state exists?" By insisting on secularist uniformity within its system of higher education the state was gainsaying the American tradition that leaves individuals free to function according to their convictions. If, in pursuit of shared religious convictions, people join to maintain a college, why should the state deny it the funds necessary to survive?[212]

Ewald Nyquist had in the meantime succeeded to the office of commissioner, and it was unfortunate for the college that he was a Catholic both knowledgeable and sympathetic. Whether because he felt a need to prove himself biddable within the political arena, or because he sensed that the college had undertaken a change more in symbol than in substance, he denied the application and declared CNR ineligible for Bundy money. Four months later the college sued successfully, but the commissioner's appeal took the lawsuit into the Appellate Division, and into December 1971, three years after Nyquist's decision.[213]

He defended his conclusion, "based not on any single factor, but rather upon an understanding of the institution as a whole." A close reading of various college publications showed that CNR presented itself within the four-hundred-year-old tradition of Christian education launched by Saint Angela Merici, and it was presided over by the Ursulines, and peopled top to bottom by a predominance of Catholics with Catholic theology, clergy, worship, piety, charitable activism, and symbolism. It called itself a "Catholic College," and that is what it obviously was. The trial judge found for the college on the procedural ground that the college had had too little opportunity to choose and interpret the facts.

The college uttered great disavowals in its appeal. All of the fragmentary facts assembled by the commissioner, it argued, amounted to no more than this: "that there is a kind of presence, hard to define but felt by the members of the academic community and it is hoped that at New Rochelle it is a Christian presence." Sister Mary Robert, with her implacable candor, had said in her affidavit:

652

"We hope that a student who comes to us a Catholic remains a Catholic." Her true sense, she assured the court, was "that every girl who comes with any religious conviction will not graduate with it weakened, and that all students will find their sense of values sharpened." The commissioner had noted that wherever "the church" appeared in college documents, e.g., in religious studies course descriptions, it invariably referred to the Catholic Church. Not so, as a New Rochelle religious studies instructor explained: "the word 'church' was not limited to the Roman Catholic Church either viewed in its hierarchical structure or all its adherents confessing its doctrines, nor to all Christians, nor to those who profess any Christian denomination but rather to all peoples of good will everywhere." As for church control, these proceedings made clear where final control and authority lay for the college: with the State of New York, not with the Catholic Church. The college's defense ended with a ringing assertion that it would accept a recent definition by Justice Brennan (then the U.S. Supreme Court's most ardent opponent of funding through religious institutions). "Sectarian institutions," he had written, "have a purpose or function to propagate or advance a particular religion." Since that was not true of New Rochelle, the brief insisted, "the College qualifies for the grant."[214]

A unanimous bench found for the college on appeal, influenced by some very important and very recent decisions of the U.S. Supreme Court. First, as for the U.S. Constitution's First Amendment: the grant to New Rochelle had a secular purpose (to support higher education), a primary effect that would neither advance nor inhibit religion, and it avoided excessive entanglement through the state nosing about in church matters. Therefore it passed muster at the federal level. Second, as for the Blaine Amendment, the court noticed that the New York Constitution forbade grants to an institution "in which *any* denominational tenet or doctrine is taught." Take that literally, and most New York universities and colleges, including many units of SUNY and CUNY, would have their state funding cut off. What the constitution must be understood as forbidding is "to teach a doctrine of a particular religious denomination to the exclusion of other denominations." New Rochelle's adjunct rabbis and Protestant minister cleared the college of that charge. Was Catholicism somehow conveyed outside the classroom, perhaps in prayer, or by the Ursuline presence? The same reasoning was repeated: a tough stand on this would touch many campuses, not just New Rochelle. Thirdly, the Blaine Amendment also proscribed aid to campuses under religious control. Here the court drew on recent precedents that sharply distinguished elementary and secondary schools from colleges and universities. When the students are immature, administrative control and a religiously pervasive "atmosphere" probably constitute religious control or denominational direction. But since "college students are less impressionable and less susceptible to religious indoctrination," a similarly solicitous administration and a similarly pervasive religious atmosphere would probably not constitute "control."[215]

New Rochelle's struggle to claim the Bundy money was in some respects a moment of truth for the college. For its president it was a time of anguish. Shortly after the Nyquist refusal she wrote in protest to the chancellor of the New York system. Bard College, she observed, with explicit patronage from the Episcopal Church, and with the prominent former rector of an Episcopal parish as president and an Episcopal bishop as trustee *ex officio* and as chancellor, and with Sunday worship from the *Book of Common Prayer,* had been declared a qualified recipient without ado (as had its fellow Episcopal progeny, Hobart and William Smith). Also on the roster of fifty-two institutions given immediate approval she could find Alfred, Colgate, Keuka, Rochester, and Vassar; Elmira and Hamilton; Hartwick; Saint Lawrence; and Syracuse: all of them progeny of the Baptists, Presbyterians, Lutherans, Universalists, and Methodists, respectively. There is no evidence that she took even oblique satisfaction from the fact that the commissioner saw the Catholics as succeeding in its commitments where these others had apparently lapsed.[216] To Nyquist himself she grieved that "by denying aid the State Education Department has created such grave internal problems for administrators of church-related colleges. . . . The inevitable discontent and even outspoken resentment and criticism of the presence of religious [congregations] as a cause of lack of state aid has aggravated the situation on some campuses and has intensified the problems of administration still more." In this thwarted state of mind she could take no comfort when Nyquist, in an attempt to console her somewhat, replied: "As a matter of fact, it seems to me that any institution that calls itself a 'Catholic' college is ineligible under the Bundy program. Manhattanville, Fordham and St. John Fisher I [more recently] declared eligible because to me they are now secular institutions and no longer Catholic colleges."[217]

Under the pressures of the crisis Falls had emerged with the view that if New Rochelle gave a professionally competent education by all the academic standards New York wanted to apply, then it was none of the state's business how religious were the environment, motivation, or faith which delivered the product. If New Rochelle could teach the ABCs, then New York should mind its p's and q's. This, of course, was the law which did apply when governmental agencies purchased services from such institutions. Religious agencies could contract with a state to raise orphans, provide milk, welcome refugees, or lease property, but might not receive unrestricted, general grants.

This view and her sense of injustice she expressed freely in her correspondence and in her statements to the college community. One must infer that it was task-oriented lawyers, not reflective Ursulines like Sister Mary Robert, who drafted the pleadings which argued so lyrically that Angela Merici, Irene Gill, Mary Xavier Fitzgerald, Mary Aquinas O'Reilly, and their many colleagues and supporters at New Rochelle had given their lives, not for anything so narrow and sectarian as advancing the faith of Catholics, but to promote values for people of good will.

Mental Reservation

It was a trustee, Sister Borgia, who made what may have been the most remarkable observation during this imbroglio. In the midst of an extended board discussion about "secular" and "sectarian," she simply concluded that their own self-understanding was, after all, more important than their public vocabulary.[218] She was giving clear voice to the widespread belief that the institutions could maintain one identity privately and another publicly. The college's self-presentation as a secular school infused with a faint religious scent was, of course, a bit of a scam, but a scam which would in a brief time dissolve because what was said publicly actually became true. Nyquist knew well what everyone involved in the litigation had to know: that the College of New Rochelle was a Catholic school run by Catholic nuns and taught by Catholic nuns and their lay colleagues for Catholic women. Nyquist seemingly lacked the gregarious mendacity which has piloted other, more political professionals through the political straits of New York public life. He wished the sisters could have had the grant (and they knew it), but by law he had to withhold it from them. Everyone else involved wanted them to have it as well, and saw that they got it despite the law.

If, for some of those, it was an impious scam, for the nuns it was a pious one. It was also much more dangerous, for the sisters were not in the habit of saying things they did not believe. In that brief, soul-warping time they brought themselves to testify that they meant no more than to purvey undetermined "values" to people of good will. No more than that. What was risky for the sisters was that from this moment on, what they (or their legal counsel) had sworn to be true, they not only made themselves believe to be true, but began to arrange for it to become true. And they succeeded. In a desperate departure from discipline and character they allowed themselves to let their public vocabulary float free of their own shared self-understanding, believing that an internal truth must survive an external prevarication. They had too little experience of imposture to anticipate what then happened: their public vocabulary proved to be much more important than their self-understanding. And they were the only ones who were deceived. Sister Borgia (of the delicious name) was more candid than she knew when she spread her whimsical insight on the minutes.

Within the CNR board there was one person who seems to have sensed what was at stake as the college was readying itself to plead and promise that it was not — or, at the least, it promised not to be any more — Catholic. The chairman, William J. Stoutenburgh, had questioned the effect that the lawsuit would have on New Rochelle's future status as a Catholic school, and abstained on the vote to proceed with the lawsuit.[219]

This struggle for funding was quite enough to dominate the sensibilities of the college at the time, but other realities were also in motion. The academic year 1969-70 was a gruesome one for Sister Mary Robert. Applications and matriculations were continuing to sink below the level of maintenance. She had appointed a Coeducation Committee, which reported that the decline showed no signs of abating. "Many of the better women's colleges appear to be losing their best candidates to the coed school." The committee confessed, however, that they were not yet sure that being a single-sex college was what explained the absence of students at CNR. After two years of dithering they concluded that more study and research were needed.[220] But the process they were reluctant to cope with was accelerating as they studied it. Women's colleges in America were reduced in number by one-quarter from 1960 to 1969; in the next two years they would be depleted by another 30 percent.[221] The financial affairs of the college went into fibrillation in 1969-70, and by year's end it would have collapsed into a deficit of nearly a half-million dollars. The college could not possibly endure another year like that.

Just as she was sending off the fateful application for the Bundy money, Sister Mary Robert announced she would resign after commencement in the spring. Possibly to leave behind a painful era in her life, she chose that as the time to resume her baptismal name and became Sister Theresa Falls. The presidential search committee, in the spirit of the times, recommended advertising for "the best possible president," whether "male or female, lay or religious, white or black, Catholic, Protestant, or Jew." This seemed to race ahead of the times, and the trustees deleted the references to race and religion. There was some staff reduction to be done, and the board thought this was man's work, so they chose one of their own number. Joseph McMurray, then the president of Queen's College (in CUNY), was a manager, not an educator; he had never earned a terminal degree. It took half of his intended first year of office for him to free himself from his commitments to Queens, and for the college to purchase an expensive new president's house. McMurray did reduce the payroll in timely fashion. He was also on duty to welcome the final Bundy verdict and the first Bundy check, and he expressed public satisfaction that "At no time did we deny the deep Catholic tradition of the College of New Rochelle."[222] His presidency was a season of uncertainty for the Ursuline community, whose demographic future was aggravated by some immediate financial needs which the college regarded as an unwelcome competition for the same dollars.[223] McMurray departed for a business venture after one and a half years in office, and there was an easy consensus that Sister Dorothy Ann Kelly, after five years as dean and acting president, should take over. She began by telling the board that the deficit had now soared to more than half again what it had been when Sister Theresa had left the presidency.[224]

The unresolved business at New Rochelle was whether or not to become coeducational. The new president's inaugural address — an eloquent and exquisitely balanced evaluation of the women's movement — announced implicitly where her preference lay, and soon the decision was taken, informally but definitively, to persevere as a women's college.[225] It was unfortunate that too few young women shared Sister Dorothy Ann's insights and preferences. Nevertheless she would find means to save the college.

656

A Suburban College Becomes an Urban University

The Art Department had been gaining in talent and ebullience, and in 1968 they persuaded the board to allow them to offer graduate courses targeted at teachers in the region who might thereby upgrade their certification. By the time a new charter amendment entitling CNR to offer graduate degrees had been secured in 1970, a much wider market had been discovered. The new Graduate School (GRS) offered the M.S. in art education, then in reading and language arts, then in therapy and special education. By the end of Sister Dorothy Ann's first year there were more than a thousand students enrolled . . . and paying tuition. Since they were mostly studying part-time, the enrollment head count was considerably greater than the actual numbers in courses, but the college had found a new, tuition-driven service based on its regular faculty.

In 1972 another initiative, destined to become much larger in vision and dimensions, was begun at the recommendation of several faculty members. West-chester seemed to house a large number of young wives whose education had been foreshortened by either marriage or work, and who seemed to be a potential clientele for adult education. This would not put them into the classroom and the curriculum alongside girls the age of their daughters, but it would be more sub-stantial than conventional extension offerings like leather making or income-tax preparation. A School of New Resources (SNR) was begun, which offered students thirty credits up front for a reflective portfolio of their "life experiences," and then agreed to go out and hire moonlighting teachers or professionals to teach whatever courses students were willing to sign up for in advance. This drew 330 students the first year, and soared to 527 the next. At that point the SNR was already a profit center for the college. A labor union in Manhattan heard of it, and soon another branch of SNR was functioning at the headquarters of District Council 37 of the American Federation of State, County, and Municipal Employees, which guar-anteed tuition for its members. Others would be added in the South Bronx; at Co-Op City, an enormous public housing complex in the North Bronx; at a seminary in Chelsea; at Bedford-Stuyvesant in Brooklyn; and at their own Rosa Parks Campus in Harlem. Today there are nearly ten times as many students in these SNR satellite schools as in the traditional undergraduate school.

In 1976 a School of Nursing (SON) was opened. At first it served RNs who were expected to earn their baccalaureates as a required credential. Then there were nurses who sought specialized certification, and eventually a full-scale program: graduate, undergraduate, and extension.

The School of Nursing added students to the college's basic undergraduate courses, and the Graduate School was an added client for the services of some faculty. Thus they both allowed the college to use its permanent faculty more efficiently. The financial dynamic of the college had already shifted away from its traditional unit, which soon needed a name of its own since the "College" was now a conglomerate. It was being called, awkwardly, "the traditional college" or "the regular college," and now became the School of Arts and Sciences (SAS). By 1973 the SAS enrolled a minority of the students and was bringing in a minority of the revenue. Yet by 1973 the cumulative deficit was the largest ever.

Financial stability was slow in coming, partly because the college's meager surpluses took so long to retire the debt, partly because so much deferred maintenance was waiting to visit old obligations on the recently rescued budget, and partly because the SNR, the great hope of the exchequer, nearly went under. The treasurer was puzzled one day to find that the SNR had accumulated more than $200,000 in delinquent and defaulted debts. There was a high evaporation rate in the student clientele, and many who had enrolled in hopes of upgraded employment afterward, but had dropped out after a few courses, simply walked away from the loans they had taken to pay their tuition and from the bills for tuition that had not been paid.[226]

New Rochelle felt the need then to review its priorities. In her first annual report the president identified three key questions for the Long Range Planning Committee in 1973:

> Should CNR continue to favor the tradition of "liberal arts" or move toward more professional and technical training?
> Should CNR remain a women's college in its four-year traditional degree program?
> Should CNR continue to try to express a commitment to values associated with Christianity?[227]

Looking back now with more perspective than was allowed the committee then, one can see that survival was at stake. The documents of the time repeatedly assert that the purpose at CNR had never been "mere survival," but when has survival ever been mere? The evidence of the time asserts that it was an urgent worry. Also, the longer CNR was engaged in long-range planning, the clearer it became that the college was being driven by the priorities of its clientele, not the plans of its governors.[228]

Traditionally the Ursulines had set out to educate fee-paying Catholic women in the liberal arts, and had gone out of their way to bring in students from poorer homes. This model was never taken as an absolute, for various modest exceptions were allowed. CNR had always managed to include students who worked their way through, had welcomed some non-Catholics, had eventually allowed some men (faculty and staff children) to take classes (but not to qualify for degrees), and had provided some vocational training to help graduates earn a living.

A Rhetoric of Continuity, a Chronicle of Change

In the main, the four traditional descriptors of the college referred to social class (integrated), church (Catholic), gender (women), and curriculum (liberal arts and sciences). For Mother Irene and her successors, church and gender would probably have been inseparable: they worked to give a Catholic education and formation to women. Curriculum would have come next, because a liberal education was what gave women the most powerful advantages in society. Sister Dorothy Ann had not mentioned class, which would have been maladroit in public, but it was always a factor. However, to the extent that they could make financial aid available, the Ursulines usually preferred to have a student body that wholesomely mingled the classes.

What has emerged at New Rochelle, more by market forces than by policy, eventually resulted in the college's service to a radically new clientele, with respect to all four of its traditional characteristics.[229]

As for class, the clientele is now mostly poor. When Sister Dorothy Ann assumed the presidency of the college, students were mostly either tuition-paying or able to pay for their education with part-time work. As it turned toward the poor and the underclass, New Rochelle developed one of the most capable and astute offices of financial aid in the region. In a metropolitan area where richly funded, low-tuition state campuses are as numerous as firehouses, CNR has been a successful competitor because it has somehow befriended its students and guided them through the mysteries of grantspersonship. For decades now, three-quarters of all tuition derives from federal or state funds.[230] The School of New Resources is explicitly directed to the ethnic poor, so much so that its very existence was threatened recently when New York rules forbade welfare recipients from attending full-time college programs. Even the School of Arts and Sciences student body is now 53 percent minorities, compared with 71 percent for the entire CNR enrollment. Most receive financial aid, and nearly 90 percent of them work an average of twenty hours a week.[231] Clearly the class profile at New Rochelle is drastically changed from what it was. It undercuts the accusation made by one unhappy SNR faculty member's lawyer: "The black school is subsidizing the lily white country club."[232] The SNR clearly subsidizes the SAS, but the latter is no longer a white preserve.

The SAS is still technically an undergraduate program for women only. But it accounts for only 7 percent of the CNR enrollment; all the rest is coed. Still, though the formal orientation of the other schools in the college cannot be explicitly feminist, the fact that 86 percent of their students are female ensures that the college remains overwhelmingly peopled by women. The gender orientation is thus somewhat intact, even though in effect the College of New Rochelle did what it thought it did not do: since SAS shares classes with some other programs, CNR became a coeducational school. So now the college literature is properly studded with "he/she's."

As regards curriculum, the Graduate School and the School of Nursing are, of course, entirely professional. The SAS, whence all vocational courses were once banished, now lists as its largest departments, in order of the number of degrees awarded: Communication Arts, Business, Art, and Psychology. At the bottom of the list one finds many of the traditionally liberal disciplines: biology, chemistry, history, classics, mathematics, American studies. It is a rare year when either philosophy or theology boasts of a single graduate. The SAS matriculants these days do not rank so high academically in their national cohort, and have required considerable remedial work. Usually this predicts a lower interest in the liberal arts.[233]

It is difficult to estimate how, if at all, the enormous SNR makes the liberal arts available. There has always been a policy of open admissions. In lieu of curriculum, each degree candidate must complete an entrance seminar ("Experience, Learning and Identity"), one course in English at any competency level, one course in mathematics, two core seminars (chosen from "American Experience," "Human Body," "Science and Human Values," and "Urban Community"), two degree-planning courses ("Career/Interest Review" and "Designing the Future"), and one exit seminar ("Ways of Knowing"). Several months in advance of each semester a list of possible courses is posted, and those which have an economically viable advance subscription will be made available. The entire faculty is composed of part-time professionals, and this mode of registration ensures that no salary commitments are made before they are covered by pre-enrollment. The menu included these and other course titles: "Physiology of the Reading Process," "The Woman as Hero," "Psychology of the Occult Life Experience," "Gerontology," "Human Communication," "Functional Pedagogy of Mathematics and Physical Science," "Current Themes of Black Literature," "Elements of Western Culture," "Art in Our Lives," "Birth to Adolescence," "Liberation and Oppression," and "American Literary Masters." Possibly in response to the strong criticism from the accrediting visitors, SNR courses now include such basics as "Introduction to Sociology," "College Algebra," "Art of Film and Television," "Early Childhood Education: Theories and Methods," and "20th Century Fiction." Proposed courses that failed to secure enough enrollment included "Small Business Management," "Psychological Aspects of AIDS," and "Introduction to Mass Media." Thus there may be some liberal courses, but no liberal education, understood as a progressive initiation into a liberal discipline. Liberal education has been displaced, if not extinguished, by professional training and remedial studies. It is fair to say that it survives only as a refugee in the School of Arts and Sciences. The academic texture of the SNR took a beating from the accreditation team, but somehow survived.[234]

The college's public rhetoric has tended to make a virtue out of necessity when reporting these great shifts in the nature of its community, culture, and education. For example, the daring bid to draw in some much-needed tuition-paying Westchester housewives in 1968 was described as "the College's reawakened sense of service." The market turn toward vocational and noncurricular education was claimed in 1974 to be a result of long-range planning. "The College has a twofold purpose: to promote both the quest for meaning in life and a commitment to academic excellence. . . . the pursuit of 'meaning in life' requires the raising and examination of questions which 'help an individual to develop convictions based on values,' and the 'academic excellence' of a program has to be judged at least in part by its responsiveness to social needs. Thus the college seeks to interweave the threads of quality education and responsiveness to the needs of society into the pattern of all its programs."[235] Within the degraded rhetorical tradition of American higher education, this ranks with the literary masters.

But the most thorough change, accompanied by the most glutinous discourse, has affected the Catholic character of New Rochelle. To begin with, there was the Ursuline community. In the mid-1950s, the nuns constituted half of the faculty and held the presidency and two-thirds of the seats on the board. The college enjoyed the services of about forty of them. Ten years later their presence was still strong: thirty-six out of eighty-one full-time faculty were Ursulines. But by the 1970s, when the college was in travail, so too were the nuns. In 1970 their province was withdrawing personnel from schools it could no longer staff. At the same time the college was anxious for its own financially threatened future, and cast a less appreciative eye upon the Ursulines now that they were not going to provide so much professionally competent and religiously dedicated service, and rebate their salaries as well. The Ursulines were having a crisis of their own. They were working to free themselves from a restrictive communal life, and they developed a lush but ambiguous vocabulary to depict in communitarian terms a life which basically yearned to be individualist. They aspired to the life of single professional women. The college had similar inclinations, wishing to be indistinguishable from Wellesley or Smith. Each wanted the feel of continuity and fidelity, while moving away from the manners and obligations of the past. By 1974 the proportion of sisters among the faculty had dropped to one-quarter, with an equal number in administration. Though few, they were quite accomplished: they held doctorates from Fordham, Maryland, Georgetown, Laval, Harvard, Catholic, and Notre Dame.

In 1975 the Ursulines at the college had formed their own association, and were holding strained colloquies with representatives of the trustees. These led to formal expressions of "mutual respect and confidence," a sure sign that all was not well. By this point the college no longer had a preferential hiring policy in favor of Ursulines, and such younger nuns as might be available for professional service (only one or two women were then entering the province each year) seemed inclined to more activist callings with vocational master's degrees. The point had been made clear when five untenured faculty failed to receive renewal contracts, and two of them were Ursulines.[236] The committee assigned to define and evoke "Ursuline presence" without Ursulines resorted to alchemy, and wrote of "a vital core of committed women . . . bearers of the Ursuline tradition." It was that kind of tradition they "wished to maintain" at the college[237] . . . yet obviously could not. Today there are four Ursulines in the administration (out of 110), three on the SAS faculty (out of 77), two on the GRS faculty (out of 128), and none on the nursing faculty.

When Sister Dorothy Ann Kelly took up the presidency in 1972, Catholics constituted about 94 percent of the student body. Today, among the "traditional" students (the SAS and the undergraduate students of nursing) Catholics make up 55 percent, and their proportion continues to decrease.[238] The rest of the student body — that is, 84 percent of the enrollment, in graduate and professional programs and the SNR — are never canvassed as to their religious membership, and Catholics are believed to be scarce among them. Thus Catholics may provide only somewhat more than 10 percent of the students being educated by CNR.

A national survey indicates that some of the shifts in the CNR traditional student population diverge from those in comparable Catholic women's colleges. Across the span of the 1970s and 1980s, for instance, the proportion of Catholics actually increased in those colleges: from 76 to 82 percent. Selectivity also changed: at the start of this two-decade period in the Catholic women's colleges 24 percent of the incoming students reported their average high school grades were A, and by the end they were enrolling 40 percent A students. In sharp contrast, New Rochelle began with 54 percent A students, but ended with only 22 percent. Attitudinal changes were also of interest. CNR's traditional students emerged as strongly in favor of both capital punishment (76 percent) and busing (61 percent), which might seem puzzling; and two decades earlier they opposed both (85 percent and 40 percent). Their support for legal abortion rose from 43 to 71 percent, and those who thought "sex OK if people like each other" increased from 29 to 50 percent. Their peers on other Catholic campuses moved to stronger support for busing but much less enthusiasm for capital punishment, legal abortion, and "liking" as the moral basis for OK sex.[239]

The same realities may be seen from another angle. The year New Rochelle applied for a New York State grant, the Department of Religious Studies was staffed by seven regular faculty members and six lecturers. Today Religious Studies (no longer a department but joined with Philosophy) in the SAS is staffed by one regular faculty member and two adjuncts. The minimal curricular requirement of three credits (then in theology) in 1969 was effectively eliminated in 1973. The department understands its task, no longer as studying religion to understand God, but to understand humanity.[240] The faculty has stated that since "religious faith, as such, transcends any particular value system," CNR's "religious heritage" manifests itself academically in the "universal moral dimension" present in all their courses, and a vague "religious-based presence" and an "intangible but real atmosphere" associated with "concern for the individual."[241] This could not be said to be hard-edged.

Since CNR does not now deal with faculty in respect of their faith, no one knows how many might be Catholics at present. One study of American colleges founded by Catholic women's orders reports that from 1965 to 1986 Catholics on their faculties decreased from 87 to 68 percent.[242]

The trauma of the Bundy struggle seemed to guarantee that the adjective "Catholic" would never again precede the noun "College" at New Rochelle. Sister Dorothy Ann claimed several years afterward that the only "compromise" CNR made in qualifying for the state funds was to refrain from calling itself a "Catholic College." This remark in retrospect, however, sounds like "peace in our time" in 1938.

The Bundy affair has raised the question about how earnest either the State Education Department or the Catholic educators were about the substantial effects of their negotiations. Even the Gellhorn Report described its task as having Fordham "treated as though it were nonsectarian."[243] Sister Dorothy Ann would describe it minimally: "Dependence on state and federal funding has sharply increased, and with this involvement has come some curtailment of freedom to articulate religious identity."[244] The Catholic educators conveyed their sense that the state officials, for whatever reasons, required conformity in matters that could safely be yielded. Said Kelly: "Our inclusion (and that of any other church-related college in New York State) was conditional upon our not being Church-controlled nor proselytizing. We were requested not to use 'Catholic' to describe ourselves because to New York State 'Catholic' meant that we were Church-controlled and proselytizing. Rather, we could use words like Ursuline, Jesuit, Judaic-Christian, etc."[245] The campus was beginning to admit obliquely that the Bundy compromise was one of dissimulation: it was their public expression, not their private conviction, that was stilled. But by that time it was becoming noticeable that by becoming private the communal faith was becoming evanescent: what is known in the trade as a "heritage."

Whenever discourse drifts onto the topic of religion, the idiom seems to blur. In her first presidential report, calling for a redefinition of New Rochelle, Sister Dorothy promised: "The abiding objective of the College of New Rochelle is to provide the undergraduate student with the opportunity to develop a core of values, to establish a set of convictions about the meaning of life, to acquire the intellectual tools with which to face the tasks of life responsibly." That might also have been said only a few miles away at West Point, save that here the subject did turn to religion: "Those who are searching for a deepening of religious convictions, or a discovery of them, will find at CNR a positive, accepting attitude which respects freedom and fosters personal responses."[246] The college, one infers, would defer to piety, but not provide it or witness to it. "Religion" would not be a varsity activity, or even an intramural one, but a pickup game.

Though the three issues (curriculum, gender, and church) were put on the table by the president in 1973 for purposes of long-range planning, none of them was ever explicitly resolved — not, in any case, by resolve of the college. Not nearly enough tuition-paying Catholic women could be found in the vicinity who sought a Catholic, single-sex, liberal education. The only choice New Rochelle might realistically have made then was to have become coeducational: on its own, or by merger with Iona College across town. But of all such possible choices, the one that was pragmatically possible was emotionally unthinkable. For want of that one decision, all the others were taken out of the college's hand, and by relying upon the main chance and determined and resourceful efforts to find any students who would enroll, New Rochelle has survived. The human body is said to replace its cells gradually over the course of seven years, and its identity survives throughout the change. New Rochelle survives, but it is not the same college.

Was the Loss of Catholic Character a Financial Necessity?

This has often been blamed — by any who thought it a matter of blame or regret — on the imperatives of the Bundy money. But it has been repeatedly denied by the people responsible.[247] In the case of New Rochelle, the predominantly lay board, the dissociation from the Ursulines, the waning centrality of theology and philosophy, the desire to recruit more non-Catholic students and faculty, the embarrassment about the "old ways" — all were under way before state funding was imagined. What the Bundy crisis did was provide a public emergency that invited the college to justify aloud what it had begun to do *sotto voce*.

Consider the full-page advertisement in *Time* magazine in 1967:

> The College of New Rochelle offers thorough and many-faceted training for the pluralistic, ecumenical, post-Vatican II life today's young girl will live.
>
> Now, as you sit there reading this in Maine, Virginia or Illinois, you may ask yourself, "Why do they want my daughter, from so far away?" She'll bring with her to campus the outlook and values of her own part of the country. Frankly, we find that mixing girls from East, West, North and South, Catholic and non-Catholic, sets up an informal learning situation which helps the girls, helps us.

The copy begins with a disclaimer that CNR had quite enough money and quite enough girls, which in 1967 was not at all the case: no need for such an expensive ad were it so. The college was appealing to a wider constituency. It would certainly have been wonderful to be a national campus filled with accents from Orono, Lynchburg, and Peoria, but New Rochelle wasn't really that bothered about its regional homogeneity. It was certainly not uneasy about being a school for women only. But it was disquieted about being perceived as Catholic, because of stereotypes in the academy and the culture. In the wake of Vatican II the campus discovered in itself an anxiety to become pluralistic, ecumenical, and post-Vatican II. The future which was confidently held before the college community was one without absolutist theology, authoritarian clergy, censorious and ingenuous nuns, narrow-minded and provincial students, ghetto-minded and nay-saying academics. The history of New Rochelle, fairly read, certainly did not qualify it as a case study in that sort of stale anti-intellectualism or prejudice. Yet this summons to a fresher future was the melody line sung above an *obbligato* of embarrassment, a very mild form of what Jews call self-hatred.

Catholic intellectual John Cogley's confessional article, "The Future of an Illusion," was much read and quoted on the campus during those days:

> The idea of the Church's conducting something identifiable as a "Catholic university," in the sense that Marquette, St. Louis, Fordham, Notre Dame, Georgetown and the Loyolas are today called Catholic universities, will one day seem as anachronistic as the papal states, the error-has-no-rights "Catholic State," the

Catholic penitentiary, or the Catholic bank. . . . The age-old links are crumbling
. . . modernity has triumphed . . . I am convinced that, like the contemporary
state, (higher learning) too is now rooted in the secular, the rational, the scientific
and a common pluralistic culture. Though it once may have been, the common
culture of the world we live in is no longer grounded on Revelation or ecclesiastical foundations. Religion, specifically Christianity, is an important factor in
the common culture but it is no longer a presiding principle.

We have no choice but to live by this learning if we hope to act in the real
world of the here-and-now. Long ago . . . I recognized that I personally had
become a very "secular" man. . . . I discovered, for example, that others also
looked elsewhere than to the Church for their actual cultural values, political
wisdom, social identification, and a personal link to the future. . . . One group
repudiated contemporary cultural values, contemporary political experience, and
the identity modernity confers, regarding them as expressions of rank "secularism." The other argued for the end of what they believed to be illusion.[248]

Sociologist Robert Hassenger weighed in with a reminder that Catholic-
college graduates had of late been abundantly successful in winning national
graduate fellowships. Readers in New Rochelle would not have missed his report
that several Catholic women's liberal arts colleges had tested high for intellectuality
and social concern. Hassenger tended to agree with David Riesman that a certain
"anti-authoritarian romanticism" was afoot among Catholic academics. "They
appear to believe that all of the problems of Catholic universities would disappear
if only they were laicized." Lay trustees, then being hastily recruited and seated,
might "be even more likely than religious to turn out what Riesman calls 'patriotic,
sports-loving, smooth but unsophisticated young women and piously protected,
"feminine" young women.' "[249]

As the college muted its Catholic identity, people began to notice, and to
react. Perceptions differed considerably. Sister Emmanuel McIver spoke to the issue
at an alumni symposium. One woman had expressed impatience with the way her
friends were apologizing for going to a small Catholic school, or for teaching in
one. She had misgivings about the "secularity" some schools now seemed to be
lusting for. Sister Emmanuel assured her that "we try to give it a more positive
connotation. By secular we don't mean the denial or antithesis of everything that
is religious. It's a mentality or a mind set really that tends to see the good and does
not offer impossible options: God or this world. The faith *or* technology. Immersion
in the political world *or* integrity." To prepare students to live in a diverse and
pluralistic world, "we have an obligation to respond by creating more pluralism
and more diversity within the institution. . . . It is impossible today to teach a valid
theology course simply from the point of view of Roman Catholicism. You are not
even doing the service of education properly when you do that."[250]

This led one senior to report that along with the others in attendance she was
anxious for the college to become coed and secular, and work toward diversifica-

tion. But "if increasing the enrollment means a loss of this spirit (and this is often the case) then I would rather see New Rochelle remain a small (cut the 'Catholic') women's college."[251]

Not everyone thought it wise to "cut the 'Catholic.'" A public relations consultant was hired in 1974 to help recruit students for the SAS. Since the SNR and GRS were "carrying" the entire college, he warned them not to be slack in their efforts to make the old undergraduate program strong and self-supporting. "Momentarily," he wrote, "the College seems to be without an image, without a clear-cut expression of what it is and where it is heading. Members of the admissions staff are not sure whether they should present the College as a Catholic institution, a sectarian institution, or what. These people definitely need 'a party line.'"[252] This was advice no one was then prepared to take: not just because of legal encumbrances on state aid. The consultant did not perceive that the people at New Rochelle did know whither and whence they were heading, and "Catholic" had come to evoke everything the college was happy to have left behind. New Rochelle had reached a turning point where the academy and its culture replaced the church and its culture as its primary environment. Many on campus thought that the college was moving from subjection to autonomy, but neither side of that belief would prove true.

"The Mission of the College Has Changed Very Little . . ."

During the earlier years of CNR's existence the Catholic women educators had been able to develop a stronger and more unapologetic sense of their distinctive mission than had their peers at the secular women's colleges. But the 1960s and 1970s were telling a different story, one of confusion and loss of nerve.[253] Sister Alice Gallin, who had been dean at the college and would become the executive director of the Association of Catholic Colleges and Universities, offers an illustration of this confusion. She observed in 1977 that what had happened locally was no local event:

> There has been genuine confusion about ecumenism, ecclesial self-understanding, and the Christian's relation to the modern world in the wake of Vatican II. *This has meant that mistakes have been made in the effort to seem more "open" to others. We have witnessed efforts to devalue our own tradition so that we might show a new awareness to the truth of other traditions.* The confusion over the identity of the Catholic college can only be understood within the context of the general identity crisis of the broad Catholic community. . . .
>
> *Some of [our institutions] have even over-reacted in order to prove their secularity. . . . Enriching one's understanding of the world by bringing it under the light of the Gospel is a worthwhile enterprise, but for many on Catholic campuses it has been repudiated. In some cases, the rituals and teachings of*

other religions are accepted with greater ease than are the celebrations of the Catholic community.

When Sister Alice's remarks reappeared one year later for the New Rochelle community, the passages here italicized had been removed. In retrospect, her interpretation of the detachment from the church became more and more benign. Her most recent account offers a reason for her optimism: "The consequent changes in self-identification and self-understanding (which are reflected in Catholic mission statements) have been labeled by some as 'secularization.' I disagree with this characterization. The fundamental movement . . . is toward inculturation, a process that is itself a necessary prerequisite to evangelization."[254] This sounds very much like Sister Borgia's hope that the college might publicly present itself as secular while privately conserving its Catholic identity. After years of "inculturation" — emulating Radcliffe and Vassar, Wellesley and Smith, and then Hunter College and Bronx Community College, all the while ingesting their commitments and convictions — for New Rochelle to possess the nerve and the knack to prevail evangelically on them all to adopt Christ as their master teacher would be no more plausible than for Lot's wife to forsake her salty vigil over Sodom and Gomorrah and resume her journey.

New Rochelle at the turn of the 1970s was served by an Ursuline community that was reduced in numbers but possessed of admirable academic credentials. Their style combined dignity with liberality, their supple disciplinary policy showed less signs of wear than at many similar campuses. The administration had been encouraging to a fault toward faculty and students. Any crimp on academic freedom by then lived in the barely remembered lore of the past. Any talk of theological absolutism or Vatican hegemony was something they were reading about in history books. This was no "priest-ridden, unthinking mob." Of all generations at New Rochelle this one had seen Catholic and catholic, academic rigor and social responsibility, liberal studies and professional apprenticeship, piety and worldliness more wholesomely merged than any other generation. The tone of those who would lay aside the college's religious identity, instead of liberating it from the naïveté which women's colleges were known by outsiders to suffer (and Catholic women's colleges were thought to suffer it more than others), only gave voice to the one serious naïveté that did afflict CNR. They were naive about the American academy itself, and imagined Dartmouth without dogma and Mount Holyoke as multicultural.

Edward O'Keefe has said that the Bundy money was not a cause of major change, but "a powerful catalyst in the change process enticing Catholic colleges and universities to move faster in the direction of secularization than they would have otherwise." The money provoked the schools to become officially secularized, he writes, but the outcome is that they are, in fact, nonsectarian, no longer projects vitally enlivened by the heart of the church.[255] It is surely true that the prospect of losing the Bundy money brought the college to full alert. But the larger force which drew nuns, faculty, trustees, students, and alumnae into the great mental reservation which would eventually set them adrift from CNR's Catholic past was a strange and untimely persuasion that the mind's work on their campus would thereby become more honest. The evasions that facilitated and justified the creed-change operation suggest the contrary.

Sister Dorothy Ann has always protested that "the mission of the College has changed very little." But its mission is then reductively described: "Devoted to its Catholic heritage, this College remains deeply concerned with the notion of continuing to provide access to all those who are equal to the challenges of higher education."[256] This is surely the case, as regards access. But that the access is to a Catholic education is not surely the case.

On one occasion the president reported: "The College of New Rochelle is striving for a goal which is not common in higher education today: a combination of academic excellence, religious commitment and extended access."[257] Even more boldly:

> For the College of New Rochelle as an institution, the challenge is how to be faithful to our mission; to our religious heritage; to the nurturing of religion in an ecumenical way; to educating fully in an atmosphere of respect for each person and each person's desire to be all that she and he can be.[258]

In an earlier day "religious commitment" meant that the campus community drew its corporate life from the Catholic Church, and that senior scholars were at pains to induct junior members into that intellectual perspective in a way that would make them appreciative yet critical. But now there is no more possibility of anything so explicit. Religion without a church is as vacant a notion as a culture without a community. Even the Smith College formula from yesteryear would now be too confessional for usage at New Rochelle: "While the fundamentally religious interest of the founder is stressed, the college is kept clear of entanglement with institutional Christianity, and the only prescription is the pervading of instruction by the spirit of the gospel of Jesus Christ." Replace that last phrase with an allusion to pervading human values, and it might work.

Academic discourse, as those continuously exposed to it can come to forget, requires a critical reading if one is to avoid serious misunderstanding. At New Rochelle, for instance, when the mission statement of 1971 and 1981 was circulated for comment before a recent reaccreditation visit, a number of faculty expressed their uneasiness with its reference to "the highest standards of excellence and educational growth." Objected one faculty member: "I feel that academic standards are considerably lower than they were when I was a student here." A nun wrote: "We have lowered our standards of excellence to survive." The text was nevertheless retained.

As the enterprise has changed significantly, even drastically, a craving for continuity requires that the most obvious departures from the past be described in terms of familiarity and continuity. One senior Ursuline described New Rochelle's "unchanging values cast in a contemporary frame adjusting to the ever-recurring new needs of the educable society." On the contrary, the evidence suggests that the demography of its student populations may have changed less than its values.[259]

This transformation is evoked and embodied by a recent display in the CNR Gill Library, dedicated to Mother Irene Gill, the foundress. An endowed purchase fund dedicated to ecology and feminism had enabled the college to acquire new books on those subjects — or subject, since the lengthy written rationale for the display explained that the two issues really merge into ecofeminism. Prominent in the display were books by Peter Singer, an ethicist interested in animal rights and liberation who argues eloquently that parents are morally more free to destroy their unwelcome unborn and newborn children than to kill their household pets. The recognizably Catholic authors in the collection seemed to have written on the goddess, and there was also a husky representation of lesbian motifs in the display. The exhibit was inculturated: it might have fit congenially into library showcases at Smith, Wellesley, or Radcliffe. But only at New Rochelle could the alumna memorialized by the purchase fund have been described thus:

> In 1951, Liz founded the Paraclete Book Center, which has been an oasis through the years for scholars, liturgists, theologians et al. She herself was a scholar, teacher and lover of learning. In the resources Liz made available at the Center, she played a prophetic role in the Church and in individual lives.

It is difficult to imagine any of these books on sale at a Paraclete Book Center. It was obviously important for patrons to imagine that that good woman's "inspirational work" had somehow begotten this bestiary. But such fiction of spiritual continuity allows CNR to carry on.

SAINT MARY'S COLLEGE OF CALIFORNIA

The Brothers of the Christian Schools, known as the Christian Brothers, have long been the largest group of Catholic men vowed exclusively to a ministry of education. In this country, besides dozens of secondary schools, they currently sponsor seven universities and colleges:

1853	Manhattan College	Riverdale, N.Y.
1859	College of Santa Fe	Santa Fe, N.Mex.
1863	La Salle University	Philadelphia, Pa.
1863	Saint Mary's College of California	Moraga, Calif.
1871	Christian Brothers University	Memphis, Tenn.
1912	Saint Mary's University of Minnesota	Winona, Minn.
1930	Lewis University	Lockport, Ill.[260]

Christian Brothers, Teachers of the Poor

A century after the Jesuits were founded in France and the Ursulines in Italy, the province of Champagne in France gave birth to the Frères des Écoles Chrétiennes (FSC), the Brothers of the Christian Schools.[261] Jean-Baptiste de La Salle was born to an affluent father and a noble mother in Reims in 1651, and in the very unreformed French church he was set on his way to what he might then have considered an enviable ecclesiastical career. He was formally tonsured into clerical status at the age of ten, appointed a canon (a well-salaried member of the governing body of the cathedral) when he was fifteen, awarded his M.A. at eighteen, ordained priest at twenty-six, and awarded his doctorate in theology at twenty-nine. At the age of twenty-eight he initiated a sharp swerve from that comfortable sinecure by offering the hospitality of his large home to a group of poor young schoolteachers. Four years later he resigned all of his emoluments and threw in his lot with these indigent men, whom he had led to think of themselves as dedicated servants of the poor. Knowing that most lay initiatives for men in the church, e.g., the monastic and mendicant movements, had eventually become clericalized and thereby compromised in their zeal, he insisted that the brotherhood wear a stylized, rough country smock as their habit, to assert their puzzling claim to be a dedicated brotherhood of vowed laymen, neither clerical nor secular.

During the nearly four decades in which he would lead his brothers, La Salle formulated communal policies that were innovative, and contentious. Most of France's parochial schools then were staffed by a solitary teacher. The brothers refused to isolate one another by accepting solo appointments, and directed their ministry to an urban clientele so as to live together and find work nearby, thereby serving a more desperate sort of poverty than was found in the agricultural country-side. They bound themselves by vow to educate the children of the poor and of semiskilled artisans, and never to charge them for tuition. Thus any parish which invited them had to accept full financial responsibility for the school. The learning environment created by the brothers was both disciplined and amiable, and despite themselves they began to attract the children of the bourgeois away from the established church schools, which were supported by fee-paying pupils and therefore resented the loss of income. The brothers insisted on treating these pupils of mixed class and manners as an integrated clientele, extraordinary in France at the time. La Salle was determined to offer bright youngsters the manners and training needed for good employment, and when his schools included instruction in mathematics and writing — over which the Guild of Writing Masters enjoyed a royal monopoly for their training of future civil servants — the brothers aroused the Guild's violent opposition. It was common practice for the better schools to place Latin in the center of their curriculum, but La Salle's determination to keep his brothers at a distance from anything that might draw them into the sphere of influence of the clergy stiffened his refusal to allow Latin texts to be taught or even shelved in his schools.

The Christian Brothers resisted conformity to any establishment. Their educational innovations repeatedly haled them into the civil courts, and their austere aloofness from the financial blandishments of clerical status put them so far ahead of canon law that for centuries they could not be fitted into any known category of religious order, so they were called an Institute: a category of their own. Nevertheless — or perhaps therefore — they would become the largest single religious community in the Catholic Church devoted exclusively to education. They numbered 100 in 1719 when Jean-Baptiste died, and would increase to nearly 17,000 working in eighty countries by the middle 1960s. In their native France they traditionally offered elementary education, and in their vocational training of the poor they excelled at vernacular, rather than classical, studies.

A Success in America, but Not for the Poor

In America they would undergo a revolution that reversed many of La Salle's foundational policies. The Christian Brothers' first foundation in the United States (1845) was Calvert Hall in Baltimore. We shall observe them at work, however, not on the eastern seaboard, but in California.[262]

Joseph Sadoc Alemany, O.P., had served for ten years as a Spanish missioner in Ohio, Kentucky, and Tennessee when he was chosen to preside over the church in California in 1850, the year it joined the Union. As bishop of Monterey, soon archbishop of San Francisco, he disposed of only twenty-two priests to serve 260,000 square miles, so he set about recruiting and training a native clergy. The Jesuits soon established colleges in Santa Clara (1851) and San Francisco (1855), but Alemany the Dominican never entrusted this task to them.[263] Several intrepid priests of his diocese trekked across the hill country, through rough settlements like Yankee Jim's, Rabbit Creek, and Poker Flat, and collected a remarkable amount of gold from the Irish miners there, and in 1863 opened Saint Mary's College (SMC) in the Mission District south of San Francisco. The priests had less success as educators, however. Alemany made repeated efforts to attract the Christian Brothers to California, but he was only one among their many suppliants. Eventually he went to Rome and persuaded Pius IX to use some papal leverage on his behalf. Thus in 1868 he welcomed the first contingent of nine from Baltimore, led by Brother Justin McMahon, late president of Calvert College. The brothers arrived to take over Saint Mary's, whose enrollment they saw grow quickly from 35 to 250, served by a faculty that swelled from two to twenty-four. Justin was adept at dealing with the legislature and with San Francisco society, and with the help of the latter he obtained from the former a charter in 1872. Saint Mary's soon boasted the largest enrollment in the state, outstripping even the University of California in Berkeley.[264]

Justin raised more than $100,000 to open a high school in Oakland (which quickly enrolled 700 pupils), and Brother Bettelin McMahon, his successor as president (and his half brother), later founded a string of feeder schools in Oakland, San Francisco, Santa Cruz, San Rafael, Sacramento, Portland, Vancouver, and Walla Walla. Unfortunately the archdiocese had incurred a staggering mortgage in building Saint Mary's College. The brothers were not able to accumulate a working surplus large enough to retire or even reduce the mortgage. Eventually in 1889 the college left the archdiocesan property and built its own "brickpile" in Oakland, helped by the contributions of the poor and the austerities of the brothers.

Their establishment in the United States had drawn the brothers into secondary schooling, and now they were moving into college work. Though their California constituency was heavily Irish and working-class, the college's nondegree, "commercial" course was not its primary program. SMC offered both a classical and a scientific curriculum, partly so as to educate future priests, and partly because Greek and Latin were seen as essential disciplines for the best education and were often a requisite for a college charter. The brothers were still honoring the founder's original determination to serve the poor, but the formula worked out in France seemed maladapted to California. The poor in this country more easily aspired to education and to professional careers, where the economy enabled some of them to pay the necessary fees, and they would not think of enrolling in a school or college publicly designated "for the poor." So students of diverse economic circumstance needed access to the full range of their programs. The brothers encouraged those with the talent and interest to enroll in their classical program. And they taught them Latin. To do this they sidestepped La Salle's old prohibition against ever teaching the classical languages. Brother Justin had consulted his confessor before ignoring both the letter and the spirit of this rule. In the East the brothers did conduct vocational and correctional schools, but their college and preparatory schools in California were drawn in this very different direction.

The brothers had shed their clodhoppers and had stylized the rustic smock reminiscent of France, where they had been known as *les frères ignorantins.* But the brothers in California, who often had to begin their teaching careers without high school diplomas and served in the college as self-taught scholars, were making bricks without straw. After the turn of the century only three or four of the twenty brothers at SMC held degrees, most likely earned before they entered the Institute. By then the college had contributed twenty-six priests to the local church (the high school in Oakland claimed forty priests), but had provided the Institute with only six brothers. The brothers themselves were living lives of exemplary poverty, yet their mission was no longer one of service simply to the poor. They had ambition for their schools, and for the education they were able to offer. The energetic and largely Irish constituency in a Catholic-hostile California seemed to be a community worthy of their labors. And as those Irish also became ambitious for their children, and able to finance the ambition, the FSC schools were happy to become bourgeois.

Saint Mary's College offered formidable competition to the colleges in Santa Clara and San Francisco, and various Jesuits periodically and vindictively reported SMC's deviant liberal arts curriculum to the *régime,* as the brothers' world headquarters was called.[265] Finally, their General Chapter of 1894 reaffirmed the explicit prohibition against the teaching of Latin. The American bishops, who needed Latin in their high schools both for academic credibility and for the preparation of clerical candidates, sent urgent requests for reconsideration, but the Institute did not budge. Bishop Byrne of Nashville was sent by the bishops to argue their case directly in Rome. To support their plea he conducted a survey of the American brothers and found that about eight hundred out of one thousand wanted the classics taught in their academies and colleges. This finding provoked, rather than persuaded, the (mostly) French authorities. To them it appeared that the Americans were catering primarily to the bourgeoisie and, by gaining proficiency in Latin, a particular prerequisite for the clergy, they were compromising their chosen status as laymen. Thirteen American brothers whom they perceived to be covertly allied with the grieving bishops were purged for thus having appealed to Rome over the heads of the *régime*. Justin and Bettelin were prime targets. Both were summarily relieved of high responsibilities and sent into exile: one to an orphanage, the other to a boarding school in southern France. The others were strewn as far as Algeria.

The "Latin Question" had enflamed a complex of stresses within the Institute: French versus Irish, British, and Americans; simplicity versus sophistication; conservatism versus liberalism; religious loyalty versus professionalism. The *régime*'s tenacity drew on the Institute's historic determination to assert its dignity and independence as an organization of laymen in the church; if that was infused with a certain anticlericalism, no one should have been surprised. The first brothers had lived in a stratified French society and joined the poor in their poverty and, perhaps, in some of their resentment. That classist attitude lived on at the Institute's headquarters, and the men there thought of it as one of the strong elements of unity in their brotherhood. Their American confreres now seemed to them to be dividing into two castes. The brothers who favored liberal education were too much at their ease with affluent benefactors, powerful legislators, and secular academics, and appeared to the French to consider themselves more refined than the brothers doing the traditional work in vocational and correctional schools. What the brothers in France saw as a class divide, the American brothers saw as an open border. A liberal education was an obvious portal through that frontier into opportunity, and the brothers thought it no compromise if they could draw student after student across it, into self-betterment.

The trauma within the Institute over the Latin Question cast the California District into decades of passive-aggressive stagnation. Latin and Greek continued to be offered at the college, though they were taught after hours, across the street, and by a layman (and sometimes on the sly by a brother). Ironically, the ban was imposed at the very time that Charles Eliot was leading American higher education away from the classical tradition, and Saint Mary's was unintentionally timely in diversifying its curriculum. Bernard Kelly, one of the exiled brothers, returned to SMC to run a new School of Applied Science, including metallurgy, hydraulics, assaying, and mining. Art and industrial arts were added before the Great War, and in the 1920s a School of Foreign Trade and a School of Education were opened. SMC had become a campus of vocationalism, albeit a sophisticated vocationalism.

The brothers themselves had been the mainstay of the faculty, though these newer applied disciplines lay beyond their usual competence and required techni-cally skilled lay colleagues. But even the humanities and basic sciences required more academic preparation on their part. Beginning in 1917 one brother per year was freed of his duties and sent off for graduate study, to the Catholic University of America, Columbia, Notre Dame, or Berkeley. By 1926 the district was able for the first time to send off two younger student brothers to begin undergraduate studies even before their first teaching assignments. But through the 1930s the need for teachers would cause the younger men to be given assignments soon after beginning their college studies, which then had to be completed by years of night classes and summer schools. And by this time laymen had become more numerous than the brothers on the college faculty.[266]

The one subject which any brother, however educated, was deemed capable of teaching was religion. There had been a low-intensity resistance to theology in the Institute, out of wariness of any studies that might cause a draw toward the priesthood. Therefore virtually all theological study was done out of multivolumed catechisms. Not until 1960 would the first Christian Brothers study theology aca-demically, and most of those later departed from the Institute, possibly confirming the earlier misgivings.

Three successive archbishops of San Francisco continued appeals to the brothers' superior general, to the Roman Curia, and to three popes, but the ban against Latin remained obstinately in place until 1923, when the General Chapter convened in Rome and received the unwelcome surprise of a directive from Pius XI that they should teach the classical languages as something needed by the local churches. The pope then consummated their surprise by adding a further injunction. They should continue to direct their educational initiatives "especially to poor children," but also "even in behalf of the well-to-do classes."[267] This papal deci-sion, which on the face of it granted the American brothers what they had long requested, only reinforced the ambiguity of their situation with regard to their founding purpose. The directive's importance as the final resolution of the Latin Question obscures its larger significance as a confirmation of what to Saint John (Jean-Baptiste de La Salle had been canonized in 1900) would have been a far more significant departure from the Institute's foundational charism, the education of the poor.

But events moved underfoot. During the early 1900s the Institute experi-enced a reduction in their recruitment. Meanwhile some of the most gifted and professionally prominent brothers resigned from the Institute. American parish priests found that the women's religious orders could provide more plentiful, economical, and compliant teachers than could the Christian Brothers or other religious communities of laymen, and the brothers were now withdrawing from virtually all elementary schools. The 1920s and 1930s were a bad season for their morale. To make matters worse, a cleavage based on age and opportunity began to appear. As the younger men aspired to standard academic credentials, the older brothers grumbled that they imagined themselves better than their elders who had born the heat of the day.

The depression years struck the college even more painfully. The "old brick-pile" in Oakland proved inadequate to expanding needs, and after a devastating fire SMC built an entirely new, mission-style campus over the crest of the hills behind Oakland and Berkeley, on a large tract beside the newly developing town of Moraga. The move was financed by bonds backed by virtually all the real estate the Institute owned in the region, and a default in the service on that debt led to bankruptcy. The campus was sold at auction in 1937, but the archdiocese quietly bought it and allowed the brothers to liquidate that debt eventually out of new revenues from their winery, by then the largest in Napa Valley.[268]

Saint Mary's bravely and gratefully celebrated its diamond jubilee in 1938. Brother Matthew McDevitt, college historian, posts these reminiscences in his account of it:

> Practically every speaker expressed or implied that religion was preeminent in the life of the faculty and students. Catholicism was not merely taught every day, it was taught every hour in every day. There was a religious atmosphere in dormitory, library, laboratory, playing field as well as in classroom; prayer began and ended every exercise, rising, retiring, studying, playing and eating. Although there was frequent recourse to prayer, students unanimously testified that there were few or no religious freaks, reformers or prophets. The campus was singularly free of saintly fanatics. Worship of God was accepted as naturally as eating, drinking or walking. It was accepted as a matter of course that the supernatural life of man had to be sustained by prayer as his natural life was supported by food and drink.[269]

The college was Catholic then because most of its faculty and students were Catholics, and because the Christian Brothers directed it. Neither the curriculum nor the Religion Department had yet done much to make the religious dimension of SMC more inquiring or sophisticated.

Struggle between the Liberal Arts and Vocational Studies

But the educational tone of the campus would soon change. Most American colleges and universities were rejuvenated by World War II through the postwar influx of veterans subsidized by the GI Bill, and profitable military training programs. In the case of SMC the first gesture toward renewal occurred improbably in 1941. With the ebullient patronage of a new president, Brother Austin Crowley, the "Great Books" method devised by Mortimer Adler and Robert Maynard Hutchins at the

University of Chicago and canonized at Saint John's College in Maryland was transplanted to Moraga by the creation of the Collegiate Seminar, years before various other campuses did the same. Then in 1943, when most of the students and many of the faculty — especially the laymen in technical subjects — were off to war, leaving a regular student enrollment of perhaps one hundred, the Schools of Arts and Letters, Science, and Economics were all conflated into a School of Liberal Disciplines. Every student (except those in the Navy programs) studied the Great Books (in translation), and the seminar format replaced class lectures until the end of the war. By offering a purely liberal education, the college had veered as far as possible from La Salle's mission to offer vocational training. Yet it was the Collegiate Seminar which first blended a religious idiom into the common forum of intellectual discourse at SMC. In the mid-1950s a four-year major centered on the seminars reemerged (now known as the Integral Program). At this same time the younger brothers began to be sent off to earn terminal degrees as part of the regular cycle of their training. As of yet, nearly half of the older brothers in the district did not hold even the baccalaureate. For the first time in its history the college had a president, Crowley, with an earned doctorate.

The 1950s were for Saint Mary's a time of "trickling increment." The location of the campus in the foothills east of San Francisco Bay put it beyond public transportation, and thus the college was dependent upon boarding students. The GI Bill brought veterans in good number, but after that the enrollment stabilized and was slow to increase. Annual subsidies from Mont La Salle Vineyards (later marketed under the Christian Brothers label) were essential to survival.

The decade of the sixties would be a long season of difficulty and decline at Saint Mary's: a decline in curricular definition, faculty continuity, the leadership of the Christian Brothers, confidence in the Catholic character of the college, student satisfaction and behavior, enrollment, and financial viability. Choices were made which at the time seemed critical to the survival of Saint Mary's. Their eventual outcomes, however, have made it difficult for Saint Mary's to remain intact.

Since World War II the curricular offerings at Moraga had been a mixture of the liberal and vocational, both sectors of which had their practitioners and advocates. The core curriculum with wide distribution requirements in the liberal disciplines was still privileged, and the college advertised itself as liberal. In a national educational environment that was then becoming more vocational, Saint Mary's tried to market its principal offerings, the humanities and basic sciences, for their ultimate vocational value. Thus the 1962-64 *Catalogue* would say:

> More than ever before, the liberally educated man is needed in the world today. He is needed in the professions, in government, in foreign service, in science and technology, in business and industry. He is needed for his clear mind, his powers of reasoning, his ability to communicate. He is needed for his perspective, his breadth of vision, and his creativeness.[270]

The 1964-66 *Catalogue* seemed to reflect an even more purist stance:

> While the College believes that its programs provide an excellent foundation for careers in the professions, in public service and in business, it does not direct its primary efforts toward the development of technical proficiency. Rather it seeks to bring its students into full, active possession of their intellectual, cultural and human heritage.[271]

Whatever the theory, the delivery of this intellectual heritage was meeting with increasing student discontent. It focused particularly on philosophy, which was loyal to the modern revival of the thought of Thomas Aquinas, and on theology, which was taught at an academic level beneath that of other departments. By the time the students began to grumble out loud about these deficiencies, as students on every campus were doing in 1968, their criticisms were largely directed at these two departments, but their larger agenda was the abolition of all required subjects or courses. A faculty anxious to show their openness to student advocacy responded with singular ardor. For example: a student representative testified to the Academic Council that he found the doctrinaire and "distinctively Catholic approach" in the Department of Philosophy "hard to take." His first preference was to replace it with "involvement in concrete realities, such as the poverty program, civil rights, peace movement, etc." Failing that, he might settle for a three-credit reduction. The request was grounded on what he assured the faculty was the students' "primary interest and concern" to be liberally educated. The college's philosophy requirement for all liberal arts students was then seventeen credits: thought to be the largest in the country. The Academic Council unanimously forwarded this proposal to a faculty referendum for approval, emphatically attesting that the "healthy and desirable" student grievance had "substantial merit" and had been presented "in a cogent, persuasive manner." The course reduction would be "salutary" for the philosophy faculty (then perhaps the most qualified in the college).[272]

The failings of the curriculum were ascribed to unhealthy aspects of its Catholic tradition. As the campus chaplain described it, the local notion of "Catholic" was unhappily authoritarian:

> If by "Catholic" college we mean one which receives its heritage of education from universal sources of human wisdom and culture and seeks likewise to be of universal service, [fine. But around the campus] it seems to mean a very closed, selective, rigidly disciplined type of training that is based upon a monolithic philosophy and theology and having a blindly obedient monolithic religious practice to match. . . . My main concern? Freeing people wherever possible so that they can make more and more choices that are truly their own. Only choices that are a person's own have any value; and only such actions as are free are of maturing and educating quality. I think that as a priest I have opportunities both within the traditional ministry and outside of it to free college students from their

own emotional hang-ups, and sometimes from external academic impositions so that they grow by experiencing their own extending of self.[273]

This was very 1968. The campus newspaper complained that Catholicity at Saint Mary's meant forcing students to take courses "in which there is no real academic incentive or excitement. We are reminded by the college that theology is central to all of man's intellectual endeavors; yet theology is presented by the College in little unbearable packages, totally isolated from the other fields of study."[274]

The year 1968-69 saw a series of faculty meetings wherein the members deliberated in the presence of an intimidating throng of students. The liberally educated among the faculty may have sensed faint overtones of Paris in 1794 and Moscow in 1937. A proposal to abolish all grades does not seem to have rallied much support, but the abolition of all curricular requirements was argued at great length. The minutes record various arguments in favor:

> that a Christian spirit of freedom and personalism, and the need for maturity and self-direction, necessitates that requirements be abolished — other than a require-ment that students seek (though not necessarily follow) a faculty member's advice; that a Christian college should build true Christianity by encouraging freedom rather than constraint; . . . that to make study a joy and to counter the alienating regimentation of modern life, the students should experience freedom in college; that counter-arguments appealing to the wisdom of the faculty are weakened by the apparent failure of this wisdom in our society . . .[275]

The final decision was to retain only one obligatory course in the curriculum: anything taught by the Government Department to satisfy the civics requirement of the State of California. No philosophy was thenceforth required, and the only provision for theology was that two of the eight required Collegiate Seminars (to be chosen by the students from a large and variegated list) would have to deal with theological Great Books and be led by members of the Theology Department.

According to Dean Rafael Pollock, the decisive argument for sweeping away the college curriculum was that the existing structure had no demonstrable or easily arguable relationship to the ends of liberal education: "It is not evident how coverage of material in language, mathematics, philosophy, theology, history and so forth will tend to foster such liberal goals as a mature, inquiring mind, intellectual discipline, commitment to wisdom and to truth, enlightened understanding of the Christian heritage."[276]

1968: Is the College Catholic?

It was a student journalist who redirected some of the campus concern away from curriculum to the faculty when he interviewed the dean. He was unsettled by Pollock's claim that a "truly Catholic college" ought purposely to hire non-Christians on the ground that it was sufficient they be qualified teachers. The reason given for Pollock's policy was that the spiritual lives of academics were distinct from their intellectual lives. The dean doubted his own ability to verify who was Christian, though he said he could identify a number of faculty members who were "un-Christian."[277]

Frank Ellis, chairman of the much-maligned Department of Philosophy, joined the debate. Since 95 percent of the student body were Catholics, said Ellis, they had not chosen SMC by coincidence, but obviously because they thought it was a Catholic college. The Catholicity, he inferred, had to permeate the shared, public enterprise of the college, and not be something private and devotional off to the side. The Christian Brothers could not assure it by their numbers, for now they were too few. Nor by their ownership, which was only legal, and remote from the educational process. Only the faculty could make Saint Mary's Catholic, by the solidarity of their intellectual lives and their spiritual lives, by reason and faith coalescing into a single wisdom that fosters both understanding and salvation.

Ellis recounted his own surprise when he had discovered from a retired professor at the University of Southern California that USC was, "in some sense of the word, a Methodist University." Over the years it had obviously lost its religious character, whose last relicts were a chaplain on campus, some courses in religion, and one Methodist clergyman on the board.

> What in all of this I found disturbing was that, so the professor told me, the secularization of the school over the years was something that just happened rather than something that was foreseen and chosen. I would not like to see Saint Mary's go that route. But insofar as we ourselves are unclear about our identity as a Catholic college, what is there to prevent it?[278]

One response to Ellis came from a Marxist colleague in the Department of Classics who denounced any regressive aspirations by the faculty to mold their students according to their own thoughts (he was evidently not an orthodox Marxist). He encouraged the appointment of (other) atheists to the faculty, whose scrutiny of Catholic life would be most likely to unmask its authoritarianism, illusions, and ideology.[279]

Dean Pollock returned to testify how impossible it was for him as an administrator to appraise the religious integrity of anyone, since church membership was no gauge of how a colleague would behave. The transformation of USC (whose student body had now become predominantly Catholic) was a harbinger of the inevitable for places like SMC, because the chief historical reason for Christian groups to want colleges of their own was their now defunct sense "of being beleaguered by an alien and, often, hostile, culture." Saint Mary's, he advised, must now retain its identity by finding "a valid new meaning for the idea of a Catholic college." Most formerly Christian colleges had severed their original connection because an increased sophistication put them at odds, not with the public culture, but with their rigidly sectarian sponsoring church. That would not be the case with Catholics. They were being led by the church itself to a more liberal self-understanding. But the church needed to be redefined as including all people of goodwill, not just formal Catholics, and in serving this larger community the college would embody a larger consciousness and purpose.[280] There was clearly no agreement possible between Pollock and Ellis, and those who joined in their polar views.

This debate about whether Saint Mary's needed a Catholic faculty in order to be a Catholic college was moved to a higher level of intensity when Professor Ronald McArthur publicly accused the college of offering an education that was neither liberal nor Catholic. Like most of its peer schools, SMC claimed to offer all that secular education had, and something more, by requiring courses in philosophy and theology. But to remain respectably within the canons of the American academy (which most Catholic educators saw as essential if they were to stay in business), the college had forfeited any confidence in the ability of a shared faith to organize and unify higher education. There was no trust in an interrelationship of truths whereby some were tributaries of others, so the curriculum remained a disjointed set of treatises instead of a collegial inquiry into a coherent wisdom. Without any philosophical trust in demonstrable truth beyond what is empirically measurable, the Catholics at Saint Mary's had become as unable as their secularized academic colleagues to engage in disciplined scholarship that might agree reliably upon master truths. Worse, they had been duped by the dogma of academic freedom (the modern academy's only admitted dogma) and had subverted their professional peer assessments by excluding all reference to ulterior truth or error.

According to McArthur's indictment, academics had immobilized their natural capacity to discriminate truth from error and right from wrong once they accepted the modern axiom that the deepest insights were a matter of private preference, not corporate discernment. Those responsible for ostensibly Catholic colleges and universities had become embarrassed to confess reliance upon a divinely imparted revelation developed within a graced church. Inevitably they had lost the conviction that their collegial intellectual effort would obviously require membership in the Catholic Church: the fellowship that was the beneficiary of this privileged and emergent understanding.[281]

Educators, he argued, had largely abandoned the traditional understanding of learning begun in the array of intellectual arts and fruiting in wisdom, which trusts itself to learn from experiential discovery, the discipline of a master, and the revelation of God within the church.

They give the contrary impression that all serious thinking about the important things has been abandoned for a series of specialties whose principles and con-

clusions are beyond questioning; the illusion is given that certain questions are
nobody's concern, and that the only task left us is to multiply the fruits of science
and change our lives.

A closer look shows that the university is in some sense alienated from the
mainstream of ordinary experience, and that its different departments are composed not so much of thinkers as of technicians who are unable, except with
small talk, even to speak with those who are teaching other disciplines, while
their members are nevertheless proclaiming universal truths about democracy, or
civil rights, or world peace.[282]

This was quite a thrashing for Saint Mary's, from within its own faculty. As
Vice President Raymond White puts it, "The College was unwilling (and probably
unable) to elevate theological study to the position of pre-eminence demanded by
Dr. McArthur."[283] Indeed, the Department of Theology was just then in the process
of becoming the Department of Religious Studies, and the Western Association
reaccreditation team traced this with satisfaction to "some ambiguity over mission." They were responding "to pressures for change by shifting their emphasis
from sectarian theology to a more ecumenical evaluation of religion in general and
Christianity in particular."[284]

Even in the most secure of times a conflict this fundamental might have tried
a small college's endurance to the breaking point. But Saint Mary's College was
approaching desperation, and at that moment lacked both the intellectual assurance
and the institutional stability to be engaged by this challenge. McArthur was joined
by several other dissidents, including several of the brothers, and they soon set
about founding Thomas Aquinas College in Santa Paula, California. It opened in
1971.

The Brothers Begin to Wane

The Christian Brothers were fading as the guardians of the college's identity. It
had long been the brothers' services offered gratis that kept the college in existence.
There was an abiding but private sentiment among some brothers that their lay
colleagues did not share their dedication or their educational vision. One of them
put it this way in an unpublished history of SMC back in 1915:

> It bodes ill for an institution like Saint Mary's to have to revert to the necessity
> of hiring men for its work. The evil will never be eliminated in its entirety, but
> the conditions [*sic*] effect on a student body and on the mind of the institution
> is such as to warrant the number of secular professors be kept at a minimum.[285]

Indeed, as late as 1946 the General Chapter of the Christian Brothers had spoken
of lay colleagues as a "necessary evil."[286]

681

Lay faculty had originally been hired to teach the applied, vocational, and professional subjects, but then they had taken their place also among the liberal disciplines. When one considers that lay teachers had been strongly in the majority since the late 1920s, and that the dean of the college was a layman, their role could hardly be described as merely to "assist the brothers." Though the official literature would go on describing the brothers as responsible for the character of the college, by the early 1960s the lay presence was acquiring an obvious influence, not only through the passive bulk of numbers but through the active force of leadership and initiative.

This was fortunate for the college, because the membership of the Christian Brothers, then swelling to nearly 17,000 in 1965, would abruptly begin to diminish, through the resignation of nearly one-third that number within a decade, and a drastic reduction in recruitment.[287] Manpower projections promised that professionally qualified brothers would now become scarce at Moraga. And even the few who would emerge as potential faculty would now have to compete with an abundance of newly minted Ph.D.s eager for employment. The records of the college display several of the senior brothers as very influential in the late sixties, but they would not be replaced. The younger brothers, whose drive for professional respect was also unavoidably influenced by the American academic doctrine that faith is to scholarship what snake handling is to medicine, would become increasingly reluctant to act as if the Catholic character of the college were any of their special concern. At the beginning of the 1960s the rebate from their salaries had amounted to a considerable 17 percent of the annual budget, but by 1969 it was only half of that.

This cultural shift was being carried on before the eyes of a student body whose profile was male, Caucasian, Catholic, B average, and upper-middle class.[288] The fact that very few of them said they had chosen SMC because it was a Catholic college may suggest that coincidence did actually play a large part in the matriculation process at Moraga. But another, newer fact — that for whatever reason fewer and fewer students were coming each year — was engendering a crisis whose pragmatic urgencies would outshout this gentle, academic tête-à-tête.

The California systems of state universities and colleges were aggressively marketing a high-cost (to the taxpayer) but low-price (to the student) education that was rivaling Nelson Rockefeller's New York systems. Economic disincentives at Saint Mary's put enrollments into a long decline in the 1960s. The traditional liberal arts emphasis in the college was of little or no interest to the new population then beginning to flood campuses elsewhere. Much of the educational growth in the 1960s was in career-related programs, whose clientele tended to be urban. Saint Mary's enjoyed a lovely rural campus, but its remote location put it beyond the reach of most commuter students from the cities around the Bay.

Also, single-sex campuses had become unappealing. Most Catholic schools were finally changing over to coeducation. Applicants who enrolled at Moraga knew they were going to a campus that was without any women in residence, or even accessible nearby for evening or weekend socializing. Not only did fewer enroll, but retention became such a problem that some classes would lose nearly two-thirds of their membership between freshman and senior years. Student behavior on campus had become noticeably more loutish as the 1960s unraveled. The college met this challenge by decreeing that its accountability for student conduct was limited to matters academic.

The Ordeal of the Early Seventies

Saint Mary's had dedicated itself to a clientele that was fairly narrow in its definition: Catholic, middle-class and upward, male, willing and able to board in the country. The manifold discontinuities of the 1960s inevitably ate into the heart of the college finances, and from 1963 onward each year ended in deficit. This appeared ominous enough in 1969 for the Christian Brothers' District to reaffirm its support by a grant of perhaps $600,000 and an interest-free loan of possibly $1 million.[289] The mood in the district was ready for a decisive change in the captaincy of its flagship campus, and one of SMC's experienced trustees, Brother Mel Anderson, was chosen. It was a bold choice. He was a high school principal who held no degree higher than the baccalaureate. But his term of service would be the longest and the most accomplished since Brother Justin's time.

Some indices of the college's well-being at the outset of the Anderson era were strongly encouraging. The vineyard moneys were used to refurbish residential facilities and classrooms. A federal grant was quickly secured for a college union. Fund-raising plans for a new science facility and other plant priorities were announced. The campus was modestly relandscaped. Ardent recruitment efforts brought more brothers on campus, increasing their presence to 30 percent of the faculty, the best ratio in years. Saint Mary's almost immediately decided to admit female students, with the hope of both improved enrollment and "more refined" campus manners. The enrollment increased by one-third after Brother Mel's first two years in office. It was expected that within four years the female students would constitute half of the student body. Despite the college's unrelieved string of fiscal years in deficit, much of the new tuition bounty was used to bring in new faculty, administrators, and students. Special preference for blacks and Chicanos, activated in the late 1960s, was intensified.

In the third year of Brother Mel's presidency, however, Saint Mary's College erupted into hostility and ugliness. Minority students were in the center of the turmoil.[290] During the 1960s the college had gradually lost control of student behavior, on and off campus. The surge in minority presence in the student body, along with widespread alcohol abuse and drug use, and the incendiary student insurrection ignited at nearby Berkeley, exacerbated tensions over student behavior here as everywhere, and the traditionally more composed lifestyle at Moraga was put under unusual strain. The president reacted quickly. The *Catalogue* was quickly purged of the disclaimer which, as he put it, "once implied the abdication of our responsibility for a student's non-academic life once he enrolled in the College."[291] The black dean of students was seemingly unprepared to be the intrepid activist Brother Mel wanted, and on the last day of 1971 he was sent a notice that his contract would not be renewed. The spring semester saw vehement campus protests against this decision. In the meantime, a new academic vice president foresaw that the enrollment, which was at an all-time high, would probably slump the next fall (as it would across the nation), and he began to issue nonrenewal notices to faculty members. One of them was a recent black appointee, an activist whom many considered a rabble-rouser. By now all the campus constituencies were aroused. A special faculty meeting was called, and when the student body decided to attend as well, they all ended up in the gymnasium for two days of declamation and commotion. The faculty adopted forceful resolutions against any economic measures that would reduce the faculty, minority presence on the faculty, or ethnic courses. Indeed, they demanded more minorities and women on the faculty and more financial aid for minorities. The only gesture made toward budgetary relief was a resolution to phase out intercollegiate sports. Days later the students joined in all the faculty demands save one: they wanted to keep varsity sports.

The basketball team, with strong black membership, joined in with a strike. Then a group of minority students settled down in the chapel for a fast and vigil. Brother Mel and other administrators sat down with them to work out some sort of agreement, and after a week in the divine presence the students emerged with some mild concessions. The trustees heard out delegations from the black and Chicano students and brought in a black consultant to appraise the SMC situation. A ten-day campus visit yielded a report that spoke of communication, credibility, racism, polarization, leadership, and other realities which some trustees took to be a resident vocabulary likely to have appeared in all studies done by their consultant.

Brother Mel later recalled the ordeal of the early 1970s:

> When I came into office in 1969, the College had approximately 900 male students, the country was in turmoil with the Vietnam War, the draft, the civil rights movement, the Free-Speech movement, spawned on neighboring Sproul Plaza, the love-ins and be-ins in Peoples' Park, the Kent State massacre and proclamations by the skeptics that God was dead. The faculty was deeply divided on many of these issues, and as a naïve, novice president appointed to captain this academic ship in a stormy sea of unusual disquietude there were a number of times when I felt that the wheel of the ship was disconnected from the rudder.[292]

By 1974 minority students constituted one-fifth of the student body, largely because the administration had been determined to achieve that ratio well before 1971-72. The president's view was that Saint Mary's turmoil arose, not from a lack of communication, but from a deep and well-expressed conflict. "There has been communication, and such communication both by word and deed has more clearly delineated the differences which cause the tension."[293]

In September of 1972 the enrollment shortfall was 20 percent, more than twice what had been forecast. Staff reduction was now even more likely and did ensue. For a small, unendowed college with a long-accumulated debt, kept open only by dint of annual subsidies from the Christian Brothers, there was no alternative. But a small group of faculty began to agitate for unionization, faculty governance, grievance procedures, and job protection.[294]

The expressed view of the dissidents was that the Christian Brothers lacked managerial talent. Anderson, however, saw neither finance nor governance to be the real issue. He exerted himself to convince the board that the contest was religious *Realpolitik,* a "life and death struggle for the College."

> A faculty group, in the minority but still strong, is intent, for various reasons, on wresting control of the College from the Christian Brothers. Present demands for an increased faculty role in governance have been chosen as an appropriate means of achieving that end. . . .
>
> The last decade has shown how quickly a Catholic College like SMC can acquire a considerable number of faculty members who view its Christian commitment with contempt.[295]

> There is a number of faculty personnel who were hired with a philosophy which could be termed antithetical to what was a traditional hallmark of a Saint Mary's Catholic education. Further, due to a rapid expansion, many who had no strong philosophy, but were not imbued with the Saint Mary's traditions also joined the faculty and were not initiated into the Saint Mary's educational program. . . . There are also those among the faculty who know better than to attack Catholicism, who adopt certain other slogans which sound quite acceptable on the surface but underlying what they say is a position which is quite secularistic and non-Christian.[296]

Brother Mel took the opposition very seriously indeed, and saw its underlying aims as a mortal danger. But it was not his style to admit or portray the terms of the struggle publicly. He seems to have been tempered to a new and stubborn strength during the course of these conflicts, but it was an inward strength, with considerable public reserve. He would eventually prevail on the issues as they lay on the table publicly. It is not so clear that he prevailed in what mattered most to him.

When he took office he dealt with the brothers in the District about their grumbling that Saint Mary's was no longer a Catholic college, no longer a Christian Brothers college. He ascribed their annoyance to the recent downgrading of philosophy and religious studies and defended those changes, arguing that Aristotle and Aquinas alone were an insufficient foundation for Catholic philosophy and theology, and that in any case the required courses had been taught so as to "deaden rather than inspire."[297]

Anderson's determination to renew the college took into account that 20 percent of the student body and "many" of the faculty were not Catholics. He defended the recent changes on campus:

> Those who feel that compulsory attendance at Mass meant vital Catholicism will be disappointed. Further, those who believe that required religion or theology courses taken each semester make for a Catholic college will also be disappointed. Likewise, those who measure Catholicism by a required curriculum in Scholastic philosophy or by the athletic teams going to communion on game days, or a compulsory annual retreat or nightly room checks will be dismayed. . . .
>
> The care exercised in presenting Catholicism as intelligent, vital, honest and free is the main function of the College as Catholic. The religious spirit on the campus emanates from several sources, and much depends on the quality of those sources. Such a spirit will inspire a free choice of Christian commitment within the Catholic fold, and will be a source of inspiration to others. Among the sources of spirit are: the visible religious spirit of the Brothers (and a significant number of Brothers as well), the spirit of the scholastic Brothers [students in training], the quality of the theology courses, the quality of the liturgy and retreats, the competence of the counseling program, the Christian attitude of many on the lay staff, and the commitment of the administration to justice and charity in fulfilling its overall mission, as well as its priorities in the area of an intellectually competent theology faculty and religious services.[298]

In 1972 Anderson's report to the brothers alluded in mildest terms to the bitter conflicts just passed:

> [A Catholic college] should be composed of scholarly men dedicated to seeking the truth, especially that revealed by God and preserved by the Church. This view does allow for opinions other than Catholic or different from traditional SMC liberal arts programs, and always on the level of serious academic pursuit. We cannot deny the existence of secular or even hostile views and the need to investigate them is clear. The important consideration, however, is that the atmosphere of the College be one of a community of scholars seeking the truth as illuminated by the Incarnation.[299]

In 1974 the brothers at SMC were surveyed on their views about the college, and they were much more forthright than Brother Mel (perhaps because their responses were anonymous) about its troubles. They deplored the lack of unity among the faculty, and even among themselves, noting a resulting tendency to equivocate about the Catholicity of the college and about its liberal arts orientation. Their most repeated concern was secularization, and their great worry was the religious disinterest being shown by their lay colleagues. One wrote: "Faculty needs conversion or replacement!"[300]

Meanwhile the college was enduring a boycott from its traditional clientele. Black student disruptions on campus, aired widely in the media, were blamed for an enrollment shortfall of one-third.[301] The lowest admissions yields in years continued to bring down the enrollment totals, and to necessitate still more faculty cutbacks. The accumulated deficit in the operating fund continued to deepen.

Professional Programs Balance the Budget

In 1974 Brother Dominic Ruegg, a classicist with a theological background, was installed as academic vice president. Throughout his four years in office the background discord of bad feelings between faculty and administration continued. Brother Dominic came to his task persuaded that while a sizable majority of the faculty and administration could not be persuaded to define Saint Mary's as anything but a liberal arts college, there were in fact not enough students interested in a liberal arts education on their campus to keep it open. He rapidly transformed the college before anyone noticed quite what he was doing. He revitalized programs in communications and English as a second language and restored accounting to the curriculum. SMC opened programs for nontraditional students, in conjunction with a national educator in the field. The Western Association of Schools and Colleges (WASC), the regional accrediting body very strongly under the influence of the University of California and California State College systems, compelled the college to withdraw from programs more than fifty miles from campus, in Arizona and southern California. But then, in conjunction with local business leaders, an executive M.B.A. program was opened nearby that enrolled eighty students on the first day. Extended Education, for adults seeking to complete bachelor's degrees in business administration and health administration in locations around the Bay Area from Sacramento to San Jose, quickly achieved high enrollment. An Oakland hospital joined in a shared nursing degree program; a Walnut Creek bank sponsored an International Institute of Banking and Finance, which lasted only a few years but left as its legacy a master's program in the School of Business. There was a bachelor's and master's Program in Health, Physical Education and Recreation. Graduate degree programs were added in Psychology, and Educational Administration and Supervision. There was a certificate program for paralegals. By adding more than half as many graduate and off-campus students as in the traditional program, these new ventures allowed new faculty to be hired and even yielded a cash surplus to the treasury.[302]

Little of this proliferation was the result of faculty initiative. Indeed, for ideas, design, and personnel the administration looked elsewhere. The chief administrators, on the *qui vive* because their traditional student body was seemingly vanishing, grew accustomed to making entrepreneurial decisions without much faculty consultation. A peevish faculty, in turn, became more difficult to consult since faculty meetings were attended by few, and they the more fractious and publicly uncooperative. It was an awful decade, marked by a loss of one-quarter of the faculty in 1974 alone. The faculty teaching load was raised to eight courses per year. There were several competing attempts to unionize the faculty, a censure by the AAUP over procedural violations in several personnel decisions, and a decision by WASC, first to monitor the campus at two-year intervals and then to lower the college's accreditation to probationary status ("there exists such a serious division of opinion among the trustees, administration, and faculty concerning institutional purposes and goals as to jeopardize the stability of the College and its capacity to maintain adequate controls over the quality of its programs").[303]

For Saint Mary's, 1979 would finally be a time of relief. The AAUP censure was lifted; a revised goals statement emerged with consensual reports from all constituencies; fifteen years of accumulated deficits were removed and the operating fund showed a slight surplus; faculty teaching loads were down and salaries were up; enrollment figures had surged; the new vocational programs were mostly thriving and the traditional undergraduate program had begun to reclaim its constituency; three new buildings had been built and six renovated; and an extensive survey of administrators and faculty showed that both constituencies agreed, more positively than on any other matter of common concern, that "However else it may change, Saint Mary's College must remain faithful to its Catholic tradition."[304] A visitation team from WASC that year sent back a highly complimentary report, and the college's accreditation was freed of the stigma of probation.

The prospect of closure had concentrated minds in Moraga wonderfully. The reactions of the administration were unilateral but constructive, while those of the faculty tended to be resentful and obstructive. Yet the restoration of fiscal health proved soothing to all, and the college began to go about its business as a community once more.

The 1980s were years of consolidation after the perilous 1970s. Brother Mel's twenty-fifth anniversary in the presidency in 1994 highlighted the new stability and, indeed, the heartening promise of the college. During his presidency the enrollment has quadrupled to four thousand: half are traditional students and half the new, nontraditional constituencies. The endowment has surged from $1.8 million to $28 million. The faculty has swelled from less than one hundred members to well more than twice that number. The fabric of the college now includes more than twice as many buildings, and the trustees are presently looking at construction priorities estimated to cost about $70 million.

Then, just as Saint Mary's was feeling the bracing hope of this age in her life, the most recent WASC team in 1993 let fly with a tomato to the face:

> The team observes that the liberal arts, Catholic and Lasallian traditions which are used to define the character of Saint Mary's College are appropriate and laudatory and consistent with WASC standards. However we found little evidence that these traditions are truly guiding the institution.[305]

Once again it was the outside accreditors who confronted them with an apparent defection from their announced purposes. For years now the college literature has invoked the traditional triad of descriptors — liberal arts, Catholic, Lasallian — but as it enjoys a crescendo of ostensible success, the visitors point the finger at a blurred — possibly deceiving — statement of purpose. It might be difficult to reckon which would be the more damaging: deception or self-deception.

There is plenty of evidence on the record to allow one to assess the authenticity of Saint Mary's triple standard. The three categories have no canonical ranking and appear in various orders, sometimes to make a point but often not.

Is Saint Mary's Lasallian?

Let us begin with the claim to be Lasallian. The brothers' schools in the United States had been caught between the conflicting expectations of their two constituencies. Despite the early experience of most Catholic immigrants in the working class, pupils in the parochial schools have manifested a strong desire for social and economic advancement, and their families looked to church schools for their academic (and therefore socioeconomic) advantages. The sponsoring clergy and religious, on the other hand, promoted the schools for their ability to build religious commitment and initiate their pupils into an understanding of Catholic belief. The brothers, who by their own commitment wanted to offer both a religious and moral initiation and a sound academic training, were perhaps inattentive to the fact that in the long pull the laypeople's priorities had more gravitational pull than those of the clergy and orders. Many of the brothers' schools tended to enroll the children of the professional classes. One tactic for honoring the Lasallian duty to serve the poor was the offer of scholarships. In 1950, for instance, 43 percent of the students in their (mostly secondary) schools in North America were given tuition scholarships. But by the late 1960s that had been reduced to 21 percent.[306]

During the period of Saint Mary's crisis and transformation the brothers have been obliged to reconsider their calling, and how they can serve authentically under such drastically changed circumstances. At a historic General Chapter in 1967, just after the Second Vatican Council had bidden religious orders review their distinctive missions, the brothers adopted what they believe to be their most authoritative statement of principles: *The Brother of the Christian Schools in the World Today: A Declaration.* The *Declaration* understandably accepts La Salle's founding injunction: they are to educate the poor. But the obvious incongruity was that in so many of the countries in which the brothers worked, free education was already provided by the government. Granted that the brothers might aspire to offer a better education, because it would be Catholic and because they would be especially dedicated teachers, there were few sources of financing that would allow them to offer it gratis to the poor. Therefore most of them could not educate the poor: as at Saint Mary's, they educated those who could pay or borrow enough to pay for their education.

The *Declaration* tries to explain why this is no deviation from their vocation. La Salle, it explained, founded the Institute to educate "with special preference for the poor." The poor are then described as "those whose poverty hinders their development as persons or their aptitude to receive the message of salvation revealed in Jesus Christ." That might have been an especially insightful perception of the truest poverty, which is perhaps more a problem for the very affluent than for the indigent. But the Chapter was engaging in artful dodging, not prophetic wisdom. The *Declaration* refers to "different historical and sociological contexts" and warns that it would be wrong to define "the poor only from an economic point of view," for "this puts much of the work we are doing under suspicion . . ." Even in the present school enrollments, our students "can become sensitive to the problems of the poor." Obviously anticipating that some brothers might see this as evasive, the text proposes another variant on poverty: the "poverty of frustration." That required a fairly lengthy profile, since it was not your crude, economic sort of poverty:

> The poverty of frustration is generally a product of injustice, of physical and social evils, or of personal insufficiency or failure. This form of poverty consists in the impossibility of certain people, groups, or persons to obtain a standard of living which would allow them real freedom. They live in a kind of slavery from which they cannot free themselves because of the deprivation in which their material and cultural poverty holds them. Often experienced as an absence of love in one's life and accompanied by a struggle to survive, such a situation prevents the human person from developing according to his proper dignity. The poverty of frustration is an evil which we have to fight.[307]

Any brother at Saint Mary's reading this literally might conclude that the college would be better placed in the most affluent spots around the Bay, like Tiburon or Oakville, where crushing economic affluence creates frustrations more acute and subtle than anything likely to be felt in Moraga. But the *Declaration* was trying to make its peace with a historical development it could not justify. La Salle had not mentioned a "preference" for the poor; they were the *only* people he wanted his brothers to serve. And he did not need to characterize it this preciously to fend off suspicion because his brothers really were working with the hardheaded children of the just plain moneyless poor.

The man most responsible for shaping the *Declaration* had hoped that it might convert the brothers once again to the actual service of the literally poor.[308] It seems to have had the opposite effect. A recent commentary on the *Declaration* offers the satisfaction that even without poor students they can have "an environment of care and respect for persons, where students feel wanted and respected as individuals . . ."[309] It might have been anticipated that this recent attempt to reinterpret the charism of the founder, drawing on the insights of Harvey Cox and Matthew Fox, Dante and Robert Bly, Black Elk and Frederick the Great, might reveal insights that Jean-Baptiste de La Salle could never have known in advance.

One scholar who studied the FSC schools closely was immediately critical of their abandonment of this primal dedication: "For the clients of the schools, and for those who teach in them, the intent of the church to serve the poor is of lower priority than the desire to continue to offer high quality education to children of higher economic position." That supports, in the author's view, "essentially a secular view of the Church school."[310] Brother John Johnston, an American who was elected vicar general (second in authority in the Institute) in 1976, addressed a large gathering of Christian Brothers from all over North America at Moraga in 1984. La Salle, he reminded his brethren, was driven by God's "love and concern for poor and neglected youngsters. . . . Thank God our First U.S. Regional Chapter declared unambiguously, *'By the word poor, we mean the economically poor.'* This no-nonsense stance does not, however, conflict with our grand tradition of reaching out to all *'down and outers'* — youngsters with behavior problems, the handicapped, the retarded, the emotionally disturbed, the intellectually slow, etc." He spoke of victims, those most in need, and many other types of affliction that were not affirmative-action categories in the FSC schools' admissions offices. Johnston subsequently became superior general and has apparently made his peace with the fact that, even after "every effort to welcome the economically poor and members of minority groups," their principal service to the poor would consist in sensitizing the affluent. "Our centers of higher education must make organized efforts to help students know and understand the world, recognize their prejudices, become familiar with the major issues, know the position of the Church on social issues, have structured opportunities for community service at home and abroad."[311]

In the United States the primary clientele for the brothers' schools have come to be neither the poor nor the working classes, but the children of professionals and executives. When this finally raised the question of fidelity to the original charism and obligation of their Institute, and "put much of the work they were doing under suspicion," there was an anxious resort to various defensive phrases. They were educating "the poor in spirit" or "with special preference for the poor" or those who suffered from "poverty of frustration." Or they were educating the affluent to have a care for the poor. In time the soft and friable rhetoric crumbled into talk of "care and respect for persons."

The depressing demographics of the brothers were a companion issue of concern alongside that of their calling to serve the poor. In the 1980s the Institute's membership was only half what it had been in the middle 1960s.[312] The brothers on the SMC faculty were increasing in age and decreasing in numbers and proportion. Today the brothers constitute 11 percent of the active undergraduate faculty, but if one scans the full SMC faculty they make up only 5 percent. None is a chairman or a dean. The brothers have virtually no presence in the nontraditional and graduate programs which now enroll half of the student body and present well more than half of the candidates for degrees. Their presence on the faculty is unlikely to increase, for there is now no member of the sponsoring district engaged in training for academic work.[313] Their annual financial contribution has shrunk correspondingly. Back in 1961 their annual rebate had contributed 17 percent of the annual budget; by 1987 it had sunk to 1 percent.[314] Lay teachers have long dominated the faculties of their colleges in the United States.

Brother John Johnston called for a sober look at their future. "The traditional model of FSC-lay collaboration has virtually collapsed everywhere. It neither can nor should continue to exist. It is not merely a question of a diminished number of brothers. It is more the call to full apostolic participation of all Christians." The brothers now had to challenge and invite their colleagues to consider their own profession a vocation, an apostolic calling, a life consecrated to the gratuitous service of the down-and-outers. These lay collaborators would have to be excellent teachers, but more than teachers: loving men and (now) women. Their zeal would need to be more potent than their professionalism: "Zeal involves an ardent desire to help young people grow in the spirit of Christianity."[315]

After several years as superior general Johnston would acknowledge that the Institute seemed headed toward extinction,[316] but this persuaded him that it was their lay colleagues who must be the ultimate Lasallians: their institutions would no longer be "Brothers' Schools" but "Lasallian Schools." However things stood in the seventy-three institutions of higher education sponsored worldwide by the Christian Brothers, at Saint Mary's College of California the hope of this otherwise very sober man might seem at best visionary, and at worst illusory. The prospect of a zealous fellowship of allied scholars, a Lasallian Family Movement, generously offering a confessional education to young people stranded on the lower slopes of opportunity and capability, was not simply an attempt to put a good face on fate. Vatican II had mandated activist, professional service by the laity before the falloff in the brothers' membership. Thus at Saint Mary's they would be seen, no longer as "a necessary evil," but as active collaborators. Yet this was a Saint Mary's where one brother had complained that one would have to fire 90 percent of the faculty in order to make SMC Catholic again. As for the brothers, many had already forsaken any role "to give spirit, support, vigor, and zest, to move to action, to encourage" their lay colleagues (in Johnston's words), such that one campus survey had to nudge the brothers to make a greater effort simply to join in public worship on campus with their colleagues.[317] This was not likely to be a campus where a predominantly non-Catholic faculty was going to catch fire with the Lasallian spirit.

Despite the unreality of the suggestion that the associated laypeople become the backup guarantors of Saint Jean-Baptiste de La Salle's charism — indeed, *because* of its unreality — various brothers turned their imaginations to describing the defining elements of such an educational project.

Brother William Mann discerned six "values and characteristics" of a Lasallian school:

1. a community of believers committed to gospel and church
2. a curriculum suited to students' needs
3. preparation for productive citizenship
4. students helped to see the world with eyes of faith, critical thinking and self-esteem
5. the educational example of teachers, as a community
6. a disciplined learning environment[318]

The reader will surely notice that the "Lasallian" education closely resembles the "Ignatian" education which laypeople were expected to maintain when there were no Jesuits available. And when Mann was fantasizing how a faculty and staff who were not Catholic might find the will and the way to make a school Lasallian, the notion was unreal. It immediately unraveled. Johnston himself has recently begun to adopt the more generic language he had previously avoided. The brothers could sponsor, not Lasallian schools, but Christian schools, and he itemizes their seven "clearly defined characteristics":

1. Respect for each student as a unique person
2. Spirit of community
3. School of quality
4. School that is Catholic
5. Solidarity with the poor
6. Teachers: men and women of faith and zeal
7. Organized around the story of de la Salle[319]

Ronald Isetti, a veteran historian at Saint Mary's, anticipates the day when there will be only a nucleus of Catholics, and they very likely as disunified as the brothers have often been. In the hope of some spiritual fellowship that might be possible without a sponsoring community or a communion, Isetti has listed some "general ideas or principles about our religious tradition on which most of us, Catholics and non-Catholics alike, can achieve some measure of consensus":

1. sacramentality: cultural achievements are outward signs of inward spiritual realities
2. contemplation: leisure is a higher activity than work
3. social justice: poverty goes beyond wealth; the common good beyond individual gain
4. unitary knowledge: faith and reason are compatible
5. inculturation: the church must adapt its message and practice to different cultures[320]

The degenerating fantasy — of a Lasallian, or Christian, or ecumenical endeavor without a sponsoring communion or community — shows how degradable is a religious consensus that is not the product and possession of an existential communion with its own discipline and fellowship. The term "Lasallian," which once invoked that very specific vocation, survives as a mantra that dissipates purpose rather than focusing it. As California poet laureate and erstwhile SMC English professor Robert Hass used to ask, "What does Lasallian mean this year?"

Is Saint Mary's Built on the Liberal Arts?

One of the most aggravated points of conflict among the SMC academics was whether or not the college ought to persevere as primarily dedicated to the liberal arts. The very early association with the Great Books movement, and the brief period during World War II when virtually nothing but liberal studies were taught in the college, had begotten a good number of faculty who were immovable in their dedication to a pure curriculum of arts and sciences (for some, it was to arts alone): no social sciences, no education or business or other professional training. During the 1970s this had become a point of sullen division that rent the Christian Brothers on campus into two intransigent factions. The liberal versus applied, elite versus populist split among the brothers was repeating the old Latin versus vernacular divide.[321] Even the WASC visitation teams mentioned this delicately as an especially unbecoming example at that trying moment in the college's life.

By the end of the decade it was empirically clear that Saint Mary's could not have survived as a liberal arts college. It had become what the academy calls a "comprehensive" college, serving a clientele that had much wider wants. To be sure, all undergraduates were required to have a basic initiation into the liberal disciplines, and to join in eight semesters of Great Books in the Collegiate Seminar. Yet in 1979 a newly constructed goals statement, their consensual covenant with the future, included this keynote passage:

> The College seeks to keep itself particularly qualified for liberal arts education — attempting in all programs to provide for the academic and career needs of its students as far as that is compatible with the spirit of the liberal arts. . . .[322]

This attempt to blend career studies and liberal arts was fishy. So was the self-study for the accreditation visit that year:

> Though the College has widened its educational horizons and services, the spirit and method of the liberal arts for the most part remains the animating and supportive spirit in the academic endeavors of the College.[323]

694

The WASC evaluators noticed the double-talk and asked why, if the liberal arts were truly so central to the college, there was no sign of them in the off-campus and nontraditional programs?

As written, the St. Mary's Goals do not clearly state the Primary Goal or Goals to the extent that they can be employed in academic planning. They do suggest that St. Mary's College wants to be, is trying to be a Catholic liberal arts college of the highest order, one with high standards of religious purpose and of academic scholarship. If so, then should not all activities, all programs be permeated to some extent with the spirit, but also some of the content of both religion and the liberal arts?[324]

The visitors found no fault with the college's goals and purpose; their complaint was "that the design and implementation of some programs do not yet fulfill St. Mary's own expressed goals."[325] One college administrator admitted: "Having found itself unable to redefine the College in terms of its expanded educational programs, the Goals Committee had chosen to take the position that virtually any activity undertaken by Saint Mary's can be considered an expression of its traditional work as a Catholic liberal arts college."[326] Several of the brothers who were most adamant about liberal studies saw what the WASC evaluators had seen. They left the college, and some even left the Institute, at least in part because they saw that Saint Mary's was never likely to be what they had hoped. But those who stayed found many ways to imagine that things *were* what they had wished. For instance, by an almost whimsical contortion of academic idiom the SMC School of Liberal Arts also includes Departments of Anthropology/Sociology; Art; Communications; Government; Health, Physical Education and Recreation; Performing Arts, Music, Dance and Theatre; and Women's Studies.

The effectual presence of the authentic liberal arts at Saint Mary's is very modest indeed. There is a relatively small cadre of faculty at Saint Mary's who argue ardently, persistently, and articulately that this is all Saint Mary's should be doing. But it is difficult for their advocacy to find an audience on a campus where, for instance, the faculty has persistently refused to reintroduce a required course in philosophy, and where by a recent reckoning less than 1 percent of the degrees awarded were in philosophy and religious studies combined, compared with 49 percent in business administration and management.[327] The flame has never been snuffed out. The Collegiate Seminar has survived as a vigorous liberal exercise required of all undergraduates and faculty, who today explore together Sophocles, the New Testament, Augustine, Chaucer, Luther, Descartes, Mary Wollstonecraft, Karl Marx, Octavio Paz, and Toni Morrison.[328] To this day all undergraduates still take four courses in the Collegiate Seminar, and (perhaps more importantly) the general faculty rotate through the tasks of leadership in the seminars.

In order to continue claiming the liberal arts as an essential element of its character, the college has had to manufacture its own meaning of the expression.

"Liberal arts" is understood as critical thinking, a perception of ultimate values, and of the theoretical underpinnings in any discipline. An official example can be seen in the school's own literature, which identifies it with "the integration of faith and reason . . . critical independent thinking . . . that liberation of the mind and acquisition of those intellectual habits and values that lead one to truth . . . skills in analyzing, in synthesizing, and in spoken, written and symbolic communication . . . to perceive pattern in complexity, to render reasoned judgments, and to make wise choices under conditions of uncertainty."[329] The dean of the School of Economics and Business Administration (SEBA) sees a "liberal arts disposition" in his faculty when they "emphasize an understanding and examination of the principles underlying a given field rather than simply an accumulation of a body of factual information and analytical techniques."[330]

This is a traditional description, not of the liberal arts, but of their desirable benefits. Likewise, an economist discovered at an SMC summer institute that "the 'liberal arts' reflect, most importantly, an attitude toward learning and living based on a consciously chosen set of values . . . a capacity for critical inquiry . . . analytical reasoning capability and . . . ability to communicate . . ."[331]

It has long been clear that Saint Mary's has had neither the will nor the way to be a liberal arts college. As with "Lasallian," for the "liberal arts" to be claimed as a pervasive and elemental descriptor of Saint Mary's College has required it to be reduced in meaning to thoughtful inquiry and communication. Thoughtful inquiry and communication, it need hardly be said, are a benefit, not a deficit, for a college. But a college which describes itself in such diminished sense may not be thoughtful enough in its inquiry and communication.

Is Saint Mary's Catholic?

The third descriptor, Catholic, is the most important for our inquiry, and it has been the most important in the college's own internal conversation. During Brother Mel's term of service Catholics have been variously reported as having been reduced from about 96 percent to about 60 percent of the student body.[332] The recent reports derive from a survey administered only to freshmen in the traditional undergraduate program, omitting transfers, graduate students, and matriculants in the many vocational and professional programs, all of which may well have a considerably lower proportion of Catholics. It is not unlikely that Catholics now represent a minority of those whom Saint Mary's educates.

At the outset of his administration Brother Mel spoke of "many" members of the faculty who were not Catholics. The college's recruitment literature once specified: "The College seeks faculty members who are committed Catholics or who respect this commitment." But by 1982 Brother Mel reported to the brothers that of the full-time faculty "less than half are Catholic, and some of those who are Catholics are so in name only. While it is clear that many non-Catholics are

696

highly respectful of the Catholic traditions of the College, it is also clear that many are oblivious of the Catholic spirit, or even hostile to certain Catholic views." The brothers' efforts on campus were made difficult "by the anxieties of those already on the faculty who may find a movement to 'Catholicize' the faculty a disturbing one, by the sincere convictions of some who believe that the concepts Catholic and university are incompatible, [and] by those whose orientation is toward a secular collegiate model." Administration efforts to encourage more Catholic appointments were often blunted by the departments whose definition of "the best possible candidate" excluded his or her religious commitments — sometimes even in the case of a Christian Brother. A provision that faculty in the Department of Religious Studies would teach nothing contrary to the teaching of the church had been removed from the contracts in deference to the displeasure of the American Association of University Professors.[333] The very articulate and committed Catholic faculty are much thinned out by retirement, and their conversations about Saint Mary's as a Catholic place have tended to be conducted in smaller and smaller circles.[334]

One administrator who deals with incoming faculty reports his impression that about 40 percent of them are Catholics. Dean Epstein's comment on his School of Economics and Business Administration may reflect a more general sense that it would be indelicate to inquire into the religious predilections of the faculty:

> Save for those few individuals who are, by some definition, practicing Catholics or have been educated in the Church (I do not know who these individuals are), the Catholic character of Saint Mary's is not doctrinally or theologically based for SEBA faculty members. Most faculty would be hard put to identify, let alone comment upon, which particular strands of nearly 2,000 years of Church history, doctrine or practice (save for Lasallian heritage) define Catholicism at the College.[335]

The college says it is Catholic, but that seems to be a function which for many years has never been brought to bear in any systematic way upon those who would be most able either to assure or stymie it. Paul Giurlanda, chairman of the Department of Religious Studies, has commented wryly on this.

> We teach in an institution founded by the Archbishop of San Francisco, but which has not for a long time required baptism in the Catholic Church of either its students or its faculty. Increasingly, its students and faculty are not Catholic, nominally Catholic, or even somewhat anti-Catholic. We hire computer programmers, experts in finance, literary deconstructionists, coaches, and what have you — all without regard to their faith. We recruit students for our sports teams for their athletic ability, not their religious profession. We start graduate programs in various professional arenas, all without regard to religion. And one day we wake up and find ourselves in an institution more and more secular in tone. Some

of us are as shocked as Claude Rains in the classic movie *Casablanca* when he hears that gambling is going on in Rick's Cafe.[336]

There are other signs that in some important sectors of Saint Mary's life, Catholicism is an awkward issue. For instance, in some of its publications the official nondiscrimination statement includes "religion" as one of the aspects of students and employees which it pledges never to consider in its dealings with them. The criteria for promotion and tenure, however, begin rather grandly:

> Faculty members at Saint Mary's College are participants in an intellectual, social, and spiritual community committed to ensuring that the College be an outstanding Catholic institution of higher education, dedicated to developing students' capacities for responsible independent thought, spiritual growth, active citizenship, and a productive life.[337]

The only specified duty of faculty in this regard is "to respect the religious commitment of the college," not to join in it.[338]

Brother John Johnston speaks for the Institute when he gives both a minimal and a maximal expectation of faculty:

> As difficult as it may be, we must do all we can to cultivate a faculty and staff of grand quality — Catholic or not — who accept the Catholic philosophy of the school and who are, at the very least, not obstacles to its implementation. But to be realistic, if we want an institution that is truly Catholic in tone and substance, we need a solid corps of men and women who are transparently committed Catholics of faith and zeal. This orientation must be reflected in our recruiting and hiring practices.[339]

The college seems to have despaired of recruiting transparent commitment, however, and to be willing to settle for nonobstruction. In 1995 the college was engaged in a major *New Century Report,* to serve as its guide for development into the 2000s. Written for its benefactors rather than for its accrediting peers, the document had more to say on the topic of religion, and Brother Mel reports faculty reaction:

> When we use such phrases as "Saint Mary's is committed to . . ." or "universities are totally committed to . . ." the implication is that enough individuals in the college or university subscribe to and act upon the commitment so stated and that their collective commitment will in some recognizable way characterize the spirit and vision of the college or university.
>
> It is at this point that the conversation may become worrisome to a number of faculty members. I have heard via the grapevine that for some the publication of the draft Mission Statement signaled the beginning of an in-house "inquisi-

tion." I found that observation to be amusing. However, if you see me carrying bundles of wood to one of the quads, perhaps you may have cause to fear.[340]

The first draft was rather conventional, though mentioning Jesus Christ and the Eucharist. The text eventually took on a more confessional tone, and was depicted as a retreat to the past. It aroused fear of an imposed orthodoxy and violations of academic freedom. Gay and lesbian faculty are said to be unsettled, and among many of the faculty there is an unusual level of nervousness.

Academics are more prone than many to be spooked by public statements drawn up for fund-raising purposes. This one, not surprisingly, relates the SMC mission to the "three traditions." Two of them are treated in the reductive language that has become standard. Liberal arts education leads scholars "to probe deeply the mystery of existence, to wonder about the nature of reality, look twice, ask why, seek not merely facts but fundamental principles . . ." Being Lasallian, Saint Mary's offers people "from different social, economic, and cultural backgrounds . . . its awareness of the consequences of economic and social injustice and its commitment to the poor." Not too much imposed orthodoxy there.

The real agitation is fired by the Catholic paragraph:

> Saint Mary's College holds that the mystery which inspires wonder about the nature of existence is revealed in the Person of Jesus Christ giving a transcendent meaning to creation and human existence. Nourished by its Christian faith, the College understands the intellectual and spiritual journeys of the human person to be inextricably connected. It promotes the dialogue of faith and reason; it builds community among its members through the celebration of the Church's sacramental life; it defends the goodness, dignity and freedom of each person, and fosters sensitivity to social and ethical concerns. Recognizing that all those who sincerely quest for truth contribute to and enhance its stature as a Catholic institution of higher learning, Saint Mary's welcomes members from its own and other traditions, inviting them to collaborate in fulfilling the spiritual mission of the college.[341]

Perhaps there is not much here to arouse most faculty members; indeed, even to keep them awake. But later the *Report* tells of "passionate discussions" and makes some unprecedented recommendations:

> a new formal policy that among qualified candidates for academic positions, preference will be given to those who are more deeply informed by the traditions of Catholicism, Lasallianism, and the Liberal Arts;
> improvements in the way that new and current faculty and their families are introduced to, educated in, and involved with the Catholic tradition at Saint Mary's;
> special efforts to reach out to Catholic students and for admissions standards

that reflect the College's historical role in serving the Catholic working class;

a review of residence hall regulations for their propriety and effectiveness in view of promoting both the Catholic and Lasallian spirit on campus;

creation by academic units like Fine and Performing Arts, and Economics and Business Administration, and Health Care Management of courses to appraise historic Catholic contributions to their disciplines.[342]

Here, after years of diffidence and double-talk about Catholic personnel, commitments, and culture, the college would propose some startling changes, and it is possible that after so many years of academic evasion this may galvanize the increasing majority of the faculty whose indifference may now be converted to opposition.

For that undefined number who see this as an *auto-da-fé,* there was one clear signal that these recommendations need not be taken too much to heart. At the very time that these "passionate" deliberations were under way, the academic vice president, himself a theologian, circulated a new protocol for the hiring process. Beginning with the preamble, "Faculty are the heart of this college," and stiffened by the reminder that the hiring decision "is one of the most crucial means by which we perpetuate who we are and how we assure that the values which are at the heart of our Saint Mary's College community will be passed down by those who follow us," the reader is presented with a thorough handbook of instruction on how to interview and draw out prospects. Its twelve pages systematically suggest how to make the first contacts by phone, book lodgings, put spouses (or significant others) in contact with realtors, draw prospects out about their personal reading, get access to their course evaluations, etc. For the campus interviews there is a long protocol for inquiring into significant involvement in the liberal arts, and knowledge, commitment, or openness to the Lasallian tradition. Then, when the reader is ready for the third traditional value, also known as Catholicity, one tumbles instead into a black hole entitled "Value-Centered Focus."

Is this candidate someone who shows real interest in pursuing value questions, puzzling through systems of value which may not necessarily be his or hers, critically evaluating conflicting worlds of meaning, and evidencing commitment to the application of one or more sets of values, particularly for the benefit of others?

We are a college which encourages students and faculty to raise essential questions, even when they are uncomfortable. "How is it best to live?" "What is a just society?" "What ethical standards are appropriate to this problem?" Long before terms like "mentoring" came in vogue, Saint Mary's College was a place where students regularly learned both academic subjects and the importance of choosing their values, particularly as stimulated by faculty and administrative example.[343]

It is difficult to imagine that any faculty member upset at the prospect of a preference by Saint Mary's for colleagues more deeply informed by the traditions of Catholicism, just as by disciplined scholarship and a dynamic classroom style, could fail to be reassured by this clear signal that for faculty prospects to be seriously Catholic was nothing the administration really wanted to know about.

Brother Luke Salm, a wise and faithful educator through his long life, sees "painful ambiguity" in this helter-skelter rhetoric that the American brothers have indulged in during this time of confusion.[344] It is that, and harmful too. The service of the poor, the liberal arts, and Christian education in the Catholic Church have all been reinterpreted in such a way that none of the three undertakings, which the Christian Brothers had claimed as central to their purposes, retained much meaning. If training a clerk in banking procedures is the same as educating a youngster to read Aeschylus, because both happen on the same campus supposedly committed to the liberal arts; and if exegeting Jeremiah is the same as exegeting the Federalist Papers, because both deal with created reality and all reality is incandescent with God's presence; and if educating a Catholic is the same for a Catholic as educating a Buddhist because both appreciate values (as, indeed, does the Aryan Nation), then Saint Mary's College is committed to a tradition so undefinable that it could never be violated. Also, it could never be meaningfully discussed.

Catholics, practitioners of the liberal arts, and Christian Brothers are being displaced as the guarantors of the constancy of Saint Mary's College. Less by intention than by providence, Saint Mary's fidelity to its own character was traditionally protected by its modest means. When circumstance threatened to swamp the school, it turned to new constituencies and stumbled into the beginnings of prosperity and the professional proficiency that prosperity could provide. There was at the time no apprehension that the Catholic faith, the liberal arts, and the gratuity of the brothers might all be vulnerable to this new prosperity and professionalism, and that they cannot thrive except by the fidelity, humility, and temperance that they respectively and jointly require.

Disintegration of Discourse

As the Catholic, liberal, and Lasallian identity — or identities — of Saint Mary's became compromised, they were simply reduced in meaning to provide a fictitious assurance that the more things changed, the more they were the same. Which they were not. Thus one could describe SMC as Catholic and claim no more than an interest in social justice or values, without any sense that the Catholic faith had some peculiar hair-raising doctrines about social justice, and some very costly values. One could describe SMC as a liberal arts college and claim no more than systematic habits of thought, without any of the depth that Sophocles or Dante or Nietzsche or Newton might make possible. One could describe SMC as Lasallian and claim no more than that acquisitive young people in California might be made mildly inquisitive about the poor people who could afford only Cal State. Vital realities were confused with their derivatives. The old identities were described as an inheritance, but it was a strange legacy: it was left unclaimed because of all the liens attached.

Thus there was a decisive change, but without a decision.

By all accounts the old divisions within the Saint Mary's brothers and faculty remain alive and intense. This has produced some strange situations. For instance, some ten years ago WASC began to formulate a policy that one of the factors in an authentic college or university was diversity. By this WASC did not commend to member institutions that they purposefully mingle dull students with bright, or foreign with domestic. The requisite diversity was originally to be one of ethnic, social, and economic backgrounds. The more WASC discussed it, the more persuaded they became that academic quality was inextricably linked to such diversity. And the more they discussed it the more their consciences were enlarged, and so eventually they also commended diversity of gender, age, religious belief, disability, sexual orientation, color, political belief, interest in the arts and in athletics, and regional and national and immigrant backgrounds. That all these diverse constituencies might be properly shuffled into the deck required the most frantic affirmative action, and sometimes voluntary compliance was frantically enforced. Experience quickly showed that the policy not only brought to campuses diverse kinds of students who had previously been underrepresented, but it infused them with a new desire to assert themselves and claim further public recognition for their own category, and to demand that various academic disciplines and courses and requirements and syllabi and vocabulary and dogmas be inclusively revised to avoid giving them offense.[345]

Saint Mary's responded affirmatively and secured a $750,000 grant from the Irvine Foundation to support its "Celebrate Diversity" initiative. Minority students quickly doubled and have held at about one-quarter of the student body (that is, the annually surveyed, traditional student body). This caused some relief by slightly reducing the very disproportionate number of students who came from homes with incomes above $100,000 (10 percent nationally, 30 percent at SMC), but some discomfort when attitudinal surveys detected some shifts to the right.[346]

The WASC policy had been explicit in providing two exemptions from the optional yet very obligatory diversity policy. Colleges might choose to admit students of only one gender. Also, "a college that requires adherence to a particular religious faith as a requirement for admission need not give up that requirement in order to increase its diversity."[347] This provision went far beyond the law, which acknowledged the right of schools to include religion in their personnel decisions simply by claiming to be religiously affiliated. WASC would allow that freedom only to institutions which refused admission and appointments to all but members of their sponsoring faith. Saint Mary's had never wanted to admit only Catholics in the way that Mills, for example, admitted only women (undergraduates). Indeed, it never missed an opportunity to reaffirm how welcome non-Catholics were.

Brother Mel, along with many other WASC presidents, disliked the policy. He quietly testified against it but made little objection in public. What was objectionable, he explained, was not the call for more diversity, but the intrusiveness of the policy.[348]

The voices that were raised against this particular policy were not loud on the Moraga campus. But they have been clear. One young philosopher challenged the entire Celebrate Diversity project, with its implied obligation for Saint Mary's "not only to be more understanding and accommodating to the customs and expectations of the various cultural groups to which our students belong, but also . . . to redesign the syllabi with the end in mind of 'celebrating' them."[349] Despite the fact that Catholics were no longer dominant among the faculty or student body, if Saint Mary's was committed to being Catholic "it would be a mistake to celebrate a pluralism of religions." The logic of his rebuke was that the only ground on which Catholics can rightly appreciate the hand and voice of God in other religious traditions is the tradition of Christ handed down through the apostles in their own Catholic Church:

> It therefore should be apparent that there is no such thing as a Catholic "celebration of (religious) diversity," if one means by this the refusal to subject pluralism to a judgment of relative truth and value. To embrace a Catholic notion of religion is to reject the bourgeois "liberal" notion which begins with the leveling of all "religions" to a common genus, perhaps with no greater aim than to avoid offending any of the parties . . . But, in truth, there is at least one notion of religion which this liberalism cannot include in its program: Catholic religion. The two shall always be at odds and Catholic schools are faced with the necessity of choosing their identity. . . .
>
> We can celebrate the exigencies of education within the context of capitalist competition and thus make a lot of hay over the fact that there is no overriding consensus on our campus as to what constitutes truth. We can celebrate an intolerant tolerance that proclaims all dogmatism out of bounds, except, of course, that particular and thoroughly uninteresting one. Or we can celebrate the Catholic, Lasallian, and liberal arts traditions that lie at the heart of St. Mary's.[350]

One trustee, a Christian Brother, took a similarly critical line. "If all colleges and universities — Catholic, Mormon, Protestant, Jewish, Islamic, any faith — are required to be pluralistic in deed as well as thought, then our society has actually lost its pluralism."[351]

Meanwhile the Department of Religious Studies emerged as another center of resistance to infra-campus multiculturalism. Its full-time staff is composed entirely of practicing Catholics, the majority of whom are Christian Brothers or former brothers who have remained on the faculty on apparently very amiable terms. When Brother Mel roused them (then the Department of Religion) from their traditional teaching of catechism and conferred the new title as a badge of professional advancement, the faculty never really adopted the mode of the profession, which was to relativize Catholicism as one of many religions. Instead, rejecting what the chairman calls the "vulgar relativism" usually implied by the "Religious Studies" nomenclature, they corporately accept the validity of the Catholic Church as their methodological starting point, expound its traditions critically, and seek to offer an array of courses to study other Christian and non-Christian religions. It would be better now, says the chairman, to call themselves a "Department of Theology."[352]

One Christian Brother in the department, however, has made a proposal in a different spirit. La Salle had sent his brothers to give a "Christian education," but that does not mean religious instruction, Brother Michael Meister argues. "If we believe that the created world is good, that it is the place where God's presence is sacramentally mediated, and that we ourselves are God's ambassadors, then everything we do has a place in this fundamental perspective." Nor, he says, would it require Catholic students to qualify as a "Catholic education." Since God is at work everywhere, not just within the church, a true ecumenism would "collaborate with all people of good will" (thus the *Declaration*). " 'Good will,' however, is not merely a euphemism by which we identify 'nice people.' Rather, it says something about a person's appreciation for values, recognition of the realm of the sacred in our midst, and aspiration for union with a higher power . . ."[353] This is obviously beyond "nice." And far from theology.

No one seems to have gone on the offensive strongly enough to claim that Saint Mary's would best serve true national diversity by reinforcing its own distinct identity through preferential recruitment of Catholics. No one, that is, until the *New Century Report* now under active consideration proposed that the triad of identifiers should become salient considerations in faculty appointments, student admissions, syllabus construction, and student rule-making. The board of trustees gave quick approval to the one-page mission statement, which speaks beautifully but not so pointedly. The attached recommendations, which would grip campus policy with a firm and innovative grasp, have been scheduled for a long season of sixteen hearings before final consideration. Quite clearly the college still has an inner core (or "corps") of articulate and committed Catholic faculty, who tend to be the same defenders of the liberal arts and of an effective Lasallian vocation to serve the poor. Their more numerous colleagues have usually been more indifferent than opposed. This unusual initiative to repeople the administration and faculty and student body with scholars who would move the college to be confessionally what it has long claimed to be but long gainsaid, will be strenuous. If the proposal carries, it might be a decisive change, with a decision.

If it fails, there will be more "painful ambiguity." But perhaps no more.

THE CATHOLIC TRAJECTORY

The stories of these three institutions display many common features. They have been sponsored by three religious orders with long records of prominence in Catholic education: the Jesuits, the Ursulines, and the Christian Brothers. The three founders of these orders had all left behind classic texts on education: Ignatius' *Constitutions* and the derivative *Ratio Studiorum,* Angela's *Règlements,* and La Salle's *The Conduct of the Schools* and *Meditations for the Time of Retreat.* All three schools were the flagship ministries of their orders' local provinces. Because the presidents of most Catholic colleges also usually served as superiors of their local religious communities, their terms of office were curtailed by the general law of the church, and so until the 1950s the stories of Catholic schools tend less to be a function of leading personalities than do the other institutions we study in this volume. In their early years the priests, sisters, and brothers managed to offer capable academic service despite their lack of university credentials, but their orders eventually made professional preparation a high priority and exerted themselves to train their prospective academics at leading graduate schools in America and abroad.

All three announced from the start that they welcomed applicants who were not Catholics, and they expected non-Catholics to be reasonably comfortable as a small minority of the enrollment. All three have drawn their students primarily from the nearby metropolitan population. Their traditional clientele were Catholics: predominantly Irish Catholics, who abounded in Boston, New York, and the Bay Area. All three orders sponsored secondary schools in their regions, which served as important feeder schools. The colleges were the object of considerable if occasional disdain by regional Protestant or secular institutions, but all three enjoyed the support and patronage of individual educators and educational executives. All three began as single-sex schools and all three have become to some degree coeducational, usually in stages, since the Second World War. All three articulately professed to offer a liberal education now surrounded by numerous vocational programs, without any admission of having abandoned their original undergraduate curriculum.

A Fourfold Crisis in the Sixties

In these case studies we see how Catholic universities and colleges underwent a common convulsion — between 1965 and 1975, though its entailments have emerged slowly ever since — which has substantially altered their character. Many elements of the transformation have been successful. The outcome thus far, however, has been a loss of Catholic identity. In each instance the college which emerged from the crisis is not the college which entered the crisis.

In the middle 1960s the sponsoring religious orders all faced a sudden and continuing drop in recruitment, just as they began to lose a large portion of their most mature, highly trained load-bearing members. Ever since the 1920s lay colleagues had been added to service the collegiate expansion, which ran well ahead of the orders' personnel capacity. The extravagant growth of most religious orders after World War II, lasting into the midsixties, had so augmented the presence of priests, sisters, and brothers on their campuses, and had allowed the young recruits to be academically trained as never before, that there was an expectation that the religious communities would go on serving as the frame which gave the colleges and universities their shape. But by the midsixties unwelcome projections showed that the orders would not be able to provide enough personnel to provide either the teachers or the administrators to dominate or animate their institutions. Thus all three of these schools were thrown into crisis, as to both their survival and their Catholic character, by the internal breakdown of their sponsoring congregations.

A second crisis was financial. Catholic schools began to deplete their current funds by a succession of annual deficits, beginning in the early 1960s. Their endowments were insignificant, and their threatened exclusion from public funding sources which subsidized most of their rivals made it plausible that they might not survive the decade. All three of these schools came within scorching distance of financial catastrophe. The Catholic colleges and universities had been eleemosynary institutions, primarily because of the professional services offered without salary by the sponsoring religious orders. The precipitate withdrawal of that great subsidy was what converted the first crisis so quickly into the second.

A third crisis then made the Catholic educators even more discouraged. Federal and state policies, supposedly neutral toward religion, took a sudden and prejudicial turn devastating to the Catholic colleges and universities. An aggressive development in the state educational systems now began to provide — for low rates of tuition, on multiple campuses conveniently located, at various echelons of educational development — abundant postsecondary educational opportunities that were intended to enroll a greatly increased share of the population. State competitors now began to draw away the traditional clientele of all three institutions: their charges were much less, their campuses usually much better appointed, and their faculty much better paid. Furthermore, mounting requirements in educational qualifications for many types of employment caused a surge of interest and enrollment in vocational degree programs. Our three schools found that their traditional undergraduate offerings were no longer likely to expand, and indeed would suffer enrollment shrinkage. Their faculties, who were for the most part loath to redefine their institutions, offered no enthusiastic support for the addition of vocational courses and programs. The fact that the Catholic population in the United States was just then moving upward socioeconomically, however, and aspiring to more education and professional training, meant that they would be inclined to welcome these opportunities.

At the same time the federal government was just beginning to make funds available to higher education, for student scholarships, grants, and loans; for research support; for building construction. But while state and other independent schools could qualify for such aid, various constitutional barriers were menacing the ability of religiously committed schools to qualify for these funds. In states like New York, which had further constitutional barriers to prospective state assistance for church-sponsored schools, the melancholy for these Catholic colleges and universities was even darker. By the time major litigation had resolved the issue mostly in their favor in the mid-1970s, many of these schools had either closed or forfeited their effective resolve to remain Catholic. As the well-documented (and nationally influential) struggle in New York State shows, though, the Catholic colleges and universities began by proving they were not church controlled, and soon were making the further argument that neither their clientele, their personnel, their education, or their campus culture was compromised by Catholic influence. As we have seen, this allowed them to secure more from the state but obliged them to surrender far more to the culture.

The fourth crisis was more internal, more motivational, and it powerfully affected the way Catholic educational leaders responded to the academy. Internal criticism and dissent among Catholics, so zestful during the nineteenth century, had been damped at the threshold of the twentieth, and it burst forth with pent-up force in the late 1950s. Catholics were displeased with their hymns; their saints; their curia; their liturgy; their concordats; their journalism; their ethnic parishes; their architecture; their aloofness from Masons, cremation, and Baptist prayers at high school graduations; their fish on Friday; their Thomism and their Bible translations; their sisters in heavy serge habits and headgear; their clericalism; their sacred art; their church histories; their reproductive rate; their seminaries; their maladaptive missionary style . . . and their parochial schools and colleges. The sense of shame was stronger still among the higher education leaders, for they were smart enough to have gone to Stanford, the Sorbonne, MIT, and Oxford, but their generation had been sent instead to the Gregorian, Catholic University, Michigan, and Notre Dame. They were gratified but surprised to find themselves easily accepted as colleagues by their sophisticated peers who had gone to those tonier places and were now presiding over them. The Catholics didn't ask for their autographs at the ACE meetings, but they came home dreadfully aware of being in the bush leagues. Because they had never been at home at Harvard or Yale or Johns Hopkins, they couldn't appreciate the native strengths of their own system or even dare guess at some of the strains of chronic anemia in the Ivies. So when John Tracy Ellis (Ph.D., Catholic University), who also hadn't trained in the major leagues, told them Catholics had no intellectual life, they believed him, but when Andrew Greeley (Ph.D., University of Chicago), who *had* got the big diploma, said Ellis was way out of date and that Catholic students were testing quite high for intellectuality, he went on about it for more than fifteen years and they still wouldn't believe him.[354] They needed Renewal in the church and Excellence on the campuses, and the National Council of Churches was their model for the one while the Association of American Universities was their model for the other. Having the

Word of God and the oldest continuous scholarly tradition in the world, being limbs of the body of Christ, and being washed in the blood of the Lamb had no academic yield. A fatter balance sheet was better to read, and a better library budget more reassuring; a membership in the National Academy was more helpful and a Ford grant more refreshing. In a word, the Catholics, especially the educators, were in the onset of their pietist phase and enjoying the flush of self-hatred. With a thirst like that of W. C. Fields emerging from a sojourn in dry Kansas, and an innocence of Pecksniffian profundity, they were ready to seize the day, to imitate their betters.

There was a complex and impulsive response to this compound crisis, within the ambit of two or three years. First, the three institutions studied here were put in the hands of new presidents and thereafter the orders gave unprecedented deference to the presidents' initiatives. The presidents had two priorities. The first was to get access to government funding, and they were anxious for it to be done speedily. The constitutional issue seemed to require emancipation from the authority of ecclesiastical oversight, and the presidents quickly persuaded their orders to renounce their tutelary, supervisory, and even proprietary rights. Their second priority was to move into the burgeoning new market of vocational education, and they quickly opened programs and hustled a new clientele: commuter and satellite-campus students, emancipated parents, and second-career and requalifying professionals. The decisive criterion was that each new program had to turn a net profit, unlike the traditional departments whose survival depended upon their solidarity with the entire undergraduate curriculum.

They succeeded in both matters. Their access to governmental programs was eventually vindicated: so well that it is less clear in retrospect that the colleges needed to be yielded up by their religious orders. Not only did they succeed with their new educational ventures, they managed to establish programs for an urban, disadvantaged clientele that were more imaginative, more serviceable, and more affordable (with abundant government tuition support) than what their respective state institutions were able to offer. The presidents were able to bring a sense of urgency, an activist style, an entrepreneurial boldness, and a capacity for fund-raising that saved each of the three schools from possible bankruptcy. All three presidents have remained long in office, and have led their institutions into financial stability and, in fact, comparative affluence.

Responses and Unforeseen Results

Other results followed from their rapid initiatives: results that were not foreseen, acknowledged, or acknowledgeable. They have compromised the Catholic character of the three institutions; more soberly said, they have doomed it.

The faculties have changed. The new disciplines have brought new people, with different credentials and backgrounds and identities and loyalties (and pay scales) than the traditional faculty. The new vocational units have tended to function as independent outrigger schools, with relatively little amalgamation into the old campus cultures. The younger members of the traditional faculties, hired when the budget was able to pay more than their elders had received (or perhaps were still receiving), naturally saw themselves more as denizens of a national guild than as partisans of a local campus. Both changes have yielded a total faculty much more inclined to centrifugal, individualist attitudes.

The students have changed too: in age, class, and gender. They no longer form a single student body. Or, to put it otherwise, the students in the traditional arts and sciences schools still regard themselves as the student bodies, though they form only a portion — indeed, a small portion — of the student bodies.

By the time major litigation had resolved the funding eligibility issue mostly in their favor in the mid-1970s, many of these schools had either closed or forfeited their effective resolve to remain Catholic. As the well-documented and nationally influential struggle in New York State shows, though, the Catholic colleges and universities began by proving they were not church controlled, and soon were making the further argument that neither their clientele, their personnel, their education, nor their campus culture was compromised by Catholic influence. As we have seen, this allowed them to secure more from the state but obliged them to surrender far more to the culture.

The new presidents are more professional than their predecessors. They tend to form closer bonds with fellow educators than with fellow religious, with alumni than with students, with donors than with scholars. They have had to rely more on the counsel of their lawyers and bankers than on that of their fellow Jesuits, Ursulines, or Christian Brothers. Though the salient reason put forward for rewriting their charters and bylaws was to gain equal access to governmental funds, there was an uncommon satisfaction in becoming the most independent, least accountable college presidents in the country. Legally they were responsible to their boards, but for a while at least their boards were responsible to them. For at least an academic generation, and possibly longer, the presidents have been and will be sovereigns. The price of this is that in many important respects they reign but no longer rule. Their faculties, of which the recent presidents have not had the opportunity to be scholarly peer members, have been quietly transformed otherwise than in their indifference to the Catholic character of their colleges. They have quietly been gathering to themselves the inertial political force which comes with affluence, security, and successor presidents less able to seize the main chance. The presidents' service to their institutions, which at that crucial moment of destiny was determinative for the survival of BC, CNR, and SMC, may prove to have been comparable to the unique service provided by the male praying mantis, upon whom the female lunches just after he has performed his momentary yet essential role in the prolongation of the species. It will not affect the presidents as individuals, but as delegates of their religious orders.

A 1983 sociological study of Loyola University of Chicago invites comparisons with the three Catholic schools studied here. Loyola had revised its identity in the early 1970s to become a "non-denominational" university, by changing its governance, curriculum, and finances. To present itself in this new identity and at the same time to reassure its traditional clientele, Loyola's corporate rhetoric was restated in newly ambiguous language, replacing references to being "Catholic" with a rationale that was "Jesuit-yet-independent." The only on-campus constituency who affirmed a constant identity, who saw Catholicity as Loyola's chief advantage, was the Jesuits, especially the older ones. But they expressed their appreciation for its liberal arts benefits in the new vocabulary of the Arrupe period — "being a person for others," "with a passion for justice," "responsible to history," etc. The administrators, the faculty, and the undergraduates, in that order, displayed a steadily diminishing interest in Loyola as Catholic, except as described in newer generic, humanitarian terms. Interest in a Catholic Loyola fell into nearly total insignificance among the non-Catholics among them (who then constituted 24 percent of the administrators, 29 percent of the students, and 43 percent of the faculty). The Catholic influence in the student body, however, was far more depleted than this figure would suggest. Students at Loyola were now primarily concerned to obtain academic credentials for their careers. Their alienation from the priorities of the church (unless framed in diffuse generalities) had, over the previous two decades, become so pronounced that "Catholic students would probably have destroyed the viability of the denominational approach at Loyola regardless of other factors."[355] Thus the Jesuit community found itself ringed by concentric rings of associates for whom the recent generic self-description, supposedly intended to enucleate the most dynamic purposes of the gospel, functioned quite contrarily. "Jesuit-yet-independent," which was meant to mean that the school would be the same, yet out of its own convictions, and not under any religious authority, made it clear instead that, having freed itself from Jesuit and Catholic governance, Loyola found itself with neither authority nor convictions.

Philosophy and Theology Benched

The reliance upon philosophy and theology as guys for the undergraduate experience was ended in this same period. In 1967 James Trent published his findings that Catholics were chronically underrepresented in higher education, and that those who did enroll in Catholic institutions, despite their superior academic aptitude, routinely manifested both a remarkably low intellectual disposition when they arrived and a low intellectual development in college and afterward. Some of Trent's suppositions were questionable, and some of his findings would soon be reversed, but one criticism was most timely: "There is a striking deficiency noted in the Catholic colleges' current performance of the special role they have embraced in the past — presentation of theology and philosophy. Although the primary purpose of these colleges historically has been to maintain the faith, the colleges have not carried out this purpose in a scholarly, intellectual manner . . ."[356] Yet 1967 was exactly the time when a freshet of young Catholic philosophers and theologians was becoming newly available: they were more numerous than ever (now most were laity), and more sophisticated in their training (they now studied at the most scholarly universities). Their arrival, however, occasioned a double enigma. It was just then, in the latter 1960s when the long-awaited personnel became available, that philosophy and theology were all but removed from their intellectually relational role in the curriculum. And it was just then that the new scholars would bring from the secularized graduate schools a conviction that their philosophy or theology would be severely compromised if required to schmooze with Catholic faith.[357] Other philosophies and other theologies grounded on other faiths, secular and proselytizing, caused them less self-consciousness. Within a few years candidates from Catholic graduate programs would be manifesting an even more dogmatic obedience to this view. The arrival of the long-awaited scholars in these two critical disciplines proved to be a countermessianic moment for the Catholic educational world. It was, however, only one aspect of a larger event, for it was just when the Catholic campuses first came into possession of the resources for excellence which they had always hoped for, that their definition of excellence denied any essential place to the Catholic Church or its faith.

The liberal disciplines and the liberal curriculum were perhaps not essential to a Catholic education. But their swift and thoughtless demise at these colleges looms large in their stories as an important sign and element of their failure of nerve. The Catholic educators were now without conviction that the Catholic identity of their colleges was academically centered. The religious and the curricular shifts were therefore accompanied by the same shifty rhetoric.

Our three study schools, which thirty years ago had all they could do to survive, are now aspiring to thrive, and their notion of thriving involves success on the academy's terms. Faculty credentials, varsity victories, campus amenities, labs and libraries, fellowships and scholarships, academic excellence and capital solidity: these are all elements of a progressive success. There is little thought, even in the public relations office, that Boston College once actually had some advantages over Harvard that are listed on a different table of excellence, or that New Rochelle had left Vassar behind in ways that only CNR could understand, or that Saint Mary's offered a better education for Catholics than Santa Cruz.

The only possible preeminence the schools might once have claimed was that they were Catholic. Their more common expressions of pride have referred to family spirit, or alumni affection, or lovely location, or lifelong friendships. In a (new and vulgar) word: "caring." There was no instinct of pride in being Catholic. The faculty were gratified as they began to succeed in hiring qualified and willing non-Catholic colleagues, and gratified when their students were hired at non-Catholic universities. It was as if they had really come to believe the darkest thoughts of Charles Eliot, or of the Saint Mary's student who found the "distinctively Catholic approach" in philosophy "hard to take" and wanted to replace it with "involvement in concrete realities, such as the poverty program, civil rights, peace movement, etc."

Being Catholic No Part of Academic Excellence

Accordingly, for twenty or thirty years now this university and these colleges have not had the nerve or inclination to consider that to be Catholic was one of the defining credentials to be an educator on their campuses. It is not a public value. A recent survey of ACCU universities and colleges shows that though 90-100 percent of them identify their institutions as Catholic in faculty recruitment notices, only 2-7 percent specify any preference for Catholic faculty, and only 2-11 percent attempt to have a predominantly Catholic faculty. Most ACCU institutions (60-68 percent) say that they "hire the most qualified faculty regardless of religion."[358] This raises the obvious question: In what sense can a college or university qualify itself as Catholic if being Catholic plays no part in the qualifications of its faculty?

The College of Notre Dame (California) recently advertised for a new vice president for academic affairs. The college claimed to be private, independent, coeducational, small, friendly, dynamic, and committed to the development of the individual student. The only two references to "Catholic" are more disavowals than claims:

> While Catholic in heritage since its founding more than 145 years ago by the Sisters of Notre Dame de Namur, the College attracts students, faculty, and staff from diverse ethnic and religious backgrounds and supports the free exchange of ideas and beliefs. . . . While the Vice President need not be Catholic, an affirming religious commitment, strong academic credentials, and significant academic administrative experience in a small-to-mid-size independent college or university are essential. The Ph.D. or its equivalent is required, as is the need for educational vision and successful leadership experience . . .[359]

It is clear that no candidate without a Ph.D. could plead an "affirming academic commitment" in its stead, and that 145 years of experience have made Notre Dame eager to be more academic and less Catholic, and fairly well persuaded that those two aspirations reinforce each other. Being Catholic becomes a handicap, rather than a neutral or even positive credential. Being Catholic not only carries with it no strategic intellectual community or liberating perspective; it seems only to be an intellectually compromising association.

Christopher Jencks and David Riesman presciently warned in 1968 that Catholics would probably have to dissent from conventional methods of faculty selection: "Surely the idea of a Catholic college or university implies some deviation from this narrowly professional and secular standard for choosing the membership of the community, some commitment to judging the human and more especially the moral qualifications of those who will teach the young. A secular university escapes this challenge by saying that it cannot pass valid judgments on such matters, except perhaps in extreme cases. If a Catholic institution takes the same position, however, what is left of the Church's pastoral commitments?"[360]

712

The point, perhaps, needed to be put more sharply. The credential in question would be a public one, not private. Dynamic membership in the Catholic communion is a primary professional qualification for any academic on a Catholic campus, and any campus whose faculty disclaims the capacity, the interest, or even the legitimacy of appraising this along with other credentials is as out of place as a paraplegic in a fire department.

Though the stories told above do not tell of responsible educational officers purposely and professedly drawing their institutions away from their Catholic identity, the estrangement did not come by happenstance. By the years that were so critical for all three institutions, 1965-75, Catholic educators were ready to say out loud what they meant to do. The only thing lacking to their consciousness was a sense of what must then follow. "The Church's Ministry in Higher Education" was the theme of a conference at the Duke Divinity School in 1978, and Methodist John Westerhoff took the occasion to suppose that the only legitimate justification for church-related colleges was "the intellectual love of God. . . . It is not enough to say that religion is taught, religious organizations supported, or religious services provided. Indeed, it is faith, and not religion, that is of primary concern for Christians." Sister Alice Gallin, O.S.U., late of New Rochelle, and then a Catholic educational executive, replied directly that her understanding of the "gift from God which enables us to say 'I believe' " was that it was entirely private, individual, not able to be taught or institutionally fostered. "I think, on the contrary, that the only legitimate goal of a college or university is an 'educational' purpose, i.e., to empower students to develop habits of mind such as analysis, criticism, synthesis, disciplined thinking. The intellectual virtues which enable us to pursue knowledge and wisdom have a justification of their own." Fostering faith would require a faculty willing and able to do so, and colleges "must be extremely cautious in trying to develop a faculty conducive to our central purpose" because that might aim at a "conformity of view" which would fall afoul of academic freedom.[361] With perhaps no sense of the irony in it, a Catholic was explaining to a Methodist how faith was private, affective rather than intellectual, fit only to be spoken of in church. It was a long time since her predecessors had thought that what was said in their educational community *was* said in church. Hers was no peculiar notion, that faith and the love of God are too private to inspirit the intellectual responsibility and enterprise of a Christian educational community. As one Catholic president put it, speaking of his Catholic faculty: "Their faith is their business just as someone's lack of it is his." Once their faith became thus privatized, obviously it could no longer be a communal enterprise.

The written record offers almost no evidence of educators on these campuses who openly advocated secession from the Catholic Church; or who saw that their faith and the public culture, especially the culture in the American academy, were at daggers drawn, and said they were willing to take sides; or who finally realized that the choice had effectively been made, to the forfeit of the faith, and confessed (with chagrin or with relief) that it was the only realistic choice. There has been no open rejection. Instead, the alienation from the Catholic faith community and its inherited intellectual tradition has been too baleful to notice, let alone admit publicly, let alone own as an advantage.

A Rhetoric of Fantasy

Throughout the time when decisions were being made seriatim that guaranteed the disestablishment of the Catholic Church, faith, and culture on these campuses, various persons who somehow sensed the change under way engaged in a communal, becharming, mantric recitation which assured them and others that it was not really happening. The elaborate, repeated, amazing assurances that the liberal arts continued to be the traditional center of education on all three campuses, recited until it was finally obvious that the liberal arts had become respected eccentrics at schools whose livelihood — whose existence — now depended on job-related training, are an instructive parallel to all the bewildering discourse about how to have a Catholic school without Catholic teachers, Catholic students, or sponsoring Catholic intellectual community.

The Jesuits at Boston College and elsewhere encouraged the fantasy that their lay colleagues would keep the flame of Jesuit education alive. How could men who had undergone so disciplined an education and formation for fifteen or more years; who lived lives of pledged poverty, chastity, and obedience; who served as a company and not as solo practitioners; who were inspired by a founder and a series of normative witnesses and expositors of what they as a Society were to live for — how could such a groomed and profiled fellowship be relieved of this awesome responsibility to interpret and apply the Jesuit spirit, by people most of whom the Jesuits had not even felt free to interrogate as to their religious loyalties? References to an abstract "Jesuit mystique" as a replacement for concrete Jesuits was a gambit very similar to the replacement of the existential "Catholic Church" by the hypothetical "Judaeo-Christian tradition." Just as Gerard Manley Hopkins's "just man justices," so the Jesuit "Jesuits." No one but Jesuits can do what Jesuits do. And what they do, they must do as a company.[362]

There was a misbegotten rhetoric evidently meant to disavow precisely what was simultaneously being assured. It was just when the Jesuits, Ursulines, and Christian Brothers were known to be vanishing that they began to describe in meticulous detail their singular and distinctive educational traditions . . . that they were no longer going to be able or willing to perpetuate. Diversity became a touted cultural imperative on these campuses, at the very time that their distinctive identity was being titrated to the point where they could not possibly initiate their students into a traditional culture that might both enhance and contend with the national diversity.

In this insecure era when the members of the sponsoring religious orders should see more clearly than their lay colleagues how rapidly their ministry is

714

degenerating into just a job, it is the Catholic religious on these campuses who seem most anxious to justify and rationalize the status quo — which, when it slides, inevitably carries them to the bottom of its angle of repose. The presidents and their allies seem to have presided in the manner of those mayors of the city of New York who managed to see out their terms of office through a series of defalcations that made municipal bankruptcy inevitable: they simply postponed it until after their terms had been completed.

Father Arrupe, the Jesuit superior general, had raised a larger question than perhaps even he realized in 1967: "Why should the Society of Jesus permit its name to be identified with an institution in which the responsible superiors of the Society can exercise no authority?" A few weeks after the Land O'Lakes Statement, Arrupe was to have had an even deeper puzzlement, for the issue was much larger than the Jesuits. The American presidents, in order to secure their autonomy, had been arguing that their universities and colleges were fully and obviously Catholic, and should thus belong to the IFCU, and be considered Catholic institutions for eleemosynary purposes. At the same time they insisted that they were legally institutions of the state, and thereby not subject to the church. This, they hoped, would allow them to secure to themselves the patronage and munificence of the Catholic people, and the grants and loans of the government, while protecting themselves from supervision, regulation, or even appraisal by either authority. The Land O'Lakes Statement simultaneously proposed an advantageous asymmetry between its intercourse with church and with state — in that most Catholic institutions were chartered or incorporated by the latter, not the former — but also a symmetry, in that both were considered "authorities external to the academic community." Thus, they said, it was very significant that they held no charter from the church, and not very significant that they did hold charters from the state. The church was held off for want of any legal warrant, and was told that she was nevertheless obliged to acknowledge that all these colleges and universities were in quiet communion with her; the state was being thanked for its charter and its funding, but held at arm's length by a claim of academic immunity. There were rights at stake: the schools claimed the right to Catholic identity and Catholic philanthropy, and also the right and duty to counsel, teach, and criticize the church. They acknowledged no right the church might have to counsel, teach, or criticize them. Arrupe took some time to realize, after authorizing the alienation of the Jesuit colleges and universities in the United States, that they really meant to claim Jesuit identity and recognition without acknowledging Jesuit responsibility. His response was weak, in the form of an ineffectual query. The church has been slower still in both its assessment and its reactions.

As the events took their course, the colleges and universities have not been all that immune to civil authority. No sooner had they begun to accept governmental aid than they were obliged to follow governmental regulations — of all sorts. But the further roll of events would show definitively that the Catholic colleges and universities did not emerge as autonomous. It would be the "academic community" whose immunities they claimed and whose authority they had negligently accepted, to whose sovereignty they would eventually have to bend the knee.

Less than two weeks after the pivotal Land O'Lakes Conference in the summer of 1967 Neil McCluskey, the Jesuit who had served as its secretary and amanuensis, said this:

> It would be absurd to set in motion a train of circumstances that would empty our institutions of the very reason for their existence. One can look in any direction today and see great institutions that began with a firm religious commitment — Harvard, Yale, Columbia, Southern California, Chicago, Amherst — and have lost all but symbolic vestiges of their Christian origin. Those who push these examples, however, lack confidence in the kind of machinery that could be established to guarantee a perpetuity of the original commitment by the [religious] order.

Along with legal "machinery" he called for Catholic institutions "to articulate a distinctive philosophy to justify their present existence . . . to win solid support from the public they serve, to say nothing of the larger public." His miscalculation was twofold. The presidents' "machinery" could not rival the church in guaranteeing perpetual religious commitment; and since the philosophy they did articulate sought the approval less of the public they were to serve than of the "larger public," they would eventually win the support of the former to finance institutions to the taste of the latter.[363]

Charles Curran, whose disposition to teach Catholic theology had been a matter of contention between him and the Catholic University of America, has provided an answer to the question, "What is a Catholic college?" in a way that is quite representative of what many Catholic educators have been saying to themselves by way of reassurance. He cites "three distinctive aspects of the Catholic tradition" that must identify a truly Catholic college or university. Catholicism is open to all peoples; it is open to all cultures; and it beholds the divine within the human. Conversely, then, it would be sectarian were the church to consider its members in every land to compose a distinct people unto themselves; or take its revealed insights and create a graced culture that might be critical of other cultures; or claim to evaluate humanity by what it sees in Jesus. Curran's reductive Catholic college "is not a worshipping community but an intellectual community"; it seeks in its intellectuals a "willingness to accept the milieu" more than a religious or a Catholic faith, and to protect that milieu from the secularization he readily acknowledges "is the primary temptation for the Catholic" as he is given to understand the Catholic, he advises the institution to "continue to talk about its vision and mission." He does not explain why they would be interested enough to do so.[364]

NOTES TO CHAPTER 6

1. Only baccalaureate-granting institutions are included. Numerous institutions have withdrawn their names from the association, either decisively or ambiguously. Some have apparently done so in virtue of a decision to discontinue any public claim to be Catholic: College of Saint Francis and Saint Xavier University (Illinois); University of New England (Maine) (formerly Saint Francis College); Lynn University (Florida) (formerly College of Boca Raton, formerly Marymount College); Villa Julie College (Maryland); Aquinas College and Marygrove College (Michigan); Maryville University of Saint Louis and Webster College (Missouri); Belmont Abbey College (North Carolina); Daemen College, D'Youville College, Manhattanville College, Medaille College, Mercy College, and Saint Joseph's College (all of New York); Heritage College (Washington) (formerly Fort Wright); Marylhurst College (Oregon); and Duquesne University (Pennsylvania). There is considerable and perhaps purposeful ambiguity involved, since several of these still list themselves in the official *Catholic Directory*. Some new foundations may think the ACCU itself too ambivalent about Catholic identity: Thomas Aquinas College (California), Magdalen College and Thomas More College (New Hampshire), Christendom College (Virginia).

2. A partial list is still a galaxy: Saint Bernard, Immaculate Heart, Lone Mountain, Loretto Heights, Annhurst, Dunbarton, Saint Benedict, Marycrest, Le Clerc, Mundelein, Marymount, Nazareth, Villa Madonna, Saint Vincent's, Ursuline, Saint Mary's Dominican, Our Lady of Mercy, Mount Saint Agnes, Saint Joseph, Cardinal Cushing, Newton College of the Sacred Heart, Saint Theresa, Saint Teresa, Mount Saint Mary, Good Counsel, Duchesne, Sacred Heart, Our Lady of Cincinnati, Mary Manse, Saint John, Catholic College of Oklahoma, Villa Maria, Our Lady of Victory, Saint Mary's, Saint Mary of the Plains, and Saint Mary-of-the-Wasatch. Some of these names have disappeared when the colleges closed; others, when they merged.

3. Joseph A. Tetlow, S.J., "Churches and Colleges: Recapturing the Great Tradition," *America* 141 (29 December 1979): 423.

4. Edward J. Power, *A History of Catholic Higher Education in the United States* (Milwaukee: Bruce, 1958), 139-43.

5. Peter McDonough, *Men Astutely Trained: A History of the Jesuits in the American Century* (New York: Free Press, 1992), 14, 91, 266.

6. Allan P. Farrell, S.J., "Four Hundred Years of Jesuit Education," *Jesuit Educational Quarterly* (hereafter cited as *JEQ*) 3 (December 1940): 117-27.

7. George Ganss, S.J., *Saint Ignatius' Idea of a Jesuit University* (Milwaukee: Marquette University Press, 1956).

8. Robert Emmett Curran, S.J., *From Academy to University, 1789-1889*, vol. 1 of *The Bicentennial History of Georgetown University* (Washington: Georgetown University Press, 1993), 1-56.

9. James W. Sauvé, S.J., "Jesuit Higher Education Worldwide," in *Jesuit Higher Education: Essays on the American Tradition of Excellence*, ed. Rolando E. Bonachea (Pittsburgh: Duquesne University Press, 1989), 161-63; also "Introduction," 6. From the sixteenth century the Society seems to have dedicated the same proportion of its personnel — one-third — to education. John W. Donohue, S.J., *Jesuit Education* (New York: Fordham University Press, 1963), 4.

10. Clandestine, not civilly, but ecclesiastically. The papal suppression of the Jesuit order was never put into effect in parts of Prussia and Russia, and in 1804 the Jesuit father general operating in Russia gave quiet approval to an informal reorganization of the order in Maryland. Georgetown was immediately put into their care.

11. N[oah] Porter [the Younger], *The Educational Systems of the Puritans and Jesuits*

Compared: A Premium Essay written for "The Society for the Promotion of Collegiate and Theological Education at the West" (New York: M. W. Dodd, 1851), 70. Further, p. 91: "the Jesuit society, in respect to the principles on which it is based, the character which it would form, and the services for which it would fit the man, nay, even in respect to its notions of what Christianity and education are, is altogether opposed to the views which we hold of education, of manhood, of freedom, of the authority of reason, and of the first principles of the religion of Christ." Porter was then professor of moral philosophy, later president, at Yale. I am grateful to Philip Gleason for having brought this book to my attention.

12. Charles F. Donovan, S.J., David R. Dunigan, S.J., and Paul FitzGerald, S.J., *History of Boston College: From the Beginnings to 1990* (Chestnut Hill: University Press of Boston College, 1990), 1-31. Much of the Boston College story to follow depends upon this helpful history. The College of the Holy Cross, founded in Worcester twenty years earlier, had a different charter that made it an exclusively Catholic college.

13. During the period of their suppression the Jesuits saw their school endowments, which had enabled them to offer education gratis, confiscated by hostile civil regimes. When they opened the Washington Seminary in 1820 with the primary purpose of educating their own young recruits, these candidates earned their own expenses by tutoring younger, fee-paying lay pupils. When the superior general learned that youngsters were paying tuition in one of the Society's schools, he immediately threatened to close it. But no stable source of financial support ever reappeared. In 1833 papal encouragement finally led the Jesuit general to permit schools to levy charges when necessary, and with very few exceptions the schools and colleges in America have charged for tuition. See Gilbert J. Garraghan, S.J., *The Jesuits of the Middle United States,* vol. 1 (New York: America Press, 1938), 304-8.

14. Donovan, Dunigan, and FitzGerald, 27-58.

15. Brochure of Boston College and the Young Men's Catholic Association, issued as a souvenir of the annual reunion, Monday, 5 February 1894. M. J. Lavelle speaks of the Protestant YMCAs as "inroads of the enemy upon our ranks." "Catholic Young Men's Societies," *Catholic World* 47 (June 1888): 403. These items were graciously provided by Philip Gleason.

16. This was typical practice in the Catholic schools: Power, *History of Catholic Higher Education,* 114-15.

17. Philip Gleason, *Contending with Modernity: Catholic Higher Education in the Twentieth Century* (New York: Oxford University Press, 1995), 29-38.

18. In 1898 BC's college division enrolled 186 students. Comparable enrollments that same year: Purdue 60; Alabama 120; Tennessee 179; Rutgers 162; New Hampshire 75; Rhode Island 67; Fordham 140. Charles F. Donovan, S.J., *Student Enrollment in the Nineteenth Century,* Occasional Papers in the History of Boston College (January 1984).

19. *Boston College Catalogue, 1894-95,* 4-5. The text, which survived through various rewrites and was later accompanied by a more explicitly religious statement on "spiritual training," remained in use until the 1952-53 catalogue. The next year it was replaced with a terse section on "The University Objective," identified as that laid down by Pius XI in his Encyclical on Christian Education: "To cooperate with divine grace in forming the true and perfect Christian." This was exegeted by a brief paragraph as terse (and as dense) as the statement by Brosnahan had been expansive: "As an institution of higher learning, Boston College has as its objective the conservation, the extension, and the diffusion of knowledge by means of the schools, colleges, institutions, and resources of the University with the purpose of imparting, in the tradition of Christian humanism, an understanding of the unity of knowledge, an appreciation of our intellectual heritage, a dedication to the advancement of learning, and a sense of personal and social responsibility as all of these are known in the light of reason and of Divine Revelation." *Boston College Catalogue, 1953-54,* 5. The Irish boys from Boston had a lot waiting for them, in either age.

20. Charles W. Eliot, "Recent Changes in Secondary Education," *Atlantic Monthly* 84 (October 1899): 436-37, 443.

21. Timothy Brosnahan, S.J., *President Eliot and Jesuit Colleges* (reprinted from *Sacred Heart Review,* 13 January 1900). Neither Eliot nor Brosnahan seems to have noted that the "colleges" which Jesuits had traditionally conducted, and for which the Jesuit matrix of studies had been devised, were often only the preparatory segment, or academy, of what might (or might not) mature into the full seven-year college. The *Ratio* would inevitably require serious revision as their educational institutions matured into full colleges and then universities. But that adjustment came slowly. And since it was pushed by the give-and-take of everyday experience, it was modified even more slowly in theory than in practice.

BC's history remembers a moment of sweet justification. Samuel Eliot Morison, Harvard's celebrated historian who would accept an honorary degree from the Jesuit university in 1960, had written: "It is a hard saying, but Mr. Eliot, more than any other man, is responsible for the greatest educational crime of the century against American youth — depriving him of his classical heritage." Morison, *Three Centuries of Harvard* (Cambridge: Harvard University Press, 1936), 389-90; Donovan, Dunigan, and FitzGerald, 109.

22. All but one piece of the correspondence was publicly released by Mullan and reproduced in the *Boston Globe,* 25 June 1900, 4.

23. "Catholic Colleges: A Significant and Successful Meeting in Chicago," *(Boston) Pilot,* 22 April 1899, 1, 5. See Kathleen Mahoney, *"Fin-de-Siècle* Catholics: Insiders and Outsiders at Harvard," *U.S. Catholic* 13, no. 1 (winter 1995): 19-48.

24. Professor Post, "Plea for Western Colleges," *First Report of the Society for the Promotion of Collegiate and Theological Education at the West,* 1841, 21. See C. Harve Geiger, *The Program of Higher Education of the Presbyterian Church in the United States of America: An Historical Analysis of Its Growth in the United States* (Cedar Rapids, Iowa: Laurance Press, 1940), 58.

25. Annual Report, Board of Education, Presbyterian Church, U.S.A., 1848, 51; E. P. Tenney, *The New West as Related to the Christian College,* 1879, 56-59; Daniel Rice, *A Plea for Higher Education and for Macalester and Albert Lea Colleges* (pamphlet), 1882, 5. All these are cited in Geiger, 59.

26. William Barnaby Faherty, S.J., "Nativism and Midwestern Education: The Experience of Saint Louis University, 1832-1856," *History of Education Quarterly* 8, no. 4 (winter 1968): 447-58.

27. "Notices of the Papal Church in the United States," *Quarterly Review* 2, no. 7 (February 1830): 189-99; "View of Roman Catholics in the United States," *Quarterly Review,* May 1830, 220-29.

28. Brosnahan, 30.

29. See also "Boston College and Harvard University," *Woodstock Letters* 29 (1900): 143-44, 337-39, 342-46.

30. It had already been observed in 1939 that Jesuit schools, because they serviced eighteen out of the country's twenty largest metropolitan centers, had been proliferating professional schools. At that time Jesuit schools maintained thirty-two professional schools; all other Catholic schools combined had only twelve; of all graduate students in Catholic schools the Jesuits enrolled 60 percent. Charles M. O'Hara, S.J., "The Expanse of American Jesuit Education," *JEQ* 2 (June 1939): 14-18.

31. *Boston College Catalogue, 1951-52.*

32. Andrew C. Smith, S.J., "The Requirement for the A.B. Degree in Jesuit Colleges," *JEQ* 11, no. 1 (June 1948): 35-40; *Proceedings of the Santa Clara Institute for Jesuit College Deans,* ed. Andrew C. Smith, S.J. (Jesuit Educational Association [JEA], 1955), 70, 90.

33. Philip Gleason, *Keeping the Faith: American Catholicism Past and Present* (Notre Dame: University of Notre Dame Press, 1987), chaps. 7 and 8; Gleason *Contending with Modernity,* 105-45, 297-304.

34. For example, the *Boston College Catalogue, 1951-52,* records that of the nonmilitary

faculty, one-third were Jesuits and two-thirds laity; 43 percent of the Jesuits held the doctoral degree, 23 percent of the laity. Since the professional schools had few Jesuits, and at that time their terminal degree was not a doctorate, these comparisons do not tell the full story. In Arts and Sciences, where Jesuits represented 46 percent of the faculty, 45 percent of their number had doctorates as opposed to 36 percent of the lay faculty. According to the catalogue for 1973-74, Jesuits then constituted only one-eighth of the total faculty; 59 percent of them held doctorates, whereas the rate among the lay faculty was 69 percent. (These figures do not include the Law School.)

35. The fortunes of philosophy at Georgetown were quite comparable. In 1962, twenty-five credits were required, which was reduced to eighteen in 1963, twelve by 1967, and six by 1970. Philosophy had originally dominated the senior year, and was moved back to the underclass years. When philosophy and theology finally became general education requirements, they were given exceptionally banal descriptions in the catalogue. John B. Brough, "Philosophy at Georgetown," in *Georgetown at Two Hundred: Faculty Reflections on the University's Future,* ed. William C. McFadden (Washington: Georgetown University Press, 1990), 109-41.

36. BC also reported the numbers of students who had decided to pursue priestly vocations: thirteen for the Jesuits, eleven for other religious orders, and thirty-five for diocesan service.

37. Archives of the JEA, box 33, file "Statistics: Various Schools." The JEA papers, as well as those of its successor, the Association of Jesuit Colleges and Universities (AJCU), are kept in the John J. Burns Library, Boston College (BCA).

38. "Jesuit Educational Association: Proceedings of the Institute for Jesuit Deans," ed. Wilfred M. Mallon, S.J., printed for private circulation (Regis College, Denver; 3-13 August 1948), 244, AJCU.

39. Papers of Edward B. Rooney, S.J. (hereafter cited as EBR; Rooney was the president of the JEA, 1937-66), "Final Report on Meeting of Jesuit Institutions of Higher Education, International Center for Jesuit Education, Rome, 5-8 September 1968," Appendix, 31-7-2-2, JEA, BCA.

40. See correspondence (1952-53) between Rooney and Andrew L. Bouwhuis, S.J., librarian of Canisius College, box 34, file "Lay Faculty in Jesuit Schools," JEA, BCA.

41. Box 34, file "Lay Faculty in Jesuit Schools," JEA, BCA; Presidents' Papers: box 18, file 6, Michael P. Walsh, S.J. (Walsh's papers hereafter cited as PP/MPW), University Archives (UA), BCA.

42. Robert F. Harvanek, S.J., "The Objectives of the American Jesuit University — A Dilemma," *JEQ* 24, no. 2 (October 1961): 69-87. In 1967 Harvanek would be appointed provincial superior of the Chicago Province.

43. Jesuit leadership in Rome had been pressing the American provincials to ascertain whether their colleges and universities, throughout such pell-mell expansion, were succeeding in remaining Jesuit. Harvanek was chairman of a select committee put to studying that, and their evolving conviction was that the American Jesuits had the resources to support no more than three good universities. This suggestion, with its implied solicitation of the order's authority to control and coordinate the schools, was anathema to the presidents. Harvanek was encouraged to publish the mind of the committee as a merely personal article, and great was the wrath of the presidents when it appeared. Walsh was chosen as the one to express their convictions. Paul FitzGerald, S.J., *The Governance of Jesuit Colleges in the United States, 1920-1970* (Notre Dame: University of Notre Dame Press, 1984), 158-66.

44. Michael P. Walsh, S.J., "The Real Meaning of Jesuit Manpower Availability," *JEQ* 16, no. 4 (March 1964): 197-204.

45. Richard M. Freeland, *Academia's Golden Age: Universities in Massachusetts, 1945-1970* (New York: Oxford University Press, 1992), 259.

46. Joseph A. Becker, S.J., "Changes in U.S. Jesuit Membership, 1958-1975, I: The Statistics and a Tentative Analysis," *Studies in the Spirituality of Jesuits* 9, nos. 1-2 (January and

March 1977): 1-104. This was a derivative report from a larger study of the Society encouraged by Father Pedro Arrupe soon after his election as general of the Society in 1965. See Becker, *The Re-Formed Jesuits,* I (San Francisco: Ignatius Press, 1992). Harvanek was one of those invited to comment on Becker's findings, and he faulted the unreflective expansion of the 1950s for having contributed to "the collapse of credibility of the system of structures and to the assertion of freedom." The devouring needs of the booming ministries caused many men to be poorly assigned, and the dominance of higher education caused the doctorate to become the ultimate goal of many young Jesuits. "Priesthood was desired, but to some it seemed to be valued more as a context or condition of professorship rather than a goal itself."

> Father Becker asks: What went wrong in the 60s? I suggest that part of the answer might be: We expanded in the 1950s beyond the capacity of the Society in the United States to maintain its interior spirit, its diversity of apostolates, and its mobility to respond to the needs of the changing culture and Church. Perhaps the most important of these was the Society's inability effectively to continue its concern for and recognition of the spiritual and personal capacities and needs of Jesuits, especially Jesuits in the process of incorporation, but also those already in the field.
>
> Harvanek, "Reflections on Father Becker's Account of the Change in Numbers of Jesuits from 1958-1975," *Studies in the Spirituality of Jesuits* 9, nos. 1-2 (January and March, 1977): 118-19.

47. Jerry Pokar, "Jesuit Identity: The Conversation Continues," *(John) Carroll Alumni Journal,* November 1993, 1.

48. Arthur F. McGovern, S.J., "Jesuit Education and Jesuit Spirituality," *Studies in the Spirituality of Jesuits* 20, no. 4 (September 1988): 2; Thomas F. Troy, "Jesuit Colleges without Jesuits?" *Commonweal,* 25 October 1991, 606.

49. Thomas E. Hennessy, S.J., letter, *Conversations on Jesuit Higher Education* (hereafter cited as *Conversations*), fall 1993, 6.

50. Walsh to John V. O'Connor, S.J., 17 March 1965, box 18, file 6, PP/MPW/UA/BCA.

51. These men had been beneficiaries of policy statements from the Jesuit general, urging the American provinces to make special arrangements to prepare their more promising men for academic work. Included were: encouragement toward doctoral studies, endowed funds to support higher studies, stable incumbencies to allow teachers to accrue seniority, freedom for academics from extraneous pastoral responsibilities, and membership in learned societies. On the other hand, it would be their generation that shrugged off important elements in the policy: shared planning and resources among the provinces, and a rule that lay teachers usually and lay deans always ought to be Catholics. John Baptist Janssens, S.J., "Instructio pro Assistentia Americae de Ordinandis Universitatibus, Collegiis, ac Scholis Altis et de Praeparandis Eorundem Magistris," *JEQ* 11, no. 2 (October 1948): 69-86.

52. This was a conviction expressed earlier by Philip Carey, S.J., one of the men trained in labor relations, a specialty in which Jesuits achieved a strong level of professional competence in the middle years of the century. He was passing on to Rooney anonymous grievances:

> In Boston College there has been some dissatisfaction over salaries of lay professors. A faculty club was formed originally for social purposes but it soon came to be a discussion group for grievances. A study was made on salaries and the group waited on the Rector to present their case. They said they got no action. They state that they were told to disband the club. This they have refused to do. Several of the better men have left the College. They are very bitter. . . .
>
> Jesuit administrators often do not comprehend the limitations and powers inherent in a position of University Administration. They understand well how to be a High School Prefect, or perhaps a good Rector. But the operation of committee systems is quite novel to them and they ignore the knowledge and skill of the departmental staffs too frequently.

Carey to Rooney, April 1954, box 34, file "Lay Faculty," JEA/BCA.

53. A. W. Crandell, S.J., to Presidents of Jesuit Colleges and Universities, 16 December 1966, box 33, file "Permissions," JEA/BCA.

54. The following account is heavily indebted to FitzGerald, *Governance*. FitzGerald was chairman of history and then dean of the graduate school at Boston College. He served the Jesuit Educational Association as chairman of its Commission on Graduate Schools, and then as vice president and staff member. He ended his career as BC archivist.

55. John Tracy Ellis, *American Catholics and the Intellectual Life* (Chicago: Heritage Foundation, 1956).

56. Freeland, 251-52, 275-76.

57. Rooney was convinced that the presidents had ignored the province prefects, intimidated their provincials, and bypassed him. In his 1965 colloquy with Pedro Arrupe he characterized the presidents (as in his personal notes): "They seem to think only of their own institutions . . . to be working for unlimited expansion (hidden expansion also) . . . to resist any 'seeming interference' by Provincial or Society authorities . . . money mad." He used the occasion to lobby for his transfer to a position supervising Jesuit education internationally. Rooney, "Personal Memorandum of Conference with Very Reverend Father General Pedro Arrupe, S.J., Monday, September 20, 1965, at Curia, Rome, Italy," box 20, file "V. Rev. Fr. Asst, Fr. Vicar," JEA/BCA.

58. Papal charters and status had been issued to three universities (Georgetown [1833], Catholic [1889], and Niagara [1956]), as well as to various seminaries: the Sulpicians in Baltimore (1822), all those of the Jesuits (1932-34), Jesuit-taught Mundelein in Chicago (1929), and the Dominicans in Washington (1941).

59. See large bundle of correspondence, 1955-65, box 8, file "Spellman," JEA/BCA.

60. James Jerome Conn, S.J., *Catholic Universities in the United States and Ecclesiastical Authority* (Rome: Editrice Pontificia Università Gregoriana, 1991), 52-115.

61. Box 34, JEA/BCA.

62. The *Maryland* case, *Horace Mann League v Board of Public Works of Maryland,* disqualified many religious colleges as too sectarian to receive state grants, 242 Md 645, 220 A2d 51 (1966). That was the first case which so alarmed the Catholic educators. A later case which took the issue up through the federal courts led to a more agreeable conclusion, *Roemer v Board of Public Works of Maryland,* 426 US 736 (1976). Similar judgment had meanwhile been given in the *Connecticut* case, *Tilton v Richardson,* 403 US 672 (1971). In the interval between 1966 and 1976 there was considerable unresolved fear among Catholic and other religious educators about the degree to which governmental assistance would be available only on condition of forfeiture of all meaningful religious commitment by their colleges and universities.

63. William F. Kelley, S.J., *The Jesuit Order and Higher Education in the United States, 1789-1966: Report to the 31st General Congregation, Society of Jesus, 8 September 1966* (JEA, Commission for the Study of American Jesuit Higher Education).

64. The notion that Catholics could make good ethical sense to those who did not share their faith was familiar from both Jesuit mission theory and neo-Thomism. It would provide solace for the Jesuit presidents when faced with the complaint that their colleges and universities were increasingly serving non-Catholics.

65. *Documents of the 31st and 32nd General Congregations of the Society of Jesus,* ed. John Padberg, S.J. (Saint Louis: Institute of Jesuit Sources, 1977), Decrees 28-29; 227-42.

66. Pedro Arrupe, S.J., "The Jesuit Apostolate of Education," *JEQ* 29, no. 1 (June 1966): 5-11.

67. FitzGerald, 197-98.

68. Raymond J. Swords, S.J., chairman of the presidents group, reporting to the JEA on

their activities, April 1966 to April 1967, box 10, file 1: "Correspondence JEA," PP/MPW/ UA/BCA.

69. Fred M. Hechinger, "A Catholic College Becoming Secular," *New York Times,* 12 January 1967, 1; Hechinger, "A College Goes Secular," *New York Times,* 15 January 1967, E13; editorial, "Settling the Dust at Webster College," *America* 116 (28 January 1967): 138; Vincent McCorry, S.J., "The Grennan Affair," *America* 116 (28 January 1967): 149-50; letters, *America* 116 (4 March 1967): 298; "Statement by a College President," *America* 116 (4 March 1967): 301; editorial, "Webster College," *Commonweal* 85 (27 January 1967): 442; Daniel Callahan, "A Crisis in Catholic Education," *New York Times Sunday Magazine,* 23 April 1967, 24; Thomas E. Blackburn, "Where Is Webster College Going?" *National Catholic Reporter,* 25 February 1968, 1-2; Helen Sanders, S.L., *More Than Renewal: Loretto before and after Vatican II, 1952-1977* (Nerinx, Ky.: Sisters of Loretto, 1982), 127-51; Ms. Christine Kemmerer, director of institutional analysis, Webster University, interview with the author, 19 September 1995.

Sister Mary Emil, I.H.M., then president of Marygrove College in Detroit and the foundress of the influential Sister Formation program that gave so many women access to higher education, was not amused by the Grennan claims. "Marygrove College would suffer a loss of freedom if it imitated Webster. A private and Catholic college which is owned and operated by a congregation of Sisters enjoys a freedom from establishment control which is actually greater than that characterizing any other type of institution in higher education today. A college of our type is neither Church-supported nor Church-controlled, neither state-supported nor state-controlled." News release, Marygrove College, 16 January 1967.

70. [Michael P. Walsh, S.J.], "The Objectives of a Catholic University" (revised schema), Appendix "C," Minutes of JEA Commission on Colleges and Universities, 27 March 1967, box 34, JEA/BCA. Walsh was chosen as drafter because of his convocation address in the autumn of 1966 which served as the template of their much briefer consensus document: "Why a Catholic University?" *Boston College Alumni News,* winter 1967, 2-5. In that text, too, reflective faith is an undertaking, not of and by the Catholic university as a believing community, but of Catholics who find there a place which allows them "a free and open religious life."

71. FitzGerald, 203-5.

72. "Statement on the Nature of the Contemporary Catholic University," in *The Idea of the Catholic University,* 23 July 1967.

73. Minutes of the Trustees of Boston College, 13 November and 14 December 1967, UA/BCA.

74. Minutes of the Trustees of Boston College, 10 and 25 January and 3 February 1968, UA/BCA.

75. Walsh to John O'Connor, 25 March 1968, box 18, file 6, PP/MPW/UA/BCA; 28 February 1969, papers of the Board of Governors, box 9, UA/BCA (*sic* FitzGerald, 207 n. 93). Walsh suggested, after all the changes had been made, that the legal theory on which the BC governance change had been grounded should be further investigated lest it impose problems on other Jesuit institutions who were later going to rely upon it. A fair and summary account of the canonical argument of John J. McGrath used by the Jesuits, and others rebutting it, is given by Conn, 194-206.

76. "Foundation Statements and Articles Relevant to the Jesuit Community at Boston College," effective 1 September 1968, box 2, file "Boston College," Papers of the Association of Jesuit Colleges and Universities (AJCU), BCA. The Jesuit Community at Boston College, unlike the Trustees of Boston College (BC's corporate title), is civilly incorporated as a religious corporation; that is, any future litigation involving it must be decided by the civil courts on the basis of canon law and the constitutions and rules of the Society of Jesus.

77. "Final Report on Meeting on Jesuit Institutions of Higher Education, September 5-8, 1968," International Center for Jesuit Education, 31-7-2-2, EBR/JEA/BCA.

78. The final form of the report appeared as Walter Gellhorn and R. Kent Greenawalt, *The*

Sectarian College and the Public Purse: Fordham — A Case Study (Dobbs Ferry, N.Y.: Oceana Publications, 1970).

79. Minutes of JEA Commission on Colleges and Universities, 11-12 January 1969, box 34, JEA/BCA.

80. Fordham University Revised Statutes, 1950, I, 4, 1.

81. Gellhorn and Greenawalt, 74 n. 161; quotation from Christopher Jencks and David Riesman, *The Academic Revolution* (New York: Doubleday, 1968), 400.

82. Conn, 174-80.

83. Charles M. Whelan, S.J., "Catholic Universities and the Gellhorn Report," *America,* 16 November 1968, 474-79. Laurence McGinley, S.J., former president of Fordham and now a consultant for the New York Archdiocese, circulated copies of the Whelan article to Catholic presidents in the area, box 6-17-2, College of New Rochelle Archives (CNRA).

84. Fordham's outstanding current debts had increased, through years of fiscal deficit, to the point where they equaled the endowment. McLaughlin's last desperate move was in October 1969, when he announced that faculty, students, and administrators should share equal responsibility for preparation of the university budget. His resignation came during the subsequent Christmas vacation. McLaughlin, "Memorandum to All Members of the Fordham University Community," 10 October 1968, box 6-17-2, CNRA.

85. Ladislas M. Örsy, S.J., "A Catholic Presence," *America* 120 (5 April 1969): 396-97. The essay was brief, and offered no view on whether the Society of Jesus could be Catholic.

86. Paul J. Reiss, "Faculty and Administration: The Jesuit-Lay Character," in *Perspectives in Jesuit Higher Education,* papers prepared for the JEA Denver Workshop, ed. Eugene E. Grollmes, S.J., Robert F. O'Brien, S.J., and Daniel A. Degnan, S.J. (Washington: JEA, 1969); also in *JEQ* 32 (October 1969). Walsh was responsible for the organization of the Denver Workshop.

87. Edmund G. Ryan, S.J., "Jesuit Presence on Campus: Today and Tomorrow," 7, in *Perspectives in Jesuit Higher Education.*

88. *Proceedings of the JEA Denver Workshop on Jesuit Universities and Colleges: Their Commitment in a World of Change,* ed. Eugene E. Grollmes, S.J. (Washington: JEA, 1969), 28.

89. Charles F. Donovan, S.J., BC academic vice president 1961-68, senior vice president and dean of the faculties 1968-79, university historian 1979-, in *Proceedings of the JEA Denver Workshop,* 23. Ten years later he reframed that memory:

> In the early '60s sometimes candidates would mention they were not Catholic or ask how much freedom they would have in a Catholic institution. I usually referred them to someone, where possible in the same discipline, who I happened to know was not Catholic, to check the experience of non-Catholic professors here. For a long time now such questions have not been raised during recruitment interviews. I have taken this to mean that the style and atmosphere of Boston College are well known today and people with at least basic sympathy with the value concerns of the institution know they would be comfortable here. I have always assumed such sentiments on the part of candidates by the very fact of their interest in a position at the University.
>
> Donovan, "A Cheerful Reminiscence," *Boston College Magazine,* June 1979, 14.

90. "Statement on the Distinctive Characteristics of Jesuit Higher Education," in *Guidelines for Jesuit Higher Education: The Consensus Statements, Recommendations, and Committee Reports of the JEA Denver Workshop,* ed. Eugene E. Grollmes, S.J. (Washington: JEA, 1969), 6.

91. Minutes of JEA Commission on Colleges and Universities, 10-11 October 1969, box 34, JEA/BCA. It was not easy for the provincials to realize that their role as board of governors had become anomalous: the presidents had effectively removed the institutions of higher education from their governance — collectively as a board, and individually as superiors. In 1972 the

provincials, no less defensive about their individual autonomy than the presidents were about theirs, formed their own unit for joint action, the Jesuit Conference.

92. Joseph A. Tetlow, S.J., "The Jesuits' Mission in Higher Education: Perspectives and Contexts," *Studies in the Spirituality of Jesuits* 15, no. 5–16, no. 1 (Saint Louis: American Assistancy Seminar, November 1983 and January 1984): 66.

93. Minutes of JEA Commission on Colleges and Universities, 10-11 January 1970, box 34, JEA/BCA.

94. FitzGerald, 216-17; Minutes of JEA Commission on Colleges and Universities, 10-11 October 1970, box 34, JEA/BCA.

95. "Statement of Jesuit Presidents to Provincials," Appendix A, Minutes of AJCU Board of Directors, 12 April 1971, box 5, AJ-90-02, AJCU/BCA.

96. In the early years of their new autonomy, the presidents of the three largest Jesuit universities would be turned out of office by their boards for having virtually liquidated their endowments through improvident management.

97. Freeland, 255-57.

98. Joseph Gallagher, consultant, "The Effect of Selected Variables on the Financial Development of the Jesuit Colleges and Universities," box 7, AJ-90-02, AJCU/BCA. Gallagher's findings were treated with suspicion at the annual board meeting of the AJCU Conference of Jesuit Advancement/Alumni Administrators, July 1972. But a six-year "Summary of Jesuit College and University Private Support" prepared by Donald Ross at Marquette and circulated by AJCU on 3 August 1973 shows alumni dollar totals (not restricted to annual fund) at Holy Cross about half again as much as at BC. BC's dollar total that year was exceeded by six other institutions. As late as 1981, nine years after Joyce had stepped down, BC alumni giving had risen to 19 percent, but was still much surpassed by the 46 percent at Holy Cross (as were all the other Jesuit colleges and universities that year). Georgetown received contributions from only 20 percent of its graduates. See "A Comparison of Twenty-Eight Jesuit Colleges and Universities in America by Percent of Alumni Donors," 1981, box 10, file 7, JA-89/AJCU/BCA.

99. Andrew M. Greeley, in a didactic tale told in 1969 about four unidentified Jesuit institutions, singled out Boston College, "Institution D," as a "miracle school" which had surged forward under the Walsh regime. Despite its plummeting balance sheet in three successive years, which would tumble far further in 1970, he praised the vigorous expansion and reform, while seeing its future as "cloudy." It was so, but for reasons only foreshadowed in the balance sheet. *From Backwater to Mainstream: A Profile of Catholic Education* (New York: McGraw-Hill, 1969), 154-57.

100. Donovan, Dunigan, and FitzGerald, 395; Martin F. Nolan, "Boston College Groans and Grows," *Boston Sunday Globe Magazine,* 13 June 1971, 24.

101. The figures here refer to 1973-74, the second year of the Monan presidency. That year's faculty lists were published in combined form, whereas previously they had been available only by schools, with considerable overlap. An earlier, modest Jesuit presence in the professional schools had abated, but this may have been by discontinuance of an older practice of appointing some lesser-credentialed Jesuits (who taught basic humanities requirements) to those schools where they served, and not to their disciplinary departments in Arts and Sciences.

102. *Project 1: The Jesuit Apostolate of Education in the United States,* ed. James L. Connor, S.J., John W. Padberg, S.J., and Joseph A. Tetlow, S.J., vol. 2 (Washington: The Jesuit Conference, 1974): 2-3, 27, 45, 53.

103. The output of Jesuit college and university policy statements in the 1970s and 1980s was prodigious. One collection alone has ninety such documents. Those in the next pages without citation are found in either "Source Book: Jesuit and Catholic Aspects of American Jesuit Colleges and Universities," compiled in 1983 by Barry McGannon, S.J., copy at AJCU; or box 2, files 1-3: "Goals Statements," AJ-90-01/AJCU/BCA.

104. "Heritage and Vision: The Jesuit Character of Marquette University," Report of the

University Committee on Collaboration, 24 July 1987; Arthur F. McGovern; Robert A. Mitchell, S.J., "What It's All About: The Five Traits of Jesuit Education," *Boston College Magazine,* fall 1989, 19; National Seminar on Jesuit Higher Education, "Raising Questions, Encouraging Conversations, Inviting Responses," *Conversations* 1 (February 1992): 6-11; Steven M. Barkan, "Jesuit Law Schools: Challenging the Mainstream," *Conversations* 3 (spring 1993): 7-15; Stephen C. Rowntree, S.J., "Ten Theses on Jesuit Higher Education," *America* 170 (28 May 1994): 6-12; Joseph J. Feeney, S.J., "Can Jesuit Higher Education Survive in a New Century?" *America* 170 (28 May 1994): 14-19; Ronald Modras, "The Spiritual Humanism of the Jesuits," *America* 172 (4 February 1995): 10-32.

105. Peter-Hans Kolvenbach, S.J., "The Jesuit University Today," *Meeting of University Presidents and Rectors,* 4-9 November 1985, Rome (Frascati), Italy (Rome: International Center for Jesuit Education, n.d.), 16.

106. Paul C. Reinert, S.J., and Paul Shore, "The Catholic University's Recognition of Mystery," *America* 172 (27 May 1995): 35.

107. George A. Aschenbrenner, S.J., *The Jesuit University Today* (Scranton: The Scranton Journal, 1982). See also "Preamble to the Constitution of the Jesuit Secondary Education Association" (1970), in *foundations,* ed. Carl E. Meirose, S.J. (Washington: Jesuit Secondary Education Association, 1994), 4; William McInnes, S.J., "How Can a Provincial Tell a Jesuit College?" Appendix IV, Minutes of the AJCU Board of Directors, 13-14 January 1973, box 5, AJ/90/02/AJCU/BCA; Loyola [New Orleans] Character and Commitment Statement (1980), in "Source Book"; Raymond A. Schroth, S.J., "Tough Choices on Campus," *Commonweal* 133 (28 March 1986): 171; Brian E. Daley, S.J., " 'Splendor and Wonder': Ignatian Mysticism and the Ideals of Liberal Education," *Presence* 1, no. 1 (Loyola in Maryland: fall 1987): 116-18; Timothy S. Healy, S.J., "The Ignatian Heritage for Today's College," *America* 137 (5 November 1977): 304-6; Healy, "Probity and Freedom on the Border: Learning and Belief in the Catholic University," *America* 163 (7 July 1990): 10; James P. M. Walsh, S.J., "Saint Ignatius's Way of Proceeding: The Spiritual Exercises," in *Georgetown at Two Hundred,* 265-80; Reinert and Shore, 34. Most Jesuit campuses now have officers charged with "Jesuit mission," in the hope that such weekend experiences will prepare lay colleagues so that "should a time come when there are no Jesuits at the University, the institution could still be identified as 'Jesuit.' . . ." James E. Flynn, S.J., "Sustaining the Founding Spirit: Institutional Identity and Mission," *Review for Religious* 30 (January-February 1991): 124.

108. Box 34, file "Dual Control of Administration," JEA/BCA.

109. Alfred de Souza, [S.J.], "The Aims and Objectives of Jesuit Education," JEA Seminar, Shembaganur, 15-21 May 1971, box 24, JEA/BCA.

110. Robert S. Miola, "A Word from the Editor: What Makes a Jesuit College Different?" *Presence* 1, no. 1 (fall 1987): inside front cover.

111. "Aims and Objectives of Jesuit Education," JEA Seminar, Shembaganur, 15-21 May 1971, box 24, JEA/BCA.

112. Healy, "Ignatian Heritage for Today's College," 304.

113. *Documents of the 31st and 32nd General Congregations of the Society of Jesus,* Decree 4, par. 2, 411. For an antecedent, see Arrupe, *Men for Others: Education for Social Justice and Social Action Today* (Washington: Jesuit Secondary Education Association, 1974), in which he draws on the 1968 Medellin conference of Latin American bishops, and the 1971 Synod of Bishops ("Action on behalf of justice and participation in the transformation of the world fully appear to us as a constitutive dimension of the preaching of the Gospel"), and insists that personal conversion "is only the root, the beginning of a renewal, a reform of the structures at the 'periphery' of our being, not only personal but social." American Jesuits often allude to this call to be "men for others." A nearer antecedent was a 1971 meeting of the Jesuit National Leadership Project (created by the provincials), known as the Fordyce House meeting, which called for corporate conversion and radical renewal in the church by reform of "sinful structures which oppress the poor." In

support of such an academic task, see Michael Buckley, S.J., "The University and the Concern for Justice: The Search for a New Humanism," *Thought* 57, no. 225 (June 1982): 219-33.

114. A studious and well-documented scholarship concerning the Ignatian educational tradition was frequently drawn upon during this period, though without obvious effect. Ganss, *Saint Ignatius' Idea,* 191-201; Ganss, *The Jesuit Educational Tradition and Saint Louis University* (Saint Louis: Institute of Jesuit Resources, 1969), 19-23; Allan Farrell, S.J., *The Jesuit Code of Liberal Education: Development and Scope of the Ratio Studiorum* (Milwaukee: Bruce, 1938); Arthur A. O'Leary, S.J., "Tests of a Good Jesuit College," *JEQ* 2, no. 4 (June 1939): 33-36. John A. LaFarge, S.J., to Zacheus Maher, S.J., then general assistant for the American Assistancy, 24 August 1943, quoted in McDonough, *Men Astutely Trained,* 199; Janssens, 77-78; Matthew J. Fitzsimons, S.J., "Objectives of a Jesuit College," *JEQ* 11, no. 4 (March 1949): 229-41; Fitzsimons, "The 'Instructio': 1934-1949," *JEQ* 12, no. 2 (October 1949): 69-78.

115. Walsh, "Criteria for Jesuitness," Appendix II, Minutes of the AJCU Board of Directors, 8-9 October 1971, AJ-90-02/AJCU/BCA; Minutes of the AJCU Board of Directors, 8-9 January 1972, 3-5, reporting a floor discussion by the presidents of Walsh's brief "operational" draft, is soon awash with amendments suggesting that "the term Jesuit needs clear description and explanation," "need for personal interest in students, etc., which is traditionally Ignatian," "unity on affective level," "the notion of Jesuit 'toughness,' " etc.

116. "Report of Boston College Prepared for the Commission of Institutions of Higher Education of the New England Association of Schools and Colleges on the Occasion of the Re-evaluation of 1976" (1975), box 2, file "Institutional Goal Statements," JA-90-01/AJCU/BCA. BC chose (and chooses) not to claim its legal right available to religiously affiliated colleges to take religion into consideration in the hiring and appointment of faculty and administrators and in the admission of undergraduates.

117. Gabriel-Marie Cardinal Garrone to the presidents of Catholic universities and the directors of Catholic institutions of higher learning, 25 April 1973, in *Periodica* 62 (1973): 659-61.

118. John W. Donohue, S.J., "Green Light for Universities," *America* 129 (21 July 1973): 29.

119. Pedro Arrupe, S.J., "The Jesuit Mission in the University Apostolate," address to Jesuit Academic Directors of Universities (Rome, 5 August 1975), in *Other Apostolates Today,* ed. Jerome Aixala, S.J. (Saint Louis: Institute of Jesuit Sources, 1981), 80-95.

120. Arrupe, "The Image of the Jesuit University President," in *Other Apostolates Today,* Appendix XV.

121. It was a familial Jesuit custom, derived from the Latin, to refer to themselves by the capitalized possessive pronoun *Nostri.* Fellow Jesuits were Ours, and their schools were Ours.

122. Kolvenbach, 9. John Paul II told them: "Your Universities and Higher Institutes, then, must guarantee and promote — as the first priority above all else — their character as Catholic academic centers which participate in the evangelical mission of the Church. . . . recognizably Catholic, and recognized for their academic quality." Kolvenbach, 92, 94.

123. Simon Decloux, S.J., "Jesuits in Formation; Jesuit Personnel," *Meeting of University Presidents and Rectors* (Frascati Conference), 122.

124. Michael Walsh specified two types of faculty in the BC theology department: "some committed Catholics for undergraduate courses and then some of a different type for electives and future graduate programs." Walsh to Donovan, 9 September 1966, box 26, file 6, AVP Files/CFD/RG16/UA/BCA.

125. David Riesman, "Reflection in Catholic Colleges, Especially Jesuit Institutions," *Journal of General Education* 34, no. 2 (summer 1982): 106-19. Riesman also remarked, almost in passing, that "the principal institutions of educational commitment in Catholicism tend to be the secondary schools."

He was also sympathetic to the Catholics' continued (but now flagging) determination to sponsor single-sex schools, especially on the secondary but also on the postsecondary level. Many young women had suffered from coeducation, "particularly when the peer culture is uncontrolled by adult authority and when the young people are thrown at each other, socially, sexually, and pharmacologically."

126. In 1952 Harvard's president, James B. Conant, a distinguished scientist of narrow philosophical perspective, publicly deplored the existence of private and parochial schools because they threatened the democratic unity of the country. Father Maxwell, then in his first year as president, and Father Rooney (much the more urbane of the two) both berated him. Maxwell, "BC Alumni Communion Breakfast," 19 April 1952, box 8, file "Speeches 1951-52," Papers of Joseph R. N. Maxwell, S.J., CFD/RG16/PP/UA/BCA; Rooney, "Address to Fordham Alumnae Meeting," 19 May 1952, 31-7-18-32, EBR/JEA/BCA. Professor David Riesman, as already mentioned, clashed with his president over the same issue.

127. In numbers of doctorates awarded, BC ranks twenty-fourth among all independent universities (for the period 1977-86). In percentage of graduates, however, it comes in fifty-second place and is outranked by Saint Louis, Fordham, Georgetown, and Loyola of Chicago. *Baccalaureate Origins of Doctorate Recipients, 1920 to 1986*, a ranking by discipline of doctoral-granting, private universities (Offices of Planning and Institutional Research, Georgetown University and Franklin and Marshall College, April 1989).

128. *(Boston) Business Journal* 15, no. 1 (17-23 February 1995): 1; Monan, Annual Faculty Convocation Address, 6 September 1995.

129. "On the Jesuit and Catholic Character of Boston College," a contribution from the Jesuit Community to the University Academic Planning Council, July 1995, n. 7. Brian E. Daley, S.J., a distinguished theologian serving at nearby Weston College, the Jesuit theologate, in his own very theoretical treatise on the matter, requires of laypeople collaborating with Jesuits in their universities only "a readiness to enter into serious conversations about the ultimate meaning of what the institution does, to ask hard questions about the implicit human values of curriculum, research and student life, and to hold the university's leadership accountable for practicing what they preach — for letting the vaunted ideals of the Christian gospel really make a difference, really transform the institution into something distinctively and selflessly humane." "Christ and the Catholic University," *America* 169 (11 September 1993): 14.

130. Charles F. Donovan, S.J., interview with the author, 11 August 1995.

131. In Maxwell's day the Jesuits had composed 30 percent of the faculty. Non-Catholics then already constituted 16 percent of the faculty and administration. This matched exactly the 16 percent of the student body who were not Catholics. Today it is believed to have been reversed: some suppose the student body comprises 80 percent Catholics, and the faculty 20 percent Catholics. Box 34, file "Lay Faculty in Jesuit Schools," JEA/BCA; surmise reported by Peter J. Kreeft, professor of philosophy, interview with the author, 13 September 1995.

132. A recent survey of Jesuit schools, Monan recalled, has reported that 30 percent of the students come from families with incomes of more than $100,000.

133. Information provided by the dean of enrollment management from the Cooperative Institutional Research Program (CIRP) administered annually by the American Council on Education (ACE). The present decline seems to run at about 1 percent per annum.

As one BC administrator notes, religious affiliation is one statistic that is not eagerly monitored on campus. Boston College does not conduct its own survey to ascertain the religious preferences of its student body. When it receives its annual table of institutional information from the ACE/CIRP survey and prepares excerpts for circulation among campus administrators, this statistic is omitted.

The national Jesuit educational office has a similar agnosticism on this subject. The AJCU scours its member institutions for all manner of useful information, which it then reports back to them in comparative tables. There have been reports on capital fund drives in progress, ethnic minority enrollments, undergraduate transfers, food service vendors, fringe benefits, Pell Grants, student loan default rates, market values of endowments, Jesuit community rebates — in more than 350 fact files compiled over the years. One subject has not been dealt with since 1970 (though it was a regular subject in the earlier JEA surveys): the proportion of Catholics among students, faculty, or administration.

134. Freeland, 287-88.

135. Protestant theologian Langdon Gilkey was the source chosen for this account of what it means to be Catholic.

136. "Goals for the Nineties: The Report of the University Planning Council," Boston College, January 1986, 1-21.

137. "The Catholic and Jesuit Identity of Boston College," subcommittee report for the University Planning Council, "Goals for the Nineties" (1986), BC-87-8/RG 1.15/UA/BCA.

138. "What It Means to Be Catholic and Jesuit," *Boston College Biweekly,* 6 October 1988, 8.

139. Joseph A. Appleyard, S.J., "Beyond the Thin Black Line," in *Assembly 1989: Jesuit Ministry in Higher Education* (Washington: The Jesuit Conference, 1990), 23-32; also in *Presence* (Loyola College in Maryland), 1990, 12-16.

140. Judith Wilt, "Catholic, Feminist, Ubiquitous," *Boston College Magazine,* winter 1993, 26-31.

141. The Jesuit Community at Boston College, "Making Old Words Live: Jesuit Education at Boston College," *Heights,* 15 October 1974, 9-12. Joseph Appleyard is said to have been the principal drafter.

142. The Jesuit Community at Boston College, *Jesuits and Boston College: Six Propositions for a Conversation,* September 1994.

143. "On the Jesuit and Catholic Character of Boston College, A Contribution from the Jesuit Community to the University Academic Planning Council, July 1995."

144. Michael J. Buckley, S.J., "The Catholic University as Pluralistic Forum," *Thought* 46, no. 181 (June 1971): 200-212; Buckley, "Concern for Justice," 228; Buckley, "Jesuit, Catholic Higher Education: Some Tentative Theses," *Review for Religious,* May-June 1983, 339-49; Buckley, "The Catholic University and Its Inherent Promise," *America* 168 (29 May 1993): 14-16.

145. Neenan's reason for ignoring the religious commitments of faculty has left behind the earlier view — widespread for years at BC — that there were legal obstacles to considering them. In 1964 the BC director of admissions believed that creed, like race and color, was a matter in which BC was not permitted to take an interest. Edmond D. Walsh, S.J., to Michael P. Walsh, S.J., box 7, file 2, PP/MPW/UA/BCA.

146. Liz Kowalczyk, "Diversity Challenging BC Tradition," *(Boston) Patriot Ledger,* 2 May 1994.

147. John L. Mahoney, Rattigan Professor of English, memorandum, 26 May 1995; interview with the author, 14 September 1995.

148. Preliminary announcement in the *(Boston) Pilot,* 5 September 1864.

149. Thomas E. Wangler, "The Religious Goals and Curriculum of Boston College: 1864-1900," in *Inscape: Studies Presented to Charles F. Donovan, S.J.,* ed. M. J. Connolly and Lawrence G. Jones (Chestnut Hill: Boston College, 1977), 211-21.

150. Frank D. Schubert, *A Sociological Study of Secularization Trends in the American Catholic University: Decatholicizing the Catholic Religious Tradition* (Lewiston, Maine: Edwin Mellen, 1990). Religious sociologist Peter Berger directed Schubert's research.

151. Schubert's method is simple, and perhaps incapable of identifying Catholic-perspective courses that were narrow and uncritical and others listed as mixed- or secular-perspective but taught by a critically Catholic intructor.

152. If the study is to be credited, the Catholic University of America was slowest of the three to enter the trend but, once having begun, seems to have done so with a vengeance.

153. Ganss, *Saint Ignatius' Idea,* 186-87.

729

154. J. Donald Monan, S.J., "Faculty and the Formative Educational Role," *Current Issues in Higher Education* 13, no. 1 (summer 1992): 21-25.

155. David J. O'Brien, "The Jesuits and Catholic Higher Education," *Studies in the Spirituality of Jesuits* 13, no. 5 (November 1981): 25. Jesuit response has been vigorous. As Leo Klein, S.J., then Xavier University's vice president for religious development, put it: "The closer one gets to the truth, the closer one gets to God." Bill Noblitt, "First Words," *Xavier,* summer 1993, inside front cover.

O'Brien shifts about. When the Jesuits claim they want distinctiveness and a place of their own, he derides the aspiration. Catholics are now "too far inside this culture" to wish for "a supposedly distinctive Catholicism." He approves of Buckley's Jesuit Institute, but with faint praise: it is reasonable "to build a vibrant Catholic intellectual community within a school," O'Brien says, only because it would be folly to try to reclaim Boston College itself as Catholic.

> Separate incorporation, professionalization, internal diversity, all make it difficult to articulate a compelling Catholic position *for the Catholic university as a whole.* To the extent one disdains the loss of control (and the bland mission statement) that comes with the increased numbers of non-Catholic faculty and staff, and demands that explicit Catholic ideals be placed at the center and in possession of the institution, then the problem of a Catholic identity leads to a solution which can only sound sectarian and restorationist, whatever the intention.

> "A Collegiate Conversation: Prof. O'Brien to Father Buckley," *America* 169 (11 September 1993): 19. See also O'Brien, "Conversations on Jesuit (and Catholic?) Higher Education: Jesuit Sì, Catholic . . . Not So Sure," *Conversations* 6 (fall 1994): 4-13.

156. Martin Tripole, S.J., *Faith beyond Justice: Widening the Perspective* (Saint Louis: Institute of Jesuit Sources, 1994), 135-38.

157. In the backwash of GC32 some capitulants cautioned that "justice" could wrongly be taken as a secular concept, despite the expressed caveat: "There can be no promotion of justice in the full and Christian sense unless we also preach Jesus Christ and the mystery of reconciliation He brings. For us, it is Christ who, in the last analysis, opens the way to the complete and definitive liberation of men" (GC32, Decree 1, 27). Justice, they argued, is uniquely discerned and distinctively pursued by the eyes of faith, and much of the talk about justice seemed to be in forgetfulness of faith. Francisco Ivern, S.J., "Our Mission Today: The Service of Faith and the Promotion of Justice," in *Conferences on the Chief Decrees of the Jesuit General Congregation XXXII,* ed. George Ganss, S.J. (Saint Louis: Institute of Jesuit Sources, 1976), 121-46.

158. Joseph Flanagan, S.J., "The Jesuit University as a Counter-Culture," 1989, manuscript, JA 89-01/AJCU/BCA.

159. Catholic institutions reported a drop from 79 to 67 percent in Catholics among their faculties between 1960 and 1970. BC was thus typical in this respect. James Michael Galvin, C.M., "Secularizing Trends in Roman Catholic Colleges and Universities, 1960-1970" (Ed.D. diss., Indiana University, 1971), 55.

160. Gregory Francis Lucey, [S.J.], "The Meaning and Maintenance of Catholicity as a Distinctive Characteristic of American, Catholic Higher Education: A Case Study" (Ph.D. diss., University of Wisconsin-Madison, 1978).

161. William P. Leahy, S.J., *Adapting to America: Catholics, Jesuits, and Higher Education in the Twentieth Century* (Washington: Georgetown University Press, 1991), 156. This was his doctoral dissertation at Stanford University in 1986.

162. Leahy, "At First Glance," interview article in *Boston College Magazine,* winter 1995, 49.

163. Leahy, *Adapting to America,* 156.

164. "Jesuits and University Life," in "The Interim Documents of General Congregation 34 of the Society of Jesus," 4.3, *National Jesuit News,* April 1995, 34.

165. R. Bruce Douglass, "The Academic Revolution and the Idea of a Catholic University," in McFadden, ed., *Georgetown at Two Hundred,* 45.

166. Joseph A. O'Hare, S.J., Commencement Address, Fordham University, 18 May 1996, copy provided by Fordham University.

167. Walsh, excerpts from recorded autobiographical interviews with Richard Freeland, in Ben Birnbaum, "Testament: The Walsh Tapes," *Boston College Magazine* 57,2 (Spring 1997): 23, 25.

168. Richard M. Freeland, *Academia's Golden Age: Universities in Massachusetts, 1945-1970* (New York: Oxford University Press, 1992), 259.

169. Peter Maurice Waters, *The Ursuline Achievement: A Philosophy of Education for Women* (North Carlton, Victoria, Australia: Colonna, 1994); Marie de Saint Jean Martin, O.S.U., *The Ursuline Method of Education* (Rahway, N.J.: Quinn & Boden, 1946).

170. The history of the College of New Rochelle is briefly told in a commemorative volume by James T. Schleifer, *The College of New Rochelle: An Extraordinary Story* (Virginia Beach: Donning Publishers, 1994). Personal memoirs of the early days have also been left behind by various Ursulines. See Irene Mahoney, O.S.U., "Reflections on Mother Irene" (1988); Mother Xavier Fitzgerald, O.S.U., "Memoirs"; Mother Ignatius Wallace, O.S.U., "Memoirs"; Mother Jane Frances Cuddy, O.S.U., "History of the College of New Rochelle" (ca. 1940); Sister Gertrude (Elizabeth) Farmer, O.S.U., "Biography of M. Irene Gill" (1968); Sister Thomas Aquinas O'Reilly, O.S.U., "History of the College of New Rochelle, 1904-1974" (1977), later published as "Looking Backward: The College according to Quiney," *College of New Rochelle Quarterly* 55, no. 3 (December 1978): 9-15; Mary Russo, O.S.U., "A History of the Eastern Province of the United States of the Roman Union of the Order of St. Ursula, 1535-1989" (New Rochelle, 1989). These unpublished materials are to be found in the College of New Rochelle Archives (CNRA), boxes 5-14-4, 5-15-1, 2, 3, 4, 5.

171. The earliest of the Catholic women's colleges announced in the first prospectus of its academy: "As members of the Institution profess the Catholic religion, the exercises of religious worship are Catholic; but members of every other religious denomination are received; of whom it is only required that they assist with propriety and decency at the public duties of religion." "Convent and Academy of the Sisters of Providence," 9 October 1841, Sisters of Providence Archives, Saint Mary-of-the-Woods, Indiana.

172. Eileen Mary Brewer, *Nuns and the Education of Catholic Women, 1860-1920* (Chicago: Loyola University Press, 1987), 15.

173. Cynthia Farr Brown, "Leading Women: Female Leadership in American Women's Higher Education" (Ph.D. diss., Brandeis University, 1992). Brewer, whose study concerns secondary, not collegiate, education, observes that convent schools inducted their pupils into the withdrawn, orderly, submissive life of the sisters. The colleges, whatever their traditions of modesty and propriety, were much more a compromise between the youthfulness of the students and the decorum of the women religious. But one Brewer observation may be equally applicable to them:

> Although the sisters and their former students rarely questioned male authority in the church, in the home, or in the workplace, they managed to construct a separate female world for the ostensible purpose of spiritual sustenance and church work. In convents, sodalities, alumnae associations and other religious organizations, these women assumed leadership positions and exercised talents without need or desire for male intrusion. While remaining perfectly faithful to the church, they transcended the roles assigned them and looked to each other for support and affirmation. At a far deeper level than their politically active Protestant counterparts who formed women's rights groups and backed female

suffrage, many Catholic women thoroughly yet unintentionally rejected male domination by choosing to live in an all-female society. Nuns provided their female co-religionists with examples of productive, happy lives without the benefit of husbands and family.

Brewer, 136.

174. *College of Saint Angela Bulletin, 1906-1908,* 8. In 1900 Ursulines throughout the world were invited to join in a single congregation known as the Ursulines of the Roman Union. The autonomous Community of Saint Teresa joined, and found itself a member of the Eastern Province of the United States. Mother Irene, who would serve several terms as provincial superior, brought the headquarters to New Rochelle.

175. Sister M. St. Mel Kennedy, O.S.F., "The Faculty in Catholic Colleges for Women," *Catholic Educational Review* 59 (1961): 289-98. That year 25 percent of all newly appointed faculty throughout the country possessed earned doctorates.

176. One notable exception was the college's acquisition of its first, historic building, Leland Castle. Mother Irene had purchased it from Adrian Iselin, Jr., who then became a charter trustee. Her blandishments eventually persuaded him to forgive the outstanding remainder of the purchase price, making him their earliest and most generous benefactor.

177. Joseph Gerard Brennan, *The Education of a Prejudiced Man* (New York: Scribners, 1977), 65. Brennan served in the Navy, then taught at Barnard College, and concluded his career on the faculty of the U.S. Naval War College.

178. *CNR Bulletin, 1944-45,* 89.

179. Transcript of a faculty meeting, 14 November 1951, CNRA, box 2-4-1.

180. The text goes on to explain that students coming from state schools were provided with an extra, "remedial" course in theology (as "Christian doctrine," later "religion," had just come to be called). The students called this course "Idiot Theology." "Data Presented for Consideration of the Commission on Institutions of Higher Education, Middle States Association of Colleges and Secondary Schools, by the College of New Rochelle," December 1955, A3, 8, CNRA, box 2-4-1. The Middle States reevaluation contained a suggestion that the Ursuline Order and the College of New Rochelle might better be separately incorporated, managed, and audited. The board began to follow through on this suggestion, but then the idea was dropped until the 1970s.

181. Oona Burke, "New Rochelle: A Famous Ursuline College for Women Stresses Participation in the Liturgical Life," *Jubilee,* June 1958, 6-13.

182. "Data Presented for Consideration" (1955), 22.

183. Statements of Thomas J. Darby, Thomas F. Maher, Thomas Moriarty, and John J. Quinn, November/December 1956, CNRA, box 3-8-5, file "Laity vs. Clergy: Academic Freedom." It is of interest that in this same period a lecture series brought to campus such independent thinkers as John Courtney Murray, S.J., Heinrich Rommen, Msgr. Reynold Hillenbrand, William Lynch, S.J., and John Corridan, S.J.

184. M. D. Ann [Mother Dorothy Ann Kelly, O.S.U.], "Unity in Our Concept of the CNR Ideal," September 1960, CNRA, box 7-19-1.

185. Office of Student Affairs Survey, Lent 1960, CNRA, box 29-107-2, "Campus Questionnaires, Surveys."

186. John J. Meng, "Catholics Face a New Frontier," CNR commencement address, 5 June 1961, CNRA, box 6-17-21.

187. "Data Presented for Consideration of the Commission on Institutions of Higher Education, Middle States Association of Colleges and Secondary Schools, by College of New Rochelle, December 1965," 2, CNRA, box 2-4-4.

188. This merited special praise from the visitation team: "Evaluation Committee Report, Middle States Association of Colleges and Secondary Schools," March 1966, 9, CNRA, box 2-4-4.

189. Admissions Task Force (James Middleton and Sr. Mary Alice [Gallin, O.S.U.]),

Memorandum to administrators with tentative report, June 1969, 2, CNRA 13-37-6; "Admissions Study"; Mother Jean Marie Casey, "Admissions and Enrollment Report to NCEA," 1965, CNRA, box 6-18-1, "Surveys."

190. Barbara Wismer McManus, '64, "Riding the Winds: CNR in the 1960s and 1990s," *CNR Quarterly* 67, no. 3 (summer 1995): 5.

191. *Time,* 4 August 1967, 86. The copy is drafted with adman's hyperbole: there were then about as few girls from the West and South as there were non-Catholics.

192. Various minutes and drafts, 1965-66, CNRA, 6-17-2, "A-B." These proceedings were within memory of the first layman appointed to the theology faculty, John Blakeley, whose departure was ascribed to shaky orthodoxy. One student of the time commented: "To my mind, he was no more radical than Mother Emmanuel." McManus, 4.

193. Schleifer, 87.

194. Mary Ellen Goodman, "Report to the Bundy Committee," 17 August 1967, Hesburgh Papers (CPHS) 127/11, University of Notre Dame Archives (UNDA).

195. There was a strong postmortem consensus that the proposed constitution was rejected on economic grounds as containing various provisions that would foster tax increases. Most commentators believed the provision removing the ban on aid to religious higher education would surely have succeeded, as Catholics were assured it would be, in a separate referendum. Peter Kihss, "Defeat of the Charter Attributed to Economic, Not Ethnic, Factor," *New York Times,* 9 November 1967; Sydney W. Schanberg, "Partisan Fight Shaping Up on Salvaging of Charter," *New York Times,* 9 November 1967; Schanberg, "Now What for New York Constitution?" *New York Times,* 12 November 1967; "The Proposed 1967 New York State Constitution: A Brief Political History," report by Research Institute for Catholic Education in New York State, 15 November 1967, CNRA, box 6-17-21.

196. Maximilian W. Kemper, Memorandum to the Select Committee, 7 August 1967, CPHS 127/16, 22. UNDA. Kemper read the first *Maryland* decision, *Horace Mann League v Board of Public Works of Maryland,* as having given the federal Constitution an interpretation as anti-religious as New York's "Blaine Amendment."

197. Sister Mary Robert Falls, O.S.U., to McGeorge Bundy, 17 July 1967. Her letter is a reply to Bundy's request for her understanding of the broad issues, and was sent two months after his desired deadline, implying that it was not casually drafted.

198. Here the committee was borrowing from Justice Frankfurter's separate opinion in *McGowan* v. *Maryland* (1961) and from its understanding of the later *Horace Mann League* case.

199. *New York State and Private Higher Education,* Report of the Select Committee on the Future of Private and Independent Higher Education in New York State (Albany, January 1968), 48-51. In its earlier draft the committee had used another descriptor for institutions to be excluded from the program: those "whose controlling purpose is religious indoctrination." Draft Report, November 1967, 35, CPHS 127/25, UNDA.

200. Former Judge Charles Desmond; Minutes of a special meeting of the Conference of Catholic Colleges and Universities, State of New York, 15 October 1968, CNRA, box 6-17-2.

201. "Implementing Non-Public College Aid," Staff Report Number 2, State Education Department, the University of the State of New York, 26 June 1968, 2-4, CNRA, box 6-17-2; Francis H. Horn, president of the Commission on Independent Colleges and Universities (of the State of New York), "Memorandum to Presidents of the Commission's Constituent Members," 23 July 1968, 5, CNRA, box 6-17-2, file "Internal A-B."

202. "Private Institutions Showing Decrease in Enrollment, 1966-1967," Report to the Select Committee, November 1967, CPHS 127/25, UNDA.

203. Falls to Bundy, 17 July 1967, 1, CNRA, box 6-178-2.

204. Falls to Sister M. Celeste Shaugnessy, O.S.U., 11 July 1968, CNRA, box 6-17-2; also, Falls to Earl J. McGrath, director of the Institute of Higher Education at Teachers College, 4 February 1967, CNRA, box 6-17-2.

205. Alice Gallin, O.S.U., "The Contribution of Religious Commitment to Education," *NICM Journal* 2, no. 4 (1977): 36.

206. Horn, 6.

207. Timothy S. Healy, S.J., "Introduction," in Gellhorn and Greenawalt, 2. Healy, late of Fordham and later of Georgetown, was then serving as vice chancellor for academic affairs at the City University of New York. His own views on assimilation were then in flux.

208. James E. Allen, Jr., to Chief Executive Officers of Institutions of Higher Education, 12 August 1968, CNRA, box 6-17-2.

209. James M. Demske, S.J., president of Canisius College and of the Conference of Catholic Colleges and Universities of the State of New York, to "Members of the CCCUNY who have applied or will or may apply for the State grant," 4 November 1968, CNRA, box 6-17-2.

210. Admissions Task Force, "Memorandum," 1969.

211. The institutions applying for Bundy money reported on average that 4 percent of their income came from such rebates by their sponsoring religious communities: Edward Michael O'Keefe, "The Influence of New York State Aid to Private Colleges and Universities" (Ph.D. diss., New York University, 1974), 109.

212. "Constitutional Eligibility of the College of New Rochelle for State Aid Pursuant to Chapter 677 of the Laws of 1963," mailed on 9 September 1969, CNRA, box 3-8-4.

213. *College of New Rochelle* v *Ewald B. Nyquist,* 37 App Div 2d 461, 326 NYS 2d 765 (1971). Copies of the record on appeal and of appellate briefs for both parties were kindly provided by Thomas A. Conniff, Esq., of Cusack and Stiles, New York, who is the surviving member of the college's litigating team.

214. *College of New Rochelle* v *Ewald B. Nyquist,* New York Supreme Court, Appellate Division, 1971, Brief of the College, 11-13, 29, 38-39.

215. The law on which the court rendered judgment had just been defined by *Board of Education* v *Allen,* 392 US 236 (1968); *Walz* v *Tax Commission,* 397 US 664 (1970); *Lemon* v *Kurtzman,* with *Earley* v *DiCenso,* and *Robinson* v *DiCenso,* 403 US 602 (1971); *Tilton* v *Richardson,* 403 US 672 (1971).

216. Falls to Joseph W. McGovern, chancellor of the Board of Regents, 19 January 1970, CNRA, box 3-8-1-4.

217. Falls to Nyquist, 20 February 1970, CNRA, box 6-17-2; Nyquist to Falls, 2 March 1970, CNRA, box 3-8-4. In 1973 the College of New Rochelle would honor Ewald Nyquist with an honorary doctorate.

218. Minutes of the Board of Trustees, 20 March 1969, CNRA, box 3-9-2. Some sense of the confused and energetic self-definition preoccupying the CNR community at the time regarding "secularity" can be found in "Thinking about the Unthinkable Question," *Alumnae News* 46, no. 1 (1969): 2-11; Nancy Quirk Keefe, "Who's in Charge Here?" *Alumnae News* 46, no. 2 (1969): 5-10; "President's Report," *Alumnae News* 48, no. 4 (winter 1971-72): 1-19.

219. Minutes of the Board of Trustees, 15 May 1970, CNRA, box 3-9-2. The vote to go forward with litigation was 15-0-1.

220. "Report by the Coeducation Committee of the College of New Rochelle," 21 May 1970, CNRA, box 3-9-2.

221. By 1980 only 39 percent of those existing in 1960 would survive. Their overall enrollments (by head count), however, were destined to increase throughout the 1970s. Catholic, or "Catholic," colleges would constitute 44 percent of the total. Women's College Coalition, *Profile II: A Second Profile of Women's Colleges — Analysis of the Data* (Washington, 1981); also "Some Statistics on Women's Colleges" (1995).

222. Joseph P. McMurray, "Memorandum to Alumnae, Parents and Friends," 21 January 1972, CNRA, box 3-8-4.

223. James B. Makos, assistant to the president, to McMurray, 5 October 1970, CNRA, box 6-18-5.

224. Dorothy Ann Kelly, O.S.U., "Report to the Board of Trustees," 27 September 1972, CNRA, box 7-19-1.

225. Kelly, "Women in the 70s," *Alumnae News* 50, no. 1 (March 1973): 5-8.

226. The Middle States evaluation team in 1974 sent the college a stern admonition to use more responsible financial controls in both the SNR and the GRS. "Evaluation Committee Report, Middle States Association of Colleges and Secondary Schools," December 1974, 15, CNRA, box 2-4-6.

227. Kelly, "Report of the President," *Alumnae News* 50, no. 3 (September 1973): 1.

228. Kelly, "More Than Survival," Report of the President, *Alumnae News* 52, no. 3 (September 1975): 1; Memorandum from the Ursuline Trustees of CNR to the Ursuline Provincial Council, 22 April 1976, CNRA, box 3-9-4.

229. Ms. Joan Bristol, vice president for student services, and Sr. Frances Lyle, O.S.U., assistant registrar, have provided several of the demographic statistics presented here.

230. Dr. Ronald Pollack, director of financial aid, interview with the author, 20 November 1995.

231. Sister Frances Lyle, O.S.U., assistant registrar, interview with the author, 27 November 1995; "College of New Rochelle Self-Study Report for the Commission on Institutions of Higher Education, Middle States Association of Colleges and Schools," January 1992, CNRA, box 2-5-4.

232. Steven Greenhouse, "Bias Charged against Branch-Campus Faculty," *New York Times,* 19 February 1997, B3.

233. "Report to Middle States," 1992, Appendix XV, "SAS Core and Physical Education Curriculum."

234. The evaluation team for the 1982 reaccreditation was scathing in its criticism of the SNR. Commending the college for its attention to "this underserved and often disadvantaged clientele," it nonetheless faulted the SNR for trying to carry so many students on nearly a full-time class load when two-thirds of them were fully employed. The life experience portfolios were "not analytical and not consistently and specifically related to course, curricular or degree objectives," there was no curricular coherence or disciplinary progression in the courses offered, there were no faculty available as mentors, there had been no redesign of the program though the art of adult education had progressed during its first ten years of existence. The program, in sum, lacked academic credibility enough to vouch for the integrity of the degree. "Evaluation Committee Report, Middle States Association of Colleges and Schools," March 1982, 7-10, CNRA, box 2-5-1.

235. "Data Presented for Consideration of the Commission on Institutions of Higher Education, Middle States Association of Colleges and Secondary Schools, by the College of New Rochelle," October 1974, 2-3, CNRA, box 2-4-6.

236. Eleanor B. Wymard, "An Academic Profile: Laywomen in Women's Catholic Colleges," *Commonweal* 14, no. 21 (14 October 1977): 655.

237. Minutes of the Board of Trustees, 15 May 1975, CNRA, box 3-9-3.

238. A 1974 survey reported that 75-80 percent of the students identified themselves as Catholics. Kitty Karol, "Religion on Campus: Changed Since '04," *Tatler,* 4 October 1974.

239. "Trends for 1971-1989," in the American Freshman and Follow-Up Survey (CIRP), nationally administered by the UCLA Higher Education Research Institute on behalf of the American Council on Education. "College of New Rochelle Self-Study Report for the Commission on Institutions of Higher Education, Middle States Association of Colleges and Schools," January 1992, Exhibit L.

240. Report of Religious Studies Department, "College of New Rochelle Self-Study Report for the Commission on Institutions of Higher Education, Middle States Association of Colleges and Schools," January 1992, Exhibit K.

241. Statement approved by the SAS and SNR faculty, 22 November 1988, "College of

New Rochelle Self-Study Report for the Commission on Institutions of Higher Education, Middle States Association of Colleges and Schools," January 1992, Exhibit J.

242. Stephen J. Sweeny, "State Financial Assistance and Selected Elements Influencing Religious Character in Catholic Colleges Sponsored by Women Religious" (Ph.D. diss., New York University, 1991), 70. There is great deviation in the sample. Copy courtesy of the author, senior vice president for academic affairs at CNR, and president as of 1997.

243. Gellhorn and Greenawalt, 30.

244. Kelly, "A College Has Three Lives . . . ," Report of the President, *College of New Rochelle Quarterly* 56, no. 4 (fall 1979): 16.

245. Kelly, "Legacy of the Past and Promises for the Future," address at the 1992 alumnae/i weekend, in *College of New Rochelle 1992 Annual Report,* 9.

Presidents of Catholic colleges and universities in New York later claimed that all of the changes they had enacted would have been made even without the Bundy restrictions, except for the suppression of "Catholic" in their catalogues. Edward F. Maloney, S.J., "A Study of the Religious Orientation of Catholic Colleges in New York State from 1962 to 1972" (Ph.D. diss., New York University, 1974), 117-18.

246. Kelly, "Report of the President," *Alumnae News* 50, no. 3 (September 1973): 2.

247. Schleifer, 89; Maloney, 118; O'Keefe, 3, 134; Sweeny, 156; Gallin, "The Contribution of Religious Commitment," 42; Kelly, "A College Has Three Lives," 16.

248. John Cogley, "The Future of an Illusion," *Commonweal,* 2 June 1967, 310-16.

249. Robert Hassenger, "A Question of Distinctiveness," *Commonweal,* 19 April 1968, 134-36.

250. Sister Emmanuel McIver, O.S.U., in "Thinking about the Unthinkable Question," *College of New Rochelle Alumni News* 46, no. 1 (1969): 5-8.

251. Lynda Georgianna, in "Thinking about the Unthinkable Question," *College of New Rochelle Alumni News* 46, no. 1 (1969): 11.

252. Luther H. Hoopes, of Interpreting Institutions, to Katherine V. Henderson, dean of SAS, 14 November 1974, enclosing "Observations and Ideas," 2, CNRA, box 13-37-6.

253. Brown, 406-58.

254. Gallin, "The Contribution of Religious Commitment," 42; revised and published the next year for the campus community: "A Question of Identity: A Personal Perspective on the 'Catholic College,' " *College of New Rochelle Quarterly* 55, no. 3 (December 1978): 20-24; "Catholic Higher Education Today — The Challenges of Ambiguity," *Cross Currents* 43, no. 4 (winter 1993/94): 485. Gallin admits that Catholic colleges today tend to define themselves differently to satisfy the contrary demands of different audiences, in a manner she calls "ambiguous." Her examples portray them as "equivocal."

255. O'Keefe, 3, 135.

256. Kelly, in *Report of the President,* 1989, 5.

257. Kelly, "For the Sake of the Future," Report of the President, *College of New Rochelle Quarterly* 58, no. 3 (fall 1981): 16.

258. Kelly, "Legacy of the Past," 1992, 10.

259. "College of New Rochelle Self-Study Report for the Commission on Institutions of Higher Education, Middle States Association of Colleges and Schools," January 1992, Exhibit A.

260. Some other colleges formerly directed by the Institute but now either closed or functioning only as secondary schools include Christian Brothers College in Saint Louis; Rock Hill Normal Institute in Ammendale, Maryland; Calvert Hall in Baltimore; and Saint John's College in Washington. The University of Scranton was theirs from 1888 until 1942.

261. For foundation of the Christian Brothers, also known as the de La Salle Brothers, see Luke Salm, F.S.C., *This Work Is Yours: The Life of Saint John Baptiste de La Salle* (Romeoville, Ill.: Christian Brothers Publications, 1989).

262. Much of what follows is grounded on Brother Matthew McDevitt (F.S.C.), *The First*

Century of St. Mary's College (Moraga: Saint Mary's College of California, 1979), and Ronald E. Isetti, F.S.C., *Called to the Pacific: A History of the Christian Brothers of the San Francisco District, 1868-1944* (Moraga: Saint Mary's College of California, 1979).

263. Raymond Joseph White, "The Effects of Internal Goals and External Pressures in the Development of a Catholic Liberal Arts College" (Ph.D. diss., University of California, Berkeley, 1981), 9-18. White was then director of internal research at Saint Mary's College, and is now vice president for administration.

264. White, 44, 49.

265. Jesuits at the time were by rule forbidden to teach vocational subjects, just as the Christian Brothers were forbidden to teach classical subjects. Power, *History of Catholic Higher Education*, 98; Power, *Catholic Higher Education in America* (New York: Appleton-Century-Crofts, 1972), 184-87.

266. In 1930 laymen outnumbered brothers on the faculty eighteen to twelve. White, 78.

267. Isetti, *Called to the Pacific*, 243-44.

268. Even so, it would not be until 1963 that the college was finally freed from debt, at which time it began a series of annual deficits that would accumulate another great debt. White, 168, 179.

269. McDevitt, 222.

270. P. 18.

271. P. 2.

272. Minutes of the Academic Council, 9, 22, and 27 May 1968; Rafael Alan Pollock, dean of the college, Memorandum to the Faculty, 28 May 1968, Saint Mary's College of California Archives (SMCA).

273. "The Interview: Garvey on Anything," *Saint Mary's Collegian*, 1 March 1968, 3. The chaplain reported that he was himself thinking of studying for a higher degree in the social sciences.

274. Unsigned editorial, *Saint Mary's Collegian*, 15 March 1968, 4.

275. Minutes of Faculty Meeting, 2 April 1969, SMCA.

276. Dean Pollock, Memorandum to Brother Michael Quinn, F.S.C., president, 28 May 1969, SMCA.

277. Mike McLean, "The Question of Uniqueness, of a Reason to Be, of Ceasing to Be," *Saint Mary's Collegian*, 15 March 1968, 4.

278. Frank Ellis, "Ellis Discusses the Catholicity of the College," *Saint Mary's Collegian*, 29 March 1968, 8.

279. A[lbert] Dragstedt, letter to the editor, *Saint Mary's Collegian*, 26 April 1968, 4. See also Ronald P. McArthur, "McArthur Responds to Dragstedt, Ellis," *Saint Mary's Collegian*, 17 May 1968, 11.

280. "The Interview: Pollock on Catholicism," *Saint Mary's Collegian*, 26 April 1968, 7; "Pollock Continued from Last Issue," *Saint Mary's Collegian*, 17 May 1968, 7.

281. [Ronald P. McArthur, Marcus Berquist, John W. Neumayr, and Edmund Doland, F.S.C.], *A Proposal for the Fulfillment of Catholic Liberal Education* (San Rafael, Calif.: Thomas Aquinas College, 1969). This treatise, known as the founding document of Thomas Aquinas College, has been amended and repeatedly reprinted with diverse introductions, most recently in 1993.

282. Ronald P. McArthur, *The Roots of Modern Education* (*The Intercollegiate Review*, 1968), by permission of the author.

283. White, 97.

284. Western Association of Schools and Colleges [WASC], "Report on Visit to Saint Mary's College," October 23, 24, 1969, 15, SMCA.

285. Brother Cyril Ash, F.S.C., "History of St. Mary's College" (1915), 95; quoted in White, 77.

286. "Documentation: The General Chapter and the Lasallian Family," *Educational Per-*

spectives 11, no. 2 (spring 1994): 40. On the other hand, the lay faculty served with very scanty salaries, and with long loyalty, and deserved what was said in public of them in 1943: "A distinguished staff of lay teachers, recruited over a period of years, assist the brothers in various departments, such as history, philosophy, literature and science." *The Making of Men: The Meaning of Education at St. Mary's College* (Moraga: Saint Mary's College, 1943), 6; quoted in White, 79.

287. Luke Salm, F.S.C., *A Religious Institute in Transition: The Story of Three General Chapters* (Romeoville, Ill.: Christian Brothers Publications, 1992), 11, 35; William Edward Mann, F.S.C., *The Lasallian School: Where Teachers Assist Parents in the Education and Formation of Children* (Narragansett, R.I.: Brothers of the Christian Schools–Long Island-New England Province, 1991), 9, 36.

288. "Poll Depicts Saint Mary's Man," *Saint Mary's Collegian,* 15 March 1968, 1. This was possibly the first year Saint Mary's had participated in the annual ACE/CIRP freshman survey.

289. Minutes of the Board of Trustees, 24 April 1969, 26-27, SMCA. This financial pledge occasioned a lengthy discussion by the trustees about what it meant for SMC to call itself Catholic, or Christian. Included were the issues of theology and philosophy in the curriculum, and Christian and non-Christian faculty (also no longer Catholic and non-Catholic), and the need for explicit public policy statements.

290. For the events of 1969-72, see "SMC Self-Evaluation Study for WASC," 1975, 136-43, SMCA.

291. Anderson to the Christian Brothers of the District, 23 July 1970, 3, SMCA.

292. Brother Mel Anderson, F.S.C., "Remarks on Accepting the 'Pro Ecclesia et Pontifice' Medal, *Educational Perspectives* (SMC) 12, no. 1 (fall 1994): 3.

293. Anderson to the Board of Trustees, 28 August 1972, SMCA.

294. Memorandum of faculty members Frankel et al. to Anderson, "Increased Faculty Participation in the Government of Saint Mary's College," August 1972, SMCA.

295. Anderson to the Board of Trustees, 19 September 1972; Anderson to the Board, "Commentary on Proposal Submitted by Professors Frankel, et al.," 19 September 1972, SMCA.

296. Anderson to the Board of Trustees, 28 August 1972, SMCA. Anderson rarely if ever expressed in public his conviction of how serious and uncompromisable a conflict was being raised by the faculty dissidents. In his welcoming address to the faculty that same month, he simply announced forthcoming conversations regarding increased faculty representation in decision making, and quoted Vatican II:

> [The Catholic school's] special function is to create for the school community a special atmosphere animated by the Gospel spirit of freedom and charity, to help youth grow according to the new creatures they were made through baptism, as they develop their own personalities, and finally to order the whole of human culture to the news of salvation so that the knowledge the students gradually acquire of the world, life and man is illumined by faith.

11 September 1972, SMCA.

297. Anderson to the Christian Brothers of the District, 23 July 1970, SMCA.

298. Anderson to the Christian Brothers of the District, 1 September 1971, SMCA.

299. Anderson to the Christian Brothers of the District, 1 September 1972, SMCA.

300. Questionnaire given to Christian Brothers at SMC, March 1974; results circulated by Anderson to brothers, 10 January 1978, SMCA.

301. White, 181.

302. Brother John Anthony (previously Dominic) Ruegg, F.S.C., interview with the author, 7 February 1996; "SMC Self-Evaluation Study for WASC," 15 November 1979, 16-18, SMCA.

303. "WASC Re-accreditation Team Reports," 1975, 1977; "St. Mary's College (California)," *AAUP Bulletin,* spring 1976, 70ff.; Brother William Beatie, F.S.C., academic vice

president, Memorandum to Board of Trustees, 20 September 1979; Minutes of the Faculty Assembly, 1977-78; Kay J. Andersen, executive director of WASC, to Brother Mel Anderson, 27 February 1976, and 27 February 1978 (placing SMC on probation); "WASC Interim Report on Probation, Revised August 1977," SMCA.

304. "SMC Self-Evaluation Study for WASC," 15 November 1979; "Report on Interpersonal Relations, Saint Mary's College," June 1979, 28, SMCA.

305. WASC reaccreditation team report, transcript of the exit interview, in Memorandum of Academic Vice President William J. Hynes, 4 March 1993; Hynes, "Excerpts from May 17, 1993 Address, 'Academic State of the College,' " *Educational Perspectives* 11, no. 1 (fall 1993): 32.

306. Largesse in the San Francisco District was not so abundant, amounting to 8 percent and 7 percent at those respective times.

307. "The Brother of the Christian Schools in the World Today: A Declaration," §§6, 13, 28-29, in *The "Declaration": Text and Contents,* ed. Michael F. Meister, F.S.C. (Landover, Md.: Christian Brothers Conference, 1994), 289, 295-96, 310-11.

308. Michel Sauvage, F.S.C., "The 'Declaration': Refoundation or Renewal?" in *The "Declaration,"* 209.

309. Meister, "Reflections on the Sacrament of Education," in *The "Declaration,"* 48.

310. William Ammentorp, *The Committed: A Sociological Study of the Brothers of the Christian Schools* (Winona, Minn.: Saint Mary's College Press, 1968), 111.

311. Brother John Johnston, F.S.C., "Lasallian Educational Ministry," paper prepared for delivery at the United States/Toronto Regional Convention, Saint Mary's College of California, 11 August 1984; Johnston, "The Christian Brothers and the Apostolate of Higher Education: Some Reflections," an invited address on the SMC campus to presidents and rectors of brothers' institutions of higher education, 13 July 1992, *Educational Perspectives* 10, no. 1 (fall 1992): 22-29.

312. Mann, 36.

313. Ms. Barbara Nicholson, director of personnel services, interview with the author.

314. At one crucial point it had been the brothers' loan of $2 million that had saved the college from bankruptcy. By the 1980s, when the brothers were preparing to forgive that loan, their patronage was not well remembered.

315. Johnston, "Lasallian Educational Ministry."

316. See Sauvage, 219.

317. "Report of the Interpersonal Relations Committee," May 1977, 7, SMCA.

318. Mann, 20. See also Regional Educational Committee of the Christian Brothers, *Characteristics of Lasallian Schools* (Landover, Md.: Christian Brothers Conference, 1986).

319. Johnston, "The Christian Brothers."

320. Ronald Isetti, *The Catholic Character of Saint Mary's College: Intellectual Tradition or Christian Service,* Professor of the Year Address (Moraga: Saint Mary's College of California, 23 March 1994), 8-9.

321. Ronald Isetti, professor of history, interview with the author, 6 December 1995.

322. *Saint Mary's College Bulletin, 1979-81,* 7.

323. "SMC Self-Evaluation Study for WASC," 15 November 1979, 52, SMCA.

324. "WASC Re-accreditation Team Report," 1980, 20; see also 5, 13, 20-23, SMCA. There is evidence that this embarrassing admonition was taken to heart. The Extended Education students, who are nontraditional transfer students seeking a degree, must have fulfilled the same basic course requirements as traditional undergraduate transfer students. To assure comparable liberal studies and religious studies components in their curriculum, the Critical Perspectives Department, working in tandem with the Collegiate Seminar, provides them with trained part-time faculty who teach Great Books Seminars, and Great Lives Seminars in lieu of religious studies. Jeanne Foster, chair of the Critical Studies Department, interview with the author,

7 February 1996; Foster, *Critical Perspectives Student Guide,* October 1994. The provision of these basic requirements does not, of course, convert Management and Health Services Administration into liberal arts.

An earlier policy statement adopted by the board of trustees at the beginning of Brother Dominic's expansion program had been more candid:

Saint Mary's College historically has been a small, residential, primarily liberal arts Catholic college. She should remain true to this heritage which must always be the core and thrust of her educational program. Nevertheless, because of her favored position in Contra Costa County, she should also develop other quality educational endeavors which not only complement what she is but which also provide a wider service to the community:

1. In-service and continuing education.
2. Graduate Division.
3. Cooperative Programs with recognized educational institutes which would like their students to have a liberal arts component in their education.

Minutes of the Board of Trustees, 2 December 1974, 163, SMCA.

While the expansion was still under way, some on campus noticed that theory continued to ignore practice: "Questions raised more than fifty years ago have yet to receive definitive answers: Should we adopt a strict or flexible interpretation of what is meant by the liberal arts? Where is the coherent educational philosophy that embraces professional programs, the liberal arts, and programs emphasizing social consciousness?" ("Report of the Interpersonal Relations Committee," May 1977, 5, SMCA).

325. "WASC Re-accreditation Team Report," 1980, 23, SMCA.

326. White, 189-90.

327. "Degrees Granted, 1988-1992," Office of the Registrar, 24 November 1992; "SMC WASC Self-Study Report," December 1992, 34, SMCA. In 1983-84, only 15 percent of degrees awarded were in the traditional liberal disciplines. "SMC Self-Evaluation Study for WASC," July 1985, Sec. 6, 10-18, SMCA. The visiting team remarked on "the evident lack of a sense of institutional identification with new directions in the College," whose faculties and purposes had not been incorporated into the college's inner life. "WASC Re-accreditation Team Report," 14-17 October 1985, Standard Two: Purposes, 9-10, SMCA.

328. For a while the Collegiate Seminar was discontinued, but its format was essentially preserved during the interim in the "World Classics," a required course for all students (sixteen credits for students in Liberal Arts, and eight for those in Science or Economics).

329. "Mission Statement for the School of Liberal Arts," in Saint Mary's College of California, *Report of the New Century Committee,* submitted to the Board of Trustees, 1 November 1995, 32.

330. Edwin M. Epstein, "SEBA and the College's Catholic, Lasallian, Liberal Arts Character: A New Dean's Perspective," *Educational Perspectives* 12, no. 2 (spring 1995): 23-24.

331. Asbjorn Moseidjord, in "Liberal Arts Institute: Three Perspectives," Saint Mary's College of California *Faculty News* 16, no. 1 (fall 1995): 2.

332. For the late 1960s, see White, 108 (96 percent); also the similar estimate by Ellis, above. For recent years, see Brother James Leahy, F.S.C., "Final Draft of the Self-Study of the Department of Religious Studies," 7 May 1992, 5, SMCA (±70 percent); "SMC Self-Evaluation Study for WASC," December 1992, 82, SMCA (±60 percent); Hynes, "A Closer Look at SMC Undergraduates: Astin Exit Data," 18 May 1994, 5, SMCA (the senior class had entered with 69 percent and was exiting with 62 percent).

333. Anderson, "Report on the Catholicity of Saint Mary's College to the Sixth District Chapter, District of San Francisco, 1982," 15-16, quoted by permission of the District Archives.

334. For instance, after the visit to the United States by John Paul II in 1987, the faculty discussed his address to Catholic higher education in a very sophisticated symposium. Participants

were from the Departments of Mathematics, English, Philosophy, Biology, and Religious Studies. One of the participants took what was for the time a remarkable position, grounding a Catholic college on a sacramental unity but not on the church:

> What makes Catholic to be Catholic is not a sentiment or attitude, not a technique or a method, not even a "confession" to a sort of system of dogmas or code of morals: it is, rather, sacramental incorporation through liturgical worship in the Person and Action of Christ to the Father in the unity of the Holy Spirit.
>
> Consequently, while Saint Mary's College is manifold in schools and programs and pluralist in religious orientations of members of the community, the principle of unity is the mystery celebrated in the liturgy; a unity of studies which preserves the diversity of subject matter and method; a unity of persons through cooperation in a common endeavor whose explicit mission is the education in Christ of the whole person but which may be implicitly engaged under the sign of justice or of truth or of benevolence or other divine names for the "God of Abraham, God of Isaac, God of Jacob," God of Jesus of Nazareth.
>
> Joseph Lanigan, Department of Philosophy, presented 14 April 1988, SMCA/Catholicity.

335. Edwin M. Epstein, "SEBA and the College's Character," 20-22. Epstein understands the Lasallian heritage reductivistically as "the professor's deep-felt commitment to the teaching function and to mentoring the development of our students not simply in a narrow academic sense but as 'whole human beings.' "

336. Paul Giurlanda, "Seven Ways of Looking at the College, or 'Why We Are Not Cal State Hayward . . . Yet,' " *Educational Perspectives* 11, no. 2 (spring 1994): 17.

337. *Faculty Handbook,* 2.6.1.

338. *Faculty Handbook,* 2.9.1. This requirement of "respect" has been tagged for review because of vagueness: "SMC Self-Evaluation Study for WASC," December 1992, 81, SMCA.

339. Johnston, "The Christian Brothers," 29.

340. Anderson, "Remarks to the Faculty, 9 September 1994," *Educational Perspectives* 12, no. 2 (spring 1995): 2-3.

341. "Saint Mary's College Mission Statement," Report of the New Century Committee, 11.

342. "Highlights," Report of the New Century Committee, 17-18.

343. William J. Hynes, professor of religious studies and academic vice president, "Guidelines for the Proactive Recruiting of Faculty," 15 May 1995.

344. Salm, *A Religious Institute in Transition,* 258.

345. Sister Magdalen Coughlin, president of Mount Saint Mary's College, Los Angeles, chair of the WASC Commission's Committee on Diversity, Memorandum to Presidents and Chief Executive Officers, 31 August 1992, SMCA.

346. Hynes, "Saint Mary's College Freshman Profile," 1 September 1992, SMC.

347. Coughlin, Memorandum, 6-7, 16.

348. Accrediting associations, Brother Mel observed with irony, were very concerned about the intrusion of the federal government, and now were adding to their own requirements in order to forestall national, and perhaps nationalized, accreditation. Minutes of the Board of Trustees, 19 January 1994, 923, SMCA; "Brother Mel's Twenty-Five Year Presidency: Expressions of Appreciation," *Educational Perspectives* 11, no. 2 (spring 1994): 2.

349. See "Celebrating Diversity: SMC Annual Report, 1992-1993 Academic Year."

350. Wayne H. Harter, "St. Thomas and the Infidels," *Educational Perspectives* 11, no. 2 (spring 1994): 23-29.

351. Brother Louis De Thomasis, F.S.C., "Addressing the Social, Political and Ideological Issues at Catholic Institutions of Higher Learning," *Educational Perspectives* 10, no. 2 (fall 1992): 38. De Thomasis was president of Saint Mary's College, Minnesota.

352. Paul Giurlanda, "A Theology Department at Saint Mary's College?" *Educational Perspectives* 13, no. 1 (fall 1995): 20-23. In a 1995 announcement of a faculty position, the department stated: "Our department focuses on the Catholic Christian tradition in its courses, which are taught from an ecumenical perspective and in the spirit of the Second Vatican Council and we seek applicants who share this tradition."

353. Meister, "Reflections," 56, 46. Meister is an assistant professor of religious studies at Saint Mary's.

354. Philip Gleason, "A Look Back at the Catholic Intellectualism Issue," *U.S. Catholic Historian* 13, no. 4 (fall 1995): 19-37.

355. Donald R[obert] LaMagdeleine, "The Changing American Catholic University" (Ph.D. diss., Loyola University of Chicago, 1984), 194.

356. James W. Trent, with Jenette Golds, *Catholics in College: Religious Commitment and the Intellectual Life* (Chicago: University of Chicago Press, 1967), 307.

357. George Marsden, *The Soul of the American Academy: From Protestant Establishment to Established Nonbelief* (New York: Oxford University Press, 1994).

358. Judith A. Dwyer and Charles E. Zech, "ACCU Survey of Catholic Colleges and Universities: Report on Faculty Development and Curriculum," *Current Issues in Catholic Higher Education* 16, no. 2 (winter 1996): 1-24.

359. *Chronicle of Higher Education,* 15 November 1996, B89.

360. Jencks and Riesman, 400.

361. John H. Westerhoff, "In Search of a Future: The Church-Related College," in *The Church's Ministry in Higher Education,* ed. Westerhoff (New York: United Ministries in Higher Education, 1978), 195-206; Sister Alice Gallin, O.S.U., "A Response," in *The Church's Ministry,* 207-15.

362. See William J. Richardson, S.J., "The Distinctiveness of Jesuit Higher Education," in *Catholic Colleges and the Secular Mystique,* ed. Eugene Grollmes, S.J. (Saint Louis: B. Herder, 1970), 148-79.

363. Neil J. McCluskey, S.J., "Relevance and the Future of Catholic Education," summer commencement address, 4 August 1967, University of Notre Dame, UNDA.

364. Charles E. Curran, "What Is a Catholic College?" in *History and Contemporary Issues: Studies in Moral Theology* (New York: Continuum, 1996), 201-15.

CHAPTER 7

The Evangelicals

David Riesman, as we have seen in the previous chapter, allowed that "there is no question that the best private institutions, and I do not in this respect include my own [Harvard], have been able to maintain an ethos which assures what the Jesuits and the French would term a certain degree of 'formation' among their under-graduates." If, for the Catholics, Riesman inclined to flattery in this matter, to the institutions we must now study he exhibited a certain disdain. "Most Catholic colleges are not religious in the sometimes claustrophobic manner of what one might term the 'committed Christian' colleges, or of the Protestant evangelical ones."[1]

Though many (but not all) colleges and universities which call themselves "evangelical" and "committed Christian" are affiliated with denominations (some with plural affiliations), like evangelical churches they are usually joined more by a common style than by a common denomination. That style is typically biblical in preaching, mildly Wesleyan or Calvinist in theology, congregational in polity, conservative in ethics and politics, enthusiastic and informal in ritual, cautious toward the regnant culture, plain in manners. Most schools that identify themselves as evangelical have been more influenced by their fellows within this genre than by denominational sister-institutions. Thus in studying them we do well to allow them to identify themselves.

In recent years many of them have formed their own association: the Coalition for Christian Colleges and Universities (CCCU), now numbering ninety members.

1823	Union University	Jackson, Tenn.
1826	Mississippi College	Clinton, Miss.
1839	Erskine College	Due West, S.C.
1846	Taylor University	Upland, Ind.

This essay was researched and written in 1996, and the statistics and facts it reports as current derive from the latest sources then available.

1848	Geneva College	Beaver Falls, Pa.
1860	Wheaton College	Wheaton, Ill.
1866	Milligan College	Milligan College, Tenn.
1866	Roberts Wesleyan College	Rochester, N.Y.
1867	King College	Bristol, Tenn.
1871	Bethel College	Saint Paul, Minn.
1873	Spring Arbor College	Spring Arbor, Mich.
1876	Calvin College	Grand Rapids, Mich.
1878	Southwest Baptist University	Bolivar, Mo.
1882	Northwestern College	Orange City, Iowa
1882	Nyack College	Nyack, N.Y.
1883	Belhaven College	Jackson, Miss.
1883	Houghton College	Houghton, N.Y.
1883	University of Sioux Falls	Sioux Falls, S.Dak.
1887	Bethel College	North Newton, Kans.
1887	Campbell University	Buies Creek, N.C.
1887	Cedarville College	Cedarville, Ohio
1887	Sterling College	Sterling, Kans.
1889	Gordon College	Wenham, Mass.
1890	Asbury College	Wilmore, Ky.
1890	Whitworth College	Spokane, Wash.
1891	George Fox College	Newberg, Oreg.
1891	North Park College	Chicago, Ill.
1891	Seattle Pacific University	Seattle, Wash.
1892	Greenville College	Greenville, Ill.
1892	Malone College	Canton, Ohio
1894	Goshen College	Goshen, Ind.
1895	Northwest Christian College	Eugene, Oreg.
1897	Huntington College	Huntington, Ind.
1897	Trinity International University	Deerfield, Ill.
1898	Dallas Baptist University	Dallas, Tex.
1899	Azusa Pacific University	Azusa, Calif.
1899	Bluffton College	Bluffton, Ohio
1899	Southern Nazarene University	Bethany, Okla.
1901	Trevecca Nazarene College	Nashville, Tenn.
1902	Northwestern College	Saint Paul, Minn.
1902	Point Loma Nazarene College	San Diego, Calif.
1906	Abilene Christian University	Abilene, Tex.
1906	Campbellsville College	Campbellsville, Ky.
1906	Oklahoma Baptist University	Shawnee, Okla.
1906	Southern Wesleyan University	Central, S.C.
1907	Olivet Nazarene University	Kankakee, Ill.
1908	Biola University	La Mirada, Calif.

1908	Tabor College	Hillsboro, Kans.
1909	Bartlesville Wesleyan College	Bartlesville, Okla.
1909	Messiah College	Grantham, Pa.
1912	East Texas Baptist University	Marshall, Tex.
1913	Northwest Nazarene College	Nampa, Idaho
1914	Colorado Christian University	Lakewood, Colo.
1916	Montreat College	Montreat, N.C.
1917	Anderson University	Anderson, Ind.
1917	Eastern Mennonite University	Harrisonburg, Va.
1918	Eastern Nazarene College	Quincy, Mass.
1918	Lee College	Cleveland, Tenn.
1919	John Brown University	Siloam Springs, Ark.
1920	Indiana Wesleyan University	Marion, Ind.
1920	Southern California College	Costa Mesa, Calif.
1921	Simpson College	Redding, Calif.
1927	The Master's College	Santa Clarita, Calif.
1928	Pacific Christian University	Fullerton, Calif.
1930	Bryan College	Dayton, Tenn.
1934	Northwest College	Kirkland, Wash.
1935	Western Baptist College	Salem, Oreg.
1937	Warner Pacific College	Portland, Oreg.
1940	Westmont College	Santa Barbara, Calif.
1941	Cornerstone College	Grand Rapids, Mich.
1941	Williams Baptist College	Walnut Ridge, Ark.
1944	Fresno Pacific College	Fresno, Calif.
1946	LeTourneau University	Longview, Tex.
1947	Bethel College	Mishawaka, Ind.
1948	Grace College	Winona Lake, Ind.
1949	Grand Canyon University	Phoenix, Ariz.
1950	California Baptist College	Riverside, Calif.
1952	Eastern College	Saint Davids, Pa.
1955	Covenant College	Lookout Mountain, Tenn.
1955	Dordt College	Sioux Center, Iowa
1955	Evangel College	Springfield, Mo.
1959	Trinity Christian College	Palos Heights, Ill.
1963	Judson College	Elgin, Ill.
1964	Mount Vernon Nazarene College	Mount Vernon, Ohio
1966	Mid-America Nazarene College	Olathe, Kans.
1968	Palm Beach Atlantic College	West Palm Beach, Fla.
1968	Warner Southern College	Lake Wales, Fla.[2]

Members of the Coalition must be regionally accredited arts-and-sciences institutions. There are three other criteria:

1. A public mission based upon the centrality of Jesus Christ and evidence of how faith is integrated with the institution's academic and student life programs.
2. A continuing institutional hiring policy which requires of each full-time faculty member and administrator personal faith in Jesus Christ.
3. Institutional fund-raising activities which are consistent with the standards of the Evangelical Council for Financial Accountability and demonstration of responsible financial operations.[3]

Despite the fact that these institutions are predominantly rural and poorly endowed, through the Coalition they have been energetically involved in cooperative study programs foreign and domestic, in professional development of administrators, and in the recurring review of their religious authenticity. Various studies agree that student religious affirmation is significantly enhanced by the CCCU schools.[4] For some acquaintance with the variety within this group, we offer two case studies, of two institutions from very different traditions.

AZUSA PACIFIC UNIVERSITY

The spiritual descendants of George Fox, the Society of Friends, came to be called Quakers in Pennsylvania and the southern tidewater locales where they were first clustered. They were a "peculiar people," whose reverence for the Inner Light begot customs and moral imperatives that set them purposely apart. But as they fanned out westward in nineteenth-century America they came under the powerful influence of the evangelical force field of the Methodists, Presbyterians, and Baptists, which dominated so much of what was then the West but would eventually be the central region of the country. Their conversation about Jesus, traditionally flattened by Fox's generic vocabulary, began to be roused by the Gospels and their energetic revivalist preachers. The Quaker fabric was finally rent by schism, as they reproduced within their own membership some of the classical Reformation and Pietist wrangles: Did revelation come primarily through the Scriptures or through the inspired believer? Were good works wheat or tares in the Christian meadow? Were other denominations their allies or their competitors? Was sacramental worship a heresy or an enrichment? One wrangle that had been especially rambunctious among Calvinists concerned sanctification: Was freedom from sin ever possible in this life? And if so, was it conferred as a concomitant of justification, as its swift sequel, or as a slowly unfolding gift? The larger party within the Friends came to be assimilated to the Protestant evangelicals, with an appetite for strong talk about original sin, eternal punishment, and atonement. They were sometimes called perfectionists, and many of them eventually aligned themselves with the Holiness movement, which believed that their conversion and reception of the Holy Spirit definitively freed them not only from their past sins but also from any inclination to sin.[5] The Holiness tradition was patron to other schools, such as Anderson and Asbury, Taylor and Wheaton.

The evangelicals also differed from traditionalist Friends by their new interest in education; Haverford in the East and Earlham in the Midwest were colleges of their persuasion. California was a strong outpost of the movement, and the evangelicals there were considerably influenced in their piety and polity by the fundamentalist upsurge. Within that relatively anti-intellectual atmosphere educational energies tended more enthusiastically toward Bible colleges than to the arts-and-sciences model. It was thus a small knot of evangelical Friends gathered in prayer at Whittier, in the backwash of powerful evangelistic meetings led by an emissary of the National Holiness Association, who decided to open such a school in 1899, which they would call the Training School for Christian Workers (TSCW).[6]

The Training School for Christian Workers

The Training School began in a private home with two students; by the end of the year they had become twelve. The first four principals were women, and seasoned evangelists; men held the chairmanship of the board and were called superinten-dents. Male/female ratios were 5:4 on the board of trustees, but 5:7 among the "resident instructors" and 4:8 in the first group of students. The intended clientele were those "who felt a Providential demand for Pentecostal, Biblical, and practical instruction for those called of God as labourers in His Vineyard." While not anti-intellectual, it was a place where the instruction of the heart and spirit clearly had the edge over anything "academic" in the educational sense of the term.

> It is specially desired to make this school a place of inspiration, as well as of education; a place of gendering spiritual enthusiasms; a place of implanting, and then of the out-working of holy fires. . . .
>
> Knowledge about God is wonderfully increased. We would not mistake think-ing that by searching we shall "find out God." It is to the obedient soul He reveals himself. We would study not so much for the head as for the heart, that we may secure transformed spirit-filled lives. . . . We would see [the school] inspiring faith in God, rather than imparting creeds. We would rather see its pupils and teachers . . . at the mouth of the cave, listening to the still small voice, than engrossed by the demonstrations, and storms, or earthquakes of human artifices. . . .
>
> While the majority of those interested in this school are of one denomination, the teaching corps embraces persons from several churches, and these are selected because of merit and qualifications, without regard to sect. All thoroughly evan-gelical Christians are welcome to its privileges. We wish to help fulfill Christ's prayer that "they may all be one."[7]

During its first decade of existence the regimen was straightforward:

> Scholastic standards were not high; only an elementary education was required for admission. All the courses were strictly religious in content except for "medicine and nursing" (taught by an M.D.), music, physical culture and Spanish. . . .
>
> The daily routine was typical for schools of its type. During breakfast all present sang hymns and recited Scripture. After morning devotions, everyone did his assigned share of the housework. Then, after the students had gone to their rooms for the "quiet hour," classes began. During the rest of the day they engaged in various types of evangelistic endeavors.
>
> There were many prayer meetings including one on Monday evening especially devoted to giving the students an opportunity to "seek the blessing." Sometimes the 5 a.m. Thursday prayer meeting would last until 9 a.m. On the weekends the students engaged in home missionary activity.[8]

The school led a vagabond existence in order to grow, moving its premises to East Los Angeles, then downtown Los Angeles, and then Huntington Park. In its tenth year enrollment rose from fifty to ninety-six. No public transportation meant few commuter students, but they managed to keep enlarging their residential capacity.

William P. Pinkham, a national figure in the Society of Friends, was brought to the TSCW presidency in 1909. By this time the terms of estrangement within the Society of Friends had been modified. The traditionalists, more responsive to the civic culture, had been moving into Unitarianism, and from there rapidly into modernism. The evangelicals had moved in the opposite direction and were in the midst of a fundamentalist fascination with theological controversies. Pinkham's aversion to the Unitarian and modernist ideas "slowly but unmistakably creeping into the church" had embroiled him in hostilities between two partisan journals, the *Evangelical Friend* and the *American Friend.* The editor of the former demanded of his counterpart at the latter an explicit statement of his faith about such issues as the divinity of Jesus, his virgin birth and propitiatory death, the loss of righteousness in Adam, scriptural inspiration, justification through faith, and eternal punishment and blessedness. The modernist editor refused "to be entangled in the complicated mesh of metaphysical theology," and claimed for himself a religion "concerned first and last with the heart's attitude to God and the life which springs out of this attitude . . . [not] with questions of ritual and ceremony and traditional doctrines."[9]

Strong in the Holiness Tradition

Pinkham made the school a center of loyalty to the evangelical party. His eventual successor in 1919, Eli Reece, was even more heated in his contempt for the Quakers who wanted to let attitudes supply for beliefs. Anyone who accepted the modernist view, he said, "has elasticity enough in his conscience to start a rubber factory; and ought not to be allowed to run at large . . . Bible penknifers, miracle rejectors, God minifiers, man magnifiers, hell expungers and those with animal ancestors belong to another family altogether and are on a road which leads to a different place than that which inspired the activities and hopes of the martyrs and early Friends."[10]

It was in this tendentious climate that Pinkham began to design the Training School's first sequence of studies leading up to "graduation." The Scriptures would remain central, but it became clearer that they were being examined within a tradition of interpretation. Coursework in philosophy and theology emerged, supported by work in English, church history, elocution, rhetoric, and history or science. The catalogue began to situate the school in relation to other colleges, rather than in contrast to them. "There is no reason why a special school devoted to the above purpose should not exist apart from the colleges, any more than that agricultural schools, or art schools, or schools of elocution or music, or theological seminaries should not exist except as departments of the college or university."[11] Pinkham's in-house discourse, however, was more reassuringly traditional. The purpose of the endeavor was "God's great work of saving men, of unfurling the Gospel banner *everywhere,* of defending and promulgating the great and imperishable doctrines of the Book at home and in other lands, of hastening the coming of the Lord." In 1912 he was pleased to report to the Training School Association (the school's patrons and corporate titleholders) that "every student boarder now witnesses to a definite experience of sanctification," and was correspondingly disappointed the following year to admit that there was "at present some exception to this."[12]

Eli Reece succeeded Pinkham with accolades for his "efficient and Spirit-filled" faculty who were offering a program unlike anything else west of the Rockies. He reassured his clientele that the TSCW need make no apologies for its work, but then expounded at some length as its apologist. The faculty offered "not only 'a guarded Christian education,' but a spiritual ballast that will steady that education amidst the storms of adversity and doubt, which are wrecking thousands on life's sea."

> Special care is exercised that no form of unsound teaching — such as "destructive criticism" or "The New Theology" — neither any phase of fanaticism shall be allowed a hearing in any classroom or chapel. . . . Our staff of teachers is chosen without direct reference to special denominational preference, but we are very careful to know that they see eye to eye on the great essential truths.[13]

Reece then proceeded to rehearse a long roster of the contested evangelical beliefs. As the 1920s, the decade of confrontation between fundamentalism and modernism, drew near, the identity of the Training School was turning somewhat to the right, from evangelical toward fundamentalist. But curricular development was increasingly stimulated by this intellectual controversy.[14] Psychology, comparative religions, and pastoral theology appeared in the curriculum; Reece then added Greek, logic, and general science, and there was a first proposal of electives. But this was no surrender to the norms of academe. The relations then between academic and religious aspects of the TSCW program are evident in the way the four graduation requirements are presented. The academic requirement — one year of attendance plus the required credits — is stated without any requisite excellence. The other three, by contrast, are all accentuated by their modifiers: deportment "above reproach," a spiritual life "genuine and growing," and Christian service "satisfactory and helpful."[15]

Despite a series of short-term presidents after Reece, the Training School came increasingly to be a sanctuary for both evangelicals and fundamentalists in the Quaker disputes in California and nationally. The conservative Quaker party succeeded in restoring a creedal requirement to official policy at the California Yearly Meeting, only to be thrust into a minority role once the liberals achieved dominance. TSCW joined a federation of regional Holiness colleges, and was well represented in the National Holiness Association. By the mid-1920s the school was committed to work toward a full four-year program and the awarding of degrees, and supported a national association to accredit "orthodox" colleges. Both ideas would require two more decades for fulfillment.

By its thirtieth year, 1928-29, the Training School could boast of nine denominations represented in its student body, seven "distinct races," three city mission bands, one ladies' octet, but only forty-seven students: less than half the enrollment twenty years before. The president somehow managed to tell the Training School Association that it had been "one of the most successful years in its history."[16] The following year the president noted with satisfaction that nearly 30 percent of the students were high school graduates, reckoned to be the highest percentage yet.[17] If these were the indices of success, then success continued unrelieved through the 1930s.

In 1931 the first non-Friend president took office, and this understandably marked a moment of estrangement between the denomination and the school. David H. Scott was a Holiness missionary who had taken no prominent role in the late controversies, and two years earlier the National Holiness Church had adopted the TSCW as its official school. In subsequent documents the institution would be called "interdenominational." The Quaker subsidies were discontinued, and Quaker loyalties were further blurred in 1937 when William Kirby, a determined evangelical who had been dismissed as a pastor by the liberal Whittier Quarterly Meeting, was selected for the TSCW presidency. The Great Depression was all the starker for this school which had already been walking the margin. Yet the president could doggedly note: "Again and again the Holy Spirit has been poured out upon our classes and chapel services tendering and melting all before it, resulting in confessions to one another and of restitutions thus keeping a beautiful spirit of brotherly kindness existing in our body."[18] As the decade of the thirties began to set, the TSCW was still an unaccredited Bible college, with three small classes of regular students and the expectation that two-thirds of each freshman class would evaporate before their time to be seniors.

Cornelius Haggard, 1939-75

All things began to change in 1939, when the TSCW elected a twenty-seven-year-old president who would serve for thirty-six years.[19] Cornelius Haggard had been a student at TSCW, and soon afterward served as the school's bookkeeper (he taught that craft as well). He had been a member of the Nazarene Church who answered an altar call at the age of sixteen. Later he worshiped with the Friends, and after their rift with the TSCW he was ordained in the new Interdenominational Evangelistic Association. He earned a degree at the Los Angeles Baptist Seminary, served as pastor to Temple of Truth and to Baptist and Pilgrim Holiness congregations, and eventually accepted an invitation to join the Free Methodists. Thus Haggard became a personal paradigm of the multidenominationalism which he would bring to his school.

Haggard quickly determined his school should be upgraded into a college, an ambition that was immediately expressed in the first of many name changes and mergers: Pacific Bible College ([PBC], 1939), Azusa College (1957), Azusa Pacific College (1965), and Azusa Pacific University (1981). Other denominational sponsorships on and off through the years have included the World Gospel Mission, the Oriental Missionary Society, the United Missionary Church, the Salvation Army, the Wesleyan Methodist Church, the Missionary Church Association, the Brethren in Christ, and the Evangelical Methodist Church.

Haggard had put himself through the University of Southern California while working at a job and serving as pastor to various congregations. He received his own A.B. two weeks after being elected president in 1939, then earned an M.A. in 1942 and a Th.D. one year later. His presidency infused a similar dogged determination into the college. By 1943 the board agreed to enlarge the course of study to four years, and soon they were awarding degrees in theology and religious education. Huntington Park became a poor provider of students once the patronage of the significant Quaker population there had chilled, and Haggard harried his board until they authorized a move out to the town of Azusa (1946). Bible colleges had no means of academic standardization and recognition, and in 1947 he was one of the founders of the Accrediting Association of Bible Institutes and Bible Colleges (PBC was one of eighteen Bible schools accredited that first year), which was quickly recognized by the U.S. Department of Education. The uphill climb toward regional accreditation was steeper and longer. By 1961 Azusa College (renamed despite objections to dropping "Bible" from the title) was accepted by the State of California for teacher training and certification. The Western Associa-

tion was demanding that Bible colleges sweep aside their extensive Bible requirements in order to gain accreditation; Haggard and his board resisted, and in 1964
he was delighted to have the college fully accredited without sacrificing a single
credit hour of Bible in the curriculum.

To expand and upgrade simultaneously required fund-raising of a magnitude
the little college had never before dared. Haggard with his relentless smile plowed
new fields, then went over the same furrows again, and managed to fund an entirely
new campus, extensive housing, a library, and a gymnasium. He founded a 50/50
Club: members pledged to set aside 50¢ each week, fifty weeks a year, for the
college. The club persevered even after Haggard's death, and by 1982 had contributed $500,000.

Haggard was an indefatigable recruiter of students. Of an early evening he
would ride a tram out to the end of the line, and with a pocketful of thirty dimes
he would head for a public telephone. He carried a card with a list of local prospects
and would spend an hour or more phoning them to press the advantages of an
education at his college. Thirty calls later he would walk back to the tram and ride
home. His office was always open without appointment to on-campus people, and
his pastoral interest in the students he had recruited was an active force in sending
many of them into missionary work.

Pursuit of Accreditation

Pursuit of the status of an accredited college naturally began to lean in a different
direction, but it is remarkable how steadily Haggard managed to pursue the new
agenda without apparently forfeiting the older one. The year of his election, the
college was still publishing the same nine "cardinal points of doctrine" which the
incorporating members of the Training School Association had signed as their
personal beliefs forty years earlier. The "Doctrinal Standard" included the Trinity;
the deity and virginal birth of Jesus; plenary inspiration of the Scriptures; the fall
and total depravity, judgment, and eternal punishment of sinners; justification by
faith through Jesus' substitutionary sacrifice; "The Entire Sanctification of Believers through the atoning Blood of Jesus Christ as a second definite work of grace,
evidenced by the Baptism of the Holy Ghost" (the signature item in the creed of
Holiness people); the imminent coming of Jesus' reign on earth; and speedy evangelization as the imperative of the age. The college put itself forward as "strictly
a Bible School" where "only the Word of God is taught," along with ancillary
disciplines.[20] Intra-Quaker conflict had aroused the earlier controversial interest in
theology through the 1920s, but when that controversy subsided, and Quakers
became a minority of the variegated clientele of the TSCW, the Holiness motif
came once more to the fore. Despite insistence on the Doctrinal Standard, interest
in theological inquiry withered.

The style of the college remained continuous. In his first annual report

752

Haggard reported the salient statistics. As best calculated, in the past forty years 18 percent of the graduates had gone to the foreign missions; 23 percent to ministry at home; and 26 percent were working in Sunday schools and the like. "The sun never sets" on their active work, he would say. He enumerated the many missionary involvements of the current student body (still only 100 students in 1940). The Male Quartet afforded special satisfaction. It had performed 214 times (twice on the radio), sung for 17 denominations in 42 towns, memorized 44 songs and sung 670. One other index of the piety of the time was the syntax of the college rules, which were headlined "Our Creed," to which the students would "consecrate ourselves." Sample items:

> In Christian consideration for others, we will keep out of the halls after 10:00 p.m.
>
> We will not rearrange furniture in the rooms.
>
> Since we as Christian young people regard as sacred the social relations between young men and young women, we will avoid accompanying the opposite sex except under social privilege conditions. We will not loiter together in the buildings, or about the campus.
>
> We will uphold the standards of holiness in appearance and conduct so "that we might walk worthy of the Lord unto all pleasing."[21]

With the country plunged into war on two fronts, no appeals were required at the college for loyalty to the nation. But patriotism was not the overriding loyalty there that it was most other places. Since the usual effect of any extended war "is such a lowering of standards as to result in moral ruin," the PBC people were summoned to quite different battle lines, to "an all-out frontal attack against the hordes of darkness by the soldiers of Christ." Haggard strongly doubted that soldiers of the United States were finding God in the foxholes. "It is a mistake to suppose that the men are turning back to organized religion. They look on the churches as social clubs . . . smothered in respectability and enervated by timidity . . . led chiefly by parsons more intent to please the congregation than to blurt out the disconcerting will of God." Exemption from military service for ministerial trainees may have had something to do with sustained enrollments at the college, but the rise from 71 students when Haggard took over to 164 four years later implies that somehow this very different sort of campus was more attractive than ever. The students represented eighteen denominations (except for the 26 who reported "none"), the largest being Nazarene, Pilgrim Holiness, Free Methodists, Friends, and Mennonite Brethren.[22]

Once PBC set itself on the path toward academic collegiate status, it began to modify its self-understanding and public self-representation. The 1944-45 *Catalog* discontinued the customary notice that PBC was "strictly a Bible School" where "only the Word of God is taught" along with ancillary disciplines. It was now a "Bible *College,*" and its purpose was to provide "that body of knowledge considered essential for the task of Christian leadership and to an appreciation of the finest contributions to scholarship." It began to require high school graduation as a prerequisite, and to suggest that degree-seeking students might take their Bible courses at PBC and then complete further curricular requirements and receive their degrees elsewhere. The Doctrinal Standard, the reliance on the Holy Spirit for a wholesome Christian life and knowledge of the Christian mysteries, the prayer meetings and evangelistic fieldwork — all continued intact. The college was willing to accept Christians who were not well developed in their faith, but "they must have a willingness to yield themselves to God's will as it is revealed to them." The college reserved to itself the right to advise them to leave if their notion of God's will veered too far from what had been revealed to the faculty.[23]

By 1945, when the college was preparing to award its first six degrees, the B.Th. in theology and the B.R.E. in religious education, and when the first veterans were coming back to study with GI educational benefits, the enrollment had again soared, to 199, and a development officer had been hired. In the midst of these expansive plans, Haggard was still issuing warm thanks in his annual report to "the consecrated saints" who contributed fruit, vegetables, and fish, and chairs for the classroom. PBC was far from affluence. He was much pleased by the swelling numbers, but more so by their character. He glossed his annual message with this handwritten notation: "We have prayed that He would permit only those who should come to do so — and keep away any he should not. We feel he has answered."[24]

Taking On the Color of Their Surroundings

With the purchase of the Azusa property in 1945 (after a month of prayer and a day of fasting), and the move in 1946, the college was set to expand even more rapidly (though the distance from Los Angeles would draw down the enrollment at first). Part of the property was developed as a plant nursery to provide both PBC and its students with sources of further income. The college which, when Haggard took office, had not a single full-time faculty member, now had a staff of nineteen, six of whom were full-time administrators and four, full-time teachers. God was duly and explicitly thanked for the abundance of surplus war materiel and the low price of beef on the hoof.[25] As some of the smaller Holiness denominations showed some interest in affiliating with PBC, Haggard thought of Cal Tech and MIT as models of what they might create in Azusa for professional training, on both the undergraduate and postgraduate levels. But he bethought himself of the

> ever present danger of taking on the color of our surroundings. For us to keep simple in matters of living, holy in character, ethical in conduct and uncontaminated by the moral pollution around us is absolutely essential. There is also the

danger of the loss of the Holy Spirit from our individual lives and from our program as a whole so that there is a form of godliness devoid of the power of the Holy Spirit. There are still other dangers such as falling into the spirit of Pharisaism and legalism in our approach to the problem of Christian living; of substituting loyalty to a program for a personal devotion to Jesus Christ and His cause; of neglecting to emphasize the fundamental principles that have made us what we are.[26]

Haggard's prayer to be sent the right students seems to have been honored. The *Student Handbook* from those postwar days leaned heavily yet cheerfully on manners and decorum.

We are happy that we have a fine swimming pool for your enjoyment. However, in order that our hours of recreation may be spent in a manner which will be above reproach to those watching our lives, we ask students to observe the following regulations:

1. Bathrobes must be worn to and from the pool. Bathers will return to their room shortly after leaving the pool.
2. Girls, no two-piece bathing suits, please.
3. No one may go in swimming *alone*. This is for your protection. At least two persons must be in the pool at the same time.
4. And please, no audience of the same sex.
5. Schedules, which will alternate each week, will be posted on the bulletin board. . . .

The daily chapel is a devotional period — a time of soul enrichment, and as such, is required of all students. It presents an opportunity to learn the refinements of listening with courtesy and attention. Never laugh if someone on the platform makes a mistake. Show such an appreciative attitude that P.B.C. chapel will be remembered by guest speakers as a place where it is a pleasure to speak. Come in the spirit of prayer and worship. . . .

Break your bread before buttering it. Never put your knife in your mouth. (You knew that before, didn't you?) And don't lean it gang plank fashion against your plate; place it across the right side of the plate with the sharp edge toward the center. . . .

Any demonstration of affection is considered improper. And this includes our married students on campus, for visitors would not understand. . . .

As you are courteous and gracious, then not only you, but the whole College is elevated in the estimation of the public. Those school sweaters tell on us — let's keep our reputation high.[27]

Accreditation as a Bible College would bring in its wake various other forms of professional acceptance. The PBC was now listed by the California Department of Education and the New York Board of Regents, and its credits in secular subjects were now transferable; its program qualified as the undergraduate component of training for Army chaplains; the Veterans Administration approved PBC for GIs and the Immigration and Naturalization Service for nonquota immigrants; the Civil Service Commission declared its graduates eligible for civil service examinations. What it lacked, and what Haggard was determined to win, was regional accreditation for its degrees.[28]

As the years passed, the conduct rules tended to become more procedural, and more didactic. The obligation to attend chapel was no longer simply asserted; it was enforced. Now seats were assigned and absences calculated. Christian service required weekly reports, on prepared blanks. Appropriate dress received four pages of very explicit treatment. An excerpt:

> If you were aware of how much your actions reflect upon your parents — good or bad — you would act more carefully. This is particularly true concerning table manners. Of course you'll find those who don't eat correctly, or follow the rules you'll read (and we hope *learn to use*) during the first semester — but the school will be better for your trying to help one another.
>
> Take this matter of wearing the appropriate thing at the right time. A girl on an Arizona turkey ranch loved to slit turkey throats Thanksgiving time. She bought a beautiful filmy picture hat — which, because she loved it, she wore on the job. It soon looked it. No sense of the "right thing at the right time."
>
> PBC is a training school for Christian workers. We hope to teach you how to do the right thing at the right time in a gracious manner. (Yes, the faculty *has* temptation to discouragement for some of you part of the time!) But actions are important. It's easy to become so sloppy and careless that we fail to see the harmful effects it may have. A pastor's wife habitually wore shorts in the parsonage. If a visitor dropped in for prayer or a visit, it was his hard luck. (Incidentally, her husband didn't receive a call for the next year. She may still be wondering why.)[29]

As the 1950s yielded to the 1960s, Dr. Haggard became increasingly inclined to mourn publicly over the larger cultural dissolution of America. His authority of choice on "this fermenting society being leavened by the yeast of sin" was J. Edgar Hoover.[30] This meant that he became explicit on crime statistics, but it is remarkable how little Christian theology entered into his threnody over "a world gone money-mad, pleasure-mad, war-mad."

As the college matured academically (dropping "Bible" from its title in 1957) and aspired to full accreditation, there was no longer the incentive to describe itself as "totally different" from the institutions whose recognition it was so effortfully seeking. The new self-understanding was that Azusa College (AC) offered exactly what other colleges offered, but also "something the other schools cannot give," "AN ADDED PLUS," a "spiritual dynamic."

Azusa College provides all the general education in arts and sciences required in a liberal arts college plus a concentration of Bible and Theology — the most liberalizing of all areas of knowledge.

To this theoretical training, Azusa College provides the added plus of practical experience, so that the theory of the classroom is immediately put to use on gospel teams and in teaching, preaching and other ministries so that one learns not only by hearing but even more effectively by doing.

This academic program is administered by a trained consecrated faculty equivalent to any faculty in any college or university. But this faculty is Spirit-filled with a personal concern for the well being of every student.

This academic program is implemented by its setting among challenging Christian young people where there is none of the cynicism and skepticism that is so debilitating on the secular campuses of our large colleges.[31]

The president was continually effervescent. Year after year was "the best year" the college had ever had. He assiduously reported to his board how many books were checked out of their library annually by comparison with other, already accredited, colleges, and how his faculty were working to bring their credentials up into the zone of Western Association respectability, while admitting, "Some of you have asked, 'When will the Gymnasium be done?' I don't know. We praise God for what was achieved both last year and this summer but as I have indicated, we again need a miracle. We are out of funds."[32] The unrelenting drive for recognition had made a difference. In earlier years he was persuaded that his faculty was as good as could be on the school's own terms, and was not so disposed to call their Spirit-filled personal concern an added plus; their degrees then looked more like the add-on. The energetic and ambitious drive for accreditation seems to have enhanced his — and probably his colleagues' — determination to be judged by the standards of their intended peers, and not found wanting. Understandably, they were beginning to absorb the norms of the academy.

Recognition at Last

Haggard's overtures finally persuaded the Western Association of Schools and Colleges (WASC) to send a small team for an exploratory visit in 1960. Their judgment was that an accreditation inspection would be premature. The college's stability at the time was still parlous. There were only 200 full-time students, hardly more than in 1945, and the fact that only thirty-two degrees were awarded annually implied that the student body had a heavy dropout rate.[33]

In 1963 a formal request for accreditation was accompanied by AC's self-study report. By this time the full-time enrollment was considerably lower (164), with a full-time faculty of seventeen, five of whom held the doctorate.[34] Azusa had taken advantage of a well-funded state campus nearby, Citrus (Junior) College, to which its students had easy and inexpensive recourse for all science, history, government, and foreign language instruction. The range of courses there was far wider than AC could ever hope to provide and, it was noted, "the horizons of students are broadened by bringing them into active contact with a secular public instruction." In an earlier day the Citrus students would have been expected to have *their* horizons widened by the contact.

In its description of the faculty appointment process, the self-study is strikingly mainstream. The four basic criteria are ranked in order: academic competence, instructional ability, mature personality, and Christian commitment. Internally it was the last criterion which had been most attentively appreciated. But the account offered to the examiners naturally stated matters in the more conventional way, since the quest for accreditation was an uphill trek. The self-study never even mentions that candidates must subscribe to the Doctrinal Standard. Instead there are indistinct references to "general attitude," and "commitment to the educational philosophy of the college."[35]

The same accommodation is found in the student life report. The college philosophy is said to foster growth that is intellectual, social, emotional, and spiritual. A report to any other group would have put the last criterion in first place. In a list of nine specific goals, the preparation of missionaries is never mentioned.[36]

The WASC survey committee was somehow given the erroneous impression that the college intended to reduce its Bible and theology requirements, "to attract a wider selection of students." They noted the need for academic upgrading. AC seniors tested in the lowest quartile of the national college population in standardized tests, and lowest of all in the humanities (eighteenth percentile). The grades they earned at Citrus College were quite low, e.g., a mean GPA of 1.1 in U.S. history. WASC made some explicit demands: faculty salaries had to be abruptly raised, and the administration had to begin consulting the faculty about the curriculum. But they did finally recommend approval.[37]

In 1964 Azusa College thus became the first Bible college to achieve regional accreditation without substantially changing its curriculum. Haggard saw this as providing inspiration to the three-hundred-odd Bible schools "tempted to jettison their Bible and Theology offerings and to compromise their spiritual ministry for secular recognition." Today about 40 percent of the Bible colleges have secured regional accreditation.[38]

No one could have predicted what would follow from accreditation. The enrollment immediately increased by 50 percent, and showers of fiscal blessing flowed in abundance. President Haggard grew effulgent in his imaginings for the future: more of everything. Yet these successes, he quickly warned, had thrown the college into crisis. Students were now coming — even to Bible and Christian colleges — with much less sense of a divine call. Furthermore, their families and churches were sending them off ill prepared. It now fell entirely to the college to transform the lives of its students. And that mission would now be harder.

We will determine this year whether (with our material growth and academic recognition) we meant what we have said across the years regarding our commitment to a unique ministry of challenging young people to Christian life and service. As a "have not" institution it was easy to thus rationalize for students who did not have the same commitment automatically enrolled at secular colleges. Now with the academic recognition it will be all too easy to succumb as so many have to a mere academic program. . . .

We have an added plus of spiritual contribution. In order to make this spiritual contribution every member of the faculty and staff must have and maintain a radiant and victorious Christian experience. . . . To that end our cooks must cook because God has called them to do so. Our secretaries must type letters because God has called them to do so. Our maintenance men must maintain a beautiful campus because God has called them to do so. And every member of the faculty and staff and Administration must do his work because God has called him to do so.[39]

And the Success It Brought

Students crowded in well beyond even Haggard's dreams; between the two WASC surveys in 1963 and 1966 they had increased by 250 percent. The faculty had doubled, as had their academic credentials. The second visiting team noted with interest that the Azusa Pacific College (APC, since 1965) faculty had engaged in a searching redefinition of their specific objectives. At the tail end of the list, after eighteen "Academic," "Personal," and "Social and Cultural" objectives, came the three "Spiritual" objectives:

1. To help each student develop a vital and vibrant faith in keeping with our motto, "God First."
2. To assist each student to achieve a meaningful Christian philosophy of life in the light of our Christian heritage.
3. To train students for Christian life and service.[40]

There is little sign of a radiant and victorious Christian experience here. Something was changing, something more than the enrollment or the annual budget.

This WASC visitation led to a reaffirmation of regional accreditation, but California state accreditors joining in the same visit unanimously recommended against allowing APC to grant the standard teaching credential. The heavy general education requirements, plus so many in biblical studies, seemed to leave no room for both an academic major and the necessary (and numerous) education courses. The clear imperative was that APC's unusual Bible requirement would have to yield.[41] APC sent a ferocious reply to the state board of education, accusing the visitors of misreading the documents submitted, of presuming to dictate institutional philosophy and objectives, and of attempting to subvert Bible studies, "our institutional uniqueness and *raison d'être.*"[42] The state board, unaccustomed to such back talk from its suppliants, sent down a high administrator for a second fact-finding visit, gulped, eventually issued the accreditation, and invited the truculent author of the APC letter onto its roster of examiners.[43] This was the old spirit.

The momentum started by the accreditation simply surged on and on. Financial support came in for a new campus, handsome new buildings, student aid, and moderately attractive faculty salaries. Grants were awarded — and without any rancorous remarks in local evangelical circles about tainted government funds. Credentialed faculty arrived, missing departments in the mainline arts-and-sciences disciplines were created and staffed, and the enrollment kept growing.

Did APC continue to keep its soul intact under the vigilant and worried eye of Cornelius Haggard? Or did it take its ease in academe? The assertive selfconfidence exhibited to the State of California's educational establishment would suggest that the college still had a strong sense of its calling, and would survive the end of its "have-not" days without succumbing to a "mere academic program."

The college *Catalog* in 1970 greeted new students with the question: "But what is Azusa Pacific College?" It was evidently no longer a trainer of missionaries.

> **Azusa Pacific College is you, the student.** You more than anyone else creates [*sic*] the reason for the existence of Azusa Pacific College. You are considered a worthwhile individual, a person, one who must be allowed the freedom to wrestle with the important ideas of life — ideas faced by every generation and those unique in your generation. It is realized that the most constructive learning possible is that which takes place within the context of guidance and advice. It is defined guidelines that allow real freedom. You, the student, are given the responsibility to experience and enjoy the freedom here at Azusa Pacific College. . . .
>
> **Azusa Pacific College is a belief.** It is this belief that a college committed to both the person and work of Jesus Christ can and does provide an education and an environment that is unique to this day and age. It is this educational experience that confronts the inner needs of man as well as the needs of his society. The future of this world will depend more on the individual with this type of education.

Chapel (three times a week) was now "a varied, thought-provoking encounter," and vespers (Wednesday evenings) "are conducted in a relaxed setting." All information beyond those laconic descriptions concerns how to certify that one has indeed fulfilled those requirements, and the increasing fines for delinquency. Local churches are also commended for Sunday mornings, "to keep your spiritual growth active and real." One other congregational activity, listening to invited speakers, evokes the only harsh note on the page. "The college is interested in speakers who are loyal Americans, not advocating civil disorder or disobedience. Extremists are to be avoided. Students are expected to be courteous to all speakers invited to the campus. Visible or audible reaction to speakers will not be permitted unless debate is scheduled or the speaker solicits student reaction."

Drugs, reckless driving, drinking, gambling, smoking, vandalism, criminal activity, and "immoral conduct" constitute the shortlist of misconduct, which faces a judicial process almost as complex as the California Code of Criminal Procedure. Though self-discipline and freedom are the new motifs of life on campus, appropriate dress continues to be dealt with: still with whimsy, but in a different tone:

> We do not expect to maintain a continual California Centennial Pageant as far as women's dress is concerned but we do expect APC coeds to dress appropriately for every occasion. We want our coeds to look attractive and feminine at all times. Certainly we are aware of the current fashions (did you hear about the weeping little boy, who when told by his mother to "take hold of my skirt," replied tearfully, "I would, but I can't reach it"?), but we do have a few fashion guidelines of our own.[44]

So dress codes are still in. But the new accepted skirt length is four inches above the knee. Above.

The Essence Restated

This is clearly not Berkeley in 1970, but neither is it Azusa back in 1960. It is wholesome, intentionally wholesome. The 1970 WASC visitors caught the spirit well, in their comments on APC's aims and objectives:

> The catalogue states that above all else Azusa Pacific College [in the muted words of the newly wrought objectives] "seeks to train its students for Christian life and service." The concept of service was emphasized by the Chairman of the Board of Trustees who asked "if Christians aren't going to be involved in community affairs, who are?"
>
> The Committee agrees that Azusa Pacific College achieves its stated purpose admirably. The strong emphasis on work in music and in speech backs up the heavy course requirements in religion. Increased emphasis in the areas of counseling, psychology, sociology and other behavioral-science orientated subjects may increase the effectiveness of graduates for community service. The present co-curricular activities strongly support this.[45]

APC was clearly interpreted in terms that made perfect sense to its WASC peers. Their students are wholesome; and they do community service.

What had become of the old president, who always began his letters with the salutation: "Greetings in the precious name of Jesus!" and who three decades earlier had pledged himself to the original objective: to make the school "a place of inspiration, as well as of education; a place of gendering spiritual enthusiasms; a place of implanting, and then of the out-working of holy fires"? Cornelius Haggard was only fifty-nine years old in 1970, but his health was stinted and the impetus of administration was largely sustained by his cabinet of officers. His regular messages at board meetings tended more and more to be roving commentaries on higher education and/or lower culture, followed by compact factual reports from his deputies. His evangelical vision persisted, but its focus suffered from farsightedness.

One must ask whether a good part of the newly presented Azusa Pacific is simply an increase of sophistication. There is no reason why the language of the tent meetings had to remain the discourse of the college as it succeeded in sharing a higher culture with its community. The place had quickly become a more professional operation. Haggard had taken responsibility for a Bible school with seventy-one students that he wanted to make into missionaries, and for twenty-five years he had striven to win academic recognition for his school. He succeeded, and on what seemed to be very accepting terms for this school of Holiness tradition, with its zeal for Christ. At the moment of accreditation the student body was still very small: hardly more than twice the number he began with. But from that moment the forces of expansion — and of transformation — assumed an impetus of their own, and Dr. Haggard in some respects had to stand out of the way and let them roll. In the first six years after accreditation both the revenues and the gross assets of the college quadrupled. That suggests how much momentum there was.

In 1974, one year before the president's death, the college completed a two-and-a-half-year process and adopted a planning paper in which the faculty, administration, and trustees all had a hand. "The Essence of Azusa Pacific College" was considered provisional, and thus confidential. Several of its provisions signaled large changes for APC: a more specific interest in liberal arts (not previously an explicit priority), another in professional studies, and a third in postgraduate education. As recently as 1970 the WASC visitors had observed that "Azusa Pacific is not vocationally oriented and shows little inclination to change in this direction. Development of an extended graduate program likewise is not one of the stated goals. Administration and trustees appear to realize this would have to be done at the expense of the present undergraduate effort."[46] But by 1974 that was no longer so, though the college was keeping its intentions quiet. In a very short time programs in nursing, business administration, and education would be thriving, and graduate degree programs both on campus and overseas would be in place.

Just as interesting in this confidential planning document on the college's "Essence" was the manner in which the religious purposes were expressed. Religion was ranked as the first among all purposes and entitled "Christian Perspective." Christian perspective was not an "added plus," but it could hardly have been formulated in more tedious terms . . . the prose which only an academic could love:

> Christian Perspective. Within the framework of the Christian college tradition, Azusa Pacific College serves its students and constituency by striving:
> 1. To provide an environment conducive to spiritual commitment consistent with conservative evangelical Christianity.
> 2. To help the student understand and respond to the redemptive message of the Bible and to apply that response to life in the modern world.
> 3. To acquaint the student with the Christian faith and to contrast the heritage derived from it with selected world traditions and some proposed modern alternatives to religion.
> 4. To integrate Christian theological emphases with other disciplines.[47]

The faculty had evidently come into its own and begun their articulation of the religious mission of the college. Here was no Pentecost.

Cornelius Haggard's thirty-six-year presidency would be closed by his death in August 1975. In his last semester the regular WASC visitation took place. The college was naturally commended for the highest enrollment and the largest operating surplus in its history. After having been exposed to the full text of the "Essence Statement," the visitors recommended still more self-study, lest the college's spiritual commitments, academic integrity, and financial health become destabilized. It was an uneventful accreditation visit.[48] In his last presentation to the board the president passed on a contemporary comment about Protestant colleges:

> Some will doubtless become non-sectarian and absorb the overflow of students looking for brand name labels. Others will probably be driven to the wall and after much soul searching will try to sell themselves to the state. A few may combine with other neighboring institutions and a few will doubtless close their doors. . . . Lacking the resources to build a clientele on the basis of academic distinction, the location to build it on the basis of physical convenience, the connections to build it on the basis of social snobbery, and the competence to build it on the basis of professional training, they will cling to their religious labels in order to escape modernity.[49]

Haggard was held by a sincere and ardent concern lest the college for which he had so prodigiously labored default on its divine calling, but since the triumph of 1964 he no longer had perspective or energy enough to direct its inner dynamics. For instance, there was something more significant to report about the student body than its heartening size. The largest denominational representation had now become Baptist. In fact, Baptists were much more numerous than students from all the seven supporting denominations combined. The student body now included Calvinists and Lutherans. Catholics, who in the Training School's early years were the population whom the mostly Quaker alumni were primarily sent out to Christianize, were now more numerous at Azusa Pacific than Friends. And the second-largest group, right after the Baptists, were those who reported no church membership. Something had happened. Anyone with half a suspicion in 1975 could have resolved that doubt by scanning the *Catalog*. The first two paragraphs dealing with the "Objectives of the College" are framed in the classical vocabulary of past-perfect institutional Christian faith:

> Azusa Pacific College has a spiritual heritage which is rooted deeply in the Christian tradition and which has been transmitted through more than a half century of higher education. In keeping with this heritage, the college as one of its principal objectives seeks to train its students for Christian life and service, assist them to achieve a meaningful Christian philosophy of life, and help them develop a vital and active faith during their tenure at the college.
>
> More specifically, Azusa Pacific College seeks to acquaint the student with the essential nature of religion as discoverable in human experience and provide him with a practical experience in applying Biblical truth in a variety of avenues of Christian service. The student should arrive at a reasoned defense of his faith through a sound knowledge of Christian theology. It is also important that each student acquire the theoretical tools necessary to successful service in the task of world evangelization.

"Heritage," "rooted," "tradition" — rhetorical fingerprints of a communal faith gone flat — prepare one to study "the essential nature of religion," which is quite a different business from being a disciple of the faith once delivered to the saints. The graduation requirements still include a hefty allotment from the Department of Philosophy and Religion: thirty-three credits. But one hardly knows what to think of one of the other graduation requirements: "Each student must give evidence of a genuine spiritual life."[50] This is not to suggest that in its decade of boisterous growth the college had become a godless simulacrum of its rustic, original self. But when chapel is justified because "This is the only time the whole body is together," and Christian faith is decomposed into "such ideals as individual worth, personal values, mutual respect, forgiveness, unconditional love, honesty, purpose, priorities and so on," little sense seems to remain of a specific tradition of particular discipleship.[51] This is not a manifesto that has been suitably enlarged for acceptance by a more widely recruited community; it has gone limp. The first TSCW community was a community in spite of not belonging to a single church or even denomination. But eventually, without a church or even a denomination to sustain it, the college's identity was somehow bleaching out in the California sun.

These dilute allusions to Christian conviction and commitment seemed to predominate when the college was speaking out in the open: promotionally, to the public at large, but also to its own constituency. When the college was in the mode of piety, however, when it had its pulpit voice — then its expressions of faith remained lively. The old doctrinal statement, for instance, which had descended through the years — retouched from time to time but substantially intact — had actually grown, and still had to be subscribed to each year by each trustee and employee:

Statement of Faith

We believe the Bible to be the only inspired, infallible, authoritative word of God.

We believe there is one God, eternally existent in three persons — Father, Son, and Holy Spirit.

We believe in the deity of our Lord Jesus Christ, in His virgin birth, in His sinless life, in His miracles, in His vicarious and atoning death through His shed blood, in His bodily resurrection, in His ascension to the right hand of the Father, and in His personal return to power and glory.

We believe in the fall of man and his consequent total moral depravity, resulting in his exceeding sinfulness and lost estate, and necessitating his Regeneration by the Holy Spirit.

We believe in the present and continuing ministry of Sanctification by the Holy Spirit by whose infilling the believing Christian is cleansed and empowered for a life of Holiness and Service.

We believe in the resurrection of both the saved and the lost; those who are saved to the resurrection of life and those who are lost to the resurrection of damnation.

We believe in the spiritual unity of believers in our Lord Jesus Christ.

And then in recent years came this supplement, which spoke in a new voice:

While the College stands firmly on these truths, it considers the spirit of equal importance to the letter. It lays as much stress on the Christian character of the messenger as upon the orthodox correctness of his message.

These fundamentals are held to be essential:

Wholehearted love toward God and Man

Christian fellowship among believers

Scriptural separation from the world

Victory through the indwelling Christ

Unswerving loyalty to Christ as Lord

Consecration for rugged, sacrificial service

The leadership of the Holy Spirit for the believer and the church

A living, working faith in the promises of God for spiritual, physical, and temporal needs

Zealous witnessing for Christ

Until the college had achieved public success, Cornelius Haggard and his associates saw its intellectual task in modest terms, as part of an overall mission which was religious. But once the college had won its struggle to be accepted by all other accredited colleges as their peer, the Christian aspect of APC was now an "added plus," and from this time onward the college looked in one direction for its religious inspiration and in another for its academic standards. During that successful struggle was when something critical had happened.

A New Regime

In 1976 APC had a new president: Paul Sago, a successful Church of God minister and a college development officer. He immediately severed its old affiliation with the Accrediting Association of Bible Colleges, which it had maintained concurrently with its regional accreditation.[52] Growth continued, especially in the newer programs. In 1979-80 the total enrollment (body count) was 3,621, of whom less than half were in on-campus programs.[53] WASC had been critical of many of these new satellite programs in both 1975 and 1977, believing them to be awarding credits and degrees on terms inappropriately lighter than was customary. The college deflected the criticism, arguing that there were at least some accredited institutions whose standards were lower.

One WASC criticism was of an entirely different nature. WASC suggested that APC reconsider the fact that some students were not expected to maintain the commitment to Christ and to Christian service. The college replied that "While undergraduates are asked to adhere to institutional values and standards while in residence, no such requirement is placed upon graduate students."[54] APC had in a very brief span of time generated graduate (actually, professional) programs that were financially very successful though, in the view of the WASC visitors, skimpy in their requirements.[55] The fact that a minority of the student body were now expected to join in the commitments that APC had previously considered its *raison d'être* raised the question, and raises it still: Could the college run a large, primarily cash-producing, vocational program without compromising the religious integrity of its traditional education?

President Sago set everyone to work once more on the Essence Statement, to produce a definitive text for public use. The "Statement of Faith," a heavily re-edited version of the old Doctrinal Standard, would continue to be published and reaffirmed, but it would now be upstaged by the much lengthier, smoother "primary document." It was meant to state the "distinctives" of the college, though couched in terms meant to minimize difference. It was, after all, to speak for *all* persons in the college. Readers were told that it was not a goals statement: it set forth who APC people *already were,* more than what they should now accomplish. It was, however, a serious redefinition of APC's tradition. Religiously APC now claimed to function "with a tradition of Wesleyan evangelical Christianity" ("broadly Wesleyan," explains one exegete). That its members "show love toward God (holiness of heart) and love toward each other (holiness of life) which . . . encourages us to abandon those distinctions that divide us" is about the only allusion to its Holiness origins. The Training School origins are also evoked by the claim "to share our faith unashamedly; disciple other Christians; participate in missionary endeavors." But the characterization of the college as in any way distinctive religiously was at an all-time low. The Christian character is chock-full of rhetorical nougat that is mouth-watering and contemporary: "critical open-mindedness . . . complexity and ambiguity . . . respect for, and cooperation with those of all cultures . . . a creative Christian style of life . . . struggle, risking, and confrontation . . . values clarification . . . life-long nurture of our physical selves . . . the unique worth of every individual." The picture of this broadly Wesleyan place is one of welcoming amiability, mostly moral Christianity, and unrelenting positivity.[56] The new Essence Statement existed alongside the older "Objectives of the College" for a while, until the rhetorical mass became uncomfortable, and then the latter was retired from service.

In 1981 the burgeoning postgraduate programs prompted the college to claim a higher rank and name: Azusa Pacific University (APU). The family income of its students became more comfortable, and their high school grade average now surpassed the national average (83 percent earned over 2.0, compared to 77 percent nationally). The programmatic proliferation on campus was such that only two or three out of nine faculty divisions operated within the disciplines of the traditional arts and sciences. And it was finally being admitted out loud that about the most APU could do for the spiritual integration of its adult off-campus clientele was to make sure they all had copies of the Essence Statement.[57]

When the WASC visitors came round to examine this greatly grown and articulated university in 1981, they reported an absence of vitality. It became immediately obvious, they said, in the way APU had recounted its own past:

> The first and only curriculum for some 40 years was a study of the Bible. The report states simply that beginning in 1939 students embarked on a four-year course which ended with the first group of graduates in 1944. There is no reference to what may have been a heavy amount of creative tension between the objectives of higher education and training for Christian living. . . . In this factual reporting of history [the self-study], the essence of a struggle between Christianity and general education is concealed. It is possible that this is the lid on conflict and ways of handling it which today is a stifling factor in the development of the institution.

The visitors opined that what the new lack of clarity and candor was repressing must be "the fervor on the part of the faculty and leadership to ensure academic freedom and a sharing of real power with the faculty." Behind some of their animus was an annoyance that the college had declared itself a university in such a way as to elude any review by WASC, which would have been bound to point out that it was a premature move in the absence of several necessary improvements.

The report continued with spleen. The Essence Statement, said the evaluators, continued to speak of a liberal arts institution, without due notice that most of its students were now in professional study tracks. There was no unified quality assurance for graduate faculty and programs. There was still a measure of degree inflation, and faculty salary deflation. Despite published standards and a complex process of admissions, in the past two years only twenty-nine out of more than eight hundred applicants had been turned down. The chief gravamen of the visitation report was that APU now had two very different clienteles: one of late adolescents and another of young professionals. Both the learning process and the holistic development which combined to form APU's distinctive sense of "education" were designed for and offered to the first, traditional clientele, while the young professional students were given an education that was insufficient on both grounds: in their educational enhancement and in their personal development.

Even the most traditional unit on campus, the Department of Philosophy and Religion, came in for a scourging: it was offering a philosophy major without a single faculty member assigned full-time to that discipline. The university library holdings were inadequate. Enrollment in its graduate program had diminished year by year.[58]

After such a critical review, accrediting associations normally arrange an interim visit sooner than the normal schedule would require, and by 1984 the university had many adjustments to report. All constituencies were reported hard at work revising the Essence Statement to take account of APU's dual educational "thrust." (In the end, however, the only notable revision would be the deletion of the first paragraph that had located APU in the tradition of Wesleyan evangelical Christianity. Henceforth they would be unlocated Christians.) On other matters there had been much pulling up of socks. The central problem, as the interim visitors observed, had been that in the 1960s Azusa Pacific had "moved with aggressive determination if not consistent good judgment into marginal academic programs and risky fields of endeavor. Some of these activities were poorly funded, understaffed, and difficult to monitor." Now, with so many positive responses to the WASC criticisms, the 1984 visitors' report (a sweetheart document; the visitation team was chaired this time by a good friend) was intent instead that APU be "not seen as narrowly sectarian, but, rather, as a caring, serving, ecumenical community motivated by the biblical heritage and church history so clearly laid out in those mission statements."[59] One innovation, more an in-house initiative than a response to outside suggestion, was a unilateral decision on the part of board and administration to discontinue awarding tenure. Instead, all faculty would thenceforth be offered "flexible" (i.e., temporary) contracts for one, three, or five years. In an institution where the very heavy workload inevitably lengthened the time required to earn a terminal degree by young faculty who lacked it at the time of first hire, this gave the institution more flexibility in retaining those who did succeed, and letting the others go.

During Dr. Sago's last year in the presidency, 1988-89, demographic shifts in the denominational makeup of the enrollment were continuing. Baptists were still the largest single denomination: 16 percent. Catholics had become the second-ranking denomination, with 6 percent. The five sponsoring denominations together provided only 3 percent.[60]

APU wanly reported to WASC that it was "still maintaining the spiritual dimension of its heritage." The postgraduate programs had been shaken down and a few phased out, and the undergraduates once again composed the majority of the enrollment. The operating budget was four times what it had been when President Sago arrived twelve years earlier, and there was no accumulated deficit. Some handsome permanent buildings had been added. One very interesting program, Operation Impact, was attracting attention at the time. Since 1973 the school had offered a master's program for American missionaries overseas, combining annual faculty site visits and on-campus tutelage during home leave. There were fifteen authorized sites, such as Costa Rica, Bolivia, the Philippines, Papua New Guinea, and the Ivory Coast. Somewhat more than two hundred people were enrolled, and the program managed to graduate about two dozen each year. The university was not in it for the income, for it usually ran in the red. But it was valuable as one of its few remaining involvements with missionaries. Those at the center of the university still cared for their old clientele, and this was one of the few corners in their program directly designed for conservative evangelicals.[61]

Two distinguished educators, both brought up in evangelical Protestantism and then providing leadership at the Carnegie Foundation for the Advancement of Teaching, Ernest Boyer and Warren Bryan Martin, had been strategically helpful to the university by chairing, respectively, the WASC visitation committee that recommended accreditation in 1964 and the one that succored the university in 1984 after the thrashing of 1981. The Foundation offered its consultancy to evaluate APU's progress, and turned its attention to the "special mission" of blending intellectual and spiritual values on campus. Not much attention, though. It did recommend an orientation procedure for adjunct faculty, who were evidently still on the outside looking in at its Christian character. A more curious suggestion was that, for the sake of "rational Christianity," APU create an academic honor code. "If it works, at least fitfully at Princeton and other universities, it should be possible for a program of Christian honesty in all aspects of campus life to be successful in an environment committed to Christian values."[62] That both raised and begged the question: Was there a Christian community at Azusa with enough solidarity of conscience and purpose to accept the responsibility for mutually defended honesty? Azusa Pacific University never followed through on the visitors' suggestion.

The Felix Presidency

In 1990 APU welcomed a new president: Richard E. Felix, raised in a Nazarene and Pilgrim Holiness family, Ph.D. from Notre Dame, and president of Friends University in Wichita. Felix would consolidate the efforts to make APU an even more professional campus. Granted the university's ingathering of a student population ever more different from the revivalist, Pentecostal community it had served until after World War II, it became natural for APU to define herself with less angularity. One can see this trend in the rewrite of the "Fundamentals" adjoined to the authoritative Statement of Faith, which all trustees and employees must sign annually. There was an aggressive tone in 1975 that had been softened by 1991:

1975	1991
• Wholehearted love toward God and Man	• Caring, effective love both to God and man
• Christian fellowship among believers	• A Christ-like unity and acceptance between believers
• Scriptural separation from the world	• A lifestyle dedicated to God's will in society
• Victory through the indwelling Christ	• A growing, victorious state of mind because of the indwelling Christ
• Unswerving loyalty to Christ as Lord	• A daily affirmation of Christ as Lord
• Consecration for rugged, sacrificial service	• A willingness to serve the Lord, even if it means sacrifice
• The leadership of the Holy Spirit for the believer and the church	• A desire to be more sensitive to the personal work of the Holy Spirit
• A living, working faith in the promises of God for spiritual, physical, and temporal needs	• A working faith in God's promises for all needs and daily life situations
• Zealous witnessing for Christ	• A witness for Christ without hypocrisy
	• A firm committed desire to be God's person.[63]

The rhetorical shifts here, not unlike those in the *Good News Bible,* avoid language redolent of old-time religion and may help some nontraditionalists to feel at home. At APU there is now a religious purpose to be served that had not been present in earlier days: the inner coherence of a student body that is no longer of a single faith community, despite the explicit duty to show mutual respect across denominational frontiers. The institution had never served a church or a denomination, but it had served a multidenominational movement. Now, even that coagulant is dissolving. Therefore the more generic the religious discourse, the more accommodating the university. These conditions make faith and theology more vulnerable to being displaced by an attitude and an ideology.

Felix came just as a majority of the full-time faculty, for the first time, held earned doctorates. Their workload was quite high: nine courses per year. Half the faculty were part-time teachers, some of whom also held full-time teaching jobs elsewhere; while part of the full-time APU faculty also held part-time jobs elsewhere to supplement their incomes.

There were some basic problems of quality that still needed to be addressed. APU still had virtually open admissions. Students in the traditional liberal arts and sciences remained a small minority, greatly outnumbered by those in vocational and professional training. The three largest baccalaureate programs were business, psychology, and music. Religion, which had been second largest five years earlier, awarding thirty-five A.B.s, now handed out only eight.

When the students began to complain of what WASC had long pointed out — that adjunct faculty were never evaluated or initiated with their religious fellowship in mind — recruitment interviews and orientation programs were adjusted. No records of the church affiliation of faculty were kept, though all annually signed the Statement of Faith. Students, on the other hand, did not need to be Christians, but they had to sign a "Statement of Agreement with Institutional Policy," attend chapel, and take the required course load in Bible and religion.[64]

In the one major accreditation visit since Dr. Felix took office, most concerns were financial. The visitors now perceived faculty concern for the problem that WASC had repeatedly pointed out: as APU expanded its postgraduate programs, it was not infusing them with the Christian mission of its undergraduate programs.[65] Cornelius Haggard, despite his apparently single-minded drive to obtain academic recognition for his little school, had been greatly apprehensive that by submitting itself to WASC standards and influence, largely controlled by educators presumably contemptuous of what he and his evangelical comrades held precious, Azusa Pacific would be forfeiting its identity and consigning itself to eventual secularization. Indeed, the Western Association of Schools and Colleges, at least in recent years, has been more forceful than other regional accrediting agencies in imposing a liberal ideological agenda upon its member colleges and universities. But the record shows that in the case of Azusa Pacific, to the contrary, it has been WASC that repeatedly nagged AC/APC/APU for gainsaying its own religious program (the 1981 visitation was an exception). WASC has coaxed and commended countless measures of modernization, adaptation, sophistication. But when, on any of these pretexts, the visitation teams detected what they considered an inclination to dilute or dissipate or — as is most often the case among academics — double-talk its religious program, WASC played the role of conscience, at times more doggedly and effectively than Haggard himself did or Haggard *redivivus* might have done.

It has been Azusa, not WASC, that tended repeatedly to reconstrue Christian faith in terms that appealed to a wider clientele but thinned its substance.

Today Azusa Pacific University is established and thriving. It has a College of Liberal Arts and Sciences, five professional schools, and forty-six degree programs. It grants the B.A., B.S., B.S.N., M.A., M.S., M.S.E., M.B.A., M.H.R.D., M.Mgt., M.Ed., M.F.T., M.M., M.S.M., M.Div., and Ed.D. (with Psy.D. and D.Min. soon to come). Enrollment is 4,601 (full-time equivalent = 3,567), which makes it the third- or fourth-largest member of the Coalition for Christian Colleges and Universities. The undergraduate/postgraduate ratio is 3:2; one-quarter of the students are from ethnic minorities. The plant includes two campuses and eleven domestic off-campus sites, more than sixty buildings, and gross assets of about $70 million, while annual operations are budgeted at more than $50 million. The endowment exceeds $7 million, with $9 million more in annuities and trusts held as prospective endowment. Annual growth was running at 5 percent, and now seems firm at 10 percent. It is all a long way from two students in Philena Hadley's house a century ago.

Full-time teaching faculty number 169, and 98 hold the doctorate. Far more important: it is ardently and credibly claimed that virtually all faculty members at Azusa Pacific regard their jobs as a ministry. What is more, they seem easy about saying this out loud.

Who are the students? Nearly 90 percent of the undergrads were A and B students in high school (though few of them got a hernia from their homework); for almost all who came, APU was their first choice (primarily, they claim, for its religious orientation). Well over half plan to earn postgraduate degrees. They are not poor: more than half come from families with income of more than $50,000. Sixty-one percent of the students report a religious affiliation; of them, the Baptists (16 percent), Disciples of Christ (11 percent), and Catholics (9 percent) are the largest cohorts, with the Catholics rapidly increasing. More than 90 percent report being born-again Christians. They test out as strongly conservative in social attitudes.[66]

There are points of stress within this story of burgeoning growth. The faculty is understaffed, and as a result a large portion of the courses, especially the service courses, are taught by part-time adjuncts. To illustrate: the Department of Religion and Philosophy, which has taught twenty thousand students in the past five years (there is an eighteen-credit requirement for all undergraduates), has eleven full-time faculty and must scour the region for fifteen to twenty adjuncts. Each full-time teacher is assigned twenty-seven course-hours per year, a very heavy but not unusual workload.[67] Aggravating this still more is the possibility for faculty to undertake another twelve hours of teaching for supplemental income at either APU or some other campus, such that a twenty-one-hour per-semester maximum is not uncommon. Another point of stress: 30 percent of the students drift away between the freshman and sophomore years.[68]

Partly because of this dearth of regular faculty, and partly because of student interests, APU does not have a liberal studies program at its heart. Less than one-third of the undergraduates choose their major subjects from the traditional arts and sciences. Those departments are able to offer only basic surveys, with few advanced courses, while vocational programs offer a wide array. For instance, in the fall semester of 1996 Philosophy offered six undergraduate courses in thirteen sections, and History offered eleven courses in sixteen sections; Music offered forty-five courses, and Nursing offered twenty-three courses in fifty-nine sections.

Also, faculty and staff salaries are low. Almost all undergraduate applicants who apply are admitted; in fact, more students are admitted each year than submit complete credentials. Thus there can be little or no selectivity. The university is committed to partial tuition grants to faculty families and to dependents of those in ministry (together equaling more than a million dollars in 1995-96), and also to merit scholarships for all matriculants with successful high school grade averages (nearly $2.4 million), two commitments which constitute a heavy claim on the annual budget.[69]

It is likely that these deficiencies are due to strategic decisions to apply the new moneys recently available. It also seems likely that steady growth will continue, with slow but sure betterment of the teachers and the teaching.

Does APU Have an Identity?

A distinct but related question regards the religious identity of Azusa Pacific University. At present there are numerous factors in place meant to assure the Christian character of the place. At the time of their appointment, and annually thereafter, all the senior members — trustees, administrators, faculty, and staff — subscribe to the Statement of Faith, descended from the old, rugged Doctrinal Standard. Faculty who no longer subscribe to the statement are expected to resign from the institution.[70] They are also expected, without exception, to be active members of a local church, and the faculty and administrators are looked for to participate with decent frequency in the thrice-weekly chapel services on campus. Students need not be Christian, but they are met even before arrival with reiterations of APU's identity as a Christian university, and are promised an education that puts "God First" and integrates Christian attitudes and evangelical practices into the intellectual project. Every student is required to take eighteen credits of religion and philosophy, to attend chapel regularly (ten absences a semester are allowed for), and to engage in student ministries or community service projects (e.g., prison ministry, Habitat for Humanity, visiting teenage mothers and elderly shut-ins) at least fifteen hours per semester. In addition there are plenty of outreach programs available for afternoons, weekends, vacations, and summers. Misconduct for students includes the evangelical imperatives (sex, alcohol, drugs, smoking), plus more modern proscriptions against hazing, harassment, and weaponry.

APU is clearly more forthright about its religious identity than any institution studied in previous chapters except Concordia University. The measures taken to recruit faculty who join in the dedication, and to attract and cultivate a student body in a shared faith, have produced a campus population, senior and junior, with less ambiguity and equivocation toward Christianity than in the foregoing case studies. Studies, volunteer service, evangelism, and worship are amalgamated with purpose and instinct. The claim to be a Christian college is fairly made.

There is serious cause for concern about the future, however. Azusa Pacific turns only a casual eye and a light hand to issues of contemporary juvenile style. So there are bare female midriffs and male earrings, and enough hair to sustain a shampoo factory. Staff members in the know speak disappointedly of student sex nowadays that was never dreamed of in the past. This symbolizes some wear and tear in the Holiness tradition. It is certainly no hand-me-down from the days when one Holiness denomination was wrenched by schism over the morality of wearing neckties, or from the days when Cornelius Haggard and his wife forwent wedding bands as ostentatious and worldly. As we have seen, the religious discourse of the campus has been repeatedly rewritten over the years: another sign of the times, and of Azusa Pacific moving with the times.

But to identify a lapse in the tradition by these signs of worldliness is misleading. It was under Haggard's grand and gifted leadership years ago that an unwitting but decisive break was made in the tradition. Haggard was no academic, no scholar. He was a preacher and a pastor, and he was the heart of Pacific Bible College. He wanted to make "College" as true as "Bible." He set out to make his school deserving of accreditation, and in order to justify PBC to the academy he accepted the academy's agenda as primary, and justified his Christian agenda as "an added plus." It was a frequent expression for him, but he could not have known its performative power. For if faith and piety were an added plus, then they were restricted to being patronal concomitants of academic activity, not components of it. He would speak sometimes of how Christian faith might enhance the various disciplines, but he did not imagine that the faith might also be a critic and corrective in the very business of scholarship. What this did was accentuate a problem that already troubled the evangelicals, especially those of the Wesleyan wing: their faith tended more and more to fasten itself upon moral integrity, and less upon intellectual perspicacity. These evangelicals had little theological interest or tradition, and without that even their moral earnestness became jeopardized, especially in the Wesleyan tradition, because, after mistaking morals for faith, they were at risk of mistaking manners for morals. After that it was all the easier to fall into the misunderstanding "which makes it possible to call a hotel and a college Christian because neither of them has a bar!"[71] Thus, in the absence of theological energy, even their moral convictions could soften into preferences governed more by class than by Christian conviction. Haggard was a man confident in the Lord, but perhaps not confident enough to think that his college might eventually do its academic work even better than many of its accredited neighbors . . . precisely because of the intellectually clarifying power of the church's faith.

Even today, some of the most dynamic units of APU's program are off-to-the-side activities which continue the missionary calling of the Training School. Operation Impact is one example already mentioned: an imaginative program to educate missionaries on-site across the world. Here is a unit where APU's inner circle can unfurl their faith unconditionally. Today no one on campus even knows how many alumni work as missionaries, because the alumni office does not classify or code graduates by that designation. It is thought that perhaps five hundred to one thousand alums now do that work. But the Office of World Missions (OWM), headquartered on campus, helps from three hundred to five hundred students each year to take a hand in the missionary effort and sends fifty to seventy APU students on longer exploratory journeys to Russia, Romania, Tanzania-Kenya, Haiti, and Ecuador. The office maintains a close bond with the Department of Global Studies, which is intended to prepare students to promote God's truth and justice in the world. On a much wider scale the OWM runs a national program that sends seven thousand people on short-term youth projects, mostly into Mexico. InterVarsity Fellowship sponsors a triennial mission meeting for twenty thousand college students, and OWM is aiming to replicate this for high school students.[72] Here, in a unit whose professionalism is not expected to vindicate itself on grounds that make sense primarily to the academy, there is a focus and an easy sense of skilled identity which cannot be matched in some of the academic units. It ignores the doctrine that faith is an "added plus."

There was another, even more serious problem dating back to the Haggard regime which has become a potential destabilizer at Azusa: its lack of a sponsoring church — by which is meant a vital and functioning communion of congregations.

The old Training School was the creation of Holiness people. The first American colleges had been founded by the New England Congregationalists and the Atlantic Presbyterians, and they served the colonial and federal elites. They were gradually invested with a strong and secular liberalism, and eventually retained only so much of their religious drive as was socially commodious. The second wave, composed largely of revivalist groups — notably the Methodists, Baptists, and Friends — originated in England and swept past the Appalachians to dominate the West. They followed the elite schools at a distance, and with lesser resources, but eventually made their turn toward respectability and a secular professionalism. They were assimilated to the elite and joined in the aspiration to train the gentlemen of their respective vicinities. After the Civil War the Holiness movement, which was an indigenous iteration of the earlier European Pietism, recoiled from what members saw as the lowered moral tone of the churches and the predominantly rationalist tone of the prevailing Calvinism, and in reaction they accentuated religious feeling (over doctrine), moral optimism, and simplicity of manners: "ardor over order," as some say.[73] Orthopathy over orthodoxy. The movement was so widespread and well networked that for a while it formed a single field of imagination and interpretation. Since it regarded specific church identity as relatively unimportant, the movement begot many new denominations, all very American and Western. Cornelius Haggard, who was born when the Training School was still a youngster, was able to move and preach in a wide variety of churches without much change of his Christian style, because the Holiness movement was still strong enough (though then waning) to maintain that united field. So, too, his college was able to gather teachers and students from various denominations into a single allegiance. The Holiness movement was so united that it became the functional equivalent of a denomination. But denominations are not churches, and in time, for want of preservation and renewal, the Holiness movement decomposed.

Does APU Have a Community?

Today the Holiness movement, like New England Puritans, is history. The university has chosen, out of its past, a single Christian identifier: "Wesleyan." Not even "Wesleyan Holiness," nor "Arminian," but the most nonecclesial, vague, and indistinct modifier of them all. In publications where categories must be used, APU calls itself "interdenominational/nondenominational." That is a precise statement. In early years, though it said it was open to all evangelicals and was indifferent to specific church membership, that was because almost everyone who came belonged to that same movement. Thus for many years the college was functionally, though not formally, denominational, even sectarian. You had to be an insider in the movement really to belong there. But as that movement dissolved, and as a finally "successful" college began to grow, its intake was increasingly market driven, to the point where now Calvinists and Catholics are nesting on campus. It is so interdenominational that it is now nondenominational.

The presumption behind APU's religious self-understanding is that there is a generic, biblical Christianity which preserves a durable piety all can share. One means intended to assure this continuity is the Statement of Faith. By virtue of having subscribed to it, all the senior people sense a working solidarity of faith. But there are two large families of evangelicals: those descended from the Wesleyan tradition, whose religion has been centered upon experience and feeling, and those descended from the Calvinist tradition, whose religion has been centered upon defined creed. The former have tended to be nondenominational; the latter, multidenominational. The same is true of the colleges they have sponsored. The Wesleyans spoke of inspiration, enthusiasm, joy, and they easily spoke of all Christian believers as really one. The Calvinists spoke of fidelity and duty, and had a stronger sense of the distance between the saved and the lost (who included not a few Christian believers).[74] The school we are studying here is indeed Wesleyan, not in descent of doctrine, but in fellowship of feeling.

At Azusa Pacific the Doctrinal Standard/Statement of Faith has probably functioned less as a creed than as a formal device whereby a fellowship much more obviously drawn by feeling than defined by faith has been able to enact its fellowship. A remark of President Felix perhaps states more pointedly what the university really demands from its teachers: "The message to them all is that they have to love Jesus, teaching, and themselves." But they are not members of a common church. As one faculty member put it but all might have: "we are members of a local community, a neighborhood; an educational community, Azusa Pacific University; a religious community, our local churches; and a nation, the United States of America."[75] This has been a problem for APU. At one time, when it was the large movement and not a local church which gave this school its culture, the movement controlled. But it was not really a denomination, nor a church, nor the church, any of which might have been a more durable cultural contender with both nation and academy.

William Yarchin, chairman of the Department of Religion and Philosophy, believes that despite their multiplicity of denominational identities, the APU type of evangelical churches today tend to share a close common culture. Like today's grocery stores, they all look the same inside, and purvey the same commodities. Their teaching, even in the absence of an assertive doctrine and authority, tends somehow to be uniform. Their ministry and fellowship are assessed mostly by their size (big) and their style (glitz). Also, there is no admission of any difference between Scripture and doctrine: the doctrine is said to be derived entirely from Scripture. But the subjects of interest that are pursued in Scripture are themselves determined by contemporary doctrinal emphases. Thus Yarchin, and wisely.

Because these evangelicals do not function as a church or even a denomination, and do not take it as an evangelical task constantly and corporately to re-discern and re-state and re-apply and re-defend the faith once delivered to the saints, as individuals and as congregations they are pulled in and out like kelp on the irresistible tides of the public culture. Another Azusa teacher wryly portrayed the prejudices of a typical American student encountering someone like her: "It's a double bind — not only am I a professor (i.e., scholar, liberal, intellectual, impractical), but I am also an evangelical Christian (i.e., conservative, religious, Republican)."[76] There is much truth to the caricature. For the typical American needs to figure out whether she is in thrall to the (liberal) academic culture, or to the (conservative) national culture (both of which are liberal historically). For the mainline churches it has been the liberal culture; for these evangelicals it has been the conservative one. As one Azusa faculty member remembers it, during the Iran-contra hearings photos of Ollie North were strewn about the campus offices as icons of devotion. A quarter-century earlier Cornelius Haggard, J. Edgar Hoover's adherent, had made much the same point to the accreditors: "Academically, we plan to prepare students to succeed in life. . . . Morally, we are committed to inculcating those moral and spiritual values and virtues which have made America great . . . Patriotically, we are 'squares.' "[77]

The Play's the Thing

Azusa Pacific's ambiguous position finds a mime in its music. The most developed and far-reaching missionary activity of the student body is carried on the medium of music. Music, explains Dean Don Grant (onetime academic vice president of the university), is central to the vitality of most "Christian colleges," and of most evangelical churches. At APU there are 140 music majors and more than four hundred students active in fifteen ensembles: the University Choir and Orchestra (their varsity groups), two female choral groups and one male, a Jazz Ensemble, Concert Band, smaller orchestra, Brass Quintet, Oratorio Choir, Handbell Choir, String Trio, and many ad hoc small groups. Their performances are APU's chief recruiting device. The University Choir and Orchestra will typically have seventy-five or more bookings a year. Their recordings are exquisite. They may perform with the Long Beach Pops or at the Hollywood Bowl, or with Billy Graham. But their staple is Sunday evening concerts in regional churches. Evangelistic music as a genre was once described as "bad as the worst jazz and hillbilly music in a cheap music hall." Not so at APU. The artistry in this musical endeavor is impeccably tasteful: professional acoustics; lush costuming and sleek grooming; repertory that combines sacred classics, liturgical pieces, spirituals, and light contemporary (with rare outbreaks of soft corn); but not much secular music. The programs may begin and end with a prayer, and they are often staged in sanctuaries, but they are not worship services. Both the idiom and the presentation are meant to give relish to religious feelings. And, like all the liturgical arts, they have a seductive side as well when the sheer beauty of the medium can distract from prayer instead of enhancing it. It, too, can drown out the still, small voice.

Azusa Pacific is about as good as it gets in offering religious mood music for the Skyline Wesleyan Church, the Rolling Hills Covenant Church, and the Pomona First Baptist Church, all moved with concord of sweet sounds. But it is also an amiable sponsor of that other music which will attract young people. That music — rap, rock, reggae — hath no charms to soothe a savage beast, but it is a first draw upon the youngsters to whom APU wants to offer an attractive gospel. The campus is thus host to another musical brigade, with a dress and grooming code the polar opposite of the School of Music's disciplined choristers upon whose cheeks not a straying sideburn is to be seen ("The Gates of Heaven open wider than the gates of Azusa Pacific College," chuckles Dean Grant). With the mien of Rasputin, the garb of Emmett Kelly, and the sonic boom of Madison Square Garden, these musicians — every bit as gifted as their official, decorous counterparts — offer an outreach in another direction.

When a large storage building became vacant, the university made it over to what they call the Warehouse Ministry. They fill it with heavy metal music under Christian lyrics and invite in the teenagers of the area. Crowds have reached two thousand, and they are hoping for twice that many. For a dozen years now they have staged a "Night of Champions." They bring in about sixteen hundred high school athletes of the area and have their own athletes demonstrate fundamentals. (Well they might: APU has won thirteen national championships in the National Association of Intercollegiate Athletics, has sent a dozen athletes into professional sports, and saw its Olympians win five medals in the 1992 Summer Games at Barcelona.) Then off to the Warehouse, where Rosie Greer and Raghib "the Rocket" Ismail have made cameo appearances — and pitches for Jesus. Then, the Music.

The question arises: Do the Christian lyrics set the tone for the event, or the contemporary music with its strong (and quite different) associations? At the recent Night of Champions, security officers had to frisk everyone at the gate, and as the music got under way the youngsters naturally began to dance. Dancing is one of the activities traditionally avoided in the Holiness tradition, conjoined as it has been historically with alcohol, flirtation, and all that. Administrators winced, but later explained they couldn't "draw the line." APU says publicly that it wants to make music for the masses, not just high-brow stuff, and this is part of that calculated missionary risk.

The light-handed policy was recently put under great strain. In the last set at a Warehouse Ministry event one singer ignored the program and did a long song, "My Funny Valentine," featuring an extended soliloquy on masturbation. Someone eventually cut the power to the amplification system. When the excitement waned and the last group prepared to conclude the evening, their leader tested the restored microphone by reciting "testicles, testicles," instead of "testing, testing." The admissions staff, who had a stake in the night's events, walked out, and the Warehouse Ministry was guaranteed its place in history. The latter offender, leader of Cranium, a "ministry band," apologized in the student newspaper but stoutly defended his group's scripted lyrics. "We hold Christ, love and the struggles and victories in the walk of faith as the core of our music and lyrics." The man who had begun the ruckus sounded somewhat less repentant. "I enjoyed speaking the ugly word, and letting people know that they need not hide from the reality of their habits in this area. . . . I've spent most of my life in a 'church family' where I was trained to cater to others' feelings. Since then, I've adopted a more blatant way of proposing ideas without the candy coating." This young man was featured a week later in a student news story on the succeeding moral issue on campus: tattooing and body piercing. He had recently had his tongue bored to carry a miniature stainless steel barbell. "I have a friend who has one and I thought it looked cool and I liked the option of having it concealed."[78] Tongue and barbell appeared in the paper, photographed at closest range, without the candy coating. The ministries were disciplined, but only by being made ineligible to participate in the annual musical awards event before graduation. President Felix was obliged to send out hundreds of letters disavowing the turn of events.

Some who reflected on these happenings pondered the fact that the director of the premier University Choir is the father of the transfixed son who took it as his Warehouse Ministry to allay juvenile sexual guilt. But one professor's reminiscence looked more largely at this moral tale: "The greatest worry for our administration is that APU might come to be regarded as liberal."[79] Ought he to have enlarged his concern and pondered whether the undeniably presentable semipro musical groups disciplined and led by the faculty might be drawing Azusa Pacific into an equal or even stronger cultural undertow than the high jinks of the heavy metal bands led by the students?

Holiness

The tradition that modest manners are a needed safety rail around a well-moored morality is much older than either Pietism or American evangelicalism. A community with a Holiness history, where faith is planted in sensibilities, would need to know what the tradition had anciently learned: that manners can both protect and subvert. If there be instability in APU's piety, it may be because its conservative mannerism is enlivened less by attentiveness to the gospel than by submission to a conservative sociopolitical culture.

Leona Nelson, in her perceptive study of the secularization process in another Holiness college, has noted what we have seen in the case of many of the Methodist and Baptist schools (descendants of an older European Pietism) before they finally were assimilated to their more elite Congregationalist and Presbyterian elder institutions: they were held back for a while by the "fear of losing the support and loyalty of the smaller, more orthodox churches throughout the Movement upon which the college depends for a great source of its income and for most of its students." When they did choose another first loyalty to replace Christian faith, it was both sociopolitical (the liberal culture of the elite) and academic (the liberal culture of the academy). But as the later-founded evangelical colleges were being drawn away from their primarily religious thrust, it was in a conservative direction, to seek the advantages of class and power of a conservative clientele. They would manifest the possibility of an at least initially conservative secularization.[80]

Decorum is to APU's perceived advantage. The veteran registrar, when asked why she thought women were outnumbering men on campus (the present ratio among undergraduates is already 3:2, and women are increasing at twice the rate of men, and are academically the more capable), reckoned that many parents think of a Christian college as a much safer environment than the state campuses and are more inclined to want (and to pay for) that safety for their daughters than to think it needful for their sons.[81] A preoccupation with decorum emerges from some of the regulations. The school has always excluded alcohol and tobacco as primeval evangelical prohibitions, but in recent regulations alcohol and drugs are forbidden, not primarily on moral grounds but as offenses against the Federal Drug-Free Workplace Act and the Drug-Free Schools and Communities Act. Smoking is forbidden "for health and safety considerations."[82] The old stricture on invited speakers ("loyal Americans, not advocating civil disorder or disobedience. Extremists are to be avoided'') was long ago retired, but students are still advised "to invite speakers/presenters to chapel, assemblies, and activities who will contribute positively to the spiritual goals of the university. Primary consideration is given to those of the evangelical Christian faith."[83] The *Faculty Handbook* enjoins harmony, a spirit of unity, without animosity or disrespect. "Matters which have the potential for creating dissent should be treated with the utmost caution, and care should be taken to confine confidential, professional issues to faculty circles."[84]

In one sense, these should not traditionally be matters of concern at a Holiness institution, because a central tenet of that tradition was that God not only forgave the sins of the converted sinner but also gave definitive sanctification by purging him or her of all inclination to sin. As another Holiness college used to put it: "We feel it right to say that no person will be allowed in the school but such as are thoroughly consecrated to God, dead to sin, utterly dead to 'youthful lusts' and whose life in Christ is established and blameless."[85] The contemporary view at APU is different. As Richard Felix explains: "APU wants to follow holiness, but hasn't yet achieved purity. Some selfishness still clings." Don Grant seems to say the same: APU is a "redemptive society. It is not perfectionist, though it says out loud what is not acceptable." Considering the university's founding community, these are doctrinally revisionist statements. But there is greater significance in the fact that the program of conformable conduct avoids public presentation in religious terms. It is said out loud, but apparently no longer as something redemptive. That does not mean they must "uphold the standards of holiness in appearance and conduct so 'that we might walk worthy of the Lord unto all pleasing,' " and explain themselves as in yesteryear. But what has replaced that lovely and now quaint discourse may not be a translation or even a paraphrase. It may be a change. Haggard's own warning may have been vindicated: they are "taking on the color of their surroundings." They may be making room for the dreaded God minifiers and man magnifiers.

The Holiness Quakers who begot the Training School a century ago saw as their great nemesis the modernist Quakers, born out of the same evangelical movement but more intellectually disposed. The Holiness mode was fundamentalist and innocent of much learning. The modernists were deferential toward academics but very vague in their belief and vision of social reform. As APU acquires financial stability and academic momentum, its strongest temptation may be a latter-day modernism, which has in the meantime acquired some suaver forms than when William Pinkham and Eli Reece raged so angrily against it.

There is no open evidence that the ethos at APU has followed the call of Norman Vincent Peale to equate free enterprise with Christianity. But it has prospered, and looks to prosper more. APU sups with the powerful. Its people have style. Class, too.

DORDT COLLEGE

U.S. Highway 75 strides straight down the west side of Iowa, seemingly resolved to persevere all the way to Tierra del Fuego. But then, in the midst of Sioux County, it passes through a small town where, like any wayfarer, it slows down, then pauses, to look about. There U.S. 75 suddenly takes on the name and duties of Main Avenue, the only thoroughfare in Sioux Center with a proper name: the other avenues (and they are few) are numbered to left and to right, and the numbered streets are woven through them east to west. The spires of the town are its three water towers; its two lesser steeples, the grain elevators. Beside the band shell in the tiny park is the town monument. It is no likeness of a boy who perished at the Marne or on Tarawa, or of a homesteading family on a prairie schooner, or even of a stolid Sioux warrior. It is a bronze effigy of the eldest of all local heroes: Old Blue Stem, the thick, reedlike grass that used to wave six feet tall in a dry prairie ocean that rolled across the central plains right up into Minnesota.

The signs along Main Avenue display only one sort of name: Wassink, Van der Ploeg, Ver Hoef, Roelofs, Driesen. These people are Dutch. Banks and insurance companies and financial advisers are abundant along that avenue. Very Dutch. The message board of the motel at the northern edge of town announces, not "Happy Honeymoon, Ken and Darlene" or "Sioux Center Welcomes Ortho/Iowa," but instead "Property Tax Evasion Is a Crime." Very serious. Beside the door at Holiday Lanes, the bowling alley where livestock men meet for heavy breakfast from six o'clock on, a poster advertises a Chemical Awareness Meeting for mothers and kids: not about pot or crack or coke like everywhere else, but about laundry bleach and fertilizer. Very wholesome. The local citizens laid out $98,000 a few years ago for an exotic mega-machine that daily sweeps the streets and vacuums the gutters and buffs the toenails of the town. Very clean. The yards are severe and the houses not very attractive, but most of them have their old wood clapboard sheathed neatly now under aluminum or vinyl siding. Sioux Center is a tidy and orderly place. As Dutch as Hilversum.

The Dutch migrations to northwest Iowa began to arrive in 1871: from the Netherlands, and from earlier sojourns in Minnesota, Wisconsin, and even nearby Muscatine and Pella. The First Reformed Church and the mails appeared in 1877; a survey and town plat in '81; the railroad in '89; a bank and saloons, a marshal and a jail, in '90; incorporation and temperance unions in '91; the first fire engine in '93; and the separation of the Dutch Reformed from the Reformed Church in '99.[86]

The Homestead Act of 1862 had offered cheap and plentiful land in the West, but these Dutch came in search of more than land; many had left land behind. They wanted a society of their own, a home they could have all to themselves. Those who had left the Netherlands were leaving one of the most crowded countries in the world, but it had not been confining until 1806 when the state had established common schools, and 1816 when it took the Dutch Reformed Church under its established control. These migrant Calvinists were breakaways. Those who came first from the Netherlands were determined to be free of a totalitarian state which imposed its doctrinaire liberalism on them and their children. Those who abandoned their first homes in the New World came to get away from another oppressive culture: that of the Americans, with their culture and their schools. These Dutch were a people who wanted to order their lives in their own way.

The Netherlands had been strongly infused with the Enlightenment, one of whose dogmas was that there should be no religious dogmas (unless stated in the most meaninglessly generic terms), since distinctive religious beliefs had so manifestly disrupted the capacity of the nation-states to subdue their peoples. The law of 1806 which created common schools throughout the nation bade them all teach a religion that was Christian but not sectarian: a Christianity which omitted all that was clear or controversial. There was no room for a Christianity that was tenacious about divine revelation and its moral claims. Some of the Reformed Dutch were very tenacious about their beliefs, and began to suspect that what the schools really meant to purvey was a divinely authorized state, a political ideology, a secular culture.

The establishment and domestication of the Reformed Church in 1816 by the state provoked a new surge of confessional renewal among both orthodox Calvinists and Catholics. When the middle class was eventually given the vote, this gave them enough political strength to assert their own educational imperatives. Guillaume Groen Van Prinsterer and his protégé, Abraham Kuyper, would found a new political party, the Antirevolutionary Party; a new secessionist free church, the Reformed Churches in the Netherlands; and a new center of higher learning, the Free University of Amsterdam. Kuyper edited *De Heraut,* founded *De Standaard,* two weekly newspapers, and wrote for both for half a century. He was also an active supporter of a Calvinist labor movement. These two men were largely driven by convictions first enunciated by Groen Van Prinsterer.

> He argued that efforts to force uniform education on all citizens in an attempt to achieve national unity were ill-founded and violated God-given rights. The result of such government interference, according to Van Prinsterer, was to force on all a system of education in which a vague, Deistic religion couched in Christian terms functioned as the guiding worldview. In Van Prinsterer's eyes, the state schools had fallen prey to the principles of the French Revolution: . . . "between freedom of conscience, freedom of worship, and freedom of education there existed an indissoluble connection."[87]

Kuyper, who would exercise the greatest influence on the Dutch emigrants to America, put it this way:

> For the sake of tolerance the [liberal elite] seeks to remove every conviction that raises itself above the superficial.. . . . A specific, settled conviction is in its eyes

a "prejudice," an "outdated," an "immoderate notion." . . . Tolerance, yes, but tolerance out of indifference, out of superficiality, out of lack of principles. . . . It is the undermining of any solid conviction, under the slogan of the struggle against witch-hunts and sectarian conflict and religious hatred.[88]

As a student Abraham Kuyper had been a flippant liberal who rejected a transcendent God, the divinity of Jesus, the reality of miracles, and the authority of the Bible. After conversion through the influence of his fiancée, he became a pastor, theologian, journalist, politician, prime minister, and cultural paladin of the Netherlands. Kuyper's coalition of nonestablished Calvinists and minority Catholics was able to create a collaborative political majority in a country that was then a Calvinist stronghold. Since the days of John Calvin himself, the Reformed movement had often been directly involved in political symbiosis with the civil power. For Calvin it had seemed a necessary expedient; but for Kuyper it became also a matter of religious conviction.

Man had been given the "cultural mandate" to subdue the earth, and only those properly endued with God's Spirit and Word (i.e., the Reformed) could rightly understand the ultimate purposes of creation and lead collaborative efforts with unbelievers to develop a culture that fostered those purposes. As Kuyper read his history, overall sovereignty belongs to God alone, and has been delegated in its fullness to one man only: Jesus. Other humans receive the authority to compel obedience only within specific spheres.

> There is accordingly a realm of nature in which its sovereign works formatively according to fixed laws. Similarly there is a realm of the personal, of the family, of science, of social and ecclesiastical life — each of which obeys its own laws, and each of which stands under its own supreme authority. There is a realm of thought where only the laws of logic may rule. There is a realm of conscience where no one may issue commands sovereignly but the Holy One Himself. And finally there is a realm of faith where only the person himself is sovereign who through faith dedicates himself in the depths of his being.[89]

Sharpened by the political struggle in Holland which required more than a century of conflict to liberate education from the state and its ideology, Kuyper's philosophy saw the totalitarian state as history's villain. With an endless passion for domination Caesar had continually intruded to impose his will upon every other enterprise. Because the state was responsible for justice, Kuyper was willing to acknowledge its authority to police relationships between the several spheres. But the state could rightly only discern, and not decide, what those interrelations properly were. But although Kuyper deferred to the professional competence of believers in their respective spheres, he assumed it was the church that understood all this and dominated the discernment process.

He seemed to entertain little worry about those who preside over the church.

That is understandable in a country where religious division had thwarted every church's temptation to civil influence. Yet in a homogeneous society (which did not then exist in the Netherlands but which the Dutch immigrants would provide for themselves in pockets of the New World) where it was really the church that provided the master ideology for all institutions and their interactions — even for the state, as Kuyper himself was doing — how could the religious leaders be kept from usurping the rightful sovereignty of all other spheres, such as education, science, or finance? The theory was that in a unitary society a close-knit Reformed *people* would rule all their institutions, the church included. Kuyper shows only mild concern that churchmen with that much say-so would be inclined to intrude their religious predilections into secular spheres of activity. He shows no concern whatever about a wholly different, sinister, long-term prospect: that the church, if authorized to describe the rationale and the moral guidelines for the mercantile, fiscal, political, educational, artistic, and social projects of such a sober and thrifty people, would be inexorably beguiled to shape its wisdom to its secular constituencies. That would have been a worry of a different sort: that a magisterial Reformed church might become, not a bully, but a shill.

The Dutch Calvinists whom we encounter in Sioux Center belong to the Christian Reformed Church in North America (CRC). As Americans they showed no disposition to fawn on the sovereignty of the state. One early intimation of their primary loyalties was a disinclination to be American flag–wavers. The *Sioux County Herald* carried a last-minute report from its Sioux Center correspondent on 30 June 1887: "We are obliged to withdraw the announcement of our Fourth of July celebration made last issue, simply because the idea of a celebration did not seem to be in accordance with the religious notions of some of our brethren in the church . . ."[90]

Dordt College is an institution begotten by and for this close society of Dutch people in America. It is very Dutch, very Christian Reformed, and very much at home in Sioux Center. There are thirteen Christian congregations in town, and the four Christian Reformed churches now count about half the town's five thousand people as members. Three other Reformed churches enroll much of the remaining population.

The flagship campus of the CRC is Calvin College (with its associated seminary) in Grand Rapids. Dordt College was founded by CRC members, mostly those west of the Mississippi and from Canada. Since their tiny Grundy College (Iowa) had closed in 1934, an Iowa-based movement had planned another junior college for the West, "to give young people an education that is Christian[91] not merely in the sense that devotional exercises are appended to the ordinary work of the college, but in the larger and deeper sense that all class work, all the students' intellectual, emotional, and imaginative activities shall be permeated with the spirit and teaching of Christianity."[92] This suggestion had an uphill journey toward realization, however, since it required official cognizance within the church. CRC practice is to refer all proposals to committees, and this proposal had to endure thirteen such committals; that it required only twenty years suggests a swifter course through each committee than usual. What handicapped this proposal was that it would create a competitor for Calvin College. The Calvin trustees were repeatedly asked for their opinion of the project and they naturally, and repeatedly, recommended that it be dropped.[93]

The CRC was always in a bit of a bad conscience about Calvin College. In defiance of all its Kuyperian doctrine about church and school as distinct spheres, Calvin was an official creature of the church. If the Synodical Tract Committee and Back to God radio broadcasts and Calvin Seminary were all denominational undertakings, that made sense: they were all directly religious activities. But "sphere sovereignty" properly required that Calvin College, in the sphere of education, be run entirely by CRC *people,* yet not by the Christian Reformed *Church.* The problem was that no system of fund-raising had been found to equal the annual "quota" system, whereby strictly denominational enterprises were costed out and then assessed pro rata to each congregation, and thence to each member family. What kept the proprietorship of the college in the church was the church's effectiveness as a taxation agency. The folks at Calvin were understandably worried that if their doctrinally dodgy but fiscally reliable status were to be shared with other institutions, the increased tax burden could provoke a reform of the Reform that might throw Calvin on its own resources.[94] What caused their western competitors to persist in their determination to found a new junior college was their large network of local Christian schools, elementary and secondary, which needed CRC-educated teachers. Their young men and women who went east to Calvin with that vocation in mind tended not to return after graduation. As it became clear, however, that the Iowa classes (in CRC nomenclature, a church district is called a "classis") would not be able to have their Calvin assessments reduced to compensate for their support of a new local junior college, they began to withdraw their sponsorship from the project. This was largely due to the influence of their ministers, mostly Calvin alumni and newcomers to the western region, whose responsibility it would have been to elicit all that new money. In the end it was the affluent and generous Classis Sioux Center that picked up the initiative and opened Midwest Christian Junior College in 1955.

Right away a conflict rose to the surface, between a faculty that pursued the stated purpose — to run a two-year school for teacher certification — and a board that had quietly dilated its ambitions and now wanted a four-year liberal arts college. The board prevailed. They changed the name in 1956 to Dordt College, purged the faculty, and installed one of their fellow trustees, the like-minded local minister B. J. Haan, as president.[95] CRC clergy must resign from the ministry if they leave the pastorate. Haan's board and classis wanted him to retain his ministerial status on two grounds: Dordt's work was to train ministers and teachers, "vocations which are immediately vital to the life of the church"; and the president of Calvin College already enjoyed this privilege. The annual Synod was not much disposed to allow that Dordt College could be likened to a pastoral ministry of Word and sacrament, but three committees and three years later synod resolved the matter in Haan's favor and granted the exception.[96] Animating this conflict was a larger, unresolved issue: Was a college whose identity, board, faculty, and student clientele were Christian Reformed an undertaking of the church, or an undertaking of its members somehow acting apart from the church? And did it make any difference? Meanwhile Dordt suffered another serious rebuff from Calvin College, as a reminder that there could be as much rivalry as sovereignty within the spheres. Early in the accreditation process Dordt had to secure the endorsement of three accredited institutions in the North Central Association. It naturally turned to its elder sister in Grand Rapids, and was refused.[97]

Synod was continually asked by Classis Sioux Center to allow some reduction (20 percent was suggested) in the Calvin assessments for any congregations supporting the new college. Synod refused: the church could not support what the church did not control. The classis responded that the church was built on the policy that schools were to be controlled by independent societies of people who were also CRC members, but not by Synod. Synod's fear was that if this principle were followed consistently, and Calvin were given its independence, Calvin would inevitably go the way of other church-sponsored colleges. Untold committees later, synod granted a compromise: the assessment for Calvin would no longer be uniform throughout the church; it would vary according to the proportion of local young people enrolled. The family quota per annum for Calvin immediately fell to $11.00 in Iowa, while that in Grand Rapids rose to $21.50. But the wrangle had shown that in defiance of the Kuyperian doctrine that the various spheres were all to be autonomously sovereign, the church really functioned as the *capo di tutti capi.*

Granted this much relief, the sponsors of Dordt — who, by an important legal fiction, were not the regional congregations but their members — decided it was time to upgrade to a degree-granting college. The 35 students enrolled in 1955 had increased to 280 by 1962, the year Reverend Haan's ministerial status and the financing compromise were both finally conceded. What forced the issue, however, was a decision of the Iowa Department of Public Instruction to discontinue awarding teacher certification after only two years of college. To supply its Christian schools with teachers, Dordt now had to grant baccalaureates. Dordt soon proved to be even more attractive as a four-year college: by the end of the 1960s its student body would number 870.

In the meantime, however, the college undertook to define itself, an arduous and compulsive task which would be repeated at close intervals. This process of self-definition disclosed an unusual capacity and even appetite for turgid, exhausting ideology. The first product was *The Educational Task of Dordt College,* adopted in 1961.[98] Encased within rambling accounts of the doctrine of Kuyper and other influential CRC worthies was a table of seventeen propositions. For many colleges this would have been a staggering length, but it has turned out to be the briefest of all such mission documents at Dordt. It begins, as would all its successors, by identifying the Scriptures as the most fundamental guide: "That Word of God is divinely inspired, the infallible and only rule for faith and practice." It then identifies successive authorities whereby the Scriptures are to be understood: first Calvin's *Institutes of the Christian Religion* (1536); then the three CRC "Forms of Unity," the Belgic Confession (1561), the Heidelberg Catechism (1563), and the Canons of Dort (1618-19); and lastly the seventeen local propositions. All members of the faculty must naturally hold membership in the CRC and subscribe to all these authorities.

There is a lumbering logical sequence to the seventeen propositions; their bearing on the college can be seen in these excerpts:

2. Man, created in God's image, possesses the faculties necessary for the explication of meaning which is implicit in the universe, and for the understanding of the relationships between the various spheres of life and their ultimate relationship to the sovereign creator. . . .

3. Man, created in God's image, is God's vice-gerent representative king in the universe and is given the mandate, often called the cultural mandate, to subdue the earth bringing all things to serve God's glory. This calls man to the task of searching out all things and relationships, leading to the proper development of God's creation to its appointed goal. . . .

7. The redemptive work of Christ has cosmic significance. He not only restores fallen man to his kingly position and activity; Christ also, as the new representative head and king of creation, by His atonement provides the basis for the restoration of the cosmos. By the restoration of man through the regenerative work of His Spirit, He enables man to understand and interpret His special revelation, the Holy Scriptures. Through the medium of the Scriptures man can interpret himself and all of nature (cosmos) in the context of sin and Christ's redemptive work. Man can cooperate with Christ's Spirit in the transformation of nature, leading all of creation to its consummation, ultimately achieved in the renewal of all things when Christ returns.

Unregenerate man cannot discern the pattern of larger spiritual and transcendent meanings. But he too under the blessing of Christ's re-creation can find moments of truth in the various realms of human endeavor. He may, for example, accomplish great things in the sciences or in the arts. But it is the Christian alone who finds for these truths their ultimate meaning and reference. This is the broadest educational task. . . .

12. God's kingdom is divided into specific spheres. There are spheres of education, state, church, home, mercy, labor, etc. Each sphere has its distinct task. What belongs to one sphere should not, normally, be transferred to another sphere. Each sphere wherever necessary should have its own society for the implementation of its task. The church, though in a sense a part of the kingdom, holds a unique position in the kingdom in that it speaks to all spheres, delineating the principles of God's Word as they apply to them. . . .

15. The subject matter for education is the entire universe, nature and man.

This is often called God's general revelation in distinction from His special revelation, the Bible, made necessary by sin. The latter is basic to the understanding of meaning in the former. . . .

17. Education is specifically a kingdom sphere properly sponsored by a society of the covenant community. Yet it stands more closely to the instituted church in its relationship to the other spheres of the kingdom in that it too is fundamental to all spheres. It is preparatory to virtually all kingdom activity. Even the institutional church depends upon the sphere of education for the execution of her task. This explains the instituted church's serious concern relative to the education of her youth. Without education her task cannot be performed. Without a Scripturally oriented education for her youth, the effective realization of her responsibilities is critically endangered. . . .[99]

More plainly put: All aspects of creation are knowable, and God would have humans use this knowledge to govern creation and restore it. Those he redeems enjoy the revealed understanding of Scripture and the direction of the Spirit for this work. All disciplines and competencies have their own special cogency, but Christians enjoy an advantaged perspective on creation. The church is therefore needed for a coherent, enlightened, and transformative education, and the church is served by such education to help pass on this insightful savvy. Even untransformed people can be allies in repossessing creation, though their understanding of themselves and of creation is nearsighted and partial.

The double doctrine — that the various elements and institutions in the cosmos are distinct spheres of endeavor, and that Christians have a privileged competence in them all — was elaborated for a situation in which the "covenant community" (Reformed Christians) was in charge. At Dordt that was largely the case. There was a civil government, but the college's constituency felt self-sufficient enough to regard it as remote, and therefore its sovereignty felt benign. There would be some strong misgivings in the middle 1960s, however, when the college brought home its first federal grant to build its first dormitory. Dordt's defense was that since it provided a benefit for the state, it was only fair to accept some aid from the state. CRC people worried, however, whether this involvement (possibly creating a dependence) might be an infringement on sphere sovereignty.

In an entirely different context a fundamentally deferential attitude toward the state was emerging in Sioux Center. Dordt students joined the national protest against the war in Vietnam and demonstrated in the town park. They were addressed by a faculty member who told them it was their responsibility to support the authority of the government God had placed over them. "The person who burns his draft card or, infinitely worse, himself, in the name of a baseless 'morality' or because he is opposed to evils such as war, is not serving the cause of goodness." The student newspaper approvingly noted that "this showing of patriotism and respect for authority did much to enhance the name of Dordt College as a Christian college." No one seems to have remembered that snubbed Fourth of July back in

'87. No one seems to have asked whether the U.S. government were really an undertaking of the covenant community for the kingdom. This was no *Mene, Mene, Teqel, Parsin* to make a regime tremble. This was only sphere sovereignty writ blurrily.

In 1965, when Dordt graduated its first four-year class, it had a student body that was 95 percent Christian Reformed. Evaluators of the North Central Association were impressed that Dordt had never had a year in the red (half its income then came from church contributions), and that it had already attracted National Science Foundation research grants for undergraduate research. Reservations were noted: three-quarters of the faculty were Calvin graduates; all CRC applicants were admitted; 30 percent of the freshmen failed to return the next year; and most students were preparing to teach in elementary or secondary schools. But the college was given candidate status toward accreditation.[100]

The North Central visitors had suggested that Dordt might find it timely to expand its 1961 statement of purpose, and to this end President Haan took pen in hand and was delivered of a fifty-eight-page behemoth: *Scripturally Oriented Higher Education.*[101] It offered a history of the college's founding; generous quotations from orthodox neo-Kuyperian literature; a cosmic account of the struggle between the kingdom of Christ and Satan; a treatise on the delicate (and sometimes contentious) relationships between sovereign families, governments, churches, and their schools; and various specifics about how the Dordt curriculum fit the needs of the kingdom. The persevering reader was given an extensive exposure to ultimacy. By this time, however, it should have been clear that while there were numerous and attractive quotations from Scripture, the intellectual construct on which they hung was about eighteen centuries younger than the New Testament.

With its much-expanded manifesto in hand, Dordt made formal application for accreditation in 1968. By this time it could claim for its constituency ninety-eight congregations, 7,850 families, and 35,423 CRC members in Iowa, Minnesota, the Dakotas, and Manitoba. This sponsoring group composed the corporate Society that each year produced electors who in turn chose the board of trustees. The baptismal rolls of the entire CRC happily forecast a college-age population of 28,000 by 1975, half of whom were expected to enroll, and most of those were expected to go to Calvin, Dordt, or their newest peer (and competitor), Trinity Christian College in Palos Heights, Illinois. Three smaller Calvinist churches without colleges had also commended Dordt to their own memberships: the Orthodox Presbyterian Church, the Reformed Church in America, and the Protestant Reformed Church. North Central was offered *Scripturally Oriented Higher Education* reduced to its barest essentials in eighteen pages to explain this distinctive system in which, since "Christ-believing parents do not accept parochial (church) or public (state) sovereignty in the sphere of education, they have founded private, covenant-communion-controlled schools where formal education can be conducted freely in obedience to the authority of God's Word . . . under the authority of God — delegated to parents, board of trustees, college president, deans and faculty, in that order." The self-study submitted to NCA made it clear that in this symbiosis of freedom and obedience, a teacher whose views became "antagonistic to the confessions and creeds upheld by the College would be expected to resign or he will be dismissed." One naturally lived in a compressed atmosphere beneath so many layers of delegated authority.

The college's aspiration in offering a liberal education was to offer its *sine qua non,* liberation in Christ. For example, Dordt showed North Central it was not at all spooked by that post-Darwinian rowdy, science. "The Christian's universe is a universe which is not based on chance; consequently, scientific effort can be meaningful. There is also no restriction on scientific exploration. It must run the gamut from the nucleus of the atom to the outer reaches of space, because man is under mandate to subdue the 'earth.' "

The faculty still had the same weaknesses: less than one-third held the doctorate; more than four-fifths were Calvin alumni. A new and interesting factor now came to light, however: the thirty-five teaching faculty boasted of 231 years of previous teaching experience at the elementary or secondary level. Teaching positions had by then claimed 150 alumni, and exactly the same number had gone to graduate schools as had entered the CRC seminary at Calvin: 19.[102]

The North Central evaluators reported on their visit with some incredulity. The largest part of their observations were positive, even commendatory. But they expressed severe misgivings about the religious mode of the school. "If Dordt College," they said, "is not an extension of the church then it is a church-college with heavy emphasis on the first term of that equation." The strong atmosphere of commitment, they said, was compromised by its reliance upon authority.

> In most of the classes visited, there was a heavy reliance upon explication of the material under discussion in terms of accepted doctrinal statements. Less attention was directed to the discipline as discipline than to a discipline as it relates to religious dogma.

In one class, they reported,

> students read the lecture which had been previously distributed to them, as it was read to them by a faculty member in sociology. The lecture dealt with the racial problem in the United States and gave the faculty member's interpretation of scripture as he saw it relating to social unrest. The presentation could be perceived as being unscientific at best and anti-intellectual at worst.

Notwithstanding their inability to elicit any faculty complaints about academic freedom, they observed that "the probability is high that such conflict will arise." In this they seem to have been mistaken. What they sought in vain was "the motivation to question and examine assumptions and ideas" in an atmosphere of "disciplined inquiry and challenge." It appears that the faculty was no more disposed than the administration or board to be embarrassed by this. They had all accepted letters of appointment which stipulated that they had already accepted the many-layered authoritative documents, from Genesis to Haan.[103]

A second North Central concern was the "very unorthodox relationship" between the governing body and the college. Candidates for faculty appointment were regularly interviewed by the trustees and even by members of the wider Society. The evaluators were correct to say that this was an unheard-of participation in what was traditionally a professional prerogative of the faculty and administrators. But they had probably never seen a college whose sponsoring community was so serious about the authentic continuity of its faith and culture.[104]

What the North Central visitors encountered was a culturally homogeneous community such as they are likely never to have seen, especially on a college campus. Even more strange to them must have been the confident, prolix ideology that offered to make sense of everything they were doing together. Most of all, it must have defied all experience to find a college where there was so little ferment . . . in 1968.

Accreditation was granted, but three years later another team came to visit, and they, too, were affronted by the distinctiveness of the college, which they readily admitted could boast of high cohesiveness and morale and a supporting constituency whose members were even ready to hold college bonds at low interest to allow the debt to be retired slowly and securely. Their eyebrows, however, were lifted at the need for the president to consult his board before admitting any student not of the affiliated denominations. Was Dordt that isolated, and of its own choice? Once again they fastened upon a lack of inquisitiveness, but they reported this time that they had seen several instances of "good faculty effort to evoke discussion, against some odds of student reluctance." "At Dordt," they surmised, "a faculty member may be a devil's advocate, but he must make clear that he is not in league with the devil." Why so? Because, as one chairman put it, inquiry was so closely and explicitly directed by the faculty, and was being constantly monitored for its doctrinal familiarity. As a result "the College is less effective than it should be in causing students to probe the meaning of their outlook and the merits of its alternatives."

The visitors readily admitted that no college is without ideology. What perplexed them about Dordt was that it was so deviant in its ideology. "The idea that subject matters of liberal studies should be enjoyed for their own sake and that students should come to be highly motivated to pursue these studies competently without regard to their possible further uses is an idea so commonly postulated in American higher education as to be widely regarded as normative. But Dordt rejects this postulate."[105] Why should it be such drudgery to renew the cosmos?

Apparently the North Central visitors in 1971 were unaware of a severe disturbance in the cohesiveness and morale of the college at the time. An entire legion of devil's advocates was busy provoking the confidence of the entire church. It had all begun in Canada. The CRC people in Canada were generally of more recent immigration from the Netherlands. Their sector of the church has been more inclined to wrangle about their faith than their brethren in the United States. That had been noticed at Dordt, because the Canadians who came south to teach or to study typically brought with them a more independent spirit and unfettered tongue. In the late 1950s a group of Canadian CRC scholars had formed the Association for the Advancement of Christian Scholarship (AACS), which found inspiration in the work of Abraham Kuyper but drew from it a more critical philosophy than what had been traditional. Internal dissent had never been a recreational activity among the Christian Reformed people in the United States, but now Canadian scholars with appointments at Calvin, Trinity, and Dordt were criticizing their American hosts. The church, claimed the AACS, was entirely too uncritical of its surrounding culture and its evil structures. And it had no coherent method for bringing the Scriptures to bear on the various academic disciplines. Salvation was conceived of so individualistically that its communal and social implications were being ignored.

> Is the education in our Christian schools really God-centered education, or is it really secularistic education with some Bible texts attached? Suppose we removed chapel exercises from our schools, how much distinctively Christian education would there be left?

One faultfinder described the Christian schools as "isolation wards" where "a Christian curriculum means sprinkling a little Jesus on top of a secular curriculum."

It was the conservatives in an already conservative CRC whose wrath was most articulately aroused, and it was natural that they stigmatized the AACS critics with the most damaging possible accusation: that they were "liberals" (in Christian Reformed circles this is as harsh as it gets).

The governing bodies at Dordt College and Trinity Christian College both moved to quench the controversy, but in different directions. Trinity declared that "as an independent educational institution, subject only to God and His revelation in His infallible written Word, as defined in the historic Reformed confessions . . . we reaffirm our historic independence from any man-made philosophic system." This simply ignored the massive systemic cantilever constructed by the church whereby to erect its doctrines upon the Scriptures. At Dordt the trustees took a more procedural approach, to avoid taking a stand on the issues. It was unrest itself, and potential harm to the college's good name, that worried them. The usual resort was made to a committee — indeed, to the usual succession of committees. Faculty members in the AACS were interrogated to smoke out their views on just about all the central elements of Christianity. Some observers noted a special Dordt animus toward their criticisms of governmental policies (i.e., the Vietnam War); Americans resented Canadians who enjoyed U.S. hospitality "only to cast judgment upon its government." In the end, both schools purged themselves of dissidents, but by taking opposite sides. At Trinity the conservatives prevailed and the AACS spokesmen were eased out. At Dordt President Haan finally targeted the conservative critics, whose bitter accusations of heresy showed them less likely to compose differences amicably. Their appointments were allowed to expire, and several other faculty members voluntarily departed.[106]

By designating the conservative troublemakers as contumacious rather than as doctrinally awry, President Haan and his associates took the wiser path. It is not clear that they enjoyed the exegetical or theological competence to arbitrate the controversy, or the stomach for it. But for want of any intellectual resolution, it proved to be a glooming peace. Dordt had still to wrestle with the youngish accusation of James Schaap, an articulate student of the sixties who would become an articulate professor of the nineties: that Dordt "was losing, semester after semester, real leaders of tomorrow because 'something' here attempts to scissor them into a pretty little string of cut-out paper men."[107] Dordt's problem was not that no explanations were offered, but that a tradition of exhaustive explanations may not have enjoyed enough power of deep, motivating conviction.

Invitation to the Dance

One public issue that provoked lengthy investigation and elaborate explanation may offer some insight into what was special about Dordt. The great issue of dancing provides a showcase of change in campus mores. Student insistence that restrictions on their behavior be modified or eliminated was one of the most salient forces against the church-college tradition on campuses in the 1960s and 1970s, but at Dordt the student revolution seemed to go more smoothly. The rules, to be sure, were conservative: beards, blue jeans, films, dancing, drinking, smoking were all regulated (by being excluded). And all were changed, but in Dordt's own way. Dordt's own way was very resolute, very slow, and very sensible. It was not simply because Dordt's students were themselves quite conservative that change came with grave and stately pace.

Dancing had always been one of the three issues of manners in the evangelical tradition. It was traditionally condemned because men who went dancing didn't always come home with their wives. Cards were also condemned because men who gambled didn't always come home with their wages. Drinking was the third thing condemned, because men who drank didn't always come home. Scripture was difficult to invoke on these matters, because dancing and drinking were obviously a hearty part of life in Israel and the early church, and gambling was not much of an issue for those archetypal folks.

The Synod of 1926 had been asked to "utter a strong warning against worldliness and take a definite stand against the popular evils of card-playing, theater-attendance [including cinema] and dancing." The committee workup required two years, and offered a report that as usual was preambled in the vertiginous considerations of eternity: "Man's chief end is the glorification of God . . . It follows also that our amusements should also glorify God." Synod took the traditionally dim view of "this familiar trio" and instructed local churches to examine prospective members "as to their stand and conduct in the matter of worldly amusements, and, if it appears that they are not minded to lead the life of Christian separation and consecration," to refuse them admission. Theoretically that did not compel total abstinence. Practically, as a later synod acknowledged, it "led many people to believe that our Church condemned the 'familiar trio' as worldly above anything else and made non-participation a shibboleth of membership." The effective ban sat heavily on some, and overtures for review had to be dodged by synods in 1932, 1940, 1944, 1949, and 1951. As one very cogent appellant expressed the grievance, the church had no right to forbid any amusement without a clear divine mandate from Scripture. "When the rulers in the Church make laws they sin against Christ and against his Church by 'binding and compelling the conscience' of the members of the Church and lording it over the charge allotted to them." The synodical defense was that it cleaved to its policy "not to itemize and catalogue a list of particular sins." Thus did Synod manage to wring a lot of specific prohibition out of its inexact grouch.

Finally the Synod of 1966 was presented with a massive report weighted by long treatises on the Christian in the world, worldliness, and Christian liberty; a critical review of film as an art form and Hollywood in particular; a sociological survey of how much cinematic abstinence the consistories (congregational ruling bodies) were currently demanding (total, 35 percent; discriminating, 55 percent; neither, 10 percent); and a sociological survey of what the laity were doing (most members had gone to the movies, but not often enough to keep Hollywood solvent). Buried in the report was a set of telling statistics: 83 percent of the laity thought the church did have an official stand on movies, and only 15 percent thought it was any of Synod's business. Synod concluded from this that cinema and television were "a legitimate cultural medium" and that Christians ought to be discriminating about what is good and evil in them.[108]

Three years earlier student editors had been publicly commending Dordt for holding fast to its disciplinary code on drinking and curfew. "Rules," said one, "are necessary to keep Dordt Christian." Here was no Berkeley. Indeed, in the later 1960s the student body favored Nixon for president by 75 percent, and a majority favored intensifying the bombing on North Vietnam. There was grumbling, however, about the quality of films that got past the campus censor, after a recreational innovation in 1964. This was also the year when dancing became a public issue: not ballroom or modern dancing, but "square-skipping," as square dancing was called locally. Back in 1949 Classis Sioux Center had banned it, but in 1969, prodded perhaps by Synod's deference to local rule making, the Dordt student council prevailed upon the classis to rescind the ban.

Classis Hamilton (Ontario) appealed to Synod in 1971 to rule on dancing, because their young people were already doing it, and that irked their nay-saying elders. The complexity of the issue, the classis pleaded, was beyond its local competence. The neighbors in Dundas, north of Toronto, heaped scorn on the

Hamilton overture, since "it is common knowledge that historically dancing in any form has proven to break down rather than build up Christian life, home and church." The Hamilton overture theologically traced dancing from Miriam and her women joyfully boogying their way across the Red Sea, to David frisking before Jehovah with all his might, and Salome belly dancing for big tips. Quickly surveying the culture dominant, the Hamilton overture then ethically appraised the frug, the twist, and other pelvic-crucial modalities of the dance. An "exploratory" questionnaire to their youth had revealed that 55 percent of those responding admitted to dancing; but only 40 percent had responded. Since significantly more men than women claimed they danced, some of the women were presumably fatigued. The analysis of the survey went on for pages, to be followed by considerations of moral stress from rock and roll, and from lascivious lyrics: "I'm hungry for your loving . . . I am going to do what I want to do . . . I don't care if I break some rules." The sexual stimulus associated with dancing which the faithful in Dundas had surlily invoked was lengthily considered but finally rejected as not conclusory.

> Young people have little patience if we try to curb their freedom while they are trying to find answers to things that are morally right and socially acceptable. Free social contact between the sexes is both good and enjoyable and ought not to be interpreted in the first place as an activity to satisfy their erotic impulses.

Could dancing ever be wholesome? With proper instruction, vetted lyrics and music, decent settings, ubiquitous chaperones, a curb on hugging and cheek-to-cheek dancing, and ultimate supervision by the One who can search the heart and the reins: Yes. In its peroration Classis Hamilton gave a wave of the arm to all the theological argumentation undergone *in re* worldly amusements five years earlier. Synod, however, in its relatively curt response, would grant no more than that the 1966 balance between Christian involvement in the world and freedom in the world was a good guide to follow in the matter of dancing.[109]

Calvin College was ready to take that as its cue. A very conservative watchdog group, the Association of Christian Reformed Laymen, had been angered in 1966 by a church choir which offered a rhythmic ritual dance interpretation of the Lord's Prayer, and again in 1969 when a Calvin fine arts group presented creative dances for passages from the Beatles' *Sgt. Pepper* album and Beethoven's Ninth Symphony. Then a fortnight later a liturgical dance on the theme of creation had to be moved out of chapel into a concert setting. Great outrage ensued, however, when critics denounced the Calvin Seminary Choir for singing the traditional folk carol "Lord of the Dance," seemingly for having proffered the sacrilegious suggestion that Jesus himself had danced. The issue was still inflamed.

But by 1975 the Calvin board invited Trinity and Dordt to join them in adopting guidelines for supervised dancing amenable to the synodical documents of 1966 and 1971, thereby hoping to present a united defense against such vigilant critics. The Dordt trustees owed them no favors and refused their assent. After two more years of self-encouragement the Calvin board took the step on its own, but delayed its effect by one full year to allow the storms to blow over. Then, aware that they were slipping on the dance dust and likely to lose their footing, Calvin College did the equivalent of appealing to Caesar: they asked Synod in 1977 to justify what they, Calvin, had already done.[110] Three years later a synodical committee filed its report, "Dance and the Christian Life," which must be the most magisterial study of this moral problem ever published. They reviewed the repeated eruptions of the question in Synod, and its seemingly endless capacity to recur. Scripture was even more thoroughly scouted, and once again all the biblical figures paraded by: David whirling, lambs gamboling, the daughters of Shiloh writhing, the priests of Baal limping, victors stomping . . . with castanets, lutes, harps, lyres, cymbals, sackbuts, and shofars. The story was carefully told of a newly ascetical church which was at its ease with rustic village festivals and chaste wedding feasts but had begun to be squeamish about the lascivious forms dance could take in the entertainments of the degenerate rich. Tough Reformers like Luther and Knox had abided some dancing. "John Calvin, however, declared himself foursquare against dance. He believed that dancing aroused passion and invited promiscuous relationships. To anyone who denied being bothered by such passions Calvin would reply, 'You are mocking God.' Despite Calvin's great vision for renewal of commerce and education, in his Geneva dance and drama were stricken from the Christian cultural life." As the story glides and shuffles on, the ebullient fox-trot and Charleston eventually give way to the sleaze of the dive and dance hall. Then, after an exhaustive theological review of the issue, the report simply ascribes to the church enough sense, taste, and memory to tell the difference between wholesome and degrading fun. The committee did not have the nerve to solicit Synod for the approval Calvin had hoped for, but asked only that their report be circulated for two years of wider consideration. This was now 1980. Well might the trustees of Calvin have complained: We piped to you and you did not dance.[111]

Back again came the report in 1982, even longer than before, but with a new turn. "While the Christian community tends to ask synod to define for it to what extent participation in dancing is permissible, it is the task of the community itself to develop a discriminating maturity which enables it to answer the redemptive question: Not whether or not we may participate, but, can this dance be redeemed, and what, in our own attitudes, milieu, and lifestyles, must happen to incorporate dance into a focused Christian life." Schools, churches, and families were bidden to sponsor dancing, not merely permissively or grudgingly, but responsibly. Synod was not quite prepared to say "gaily."[112]

In 1982, the year of Synod's permissive decision, President Haan retired and was succeeded by Rev. John B. Hulst, sometime pastor of the Orange City CRC, then trustee, Bible teacher, campus pastor, and dean of students at Dordt. Hulst would not quickly lead Dordt soft-shoeing through the newly opened doors. He was a *non-danseur*. Two years later, in 1984, the board of trustees would make a decisive move: it had received a recommendation from its Advisory Council on the Dance that a task force be appointed to develop a plan for Dordt College to teach (1) "Perspectives on Dance" and (2) "Dance Rhythm Skills." The board, in furtherance of the college's mandate to advance the claims of Christ *over all areas of life,* urged the college community to "redeem" the area of dance. But not abruptly. The board began to study the issue: this study would last five years. Along the way an essay by a young philosopher in the Dordt faculty journal would speak of dancing as an issue still sensitive and unresolved. Some course offerings in dance, he thought, would be one way to lead off.[113]

In the same proceedings Synod issued a much brisker moral declaration on the "Just War" with much swifter dispatch.[114]

It was in 1989-90 that President Hulst finally released an actual "Dance Policy" to Dordt College. Every sponsoring committee was asked to specify on the standard proposal form "how this event is going to be an expression of Christian growth." Music and lyrics required prior approval, and the music guidelines warned against promiscuity, lewdness, sadism, masochism, profanity, narcissism, "self-ism," nihilism, substance abuse, antisocial behavior, civil disobedience, undue flippancy, sarcasm, etc. "Songs which militate against loving God above all and neighbor as self will not be approved." Twenty-two paragraphs gleaned from synodical minutes offered further guidance. Thus, only twenty-five brief years after square-skipping was openly requested, Dordt was prepared to bring back to campus all the students who had been rocking in the regional taverns: to redeem the dance, and to experience what one of the earlier synods is remembered to have called "playfulness." In 1994 Hulst would report to his board with evident relief that despite all the discussion pro and con, "the dance has been a very positive, beneficial, and popular" social activity . . . "up to this point at least." The Dance Committee, he admitted, had been encouraging a variety of ethnic dances, but without enthusiastic response.[115] The two course offerings publicly announced back in 1985-86 had still not materialized by 1995-96.[116] Campus pastor Rev. Donald Draayer, who was a freshman at Dordt when Classis Sioux Center had first tried to lift the ban on square-skipping in 1969, now chairs the Dance Committee, and is as up-to-date on lyrics as anyone in Sioux County.

This invitation to the dance is a saga that illustrates the inveterate conservatism of an ethnic, agrarian community whose comfort with change was frail. One begins to suppose that the constantly repeated theological treatises which inevitably were replayed *da capo* from Genesis 1 were not what finally moved the sensibilities and judgment of the CRC from traditional resistance to dutiful (and wholesome) acceptance. All along there are glimpsing reminders that the young people have gone their own way, and may be out there right now dancing God-knows-what or -where. But the difficulty was manifest: a community of elders whose imaginations were fired by stray images of graceful Fred Astaire and Ginger Rogers being bumped aside by disgraceful Elvis and the Grateful Dead and then John Travolta, somehow could not bring to bear the wholesome imagination and taste without which the entire issue was as unlikely of sound resolution as their trying to work out a nuclear defense policy. Somehow the biblical and theological treatises seem not to have been moving the community as was believed. The sensibilities were not attuned, or perhaps not trusted, because of the tradition of lengthy rationalization.

What Would Expansion and Diversity Do for Dordt?

The lengthy saga of the dance deliberations is also instructive because it displays a community of close mutual understanding. In almost any other church the petitioners would have manifested an end of their patience, an exasperation. But deliberation to the point of consensus is an accepted part of CRC tradition. Also, those who engaged in the ponderously deliberate exercise of authority were confident enough to avert their gaze from those borderers who were impatient, and quietly enjoyed a few dances on the side in a way that they credibly combined with loyalty to the church in other issues. The church is even more remarkable in its shared loyalty than in its legislation — provided, of course, that the difference be in the area of morals, not in the area of doctrine. Dordt College has been able to absorb stresses that would have fractured other campuses, because it is a college of this church. But what if that religious and ethnic solidarity were forfeited or compromised?

What are the prospects for Dordt College as a project of the Christian Reformed community, which says it is determined to be distinctive? Dordt enjoys a stable clientele, who are religiously the members of the Christian Reformed Church in North America and ethnically of Dutch descent. Residentially they are found mostly clustered in areas where they can enjoy a homogeneous community, and sometimes dominance over local society. Their annual collections and assessments contribute significantly to the Dordt budget. The board of trustees, more than perhaps any other we have studied, is truly representative of the college's clientele. It has been steadily supportive financially, and dependably so in various moments of abrupt need.

Yet facts do challenge intentions. In 1979 the King's University College was opened with CRC participation in Alberta, followed by Redeemer College (1984) in Ontario. These naturally attracted some of the Canadians who would have journeyed down to Dordt, and from 1979 Dordt enrollment declined from its peak (1,218). Virtually every applicant was admitted, yet the enrollment sagged by one-quarter of what it had been in the latter 1970s. The religious makeup of the student body remained constant. About 90 percent were Christian Reformed, 7 percent were from other Reformed churches, and only 3 percent were "other." A decision was reached in the early 1980s to admit more non-CRC students. This was done, it was said, to bring in a welcome diversity, but the imperative was to keep the enrollment stable. Those diverse students never came, however, because they failed to apply.[117] Efforts were made to retain more of those who did enroll, but at the end of the 1980s one-quarter of Dordt's freshmen were still evaporating before the sophomore year. The college was graduating only half of its matriculants within four years.[118]

Though the enrollment has returned to its previous peak of 1978-80, then 92 percent of the students were from the CRC, and now only 75 percent are. It seems clear that the church cannot provide students sufficient to sustain Dordt's basic enrollment. This deficit is apparently going to be worsened by expected defections from the CRC constituency over issues such as the ordination of female clergy. But long-range planning calls tentatively for an enlargement (by one-quarter) of the student population in the near future, to be achieved by the admission of applicants from a variety of churches. The campus, says President Hulst, "will have a noticeable international and ethnic presence," which forecasts another source of variety. Granted that Dordt has hitherto been noticeably 100 percent white, that may effect some visible change.

The desired growth is not chosen in order to diversify the student body; it is accepted in order to strengthen the college's financial stability. Events may show that this policy decision is no more realistic than the one in the early 1980s, because diverse other students will not be attracted to Dordt. But if for some reason the college should succeed in recruiting, enrolling, and retaining new blood in significant proportion, how would this campus accommodate 25 percent truly different students, or even 5 percent? Even a modest contingent of newcomers inclined to ask "Why?" in all directions, and to allege their own convictions as worthy alternatives (and to expect a decision before they graduate), might dislodge the settled homogeneity of the Dordt campus more than is now anticipated. Planning documents speak of diversity (not yet Diversity) with no evident worry that it might prove more obnoxious than what comes down on the afternoon breeze from the stockyards to the north.[119]

A Distinctive Student Body

Who are the learners that people this unusual campus? Today, despite some softening of its distinctiveness, the student population at Dordt is still highly profiled, and highly untypical of its generation across the nation. CRC members constitute 75 percent of the student body; other Reformed churches now claim 13 percent, and 12 percent are "other."[120] Only 2 percent report parents who are divorced or separated, by contrast with about half of their national peer group. More than 60 percent have known a working father and a homemaker mother. The median parental income of their families is about $45,000. About one student in four comes from a farm family, and most from towns of modest population. Their academic preferences are mostly vocational. The most populated academic fields are elementary education, business administration, agriculture, and engineering. While 240 have chosen teacher training, there are only 9 studying theology and 8 philosophy.

These are not like their national contemporaries who have spent 22,000 hours in front of a television, developed their central motor skills on Atari and Nintendo, and cruised the malls as their village greens, and only 20 percent of whom define "family" as relatives. The Dordt students are indeed different. Ninety-eight percent say that Jesus Christ is their Lord and Savior; 96 percent attend church weekly. They claim they received their core values first from their family, second from their church, and least of all from the media (less than 1 percent of those responding even listed the media among their first two choices). About 85 percent say their most important social objective is to raise a family; 59 percent identify themselves as conservatives and 6 percent as liberals; 9 percent discussed politics in the past year and 50 percent discussed religion; two-thirds chose Dordt primarily because of its religious affiliation; less than 2 percent think abortion should be legal (versus 46 percent in Protestant colleges and 51 percent in more academically selective Protestant colleges), and 3 percent agree that sex is "OK if people like each other" (versus 30 percent and 32 percent, respectively).[121] Students and faculty both attend chapel twice weekly. About a third of the student body is there. Attendance has always been "mandatory" but never sanctioned. Students lead extemporaneous prayer unselfconsciously and devoutly. The music is carefully done in the evangelical manner, but also unselfconsciously. This is a community that prays easily together.

The student newspaper finds campus restrictions on drinking obnoxious, while at the same time the students are staging an energetic Alcohol Awareness Week. The music at a poorly attended outdoor dance was so raucous that children of the town seven blocks away could not sleep, and it was shut down at only 10·30. Another dance, with endless grub and a DJ who used only Christian music, was pronounced "real cool": "there should have been a little more variety [in the music] than just all Christian, though it wasn't necessarily bad." The student editor berates students for their political apathy and ignorance of public affairs; a student correspondent delivers himself of a long defense of his constitutional right to keep a hunting arsenal. One student group heads to Minneapolis for a weekend of culture, and takes in both Becket and Shakespeare at the Guthrie. A recent Bon Jovi album gets a yawning review: "The opening track, 'Hey God,' is basically Jon Bon Jovi himself, questioning why the things that happen in the world really happen. Why does God let those things happen? Sorry, Jon, it's been done. So have the harmonies, guitar riffs, and lyrics in many of the songs." A "Big Tent Revival" by Geoff Moore and the Distance is reported. "The concert was a rousing, yelling, screaming success."[122]

Of all institutions studied, Dordt has in its students the most closely shared culture, and the most quiet possession of the campus community by a Christian communion. The tidewaters of change, however, are beginning to lap at their feet.

And a Distinctive Faculty

All faculty members and administrators must be members of the CRC. For those who come from elsewhere ecclesially, there is the expectation that within their first two years they and their families will have found a home in one of the local CRC congregations; less than a dozen of the present faculty have come under that proviso. The ideology of the college is made known in all its abundance to faculty recruits, whether CRC veterans or newcomers.[123] All faculty members are interviewed by the executive committee of the board of trustees before their first appointment, and by the full board before their first contract expires. When NCA evaluators in 1968 criticized this involvement as "unorthodox," and further objected to trustee participation with administration and faculty on issues of student discipline and religious life for not following "the ordinary channels in the typical administrative hierarchy," Dordt ignored the evaluators in the belief that what they already had was better than the typical board whose only task was to raise money.[124]

Nevertheless, by putting a good face on prospective diversity in the student body the college now invites speculation that diversity might be appropriate for the senior members of the college as well. The Long-Range Planning Committee has quite recently been considering that Dordt may open its faculty ranks and thus its identity to the "broader — especially Reformed — church community." A faculty member then might belong to a church that endorsed beliefs "such as," but not the same as, the three "Forms of Unity," and "support" but not really profess the actual CRC tradition.[125] No matter how daintily stated, this elective approach to religious solidarity, once begun, would be almost impossible to limit, either in anticipation or in realization.

That may be yet to come. There is already among the CRC faculty, however, some good-natured indifference toward the particulars of the Reformed confessions to which they are all obliged to subscribe. The CRC itself has recently had to deal with misgivings over a passage in the Belgic Confession: "we detest the Anabaptists and other seditious people" for their refusal to serve in the armed forces. CRC people with Mennonites or conscientious objectors as friends were reluctant to join in that detestation, and proposed alternative phrases: "We detest *all those . . .*" or "We *denounce* Anabaptists . . ." or "We *reject their error.*"[126] Similar twinges about the traditional professions compromise the force of their unanimous acceptance by the faculty. Some Dordt faculty members admit to misgivings or disbelief regarding various items in the confessions, and there seems to be a general understanding that such reservations are common, and to be expected. It may be that mental reservations of this sort leave intact the greater matters at the heart of the Calvinist canon: unconditional election, limited atonement, total depravity, irresistible grace, and perseverance of the saints. But the elaboration and enforcement of explicit formulae of belief are close to the soul of the Reformed denominations, and a readiness to sit lightly to these texts may be symptomatic of a more generalized nonchalance.

The Dordt faculty are very Dutch, but at least since the AACS fracas they have rarely manifested that free-spoken earnestness one associates with the Reformed tradition. Accreditation teams regularly express their wonderment at the fact that tenure on this campus is only a metaphor, at least legally, since faculty who have been given definitive acceptance are given five-year rolling contracts, which are continually reissued during their third year after reaffirmation of satisfactory service, but would be allowed to expire in the absence of such satisfaction. Despite this insecurity, the Dordt faculty is unusual for its longevity, and for its lack of grievances about academic freedom.[127] It is quite common for evangelical colleges to claim that they integrate faith with learning. Dordt faculty have clearly taken that mandate to heart, in testimony whereof they have been publishing a spate of show-and-tell articles in *Pro Rege,* the faculty journal: "Engineering in Reformed Perspective," "A Case for Free Enterprise, Radio and the Christian Broadcaster," "The Contributions of Women's Studies to a Christian World View," "Christian Astronomy vs. Secular Astronomy," "Where a Christian Theatre Consortium Might Decide to Go," "A Biblical Framework for Biology," "The Agricultural Crisis in Context: A Reformational Philosophical Perspective," "Can Christians Accept Capitalism?" A reader quickly notices, however, that Scripture is not at all the source for these ventures at integration. Nor are they very theological.

Serviceable Insight

Dordt College may be where Azusa Pacific University was in the later 1960s, and where Concordia, River Forest was in the later 1970s. Both schools had a strong religious solidarity on their campuses, joining both faculty and students. Both then faced the prospect of diversification: Azusa Pacific because of its success, River Forest because of a shortfall. In both cases they seized the main chance: one, under a president who was uninterested in the religious tradition; the other, under a president who was too pressed to anticipate the results. Both have thus far retained faculties who strongly share the religious tradition native to the school, and have student bodies increasingly balkanized into those who share it and those who are indifferent. Both institutions, each in its own way, are now left with an instability: they have asked into their midst an awkward proportion of junior and senior people who do not belong religiously, and are becoming less supportive, even less tolerant.

It is far from clear that Dordt is going to be successful in diversifying. Sioux Center lacks some of the blandishments of Azusa, to note but one difference. But, whatever the outcome, what is at stake in Dordt's desire to grow and improve through diversification?

The college has already experienced one significant shift, which it stumbled into without its traditional deliberation.

Fibrillation in the budget during the early 1980s when the enrollment was falling persuaded the college to look for special programs that might enhance its draw. The top three fields (in enrollment) were already elementary education, business administration, and physical education, and the array of vocational majors was expanded to attract more students: accounting, agribusiness, agriculture, art, communication, engineering, and social work were added, along with many preprofessional programs: pre-agriculture, pre-dental, pre-legal, pre-medical, pre-nursing, pre-optometry, pre-pharmacy, pre-physical therapy, pre-seminary, and pre-veterinary.

Dordt did not follow the usual syndrome of asserting all the more vigorously that it was indeed a liberal arts college, meanwhile becoming a largely vocational school. It had just previously wrung from the Calvinist tradition what would serve as a new justification. In 1979 a third Dordt statement of purpose emerged (after five years' gestation), and it spoke as before of a covenant people charged by the Creator to extend his rule by living obediently under his laws (the theme of obedience is a strong motif), restoring humankind to fellowship with God, and subduing the earth. Education, especially within a culture as complex and deceptive as the North American, is one strategy for fulfilling this cultural mandate. Thus far the statement is utterly familiar, but then it swerves off in a new direction:

> [Christian colleges] can no longer be satisfied with the transmission of abstractions. They must provide the kind of insight that enables Christians to carry out their task effectively in a complicated world. Whereas the majority of North American educational institutions transmits little more than the kind of insight that contributes to secularization and fosters individualism, it is the educational task of Dordt College to provide genuinely Christian, that is, truly *serviceable insight* . . . to discern the will of God for any situation and to develop the capacity to implement it. . . . For that reason, practice or skill is not to be separated from its imbeddedness in the wider structural context to be theoretically understood: nor is the theoretical understanding of God's creation to be divorced from the mental capacity to implement the will of the Lord in everyday situations. . . . Dordt, as a Calvinistic institution in the tradition of the Reformation, seeks to instill the ability to discern the spirits and to engage in genuinely reforming cultural activity.[128]

Dordt was giving this theory some new flesh by establishing two new academic programs rarely found in small colleges, but quite right for her clientele. Agriculture was added in 1978 and engineering in 1980, and in both cases the college went out of its way to say that they were intentionally shaped to fit the "cultural mandate" to redeem all sectors of culture, natural and technical, for Christ. A quarter section of land north of town was purchased and fitted out as the Agricultural Stewardship Center, for both animal husbandry and dairy, and for crop raising.

The Department of Agriculture (Dordt's, not Washington's) promoted stewardship as the dominant principle governing the farming of God's good earth.

It urged evaluating every hybrid and every fertilizer for its long-term effect on life, health, and soil. It regarded people as caretakers of God's gifts, but identified God's soil and livestock as the farmers' domain. It suggested that the creation would be renewed by the Spirit working through God's servants, and must not be used, abused, and desecrated. Some secular writers have faulted Christian farmers for "subduing" God's earth too zealously in response to the cultural mandate, but if these critics had been aware of Dordt's approach to agriculture, they might not have made such a charge.[129]

When North Central came calling again in 1981, "serviceable insight" was writ large across the college's self-study. But it was doubtful that Dordt had the resources to provide serviceable insight. The departments, courses, and choices of major field were manifold. But teaching resources were so thin that, except in certain technical and professional programs, students had restricted access to advanced level courses, which was where the development of insight, perspective, and critical analysis would become possible.

Is "serviceable insight" primarily a public relations turn-of-phrase? For the educational encounter to beget effective insights it has to activate the student's critical independence, which is not so easily done in a wisdom community where the teacher/student relationship evokes the cosmic obedience demanded for Christ's kingdom. This difficulty is recognized at Dordt, at least in theory. A strategic planning document, which appears about as complex as the repair manual for a nuclear power plant, puts it this way:

> If Dordt students are to become reforming servant-leaders, they must have opportunity to challenge unexamined, tradition-bound ways of doing things. Applied theory of this kind cannot be done in practicums where the outside, contracted agency sets the parameters of the workplace and defines too much the learning experience.[130]

Dordt's extensive assessment program raises questions about the still predominantly tradition-bound ways of doing things on campus. Alumni testify that they learned to work independently at Dordt, yet "clarifying values" is a skill in which the students test poorly; indeed, that skill seemingly declines between freshman and senior years.[131] A recent academic profile shows Dordt students with average critical skills; but considering the college's explicit ambitions in this matter, and the low selectivity of schools in the comparison group, that is not a satisfying average.[132]

Serviceable insight, like the faith it stands on, is said to be grounded upon an understanding of the Bible. Philosophy and theology would be the disciplines-in-chief to develop a student's capacity to integrate the knowledge available in the Bible, and also to derive the intended benefits from coursework in other disciplines. Yet those two subjects, confided to one small department, are accessible in very limited courses. In the Dordt *Catalog* the Dutch Department offers about as many courses as Philosophy; Agriculture twice as many; Business thrice as many; Education four times as many. In the general curriculum all that is required in these two crucial disciplines are either two very basic theology courses or one each in theology and philosophy. Granted the repeated claim that the Bible is the fundamental source of Christian faith and critical insight, it is astonishing to find that the basic course on the Bible, the only one all students must take, offers little exposure to a contextual reading of the books themselves, but tends to be organized ideologically around the traditional Calvinist motifs. Students are hardly into the third chapter of Genesis before they must cut to the credo and the cosmology.

The drawback to all this is that whatever serviceable insights Dordt students can eke out of the program would have to derive more from professorial hearsay than from student inquiry, since so little opportunity is given for ruminatory and knowledgeable access to the great texts and inspired minds themselves. This touches upon one of the special characteristics of the college: that it offers plug-and-play ideology which students (and, perhaps, faculty) have little opportunity to appraise, engage, or appropriate.[133] The freedom is probably more restricted by the budget than by the tradition. If, as NCA evaluators have warned, the instruction at Dordt has tended to come encased within a familiar ideology, it is unlikely to instill in students the art and skills of disciplined inquiry and challenge, and thus to make them carry away major insights as their own.[134]

Dordt in Crisis

The "serviceable insight" episode is sobering. The college made some swift moves to recoup its viability and, being Dordt, offered a rationale. The financial viability was restored, but the viability of the character of Dordt College probably suffered. Serviceable insight in these professional programs requires a strength in the basic liberal programs which the college has not yet attained. And its desire to have succeeded may well conceal from them the degree to which they have not done so.

All the more reason to recognize that Dordt now faces destiny. One might ask, as others have, what Azusa Pacific and Concordia, River Forest could have done otherwise. If Cornelius Haggard had wanted to keep Azusa Pacific as a Holiness school, it would still be relatively small. If Concordia were truly determined to be an unambiguously Missouri Synod school, it would have shrunk. Neither could have claimed even the name of "university." The churches, denominations, and traditions have limits on the degree to which their members will support hallmark colleges with students and offerings. It is up to them whether or not they want colleges and universities enough to sponsor them adequately. If they do, they have a right to expect that the educators treat them as a trust. The Christian Reformed people in Dordt's supporting region have been more sincere in their support than the ecclesial clientele of most colleges and universities in this study.

Dordt is always going to be small if it is Christian Reformed. It will lack many amenities. It will be weak in internal liveliness, skirmishes, and friction with the church. But if the church grows Dordt will mature, and the church may allow Dordt to provoke it to renew itself. If the Dordt faculty were motivated enough, they would be engaged more vitally with the Christian tradition of the past and more creatively with the very unchristian tradition of the present.

If, on the other hand, Dordt were to follow the wheel tracks of most other colleges and universities in this study and in some remarkable way entice all manner of young scholars to Sioux Center, it will become another kind of college: better in some aspects, and for a short while probably better as Christian Reformed, due to the admixture of amiable dissidents. But their parabolic trajectory would soon pass through that high, slow, weightless curve of optimal function and fall down inexorably into what none of its sponsors or present scholars ever wanted. Being Reformed, and not very Pietistic, Dordt would do that with much less reductive good cheer. They would probably continue to talk as they always have, and to turn out mission statements like the one for KDCR-FM, the Dordt College radio station, which is several times as long as the Athanasian Creed. But these papers would no longer have any grip on the Dordt people's minds or imaginations.

If that change were resisted with some fire and determination, the college would have to bite the heels of its constituency and persuade them willingly to fund and people a college that would send their children home as faithful disturbers of the peace.

A Peculiar Problem

Most of the crucial institutional decisions that detached colleges and universities in this study from their churches were made pragmatically, with light ideological forethought but heavy ideological justification afterward. Dordt is different. But Dordt still faces one old issue that is unresolved, and could make a difference. We must revisit the dispute of 1971, when the AACS scholars provoked a crisis over how the church should treat the culture.

Mainline Calvinist doctrine shared the Lutheran dismay for the unchurched world as perfused with sin. Calvinists believed that the Reformed fellowship of the saved, the regenerate, was the beneficiary of God's grace in Christ, and that the church was surrounded by a world which found their Christian undertakings repugnant. The full energies of the elect would thus be called upon for their own salvation and for the offering of salvation to others. On that view God's grace was directed away from the world and its culture, and toward Christ's kingdom. This view has been given various names in CRC usage; here we name it a "confessional" stance toward the world. Some have called this view the "anabaptist vision," because it believes creation to be so destroyed by sin that God will replace it, not redeem it. The people in northwest Iowa had come a long way to have as little as possible to do with the public culture, and they were inclined in this confessional direction, which helped stiffen their determination to have their own separate schools.

Abraham Kuyper's public experience and teaching had led him to formulate a counterposition, which enjoyed great authority in some CRC circles. He held that in addition to the "particular grace" provided through Jesus and the Bible and the church to save those predestined, God offered "common grace" to others. Common grace could not enter the soul to save a person, but it could envelop a person and, without making him or her good, allow the person to accomplish good. It thereby allowed fruitful collaboration between the regenerate and the unregenerate. Even at the hands of unregenerate sinners, culture is capable of being good in some measure, and of being bettered, and that enterprise is worthy of collaboration by the elect. Common grace, these Christian Reformed thinkers taught, restrains sin and sin's consequences, so that creation and society, nature and culture, family and institutions, insight and history can actually progress. The CRC members were thus encouraged to make common cause with outsiders, to be their energetic partners in a public culture. The distinctive advantage and contribution of the regenerate in this collaboration was that they alone, by dint of God's particular grace, could understand the final purposes and significance of these shared endeavors. But the terms of collaboration, it seemed, could not be distinctively Christian because that uncommon grace, faith, was not shared. Creation had its own intrinsic, divinely established structures which could be studied and known, by the elect and the unregenerate alike. The realm of thought must submit to the logic of logic alone; the realm of science must submit to empirical evidence alone; the realm of the state is stipulated by the rules of justice alone.[135] Most of the Christian Reformed people in northwest Iowa didn't follow these lengthy arguments too closely, but from what they knew of the common grace crowd, it sounded like just one more attempt to fraternize with the godless.

Along came the AACS scholars. They were critical in both directions. The confessional view did not suitably acknowledge what God had revealed in and through nature, or that unbelievers were capable by God's grace of gaining some access to that revelation. They were critical of the common grace view (or at least what had become of it since it left Kuyper's hands), because it was naive in disregarding how distorted nature had become, and how denatured were the various cultural traditions in society. The dispute which blew up at Dordt was in some respects a comedy of errors, since the "reformational" view of the AACS people was much more critical of what had become of the common grace view than of the locally popular confessional view.

The AACS view, which they called "reformational," recognized the common grace theory as very similar to the Aristotelian-Thomistic view of nature and grace, whose disciples were easily led to imagine that grace was little more than nature in good running order. Common grace partisans (whom they accused of distorting Kuyper's more discriminating theory) believed their Christian faith provided them with no perspective or critical wisdom that would allow them to question and engage the very axioms and suppositions of the dominant culture. They did not look to Christ's word or Christ's Spirit to confer any radical or transcendent criteria for discernment in statecraft or the economy or race or family or labor-management relations or biology or civil engineering or urban planning. If, said the reformational people, Christian energies in the world and its cultures must be restricted by the limits of what makes sense to nonbelievers, then Christians are most likely to be co-opted into the perspective of their secular collaborators.

The common grace theory, however, is much more simply and cogently explained than the reformational theory, and is very attractive to those who want to make their way in the world. The reformational theory has proven very tangled and complex in the hands of its promoters. If that should continue, then the more accommodationist common grace view is likely to return to the fore and lead the more educated Christian Reformed people, including the graduates of Dordt College.

The justification for a college that is home to a professing community is that they would be elaborating there a critical judgment about the many subjects they study and the culture of their nation and world. Without that, both faculty and students, whatever their apparent isolation, will be helplessly permeable by the dominant cultures of the academy and the nation. Sequestration is never helpful unless those gathered in close fellowship are intently working together to understand and to judge both the integrity and the folly within their own communion, and also in the world that surrounds them.[136]

The Reformed churches have a long tradition of brawny discourse. The CRC is no exception. The virtue in all that brawling is that these people take the truth seriously. There is a discouraging contrast between that discourse (or at least its most redemptive moments) and the mild, even timid, discourse which is not spirited enough to appropriate Christian insight and use it to be both creative and critical within the several disciplines of scholarship. It is not clear that anyone really trusts "particular grace" enough to believe that the church can articulately and provocatively identify and describe, on its own Christian terms, the pathologies that consume the public culture. The nerve and verve that have embittered some intramural Christian debates might better be spent on scholarly extramural appraisal of the nation, society, and culture.

The educational training of the faculty, their workload, and inhibitions on their internal debate make it unlikely that Dordt's educators will have enough theological insight or inclination to awaken and inspire their students' minds to distinguish what is fraudulent from what is prophetic, what is seductive from what is sound.

THE EVANGELICALS

There are some obvious contrasts between Wesleyan Azusa Pacific University and Calvinist Dordt College. Unlike the Holiness people, the Reformed have a devout belief in the perduring presence of sin and in the inclination to further sin in their own lives. At Azusa Pacific there is glitz, or the hope of glitz, while Dordt is homely. The one religious tradition lives as determinedly in sensibility as the other does in rationality. Azusa's founders were as wary of the world as Dordt's founders were assured of their independence within it. In the Azusa tradition philosophy and theology are not supposed to be important, but they are; in the Dordt tradition they are supposed to be much more important than they actually are. Azusa Pacific is so multidenominational that it is nondenominational; Dordt is denominational beyond all quibble.

Both institutions are the product of the devotion of faithful people of modest monetary means. Both have benefited from the patronage of people who did not understand their faith to depend on learning, and now both are sustained and led by people who want them to become very learned indeed. Both carry the hopes of people who believe in Jesus, and who cannot imagine how they could thereby offer any embarrassment to their respective campuses.

Both know that most colleges and universities have gone the way of all the earth, and worry that this same fate may be stalking them. It may.

NOTES TO CHAPTER 7

1. David Riesman, "Reflections on Catholic Colleges, Especially Jesuit Institutions," *Journal of General Education* 34, no. 2 (summer 1982): 109.

2. This roster omits three Canadian members.

3. CCCU, *1995-96 Resource Guide for Christian Higher Education.* Institutions sympathetic to the CCCU's purposes but unable to fulfill its requirements may seek affiliate status. The Coalition grew out of a twelve-member (now thirteen) Christian College Consortium (founded in 1971) in 1976.

4. Gary Lyle Railsback, "An Exploratory Study of the Religiosity and Related Outcomes among College Students" (Ph.D. diss., University of California, Los Angeles, 1994); Robert Melvin Hubbard, "Institutional Goals and Institutional Functioning of Selected Denominational and Non-Denominational Private Four-Year Liberal Arts Colleges" (Ed.D. diss., Boston University, 1984).

5. Thomas D. Hamm, *The Transformation of American Quakerism: Orthodox Friends, 1800-1907* (Bloomington and Indianapolis: Indiana University Press, 1988). The evangelical Orthodox Friends gradually overbore the Hicksite and Wilburite minority through the course of the nineteenth century, until both the liberal and the conservative branches produced modernist variants that became normative in the twentieth century, when creedal controversies were muted by a moral agenda that was largely secular and liberally sociopolitical, a worship that returned to the simplicity but not the faith of George Fox, and a doctrine that eschewed doctrines.

6. Much of the school's history as recounted here is indebted to Charles H. Brackett, "The History of Azusa College and the Friends, 1900-1965" (M.A. thesis, University of Southern California, 1967), copy in Azusa Pacific University Archives (APUA). The Friends Bible Institute and Training School founded by Holiness Quakers in Cleveland in 1892 was the prototype followed by the TSCW in Whittier and others in Oregon, Kansas, Indiana, and elsewhere in the West; see Hamm, 160-61.

7. *Catalogue and Prospectus of the Training School for Christian Workers, 1900 01,* APUA.

8. Brackett, 54-55.

9. Brackett, 68-69.

10. Brackett, 87-88.

11. *Training School for Christian Workers Catalogue, 1909-10,* 12-13, 5.

12. William P. Pinkham, "Annual Report of President," 2 June 1913, APUA.

13. *Training School for Christian Workers Catalogue, 1918-19,* 12-15.

14. Eli Reece, "Annual Report of President, 1921-22," manifests an intensified apocalypticism. Referring to certain internal stresses among the students, he writes:

> Fruit-growers and farmers tell us that new and worse pests are all the time arriving and multiplying until continual vigilance is not sufficient to exterminate them; so with the work of God; as satan knowing that his time is short is multiplying his schemes and devices especially upon such places as this where workers are being prepared to attack his strongholds. Only by continuous prayer and praise have we kept the victory.

An entirely different aspect of TSCW life, its student health care program, is likewise construed in religious terms. Though the prospective missionaries were given basic instruction in hygiene, first aid, and public health, the school had no funds to provide medical care. Instead, serious health needs were submitted to prayer, and healings were reported from time to time. In this report Reece writes that student health had been good, with no serious illness, "several having experienced the health from the Lord for their bodies." For a similar treatment of health as an element of religion at Anderson University, a Church of God college, see Leona Nelson, "The Secularization of a Church-Related College" (Ph.D. diss., University of Chicago, 1953), 101.

15. *Training School for Christian Workers Catalogue, 1918-19,* 22.

16. Ray L. Carter, "President's Report to the Training School Association, 6 May 1929," APUA.

17. Carter, "President's Report to the Training School Association, 5 May 1930," APUA.

18. David H. Scott, "President's Report to the Training School Association, 1932," APUA.

19. For biographical information on Cornelius P. Haggard, see Emma L. Haggard, *The Intrepid Builder* (Glendora, Calif.: Thaddeus Foundation, 1983).

20. *Pacific Bible College Catalogue, 1939-40,* 9, 12-13.

21. Cornelius P. Haggard, "President's Annual Message, 1940," APUA.

22. *Bulletin of the Pacific Bible College* 31, no. 3 (March 1942): 1; Haggard, "President's Annual Message, 1944," APUA.

23. *Pacific Bible College Catalog, 1944-45,* 8-11.

24. Haggard, "President's Annual Message, 1945," APUA.

25. Haggard, "President's Annual Message, 1946," APUA.

26. Haggard, "President's Annual Report, 1947," APUA.

27. *Pacific Bible College Student Handbook, 1947-48,* 18-22.

28. Haggard, "President's Annual Report, 1949," and "1950," APUA.

29. *Pacific Bible College Student Handbook, 1957-58,* 16-17.

30. See, e.g., his annual reports in 1944, 1959, 1963, APUA.

31. Haggard, "President's Annual Report, 1959," "1963," APUA.

32. Haggard, "President's Annual Report, 1959," APUA.

33. Earl V. Pullias and Mitchell P. Briggs, for the Commission on Membership and Standards, WASC, Report on preliminary visit at Azusa College, 29 July 1960, APUA.

34. Of these five, however, WASC would point out that four did little or no teaching; Haggard, "Report of the President, 19 November 1963," 4, APUA.

35. Another extraordinary feature of the college only hinted at in the report is that the C. P. Haggard Educational Foundation had contributed more than $26,000 to the college; readers would have no way of knowing that these were contributions made over the years from the president's extremely meager salary.

36. Self-Study Report of Azusa College to the Western Association of Schools and Colleges, February 1963, vi, viii, 9-10, 26, APUA.

37. WASC Survey Report of Azusa College, 28 February and 1 March 1963, 1, 10, APUA.

38. Karen Longman, vice president of the CCCU, interview with the author, 6 March 1996.

39. Haggard, "Report of the President, 17 November 1974," APUA. The faculty, whose salaries had just been raised 37 percent to satisfy WASC, may have had the hardest time of it.

40. Self-Study Report of Azusa Pacific College for WASC and California State Board of Education, September 1966, APUA, ix, A-3. The Accreditation Association of Bible Colleges joined as a third agency in the visitation.

41. WASC Visitation Report for Azusa Pacific College, 31 October–1 November 1966; California State Board of Education Visitation Report for Azusa Pacific College, 31 October–1 November 1966, APUA.

42. "Analysis of Certain Aspects of the Report of the Visitation Team for Azusa Pacific College to the Committee on Accreditation of the California State Board of Education, Presented by Azusa Pacific College, September 1967," APUA/378.794/A9972ac/1967A. The anonymous drafter was Dean Malcolm R. Robertson.

43. Malcolm R. Robertson, dean and professor emeritus, interview with the author, 14 March 1996.

44. *Azusa Pacific College Catalog, 1970-71,* n.p., APUA.

45. WASC Visitation Report for Azusa Pacific College, November 1970, 3, APUA/378.794/A9972ac/1970A.

46. WASC Visitation Report for Azusa Pacific College, November 1970, 3, APUA.

47. "The Essence of Azusa Pacific College," approved by the board of trustees 19 February 1974, circulated with covering memorandum by Stan Frame, 1, APUA.

48. Self-Study Report of Azusa Pacific College for WASC, February 1975; WASC Visitation Report for Azusa Pacific College, February 1975, APUA/378.794/A9972ac/1975A.

49. Haggard, "Report of the President, 20 May 1975," APUA.

50. *Azusa Pacific College Catalog, 1975-77*, 10.

51. *Azusa Pacific College Catalog, 1975-77*, 16.

52. Minutes of the Executive Board, Azusa Pacific College, 15 September 1976, APUA.

53. Paul E. Sago, "Report of the President, 16 October 1979," 3, AUPA.

54. "A Response from Azusa Pacific College Relating to Selected Items in the Western Association of Schools and Colleges' Report on Off Campus and Contractual Programs, 20-22 October 1977," APUA.

55. One new venture, the Universal College, was designed to educate off-campus students, e.g., military personnel, with prerecorded videocassettes, up to the A.A. degree, and its enrollments were at this time thought to be heading toward two thousand. It is very difficult to imagine that those consumers would have been, or would be, integrated into the college's religious ethos.

56. The Essence Statement, as finally approved in October 1979, appears with a series of faculty and staff commentaries in the *Proclaimer* 3, no. 5 (October/November 1980).

57. Self-Study Report of Azusa Pacific College for WASC, 15 June 1981, 13, 15, 74, 81, APU/378.794/A9972ac/1981.

58. WASC Visitation Report for Azusa Pacific University, October 1981, 1-9, 23-25, 42, APUA/378.794/A9972ac/1981B.

59. Self-Study Report of Azusa Pacific University for WASC Interim Visit, 28 November 1984, APU/378.794/A9973ac/1984; WASC Interim Visitation Report for Azusa Pacific University, 28 February–1 March 1985, 2, 15, APUA.

60. The second-largest group (9 percent) call themselves "Christian"; technically this is a short name for Disciples of Christ (the Christian Church), but for APU students it probably meant the same as "nondenominational." Catholics, then, would be the third-largest denominational representation.

61. Self-Study Report of Azusa Pacific University for WASC Visit, 1 November 1988, 12-21, APU/378.794/A9973ac/1988.

62. The Carnegie Foundation for the Advancement of Teaching, "A Community of Teaching and Learning: Striking the Balance: Report to Azusa Pacific University," December 1988, 12, APUA/378.794/A9973co/1988. APU policy asserts that academic integrity is the responsibility of each student, but does not expect students to answer for honesty communally. *APU Student Handbook, 1995-96*, 10.

63. *Azusa Pacific University Catalog, 1991-92*, 10.

64. Self-Study Report of Azusa Pacific University for WASC Visit, October 1991, APUA.

65. Stephen S. Weiner, executive director of WASC, to Felix, 3 March 1992, APUA.

66. APU Registrar's Report, fall 1995; ACE/CIRP Freshman Survey, 1995. The denomination "Christian" may create a misleading statistic, since some respondents may have taken it as the designation of the Christian Church, informally known as the Disciples of Christ, and others may have understood it as a generic, nondenominational designation for Christians. See n. 61 above.

67. A recent survey of members of the CCCU and a comparable group of small state institutions showed an average assignment of twenty-five course-hours per year. Ann C. McPherren, "Faculty Workload: Hours and Activities in Christian College Coalition and Small Public Universities," *Research in Christian Higher Education* 1, no. 1 (summer 1994): 89-105.

68. Matt Browning, director of student services, interview with the author, 13 March 1996. He explains that this wastage rate is about average for similar schools.

69. According to information provided by Mrs. Diane Lejeune, director of student financial services.

70. *APU Faculty Handbook, 1995,* V.F.

71. Robert G. Mickey, "Questions about the Christian College," *Christian Scholar* 41 (March 1958): 17-18.

72. Joseph W. Handley, Jr., director of the Office of World Missions, interview with the author, 14 March 1996.

73. Nelson, 11-14.

74. I am indebted to Professor Merle Strege of Anderson University for improving my clarity on this point.

75. David Weeks, professor of political science, "Politicizing the Classroom: Promoting Community with Civic Education," in *In Celebration of Scholarship: Azusa Pacific University, Integrating Faith and Reason,* ed. James L. Hedges (Azusa: Azusa Pacific University, 1995), 26-27.

76. Roxane Salyer Lulofs, professor of communication, "Temptations of the Scholarly Life," in *In Celebration of Scholarship,* 3.

77. Haggard, "Report of the President, 21 November 1972," 3.

78. Sarah Pittenger, "Tongues and Other Pierceable Parts," *Clause,* 23 February 1996, 6-7. APU being what it is, the article also featured the tattoo on a graduate student's back, superimposing the Greek letters Chi and Rho, an ancient Christian logo for Christ, to "remind me of who I am and what I'm about."

79. Another incident illustrates this. At an annual good-fun APU event, the "Mugging," the president scoops out ice cream for all the students who bring their (beer) mugs to the party. After the heavy metal music had taken over one of these events, the students maneuvered Felix out onto the floor and tried to coax him to dance. There are many evangelical Christian high schools that now sponsor dances, but this was an awkward enough situation that when a photo got into the press it caused some stir in the APU constituency.

80. Nelson, 2-3. See also Channing Matthew Briggs, "George Williams College, 1925-50: A Study in Institutional Change" (M.A. thesis, University of Chicago, 1952); John T. Flint, "Kent State — From Normal School to University: The Study of an Institution in Process" (M.A. thesis, University of Chicago, 1951).

81. Jeanette Brookins, registrar, interview with the author, 13 March 1996.

82. *APU Faculty Handbook, 1995,* V.U.3 and 6; *APU Student Handbook, 1995-96,* 36.

83. *Student Handbook, 1995-96,* 5.

84. *Faculty Handbook, 1995,* V.A.2, "Unity and Loyalty."

85. *Catalogue of Anderson College and Seminary,* 1925, 6-7; quoted in Nelson, 71.

86. Mike [Marlin] Vanden Bosch, professor of English, *A Pocket of Civility: A History of Sioux Center* (Sioux Falls, S.Dak.: Modern Press, [1977?], 1-31; Peter B. Mouw, *1891-1976: Sioux Center's First 75 Years* (Sioux Center: 75th Anniversary Committee, 1976), Dordt College Archives (DCA).

87. Wayne Allen Kobes, professor of theology, "Sphere Sovereignty and the University: Theological Foundations of Abraham Kuyper's View of the University and Its Role in Society" (Ph.D. diss., Florida State University, 1993), 37-38. Kobes is professor of theology at Dordt College. The treatment of Kuyper here is much indebted to his dissertation. See also Charles Glenn, Jr., *The Myth of the Common School* (Amherst: University of Massachusetts Press, 1988), 109-12.

88. Glenn, 247.

89. Abraham Kuyper, "Souvereiniteit in Eigen Kring" (Sphere sovereignty), dedicatory address for the Free University of Amsterdam, 1880, translation in Kobes, 283.

90. Vanden Bosch, *A Pocket of Civility,* 35. Dordt College's first president recalled in his memoirs how patriotic sentiment in central Iowa during World War I had forced his father's church to worship in English and had led to arson attacks on several of their "anti-American" Christian schools. B[ernard] J[ohn] Haan, *A Zeal for Christian Education* (Sioux Center: Dordt College Press, 1992), 16.

91. CRC usage tends to give the word "Christian" a proprietary sense, as pertaining to their community. Thus, a "Christian school" is an elementary or secondary school under Christian Reformed auspices.

92. Mike [Marlin] Vanden Bosch, *The History of Dordt College: The B. J. Haan Years* ([Sioux Center]: Dordt College Press, 1990), 11. Along with Haan, *A Zeal for Christian Education,* this book has been a major source for much of the historical background that follows.

93. While the public reason cited for a junior college in the West was geographical expediency, there was a quiet ideological agenda involved, since the Dordt faction represented a critical displeasure with a perceived deviancy in Grand Rapids from the authentic Kuyperian tradition. Haan, 72-73.

94. Indeed, it had been a determined campaign by Calvin College that had diminished and then destroyed the thriving Grundy complex of a four-year high school, two-year college, and three-year seminary.

95. The college's namesake was the Synod of Dordrecht (anglicized to Dort), one of the grand sortings-out among Calvinists of the perennial wrangle over how God is both just and merciful.

96. Vanden Bosch, *The History of Dordt College,* 69-71; CRC, *Acts of Synod, 1962,* 34-35, 505.

97. Haan, 102.

98. Haan, 106, reports that the document drew heavily on Kuyper's *Encyclopaedie der Heilige Godgeleerdheid.*

99. *The Educational Task of Dordt College,* 1961, DCA/Do/D/1.

100. North Central Association of Colleges and Secondary Schools [NCA], Visitation Report, 24-25 May 1965, 1-2, 5-9, DCA/Do/M/1.

101. *Scripturally Oriented Higher Education* (Sioux Center: Dordt College, November 1967), adopted by the faculty and the board of trustees in 1968, DCA/Do/D/1.

102. Dordt College, Self-Study for Visitation by NCA, 1968, DCA/Do/M/1.

103. Dordt College, *Faculty Handbook,* 1968-69, III-14, DCA/Do/E9.

104. NCA, Visitation Report on Dordt College, 9-10 December 1968, 1-4, 8, DCA/Do/M/1.

105. NCA, Visitation Report on Dordt College, 2-4 May 1971, 2-3, 5, 8-10, DCA/Do/M/1.

106. Vanden Bosch, *The History of Dordt College,* 131-87, gives a very thorough chronicle of the controversy. Quotations are from 136, 141, 142, 149.

107. James C. Schaap, in the *Dordt College Diamond,* 1 November 1968, quoted in Vanden Bosch, *The History of Dordt College,* 189. Schaap, a professor of English and a heavily published fiction writer, has been on the faculty since 1976.

108. CRC, *Acts of Synod, 1966,* 32-36, 316-61.

109. CRC, *Acts of Synod, 1971,* 139, 609-23.

110. Much of this documentation can be found reproduced in *A Handbook of C.R.C. Issues: Winds of Change, Frustration of Protest, the Victorious Church [1968-78],* by Association of Christian Reformed Laymen (Grand Rapids, [1978]), 43-45, 412-20, 578-82, DCA.

111. CRC, *Acts of Synod, 1980,* 78-81, 448-66.

112. CRC, *Acts of Synod, 1982,* 86-91, 556-75.

113. John H. Kok, "Dance: Playful Praise," *Pro Rege* 16, no. 1 (September 1987): 15-22.

114. CRC, *Acts of Synod, 1982,* 102-6, 615-18, 621.

115. John B. Hulst, Report of the President, 1993-94, 19, DCA/Do/B/2b.

116. Hulst, Report of the President, 1985-86, 28, DCA/Do/B/2b.

117. Hulst, Report of the President, 1985-86, 11, DCA/Do/B/2b.

118. Dordt College, Self-Study for NCA Visitation, January 1981, 82; Self-Study for NCA Visitation, July 1991, 49, 55; Hulst, Report of the President, 1990-91, 7-8. It is noteworthy that the assessments and other contributions from Christian Reformed churches fluctuated: in 1976-77 they brought in 10 percent of the total income; by 1991-92 it would be only 6.4 percent. Even so, by the end of the decade the church was contributing twice as much subsidy per student to Dordt as it was to Calvin College. In 1993-94 Dordt's church support in dollars declined to what it had been twenty years earlier. Lyle Gritters, Dordt's vice president for advancement, reported in 1988 that if denominational quotas, which are optional for Dordt but obligatory for Calvin, had been met, the Dordt receipts might have been doubled. Gritters, "CRC Quota Support for Christian Higher Education," reprint of articles in Dordt College *Voice,* courtesy of the author. See also Cerry Ebbers, Memorandum to Board of Trustees, 28 February 1992, DCA; Hulst, President's Report: To the Dordt Community, 1993-94.

119. Hulst, Report of the President, April 1995, 3, DCA/Do/B/2b. In his contemporaneous report to the annual Synod, Hulst moved this disclosure from first to last place in his agenda and offered assurance that diversity on campus would not affect "unity of perspective" or "Reformed distinctiveness." His text did not indicate whether he did or could imagine what this would involve. Hulst, "Dordt College," *CRC Agenda for Synod, 1995,* 250-51; likewise, to benefactors, Report of the President, 1995 [7, 11].

120. Registrar's Report, 1995-96.

121. Cooperative Institutional Research Program [CIRP/ACE], Freshman Survey for 1995; Moes, "Report on Assessment Activities, 1993-94"; Donald G. Draayer, Dordt campus pastor, "Brokenness to Wholeness: A Design for Christian College Campus Ministry in the 1990s" (D.Min. diss., Fuller Theological Seminary, 1996), courtesy of the author; Registrar's Report, 1995-96.

122. *Dordt College Diamond,* 29 September 1995, 2 November 1995, 4 April 1996.

123. Inquirers are sent the two most recent mission statements, *The Educational Task of Dordt College* and *The Educational Framework of Dordt College,* and are asked for explicit written responses to them. Applicants are then told:

> The Dordt College community confesses that the Scriptures are the Word of God. As God's infallibly and authoritatively inspired revelation, the Bible reveals the way of salvation in Jesus Christ, requires a life of obedience to the Lord, and provides the key to understanding, to finding and interpreting purpose in life. The educational philosophy of Dordt College is based upon what historically is known as a Reformed (Calvinistic) worldview.

124. NCA, Visitation Report on Dordt College, 9-10 December 1968, 3-4, DCA/Do/M/1.

125. "Relationship of Dordt College to the Instituted Church," in Report of the Long-Range Planning Committee, 3 April 1996.

126. Belgic Confession, art. 36; CRC, *Acts of Synod, 1982,* 44, 615; *1983,* 277-79, 362, 576, 647-48; *1984,* 441, 609.

127. As already noted, Azusa Pacific University discontinued granting tenure some years ago. A 1983 study of academic freedom at CCCU colleges reported that faculty had little sense of having had their freedom violated, despite the usual requirement that their teaching respect the theological commitments of the institutions. They also thought the tenure system was not a particularly critical or necessary protection for their freedom. Barry L. Callen, "Faculty Academic Freedom in Member Institutions of the Christian College Coalition" (Ph.D. diss., Indiana University, 1983), 138; copy on file at the CCCU.

128. *The Educational Task of Dordt College* (1979), 8-9, 11, emphasis added.

129. Vanden Bosch, *The History of Dordt College,* 219. Actually, the agricultural venture began in the hands of very traditional stockmen and worked with all its mind and soul to achieve

and teach high output. It required time and patience for the administration to realize this and initiate some environmentalist course correction.

130. "Report of the Task Force on Special Academic Programs and Services," 14, in Strategic Planning Documents Prepared for the Commission on Institutions of Higher Education of the North Central Association of Colleges and Schools, July 1991.

131. Dordt College, Self-Study for NCA Visitation, July 1991, 155-58.

132. Paul Moes, director of assessment, "A Brief Summary of Assessment Activities and Results at Dordt College, Presented to the Faculty, Spring Semester, 1995"; Moes, "Report on Assessment Activities and Results at Dordt College 1993-1994," 10 January 1995. Both items, courtesy of the author.

133. Dordt College, Self-Study for NCA Visitation, January 1981, 102-15.

134. NCA, Visitation Report on Dordt College, 9-10 December 1968, 8, DCA/Do/M/1. The NCA visitors recalled the earlier observation that the classroom seemed to operate on an authority model with little discussion, but found faculty who were now committed to "breaking through the passivity and dependence on authority which characterize many students." NCA, Visitation Report on Dordt College, 6-8 April 1981, 7, DCA/Do/M.

135. This doctrine resembled two other doctrines that were beginning to receive new attention from two other communities at the same time. The Jewish doctrine of the so-called Covenant of Noah provided an intelligible code of integrity for Gentiles that was independent of but congruent with the Mosaic Law. The Catholic doctrine of natural law provided an intelligible code of integrity for non-Christians that was independent of but congruent with the gospel. Both communities, Jewish and Catholic, believed that these codes had been revealed to them, but that they made perfect sense on their own merits and had a persuasive cogency about them which would sustain a system of moral duty for all peoples. This duty fell short of what the believers knew and accepted through faith, yet it was sound and adequate enough for those outside revelation. Those within the covenants of Moses and Jesus could take those lesser moral visions as a common enough ground on which they could have a shared understanding and cultural enterprise with outsiders.

136. See H. Evan Runner, *The Relation of the Bible to Learning,* 5th ed. (Jordan Station, Ontario, Canada: Paideia, 1982); James D. Bratt, "The Dutch Schools," in *Dutch Reformed Theology,* ed. David F. Wells (Grand Rapids: Baker, 1989), 13-32; "Relationship of Dordt College to the Instituted Church," 3 April 1996.

CHAPTER 8

The Story within the Stories

Until the later nineteenth century it was conventional for colleges in the United States to be identified by association with a Christian church.[1] Their founding, faculty, students, funding, piety, morality, and religious study (but not much other study) were braided together into a cord that tethered college to church. Yet we have seen that this church-college relation could be feeble on the brightest of days, and in the longer judgment of history the churches may be more harshly judged for continuing to claim colleges than for nagging them.

When we say a college was founded by a church, we speak more analogically than literally. Some of these colleges were founded by the initiative of local communities, like Lafayette. Others were founded by church initiative, e.g., Gettysburg, Virginia Union, New Rochelle, and Ohio Wesleyan. Others, by a combination of church and citizens, like Linfield, or by a group of locals who were both church and citizenry, like Dordt. Millsaps sprang from the wish of a church and the wherewithal of a single benefactor.

Despite these variations of sponsorship and initiative and motivation, the early educators themselves were usually people in ministry. There were always some preachers, priests, pastors, and nuns more disposed or able to teach than to preach. It was a natural work for them. Many who did accept calls to the pastorate traditionally supplemented their income by taking in students. The full-time tutors of the gentry were often in holy orders. Since the older churches and denominations expected some level of literacy in their clergy, and since even the newer, anti-intellectual movements turned in that direction after their first polemics were spent, most ministers were equipped to teach at some level. Lawyers and doctors, apothecaries and surveyors, bankers and journalists may have shared the same elementary training, yet they were not expected to be schoolmasters. The tutelary function of the teacher was conventionally assumed to be well suited to the Christian minister. Perhaps the recompense for ministry was poor enough to lessen the risks of a change to the classroom.

It is a commonplace that most of these institutions were begun, as the sponsors of Davidson put it, "for securing the means of Education to young men within our bounds of hopeful talents and piety, preparatory to the Gospel ministry" (1845). Dartmouth reckoned that a quarter of its early graduates had followed that path to ministry (1877); Gettysburg, 56 percent (1882); Lafayette, 14 percent (1889); Millsaps counted 36 percent (1902); St. Olaf, 29 percent (1924); Azusa Pacific, 31 percent (1940). The expectation, however, was that prospective parsons would not come in crowds. Therefore the founders counted on young people interested in the law and in medicine and in other skilled professions to come along as well. The common curriculum was intended for them all, as well as for the children of the gentry, who would need it to administer their estates with dignity.

Not a single college studied here was opened with the proviso that only students of the affiliate church or denomination were welcome. To the contrary, most legislatures imposed nondiscrimination in the charters they granted. Thus Ohio Wesleyan was "forever to be conducted on the most liberal principles, accessible to all religious denominations and designed for the benefit of our citizens in general." Some sponsors were quite vexed by such unsolicited amendments but in time found them providential, and their promotional literature eventually made a large point of saying that they were ready to serve students of any faith. New Rochelle said it simply: "Members of all denominations received." Some Protestant colleges drew the line at Catholics, Jews, and Unitarians, and encoded this unwillingness in their positive welcome to "all evangelical Christians." But that is because they did not expect to need Catholics or Jews or Unitarians. When they did, they admitted them. When they needed them badly, they welcomed them.

There was another natural linkage between the church and the early college. In the eighteenth century, and in rural areas until the end of the nineteenth century, the territorial and state governments secured their revenues from land sales, tolls, fees, poll taxes, monopolies, and fines. Taxation was viewed with ardent hostility by the citizenry, as were all appropriations which might augment it. We have read of several timely state grants to some of these colleges in their infancy, but they were usually without an encore. The only social entity which had a regular claim upon household incomes was the church. Therefore almost all these attempts to open a college (including the begging journey by two priests who dunned the Irish gold miners at Yankee Jim's, Rabbit Creek, and Poker Flat for Saint Mary's) have been addressed to the patronage of sponsoring churches. There was the added likelihood that congregations who were persuaded to send students, especially students with ministry in mind, might also send contributions in the form of scholarships.

Early Protestant colleges initiated their students into the piety and the discipline of a parson's household; the model for the Catholics was that of pupils in conventual schools. Their mentors held them to it until the late nineteenth and early twentieth century, when the students noticed the faculty furtively defecting from their role as disciplinary models and agents. The students began to badger the administration to alleviate their devotional duties and behavioral restrictions, item

820

by item. The long pressing and yielding, voiced by rhythmic argument and obnox-
iousness, was comparable, in its stubborn importunity-and-resistance, to the yielding by the British monarchy to parliamentary rule. One of the social forces that
came to distinguish and divide administrators from faculty professionally was the
way the latter soon left responsibility for student piety and morality in the hands
of the former. It was later, when the administrators in their turn created a class of
religious functionaries — chaplains, Y secretaries, deans of students, et al. — to
relieve them, too, of those responsibilities, that ecclesial piety and discipline were
shown to be only loosely and incoherently bound to the central purposes of the
colleges.

Students found little nourishment for their Christian faith in the classical
curriculum which held fast until the latter nineteenth century. Emerson called it
"an old granny system." As one Pennsylvania legislator put it in his harangue
against a charter for Lafayette: "The knowledge of all the dead languages, would
not furnish a single idea, that could not be communicated in English . . . and [has]
added no more to scientific knowledge than the croaking of frogs" (1825). Lafayette's most celebrated professor, Frederick March, agreed, and deplored the failure
of American colleges to follow the Renaissance, which had studied the early
Christian writers and "never imagined it possible that the best years of youth should
be spent in mastering the refinements of a mythology and life which at first they
feared and loathed, and which at last became as remote and unreal to them as the
Veda is to us. . . . It is strange that our children should spend years on the faint
Homeric echoes of Virgil, and commit to memory the graceful epicureanism of
Horace, and never see the *Dies Irae*" (1874). It was in the mid–twentieth century
that Will Herberg was asking his Christian friends why they had ever clung to such
"a thinly Christianized version of the Greek ideal of intellectual self-realization. . . .
If man's good was the 'life according to reason,' as it was in the classical-humanistic
ideal, then a liberal education along academic lines was obviously appropriate; but
how appropriate was it, indeed what sense did it make, if man's good was what
the Christian faith must hold it to be — to know and do the will of God?" (1961).

The Christian faith was not studied academically in the American colleges,
even after Charles Eliot had succeeded in annihilating the classical curriculum.
On Protestant campuses where all belief was ascribed to the Scriptures, there was
no respectable Bible study. The lecture series on moral philosophy customarily
delivered by nineteenth-century Protestant college presidents to their seniors dealt
in apologetics and relied upon Scottish commonsense philosophy, but did not
customarily drift into disciplined exposition of the faith itself. On those Protestant
campuses which expected more of conversion than of right belief, learning and
religion could be mutually exclusive: classes would have to be suspended for
days or weeks when religion got into full cry. On the Catholic campuses, where
the church with her theologians was hailed as the mistress of faith, the catechism
was the only book to come off the shelf for religion class. The serious study of
religion was left for later, for the seminaries, where the respective scholasticisms

821

of the seventeenth and eighteenth centuries were opened for learning, to no great benefit. The absence of vital theological inquiry was sure evidence that there was no faith studiously and strenuously enough engaged to validate the marketing claim that the campuses were "permeated" by it. One who doubts the stagnation of theology ought to read the intradenominational debates over the most vital subject of the nineteenth century — slavery. It is likely that the occasional debate with religious implications staged by the students in their own literary societies was better sourced and more theologically speculative than what occurred in their academic recitations.

The colleges and universities in the United States grew in youthful age, if not in wisdom and grace, in an era when the Christian churches were conspicuously unprovided with the very faculties the church would require to be a patron of higher learning. Yet in the last hundred years many of the prerequisites to faith seeking and sparring for understanding have developed. The informative disciplines of history and politics, the interpretive disciplines of philosophy and exegesis, and the imaginative disciplines of natural science, sociology, and economics, have enjoyed a steady maturation. Within the Christian communions, along with re-newals of piety and liturgy, there has been remarkable development in the inter-pretation of Scripture and the rest of the corpus of tradition, in both positive and speculative theology, and in the capacity in the various churches to sustain a dialectic that is both authoritative and forthright, intramurally and extramurally. Just when the churches were developing these manifold powers to engage in broad-spectrum, scholarly, and critical discourse, however, a great failure of nerve devastated their capacity to be worthy patrons of higher education. Just when scholars had begun to be equipped to teach serious theology, colleges and univer-sities implicitly decided that serious theology was not appropriate. This promise of theology as a mature discipline seemed to occur on the very eve of the defection by each denominational cadre of colleges and universities from the claim or aspira-tion to teach it. For the liberal Protestants this was occurring around the turn of the century; for the Catholics it awaited the 1960s.

It does not require a Marxist historian to ascertain that the religious identity of most of these colleges was, as they began, circumstantial and indirect. The teachers were ministers for whom this was a preferred or more available alternative to preaching. The colleges were identified with a church or denomination, usually but not always that of the president, with the expectation that patronage (in students and grants) would be forthcoming. The students were primarily recruited from within the sponsoring church or denomination, but the college's catchment zone was determined more by its geographical radius than by that of orthodoxy. Even under the most ecclesially attentive patronage, like that of the Missouri Lutherans, Christian Reformed, and Catholics, colleges were ready to accept the fees of all who could accept them.

It is fair to say that while every one of these colleges was from the start identified with a specific church, denomination, or movement, there was no manifest intensity in that identification, no very express concern to confirm or to be intellectually confirmed or critical within the particular faith of their communion. There was hardly any expectation that the *quality* of faith in the church stood to be strongly served by its colleges. It was the piety that they thought they knew how to serve.

Yearning to Be Free

It required only the possibility of emancipation-and-survival to provoke the educators' preference for autonomy. The cordage that held college and church together began to unravel.

Access to independent funding often provided the first inspiration to the colleges that they might stand on their own. The patronage of the churches was often stingy, and their chosen trustees were sometimes there more to be humored than to help. As the colleges gained in sophistication and financial stability, they naturally suffered church fools less gladly. These mutual disservices tended to loosen their liaisons of convenience. For some colleges effective emancipation came in the form of a sudden, large benefaction. Major Millsaps emancipated his namesake from the very start, D. K. Pearsons did it for Beloit, Ario Pardee for Lafayette, Maxwell Chambers and then the Dukes for Davidson, the Reynolds family for Wake Forest, and Carnegie for several of them. Once the annual scrabbling for students and solvency could be relieved, and patient growth begun, the colleges naturally began to think themselves less answerable to the churches. As the president of Brown University is said to have put it: "When I speak in Baptist churches and their mission boards, Brown is a church-related university. When I speak to the officers of the educational foundations, Brown is a *university*."

Alumni also came along as an emancipating asset for the colleges. It took years for them to fructify as substantial contributors. But from earliest times some of them had been achieving prominence and affluence in their own right, and the more successful alumni tended to migrate away from the rural constituency surrounding the country colleges and to cluster in the large cities. From the middle of the nineteenth century they began to pester their *almae matres* for representation on their boards, and to be given some statutory seats, and then more seats. Davidson began to choose alumni trustees in 1876, Lafayette in 1888, Beloit in 1903, Linfield in 1926. At first alumni were given only the privilege of nominating; later they secured the power to elect. By 1909 alumni trustees controlled the Dartmouth board. This seriously undercut the traditional trusteeships, which had been denominational and regional when they represented the sponsoring church judicatories.

One feature of the emancipation process which took a long time to develop was the definitive marginalization of theological discourse. After the Civil War, as college and university teachers began to receive graduate training, and libraries and laboratories were enlarged, and learned societies and journals nurtured disciplinary guilds, and as vocational prospects heightened student interest in the newer studies, academic disciplines began to mature, to ramify, to divide, and to contend for more room within the student curriculum. This usually had the effect of shouldering academic religion aside. Already in 1861 President Kirkpatrick of Davidson saw this under way: "There is a tendency in all literary institutions to eliminate by degrees the religious elements if any have been incorporated in their primary schemes. I am constrained to say that I fear that such a tendency has been developed . . . in consequence of the desire, and a very natural one it is, on the part of the several instructors to obtain each more time for the special studies of his department."

The postbellum study of religion did not enjoy a competitive season of development on these college campuses. Kant and Hegel, Strauss and Ritschl, Renan and Nietzsche, Mill and Marx, Darwin and Huxley had all kicked loose a great avalanche of doubt regarding the authenticity and historicity and interpretation of traditional Christian belief, and by the 1870s American Christians were becoming polarized. Many conservatives swung out and became angry confessionalists; and liberals often became modernists. New colleges were founded by polarized constituencies who refused to patronize the older ones. Seminaries had long since been founded because colleges were gone astray (Andover in the face of Harvard, Princeton Seminary rather than the College of New Jersey [Princeton]), but now counterseminaries were opened. After the Lutheran General Synod split, for instance, the seminary in Philadelphia was founded to rival the one in Gettysburg. New journals were founded to grapple with the established ones. George Peterson has narrated the convulsions at Amherst, Bowdoin, Dartmouth, Union, Wesleyan, and Williams, where an early ascendancy of the liberals was followed by an orthodox restoration, and then, in the late 1880s and early 1890s, by a forceful overthrow by progressives.

But after several decades of hostilities, academics and divines were so wearied by the polemics that there was an ennui, a distaste for dialectical religious inquiry. The effect of this was not simply to marginalize theological expression, but to reconstrue the colleges' own self-understandings as Christian. The word "sectarian" had always been a no-go word on the campuses: it had first meant an inhospitable sponsoring church or denomination. After the dust had settled, "sectarian" had become a word of sharper offense because it evoked the painful animosities of old religious quarrels. In its newer sense, "sectarian" denoted any doctrinal preoccupations that spoiled the religious, devotional, and behavioral commonplaces which the modernists took as cultural lozenges. But some of their adversaries were also in need of a more soothing rhetoric. The Calvinists were heavy with the cudgels during this struggle, for they had the most emphatically explicit doctrinal structure to defend. The liberal wing of the Calvinists who survived the polemics were particularly leery of any further doctrinal dispute, and it was they who led the way into a newly evasive rhetoric.

Asa Dodge Smith of Dartmouth offers a fair representation of the older, hearty blather:

> The College . . . should be distinctly and eminently *Christian*. Not in the narrow, sectarian sense — that be far from us — but in the broadest evangelical view. . . . Christianity is the great unity. . . . All things are Christ's; all dominions, dignities, potences; it is especially meet that we say, to-day, all institutions. It is the grossest wrong practically to hold otherwise. It is loss, too, and nowhere more palpably than in the educational sphere. It is no cant saying to affirm, and that in a more than spiritual sense, that in Christ "are hid all the treasures of wisdom and knowledge." At His throne the lines of all science terminate; above all, the science that has man for its subject. Of all history, for example, rightly read, how is He the burden and the glory! (1863)

After the theology wars, as Peterson puts it, evangelical religion would be "replaced by a more gentle, more rational, and more socially minded Christianity." Congregationalists led the way. Gun-shy liberals learned to talk religiously without giving offense, by saying much and affirming little. Secretary Bliss out in the West was determined to open a Christian school whose only definitions were "non-sectarian," "non-ecclesiastical," "non-polemical," and "liberal-minded" (1881). The word "Christian," he explained, "is a term of very wide meaning." Professor Porter at Beloit turned away from all dispute: "I sometimes think it is the last stage of grace when a man has as much respect for another's convictions as for his own." William Jewett Tucker, roughed up at the Andover heresy trial, wanted never to speak of any "distinctive tenets," which would be sectarian, but only of "those fundamental obligations and incentives of religion in which we are all substantially agreed" (1909). Tucker was describing Dartmouth exactly as Horace Mann had described the state elementary and secondary schools, which were to teach values and a worldview "on which all reasonable men agree," by which Mann confidently meant the "pure religion of heaven," Unitarianism.[2] Tucker looked past the "content of faith" to the "tone of faith"; it was not what one believed, but how — indeed, how becomingly. "Formerly the distinction was, Is a man orthodox or heterodox? To-day the distinction is, — Is a man an optimist or a pessimist? Our religious beliefs and denials are experienced in shades and colors rather than in sharp and rigid outlines" (1910). Hopkins, Tucker's protégé, cut this to half strength with neutral spirit and put forward "friendliness and good will" as "the essence of the religion Jesus taught" (1921). Young men were initiated into the evangelical YMCA by affirming "the Christian ideals of character and service," which amounted to "clean living and all-around manhood" (1919).

This is what happened to the denominations most affected by the strains of the 1880s and 1890s. But this same polarizing struggle was visited upon the churches and their colleges again in the fundamentalist controversy of the 1920s, when it struck others who had had less grief earlier. The Missouri Synod entered into long crisis in the 1960s; the Catholics, who had been waved off from modernism after the turn of the century, entered their crazy season in the 1960s and 1970s; and the Southern Baptists, in the 1980s. Usually when the heavy weather struck the churches, the colleges felt their affiliation to be a burden, and through a variety of maneuvers drew themselves beyond arm's length. One must say "felt" rather than "found," because the ecclesial interferences alleged by the colleges were more by way of anticipation than of realization. Somehow the turbulence required by religious fidelity and self-definition became so distasteful, so mortifying, that these colleges found it preferable to lay serious religious studies aside. Why that was so, we must presently try to determine.

Primacy of the President

In many of these stories the critical turn away from Christian accountability was taken under the clear initiative of a single president. Our first narrative offers a strong example. William Jewett Tucker, determined to liberate Dartmouth from all that Samuel Colcord Bartlett had stood for, was a modernist, a social reformer and a gentleman, religiously observant but not religiously motivated. He led his college to be the same. But because he and his generation continued steadfastly in their religious observance, it was not clear to him or to most of them quite what he was doing. It usually became clear later, on another president's watch, when there was neither conviction nor observance extant, that the purge of Christian purpose was there to be seen. Thus what began under Tucker (1893-1909) became visible and determinative during the regime of Ernest Hopkins (1916-45). This same two-stroke pattern applies largely to Eaton (1886-1917) and Maurer (1924-42) at Beloit, Henry Hanson (1923-52) and Glassick (1977-90) at Gettysburg, Martin (1958-68) and Spencer (1968-84) at Davidson, Bergethon (1958-78) and Ellis (1978-90) at Lafayette, Finger (1952-64) and Harmon (1978-) at Millsaps, Scales (1967-83) and Hearn (1983-) at Wake Forest, Dillin (1943-68) and Bull (1992-) at Linfield, Walsh (1958-68) and Monan (1972-96) at Boston College, Falls (1963-70) and Kelly (1972-97) at New Rochelle. St. Olaf underwent considerable estrangement from the church under both the Rand (1963-80) and the Foss (1980-85) administrations, but the process may have been checked somewhat under George (1985-94). The Lutheran dynamics at Concordia were none the better for the Zimmerman presidency (1973-83), and under Krentz (1983-) it is not clear that they improve. Saint Mary's seems unrecoverably changed during the long Anderson (1969-97) regime, but the energy of Catholic activists buffers some of that change for the present. At Azusa Pacific the many compromises under Sago (1976-89) may be reversed by Felix (1990-), but that is not yet clear.

This salient role of the president is not so clear in the way some colleges have become estranged from their religious identities. At Ohio Wesleyan the process is now complete under President Harmon, but it is difficult to identify any moment of critical turn; the process was long and continuous. At Virginia Union the relation with the American Baptist Churches was so compromised by a benevolently racist patronage of blacks by whites that the severance from Baptist sponsorship left behind little affective or effective desire for the university to be intentionally Baptist, even by relation to its two neighboring black conventions. Dordt continues on: with difficulties, but thus far without crisis.

With very few exceptions, the presidents who have been the strategists of religious alienation have been large souled, attractive, and trusted. They typically felt that their institutions were somehow confined, stifled, or trivialized by their church or denomination or order, and at a critical moment they greatly enhanced the professionalism, resources, and clientele of their colleges. As they enacted a new age on their campuses, they tended to point out the deficiencies of the past, though only as a foil for what they proposed as a future. They rarely criticized the religious sponsorship openly. There was usually no rhetoric of rejection, no break-away surge, no praise of secularization, except perhaps among the Catholics. Even when there was a secession from formal oversight by church authorities, such as at Lafayette, Wake Forest, and Boston College, the claim and the belief were that the institution would of course remain as Presbyterian, Baptist, or Catholic as ever. Indeed, all change was supposed to be gain, without a sense of loss.

The Breakaway from Governance

Though the early interaction between colleges and churches was more circumstantial than vital, there came a time when the colleges broke away. What constitutes that critical turn away from religious affiliation? It is tempting to identify it with the moment when the sponsoring church was removed from college governance. In many institutions there were, from the time of foundation, some rights to governance vested in a synod, conference, convention, board, religious order, or other denominational body, from which the college or university somehow freed itself. Millsaps, Ohio Wesleyan, Wake Forest, Virginia Union, and Boston College are instances of this. Lafayette had given over such rights and later took them back. The self-perpetuating boards at Dartmouth, Beloit, Linfield, and Gettysburg had by their preference, not by any obligation, been dominated by members of their sponsoring denominations until, at once or over time, they turned away from that association. Davidson, St. Olaf and Concordia, and Saint Mary's all continue to have their respective presbytery, synod, or institute variously empowered in their governance, yet to strikingly different effect. Azusa Pacific, truly multidenominational all along, has never had governance ties with any denomination; Dordt remains peaceably under governance which is effectively but not legally denominational. The fact that these last two institutions, which are ostensibly polar opposites with regard to their governance, are so similarly stable thus far in their religious commitments reminds us that legalities illustrate but need not control the character of colleges.

827

There is no single pattern for these disengagements. In some cases it was the work of a single meeting. This was usually because, although the judicatory held powers from the charter (typically, to influence the selection of board members), it was the board itself that had the power to amend the charter and thus withdraw those powers. On other occasions the disengagement required mutual agreement, and it required years, sometimes decades, to achieve. In very few instances was the breach a reaction to direct harassment by the churches, though the presidents at Dartmouth, Wake Forest, and Virginia Union had their stories to tell. The church representatives offended more by ineptitude than by intrusion. Often the menace they presented was not that they were bent upon imposing their policies on the educators, but that they held residuary policy powers without the apparent competence to use them constructively.

There was the further problem that they held these powers, not because the colleges respected the churches' confidence or oversight, but because they needed the churches' money. Some institutions walked away in order to qualify for better money: Dartmouth and Beloit had their eye on Carnegie awards, and Lafayette, Boston, Millsaps, and New Rochelle six decades later were standing in the need of grants. But some of the mainline Protestant denominations who had been such listless financial patrons in earlier days chose to take no offense at being disempowered, and actually increased their subsidies after disenfranchisement, thereby offering the paradoxical sight of denominations sinking into poverty just as their former colleges were uncorking the champagne. Religious severity and economic advantage, imagined or real, may have provided the occasion, and sometimes the pretext, for these *coups d'école,* but not their cause, not their deeper explanation.

There is no simple equivalence between church participation in college governance and an effective symbiosis between them. Some informal or customary relations have been among the more lively. St. Olaf was thick with friendly synods in the years before formal affiliation. The absence of Ursulines from their own college's board throughout its early years in no way distanced New Rochelle from the order. And no authority in the Baptist State Convention of North Carolina could have held Wake Forest to being Baptist if the faculty and/or the students had not been active Baptists. These stories of legal estrangement are important sidebars to the main story of alienation, but they are not the main plot.

The Faculty Loses Interest

College and university histories are in large part given their bearings by official policy documents. But academic kind cannot bear very much reality, and their public declarations are often poorly indicative of what is really under way. Whatever presidents and trustees do, whatever be the market forces imposed by those who pay (students and benefactors), the inertial force of these institutions is in their faculties. And in our saga, the faculty was the first constituency to lose interest in their colleges being Lutheran or Catholic or Congregational. The faculty shifted from clerical to lay status before the presidency did. The faculty resided farther from their students, became dissociated from responsibility for their moral discipline and from partnership in their piety. The faculty became more interested in their own academic disciplines (already in the early days when most teachers had to teach several disciplines), then exclusively so. As the disciplines, their literatures, their research, and their academic appointments broke out into ever more specificity, the professional identity and interest of each faculty member became accordingly more narrow. Faculty became more specified, which made it more likely that one might move between institutions to enjoy a more advantageous "fit" in a more specified situation. Thus in 1870 Mr. Jones might hold the professorship of mathematics, with responsibilities anywhere in the natural sciences; his son, Mr. Jones, might be hired in 1900 as professor of chemistry; his son, Dr. Jones, in 1930 might teach only organic chemistry; his son, Dr. Jones, might specialize in polymer chemistry by 1960; and his daughter, Dr. Jones, would in 1990 be hired as a protein chemist. And she might migrate through three or four institutions to find the best home for her special competence, unlike her great-great-grandfather who had taught at one college all his life. The self-understanding of the teacher was slowly detaching itself from the colleagueship where he or she taught and fastening itself to the colleagueship of the discipline, and also of the teaching profession as that became more tangibly organized. The teacher thereby came to love his or her career more than his or her college. And if the college identified itself as Reformed or Universalist, whether confessionally or only nominally, the teacher no longer did. The faculty were expected to be as ardent as clergymen, but that ardor began its long cooling into indifference.

Because stridency is usually no help to a career, the growing indifference of the professorste to the religious identity of the colleges was usually expressed by silence and absence. At first they took the religious character of the college for granted, or even as a saving grace; but it became an aspect, like the food service, which did not require their management. In that mode they might attend chapel, but no longer be called upon to lead the prayers. Later the religious aspect would take on the weight of a burden, and they would find reasons not to go to chapel. Later still, they needed no reasons. And if in early years they would be chided for it, the chiding rarefied, then ceased. Then it became a matter of indifference in the evaluation of prospective colleagues, though for some years the subject of religion might continue to be raised in the interview with the president or, later, the dean. But those exchanges quickly became stylized: the president's question would be framed in increasingly helpful, i.e., indistinct, terminology, and would lead dialectically to an answer that was an equally indistinct affirmation. As the process worked its way closer toward its term, those conversations brought forth affirmations in tones that shifted from assurance to nonchalance, to impatience, and then to affront. By that time the requisite faculty solidarity with the character of the college would have been significantly reduced as to both noun and verb. The identity would slide from Methodist to evangelical, to Christian, to religious, to wholesome, to "the goals of the college" which by then were stated in intangible terms. The required affirmation would devolve from active membership in the sponsoring church or denomination to nominal membership, to acceptance of the college's own faith statement, to silent tolerance of the ill-specified purposes of the institution.

To illustrate: though Davidson College was chartered to ignore the religious denominations of its students (1838), the faculty had to take the same "vows" as Presbyterian clergy, accepting the authority of the Scriptures and of the PCUS. The college explained this requirement candidly: "When religion sets up a distinctive claim to attention; when it demands a separation from the fashionable customs of the world, and administers unequivocal reproof for particular faults, then, it becomes an unwelcome intruder; and, if its rights are not made an inherent part of the institution, it will be ejected." But to avoid the taint of sectarianism, Presbyterian Davidson said it claimed only "the broad principles of revealed religion" (1845). Later, however, the ideal Davidson professor was being described as a "Christian gentleman" who never smoked, swore, or sipped (1904). It was significant that those qualifications were behavioral, not ecclesial; they stipulated the desired effects, not their desiring cause. As competent Presbyterian teachers became harder to hire, Davidson became "much more concerned that a man shall be a positive Christian and exercise Christian influence over young men, and that he shall be orthodox in all the great fundamental truths of Scripture" (1921). In 1938 the ordination vows were still being administered, but only to tenured professors. By 1945 one-fourth of the tenured professors (except in Bible and philosophy) might belong to any evangelical church, yet the same vow was still — awkwardly — exacted of them all. Years of low-grade anguish followed, while the reproach of "sectarian" festered within the college's soul like a splinter, until all faculty except the professors of Bible and philosophy were bound only to a vague vow that anyone but a Rosicrucian could accept (1957). By 1964 Davidson saw its loyalty reaching "beyond the bonds of denomination to the Christian Community as a whole," and looked for "genuine spirituality," "humane instincts," and "Christian character" in its faculty — an update of the nonsipping gentleman. Incoming faculty were required only to belong to an evangelical church, accept the Bible as revealing God's will, and approve a filmy statement of purpose. An exposé in the *New York Times* shamed Davidson into removing all its vows, but "in no way lessened the college's commitment to Christian purpose" (1965). By 1972 Davidson faculty members had to appear "prepared conscientiously to uphold and increase its effectiveness as an institution of Christian learning," and in order to be tenured they had to be members of some Christian church. A strident voice from the Department of Bible and Religion denounced this contentless obligation as "a direct contradiction of our public espousal of an open and unlimited search for truth," and insisted Davidson emerge from its "pious isolation" and fearlessly welcome adversaries. The board then timidly authorized an occasional "reverent seeker" who would respect the Christian tradition without accepting it (1974). Then came Ronald Linden. A newly hired young Jewish political scientist, neither reverent nor seeking, he scorned Davidson's hiring policies as "morally repugnant" and had his job offer withdrawn. After an inferno of protest the trustees asked only that faculty be tolerant, if they could not be accepting (1977). In 1994 there were new proposals that the president and trustees need not be Presbyterians. The argument was once more framed by the same censorious theologian: to remain a self-consciously church-related college, Davidson must welcome faculty regardless of religious conviction. A critical mass of scholars "committed to our heritage" would somehow appear spontaneously and manage to maintain some kind of "relation to the Christian faith." Whatever that faith is imagined to be, it is clearly no longer one that "demands a separation from the fashionable customs of the world, and administers unequivocal reproof for particular faults." When the trustees' decision came down in 1996, intended to define and invigorate the college's relationship with the Presbyterian Church (U.S.A.) in North Carolina, it determined that the president was the only person on the Davidson campus who would henceforth have to belong to that church. Here the much-invoked notion of "critical mass" was compressed to its absolute and mirthful minimum.

"Sectarian" was a reproach that never lost its power to unnerve the Davidson authorities. From the very beginning, it would seem, they could find no grounds for believing that a fellowship of scholarly Presbyterians might claim or offer any defensible educational advantage, what Marsden and Longfield call a "determinative perspective." One is reminded of the Lutherans' astounding belief that a college that was homogeneous in its theism could find no effective place in a society that is pluralistic. The self-doubt about "sectarianism" has been surpassed recently by the Catholics, who seem persuaded that a fellowship of scholarly Catholics would be at an actual disadvantage. The Jesuit presidents argued that to prepare Catholics for public witness their colleges should be as pluralistic inside as the society outside. The Jesuit community at BC took it as their duty to replicate the diversity of the public culture on their campus. Jesuit father William Byron, who presided over both Scranton and Catholic Universities, has also argued on behalf of diversity: "It would not be a good thing to have an all-Catholic board, an all-Catholic administration, faculty, staff and student body."[3] No one cautions against a board composed entirely of Americans, or a faculty composed only of publishing scholars, or a student body in which every member could write effectively. A shared faith seems to be the only hazardous affinity.

Ursuline sister Alice Gallin, sometime executive secretary of the Association of Catholic Colleges and Universities, has made the more radical claim that shared faith has no business sponsoring education:

My theological understanding of faith, and the obedience which is consequent upon it, is that it is a gift from the Lord which enables us to say "I believe." . . . I do not see how it can be the ground for the institution's existence. I think, on the contrary, that the only legitimate goal of a college or university is an "educational" purpose, i.e., to empower students to develop habits of mind such as analysis, criticism, synthesis, disciplined thinking.

In a word, the church, understood as the communion of those who confess together the same faith, cannot rightly sponsor — or perhaps even endure — disciplined, principled inquiry.

Faith is thus not expected to enable anyone to say "I know" or "I understand" or "I contend." If, as she argues, Catholic convictions are so private and individualistic that the church cannot rely upon its faith for any characteristic analysis, criticism, synthesis, or disciplined thinking, then Boston College's academic vice president makes perfect sense to say that his faculty's faith has no bearing on their intellectual calling: "It's inappropriate to ask a job candidate their religion. When we're hiring an economist, we're interested in hiring the best economist." This reflects the same attitude as the Thomist inclined to say he was a philosopher "who happens also to be a Catholic."[4] The intellectual irrelevance of faith was as clearly stated by Beloit's President Maurer: "The warrant of religion is twofold: to speak to the moral conscience of the scholar, but to refrain from confronting his intellect." If Catholic faith can offer no insightful element of perfection to the practice and critique of economics, then Boston College should have neither the wish nor the ambition to present itself as an undertaking of Catholic scholars.

Yet it is a Catholic theologian at Saint Mary's who offers the wryest comment on how the faculty ceased to be a fellowship of faith:

> We hire computer programmers, experts in finance, literary deconstructionists, coaches, and what have you — all without regard to their faith. We recruit students for our sports teams for their athletic ability, not their religious profession. We start graduate programs in various professional arenas, all without regard to religion. And one day we wake up and find ourselves in an institution more and more secular in tone. Some of us are as shocked as Claude Rains in the classic movie *Casablanca* when he hears that gambling is going on in Rick's Cafe.

The flight from "sectarianism," in its most modern surge since World War II, has blended into a more general change within American higher education. Campuses of every sort — urban universities, commuter colleges, liberal arts colleges, technical schools, church-related colleges and universities, branch campuses, evening schools — all began to fill out their programs and diversify their offerings. In their competitive drive to appeal to all available students, the single-gender schools became coed, liberal arts campuses pullulated vocational training, technical schools began to offer general education, universities added on more professional schools, junior colleges began to build up baccalaureate programs, undergraduate campuses begot graduate courses, then programs, then degrees. The result was paradoxical:

the competitive drive to replicate all possible diversity within each campus caused a sharp decline in diversity between them. The Carnegie Commission on Higher Education warned of "a trend towards homogenization." This was doubly paradoxical, because the academy had accepted the questionable task of socializing American youth, but then created an on-campus culture that was increasingly unresponsive to the needs of its sponsoring cultures. The universities and colleges created a culture of their own, stubbornly submissive to the professional predilections of the academic professionals.[5] This was the context in which so many Christian colleges and universities became ashamed of their mandate to house, serve, and criticize their sponsoring communities. To justify it they invoked the need for diversity, thereby depriving their churches of their intellectual ateliers, and depriving the nation of diverse campuses.

Owen Chadwick has argued eloquently that the drive to secularize European society in the nineteenth century was itself taken to be a religious process. "Most of the men who tried to separate the Churches from the State, wanted to make society more Christian even while they made the State more secular." Next they assailed the churches themselves, but generally not religion itself. They proposed, instead, less compromised objects for human homage: civilization, rational inquiry, communism, science, fatherland. Many, like Tolstoy, attacked the Christian churches in the name of Christ but absolutized what they took to be the old Christian morality, now freed from the old Christians and their creeds. Chadwick's remark about Voltaire and Rousseau powerfully evokes what we have seen in these case studies: they "had not overturned the Church but replaced it. They, the philosophers, were the new Papacy which France gave to the world; stripping the essentials of the old religion and reforming it for us. Christianity secularized but still Christianity."[6] So many of the academics in our chronicle withdrew their campuses from the reach of their churches, imagining or saying they were doing a favor to both church and academy. In doing so, most often they were not liberating learning from an authoritative master-perspective. Under cover of the usual banalities — "Judaeo-Christian values," "the broad principles of revealed religion," etc. — they were usually just transferring their credence to those old divine surrogates: civilization, rational inquiry, communism, science, fatherland.

Patterns That Repeat

Almost without exception a rhetoric of concern began on these campuses just as the critical turn had been made. When the covenants and statements of purpose and conferences on the church relationship were produced, they served as a distraction from the fact that the turn had already passed the point of no return. It was common for educators and church executives to express their concern that their college *could*, or *might*, follow others into secularity, a decade or so after such misgivings had become useless. From another point of view they were not quite useless, because their real function was to provide cover and time for the new commitment to take hold. Also, these vision statements and preambles to bylaws invariably addressed outcomes instead of causes. For instance, they easily spoke of the college persevering in its offer of Christian values, but never of hiring those who could and would do the offering. While working on the menu they declined to hire a cook.

The impetus for many of the critical turns was the fear or threat of main force by the church, usually through whatever access it had to governance or the budget. Yet they were almost always false scares. The clearest example is offered by the Catholics, who gave great amplification to miscellaneous grumblings from Rome so that their leap over the wall (which was invariably approved by nearby religious authorities) would be shown to best advantage in the eyes of the academy and of government funders as the right move to be truly independent, and answerable to no one.

There was some paradox in that. It became a commonplace to classify both church and state as outside forces whose inclination to meddle in the academy must be fearlessly resisted. The church has compliantly withdrawn to an impotent distance, while civil authorities at every level now make no apology for imposing their laws and regulations on zoning, gender and ethnic imperatives for enrollment, occupational safety, hiring and faculty appointments, the positioning of chapels, the array of varsity sports, et cetera. Colleges that for fifty years have refused to disclose to their patronal presbyteries how many Presbyterians they enroll are faithfully reporting to the federal government how many students of Samoan extraction they enroll.

But the greatest outside authority to which all these colleges in our study now defer is that of the academy itself. When the Western Association of States and Colleges told Saint Mary's it could not prefer Catholics in faculty hiring, the college felt forced to acquiesce. Meanwhile the sponsoring Christian Brothers were strongly distressed that the faculty included so few authentic Catholics, but to them the college did not feel forced to acquiesce.

The critical turn, as we have seen, often involved forcing those who spoke for the church out of college governance. Whatever the reason for each college's move, the reason publicly given was that the college would be fatally compromised if it were subject to any outside authority (no one ever seems to have asked what that might mean for state colleges and military academies). When the colleges adamantly refused to be answerable to their maternal churches through governance, it would still have been possible for the churches to engage in their own accreditation. If the regional associations, the nursing profession, the bar association, the chemical engineers, and so many other associations of shared interest insisted on determining whether the colleges and universities passed muster from their perspective, the churches might have done the same. When the Jesuit colleges threw off the authority of the provincial superiors, the latter did propose in 1969 that criteria of "Jesuitness" be published, and that a regular accreditation procedure should then verify whether each college qualified. The presidents were acutely troubled by that prospect, and successfully insisted that their institutions be acknowledged as authentically Jesuit on their own say-so. The Jesuit presidents' fears might have been allayed had they studied the University Senate, which since 1892 has set standards for, and accredited, Methodist schools. In recent years the Senate has disciplined various institutions for financial mismanagement and athletic scandal, but never for religious default. As long as "church relatedness" is assessed by the "common core of values rooted in the Judaeo-Christian heritage and the tenets of a free democratic society," no such discomfort is likely.

One other recurring feature in the process of emancipation has been the singular role played by Catholics. We have seen the uniquely widespread antipathy to the Catholic expansion in higher education by Protestant educators and churchmen of yesteryear. Today Catholics compose the largest undergraduate groups at Dartmouth, Beloit, Lafayette, Ohio Wesleyan, Linfield, Wake Forest, and Gettysburg, in addition to Boston College and Saint Mary's; they are now probably the second-largest cohort at Davidson, St. Olaf, Concordia, and Azusa Pacific, and the third-largest at Millsaps and Virginia Union. Only at New Rochelle and Dordt are they insignificant numerically. There are three times as many Catholics as Lutherans at Gettysburg, and twice as many Catholics as Baptists at Linfield. At Ohio Wesleyan the Catholics have been the dominant group for more than twenty years. At Lafayette they have taken over the handsome college chapel. Throughout the nation, 30 percent of all freshmen now report themselves as Catholics.[7] In the years when Protestant colleges assumed that their chapel services were universally acceptable, it was often the Catholics, who had not yet crossed the threshold of Pietism, Judaco-Christian values, and "the broad principles of revealed religion," and had not yet learned to take offense at accusations of sectarianism, that tended to say they had no intention of fulfilling any alien chapel requirement. Since they then had more financial clout at college than the intrepid but lonely James Foley who came to Beloit in 1866, the rules soon bent for them, and once that exception was made it was difficult to hold the line on anyone else. But many Catholics are now card-carrying pietists, and have become less inclined to consider their own colleges as the right choice. By lowering the enrollments there they have provoked formerly Catholic colleges to turn to a market wherein religion is insignificant, as in the case of New Rochelle. Thus theirs has been a doubly secularizing influence.

Of all the colleges studied, only a handful now enroll an undergraduate majority from their founding church: Boston College, Dordt, Saint Mary's, Virginia Union, and St. Olaf.

A Transfer of Identity from Church to Nation and Guild

Throughout the period we have been studying, both the Protestant churches and denominations and the Catholic Church were suffering from theological traditions whose metabolic rate and vital signs were near moribund. The most formidable theological renaissance among Protestants, the neo-orthodoxy of Reinhold and H. Richard Niebuhr and of Paul Tillich, burnt down to the cinders of death-of-God and process theology. The Catholic theological renaissance energized by Vatican II is also dead-ending in the hands of some who live by the reforms but not the fidelities. For want of a vital theological stimulus over the years, the colleges could have no access to an energized and critical faith. In colleges whose patronal faith was at least historically self-conscious and not too distorted by polemic, sound scholarship could offer some access to Christian tradition. But they usually lacked a critical philosophical tradition as well, even an interest in philosophy or history, so these colleges were innocent of the important languages whereby the discourses of faith and worship and theology could be made conversant with those of the other academic disciplines. One result of the narrowing definition of each faculty member's academic interests was an education that might include very little of the history, philosophy, and theology required to give them a disciplined perspective on their own scholarly pursuits. This was perpetuated by their isolation as teachers. On the typical campus a typical student might be studying and discussing medieval philosophy, modern drama, advanced calculus, the Hebrew prophets, and constitutional law, to be followed the next semester by another medley of disciplines, while the typical faculty member would be teaching and discussing a single discipline, semester after semester. The almost inevitable result among the family was inquiry without any conscious perspective, not just a perspective of faith. If the faith of the Christian sponsors was really "permeating" these colleges, it was more like mildew than grace.

Lacking the thoughtful critique of the world and its cultures (and of the church) which the Christian faith was reputedly responsible to provoke, the colleges were helpless to prevent their sense of religious self-identity from degrading into one of morals, then piety, then manners, then class or ethnicity or nationalism. When the Jesuit community invokes Ignatian spirituality to appraise all "culture in and around us as graced at its core by God's self-giving" and "discloses God drawing all that is of our world and all that is human into God's own life," the traditional Christian cultural critique has been blunted. Often religious sponsors had so low a sense of church that they could supply their colleges with no communion of sound and thoughtful piety, but only a weak, unreflective, and unself-renewing set of observances. Thus the president at Lafayette could say: "The chapel service gives an opportunity to touch all the students with educational matters of importance which cannot be stressed in the full schedule of the classroom: The observance of great anniversaries; the explanation of great events; as the recent eclipse of the sun (April 28, 1930); contact with fine music, appreciation of which added to any man's life; initiation of members of the honor societies of the college and other student ceremonies."

Lacking (in most instances) the support of a church or denomination that had retained a sense of prophetic independence, the colleges were the more easily suborned by nationalism and its half brother, the jingoism of the academy. We have seen how the colleges began to use patriotic language. It was as if they were looking for a new larger community to serve, now that they no longer spoke of serving Christ or the church. Maurer at Beloit said this: "Faculties in the colleges should be made up of men with a social spirit, men who love America, who are good citizens, who respect the American people. . . . Having that sort of man on our faculties, we should let him alone" (1936). Valentine said Gettysburg educated students "for their place and duties in both society and the State" (1882); his successor Hanson saw religious education as patriotic, preparing students for civil society (1934); Langsam, his successor, said they were producing effective Christian citizens and leaders for tomorrow (1952); Mohn saw St. Olaf helping to meld the German Lutherans into America, and offering learning "worthy of our record as a nation" (1889); the New Rochelle graduates were told in 1961, "We now have a chance to demonstrate that American Catholics are . . . thinking, intelligent Americans with the welfare of the country they love at heart." Cornelius Haggard in Azusa warned his students away from "the moral pollution around us" (1947), but was "committed to inculcating those moral and spiritual values and virtues which have made America great. . . . Patriotically, we are 'squares'" (1972). In Sioux Center, the Christian Reformed had wanted no part of any Fourth of July celebration in 1887, but eighty years later they were mighty impatient with the "immoral" opposition to the Vietnam War, which they blamed on subversive influence by their Canadian brethren. This intensified patriotism was being readied to exalt the nation as beneficiary of the primary loyalty which had traditionally been accorded to church. No one anywhere was worried that to be American might be more sectarian than being Methodist.

The elements of the slow but apparently irrevocable cleavage of colleges from churches were many. The church was replaced as a financial patron by alumni, foundations, philanthropists, and the government. The regional accrediting associations, the alumni, and the government replaced the church as the primary authorities to whom the college would give an accounting of its stewardship. The study of their faith became academically marginalized, and the understanding of religion was degraded by translation into reductive banalities for promotional use. Presidential hubris found fulfillment in cultivating the colleges to follow the academic pacesetters, which were selective state and independent universities. The faculty transferred their primary loyalties from their college to their disciplines and their guild, and were thereby antagonistic to any competing norms of professional excellence related to the church.

Why did these emancipations, which were to be radical and apparently irreversible, convey to their sponsors little sense of drastic change, and no sense of loss? Usually, though not always, the change of a college or university's character went largely unnoticed because of the stability of the cultural symbols, which altered more slowly. The replacement of the church-related faculty may already have been practically complete, while the student body continued to be recruited from the traditional clientele. The fund-raising actually intensified its appeal to believing contributors whose principal attachment to the institution was their belief that it represented all they had hoped for: real learning linked to real piety. All gain with no loss. Often a new chapel was built or the old one transfigured just in time to be a mausoleum for the faith of the past. The reductive slogans that we have heard from all these schools were intended — unwittingly, of course, as was so much else — to reassure the native constituency that the aspirations of the past were being realized better now. The linguistic generalities had to be stretched ever more broadly to relate realities that were diverging farther each year. The period of transition which looked to, and ensured, a radically different future was usually characterized by a celebration, in the fabric of the campus and the rhetoric of its managers, of continuity with the past.

The crucial issue was whether the college as a professional subcommunity of the church could address its intellectual pursuits with an insight, and a tradition, and a communal dynamic that are privileged. In the perspective that became dominant, that would be an unacceptable aspiration. It assumes that a church is privileged, and "sectarian" is the epithet for that kind of presumption. After being frightened off any self-identification as Presbyterian or Reformed or Episcopal or Congregational, the college began to replace its church with a descending succession of acceptably inclusive identifiers, increasingly hospitable to all denominations, and after a while, to atheism as well. In the course of this thinning sense of self, as the religious lineaments became less substantial, it has been natural for the college community to gather about other, more empathetic, identities. Identities of class, of ethnicity, and of nationality easily moved in to accompany religion, and then to help ease it aside.

The Pietist Instability

The pattern of devotional piety and the discipline of a moral life were foundational aspects of the Christian colleges which finally waned and vanished. Vital theological reflection was something missing from the start, then became available only when Christian devotion and discipline had all but vaporized, and for want of them died quickly of embarrassment. One might well infer that none of the three — piety, morality, or theology — has much stability without the others. But there is a fourth, catalytic, element in the Christian character of the colleges, one equally needed for their symbiotic flourishing, and that is the church, a historically continuous community with its own mind and way of life. The early church-relationships of the colleges, as we have remarked, were mostly adventitious. These many pages have given no more than a suggestion of the many peevish moves by judicatories to lessen or stop their subsidies to their affiliate colleges, and of the devious and snooty resistance by educators when their Christian authenticity was being questioned.

But this domestic bickering only mildly subverted the relationship between churches and colleges. More important in their estrangement was the subversive influence of Pietism. The original outbreak of the Pietist instinct was reformist. Men like Johann Arndt (1555-1621), Philipp Jakob Spener (1635-1705), August Hermann Francke (1663-1727), and Gottfried Arnold (1666-1714) deplored how thoroughly their Protestant churches had backslid from the sixteenth-century Reformation. Hardly a century had passed before the magistrates of the church had reconstructed another hierarchy, the theologians had reconstructed another pedantic scholasticism, and the ministers had disabled the reformed worship by formalities that smothered sincere spontaneity. Within both major Reformation traditions, Lutheran and Calvinist, this prophetic complaint was voiced at the same time. Together they incited another reformation (the third, if one counts the late medieval and early Renaissance outburst of mendicant, pacifist, and devotional lay reforms as the first). For America the Pietist reformation was very important, for the Congregationalists, Baptists, Methodists, and Quakers were among its progeny. Also, it was the follow-up American pietisms (when applied to later movements the term is used analogously, which we shall signify by lowercasing it), in the Great Awakening of the eighteenth century and the Second Great Awakening of the nineteenth century, that begot dozens of new, native-born denominations in the United States. If one takes these pietist outbreaks as a template that also largely matches the Catholic experience after the Second Vatican Council, the pattern will be even more generally explanatory.

The Pietists propounded the primacy of spirit over letter, commitment over institution, affect over intellect, laity over clergy, invisible church over visible, and they looked to the earliest Christian communities for their models. By holding up the simpler beginnings of the Christian faith as their model, they were able to isolate the original meaning and authentic dynamism of many elements of Christian life that had subsequently been adapted and amended beyond recognition, and seemed spent. This return to origins begot a strong ecumenism which encouraged Lutherans and Calvinists in the movement to reach over the fences of their respective quarrels, and even elicited an occasional amiable word for their common adversary, the Catholics.

The Pietist reform and its later pietist iterations react to a dispirited and sclerotic church, and direct their impatient energy to a redefinition of ancient institutions. They reach back both imaginatively and historically to the original sense and inspiration of church order, worship, discipline, preaching, and theology. If they have further strength they may also deliver a prophetic critique of the family, the civil powers, the classes in society, the relations of nations and peoples, and the stewardship of property. The pietist knack is to confront a snarled tangle of custom, construal and protected interests, and to point a prophetic finger at the obscured nucleus of truth within. Thus pietists are inveterate simplifiers. They are poetic, as Jeremiah and Jesus and Francis were. They break out with zinging one-liners that raze institutions to rubble, only to raise them to a life renewed. They leave people with a restored sense of purpose, priority, the "point of it all." The authentic pietist speaks to a generation whose life in the church has been hopelessly disordered and makes clean sense of the gospel that is ever ancient, ever new. For them it is a deliverance.

But pietists also have a second-generation audience, who now know little or nothing of the tradition. To them, this reformed presentation is wondrously clear, preciously simple, and cogent because so easily comprehended. But they are easily misled. They grasp the "point," but not the "all." And they can come to imagine that the point is all there is. John Wesley was a Pietist. He uttered illuminating and arresting insights that were meant to purify the priorities of his church, the Church of England. But others who came after took the new without the old and created something much simpler, the Methodist church, which had a cleaner voice but fewer overtones and echoes. William Rainey Harper passed for a pietist already on the slide: for him "the essence" of the teachings of Jesus and Israel's inspired prophets and sages was "fear of the Lord," "belief in and acceptance of One who has power to help." He was offering this essence, not as an interpretive key to understanding the prophets, the sages, and the Gospels, but as a slogan to replace them. The devolution was usually rapid. Frederick Robertson was a pietist who held to and refreshed the tradition; his devotee William Jewett Tucker was a liberal indifferentist who discarded the tradition but retained its pieties; and his disciple Ernest Hopkins was the rationalist who believed in none of it.

A pietist directly addresses people who have inherited a confused tradition, and when he or she says that "all property is God's," or that "we are all brothers and sisters and call no man teacher," and that "it is all summed up in love," the short saying is like a single wink from Alec Guinness near the end of a complex film, a wink that suddenly makes sense of it all to the attentive viewer. But to a patron who walked into the theater in the midst of the final reel the wink might as well be a flirtatious come-on, for it is all the newcomer can see. To someone who has absorbed the lore of Ananias and Sapphira, the martyrdom of Lawrence, Antony in the desert of Egypt, Augustine on grace, Gregory the Great on pastoral care, Bede on the conflict of Celtic and Anglo-Saxon Christianity, John Damascene's dialogue between a Christian and a Saracen, Maximos the Confessor on charity, Julian of Norwich on the divine love, besides some of Dante and Anne Hutchinson and Dean Swift and Berdyaev and Marx . . . to such a listener the pietist's dense toss-off, "How could I own anything?" is enough to set her ears ringing and rearranging down the years. By contrast, to someone whose head is so empty as to make confusion impossible, for someone who is starting from an intellectual ground zero, the toss-off could be a quip that becomes the cornerstone of a new and lethally naive *Weltanschauung*. This ability of the unformed addressee to receive what the pietist intended as a restorative insight, and to mistake it as a freestanding truth instead, and thereby to take in hand terribly less than was handed on, is what has made pietist reforms so powerfully clichéd and unstable.

Pietism was driven by fervor, and even in the hands of scholars it was naive about history: it underestimated the need of Christianity to grow through time and circumstance, and its ability to modify or molt older forms without renouncing their purposes. The emphasis on spirit, enthusiasm, and unmediated grace repressed any strong sense of the visible church as an incarnate undertaking, as the body of Christ. Thus what began as ecumenical fraternization often disintegrated into endless fission. The newer denominations, unlike the older churches, often owed their birth to a single quarrel or a single charismatic figure rather than a thoroughgoing reading of the gospel. Admittedly, the newer generation was much less likely to take up the sword over sprinkling versus immersing as men of old might have done over supralapsarianism versus infralapsarianism. But eventually pietism persuaded itself that the individual, and perhaps the local congregation, is the only authentic bearer of the adjective "Christian." By the time pietism had devolved this far, it could not possibly be the sponsor of a stable sense of church. Its doctrine was also very transient, for its foundational insights, once they were imagined to be free-floating concepts instead of the manifold convictions that a continuous community had been inspired to wring from its strenuous experience, became banal commonplaces. Once pried out of their history and their church, they had no capacity to endure much history or church. So they begot piety unsustained by morality, church without theology, preaching without sacrament, community without order. They would inevitably have a short half-life.

As the pietist renewal degraded, it seemed to devolve in two different ways. People determined to persevere as Christians developed a liberal piety whose wisdom had to be framed so broadly as to lack all depth. It had all the pungency of a cliché. Liberalism, in this religious mode, could be infectiously tedious.

There was another, quite contrary pattern among those whom the pietists gave a great distaste for church. Pietist historians had narrated how much conflict and violence had been begotten by ecclesial differences. And while their hope for the future was to repristinate Christian faith and free it from those old animosities, their reading of the Christian past was one of chagrin and contrition. There were others, far less enthusiastic than they for Jesus, who looked over their shoulders at this same sad history and saw it as Europe's folly. All those quarrels over the *homoousios* and *homoiousios,* Communion from the cup, predestination, apostolic succession, total depravity, infant baptism, and so much else, persuaded this generation that all the bickering had been no more important than the tithing of anise and cumin. Indeed, they thought, those were all unresolvable quarrels, because they could appeal to nothing stronger than unverifiable opinion. Thus the credibility vacuum created by pietism came naturally to be filled by rationalism, which proffered a more peaceable life by refusing to discuss anything beyond what could be resolved consensually by appeal to empirical evidence.

Rationalism, the whelp of pietism, was misbegotten. It was anything but pious. Out of little more than habit it provided itself with Deism, the religious equivalent of safe sex. Deists offered their compliments, if not their praise, to the godhead, if not to God, who was on display in creation, though certainly not in redemption. For those who liked their Deism in costume, there was Freemasonry. But whether it was god without garb or garb without God, Deism was little more than deviancy. For rationalism was Christianity's enemy. Its explicit grudge was directed at Christianity's partisan belligerents who had disturbed the peace with their gang wars. But in time the deeper odium came to light, and it was not for the warring Christians. It was for Christ: God who walked in Galilee, and who disturbingly still held the first allegiance of people in Gloucestershire and Ghana, Goa and Göteborg, Guadalajara and the Gironde. The rationalists were not without their own allegiance. Having blamed Christianity for the wars of religion that had made Europe despair of peace, they turned instead to the nation-states, provided they be governed by rational politics in the hands of people with no rival loyalties. Thus those gentlemen in Virginia, who on Sundays paid their respects to the Great Artificer, shunned more serious religions as "factions" whose loyalties threatened the Great Loyalty of the state. Rationalists with civic clout were mostly gentlefolk, and could thus be excused somewhat for not having noticed that those wars of religion had had more than a little to do with nationality, and ethnicity, and class, and commerce. It also escaped their notice how easily their own national loyalties were reinforced by race and class: reinforced in ways that always placed them well uphill and upwind from those to whom the Divine Architect had inscrutably given a lesser measure of Fortune, yet expected the fullest measure of loyalty to the People.

Pietism as It Affected the Colleges

The pietist view eventually shared by these various denominations and churches was that religious endeavors on campus should be focused upon the individual life of faith, as distinct from the shared labor of learning. Religion's move to the academic periphery was not so much the work of godless intellectuals as of pious educators who, since the onset of pietism, had seen religion as embodied so uniquely in the personal profession of faith that it could not be seen to have a stake in social learning. The radical disjunction between divine knowledge and human knowledge had been central to classical Reformation thinking, and its unintended outcome was to sequester religious piety from secular learning. The older, pre-Reformation view, that faith was goaded by revelation to seek further understanding, and that learning itself could be an act of piety — indeed, the form of piety proper to a college or university — succumbed to the view that worship and moral behavior were to be the defining acts of a Christian academic fellowship. Later, worship and moral behavior were easily set aside because no one could imagine they had anything to do with learning.[8]

The inquiries of science created a mode of learning that was self-consciously and aggressively autonomous, and its practitioners soon found "sectarian faith" to be an offensive foreign body on campus. They prevailed, and mainline Protestant academics ratified their victory by insisting that faith might be grounded on private affect, not communal inquiry. They willingly forwent any crucial concern for the work of the intellect, and accepted comfortably enough that religious enterprise at a college or university might direct itself to the welfare of the learners but not to that of the learning. Evangelical Protestants and Catholics would later be drawn into this same attitude and its inexorable sequelae.

The critical turn of allegedly Christian colleges and universities in the United States has been a modern rerun of the degradation of an unstable pietism through liberal indifferentism into rationalism. The prototypical colleges happened to be staffed by clergy and somewhat subsidized by churches, and to be ordered by a piety and a discipline that were taken for granted by those clergy and those churches. Whether it was the Congregationalists at Dartmouth or the Presbyterians at Lafayette or the Methodists at Ohio Wesleyan or the Baptists at Wake Forest or the Lutherans at Gettysburg, the religious mode was pietism in its first stage: each person ultimately alone in the hand of God, construing the faith in simplicity, praying in open fellowship, and confident of solidarity with most other right-minded Christians. Even the Calvinists and Lutherans had muted some of the controversial emphases of their heritages, or moved them off to the edge, as of less importance, even bothersome. Thus, from the very start, the educators did not imagine themselves to belong to a communion that had credibly received a faith once delivered to the saints, a faith which bound them in closest fellowship to all those who had shared it since the apostles, and which would allow them, the more educated they became, to become all the more able to share judgments, both constructive and critical, of their country, their culture, and their church itself. By being reduced to simplistic rudiments, their faith was not ready to rush to any such judgment.

This was not so true of the evangelicals or the Missouri Synod Lutherans, or of the Christian Reformed, or of the Catholics. They sometimes stood apart, and rather enjoyed outright nonpietism. One thinks of St. Olaf's dedication to "preserve the pupils in the true Christian faith, as taught by the Evangelical Lutheran Church and nothing taught in contravention with the Symbolum Apostolicum, Nicenum & Athanasianum; the Unaltered Confession delivered to the Emperor Charles the Fifth at Augsburg in Germany in the year of our Lord 1530 and the small Catechism of Luther" (1874), and of Azusa Pacific president Eli Reece's orthodox invective against "Bible penknifers, miracle rejectors, God minifiers, man magnifiers, hell expungers and those with animal ancestors" (±1919). But those Lutherans, Reformed, and Catholics would, each in their own climacteric, enter the ambit of pietism. A memorable illustration of this is provided by a modern Catholic creed:

Affirmation of Faith

I believe in people, and in a world in which it is good to live for all humankind; and that it is our task to create such a world.

I believe in equal rights for all people — in love, justice, fellowship, and peace. I must continually act out these beliefs.

I am inspired to do so because I believe in Jesus of Nazareth, and I want to orient my life to him.

In doing so, I believe that I am drawn into the mysterious relationship with the one, whom he called his Father.

Because of my belief in Jesus, I make no claims to exclusivity.

I shall work together with others for a better world because I believe in the community of the faithful, and in our task to be the salt of the earth and the light of the world.

But all of this in humility, realizing my own shortcomings every day.

And I believe in the resurrection — whatever it may mean. Amen.[9]

The colleges of the pietists who would later be called "mainline" Protestants usually had a very slow early development. But once their enrollments and finances were stabilized, and they were less in need of the only things their churches or denominations had been asked to provide — students and subsidies — they naturally let those relationships atrophy as they entered into a more principled indifferentism.[10] What they needed was precisely what they lacked: learned and articulate believers who were not only open to all truth, but possessed of advantages in approaching all truth: graced master insights, an interpretive community, and an authentic tradition. The great need was not to equalize all truths but to order them.

The Christian character of the colleges was rarely vitally resident in its academics, and had to live an eccentric existence in chapel, in volunteer service, and in clean living and all-around manhood. It was "the added plus." Though the bond holding college to church was never sturdy, and had been unraveling, the educators grew self-conscious as they began to move away, and needed to reassure their clientele and themselves that the college itself would maintain the old religious benefits: "friendliness and good will"; "a more gentle, more rational, and more socially minded Christianity"; student conduct "in harmony with the Golden Rule, and the behavior of gentlemen"; "Christianity, in all its essential doctrines," taught "without interfering with anyone's conscience" — whatever it all might mean. The worm was in the wood.

The pietist organism, which eventually found cogent belief toxic, was producing its unmistakable rhetorical symptoms. Ohio Wesleyan's charter provided that it was "forever to be conducted on the most liberal principles, accessible to all denominations, and designed for the benefit of our citizens in general." Much later Herbert Welch, who went on from being president to being a bishop, said: "The Christian college, in short, is one whose ideals and aims are determined by the great conceptions of life which we count distinctively Christian." Were one to read these apart from their historical context, one might imagine that OWU was claiming a distinctiveness in 1916 that it had disavowed in 1842. Quite the contrary: in 1842 the Methodists in Ohio would have admitted, at least privately, that there were some denominations with whom they did have some serious differences. In 1916 Bishop Welch may have thought anyone demented who did not share in his great, distinctively Christian conceptions. They were distinctive of a Christianity which was so appealing because it had been reduced to indistinct clichés. On this view of Christian faith, Gettysburg could coherently say in 1916 that the absolute requirement for a faculty appointment is that one be "a Christian gentleman of the highest type." What was said at Millsaps in the midst of charter revisions in 1985 may be read in the same genre: "The college's purpose and mission does not include teaching doctrine or demanding conformity, but rather operates from a core of truth which is affirmed with all Christian people." Millsaps' perfect refrain to this is a stanza of academic platitudes: "dignity and respect, trust and mutual support, sense of national heritage and global consciousness, affecting the state with the best of Church and higher education values."

When old Aaron Chapin, once a Presbyterian, stood up in the Congregational church at Beloit and shut down a tiresome debate by saying, "Congregationalism is common sense," those who knew all the wrangles and crises between the two half-sister denominations might take his aphorism as an interpretive insight. But many who stood at a distance from that history could take it for a reductive definition of Congregationalism as a sort of no-nonsense, frontier comradeship and — this is the point — little more.

To study these stories one must be able to distinguish simple pieties from those which are terse but profound. The narratives in this study abound in simplicities. Unfortunately, many are of the former kind: simple outside and simple inside. If it is a self-standing whole, a simple statement can be so uncomplicated that it speaks beguilingly to people who wrongly assume that it is the private entrance to a great store of wisdom. When Andrew Carnegie and his deputy, Henry Pritchett, said they wanted religion without dogmas or churches or man-made theology (1908-9), they were eager for simplicity, for a program without echoes or overtones. Or meaning.

In the case of the Christian colleges and universities, the pietist slide into liberal indifferentism was usually accomplished early — when the founders used promotional language, not just to make all Christian students feel welcome, but to make them all feel equally at home. To do this they offered public accounts of their enterprise which in other hands at other times might have been penetrating insights, but in their hands became banalities. That listless genre, often compromised by duplicity, lasted for years without further degradation, perhaps because like all conventional white lies it was understood by its clientele. Samuel Schmucker gave himself away when he said at the outset that "the college he aimed at was to be un-sectarian in its instruction, but at the same time to be prevailingly under Lutheran influence and control" (1831). But Gettysburg was a beneficiary of Pietism, and gradually Schmucker's college did become unsectarian, by a reductive shrinking of the corporate faith to whatever every student would abide. That was something serious Lutherans could have no lasting drive to influence or control.

From Indifferentism to Rationalism

Once the colleges had settled into the indifferentism their inclusivist language expressed, they were within reach of that more degraded and more incisive form of liberalism: rationalism. Rationalism in the United States has not diffused evenly, but has accumulated as toxins do in certain organs of the culture, lately including the federal judiciary, the state ("public") schools, and the universities. Recent constitutional jurisprudence has strongly favored rationalism and its discovery that any serious and public Christianity must be a threat to intellectual comity and national solidarity. But an even stronger enhancer of rationalism for the colleges we have studied was the academy and its culture. When the church colleges and universities made their way upward — as they thought — and emancipated themselves from what had been the indolent oversight of their pietist parents, they had no ambition more compelling than to enjoy the hospitality of the secular academy. Before long they were at close range, exclaiming on how big the academy's eyes were, how long her ears, how awesome her teeth. The colleges had freed themselves from "encroachment" by the church, now seen as an "external authority," an "outside interest." Chapel, long degraded into assembly, was gone. Religion was replaced by not-very-religious studies. The native faculty who had shared faith with the college were succeeded by a faculty whose faith was now mutually regarded as a topic of conversation inappropriate between academics. There was a new "unashamed," "unabashed," "unapologetic" vocabulary that invoked "a virile, rugged, red-blooded manhood, which is passionately loyal to the worthwhile ideals," "critical mass," "core of values," "growth in self-acceptance," "Judaeo-Christian tradition," "heritage," "values," "all truth is of God," and "an intangible but real atmosphere" associated with "concern for the individual."

Caring.

When this process had run its course among mainline Protestants, Catholics suddenly entered the pietist experience and have been making their way much more swiftly through indifferentism into rationalism. Certain other holdout churches may have been entering the cycle more recently. The process moves along more surely than it appears. A college or university may have irreversibly descended into the terminal phase, while concerned folk on campus are still openly expressing their distracted worry that someday, somehow, if they are not attentive, the place "could" give way.

One of the persuasions of pietism was that there is a solo Christianity: engendered, nourished, and revitalized in the individual. This generic and lonely discipleship does not come through the church, and it can regard all churches the way a consumer sizes up competing vendors. The major characters we have depicted here would never imagine that Christian faith without the Christian church is like a seed which falls on the rock, sprouts in a crevice of rainwater, then wilts under the heat of the next sun. But they encouraged many of these colleges to claim the benefits of Christian communion without the communion itself. Thus President Warren about Ohio Wesleyan: "I don't think it has lost its religious identity altogether. . . . we still carry many elements of the Methodist tradition; that ethos still influences a belief in the democratic process, a concern for the disadvantaged, a commitment to the education of all persons." Wake Forest claims certain inheritances from its Baptist "background": insistence on the separation of church and state, a feisty academic freedom, the mutual critique of reason and revelation. But such an "ethos" no longer vitalized and shaped by its mother faith is already in the process of decomposition. And without any vital participation in the Baptist give-and-take, Wake Forest has no stable way authentically to refresh these inherited insights.

Colleges and Churches Jointly Responsible

Our stories have been recounted from the vantage point of the campus, and one could gain the impression that the separation from the churches was initiated and achieved by the educators alone. That would be a mistake, for the dynamics of separation were two-sided. The degradation of pietism to indifferentism was an initiative from within the churches. Authentic ecumenism discovers wholesome elements of Christian faith or piety in another communion, admits their authenticity, and takes them as incentives to emulation and self-renewal. Authentic reform is the rediscovery of wholesome elements in a church's past which have been lost, and takes them as cues for renewal. Degradable pietism is wrongly confused with both ecumenism and reform by its promoters, but it proceeds from the contrary instinct. It does not reappropriate elements of the faith that had been neglected or misunderstood because of past antagonisms and distorting polemics. Instead, it moves to deactivate controversial features within one's own communion in order to broker a shared agreement on the "basics," first with other communions, but then with the wider society which neither knows nor desires a communion of faith. Another, more stable instinct might value and renew the elements of piety for their intrinsic coherence within a matrix of revealed and pondered faith. The pietisms we have seen at work here tend to slough off those elements of piety that were compromised by a contentious history. Thus it is not surprising that the process of degradation paradoxically first lets go of the "basics" (indifferentism) and then lets go of the church (rationalism). Yet, it must be repeated, this self-destructive pathology arose first within the churches, not within the colleges.

Another negative influence from within the churches has been a variety of embittered and pugnacious *bêtes noires,* conservatives who have targeted and harassed the educators who were trying to upgrade their colleges, and by their rancor assured the latter of widespread sympathy. In the story of the defection of Vanderbilt University, told elsewhere, Bishop Elijah Hoss — academic, journalist, and member of the Vanderbilt Board of Trust — became an unremitting scourge of James Kirkland, whose contempt for traditional piety was drawing the university away from Methodism.

> Bishop Hoss, who was one of the few to intuit the destination for which Chancellor Kirkland was bound, happened to be a strident, impassioned, and unattractive antagonist, who defined the issues in so anti-intellectual a way that he strengthened Kirkland's credibility among those who sought an institution of rigorous learning. As often happens, the church was served by officers to whom advanced learning was an unknown. Hoss was the very incarnation of that to which an ambitious company of scholars would not wish to be accountable.[11]

Edwards A. Park, Ethelbert Dudley Warfield, William Jennings Bryan, those fundamentalist rural pastors from the hills of North Carolina, Cecil Ray, Jacob A. O. Preus, and Cardinal Pizzardo are figures in our stories who likewise thought they saw godless, secessionist mischief among the educators. But they were so maladroit, so obviously distrustful of innovative scholarship, that their antagonism only enhanced the public credibility of those they distrusted. Thus the churches were at fault in their inability to raise up a more prophetic and learned criticism of their centrifugal colleges and their leaders.

Also, after their institutions had severed all interactive relations, the churches have speciously continued to claim them as their own. Thus the Congregationalists restored Harvard, Yale, Dartmouth, Smith, Bowdoin, and other old defectors to their published list of institutions in 1940, later removed them again, and astonishingly reinstated them a second time in 1960. Years after Boston, Wesleyan, Albion, Allegheny, Southern California, Northwestern, Lawrence, and Westminster began publicly to present themselves as "private and non-sectarian," and to ignore requests by the church's University Senate for information, they were still doggedly included on the Methodist lists. The American Baptists were listing the University of Chicago as late as 1964, on the absurd pretext that "the question of official policy concerning relationship is open for continuing consideration" (certainly not in Hyde Park). Denominational executives for most of the churches studied here admit privately that many (in some instances, almost all) of the colleges listed regard their affiliation as a dead letter, and in some instances an annoyance, yet in many cases they still receive modest annual subsidies from the churches, which justify their continued listing. The churches apparently find some measure of reflected glory in these anachronistic affiliations, but they thereby forfeit their duty and ability to discern what it really might mean to be a limb of the church. Some faculty at St. Olaf say that Presidents Rand and Foss had all but severed the ties with the church when Mel George came along and strove to reverse the trend. They believe that the ELCA educational executives actually favored a secularized model and disfavored his restorationist efforts.

The churches have been heavily complicit in the defection of most colleges from any effective Christian sponsorship. One sign of their co-responsibility is their astounding co-creation of a remarkably degraded rhetoric. As this study has so often noted, the divorce between colleges and churches has been befogged by vision statements, mission statements, goals statements, statements of purpose, covenants, bylaws, catalogue blurbs, reports from seminars and retreats, conversations, and other bilious prose which surge in greatest abundance just when the critical turn has been made, just when there is no longer any realistic possibility of restoration. Thus "The Jesuit University as a Counter-Culture" is circulated after it becomes irrefragably certain that the university has succumbed to the culture. The Methodist Board of Higher Education announces that its colleges will take on the task of evangelizing the United Methodist Church and sensitizing it "to intellectual, moral and value-centered issues . . . to affirm a universal gospel for a universal community," by which time the colleges could not care less.

Reductionist rhetoric pours forth in a swill of non-sense. Ernest Hopkins says of Eleazar Wheelock: "The founder's altruistic purpose of converting the heathen savage to the glory of God becomes in modern parlance a desire to convert society to the welfare of man. Either purpose requires the highest idealism, and the highest idealism is the purest religion, the symbol of which is God and the manifestation of which is the spirit of Christ." Muhlenberg College says its traditions as a church-related college do not require a shared Lutheran faith, worship, or morality. Instead (not also, but instead) they entail "a respect for persons who differ, a readiness to engage open-mindedly in a corporate search for truth, and attentiveness to the role of values in the educational task . . . the growth of students as whole persons . . . a willingness and capacity, at times and in ways appropriate to an academic community, to treat fairly the Christian point of view."

Educators anxiously disclaim any distinctive Christian vision. William Rainey Harper's "essence" of Jesus and the prophets, "fear of the Lord . . . belief in and acceptance of One who has power to help," is one example. Lafayette's Wenzlau soars on a wave of confusion: "No student or other individual is required to adopt or accept the University's set of values or any particular value or value system. However, the person must be responsible for actions taken based on whatever values or value system the person employs especially when those values are not consistent with those of the University." What if it is Bugsy Malone who enrolls, instead of Tom Playfair? The Boston College Jesuits confusedly argue that BC serves a pluralist society, not by being a distinctive institution with its own convictions and commitments, but by being a characterless amalgam of diversity: "a pluralist society requires institutions which are effectively pluralist in outlook." BC will thus offer its students, not the beat of a different drummer, but the dissonance of a band without a score. New Rochelle struggled valiantly to describe its concerns as meaninglessly as possible: "values which motivated the founding . . . openness to the shape of the future . . . quest for meaning in life . . . sensitivity to human dignity . . . growth in self acceptance."

This degraded rhetoric in which both colleges and churches have indulged is more delusional than deceitful. It bespeaks an ardent conviction that the colleges' educational purposes have remained the same, only now they are being pursued more sagaciously. Those who speak this way are being beguiled more than anyone who cares to listen. Both educators and church officers have been persuaded that their churches have no intellectual insight or critical gift that would distinguish them as academic mentors. To sidestep embarrassment they must reduce their description of the colleges' ambitions and the churches' expectations to secular bafflegab. This strange discourse deserves a Pascal to describe it, for it has been providing the background music to distract everyone but cantankerous critics from watching the critical swerve from pietism directly into indifferentism and then into the academic variant of rationalism.

An End or a Beginning

The process of alienation which these stories have narrated, and which this study has surely only partially understood, has produced colleges and universities that, in their otherwise successful pursuit of intellectual sophistication and competence, have accepted one great change. It is a change they might not, on reflection, have intended. As we have seen, however, reflection was lacking, and was nervously replaced with rhetoric.

The rhetoric generated by these innovating academics has invariably adopted the academic motif of intellectual freedom, patient research, evidence-based judgment, and rational argument. The implicit image is of free agents engaged in free inquiry and free conclusions. Naturally a Christian church which offers the gospel for conviction and commitment exacts an intellectual loyalty that makes it a meddling patron of education thus understood. Rational discourse in the contemporary academy believes — or says — that it can abide no prior convictions, commitments, or loyalties. But Christian scholars, to be at home in this kind of academy, need not actually forswear their faith. All they must do is agree to criticize the church by the norms of the academy, and to judge the gospel by the culture. And most of them have burnt that incense when bidden.

What the academicians ignore, partly because they do not wish to know it and partly because their Christian colleagues have so feebly manifested it, is that the gospel within the church has continually been at the center of intense and critical dialectic: textual, hermeneutical, historical, intercultural, philosophical, theological. Further, the church has steadfastly recognized the revelatory powers of inspiration, witness, repentance, and communal conflict within and without, as a stimulant to continuous redefinition and purification. These are intellectual resources about

850

which the contemporary academy, for the most part, has only crude and tendentious intimations.

Christian scholars knowledgeable in the long dialectical tradition of their faith know that it has zestfully grappled with criticism in diverse cultures and centuries. It has been able to learn: often when it was right, and also from when it was wrong. If Christian scholars have the insight and the nerve to believe that the gospel and its church are gifted, that together they offer a privileged insight, a "determinative perspective," then they will be grateful to grapple some more, using the very insights of the gospel to judge critically both the church and the academy and the culture.

But if they lose their nerve and are intimidated by their academic colleagues, as is true of most of the characters in these stories, they, too, will end up judging the church by the academy and the gospel by the culture. In time, they will probably lose the capacity to tell them apart. They will fail to judge the academy, or to notice intellectuals who are in thrall, not free; argument that is not rational; judgments that have become dogmas roughly enforced.

Readers who have seen this story through thus far will naturally wonder whether this is the end: the end of Christian colleges and universities. They may be annoyed with a book that portrays Christian higher learning as sympathetic yet somehow fated to succumb. The author does not believe that sophisticated learning is like wealth and power, those inexorable corrupters of authentic faith. Yet these stories do imply that higher learning, if not an irresistible seducer, is still a very able one. The mind's affluence does seem at least as beguiling as that of the body. There was, in the stories told here, little learned rage against the dying of the light. Yet this book is written in the belief that the ambition to unite "knowledge and vital piety" is a wholesome and hopeful and stubborn one. It is a shame that so much of yesterday's efforts has become compost for those of tomorrow.

Readers may have expected instruction on how to avoid the failures of the past (and present). But that is not the purpose of this book. The failures of the past, so clearly patterned, so foolishly ignored, and so lethally repeated, emerge pretty clearly from these stories. Anyone who requires further imagination to recognize and remedy them is not up to the task of trying again, and better.

NOTES TO CHAPTER 8

1. Though most colleges first functioned at the preparatory level of the academy and many later developed into universities, they were typically founded with the title of "college," which for simplicity's sake we shall now use to refer to all these institutions. Also, though churches and denominations are different forms of Christian fellowship, we shall now use only "church" for simplicity's sake.

2. Charles L. Glenn and Joshua L. Glenn, "Making Room for Religious Conviction in Democracy's Schools," in *Schooling Christians: "Holy Experiments" in American Higher Education,* ed. Stanley Hauerwas and John H. Westerhoff (Grand Rapids: Eerdmans, 1992), 88-114.

3. William J. Byron, S.J., *Quadrangle Considerations* (Chicago: Loyola University Press, 1989), 22.

4. Alasdair MacIntyre, "How Is Intellectual Excellence in Philosophy to Be Understood by a Catholic Philosopher? What Has Philosophy to Contribute to Catholic Intellectual Excellence?" *Current Issues in Catholic Education* 12, no. 1 (summer 1991): 48.

5. Richard M. Freeland, *Academia's Golden Age: Universities in Massachusetts, 1945-1970* (New York: Oxford University Press, 1992), 3, 114-19; Lenore O'Boyle, "Learning for Its Own Sake: The German University as Nineteenth Century Model," *Comparative Studies in Society and History* 25, no. 1 (January 1983): 3-25; Robert Birnbaum, *Maintaining Diversity in Higher Education* (San Francisco: Jossey-Bass, 1993).

6. Owen Chadwick, *The Secularization of the European Mind in the Nineteenth Century* (Cambridge: Cambridge University Press, 1975), 93, 156.

7. Catholics constitute the largest denominational group in all U.S. colleges and universities taken together. L. J. Sax, A. W. Astin, W. S. Korn, and K. M. Mahoney, *The American Freshman: Norms for Fall 1995* (Los Angeles: Higher Education Research Institute, University of California, Los Angeles, 1995). Sixty years earlier, Catholics made up the second-largest cohort (second to Methodists), with 15 percent. Gould Wickey, "A National Survey of the Religious Preferences of Students in American Colleges and Universities, 1936-1937," *Christian Education* 21 (1937): 49-55.

8. This has been very cogently argued by Henry C. Johnson, Jr., "Down from the Mountain: Secularization and Higher Education in America," *Review of Politics* 54 (fall 1992): 551-88.

9. "Affirmation of Faith" used at Eucharist by a Call to Action group in Wichita, Kansas.

10. For an account of how this matches the experience of the churches themselves, see Benton Johnson, Dean R. Hoge, and Donald A. Luidens, "Mainline Churches: The Real Reason for Decline," *First Things* 31 (March 1993): 13-18.

11. James Tunstead Burtchaell, C.S.C., "The Alienation of Christian Higher Education in America: Diagnosis and Prognosis," in *Schooling Christians,* 144-45; also as "The Decline and Fall of the Christian College," *First Things* 12 (April 1991): 16-29; 13 (May 1991): 30-38.

Index